SEVENTH EDITION

PETER CONRAD

Brandeis University

WORTH PUBLISHERS

Acquisitions Editor: Valerie Raymond
Developmental Editor: Erik Gilg
Marketing Manager: John Britch
Production: Print Matters, Inc.
Production Manager: Barbara Anne Seixas
Art Director and Cover Designer: Barbara Reingold
Composition: Compset, Inc.
Printing and Binding: R.R. Donnelly & Sons Company

ISBN: 0-7167-0998-8 (EAN: 9780716709985)

Printed in the United States of America

First printing, 2004

Credits begin on page 565, and constitute an extension of the copyright page.

Worth Publishers
41 Madison Avenue
New York, NY 10010
http://www.worthpublishers.com

Contents

Preface

In the past five decades, medical sociology has grown from a small subspecialty to a major area of scholarly and student interest. Twenty-five years ago, when we first envisioned this book, there were few good teaching resources and none from a critical perspective. The first edition of *Sociology of Health and Illness: Critical Perspectives* was published in 1981 and it has been revised numerous times, culminating with this seventh edition. From the beginning, I was (and remain) committed to drawing on diverse sources: Articles are primarily by sociologists, but also by public health specialists, health activists, feminists, and social critics. Criteria in choosing selections are that they be interesting, readable, and make important sociological and conceptual points about health and health care. For each section, I provide substantive introductions that contextualize the issues at hand and highlight each selection's main points.

There are few areas in society changing as rapidly as the health care system. Health costs have risen more rapidly than virtually any other part of society, new treatments and technologies continually become available, more people have become "uninsured," professional power has declined while corporate power has increased, and pressures remain on the health care system to change in ways that are not always in the patients' interest. While health and medical care do not stand still for our sociological study, it is possible to examine the health system as it is being transformed.

The seventh edition of the book reflects the continuities and changes in the sociology of health and illness. Only seven articles remain from the original edition; the other forty-two were added in subsequent editions as older selections were dropped. When I produced the first edition, issues like environmental disease, HIV–AIDS, neonatal infant care, wellness programs, rationing, genetics, managed care, and alternative medicine had not yet moved to the fore, but they are all central to this edition.

While I maintain the overall framework that has characterized the book since its inception, changes in health and medicine are reflected in this new edition. There are eleven new selections, and two others have been revised and updated. These selections provide greater coverage of the social determinants of disease and death, AIDS and its stigma, the experience of a contested illness, the impacts of managed care medicine and doctoring, the expansion of biomedicalization, and the Canadian health system as a model for American reform. There are several new topics: the impact of alternative medicine, the communications about illness on the Internet, and the increasing influence of the pharmaceutical industry for health and health care. Three new articles were written especially for this volume: a fresh analysis of sex differences in mortality, an original replication of Victor Fuch's classic study "Tale of Two States," and an updated look at the National Health Service. Throughout the volume, I continue to believe that a critical and conceptual sociological orientation is necessary to understand the problems with our health care system. The book's purpose continues to be to help students better understand issues underlying our health care dilemmas and to promote an informed discussion on the potential changes in health and health care.

Acknowledgments

I am grateful to the many colleagues and adopters who have been kind enough to share their reactions to previous editions and whose comments have helped to strengthen this edition. I especially want to acknowledge one reviewer who rightly suggested that a medical sociology text for the twenty-first century should include discussions of alternative or complimentary medicine and an examination of the role of the pharmaceutical industry. I only wish there were space to include the many other worthy suggestions I received. I want to thank colleagues and friends Stefan Timmermans, Phil Brown, Chuck Bosk, Susan Bell, and Donald Light, who are always willing to share their expertise on the changing state of medical sociology. An ongoing dialogue with Libby Bradshaw, a physician committed to examining the social context of medical care who is also my wife and partner, helps keep me honest in relation to medicine while sharing many critical perspectives. Heather Jacobson deserves particular thanks. She has served as my research assistant on both the sixth and seventh editions of this book and done so with thoughtful comments, impeccable organization, and continual good energy. She has contributed in many ways to making this a stronger book. Finally, thanks to the folks at Worth Publishers, who are commited to producing high-quality texts and do all those small things to help facilitate that goal.

General Introduction

Three major themes underlie the organization of this book: that the conception of medical sociology must be broadened to encompass a sociology of health and illness; that medical care in the United States is presently in crisis; and that the solution of that crisis requires that our health care and medical systems be reexamined from a critical perspective.

TOWARD A SOCIOLOGY OF HEALTH AND ILLNESS

The increase in medical sociology courses and the number of medical sociological journals now extant are but two indicators of rapid development in this field.[1] The knowledge base of medical sociology expanded apace so that this discipline moved in less than two decades from an esoteric subspecialty taught in a few graduate departments to a central concern of sociologists and sociology students (Bloom, 2002). The causes of this growth are too many and too complex to be within the scope of this book. However, a few of the major factors underlying this development are noted below.

The rise of chronic illness as a central medical and social problem has led physicians, health planners, and public health officials to look to sociology for help in understanding and dealing with this major health concern. In addition, increased government involvement in medical care has created research opportunities and funding for sociologists to study the organization and delivery of medical care. Sociologists have also become increasingly involved in medical education, as evidenced by the large number of sociologists currently on medical school faculties. Further, since the 1960s the social and political struggles over health and medical care have become major social issues, thus drawing additional researchers and students to the field. Indeed, some sociologists have come to see the organization of medicine and the way medical services are delivered as social problems in themselves. In recent years, sociologists have been deeply involved in research on how to prevent HIV-AIDS and best stem the AIDS epidemic.

Traditionally, the sociological study of illness and medicine has been called simply medical sociology. Straus (1957) differentiated between sociology "of" medicine and sociology "in" medicine. Sociology *of* medicine focuses on the study of medicine to illuminate some *sociological concern* (e.g., patient–practitioner relationships, the role of professions in society). Sociology *in* medicine, on the other hand, focuses primarily on *medical problems* (e.g., the sociological causes of disease and illness, reasons for delay in seeking medical aid, patient compliance or noncompliance with medical regimens). As one might expect, the dichotomy between these two approaches is more distinct conceptually than in actual sociological practice. Be that as it may, sociologists who have concentrated on a sociology of medicine have tended to focus on the profession of medicine and on doctors and to slight the social basis of health and illness. Today, for example, our understanding of the sociology of medical practice and the organization of medicine is still more developed than our understanding of the relationship between social structure and health and illness.

One purpose of this book is to help redress this imbalance. In it, we shift from a focus on the physician and the physician's work to a more general concern with how health and illness are dealt with in our society. This broadened conceptualization of the relationship between sociology and medicine encourages us to examine problems such as the social causation of illness, the economic basis of medical services, and the influence of medical industries, and to direct our primary attention to the social production of disease and illness and the social organization of the medical care system.

Both disease and medical care are related to the structure of society. The social organization of society influences to a significant degree the type and distribution of disease (Kawachi et al., 1999). It also shapes the organized response to disease and illness—the medical care system. To analyze either disease or medical care without investigating its connection with social structure and social interaction is to miss what is unique about the sociology of health and illness. To make the connection between social structure and health, we must investigate how social factors such as the political economy, the corporate structure, the distribution of resources, and the uses of political, economic, and social power influence health and illness and society's response to health and illness. To make the connection between social interaction and health we need to examine people's experiences, face-to-face relationships, cultural variations within society, and in general how society constructs "reality." Social structure and interaction are, of course, interrelated, and making this linkage clear is a central task of sociology. Both health and the medical system should be analyzed as integral parts of society. In short, instead of a "medical sociology," in this book we posit and profess a *sociology of health and illness*.[2]

THE CRISIS IN AMERICAN HEALTH CARE

It should be noted at the outset that, by any standard, the American medical system and the American medical profession are among the best in the world. Our society invests a great amount of its social and economic resources in medical care; has some of the world's finest physicians, hospitals, and medical schools; is no longer plagued by most deadly infectious diseases; and is in the forefront in developing medical and technological advances for the treatment of disease and illness.

This said, however, it must also be noted that American health care is in a state of crisis. At least that is the judgment not of a small group of social and political critics, but of concerned social scientists, thoughtful political leaders, leaders of labor and industry, and members of the medical profession itself. But although there is general agreement that a health-care crisis exists, there is, as one would expect, considerable disagreement as to what caused this crisis and how to deal with it.

What major elements and manifestations of this crisis are reflected in the concerns expressed by the contributors to this volume?

Medical costs have risen exponentially; in four decades the amount Americans spent annually on medical care increased from 4 percent to nearly 14 percent of the nation's gross national product. In 2003, the total cost was over $1.6 trillion. Indeed, medical costs have become the leading cause of personal bankruptcy in the United States.

Access to medical care has become a serious problem. An estimated 43 million people have no health insurance and perhaps an equal number are underinsured, so that they do not have adequate financial access to health care when they are sick. American health care suffers from "the inverse coverage law": the more people need insurance coverage, the less they are likely to get it (Light, 1992).

Increasing specialization of doctors has made *primary-care* medicine scarce. Fewer than one out of four doctors can be defined as primary-care physicians (general and family practitioners, and some pediatricians, internists, and obstetrician-gynecologists). In many rural and inner-city areas, the only primary care available is in hospital emergency rooms, where waits are long, treatment is often impersonal, continuity of care is minimal, and the cost of service delivery is very high.

Although the quality of health and medical care is difficult to measure, a few standard measures are helpful. *Life expectancy,* the number of years a person can be expected to live, is at least a crude measure of a nation's health. According to United Nations data, the U.S. ranks seventeenth among nations in life expectancy for males and twentieth for females. *Infant mortality,* generally taken to mean infant death in the first year, is one of our best indicators of health and medical care, particularly prenatal care. The U.S. ranks twenty-eighth in infant mortality, behind such countries as Sweden, Finland, Portugal, Canada, Japan, and the United Kingdom (United Nations Demographic Yearbook, 2002).

Our medical system is organized to deliver "medical care" (actually, "sick care") rather than "health care." Medical care is that part of the system "which deals with individuals who are sick or who think they may be sick." Health care is that part of the system "which deals with the promotion and protection of health, including environmental protection, the protection of the individual in the workplace, the prevention of accidents, [and] the provision of pure food and water. . . ." (Sidel and Sidel, 1983: xxi–xxii).

Very few of our resources are invested in "health care"—that is, in *prevention* of disease and illness. Yet, with the decrease in infectious disease and the subsequent increase in chronic disease, prevention is becoming ever more important to our nation's overall health and would probably prove more cost-effective than "medical care" (Department of Health and Human Services, 2001).

There is little *public accountability* in medicine. Innovations such as Health Systems Agencies, regional organizations designed to coordinate medical services (now defunct), and Peer Review Organizations, boards mandated to review the quality of (mostly) hospital care, had limited success in their efforts to control the quality and cost of medical care. (The incredible rise in the number of malpractice suits may be seen as an indication not of increasing poor medical practice but of the fact that such suits are about the only form of medical accountability presently available to the consumer.) Numerous other attempts to control medical costs—in the form of Health Maintenance Organizations (HMOs), Diagnostic Related Groups (DRGs), evidence-based medicine, and "managed care"—have also largely failed. The most significant attempt, "managed care," is changing how medicine is delivered. But it is not yet clear if it controls costs, and it is most unlikely to increase public accountability.

Another element of our crisis in health care is the *"medicalization"* of society. Many, perhaps far too many, of our social problems (e.g., alcoholism, drug addiction, and child abuse) and of life's normal, natural, and generally nonpathological events (e.g., birth, death, and sexuality) have come to be seen as "medical problems." It is by no means clear that such matters constitute appropriate medical problems per se. Indeed, there is evidence that the medicalization of social problems and life's natural events has itself become a social problem (Zola, 1972; Conrad, 1992).

Many other important elements and manifestations of our crisis in health care are described in the works contained in this volume, including the uneven distribution of disease and health care, the role of the physical environment in disease and illness, the monopolistic history of the medical profession, the role of government in financing health care, inequalities in medical care, the challenge of self-help groups, the role of the Internet, and possibilities of health care reform. The particularities of America's health crisis aside, most contributors to this volume reflect the growing conviction that the social organization of medicine in the United States has been central to perpetuating that crisis.

CRITICAL PERSPECTIVES ON HEALTH AND ILLNESS

The third major theme of this book is the need to examine the relationship between our society's organization and institutions and its medical care system from a "critical perspective." What do we mean by a critical perspective?

A critical perspective is one that does not consider the present fundamental organization of medicine as sacred and inviolable. Nor does it assume that some other particular organization would necessarily be a panacea for all our health-care problems. A critical perspective accepts no "truth" or "fact" merely because it has hitherto been accepted as such. It examines what is, not as something given or static, but as something out of which change and growth can emerge. In contrast, any theoretical framework that claims to have all the answers to understanding health and illness is not a critical perspective. The social aspects of health and illness are too complex for a monolithic approach.

Further, a critical perspective assumes that a sociology of health and illness entails societal and personal values, and that these values must be considered and made explicit if illness and health-care problems are to be satisfactorily dealt with. Since any critical perspective is informed by values and assumptions, we would like to make ours explicit: (1) The problems and inequalities of health and medical care are connected to the particular historically located social arrangements and the cultural values of any society. (2) Health care should be oriented toward the prevention of disease and illness. (3) The priorities of any medical system should be based on the needs of the consumers and not the providers. A direct corollary of this is that the socially based inequalities of health and medical care must be eliminated. (4) Ultimately, society itself must change for health and medical care to improve.

While economic concerns have dominated the health policy debate since the 1980s, the development of critical perspectives on health and illness are central to the reform of health care in the twenty-first century (Mechanic, 1993). Bringing such critical perspectives to bear on the sociology of health and illness has thus informed the selection of readings contained in this volume. It has also informed editorial comments that introduce and bind together the book's various parts and subparts. Explicitly and implicitly, the goal of this work is to generate awareness that informed social change is a prerequisite for the elimination of socially based inequalities in health and medical care.

NOTES

1. Until 1960 only one journal, *Milbank Memorial Fund Quarterly* (now called *Milbank Quarterly*), was more or less devoted to medical sociological writings, although many articles on medicine and illness were published in other sociological journals. Today five more journals focus specifically on sociological work on health, illness, and medicine: *The Journal of Health and Social Behavior; Social Science and Medicine; International Journal of Health Services; Sociology of Health and Illness; Health.* So do the annual volumes *Research in the Sociology of Health Care* and *Advances in Medical Sociology.* Such medical journals as *Medical Care* and *American Journal of Public Health* frequently publish medical sociological articles, as do various psychiatric journals.
2. Inasmuch as we define the sociology of health and illness in such a broad manner, it is not possible to cover adequately all the topics it encompasses in one volume. Although we attempt to touch on most important sociological aspects of health and illness, space limitations preclude presenting all potential topics. For instance, we do not include sections on professional socialization, the social organization of hospitals, and the utilization of services. Discussions of these are easily available in standard medical sociology textbooks. We have made a specific decision not to include materials on mental health and illness. While mental and physical health are not as separate as was once thought, the sociology of mental health comprises a separate literature and raises some different issues from the ones developed here.

REFERENCES

Bloom, Samuel W. 2002. The Word as Scalpel. New York: Oxford University Press.

Conrad, Peter. 1992. "Medicalization and social control." Annual Review of Sociology. 18:209–232.

Kawachi, Ichiro, Bruce P. Kennedy, and Richard G. Wilkerson. 1999. The Society and Population Health Reader: Income Inequality and Health. New York: The New Press.

Light, Donald W. 1992. "The practice and ethics of risk-rated health insurance." Journal of American Medical Association. 267:2503–2508.

Mechanic, David. 1993. "Social research in health and the American sociopolitical context: The changing fortunes of medical sociology." Social Science and Medicine. 36:95–102.

Sidel, Victor W., and Ruth Sidel. 1983. A Healthy State. rev. ed. New York: Pantheon Books.

Straus, Robert. 1957. "The nature and status of medical sociology." American Sociological Review. 22 (April): 200–204.

U.S. Department of Health and Human Services. 2001. Healthy People 2010. Washington, D.C.: U.S. Government Printing Office. (www.healthypeople.gov/documents)

Zola, Irving Kenneth. 1972. "Medicine as an institution of social control." Sociological Review. 20:487–504.

PART 1
THE SOCIAL PRODUCTION OF DISEASE AND ILLNESS

Part 1 of this book is divided into five sections. While the overriding theme is "the social production of disease and the meaning of illness," each section develops a particular aspect of the sociology of disease production. For the purposes of this book, we define *disease* as the biophysiological phenomena that manifest themselves as changes in and malfunctions of the human body. *Illness,* on the other hand, is the experience of being sick or diseased. Accordingly, we can see disease as a physiological state and illness as a social psychological state presumably caused by the disease. Thus, pathologists and public health doctors deal with disease, patients experience illness, and ideally clinical physicians treat both. Furthermore, such a distinction is useful for dealing with the possibility of people feeling ill in the absence of disease or being "diseased" without experiencing illness. Obviously, disease and illness are related, but separating them as concepts allows us to explore the objective level of disease and the subjective level of illness. The first three sections of Part 1 focus primarily on disease; the last two focus on illness.

All the selections in Part 1 consider how disease and illness are socially produced. The so-called *medical model* focuses on organic pathology in individual patients, rarely taking societal factors into account. Clinical medicine locates disease as a problem in the individual body, but although this is clearly important and useful, it provides an incomplete and sometimes distorted picture. In the face of increased concern about chronic disease and its prevention (U.S. HHS, 1991), the selections suggest that a shift in focus from the internal environment of individuals to the interaction between external environments in which people live and the internal environment of the human body will yield new insights into disease causation and prevention.

The Social Nature of Disease

When we look historically at the extent and patterns of disease in Western society, we see enormous changes. In the early nineteenth century, the infant mortality rate was very high, life expectancy was short (approximately forty years), and life-threatening epidemics were common. Infectious diseases, especially those of childhood, were often fatal. Even at the beginning of the twentieth century the United States' annual death rate was 28 per 1000 population compared with 7.3 per 1000 today, and the cause of death was usually pneumonia, influenza, tuberculosis, typhoid fever, or one of the various forms of dysentery (Cassell, 1979: 72). But patterns of *morbidity* (disease rate) and *mortality* (death rate) have changed. Today we have "conquered" most infectious diseases; they are no longer feared and few people die from them.

Chronic diseases such as heart disease, cancer, and stroke are now the major causes of death in the United States (see Figure 1-3).

Medicine usually receives credit for the great victory over infectious diseases. After all, certain scientific discoveries (e.g., germ theory) and medical interventions (e.g., vaccinations and drugs) developed and used to combat infectious diseases must have been responsible for reducing deaths from those diseases, or so the logic goes. While this view may seem reasonable from a not too careful reading of medical history, it is contradicted by some important social scientific work.

René Dubos (1959) was one of the first to argue that social changes in the environment rather than medical interventions led to the reduction of mortality by infectious diseases. He viewed the nineteenth-century Sanitary Movement's campaign for clean water, air, and proper sewage disposal as a particularly significant "public health" measure. Thomas McKeown (1971) showed that biomedical interventions were not the cause of the decline in mortality in England and Wales in the nineteenth century. This viewpoint, or the "limitations of modern medicine" argument (Powles, 1973), is now well known in public health circles. The argument is essentially a simple one: Discoveries and interventions by *clinical medicine* were not the cause of the decline of mortality for various populations. Rather, it seems that social and environmental factors such as (1) sanitation, (2) improved housing and nutrition, and (3) a general rise in the standard of living were the most significant contributors. This does not mean that clinical medicine did not reduce some people's suffering or prevent or cure diseases in others; we know it did. But social factors appear much more important than medical interventions in the "conquest" of infectious disease.

In the keynote selection in this book, John B. McKinlay and Sonja M. McKinlay assess "Medical Measures and the Decline of Mortality." They offer empirical evidence to support the limitations of medicine argument and point to the social nature of disease. We must note that mortality rates, the data on which they base their analysis, only crudely measure "cure" and don't measure "care" at all. But it is important to understand that much of what is attributed to "medical intervention" seems not to be the result of clinical medicine per se (cf. Levine et al., 1983).

The limitations of medicine argument underlines the need for a broader, more comprehensive perspective on understanding disease and its treatment (see also Tesh, 1988), a perspective that focuses on the significance of social structure and change in disease causation and prevention.

REFERENCES

Dubos, René. 1959. Mirage of Health. New York: Harper and Row.

Levine, Sol, Jacob J. Feldman, and Jack Elinson. 1983. "Does medical care do any good?" Pp. 394–404, in David Mechanic (ed.), Handbook of Health, Health Care, and the Health Professions. New York: Free Press.

McKeown, Thomas. 1971. "A historical appraisal of the medical task." Pp. 29–55 in G. McLachlan and T. McKeown (eds.), Medical History and Medical Care: A Symposium of Perspectives. New York: Oxford University Press.

Powles, John. 1973. "On the limitations of modern medicine." Science, Medicine and Man, 1: 1–30.

Tesh, Sylvia Noble. 1988. Hidden Arguments: Political Ideology and Disease Prevention. New Brunswick, NJ: Rutgers University Press.

U.S. Department of Health and Human Services. 1991. Healthy People 2000: National Health Promotion and Disease Prevention Objectives. Washington, D.C.: U.S. Government Printing Office.

U.S. Department of Health and Human Services. 1998. Health, United States 1998, with socioeconomic status and health chartbook. Washington, D.C.: U.S. Government Printing Office.

1 Medical Measures and the Decline of Mortality

John B. McKinlay and Sonja M. McKinlay

. . . by the time laboratory medicine came effectively into the picture the job had been carried far toward completion by the humanitarians and social reformers of the nineteenth century. Their doctrine that nature is holy and healthful was scientifically naive but proved highly effective in dealing with the most important health problems of their age. When the tide is receding from the beach it is easy to have the illusion that one can empty the ocean by removing water with a pail.

R. Dubos, Mirage of Health, *New York: Perennial Library,* 1959, p. 23

INTRODUCING A MEDICAL HERESY

The modern "heresy" that medical care (as it is traditionally conceived) is generally unrelated to improvements in the health of populations (as distinct from individuals) is still dismissed as unthinkable in much the same way as the so-called heresies of former times. And this is despite a long history of support in popular and scientific writings as well as from able minds in a variety of disciplines. History is replete with examples of how, understandably enough, self-interested individuals and groups denounced popular customs and beliefs which appeared to threaten their own domains of practice, thereby rendering them heresies (for example, physicians' denunciation of midwives as witches, during the Middle Ages). We also know that vast institutional resources have often been deployed to neutralize challenges to the assumptions upon which everyday organizational activities were founded and legitimated (for example, the Spanish Inquisition). And since it is usually difficult for organizations themselves to directly combat threatening "heresies," we often find otherwise credible practitioners, perhaps unwittingly, serving the interests of organizations in this capacity. These historical responses may find a modern parallel in the way everyday practitioners of medicine, on their own altruistic or "scientific" grounds and still perhaps unwittingly, serve present-day institutions (hospital complexes, university medical centers, pharmaceutical houses, and insurance companies) by spearheading an assault on a most fundamental challenging heresy of our time: *that the introduction of specific medical measures and/or the expansion of medical services are generally not responsible for most of the modern decline in mortality.*

In different historical epochs and cultures, there appear to be characteristic ways of explaining the arrival and departure of natural vicissitudes. For salvation from some plague, it may be that the gods were appeased, good works rewarded, or some imbalance in nature corrected. And there always seems to be some person or group (witch doctors, priests, medicine men) able to persuade others, sometimes on the basis of acceptable evidence for most people at that time, that they have *the* explanation for the phenomenon in question and may even claim responsibility for it. They also seem to benefit most from common acceptance of the explanations they offer. It is not uncommon today for biotechnological knowledge and specific medical interventions to be invoked as *the major reason* for most of the modern (twentieth century) decline in mortality.[1] Responsibility for this decline is often claimed by, or ascribed to, the present-day major beneficiaries of this prevailing explanation. But both in terms of the history of knowledge and on the basis of data presented in this paper, one can reasonably wonder whether the supposedly more sophisticated explanations proffered in our own time (while seemingly distinguishable from those accepted in the past) are really all that different from those of other cultures and earlier times, or any

This paper reports part of a larger research project supported by a grant from the Milbank Memorial Fund (to Boston University) and the Carnegie Foundation (to the Radcliffe Institute). The authors would like to thank John Stoeckle, M.D. (Massachusetts General Hospital) and Louis Weinstein, M.D. (Peter Bent Brigham Hospital) for helpful discussions during earlier stages of the research.

more reliable. Is medicine, the physician, or the medical profession any more entitled to claim responsibility for the decline in mortality that obviously has occurred in this century than, say, some folk hero or aristocracy of priests sometime in the past?

AIMS

Our general intention in this paper is to sustain the ongoing debate on the questionable contribution of specific medical measures and/or the expansion of medical services to the observable decline in mortality in the twentieth century. More specifically, the following three tasks are addressed: (a) selected studies are reviewed which illustrate that, far from being idiosyncratic and/or heretical, the issue addressed in this paper has a long history, is the subject of considerable attention elsewhere, attracts able minds from a variety of disciplines, and remains a timely issue for concern and research; (b) age- and sex-adjusted mortality rates (standardized to the population of 1900) for the United States, 1900–1973, are presented and then considered in relation to a number of specific and supposedly effective medical interventions (both chemotherapeutic and prophylactic). So far as we know, this is the first time such data have been employed for this particular purpose in the United States, although reference will be made to a similar study for England and Wales; and (c) some policy implications are outlined.

BACKGROUND TO THE ISSUE

The beginning of the serious debate on the questionable contribution of medical measures is commonly associated with the appearance, in Britain, of Talbot Griffith's (1967) *Population Problems in the Age of Malthus*. After examining certain medical activities associated with the eighteenth century—particularly the growth of hospital, dispensary, and midwifery services, additions to knowledge of physiology and anatomy, and the introduction of smallpox inoculation—Griffith concluded that they made important contributions to the observable decline in mortality at that time. Since then, in Britain and more recently in the United States, this debate has continued, regularly engaging scholars from economic history, demography, epidemiology, statistics, and other disciplines. Habakkuk (1953), an economic historian, was probably the first to seriously challenge the prevailing view that the modern increase in population was due to a fall in the death rate attributable to medical interventions. His view was that this rise in population resulted from an increase in the birth rate, which, in turn, was associated with social, economic, and industrial changes in the eighteenth century.

McKeown, without doubt, has pursued the argument more consistently and with greater effect than any other researcher, and the reader is referred to his recent work for more detailed background information. Employing the data and techniques of historical demography, McKeown (a physician by training) has provided a detailed and convincing analysis of the major reasons for the decline of mortality in England and Wales during the eighteenth, nineteenth, and twentieth centuries (McKeown et al., 1955, 1962, 1975). For the eighteenth century, he concludes that the decline was largely attributable to improvements in the environment. His findings for the nineteenth century are summarized as follows:

> . . . the decline of mortality in the second half of the nineteenth century was due wholly to a reduction of deaths from infectious diseases; there was no evidence of a decline in other causes of death. Examination of the diseases which contributed to the decline suggested that the main influences were: (a) rising standards of living, of which the most significant feature was a better diet; (b) improvements in hygiene; and (c) a favorable trend in the relationship between some micro-organisms and the human host. *Therapy made no contributions, and the effect of immunization was restricted to smallpox which accounted for only about one-twentieth of the reduction of the death rate.* (Emphasis added, McKeown et al., 1975, p. 391)

While McKeown's interpretation is based on the experience of England and Wales, he has examined its credibility in the light of the very different circumstances which existed in four other European countries: Sweden, France, Ireland, and Hungary (McKeown et al., 1972). His interpretation appears to withstand this cross-examination. As for the twentieth century (1901–1971 is the period actually considered), McKeown argues that about three-quarters of the decline was associated with control of infectious diseases and the remainder with conditions not attributable to microorganisms. He distinguishes the infections according to their modes of transmission (air-, water- or food-borne) and isolates three types of influences which figure during the period considered: medical measures (specific therapies and immunization), reduced exposure to infection, and improved nutrition. His conclusion is that:

> The main influences on the decline in mortality were improved nutrition on air-borne infections, reduced exposure (from better hygiene) on water- and food-borne diseases and, less certainly, immunization and therapy on the large number of conditions included in the miscellaneous group. Since these three classes were responsible respectively for nearly half, one-sixth, and one-tenth of the fall in the death rate, it is probable that the advancement in nutrition was the major influence. (McKeown et al., 1975, p. 422).

More than twenty years of research by McKeown and his colleagues recently culminated in two books—*The Modern Rise of Population* (1976a) and *The Role of Medicine: Dream, Mirage or Nemesis* (1976b)—in which he draws together his many excellent contributions. That the thesis he advances remains highly newsworthy is evidenced by recent editorial reaction in *The Times* of London (1977).

No one in the United States has pursued this thesis with the rigor and consistency which characterize the work by McKeown and his colleagues in Britain. Around 1930, there were several limited discussions of the questionable effect of medical measures on selected infectious diseases like diphtheria (Lee, 1931; Wilson & Miles, 1946; Bolduan, 1930) and pneumonia (Pfizer and Co., 1953). In a presidential address to the American Association of Immunologists in 1954 (frequently referred to by McKeown), Magill (1955) marshalled an assortment of data then available—some from England and Wales—to cast doubt on the plausibility of existing accounts of the decline in mortality for several conditions. Probably the most influential work in the United States is that of Dubos who, principally in *Mirage of Health* (1959), *Man Adapting* (1965), and *Man, Medicine and Environment* (1968), focused on the nonmedical reasons for changes in the health of overall populations. In another presidential address, this time to the Infectious Diseases Society of America, Kass (1971), again employing data from England and Wales, argued that most of the decline in mortality for most infectious conditions occurred prior to the discovery of either "the cause" of the disease or some purported "treatment" for it. Before the same society and largely on the basis of clinical experience with infectious diseases and data from a single state (Massachusetts), Weinstein (1974), while conceding there are some effective treatments which seem to yield a favorable outcome (e.g., for poliomyelitis, tuberculosis, and possibly smallpox), argued that despite the presence of supposedly effective treatments some conditions may have increased (e.g., subacute bacterial endocarditis, streptococcal pharyngitis, pneumococcal pneumonia, gonorrhea, and syphilis) and also that mortality for yet other conditions shows improvement in the absence of any treatment (e.g., chickenpox). With the appearance of his book, *Who Shall Live?* (1974), Fuchs, a health economist, contributed to the resurgence of interest in the relative contribution of medical care to the modern decline in mortality in the United States. He believes there has been an unprecedented improvement in health in the United States since about the middle of the eighteenth century, associated primarily with a rise in real income. While agreeing with much of Fuchs' thesis, we will present evidence which seriously questions his belief that "beginning in the mid '30s, major therapeutic discoveries made significant contributions independently of the rise in real income."

Although neither representative nor exhaustive, this brief and selective background should serve to introduce the analysis which follows. Our intention is to highlight the following: (a) the debate over the questionable contribution of medical measures to the modern decline of mortality has a long history and remains topical; (b) although sometimes popularly associated with dilettantes such as Ivan Illich (1976), the debate continues to preoccupy able scholars from a variety of disciplines and remains a matter of concern to the most learned societies; (c) although of emerging interest in the United States, the issue is already a matter of concern and considerable research elsewhere; (d) to the extent that the subject has been pursued in the United States, there has been a restrictive tendency to focus on a few selected diseases, or to employ only statewide data, or to apply evidence from England and Wales directly to the United States situation.

HOW RELIABLE ARE MORTALITY STATISTICS?

We have argued elsewhere that mortality statistics are inadequate and can be misleading as indicators of a nation's overall health status (McKinlay and McKinlay, forthcoming). Unfortunately, these are the only types of data which are readily accessible for the examination of time trends, simply because comparable morbidity and disability data have not been available. Apart from this overriding problem, several additional caveats in the use of mortality statistics are: (a) difficulties introduced by changes in the registration area in the United States in the early twentieth century; (b) that often no single disease, but a complex of conditions, may be responsible for death (Krueger, 1966); (c) that studies reveal considerable inaccuracies in recording the cause of death (Moriyama et al., 1958); (d) that there are changes over time in what it is fashionable to diagnose (for example, ischaemic heart disease and cerebrovascular disease); (e) that changes in disease classifications (Dunn and Shackley, 1945) make it difficult to compare some conditions over time and between countries (Reid and Rose, 1964); (f) that some conditions result in immediate death while others have an extended period of latency; and (g) that many conditions are severely debilitating and consume vast medical resources but are now generally non-fatal (e.g., arthritis and diabetes). Other obvious limitations could be added to this list.

However, it would be foolhardy indeed to dismiss all studies based on mortality measures simply because they are possibly beset *with known limitations.* Such data are preferable to those the limitations of which are either unknown or, if known, cannot be estimated. Because of an over-awareness of potential inaccuracies, there is a timorous tendency to disregard or devalue studies based on mortality evidence, even though there are innumerable examples of their fruitful use as a basis for planning and informed social action (Alderson, 1976). Sir Austin Bradford Hill (1955) considers one of the most important features of Snow's work on cholera to be his adept use of mortality statistics. A more recent notable example is the study by Inman and Adelstein (1969) of the circumstantial link between the excessive absorption of bronchodilators from pressurized aerosols and the epidemic rise in asthma mortality in children aged ten to fourteen years. Moreover, there is evidence that some of the known inaccuracies of mortality data tend to cancel each other out.[2] Consequently, while mortality statistics may be unreliable for use in individual cases, when pooled for a country and employed in population studies, they can reveal important trends and generate fruitful hypotheses. They have already resulted in informed social action (for example, the use of geographical distributions of mortality in the field of environmental pollution).

Whatever limitations and risks may be associated with the use of mortality statistics, they obviously apply equally to all studies which employ them—both those which attribute the decline in mortality to medical measures and those which argue the converse, or something else entirely. And, if such data constitute acceptable evidence in support of the presence of medicine, then it is not unreasonable, or illogical, to employ them in support of some opposing position. One difficulty is that, depending on the nature of the results, double standards of rigor seem to operate in the evaluation of different studies. Not surprisingly, those which challenge prevailing myths or beliefs are subject to the most stringent methodological and statistical scrutiny, while supportive studies, which frequently employ the flimsiest impressionistic data and inappropriate techniques of analysis, receive general and uncritical acceptance. Even if all possible "ideal" data were available (which they never will be) and if, after appropriate analysis, they happened to support the viewpoint of this paper, we are doubtful that medicine's protagonists would find our thesis any more acceptable.

THE MODERN DECLINE IN MORTALITY

Despite the fact that mortality rates for certain conditions, for selected age and sex categories, continue to fluctuate, or even increase (U.S.

Dept. HEW, 1964; Moriyama and Gustavus, 1972; Lilienfeld, 1976), there can be little doubt that a marked decline in overall mortality for the United States has occurred since about 1900 (the earliest point for which reliable national data are available).

Just how dramatic this decline has been in the United States is illustrated in Fig. 1-1 which shows age-adjusted mortality rates for males and females separately.[3] Both sexes experienced a marked decline in mortality since 1900. The female decline began to level off by about 1950, while 1960 witnessed the beginning of a slight increase for males. Figure 1-1 also reveals a slight but increasing divergence between male and female mortality since about 1920.

Figure 1-2 depicts the decline in the overall age- and sex-adjusted rate since the beginning of this century. Between 1900 and 1973, there was a 69.2 percent decrease in overall mortality. The average annual rate of decline from 1900 until 1950 was .22 per 1,000, after which it became an almost negligible decline of .04 per 1,000 annually. Of the total fall in the standardized death rate between 1900 and 1973, 92.3 percent occurred prior to 1950. Figure 1-2 also plots the decline in the standardized death rate *after* the total number of deaths in each age and sex category has been reduced by the number of deaths attributed to the eleven major infectious conditions (typhoid, smallpox, scarlet fever, measles, whooping cough, diphtheria, influenza, tuberculosis, pneumonia, diseases of the digestive system, and poliomyelitis). It should be noted that, although this latter rate also shows a decline (at least until 1960), its slope is much more shallow than that for the overall standardized death rate. A major part of the decline in deaths from these causes since about 1900 may be attributed to the virtual disappearance of these infectious diseases.

An absurdity is reflected in the third broken line in Fig. 1-2 which also plots the increase in the proportion of Gross National Product expended annually for medical care. *It is evident that the beginning of the precipitate and still unrestrained rise in medical care expenditures began when nearly all (92 percent) of the modern decline in mortality this century had already occurred.*[4]

Figure 1-3 illustrates how the proportion of deaths contributed by the infectious and chronic conditions has changed in the United States since the beginning of the twentieth century. In

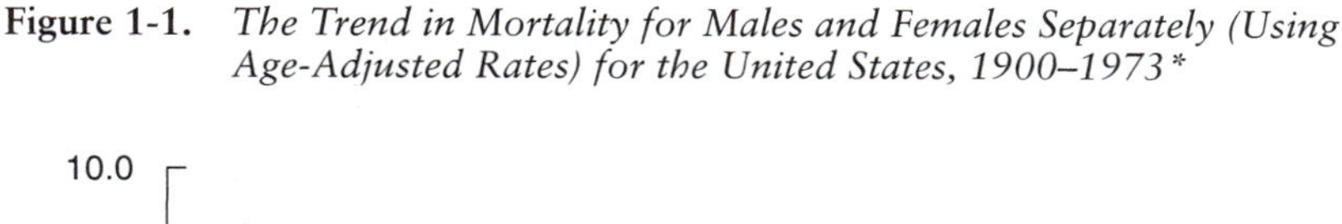

Figure 1-1. *The Trend in Mortality for Males and Females Separately (Using Age-Adjusted Rates) for the United States, 1900–1973**

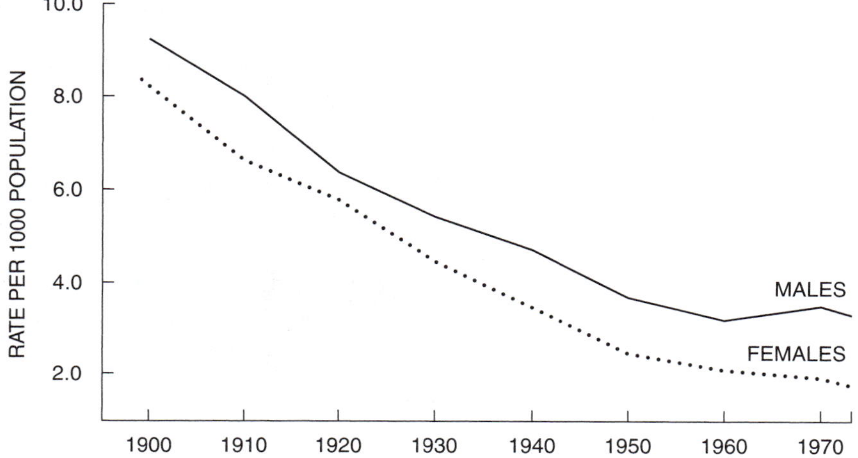

* For these and all other age- and sex-adjusted rates in this paper, the standard population is that of 1900.

Figure 1-2. *Age- and Sex-Adjusted Mortality Rates for the United States, 1900–1973, Including and Excluding Eleven Major Infectious Diseases, Contrasted with the Proportion of the Gross National Product Expended on Medical Care*

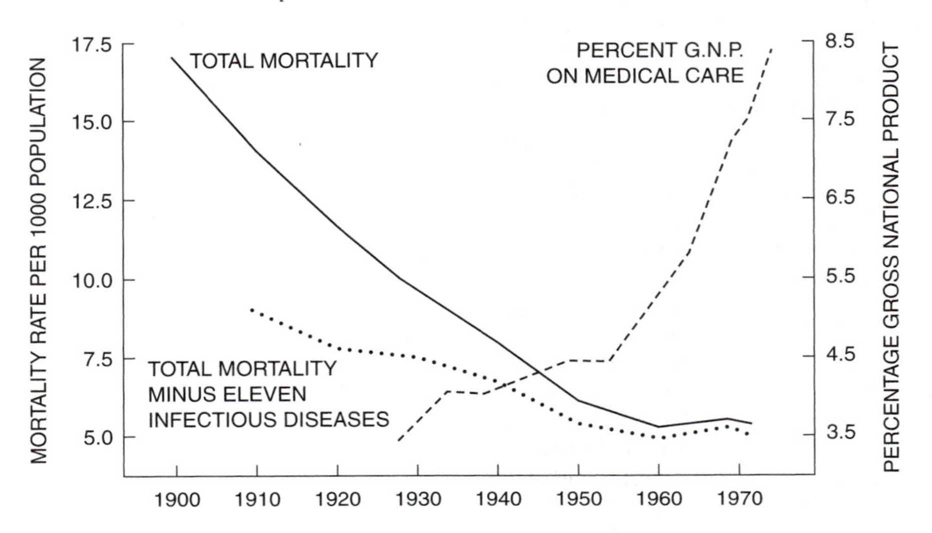

Figure 1-3. *Pictorial Representation of the Changing Contribution of Chronic and Infectious Conditions to Total Mortality (Age- and Sex-Adjusted) in the United States, 1900–1973*

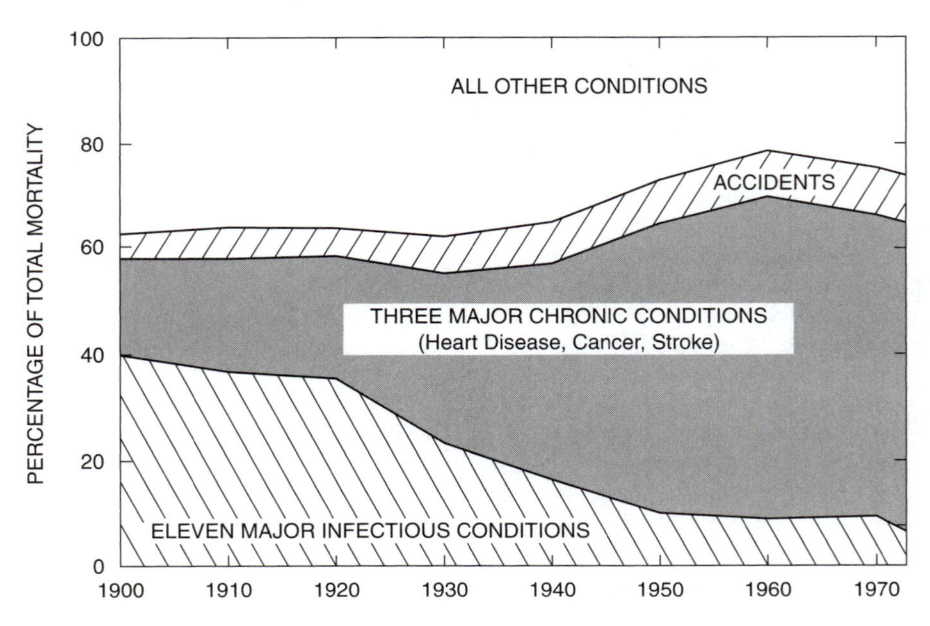

1900, about 40 percent of all deaths were accounted for by eleven major infectious diseases, 16 percent by three chronic conditions 4 percent by accidents, and the remainder (37 percent) by all other causes. By 1973, only 6 percent of all deaths were due to these eleven infectious diseases, 58 percent to the same three chronic conditions, 9 percent to accidents, and 27 percent were contributed by other causes.[5]

Now to what phenomenon, or combination of events, can we attribute this modern decline in overall mortality? Who (if anyone), or what group, can claim to have been instrumental in effecting this reduction? Can anything be gleaned from an analysis of mortality experience to date that will inform health care policy for the future?

It should be reiterated that a major concern of this paper is to determine the effect, if any, of specific medical measures (both chemotherapeutic and prophylactic) on the decline of mortality. It is clear from Figs. 1-2 and 1-3 that most of the observable decline is due to the rapid disappearance of some of the major infectious diseases. Since this is where most of the decline has occurred, it is logical to focus a study of the effect of medical measures on this category of conditions. Moreover, for these eleven conditions, there exist clearly identifiable medical interventions to which the decline in mortality has been popularly ascribed. No analogous interventions exist for the major chronic diseases such as heart disease, cancer, and stroke. Therefore, even where a decline in mortality from these chronic conditions may have occurred, this cannot be ascribed to any specific measure.

THE EFFECT OF MEDICAL MEASURES ON TEN INFECTIOUS DISEASES WHICH HAVE DECLINED

Table 1-1 summarizes data on the effect of major medical interventions (both chemotherapeutic and prophylactic) on the decline in the age- and sex-adjusted death rates in the United States, 1900–1973, for ten of the eleven major infectious diseases listed above. Together, these diseases accounted for approximately 30 percent of all deaths at the turn of the century and nearly 40 percent of the total decline in the mortality rate since then. The ten diseases were selected on the following criteria: (a) some decline in the death rate had occurred in the period 1900–1973; (b) significant decline in the death rate is commonly attributed to some specific medical measure for the disease; and (c) adequate data for the disease over the period 1900–1973 are available. The diseases of the digestive system were omitted primarily because of lack of clarity in diagnosis of specific diseases such as gastritis and enteritis.

Some additional points of explanation should be noted in relation to Table 1-1. First, the year of medical intervention coincides (as nearly as can be determined) with the first year of widespread or commercial use of the appropriate drug or vaccine.[6] This date does *not* necessarily coincide with the date the measure was either first discovered, or subject to clinical trial. Second, the decline in the death rate for smallpox was calculated using the death rate for 1902 as being the earliest year for which this statistic is readily available (U.S. Bureau of the Census, 1906). For the same reasons, the decline in the death rate from poliomyelitis was calculated from 1910. Third, the table shows the contribution of the decline in each disease to the total decline in mortality over the period 1900–1973 (column b). The overall decline during this period was 12.14 per 1,000 population (17.54 in 1900 to 5.39 in 1973). Fourth, in order to place the experience for each disease in some perspective, Table 1-1 also shows the contribution of the relative fall in mortality after the intervention to the overall fall in mortality since 1900 (column e). In other words, the figures in this last column represent the percentage of the total fall in mortality contributed by each disease after the date of medical intervention.

It is clear from column b that only reductions in mortality from tuberculosis and pneumonia contributed substantially to the decline in total mortality between 1900 and 1973 (16.5 and 11.7 percent, respectively). The remaining eight conditions *together* accounted for less than 12 percent of the total decline over this period. Disregarding smallpox (for which the only effective measure had been introduced about 1800), only influenza, whooping cough, and poliomyelitis show what could be considered substantial declines of 25 percent or more after the date of medical intervention. However, even under the somewhat unrealistic assumption of a constant (linear) rate of decline in the mortality rates, only whooping

Table 1-1. The Contribution of Medical Measures (Both Chemotherapeutic and Prophylactic) to the Fall in the Age- and Sex-Adjusted Death Rates (S.D.R.) of Ten Common Infectious Diseases and to the Overall Decline in the S.D.R., for the United States, 1900–1973

Disease	Fall in S.D.R. per 1,000 Population, 1900–1973 (*a*)	Fall in S.D.R. as % of the Total Fall in S.D.R. $(b) = \frac{(a)}{12.14} \times 100\%$	Year of Medical Intervention (Either Chemotherapy or Prophylaxis)	Fall in S.D.R. per 1,000 Population After Year of Intervention (*c*)	Fall in S.D.R. After Intervention as % of Total Fall for the Disease $(d) = \frac{(c)}{(a)}$	Fall in S.D.R. After Intervention as % of Total Fall in S.D.R. for All Causes $(e) = \frac{(b)(c)\%}{(a)}$
Tuberculosis	2.00	16.48	Izoniazid/ Streptomycin, 1950	0.17	8.36	1.38
Scarlet Fever	0.10	0.84	Penicillin, 1946	0.00	1.75	0.01
Influenza	0.22	1.78	Vaccine, 1943	0.05	25.33	0.45
Pneumonia	1.42	11.74	Sulphonamide, 1935	0.24	17.19	2.02
Diphtheria	0.43	3.57	Toxoid, 1930	0.06	13.49	0.48
Whooping Cough	0.12	1.00	Vaccine, 1930	0.06	51.00	0.51
Measles	0.12	1.04	Vaccine, 1963	0.00	1.38	0.01
Smallpox	0.02	0.16	Vaccine, 1800	0.02	100.00	0.16
Typhoid	0.36	2.95	Chloramphenicol, 1948	0.00	0.29	0.01
Poliomyelitis	0.03	0.23	Vaccine, Salk/ Sabin, 1955	0.01	25.87	0.06

cough and poliomyelitis even approach the percentage which would have been expected. The remaining six conditions (tuberculosis, scarlet fever, pneumonia, diphtheria, measles, and typhoid) showed negligible declines in their mortality rates subsequent to the date of medical intervention. The seemingly quite large percentages for pneumonia and diphtheria (17.2 and 13.5, respectively) must of course be viewed in the context of relatively early interventions—1935 and 1930.

In order to examine more closely the relation of mortality trends for these diseases to the medical interventions, graphs are presented for each disease in Fig. 1-4. Clearly, for tuberculosis, typhoid, measles, and scarlet fever, the medical measures considered were introduced at the point when the death rate for each of these diseases was already negligible. Any change in the rates of decline which may have occurred subsequent to the interventions could only be minute. Of the remaining five diseases (excluding smallpox with its negligible contribution), it is only for poliomyelitis that the medical measure appears to have produced any noticeable change in the trends. Given peaks in the death rate for 1930, 1950 (and possibly for 1910), a comparable peak could have been expected in 1970. Instead, the death rate dropped to the point of disappearance after 1950 and has remained negligible. The four other diseases (pneumonia, influenza, whooping cough, and diphtheria) exhibit relatively smooth mortality trends which are unaffected by the medical measures, even though these were introduced relatively early, when the death rates were still notable.

It may be useful at this point to briefly consider the common and dubious practice of projecting estimated mortality trends (Witte and Axnick, 1975). In order to show the beneficial (or even detrimental) effect of some medical measure, a line, estimated on a set of points observed prior to the introduction of the measure, is projected over the period subsequent to the point of intervention. Any resulting discrepancy between the projected line and the observed trend is then used as some kind of "evidence" of an effective or beneficial intervention. According to statistical theory on least squares estimation, an estimated line can serve as a useful predictor, but the prediction is only valid, and its error calculable, within the range of the points used to estimate the line. Moreover, those predicted values which lie at the extremes of the range are subject to much larger errors than those nearer the center. It is, therefore, probable that, even if the projected line was a reasonable estimate of the trend after the intervention (which, of course, it is not), the divergent observed trend is probably well within reasonable error limits of the estimated line (assuming the error could be calculated), as the error will be relatively large. In other words, this technique is of dubious value as no valid conclusions are possible from its application, and a relatively large prediction error cannot be estimated, which is required in order to objectively judge the extent of divergence of an observed trend.

With regard to the ten infectious diseases considered in this paper, when lines were fitted to the nine or ten points available over the entire period (1900–1973), four exhibited a reasonably good fit to a straight line (scarlet fever, measles, whooping cough, and poliomyelitis), while another four (typhoid, diphtheria, tuberculosis, and pneumonia) showed a very good quadratic fit (to a curved line). Of the remaining two diseases, smallpox showed a negligible decline, as it was already a minor cause of death in 1900 (only 0.1 percent), and influenza showed a poor fit because of the extremely high death rate in 1920. From Fig. 1-4 it is clear, however, that the rate of decline slowed in more recent years for most of the diseases considered—a trend which could be anticipated as rates approach zero.[7]

Now it is possible to argue that, given the few data points available, the fit is somewhat crude and may be insensitive to any changes subsequent to a point of intervention. However, this can be countered with the observation that, given the relatively low death rates for these diseases, any change would have to be extremely marked in order to be detected in the overall mortality experience. Certainly, from the evidence considered here, only poliomyelitis appears to have had a noticeably changed death rate subsequent to intervention. Even if it were assumed that this change was entirely due to the vaccines, then only about one percent of the decline following interventions for the diseases considered here (column d of Table 1-1) could be attributed to medical measures. Rather more conservatively, if we attribute some of the subse-

Figure 1-4. *The Fall in the Standardized Death Rate (per 1,000 Population) for Nine Common Infectious Diseases in Relation to Specific Medical Measures, for the United States, 1900–1973*

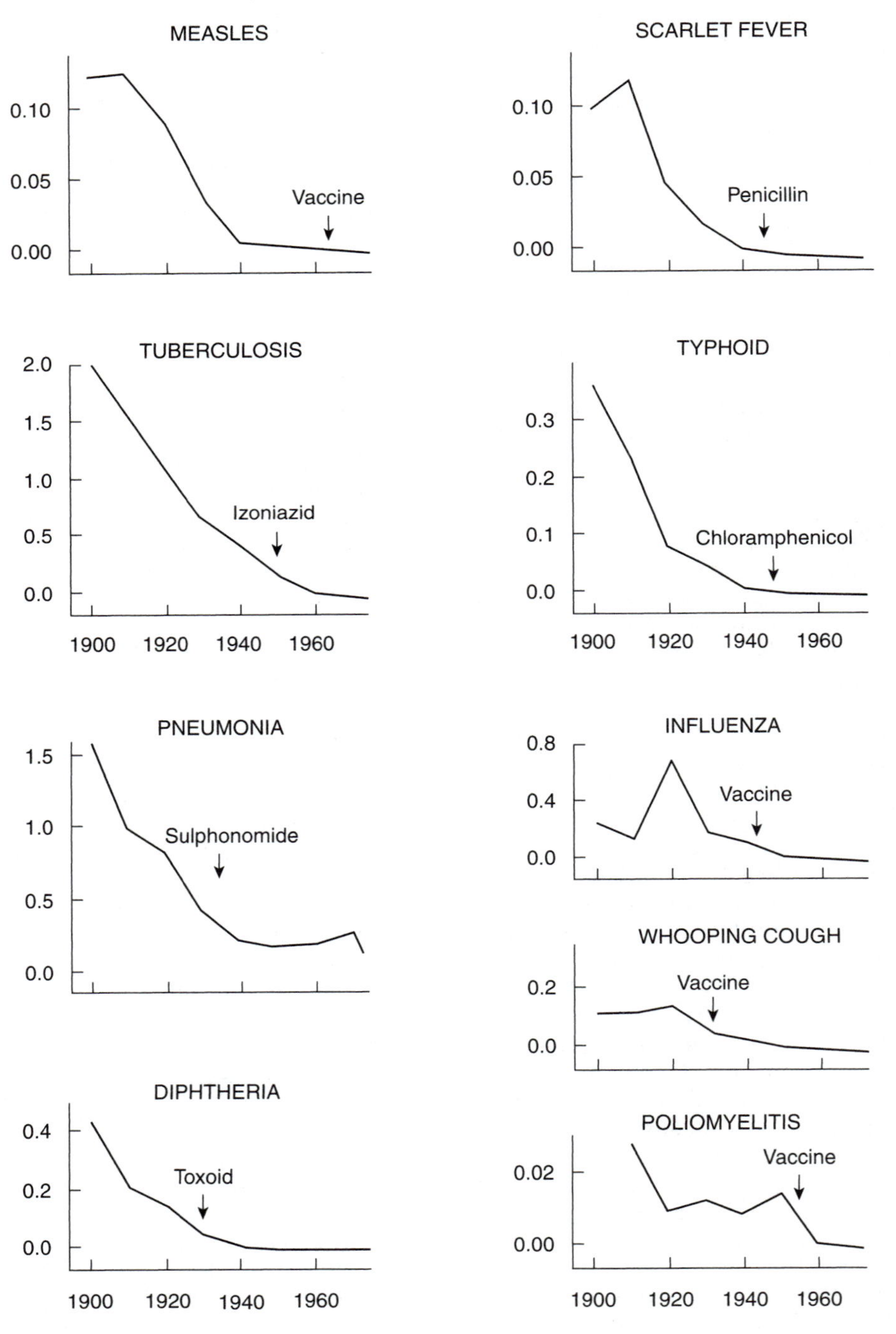

Table 1-2. Pair-wise Correlation Matrix for 44 Countries, between Four Measures of Health Status and Three Measures of Medical Case Input

Variable		Matrix of Coefficients							
1.	Infant Mortality Rate (1972)								
2.	Crude Mortality Rate (1970–1972)	−0.14							
3. (a)	Life Expectancy (Males) at 25 years	−0.14	−0.12						
3. (b)	Life Expectancy (Females) at 25 years	−0.12	0.04	0.75					
4. (a)	Life Expectancy (Males) at 55 years	−0.01	0.10	0.74	0.93				
4. (b)	Life Expectancy (Females) at 55 years	−0.13	0.01	0.75	0.98	0.95			
5.	Population per Hospital Bed (1971–1973)	0.64	−0.30	0.05	−0.02	0.17	0.0		
6.	Population per Physician (1971–1973)	0.36	−0.30	0.11	0.04	0.16	0.07	0.70	
7.	Per Capita Gross National Product: In $U.S. Equivalent (1972)	−0.66	0.26	0.16	0.18	0.07	0.22	−0.56	−0.46
	Variable (by number)	1	2	3a	3b	4a	4b	5	6

SOURCES: 1. *United Nations Demographic Yearbook: 1974,* New York, United Nations Publications, 1975. (For the Crude and Infant Mortality Rates). 2. *World Health Statistics Annual: 1972,* Vol. 1, Geneva, World Health Organization, 1975, pp. 780–783. (For the Life Expectancy Figures). 3. *United Nations Statistical Yearbook, 1973 and 1975,* New York, United Nations Publications, 25th and 27th issues, 1974 and 1976. (For the Population Bed/Physician Ratios). 4. *The World Bank Atlas,* Washington, D.C., World Bank, 1975. (For the Per Capita Gross National Product).

quent fall in the death rates for pneumonia, influenza, whooping cough, and diphtheria to medical measures, then perhaps 3.5 percent of the fall in the overall death rate can be explained through medical intervention in the major infectious diseases considered here. Indeed, given that it is precisely for these diseases that medicine claims most success in lowering mortality, 3.5 percent probably represents a reasonable upper-limit estimate of the total contribution of medical measures to the decline in mortality in the United States since 1900.

CONCLUSIONS

Without claiming they are definitive findings, and eschewing pretentions to an analysis as sophisticated as McKeown's for England and Wales, one can reasonably draw the following conclusions from the analysis presented in this paper:

In general, medical measures (both chemotherapeutic and prophylactic) appear to have contributed little to the overall decline in mortality in the United States since about 1900—having in many instances been introduced several decades after a marked decline had already set in and having no detectable influence in most instances. More specifically, with reference to those five conditions (influenza, pneumonia, diphtheria, whooping cough, and poliomyelitis) for which the decline in mortality appears substantial after the point of intervention—and on the unlikely assumption that all of this decline is attributable to the intervention—it is estimated that at most 3.5 percent of the total decline in mortality since 1900 could be ascribed to medical measures introduced for the diseases considered here.

These conclusions, in support of the thesis introduced earlier, suggest issues of the most strategic significance for researchers and health care legislators. Profound policy implications follow from either a confirmation or a rejection of the thesis. If one subscribes to the view that we are slowly but surely eliminating one disease after another because of medical interventions, then there may be little commitment to social change and even resistance to some reordering of priorities in medical expenditures. If a disease *X* is disappearing primarily because of the presence of a particular intervention or service *Y*, then clearly *Y* should be left intact, or, more preferably, be expanded. Its demonstrable contribution justifies its presence. But, if it can be shown convincingly, and on commonly accepted grounds, that the major part of the decline in mortality is unrelated to medical care activities, then some commitment to social change and a reordering of priorities may ensue. For, if the disappearance of *X* is largely unrelated to the presence of *Y*, or even occurs in the absence of *Y*, then clearly the expansion and even the continuance of *Y* can be reasonably questioned. Its demonstrable ineffectiveness justifies some reappraisal of its significance and the wisdom of expanding it in its existing form.

In this paper we have attempted to dispel the myth that medical measures and the presence of medical services were primarily responsible for the modern decline of mortality. The question now remains: if they were not primarily responsible for it, then how is it to be explained? An adequate answer to this further question would require a more substantial research effort than that reported here, but is likely to be along the lines suggested by McKeown which were referred to early in this paper. Hopefully, this paper will serve as a catalyst for such research, incorporating adequate data and appropriate methods of analysis, in an effort to arrive at a more viable alternative explanation.

NOTES

1. It is obviously important to distinguish between (a) advances in knowledge of the cause and natural course of some condition and (b) improvements in our ability to effectively treat some condition (that is, to alter its natural course). In many instances these two areas are disjoint and appear at different stages of development. There are, on the one hand, disease processes about which considerable knowledge has been accrued, yet this has not resulted (nor necessarily will) in the development of effective treatments. On the other hand, there are conditions for which demonstrably effective treatments have been devised in the absence of knowledge of the disease process and/or its causes.
2. Barker and Rose cite one study which compared the ante-mortem and autopsy diagnoses in 9,501 deaths which occurred in 75 different hospitals. Despite lack of a concurrence on *individual* cases, the *overall* frequency was very similar in diagnoses obtained on either an ante-mortem or post-mortem basis. As an example they note that clinical diagnoses of carcinoma of the rectum were confirmed at autopsy in only 67 percent of cases, but the incorrect clinical diagnoses were balanced by an almost identical number of lesions diagnosed for the first time at autopsy (Barker and Rose, 1976).
3. All age and sex adjustments were made by the "direct" method using the population of 1900 as the standard. For further information on this method of adjustment, see Hill (1971) and Shryock et al. (1971).
4. Rutstein (1967), although fervently espousing the traditional view that medical advances have been largely responsible for the decline in mortality, discussed this disjunction and termed it "The Paradox of Modern Medicine." More recently, and from a perspective that is generally consistent with that advanced here, Powles (1973) noted the same phenomenon in England and Wales.
5. Deaths in the category of chronic respiratory diseases (chronic bronchitis, asthma, emphysema, and other chronic obstructive lung diseases) could not be included in the group of chronic conditions because of insurmountable difficulties inherent in the many changes in disease classification and in the tabulation of statistics.
6. In determining the dates of intervention we relied upon: (a) standard epidemiology and public health texts; (b) the recollections of authorities in the field of infectious diseases; and (c) recent publications on the same subject.
7. For this reason, a negative exponential model is sometimes used to fit a curved line to such data. This was not presented here as the number of points available was small and the difference between a simple quadratic and negative exponential fit was not, upon investigation, able to be detected.

REFERENCES

Alderson, M. 1976. *An Introduction to Epidemiology*. London: Macmillan Press, pp. 7–27.

Barker, D.J.P., and Rose, G. 1976. *Epidemiology in Medical Practice*. London: Churchill Livingstone, p. 6.

Bolduan, C.F. 1930. *How to Protect Children From Diphtheria.* New York: N.Y.C. Health Department.

Dubos, R. 1959. *Mirage of Health.* New York: Harper and Row.

Dubos, R. 1965. *Man Adapting.* New Haven, Connecticut: Yale University Press.

Dubos, R. 1968. *Man, Medicine and Environment.* London: Pall Mall Press.

Dunn, H.L., and Shackley, W. 1945. *Comparison of cause of death assignments by the 1929 and 1938 revisions of the International List: Deaths in the United States, 1940 Vital Statistics—Special Reports* 19:153–277, 1944, Washington, D.C.: U.S. Department of Commerce, Bureau of the Census.

Fuchs, V.R. 1974. *Who Shall Live?* New York: Basic Books, p. 54.

Griffith, T. 1967. *Population Problems in the Age of Malthus.* 2nd ed. London: Frank Cass.

Habakkuk, H.J. 1953. English Population in the Eighteenth Century. *Economic History Review,* 6.

Hill, A.B. 1971. *Principles of Medical Statistics.* 9th ed. London: Oxford University Press.

Hill, A.B. 1955. Snow—An Appreciation. *Proceedings of the Royal Society of Medicine* 48:1008–1012.

Illich, I. 1976. *Medical Nemesis.* New York: Pantheon Books.

Inman, W.H.W., and Adelstein, A.M. 1969. Rise and fall of asthma mortality in England and Wales, in relation to use of pressurized aerosols. *Lancet* 2:278–285.

Kass, E.H. 1971. Infectious diseases and social change. *The Journal of Infectious Diseases,* 123(1): 110–114.

Krueger, D.E. 1966. New enumerators for old denominators—multiple causes of death. In *Epidemiologial Approaches to the Study of Cancer and Other Chronic Diseases,* edited by W. Haenszel. National Cancer Printing Office, pp. 431–443.

Lee, W.W. 1931. Diphtheria immunization in Philadelphia and New York City. *Journal of Preventive Medicine* (Baltimore) 5:211–220.

Lilienfeld, A.M. 1976. *Foundations of Epidemiology.* New York: Oxford University Press. pp. 51–111.

McKeown, T. 1976a. *The Modern Rise of Population.* London: Edward Arnold.

McKeown, T. 1976b. *The Role of Medicine: Dream, Mirage or Nemesis.* London: Nuffield Provincial Hospitals Trust.

McKeown, T.; Brown, R.G.; and Record, R.G. 1972. An interpretation of the modern rise of population in Europe. *Population Studies* 26:345–382.

McKeown, T., and Record, R.G. 1955. Medical evidence related to English population changes in the eighteenth century. *Population Studies* 9:119–141.

McKeown, T., and Record, R.G. 1962. Reasons for the decline in mortality in England and Wales during the nineteenth century. *Population Studies* 16:94–122.

McKeown, T.; Record, R.G.; and Turner, R.D. 1975. An interpretation of the decline of mortality in England and Wales during the twentieth century. *Population Studies* 29:391–422.

McKinlay, J.B., and McKinlay, S.M. *A refutation of the thesis that the health of the nation is improving.* Forthcoming.

Magill, T.P. 1955. The immunologist and the evil spirits. *Journal of Immunology* 74:1–8.

Moriyama, I.M.; Baum, W.S.; Haenszel, W.M.; and Mattison, B.F. 1958. Inquiry into diagnostic evidence supporting medical certifications of death. *American Journal of Public Health* 48:1376–1387.

Moriyama, I.M., and Gustavus, S.O. 1972. *Cohort Mortality and Survivorship: United States Death—Registration States, 1900–1968.* National Center for Health Statistics, Series 3, No. 16. Washington, D.C.: U.S. Government Printing Office.

Pfizer, C., and Company. 1953. *The Pneumonias, Management with Antibiotic Therapy.* Brooklyn.

Powles, J. 1973. On the limitations of modern medicine. *Science, Medicine and Man.* 1:2–3.

Reid, O.D., and Rose, G.A. 1964. Assessing the comparability of mortality statistics. *British Medical Journal* 2:1437–1439.

Rutstein, D. 1967. *The Coming Revolution in Medicine.* Cambridge, Massachusetts: MIT Press.

Shryock, H., et al. 1971. *The Methods and Materials of Demography.* Washington, D.C.: U.S. Government Printing Office.

The Times (London). 1977. The Doctors Dilemma: How to Cure Society of a Life Style That Makes People Sick. Friday, January 21.

U.S. Bureau of the Census. 1906. *Mortality Statistics 1900–1904.* Washington, D.C.: Government Printing Office.

U.S. Department of Health, Education and Welfare. 1964. *The Change in Mortality Trend in the United States.* National Center for Health Statistics, Series 3, No. 1. Washington, D.C.: U.S. Government Printing Office.

Weinstein, L. 1974. Infectious Disease: Retrospect and Reminiscence. *The Journal of Infectious Diseases.* 129 (4):480–492.

Wilson, G.S., and Miles, A.A. 1946. In Topley and Wilson's *Principles of Bacteriology and Immunity.* Baltimore: Williams and Wilkins.

Witte, J.J., and Axnick, N.W. 1975. The benefits from ten years of measles immunization in the United States. *Public Health Reports* 90 (3):205–207.

Who Gets Sick? The Unequal Social Distribution of Disease

Disease is not distributed evenly throughout the population. Certain groups of people get sick more often, and some populations die prematurely at higher rates than others. The study of what groups of people get sick with what disease is called *epidemiology* and has been defined by one expert as "the study of the distributions and determinants of states of health in human populations" (Susser, 1973: 1). By studying populations rather than individuals, epidemiologists seek to identify characteristics of groups of people or their environments that make them more or less vulnerable to disease (*morbidity*) or death (*mortality*).

A growing body of research has found significant associations between a range of social and cultural factors and the risk for disease and death. The term *social epidemiology* has been adopted by some researchers to emphasize the importance of social variables in the patterning of disease. By focusing on the connections between social processes and the risk for disease, the study of social epidemiology provides the social scientist with an important opportunity to understand more fully the relationship between society and the individual. Among the historical predecessors of today's social epidemiology was the emergence in the nineteenth century of "social medicine" with a number of important studies in Western Europe. In England, Edwin Chadwick studied the death rates of populations and identified relationships between disease and social problems—most notably poverty—thus laying an important foundation for the developing Public Health Movement (Chadwick, 1842). Another early investigator in social medicine was Rudolf Virchow, who was asked by the Prussian government to study the causes of a terrible typhus epidemic. His pioneering research identified connections between disease and a number of social factors, including the economy, conditions of work, and the organization of agriculture (Virchow, 1868, 1879, in Waitzkin, 1978).

The readings in this section examine selected associations between the distribution of disease and social variables, including social class, race, gender, and lifestyle. These studies highlight the relevance of a social epidemiological perspective and point to several promising directions for future research.

In the United States, one of the most striking and consistent patterns in the distribution of disease is its relationship to poverty. By and large, death and disease rates vary inversely with social class; that is, the poorer the population, the higher the risk for sickness and death (Najman, 1993). While it has been known for well over a century that poor people suffer from more disease than others, just how poverty influences health is not yet well understood. And the situation is not getting better. Despite an overall decline in death rates in the United States, the poor are still dying at higher rates than those with higher incomes, and the disparity between socioeconomic groups has actually increased (Pappas, Queen, Hadden, and Fisher, 1993). Some have suggested that the unequal distribution of income in a society, rather than only poverty, has a negative impact on health (Wilkinson, 1994). Other recent evidence notes that there is a continuous impact of social class on health (Adler, Boyce, Chesney, et al., 1994); that is, the health effects of socioeconomic status extend to all classes along a gradient from the lower to higher classes, although with more negative impacts in the lower classes. While the research is becoming more sophisticated and subtle, the evidence of the impact of social class on health remains stronger than ever (Robert and House, 2000). In "Social Class, Susceptibility, and Sickness," S. Leonard Syme and Lisa F. Berkman explore the relationship between social class and sickness, reviewing the evidence of the influence of stress, living conditions, nutrition, and medical services on the patterns of death and disease among the poor. They focus on how the living conditions of the lower class may compromise "disease defense systems" and engender greater vulnerability to disease.

In American society, race and class are highly associated in that a disproportionate number of African Americans and other minorities are living in poverty. In general, African Americans have higher morbidity and mortality rates than do whites and a shorter life expectancy (71.7 compared with 77.4 in 2002). Although the infant mortality (death before the age of one) rate in the U.S. has declined dramatically in this century, it remains twice as high among African Americans than whites. *The Report of the Secretary's Task Force on Black and Minority Health* stated that minorities had 60,000 "excess" deaths annually (U.S. Department of Health and Human Services, 1986). There is some evidence that middle-class African Americans and whites have rather similar mortality rates (Schoendorf et al., 1992), but that blacks living in poverty have much worse health outcomes. In "Excess Mortality in Harlem," Colin McCord and Harold P. Freeman show how the intertwining of race and social class can have a devastating impact on health. Harlem, an area of New York City, is 96% black with 40% of its residents living below the poverty line. The mortality rate in Harlem, adjusted for age, was the highest in New York City—more than double that of whites and 50% higher than the national average among African Americans. Although Harlem is located in the midst of a modern, sophisticated, and wealthy city, the death rates for its inhabitants between the ages of 5 and 65 were worse than their peers' in Bangladesh, one of the poorest countries in the world. The logical conclusion to be drawn from this fact is that social conditions and the state of health of the population in certain impoverished inner-city areas engender health outcomes equivalent to those encountered in the third world.

Another interesting and consistent pattern is the difference between the distribution of disease and death in men and women. Women have higher illness rates than men, while men have higher death rates. (Such comparisons rely on "age-adjusted" samples in order to eliminate the effects of age on gender differences.) There is a great deal of disagreement about the explanation for these patterns, including debates over whether women actually do get sick more often than men or whether they are more likely to report symptoms or seek medical care (e.g., Muller, 1991; Waldron, 2000; Gove and Hughes, 1979). The growing feminist scholarship on women's health and the more recent epidemiological interest in studying patterns of physical disease in female populations have begun to clarify the debate. It now appears that women *do* in fact have higher rates of sickness than men *and* that they are more likely than men to report symptoms and use medical services (Wingard, 1982).

Ingrid Waldron re-examines these findings in "Gender Differences in Mortality: Causes and Variation in Different Societies." It has long been recognized that in American society women live longer than men; currently, women live just over five years longer than men. But in countries like Russia, the difference is 13 years, while in Pakistan it's less than one. Waldron shows how the different social and cultural situations for women and men in different societies affect life expectancy and mortality. For example, it is well known that men's greater propensity to risky behaviors (e.g., smoking, drinking, occupational hazards) affect male longevity; it is also true that changing women's and men's behaviors narrowed the gap of life expectancy in developed countries (cf. Trovoto and Lalu, 2001). Waldron's article raises the question of how changes in gender roles will continue to affect the ratio of male to female deaths. But the question is not only how long people live, but how healthy their life expectancies will be (Crimmins and Saito, 2001).

It is important to note that *intergender* differences (that is, differences between male and female populations) may mask significant *intragender* patterns (that is, patterns among men or among women). In fact, there is evidence that the distribution of disease and death within male and female populations is patterned by other social factors, and importantly, that these patterns differ for men and women. Social class, race, age, marital status, presence and number of children in the home, and employment outside the home have all been found to be associated with rates of disease within male and female populations, accounting for at least some of the differences between the sexes (e.g., Bird and Rieker, 2000; Waldron, 2000).

In the fascinating selection "A Tale of Two States," Victor R. Fuchs compares the health of the populations of two neighboring states in the 1960s: Nevada and Utah. While similar in many ways, these populations have very different patterns of death. Fuchs argues that the explanation for this difference is to be found in the lifestyles of each of the populations and that these lifestyle differences are the result of the cultural environments, values, and norms of each of the populations.

Victor Rodwin and Melanie J. Corce-Galis examine similar data nearly three decades later in "Population Health in Utah and Nevada: An Update of Victor Fuchs' Tale of Two States" and find remarkably similar results. They conclude that Utah's distinctive social characteristics, including community and family stability, a relatively homogeneous population, and fewer risky health behaviors, are among the social factors that make its residents healthier.

The findings of these authors and the developing social epidemiology to which they contribute challenge the traditional medical model by seeing social factors as part of the process of disease production. While not dismissing the possibility that some biological processes contribute to the risk for disease among some groups, the bulk of the evidence supports a view that much of the epidemiological significance of race, gender, and age results from the social and cultural consequences of being, for example, a black, a woman, or an elderly person.

The importance of social processes in disease production is also supported by the consistent findings of the significance of social networks such as community and family ties and stress. Included in the definition of *stress* are the chronic stresses of jobs, family obligations, and economic pressures, and the stress produced by the relatively rare "stressful life events" (Dohrenwend and Dohrenwend, 1981; Kessler and Workman, 1989). These stressful events are the more dramatic and unusual occurrences, such as divorce, job loss, or the birth of a child, that produce major changes in people's lives. These researchers have found a consistent connection between these events and the individual's vulnerability to disease. Social networks and stress have been found to be associated with the development of physical diseases (e.g., coronary heart disease, hypertension) as well as psychological disorders (e.g., depression) (see for example, Berkman et al., 2000; Dohrenwend and Dohrenwend, 1981).

Clearly, there is a need for a new and broader conceptualization of disease production than the traditional medical model can provide. Attention must shift from the individual to the social and physical environments in which people live and work. The development of an adequate model of disease production must draw on the conceptual and research contributions of several disciplines not only to identify the social production of diseases, but to elaborate this process and provide important information on which to base effective primary intervention and prevention strategies.

REFERENCES

Adler, Nancy E., Thomas Boyce, Margaret A. Chesney, Sheldon Cohen, Susan Folkman, Robert L. Kahn, and Leonard Syme. 1994. "Socioeconomic status and health: The challenge of the gradient." American Psychologist. 49:15–24.

Berkman, Lisa F., Thomas Glass, Ian Brissette, Theresa E. Seeman. 2000. "From Social Integration to Health: Durkheim In the New Millenium." Social Science and Medicine. 51:843–857.

Bird, Chloe E., and Patricia P. Rieker. 2000. "Sociological explanations of gender differences in mental and physical health." Pp. 98–113 in Chloe E. Bird, Peter Conrad, and Allen M. Fremont (eds.), Handbook of Medical Sociology, Fifth edition. Upper Saddle River, N.J.: Prentice-Hall.

Chadwick, Edwin. 1842. Report on the Sanitary Condition of the Labouring Population of Great Britain. Reprinted 1965. Edinburgh: Edinburgh University Press.

Crimmins, Eileen M. and Yasuhiko Saito. 2001. "Trends in healthy life expectancy in the United States, 1970–1990: Gender, racial and educational differences." Social Science and Medicine 52: 1629–41.

Dohrenwend, Barbara S., and Bruce P. Dohrenwend, eds. 1981. Stressful Life Events and Their Contexts. New York: Prodist.

Gove, Walter, and Michael Hughes. 1979. "Possible causes of the apparent sex differences in physical health: An empirical investigation." American Sociological Review. 44:126–146.

Kessler, Ronald C., and Camille B. Workman. 1989. "Social and psychological factors in health and illness." Pp. 69–86 in Howard Freeman and Sol Levine (eds.), Handbook of Medical Sociology. Englewood Cliffs, N.J.: Prentice-Hall.

Muller, Charlotte. 1991. Health Care and Gender. New York: Russell Sage.

Najman, Jake M. 1993. "Health and poverty: Past, present and prospects for the future." Social Science and Medicine. 36:157–166.

Pappas, Gregory, Susan Queen, Wilbur Hadden, and Gail Fisher. 1993. "The increasing disparity in mortality between socioeconomic groups in the United States, 1960 and 1986." New England Journal of Medicine. 329:103–09.

Robert, Stephanie A. and James S. House. 2000. "Socioeconomic Inequalities in health: An enduring sociological problem." Pp. 79–97 in Chloe E. Bird, Peter Conrad, and Allen M. Fremont (eds.), Handbook of Medical Sociology, Fifth edition. Upper Saddle River, N.J.: Prentice-Hall.

Schoendorf, Kenneth C., Carol J.R. Hogue, Joel Kleinman, and Diane Rowley. 1992. "Mortality among infants of black as compared with white college-educated parents." New England Journal of Medicine. 326:1522–1526.

Trovato, Frank and N. M. Lalu. 2001. "Narrowing sex differences in life expectancy: Regional variations, 1971–1991." Canadian Studies in Population. 28:89–110.

United States Department of Health and Human Services. 1986. Report of the Secretary's Task Force on Black and Minority Health. Washington, D.C.: U.S. Government Printing Office.

Virchow, Rudolf. 1958. Disease, Life and Man. Tr. Lelland J. Rather. Stanford: Stanford University Press.

Waitzkin, Howard. 1978. "A Marxist view of medical care." Annals of Internal Medicine. 89:264–278.

Waldron, Ingrid. 2000. "Trends in gender differences in mortality: Relationships to changing gender differences in behavior and other causal factors." In E. Annandale and K. Hunt (eds). Gender Inequalities in Health. Buckingham: Open University Press.

Wilkinson, Richard G. 1994. "The epidemiological transition: From material scarcity to social disadvantage." Daedalus. 123:61–78.

2 SOCIAL CLASS, SUSCEPTIBILITY, AND SICKNESS

S. Leonard Syme and Lisa F. Berkman

Social class gradients of mortality and life expectancy have been observed for centuries, and a vast body of evidence has shown consistently that those in the lower classes have higher mortality, morbidity, and disability rates. While these patterns have been observed repeatedly, the explanations offered to account for them show no such consistency. The most frequent explanations have included poor housing, crowding, racial factors, low income, poor education and unemployment, all of which have been said to result in such outcomes as poor nutrition, poor medical care (either through non-availability or non-utilization of resources), strenuous conditions of employment in non-hygienic settings, and increased exposure to noxious agents. While these explanations account for some of the observed relationships, we have found them inadequate to explain the very large number of diseases associated with socioeconomic status. It seemed useful, therefore, to reexamine these associations in search of a more satisfactory hypothesis.

Obviously, this is an important issue. It is clear that new approaches must be explored emphasizing the primary prevention of disease in addition to those approaches that merely focus on treatment of the sick (1). It is clear also that such preventive approaches must involve community and environmental interventions rather than one-to-one preventive encounters (2). Therefore, we must understand more precisely those features of the environment that are etiologically related to disease so that interventions at this level can be more intelligently planned.

Of all the disease outcomes considered, it is evident that low socioeconomic status is most strikingly associated with high rates of infectious and parasitic diseases (3–7) as well as with higher infant mortality rates (8,9). However, in our review we found higher rates among lower class groups of a very much wider range of diseases and conditions for which obvious explanations were not as easily forthcoming. In a comprehensive review of over 30 studies, Antonovsky (10) concluded that those in the lower classes invariably have lower life expectancy and higher death rates from all causes of death, and that this higher rate has been observed since the 12th century when data on this question were first organized. While differences in infectious disease and infant mortality rates probably accounted for much of this difference between the classes in earlier years, current differences must primarily be attributable to mortality from non-infectious disease.

Kitagawa and Hauser (11) recently completed a massive nationwide study of mortality in the United States. Among men and women in the 25–64-year age group, mortality rates varied dramatically by level of education, income, and occupation, considered together or separately:

> For example . . . white males at low education levels had age-adjusted mortality rates 64 per cent higher than men in higher education categories. For white women, those in lower education groups had an age-adjusted mortality rate 105 per cent higher. For non-white males, the differential was 31 per cent and, for non-white females, it was 70 per cent. These mortality differentials also were reflected in substantial differences in life expectancy, and . . . for most specific causes of death. . . . White males in the lowest education groups have higher age-adjusted mortality rates for every cause of death for which data are available. For white females, those in the lowest education group have an excess mortality rate for all causes except cancer of the breast and motor vehicle accidents.

These gradients of mortality among the social classes have been observed over the world by many investigators (12–18) and have not changed materially since 1900 (except that non-whites, especially higher status non-whites, have experienced a relatively more favorable improvement). This consistent finding in time and space is all the more remarkable since the concept of "social class" has been defined and measured in so many different ways by these investigators. That the same findings have been obtained in spite of such methodological differences lends strength to the validity of the observations; it suggests also that the concept is an imprecise term encompassing diverse elements of varying etiologic significance.

In addition to data on mortality, higher rates of morbidity also have been observed for a vast array of conditions among those in lower class groups (19–28). This is an important observation since it indicates that excess mortality rates among lower status groups are not merely attributable to a higher case fatality death rate in those groups but are accompanied also by a higher prevalence of morbidity. Of special interest in this regard are data on the various mental illnesses, a major cause of morbidity. As shown by many investigators (29–35), those in lower as compared to higher socioeconomic groups have higher rates of schizophrenia, are more depressed, more unhappy, more worried, more anxious, and are less hopeful about the future.

In summary, persons in lower class groups have higher morbidity and mortality rates of almost every disease or illness, and these differentials have not diminished over time. While particular hypotheses may be offered to explain the gradient for one or another of these specific diseases, the fact that so many diseases exhibit the same gradient leads to speculation that a more general explanation may be more appropriate than a series of disease-specific explanations.

In a study reported elsewhere (36), it was noted that although blacks had higher rates of hypertension than whites, blacks in the lower classes had higher rates of hypertension than blacks in the upper classes. An identical social class gradient for hypertension was noted among whites in the sample. In that report, it was concluded that hypertension was associated more with social class than with racial factors, and it was suggested that the greater prevalence of obesity in the lower class might be a possible explanation. The present review makes that earlier suggestion far less attractive since so many diseases and conditions appear to be of higher prevalence in the lower class groups. It seems clear that we must frame hypotheses of sufficient generality to account for this phenomenon.

One hypothesis that has been suggested is that persons in the lower classes either have less access to medical care resources or, if care is available, that they do not benefit from that availability. This possibility should be explored in more detail, but current evidence available does not suggest that differences in medical care resources will entirely explain social class gradients in disease. The hypertension project summarized above was conducted at the Kaiser Permanente facility in Oakland, California, which is a prepaid health plan with medical facilities freely available to all study subjects. The data in this study showed that persons in lower status groups had utilized medical resources more frequently than those in higher status categories (37). To study the influence of medical care in explaining these differences in blood pressure levels, all persons in the Kaiser study who had ever been clinically diagnosed as hypertensive, or who had ever taken medicine for high blood pressure, were removed from consideration. Differences in blood pressure level between those in the highest and lowest social classes were diminished when hypertensives were removed from analysis, but those in the lowest class still had higher (normal) pressures. Thus, while differences in medical care may have accounted for some of the variation observed among the social class groups, substantial differences in blood pressures among these groups nevertheless remained. Similar findings have been reported from studies at the Health Insurance Plan of New York (38).

Lipworth and colleagues (39) also examined this issue in a study of cancer survival rates among various income groups in Boston. In that study, low-income persons had substantially less favorable one and three-year survival rates following treatment at identical tumor clinics and hospitals; these differences were not accounted for by differences in stage of cancer at diagnosis, by the age of patients, or by the specific kind of treatment patients received. It was concluded that patients from lower income areas simply did not fare as well following treatment for cancer. While it is still possible that lower class patients received less adequate medical care, the differences observed in survival rates did not seem attributable to the more obvious variations in quality of treatment. Other studies support this general conclusion but not enough data are available to assess clearly the role of medical care in explaining social class gradients in morbidity and mortality; it would seem, however, that the medical care hypothesis does not account for a major portion of these gradients.

Another possible explanation offered to explain these consistent differences is that persons in lower socioeconomic groups live in a more toxic, hazardous and non-hygienic environment resulting in a broad array of disease consequences. That these environments exert an influence on disease outcome is supported by research on crowding and rheumatic fever (5), poverty areas and health (40), and on air pollution and respiratory illnesses (41). While lower class groups certainly are exposed to a more physically noxious environment, physical factors alone are frequently unable to explain observed relationships between socioeconomic status and disease outcome. One example of this is provided by the report of Guerrin and Borgatta (16) showing that the proportion of people who are illiterate in a census tract is a more important indicator of tuberculosis occurrence than are either economic or racial variables. Similarly, the work of Booth (42) suggests that perceived crowding which is not highly correlated with objective measures of crowding may have adverse effects on individuals.

There can be little doubt that the highest morbidity and mortality rates observed in the lower social classes are in part due to inadequate medical care services as well as to the impact of a toxic and hazardous physical environment. There can be little doubt, also, that these factors do not entirely explain the discrepancy in rates between the classes. Thus, while enormous improvements have been made in environmental quality and in medical care, the mortality rate gap between the classes has not diminished. It is true that mortality rates have been declining over the years, and it is probably true also that this benefit is attributable in large part to the enormous improvements that have been made in food and water purity, in sanitary engineering, in literacy and health education, and in medical and surgical knowledge. It is important to recognize, however, that these reductions in mortality rates have not eliminated the gap between the highest and the lowest social class groups; this gap remains very substantial and has apparently stabilized during the last 40 years. Thus, while improvements in the environment and in medical care clearly have been of value, other factors must be identified to account for this continuing differential in mortality rate and life expectancy.

The identification of these new factors might profitably be guided by the repeated observation of social class gradients in a wide range of disease distributions. That so many different kinds of diseases are more frequent in lower class groupings directs attention to generalized susceptibility to disease and to generalized compromises of disease defense systems. Thus, if something about life in the lower social classes increases vulnerability to illness in general, it would not be surprising to observe an increased prevalence of many different types of diseases and conditions among people in the lower classes.

While laboratory experiments on both humans and animals have established that certain "stressful events" have physiologic consequences, very little is known about the nature of these "stressful events" in non-laboratory settings. Thus, while we may conclude that "something" about the lower class environment is stressful, we know much less about what specifically constitutes that stress. Rather than attempting to identify *specific* risk factors for *specific* diseases in investigating this question, it may be more meaningful to identify those factors that affect *general* susceptibility to disease. The specification of such factors should rest on the identification of variables having a wide range of disease outcomes. One such risk factor may be life change associated with social and cultural mobility. Those experiencing this type of mobility have been observed to have higher rates of diseases and conditions such as coronary heart disease (43–46), lung cancer (47), difficulties of pregnancy (48,49), sarcoidosis (50), and depression (30). Another risk factor may be certain life events; those experiencing what are commonly called stressful life events have been shown to have higher rates of a wide variety of diseases and conditions (51–57).

Generalized susceptibility to disease may be influenced not only by the impact of various forms of life change and life stress, but also by differences in the way people cope with such stress. Coping, in this sense, refers not to specific types of psychological responses but to the more generalized ways in which people deal with problems in their everyday life. It is evident that such coping styles are likely to be products of environmental situations and not independent of such factors. Several coping responses that have a wide range of disease outcomes have been described. Cigarette smoking is one such coping response that has been associated with virtually all causes of morbidity and mortality (58); obesity may be another coping style associated with a higher rate of many diseases and conditions (59,60); pattern A behavior is an example of a third coping response that has been shown to have relatively broad disease consequences (61). There is some evidence that persons in the lower classes experience more life changes (62) and that they tend to be more obese and to smoke more cigarettes (63,64).

To explain the differential in morbidity and mortality rates among the social classes, it is important to identify additional factors that affect susceptibility and have diverse disease consequences; it is also important to determine which of these factors are more prevalent in the lower classes. Thus, our understanding would be enhanced if it could be shown not only that those in the lower classes live in a more toxic physical environment with inadequate medical care, but also that they live in a social and psychological environment that increases their vulnerability to a whole series of diseases and conditions.

In this paper, we have emphasized the variegated disease consequences of low socioeconomic status. Any proposed explanations of this phenomenon should be capable of accounting for this general outcome. The proposal offered here is that those in the lower classes consistently have higher rates of disease in part due to compromised disease defenses and increased general susceptibility. To explore this proposal further, systematic research is needed on four major problems:

(1) The more precise identification and description of subgroups within the lower socioeconomic classes that have either markedly higher or lower rates of disease: Included in what is commonly called the "lower class" are semi-skilled working men with stable work and family situations, unemployed men with and without families, the rural and urban poor, hard core unemployed persons, and so on. The different disease experiences of these heterogeneous subgroups would permit a more precise understanding of the processes involved in disease etiology and would permit a more precise definition of social class groupings.

(2) The disentanglement of socio-environmental from physical-environmental variables: It is important to know whether high rates of illness and discontent in a poverty area, for example, are due to the poor physical circumstances of life in such an area, to the social consequences of life in such an area, or to the personal characteristics of individuals who come to live in the area.

(3) The clarification of "causes" and "effects": The implication in this paper has been that the lower class environment "leads to" poor health. Certainly, the reverse situation is equally likely. Many measures of social class position may be influenced by the experience of ill health itself. Further research is needed to clarify the relative importance of the "downward drift" hypothesis. One way of approaching such study is to use measures of class position that are relatively unaffected by illness experience. An example of one such measure is "educational achievement" as used by Kitagawa and Hauser (11). In this study, educational level was assumed to be relatively stable after age 20 and was felt to be a measure relatively unaffected by subsequent illness experience.

(4) The more comprehensive description of those psycho-social variables that may compromise bodily defense to disease and increase susceptibility to illness: The possible importance of life events, life changes, and various coping behavior has been suggested but systematic research needs to be done to provide a more complete view of the factors involved in this process. Of particular interest would be research on the ways in which social and familial support networks (48,55) mediate between the impact of life events and stresses and disease outcomes.

The research that is needed should not be limited to the study of the specific risk factors as these affect specific diseases. Instead, the major focus of this research should be on those general features of lower class living environments that compromise bodily defense and thereby affect health and well-being in general. This research should go beyond the superficial description of demographic variables associated with illness and should attempt the identification of specific etiologic factors capable of accounting for the observed morbidity and mortality differences between the social classes.

The gap in mortality and life expectancy between the social classes has stabilized and may be increasing; the identification of those factors that render people vulnerable to disease will hopefully provide a basis for developing more meaningful prevention programs aimed toward narrowing the gap.

REFERENCES AND NOTES

1. Winkelstein W Jr, French FE: The role of ecology in the design of a health care system. Calif Med 113:7–12, 1970.
2. Marmot M, Winkelstein W Jr: Epidemiologic observations on intervention trials for prevention of coronary heart disease. Am J Epidemiol 101: 177–181, 1975.
3. Tuberculosis and Socioeconomic Status. Stat Bull, January 1970.
4. Terris M: Relation of economic status to tuberculosis mortality by age and sex. Am J Public Health 38:1061–1071, 1948.
5. Gordis L, Lilienfeld A, Rodriquez R: Studies in the epidemiology and preventability of rheumatic fever. II. Socioeconomic factors and the incidence of acute attacks. J Chronic Dis 21:655–666, 1969.
6. Influenza and Pneumonia Mortality in the U.S., Canada and Western Europe. Stat Bull, April 1972.
7. Court SDM: Epidemiology and natural history of respiratory infections in children. J Clin Pathol 21:31, 1968.
8. Chase HC (ed): A study of risks, medical care and infant mortality. Am J Public Health 63: supplement, 1973.
9. Lerner M: Social differences in physical health. *In:* Poverty and Health. Edited by J Kozsa, A Antonovsky, IK Zola. Cambridge, Harvard University Press, 1969, pp 69–112.
10. Antonovsky A: Social class, life expectancy and overall mortality. Milbank Mem Fund Q 45: 31–73, 1967.
11. Kitagawa EM, Hauser PM: Differential Mortality in the United States. Cambridge, Harvard University Press, 1973.
12. Nagi MH, Stockwell EG: Socioeconomic differentials in mortality by cause of death. Health Serv Rep 88:449–465, 1973.
13. Ellis JM: Socio-economic differentials in mortality from chronic disease. *In:* Patients, Physicians and Illness. Edited by EG Jaco. Glencoe, Ill, The Free Press, 1958, pp 30–37.
14. Yeracaris J: Differential mortality, general and cause-specific in Buffalo, 1939–1941. J Am Stat Assoc 50:1235–1247, 1955.
15. Brown SM, Selvin S, Winkelstein W Jr: The association of economic status with the occurrence of lung cancer. Cancer 36:1903–1911, 1975.
16. Guerrin RF, Borgatta EF: Socio-economic and demographic correlates of tuberculosis incidence. Milbank Mem Fund Q 43:269–290, 1965.
17. Graham S: Socio-economic status, illness, and the use of medical services. Milbank Mem Fund Q 35:58–66, 1957.
18. Cohart EM: Socioeconomic distribution of stomach cancer in New Haven. Cancer 7:455–461, 1954.
19. Socioeconomic Differentials in Mortality. Stat Bull, June 1972.
20. Hart JT: Too little and too late. Data on occupational mortality, 1959–1963. Lancet 1:192–193, 1972.
21. Wan T: Social differentials in selected work-limiting chronic conditions. J Chronic Dis 25: 365–374, 1972.
22. Hochstim JR, Athanasopoulos DA, Larkins JH: Poverty area under the microscope. Am J Public Health 58:1815–1827, 1968.
23. Burnight RG: Chronic morbidity and socioeconomic characteristics of older urban males. Milbank Mem Fund Q 43:311–322, 1965.
24. Elder R, Acheson RM: New Haven survey of joint diseases. XIV. Social class and behavior in response to symptoms of osteoarthritis. Milbank Mem Fund Q 48:499–502, 1970.
25. Cobb S: The epidemiology of rheumatoid disease. *In:* The Frequency of Rheumatoid Disease. Edited by S Cobb. Cambridge, Harvard University Free Press, 1971, pp 42–62.
26. Graham S: Social factors in the relation to chronic illness. *In:* Handbook of Medical Sociology. Edited by HE Freeman, S Levine, LG Reeder. Englewood Cliffs, NJ, Prentice-Hall Inc, 1963, pp 65–98.
27. Wan T: Status stress and morbidity: A sociological investigation of selected categories of working-limiting conditions. J Chronic Dis 24:453– 468, 1971.
28. Selected Health Characteristics by Occupation, U.S. July 1961–June 1963. National Health Center for Health Statistics, Series 10 21:1–16, 1965.

29. Abramson JH: Emotional disorder, status inconsistency and migration. Milbank Mem Fund Q 44:23–48, 1966.
30. Schwab JJ, Holzer CE III, Warheit GJ: Depression scores by race, sex, age, family income, education and socioeconomic status. (Personal communication, 1974).
31. Srole L, Langner T, Michael S, et al: Mental Health in the Metropolis: the Midtown Study. New York, McGraw-Hill, 1962.
32. Jackson EF: Status consistency and symptoms of stress. Am Sociol Rev 27:469–480, 1962.
33. Hollingshead AB, Redlich FC: Social Class and Mental Illness. New York, John Wiley and Sons Inc. 1958.
34. Gurin G, Veroff J, Feld S: Americans View Their Mental Health. New York, Basic Books Inc. 1960.
35. Langner TS: Psychophysiological symptoms and the status of women in two Mexican communities. *In:* Approaches to Cross-cultural Psychiatry. Edited by AH Leighton, JM Murphy. Ithaca, Cornell University Press, 1965. pp 360–392.
36. Syme SL, Oakes T, Friedman G, et al: Social class and racial differences in blood pressure. Am J Public Health 64:619–620, 1974.
37. Oakes TW, Syme SL: Social factors in newly discovered elevated blood pressure. J Health Soc Behav 14:198–204, 1973.
38. Fink R, Shapiro S, Hyman MD, et al: Health status of poverty and non-poverty groups in multiphasic health testing. Presented at the Annual Meeting of the American Public Health Association, November 1972.
39. Lipworth L, Abelin T, Connelly RR: Socioeconomic factors in the prognosis of cancer patients. J Chronic Dis 23:105–116, 1970.
40. Hochstim JR: Health and ways of living. *In:* Social Surveys. The Community as an Epidemiological Laboratory. Edited by I Kessler, M Levine. Baltimore, Johns Hopkins Press, 1970, pp 149–176.
41. Winkelstein W Jr, Kantor S, Davis EW, et al: The relationship of air pollution and economic status to total mortality and selected respiratory system mortality in men. I. Suspended particulates. Arch Environ Health 14:162–171, 1967.
42. Booth A: Preliminary Report: Urban Crowding Project. Canada, Ministry of State for Urban Affairs, August 1974 (mimeographed).
43. Syme SL, Hyman MM, Enterline PE: Some social and cultural factors associated with the occurrence of coronary heart disease. J Chronic Dis 17:277–289, 1964.
44. Tyroler HA, Cassel J: Health consequences of cultural change. II. The effect of urbanization on coronary heart mortality in rural residents. J Chronic Dis 17:167–177, 1964.
45. Nesser WB, Tyroler HA, Cassel JC: Social disorganization and stroke mortality in the black populations of North Carolina. Am J Epidemiol 93: 166–175, 1971.
46. Shekelle RB, Osterfeld AM, Paul O: Social status and incidence of coronary heart disease. J Chronic Dis 22:381–394, 1969.
47. Haenszel W, Loveland DB, Sirken N: Lung-cancer mortality as related to residence and smoking histories. I. White males. J Natl Cancer Inst 28: 947–1001, 1962.
48. Nuckolls KB, Cassel J, Kaplan BH: Psychosocial assets, life crisis, and the prognosis of pregnancy. Am J Epidemiol 95:431–441, 1972.
49. Gorusch RL, Key MK: Abnormalities of pregnancy as a function of anxiety and life stress. Psychosom Med 36:352–362, 1974.
50. Terris M, Chaves AD: An epidemiologic study of sarcoidosis. Am Rev Respir Dis 94:50–55, 1966.
51. Rahe RH, Gunderson EKE, Arthur RJ: Demographic and psychosocial factors in acute illness reporting. J Chronic Dis 23:245–255, 1970.
52. Wyler AR, Masuda M, Holmes TH: Magnitude of life events and seriousness of illness. Psychosom Med 33:115–122, 1971.
53. Rahe RH, Rubin RT, Gunderson EKE, et al: Psychological correlates of serum cholesterol in man: A longitudinal study. Psychosom Med 33: 399–410, 1971.
54. Spilken AZ, Jacobs MA: Prediction of illness behavior from measures of life crisis, manifest distress and maladaptive coping. Psychosom Med 33:251–264, 1971.
55. Jacobs MA, Spilken AZ, Martin MA, et al: Life stress and respiratory illness. Psychosom Med 32: 233–242, 1970.
56. Kasl SV, Cobb S: Blood pressure changes in men undergoing job loss; A preliminary report. Psychosom Med 32:19–38, 1970.
57. Hinkle LE, Wolff HG: Ecological investigations of the relationship between illness, life experiences, and the social environment. Ann Intern Med 49:1373–1388, 1958.
58. US Dept of Health, Education, and Welfare: The Health Consequences of Smoking. National Communicable Disease Center, Publication No 74-8704, 1974.
59. US Public Health Service, Division of Chronic Diseases: Obesity and Health. A Source Book of Current Information for Professional Health Personnel. Publication No 1485. Washington DC, US GPO, 1966.

60. Build and Blood Pressure Study. Chicago, Society of Actuaries, Vol I and II, 1959.
61. Rosenman RH, Brand RH, Jenkins CD, et al: Coronary heart disease in the Western collaborative group study: Final follow-up experience of 8½ years. (Manuscript).
62. Dohrenwend BS (ed): Stressful Life Events: Their Nature and Effects. New York, Wiley-Interscience, 1974.
63. US Dept of Health, Education, and Welfare: Adult Use of Tobacco 1970, Publication No HSM-73-8727, 1973.
64. Khosla T, Lowe CR: Obesity and smoking habits by social class. J Prev Soc Med 26:249–256, 1972.

3 *EXCESS MORTALITY IN HARLEM*

Colin McCord and Harold P. Freeman

Mortality rates for white and nonwhite Americans have fallen steadily and in parallel since 1930 (Fig. 3-1). Lower rates for nonwhites have been associated with an improved living standard, better education, and better access to health care.[1,2] These improvements, however, have not been evenly distributed. Most health indicators, including mortality rates, are worse in the impoverished areas of this country.[3–9] It is not widely recognized just how much certain inner-city areas lag behind the rest of the United States. We used census data and data from the Bureau of Health Statistics and Analysis of the New York City Health Department to estimate the amount, distribution, and causes of excess mortality in the New York City community of Harlem.

THE COMMUNITY

Harlem is a neighborhood in upper Manhattan just north of Central Park. Its population is 96 percent black and has been predominantly black since before World War I. It was the center of the Harlem Renaissance of black culture in the 1920s, and it continues to be a cultural center for black Americans. The median family income in Harlem, according to the 1980 census, was $6,497, as compared with $16,818 in all New York City, $21,023 in the United States, and $12,674 among all blacks in the United States. The families of 40.8 percent of the people of Harlem had incomes below the government-defined poverty line in 1980. The total population of Harlem fell from 233,000 in 1960 to 121,905 in 1980. In the same 20-year period the death rate from homicide rose from 25.3 to 90.8 per 100,000.

The neighborhood is not economically homogeneous. There is a middle-to-upper-class community of about 25,000 people living in new, private apartment complexes or houses, a less affluent group of 25,000 living in public housing projects, and a third group of about 75,000 who live in substandard housing. Most of the population loss has been in the group living in substandard housing, much of it abandoned or partially occupied buildings.

The pattern of medical care in Harlem is similar to that reported for other poor and black communities.[10,11] As compared with the per capita averages for New York City, the rate of hospital admission is 26 percent higher, the use of emergency rooms is 73 percent higher, the use of hospital outpatient departments is 134 percent higher, and the number of primary care physicians per 1000 people is 74 percent lower.[12]

METHODS

Age-adjusted death rates for whites and nonwhites were taken from *Vital Statistics of the*

United States, 1980.[13] Age-adjusted rates for nonwhites rather than blacks were used in Figure 3-1 because the deaths of blacks were not reported separately before 1970. Age-adjusted mortality rates for blacks in the United States have been slightly higher in recent years than those for all nonwhites (8.4 per 1000 for blacks and 7.7 per 1000 for all nonwhites in 1980). The age-adjusted mortality rates for Harlem in 1960, 1970, and 1980, as well as certain disease-specific death rates, were calculated from data supplied by the New York City Health Department. The U.S. population in 1940 was used as the reference for all the age-adjusted rates in Figure 3-1.

Tapes were provided by the New York City Health Department containing everything but personal identifying information from all death certificates in 1979, 1980, and 1981. Deaths were recorded by age, sex, underlying cause, health-center district, and health area. The Central Harlem Health Center District corresponds to the usual definition of the Harlem community. For our analysis, we calculated age-, sex-, and cause-specific death rates for Harlem using the recorded deaths for 1979, 1980, and 1981 and population data from the 1980 census. New York City determines the underlying cause of death by the methods proposed by the National Center for Health Statistics.[14] We used the diagnostic categories of the ninth revision of the *International Classification of Diseases.*[15] They were generally but not always grouped in the way that the New York City Bureau of Health Statistics and Analysis groups diagnoses in its annual reports of vital statistics according to health areas and health-center districts. For example, "cardiovascular disease" refers to diagnostic categories 390 through 448 in the *International Classification of Diseases,* and "ill defined" refers to categories 780 through 789.

The reference death rates we used to calculate the standardized mortality ratios (SMRs) are those of the white population of the United States, as published in *Vital Statistics of the United States, 1980.*[13] To calculate the SMRs, the total number of observed deaths in 1979, 1980, and 1981 for each age group, sex, and cause was divided by the expected number of deaths, based on the population of each sex and age group and the reference death rate. Using

Figure 3-1. *Age-Adjusted Death Rates in Harlem (1960–1980) and the United States (1930–1980)*

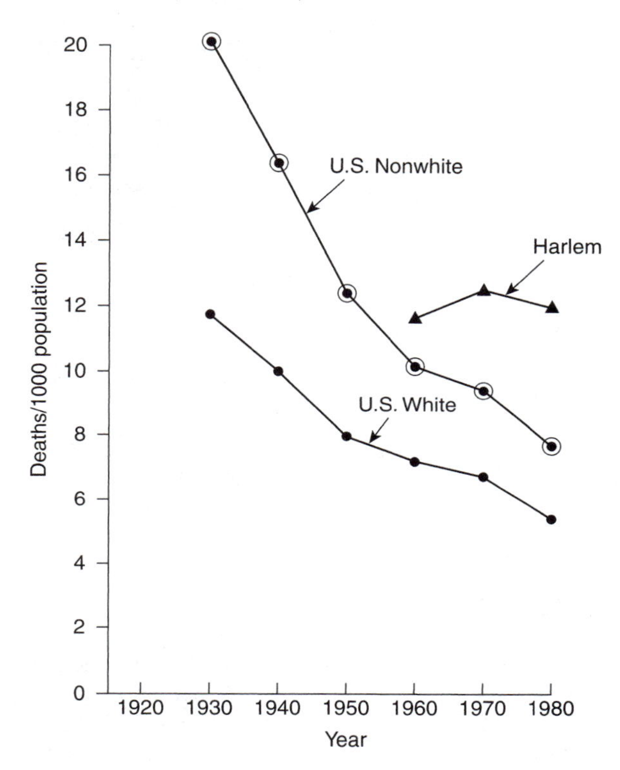

the same methods, we calculated the SMR for deaths under the age of 65 for each health area in the city with a population of more than 3000. New York City has 353 health areas, with an average population of 21,000. Only 11 have a population of less than 3000.

The survival curves in Figure 3-2 were constructed with the use of life tables. The tables for Bangladesh were from a report of the Matlab study area of the International Center for Diarrheal Disease Research,[9] modified from 5-year to 10-year age intervals. Life tables for Harlem were calculated with the same formulas and for the same 10-year intervals. Life tables for the United States are from *Vital Statistics of the United States, 1980.*[13]

Figure 3-2. *Survival to the Age of 65 in Harlem, Bangladesh, and among U.S. Whites in 1980*

Percent Alive
100
90
80
70
60
50
40
30
20
10
0
U.S. White
Bangladesh
Harlem
Male
5 15 25 35 45 55 65
Age (yr)

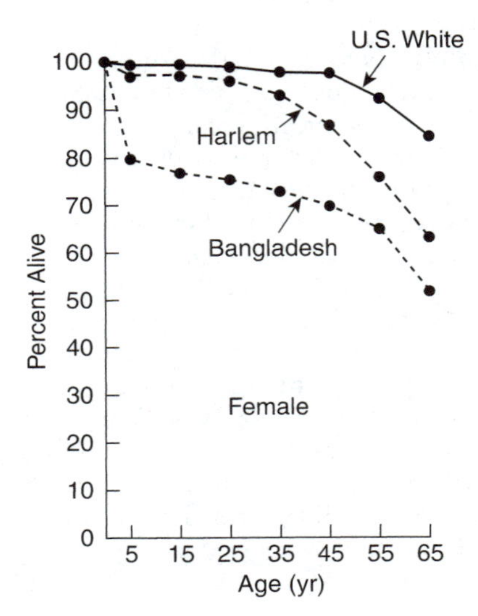

RESULTS

Since 1950, when the New York City Health Department began to keep death records according to health-center district, Central Harlem has consistently had the highest infant mortality rate and one of the highest crude death rates in the city. In 1970 and 1980, age-adjusted mortality rates for Harlem residents were the highest in New York City, much worse than the rates for nonwhites in the United States as a whole, and they had changed little since 1960 (Fig. 3-1). This lack of improvement in the age-adjusted death rate reflected worsening mortality rates for persons between the ages of 15 and 65 that more than offset the drop in mortality among infants and young children (Fig. 3-3).

Figure 3-2 shows the survival curves for male and female residents of Harlem, as compared with those for whites in the United States and those for the residents of an area in rural Bangladesh. Bangladesh is categorized by the World Bank as one of the lowest-income countries in the world. The Matlab demographic-study area is thought to have somewhat lower death rates than Bangladesh as a whole, but the rates are typical for the region. Life expectancy at birth in Matlab was 56.5 years in 1980, as compared with an estimated 49 years for Bangladesh and 57 years for India in 1986.[9,16] For men, the rate of survival beyond the age of 40 is lower in Harlem than Bangladesh. For women, overall survival to the age of 65 is somewhat better in Harlem, but only because the death rate among girls under 5 is very high in Bangladesh.

The SMRs for Harlem (Table 3-1) were high for those of all ages below 75, but they were particularly high for those between 25 and 64 years old and for children under 4. In the three years 1979 to 1981, there were 6415 deaths in Harlem. If the death rate among U.S. whites had applied to this community, there would have been 3994 deaths. Eighty-seven percent of the 2421 excess deaths were of persons under 65.

Table 3-2 compares the numbers of observed and expected deaths among persons under 65, according to the chief underlying causes. A large proportion of the observed excess was directly due to violence and substance abuse, but these

Figure 3-3. *Age-Specific Death Rates in Harlem from 1960 to 1980**

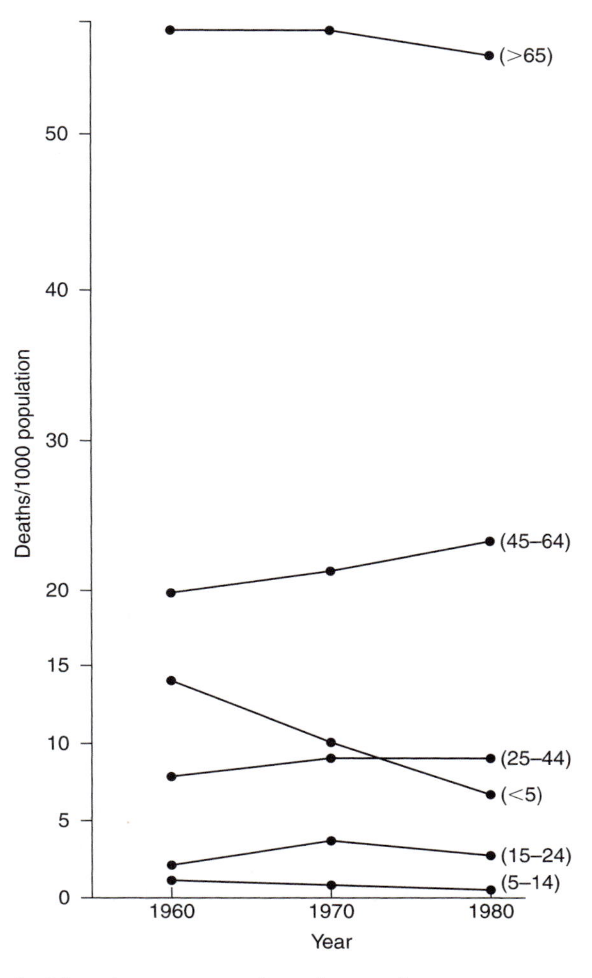

* *Note:* Age groups are shown in parentheses.

causes did not account for most of the excess. Cirrhosis, homicide, accidents, drug dependency, and alcohol use were considered the most important underlying causes of death in 35 percent of all deaths among people under 65, and in 45 percent of the excess deaths.

For people between the ages of 65 and 74 the SMRs in Harlem were much lower than those for people younger than 65. For residents of Harlem 75 years old or older, overall death rates were essentially the same as those for U.S. whites (Table 3-1). Disease-specific SMRs for people over the age of 65 were below those of younger age groups in almost every category. In several categories (notably cardiovascular disease in Harlem residents 75 or older), they were lower than in whites. This may represent the survival of the fittest in this area of excess mortality.

To estimate the number of people in New York City whose mortality rates were similar to those of people in Harlem, SMRs for persons under the age of 65 were calculated for each of

Table 3-1. Standardized Mortality Ratios for Harlem, 1979 to 1981*

Age (Yr)	Observed Deaths (No.)	Standardized Mortality Ratio	Annual Excess Deaths†
Male			
0–4	81	2.45	462
5–14	10	1.10	4
15–24	105	2.28	214
25–34	248	5.77	911
35–44	347	5.98	1401
45–54	521	3.28	1824
55–64	783	2.10	2026
65–74	727	1.23	945
≧75	747	1.001	14
Total	3569	1.72	878
Total <65	2095	2.91	948
Female			
0–4	57	2.19	291
5–14	9	1.80	17
15–24	32	1.88	48
25–34	98	6.13	330
35–44	148	4.63	510
45–54	303	3.40	927
55–64	508	2.09	973
65–74	699	1.47	968
≧75	992	0.96	−315
Total	2846	1.47	449
Total <65	1155	2.70	445

* Reference death rates are those for U.S. whites in 1980.
† Per 100,000 population in each age group.

Table 3-2. Causes of Excess Mortality in Harlem, 1979 to 1981*

Cause	Observed Deaths (No.)	Standardized Mortality Ratio	Annual Excess Deaths per 100,000	% of Excess Deaths
Cardiovascular disease	880	2.23	157.5	23.5
Cirrhosis	410	10.49	120.4	17.9
Homicide	332	14.24	100.2	14.9
Neoplasm	604	1.77	84.9	12.6
Drug dependency	153	283.1	49.5	7.4
Diabetes	94	5.43	24.9	3.7
Alcohol use	73	11.33	21.6	3.2
Pneumonia and influenza	78	5.07	20.3	3.0
Disorders in newborns	64	7.24	17.9	2.7
Infection	65	5.60	17.3	2.6
Accident	155	1.17	7.2	1.1
Ill defined	44	2.07	7.4	1.1
Renal	26	4.54	6.6	0.9
Chronic obstructive pulmonary disease	35	1.29	2.6	0.4
Congenital anomalies	23	1.21	1.3	0.2
Suicide	33	0.81	−2.5	—
All other	181	3.13	40.0	6.0
All causes	3250	2.75	671.2	100.0

* The calculations are based on the deaths of all persons—male and female—under the age of 65. The reference death rates are those for U.S. whites in 1980.

New York's 342 health areas with populations over 3000. There were 54 areas with SMRs of 2.0 or higher for persons under the age of 65. This means that these 54 health areas had at least twice the expected number of deaths (Fig. 3-4). The total population of these high-risk areas was 650,000. In 53 of them more than half the population was black or Hispanic. There was much more variation in the SMRs of the health areas predominantly inhabited by members of minority groups than in the areas that were less than half nonwhite (Fig. 3-4). White areas were relatively narrowly clustered around a mean SMR of 0.97. The SMRs for predominantly black or Hispanic health areas ranged from 0.59 to 3.95, with a mean of 1.77. The SMRs for the 10 health areas in Harlem ranged from 2.16 to 3.95.

It is believed that recent U.S. censuses have undercounted blacks and other minority groups, particularly young men. This would lead to an increase in the age-specific mortality rates used to calculate life tables and SMRs. The Bureau of the Census has estimated the scale of undercounting in various ways—the highest figure is 19 percent for black men in the 25-to-34-year-old group.[17] Because the absolute amount of the observed excess mortality in Harlem is so great, recalculation has little effect on the data presented here, but for the calculations required for Figure 3-3 and Tables 3-1 and 3-2 we increased the 1980 census population in each sex and age group by an amount conforming to the largest Census Bureau estimate of the undercounting. This produced a slight increase in the percentage shown to be still living at the age of 65 in Figure 3-2 and a slight reduction in the SMRs in Tables 3-1 and 3-2. (With this correction the SMR for male residents under the age of 65 was 2.91 rather than 3.15.)

Figure 3-4. *Standardized Mortality Ratios for Persons under 65 in 342 Health Areas in New York City, 1979 to 1981**

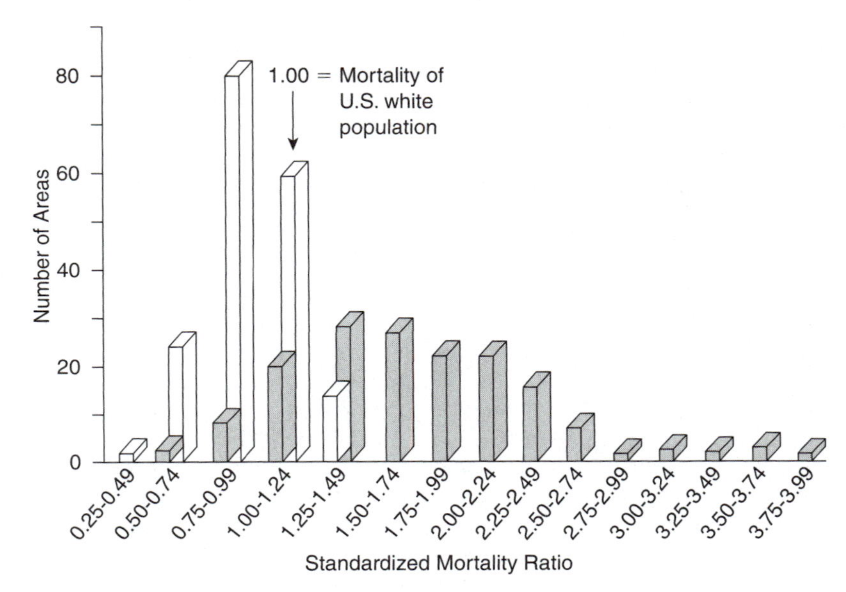

* *Note:* The shaded bars denote communities more than half of whose residents are nonwhite, and the open bars communities that are half or more white. Bars to the right of the arrow represent communities in which the mortality of persons under the age of 65 was higher than that of U.S. whites.

DISCUSSION

An improvement in child mortality in Harlem between 1960 and 1980 was accompanied by rising mortality rates for persons between the ages of 25 and 65. There was therefore no improvement in overall age-adjusted mortality. Death rates for those between the ages of 5 and 65 were worse in Harlem than in Bangladesh.

We have not attempted to calculate SMRs since 1981, because the 1980 census is the most recent reliable estimate of the population of New York City, but all available evidence indicates that there has been very little change since then. The total number of deaths in Harlem from 1985 through 1987 was 1.6 percent higher than from 1979 through 1981. According to the New York City Planning Department, the decline in Harlem's population stopped in 1980 and the total population has been growing at the rate of 1 percent per year since then.[18] If this estimate is accepted, there has been a slight drop in the crude death rate for Harlem since 1980, but not large enough to affect any of our conclusions. Since 1980 the number of deaths of persons 25 to 44 years of age has increased considerably (31 percent), and the acquired immunodeficiency syndrome (AIDS) has become the most common cause of death in this age group in Harlem and in all New York City. The number of deaths from AIDS is expected to continue to rise.

The situation in Harlem is extreme, but it is not an isolated phenomenon. We identified 54 health areas (of 353) in New York City, with a total population of 650,000, in which there were more than twice as many deaths among people under the age of 65 as would be expected if the death rates of U.S. whites applied. All but one of these health areas have populations more than half composed of minority members. These are areas that were left behind when the minority population of the city as a whole experienced the same improvement in life expectancy that was seen in the rest of the United States.[19] Similar pockets of high mortality have been described in other U.S. cities.[3,20] Jenkins et al. calculated SMRs for all deaths in Roxbury and adjacent areas of Boston that were almost as high in 1972–1973 as those reported here.[20] This area of highest mortality in Boston was the area with the highest proportion of minority groups.

It will be useful to know more about the circumstances surrounding premature deaths in high-risk communities to determine the relative importance of contributing factors such as poverty, inadequate housing, psychological stress, substance abuse, malnutrition, and inadequate access to medical care. But action to correct the appalling health conditions reflected in these statistics need not wait for more research. The essential first steps are to identify these pockets of high mortality and to recognize the urgent severity of the problem. Widespread poverty and inadequate housing are obvious in Harlem and demand a direct attack wherever they are present. The most important health investigations will be those designed to evaluate the effectiveness of measures to prevent and treat the causes of death already identified. The SMR for persons under 65 years of age may be a useful tool both to identify the high-mortality areas and to monitor the effect of measures to reduce mortality. This ratio is simpler to calculate than the years of productive life lost,[6] and the information obtained is similar.

Those responsible for implementing health programs must face the reality of high death rates in Harlem and the enormous burden of disease that requires treatment in the existing facilities. The health care system is overloaded with such treatment and is poorly structured to support preventive measures, detect disease early, and care for adults with chronic problems. At the same time, the population at highest risk has limited contact with the health care system except in emergencies. Brudny and Dobkyn reported that 83 percent of 181 patients discharged from Harlem Hospital with tuberculosis in 1988 were lost to follow-up and did not continue treatment.[21] New approaches must be developed to take preventive and therapeutic measures out of the hospitals, clinics, and emergency rooms and deliver them to the population at highest risk.

Intensive educational campaigns to improve nutrition and reduce the use of alcohol, drugs, and tobacco are needed and should be directed at children and adolescents, since habits are formed early and the death rates begin to rise immediately after adolescence. Education will have little effect unless it is combined with access to adequate incomes, useful employment, and decent housing for these children and their parents. Education can help in controlling epidemic drug use and associated crime only if it is combined with effective and coordinated police and public action. AIDS in Harlem is largely related to intravenous drug use and is not likely to be controlled until drugs are controlled, but effective education about this disease is also urgently needed.

Knowledge of the history of previous efforts to improve health in Harlem does not lead to optimism about the future. The Harlem Health Task Force was formed in 1976 because Harlem and the Carter administration recognized that death rates were high. An improved system of clinics, more drug-treatment centers, and active community-outreach programs were recommended. The recommendations have been implemented to varying degrees, but funding has been limited. The preventive and curative health care system is essentially unchanged today. Drug use has increased, and the proportion of the population receiving public assistance has increased. There has been no decrease in the death rates.

In 1977 Jenkins et al. pointed out that the number of excess deaths recorded each year in the areas of worst health in Boston was considerably larger than the number of deaths in places that the U.S. government had designated as natural-disaster areas. They suggested that these zones of excess mortality be declared disaster areas and that measures be implemented on this basis.[20] No such action was taken then or is planned now. If the high-mortality zones of New York City were designated a disaster area today, 650,000 people would be living in it. A major political and financial commitment will be needed to eradicate the root causes of this high mortality: vicious poverty and inadequate access to the basic health care that is the right of all Americans.

NOTE

We are indebted to Meril Silverstein, Chih Hwa, John Ross, and Elmer Struerning for advice and assistance. The authors alone are responsible for the calculations and conclusions.

REFERENCES

1. Manton KG, Patrick CH, Johnson KW. Health differentials between blacks and whites: recent trends in mortality and morbidity. Milbank Q 1987; 65:Suppl 1:125–99.
2. Davis K, Lillie-Blanton M, Lyons B, Mullan F, Powe N, Rowland D. Health care for black Americans: the public sector role. Milbank Q 1987; 65:Suppl 1:213–47.
3. Kitagawa EM, Hauser PM. Differential mortality in the United States: a study in socioeconomic epidemiology. Cambridge, Mass.: Harvard University Press, 1973.
4. Woolhandler S, Himmelstein DU, Silber R, Bader M, Harnly M, Jones A. Medical care and mortality: racial differences in preventable deaths. Int J Health Serv 1985; 15:1–22.
5. Savage D, Lindenbaum J, Van Ryzin J, Struerning E, Garrett TJ. Race, poverty, and survival in multiple myeloma. Cancer 1984; 54:3085–94.
6. Black/white comparisons of premature mortality for public health program planning—District of Columbia. MMWR 1989; 38:33–7.
7. Freeman HP, Wasfie TJ. Cancer of the breast in poor black women. Cancer 1989; 63:2562–9.
8. Cancer in the economically disadvantaged: a special report prepared by the subcommittee on cancer in the economically disadvantaged. New York: American Cancer Society, 1986.
9. Demographic surveillance system—Matlab. Vital events and migration tables, 1980. Scientific report no. 58. Dhaka, Bangladesh: International Centre for Diarrheal Disease Research, 1982.
10. Davis K, Schoen C. Health and the war on poverty: a ten-year appraisal. Washington, D.C.: Brookings Institution, 1978.
11. Blendon RJ, Aiken LH, Freeman HE, Corey CR. Access to medical care for black and white Americans: a matter of continuing concern. JAMA 1989; 261:278–81.
12. Community health atlas of New York. New York: United Hospital Fund, 1986.
13. Vital statistics of the United States 1980. Hyattsville, Md.: National Center for Health Statistics, 1985. (DHHS publication no. (PHS) 85-1101.)
14. Vital statistics: instructions for classifying the underlying cause of death, 1980. Hyattsville, Md.: National Center for Health Statistics, 1980.
15. The international classification of diseases. 9th revision, clinical modification: ICD-9-CM, 2nd ed. Washington, D.C.: Department of Health and Human Services, 1980. (DHHS publication no. (PHS) 80-1260.)
16. The state of the world's children 1988 (UNICEF). New York: Oxford University Press, 1988.
17. Fay RE, Passel JS, Robinson JG. Coverage of population in the 1980 census. Washington, D.C.: Bureau of the Census, 1988. (Publication no. PHC 80-E4.)
18. Community district needs, 1989. New York: Department of City Planning, 1987. (DCP publication no. 87-10.)
19. Summary of vital statistics, 1986. New York: Bureau of Health Statistics and Analysis, 1986.
20. Jenkins CD, Tuthill RW, Tannenbaum SI, Kirby CR. Zones of excess mortality in Massachusetts. N Engl J Med 1977; 296:1354–6.
21. Brudny K, Dobkyn J. Poor compliance is the major obstacle in controlling the HIV-associated tuberculosis outbreak. Presented at the Fifth International Conference on Acquired Immune Deficiency Syndrome, Montreal, June 8, 1989.

4 GENDER DIFFERENCES IN MORTALITY—CAUSES AND VARIATION IN DIFFERENT SOCIETIES

Ingrid Waldron

INTRODUCTION

Women live longer than men in all contemporary developed countries, as well as almost all contemporary developing countries (Table 1; U.N., 2003).[1] For example, in the U.S. female life expectancy is five years longer than male life expectancy. The magnitude of the gender difference in life expectancy varies considerably, ranging from a high of 13 years longer life expectancy for females in Russia to little or no gender difference in life expectancy in Bangladesh and Pakistan in South Asia. These gender differences in life expectancy reflect higher death rates for males than for females at all ages in most countries, although females have higher death rates than males at some ages in some countries, particularly in South Asia (Guralnick et al., 2000; Lopez and Ruzicka, 1983; U.N. 1998).

Gender differences in mortality have contributed to an imbalance in numbers of men and women available for marriage in some countries and considerable differences in the numbers of elderly men and women in many countries (Das Gupta and Li, 1999; Guralnik et al., 2000). For example, in Russia during the twentieth century mortality has been considerably higher for males than for females, so relatively few men have survived to ages 75 and above, and there are over three times as many women as men in this elderly age range. In the U.S., where males have had moderately higher mortality than females, the number of elderly women is 50% larger than the number of elderly men. In contrast, in the largest South Asian countries, mortality has not been consistently higher for males, and there are at least as many elderly men as women.

Because gender differences in mortality vary in different countries, this chapter reviews the patterns and causes of gender differences in mortality separately for three major groups of countries. Specifically, the three major sections

Table 4-1. Gender Differences in Life Expectancy for the Ten Largest Population Countries, 2001

	Life Expectancy		
Country	Females	Males	Gender Difference[a]
Russia	72.3	58.9	13.4
Japan	84.7	77.9	6.8
Brazil	72.0	65.5	6.5
U.S.	79.5	74.3	5.2
Indonesia	67.4	64.4	3.0
China	72.7	69.8	2.9
Nigeria	52.6	50.6	2.0
India	61.7	60.0	1.7
Pakistan	61.5	61.0	0.5
Bangladesh	61.7	61.9	−0.2

[a] The gender difference in life expectancy is the female minus the male life expectancy. (Data from World Health Organization, 2003)

analyze (1) the reasons why males have higher mortality than females in the U.S. and other developed democracies, (2) the reasons why the male mortality disadvantage is so large in Russia and some other formerly Communist European countries, and (3) the reasons why gender differences in mortality are so small in many developing countries.

Within each section, the causes of gender differences in mortality are analyzed by addressing three major questions. First, what causes of death contribute to gender differences in total mortality? Second, what biological factors and gender differences in behavior and environmental exposures influence gender differences in mortality for these causes of death? Third, how are these effects influenced by the varied cultural, economic, public health, and health-care circumstances in the countries considered?

As background for these analyses, it is useful to clarify some basic terminology and to review the basic types of biological and social influences on gender differences in mortality. Some authors distinguish between biologically based "sex differences" and culturally or socially determined "gender differences." However, this distinction is not useful for analyses of gender differences in mortality, because both biological and sociocultural causes interact to influence gender differences in mortality. Therefore, the term "gender differences" is used throughout, with no implication concerning environmental vs. biological causes of these differences. The term "sex mortality ratio" designates the male death rate divided by the female death rate, which is one important measure of gender differences in mortality.

Biological factors that contribute to gender differences in mortality include differences in reproductive anatomy and function and differences in hormones (Waldron, 1998). Hormonal differences begin before birth, with higher secretion of testosterone by the male fetus. These hormonal differences appear to contribute to gender differences in behavior and physiology, which, in turn, contribute to gender differences in mortality (Collaer and Hines, 1995; Waldron, 1995a, 1998, 2002). Another biological difference is that, in females, each cell contains a pair of X chromosomes, whereas, in males, each cell contains an X and a Y chromosome. For the many genes that are found only on the X chromosome, females have two copies and males have only one, so males are more vulnerable to X-linked recessive genetic disorders. However, most fatal X-linked recessive genetic disorders are relatively rare and thus make a small contribution to gender differences in total mortality (Waldron, 1998).

Some biological differences contribute to higher male mortality, and others contribute to higher female mortality. The relative importance of specific biological causal factors varies, depending on the cultural, economic, public health, and health care context in different countries and historical periods. For example, maternal mortality significantly increases female mortality in some developing countries but is a minor cause of death in developed countries (Murray and Lopez, 1996; Waldron, 1986a).

Gender differences in mortality are also influenced by the social environment, especially cultural expectations and socialization for male and female gender roles. In this chapter, the term "gender roles" is used broadly to refer to the social roles, behaviors, attitudes and psychological characteristics that are more common, more expected and more accepted for one sex or the other. Differences between male and female gender roles influence gender differences in health-related behaviors (such as cigarette smoking and heavy drinking) and gender differences in exposures to hazards (such as occupational accidents and carcinogens). These effects generally contribute to higher mortality for males. These effects are particularly important in developed countries, including both the developed democracies and the formerly Communist countries of Europe.

Differences between male and female roles can also contribute to gender differences in mortality by influencing gender differences in access to resources such as health care, particularly in developing countries with limited material resources. For example, because of differences between male and female roles, sons can contribute more to their parents' future well-being than daughters in some societies; correspondingly, it appears that boys receive more adequate health care than girls in some South Asian societies, and this contributes to lower mortality for boys.

In summary, some effects of gender roles decrease male mortality relative to female mortality, whereas other effects increase male mortality. The relative importance of specific effects varies in different socioeconomic and cultural circumstances.

U.S. and Other Developed Democracies

In the developed democracies, including the U.S., Western European countries, and Japan, male mortality is higher than female mortality at all ages and for almost all major causes of death (Lopez and Ruzicka, 1983; Murray and Lopez, 1996; Waldron, 1986a, 2000). For example, males have substantially higher mortality than females for coronary heart disease, lung cancer, accidents, and suicide (Table 2; Figure 1). These four causes of death account for more than half of the total gender difference in mortality in the developed democracies.

As discussed in the following paragraphs, gender differences in behavior make a major contribution to males' higher mortality for these causes of death, and the behaviors that contribute to males' higher mortality have been more expected and accepted for males. The evidence to be reviewed indicates that these gender differences in behavior are influenced not only by socialization for male and female gender roles, but also by hormonal effects. Additional topics discussed below include assessments of whether gender differences in employment and health-care utilization contribute to gender differences in mortality, brief descriptions of the contributions of several biological factors, and a summary of historical trends in gender differences in mortality in the developed democracies.

Injuries

Behaviors that are more expected or accepted for males than for females are the primary cause of males' higher injuries mortality, including accidents, suicide and homicide (Waldron, 1986a, 1997; Waldron et al., 2004). Men are much more likely than women to be employed in risky occupations such as construction and mining, so men have much higher rates of fatal occupational accidents. Males engage in more risky recreational behavior, and one consequence is males' much higher death rates for accidental drownings. Males have higher rates of fatal motor vehicle accidents because males drive more than females and males have more fatal accidents per mile driven. Males' higher rates of fatal accidents per mile driven suggest that they drive less safely, and this has been confirmed by observational studies that show that males tend

Table 4-2. Gender Differences in Mortality by Cause of Death, U.S., 2001[a]

Cause of Death	Male Death Rate	Female Death Rate	% of Total Gender Difference In Mortality	Sex Mortality Ratio
Coronary Heart Disease[b]	228.5	139.9	29	1.6
Lung Cancer[c]	75.2	41.0	11	1.8
Suicide	18.2	4.0	5	4.6
Motor Vehicle Accidents	21.8	9.3	4	2.3
Other Accidents	28.3	13.2	5	2.1
Breast Cancer	0.3	26.0	–8	0.01
Total	1029.1	721.8	100	1.4

[a] Death rates have been age-adjusted to account for gender differences in age distribution. Death rates are deaths per 100,000 population per year. Gender difference in mortality refers to male minus female death rates. Causes of death were included if the gender difference for a specific cause of death was at least 4% of the gender difference in total mortality. Sex mortality ratio refers to male divided by female death rates. (Data from Arias et al., 2003)

[b] Coronary heart disease is also known as ischemic heart disease.

[c] Lung cancer refers to malignant neoplasms of the trachea, bronchus, and lung.

Figure 4-1. *Gender Differences in Mortality in Different Regions and Countries, 1990*

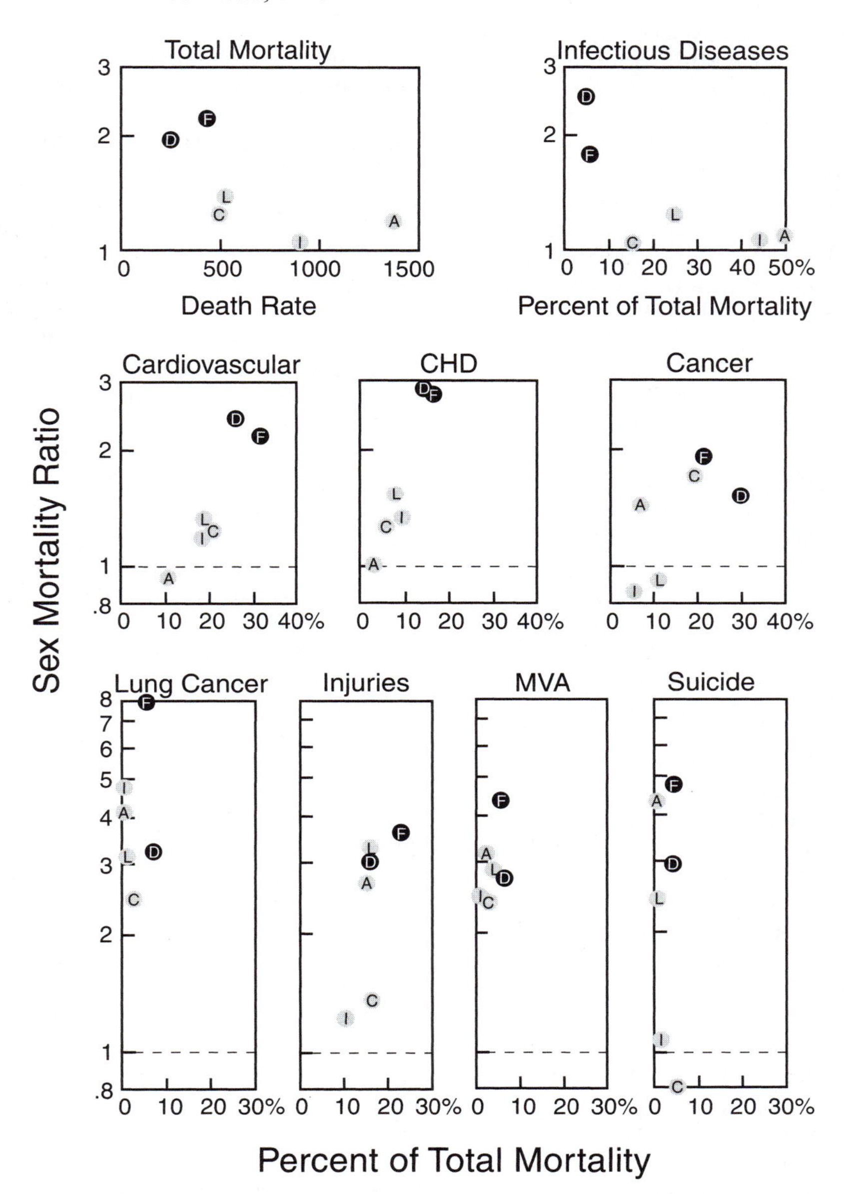

The first graph shows sex mortality ratios for total mortality in four major regions of the world and two very large countries.[5] Each subsequent graph shows the sex mortality ratios for a major cause of death or cause of death category vs. the percent of total mortality due to that cause or category.

D indicates data for developed democracies (also called established market economies, e.g., the U.S. and Japan). F indicates data for formerly Communist European countries (also called formerly socialist economies of Europe, e.g., Russia). L indicates data for Latin America and the Caribbean, A indicates data for sub-Saharan Africa, C indicates data for China, and I indicates data for India.

Coronary heart disease (CHD, also called ischemic heart disease) is one category within cardiovascular diseases. Lung cancer (malignant neoplasms of the trachea, bronchus, and lung) is one category within cancer (malignant neoplasms). Motor vehicle accidents (MVA; also called road traffic accidents) and suicide (self-inflicted injuries) are two categories within injuries. Infections include infectious and parasitic diseases and respiratory infections.

to drive faster and less cautiously than females, males more often violate traffic regulations, and males are more likely to drink and drive. Males are much more likely than females to be heavy drinkers, and this contributes to their higher mortality for multiple types of accidents, suicide, and homicide (Bloomfield, 2003; Waldron, 1986a, 1997; Waldron et al., 2004). Gun use is also much more common among males, and this contributes to higher male mortality for gun accidents, suicide, and homicide.

Males more often use guns in suicidal behavior, whereas females more often use drug overdoses (Canetto and Sakinofsky, 1998; Waldron, 1986a). Since guns are much more consistently lethal than drug overdoses, this difference in methods contributes to males' higher rates of suicide fatalities and females' higher rates of non-fatal suicide attempts. Gender differences in suicide methods are not the only factor that contributes to gender differences in suicide mortality. Another factor that may be important is that women may more often use a suicide attempt as a desperate, last-ditch plea for help, whereas men, who feel more pressure to be strong, may be less willing to plead for help and more likely to carry a suicidal act through to a fatal conclusion.

Research evidence indicates that these gender differences in injury-related behavior result from the effects of both hormones and gender role socialization. Males are exposed to higher levels of testosterone both before and after birth, which appears to contribute to their higher rates of vigorous physical activity and physical aggressiveness, which, in turn, contribute to their higher rates of injury mortality (Collaer and Hines, 1995; Waldron, 1998). In addition, differential socialization of boys and girls is widespread cross-culturally and begins as early as infancy, with greater encouragement of physical activity in male babies (Waldron, 1986a, 1997, 1998). Gender role socialization that encourages more injury-related behavior in males continues into the teenage and adult years. For example, men's drinking has often been encouraged as part of traditional male gender roles, but heavy drinking by women has been discouraged, apparently because it is incompatible with traditional female responsibilities for sexual restraint and care of young children (Waldron, 1997).

Smoking

The single most important behavioral cause of men's higher mortality has been men's higher rates of cigarette smoking and more hazardous smoking habits (Pampel, 2002; Waldron, 1986b, 1991a, 2000). In developed democracies in the second half of the twentieth century, gender differences in cigarette smoking accounted for roughly half of the gender differences in total mortality for adults, roughly half of the gender differences in coronary heart disease mortality, and about 90% of the gender differences in lung cancer mortality (Waldron, 1986b, 1995a; calculated from data in Pampel, 2002, and Peto et al., 1994).

The magnitude of gender differences in smoking has varied in different countries and historical periods (Waldron, 1991a). In the early twentieth century, cigarette smoking became widespread among men in countries like the U.S., but few women began smoking, because of strong social disapproval of women's smoking. During the mid-twentieth century, changes in women's roles were accompanied by increased social acceptance of smoking, increased smoking by women, and decreased gender differences in smoking. Between about 1965 and 1985 in the U.S., gender differences in smoking continued to decrease due to substantial decreases in men's smoking in response to accumulating evidence concerning the harmful health effects of smoking for men.

Thus, in the U.S. and some other developed democracies, gender differences in cigarette smoking increased during the early twentieth century and then decreased. These trends were a major cause of increases in gender differences in mortality during the middle decades of the twentieth century and subsequent decreases in gender differences in mortality during the late twentieth century (Pampel, 2002; Waldron, 1993, 2000). There has been a significant lag between the trends in gender differences in smoking and the trends in gender differences in mortality because the damage caused by smoking typically accumulates over many years before resulting in death.

Employment

As mentioned previously, men's more risky occupations result in much higher rates of fatal occupational injuries for men. Data for the U.S. indicate that occupational injuries are responsible for somewhat over 10% of total gender differences in fatal injuries (Waldron, 1991b and calculated from data in Arias et al., 2003, and National Center for Health Statistics, 2003). Occupational exposures to carcinogens such as asbestos appear to make a similarly small, but significant, contribution to men's higher lung cancer mortality. It has been estimated that, taken together, occupational exposures were responsible for roughly 5–10% of gender differences in total mortality in the U.S. during the late twentieth century (Waldron, 1991b).

Increases in women's employment during the second half of the twentieth century appear to have had little effect on women's mortality, in part because few women were employed in physically hazardous occupations (Pampel, 2002; Waldron, 1991b, 1993, 1995b, 2000). Therefore, the decreasing gender differences in employment have not had a significant direct effect on trends in gender differences in mortality. However, earlier increases in women's employment may have had an indirect effect on trends in gender differences in mortality. Specifically, increased employment of women may have contributed to a general liberalization of norms concerning women's behavior, including increasing social acceptance of women's smoking, which contributed to decreasing gender differences in smoking and smoking-related mortality (Waldron, 1991a).

Health Care Utilization

Gender differences in health care utilization do not appear to contribute substantially to gender differences in mortality for the most important causes of death in contemporary developed democracies (Micheli et al., 1998; Mor et al., 1990; Waldron, 1986a, 1995a, 2002). For example, women delay at least as long as men in seeking health care for symptoms of heart attack or cancer.

Biological Effects

The multiple biological differences between males and females include some that disadvantage males and others that disadvantage females. As discussed above, males' higher levels of testosterone both before and after birth appear to contribute to males' greater physical activity and aggressiveness, which in turn contribute to males' higher injury mortality. On the other hand, women have much higher breast cancer mortality, due to inherent differences between male and female anatomy and hormonal effects (Table 2; Waldron, 1986a).

There has been considerable interest in evaluating possible biological causes of men's higher coronary heart disease mortality. One major hypothesis has been that women are protected by beneficial effects of estrogens, while men's risk of coronary heart disease is increased by harmful effects of testosterone. However, research evidence has shown that both estrogen and testosterone have multiple harmful and beneficial effects on coronary heart disease mortality risk (Gyllenborg et al., 2001; Rossouw, 2002). Thus, it is important to evaluate whether, on balance, the net effect of women's hormones on coronary heart disease mortality risk is more beneficial than the net effect of men's hormones. Research findings, particularly from studies of the effects of removing the ovaries and the effects of menopause, suggest that, on balance, women's natural sex hormones reduce their risk of coronary heart disease (Gohlke-Barwolf, 2000; Merz et al., 2003; Waldron, 1995a, 2002). However, evidence concerning the effects of sex hormones on coronary heart disease risk is inconsistent and inconclusive, so the contribution of hormonal effects to gender differences in coronary heart disease mortality remains controversial (Bhasin and Herbst, 2003; Lawlor et al., 2002; Rossouw, 2002; Waldron, 1995a, 2002).[2] Other biological differences between men and women, including men's greater propensity to accumulate abdominal fat, appear to contribute to men's higher coronary heart disease mortality (Waldron, 1995a).

Biological factors that contribute to men's higher coronary heart disease mortality appear to have a larger or smaller effect, depending on environmental circumstances. Specifically, it appears that differences in sex hormones have a more adverse effect on male coronary heart disease mortality in societies with high dietary intake of saturated or animal fats, and men's propensity to accumulate abdominal fat makes a greater contribution in societies where obesity is more common (Lawlor et al., 2002; Waldron, 1995a, 2002).

Trends

Gender differences in mortality have shown considerable historical variation in the countries that are currently developed democracies (Lopez and Ruzicka, 1983; van Poppel, 2000; Waldron, 1986a, 1993). In general, gender differences in mortality were smaller and somewhat inconsistent at the beginning of the twentieth century, and the male mortality disadvantage increased during much of the twentieth century. However, the male mortality disadvantage decreased in some developed democracies during the later decades of the twentieth century.

During the nineteenth and early twentieth centuries it was relatively common for females to have higher mortality than males during childhood, the teen years and/or young adulthood (Klasen, 1998; Tabutin and Willems, 1998; van Poppel, 2000). Maternal mortality and higher female mortality for infectious diseases contributed to females' higher total mortality at these ages. Available evidence suggests that higher female mortality may have been due in part to the lower status of females, which may have resulted in less access to health-promoting resources.

During the mid-twentieth century, several trends contributed to the disappearance of higher female mortality and an increasing male mortality disadvantage (Lopez and Ruzicka, 1983; Pampel, 2002; Tabutin and Willems, 1998; van Poppel, 2000; Waldron, 1986a). Improvements in medical care and socioeconomic conditions, as well as decreases in pregnancy rates, had especially favorable effects on female mortality trends. In addition, the harmful effects of increases in men's cigarette smoking contributed substantially to the increasing male mortality disadvantage.

More recently, during the 1980s and 1990s, gender differences in mortality decreased in the U.S. and some other Western countries (Figure 2; Pampel, 2002; Waldron, 1993, 2000; Waldron et al., 2004). One important reason for these decreasing gender differences in mortality has been decreasing gender differences in some types of health-related behavior. Decreased gender differences in smoking have been primarily responsible for decreasing gender differences in lung cancer mortality. Similarly, decreasing gender differences in amount of driving have contributed to decreasing gender differences in motor vehicle accidents mortality.

Figure 2. *Trends in Gender Differences in Life Expectancy in the U.S. and Russia.*

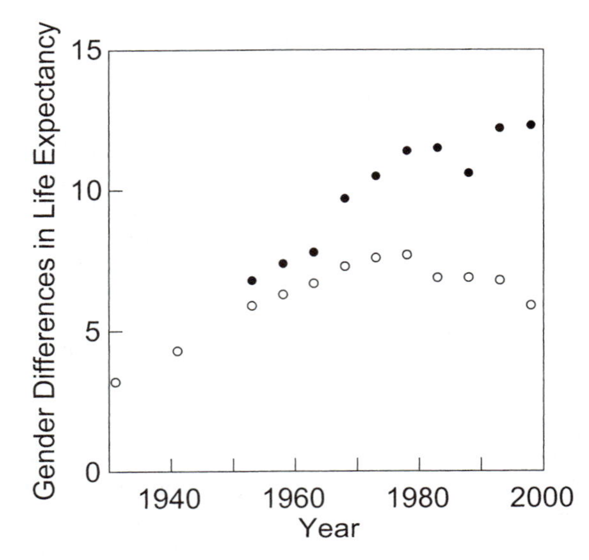

Female minus male life expectancy is indicated by open circles for the U.S. and filled circles for Russia. (Data from U.N., 2003 and Anderson, 1999)

The historical trends illustrate some of the diverse factors that contribute to variation in gender differences in mortality, including changes in gender roles, with related changes in attitudes toward women's behavior, and general societal trends, such as improvements in socioeconomic and health-care resources (Lopez and Ruzicka, 1983; Tabutin and Willems, 1998; van Poppel, 2000; Waldron, 1986a, 2000).

Russia and Other Formerly Communist European Countries

In recent decades, gender differences in mortality have been larger in Russia and some other formerly Communist European countries than in the U.S. and most other developed democracies (McKee and Schkolnikov, 2001). In Russia toward the end of the twentieth century, the male disadvantage in life expectancy reached a maximum of over 13 years, which was twice as large as the male disadvantage in the U.S. (Notzon et al., 2003). Men's mortality rates were so high in Russia that the male life expectancy in Russia was shorter than the male life expectancy in Brazil, China, or any of the other largest developing countries of Asia (Table 1).

The causes of death that contribute to males' higher mortality are similar in Russia and the U.S., but the sex mortality ratios for these causes of death are higher in Russia than in the U.S. (Table 3). Causes of death with particularly high sex mortality ratios in Russia include lung cancer, which is ten times higher for males than for females; suicide, which is six times higher for males; accidents mortality, which is four times higher for males; and liver disease and other alcohol-related mortality, which is three times higher for males.

In Russia, as in the U.S., gender differences in health-related behavior are major contributors to males' higher mortality, but with even greater gender differences in behavior observed in Russia. For example, in Russia at the beginning of the 1990s, approximately 60% of men vs. 10% of women were smokers; in contrast, in the U.S., 28% of men vs. 23% of women were smokers (National Center for Health Statistics, 2003; Notzon et al., 2003). The large gender difference in smoking in Russia is a major cause of the high sex mortality ratios for lung cancer and chronic obstructive pulmonary diseases (Table 3). Russian men also have particularly high rates of binge drinking, which contributes to their high risk of accidents, suicide, liver disease, and heart disease (Bobadilla et al., 1997; McKee et al., 2000). Women's alcohol consumption is less than one-quarter of men's, and this large gender difference in drinking is a major cause of the large gender difference in mortality in Russia.

Many of the other formerly Communist European countries also show a large male mortality disadvantage, although not as extreme as in Russia (Figure 1; Bobadilla et al., 1997; McKee and Schkolnikov, 2001; Nolte et al., 2000; U.N., 2003; Weidner et al., 2002). In these countries, gender differences in mortality are particularly large for causes of death such as lung cancer, motor vehicle accidents, and suicide. One major reason for men's mortality disadvantage is their high rates of smoking and drinking.

It appears that a major underlying cause of the large male mortality disadvantage in Russia and many other formerly Communist European countries has been the particularly adverse effect on

Table 4-3. Gender Differences in Mortality by Cause of Death, U.S. and Russia, 1994a

Cause of Death	Sex Mortality Ratios: U.S.	Sex Mortality Ratios: Russia
Diseases of Heart	1.7	2.0
Lung Cancer[b]	2.1	10.1
Chronic Obstructive Pulmonary Diseases	1.7	3.9
Chronic Liver Disease, Cirrhosis and Other Alcohol-related Causes[c]	2.6	3.2
Suicide	4.5	6.1
Motor Vehicle and Other Transport Accidents	2.3	3.7
Non-transport Accidents and Other External Causes	2.6	4.2
Total	1.6	2.1

[a] Sex mortality ratios are male divided by female age-adjusted death rates. (Data from Notzon et al., 2003)

[b] Lung cancer refers to malignant neoplasms of the respiratory system.

[c] Alcohol-related causes include chronic liver diseases and cirrhosis, alcohol poisoning and alcohol-dependence syndrome.

men's mortality of the social and economic stresses during the late Communist period and during the transition from Communism, which resulted in a substantial deterioration in economic conditions (Bobadilla et al., 1997; McKee and Schkolnikov, 2001; Notzon et al., 2003). During the late Communist period of the 1970s and 1980s, death rates tended to increase for adult males of working ages, and gender differences in mortality and life expectancy increased in Russia and many other Communist countries of Eastern Europe (Figure 2; Bobadilla et al., 1997; Nolte et al., 2000; Waldron, 1993). A further increase in the male mortality disadvantage was observed after the transition from Communist rule and the breakup of the Soviet Union during the late 1980s and very early 1990s (Bobadilla et al., 1997; Notzon et al., 2003).

One notable exception to the trends toward an increasing male mortality disadvantage occurred during the late 1980s in Russia, when government policies temporarily caused a substantial reduction in alcohol availability (Figure 2; Bobadilla et al., 1997; Weidner et al., 2002). The decrease in drinking benefited men particularly, resulting in substantial decreases in mortality for accidents, suicide, homicide, and cardiovascular diseases. Consequently, gender differences in mortality and life expectancy decreased during this brief period of reduced alcohol availability. These observations indicate that one major reason for the particularly adverse effect of societal stresses on men's mortality in Russia is that men were much more likely than women to respond to these stresses by binge drinking, with the associated increased mortality risk.

In conclusion, the data for Russia and other formerly Communist European countries suggest that men experienced more adverse health effects than women during the last decades of Communist rule and the difficult social and economic transitions after the collapse of Communism and the Soviet Union. The health effects have been particularly harmful for men in Russia, where it appears that many men have responded to recent societal stresses with increased binge drinking, which has particularly harmful effects on mortality risk.

Developing Countries

Gender differences in life expectancy and mortality vary considerably in different developing countries, reflecting the diversity of economic and cultural conditions among these countries. For example, gender differences in the largest developing countries vary from 6.5 years longer life expectancy for females in Brazil to little or no gender difference in life expectancy in Bangladesh and Pakistan (Table 1). The small gender difference in life expectancy in many South Asian countries reflects a rough balance between higher mortality for females among children and young adults and higher mortality for males at older ages (Lopez and Ruzicka, 1983; Murray and Lopez, 1996; U.N., 1998; Waldron, 1986a).

In general, gender differences in life expectancy and mortality are smaller in developing countries than in developed countries (Table 1; Figure 1). One reason is that factors that disadvantage males are counterbalanced by other factors that disadvantage females. In addition, the factors that disadvantage males have relatively less impact on total mortality in developing countries because total mortality is increased for both females and males due to the effects of inadequate material resources.

Some of the causes that contribute to higher male mortality in developed countries also tend to increase male mortality in developing countries (Table 4). For example, more males than females smoke in almost all societies, and in many developing countries gender differences in smoking are largely due to women's low rates of smoking (Anson and Sun, 2002; U. S. Department of Health and Human Services, 2001; Waldron et al., 1988). Correspondingly, men have substantially higher lung cancer mortality than women, even in developing countries or regions where there is little or no gender difference in total mortality (Figure 1). Similarly, in both developing and developed countries, males are more likely to be heavy drinkers, which increases their mortality risk (Table 4). However, these male disadvantages have less impact on gender differences in total mortality in developing countries, since smoking and alcohol-related mortality generally constitute a smaller

Table 4-4. Contribution of Major Risk Factors to Male and Female Mortality in Developed and Developing Countries, 2000a

	Developed Countries[b]		Low-Mortality Developing Countries[c]		High-Mortality Developing Countries[d]	
Risk Factors	Males	Females	Males	Females	Males	Females
Tobacco	26.3%	9.3%	12.2%	2.9%	7.5%	1.5%
Alcohol	8.0%	–0.3%	8.5%	1.6%	2.6%	0.6%
Underweight due to undernutrition	0.1%	0.1%	1.8%	1.9%	12.6%	13.4%
Unsafe water, sanitation, and hygiene	0.2%	0.2%	1.1%	1.1%	5.8%	5.9%
Indoor smoke from solid fuels	0.1%	0.2%	1.9%	5.4%	3.6%	4.3%
Unsafe sex	0.2%	0.6%	0.8%	1.3%	9.3%	10.9%
Total deaths (millions)	6.9	6.6	8.6	7.4	13.8	12.6

[a] The numbers in this table show the percentage of total mortality attributed to each specified risk factor for males and for females in each category of countries. (Data from WHO, 2003)
[b] e.g. U.S., Japan, Russia
[c] e.g. Brazil, Indonesia, China
[d] e.g. Bangladesh, India, Pakistan, Nigeria

proportion of the higher total mortality in these countries.

In many developing countries, total mortality is increased for both sexes by high rates of infectious disease mortality due to the limited availability of clean water, sanitation, nutrition, and preventive and curative health care (Table 4; Figure 1; Murray and Lopez, 1996; WHO, 2003). In some areas, girls have even less access than boys to limited health-promoting resources, resulting in higher mortality risk for girls. In some developing countries, female mortality risk is also increased by women's exposure to indoor smoke from cooking and heating fires (Table 4). In addition, risks associated with female reproductive functions contribute significantly to women's mortality risk in some developing countries with limited material resources. All of these factors contribute to smaller gender differences in mortality in developing countries. The following paragraphs summarize additional information concerning the behavioral and biological factors that influence gender differences in mortality in developing countries.

Injuries

In developing countries, as in developed countries, males have higher injuries mortality than females, reflecting the effects of many of the same differences in biology and gender role socialization discussed previously (Murray and Lopez, 1996; Waldron, 1998). In Africa and Latin America, injuries mortality is approximately three times higher for males than for females, comparable to the sex mortality ratios observed in developed countries (Figure 1). In contrast, in India and China, gender differences in injuries mortality are much smaller, with a male excess of only 20–35%.

In India, females have much higher accidental fires mortality than males, which reduces the gender difference in total injuries mortality (data from Murray and Lopez, 1996). Women's high accidental fires mortality results in part from risk of fire accidents during cooking, but apparently also includes some homicides related to dowry disputes (Das Gupta and Li, 1999).

In India and China, suicide mortality does not show the substantial male excess observed in many other countries, and this is another reason for the small gender differences in total injuries mortality (Figure 1). In India there is very little gender difference in suicide mortality, and in China women have higher suicide mortality than men. Chinese women's higher suicide mortality is due primarily to young rural women, who have substantially higher suicide rates than corresponding men (Phillips et al., 2002). It appears that, in many cases, the suicides of young rural Chinese women are impulsive responses to family conflicts that might result in non-fatal suicide attempts in Western countries, but become fatal in rural China because of ready access to highly toxic pesticides and other agricultural chemicals, as well as limited availability of medical care (Pearson et al., 2002; Phillips et al., 2002).

Biological Effects

The relative importance of specific biological factors that influence gender differences in mortality varies in different countries, depending on environmental conditions. For example, biological factors that contribute to greater male vulnerability to coronary heart disease mortality appear to have less adverse effects on males in countries where there is less consumption of saturated fats and less obesity (Lawlor et al., 2002; Waldron, 1995a, 2002). Correspondingly, sex mortality ratios for coronary heart disease are lower in developing countries (Figure 1). In addition, in developing countries, coronary heart disease is responsible for a smaller proportion of total mortality. Thus, biological effects on gender differences in coronary heart disease mortality have less effect on gender differences in total mortality in developing countries than in developed countries.

In developing countries with limited material resources, differences between male and female reproductive biology tend to increase female mortality and thus reduce gender differences in total mortality. For example, maternal mortality accounts for 5% of total female mortality in sub-Saharan Africa, although maternal mortality is less important in other regions (data from Murray and Lopez, 1996). Women who are pregnant or lactating have increased nutritional requirements and correspondingly, in developing countries with limited resources, pregnant and lactating women are less likely than men to have nutritionally adequate diets (DeRose et al., 2000). Inadequate nutrition contributes to greater vulnerability to infectious disease mortality.[3] Additional biological factors that influence gender differences in infectious disease mortality are discussed in the following section.

Infectious Diseases

Infectious diseases, including diarrheal diseases, measles, tuberculosis, other respiratory infections, and HIV/AIDS, make a much larger contribution to total mortality in developing countries than in developed countries (Figure 1; Murray and Lopez, 1996). Gender differences in infectious disease mortality tend to be relatively small in the developing countries, because factors that tend to increase male mortality are balanced by factors that tend to increase female mortality.

Hormonal and genetic effects appear to contribute to generally lower immune function in males and greater vulnerability to infectious diseases (Waldron, 1998; Wizeman and Pardue, 2001). Nevertheless, girls have higher rates of infectious disease mortality than boys in some regions, especially in South Asia and China (data from Murray and Lopez, 1996). Data for South Asia indicate that girls' higher rates of infectious disease mortality are related to less adequate health care and lower rates of immunization for girls (Hazarika, 2000; Khanna et al., 2003; Pande and Yazbeck, 2003; U.N., 1998; Waldron, 1987). It should be mentioned that complex and somewhat inconsistent patterns have been observed in research findings concerning both the postulated biological vulnerability of males and gender differences in access to health care; gender differences in nutrition have shown even more variable and inconsistent patterns (DeRose et al., 2000; Hill and Upchurch, 1995; U.N., 1998; Waldron, 1987, 1998; Wizemann and Pardue, 2001). In summary, although current evidence is not conclusive, it appears that, in regions such as South Asia and China, less adequate immunization and health care for girls can outweigh any biological advantages for females, resulting in higher infectious disease mortality for girls.

It should be noted that different types of infectious diseases are influenced by different causal factors and show different patterns of gender differences. This is illustrated by the example of HIV/AIDS, which is a major cause of mortality in sub-Saharan Africa (WHO, 2002). Due to biological differences, heterosexual intercourse with an infected partner results in a greater risk of infection for females than for males (Cohen and Eron, 2001; Nicolosi, et al., 1994). In contrast, homosexual contacts result in a much greater risk of infection for males. Males also are more likely to be intravenous (IV) drug users, which increases their exposure to HIV infection. As expected, in areas such as Africa, where the main mode of HIV transmission is heterosexual contact, over half of HIV-infected adults are women, while in areas such as East Asia and Latin America, where the main modes of transmission are intravenous drug use and homosexual contact, substantially more men than women have HIV infections (data from WHO, 2002).[4]

In summary, multiple counteracting factors influence gender differences in infectious disease mortality, and in developing countries the net result is generally small gender differences in total infectious disease mortality. The substantial contribution of infectious disease mortality to total mortality, together with the relatively small gender differences for this category, are important reasons for the generally smaller gender differences in total mortality in developing countries.

Cultural Context

As discussed above, the smaller gender differences in mortality in developing countries are due in part to the effects of limited material resources. In addition, cultural factors disadvantage females in some regions, particularly by contributing to discrimination against girls in access to health-promoting resources in regions such as South Asia. This type of discrimination appears to be related to a cultural preference for sons, who can make greater economic, social, and religious contributions to their parents' future well-being than daughters (Arnold et al., 1998; Hazarika, 2000; Hill and Upchurch, 1995; Khanna et al., 2003; Waldron, 1987).

Researchers have estimated that discrimination against females has resulted in 100 million "missing women," as indicated by the lower than expected number of females in the population in countries such as China and India (Klasen and Wink, 2003). The reduced number of females in these populations is due not only to higher than expected female mortality after birth, but also to sex-selective abortion by couples who want to ensure the birth of a son and avoid the birth of a daughter. Rates of "missing women" and excess mortality for girls are particularly high in areas with greater preference for sons and low female literacy and labor force participation (Dreze and Sen, 1995; Klasen and Wink, 2003; Waldron, 1987). These findings indicate that low status for women contributes to a female mortality disadvantage in some developing countries.

CONCLUSIONS

Gender differences in mortality and life expectancy vary considerably in different contemporary countries, ranging from a large male disadvantage in some countries, such as Russia, to a more moderate male disadvantage in most countries, including the U.S., to little or no male disadvantage in a few countries, such as Bangladesh. These variable gender differences in mortality are influenced by multiple causal factors, including biological factors (such as hormonal influences on physiology and behavior) and environmental factors (such as cultural influences on gender differences in behavior). In some cases, biological and environmental factors reinforce each other, both contributing to higher male mortality. In other cases, biological and environmental factors have counteracting effects on gender differences in mortality. The relative importance of specific causal factors varies in different environments, so the most important influences on gender differences in mortality differ between developed and developing countries.

In developed countries, males' more risky health-related behavior is one major cause of their higher mortality. For example, males' higher rates of cigarette smoking, heavy drinking, gun use, employment in hazardous occupations, and risk-taking in recreation and driving are primarily responsible for males' higher mortality for lung cancer, accidents, suicide, and homicide. For coronary heart disease, the effects of men's more hazardous smoking habits appear to be reinforced by biological disadvantages for males, including effects of sex hormones and men's greater propensity to develop abdominal adiposity.

Males' more risky health-related behavior appears to be due to both biological and cultural factors. Current evidence indicates that hormonal effects contribute to males' greater physical activity and aggressiveness, which in turn contribute to males' higher accidents and homicide mortality. In addition, gender role expectations and differential socialization of males and females contribute to gender differences in health-related behaviors. For example, in many cultures, heavy drinking by men is accepted or encouraged as an appropriate part of masculinity, whereas heavy drinking by women is discouraged, probably because it is incompatible with traditional female responsibilities for sexual restraint and the care of young children. Gender differences in smoking also reflect social expectations concerning gender-appropriate behavior. For example, in Western countries like the U.S., gender differences in smoking were much larger during the first half of the twentieth century, when few women smoked, due in large part to widespread social disapproval of women's smoking.

Culturally influenced variation in gender differences in health-related behavior has been a major cause of variation in gender differences in mortality in different historical periods and between different developed countries. For example, men's widespread adoption of cigarette smoking during the first half of the twentieth century was one major cause of increases in the male mortality disadvantage during much of the twentieth century in most developed countries. In some developed democracies, subsequent decreases in gender differences in smoking have contributed to decreasing gender differences in mortality in recent decades. In contrast, in Russia, the continuing large gender difference in smoking has contributed to the very large male mortality disadvantage in recent decades. In addition, a cultural tradition of binge drinking by men in Russia, combined with the social and economic stresses resulting from recent political and economic transitions, has had particularly harmful effects on Russian men's mortality risk.

In developing countries, gender differences in mortality have generally been smaller than in developed countries. One reason is that factors that disadvantage males have been balanced by factors that disadvantage females. In addition, several of the factors that contribute to higher mortality rates in developing countries increase mortality risk for females as much as for males. For example, in developing countries with limited material resources, environmental factors such as unsafe water and inadequate nutrition increase infectious disease mortality for both females and males.

Gender differences in infectious disease mortality are generally small in developing countries due to a balance between factors that disadvantage males and factors that disadvantage females. On the one hand, it appears that hormonal effects and X-linked immunodeficiencies contribute to greater male vulnerability to infectious diseases. On the other hand, in some developing countries, particularly in South Asia, lower rates of immunization and health care for girls increase girls' risk of infectious disease mortality. Discrimination against females and higher mortality for girls are related to a cultural preference for sons, who are able to make greater economic, social, and religious contributions than daughters to their parents' future well-being.

The multiple additional biological, behavioral, and environmental factors that influence gender differences in mortality in developing countries include some that disadvantage males and some that disadvantage females. Men's higher rates of smoking and drinking increase male mortality. However, the male excess for smoking and drinking-related mortality has less impact on gender differences in total mortality in developing countries than in developed countries, primarily because other causes of death, such as infectious diseases, contribute more to total mortality in developing countries. Factors that increase female mortality risk include high maternal mortality in sub-Saharan Africa and higher suicide rates for women than for men in China. The diversity of mortality patterns in different developing countries reflects the diversity of cultural, economic, public health, and health-care conditions in these countries.

The patterns of gender differences in mortality observed in contemporary developing countries are somewhat similar to the patterns observed in historical data for developed countries. In Western countries, gender differences in mortality were smaller in the nineteenth and early twentieth centuries, due in large part to the contributions of high maternal and infectious diseases mortality. As socioeconomic conditions and medical care improved during the twentieth century, these causes of death became less important, smoking-related mortality became more important, and the male mortality disadvantage increased during much of the twentieth century in Western countries. Similar trends are expected to contribute to an increasing male mortality disadvantage in the developing countries of Asia and Africa during the early decades of the twenty-first century (Murray and Lopez, 1997; U.N., 2003). However, any predictions concerning future mortality trends in these regions must be viewed with caution, due to uncertainty concerning the future of the HIV/AIDS epidemic. For developed countries, there is no consensus concerning future trends in gender differences, with different researchers predicting increases or decreases in gender differences in life expectancy (Murray and Lopez, 1997; U.N., 2003).

Future trends in gender differences in mortality are difficult to predict in part because these trends will be influenced by multiple future decisions of governments, organizations, and individuals. For example, if governments and organizations mount effective public health campaigns to reduce risky health-related behaviors, these may benefit males more than females, as demonstrated by previous U.S. campaigns against smoking and drunk driving, which have had a greater impact on male mortality and thus have contributed to recent decreases in gender differences in mortality (Waldron, 1991a, 2000; Waldron et al., 2004). In some cases, broader societal trends may be even more important than public health campaigns. For example, in Russia the anti-alcohol campaign during the late 1980s had only very brief success, and it appears that broader policies to reduce socioeconomic stresses will be needed to reduce excess male mortality (Notzon et al., 2003; Weidner et al., 2002). In developing countries, female mortality might be reduced by programs that improve the status of females (e.g., increased education of girls and the provision of microcredit loans for poor women to invest in tiny businesses to improve their income-earning capacity) (Dreze and Sen, 1995; Klasen and Wink, 2003).

In conclusion, gender differences in mortality have varied considerably in different countries and historical periods. Some biological differences between the sexes benefit males, and others benefit females, and the balance between these effects varies, depending on cultural and socioeconomic conditions. Similarly, the differences between male and female gender roles are more beneficial for males or for females, depending on the societal context. The health effects of male gender roles can be more beneficial when higher male status results in greater male access to health-promoting resources in societies with limited material resources. In contrast, male roles can have more harmful health effects than female roles due to greater cultural acceptance and encouragement of some types of harmful health-related behavior for males. One general conclusion, which is also supported by research concerning social class, ethnic, and international differentials in mortality, is that an individual's health-related behavior and mortality risk is very much affected by his or her social context (Robert and House, 2000; WHO, 2003).

Acknowledgments

It is a pleasure to thank Katie Eyer and Marian Sandmaier for helpful comments on previous drafts of this chapter and Chris McCloskey and Jason Wang for their help in obtaining and analyzing data.

FOOTNOTES

1. For brevity, economically developed countries are referred to as developed countries, and economically developing countries (also called less-developed countries) are referred to as developing countries. Also for brevity, the Russian Federation is referred to as Russia and the United States of America is referred to as the U.S..
2. Recent evidence indicates that the risk of coronary heart disease is slightly increased by hormone replacement therapy in postmenopausal women (Rossouw, 2002; Writing Group for the Women's Health Initiative Investigators, 2002). However, the balance between harmful and beneficial effects of hormones on coronary heart disease risk appears to vary depending on the specific hormone combination, doses, and timing, so the evidence concerning the effects of hormone replacement therapy is less relevant to understanding gender differences in coronary heart disease than the evidence concerning the effects of early loss of a woman's own endogenous hormones (Rossouw, 2002; Waldron, 1995a, 2002).
3. In addition, limited health-care resources in developing countries increase the impact of reproductive biology on women's cancer risk. Cervical cancer mortality is much higher in many developing countries than in developed countries such as the U.S., where cervical cancer mortality has been substantially reduced by early detection with Pap smears followed by effective medical treatment (IARC Working Group on Evaluation of Cervical Cancer Screening Programmes, 1986). High female mortality for cervical cancer is one reason why females have higher total cancer mortality than males in India and Latin America, despite males' higher lung cancer mortality (Figure 1, and data from Murray and Lopez, 1996).
4. Transmission via homosexual behavior and intravenous drug use has also resulted in high sex mortality ratios for HIV/AIDS in the developed democracies, and this is the reason for the relatively high sex mortality ratio for infectious diseases in these countries (Figure 1; data from Murray and Lopez, 1996, and WHO, 2002).
5. For Figure 1, sex mortality ratios (male death rates divided by female death rates) are shown on a log scale on the *y* axis. Death rates for ages 0–69 were age-adjusted based on the age distribution of the world population (calculated from data in Murray and Lopez, 1996). Data for China and India are shown separately because these two very large countries, taken together, account for more than a third of total world population.

REFERENCES

Anderson, R. N. (1999) United States life tables, 1997. *National Vital Statistics Reports*. Vol. 47, No. 28. Hyattsville, Maryland: National Center for Health and Statistics.

Anson, O. and Sun, S. (2002) Gender and health in rural China: Evidence from HeBei province, *Social Science and Medicine* 55:1 in the 039–1054.

Arias, E., Anderson, R. N., Hsiang-Ching, K., et al. (2003) Deaths: Final Data for 2001. *National Vital Statistics Reports*. Vol. 52, No. 3. Hyattsville, Maryland: National Center for Health Statistics.

Arnold, F., Choe, M. K., and Roy, T. K. (1998) Son preference, the family-building process and child mortality in India, *Population Studies* 52:301–315.

Bhasin, S. and Herbst, K. (2003) Testosterone and atherosclerosis progression in men, *Diabetes Care* 26(6):1929–1931.

Bloomfield, K. (coordinator) (2003) *Gender and Alcohol—a Multinational Study*. (www.medizin.fuberlin.de/statistik/Gender&Alcohol/).

Bobadilla, J. L., Costello, C. A., and Mitchell, F., eds. (1997) *Premature Death in the New Independent States*. Washington, D.C.: National Academy Press.

Canetto, S. S. and Sakinovsky, I. (1998) The gender paradox in suicide, *Suicide and Life-threatening Behavior* 28(1):1–23.

Cohen, M. S., and Eron, J. J. (2002) Sexual HIV Transmission and its prevention (www.Medscape.com <http://www.Medscape.com>).

Collaer, M. L. and Hines, M. (1995) Human behavioral sex differences: A role for gonadal hormones during early development? *Psychological Bulletin* 118:55–107.

Das Gupta, M. and Li, S. (1999) Gender bias in China, South Korea and India 1920–1990: Effects of war, famine and fertility decline, *Development and Change* 30:619–652.

DeRose, L. F., Das, M. and Millman, S. R. (2000) Does female disadvantage mean lower access to food? *Population and Development Review* 26(3): 517–547.

Dreze, J. and Sen, A. (1995) *India: Economic Development and Social Opportunities*. Delhi:Oxford University Press.

Gohlke-Barwolf, C. (2000) Coronary artery disease—Is menopause a risk factor? *Basic Research in Cardiology* 95(Suppl. 1):I/77–I/83.

Guralnik, J. M., Balfour, J. L., and Volpato, S. (2000) The ratio of older women to men: Historical perspectives and cross-national comparisons, *Aging Clin. Exp. Res.* 12(2):65–67.

Gyllenborg, J., Rasmussen, S. L., Borch-Johnsen, K., et al. (2001) Cardiovascular risk factors in men: The role of gonadal steroids and sex hormone-binding globulin, *Metabolism* 58 (8):882–888.

Hazarika, G. (2000) Gender differences in children's nutrition and access to health care in Pakistan, *Journal of Developmental Studies* 37(1): 73–92.

Hill, K. and Upchurch, D. M. (1995) Gender differences in child health: Evidence from the Demographic and Health Surveys, *Population and Development Review* 21(1):127–151.

IARC Working Group on the Valuation of Cervical Cancer Screening Programmes (1986) Screening for squamous cervical cancer: Duration of low risk after negative results of cervical cytology and its implications for screening policies, *British Medical Journal Clinical Research Ed.* 293 (6548):659–664.

Khanna, R., Kumar, A., Vaghela, J. F., et al. (2003) Community based retrospective study of sex in infant mortality in India, *British Medical Journal* 327:126–129.

Klasen, S. (1998) Marriage, bargaining, and intrahousehold resource allocation: excess female mortality among adults during early German development, 1740–1860, *The Journal of Economic History* 58(2): 32–467.

Klasen, S. and Wink, C. (2003) "Missing Women": Revisiting the debate, *Feminist Economics* 9(2–3): 263–299.

Lawlor, D. A., Ebrahim, S., and Smith, G. D. (2002) A life course approach to coronary heart disease and stroke, in D. Kuh and R. Hardy, *A Life Course Approach to Women's Health*. Oxford: Oxford University Press.

Lopez, A. D., and Ruzicka, L. T., eds. (1983) *Sex Differentials in Mortality: Trends, Determinants and Consequences*. Canberra: Australian National University, Miscellaneous Series No. 4.

McKee, M. and Shkolnikov, V. (2001) Understanding the toll of premature death among men in eastern Europe, *British Medical Journal* 323:1051–1055.

McKee M., Shkolnikov, V., and Leon, D. A. (2000) Alcohol is implicated in the fluctuations in cardiovascular disease in Russia since the 1980s, *Annals of Epidemiology* 11(1):1–6.

Merz, C. N. M., Johnson, B. D., Sharaf, B. L., et al. (2003) Hypoestrogenemia of hypothalamic origin and coronary artery disease in premenopausal women: A report from the NHLBI-sponsored WISE Study, *Journal of the American College of Cardiology* 41(3):413–419.

Micheli, A., Mariotto, A., Rossi, A., et al. (1998) The prognostic role of gender in survival of adult cancer patients, *European Journal of Cancer* 34(14): 2271–2278.

Mor, V., Masterson-Allen, S., Goldberg, R., et al. (1990) Pre-diagnostic symptom recognition and help seeking among cancer patients, *Journal of Community Health* 15(4): 253–266.

Murray, C. J. L., and Lopez, A. D. (1996) *The Global Burden of Disease: A Comprehensive Assessment of Mortality and Disability from Diseases, Injuries, and Risk Factors in 1990 and Projected to 2020.* Boston, Massachusetts: The Harvard School of Public Health, Harvard University Press.

Murray, C. L. and Lopez, A. D. (1997) Alternative projections of mortality and disability by cause 1990–2020: Global Burden of Disease Study. *Lancet 349*:1498–1504.

National Center for Health Statistics (2003) *Health, United States, 2003*. Hyattsville, MD: U. S. Department of Health and Human Services.

Nicolosi, A., Leite, M. L. C., Musicco, M. et al (1994) The efficiency of male-to-female and female-to-male sexual transmission of the human immunodeficiency virus: A study of 730 stable couples, *Epidemiology* 5(6):570–575.

Nolte, E., Shkolnikov, V. and McKee, M. (2000) Changing mortality patterns in East and West Germany and Poland. I: Long term trends (1960–1997), *Journal of Epidemiology and Community Health* 54:890–898.

Notzon, F.C., Komarov, Y.M., Ermakov, S.P., et al. (2003) Vital and Health Statistics: Russian Federation and United States, selected years 1985–2000. *Vital and Health Statistics* 5 (11). Hyattsville MD: National Center for Health Statistics.

Pampel, F. C. (2002) Cigarette use and the narrowing sex differential in mortality, *Population and Development Review* 28(1):77–104.

Pande, R. P. and Yazbeck, A. S. (2003) What's in a country average? Wealth, gender, and regional inequalities in immunization in India, *Social Science and Medicine* 57:2075–2088.

Pearson, V., Phillips, M. R., He, F., et al. (2002) Attempted suicide among young rural women in the People's Republic of China: Possibilities for prevention, *Suicide and Life-Threatening Behavior* 32(4):359–369.

Peto, R., Lopez, A. D., Boreham, J., et al. (1994) *Mortality from Smoking in Developed Countries 1950–2000.* Oxford: Oxford University Press.

Phillips, M. R., Li, X., and Zhang, Y. (2002) Suicide rates in China, 1995–99, *Lancet* 359:835–840.

Robert, S. A. and House, J. S. (2000) Socioeconomic inequalities in health: an enduring sociological problem, in Bird, C. E., Conrad, P., and Fremont, A. M. (eds), *Handbook of Medical Sociology*, 5th edition. Upper Saddle River, New Jersey: Prentice-Hall.

Rossouw, J. E. (2002) Hormones, genetic factors, and gender differences in cardiovascular disease, *Cardiovascular Research* 53:550–557.

Tabutin, D. and Willems, M. (1998) Differential mortality by sex from birth to adolescence: The historical experience of the West (1750–1930), in U.N., *Too Young to Die: Genes or Gender?* New York: U.N., Population Division.

United Nations (1998) *Too Young to Die: Genes or Gender?* New York: United Nations, Population Division.

United Nations (2003) *World Population Prospects, The 2002 Revision, Vol. 1: Comprehensive Tables.* New York: United Nations, Population Division.

U.S. Department of Health and Human Services (2001) *Women and Smoking: A Report of the Surgeon General.* Rockville, Maryland: U. S. Department of Health and Human Services.

Van Poppel, F. (2000) Long-term trends in relative health differences between men and women, *European Journal of Obstetrics and Gynecology and Reproductive Biology* 93:119–122.

Waldron, I. (1986a) What do we know about causes of sex differences in mortality? A review of the literature, *Population Bulletin of the United Nations* 18: 59–76.

Waldron, I. (1986b) The contribution of smoking to sex differences in mortality, *Public Health Reports* 101(2): 163–174.

Waldron, I. (1987) Patterns and causes of excess female mortality among children in developing countries, *World Health Statistics Quarterly* 40(3): 194–210.

Waldron, I. (1991a) Patterns and causes of gender differences in smoking, *Social Science and Medicine*, 32(9): 989–1005.

Waldron, I. (1991b) Effects of labor force participation on sex differences in mortality and morbidity, in M. Frankenhauser, U. Lundberg, and M. Chesney (eds.) *Women, Work and Health.* New York: Plenum Press.

Waldron, I. (1993) Recent trends in sex mortality ratios for adults in developed countries, *Social Science and Medicine*, 36(4): 451–462.

Waldron, I. (1995a) Contributions of biological and behavioural factors to changing sex differences in ischaemic heart disease mortality, in A. Lopez, G. Caselli, and T. Valkonen (eds.) *Adult Mortality in Developed Contries: From Description to Explanation.* New York: Oxford University Press.

Waldron, I. (1995b) Contributions of changing gender differences in behavior and social roles to changing gender differences in mortality, in D. Sabo and D. F. Gordon (eds.) *Men's Health and Illness.* Thousand Oaks: Sage Publications.

Waldron, I. (1997) Changing gender roles and gender differences in health behavior, in D. S. Gochman (ed.) *Handbook of Health Research I: Personal and Social Determinants.* New York: Plenum Press.

Waldron, I. (1998) Sex differences in infant and early childhood mortality: Major causes of death and possible biological causes, in U.N., *Too Young to Die: Genes or Gender?* New York: United Nations.

Waldron, I. (2000) Trends in gender differences in mortality: relationships to changing gender differences in behaviour and other causal factors, in E. Annandale and K. Hunt (eds.) *Gender Inequalities in Health*. Buckingham: Open University Press.

Waldron, I. (2002) Trends in gender differences in coronary heart disease mortality—Relationships to trends in health-related behavior and changing gender roles. In Weidner, G., Kopp, M., and Kristenson, M., eds., *Heart Disease: Environment, Stress and Gender*. Amsterdam: IOS Press.

Waldron, I., Bratelli, G., Carriker, L.,et al. (1988) Gender differences in tobacco use in Africa, Asia, the Pacific, and Latin America, *Social Science and Medicine*. 27(11): 1269–1275.

Waldron, I., McCloskey, C., and Earle, I. (2004) Trends in gender differences in accidents mortality—Relationships to changing gender roles and other societal trends. (Submitted paper)

Weidner, G., Kopp, M., and Kristenson, M., eds. (2002) *Heart Disease: Environment, Stress and Gender*. Amsterdam: IOS Press.

Wizemann, T. M., and Pardue, M.-L., eds. 2001. *Exploring the Biological Contributions to Human Health: Does Sex Matter?* Washington, D.C.: National Academy Press, Institute of Medicine.

World Health Organization (2002) *AIDS Epidemic Update: December 2002*. Geneva, Switzerland: UNAIDS and WHO. (www.who.int/hiv/pub/epidemiology)

World Health Organization (2003) *The World Health Report 2002*. (www.who.int/whr/2002/).

Writing Group for the Women's Health Initiative Investigators (2002) Risks and benefits of estrogen plus progestin in healthy postmenopausal women, *JAMA* 288 (3): 321–333.

5 A Tale of Two States

Victor R. Fuchs

In the western United States there are two contiguous states that enjoy about the same levels of income and medical care and are alike in many other respects, but their levels of health differ enormously. The inhabitants of Utah are among the healthiest individuals in the United States, while the residents of Nevada are at the opposite end of the spectrum. Comparing death rates of white residents in the two states, for example, we find that infant mortality is about 40 percent higher in Nevada. And lest the reader think that the higher rate in Nevada is attributable to the "sinful" atmosphere of Reno and Las Vegas, we should note that infant mortality in the rest of the state is almost exactly the same as it is in these two cities. Rather . . . infant death rates depend critically upon the physical and emotional condition of the mother.

The excess mortality in Nevada drops appreciably for children because, as shall be argued below, differences in life-style account for differences in death rates, and these do not fully emerge until the adult years. As [Table 5-1] indicates, the differential for adult men and women is in the range of 40 to 50 percent until old age, at which point the differential naturally decreases.

The two states are very much alike with respect to income, schooling, degree of urbanization, climate, and many other variables that are frequently thought to be the cause of variations in mortality. (In fact, average family income is actually higher in Nevada than in Utah.) The numbers of physicians and of hospital beds per capita are also similar in the two states.

What, then, explains these huge differences in death rates? The answer almost surely lies in the different life-styles of the residents of the two states. Utah is inhabited primarily by Mormons, whose influence is strong throughout the state.

Table 5-1. **Excess of Death Rates in Nevada Compared with Utah, Average for 1959–61 and 1966–68**

Age Group	Males	Females
<1	42%	35%
1–19	16%	26%
20–29	44%	42%
30–39	37%	42%
40–49	54%	69%
50–59	38%	28%
60–69	26%	17%
70–79	20%	6%

Devout Mormons do not use tobacco or alcohol and in general lead stable, quiet lives. Nevada, on the other hand, is a state with high rates of cigarette and alcohol consumption and very high indexes of marital and geographical instability. The contrast with Utah in these respects is extraordinary.

In 1970, 63 percent of Utah's residents 20 years of age and over had been born in the state; in Nevada the comparable figure was only 10 percent; for persons 35–64 the figures were 64 percent in Utah and 8 percent in Nevada. Not only were more than nine out of ten Nevadans of middle age born elsewhere, but more than 60 percent were not even born in the West.

The contrast in stability is also evident in the response to the 1970 census question about changes in residence. In Nevada only 36 percent of persons 5 years of age and over were then living in the same residence as they had been in 1965; in Utah the comparable figure was 54 percent.

The differences in marital status between the two states are also significant in view of the association between marital status and mortality discussed in the previous section. More than 20 percent of Nevada's males aged 35–64 are single, widowed, divorced, or not living with their spouses. Of those who are married with spouse present, more than one-third had been previously widowed or divorced. In Utah the comparable figures are only half as large.

The impact of alcohol and tobacco can be readily seen in [Table 5-2] the comparison of death rates from cirrhosis of the liver and malignant neoplasms of the respiratory system. For

Table 5-2. **Excess of Death Rates in Nevada Compared with Utah for Cirrhosis of the Liver and Malignant Neoplasms of the Respiratory System, Average for 1966–68**

Age	Males	Females
30–39	590%	443%
40–49	111%	296%
50–59	206%	205%
60–69	117%	227%

both sexes the excess of death rates from these causes in Nevada is very large.

The populations of these two states are, to a considerable extent, self-selected extremes from the continuum of life-styles found in the United States. Nevadans, as has been shown, are predominantly recent immigrants from other areas, many of whom were attracted by the state's permissive mores. The inhabitants of Utah, on the other hand, are evidently willing to remain in a more restricted society. Persons born in Utah who do not find these restrictions acceptable tend to move out of the state.

SUMMARY

This dramatic illustration of large health differentials that are unrelated to income or availability of medical care helps to highlight the [following] themes . . .

1. From the middle of the eighteenth century to the middle of the twentieth century rising incomes resulted in unprecedented improvements in health in the United States and other developing countries.
2. During most of this period medical care (as distinct from public health measures) played an insignificant role in health, but, beginning in the mid-1930s, major therapeutic discoveries made significant contributions independently of the rise in real income.
3. As a result of the changing nature of health problems, rising income is no longer significantly associated with better health, except in the case of infant mortality (primarily post-neonatal mortality)—and even here the relationship is weaker than it used to be.

4. As a result of the wide diffusion of effective medical care, its marginal contribution to health is again small (over the observed range of variation). There is no reason to believe that the major health problems of the average American would be significantly alleviated by increases in the number of hospitals or physicians. This conclusion might be altered, however, as the result of new scientific discoveries. Alternatively, the *marginal* contribution of medical care might become even smaller as a result of such advances.
5. The greatest current potential for improving the health of the American people is to be found in what they do and don't do to and for themselves. Individual decisions about diet, exercise, and smoking are of critical importance, and collective decisions affecting pollution and other aspects of the environment are also relevant.

These conclusions notwithstanding, the demand for medical care is very great and growing rapidly. As René Dubos has acutely observed, "To ward off disease or recover health, men as a rule find it easier to depend on the healers than to attempt the more difficult task of living wisely."[1]

NOTE

1. René Dubos, *The Mirage of Health* (New York: Harper, 1959), p. 110.

6 *Population Health in Utah and Nevada: An Update on Victor Fuchs' Tale of Two States*

Victor G. Rodwin and Melanie J. Croce-Galis

In 1974, after examining age-specific mortality rates in Utah and Nevada, health economist Victor Fuchs noted that Utah's population was healthier than Nevada's even though these states had similar densities of physicians and hospital beds.[1] Since Utah and Nevada had similar levels of average family income, urbanization, and education, Fuchs concluded that access to medical care makes only a marginal contribution to population health. He suggested, therefore, that a policy of increasing the number of hospitals and/or physicians would be of little benefit to population health. In comparison to Nevada, Utah's residents are part of a more homogeneous, predominantly Mormon state with less migration, more family stability, and fewer risky health behaviors. Fuchs' "Tale of Two States" illustrates the powerful role of lifestyle and other social determinants of population health.[2]

Do Fuchs' findings hold up after three decades? Has Utah's health advantage been maintained? Since state-level data on risk factors for disease and measures of health status that go beyond mortality are more easily available today, we present 2000 data on these indicators to shed more light on the characteristics of both states.

What did we find? Sure enough, these two contiguous states continue to share some important characteristics (Table 1). They also differ in important ways with respect to risk factors for disease, age-specific mortality rates, and a range of other health-status indicators. Thirty years later, the population of Utah continues to live longer, on average, and appears, by all measures, to be in better health than Nevada's residents.

Acknowledgment: This article grows out of a discussion with students in Wagner/NYU's "Community Health and Medical Care" class taught by Professor Rodwin. A rough draft was written by Melanie Croce-Galis and Brenda Hurtubise. Subsequently, Victor Rodwin and Melanie Croce-Galis gathered additional data and rewrote the paper. The authors thank Brenda Hurtubise for her contribution to the initial research for this article.

CONVERGENT CHARACTERISTICS

Based on the latest data available—in 2000—Utah and Nevada still share similar levels of income—whether measured by household or family units. They share similar levels of poverty, urbanization, and education. Also, Utah and Nevada have similar levels of medical resources: Utah has a slightly higher physician density; Nevada has a slightly higher hospital bed density.[3] Finally, Utah and Nevada have similar levels of health care coverage. Nevada has a slightly higher level of coverage, perhaps because it has a higher percentage of its population over the age of 65 (10.5% versus 8.5%) that are covered by Medicare.

DIVERGENT CHARACTERISTICS

One of the most striking differences between Nevada and Utah concerns patterns of community stability (Table 2). In Utah, 63 percent of the population was born in the state in contrast to only 21 percent in Nevada. Utah's Hispanic and African-American population is under 10 percent whereas Nevada's comes to 26 percent. Utah's families are characterized by lower divorce rates and its residents drink far less alcohol and smoke far less tobacco than Nevada. In summary, The Behavioral Risk Factor Surveillance Survey (BRFSS) indicates that rates of binge drinking, chronic drinking, and cigarette consumption are about twice as high in Nevada than in Utah.

POPULATION HEALTH IN UTAH AND NEVADA

Although Nevada's infant mortality rates have increased proportionately more than Utah's over the past thirty years, they continue to lag significantly in comparison to Utah (6.5 versus 5.2[4]). Age-specific mortality rates in Nevada also exceed Utah's for every age cohort (Table 3). What is more, for those 50 years of age and over, there is an *even greater* excess of death rates in Nevada in 2000 than thirty years ago.

Mortality, by selected causes, is also higher in Nevada than in Utah (Table 4). For example, the higher mortality rates from malignant neoplasms of the respiratory system and from cirrhosis of the liver probably reflect the cumulative effects of different health behaviors, noted earlier (Table 2).

Beyond the comparison of mortality differentials, we found a range of other health status indicators that reveal, in more depth, some of the ways in which Utah's residents are healthier

Table 6-1. Utah and Nevada: Convergent Characteristics

	Utah	Nevada
Socioeconomic Characteristics		
Average household income	$45,726	$44,581
Average family income	$51,022	$50,849
% Families below poverty level	6.5%	7.5%
Individuals below poverty level	9.4%	10.5%
Level of urbanization	88%	92%
Education: high school diploma or higher	88%	81%
Medical Care Resources and Coverage		
Hospital Beds *(per 1,000 pop'n)*	2.2	3.1
Physicians *(per 10,000 pop'n)*	31	29
Have some kind of health insurance coverage	86.4%	88.9%

Sources: 2000 U.S. Census; Utah Health Data Committee, Office of Health Care Statistics; Nevada Bureau of Licensure and Certification, Department of Human Resources; 2000 BRFSS Utah and Nevada.

Table 6-2. Utah and Nevada: Divergent Characteristics

	Utah	Nevada
Community Stability/Migration		
% of persons (age 5 +) that were living in same residence in 1995	49%	37%
% of residents born in state	63%	21%
Socio-Demographic Characteristics		
% African-American and Hispanic	9.7%	26.3%
% Non-Hispanic White	85%	65.2%
Family Stability		
Divorce rate	4.3 per 1,000	7.3 per 1,000
Married couple/family households	63.2%	49.7%
Risky health behaviors		
Alcohol use:		
binge drinking	10. 2%	22.6%
Tobacco use:		
Ever smoked 100 cigarettes and a current smoker?	12.9%	29.0%

Sources: 2000 U.S. Census; 1999 BRFSS, 2000 BRFSS, Nevada State Health Division: Center for Health Data and Research; Utah Department of Health: Center for Health Data; Utah Vital Statistics, Marriages and Divorces 1999 and 2000.

than Nevada's (Table 5). For example, differences in years of potential life lost (YPLL) before the age of 75 indicate that heart disease, homicides, and suicides exact far greater costs on residents of Nevada than on their counterparts in Utah. This is consistent with measures of self-assessed health status, which indicate that residents of Utah perceive themselves to be in better health than those of Nevada.

CONCLUDING OBSERVATIONS

Although Utah and Nevada share a host of convergent characteristics, Utah's distinctive features—community and family stability, population homogeneity, and fewer risky health behaviors—highlight the social factors that appear to make its residents healthier. All of these factors are influenced by the dominant Mormon

Table 6-3. Excess Mortality Rates in Nevada Compared with Utah: 1960s and 2000

Average for 1959–61 and 1966–68			2000	
Age Group	*Males*	*Females*	*Age Group*	*Males and Females*
<1	42%	35%		
1–19	16%	26%	<24	31%
20–29	44%	42%	25–34	45%
30–39	37%	42%	35–44	43%
40–49	54%	69%	45–54	65%
50–59	38%	28%	55–64	53%
60–69	26%	17%	65–74	45%
70–79	20%	6%	75–84	13%

Sources:
1960s: Fuchs in Conrad, Table 5.1, p. 50, 1974.
2000: Utah and Nevada Vital Statistics: Births and Deaths; 2000 U.S. Census.

Table 6-4. Excess of Death Rates in Nevada Compared with Utah for Cirrhosis of the Liver and Malignant Neoplasm of the Respiratory System: 1960s and 2000

Cirrhosis of the Liver and Malignant Neoplasms of the Respiratory System Average for 1966–68			Cirrhosis of the Liver 2000			Malignant Neoplasms of the Respiratory System 2000		
Age	*Males*	*Females*	*Utah Rate*	*Nevada Rate*	*Excess*	*Utah Rate*	*Nevada Rate*	*Excess*
30–39	590%	443%	6	14	133%	18	57	217%
40–49	111%	296%	Rate is per 100,000 population					
50–59	206%	205%						
60–69	117%	227%						

Sources:
1960s: Fuchs in Conrad, Table 5.2, p. 50, 1974.
2000: Utah and Nevada Vital Statistics: Births and Deaths; 2000 U.S. Census.

Table 6-5. Utah and Nevada: Health Status Indicators

	Utah	Nevada
Motor Vehicle-Related Deaths *(per 100,000 population)*	17.7	18.9
Years of Potential Life Lost (YPLL) Before Age 75	6503	8970
YPLL<75 by Cause:		
Homicides	98	397
Suicides	494	660
Heart disease	759	1581
Self-Assessed Health Status As Very Good or Excellent	61.6%	55.7%
Self-Assessed Health Status As Poor	2.4%	5.0%
Average Number of Days with Limited Activity (per 30 Days)	2.8	3.3

Sources: 1999 National Vital Statistics System, National Center for Health Statistics, Age-Adjusted YPLL<75 years per 100,000 population; 2000 BRFSS Survey (http://health2k.state.nv.us/nihds/brfss/Brfss%202000/General%20Health/genhlth.htm); Kaiser Family Foundation State Health Facts Online: United Health Foundation analysis of 2001 BRFSS.

culture in Utah and probably account for the confluence of many behavioral choices that lower Utah's mortality rates across a wide range of health risks and raise its population's health status.

Do residents of Utah have a better quality of life? Do they derive more happiness from life? We still do not have the kinds of indicators and data we might like to answer such questions. But thirty years later, Fuchs' citation from René Dubos continues to ring true: "To ward off disease or recover health, men as a rule find it easier to depend on the healers than to attempt the more difficult task of living wisely."[5]

NOTES

1. Fuchs in P. Conrad (Ed.) *The Sociology of Health and Illness* (6th ed.) (pp. 50). New York, NY: Worth Publishers, 2001. Fuchs' tale was originally published as a chapter in his book, *Who Shall Live? Health Economics and Social Change*. New York, Basic Books, 1974.
2. Evans, R.G. (1994). Why Are Some People Healthy and Others Not? NY: Aldine de Gruyter.
3. Utah/Nevada Department of Licensure, personal communication April 23, 2003. Part of the difference in divorce rate figures may be due to the fact that Nevada grants divorces to Nevada residents who have resided in the state for at least six weeks, whereas in Utah residents must have resided in the county where the divorce is filed for at least three months prior to filing; in addition, residents of Utah have a mandatory ninety-day waiting period after the filing before the divorce is granted.
4. Utah/Nevada Vital Statistics, 2000.
5. Fuchs in Conrad, 2001, p. 51.

REFERENCES

Behavioral Risk Factor Surveillance System: (http://www.cdc.gov/brfss/index.htmndividual Nevada Behavioral Risk Factor Surveillance Survey. (2000). Tobacco Use. Q: Have You Ever Smoked 100 Cigarettes and a Current Smoker (Smoke Every day and Some days). General Health Status. Self-Assessment of General Health Status. Health Insurance. Q: Do You Have Any Kind of Health Care Coverage? Retrieved 4/19/03 from the World Wide Web: http://health2k.state.nv.us/nihds/brfss/Brfss%202000/index.htm

Center for Disease Control and Prevention. Epidemiology Program Office: State Health Profiles-Tables and Maps: http://www.cdc.gov/epo/shp/maps.htm; and Kaiser Family Foundation. State Health Facts Online: I State Profiles. http://www.statehealthfacts.kff.org/cgi-bin/healthfacts.

Nevada Department of Human Resources, Bureau of Licensure and Certification. (2003). Health Facilities-Northern Nevada, Southern Nevada. Medical Facilities-Northern Nevada, Southern Nevada.

Nevada State Health Division: Center for Health Data and Research. Nevada Vital Statistics 2000. Cancer Mortality Rates by Type of Cancer, Nevada Residents, 2000. Number of Marriages and Divorces in Nevada and the United States, Selected Years, 1950 to 2000. Population Pyramid in Nevada, 2000. Retrieved 4/19/03 from the World Wide Web: http://health2k.state.nv.us/vs/2000%20Vital%20Statistics%20Report.pdf

U.S. Census Bureau. (2000). GCT-P11. Language, School Enrollment, and Educational Attainment: 2000, Nevada, Utah. Retrieved 4/19/03 from the World Wide Web: http://factfinder.census.gov/bf/_lang=en_vt_name=DEC_2000_108S_GCTP11_ST10_geo_id=04000US32.html

U.S. Census Bureau. (2000). GCT-P13. Occupation, Industry and Class of Worker of Employed Civilians 16 Years and Over: 2000, Nevada, Utah. Retrieved 4/19/03 from the World Wide Web: http://factfinder.census.gov/bf/_lang=en_vt_name=DEC_2000_108S_GCTP13_ST10_geo_id=04000US32.html

U.S. Census Bureau. (2000). Population: Race, Hispanic, or Latino and Age, 2000, Nevada, Utah. Retrieved 4/19/03 from the World Wide Web: http://factfinder.census.gov/bf/_lang=en_vt_name=DEC_2000_PL_U_QTPL_geo_id=04000US32.html

Utah Department of Health: Center for Health Data. Utah's Vital Statistics: Births and Deaths, 2000. Deaths by Age, Race, and Gender, Residents: Utah, 2000. Infant Mortality Rates by Age at Death, Residents: Utah, 1960–2000. Leading Causes of Death and Death Rates: Utah and United States, 2000. Retrieved 4/19/03 from the World Wide Web: http://www.health.state.ut.us/bvr/pub_vs/ia00/00bx.pdf

Utah Department of Health: Center for Health Data. Utah's Vital Statistics, Marriages and Divorces 1999 and 2000. Marriage and Divorce Rates, Utah and United States, 1960 and 1970–2000. Retrieved 4/19/03 from the World Wide Web: http://www.health.state.ut.us/bvr/pub_vs/ia00/99and00md.pdf

Utah Office of Health Care Statistics. (2003). Utah Hospital and Freestanding Ambulatory Surgery Center (FASC) Characteristics: 2000. Retrieved 3/13/03 from the World Wide Web: http://hlunix.hl.state.ut.us/had/index.html

Our Sickening Social and Physical Environments

. . .

In the previous section, we explored the relationship between society and the distribution of disease and death. We saw that in American society diseases are patterned by sociocultural factors, including social class, gender, race, and lifestyle. Here we continue to search for an understanding of the interface between diseases and society by examining the sociological contexts of three serious health disorders in the United States: coronary heart disease, black lung disease, and leukemia.

Social scientists have little difficulty analyzing the social nature of such problems as homicide, suicide, and automobile accidents. Less often, however, have they applied sociological perspectives to understanding the causes and prevention of diseases such as cancer or hypertension. The selections in this section share the theme that at least some of these chronic diseases have developed as a result of modern industrialization, and so are deeply connected to the organization and characteristics of social life.

According to the U.S. Department of Health and Human Services, approximately 40 percent of all deaths in 2003 were caused by diseases of the heart and circulatory system (coronary heart disease, hypertension, and stroke), and an additional 25 percent of deaths were the result of some form of cancer (National Center for Chronic Disease Prevention, 2003). These data give us a general picture of the significant impact of chronic disease on our population's health. Chronic diseases generally develop and persist over a long period of time. Their signs often go unnoticed or unidentified until they cause serious damage to the victim's body, and they usually have complex rather than simple or single causes. Medical treatment generally aims to alleviate symptoms, prevent or slow down further organic damage, or minimize physical discomfort, primarily through treatments with medications or surgery. Treatment rather than prevention is the dominant medical approach to these diseases.

Although *prevention* of chronic diseases seems to be the most logical, safe, and perhaps the most moral approach, few financial resources have been devoted in the United States to the elimination of the physical and social causes of chronic health disorders. (To the contrary, the federal government continues to subsidize the tobacco industry in the United States despite the surgeon general's warning that cigarette smoking is the leading cause of death from lung cancer and a major risk factor for other diseases.) The growing recognition of the environmental component in many chronic diseases has led some critics to question the priorities of our current medical care system, as well as the limits of its approach to the treatment, let alone prevention, of these disorders.

For example, Samuel Epstein has argued that the "epidemic" of cancer in the United States is both a medical and social issue, involving as it does a range of political and economic factors including the use of chemicals in manufacturing to increase profits, the economic and political pressures on industry scientists, and the relatively low priority given to cancer prevention research (Epstein, 1979; Patterson, 1989). If many cancers are environmentally produced and the federal government has estimated that as many as 90 percent may be so why has medical research and treatment focused on cure rather than prevention (Muir and Sasco, 1991)?

. . .

Over the last decade, toxic waste has become one of the major environmental issues facing our society. How do we dispose of dangerous materials produced as a by-product of our industrial society? What consequences do these toxic materials have for people's health and welfare? Polluting industries rarely point to the dangers of toxic waste; rather, most problems have been uncovered by community action or government intervention. In the first selection, "Popular Epidemiology: Community Response to Toxic Waste-Induced Disease," Phil Brown presents the case of the leukemia cluster in Woburn, Massachusetts. Brown shows how community initiative what he calls "popular epidemiology" with the aid of scientists uncovered the link between the corporate dumping of toxic wastes, the pollution of the drinking water, and the increase in childhood leukemia. He presents popular epidemiology as one strategy people can use to struggle against forces that create dangerous and sickening environments.

Public health analysts have long known that the physical environment can produce disease, but in recent years evidence has accumulated that the social environment may also produce ill health. For example, studies have shown that the social organization of the work environment (House and Cottington, 1984), social stress (Kasl, 1984) and social support (Cohen and Syme, 1985) can affect health status and outcome. Among the most intriguing work in this area are the studies that show the importance of social relationships to health. There is continuing evidence that individuals with few social relationships are at increased risk for disease (morbidity) and death (mortality). In "Social Relationships and Health," James S. House, Karl R. Landis, and Debra Umberson review the existing research and conclude that a significant causal relationship exists between social relationships and health. They contend the evidence is as strong as that for cigarette smoking and health in 1964, when the surgeon general issued the first report on the dangers of smoking, although the specificity of the associations is not yet as well-known. While we don't really know how social relationships affect health, it is increasingly clear that these factors need to be considered seriously in terms of etiology and prevention. This awareness is especially important because evidence exists that the quantity and quality of social relationships in our society may be declining.

In the third selection, "Dying Alone: The Social Production of Urban Isolation," Eric Klinenberg presents a dramatic and tragic illustration of the impact of an extreme lack of social relationships. In this article, he searches for the root causes of the deaths of over 700 Chicago residents during a devastating heat wave in 1995. He engages in what he calls a "social autopsy" to examine the underlying factors of why these residents died, beyond the immediate "medical" causes that would be listed on the death certificates. Klinenberg found that urban isolation combined with a culture of fear and political neglect created a "chronic" situation that made certain people particularly vulnerable to death in this disaster (see also Klinenberg, 2002). With a greater number of people living alone, many of them poor and elderly, this type of social susceptibility to disease and death may become a greater problem despite any advances in medical care.

In the final selection, "Health Inequalities: Relative or Absolute Material Standards?" Richard Wilkinson attempts to refine our understanding of the impact of social inequality on health. Using several sources of data, he finds that relative differences in economic status have a more significant impact on health and mortality than absolute levels of income or wealth. For example, being poor in country A where the income differences are high (e.g., the highest 20% of the population earns on average 12 times more than the lowest 20%) has a more negative effect on health than being poor in country B where the income differences are small (e.g., the highest 20% of population earns on average 3 times more than the lowest 20%). Even if the absolute per capita income of country A were substantially higher than country B, the mortality rates might well be higher in A. The issue here is not absolute poverty, but *relative disparity* or income gap between rich and poor that seems most significant. Sociologists have long known about the effects of relative deprivation; the key to understanding relative deprivation is to examine the comparison group. People tend to compare themselves to others within their own society, so where the income and living standard differences between rich and poor are great (like with the United States), the poor are likely to suffer from greater relative deprivation. According to Wilkinson, the adverse impact on mortality is due to the psychosocial impact of relative deprivation; it creates a chronic form of stress that is detrimental to health. Some have suggested links between social rank and physiological processes as immune function and endocrine responses to stress (see Kawachi, Kennedy, and Wilkinson, 1999). On the other hand, countries with more income equality tend to have the longest life expectancies. This expands our ideas about how social inequalities affect health and suggests that in more equalitarian societies the burden of relative deprivation is reduced.

REFERENCES

Cohen, Sheldon, and S. Leonard Syme. 1985. Social Support and Health. New York: Academic Press.

Epstein, Samuel. 1979. The Politics of Cancer. New York: Anchor/Doubleday.

House, James S., and Eric M. Cottington. 1984. "Health and the workplace." In David Mechanic and Linda H. Aiken (eds.) Applications of Social Science to Clinical Medicine and Health Policy. New Brunswick, NJ: Rutgers University Press.

Kasl, Stanislav. 1984. "Stress and health." Annual Review of Public Health. 5:319–341.

Kawachi, Ichiro, Bruce P. Kennedy, and Richard G. Wilkinson (eds.). 1999. The Society and Population Health Reader: Income Inequality and Health. New York: New Press.

Klinenberg, Eric. 2002. Heat Wave: A Social Autopsy of Disaster in Chicago. University of Chicago Press.

Muir, C. S., and A. J. Sasco. 1991. "Prospects for cancer control in the 1990s." Annual Review of Public Health. 11:143–64.

National Center for Health Statistics. 1994. Health, United States, 1994. Washington, DC: U.S. Government Printing Office.

Patterson, James. 1989. The Dread Disease: Cancer and American Culture. Cambridge: Harvard University Press.

Syme, S. Leonard. 1986. "Strategies for health promotion." Preventive Medicine. 15:492–507.

Tesh, Sylvia. 1988. Hidden Arguments: Political Ideology and Disease Prevention. New Brunswick, NJ: Rutgers University Press.

7 Popular Epidemiology: Community Response to Toxic Waste-Induced Disease

Phil Brown

Residents of Woburn, Massachusetts, were startled several years ago to learn that their children were contracting leukemia at exceedingly high rates. By their own efforts, the affected families confirmed the existence of a leukemia cluster and demonstrated that it was traceable to industrial waste carcinogens that leached into their drinking water supply. These families put into process a long train of action which led to a civil suit against corporate giants W. R. Grace and Beatrice Foods, which opened in Boston in March 1986. On 28 July 1986, a federal district court jury found that Grace had negligently dumped chemicals on its property; Beatrice Foods was absolved. The case then proceeded to a second stage in which the plaintiffs would have to prove that the chemicals had actually caused leukemia. As this part of the case was under way, the judge decided that the jury had not understood the hydrogeological data that were crucial to the suit, and on 17 September he ordered the case to be retried. Because of this decision, an out-of-court settlement with Grace was reached on 22 September 1986.[1] The Woburn families filed an appeal against Beatrice in May 1987 on the grounds that the judge was wrong to exclude evidence and effects of pre-1968 dumping from the case.

This case has received much national attention and has a number of important effects. It has focused public attention on corporate responsibility for toxic wastes and their resultant health effects. For some time now, civic activists have organized opposition to environmental contamination, and the Woburn situation provides a valuable case study which can help to understand, forecast, and perhaps even to catalyze similar efforts in the future. It has also demonstrated that the health effects of toxic wastes are not restricted to physical disease but also include emotional problems. The Woburn plaintiffs were one of the first groups of toxic waste plaintiffs to introduce such evidence in court. These data can expand our knowledge of the effects of toxic wastes as well as our understanding of the psychological effects of disasters and trauma.

Woburn also offers a valuable example of lay communication of risk to scientific experts and government officials. Citizens in other locations and situations have previously attempted to convey risks to appropriate parties. In Woburn and other recent cases, however, a more concerted effort was made, which involved varying degrees of investigation into disease patterns and their potential or likely causes. I term this type of activity *popular epidemiology.*

Popular epidemiology is defined as the process by which laypersons gather statistics and other information and also direct and marshall the knowledge and resources of experts in order to understand the epidemiology of disease. Popular epidemiology is not merely a matter of public participation in what we traditionally conceive of as epidemiology. Lilienfeld defines epidemiology as "the study of the distribution of a disease or a physiological condition in human populations and of the factors that influence this distribution." These data are used to explain the etiology of the condition and to provide preventive, public health, and clinical practices to deal with the condition.[2] Popular epidemiology includes more elements than the above definition in that it emphasizes basic social structural factors, involves social movements, and challenges certain basic assumptions of traditional epidemiology. Nevertheless I find it appropriate to retain the word "epidemiology" in the concept of popular epidemiology because the *starting point* is the search for rates and causes of disease.

In order to develop the concept of popular epidemiology, I will first provide a brief capsule of the Woburn events. Following that, I will show commonalities between Woburn and other communities in popular epidemiological investigation. Finally, I will expand on the original definition of popular epidemiology by examining in detail five components of that concept.

BRIEF HISTORY OF THE WOBURN LEUKEMIA CLUSTER

In May 1979 builders found 184 55-gallon drums in a vacant lot along the Aberjona River. They called the police, who then called the state Department of Environmental Quality Engineering (DEQE). Water samples from wells G and H showed large concentrations of organic compounds that were known carcinogens in laboratory animals. Of particular concern were trichloroethylene (TCE) and tetrachloroethylene (PCE). The EPA's risk level for TCE is 27 parts per billion (ppb), and well G had ten times that concentration. The state ordered that both wells be closed due to their TCE and PCE levels.[3]

But town and state officials had prior knowledge of problems in the Woburn water. Frequent complaints about dishwasher discoloration, bad odor, and bad taste had led to a 1978 study by private consultants. They used an umbrella screen for organic compounds and reported a carbon-chloroform extract (CCE) concentration of 2.79 mg/L, while stating that the level should not exceed 0.1 mg/L. This Dufresne-Henry report led Woburn officials to ask the state Department of Public Health (DPH) to allow the town to change its chlorination method; because they assumed that chlorine was interacting with minerals. The DPH allowed this change and in the same letter told the officials not to rely on wells G and H because of high concentrations of salt and minerals. The DPH did not mention another important piece of information it possessed: In 1975 a DEQE engineer, who had been applying a more exact screening test to all wells in the state, found wells G and H to have higher concentrations of organic compounds than nearby wells. In retrospect, he stated that the level seemed high, but "at the time I was doing research only on the method and nobody knew how serious water contamination problems could be." Thus, before the discovery of the visible toxic wastes, both local and state officials had some knowledge of problems in Woburn water and specifically in the two wells in question.[4]

The first popular epidemiological efforts also predated the 1979 well closings. Anne Anderson, whose son, Jimmy, had been diagnosed with acute lymphocytic leukemia in 1972, had gathered information about other cases by word of mouth and by chance meetings with other victims at stores and at the hospital where Jimmy was being treated. She began to theorize that the growing number of leukemia cases may have been caused by something carried in the water. She asked state officials to test the water but was told that this could not be done on an individual's initiative. Anderson's husband did not support her in this effort but rather asked the family pastor to help her get her mind off what he felt to be an erroneous idea. This development led to one of the key elements of the Woburn story, since Reverend Bruce Young became a major actor in the community's efforts.[5]

Another fortuitous circumstance occurred in June 1979, just weeks after the state ordered the wells shut down. A DEQE engineer, on his way to work, drove past the nearby Industri-Plex construction site and thought that there might be violations of the Wetlands Act. Upon investigation, EPA scientists found dangerous levels of lead, arsenic, and chromium, yet they told neither the town officials nor the public. Only in September did a Woburn newspaper break the news. At this point, Reverend Young began to agree with Anne Anderson's conclusions about the water supply, and so he placed an ad in the Woburn paper, asking people who knew of childhood leukemia cases to respond. He prepared a map and a questionnaire, in consultation with Dr. Truman, the physician treating Jimmy Anderson. Several days later, Anderson and Young plotted the cases. There were 12, with 6 of them closely grouped. The data convinced Truman, who called the Centers for Disease Control (CDC). The activists spread the word through the press and succeeded in persuading the City Council on 19 December 1979 to request the CDC to investigate. In January 1980 Young, Anderson, and 20 other people formed For a Safe Environment (FACE) to generate public concern about the leukemia cluster.[6]

Five days after the City Council request to the CDC, the Massachusetts DPH issued a report that contradicted the Young-Anderson map model of the leukemia cluster. According to the DPH, there were 18 cases, when 10.9 were expected, but the difference was not so great for a ten-year period. Further, the DPH argued that a cluster pattern was not present. Despite this blow, the activists were buoyed by growing public awareness of the environmental hazard and by popular epidemiological efforts in other places. In June 1980, Anderson and Young were asked by Senator Edward Kennedy to testify at hearings on the Superfund. Young told the hearing:

> For seven years we were told that the burden of proof was upon us as independent citizens to gather the statistics. . . . All our work was done independent of the Commonwealth of Massachusetts. They offered no support, and were in fact one of our adversaries in this battle to prove that we had a problem.[7]

On 23 May 1980 the CDC and the National Institute for Occupational Safety and Health (NIOSH) sent John Cutler to lead a team affiliated with the Massachusetts DPH to study the Woburn case. This report, released on 23 January 1981, five days after the death of Jimmy Anderson, stated that there were 12 cases of childhood leukemia in East Woburn, when 5.3 were expected. The incidence of kidney cancer was also elevated. The discussion of the data was, however, inconclusive, since the case-control method failed to find characteristics that differentiated victims from nonvictims. Further, a lack of environmental data for earlier periods was an obstacle to linking disease with the water supply.[8]

The conjuncture of Jimmy Anderson's death and the report's failure to confirm the water-leukemia hypothesis led the families and friends of the victims, along with their local allies, to question the nature of the scientific study. As DiPerna puts it, a layperson's approach to epidemiological science evolved.[9] The Woburn residents were helped in this direction when Larry Brown from the Harvard School of Public Health (SPH) invited Anderson and Young to present the Woburn data to a SPH seminar. Marvin Zelen, an SPH biostatistician present at the seminar, became interested. At this time, clusters of cancer and other diseases were being investigated around the United States, although the CDC did not inform Woburn residents of this heightened public and scientific interest in cluster studies. Moreover, the DPH issued a follow-up report in November 1981 which stated that the number of childhood leukemia deaths began to rise in the 1959–1963 period, before the wells were drilled. Assuming an average latency period of 2–5 years, the DPH report agreed that deaths should not have started to increase until 1969–1973, when in fact the rate was lower than expected.[10]

In order to elicit more conclusive data, Zelen and his colleague, Steven Lagakos, undertook a more detailed study of health status in Woburn, focusing on birth defects and reproductive disorders, since these were widely considered to be environmentally related. The biostatisticians and the FACE activists teamed up in what was to become a major epidemiological study and a prototype of a popular epidemiological alliance between citizen activists and sympathetic scientists. FACE coordinated 301 Woburn volunteers who administered a telephone survey from April to September in 1982, which was designed to reach 70% of the city's population who had phones.[11]

At the same time, the state DEQE conducted a hydrogeology study which found that the bedrock in the affected area of Woburn sloped in a southwest direction and was shaped like a bowl, with wells G and H in the deepest part. The agency's March 1982 report addressed the location of the contamination: the source was not the Industri-Plex site as had been believed, but rather W.R. Grace's Cryovac Division and Beatrice Foods' Riley tannery. This major information led eight families of leukemia victims to file a $400 million suit in May 1982 against those corporations for poor waste disposal practices, which led to groundwater contamination and hence to fatal disease.[12] A smaller company, Unifirst, was also sued but quickly settled before trial.[13]

The Harvard School of Public Health/FACE Study

Sources of data included information on 20 cases of childhood leukemia (ages 19 and under) which were diagnosed between 1964 and 1983, the DEQE water model of regional and temporal distribution of water from wells G and H, and the health survey. The survey gathered data on adverse pregnancy outcomes and childhood disorders from 5,010 interviews, covering 57% of Woburn residences with telephones. The researchers trained 235 volunteers to conduct the health survey, taking precautions to avoid bias.[14]

On 8 February 1984, the Harvard SPH data were made public. Childhood leukemia was found to be significantly associated with exposure to water from wells G and H, both on a cumulative basis and on a none-versus-some exposure basis. Children with leukemia received an average of 21.2% of their yearly water supply from the wells, compared to 9.5% for children without leukemia. The data do not, however, explain all 11 excess cases; the cumulative method explains 4 excess cases and the none-versus-some metric explains 6 cases.

Controlling for important risk factors in pregnancy, the investigators found the access to contaminated water was not associated with spontaneous abortions, low birth weight, perinatal deaths before 1970, or with musculoskeletal, cardiovascular, or "other" birth anomalies. Water exposure was associated with perinatal deaths since 1970, eye/ear anomalies, and CNS/chromosomal/oral cleft anomalies. With regard to childhood disorders, water exposure was associated with only two of nine categories of disease: kidney/urinary tract and lung/respiratory. There was no association with allergies, anemia, diabetes, heart/blood pressure, learning disability, neurologic/sensory, or "other" disorders.[15] If only the *in-utero* cases are studied, the results are even stronger in terms of the positive associations.[16]

The researchers conducted extensive analyses to demonstrate that the data were not biased. They compared baseline rates of adverse health effects for West Woburn (never exposed to wells G and H water) and East Woburn (at a period prior to the opening of the wells): no differences were found. They examined transiency rates to test whether they were related to exposure and found them to be alike in both sectors. Various tests also ruled out a number of biases potentially attributable to the volunteer interviewers.[17]

The report was greeted with criticism from many circles: the CDC, the American Cancer Society, the EPA, and even the Harvard SPH Department of Epidemiology. These criticisms demonstrate both legitimate concerns and clear examples of elitism and opposition to community involvement in scientific work. One of the legitimate concerns was the grouping of diseases into categories, despite their different etiologies. Similarly, the biostatisticians were criticized for grouping diverse birth defects under the broad heading of "environmentally associated disease."[18] The researchers argue, however, that they grouped defects because there could never be sufficient numbers of each of the numerous defects. Further, they claim that their grouping was based on the literature on chemical causes of birth defects. In fact, if the grouping was incorrect, they note that they would not have found positive results.[19] Some critics questioned whether the water model was precise enough, and whether it was independently verified.[20] Actually, the DEQE officials failed to release the water data in a timely fashion, making it impossible to obtain other validation. A more detailed model is now available, although it has been consistently hard to get funds to conduct new analyses.[21] Critics have also noted that there were increasing numbers of cases even after the wells were shut down, and that these new cases were more likely to be in West Woburn than in East Woburn. If wells G and H were the culprit, such critics ask, is it possible that there could be yet another cluster *independent* of the one studied?[22] In fact, given the chemical soup in Woburn, it is indeed plausible that this could be the case. Excavations at the Industri-Plex site produced buried animal hides and chemical wastes. A nearby abandoned lagoon was full of lead, arsenic, and other metals. A sampling from 61 test wells in East Woburn turned up 48 toxic substances on the EPA priority list as well as raised levels of 22 metals.[23]

The criticisms of most interest here are those that argue against the basic concept of public participation in science. Critics held that the study was biased precisely because volunteers conducted the health survey and because the study was based on a political goal. These arguments will be addressed below, as I develop the five elements of popular epidemiology. First, though, we will take a look at commonalities between several communities that engaged in forms of popular epidemiology.

ELEMENTS OF POPULAR EPIDEMIOLOGY

Commonalities in Popular Epidemiology

Couto studied Yellow Creek, Kentucky, where residents identified problems of creek pollution caused by untreated residential and commercial sewage. Comparing this and other locations, Couto develops a model which is a valuable starting place on which I shall expand. Couto identifies three sets of actors. The *community at risk* is the community and people at risk of environment hazards. The *community of consequence calculation* includes the public and private officials who allocate resources related to environmental health risks. The *community of probability calculation* consists of epidemiologists and allied scientists.[24]

The community at risk is where popular epidemiological action begins. In Yellow Creek the shared evidence of obvious pollution was from fish kills, disappearances of small animals, and corrosion of screens and other materials. This "street-wise or creek-side environmental monitoring" precedes awareness of health risks.[25] My interviews with Woburn residents show the same phenomenon: People noticed the water stains on dishwashers and the bad odor long before they were aware of any adverse health effects. Love Canal residents remembered years of bad odors, rocks that exploded when dropped or thrown, sludge leakage into basements, chemical residues on the ground after rainfall, and children's foot irritations after playing in fields where toxic wastes were dumped.[26] Residents of South Brunswick, New Jersey, noticed foul tasting water and saw barrels marked "toxic chemicals" dumped, bulldozed, and ruptured.[27]

The next stage in Couto's model is *common sense epidemiology,* where people intuit that a higher than expected incidence of disease is attributable to pollution.[28] As a result of such judgments, people organize and approach public officials. Another avenue, not mentioned by Couto, is taking the issue to court, for blame, redress, organizing, and legitimation. When citizens organize publicly, they first encounter the community of consequence calculation, a community that usually resists them by denying the problem or its seriousness, and even by blaming the problem on the lifestyle and habits of the people at risk.[29] This is in part due to "environmental blackmail," whereby officials fear that plants will close and jobs and taxes will be lost.

The initial shock at the existence of the toxic substances gives way to anger at the public and private officials who do little or nothing about the problem.[30] This reaction is found in residents' attitudes toward corporate and governmental officials in Woburn and in numerous other sites.[31]

. . .

We can now build on Couto's work to generate a broader model of popular epidemiology. Although my examples often involve toxic waste-induced disease, the concept of popular epidemiology clearly extends into other areas.

Popular Participation and the Myth of Value-Neutrality

Popular epidemiology opposes the widely held belief that epidemiology is a value-neutral scientific enterprise which can be conducted in a sociopolitical vacuum. Directly related to this assumption is the belief that epidemiological work should not be conducted only by experts. Those who criticized volunteer bias and political goals in the Woburn study posited a value-free science of epidemiology in which knowledge, theories, techniques, and actual and potential applications are devoid of self-interest or bias. The possibility of volunteer bias is a real concern, of course, but in the Woburn case the care with which the biostatisticians controlled for bias is noteworthy.

Beyond the methodological and statistical controls for bias are a number of other important issues. Science is limited in its practice by factors such as financial and personnel resources. Without popular participation, it would often be impossible to carry out much of the research needed to document health hazards. Science is also limited in its conceptualization of what are problems and how they should be studied and addressed. Without popular involvement there might be no professional impetus to target the appropriate questions. These aspects of popular involvement are very evident in the history of the women's health movement,[32] the occupational health and safety movement,[33] and the environmental health movement.[34] These movements have been major forces in advancing the public's health and safety by pointing to problems that were otherwise not identified, by showing how to approach such problems, by organizing to abolish the conditions giving rise to them, and by educating citizens, public agencies, health care providers, officials, and institutions. Without such popular participation, how would we have known of such hazards and diseases as DES, Agent Orange, pesticides, unnecessary hysterectomies, sterilization abuse, black lung, brown lung, and asbestos? Couto's discussion of the "politics of epidemiology" argues that the scientific assumptions of traditional epidemiology are not completely suited to environmental hazards. Epidemiologists prefer false negatives to false positives i.e., they would prefer to claim (falsely) no association between variables when there is one than to claim an association when there is none. Epidemiologists require evidence to achieve scientific statements of probability, but this need exceeds the evidence required to state that something should be done to eliminate or minimize a health threat.[35] In this view,

> The degree of risk to human health does not need to be at statistically significant levels to require political action. The degree of risk does have to be such that a reasonable person would avoid it. Consequently, the important political test is not the findings of epidemiologists in the probability off nonrandomness of an incidence of illness but the likelihood that a reasonable person, including members of the community of calculation, would take up residence with the community at risk and drink from and bathe in water from the Yellow Creek area or buy a house along Love Canal.[36]

Indeed, these are the kinds of questions presented to public health officials, researchers, and government members in every setting where there is dispute between the citizen and official perceptions. These questions bring out the metaphors and symbols employed by lay citizens in risk communication, and they stand in contrast to scientific, corporate, and governmental metaphors and symbols.

Popular epidemiology obviously challenges some fundamental epidemiological preconceptions of a "pure" study and its appropriate techniques, such as the nomenclature of disease classifications and the belief that community volunteers automatically introduce bias.[37] Such disputes are not settled primarily within the scientific community. Professional antagonism to popular participation in scientific endeavors is common. Medical sociology has long been aware that such antagonism only occasionally revolves around questions of scientific fact; it usually stems from professional dominance, institutional dominance, and political-economic factors. Professional dominance in science plays an important role here. Professionals generally do not want to let lay publics take on the work that they control as professionals, a particularly ironic situation in the case of epidemiology since the original "shoeleather" epidemiological work that founded the field is quite similar to popular epidemiological efforts. The Woburn residents' efforts are in fact reminiscent of John Snow's classic study of cholera in London in 1854. The scientific paternalism that holds that lay people cannot involve themselves in scientific decisionmaking is a perspective quite familiar to analysts of health care, and which has been widely discredited in recent years.

Further, environmental health groups challenge the canons of value-neutrality and statistical reasoning, thus undermining the core foundations of professional belief systems. By putting forth their own political goals, they may challenge scientists to acknowledge that they have their own political agendas, even if covert, unconscious, or unrecognized. Corporate legal defenses may not be in collusion with professional dominance, but there is an affinity between the two in the courtroom. Corporate attorneys make much of the challenge that citizen activists are untrained individuals who are incapable of making valid judgments regarding pollution.[38] This affinity is due to the fact that popular participation threatens not only the professional-lay division of knowledge and power but also the social structures and relations that give rise to environmental hazards.

The Activist Nature of Popular Epidemiology

Popular epidemiology is by nature activist, since the lay public is doing work that should be done by corporations, experts, and officials. Popular epidemiology may involve citizen-propelled investigation of naturally occurring diseases for which no firm is responsible. With regard to the recognition of and action around Lyme Disease in Connecticut, where a tick-borne disease was the issue, citizen activists became involved because they considered health officials to be dragging their heels in the matter. Despite such examples, however, popular epidemiology is particularly powerful when the issue is environmental pollution, occupational disease, or drug side effects. In those cases, persons and organizations are seen to be acting against the public health, often in light of clear knowledge about the dangers. The process of popular epidemiological investigation is therefore an activist one, in which epidemiological findings are immediately employed to alleviate suffering and causes of suffering.

Environmental health activists are by definition acting to correct problems that are not corrected by the established corporate, political, and scientific communities. Logically, the first step in protecting people from the hazards of toxic chemicals is appropriate corporate action, relating to the judicious use and safe disposal of toxic chemicals. It is well known that manufacturers are often lax in this sphere and frequently violate known laws and safe practices.

Given this situation, and given the fact that many corporations purchase land and factories about which they know nothing concerning their past use of toxic chemicals, public agencies present the next line of defense. These agencies include local boards of health, local water boards, state boards of health, state environmental agencies, and the federal EPA. Lay people often begin at the public agency level rather than the corporate level. As the case studies of Woburn, Yellow Creek, South Brunswick, Love Canal, and many other sites indicate, officials are often skeptical or even hostile to citizen requests and inputs.

Even when public agencies are willing to carry out studies, they often demand a different level of proof than community residents want. Further, agencies tend to undertake "pure" epidemiological research without reference to practical solutions to the problem. Moreover, even if they want to, many public bodies have no legal or effective power to compel cleanups, and they rarely can provide restitution to victims. Popular epidemiology emphasizes the practical nature of environmental health issues, and its practitioners are therefore impatient with the caution with which public agencies approach such problems. As with so many other areas of public policies, the fragmentation of agencies and authority contributes to this problem. Community activists cannot understand why more immediate action cannot be taken, particularly when they are apt to define the situation as more of a crisis than do the officials. . . .

CONCLUSION

By examining examples of popular epidemiology and by constructing a theoretical framework for it, we have shown it to be a highly politicized form of action. Popular epidemiology is also a form of risk communication by lay persons to professional and official audiences, and as such it demonstrates that risk communication is indeed an exercise of political power. In a growing number of instances, organized communities have been able to successfully communicate risk in such a way as to win political, economic, and cultural battles.

Yet there are some structural problems associated with such victories. Experts and officials may demand increasingly higher levels of proof, requiring field studies that are prohibitive in terms of time, skills, and resources. Concerted political action may win a case but not necessarily build up scientific credibility or precedence. People may fear such a result and begin to tailor their efforts toward convincing experts and officials, thus possibly diminishing the impact of their efforts on their communities.

Solutions to these structural problems are not simple; community residents will have to find ways to work on several fronts simultaneously, and we should not assume that the task is theirs alone. Academics and health and public health professionals can play an important role in informing their colleagues and government officials that there are new ways to understand risk. The public as a whole needs to work toward more stringent and actively enforced environmental legislation and regulation as well as greater social control over corporations.

We are only in the earliest stages of understanding the phenomenon of popular epidemiology. Most research has been on empirical studies of individual cases, with a few preliminary stabs at theoretical and analytical linkages. The existing and future successes of popular epidemiological endeavors can potentially play a major role in reformulating the way that lay people, scientists, and public agencies view public health problems. This is an exciting possibility and one with which by definition we can all be involved.

Acknowledgments This research was supported in part by funds from the Wayland Collegium, Brown University. This paper is a revised version of a presentation to the Boston Area Medical Sociologists meeting, 6 April 1987, where participants offered important feedback. Many of the ideas here have developed during a year-long faculty seminar at Brown University, where I have benefited from interacting with Anne Fausto-Sterling, John Ladd, Talbot Page, and Harold Ward. Other ideas and data have come from my collaboration with Edwin J. Mikkelsen on a book about Woburn. Dorothy Nelkin and Alonzo Plough provided valuable comments on the manuscript.

NOTES

1. Jerry Ackerman and Diego Ribadeneira, "12 Families, Grace Settle Woburn Toxic Case," *Boston Globe,* 23 September 1986; William F. Doherty, "Jury: Firm Fouled Wells in Woburn," *Boston Globe,* 29 July 1986.
2. Abraham Lilienfeld, *Foundations of Epidemiology* [New York: Oxford, 1976], p. 4.
3. Paula DiPerna, *Cluster Mystery: Epidemic and the Children of Woburn, Mass.* (St. Louis: Mosby, 1985), pp. 106–108.
4. *Ibid.,* p. 75–82.
5. *Ibid.,* pp. 53–70.
6. *Ibid.,* pp. 111–155.
7. *Ibid.,* p. 161.
8. *Ibid.,* pp. 164–173.
9. *Ibid.,* p. 175.
10. *Ibid.,* pp. 176–199.
11. *Ibid.,* pp. 200–211.
12. *Ibid.,* pp. 209–215.
13. Jan Schlictmann, interview, 12 May 1987.
14. Steven W. Lagakos, Barbara J. Wessen, and Marvin Zelen, "An Analysis of Contaminated Well Water and Health Effects in Woburn, Massachusetts," *Journal of the American Statistical Association.* Volume 81, Number 395 (1984): 583–596.
15. *Ibid.*
16. Steven Lagakos, interview, 6 April 1987.
17. *Ibid.*
18. DiPerna, *op. cit.,* pp. 168–169.
19. Marvin Zelen, interview, 1 July 1987.
20. DiPerna, *op. cit.,* pp. 251–273.
21. Zelen, *op. cit.*
22. Allan Morrison lecture, Brown University, Department of Community Health, 25 February 1987.
23. Lagakos *et al., op. cit.*
24. Richard A. Couto, "Failing Health and New Prescriptions: Community-Based Approaches to Environmental Risks," in Carole E. Hill, ed., *Current Health Policy Issues and Alternatives: An Applied Social Science Perspective* (Athens: University of Georgia Press, 1986).
25. *Ibid.*
26. Adeline Gordon Levine, *Love Canal: Science, Politics, and People* (Lexington, Mass.: Heath, 1982), pp. 14–15.
27. Celene Krauss, "Grass-Root Protests and Toxic Wastes: Developing a Critical Political View." Paper presented at a 1986 meeting of the American Sociological Association.
28. Couto, *op. cit.*
29. *Ibid.*
30. *Ibid.*
31. Nicholas Freudenberg, *Not in Our Backyards: Community Action for Health and the Environment* (New York: Monthly Review, 1984).
32. Helen Rodriguez-Trias, "The Women's Health Movement: Women Take Power," in Victor Sidel and Ruth Sidel, eds., *Reforming Medicine: Lessons of the Last Quarter Century* (New York: Pantheon, 1984), pp. 107–126.
33. Daniel Berman, "Why Work Kills: A Brief History of Occupational Health and Safety in the United States," *International Journal of Health Services.* Volume 7, Number 1 (1977): 63–87.
34. Freudenberg, *Not in Our Backyards, op. cit.*
35. Couto, *op cit.*
36. *Ibid.*
37. DiPerna, *op. cit.,* p. 379.
38. Krauss, *op. cit.*

8 SOCIAL RELATIONSHIPS AND HEALTH

James S. House, Karl R. Landis, and Debra Umberson

. . . my father told me of a careful observer, who certainly had heart-disease and died from it, and who positively stated that his pulse was habitually irregular to an extreme degree; yet to his great disappointment it invariably became regular as soon as my father entered the room. Charles Darwin (*1*)

Scientists have long noted an association between social relationships and health. More socially isolated or less socially integrated individuals are less healthy, psychologically and physically, and more likely to die. The first major work of empirical sociology found that less socially integrated people were more likely to commit suicide than the most integrated (*2*). In subsequent epidemiologic research age-adjusted mortality rates from all causes of death are consistently higher among the unmarried than the married (*3–5*). Unmarried and more socially isolated people have also manifested higher rates of tuberculosis (*6*), accidents (*7*), and psychiatric disorders such as schizophrenia (*8, 9*). And as the above quote from Darwin suggests, clinicians have also observed potentially health-enhancing qualities of social relationships and contacts.

The causal interpretation and explanation of these associations has, however, been less clear. Does a lack of social relationships cause people to become ill or die? Or are unhealthy people less likely to establish and maintain social relationships? Or is there some other factor, such as a misanthropic personality, which predisposes people both to have a lower quantity or quality of social relationships and to become ill or die?

Such questions have been largely unanswerable before the last decade for two reasons. First, there was little theoretical basis for causal explanation. Durkheim (*2*) proposed a theory of how social relationships affected suicide, but this theory did not generalize to morbidity and mortality from other causes. Second, evidence of the association between social relationships and health, especially in general human populations, was almost entirely retrospective or cross-sectional before the late 1970s. Retrospective studies from death certificates or hospital records ascertained the nature of people's social relationships after they had become ill or died, and cross-sectional surveys of general populations determined whether people who reported ill health also reported a lower quality or quantity of relationships. Such studies used statistical control of potential confounding variables to rule out third factors that might produce the association between social relationships and health, but could do this only partially. They could not determine whether poor social relationships preceded or followed ill health.

In this article, we review recent developments that have altered this state of affairs dramatically: (i) emergence of theoretical models for a causal effect of social relationships on health in humans and animals; (ii) cumulation of empirical evidence that social relationships are a consequential predictor of mortality in human populations; and (iii) increasing evidence for the causal impact of social relationships on psychological and physiological functioning in quasi-experimental and experimental studies of humans and animals. These developments suggest that social relationships, or the relative lack thereof, constitute a major risk factor for health rivaling the effects of well-established health risk factors such as cigarette smoking, blood pressure, blood lipids, obesity, and physical activity. Indeed, the theory and evidence on social relationships and health increasingly approximate that available at the time of the U.S. Surgeon General's 1964 report on smoking and health (*10*), with similar implications for future research and public policy.

THE EMERGENCE OF "SOCIAL SUPPORT" THEORY AND RESEARCH

The study of social relationships and health was revitalized in the middle 1970s by the emergence of a seemingly new field of scientific research on "social support." This concept was first used in the mental health literature (*11, 12*), and was linked to physical health in separate seminal articles by physician-epidemiologists Cassel (*13*) and Cobb (*14*). These articles grew out of a rapidly developing literature on stress and psychosocial factors in the etiology of health and illness (*15*). Chronic diseases have increasingly replaced acute infectious diseases as the major causes of disability and death, at least in industrialized countries. Consequently, theories of disease etiology have shifted from ones in which a single factor (usually a microbe) caused a single disease, to ones in which multiple behavioral and environmental as well as biologic and genetic factors combine, often over extended periods, to produce any single disease, with a given factor often playing an etiologic role in multiple diseases.

Cassel (*13*) and Cobb (*14*) reviewed more than 30 human and animal studies that found social relationships protective of health. Recognizing that any one study was open to alternative interpretations, they argued that the variety of study designs (ranging from retrospective to experimental), of life stages studied (from birth to death), and of health outcomes involved (including low birth weight, complications of pregnancy, self-reported symptoms, blood pressure, arthritis, tuberculosis, depression, alcoholism, and mortality) suggested a robust, putatively causal, association. Cassel and Cobb indicated that social relationships might promote health in several ways, but emphasized the role of social relationships in moderating or buffering potentially deleterious health effects of psychosocial stress or other health hazards. This idea of "social support," or something that maintains or sustains the organism by promoting adaptive behavior or neuroendocrine responses in the face of stress or other health hazards, provided a general, albeit simple, theory of how and why social relationships should causally affect health (*16*).

Publications on "social support" increased almost geometrically from 1976 to 1981. By the late 1970s, however, serious questions emerged about the empirical evidence cited by Cassel and Cobb and the evidence generated in subsequent research. Concerns were expressed about causal priorities between social support and health (since the great majority of studies remained cross-sectional or retrospective and based on self-reported data), about whether social relationships and supports buffered the impact of stress on health or had more direct effects, and about how consequential the effects of social relationships on health really were (*17–19*). These concerns have been addressed by a continuing cumulation of two types of empirical data: (i) a new series of prospective mortality studies in human populations and (ii) a broadening base of laboratory and field experimental studies of animals and humans.

PROSPECTIVE MORTALITY STUDIES OF HUMAN POPULATIONS

Just as concerns began to surface about the nature and strength of the impact of social relationships on health, data from long-term, prospective studies of community populations provided compelling evidence that lack of social relationships constitutes a major risk factor for mortality. Berkman and Syme (*20*) analyzed a probability sample of 4775 adults in Alameda County, California, who were between 30 and 69 in 1965 when they completed a survey that assessed the presence or extent of four types of social ties—marriage, contacts with extended family and friends, church membership, and other formal and informal group affiliations. Each type of social relationship predicted mortality through the succeeding 9 years. A combined "social network" index remained a significant predictor of mortality (with a relative risk ratio for mortality of about 2.0, indicating that persons low on the index were twice as likely to die as persons high on the index) in multivariate analyses that controlled for self-reports in 1965 of physical health, socioeconomic status, smoking, alcohol consumption, physical activity, obesity, race, life satisfaction, and use of preventive health services. Such adjustment or control for baseline health and other risk factors provides a conservative estimate of the predictive power of social relationships, since some of their impact may be mediated through effects on these risk factors.

The major limitation of the Berkman and Syme study was the lack of other than self-reported data on health at baseline. Thus, House *et al.* (*21*) sought to replicate and extend the Alameda County results in a study of 2754 adults between 35 and 69 at their initial interview and physical examinations in 1967 through 1969 by the Tecumseh (Michigan) Community Health Study. Composite indices of social relationships and activities (as well as a number of the individual components) were inversely associated with mortality during the succeeding 10- to 12-year follow-up period, with relative risks of 2.0 to 3.0 for men and 1.5 to 2.0 for women, after adjustment for the effects of age and a wide range of biomedically assessed (blood pressure, cholesterol, respiratory function, and electrocardiograms) as well as self-reported risk factors of mortality. Analyzing data on 2059 adults in the Evans County (Georgia) Cardiovascular Epidemiologic Study, Schoenback *et al.* (*22*) also found that a social network index similar to that of Berkman and Syme (*20*) predicted mortality for an 11- to 13-year follow-up period, after adjustment for age and baseline measures of biomedical as well as self-reported risk factors of mortality. The Evans County associations were somewhat weaker than those in Tecumseh and Alameda County, and as in Tecumseh were stronger for males than females.

Studies in Sweden and Finland have described similar results. Tibblin, Welin, and associates (*23, 24*) studied two cohorts of men born in 1913 and 1923, respectively, and living in 1973 in Gothenberg, Sweden's second largest city. After adjustments for age, baseline levels of systolic blood pressure, serum cholesterol, smoking habits, and perceived health status, mortality in both cohorts through 1982 was inversely related to the number of persons in the household and the men's level of social and outside home activities in 1973. Orth-Gomer *et al.* (*25*) analyzed the mortality experience through 1981 of a random sample of 17,433 Swedish adults aged 29 to 74 at the time of their 1976 or 1977 baseline interviews. Frequency of contact with family, friends, neighbors, and co-workers in 1976–77 was predictive of mortality through 1981, after adjustment for age, sex, education, employment status, immigrant status, physical exercise, and self-reports of chronic conditions. The effects were stronger among males than among females, and were somewhat nonlinear, with the greatest increase in mortality risk occurring in the most socially isolated third of the sample. In a prospective study of 13,301 adults in predominantly rural eastern Finland, Kaplan *et al.* (*26*) found a measure of "social connections" similar to those used in Alameda County, Tecumseh, and Evans County to be a significant predictor of male mortality from all causes during 5 years, again after adjustments for other biomedical and self-reported risk factors. Female mortality showed similar, but weaker and statistically nonsignificant, effects.

These studies manifest a consistent pattern of results, as shown in Figs. 8-1 and 8-2, which show age-adjusted mortality rates plotted for the five prospective studies from which we could extract parallel data. The report of the sixth study (*25*) is consistent with these trends. The relative risks (*RR*) in Figs. 8-1 and 8-2 are higher than those reported above because they are only adjusted for age. The levels of mortality in Figs. 8-1 and 8-2 vary greatly across studies depending on the follow-up period and composition of the population by age, race, and ethnicity, and geographic locale, but the patterns of prospective association between social integration (that is, the number and frequency of social relationships and contacts) and mortality are remarkably similar, with some variations by race, sex, and geographic locale.

Only the Evans County study reported data for blacks. The predictive association of social integration with mortality among Evans County black males is weaker than among white males in Evans County or elsewhere (Fig. 8-1), and the relative risk ratio for black females in Evans County, although greater than for Evans County white females, is smaller than the risk ratios for white females in all other studies (Fig. 8-2). More research on blacks and other minority populations is necessary to determine whether these differences are more generally characteristic of blacks compared to whites.

Modest differences emerge by sex and rural as opposed to urban locale. Results for men and women are strong, linear, and similar in the urban populations of Alameda County (that is, Oakland and environs) and Gothenberg, Sweden (only men were studied in Gothenberg). In the

Figure 8-1. *Level of Social Integration and Age-Adjusted Mortality for Males in Five Prospective Studies*

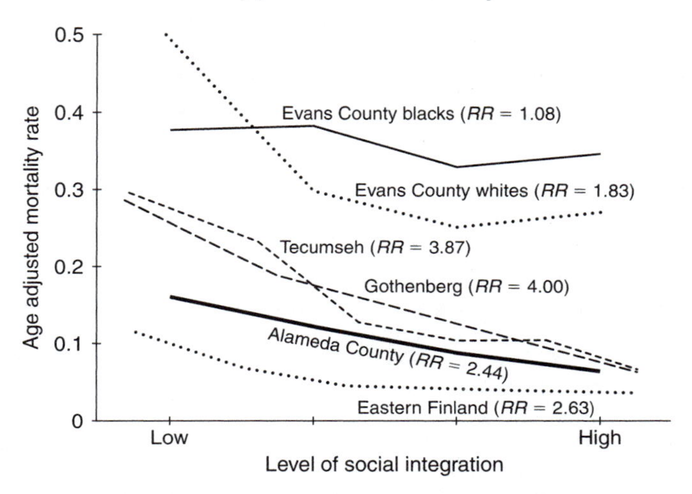

Note: RR, the relative risk ratio of mortality at the lowest versus highest level of social integration.

predominantly small-town and rural populations of Tecumseh, Evans County, and eastern Finland, however, two notable deviations from the urban results appear: (i) female risk ratios are consistently weaker than those for men in the same rural populations (Figs. 8-1 and 8-2), and (ii) the results for men in more rural populations, although rivaling those in urban populations in

Figure 8-2. *Level of Social Integration and Age-Adjusted Mortality for Females in Five Prospective Studies*

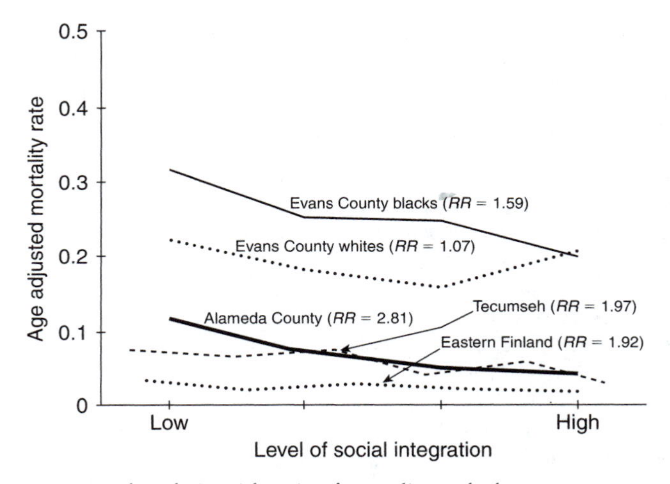

Note: RR, the relative risk ratio of mortality at the lowest versus highest level of social integration.

terms of risk ratios, assume a distinctly nonlinear, or threshold, form. That is, in Tecumseh, Evans County, and eastern Finland, mortality is clearly elevated among the most socially isolated, but declines only modesty, if at all, between moderate and high levels of social integration.

Explanation of these sex and urban-rural variations awaits research on broader regional or national populations in which the same measures are applied to males and females across the full rural-urban continuum. The current results may have both substantive and methodological explanations. Most of the studies reviewed here, as well as others (*27–29*), suggest that being married is more beneficial to health, and becoming widowed more deterimental, for men than for women. Women, however, seem to benefit as much or more than men from relationships with friends and relatives, which tend to run along same-sex lines (*20, 30*). On balance, men may benefit more from social relationships than women, especially in cross-gender relationships. Small communities may also provide a broader context of social integration and support that benefits most people, except for a relatively small group of socially isolated males.

These results may, however, have methodological rather than substantive explanations. Measures of social relationships or integration used in the existing prospective studies may be less valid or have less variance in rural and small town environments, and for women, thus muting their relationship with mortality. For example, the data for women in Fig. 8-2 are similar to the data on men if we assume that women have higher quality relationships and hence that their true level of social integration is moderate even at low levels of quantity. The social context of small communities may similarly provide a moderate level of social integration for everyone except quite isolated males. Thus measures of frequency of social contact may be poorer indices of social integration for women and more rural populations than for men and urban dwellers.

Variations in the results in Figs. 8-1 and 8-2 should not, however, detract from the remarkable consistency of the overall finding that social relationships do predict mortality for men and women in a wide range of populations, even after adjustment for biomedical risk factors for mortality. Additional prospective studies have shown that social relationships are similarly predictive of all-cause and cardiovascular mortality in studies of people who are elderly (*31–33*) or have serious illnesses (*34, 35*).

EXPERIMENTAL AND QUASI-EXPERIMENTAL RESEARCH

The prospective mortality data are made more compelling by their congruence with growing evidence from experimental and clinical research on animals and humans that variations in exposure to social contacts produce psychological or physiological effects that could, if prolonged, produce serious morbidity and even mortality. Cassel (*13*) reviewed evidence that the presence of a familiar member of the same species could buffer the impact of experimentally induced stress on ulcers, hypertension, and neurosis in rats, mice, and goats, respectively; and the presence of familiar others has also been shown to reduce anxiety and physiological arousal (specifically secretion of free fatty acids) in humans in potentially stressful laboratory situations (*36, 37*). Clinical and laboratory data indicate that the presence of or physical contact with another person can modulate human cardiovascular activity and reactivity in general, and in stressful contexts such as intensive care units (*38*, pp. 122–141). Research also points to the operation of such processes across species. Affectionate petting by humans, or even their mere presence, can reduce the cardiovascular sequelae of stressful situations among dogs, cats, horses, and rabbits (*38*, pp. 163–180). Nerem *et al.* (*39*) found that human handling also reduced the arteriosclerotic impact of a high fat diet in rabbits. Recent interest in the potential health benefits of pets for humans, especially the isolated aged, is based on similar notions, although the evidence for such efforts is only suggestive (*40*).

Bovard (*41*) has proposed a psychophysiologic theory to explain how social relationships and contacts can promote health and protect against disease. He reviews a wide range of human and animal studies suggesting that social relationships and contacts, mediated through the amygdala, activate the anterior hypothalamic zone (stimulating release of human growth hormone) and inhibit the posterior hypothalamic zone (and hence secretion of adrenocorticotropic hormone, cortisol, catecholamines, and associated sympathetic autonomic activity). These mechanisms are consistent with the impact of social relationships on mortality from a wide range of causes and with studies of the adverse effects of lack of adequate social relationships on the development of human and animal infants (*42*). This theory is also consistent with sociobiological processes which, due to the survival benefit of social relationships and collective activity, would promote genetic selection of organisms who find social contact and relatedness rewarding and the lack of such contact and relatedness aversive (*43*).

The epidemiologic evidence linking social relationships and supports to morbidity in humans is limited and not fully consistent. For example, although laboratory studies show short-term effects of social relationships on cardiovascular functioning that would, over time, produce cardiovascular disease, and prospective studies show impacts of social relationships on mortality from cardiovascular disease, the link between social relationships and the incidence of cardiovascular morbidity has yet to be firmly demonstrated (*19, 44*). Overall, however, the theory and evidence for the impact of social relationships on health are building steadily (*45, 46*).

SOCIAL RELATIONSHIPS AS A RISK FACTOR FOR HEALTH: RESEARCH AND POLICY ISSUES

The theory and data reviewed above meet reasonable criteria for considering social relationships a cause or risk factor of mortality, and probably morbidity, from a wide range of diseases (*10; 46; 47;* pp. 289–321). These criteria include strength and consistency of statistical associations across a wide range of studies, temporal ordering of prediction from cause to effect, a gradient of response (which may in this case be nonlinear), experimental data on animals and humans consistent with nonexperimental human data, and a plausible theory (*41*) of biopsychosocial mechanisms explaining the observed associations.

The evidence on social relationships is probably stronger, especially in terms of prospective studies, than the evidence which led to the certification of the Type A behavior pattern as a risk factor for coronary heart disease (*48*). The evidence regarding social relationships and health increasingly approximates the evidence in the 1964 Surgeon General's report (*10*) that established cigarette smoking as a cause or risk factor for mortality and morbidity from a range of diseases. The age-adjusted relative risk ratios shown in Fig. 8-1 and 8-2 are stronger than the relative risks for all cause mortality reported for cigarette smoking (*10*). There is, however, less specificity in the associations of social relationships with mortality than has been observed for smoking, which is strongly linked to cancers of the lung and respiratory tract (with age-adjusted risk ratios between 3.0 and 11.0). Better theory and data are needed on the links between social relationships and major specific causes of morbidity and mortality.

Although a lack of social relationships has been established as a risk factor for mortality, and probably morbidity, three areas need further investigation: (i) mechanisms and processes linking social relationships to health, (ii) determinants of levels of "exposure" to social relationships, and (iii) the means to lower the prevalence of relative social isolation in the population or to lessen its deleterious effects on health.

MECHANISMS AND PROCESSES LINKING SOCIAL RELATIONSHIPS TO HEALTH

Although grounded in the literature on social relationships and health, investigators on social support in the last decade leaped almost immediately to the interpretation that what was consequential for health about social relationships was their supportive quality, especially their capacity to buffer or moderate the deleterious effects of stress or other health hazards (*13, 14*). Many recent studies have reported either a general positive association between social support and health or a buffering effect in the presence of stress (*49*), but these studies are problematic because the designs are largely cross-sectional or retrospective and the data usually self-reported. The most compelling evidence of the causal significance of social relationships on health has come from the experimental studies of animals and humans in the prospective mortality studies reviewed above studies in which the measures of social relationships are merely the presence or absence of familiar other organisms, or relative frequency of contact with them, and which often do not distinguish between buffering and main effects. Thus, social relationships appear to have generally beneficial effects on health, not solely or even primarily attributable to their buffering effects, and there may be aspects of social relationships other than their supportive quality that account for these effects.

We now need a broader theory of the biopsychosocial mechanisms and processes linking social relationships to health than can be provided by extant concepts or theories of social support. That broader theory must do several things. First, it must clearly distinguish between (i) the existence or quantity of social relationships, (ii) their formal structure (such as their density or reciprocity), and (iii) the actual content of these relationships such as social support. Only by testing the effects on health of these different aspects of social relationships in the same study can we understand what it is about social relationships that is consequential for health.

Second, we need better understanding of the social, psychological, and biological processes that link the existence, quantity, structure, or content of social relationships to health. Social support whether in the form of practical help, emotional sustenance, or provision of information is only one of the social processes involved here. Not only may social relationships affect health because they are or are not supportive, they may also regulate or control human thought, feeling and behavior in ways that promote health, as in Durkheim's (2) theory relating social integration to suicide. Current views based on this perspective suggest that social relationships affect health either by fostering a sense of meaning or coherence that promotes health (*50*) or by facilitating health-promoting behaviors such as proper sleep, diet, or exercise, appropriate use of alcohol, cigarettes, and drugs, adherence to medical regimens, or seeking appropriate medical care (*51*). The negative or conflictive aspects of social relationships need also to be considered, since they may be detrimental to the maintenance of health and of social relationship (*52*).

We must further understand the psychological and biological processes or mechanisms linking social relationships to health, either as extensions of the social processes just discussed [for example, processes of cognitive appraisal and coping (*53*)] or as independent mechanisms. In the latter regard, psychological and sociobiological theories suggest that the mere presence of, or sense of relatedness with, another organism may have relatively direct motivational, emotional, or neuroendocrinal effects that promote health either directly or in the face of stress or other health hazards but that operate independently of cognitive appraisal or behavioral coping and adaptation (*38*, pp. 87–180; *42, 43, 54*).

DETERMINANTS OF SOCIAL RELATIONSHIPS: SCIENTIFIC AND POLICY ISSUES

Although social relationships have been extensively studied during the past decade as independent, intervening, and moderating variables affecting stress or health or the relations between them, almost no attention has been paid to social relationships as dependent variables. The determinants of social relationships, as well as their consequences, are crucial to the theoretical and causal status of social relationships in relation to health. If exogenous biological, psychological, or social variables determine both health and the nature of social relationships, then the observed association of social relationships to health may be totally or partially spurious. More practically, Cassel (*13*), Cobb (*14*), and others became interested in social support as a means of improving health. This, in turn, requires understanding of the broader social, as well as psychological or biological, structures and processes that determine the quantity and quality of social relationships and support in society.

It is clear that biology and personality must and do affect both people's health and the quantity and quality of their social relationships. Research has established that such factors do not, however, explain away the experimental, cross-sectional, and prospective evidence linking social relationships to health (*55*). In none of the prospective studies have controls for biological or health variables been able to explain away the predictive association between social relationships and mortality. Efforts to explain away the association of social relationships and supports with health by controls for personality variables have similarly failed (*56, 57*). Social relationships have a predictive, arguably causal, association with health in their own right.

The extent and quality of social relationships experienced by individuals is also a function of broader social forces. Whether people are employed, married, attend church, belong to organizations, or have frequent contact with friends and relatives, and the nature and quality of those relationships, are all determined in part by their positions in a larger social structure that is stratified by age, race, sex, and socioeconomic status and is organized in terms of residential communities, work organizations, and larger political and economic structures. Older people, blacks, and the poor are generally less socially integrated (*58*), and differences in social relationships by sex and place of residence have been discussed in relation to Figs. 8-1 and 8-2. Changing patterns of fertility, mortality, and migration in society affect opportunities for work, marriage, living and working in different settings, and having relationships with friends and relatives, and can even affect the nature and quality of these relations (*59*). These demographic patterns are themselves subject to influence by both planned and unplanned economic and political change, which can also affect individuals' social relationships more directly witness the massive increase in divorce during the last few decades in response to the women's movement, growth in women's labor force participation, and changing divorce law (*60, 61*).

In contrast with the 1950s, adults in the United States in the 1970s were less likely to be married, more likely to be living alone, less likely to belong to voluntary organizations, and less likely to visit informally with others (*62*). Changes in marital and childbearing patterns and in the age structure of our society will produce in the 21st century a steady increase of the number of older people who lack spouses or children—the people to whom older people most often turn for relatedness and support (*59*). Thus, just as we discover the importance of social relationships for health, and see an increasing need for them, their prevalence and availability may be declining. Changes in other risk factors (for example, the decline of smoking) and improvements in medical technology are still producing overall improvements on health and longevity, but the improvements might be even greater if the quantity and quality of social relationships were also improving.

REFERENCES AND NOTES

1. C. Darwin, *Expression of the Emotions in Man and Animals* (Univ. of Chicago Press, Chicago, 1965 [1872]).
2. E. Durkheim, *Suicide* (Free Press, New York, 1951 [1897]).
3. A. S. Kraus and A. N. Lilienfeld, *J. Chronic Dis.* **10,** 207 (1959).
4. H. Carter and P. C. Glick, *Marriage and Divorce: A Social and Economic Study* (Harvard Univ. Press, Cambridge, MA, 1970).
5. E. M. Kitigawa and P. M. Hauser, *Differential Mortality in the United States: A Study in Socio-Economic Epidemiology* (Harvard Univ. Press, Cambridge, MA, 1973).
6. T. H. Holmes, in *Personality, Stress and Tuberculosis,* P. J. Sparer, Ed. (International Univ. Press, New York, 1956).
7. W. A. Tillman and G. E. Hobbs, *Am. J. Psychiatr.* **106,** 321 (1949).
8. R. E. L. Faris, *Am. J. Sociol.* **39,** 155 (1934).
9. M. L. Kohn and J. A. Clausen, *Am. Sociol. Rev.* **20,** 268 (1955).
10. U.S. Surgeon General's Advisory Committee on Smoking and Health, *Smoking and Health* (U.S. Public Health Service, Washington, DC, 1964).
11. G. Caplan, *Support Systems and Community Mental Health* (Behavioral Publications, New York, 1974).
12. President's Commission on Mental Health, *Report to the President* (Government Printing Office, Washington, DC, 1978), vols. 1 to 5.
13. J. Cassel, *Am. J. Epidemiol.* **104,** 107 (1976).
14. S. Cobb, *Psychosomatic Med.* **38,** 300 (1976).
15. J. Cassel, in *Social Stress,* S. Levine and N. A. Scotch, Eds. (Aldine, Chicago, 1970), pp. 189–209.

16. J. S. House, *Work Stress and Social Support* (Addison-Wesley, Reading, MA, 1981).
17. K. Heller, in *Maximizing Treatment Gains: Transfer Enhancement in Psychotherapy,* A. P. Goldstein and F. H. Kanter, Eds. (Academic Press, New York, 1979), pp. 353–382.
18. P. A. Thoits, *J. Health Soc. Behav.* **23,** 145 (1982).
19. D. Reed *et al., Am. J. Epidemiol.* **117,** 384 (1983).
20. L. F. Berkman and S. L. Syme, *ibid.* **109,** 186 (1979).
21. J. S. House, C. Robbins, H. M. Metzner, *ibid.* **116,** 123 (1982).
22. V. J. Schoenbach *et al., ibid.* **123,** 577 (1986).
23. G. Tibblin *et al.,* in *Social Support: Health and Disease,* S. O. Isacsson and L. Janzon, Eds. (Almqvist & Wiksell, Stockholm, 1986), pp. 11–19.
24. L. Welin *et al., Lancet* **i,** 915 (1985).
25. K. Orth-Gomer and J. Johnson, *J. Chron. Dis.* **40,** 949 (1987).
26. G. A. Kaplan *et al., Am. J. Epidemiol.,* in press.
27. M. Stroebe and W. Stroebe, *Psychol. Bull.* **93,** 279 (1983).
28. W. R. Gove, *Soc. Forces* **51,** 34 (1972).
29. K. J. Helsing and M. Szklo, *Am. J. Epidemiol.* **114,** 41 (1981).
30. L. Wheeler, H. Reis, J. Nezlek, *J. Pers. Soc. Psychol.* **45,** 943 (1983).
31. D. Blazer, *Am. J. Epidemiol.* **115,** 684 (1982).
32. D. M. Zuckerman, S. V. Kasl, A. M. Ostfeld, *ibid.* **119,** 410 (1984).
33. T. E. Seeman *et al., ibid.* **126,** 714 (1987).
34. W. E. Ruberman *et al., N. Engl. J. Med.* **311,** 552 (1984).
35. K. Orth-Gomer *et al., in Social Support: Health and Disease,* S. O. Isacsson and L. Janzon, Eds. (Almqvist & Wiksell, Stockholm, 1986), pp. 21–31.
36. L. S. Wrightsman, Jr., *J. Abnorm. Soc. Psychol.* **61,** 216 (1960).
37. K. W. Back and M. D. Bogdonoff, *Behav. Sci.* **12,** 384 (1967).
38. J. J. Lynch, *The Broken Heart* (Basic Books, New York, 1979).
39. R. M. Nerem, M. J. Levesque, J. F. Cornhill, *Science* **208,** 1475 (1980).
40. J. Goldmeier, *Gerontologist* **26,** 203 (1986).
41. E. W. Bovard, in *Perspectives on Behavioral Medicine,* R. B. Williams (Academic Press, New York, 1985), vol. 2.
42. J. Bowlby, in *Loneliness: The Experience of Emotional and Social Isolation,* R. S. Weiss, Ed. (MIT Press, Cambridge, MA, 1973).
43. S. P. Mendoza, in *Social Cohesion: Essays Toward a Sociophysiological Perspective,* P. R. Barchas and S. P. Mendoza, Eds. (Greenwood Press, Westport, CT, 1984).
44. S. Cohen, *Health Psychol.* **7,** 269 (1988).
45. L. F. Berkman, in *Social Support and Health,* S. Cohen and S. L. Syme, Eds. (Academic Press, New York, 1985), pp. 241–262.
46. W. E. Broadhead *et al., Am. J. Epidemiol.* **117,** 521 (1983).
47. A. M. Lilienfeld and D. E. Lilienfeld, *Foundations of Epidemiology* (Oxford Univ. Press, New York, 1980).
48. National Heart, Lung and Blood Institute, *Circulations* **63,** 1199 (1982).
49. S. Cohen and S. L. Syme, *Social Support and Health* (Academic Press, New York, 1985).
50. A. Antonovsky, *Health, Stress and Coping* (Jossey-Bass, San Francisco, 1979).
51. D. Umberson, *J. Health Soc. Behav.* **28,** 306 (1987).
52. K. Rook, *J. Pers. Soc. Psychol.* **46,** 1097 (1984).
53. R. S. Lazarus and S. Folkman, *Stress, Appraisal, and Coping* (Springer, New York, 1984).
54. R. B. Zajonc, *Science* **149,** 269 (1965).
55. J. S. House, D. Umberson, K. Landis, *Annu. Rev. Sociol.,* in press.
56. S. Cohen, D. R. Sherrod, M. S. Clark, *J. Pers. Soc. Psychol.* **50,** 963 (1986).
57. R. Schultz and S. Decker, *ibid.* **48,** 1162 (1985).
58. J. S. House, *Socio Forum* **2,** 135 (1987).
59. S. C. Watkins, J. A. Menken, J. Bongaarts, *Am. Sociol. Rev.* **52,** 346 (1987).
60. A. Cherlin, *Marriage, Divorce, Remarriage* (Harvard Univ. Press, Cambridge, MA, 1981).
61. L. J. Weitzman, *The Divorce Revolution* (Free Press, New York, 1985).
62. J. Veroff, E. Douvan, R. A. Kulka, *The Inner American: A Self-Portrait from 1957 to 1976* (Basic Books, New York, 1981).
63. Supported by a John Simon Guggenheim Memorial Foundation Fellowship and NIA grant 1-PO1-AG05561 (to J.S.H.), NIMH training grant 5-T32-MH16806-06 traineeship (to K.R.L.), NIMH training grant 5-T32-MH16806-05 and NIA 1-F32-AG05440-01 postdoctoral fellowships (to D.U.). We are indebted to D. Buss, P. Converse, G. Duncan, R. Kahn, R. Kessler, H. Schuman, L. Syme, and R. Zajonc for comments on previous drafts, to many other colleagues who have contributed to this field, and to M. Klatt for preparing the manuscript.

9 · *Dying Alone: The Social Production of Urban Isolation*

Eric Klinenberg

There is a file marked "Heat Deaths" in the recesses of the Cook County morgue. The folder holds hundreds of hastily scribbled death reports authored by city police officers in July 1995 as they investigated cases of mortality during the most proportionately deadly heat wave in recorded American history.[1] Over 700 Chicago residents in excess of the norm died during the week of 13th to 20th of July (Whitman et al., 1997),[2] and the following samples of the official reports hint at the conditions in which the police discovered the decedents.

> Male, age 65, black, July 16, 1995:
>
> R/Os [responding officers] discovered the door to apt locked from the inside by means of door chain. No response to any knocks or calls. R/Os . . . gained entry by cutting chain. R/Os discovered victim lying on his back in rear bedroom on the floor. [Neighbor] last spoke with victim on 13 July 95. Residents had not seen victim recently. Victim was in full rigor mortis. R/Os unable to locate the whereabouts of victim's relatives . . .
>
> Female, age 73, white, July 17, 1995:
>
> A recluse for 10 yrs, never left apartment, found today by son, apparently DOA. Conditions in apartment when R/Os arrived thermostat was registering over 90 degrees f. with no air circulation except for windows opened by son [after death]. Possible heat-related death. Had a known heart problem 10 yrs ago but never completed medication or treatment . . .
>
> Male, age 54, white, July 16, 1995:
>
> R/O learned . . . that victim had been dead for quite awhile. . . . Unable to contact any next of kin. Victim's room was uncomfortably warm. Victim was diabetic, doctor unk. Victim has daughter . . . last name unk. Victim hadn't seen her in years. . . . Body removed to C.C.M. [Cook County Morgue].
>
> Male, age 79, black, July 19, 1995:
>
> Victim did not respond to phone calls or knocks on victim's door since Sunday, 16 July 95. Victim was known as quiet, to himself and, at times, not to answer the door. X is landlord to victim and does not have any information to any relatives to victim. . . . Chain was on door. R/O was able to see victim on sofa with flies on victim and a very strong odor decay (decompose). R/O cut chain, per permission of [landlord], called M.E. [medical examiner] who authorized removal. . . . No known relatives at this time.

These accounts rarely say enough about a victim's death to fill a page, yet the words used to describe the deceased—"recluse," "to himself," "no known relatives"—and the conditions in which they were found—"chain was on door," "no air circulation," "flies on victim," "decompose"—are brutally succinct testaments to forms of abandonment, withdrawal, fear, and isolation that proved more extensive than anyone in Chicago had realized, and more dangerous than anyone had imagined. "During the summer heat wave of 1995 in Chicago," the authors of the most thorough epidemiological study of the disaster explained, "anything that facilitated social contact, even membership in a social club or owning a pet was associated with a decreased risk of death" (Semenza et al., 1996: 90). Chicago residents who lacked social ties and did not leave their homes regularly died disproportionately during the catastrophe.

Three questions motivate this article. First, why did so many Chicagoans *die alone* during the heat wave? Second, to expand this question, why do so many Chicagoans, particularly older residents, *live alone* with limited social contacts and weak support during normal times? What accounts for the social production of isolation? Third, what social and psychological processes organize and animate the experiential make-up of aging alone? How can we understand the lives and deaths of the literally isolated?

DYING ALONE

If "bowling alone," the social trend reported by Robert Putnam and mined for significance by social critics and politicians of all persuasions (Putnam, 1995), is a sign of a weakening American civil society, dying alone—a fate few Americans can confidently elude—carries even more powerful social and symbolic meaning. For while in advanced societies the normative "good death" takes place at home, it is even more crucial that the process of dying is collective, shared by the dying person and his or her community of family and friends.[3] When someone dies alone and at home the death is a powerful symbol of social abandonment and failure. The community to which the deceased belonged, whether familial, friendship-based, or political, is likely to suffer from stigma or shame as a consequence, one which it must overcome with redemptive narratives and rituals that reaffirm the bonds among the living (Seale, 1995).

The issues of aging and dying alone are hardly limited to Chicago. In Milwaukee, where a similar proportion of city residents died during the 1995 heat wave (US Centers for Disease Control and Prevention, 1996), 27 percent of the decedents, roughly 75 percent of whom were over 60, were found alone more than one day after the estimated time of death (Nashold et al., n.d.). Most older people in Western societies, and particularly in the United States, place great value on their independence, a characteristic of sufficient cultural and psychological importance that people for whom independence is objectively dangerous are often willing to risk its consequences in order to remain self-sufficient. The number of older people living alone is rising almost everywhere in the world, making it one of the major demographic trends of the contemporary period. According to the US Census Bureau, the total number of people living alone in the United States rose from 10.9 million in 1970 to 23.6 million in 1994 (Wuthnow, 1998); and, as Tables 1 and 2 show, the proportions of American households inhabited by only one person and of elderly people living alone have soared since the 1950s. Dramatic as these figures are, they are certain to rise even higher in the coming decades as societies everywhere age.

Ethnographers have done little to document the daily routines and practices of people living alone,[4] but a recent study in the *New England Journal of Medicine* (Gurley et al., 1996) suggests that their solitary condition leaves them vulnerable in emergency situations and times of illness. Researchers in San Francisco, a city about one-quarter the size of Chicago, reported that in a 12 week period emergency medical workers found 367 people who lived alone and were discovered in their apartments either incapacitated or, in a quarter of the cases, dead. The victims, as in the Chicago heat wave, were disproportionately old, white and African American, with older black men most over-represented. Many of them, the researchers reported, suffered tremendously while they waited to be discovered in their homes, suffering that could have been reduced by earlier intervention but was exacerbated by the victims' isolation (Gurley et al., 1996).

In this article I examine the lived experiences of isolated Chicago residents, placing them in the context of the changing demography and ecology of the city and paying special attention to the ways in which migration patterns, increasing life-spans and changes in urban social morphology have altered the structural conditions of social and support networks. I also consider the impact of the spreading *culture of fear* that has transformed the nature of social life and community organization as well as the physical and political structure of cities. To illustrate how city residents experience these conditions and depict how they impact on the social life of the city, I return to the streets and neighborhoods of Chicago, drawing upon ethnographic research to flesh out the haunting spectre of dying alone in the great metropolis. Although we cannot speak with those who perished during the heat wave, we can look closely at the conditions in which they died and then follow up by examining the experiences of people in similar conditions today. Thus my focus moves outward from the heat wave to the years immediately following when I conducted fieldwork alongside seniors living alone in Chicago.

Table 9-1. Proportion of American households with one inhabitant.

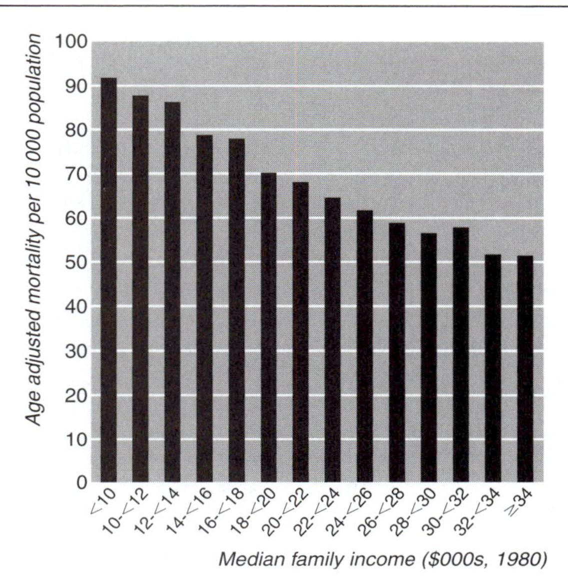

Source: The Statistical Abstract of the United States (1980, 1989, 1999), US Census Bureau.

Table 9-2. Proportion of American elderly (65+) living alone.

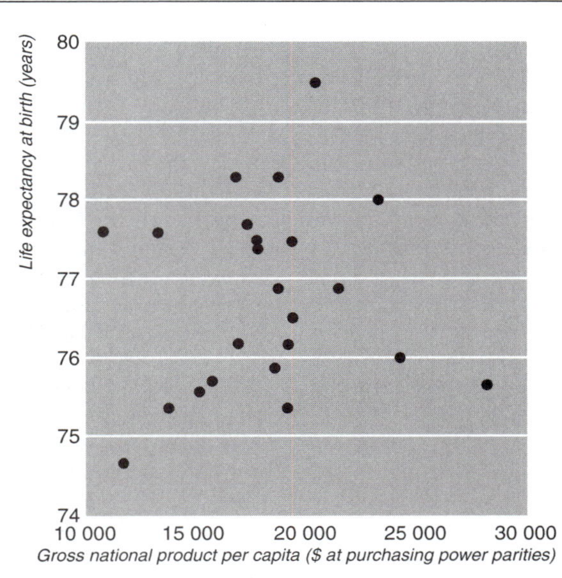

Source: The Statistical Abstract of the United States (1980, 1989, 1999), US Census Bureau.

It is important to make distinctions between *living alone, being isolated, being reclusive,* and *being lonely.* I define alone as residing without other people in a household; being isolated as having limited social ties; being reclusive as largely confining oneself to the household; and being lonely as the subjective state of feeling alone.[5] Most people who live alone, seniors included, are neither lonely nor deprived of social contacts.[6] This is significant because seniors who are embedded in active social networks tend to have better health and greater longevity than those who are relatively isolated. Being isolated or reclusive, then, is more consequential than simply living alone. But older people who live alone are more likely than seniors who live with others to be depressed, isolated, impoverished, fearful of crime and removed from proximate sources of support.[7] Moreover, seniors who live alone are especially vulnerable to traumatic outcomes during episodes of acute crisis because there is no one to help recognize emerging problems, provide immediate care or activate support networks.

It is difficult to measure the number of people who are relatively isolated and reclusive because they have few ties to informal or formal support networks or have little exposure to researchers. In surveys and censuses, isolates and recluses are among the social types most likely to be uncounted or undercounted because those with permanent housing often refuse to open their doors to strangers and are unlikely to participate in city or community programs through which they can be tracked. In academic research it is common to underestimate the extent of isolation or reclusion among seniors because most scholars gain access to samples of elderly people who are already relatively connected. One recent book about loneliness in later life, for example, makes generalizations about the prevalence of isolation and loneliness on the basis of a survey of seniors who participate in a university for the aged (Gibson, 2000) and even medical studies of isolation and health are likely to exclude people whom medical doctors and research teams never see or cannot locate. . . .

What social conditions produce isolation? And how can we understand the lived experience of isolation itself? The heat wave mortality patterns pointed to places in the city where isolation proved to be especially dangerous and suggested sites where similarly situated isolates who survived the disaster but remained alone and vulnerable to the problems stemming from reclusiveness were concentrated. In addition, the disaster illuminated a set of demographic, cultural and political conditions that are associated with isolation, forming the broader social context in which social isolation emerges.

There are four key social conditions that contribute to the production of literal and extreme social isolation: first, the aging of the urban population, particularly the increases in the population of African American, Latino and Asian seniors; second, the fear of crime stemming from the violence and perceived violence of everyday life—in extreme forms this fear can result in the retreat from public life altogether and the creation of urban burrows, "safe houses" where the alone and the afraid protect themselves from a social world in which they no longer feel secure; third, the degradation and fortification of public spaces in poor urban areas and specific residential facilities (such as senior public housing units and some single-room-occupancy hotels); fourth, the transformation in the nature of state social services and support systems such as health care, public or subsidized housing and home energy subsidies. The interaction of these conditions with poverty and the daily deprivations it entails renders poor seniors who live alone vulnerable to a variety of dangers whose consequences can be severe.

Our focus on social isolation should not obscure the fact that literal isolation is an uncommon condition. As Claude Fischer has shown, the overwhelming majority of city dwellers are integrated into personal networks that provide them with support during normal times as well as times of crisis (Fischer, 1982, 1984[1976]). There is, by now, compelling evidence that Wirth's general theory of urbanism—the thesis that city living will break down most forms of solidarity, destroying social groups and creating an anomic society and alienated, isolated individuals—is simply not true; nor is there evidence that city residents on the whole are any less socially integrated than residents of rural areas. Whether urbanites remain with their traditional ethnic groups or form new subcultural groups on the basis of shared interests and experiences (Fischer, 1975), decades of research have shown that, despite the common experience of feeling alone in crowded urban areas, in private life most city dwellers have rich and rewarding relationships and social networks (Fischer, 1982). What I want to show here, however, is that literal social isolation arises in certain situations which, although historically unusual, are becoming more common in American cities today.

"THE CLOSEST I'VE COME TO DEATH"

The first of the conditions producing extreme urban isolation and its experiential correlates is the general aging of American society and the willingness of seniors to live alone. For cities there are three specific pre-disposing factors: first, the rise in the number of seniors living alone, often after outliving their social contacts and seeing their children migrate to the suburbs or other regions of the country altering their neighborhood populations so that they feel culturally or linguistically differentiated; second, the rapid increase in the population of "very old" seniors, 85 and above, who are more likely to be both alone and frail, sick, and unable or unwilling to enter into a public world in which they often feel vulnerable and who are, in fact, an historically new group, older than all previous cohorts and subjected to a distinct set of physical constraints; and third, the increase in the population of black and Latino seniors, who are more likely than their white counterparts to live in poverty and be at risk of the related forms of vulnerability, including illness and inadequate access to health care (Ford, et al., 1992; Lawlor et al., 1993). There is a fourth implication for metropolitan areas (as distinct from central cities) which is the growth of the elderly population in the suburban ring which in general lacks the appropriate housing stock and support systems for aged and aging residents.

By 1990, one-third of Chicago's elderly population, roughly 110,000 seniors, lived alone. When a group of researchers from the Heartland Center on Aging, Disability and Long Term Care at Indiana University surveyed Chicago seniors in 1989 and 1990, they found that 48 percent of Chicagoans over 65, and 35 percent of suburbanites over 65, reported having no family members available to assist them (Fleming-Moran et al., 1991).

Pauline Jankowitz is one of the recluses I got to know during my fieldwork in Chicago.[8] Her story helps to illustrate some of the fundamental features of life alone and afraid in the city. I first met Pauline on her 85th birthday, when I was assigned to befriend her for a day by the local office of an international organization that supports seniors living alone by linking them up with volunteers who are willing to become "friends" and inviting them to the organization's center for a birthday party, Christmas and a Thanksgiving dinner every year. A stranger before the day began, I became her closest companion for the milestone occasion when I picked her up at the uptown apartment where she had lived for 30 years.

Pauline and I had spoken on the phone the previous day and she was expecting me when I arrived late in the morning. She lived on a quiet residential street dominated by the small, three and four-flat apartment buildings common in Chicago. The neighborhood, a key site of departure and arrival for suburbanizing and new urban migrants, had changed dramatically in the time she had lived there, and her block had shifted from a predominately white ethnic area in which Pauline was a typical resident to a mixed street with a sizable Asian and increasingly Mexican population. Uptown remained home to her, but she was less comfortable in it because the neighbors, whom she was eager to praise for their responsibility and good character, were no longer familiar to her. "They are good people," she explained, "but I just don't know them." Her situation is similar to that of thousands of Chicago residents and millions of seniors across the country who have *aged in place* while the environment around them changes.

The major sources of her discomfort were her physical infirmities which grew worse as she aged, a bladder problem that left her incontinent and a weak leg that required her to walk with a crutch and drastistically reduced her mobility, and her real terror of crime, which she heard about daily on the radio and television shows that she likes. "Chicago is just a shooting gallery," she told me, "and I am a moving target because I walk so slowly." Acutely aware of her vulnerability, Pauline reorganized her life to limit her exposure to the threats outside, bunkering herself in a third-floor apartment (in a building with no elevator) that she had trouble reaching because of the stairs, but which "is much safer than the first floor. . . . If I were on the first floor I'd be even more vulnerable to a break-in." With a home-care support worker, meals-on-wheels and a publicly subsidized helper visiting weekly to do her grocery shopping and help with errands, Pauline has few reasons to leave home. "I go out of my apartment about six times a year," she told me, and three of them are for celebrations sponsored by the support organization.

It is, I would learn, a challenge for service providers and volunteers to help even the seniors with whom they have contact. Pauline and I made it to the birthday celebration after a difficult and painful trip down her stairway, during which we had to turn around and return to the apartment so that she could address "a problem" that she experienced on the stairs. Pauline's grimaces and sighs betrayed the depth of the pain the walk had inflicted, but she was so excited to be going out, and going to her party, that she urged me to get us to the center quickly.

During one visit, Pauline, who knew that I was studying the 1995 heat wave, told me that she wanted to tell me her story. "It was," she said softly, "the closest I've come to death." She has one air conditioner in her apartment which gets especially hot during the summer because it is on the third floor. But the machine "is old and it doesn't work too well," which left her place uncomfortably, if not dangerously warm during the disaster. A friend had told her that it was important for her to go outside if she was too hot indoors, so she woke up very early ("it's safer then") on what would become the hottest day of the heat wave and walked towards the local store to buy cherries ("my favorite fruit, but I rarely get fresh food so they're a real treat for me") and cool down in the air conditioned space. "I was so exhausted by the time I got down the stairs that I wanted to go straight back up again," she recounted, "but instead I walked to the corner and took the bus a few blocks to the store. When I got there I could barely move. I had to lean on the shopping cart to keep myself up." But the cool air revived her and she got a bag of cherries and returned home on the bus.

"Climbing the stairs was almost impossible," she remembers. "I was hot and sweaty and so tired." Pauline called a friend as soon as she made it into her place and as they spoke she began to feel her hands going numb and swelling, a sensation that quickly extended into other parts of her body, alarming her that something was wrong. "I asked my friend to stay on the line but I put the phone down and lied down." Several minutes later, her friend still on the line but the receiver on the floor, Pauline got up, soaked her head in water, directed a fan towards her bed, lay down, and placed a number of wet towels on her body and face. Remembering that she had left her friend waiting, Pauline got up, picked up the phone to report that she was feeling better and to thank her buddy for waiting before she hung up. Finally, she lay down again to cool off and rest in earnest. Before long she had fully recovered.

"Now," she ended her story, "I have a special way to beat the heat. You're going to laugh, but I like to go on a Caribbean cruise," which she does alone and, as she does nearly everything else, without leaving her home.

> I get several wash cloths and dip them in cold water. I then place them over my eyes so that I can't see. I lie down and set the fan directly on me. The wet towels and the wind from the fan give a cool breeze, and I imagine myself on a cruise around the islands. I do this whenever it's hot, and you'd be surprised at how nice it is. My friends know about my cruises too. So when they call me on hot days they all say, "Hi Pauline, how was your trip?" We laugh about it, but it keeps me alive.

Social ecological conditions stemming from migration patterns and the widespread abandonment of urban regions have created new barriers to collective life and social support, particularly for the elderly. In *When Work Disappears* William Julius Wilson noted the significance of depopulation in poor black neighborhoods for both formal and informal social controls (Wilson, 1996: 44–5). Most scholars who have analyzed urban social support systems have focused on provision for children, but the changing demographics of the city suggest that it is increasingly important to consider how these systems work for older neighborhood residents as well. The problems are not exclusive to black and Latino communities. Since the 1950s, many white ethnic groups have experienced a sweeping suburbanization that has undercut the morphological basis for cross-generational support, leaving thousands of white seniors estranged in neighborhoods that their families and friends had left behind, out of reach during times of need but also during everyday life. As the concentration of heat wave deaths among seniors in the traditionally Polish and Slav neighborhoods on the southwest side of Chicago suggests, many of the older Italians, Slavs and Poles whose communities appeared so resilient in the work of Kornblum (1974) and Suttles (1968) have been separated from their children and extended family ties. These patterns are becoming more prevalent in Latino and African American communities as they join the suburban exodus, leaving behind older and poorer people for whom the loss of proximity to family and friends will be compounded by the relatively high rates of poverty and illness in America's so-called minority groups.

In addition to the fraying lines of social support from families experiencing generational rifts due to migration, the changing nature of friendship networks has also undermined the morphological basis of mutual assistance. For decades, community scholars have shown that many communities are no longer place-based, but organized instead around common interests and values. Advanced technology, including the telephone and the internet, ease the process of establishing connections with people in disparate places and therefore increase the probability that new social networks will develop without much regard for spatial proximity. Yet, as much research has established, certain forms of social assistance, particularly emergency care and frequent visitation, are more likely when members of a network are physically close to one another. Indeed, after the heat wave, epidemiologists found that older Chicagoans who had died during the disaster were less likely than those who survived to have had friends in the city (Semenza et al., 1996: 86). Spatial distance, in other words, imposes real barriers to social support for friends as well as family. Proximity is a life and death matter for some people, particularly for the elderly who suffer from limited mobility.

"I'LL TALK THROUGH THE DOOR"

Although old age, illness and spatial separation from her family and friends established the grounding for Pauline Jankowitz's condition, her isolation became particularly extreme because of her abiding fear of being victimized by crime. Pauline's perception of her own extreme vulnerability heightens her fear, but her concerns are in fact typical of city dwellers throughout the United States at a time when a veritable culture of fear and a powerful cultural industry based on crime have come to influence much of the organizational, institutional and political activity within the country as well as the thought and action of Americans in their everyday lives. By the late 1990s, fear of crime has taken on a paradoxical role in American urban life, on the one hand pushing people to dissociate from their neighbors and extend their social distance from strangers, and on the other hand becoming one of the organizing principles of new collective projects, such as neighborhood watch groups and community policing programs. Regardless of the form it takes, "coping with crime," as Wesley Skogan and Michael Maxfield put it in the title of their book (Skogan and Maxfield, 1981), has become a way of life for Americans in general and for residents of notably violent cities such as Chicago.

Throughout Chicago and especially in the most violent areas, city residents have reorganized their daily routines and behaviors in order to minimize their exposure to crime in an increasingly Hobbesian universe, scheming around the clock to avoid driving, parking or walking on the wrong streets or in the wrong neighborhoods, seeing the wrong people and visiting the wrong establishments and public places. In Chicago, as in most other American cities, "wrong" in this context is associated with blacks in general and young men in particular, especially now that the massive dragnet cast by the drug warrior state has captured so many young blacks and labeled them as permanent public enemies (Wacquant, 2001). Yet doing fieldwork in even the most objectively dangerous streets of Chicago makes it clear that the common depiction of city residents, and particularly those who live in poor and violent aras, as constantly paranoid and so acutely concerned about proximate threats that they can hardly move, is a gross misrepresentation of how fear is managed and experienced. "It's caution, not fear, that guides me," Eugene Richards, a senior citizen living in North Lawndale explained to me during a discussion of managing danger in the area. Eugene will walk a few blocks during the day, but he refuses to go more than four blocks without a car. Alice Nelson, a woman in her 70s who lives in the Little Village, walks during the day and carries small bags of groceries with her. "But I won't go out at night," she told me. "And if someone comes to the door I won't open it. I'll talk through the door because you never know . . ."[9]

Preying on the elderly, who are presumed to be more vulnerable and easier to dupe, is a standard and recurrent practice of neighborhood deviants and legitimate corporations, mail-order businesses and salespersons alike. Several of my informants said that turning strangers away at the door was part of their regular routine, and complained that they felt besieged by the combination of local hoodlums who paid them special attention around the beginning of the month when social security checks were delivered as well as outsiders who tried to visit or call and convince them to spend their scarce dollars. In the United States, where guns are easy to obtain and levels of gun-related violence are among the highest in the world, roughly one-quarter of households are touched by crime each year, and about one-half of the population will be victimized by a violent crime in their life-time (Miethe, 1995). The nature of the association between fear and vulnerability is enigmatic because it is impossible to establish that the lower levels of victimization are not at least partially attributable to fear which causes people to avoid potentially dangerous situations and, in the most extreme cases, pushes people to become recluses, "prisoners of their own fear," as one social worker I shadowed calls them. Nonetheless, many scholars of crime have argued that fear of crime is irrational because of the often-cited finding that the elderly and women, who are the least likely to be victimized, are the most fearful of crime. Yet ethnographic observation and more fine-grained surveys of fear can show what grounds these concerns.

First, community area or neighborhood characteristics influence levels of fear. Just as city residents tend to be more concerned about crime than residents of suburban and rural areas, African Americans and other ethnic groups who live in areas with higher levels of crime are more likely than whites to report fear of crime in surveys (Joseph, 1997; Miethe, 1995). Signs of neighborhood "disorder," such as abandoned buildings, vandalism, litter and graffiti, instill fear in local residents, whereas, as Richard Taub and his colleagues found in Chicago, neighborhood resources, such as stores, safe public spaces, and active collective life provide incentives for city dwellers to overcome their fears and participate in public activities (Joseph, 1997; Miethe, 1995; Skogan, 1990; Taub et al., 1984). Second, as Sally Engle Merry concluded from her study of a high-crime, multi-ethnic urban housing project, once residents of a particular area grow fearful of crime a vicious cycle begins: fear causes people to increase the amount of time they spend at home and reduces their willingness to socialize with their neighbors; reclusiveness increases the social distance between residents and their neighbors creating a community of strangers who grow even more fearful of each other; heightened fear leads to heightened reclusiveness, and so on (Merry, 1981).

In interviews and casual conversations conducted during my fieldwork, Chicago seniors provided their own explanations for the fear that so many criminologists and city officials seem unable to understand. Many of the seniors I got to know said that although they knew that they were unlikely to be robbed or attacked, their heightened concern about victimization stemmed from their knowledge that if they were victimized, the consequences, particularly of violent crime, would be devastating in ways that they would not be for younger people. At the economic level, seniors living on fixed and limited incomes feared that a robbery or burglary could leave them without sufficient resources to pay for such basic needs as food, medication, rent or energy. In Chicago, where hunger, under-medication, homelessness, displacement and energy deprivation are not uncommon among seniors, these are not unfounded concerns. At the physical level, seniors, for whom awareness of bodily fraility is one of the defining conditions of life, are afraid that a violent attack could result in permanent disabilities, crippling and even death. The elderly make it clear that their fears of crime are directly related to their concerns about the difficulty of recovering from crime and that their sensitivities to danger were rational from their points of view.

DEAD SPACE

A cause and consequence of this culture of fear is the degradation and fortification of urban public spaces in which city dwellers circulate. The loss of viable public space is the third condition that gives rise to literal social isolation undermining the social morphological foundations of collective social life and so giving rise to sweeping insecurity in everyday urban life. The real and perceived violence of the city has pushed Chicago residents to remake the sociospatial environment in which they live.[10] In Chicago the degradation of public space has been most rampant in the city's hyperghettos, where the flight of business, the retrenchment of state supports, the out-migration of middle-class residents, the rise of public drug markets, and the concentration of violent crime and victimization have radically reduced the viability of public spaces (Wacquant, 1994). Despite the real decreases in crime that Chicago experienced in the mid-1990s, the overall crime rate in Chicago is falling at a slower pace than in all of the other major American cities. According to the Chicago Community Policing Evaluation Consortium, a major research project directed by Wesley Skogan at Northwestern University, "the largest declines [in crime] have occurred in the highest-crime parts of the city," and "the greatest decline in gun-related crime has occurred in African-American neighborhoods" (Chicago Community Policing Evaluation Consortium, 1997: 6–8). Nonetheless the levels of violent crime concentrated in poor black areas of the city remain comparatively high, making it difficult for residents to feel safe in the streets. A study by the Epidemiology Program at the Chicago Department of Public Health showed that in 1994 and 1995 the overall violent crime rate as reported to the Chicago Police Department, a likely underestimation of the true victimization levels, was 19 violent crimes for every 100 residents of Fuller Park, the community area that had the highest mortality levels during the heat wave. Other community areas with high heat wave mortalities had similar crime levels: Woodlawn, with the second highest heat mortality rate, reported 13 violent crimes per 100 residents; Greater Grand Crossing reported 11 per 100; Washington Park, Grand Boulevard, and the near south side, all among the most deadly spots during the disaster, listed rates above 15 crimes per 100 residents as well, suggesting, as did the Illinois Department of Public Health, an association between the everyday precariousness of life in these neighborhoods and vulnerability during the heat wave (City of Chicago, 1996). In contrast, Lincoln Park, the prosperous community on the near north side, reported two violent crimes for every 100 residents, and a heat wave mortality rate among the lowest in the city (City of Chicago, 1996).

But the conditions of insecurity are hardly confined to the Chicago ghettos, and constant exposure to images and information about violence in the city has instilled genuine fear in communities throughout the city. Moreover, the depacification of daily life that is concentrated in the city's ghettos has emerged on a smaller scale in other parts of Chicago, affecting a broad set of buildings, blocks, and collective housing facilities as well as neighborhood clusters. Several studies have documented the erosion of the sociospatial infrastructure for public life in low-income barrios and ghettos, therefore I will focus here on showing the ways in which spatial degradation and public crime have fostered reclusiveness in settings, such as senior public housing units, where many of the heat wave deaths occurred.

In the four years leading up to the heat wave conditions in the city's senior public housing facilities bucked all of Chicago's crime trends. Residents of these special units experienced a soaring violent crime rate even as the overall crime levels in the Chicago Housing Authority (CHA) family projects and the rest of the city declined, forcing many residents to give up not only the public parks and streets that once supported their neighborhoods, but the public areas within their own apartment buildings as well. In the 1990s the CHA opened its 58 senior buildings, which house about 100,000 residents and are dispersed throughout the city although generally located in safer areas than the family public housing complexes, to people with disabilities as well as to the elderly. The 1990 Americans with Disabilities Act made people with substance abuse problems eligible for social security insurance and the CHA welcomed them into senior housing units as well. Unfortunately this act of accommodation has proven disastrous for senior residents and the communities they had once established within their buildings: the mix of low-income substance abusers, many of whom continue to engage in crime to finance their habits, and low-income seniors, many of whom keep everything they own, savings included, in their tiny apartments, creates a perfect formula for disaster in the social life of the housing complex.

In March of 1995, just a few months before the heat wave, the Chicago Housing Authority reported that from 1991 to 1994 the number of Part I crimes (in which the US Justice Department includes homicide, criminal sexual assault, serious assault, robbery, burglary, theft and violent theft) committed and reported within CHA housing increased by over 50 percent. "The elderly in public housing," a group of CHA tenants and advisers called the Building Organization and Leadership Development (BOLD) group reported, "are more vulnerable than seniors in assisted or private housing in that they are being victimized in many cases by their neighbors." Moreover, BOLD showed that thefts, forcible entry, armed robbery, "and other crimes of violence are substantially higher in those developments housing a large percentage of non-elderly disabled. . . . The reality appears to be that disabled youth are victimizing seniors" (BOLD, 1995).

Elderly residents of senior buildings throughout the city now voice the same complaint: they feel trapped in their rooms, afraid that if they leave they might be attacked or have their apartment robbed, and the most afraid refuse to use the ground floor common rooms unless security workers are there. The fortification of public space that contributes to isolation all over the city is exacerbated here. Most residents, to be sure, do manage to get out of their units, but they have to limit themselves to secure public areas, elevators and halls. Unable to reduce the structural conditions of insecurity in the buildings, workers at the Chicago Department on Aging recently initiated a program to help residents develop building watch groups in the senior complexes. True to its mission to enable as well as provide, the city has increased the security services in the buildings but has also encouraged the elderly and poor CHA residents to arm themselves with flashlights, cellular phones and badges to patrol their home turf. Yet while one branch of the city government prepares the seniors for a feeble battle against the conditions that another branch of the city has created, the most worried and disaffected residents of the senior buildings respond by sealing off their homes with home-made security systems designed to ward off invaders.

Concern about the proximity of younger residents and their associates who are using or peddling drugs is ubiquitous in Chicago's senior housing complexes. During an interview in her home, one woman, a resident of a CHA building on the near west side, expressed remorse that a formerly pleasant and popular patio on the top floor had been vandalized and looted by younger residents and their friends. The group had first taken the space over and made it their hangout spot, then decided to take some of the furniture and even the fire extinguishers for themselves. Some older residents, she explained to me, did not want to make a big deal out of the problem because they worried that their young neighbors would learn who had informed security and then retaliate. The fear of young people and the demonization of drug users common in contemporary American society rendered the situation more difficult, as many building residents presumed that the younger residents would cause trouble and were scared to approach them. Ultimately, the seniors have been unable to fix up the area or win it back. "Now," she sighed, "no one uses that space. It's just empty, dead."

"I NEVER HAVE ENOUGH TIME TO SEE THEM"

The current array of programs and services is insufficient to provide primary goods such as adequate housing, transportation, energy assistance, reliable health care and medication for the elderly poor, leaving private agencies and numerous charities to address gaps that they have no means to fill. Local welfare state agencies in American cities historically have lacked the resources necessary to meet the needs of impoverished and insecure residents, but in the 1990s the rise of entrepreneurial state programs that required more active shopping services from consumerist citizens created additional difficulties for the most isolated and vulnerable city residents. Studies of Chicago's programs for the poor elderly had warned officials about the dangers of residents falling through gaps in the withering safety net. After conducting a major study of Chicago's support programs and emergency services, social service scholar Sharon Keigher concluded that "city agencies are not equipped to intervene substantially with older persons who do not ask for help, who have no family, or who do not go to senior centers and congregate at meal sites. Yet, increasingly these persons—who tend to be very old, poor and living alone—are in need of multiple services" (Keigher, 1991: 12). Published as both an official city report (in 1987) and a scholarly book (in 1991), Keigher's findings were known to city agencies responsible for serving vulnerable seniors long before the heat wave. But the city government lacked both the resources and the political priorities necessary to respond to them sufficiently, and its agencies were poorly prepared for assisting needy seniors in either the heat disaster of 1995 or the struggles they take on regularly.

Government policies and procedures that limited the capacity of residents to enter programs and obtain resources they need is the fourth condition that produces literal isolation. These changes have been disproportionately destructive for the city's most impoverished residents, who have had to struggle to secure the basic resources and services necessary for survival that a more generous welfare state would provide. In a political context where private organizations provide most of the human services to elderly city residents, research must shift from state agencies and agents to include the private offices and employees through which local governments reach their constituents. Spending time alongside social workers and home care providers for Chicago seniors, it became clear that the city's incapacity to reach isolated, sick or otherwise vulnerable seniors during the heat wave was by no means an anomaly created by the unusual environmental conditions. Underservice for Chicago's poor elderly is a structural certainty and everyday norm in an era where political pressures for state entrepreneurialism have grown hand-in-hand with social pressures for isolation. Embedded in a competitive market for gaining city contracts which provides perverse incentives for agencies to underestimate the costs of services and overestimate their capacity to provide them, the agencies and private organizations I observed had bargained themselves into responsibilities that they could not possibly meet. "Most entrepreneurial governments promote *competition* between service providers," David Osborne and Ted Gaebler wrote in *Reinventing Government* (Osborne and Gaebler, 1992: 19), but competition undermines the working conditions of human service providers if it fosters efficiency but compromises the time and human resources necessary to provide quality care. "My seniors love to see me," Mandy Evers, an African-American woman in her late 20s who was on her fourth year working as a case manager, told me. "The problem is I never have enough time to get to them."

Stacy Geer, a seasoned advocate of Chicago seniors who spent much of the 1990s helping the elderly secure basic goods such as housing and energy, insists that the political mismatch between more entrepreneurial service systems and isolated seniors contributed to the vulnerability of Chicago seniors during the heat wave. "The capacity of service delivery programs is realized fully only by the seniors who are most active in seeking them out, who are connected to their family, church, neighbors, or someone who helps them get the things they need." In some circumstances, the aging process can hinder seniors who have been healthy and financially secure for most of their lives. Geer continues, "As seniors become more frail their networks break down. As their needs increase, they have less ability to meet them. The people who are hooked into the Department on Aging, the AARP, the senior clubs at the churches, they are part of that word of mouth network and they hear. I know, just from doing organizing in the senior community, that you run into the same people, and the same are active in a number of organizations."[11] Seniors who are marginalized at the first, structural level of social networks and government programs are then doubly excluded at the second, conjunctural level of service delivery because they do not always know of—let alone know how to activate—networks of support. Those who are out of the loop in their daily life are more likely to remain so when there is a crisis. This certainly happened during the heat wave, when relatively active and informed seniors used official cooling centers set up by the city while the more inactive and isolated elderly stayed home.

During the 1990s, however, not even the best-connected city residents knew where to appeal if they needed assistance securing the most basic of primary goods: home, energy and water. In Chicago, the combination of cuts to the budget for the federally-sponsored Low Income Home Energy Assistance Program (LIHEAP) and a market-model managerial strategy for punishing consumers who are delinquent on their bills has placed the poor elderly in a permanent energy crisis. Facing escalating energy costs (even before prices soared in 2000), declining government subsidies and fixed incomes, seniors throughout the city express great concern about the cost of their utilities bills and take pains to keep their fees down.[12]

Poor seniors I got to know understood that they would face unaffordable utilities costs in the summer if they used air conditioners. Epidemiologists estimate that "more than 50 percent of the deaths related to the heat wave could have been prevented if each home had had a working air conditioner," arguing that surely this would be an effective public health strategy (Semenza et al., 1996: 87). Yet the elderly who regularly struggle to make ends meet explain that they could not use air conditioners even if they owned them because activating the units would push their energy bills to unmanageable levels. But their energy crisis was pressing even during moderate temperatures. The most impoverished seniors I visited kept their lights off during the day, letting the television, their most consistent source of companionship, illuminate their rooms. Fear of losing their energy altogether if they failed to pay the bills has relegated these seniors to regular and fundamental forms of insecurity and duress. Yet their daily crisis goes largely unnoticed.

THE FORMULA FOR DISASTER

The four conditions highlighted here impose serious difficulties for all seniors. But they are particularly devastating for the elderly poor who cannot buy their way out of them by purchasing more secure housing in safer areas, visiting or paying for distant family members to visit, by obtaining private health insurance supplements or by using more expensive and safe transportation such as taxis to get out of the house or the neighborhood. Each one of the key conditions described in this article contributes to the production of the forms of isolation that proved so deadly during the heat wave and that continue to undermine the health and safety of countless older Chicagoans. But in many cases Chicago residents are subjected to all of the conditions together, and the combination creates a formula for disaster that makes extreme social, physical and psychological suffering a feature of everyday life. If aging alone, the culture of fear, the degradation and fortification of public space and the reduction of redistributive and supportive state programs continue at their current pace, more seniors will retreat to their "safe houses," abandoning a society that has all but abandoned them. Collectively producing the conditions for literal isolation, we have made dying alone a fittingly tragic end.

ACKNOWLEDGMENTS

The National Science Foundation Graduate Research Fellowship, the Jacob Javits Fellowship and a grant from the Berkeley Humanities Division helped to support research for this project. This publication was also supported in part by a grant from the Individual Project Fellowship Program of the Open Society Institute. Thanks go to Loïc Wacquant, Mike Rogin, Jack Katz, Nancy Scheper-Hughes, Kim DaCosta, Dan Dohan, Paul Willis and Caitlin Zaloom for incisive comments on earlier drafts.

NOTES

1. For a synthetic sociological account of the conditions that helped produce the historic mortality rates, see Klinenberg (1999); for an epidemiological account, see Semenza et al. (1996).
2. Roughly 70 Chicagoans died on a typical July day during the 1990s. "Excess deaths" measures the variance from the expected death rate. In assessing heat wave mortality, forensic scientists prefer the excess death measure to the heat-related death measure, which is based on the number of deaths examined and recorded by investigators, because many deaths during heat waves go unexamined or are not properly attributed to the heat (Shen et al., 1998).
3. Sherwin Nuland is among the more recent writers to discuss the modern version of the *ars moriendi*. Describing a man dying of AIDS, Nuland writes, "During his terminal weeks in the hospital, Kent was never alone. Whatever help they could or could not provide him at the final hours, there is no question that the constant presence of his friends eased him beyond what might have been achieved by the nursing staff, no matter the attentiveness of their care" (Nuland, 1993: 196).
4. There is, of course, a brighter side to the extension of the life span, which is itself a sign of significant social and scientific progress. Aging alone, as Robert Coles and Arlie Hochschild have argued, can be a rich personal and social experience, albeit one filled with challenges. In *The Unexpected Community,* Hochschild documents the active social lives of a group of Bay Area seniors who, as she emphatically stated, "were not isolated and not lonely" but instead "were part of a community I did not expect to find" (Hochschild, 1973: xiv), one that worked together to solve the problem of loneliness that proves so troublesome for the elderly. There are vital communities of older people and Hochschild's research shows how these groups come into being, portraying them once they are made. But too often readers of Hochschild are so eager to celebrate the community she describes that they forget that she chose to study Merrill Court precisely because the residents there were an exceptional case. The opening lines of her epilogue explain the goal of her project much better than do many of her interpreters. She wrote, "The most important point I am trying to make in this book concerns the people it does not discuss—the isolated. Merrill Court was an unexpected community, an exception. Living in ordinary apartments and houses, in shabby downtown hotels, sitting in parks and eating in cheap restaurants, are old people in various degrees and sorts of isolation" (Hochschild, 1973: 137). Hochschild leaves it to others to render the social worlds of the isolated as explicit as she makes the world in Merrill Court.
5. This conception of social isolation breaks from both sociological definitions of the term, which generally refer to relations between groups rather than people, and from conventional gerontological definitions of isolation, which define isolation as being single or living alone. There are, however, an increasing number of social network studies and gerontological reports that classify social integration or isolation by relative levels of social contact. Fischer and Phillips, for example, define social isolation as "knowing relatively few people who are probable sources of rewarding exchanges" (Fischer and Phillips, 1982: 22); Rubinstein classifies social integration and activity on a scale ranging from "very low range" to "high range" (Rubinstein, 1986: 172–9); and Gibson lists four types of loneliness: "physical aloneness," "loneliness as a state of mind," "the feeling of isolation due to a personal characteristic," and "solitude" (Gibson, 2004: 4–6).
6. See Gibson (2000) for a review of studies showing that most seniors who live alone are not lonely.
7. Thompson and Krause find that not only do people who live alone report more fear of crime than those who live with others, but also that "the greater sense of security among those who live with others appears to permeate beyond the home because they report less fear of crime than their counterparts" (Thompson and Krause, 1998: 356).
8. All personal names of Chicago residents have been changed.

9. Yet, as Alex Kotlowitz and teenage journalists LeAlan Jones and Lloyd Newman have shown in their accounts of growing up in Chicago's West and South Side housing projects, even young residents of the most violent urban areas are subjected to so much brutality, death and suffering that they have learned from their infancy how to organize their daily routines around the temporal and seasonal variations of the criminal economy (Jones et al., 1997; Kotlowitz, 1991). For Jones and Newman, managing fear and avoiding violence is such a fundamental part of their everyday lives that they decided to introduce and organize their book around it. "They used to shoot a lot in the summertime," Jones begins. Lloyd continues ominously, especially in light of the heat wave, "That's why I stayed in my house most of the time" (Jones et al., 1997: 31).
10. In 1995 Chicago ranked 6th in robbery and 5th in aggravated assaults among all United States cities with a population of over 350,000; in 1998 the city was the national leader in homicide, with the annual figure of 698 exceeding New York City's by about 100 even though Chicago is roughly one-third as populous; and throughout the 1990s its violent crime rate decreased much more slowly than any of the eight largest American cities (New York City, Los Angeles, Chicago, Houston, Philadelphia, Phoenix, San Diego, Dallas).
11. Internal pressures within state agencies and advocacy organizations push social workers and organizers to reward the most entrepreneurial clients with special attention. Overwhelmed with problem cases and operating in an environment where agencies must show successful outcome measures to garner resources from external funders who expect tangible results, the social workers I observed engaged in what Lipsky called "creaming," the practice of favoring and working intensively on the cases of people "who seem likely to succeed in terms of bureaucratic success criteria" (Lipsky, 1980: 107).
12. While the average Illinois family spends roughly 6 percent of its income on heat-related utilities during winter months, for low-income families the costs constitute nearly 35 percent (Pearson, 1995).

REFERENCES

BOLD (1995) "BOLD Group Endorses CHAPS Police Unit," report by the Building Organization and Leadership Development group, Chicago.

Chicago Community Policing Evaluation Consortium (1997) "Community Policing in Chicago, Year Four: An Interim Report," report by the Chicago Community Policing Evaluation Consortium.

City of Chicago (1996) "An Epidemiological Overview of Violent Crimes in Chicago, 1995," report by the Department of Public Health, City of Chicago.

Fischer, Claude (1975) "Toward a Subcultural Theory of Urbanism," *American Journal of Sociology* 80: 1319–41.

Fischer, Claude (1982) *To Dwell among Friends: Personal Networks in Town and City.* Chicago, IL: University of Chicago Press.

Fischer, Claude (1984[1976]) *The Urban Experience.* San Diego: Harcourt, Brace, Jovanovich.

Fischer, Claude and Meredith Phillips (1982) "Who is Alone? Social Characteristics of People with Small Networks," in Leticia Anne Peplau and Daniel Perlman (eds) *Loneliness: A Sourcebook on Current Theory: Research and Therapy.* New York: Wiley.

Fleming-Moran, Millicent, T. Kenworthy-Bennett and Karen Harlow (1991) "Illinois State Needs Assessment Survey of Elders Aged 55 and Over," report from the Heartland Center on Aging, Disability and Long Term Care, School of Public Health and Environmental Affairs, Indiana University and the National Center for Senior Living, South Bend, IN.

Ford, Amasa, Marie Haug, Paul Jones and Steven Folmar (1992) "New Cohorts of Urban Elders: Are They in Trouble?," *Journal of Gerontology* 47: S297–S303.

Gibson, Hamilton (2000) *Loneliness in Later Life.* New York: Saint Martin's Press.

Gurley, Jan, Nancy Lum, Merle Sande, Bernard Lo and Mitchell Katz (1996) "Persons Found in their Homes Helpless or Dead," *New England Journal of Medicine* 334: 1710–16.

Hochschild, Arlie Russel (1973) *The Unexpected Community: Portrait of an Old-Age Subculture.* Berkeley: University of California Press.

Jones, LeAlan and Lloyd Newman with David Isay (1997) *Our America: Life and Death on the South Side of Chicago.* New York: Washington Square Press.

Joseph, Janice (1997) "Fear of Crime among Black Elderly," *Journal of Black Studies* 27: 698–717.

Keigher, Sharon (1987) "The City's Responsibility for the Homeless Elderly of Chicago," report by the Chicago Department of Aging and Disability.

Klinenberg, Eric (1999) "Denaturalizing Disaster: A Social Autopsy of the 1995 Chicago Heat Wave," *Theory and Society* 28: 239–95.

Kornblum, William (1974) *Blue Collar Community.* Chicago, IL: University of Chicago Press.

Kotlowitz, Alex (1991) *There are No Children Here: The Story of Two Boys Growing Up in the Other America*. New York: Anchor Books.

Lawlor, Edward, Gunnar Almgren and Mary Gomberg (1993) "Aging in Chicago: Demography," report, Chicago Community Trust.

Lipsky, Michael (1980) *Street-Level Bureaucracy: Dilemmas of the Individual in Public Services*. New York: Russell Sage.

Merry, Sally Engle (1981) *Urban Danger: Life in a Neighborhood of Strangers*. Philadelphia, PA: Temple University Press.

Miethe, Terance (1995) "Fear and Withdrawal," *The Annals of the American Academy* 539: 14–29.

Nashold, Raymond, Jeffrey Jentzen, Patrick Remington and Peggy Peterson (n.d.) "Excessive Heat Deaths, Wisconsin, June 20–August 19, 1995," unpublished manuscript.

Nuland, Sherwin (1993) *How We Die: Reflections on Life's Final Chapter*. New York: Vintage.

Osborne, David and Ted Gaebler (1992) *Reinventing Government: How the Entrepreneurial Spirit is Transforming the Public Sector*. New York: Plume.

Pearson, Rick (1995) "Funding to Help Poor Pay Heating Bills Evaporating," *Chicago Tribune* (20 July): Metro 2.

Perrow, Charles and Mauro Guillen (1990) *The Aids Disater*. New Haven, CT: Yale University Press.

Putnam, Robert (1995) "Bowling Alone: America's Declining Social Capital," *Democracy* 6: 65–78.

Rubinstein, Robert (1986) *Singular Paths: Old Men Living Alone*. New York: Columbia University Press.

Seale, Clive (1995) "Dying Alone," *Sociology of Health and Illness* 17: 376–92.

Semenza, Jan, Carol Rubin, Kenneth Falter, Joel Selanikio, W. Dana Flanders, Holly Howe and John Wilhelm (1996) "Heat-Related Deaths During the July 1995 Heat Wave in Chicago," *The New England of Medicine* 335: 84–90.

Shen, Tiefu, Holly Howe, Celan Alo and Ronald Moolenaar (1998) "Toward a Broader Definition of Heat-Related Death: Comparison of Mortality Estimates From Medical Examiners" Classification with Those from Total Death Differentials During the July 1995 Chicago Heat Wave', *The American Journal of Forensic Medicine and Pathology* 19: 113–18.

Skogan, Wesley (1990) *Disorder and Decline: Crime and the Spiral of Decay in American Neighborhoods*. Berkeley: University of California Press.

Skogan, Wesley and Michael Maxfield (1981) *Coping with Crime: Individual and Neighborhood Reactions*. Newbury Park, CA: Sage.

Suttles, Gerald (1968) *The Social Order of the Slum: Ethnicity and Territory in the Inner City*. Chicago, IL: University of Chicago Press.

Taub, Richard, D. Garth Taylor and Jan Durham (1984) *Paths of Neighborhood Change: Race and Crime in Urban America*. Chicago, IL: University of Chicago Press.

Thompson, Emily and Neil Krause (1998) "Living Alone and Neighborhood Characteristics as Predictors of Social Support in Later Life," *Journal of Gerontology* 53B(6): S354–S364.

US Centers for Disease Control and Prevention (1996) "Heat-Related Mortality—Milwaukee, Wisconsin, July 1995," *Morbidity and Mortality Weekly Report* 45:505–7.

Wacquant, Loïc (1994) "The New Urban Color Line: The State and Fate of the Ghetto in PostFordist America," in Craig Calhoun (ed.) *Social Theory and the Politics of Identity*. Oxford: Basil Blackwell.

Wacquant, Loïc (2001) "Deadly Symbiosis: When Ghetto and Prison Meet and Mesh," *Punishment and Society* 3(1): 95–134.

Wilson, William Julius (1996) *When Work Disappears: The World of the New Urban Poor*. New York: Alfred Knopf.

Wuthnow, Robert (1998) *Loose Connections: Joining Together in America's Fragmented Communities*. Cambridge, MA: Harvard University Press.

10 HEALTH INEQUALITIES: RELATIVE OR ABSOLUTE MATERIAL STANDARDS?

Richard Wilkinson

The existence of wide and widening socio-economic differences in health shows how extraordinarily sensitive health remains to socio-economic circumstances. Twofold, threefold, or even fourfold differences in mortality have been reported within Britain, depending largely on the social classification used.[1–3] This article will illustrate some of the most important mechanisms involved in the generation of these differences.

Fundamental to understanding the causes of these differences in health is the distinction between the effects of relative and absolute living standards. Socioeconomic gradients in health are simultaneously an association with social position and with different material circumstances, both of which have implications for health—but which is more important in terms of causality? Is the health disadvantage of the least well off part of the population mainly a reflection of the direct physiological effects of lower absolute material standards (of bad housing, poor diets, inadequate heating, and air pollution), or is it more a matter of the direct and indirect effects of differences in psychosocial circumstances associated with social position—of where you stand in relation to others? The indirect effects of psychosocial circumstances here include increased exposure to behavioural risks resulting from psychosocial stress, including any stress related smoking, drinking, eating "for comfort," etc; most of the direct effects are likely to centre on the physiological effects of chronic mental and emotional stress.

Evidence from three sources suggests that the psychosocial effects of social position account for the larger part of health inequalities. If valid, this perspective would have fundamental implications for public policy and for our understanding of the pathways through which socio-economic differences have an impact on human biology.

INCOME WITHIN AND BETWEEN SOCIETIES

Despite the difficulty of disentangling material from social influences on health, it is possible to look at the relation between income and health in population groups where income differences are, and are not, associated with social status. Social stratification exists within rather than between societies. Therefore, while income differences among groups within the developed societies are associated with social status, the differences in average per capita incomes between developed societies are not. We may therefore compare the association of income and health within and between societies.

Within countries there is a close relation between most measures of health and socioeconomic circumstances. As an example, Figure 9-1 uses data from 300 685 white American men in the multiple risk factor intervention trial to show the relation between mortality and the median family income in the postcode areas in which they lived.[4] Among black men in the trial, larger mortality differences are spread over a smaller income range.[5] In Britain, there are similar gradients in mortality and sickness absence among men and women.[6, 7]

The regular gradients between income and mortality within countries contrast sharply with the much weaker relation found in the differences between rich developed societies. Figure 9-2 shows the cross sectional relation between life expectancy and gross domestic product per capita for 23 members of the Organisation of Economic Cooperation and Development (OECD) in 1993. Using data from the OECD countries reduces the influence of extraneous cultural differences by restricting the comparison to developed, democratic countries with market economies. Currencies have been converted at "purchasing power parities" to reflect real differences in spending in each country. The correlation coefficient of 0.08 shows that life expectancy and gross national product per capita are not related in this cross sectional data. Excluding government expenditure makes little difference: the correlation with private consumer's expenditure per capita is only 0.10.

Data on changes over time between countries show a weak but non-significant relation. During 1970–93 the correlation between increases in life expectancy and percentage increases in gross domestic product per capita among OECD countries was 0.30, suggesting that less than 10% of the increases in life expectancy were related to economic performance. Though the recent rise in national mortality in eastern Europe suggests that time lags may be short, the period used here allows for the possibility of longer lags.[8]

As Figure 10-2 uses data for whole countries, the contrast between it and the strong relation shown in Figure 10-1 cannot arise from sampling error. A strong international relation is unlikely to be masked by cultural factors: not only are the international comparisons confined to OECD countries, but the picture is supported by comparisons among the 50 states of the United States, where cultural differences are smaller. The correlation reported between age adjusted mortality and median incomes in the states was −0.28.[9] As with the international comparisons, social stratification mainly occurs within rather than between American states.

Income and mortality are so strongly related within societies that this relation cannot be assumed to exist between developed societies but has somehow become hidden. Its robustness within societies shows not merely in mortality data but in measures as diverse as medically certified sickness absence among civil servants and prescription items issued per head of population in relation to local rates of unemployment.[7, 10] However, the contrast in the strength of the relation within and between societies would make sense if mortality in rich countries were influ-

Figure 10-1. *Age Adjusted Mortality of 300 685 White American Men by Median Family Income of Zip Code Areas in the United States*[4]

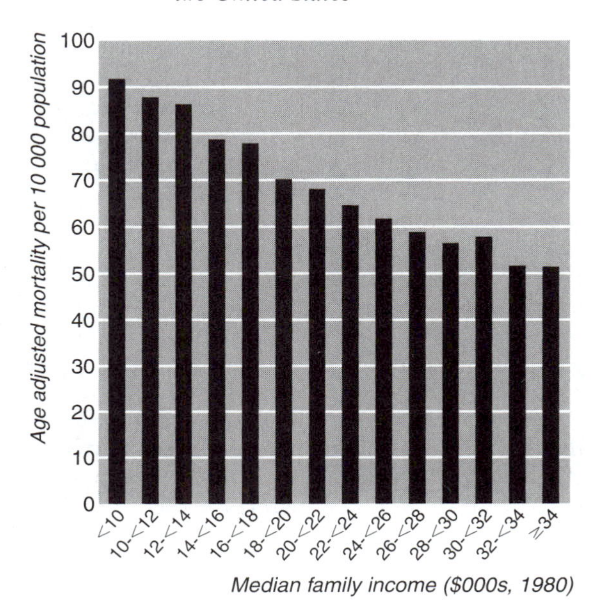

Figure 10-2. *Relation of Life Expectancy and Gross National Product Per Capita in OECD Countries, 1993 (Based on Data from OECD National Accounts 1995 and World Bank's World Tables 1996)*

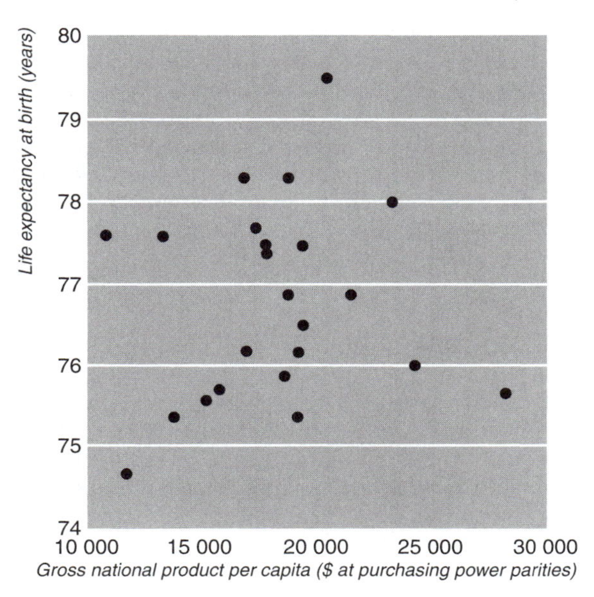

enced more by relative income than by absolute material standards.

INCOME DISTRIBUTION

A second source of evidence that relative income has a powerful influence on health comes from analyses of the relation between measures of income inequality and mortality both among developed countries[11] and among the 50 states of the United States.[12] Cross sectional data and data covering changes over time both show that mortality tends to be lower in societies where income differences are smaller, even after average income, absolute poverty, and a number of other socioeconomic factors have been controlled for. This relation has now been shown independently on over a dozen different datasets and has been reported absent only once.[11] The most plausible explanation is that mortality is lower in more egalitarian societies because the burden of relative deprivation is reduced.

The weak association between mortality and median (absolute) incomes of the 50 American states disappears when the distribution of income within each state is controlled for.[9] The correlation coefficient drops from −0.28 to −0.06, suggesting that absolute income is unrelated to mortality in the United States. Unfortunately, further exploration of the international relation between income distribution and mortality will depend on taking account of the differences in response to income surveys in different countries. Response rates vary by more than 30%, and as non-responders are concentrated particularly among the rich and poor, high non-response leads to smaller reported income differences.[13, 14]

EPIDEMIOLOGICAL TRANSITION

The third reason for thinking that health is influenced more by relative than absolute income centres on the epidemiological transition. Although absolute material standards remain important in less developed countries, there are indications that the epidemiological transition represents a stage in economic development after which further improvements in material standards have less influence on health. Not only do the infectious diseases of poor countries give way to degenerative diseases as the main causes of death, but the transition also coincides with a flattening of the curve relating life expectancy to gross domestic product per capita.[11, 15] In addition, several of the so called "diseases of affluence" (including coronary heart disease, stroke, hypertension, obesity, and duodenal ulcers) reverse their social distribution to become more common among poor people in affluent societies, reflecting that the majority of the population has risen above a minimum threshold level of living.[11,16] When those who are less well off cease to be thin, obesity ceases to be associated with social status.

A THEORY OF HEALTH AND SOCIAL POSITION?

If the association between health and socioeconomic status within societies—at least in the developed world—is not primarily the direct effect of material standards, then some might think it resulted simply from differential social mobility between healthy people and unhealthy people. However, many research reports show that this is not the major part of the picture,[17–20] and social selection is entirely unable to account for the relation between national mortality rates and income distribution.

This pushes us—inexorably though perhaps reluctantly—towards the view that socioeconomic differences in health within countries result primarily from differences in people's position in the socioeconomic hierarchy relative to others, leaving a less powerful role to the undoubted direct effects of absolute material standards. If health inequality had been a residual problem of absolute poverty it might have been expected to have diminished under the impact of postwar economic growth, and it would tend to distinguish primarily between the poor and the rest of the population—rather than running across society, making even the higher echelons less healthy than those above them (see Figure 9-1).

Need for a Theory

A theory is needed which unifies the causes of the health inequalities related to social hierarchy with the effects of income inequality on national mortality rates. At its centre are likely to be factors affecting how hierarchical the hierarchy is, the depths of material insecurity and social exclusion which societies tolerate, and the direct and indirect psychosocial effects of social stratification.[21]

One reason why greater income equality is associated with better health seems to be that it tends to improve social cohesion and reduce the social divisions.[11] Qualitative and quantitative evidence suggests that more egalitarian societies are more cohesive. In their study of Italian regions, Putnam *et al* report a strong correlation (0.81) between income equality and their index of the strength of local community life.[22] They say, "Equality is an essential feature of the civic community." Kawachi *et al* have shown that measures of "social trust" provide a statistical link between income distribution and mortality in the United States.[23] Better integration into a network of social relations is known to benefit health.[24, 25] This accords with the emphasis placed on relative poverty as a form of social exclusion, and with the evidence that racial discrimination has direct health effects.[26] However, social wellbeing is not simply a matter of stronger social networks. Low control, insecurity, and loss of self esteem are among the psychosocial risk factors known to mediate between health and socioeconomic circumstances. Indeed, integration in the economic life of society, reduced unemployment, material security, and narrower income differences provide the material base for a more cohesive society. Usually the effects of chronic stress will be closely related to the many direct effects of material deprivation, simply because material insecurity is always worrying. However, even absolute poverty has often killed through psychosocial and behavioural pathways.

Pathways

In terms of the pathways involved in the transition from social to biological processes, there is increasing interest in the physiological effects of chronic stress. Social status differences in physiological risk factors among several species of non-human primates have been identified. Animals lower in the social hierarchy hypersecreted cortisol, had higher blood pressure, had suppressed immune function, more commonly had central obesity, and had less good ratios of high density lipoproteins to low density lipoproteins—even when they were fed the same diet and social status was manipulated experimentally.[27, 28] Among humans, lower social status has also been associated with lower ratios of high to low density lipoproteins, central obesity, and higher fibrinogen concentrations.[29] In experiments in which social status was manipulated, subordinate monkeys "received more aggression, engaged in less affiliation, and spent more time alone than dominants . . . they spent more time fearfully scanning the social environment and displayed more behavioral depression than dominants."[30] Loss of social status resulting from being rehoused with more dominant animals was associated with fivefold increases in coronary artery atherosclerosis.[31]

Although research has shown that psychosocial factors are related to both morbidity and mortality, differences in reporting make international comparisons of morbidity unreliable. Nevertheless, because patterns even of self reported morbidity are predictive of mortality rates, we can probably assume that mortality differences indicate differences in objectively defined morbidity.[32, 33] Although no obvious patterns have emerged from attempts to assess international differences in the extent of inequalities in self reported morbidity when people are classified by education or social class, across countries there is a close relation between the extent of inequalities in income and in self reported morbidity.[34, 35]

RELATIVE POVERTY AND MORTALITY

Although Britain had a greater increase in inequality during the 1980s than other developed market economies,[36] the proportion of the population living in relative poverty (below half the average income) may—for the first time in two decades—have decreased slightly during the early 1990s. It now stands at almost one in four of the whole population (incomes after deducting housing costs).[37] Among children the proportion is almost one in three. Particularly worrying is the likely increase in the proportion of children emotionally scarred by the tensions and conflicts of family life aggravated by living in relative poverty. During 1982–92 there were no improvements in national mortality rates among young men (aged 20–40) and smaller improvements among younger women (aged 15–24) than at most other ages.[38] Socioeconomic differences in mortality are at their maximum at these ages, and the national trends are likely to be partly a reflection of the increased burden of relative deprivation. Among young men, deaths from suicide, AIDS, violence, and cirrhosis increased. These causes suggest that the psychosocial effects of relative deprivation are unlikely to be confined to health. As in the international data, where death rates from accidents, violence, and alcohol related causes seem to be particularly closely related to wider income inequalities, the predominance of behavioural causes may reflect changes in social cohesion.[9, 13]

Related papers are intended to illustrate some of the processes which give rise to the relation between relative deprivation and health. What comes out of several of them may not have been so different had the subject been crime, drug misuse, or poor educational performance. Important aspects of the evidence suggest that the rest of society cannot long remain insulated from the effects of high levels of relative deprivation.

REFERENCES

1. Phillimore P, Beattie A, Townsend P. The widening gap. Inequality of health in northern England, 1981–91. *BMJ* 1994;308:1125–8.
2. Goldblatt P. Mortality and alternative social classifications In: Goldblatt P, ed. *Longitudinal study 1971–1981: mortality and social organisation.* London: HMSO, 1990. (OPCS series LS, No 6.)
3. Davey Smith G, Shipley MJ, Rose G. Magnitude and causes of socioeconomic differentials in mortality: further evidence from the Whitehall Study. *J Epidemiol Community Health* 1990;44:265–70.
4. Davey Smith G, Neaton JD, Stamler J. Socioeconomic differentials in mortality risk among men screened for the multiple risk factor intervention trial. 1. White men. *Am J Public Health* 1996;86:486–96.
5. Davey Smith G, Wentworth D, Neaton JD, Stamler R, Stamler J. Socioeconomic differentials in mortality risk among men screened for the multiple risk factor intervention trial. 2. Black men. *Am J Public Health* 1996;86:497–504.
6. Office of Population Censuses and Surveys. *Registrar general's supplement on occupational mortality 1979–83.* London: HMSO, 1986.
7. North F, Syme SL, Feeney A, Head J, Shipley MJ, Marmot MG. Explaining socioeconomic differences in sickness absence: the Whitehall II study. *BMJ* 1993;306:361–6.
8. Hertzman C, Kelly S, Bohak M. *East-West life expectancy gap in Europe.* Dortrecht: Kluwer, 1996.
9. Kaplan GA, Pamuk E, Lynch JW, Cohen RO, Balfour JL. Income inequality and mortality in the United States: analysis of mortality and potential pathways. *BMJ* 1996;312:999–1003.
10. Office of Health Economics. *Compendium health statistics.* London: OHE, 1995.
11. Wilkinson RG. Unhealthy societies: the afflictions of inequality. London: Routledge, 1996.
12. Kennedy BP, Kawachi J, Prothrow-Stith D. Income distribution and mortality: cross sectional ecological study of the Robin Hood index in the United States. *BMJ* 1996;312:1004–7. (Important correction. *BMJ* 1996;312:1194.)
13. McIsaac SJ, Wilkinson RG. Income distribution and cause-specific mortality. *Eur J Public Health* (in press).
14. Wilkinson RG. Research note: German income distribution and infant mortality. *Sociology of Health and Illness* 1994;16:260–2.
15. World Bank. *World development report.* New York: Oxford University Press, 1993.
16. Wilkinson RG. The epidemiological transition: from material scarcity to social disadvantage? *Daedalus* 1994;123(4):61–77.
17. Lundberg O. Childhood living conditions, health status, and social mobility: a contribution to the health selection debate. *European Sociological Review* 1991;7:149–62.
18. Blane D, Davey Smith G, Bartley M. Social selection: what does it contribute to social class differences in health? *Sociology of Health and Illness* 1993;15:1–15.
19. Fox J, Goldblatt P, Jones D. Social class mortality differentials: artefact, selection or life circumstances? *J Epidemiol Community Health* 1985; 39:1–8.
20. Power C, Manor O, Fox AJ, Fogelman K. Health in childhood and social inequalities in young adults. *J R Stat Soc (A)* 1990;153:17–28.

21. Sennett R, Cobb J. *The hidden injuries of class.* New York: Knopf, 1973.
22. Putnam RD, Leonardi R, Nanetti RY. Making democracy work: civic traditions in modern Italy. Princeton, NJ: Princeton University Press, 1993: 102–5, 224.
23. Kawachi I, Kennedy BP, Lochner K, Prothrow-Stith D. Social capital, income inequality and mortality. *Am J Public Health* (in press).
24. House JS, Landis KR, Umberson D. Social relationships and health. *Science* 1988;241:540–5.
25. Berkman LF. The role of social relations in health promotion. *Psychosom Res* 1995;57:245–54.
26. Krieger N, Sidney S. Racial discrimination and blood pressure: the CARDIA study of young black and white adults. *Am J Public Health* 1996;86:1370–8.
27. Shively CA, Clarkson TB. Regional obesity and coronary artery atherosclerosis in females: a non-human primate model. *Acta Medica Scand* 1988:723(suppl):71–8.
28. Sapolsky RM. Endocrinology alfresco: psychoendocrine studies of wild baboons. *Recent Prog Hormone Res* 1993;48:437–68.
29. Brunner E. The social and biological basis of cardiovascular disease in office workers. In: Brunner E, Blane D, Wilkinson RG, eds. *Health and social organisation.* London: Routledge, 1996.
30. Shively CA, Laird KL, Anton RF. The behavior and physiology of social stress and depression in female cynomolgus monkeys. *Biol Psychiatry* (in press).
31. Shively CA, Clarkson TB. Social status and coronary artery atherosclerosis in female monkeys. *Arteriosclerosis Thrombosis* 1994;14:721–6.
32. Ostlin P. Occupational history, self-reported chronic illness, and mortality: a follow up of 25,586 Swedish men and women. *J Epidemiol Community Health* 1990;44:12–6.
33. Arber S. Social class, non-employment, and chronic illness: continuing the inequalities in health debate. *BMJ* 1987;94:1069–73.
34. Kunst AK, Cavelaar AEJM, Groenhof F, Geurts JJM, Mackenbach JP. Socioeconomic inequalities in morbidity and mortality in Europe: a comparative study. Rotterdam: Erasmus University, 1997. (EU Working Group on Socio-Economic Inequalities in Health.)
35. Van Doorslaer E, Wagstaff A, Bleichrodt H, Calonge S, Gerdtham U, Gerfin M, *et al.* Socioeconomic inequalities in health: some international comparisons. *J Health Econ* (in press).
36. Hills J. *The future of welfare.* York: Joseph Rowntree Foundation, 1994.
37. Department of Social Security. *Households below average income 1979–1993/4.* London: Stationary Office, 1996.
38. Tickle L. Mortality trends in the United Kingdom, 1982–1992. *Population Trends* 1996;86:21–8.

The Social and Cultural Meanings of Illness

Analysts in recent years have often drawn the distinction between disease and illness. Put simply, disease is the biophysiological phenomenon that affects the body, while illness is a social phenomenon that accompanies or surrounds the disease. The shape of illness is not necessarily determined by the disease. What an illness is involves the interaction of the disease, sick individuals, and society. To examine illness, we must focus on the subjective worlds of meaning and experience. In the next section, we explore this area when we look at "The Experience of Illness." Here, rather than focusing on individual experience, we investigate the social images and moral meanings that are attributed to illnesses.

In this perspective, we view illness as a social construction. While most illnesses are assumed to have a biophysiological basis (i.e., an underlying disease), this is not a necessary condition for something to be defined as an illness. As Joseph Gusfield (1967) notes, "Illness is a social designation, by no means given by the nature of medical fact." Thus, we can conceivably have illnesses without diseases or illnesses whose meaning is completely independent from the actual biomedical entity. In examining the social meaning of illness, we focus on the role of social and cultural values that shape the perception of a disease or malady. Illness can reflect cultural assumptions and biases about a particular group or groups of people, or it can become a cultural metaphor for extant societal problems.

Illnesses may reflect deeply rooted cultural values and assumptions. This is perhaps particularly evident in the medical definition and treatment of women and women's maladies. During the nineteenth century, organized medicine achieved a strong dominance over the treatment of women and proceeded to promulgate erroneous and damaging conceptualizations of women as sickly, irrational creatures at the mercy of their reproductive organs (Barker-Benfield, 1976; Wertz and Wertz, 1989). Throughout history we can find similar examples of medical and "scientific" explanations of women's health and illnesses that reflect the dominant conceptions of women in society. For example, a century ago common medical knowledge was replete with assumptions about the "fragile" nature of upper-class women, a nature first believed to be dominated by reproductive organs and later by psychological processes innate in women (Ehrenreich and English, 1978). Assumptions about women's nature frequently set cultural limits on what women could do. In the late nineteenth century physicians opposed granting women the right to vote on the grounds that concern about such matters would strain their "fragile" brains and cause their ovaries to shrink! The creation of the "cult of invalidism" among upper-class women in the nineteenth century—at the same time working-class women were considered capable of working long, hard hours in sweatshops and factories—can be interpreted as physicians acting as agents of social control. In this case, the physicians' use of definitions of health and illness kept women of both classes "in their place," both overtly and subtly, through a socialization process in which many women came to accept being sickly as their proper role and in which many more unquestioningly accepted the physicians' claim to "expertise" in treating women's health and sexual problems. While physicians did not invent sexism, they reflected common sexist attitudes which they then reinforced in their definition and treatment of women.

While the grossest biases about women and their bodies have diminished, the effects of gender bias on the meanings of illness are now subtler and more complex. Since the 1930s, a significant number of women's problems—childbirth, birth control, abortion, menopause, and premenstrual syndrome—have become "medicalized" (see "The Medicalization of American Society" in Part Three). While the consequences of medicalization are probably mixed (Riessman, 1983), various feminist analysts see it as an extension of medicine's control over women (see, for example, Boston Women's Health Book Collective, 1985). Looking at one example, premenstrual syndrome (PMS), we see that medicalization can legitimate the real discomforts of many women who had long been told their premenstrual pain was "all in their head." On the other hand, one consequence of the adoption of PMS as a medical syndrome is the legitimation of the view that all women are potentially physically and emotionally handicapped each month by menstruation and thus not fully capable of responsibility. Wide adoption of PMS as a syndrome could undercut some important gains of the contemporary women's movement (cf. Figert, 1995).

The current treatment of menopause provides another example of the changing medical meanings of women's disorders. Several analysts (Kaufert, 1982; McCrea, 1983; Bell, 1987) have described how menopause, a natural life event for women, became defined as a "deficiency disease" in the 1960s when medical therapy became readily available to treat it. The treatment, estrogen replacement therapy, promised women they could stay "feminine forever" and preserve their "youth and beauty." Feminists argued that menopause is part of the normal aging process and thus not an illness. They also argued that the treatment is usually unnecessary and, since estrogen has been linked to cancer, always dangerous. Recently, studies have suggested that both the meanings and experience of menopause may be culturally bound. In Japan, for example, cessation of menstruation is not given much importance and is seen as a natural part of aging, not a disease-like condition. Even the experience is different: Japanese women report few "hot flashes" but rather typically suffer from stiff shoulders (Lock, 1993). PMS and menopause provide contemporary examples of how cultural assumptions of gender can be reflected in the medical definitions of disorder, which affect the medical treatment of women.

The meaning attributed to medical problems often reflects the attitudes of a given culture. In this section's first selection, "Anorexia Nervosa in Context," Joan Jacobs Brumberg examines the cultural bases of the current epidemic of anorexia among young, middle-class women in American society. While this disorder may have biological and psychological components, Brumberg describes how it also reflects changing social expectations and roles of women in American society. Feminists have often pointed out how anorexia relates to the great preoccupation with women's weight and body image and the middle-class values placed on control and self-presentation (see Bardo, 1993). While recognizing that the cultural explanation has some limitations, Brumberg provocatively depicts ano-rexia as an "addiction to starvation" and a "secular form of perfection," a disorder that reflects the strains and ambiguities of changing gender roles in our society.

All illnesses are not created and treated equally. Certain illnesses may engender social meanings that affect our perception and treatment of those who suffer the illness. One important example of this is "stigmatized illness" (Gussow and Tracy, 1968). Certain illnesses including leprosy, epilepsy, sexually transmitted diseases, and AIDS, have acquired moral meanings that are inherent in the very construction of the illness's image and thus affect our perception of the illness and our reaction to those who have it. These illnesses carry considerable potential to stigmatize individuals, adding social suffering to physical difficulties. Frequently, as much energy must be invested in managing the stigma as the disorder itself (e.g., Lee et al., 2002).

The social meaning can shape the social response to illness. Illness can become imbued with a moral opprobrium that makes its sufferers outcasts. For example, Cotton Mather, the celebrated eighteenth-century New England Puritan minister, declared that syphilis was a punishment "which the Just judgment of God has reserved for our later ages" (cited in Sontag, 1988:92). The social definition of epilepsy fostered myths (e.g., epilepsy was inherited or it caused crime) that further stigmatized the disorder (Schneider and Conrad, 1983). Finally, the negative image of venereal diseases was a significant factor in the limited funds allocated for dealing with these illnesses (Brandt, 1985).

AIDS, perhaps more than any other example in the twentieth century, highlights the significance that social meaning has on the social response to illness. A fear virtually unprecedented in contemporary society led to an overreaction to the disease sometimes bordering on hysteria.

When AIDS was first discovered, it was thought to be a "gay disease" and thus was stigmatized and its research underfunded. (Perrow and Guillén, 1990). Although we have learned a great deal about AIDS in recent years, the image of AIDS remains fundamentally shaped by the stigma attached to it and the fear of contagion (Nelkin et al., 1991; Rushing, 1995).

In the second selection, "AIDS and Stigma," Gregory M. Herek reviews the current knowledge about AIDS-related stigma. He shows how AIDS stigma has been manifested in discrimination, violence, and personal rejection of people with AIDS (PWAs). People with AIDS, at least in developed countries, are living longer with the disease, thus the impact of AIDS stigma has a direct effect on individuals' well-being and everyday life (e.g., see Klitzman, 1997). Stigma has hindered the societal response to the AIDS epidemic and continues to impact on the lives of PWAS and their families and associates.

. . .

To understand the effects of disease in society, it is also necessary to understand the impact of illness. For it is in the social world of illness that the sick and the well must face one another and come to terms.

REFERENCES

Bardo, Susan. 1993. Unbearable Weight: Feminism, Western Culture and the Body. Berkeley: University of California Press.

Barker-Benfield, G.J. 1976. The Horrors of the Half-Known Life. New York: Harper and Row.

Bell, Susan E. 1987. "Premenstrual syndrome and the medicalization of menopause: A sociological perspective." Pp. 151–73 in Benson E. Ginsburg and Bonnie Frank Carter (eds.), Premenstrual Syndrome: Ethical and Legal Implications in a Biomedical Perspective. New York: Plenum.

Boston Women's Health Book Collective. 1985. The New Our Bodies, Ourselves. New York: Simon and Schuster.

Brandt, Allen M. 1985. No Magic Bullet. New York: Oxford University Press.

Ehrenreich, Barbara, and Deirdre English. 1978. On Her Own. New York: Doubleday.

Figert, Ann. 1995. "Three faces of PMS: The professional, gendered and scientific structuring of a psychiatric disorder." Social Problems. 42: 56–73.

Gusfield, Joseph R. 1967. "Moral passage: The symbolic process in the public designations of deviance." Social Problems. 15: 175–88.

Gussow, Zachary, and George Tracy. 1968. "Status, ideology, and adaptation to stigmatized illness: A study of leprosy." Human Organization. 27: 316–25.

Kaufert, Patricia A. 1982. "Myth and the menopause." Sociology of Health and Illness. 4: 141–66.

Klitzman, Robert. 1997. Being Positive: Lives of Men and Women with HIV. Chicago: Ivan R. Dee.

Lee, Rachel S., Arlene Kochman, and Kathleen Sikkema. 2002. "Internalized stigma among people living with HIV-AIDS." AIDS and Behavior. 6: 309–19.

Lock, Margaret. 1993. Encounters with Aging: Mythologies of Menopause in Japan and North America. Berkeley: University of California Press.

McCrea, Frances. 1983. "The politics of menopause: The 'discovery' of a deficiency disease." Social Problems. 31: 111–123.

Nelkin, Dorothy, David P. Willis, and Scott Parris. 1991. A Disease of Society: Cultural and Social Responses to AIDS. New York: Cambridge University Press.

Perrow, Charles, and Mauro F. Guillén. 1990. The AIDS Disaster. New Haven: Yale University Press.

Riessman, Catherine K. 1983. "Women and medicalization." Social Policy. 14: 3–18.

Rushing, William. 1995. The AIDS Epidemic: Social Dimensions of an Infectious Disease. Boulder, CO: Westview Press.

Schneider, Joseph W., and Peter Conrad. 1983. Having Epilepsy: The Experience and Control of Illness. Philadelphia: Temple University Press.

Sontag, Susan. 1988. Illness and Its Metaphors. New York: Farrar, Straus and Giroux.

Wertz, Richard, and Dorothy Wertz. 1989. Lying-In: A History of Childbirth in America. New Haven: Yale University Press.

11 *ANOREXIA NERVOSA IN CONTEXT**

Joan Jacobs Brumberg

The American public discovered anorexia nervosa only recently. Although the disease was known to physicians as early as the 1870s, the general public knew virtually nothing about it until the 1970s, when the popular press began to feature stories about young women who refused to eat despite available and plentiful food. In 1974, the "starving disease" made its first appearance as an independent subject heading in the *Readers' Guide to Periodical Literature,* a standard library reference tool that also provides a useful index to contemporary social issues. By 1984, the disease had become so commonplace that *Saturday Night Live* featured jokes about the "anorexic cookbook," and a comedian in the Borscht Belt drew laughs with a reference to a new disease, "anorexia ponderosa." In *Down and Out in Beverly Hills,* 1986 film audiences tittered at the predictable presence of an anorexic daughter in a lush suburban setting. Today nearly everyone understands flip remarks such as "You look anorexic." Anorexia nervosa has become common parlance, used as hyperbole by those outside the medical profession (particularly women) to comment on one another's bodies.

Our national education on the subject of anorexia nervosa can be traced to a variety of published popular sources in the decade of the 1970s. An early article in *Science Digest* reported on a "strange disease" in adolescent girls characterized by a "morbid aversion" to eating. Despite a new permissiveness in many areas of social behavior, parents in the 1960s were counseled against taking adolescent food refusal lightly or allowing it to continue. In 1970, at the outset of a decade of national education about anorexia nervosa, the press warned American parents to seek professional medical intervention as soon as possible, because there was "no safe leeway for home-style cure attempts."[1]

Newspapers as diverse as the *New York Times* and the *Weekly World News* pursued the subject in their own inimitable ways. The *Times*'s first discussion of the disease was a synthetic overview of state-of-the-art medical treatment, defined as New York City and Philadelphia clinical practice. The *World News,* a tabloid equivalent of the *National Enquirer* and the *Star*, ran a provocative banner headline—"The Bizarre Starving Disease"—and featured a horrifying picture of a 55-pound woman in shorts and a halter. While the *Times* reported a fatality rate of 5 to 15 percent, the *World News* claimed 30 to 50 percent.[2] From whatever newspaper one draws information, anorexia nervosa has been taught to a variety of people from different class and educational backgrounds since the 1970s.

The disease has always had particular salience for women and girls. Not surprisingly, the three magazines that generated the largest volume of national coverage on anorexia nervosa—*People, Mademoiselle,* and *Seventeen*—all cater to the primary constituency for the disease: adolescent and young adult women. Another important source of information about anorexia nervosa suggests that the disease has a specific class constituency. Alumnae magazines from the elite eastern women's colleges took up the cause of the disease by alerting former students to the problem of anorexia nervosa on campus. Alumnae coverage provided information on what the typical anorectic was like: intelligent, attractive, polite, demanding on herself. In effect, she was the mirror image of much of their own student body.[3]

All of the women's magazines wrote about the disease with a common sense of urgency. Without being entirely certain of the data, they spoke of "epidemics," proclaiming that there were somewhere between one hundred thousand and one million Americans with anorexia nervosa. In addition, they reported that between 5 percent and 15 percent of anorectics in psychiatric treatment died, giving it one of the highest fatality rates of any psychiatric diagnosis. Although the notion of adolescent death through compulsive starvation seemed silly to some, anorexia nervosa was becoming a growing subject of concern among mothers in private discussions and among psychiatrists in clinical practice.

In 1978, after nearly three decades of clinical experience treating eating disorders, psychiatrist Hilde Bruch (1904–1984) published a book on anorexia nervosa for lay audiences. *The Golden Cage,* based on seventy case histories, was a popular success. Bruch began by saying: "New diseases are rare, and a disease that selectively befalls the young, rich, and beautiful is practically unheard of. But such a disease is affecting the daughters of well-to-do, educated, and successful families." She explained that "for the last fifteen or twenty years anorexia nervosa [has been] occurring at a rapidly increasing rate. Formerly it was exceedingly rare." As a practicing psychiatrist in Houston, Bruch observed that most of her colleagues "recognized the name as something they had heard about in medical school, but they never saw a case in real life." By the time her book was published, Bruch claimed that anorexia nervosa was "so common" that it was a "real problem in high schools and colleges."[4] Bruch's extensive knowledge of the condition, combined with her sense of urgency about the disease, contributed to the growing cultural perception of an epidemic. In effect, anorexia nervosa was the disease of the 1970s, to be obscured only by AIDS and the accompanying specter of contagion and pollution that absorbs public attention at this moment.

THE QUESTION OF EPIDEMIOLOGY

Is an epidemic of anorexia nervosa in progress? When did the numbers of anorectics really begin to accelerate?

An increase in the number of cases of anorexia nervosa appears to have started about twenty years ago. During the Great Depression and World War II, in times of scarcity, voluntary food refusal had little efficacy as an emotional strategy and anorexic girls were a relative rarity in American clinical practice. A comment by Mara Selvini-Palazzoli, an Italian pioneer in the psychiatric study of anorexia nervosa, confirmed the relationship between anorexia nervosa and post-World War II affluence: "During the whole period of World War II in Italy (1939–1945) there were dire food restrictions and no patients at all were hospitalized at the Clinic for anorexia [nervosa]." After the war, however, "concurrent with the explosion of the Italian economic miracle and the advent of the affluent society," Selvini-Palazzoli did see hospitalizations for anorexia nervosa.[5]

By the 1960s wartime experiences of rationing, famine, and concentration camps were fading from memory. In the postwar culture of affluence many aspects of personal behavior were transformed: sexuality, relations between the generations, forms of family life, gender roles, clothing, even styles of food and eating. . . . From a psychiatrist's perspective, the postwar years brought an increasing number of adolescent female patients who used appetite and eating as emotional instruments much as they had in early childhood. In the 1960s Bruch published extensively on the subject of anorexia nervosa, and her work was a bellwether that marked the beginning of a rise in the number of diagnosed cases, a rise that became even more precipitous in the next two decades.[6]

The dimensions of the recent increase are hard to ascertain, however, because of problems in collecting and interpreting data as well as lack of standardization in diagnostic criteria. Not all patients with anorexia nervosa have exactly the same symptoms in the same degree or intensity. Not all cases present exactly the same symptoms as those elaborated in the American Psychiatric Association's *Diagnostic and Statistical Manual,* the standard reference guide to modern psychiatric disorders. The DSM-III criteria are the following: refusal to maintain normal body weight; loss of more than 25 percent of original body weight; disturbance of body image; intense fear of becoming fat; and no known medical illness leading to weight loss.[7] Yet some clinicians differentiate between primary and secondary anorexia, some favor a less stringent weight criterion, and some include hyperactivity and amenorrhea as symptom criteria.[8] There is also the matter of how anorexia nervosa is related to bulimia, the binge-purge syndrome. Until 1980, when it was listed in DSM-III as a separate diagnostic entity, bulimia (from the Greek meaning ox hunger) was only a symptom, not an independent disease. But in 1985, in DSM-III-R, bulimia obtained independent disease status; according to the newest categorization, anorexia nervosa and bulimia are separate but related disorders. In the diagnosis of anorexia nervosa, there is increasing support for subtyping anorexic patients into those who are pure dieters ("restrictive anorectics") and those who incorporate binging and purging ("bulimic anorectics" and/or "bulimarexics").[9] Who gets counted (and who does not) is never entirely clear or consistent, so that diagnostic imprecision makes the numbers difficult to assess.

Despite these problems, the evidence does suggest that we have experienced an absolute increase in the amount of anorexia nervosa over the past two decades. For example, twenty years ago the University of Wisconsin Hospital typically admitted one anorectic a year; in 1982 over seventy cases were admitted to the same institution. A retrospective review of incidence rates in Monroe County, New York, revealed that the number of cases of anorexia nervosa doubled between 1960 and 1976.[10]

In terms of the general population, however, anorexia nervosa is still a relatively infrequent disease: the annual incidence of the disorder has never been estimated at more than 1.6 per 100,000 population.[11] Still, among adolescent girls and young women there is an increasing and disturbing amount of anorexia nervosa and bulimia; by a number of different estimates, as many as 5 to 10 percent are affected. On some college campuses estimates run as high as 20 percent.[12]

Two critical demographic facts about the contemporary population of anorectics are relevant to the question of an "epidemic." Ninety to 95 percent of anorectics are young and female, and they are disproportionately white and from middle-class and upper-class families. Anorexia nervosa can exist in males but with a quite different clinical picture. The rare anorexic male exhibits a greater degree of psychopathology, tends to be massively obese before becoming emaciated, and has a poorer treatment prognosis. Moreover, the male anorexic is less likely to be affluent.[13] Anorexia nervosa is not a problem among contemporary American blacks or Chicanos; neither was it a conspicuous problem among first-generation and second-generation ethnic immigrants such as Eastern European Jews.[14] As these groups move up the social ladder, however, their vulnerability to the disorder increases. In fact, the so-called epidemic seems to be consistently restrained by age and gender but promoted by social mobility.

In a similar vein, the "contagion" is also confined to the United States and Western Europe, Japan, and other areas experiencing rapid Westernization. A description of anorexia nervosa compiled by a Russian psychiatrist in 1971 was basically a report of clinical cases drawn from outside his country. Physicians looking for anorexia nervosa in developing nations or countries of the Third World have been unsuccessful in finding it, a fact which has led to its classification as a "culture-bound syndrome."[15] In other words, the anorexic population has a highly specific social address.

In the United States, as well as in Western Europe, the growth of anorexia nervosa is due in part to heightened awareness and reporting on the part of families and doctors. Rising numbers of anorectics do reflect "diagnostic drift"—that is, the greater likelihood that a clinician who sees a very thin adolescent female with erratic eating habits and a preoccupation with weight will describe and label that patient as a case of anorexia nervosa, rather than citing some other mental disorder where lack of appetite is a secondary feature (such as depression or schizophrenia).[16] Simple anorexia—meaning lack of appetite—is a secondary symptom in many medical and psychiatric disorders ranging from the serious to the inconsequential. For some girls an episode of anorexia is mild and transitory; others, perhaps as many as 19 percent of the diagnosed cases, die from it.[17] In the 1980s there may well be a medical tendency to place temporary and chronic anorexias under one diagnostic rubric precisely because of our familiarity with the disease. Most thoughtful clinicians agree that anorectics are not necessarily a homogeneous group and that more attention should be paid to defining and specifying their psychological and physiological characteristics.

This situation reflects a basic medical reality—that there are fashions in diagnosis. In 1984 Dr. Irving Farber, a practitioner in Jamaica, New York, wrote to his state medical journal about the overdiagnosis of anorexia nervosa: "In my experience, a significant number of girls and young women who have been diagnosed by professionals, and [girls] themselves, are not suffering from this disorder." A group of physicians from the Department of Pediatrics, Long Island Jewish-Hillside Medical Center, responded that Farber's point was "well-taken," although they disagreed with his analysis of a specific case.[18]

The statistical increase in the number of anorexics over the past two decades can be explained also by the amount of media attention paid to the disorder. Anorexia nervosa has become *au courant,* an "in" disease among affluent adolescent and young adult women, a phenomenon that confirms long-standing beliefs about the susceptibility of girls to peer influence. One prominent psychologist specializing in treatment of the disorder estimates that 30 percent of all current cases are what Bruch once called "me too" anorectics. Bruch herself wrote: "The illness used to be the accomplishment of an isolated girl who felt she had found her own way to salvation. Now it is more a group reaction."[19] This mimetic or copycat phenomenon is hard to assess statistically and only adds confusion to an already complex problem in psychiatric epidemiology. In sum: although the total number of actual anorectics is hard to assess and probably not enormous, incidence of the disorder is higher today than at any other time since the discovery of the disease over a century ago. In addition, among the constituency most vulnerable to the disease, bourgeois adolescent and young adult women, there is the perception of an epidemic—a perception fueled in part by messages coming from American popular culture.

THE INFLUENCE OF POPULAR CULTURE

In a society committed to hearing nearly everyone's story, the anorectic has come "out of the closet" like so many others—homosexuals, adopted people, substance abusers, molested children, born-again Christians and Jews. To be sure, the genre of disclosure has different ideological sources and purposes. Yet the current interest in experience and our self-confessional tendencies have generated a plethora of writing about anorexia nervosa, ranging from self-help books to autobiographical accounts to adolescent fiction. This concern for personal testimony and authenticity is revealed in the fact that the American Anorexia and Bulimia Association (AA/BA), founded in 1978, maintains a daily hot line across the country that provides telephone access to a recovered anorectic.

The disclosure in January 1983 that thirty-two-year-old popular singer Karen Carpenter had died of heart failure associated with low serum potassium—a consequence of prolonged starvation—fueled interest in the disease. Carpenter's tragic death confirmed the fact that anorexia nervosa could be fatal rather than just annoying. The news media emphasized that the best and most expensive medical treatment on both coasts had been ineffective against the disease. Although Carpenter's anorexia was described as a psychiatric disorder generated by her own insecurities and personality, she was also called a "victim" of anorexia nervosa, as if the disease were totally involuntary, or even contagious.[20] Carpenter's death focused national attention on the life-and-death drama of anorexia nervosa.

In the 1980s one can experience anorexia nervosa vicariously through films as well as books. Two made-for-television movies about anorexia nervosa have been shown in prime time on the major networks. The first, *The Best Little Girl in the World* (1981), had a screenplay by New York psychologist Steven Levenkron and was promoted with an advertisement that said simply, "A Drama of Anorexia Nervosa." The adviser assumed that the disease was familiar and that its characteristic tensions and struggles generated audience involvement. At least one episode of "Fame," a program that portrays life at a select New York City high school for the performing arts, revolved around anorexia nervosa in a young student and its impact on her teachers and peers. In Marge Piercy's 1984 novel, *Fly Away Home,* the central character is a middle-aged, middle-class divorcée who is both a successful Boston cookbook author and the mother of an anorexic daughter.

Two other popular sources of information about anorexia nervosa are important for understanding the process of learning about the disease: fiction designed specifically for the adolescent market, and autobiographical accounts by sufferers. As a genre, anorexia stories are intended to provide adolescent girls with both a dramatic warning and a source of real information. The books are notable for their graphic descriptions of the anorectic's food preoccupations (for instance, never allowing oneself to eat more than three curds of cottage cheese at one sitting) and for their endorsement of medical and psychiatric intervention. In fact, the novel is used primarily as a device for getting adolescents to understand that professional intervention is imperative.[21]

In the typical anorexia story, psychiatrists and psychologists are portrayed as benign and compassionate figures whose only offense is that they ask a lot of questions. There is no real presentation of the classic battle for control that absorbs so much time and energy in psychotherapeutic treatment of the disorder. Nor is there any mention that patients with anorexia nervosa generate great anger, stress, and helplessness in the medical personnel who treat them. Clinicians report that anorectics have resorted to all of the following kinds of deceptions: drinking enormous amounts of water before being weighed; using terrycloth towels as napkins to absorb foods and food supplements; recalibrating scales; and inserting weights in the rectum and vagina. Consequently, anorectics are not popular patients, a fact confirmed by the comment of a New York physician: "Referral of an eating disorders patient to a colleague is not usually considered a friendly act."[22]

These stories are nearly formulaic: they emphasize family tensions and the adolescent girl's confused desire for autonomy and control, but they do not advance any particular interpretation of the cause or etiology of the disease. The plot almost always involves an attractive (usually 5 feet 5 inches), intelligent high school girl from a successful dual-career family. The mother is apt to be a fashion designer, artist, actress, or writer; the father is a professional or self-made man. In two of the novels the central characters say that they want to go to Radcliffe.

Naturally enough, the protagonist becomes interested in reducing her weight. Like virtually all American girls, she wishes to be slim because in American society slim is definitely a good thing for a female to be. Francesca, the principal character of *The Best Little Girl in the World,* cuts out pictures of models and orders them by thinness. Her goal is to be thinner than her thinnest picture. In each of the anorexia stories, for a number of different reasons all of which have to do with the difficulties of adolescence, ordinary dieting becomes transformed into a pattern of bizarre food and eating behavior that dominates the life of the central character. Some girls eat only one food, such as celery, yogurt, or dry crackers; others steal from the refrigerator at night and refuse to be seen eating. In one novel the parents are persuaded by their daughter to allow her to take supper alone in her room so that she can do homework at the same time. The mother acquiesces only to discover that for over a year her daughter has been throwing her dinner out the window of their Central Park West apartment.

In all of the fiction, girlhood anorexia curtails friendships and makes both parents extraordinarily tense, unhappy, and solicitous. Because the main characters are depicted as still in high school and living at home, mothers are central to the story. The fictive anorectic both dislikes and loves her mother and feels perpetually guilty about hurting and deceiving her. Mothers, not fathers, are the usual source of referral to professional help, a fact that is reflected in the real world composition of many anorexia nervosa support groups. Mothers of anorectics commonly join such groups to share their experiences; the AA/BA was founded by a mother for precisely that purpose.

Even though all of the novels move the story to the critical point of therapeutic intervention, few provide any valid information about the physical and emotional discomfort that lies ahead. In *Second Star to the Right* Leslie, age fifteen, is hospitalized in a behavior-modification program on a ward of anorectics where she is required to consume five glasses of liquid food per day or else she will be fed involuntarily. Her visits with parents and friends, as well as her television watching, are controlled and allocated on the basis of her weight. Yet the story stops short of describing the realities of forced feeding. By the end of the book Leslie wants to get well but has made little physical progress. Most of the fiction for teenagers finesses the difficult, lengthy, and often unpleasant recovery period. With only one exception, none of the fictional anorectics die.

Personal testimonials provide another compelling perspective on anorexia nervosa. Between 1980 and 1985 a number of autobiographical accounts achieved wide readership: in particular, novelist Sheila MacLeod's detailed account of her anorexic girlhood in Britain and Cherry Boone O'Neill's intimate story of her anorexia, marriage, and dedication to the evangelical Christian faith.[23] Unlike the fiction, which protects its youthful readers from the harsh realities of the recovery process, these are testimonies to extraordinary and protracted personal suffering. Few details are spared. Boone, for example, describes an incident in which her eating behavior became so bizarre that she stole slimy scraps from a dog's dish.

In the effort to educate and raise public awareness about particular diseases, some contemporary celebrities have been forthcoming about their personal health histories. Rock Hudson's 1985 deathbed revelation that he had AIDS was a powerful and poignant example; Mary Tyler Moore, a lifelong diabetic, openly identifies herself with that disease. For the purposes of our story, Jane Fonda's 1983 disclosure that she suffered from bulimia was a critical public event. Fonda's revelation that she binged and purged throughout her years at Vassar College and during her early film career had the effect of imprinting bulimia and anorexia nervosa on the national consciousness.[24] Since then, many autobiographical narratives from contemporary bulimic women have surfaced. These are among the most disturbing and unhappy documents generated by women in our time. They describe obsessive thinking about food and its acquisition; stealing food; secret, ritualistic eating; and compulsive vomiting, often with orgiastic overtones.[25] Compared to the restrictive anorectic who typically limits herself to between 200 and 400 calories a day, the bulimic may ingest as much as 8,000 calories at one sitting. The public discovery of bulimia in the early 1980s meant that anorexia nervosa no longer stood alone as the solitary example of aberrant female appetite. Rather, it was the jagged, most visible tip of the iceberg of eating disorders.

. . . The cultural explanation of anorexia nervosa is popular and widely promoted. It postulates that anorexia nervosa is generated by a powerful cultural imperative that makes slimness the chief attribute of female beauty. In casual conversation we hear this idea expressed all the time: anorexia is caused by the incessant drumbeat of modern dieting, by the erotic veneration of sylphlike women such as Twiggy, and by the demands of a fashion ethic that stresses youth and androgyny rather than the contours of an adult female body. The common wisdom reflects the realities of women's lives in the twentieth century. In this respect the cultural model, more than any other, acknowledges and begins to explain why eating disorders are essentially a female problem.

Important psychological studies by Susan and Orlando Wooley, Judith Rodin, and others confirm that weight is woman's "normative obsession."[26] In response to the question, "How old were you when you first weighed more than you wanted?" American women report a preoccupation with overweight that begins before puberty and intensifies in adolescence and young adulthood. Eighty percent of girls in the fourth grade in San Francisco are dieting, according to researchers at the University of California. At three private girls' schools in Washington, D.C., 53 percent of the students said they were unhappy with their bodies by age thirteen; among those eighteen or older, 78 percent were dissatisfied. In the same vein, a 1984 *Glamour* magazine survey of thirty-three thousand women between the ages of eighteen and thirty-five demonstrated that 75 percent believed they were fat, although only 25 percent were actually overweight. Of those judged underweight by standardized measures, 45 percent still thought they were too fat. Clinicians often refer to people with weight preoccupations of this sort as "obesophobic."[27]

The women in the *Glamour* survey confirm that female self-esteem and happiness are tied to weight, particularly in the adolescent and young adult years. When asked to choose among potential sources of happiness, the *Glamour* respondents chose weight loss over success at work or in interpersonal relations. The extent to which "feeling fat" negatively influences female psychological adjustment and behavior is only beginning to be explored. A 1984 study, for example, demonstrates that many college-age women make weight a central feature of their cognitive schema. These women consistently evaluate other women, themselves, and their own achievements in terms of weight. A 1986 study revealed that "feeling fat" was significantly related to emotional stress and other external stimuli. Obviously, being and feeling thin is an extremely desirable condition in this culture, whereas feeling fat is not: "I become afraid of getting fat, of gaining weight. [There is] something dangerous about becoming a fat American."[28]

All indications are that being thin is particularly important to women in the upper classes. (This social fact is reflected in the widely quoted dictum, attributed to the Duchess of Windsor, "A woman can never be too rich or too thin.") A study by Stanford University psychologist Sanford M. Dornbusch revealed a positive correlation between gender, social class, and desire to be thin. Controlling for the actual level of fatness, Dornbusch's data, based on a nationwide sample of more than seventy-five hundred male and female high school students, showed that adolescent females in higher social classes wanted to be thinner more often than those in the lower classes. (Not surprisingly, most obese women come from the working class and the poor.) By contrast, the relationship between social class and the desire to be thin was minimal in males. Because body preference differs among girls according to social class, those from middle-class and upper-class families are the most likely to be dissatisfied and troubled by the normal development associated with sexual maturation.[29]

According to the cultural model, these class-specific ideas about body preference pervade the larger society and do enormous harm. The modern visual media (television, films, video, magazines, and particularly advertising) fuel the preoccupation with female thinness and serve as the primary stimulus for anorexia nervosa. Female socialization, in the hands of the modern media, emphasizes external qualities ("good looks") above all else. As a consequence, we see few women of real girth on television or in the movies who also have vigor, intelligence, or sex appeal. Young girls, fed on this ideological pablum, learn to be decorative, passive, powerless, and ambivalent about being female. Herein lies the cause of anorexia nervosa, according to the cultural model.

The most outspoken and influential proponents of this model of the etiology of anorexia nervosa are feminists, often therapists, concerned with the spectrum of eating disorders that ranges from overeating to noneating. In the work of Kim Chernin, Marcia Millman, Susie Ohrbach, and Marlene Boskin-White and William C. White, the obese, the anorectic, and the bulimic all receive sympathetic treatment.[30] The tendency of these authors is to avoid casting the behavior as pathological. Instead, they seek to demonstrate that these disorders are an inevitable consequence of a misogynistic society that demeans women by devaluing female experience and women's values; by objectifying their bodies; and by discrediting vast areas of women's past and present achievements. Both overeating and noneating are a "protest against the way in which women are regarded in our society as objects of adornment and pleasure."[31]A strain of Socialist feminism, popular in women's studies scholarship, also marks these and related critiques. To wit, our society's exaltation of thin, weak women expresses the inner logic of capitalism and patriarchy, both characterized by the sexual division of labor and female subordination. In response to these brutal economic and cultural imperatives, women turn to an excessive concern with food as a way of filling their emptiness and dealing with their fear and self-hate.

Following the organizational models of the contemporary feminist movement (that is, collective consciousness raising and networking), advocates of the cultural model suggest that above and beyond psychotherapy women with eating disorders should (1) talk with other women who are similarly afflicted and (2) organize to educate the public about their problem. The AA/BA, for example, sponsors such groups in a number of different metropolitan areas. Many former anorectics and bulimics attribute their recovery to the experience of listening and sharing with others. Group therapy and peer support groups for anorectics and bulimics are common. In May 1986 in New York City, Susie Ohrbach, a leader in the feminist therapy community, organized a Speak-Out against eating disorders, an event that sought to bring the experience and pain of eating disorders to a larger audience through the presentation of personal statements and testimonials. In its most simplistic form, the cultural model suggests that merely by speaking up about sexism and subordination, women with eating disorders can cure themselves and society.

The popular feminist reading of anorexia nervosa has much to commend it. First and foremost, this interpretation underscores the fact that a total reliance on medical models is inadequate. Because of feminist sensitivity to the interrelationship of culture, gender, and food, the impact and meaning of weight obsession in women's lives is now a serious area of theory and research in the academic disciplines and in the mental health professions. Before Chernin, Ohrbach, and Millman, women's dieting and weight concerns were trivialized or interpreted as masking a strictly individual psychological problem without consideration of the ways in which culture stimulated, exacerbated, and gave shape to a pattern of problematic behaviors.[32]

This contemporary feminist analysis has a literary analogue in the writing of academic feminist critics on nineteenth-century women, medicine, and madness. Their interpretation is rooted in the study of nineteenth-century medical texts and the male physician's view, in that era, of the female body. The analysis is confined to examination of the discourses and representations that evolved in the discussion of women and their diseases in nineteenth century Britain and the United States.[33] In this mode of analysis the primary focus is on epistemology, or how we conceptualize mental disorder. Following Michel Foucault, these scholars argue that women's bodies are a locus of social control; that in the nineteenth century male-dominated medicine created nosologies that marked women as deviant; and that "female diseases" are socially constructed states that symbolize both the hegemony of scientific medicine and Victorian social constraints on women.[34] In conditions such as anorexia nervosa, where there are no discernible lumps, lesions, or germs, there are those who question whether there is a disease at all. The problematic behavior, in this case refusal of food, is interpreted strictly as a form of symbolic interaction. Thus, anorexia nervosa is painted as a young woman's protest against the patriarchy—that is, as a form of feminist politics.

The strength of this analysis is that it identifies a troubling, if not misogynistic, set of ideas about women's bodies and minds that was part of the intellectual world of Victorian medical men and, inevitably, shaped some part of their clinical practice. While I respect the contribution of feminist literary critics to our understanding of the discourse that surrounded medical treatment in the nineteenth century, I am disquieted by the tendency to equate all female mental disorders with political protest. Certainly we need to acknowledge the relationship between sex-role constraints and problematic behavior in women, but the madhouse is a somewhat troubling site for establishing a female pantheon. To put it another way: as a feminist, I believe that the anorectic deserves our sympathy but not necessarily our veneration.

Feminist insistence on thinking about anorexia nervosa as cultural protest leads to an interpretation of the disorder that overemphasizes the level of conscious control at the same time that it presents women and girls as hapless victims of an all powerful medical profession. Anyone who has worked with anorectics or read the clinical literature understands that food refusal becomes increasingly involuntary as the physiological process of emaciation unfolds. In full-blown cases of anorexia nervosa, the patient cannot eat even when she wants to. The cultural model denies the biomedical component of this destructive illness by obscuring the helplessness and desperation of those who suffer from it. After years of treatment a disheartened anorexic student wrote to me: "I too hope more than one could ever express that one day I will be well and my future will be bright and fulfilling. The frustration and fear I feel now is tremendous, as each day is a struggle for survival." This is hardly the voice of social protest.[35]

The romanticization of anorexia nervosa (and female mental disorders in general) can lead to some unwise and counterproductive therapeutic strategies. For example, in 1978 when Susie Ohrbach declared fat a "feminist issue," some took her to mean that feminists should allow themselves to get fat, thereby repudiating both patriarchal and capitalist imperatives. More recently, as the number of anorectics and bulimics has grown, some writers, in a well-intentioned but desperate attempt to dignify these all-too-frequent disorders, have tried to transform anorexia nervosa into the contemporary moral equivalent of the hunger strikes associated with early-twentieth-century English suffragists such as Emmeline and Sylvia Pankhurst.[36]

In the *Wisconsin Law Review* (1984) Roberta Dresser, an attorney and professor of law, argued that all medical and parental orders for renourishment of anorectics should be opposed on civil libertarian grounds. Dresser's intention, to make the case for minimizing state intrusion in personal medical decisions, was altogether admirable, but her understanding of anorexia nervosa was naive (in terms of both the psychology and the physiology of the disorder) and insensitive (in terms of historical precedents). Dresser based her argument on the idea, drawn from literary analysis, that "socio-cultural explanations of anorexia nervosa challenge the notion that the condition is a mental illness attributable to sources within the individual."[37] She posited that anorectics and early-twentieth-century hunger strikes were essentially the same and that anorexia nervosa is a freely chosen method of communicating and asserting power—in essence, an exercise of free will. (Dresser did not consider that anorectics may become physically unable to eat and that at some point the behavior may become involuntary.)

Although some earnestly believe that anorexia nervosa is a conscious and/or symbolic act against sexism that follows in a direct line from early-twentieth-century feminism, it is difficult from a historical perspective to see the analogy between the articulate and life-affirming political strategies of the Pankhursts and the silent, formulaic behavior of the modern Karen Carpenters.[38] The suffragists had a specific political goal to achieve, at which point food refusal ended. In contrast, the anorectic pursues thinness unrelentingly (in the same way that a paranoid schizophrenic attempts to elude imagined enemies), but she has no plan for resumption of eating. If the anorectic's food refusal is political in any way, it is a severely limited and infantile form of politics, directed primarily at parents (and self) and without any sense of allegiance to a larger collectivity. Anorectics, not known for their sisterhood, are notoriously preoccupied with the self. The effort to transform them into heroic freedom fighters is a sad commentary on how desperate people are to find in the cultural model some kind of explanatory framework, or comfort, that dignifies this confusing and complex disorder.

Finally, there is a strain of cultural analysis that implicates recent social change in the etiology of anorexia nervosa, particularly increased educational, occupational, and sexual options for women. In *The Golden Cage* Hilde Bruch suggested such a connection. In 1978 she wrote: "Growing girls can experience . . . liberation as a demand and feel that they have to do something outstanding. Many of my patients have expressed the feeling that they are overwhelmed by the vast number of potential opportunities available to them . . . and [that] they had been afraid of not choosing correctly."[39] Yet, as a sophisticated clinician, Bruch did not blame social change or feminism for anorexia nervosa. She understood that confusion about choices was only a partial explanation, for most young women handled the same array of new options with enthusiasm and optimism and did not develop the disease. Some antifeminists will still insist, however, that feminism is to blame for the upsurge in eating disorders. This interpretation usually asserts, incorrectly, that anorexia emerged for the first time in the late 1960s and 1970s, at the same time as the modern women's movement. To the conservative mind, anorexia nervosa might go away if feminism went away, allowing a return to traditional gender roles and expectations. The mistaken assumption is that anorexia nervosa did not exist in past time, when women's options were more limited.

In sum, the explanatory power of the existing cultural models is limited because of two naive suppositions: (1) that anorexia nervosa is a new phenomenon created by the pressures and circumstances of contemporary life and (2) that the disease is either imposed on young women (as victims) or freely chosen (as social protest) without involving any biological or psychological contribution. Ultimately, the current cultural models fail to explain why so many individuals *do not* develop the disease even though they have been exposed to the same cultural environment. This is where individual psychology as well as familial factors must come into play. Certainly, culture alone does not cause anorexia nervosa.

In order to understand anorexia nervosa, we must think about disease as an interactive and evolving process. I find the model of "addiction to starvation" particularly compelling because when we think about anorexia nervosa in this way, there is room for incorporating biological, psychological, and cultural components. Let me demonstrate. An individual may begin to restrict her food because of aesthetic and social reasons related to gender, class, age, and sense of style. This constitutes the initial "recruitment" stage. Many of her friends may also be doing the same thing, because in the environment in which they live being a fat female is a social and emotional liability. Being thin is of critical importance to the young woman's sense of herself. Contemporary culture clearly makes a contribution to the genesis of anorexia nervosa.

An individual's dieting moves across the spectrum from the normal to the obsessional because of other factors, namely emotional and personality issues, and personal physiology and body chemistry. If refusing food serves a young woman's emotional needs (for instance, as a symbolic statement about herself, as a bid for attention, as a way of forestalling adult sexuality, as a means of hurting her parents or separating from them, as a form of defiance), she may continue to do so because it seems like an efficacious strategy. It becomes more and more difficult to back off and change direction if the denial and control involved bring her emotional satisfaction. In some families the symptom (not eating) and the girl's emaciated appearance are overlooked or denied longer than in other families, thereby creating a situation that may actually contribute to the making of the disorder.

After weeks or months of starvation the young woman's mind and body become acclimated to both the feeling of hunger and nutritional deprivation. This constitutes a second stage of the disorder. There is evidence to suggest that hunger pangs eventually decrease rather than intensify and that the body actually gets used to a state of semistarvation, that is, to a negative energy balance. At some unidentified point in time, in certain girls, starvation may actually become satisfying or tension relieving—a state analogous perhaps to the well-known "runner's high."[40] Certain individuals, then, may make the move from chronic dieting to dependence on starvation because of a physiological substrate as well as emotional and family stresses. This is where biochemical explanations (such as elevated cortisol levels in the blood or some other neuroendocrine abnormality) come into play. The fact that many anorectics seem unable to eat (or develop withdrawal symptoms when they begin to eat regularly) suggests that something biological as well as psychological is going on.

Obviously, only a small proportion of those who diet strenuously become addicted to it, presumably because the majority of young women have neither a psychic nor a biological need for starvation. For most, even normal dieting, for short periods, is an unpleasant necessity that brings more frustration than it does satisfaction (hence the current rash of popular women's cartoons about eating as a form of forbidden pleasure and self-expression, and dieting as a futile endeavor).[41] Yet in alcohol and drug dependence and in anorexia nervosa, there appears to be a correlation between the level of exposure and the prevalence of a dependence. Simply put, when and where people become obesophobic and dieting becomes pervasive, we can expect to see an escalating number of individuals with anorexia nervosa and other eating disorders.[42] Thus, we have returned full circle to the cultural context and its power to shape human behavior.

For this study the critical implication of the dependency-addiction model is that anorexia nervosa can be conceptually divided into two stages. The first involves sociocultural context, or "recruitment" to fasting behavior; the second incorporates the subsequent "career" as an anorexic and includes physiological and psychological changes that condition the individual to exist in a starvation state.[43] The second stage is obviously the concern of medicine and mental health professionals because it is relatively formulaic and historically invariant. Stage one involves the historian, whose task it is to trace the forces and events that have led young women to this relatively stereotypical behavior pattern.

History is obviously important in understanding how and why we are where we are today vis-à-vis the increasing incidence of the disorder. A historical perspective also contributes to the debate over the etiology of anorexia nervosa by supplying an interpretation that actually reconciles different theoretical models. Despite the emphasis here on culture, my interpretation does not disallow the possibility of a biomedical component in anorexia nervosa. In fact, when we take the long history of female fasters into account, it becomes apparent that there are certain historical moments and cultural settings when a biological substratum could be activated by potent social and cultural forces. In other words, patterns of culture constitute the kind of environmental pressure that interacts with physiological and psychological variables.

. . . My assertion that the post-1960 epidemic of anorexia nervosa can be related to recent social change in the realm of food and sexuality is not an argument for turning back the clock. As a feminist, I have no particular nostalgia for what is deceptively called a "simpler" past. Moreover, historical investigation demonstrates that anorexia nervosa was latent in the economic and emotional milieu of the bourgeois family as early as the 1850s. It makes little sense to think a cure will be achieved by putting women back in the kitchen, reinstituting sit-down meals on the nation's campuses, or limiting personal and professional choices to what they were in the Victorian era. On the basis of the best current research on anorexia nervosa, we must conclude that the disease develops as a result of the intersection of external and internal forces in the life of an individual. External forces such as those described here do not, by themselves, generate psychopathologies, but they do give them shape and influence their frequency.

In the confusion of this transitional moment, when a new future is being tentatively charted for women but gender roles and sexuality are still constrained by tradition, young women on the brink of adulthood are feeling the pain of social change most acutely.[44] They look about for direction, but find little in the way of useful experiential guides. What parts of women's tradition do they want to carry into the future? What parts should be left behind? These are difficult personal and political decisions, and most young women are being asked to make them without benefit of substantive education in the history and experience of their sex. In effect, our young women are being challenged and their expectations raised without a simultaneous level of support for either their specific aspirations or for female creativity in general.

Sadly, the cult of diet and exercise is the closest thing our secular society offers women in terms of a coherent philosophy of the self.[45] This being the case, anorexia nervosa is not a quirk and the symptom choice is not surprising. When personal and social difficulties arise, a substantial number of our young women become preoccupied with their bodies and control of appetite. Of all the messages they hear, the imperative to be beautiful and good, by being thin, is still the strongest and most familiar. Moreover, they are caught, often at a very early age, in a deceptive cognitive trap that has them believing that body weight is entirely subject to their conscious control. Despite feminist influences on the career aspirations of the present college-age generation, little has transpired to dilute the basic strength of this powerful cultural prescription that plays on both individualism and conformity. The unfortunate truth is that even when she wants more than beauty and understands its limitations as a life goal, the bourgeois woman still expends an enormous amount of psychic energy on appetite control as well as on other aspects of presentation of the physical self.

And what of the future? I believe that we have not yet seen the crest of the late-twentieth-century wave of eating disorders. Although historians need to be cautious about prognostication, a few final observations seem in order.

In affluent societies the human appetite is unequivocally misused in the service of a multitude of nonnutritional needs. As a result, both anorexia nervosa and obesity are characteristic of modern life and will continue to remain so.

We can expect to see the evolution of a more elaborate medical classification scheme for eating disorders, and greater attention to distinguishing one syndrome from another. Modern medicine is built on this kind of refinement. There is also the possibility that, as eating behavior is subjected to closer scrutiny by doctors and other health professionals, more eating disorders will be identified. The new syndromes will probably be described in terms that suggest a biomedical (rather than biosocial) etiology. Some clinics specializing in weight and appetite control already advertise a specific treatment for "carbohydrate addiction."

Although eating disorders certainly deserve medical attention, an exclusive concentration on biomedical etiology obscures the ways in which social and cultural factors were implicated in the emergence of these disorders in the past century and in their proliferation today. As we approach the twenty-first century, it will surely become apparent that the postindustrial societies (the United States, Canada, Western Europe, Australia, and Japan) generate many people, not just adolescents, whose appetites are out of kilter. In effect, capitalism seems to generate a peculiar set of human difficulties that might well be characterized as consumption disorders rather than strictly eating disorders.

As Western values and life-styles are disseminated throughout the world and, in the wake of that process, traditional eating patterns disappear, anorexia nervosa will probably spread. Where food is abundant and certain sociocultural influences predominate, there will be some women whose search for perfection becomes misguided, translating into a self-destructive pathology such as anorexia nervosa. Our historical experience suggests that a society marching in a particular direction generates pschopathologies that are themselves symptomatic of the culture.

Finally, we can expect to see eating disorders continue, if not increase, among young women in those postindustrial societies where adolescents tend to be under stress. For both young men and young women, vast technological and cultural changes have made the transition to adulthood particularly difficult by transforming the nature of the family and community and rendering the future unpredictable. According to psychologist Urie Bronfenbrenner and others, American adolescents are in the worst trouble: we have the highest incidence of alcohol and drug abuse among adolescents of any country in the world; we also have the highest rate of teenage pregnancy of any industrialized nation; and we appear to have the most anorexia nervosa.[46]

Although the sexually active adolescent mother and the sexually inactive adolescent anorectic may seem to be light-years apart, they are linked by a common, though unarticulated, understanding. For adolescent women the body is still the most powerful paradigm regardless of social class. Unfortunately, a sizable number of our young women—poor and privileged alike—regard their body as the best vehicle for making a statement about their identity and personal dreams. This is what unprotected sexual intercourse and prolonged starvation have in common. Taken together, our unenviable preeminence in these two domains suggests the enormous difficulty involved in making the transition to adult womanhood in a society where women are still evaluated primarily in terms of the body rather than the mind.

Although the disorder we have examined here is part of a general pattern of adolescent discomfort in the West, anorexia nervosa ultimately expresses the predicament of a very distinct group, one that suffers from the painful ambiguities of being young and female in an affluent society set adrift by social change. Intelligent, anxious for personal achievement, and determined to maintain control in a world where things as basic as food and sex are increasingly out of control, the contemporary anorectic unrelentingly pursues thinness a secular form of perfection. In a society where consumption and identity are pervasively linked, she makes nonconsumption the perverse centerpiece of her identity. In a sad and desperate way, today's fasting girls epitomize the curious psychic burdens of the dutiful daughters of a people of plenty.

NOTES

Footnotes have been abridged, condensed, and renumbered for this volume. For complete notes, see original book.

REFERENCES

1. Carol Amen, "Dieting to Death," *Science Digest* 67 (May 1970), 27–31. A shorter version of this article appeared earlier in *Family Weekly.*
2. Sam Blum, "Children Who Starve Themselves," *New York Times Magazine* (November 10, 1974), 63–79; C. Michael Brady, "The Dieting Disease," *Weekly World News* 4 (March 22, 1983), 23. The *Star* of March 23, 1983, proposed that Britain's Diana, Princess of Wales, and her sister, Lady Sarah McCorquodale, are both anorectics. The *National Enquirer* has speculated that Michael Jackson is anorexic.
3. Between March 1974 and February 1984 the *Reader's Guide* lists almost fifty articles on anorexia nervosa.
4. Hilde Bruch, *The Golden Cage: The Enigma of Anorexia Nervosa* (Cambridge, Mass., 1978), pp. vii–viii.
5. Mara Selvini-Palazzoli, "Anorexia Nervosa: A Syndrome of the Affluent Society," translated from the Italian by V.F. Di Nicola, *Transcultural Psychiatric Research Review* 22: 3 (1985), 199.
6. Hilde Bruch, "Perceptual and Conceptual Disturbances in Anorexia Nervosa," *Psychosomatic Medicine* 24: 2 (1962), 187–194.
7. American Psychiatric Association, *Diagnostic and Statistical Manual of Mental Disorders* 69 (3rd ed., Washington, D.C., 1980; 3rd ed., rev., Washington, D.C., 1987).
8. On weight criteria see N. Rollins and E. Piazza, "Diagnosis of Anorexia Nervosa: A Critical Reappraisal," *Journal of the American Academy of Child Psychiatry* 17 (1978), 126–137. On amenorrhea see Katherine Halmi and J. R. Falk, "Behavioral and Dietary Discriminators of Menstrual Function in Anorexia Nervosa," in *Anorexia Nervosa: Recent Developments in Research,* ed. P. L. Darby et al. (New York, 1983), 323–329. On hyperactivity see L. Kron et al., "Hyperactivity in Anorexia Nervosa: A Fundamental Clinical Feature," *Comparative Psychiatry* 19 (1978), 433–440.
9. In bulimia (without anorexia nervosa) weight loss may be substantial, but the weight does not fall below a minimal normal weight.
10. William J. Swift, "The Long Term Outcome of Early Onset of Anorexia Nervosa: A Critical Review," *Journal of the American Academy of Child Psychiatry* 21 (January 1982), 38–46; D. J. Jones et al., 'Epidemiology of Anorexia Nervosa in Monroe County, New York: 1960–1976," *Psychosomatic Medicine* 42 (1980), 551–558. See also M. Duddle, "An Increase in Anorexia Nervosa in a University Population," *British Journal of Psychiatry* 123 (1973), 711–712; A. H. Crisp, R. L. Palmer, and R. S. Kalucy, "How Common Is Anorexia Nervosa? A Prevalence Study," ibid. 128 (1976), 549–554.
11. R. E. Kendell et al., "The Epidemiology of Anorexia Nervosa," *Psychological Medicine* 3 (1973), 200–203.
12. Herzog and Copeland, "Eating Disorders," p. 295; Jane Y. Yu, "Eating Disorders," *Vital Signs* (September 1986), Cornell University Health Services, p. 2.
13. Paul E. Garfinkel and David M. Garner, *Anorexia Nervosa: A Multidimensional Perspective* (New York, 1982), pp. 103, 190; Gloria R. Leon and Stephen Finn, "Sex Role Stereotypes and the Development of Eating Disorders," in *Sex Roles and Psychopathology,* ed. C. S. Wilson (New York, 1984), pp. 317–337; A. H. Crisp et al., "The Long Term Prognosis in Anorexia Nervosa: Some Factors Predictive of Outcome," in *Anorexia Nervosa,* ed. R. A. Vigersky (New York, 1977), pp. 55–65. The fact that anorexia nervosa only rarely exists in males supports the idea that cultural factors play a role in producing the disorder.
14. There are some reports of anorexia nervosa among blacks: see A. J. Pumariega, P. Edwards, and L. B. Mitchell, "Anorexia Nervosa in Black Adolescents," *Journal of the American Academy of Child Psychiatry* 23 (1984), 111–114; T. Silber, "Anorexia Nervosa in Black Adolescents," *Journal of the National Medical Association* 76 (1984), 29–32; George Hsu, "Are Eating Disorders More Common in Blacks?" *International Journal of Eating Disorders* 6 (January 1987), 113–124.
15. See Hiroyuki Suematsu et al., "Statistical Studies on the Prognosis of Anorexia Nervosa," *Japanese Journal of Psychosomatic Medicine* 23 (1983), 23–30. In general, physicians have looked unsuccessfully for anorexia nervosa in other cultures. See Raymond Prince, "The Concepts of Culture Bound Syndromes: Anorexia Nervosa and Brain-Fag," *Social Science Medicine* 21: 2 (1985), 197–203; Pow Meng Yap, "The Culture Bound Reactive Syndromes," in *Mental Health Research in Asia and the Pacific,* ed. William Caudill and Tsung-yi Lin (Honolulu, 1969), pp. 33–53; Satish Varma, "Anorexia Nervosa in Developing Countries," *Transcultural Psychiatric Research Review* 16 (April 1979), 114–115; R. Prince, "Is Anorexia Nervosa a Culture Bound Syndrome?" ibid. 20: 1 (1983), 299–300.

16. There have been a number of attempts to place anorexia nervosa within other established psychiatric categories. See for example G. Nicolle, "Prepsychotic Anorexia," *Lancet* 2 (1938), 1173–74; D. P. Cantwell et al., "Anorexia Nervosa: An Affective Disorder?" *Archives of General Psychiatry* 34 (1977), 1087–93; H. D. Palmer and M. S. Jones, "Anorexia Nervosa as a Manifestation of Compulsive Neurosis," *Archives of Neurology and Psychiatry* 41 (1939), 856. More recently, the focus has been on the behavioral signs and symptoms, and on biological similarities to depressive disorder.
17. Katherine A. Halmi, G. Broadland, and C. A. Rigas, "A Follow Up Study of 79 Patients with Anorexia Nervosa: An Evaluation of Prognostic Factors and Diagnostic Criteria," in *Life History Research in Psychopathology,* ed. R. D. Wirt, G. Winokur, and M. Roff, vol. 4 (Minneapolis, 1975).
18. *New York State Journal of Medicine* 84 (May 1984), 228. On the overdiagnosis of bulimia see George Groh, "You've Come a Long Way, Bulimia," *M.D., Medical Newsmagazine* 28 (February 1984), 48–57.
19. Quote from Steven Levenkron in the newsletter of AA/BA, based on Bruch, *The Golden Cage,* p. xii.
20. See the coverage of Karen Carpenter's death in *People Weekly* (February 21 and November 21, 1983; May 31, 1985). In the earliest accounts, low serum potassium was reported to have caused an irregularity in Carpenter's heartbeat. By 1985, the reports were that Carpenter had died of "cardiotoxicity" brought on by the chemical emetine. The suggestion is that Carpenter was abusing a powerful over-the-counter drug, Ipecac, used to induce vomiting in case of poison.
21. Some examples of novels about anorexia nervosa are Deborah Hautzig, *Second Star to the Right* (New York, 1981); Steven Levenkron, *The Best Little Girl in the World* (New York, 1978); Rebecca Joseph, *Early Disorder* (New York, 1980); Ivy Ruckman, *The Hunger Scream* (New York, 1983); Margaret Willey, *The Bigger Book of Lydia* (New York, 1983); John Sours, *Starving to Death in a Sea of Objects* (New York, 1980); Emily Hudlow, *Alabaster Chambers* (New York, 1979); Isaacsen-Bright, *Mirrors Never Lie* (Worthington, Ohio, 1982).
22. See Andrew W. Brotman, Theodore A. Stern, and David B. Herzog, "Emotional Reactions of House Officers to Patients with Anorexia Nervosa, Diabetes and Obesity," *International Journal of Eating Disorders* (Summer 1983), 71–77, and, for the comment of John Schowalter, *AA/BA Newsletter* 8 (September–November 1985), 6.
23. For personal testimonials see Sheila MacLeod, *The Art of Starvation: A Story of Anorexia and Survival* (New York, 1983); Cherry Boone O'Neill, *Starving for Attention* (New York, 1983); Aimee Liu, *Solitaire* (New York, 1979); Sandra Heater, *Am I Still Visible? A Woman's Triumph over Anorexia Nervosa* (Whitehall, Va., 1983); Camie Ford and Sunny Hale, *Two Too Thin: Two Women Who Triumphed over Anorexia Nervosa* (Orleans, Mass., 1983). The last-named work shares with O'Neill's book an evangelical Christian emphasis.
24. Fonda's experience with bulimia, although the author never used the clinical term, was described by Thomas Kiernan in *Jane: An Intimate Biography of Jane Fonda* (New York, 1973), p. 67.
25. See for example Lisa Messinger, *Biting the Hand that Feeds Me: Days of Binging, Purging and Recovery* (Moonachie, N.J., 1985); Jackie Barrile, *Confessions of a Closet Eater* (Wheaton, Ill., 1983).
26. Judith Rodin, Lisa Silberstein, and Ruth Streigel-Moore, "Women and Weight: A Normative Discontent," in *1984 Nebraska Symposium on Motivation,* ed. Theodore B. Sonderegger (Lincoln, 1985); April E. Fallon and Paul Rozin, "Sex Differences in Perceptions of Desirable Body Shape," *Journal of Abnormal Psychology* 94 (1985), 102–105.
27. See *Time* (January 20, 1986), 54, and *Los Angeles Times,* February 15 and March 29, 1984, for a report on the work of anthropologist Margaret MacKenzie. For a report of the *Glamour* survey see *Palm Beach Post,* December 26, 1985.
28. These studies are summarized in Ruth Streigel-Moore, Gail McAvay, and Judith Rodin, "Psychological and Behavioral Correlates of Feeling Fat in Women," *International Journal of Eating Disorders* 5: 5 (1986), 935–947; quoted in Ana-Maria Rizzuto, Ross K. Peterson, and Marilyn Reed, "The Pathological Sense of Self in Anorexia Nervosa," *Psychiatric Clinics of North America* 4 (December 1981), 38.
29. Sanford M. Dornbusch et al., "Sexual Maturation, Social Class, and the Desire to Be Thin among Adolescent Females," *Journal of Developmental and Behavioral Pediatrics* 5 (December 1984), 308–314.
30. Susie Ohrbach, *Fat Is a Feminist Issue: The Anti-Diet Guide to Permanent Weight Loss* (New York, 1978); idem, *Hunger Strike: The Anorectic's Struggle as a Metaphor for Our Age* (New York, 1986); Kim Chernin, *The Obsession: Re-*

flections on the Tyranny of Slenderness (New York, 1981); idem, *The Hungry Self;* Marcia Millman, *Such a Pretty Face: Being Fat in America* (New York, 1980); Marlene Boskin-White and William C. White, *Bulimarexia: The Binge Purge Cycle* (New York, 1983).
31. Ohrbach, *Hunger Strike,* p. 63.
32. Feminist analysis has begun to suggest that the medical models for understanding obesity are inadequate and that rigid appetite control and body-image preoccupations have negative developmental consequences for many women. See for example, Barbara Edelstein, *The Woman Doctor's Diet for Women* (Englewood Cliffs, N.J., 1977); C. P. Herman and J. Polivy, "Anxiety, Restraint, and Eating Behavior," *Journal of Abnormal Psychology* 84 (December 1975), 666–672.
33. For examples see Sandra Gilbert and Susan Gubar, *The Madwoman in the Attic* (New Haven, 1979); Elaine Showalter, *The Female Malady: Women, Madness and English Culture, 1830–1980* (New York, 1985).
34. See Bryan Turner, *The Body and Society: Explorations in Social Theory* (Oxford, 1984).
35. Personal communication to the author, April 1987.
36. Ohrbach's *Hunger Strike* (1986) implies in its title that anorexia nervosa is a form of political protest.
37. Dresser, "Feeding the Hunger Artists," p. 338.
38. Showalter, *The Female Malady,* p. 162, writes of the suffragists in 1912, "The hunger strikes of militant women prisoners brilliantly put the symptomatology of anorexia nervosa to work in the service of a feminist cause."
39. Bruch, *The Golden Cage,* p. ix.
40. J. Blumenthal, "Is Running an Analogue of Anorexia Nervosa? An Empirical Study of Obligatory Running and Anorexia Nervosa," *Journal of the American Medical Association* 252 (1984), 520–523.
41. I refer here to cartoons by Sylvia (Nicole Hollander), Cathy (Cathy Guisewaite), and Linda Barry.
42. Ruth Streigel-Moore, Lisa R. Silberstein, and Judith Rodin, "Toward an Understanding of Risk Factors in Bulimia," *American Psychologist* 41 (March 1986), 256–258, make a similar argument.
43. The distinction between recruitment and career evolved in conversations with Dr. William Bennett, whose command of the medical literature (and sensitivity to historical concerns) improved my understanding of the relationship between etiology and symptoms.
44. In *Theories of Adolescence* (New York, 1962) R. E. Muuss wrote, "Societies in a period of rapid transition create a particularly difficult adolescent period; the adolescent has not only the society's problem to adjust to but his [or her] own as well" (p. 164). See also Paul B. Baltes, Hayne W. Reese, and Lewis P. Lipsitt, "Life Span Developmental Psychology," *Annual Review of Psychology* 31 (1980), 76–79; J. R. Nesselroade and Paul B. Baltes, "Adolescent Personality Development and Historical Change: 1970– 1972," *Monographs of Society for Research in Child Development* 39 (May 1974), ser. 154.
45. My view of this issue complements ideas presented in Robert Bellah et al., *Habits of the Heart: Individualism and Commitment in American Life* (New York, 1986).
46. These data are synthesized in Urie Bronfenbrenner, "Alienation and the Four Worlds of Childhood," *Phi Delta Kappan* (February 1986), 434.

12 AIDS AND STIGMA

Gregory M. Herek

Ever since the first cases were detected in the United States in 1981, people with AIDS (PWAs) have been the targets of stigma. Press accounts and anecdotal reports from the early 1980s told stories of PWAs—as well as those simply suspected of having the disease—being evicted from their homes, fired from their jobs, and shunned by family and friends. Early surveys of public opinion revealed widespread fear of the disease, lack of accurate information about its transmission, and willingness to support draconian public policies that would restrict civil liberties in the name of fighting AIDS (Altman, 1986; Blake & Arkin, 1988; Clendinen, 1983; Herek, 1990).

After nearly two decades of extensive public education about HIV, one could hope that AIDS-related prejudice and discrimination would now be relics of the past. Unfortunately, this is not the case. In 1998, an 8-year-old New York girl was unable to find a Girl Scout troop that would admit her once her HIV infection was disclosed ("HIV-positive girl," 1998). In a 1997 national telephone survey, more than one fourth of the U.S. public expressed discomfort about associating with a PWA in a variety of circumstances (Herek & Capitanio, 1998). In 1996, federal legislation was enacted that singled out HIV-positive military personnel for discharge while ignoring other active-duty personnel with comparable serious medical conditions (Shenon, 1996).

Nor is the problem of AIDS stigma confined to the United States. In South Africa, an HIV-infected volunteer recently was beaten to death by neighbors who accused her of bringing shame on their community by revealing her HIV infection (McNeil, 1998). In India, AIDS workers report that people with HIV have become new untouchables who are often shunned by medical workers, neighbors, and employers (Burns, 1996). In rural Tanzania, having AIDS is often attributed to witchcraft and PWAs are frequently blamed for their disease (Nnko, 1998).

These are examples of AIDS-related stigma, a term that refers to prejudice, discounting, discrediting, and discrimination directed at people perceived to have AIDS or HIV, and the individuals, groups, and communities with which they are associated (Herek et al., 1998; see also Alonzo & Reynolds, 1995; Crawford, 1996; Herek, 1990; Pryor & Reeder, 1993). This article briefly describes current knowledge about AIDS-related stigma (or simply AIDS stigma) in the United States. It is not intended to provide a thorough literature review, but instead highlights some major findings about AIDS stigma and cites representative studies.

MANIFESTATIONS OF AIDS STIGMA IN THE UNITED STATES

AIDS is a global pandemic, and persons with HIV (PWHIVs) are stigmatized throughout the world to varying degrees. AIDS stigma around the world is expressed through social ostracism and personal rejection of PWHIVs, discrimination against them, and laws that deprive them of basic human rights (Mann, Tarantola, & Netter, 1992; Panos Institute, 1990). Although AIDS stigma is effectively universal, it takes different forms from one country to another and its specific targets vary considerably. This variation is shaped in each society by multiple factors, including the local epidemiology of HIV and preexisting prejudices within the culture. A consistent pattern is that stigma is often expressed against unpopular groups disproportionately affected by the local epidemic (Goldin, 1994; Mann et al., 1992; Panos Institute, 1990; Sabatier, 1988).

In the United States, a significant minority of the public has consistently expressed negative attitudes toward PWAs since the epidemic began and has supported authoritarian and punitive measures against them, including quarantine, universal mandatory testing, and even tattooing of infected individuals. Such attitudes have fluctuated in their prevalence, with support for punitive policies highest in the late 1980s (e.g., Blake & Arkin, 1988; Blendon & Donelan, 1988; Blendon, Donelan, & Knox, 1992; Herek, 1997; Herek & Capitanio, 1993; Herek & Glunt, 1991; Rogers, Singer, & Imperio, 1993; Schneider, 1987; Singer & Rogers, 1986; Stipp & Kerr, 1989).

Although diminished, many of the same attitudes persist today. In a 1997 national telephone survey, intentions to avoid PWAs in various situations and support for measures such as quarantine were lower than in previous years (Herek & Capitanio, 1998). Compared to a similar survey conducted in 1991, however, more respondents in 1997 overestimated the risks of HIV transmission through casual contact and perceived PWAs as deserving their condition. Approximately one third expressed discomfort and negative feelings toward PWAs (for more findings from the survey, see Capitanio & Herek, 1999; Herek & Capitanio, 1999).

AIDS-related discrimination in employment, health care, insurance, education, and other realms has been widely reported since the early days of the epidemic. PWAs have been fired from their jobs, evicted from their homes, and denied services (e.g., Gostin, 1990; Hunter & Rubenstein, 1992). Discrimination continues to occur despite legal precedents and protective legislation (e.g., Burris, 1999; Gostin & Webber, 1998).

Stigma is manifested in its most extreme form when people perceived to be infected with HIV are physically attacked. In a 1992 survey of 1,800 people with HIV, 21% of respondents reported that they had experienced violence in their communities because of their HIV status (National Association of People With AIDS, 1992; see also National Workshop on HIV and Violence, 1996).

THE SOCIAL PSYCHOLOGY OF AIDS STIGMA

A considerable amount of empirical research has focused on attitudes of the uninfected toward PWHIVs and AIDS-related policies. In these studies, AIDS stigma is conceptualized as a psychological attitude or a facet of public opinion. Even a cursory examination of the literature in this area quickly reveals that AIDS-related attitudes have been conceptualized in many different ways, including affective reactions to PWAs, attributions of blame and responsibility to PWAs, willingness to interact with PWAs, and attitudes toward laws and public policies related to AIDS (e.g., Capitanio & Herek, 1999; Herek & Capitanio, 1999; Pryor, Reeder, & Landau, 1999).

A variety of social, psychological, and demographic variables have been found to correlate with AIDS-related attitudes. Among the most consistent correlates have been age, education, personal contact with PWAs, knowledge about HIV transmission, and attitudes toward homosexuality (e.g., Gerbert, Sumser, & Maguire, 1991; Herek & Capitanio, 1997; Price & Hsu, 1992; Stipp & Kerr, 1989). Younger and better-educated respondents consistently manifest lower levels of AIDS stigma than older respondents and those with lower levels of education. Similarly, uninfected people who personally know a PWA generally manifest less AIDS stigma than others. Attitudes toward PWAs tend to be more favorable and attitudes toward AIDS-related policies less restrictive to the extent that respondents have more favorable attitudes toward gay people and are knowledgeable about the lack of risk of HIV transmission through casual social contact (Capitanio & Herek, 1999; Herek & Capitanio, 1999; Pryor et al., 1999).

Some data reveal racial and ethnic differences in AIDS stigma. Members of racial and ethnic minority groups—mainly African Americans and Hispanic Americans—appear more likely than non-Hispanic White Americans to overestimate the risks of HIV transmission through casual contact and to endorse policies that would separate PWAs from others (Alcalay, Spiderman, Mitchell, & Griffin, 1989-1990; Herek & Capitanio, 1993, 1997, 1998; Herek & Glunt, 1991; McCaig, Hardy, & Winn, 1991). Such patterns may reflect differences in the credibility that minority group members attach to official AIDS information (Herek & Capitanio, 1994), which in turn have multiple cultural and historical roots (e.g., Herek & Glunt, 1993; Stevenson, 1994; Turner, 1993).

In trying to explain the social psychology of AIDS stigma, it is useful to recognize that, as a disease, AIDS manifests at least four characteristics likely to evoke stigma (Goffman, 1963; Jones et al., 1984). First, stigma is more often attached to a disease whose cause is perceived to be the bearer's responsibility. To the extent that an illness is perceived as having been contracted through voluntary and avoidable behaviors—especially if such behaviors evoke social disapproval—it is likely to be stigmatized and to evoke anger and moralism rather than pity or empathy (Weiner, 1993). Thus, because the primary transmission routes for HIV are behaviors that are widely considered voluntary and immoral, PWHIVs are regarded by a significant portion of the public as responsible for their condition and consequently are stigmatized (e.g., Herek & Capitanio, 1999).

Second, greater stigma is associated with illnesses and conditions that are unalterable or degenerative. Since the earliest days of the epidemic, AIDS has been widely perceived to be a fatal condition (Blake & Arkin, 1988). Being diagnosed with such a disease is often regarded as equivalent to dying, and those who are diagnosed may represent a reminder—or even the personification—of death and mortality (e.g., Stoddard, 1994). New drug regimens have offered realistic hope that HIV disease may be transformed from a fatal malady to a chronic illness. Those medicines, however, are not effective for all who take them, and many PWHIVs do not have access to antiviral drugs. Thus, despite the development of increasingly effective therapies, AIDS will probably continue to be perceived as a fatal disease by most of the U.S. public for the foreseeable future.

Third, greater stigma is associated with conditions that are perceived to be contagious or to place others in harm's way. Perceptions of danger and fears of contagion have surrounded AIDS since the beginning of the epidemic (Herek, 1990), and are evident in Americans' continuing overestimation of the risks posed by casual contact (Herek & Capitanio, 1998, 1999). Fourth, a condition tends to be more stigmatized when it is readily apparent to others—when it actually disrupts a social interaction or is perceived by others as repellent, ugly, or upsetting. In this regard, the advanced stages of AIDS often dramatically affect an individual's physical appearance and stamina, evoking distress and stigma from observers (e.g., Klitzman, 1997).

Given these characteristics, AIDS probably would have evoked stigma regardless of its specific epidemiology and social history. Yet the character of AIDS stigma in the United States derives from the widely perceived association between HIV and particular sectors of the population, especially gay and bisexual men and injecting drug users (IDUs). Recognizing this fact, social psychologists have postulated several theories of AIDS stigma (Herek, 1999; Pryor et al., 1999). Many of these models describe two sources for individual's attitudes: (a) fear of AIDS as an illness and an accompanying desire to protect oneself from it, and (b) symbolic associations between AIDS and groups identified with the disease.

Instrumental AIDS stigma results from the communicability and lethality of HIV. It reflects the fear and apprehension likely to be associated with any transmissible and deadly illness. It is perhaps best illustrated by the experiences of people who acquired HIV through receiving blood products. Compared to gay men and drug users, such individuals were not previously highly stigmatized by society (although many faced some degree of illness-related stigma). After the onset of AIDS, however, they often faced rejection and isolation because of others' fears about the spread of HIV through casual contact (e.g., Kinsella, 1989).

Symbolic AIDS stigma results from the social meanings attached to AIDS. It represents the use of the disease as a vehicle for expressing a variety of attitudes, especially attitudes toward the groups perceived to be at risk of AIDS and the behaviors that transmit HIV. Historically, symbolic AIDS stigma in the United States has focused principally on male homosexuality, and much of the American public continues to equate AIDS with homosexuality to a significant extent (Herek, 1999; Herek & Capitanio, 1999). At the same time, some segments of society have had different experiences with the epidemic and, consequently, have different symbolic associations for AIDS. In the African American community, for example, AIDS has affected not only gay and bisexual men but also a substantial number of injecting drug users, with the consequence that symbolic AIDS stigma is closely related to attitudes toward the latter as well as the former (Capitanio & Herek, 1999; Fullilove & Fullilove, 1999).

THE PERSONAL IMPACT OF AIDS STIGMA

In the 1997 national survey mentioned above, more than three fourths of respondents expressed the belief that people with AIDS are unfairly persecuted in our society (Herek & Capitanio, 1998). The widespread expectation of stigma, combined with actual experiences with prejudice and discrimination, exerts a considerable impact on PWHIVs, their loved ones, and caregivers. It affects many of the choices that PWHIVs make about being tested and seeking assistance for their physical, psychological, and social needs (Alonzo & Reynolds, 1995; Chesney & Smith, 1999; Hays et al., 1993; Klitzman, 1997; Lester, Partridge, Chesney, & Cooke, 1995; Lyter, Valdiserri, Kingsley, Amoroso, & Rinaldo, 1987; Siegel & Krauss, 1991). For example, fear of AIDS stigma and its attendant discrimination may deter people at risk for HIV from being tested and seeking information and assistance for risk reduction (Chesney & Smith, 1999).

In addition to the negative effects of experiencing outright rejection and persecution, AIDS stigma has considerable impact on PWHIVs' decisions about disclosing their health status to others. Fearing rejection and mistreatment, many PWHIVs keep their seropositive status a secret (Gielen, O'Campo, Faden, & Eke, 1997; Hays et al., 1993; Klitzman, 1997). Whereas a desire to set boundaries and control others' access to information about one's personal life—including one's health status—is an important consideration (Greene & Serovich, 1996), hiding one's HIV-positive status can lead to isolation at a time when social support is badly needed (Crandall & Coleman, 1992; Johnston, Stall, & Smith, 1995). Nondisclosure may also reflect an internalizing of societal stigma by PWHIVs, which can lead to self-loathing, self-blame, and self-destructive behaviors (Herek, 1990; Klitzman, 1997). Nondisclosure to a sexual partner, especially when the PWHIV fails to ensure that safer sex guidelines are strictly followed, raises multiple ethical questions (Bayer, 1996).

The loved ones of PWAs also are at risk for AIDS stigma and its negative effects. They, too, often face ostracism and discrimination because of their association with a PWHIV. This courtesy stigma (Goffman, 1963) can leave them without adequate social support (Folkman, Chesney, & Christopher-Richards, 1994; Folkman, Chesney, Cooke, Boccellari, & Collette, 1994; Jankowski, Videka-Sherman, & Laquidara-Dickinson, 1996; Paul, Hays, & Coates, 1995; Poindexter & Linsk, 1999). Caregivers and advocates for PWAs, whether professionals or volunteers, also risk courtesy stigma, which may deter them from working with PWHIVs entirely or make their work more difficult (Snyder, Omoto, & Crain, 1999).

AIDS STIGMA AND PUBLIC POLICY

The politics of AIDS stigma have repeatedly hindered society's response to the epidemic (Panem, 1988; Shilts, 1987). Mass media were initially slow to report on AIDS, probably because of its prevalence among already stigmatized groups (Albert, 1986; Baker, 1986; Kinsella, 1989). Extensive resources that might otherwise have gone to prevention instead were needed to respond to coercive AIDS legislation whose purpose was primarily to stigmatize and punish PWAs (Bayer, 1989; Epstein, 1996; Herek & Glunt, 1993). Despite empirical data showing that needle exchange programs can play a valuable role in helping to reduce HIV transmission among IDUs without fostering increased drug use (Cross, Saunders, & Bartelli, 1998; Normand, Vlahov, & Moses, 1995; Watters, Estilo, Clark, & Lorvick, 1994), AIDS stigma and the stigma attached to injecting drug use have prevented the large-scale implementation of such programs (Bayer, 1989; Capitanio & Herek, 1999; Stolberg, 1998). Federal law and policy have consistently prevented AIDS educators from providing clear and explicit risk reduction information to individuals at risk (Bailey, 1995; Bayer, 1989; Epstein, 1996; Shilts, 1987), which probably have reduced the effectiveness of HIV prevention efforts. Indeed, some commentators have argued that stigma is the root cause of the HIV epidemic in the United States (Novick, 1997).

Recognition of the negative consequences of AIDS stigma for individuals and for public health led to the enactment of statutory protections for PWHIVs (Burris, 1999). In addition to barring most discrimination based on HIV status, HIV was exempted from traditional public health practices such as partner notification and contact tracing, a pattern labeled *AIDS exceptionalism* by some (Bayer, 1991, 1994). Moreover, whereas AIDS is a reportable disease nationwide, requirements for reporting HIV infections vary across states.

With the development of more effective treatments for HIV disease and a widespread perception that AIDS stigma has substantially declined, support for AIDS exceptionalism has diminished. National reporting of the names of HIV-infected persons is now strongly advocated by many leaders in public health (Gostin, Ward, & Baker, 1997). The assumption that stigma no longer represents a serious challenge in HIV policy may be premature, however. Given the widespread perception that people with AIDS are unfairly persecuted (Herek & Capitanio, 1998) coupled with distrust of government authorities in minority communities (Herek & Capitanio, 1994), it is possible that many people at risk for HIV infection could be deterred or delayed from being tested if they believe that their names will be reported to a government agency. Thus, a rush to institute the reporting of PWHIVs by name may have deleterious consequences for increasing HIV testing among the individuals at greatest risk for infection.

CONCLUSION

The association of stigma with disease is not a new phenomenon. Throughout history, the stigma attached to epidemic illnesses and social groups associated with them have often hampered treatment and prevention, and have inflicted additional suffering on sick individuals and their loved ones (e.g., McNeill, 1976; Rosenberg, 1987). In this sense, the AIDS epidemic has many parallels to older epidemics of cholera and plague (Herek, 1990). What differentiates AIDS from earlier epidemics is that today we have the collective insight to recognize stigma's impact on individual lives and public health, as well as the technology to scientifically study stigma and seek to reduce it (Devine, Plant, & Harrison, 1999). One of the great challenges of the epidemic in the new millennium will be to apply our insight and technology to the problem of eradicating AIDS stigma.

REFERENCES

Albert, E. (1986). Illness and deviance: The response of the press to AIDS. In D. A. Feldman & T. M. Johnson (Eds.), *The social dimensions of AIDS: Method and theory* (pp. 163–178). New York: Praeger.

Alcalay, R., Sniderman, P. M., Mitchell, J., & Griffin, R. (1989–1990). Ethnic differences in knowledge of AIDS transmission and attitudes towards gays and people with AIDS. *International Quarterly of Community Health Education,* 10, 213–222.

Alonzo, A. A., & Reynolds, N. R. (1995). Stigma, HIV and AIDS: An exploration and elaboration of a stigma trajectory. *Social Science and Medicine,* 41, 303–315.

Altman, D. (1986). *AIDS in the mind of America.* Garden City, NY: Anchor.

Bailey, W. A. (1995). The importance of HIV prevention programming to the lesbian and gay community. In G. M. Herek & B. Greene (Eds.), *AIDS, identity, and community: The HIV epidemic and lesbians and gay men* (pp. 210–225). Thousand Oaks, CA: Sage.

Baker, A. J. (1986). The portrayal of AIDS in the media: An analysis of articles in the *New York Times.* In D. A. Feldman & T. M. Johnson (Eds.), *The social dimensions of AIDS: Method and theory* (pp. 179–194). New York: Praeger.

Bayer, R. (1989). *Private acts, social consequences: AIDS and the politics of public health.* New York: Free Press.

Bayer, R. (1991). Public health policy and the AIDS epidemic: An end to HIV exceptionalism? *New England Journal of Medicine,* 324, 1500–1504.

Bayer, R. (1994). HIV exceptionalism revisited. *AIDS & Public Policy Journal,* 9(1), 16–18.

Bayer, R. (1996). AIDS prevention: Sexual ethics and responsibility. *New England Journal of Medicine,* 334, 1540–1542.

Blake, S. M., & Arkin, E. B. (1988). *AIDS information monitor: A summary of national public opinion surveys on AIDS: 1983 through 1986.* Washington, DC: American Red Cross.

Blendon, R. J., & Donelan, K. (1988). Discrimination against people with AIDS: The public's perspective. *New England Journal of Medicine,* 319, 1022–1026.

Blendon, R. J., Donelan, K., & Knox, R. A. (1992). Public opinion and AIDS: Lessons for the second decade. *Journal of the American Medical Association,* 267, 981–986.

Burns, J. F. (1996, September 22). A wretched new class of infected untouchables. *New York Times,* p. 4.

Burris, S. (1999). Studying the legal management of HIV-related stigma. *American Behavioral Scientist,* 42(7), 1229–1243.

Capitanio, J. P., & Herek, G. M. (1999). AIDS-related stigma and attitudes toward injecting drug users among Black and White Americans. *American Behavioral Scientist,* 42(7), 1148–1161.

Chesney, M. A., & Smith, A. W. (1999). Critical delays in HIV testing and care: The potential role of stigma. *American Behavioral Scientist,* 42(7), 1162–1174.

Clendinen, D. (1983, June 17). AIDS spreads pain and fear among ill and healthy alike. *New York Times,* pp. A1, B4.

Crandall, C. S., & Coleman, R. (1992). AIDS-related stigmatization and the disruption of social relationships. *Journal of Social and Personal Relationships,* 9, 163–177.

Crawford, A. M. (1996). Stigma associated with AIDS: A meta-analysis. *Journal of Applied Social Psychology,* 26, 398–416.

Cross, J. E., Saunders, C. M., & Bartelli, D. (1998). The effectiveness of education and needle exchange programs: A meta-analysis of HIV prevention strategies for injecting drug users. *Quality and Quantity,* 32, 165–180.

Devine, P. G., Plant, E. A., & Harrison, K. (1999). The problem of "us" versus "them" and AIDS stigma. *American Behavioral Scientist,* 42(7), 1212–1228.

Epstein, S. (1996). *Impure science: AIDS, activism, and the politics of knowledge.* Berkeley: University of California Press.

Folkman, S., Chesney, M. A., & Christopher-Richards, A. (1994). Stress and coping in caregiving partners of men with AIDS. *Psychiatric Clinics of North America,* 17, 35–53.

Folkman, S., Chesney, M. A., Cooke, M., Boccellari, A., & Collette, L. (1994). Caregiver burden in HIV-positive and HIV-negative partners of men with AIDS. *Journal of Consulting and Clinical Psychology,* 62, 746–756.

Fullilove, M. T., & Fullilove, R. E. (1999). Stigma as an obstacle to AIDS action: The case of the African American community. *American Behavioral Scientist,* 42(7), 1117–1129.

Gerbert, B., Sumser, J., & Maguire, B. T. (1991). The impact of who you know and where you live on opinions about AIDS and health care. *Social Science and Medicine,* 32, 677–681.

Gielen, A. C., O'Campo, P., Faden, R. R., & Eke, A. (1997). Women's disclosure of HIV status: Experiences of mistreatment and violence in an urban setting. *Women & Health,* 25(3), 19–31.

Goffman, E. (1963). *Stigma: Notes on the management of spoiled identity.* Englewood Cliffs, NJ: Prentice Hall.

Goldin, C. S. (1994). Stigmatization and AIDS: Critical issues in public health. *Social Science & Medicine*, 39, 1359–1366.

Gostin, L. O. (1990). The AIDS litigation project: A national review of court and human rights commission decisions, part II: Discrimination. *Journal of the American Medical Association,* 263, 2086–2093.

Gostin, L. O., Ward, J. W., & Baker, A. C. (1997). National HIV case reporting for the United States: A defining moment in the history of the epidemic. *New England Journal of Medicine,* 337, 1162–1167.

Gostin, L. O., & Webber, D. M. (1998). The AIDS Litigation Project: HIV/AIDS in the courts in the 1990s, part 2. *AIDS & Public Policy Journal,* 13, 3–13.

Greene, K., & Serovich, J. (1996). Appropriateness of disclosure of HIV testing information: The perspective of PLWAs. *Journal of Applied Communication Research,* 24(1), 50–65.

Hays, R. B., McKusick, L., Pollack, L., Hilliard, R., Hoff, C., & Coates, T. J. (1993). Disclosing HIV seropositivity to significant others. *AIDS,* 7, 425–431.

Herek, G. M. (1990). Illness, stigma, and AIDS. In P. T. Costa, Jr. & G. R. VandenBos (Eds.), *Psychological aspects of serious illness: Chronic conditions, fatal diseases, and clinical care* (pp. 103–150). Washington, DC: American Psychological Association.

Herek, G. M. (1997). The HIV epidemic and public attitudes toward lesbians and gay men. In M. P. Levine, P. Nardi, & J. Gagnon (Eds.), *In changing times: Gay men and lesbians encounter HIV/AIDS* (pp. 191–218). Chicago: University of Chicago Press.

Herek, G. M. (1999). The social construction of attitudes: Functional consensus and divergence in the US public's reactions to AIDS. In G. R. Maio & J. M. Olson (Eds.), *Why we evaluate: Functions of attitudes.* Mahwah, NJ: Lawrence-Erlbaum.

Herek, G. M., & Capitanio, J. P. (1993). Public reactions to AIDS in the United States: A second decade of stigma. *American Journal of Public Health,* 83, 574–577.

Herek, G. M., & Capitanio, J. P. (1994). Conspiracies, contagion, and compassion: Trust and public reactions to AIDS. *AIDS Education and Prevention,* 6, 367–375.

Herek, G. M., & Capitanio, J. P. (1997). AIDS stigma and contact with persons with AIDS: Effects of personal and vicarious contact. *Journal of Applied Social Psychology,* 27, 1–36.

Herek, G. M., & Capitanio, J. P. (1998, July). *AIDS stigma and HIV-related beliefs in the United States: Results from a national telephone survey.* Conference record of the 12th World AIDS Conference, Geneva, Switzerland.

Herek, G. M., & Capitanio, J. P. (1999). AIDS stigma and sexual prejudice. *American Behavioral Scientist,* 42(7), 1130–1147.

Herek, G. M., & Glunt, E. K. (1991). AIDS-related attitudes in the United States: A preliminary conceptualization. *Journal of Sex Research,* 28, 99–123.

Herek, G. M., & Glunt, E. K. (1993). Public attitudes toward AIDS-related issues in the United States. In J. B. Pryor & G. D. Reeder (Eds.), *The social psychology of HIV infection* (pp. 229–261). Hillsdale, NJ: Lawrence Erlbaum.

Herek, G. M., Mitnick, L., Burris, S., Chesney, M., Devine, P., Fullilove, M. T., Fullilove, R., Gunther, H. C., Levi, J., Michaels, S., Novick, A., Pryor, J., Snyder, M., & Sweeney, T. (1998). *AIDS and stigma: A conceptual framework and research agenda.* AIDS & Public Policy Journal, 13, 36–47.

HIV-positive girl unable to find a Brownie troop to call her own. (1998, December 1). *San Francisco Examiner*, p. A-20.

Hunter, N. D., & Rubenstein, W. B. (Eds.). (1992). *AIDS agenda: Emerging issues in civil rights*. New York: New Press.

Jankowski, S., Videka-Sherman, L., & Laquidara-Dickinson, K. (1996). Social support networks of confidants to people with AIDS. *Social Work*, 41, 206–213.

Johnston, D., Stall, R., & Smith, K. (1995). Reliance by gay men and intravenous drug users on friends and family for AIDS-related care. *AIDS Care*, 7, 307–319.

Jones, E., Farina, A., Hastorf, A. H., Markus, H., Miller, D. T., & Scott, R. A. (1984). Social stigma: *The psychology of marked relationships*. New York: Freeman.

Kinsella, J. (1989). *Covering the plague: AIDS and the American media*. New Brunswick, NJ: Rutgers University Press.

Klitzman, R. (1997). *Being positive: The lives of men and women with HIV*. Chicago: Ivan R. Dee.

Lester, P., Partridge, J. C., Chesney, M. A., & Cooke, M. (1995). The consequences of a positive prenatal HIV antibody test for women. *Journal of Acquired Immune Deficiency Syndromes and Human Retrovirology*, 10, 341–349.

Lyter, D. W., Valdiserri, R. O., Kingsley, L. A., Amoroso, W. P., & Rinaldo, C. R., Jr. (1987). The HIV antibody test: Why gay and bisexual men want or do not want to know their results. *Public Health Reports*, 102, 468–474.

Mann, J., Tarantola, D. J. M., & Netter, T. W. (Eds.). (1992). *AIDS in the world*. Cambridge, MA: Harvard University Press.

McCaig, L. F., Hardy, A. M., & Winn, D. M. (1991). Knowledge about AIDS and HIV in the United States adult population: Influence of the local incidence of AIDS. *American Journal of Public Health*, 81, 1591–1595.

McNeil, D. G., Jr. (1998, December 28). Neighbors kill an HIV-positive AIDS activist in South Africa. *New York Times*, p. A5.

McNeil, W. H. (1976). *Plagues and peoples*. Garden City, NY: Anchor.

National Association of People With AIDS. (1992). HIV in America: *A profile of the challenges facing Americans living with HIV*. Washington, DC: Author.

National Workshop on HIV and Violence. (1996). *HIV violence: Recommendations for the prevention and intervention of HIV-related violence*. New York: New York City Gay and Lesbian Anti-Violence Project.

Nnko, S. (1998, July). *AIDS stigma: A persistent social phenomenon in Mwanza, Tanzania*. Conference record of the 12th World AIDS Conference, Geneva, Switzerland.

Normand, J., Vlahov, D., & Moses, L. E. (Eds.). (1995). *Preventing HIV transmission: The role of sterile needles and bleach*. Washington, DC: National Academy.

Novick, A. (1997). Stigma and AIDS: Three layers of damage. *Journal of the Gay and Lesbian Medical Association*, 1, 53–60.

Panem, S. (1988). *The AIDS bureaucracy*. Cambridge, MA: Harvard University Press.

Panos Institute. (1990). *The 3rd epidemic: Repercussions of the fear of AIDS*. London: Author.

Paul, J. P., Hays, R. B., & Coates, T. J. (1995). The impact of the HIV epidemic on U.S. gay male communities. In A. R. D'Augelli & C. J. Patterson (Eds.), *Lesbian, gay, and bisexual identities across the life span: Psychological perspectives on personal, relational, and community processes* (pp. 347–397). New York: Oxford University Press.

Poindexter, C., & Linsk, N. L. (1999). HIV-related stigma in a sample of HIV-affected older female African American caregivers. *Social Work*, 44, 46–61.

Price, V., & Hsu, M. (1992). Public opinion about AIDS policies: The role of misinformation and attitudes toward homosexuals. *Public Opinion Quarterly*, 56, 29–52.

Pryor, J. B., & Reeder, G. D. (1993). Collective and individual representations of HIV/AIDS stigma. In J. B. Pryor & G. D. Reeder (Eds.), *The social psychology of HIV infection* (pp. 263–286). Hillsdale, NJ: Lawrence Erlbaum.

Pryor, J. B., Reeder, G. D., & Landau, S. (1999). A social-psychological analysis of HIV-related stigma: A two-factory theory. *American Behavioral Scientist*, 42(7), 1193–1211.

Rogers, T. F., Singer, E., & Imperio, J. (1993). The polls: AIDS—an update. *Public Opinion Quarterly*, 57, 92–114.

Rosenberg, C. E. (1987). *The cholera years: The U.S. in 1832, 1849, and 1866* (2nd ed.). Chicago: University of Chicago Press.

Sabatier, R. (1988). *Blaming others: Prejudice, race, and worldwide AIDS*. London: Panos Institute.

Schneider, W. (1987). Homosexuals: Is AIDS changing attitudes? *Public Opinion*, 10(2), 6–7, 59.

Shenon, P. (1996, February 11). Reluctantly, Clinton signs defense bill. *New York Times*, p. 12.

Shilts, R. (1987). *And the band played on: Politics, people and the AIDS epidemic*. New York: St. Martin's.

Siegel, K., & Krauss, B. J. (1991). Living with HIV infection: Adaptive tasks of seropositive gay men. *Journal of Health and Social Behavior,* 32, 17–32.

Singer, E., & Rogers, T. F. (1986). Public opinion and AIDS. *AIDS & Public Policy Journal,* 1, 1–13.

Snyder, M., Omoto, A. M., & Crain, A. L. (1999). Punished for their good deeds: Stigmatization of AIDS volunteers. *American Behavioral Scientist,* 42(7), 1175–1192.

Stevenson, H. C., Jr. (1994). The psychology of sexual racism and AIDS: An ongoing saga of distrust and the "sexual other." *Journal of Black Studies,* 25(1), 62–80.

Stipp, H., & Kerr, D. (1989). Determinants of public opinions about AIDS. *Public Opinion Quarterly,* 53, 98–106.

Stoddard, T. (1994, August 17). Don't call it AIDS. (HIV disease is more appropriate). *New York: Times,* p. A15.

Stolberg, S. G. (1998, April 21). President decides against financing needle programs. *New York Times,* pp. A1, A18.

Turner, P. A. (1993). *I heard it through the grapevine: Rumor in African-American culture.* Berkeley: University of California Press.

Watters, J. K., Estilo, M. J., Clark, G. L., & Lorvick, J. (1994). Syringe and needle exchange as HIV/AIDS prevention for injection drug users. *Journal of the American Medical Association,* 271, 115–120.

Weiner, B. (1993). AIDS from an attributional perspective. In J. B. Pryor & G. D. Reeder (Eds.), *The social psychology of HIV infection* (pp. 287–302). Hillsdale, NJ: Lawrence Erlbaum.

Author's Note: *Preparation of this article was supported by an Independent Scientist Award from the National Institute of Mental Health (K02 MH01455).*

The Experience of Illness

Disease not only involves the body. It also affects people's social relationships, self-image, and behavior. The social psychological aspects of illness are related in part to the biophysiological manifestations of disease, but are also independent of them. The very act of defining something as an illness has consequences that are independent of any effects of biophysiology.

> When a veterinarian diagnoses a cow's condition as an illness, he does not merely by diagnosis change the cow's behavior; to the cow, illness [disease] remains an experienced biophysiological state, no more. But when a physician diagnoses a human's condition as an illness, he changes the man's behavior by diagnosis: a social state is added to a biophysiological state by assigning the meaning of illness to disease (Freidson, 1970: 223).

Much of the sociological study of illness has centered on the *sick* role and *illness behavior*. Talcott Parsons (1951) argued that in order to prevent the potentially disruptive consequences of illness on a group or society, there exists a set of shared cultural rules (norms) called the "sick role." The sick role legitimates the deviations caused by illness and channels the sick into the reintegrating physician-patient relationship. According to Parsons, the sick role has four components: (1) the sick person is exempted from normal social responsibilities, at least to the extent it is necessary to get well; (2) the individual is not held responsible for his or her condition and cannot be expected to recover by an act of will; (3) the person must recognize that being ill is undesirable and must want to recover; and (4) the sick person is obligated to seek and cooperate with "expert" advice, generally that of a physician. Sick people are not blamed for their illness but must work toward recovery. There have been numerous critiques and modifications of the concept of the sick role, such as its inapplicability to chronic illness and disability, but it remains a central sociological way of seeing illness experience (Segall, 1976).

Illness behavior is essentially how people act when they develop symptoms of disease. As one sociologist notes, it includes "the way in which given symptoms may be differentially perceived, evaluated, and acted (or not acted) upon by different kinds of persons . . . whether by reason of early experience with illness, differential training in respect to symptoms, or whatever" (Mechanic, 1962). Reaction to symptoms, use of social networks in locating help, and compliance with medical advice are some of the activities characterized as illness behavior.

Illness behavior and the sick role, as well as the related concept of *illness career* (Suchman, 1965), are all more or less based on a perspective that all (proper) roads lead to medical care. They tend to create a "doctor-centered" picture by making the receipt of medical care the centerpiece of sociological attention. Such concepts are essentially "outsider" perspectives on the experience of illness. While these viewpoints may be useful in their own right, none of them has as a central concern the actual subjective experience of illness. They don't analyze illness from the sufferer's (or patient's) viewpoint. Over the years sociologists (e.g., Strauss and Glaser, 1975; Schneider and Conrad, 1983; Charmaz, 1991) have attempted to develop more subjective "insider" accounts of what it is like to be sick. These accounts focus more on individuals' perceptions of illness, interactions with others, the effects of illness on identity, and people's strategies for managing illness symptoms than do the abstract notions of illness, careers, or sick roles. Sociologists have produced studies of epilepsy, multiple sclerosis, diabetes, asthma, arthritis, and end-stage renal disease that demonstrate an increasing sociological interest in examining the subjective aspects of illness (see Roth and Conrad, 1987; Anderson and Bury, 1988; Charmaz, 1999, Gabe et al., 2002).

The first two selections in the section present different faces of the experience of illness. Fibromyalgia syndrome (FMS) is a controversial pain disorder. It is a functional pain syndrome or illness for which there is no commonly accepted medical or organic explanation. Since many people suffer from the disorder, but physicians tend to be skeptical about its organic origin, we could call it a "contested illness." Yet there are millions of individuals who suffer pain and believe they have the disorder. In the first selection, "Self-Help Literature and the Making of an Illness Identity: The Case of Fibromyalgia Syndrome (FMS)," Kristin Barker analyzes the role of self-help books in the creation of an illness identity. She shows how the lay knowledge contained in the self-help books helps individuals to validate their own illness experiences and develop an illness identity. The accounts in these books legitimate patients' identities as having an illness, even in the face of a doubting biomedicine. Patients gain great knowledge about their disorder and often become the experts on their own illness (Prior, 2003). Barker demonstrates the importance of lay knowledge and self-help communities in shaping illness identities. In recent years, the Internet, even more than self-help books, serves as an important self-help community to validate and shape illness identities (see, for example, Victoria Pitts' article on breast cancer in cyberspace in the "Community Initiatives" section).

The second reading, "The Meanings of Medications: Another Look at Compliance" by Peter Conrad, examines the important issue of how people manage their medication regimens. As part of a study of the experience of epilepsy, Conrad found that a large portion of his respondents did not take their medications as prescribed. From a medical point of view these patients would be depicted as "noncompliant"; i.e., they do not follow doctor's orders. However, from the perspective of people with epilepsy the situation looks quite different. Conrad identifies the meanings of medications in people's everyday lives, and suggests that from this perspective it makes more sense to conceptualize these patients' behavior as self-regulation than as noncompliance. By focusing on the experience of illness we can reframe our understanding of behavior and see what may be deemed a "problem" in a different light.

In the final selection, "The Remission Society," Arthur Frank introduces an important new concept based on his own experience of having had cancer (cf. Frank, 1995). With the rise of chronic illness and the advent of modern medical interventions, more patients are surviving what at one time might have been fatal illnesses. This has created a new category of "survivors" (Mullan, 1985) who are neither ill nor completely well. They have usually come through medical treatment, are often doing well, but are not "cured" in the traditional sense of the word. The populace of the remission society continues to grow, although most remain invisible to us until their condition or history becomes an issue. Their existence, however, stretches our understanding of the experience of illness and hearkens us to listen to the survivors.

Issues such as illness identity and managing medication regimens are crucial aspects of the illness experience and are independent of both the disease itself and the sick role. When we understand and treat illness as a subjective as well as objective experience, we no longer treat patients as diseases but as people who are sick. By understanding the remission society, we better begin to understand how survivors live in the liminal space between the ill and the well. This is an important dimension of human health care.

REFERENCES

Anderson, Robert, and Michael Bury (eds.). (1988). Living with Chronic Illness: The Experience of Patients and Their Families. London: Unwin Hyman.

Charmaz, Kathy. (1991). Good Days, Bad Days: The Self in Chronic Illness and Time. New Brunswick: Rutgers University Press.

Charmaz, Kathy. (1999). "Experiencing chronic illness." Pp. 277–92 in Gary L. Albrecht, Ray Fitzpatrick, and Susan C. Scrimshaw (eds.), Handbook of Social Studies in Health and Medicine. Thousand Oaks, CA: Sage Publications.

Frank, Arthur. (1995). The Wounded Storyteller. Chicago: University of Chicago Press.

Gabe Jonathan, Michael Burg, and Rosemary Ramsey. (2002). "Living with asthma: The experiences of young people at home and at school." Social Science and Medicine, 55: 619–33.

Friedson, Eliot. (1970). Profession of Medicine. New York: Dodd, Mead.

Mechanic, David. (1962). "The concept of illness behavior." Journal of Chronic Diseases. 15: 189–94.

Mullan, Fitzhugh. (1985). "Seasons of survival: Reflections of a physician with cancer." New England Journal of Medicine. 313: 270–73.

Parsons, Talcott. (1951). The Social System. New York: Free Press.

Prior, Lindsay. (2003). "Belief, knowledge and expertise: The emergence of the lay expert in medical sociology." Sociology of Health and Illness 25: 41–57.

Roth, Julius, and Peter Conrad. (1987). The Experience and Management of Chronic Illness (Research in the Sociology of Health Care, Volume 6). Greenwich, CT: JAI Press.

Schneider, Joseph W., and Peter Conrad. (1983). Having Epilepsy: The Experience and Control of Illness. Philadelphia: Temple University Press.

Segall, Alexander. (1976). "The sick role concept: Understanding illness behavior." Journal of Health and Social Behavior. 17 (June): 163–70.

Strauss, Anselm, and Barney Glaser. (1975). Chronic Illness and the Quality of Life. St. Louis: C. V. Mosby.

Suchman, Edward. (1965). "Stages of illness and medical care." Journal of Health and Social Behavior. 6: 114–28.

13 *Self-Help Literature and the Making of an Illness Identity: The Case of Fibromyalgia Syndrome (FMS)*

Kristin Barker

Approximately six million Americans are diagnosed with the pain disorder fibromyalgia and nearly all of those diagnosed are women (Oregon Fibromyalgia Foundation 2000; Wallace and Wallace 1999).[1] Fibromyalgia is not a disease but a syndrome represented by a collection of symptoms including widespread pain and a host of associated complaints, such as fatigue, headaches, sleep disorders, digestive disorders, depression, and anxiety. Yet, like chronic fatigue syndrome (CFS), which is identified by most patients, physicians, and medical researchers as either the same or a sister disorder, there are questions about the diagnostic legitimacy of FMS (Barsky and Borus 1999; Goldenberg et al. 1990; Manu 1998; Wessely, Nimnuan, and Sharpe, 1999).[2]

In biomedical lexicon, FMS is a functional somatic syndrome or an illness for which there is no organic explanation or demonstrable physiological abnormality (Manu 1998). For those diagnosed with FMS, there is typically a deeply felt contradiction between their subjective certainty of their symptoms and the inability of biomedical science to demonstrate their objective existence. This results in self-doubt and alienation among sufferers and gives impetus to the formation of the FMS self-help and support community, including the emergence of local support groups, national newsletters, Internet sites and chat groups, and self-help literature. Individuals draw upon this community to affirm the "realness" of their collective (and hence, individual) FMS experience, despite the disorder's biomedical invisibility.

The FMS self-help literature is one resource that individuals draw on in their efforts to overcome self-doubt and alienation. In this paper, I demonstrate how the FMS self-help literature contributes to this process by facilitating a collective understanding of the symptoms of FMS that gives them meaning and legitimacy. By linking an analysis of the five bestselling FMS self-help books and interviews with 25 women diagnosed with FMS, I explain how the self-help literature organizes vast and dissimilar symptoms and symptom trajectories into a diagnostically bound FMS illness identity. Further, I demonstrate how the permissive boundaries of this identity function to reduce self-doubt and alienation in a context where biomedical science is unable to make FMS visible.

Although there are specific reasons for the emergence of the FMS self-help community, self-help has become an increasingly important component of the illness experience generally (Davison, Pennebaker, and Dickerson 2000). Managed care, the erosion of community, and the populist critique of professional authority all contribute to the increase in health-related, self-help activities and resources (Borkman 1999; Burrows et al. 2000; Wituk et al. 2000). The emergence of Internet self-help communities and information devoted to illness is particularly dramatic (Davison, Pennebaker, and Dickerson 2000; Eng 2001; Oravec 2001). I contend that the processes of collective illness identity formation described here are not limited to FMS or even to other contested illnesses. Similar processes of illness identity formation occur within other health-related, self-help communities. As I discuss in the conclusion, the lay public is increasingly involved as patients (or potential patients) in collectively defining their "illnesses," raising new questions about the nature and consequences of the medicalization of social and personal problems, discontent, and distress.

THE FMS CONTROVERSY

Although medical accounts of systemic and chronic joint and muscular pain have existed for centuries, the chronic pain disorder fibromyalgia has existed as a specific diagnosis only since the mid-1970s (Clauw 1995; Goldenberg 1999). There are multiple reasons for the controversy surrounding FMS, but the most salient is its biomedical invisibility.[3] There are no objective indicators of the disorder (Goldenberg 1999). To address this lack of objectivity, the American College of Rheumatology (ACR) established criteria for the classification of FMS in 1990. The ACR diagnostic criteria include the experience of widespread pain for at least three months in conjunction with subjectively reported tenderness in at least 11 of 18 identified "tender points" palpitated during a physical exam (Wolfe et al. 1990). Moreover, for a positive FMS diagnosis other possible causes for such pain must be disconfirmed. As such, the parameters of FMS are determined by exclusion and subjectively, making it truly diagnostically anachronistic in an era of rigorous, high-tech biomedicine. Indeed, biomedical authority is premised on the use of instrumentation to make disease visible and the concurrent reduced reliance on patient's subjective evaluations (Foucault 1973; Starr 1982).

Even though the ACR criteria were established to create uniformity in FMS biomedical research, there is general recognition among patients and physicians that FMS is associated with a vast collection of symptoms and physical complaints not limited to the ACR's definition of chronic widespread pain (Copenhagen Declaration 1992; Wolfe et al. 1990; Yunus et al. 1981). Some of the common FMS symptoms are fatigue, morning stiffness, headaches, sleep problems, anxiety, depression, difficulties concentrating, swelling/numbness/tension in hands/arms/legs, dizziness, digestive problems, bowel and bladder irritability, painful menstruation, chest pain, and dryness of mouth/nose/eyes. FMS is also controversial, therefore, because of the lack of clinical uniformity in diagnostic criteria and because of the inclusion of symptoms that are extensive and ubiquitous—symptoms that, in themselves, may indicate no pathology at all or the presence of any number of medical disorders.

The elusiveness of FMS is amplified by the fact that its etiology is unknown and there are no efficacious medical treatments.[4] Like other patient complaints that cannot be traced to known organic causes and/or fail to respond to established medical treatments, FMS is identified by many physicians as "psychosomatic" or a somatic presentation of mental illness. The high rates of psychiatric co-morbidity among those with FMS increase the credibility of such claims (Hudson and Pope 1989; Wessely and Hotopf 1999). The fact that nearly all those diagnosed with FMS are women results in predictable claims that FMS is the new clinical presentation of hypochondriacity and/or hysteria (Bohr 1995, 1996; Showalter 1997). Even advocates for the diagnostic utility of FMS acknowledge the amorphous nature of the disorder. "Fibromyalgia is simply a label to use when patients have chronic, unexplained diffuse pain," says one leading FMS clinician researcher (Goldenberg 1999:781).

The biomedical uncertainty about FMS stands in sharp contrast to the subjective experiences of individuals diagnosed with FMS. The accounts of sufferers are strikingly vivid and highly compelling (Appeldoorn 1996; Gaston-Johansson et al. 1990; Helistrom et al. 1999). In most cases, the syndrome is experienced as debilitating with social, family, and work life seriously compromised and sometimes destroyed. Still, those diagnosed with FMS understand that, while they recognize their symptoms as unambiguously real, those around them (family members, friends, employers, co-workers, and the medical profession) frequently do not. The outcome of this paradox for many with FMS is that they find themselves in an epistemological purgatory in which they question their own sanity precisely because of their certainty about the realness of their experience in the face of public doubt. This epistemological purgatory is the springboard for the vast self-help and support community that has grown up around FMS. During the last decade several million women have joined local FMS support groups, exchanged information through FMS websites, and read FMS self-help literature. A central aim of this loosely organized community is to address the self-doubt and alienation among FMS sufferers by assuring them of the certainty of their symptoms because others share them.

THE CONCEPT OF ILLNESS IDENTITY

I approach FMS as a product of collective identity formation based on the experience of symptomatic suffering. To facilitate this inquiry, I advance the concept of "illness identity" by (Kleinman 1988). Collective identity formation involves the understanding of self, and affiliation with others, in terms of shared characteristics (boundaries) that mark *us* from *them* (Bourdieu 1984; Cerulo 1997; Lamont 1992; Melucci 1989). Therefore, an illness identity refers to an understanding of self, and affiliation with others, on the basis of shared experiences of symptoms and suffering. Importantly, the theoretical and methodological use of narrative in both the illness experience and identity formation literatures directs us toward the investigation of public illness narratives as cognitive resources facilitating identity formation.

In what follows, I argue that individuals work to remake their life worlds in the face of FMS. They do this, in part, by drawing on the public narratives of the FMS self-help and support community to affirm the "realness" of their experience in the face of its biomedical invisibility. To illustrate this point, I examine the role of FMS self-help literature in facilitating the creation of an FMS illness identity, or an understanding of how their symptom experience links them to others.[5] Lest I be misunderstood, I am not arguing that these books construct FMS in the absence of "real" suffering or that individuals hysterically act out the symptoms about which they read (Showalter 1997). Rather, I seek to illustrate the ways FMS self-help literature creates a public narrative onto which individuals in distress can situate their symptoms to give their illness experience structure, meaning, and legitimacy.

THE FMS SELF-HELP LITERATURE

The self-help literature on fibromyalgia is vast. A search on *Worldcat* (http://www.oclc.org/man/6928fsdb/worldcat.htm) reveals more than 150 self-help books focused on fibromyalgia, most of which have been published since 1996. The top five best sellers as measured by distribution demand in January 2000, are listed in Table 1.[6] Also included are publishers' estimates of total sales (where available). Based on both distribution demand and sales figures, one book clearly stands out as the most widely read FMS self-help book. Devin Starlanyl and contributor Mary Ellen Copeland's *Fibromyalgia and Chronic Myofascial Pain Syndrome: A Survival Manual* (referred to henceforth as *A Survival Manual*) is considered by many "fibromites" (a term introduced by Starlanyl in the text) to be the FMS Bible. *A Survival Manual* has sold more than 300,000 copies since its publication in 1996. Sales figures for all of these books significantly understate readership since many readers gain access to them through their support-group libraries rather than purchasing them individually. Because of its clear dominance I will organize this paper around *A Survival Manual,* but use all five best sellers as evidence for my claims.

Table 13-1. FMS Self-Help Books in Order of Distribution Demand, January 2000

Title	Author(s)	Sales
Fibromyalgia and Chronic Myofascial Pain Syndrome: A Survival Manual	Starlanyl and Copeland (1996)	300,000
Reversing Fibromyalgia	Elrod (1997)	73,000
Fibromyalgia: A Comprehensive Approach	Williamson (1996)	87,000
The Fibromyalgia Help Book: Practical Guide to Living Better with Fibromyalgia	Fransen and Russell (1996)	80,000
The Fibromyalgia Handbook	McIlwain and Bruce (1996)	#

Publisher refused to release sales figures.

All the top sellers summarize the main symptoms of FMS, detail disorders that are similar to and/or coexist with FMS, outline what is currently known about the potential causes of FMS, and summarize current medical treatments, including alternative medicine. Each of the books is devoted to outlining techniques for managing the symptoms and the medical, personal, and workplace struggles related to FMS. It is in this regard, after all, that the texts function as part of the FMS self-help movement. Although all five top sellers cover the general self-help advice listed above, each book has a particular therapeutic approach it promotes. In addition, the books differ in terms of the basis of their authority; some authors are medical professionals, whereas others are individuals with FMS (Devin Starlanyl is an M.D. with FMS). Finally, the books are considered to vary in terms of their legitimacy as evaluated by the FMS medical research and treatment communities, although most FMS readers do not recognize these distinctions. In spite of these variations, the books are remarkably similar in terms of their narrative composite of FMS and this narrative has important implications for shaping FMS as an illness experience.

A PERMISSIVE ILLNESS NARRATIVE: THE SYMPTOMS AND ETIOLOGY

Perhaps the single most obvious observation regarding the FMS self-help literature is the vast number of symptoms that are potentially characteristic of FMS. Formally, pain as defined by the ACR, is the sole diagnostic basis for FMS. In spite of the restricted ACR criterion, all five top sellers detail an expansive FMS symptomology. In *A Survival Manual* the reader is asked 96 questions concerning common FMS symptoms. The sheer number of FMS symptoms revealed in these questions is overwhelming. For example, readers are asked if they experience body aches, fatigue, double-jointedness, allergies, abdominal bloating, difficulty driving at night, illegible handwriting, frequent headaches, shin splints, and fluctuating blood pressure. Additional questions inquire if readers bruise easily, experience frequent frustration, and crave carbohydrates or sweets.

Although the breadth of symptoms presented in *A Survival Manual* is unmatched by other self-help books, the remaining top sellers also present an extensive FMS symptomology. For example, Williamson (1996:vii, 11–13) lists temporomandibular joint dysfunction syndrome (TMJ), sleep disorders, headaches, memory and concentration problems, dizziness, numbness and tingling, itchy and sensitive skin, fluid retention, crampy abdominal and pelvic area, irritable bowel syndrome (IBS) and diarrhea, premenstrual syndrome (PMS), muscle twitching, dry eyes and mouth, impaired coordination, urinary urgency, chest pain, and intermittent hearing loss. Many of these symptoms, plus anxiety and depression are listed in *Reversing Fibromyalgia* and *The Fibromyalgia Handbook,* while *The Fibromyalgia Help Book* adds "swelling sensation of the hands, and sensitivity to cold" (Fransen and Russell 1996:7).

Not only are many of the listed FMS symptoms very common in the general (healthy) public, but threshold levels are either not specified or so low that almost any reader could easily match his or her own experience to the symptom. For example, *The Survival Manual*'s list of question includes: "Do you ever get a stiff neck?", "Do you experience nausea?", and "Do you 'stumble over your own feet'?" (Starlanyl and Copeland 1996:83, 92, 98). In all five top sellers the presentation of common symptoms without stated thresholds of frequency or intensity sets up an illness narrative that may result in the mis- and/or over-attribution of normal physical complaints as FMS symptoms.

In addition to the sheer number of possible FMS symptoms, there are also specific symptoms listed and/or described that raise questions concerning scientific legitimacy. For example, returning to the symptoms listed in the 96 questions presented in *A Survival Manual,* some include opposite effects, or what we might call "either/or symptoms." These include opposite symptom effects within a given individual and/or among those with FMS. For example, it is noted in a discussion concerning susceptibility to infection that those with FMS sometimes don't catch any colds, but then later on, that their "immune system has no success attacking infections at all" (Starlanyl and Copeland 1996:

73). Opposite effects among those with FMS can be seen in the discussion concerning sensitivity to light where the authors claim: "Some fibromites can't go anywhere unless they wear dark glasses. Others have seasonal affective disorder (SAD) and need to experience certain amounts of daylight to prevent depression" (Starlanyl and Copeland 1996:74). In a variation on "either/or symptoms," some symptom questions cover all possible ground, a pattern seen clearly in the description of possible menstrual problems associated with FMS. "Do you have menstrual problems such as severe cramping, delayed periods, irregular periods, long periods with a great deal of bleeding, late periods, missed periods, membranous low, and/or blood clots?" (Starlanyl and Copeland 1996:93). As with the presentation of common symptoms, either/or symptoms create a permissive narrative framework for self-diagnostic confirmation.

Also related to scientific legitimacy, some of the symptoms described in the 96 questions from *A Survival Manual* are odd or paranormal. Some of the most striking examples include: "Do you attract blackflies and mosquitoes?" and "Do you have electromagnetic sensitivity?" (Starlanyl and Copeland 1996:68, 75). The later point, the authors maintain, accounts for otherwise unexplainable interference with the functioning of watches, computers, phones, and VCRs, as well as the enhanced ability of those with FMS to communicate with animals (Starlanyl and Copeland 1996:75). While none of the remaining best sellers describe paranormal symptoms, they do claim that FMS symptoms can appear and then disappear and/or appear and then move around the body. References to paranormal symptoms and to the fleeting and changing nature of symptoms, compromise scientific credibility, while they create a permissive illness narrative.

The self-help literature thus creates a highly permissive symptomological composite of FMS by presenting a vast list of common symptoms, offering no or unclear thresholds for the number or severity of symptoms, and detailing symptoms and symptom characteristics that fall outside (or on the margins) of scientific orthodoxy. Each of these aspects is captured in the following passage from *A Comprehensive Approach:*

> It is important to remember that having one or even a few of these symptoms does not necessarily mean that the diagnosis is fibromyalgia. But if you have low back pain and X-rays show no problem with your spine, and you have what appears to be a bladder infection and the tests come out negative, and you have aches and pains that come and go in various, unpredictable parts of your body—in fact, if you have any combination of symptoms described in this chapter, fibromyalgia may be the cause of your problem (Williamson 1996:13).

In addition to the complex nature of FMS symptoms presented in the self-help literature, the etiological framework uniting the symptoms under a unified diagnosis is also highly confusing. This is due, in part, to the lack of biomedical consensus concerning the cause of FMS. Amidst this biomedical uncertainty the self-help literature is fairly unrestrained in presenting etiological possibilities. This includes describing many possible causal mechanisms that have never been clinically tested and others that have received no empirical support despite substantial inquiry.[7] *A Survival Manual* mentions heredity, sleep abnormalities, "triggering events" (including physical and emotional trauma), behavioral factors, biochemical (including hormonal) changes, immune dysregulation, and environmental disturbances as some of the many possible contributing factors of FMS. The confused nature of FMS onset is captured in the following quote from *A Survival Manual:*

> In FMS, a triggering event often activates biochemical changes, causing a cascade of symptoms. For example, unremitting grief of six months or longer can trigger FMS. It's sort of life "Survivors Syndrome." Cumulative trauma, protracted labor in pregnancy, open-heart surgery; even inguinal hernia repair have all been triggering events for FMS. Life stressors can overwhelm the body's balancing act, turning life itself into an endurance contest. Note, however, that only about 20 percent of FMS cases have a known triggering event that initiates the first obvious *flare* (Starlanyl and Copeland 1996:13–14).

Similarly, from *Reversing Fibromyalgia:*

> [C]lose to 100 percent of the fibromyalgia victims I have personally worked with have all experienced a long period of undue stress or emotional trauma—

> whether it be an automobile accident, divorce, a long illness, growing up in a dysfunctional family, experiencing abuse as a child, or some other type of trauma. It is reported that these triggering events probably do not cause fibromyalgia, but rather they awaken or provoke an underlying physiological abnormality that is already existent (Elrod 1997:16).

Hence, the self-help literature presents a highly confounded etiological framework for FMS. The disorder can be triggered by multiple factors internal and external to the individual (or may not have a trigger at all) and the links between "triggers" and systemic symptoms are unspecified. Consequently, a specific etiological agent, disease onset, or trajectory is not required to confirm the existence of FMS. Together with the symptomological flexibility, the lack of a clear etiological framework creates a highly permissive FMS illness narrative.

FMS, INVISIBILITY, AND REALNESS: UNMAKING AND REMAKING THE LIFE WORLD

Each of the top-selling FMS self-help books addresses the invisibility of FMS in great detail. FMS is invisible in two interrelated ways. First, FMS patients usually look fine and so family members, friends, co-workers, and employers are often skeptical of their complaints. Second, FMS remains invisible biomedically and many physicians and other health care providers respond to those with FMS with skepticism. The ways the invisibility of FMS results in the unmaking of the individual's life world is clearly presented in the self-help literature. From *A Survival Manual:*

> As an FMS patient, you have probably been burdened with a long history of undiagnosed illness. Because your condition is more or less invisible, friends and family may not believe you when you say you hurt, so you may also be suffering from a loss of self-esteem. In other words, you may be deprived of the normal support network that forms around a chronically ill person because "you look just fine." And without the support of family and friends, you may well withdraw from others to conserve what little self-esteem and energy you have left (Starlaynl and Copeland 1996:14).

And from *The Fibromyalgia Help Book:*

> One of the most frustrating aspects of fibromyalgia is that others cannot see or feel the magnitude of the pain you are experiencing. Family or friends may remark about how well you look. This is distressingly inconsistent with how terrible you feel. . . . Thus, fibromyalgia can be described as an invisible, ongoing nightmare that others cannot see or feel. Being trapped in this nightmare may cause you to doubt your own sanity, which may contribute to depression and lead to withdrawal from society into lonely isolation (Fransen and Russell, 1996:5).

As seen in these passages, the lay and medical invisibility of FMS results in the unmaking of the sufferer's life world through the questioning of her subjective experience and the resultant social isolation. Consequently, addressing the gap between the lack of objective indicators of FMS and the subjective experiences of those with FMS is fundamental to the self-help literature. Readers are assured that they are not crazy and that FMS is real. To that end, two interrelated pieces of evidence are repeatedly cited. First, the symptoms of FMS are real because others share them. Second, these shared symptoms are the basis of an established and recognized medical diagnosis.

In the face of social invalidation and isolation, solidarity around shared symptoms confirms the realness of FMS and, therefore, serves as an important resource for remaking the sufferer's life world. This is clearly evident in the following passage from *A Comprehensive Approach:*

> Most importantly, you will know that you are not alone, and that the discomfort you experience is *not* "all in your head." . . . People with fibromyalgia feel better, mentally and physically, when they can share information and support. . . . Hearing from others with similar experiences validates you as a human being and improves your self-esteem (Williamson 1996:3–5).

The self-help literature thus presents the existence of the FMS community as affirmation of the sufferer and the sufferer as affirmation of the FMS community. *A Survival Manual* offers a language for the sense of community among those with FMS: "I coined the word 'FMily' to describe the special bond those of us who have fibromyalgia all share. We often have more in common with our fellow fibromites . . . than we do with members of our family" (Starlanyl and Copeland 1996:8).

The existence of the diagnosis, readers are told, also affirms the realness of their FMS experience. The adoption of FMS by established medical authorities is summed in defense: "The American College of Rheumatology, American Medical Association, World Health Organization, and the National Institutes of Health have all accepted FMS as a legitimate clinical entity. There is no excuse for doctors 'not believing' in its reality. It's real" (Starlanyl and Copeland 1996:13). The diagnosis itself, and being diagnosed in particular, are also key resources for remaking the life world in the face of FMS's invisibility. The naming of the symptoms becomes a type of liberation. A label, a diagnosis, after years of biomedicine's inability to offer confirmation of their subjective experiences, bestows a sense of legitimacy, a profound sense of relief, and a sense of coherence and order. The self-help literature is peppered with accounts of individuals' struggles toward, and relief upon receiving, their FMS diagnosis.

> It isn't unusual for those who are fibromyalgia patients to feel a profound sense of relief when they learn they have a recognized illness and they come to understand that it isn't progressive.
>
> If this has been your experience, you may cry with relief at not having to doubt yourself any longer. At last, someone believes you and believes in you. You really do have these symptoms, and you are no longer fighting the world alone. Debilitating self-doubt can be replaced with appropriate self-care (Starlanyl and Copeland 1996:8).

Even though the diagnosis confirms the existence of what is defined as a chronic illness that is unresponsive to medical treatment, it provides an invaluable refuge. The FMS diagnosis finally provides a narrative for talking about one's body that is in line with one's subjective sense of it. Because it captures this point so well, I quote at length from *A Comprehensive Approach:*

> Fibromyalgia was the reason for my constant muscle aches and joint pains, and for the stabbing pains that from time to time made me catch my breath to keep from crying out. I found that the crampy diarrhea I had when I was younger was probably caused by fibromyalgia. I learned that fibromyalgia was the reason I could swell up like a balloon, gaining as much as five pounds of water weight overnight, usually losing it within a day or two. My poor coordination; the knee that sometimes forgot to catch my weight, landing me in a heap on the ground; the bursitis-like pain that a doctor once told me was all in my head; the sciatica that put me in bed for three months when walking became impossibly painful, although my doctor at the time could see no reason for the pain—these things and many more are associated with fibromyalgia.
>
> I concluded that I had fibromyalgia since childhood. As a little girl, I was teased to the point of despair by schoolmates, teachers, and family for my clumsiness and poor coordination. When I told my mother about my aches, she merely replied that pain was a normal part of living and that I should stop complaining. My adulthood was no better. . . . Doctors labeled me a hypochondriac and offered tranquilizers, sleeping pills, and psychiatric referrals (Williamson 1996:2–3).

Hence, as a diagnosis, FMS creates a flexible narrative framework for making sense of extreme pain and suffering, but bends to incorporate the minor frustrations of everyday life. Its unbound nature offers a narrative in which to situate symptoms across one's life course ranging from the profound to the trivial—a childhood of suffering, abuse, and alienation; an adulthood marked by forgetting needed items at the grocery store or spilling food on a favorite outfit (Starlanyl and Copeland 1996:171, 157). The diagnostic narrative of FMS thus offers a way of "remaking" the world by creating an overarching framework that gives order and meaning to past, present, and future symptomology (broadly defined). Said more sociologically, the diagnostic narrative of FMS functions as a narrative of selfhood.

THE SPECIFIC/UNSPECIFIABLE PARADOX OF FMS

This sets up perhaps the most fascinating aspect of the FMS narrative presented in the self-help literature (and present in the FMS self-help and support communities more generally) and brings us back full circle to FMS as an illness identity. FMS is both specific and unspecifiable. Even a quick reading of any of the self-help books will reveal a tension between these two potentially contradictory claims. On one hand, the boundaries of FMS are discrete and identifiable (the ACR criteria). On the other hand, each individual's FMS is unique in terms of onset, intensity, duration, and which symptoms (beyond pain as defined by the ACR criteria) from the extensive list of symptoms are experienced. For example, from *A Comprehensive Approach*: "The important thing to remember as you read the discussion of signs and symptoms is that no two people experience fibromyalgia in the exactly the same way" (Williamson 1996:8). A few pages later in this text Williamson (1996:10) extends her point by evoking the legendary blind men and the elephant: "Fibromyalgia is a lot like that elephant. Each of us who has FM experiences it slightly differently, depending on which symptoms we find most distressing. . . . Each of us has a part of the truth, but none of us sees the whole disorder." Whereas Williamson (1996:13) tells readers they may have fibromyalgia if they have any combination of symptoms described in her book, Starlanyl and Copeland (1996:104) warn readers that even their 96 symptom questions capture "by no means all of the possible symptoms associated with FMS."

The tension between the specific and unspecific nature of FMS in the self-help literature simultaneously creates a narrative of selfhood and a collective identity. On the one hand, the self-help literature presents FMS as a vast collection of ubiquitous and vague symptoms not restricted to a specific beginning (etiology or onset), intensity (severity), or trajectory (symptom course). Nearly any combination, order, and intensity of symptoms (even normal symptoms or symptoms not presented in the text) can be situated within the FMS narrative. Beyond the ACR criteria (themselves controversial), no specific standards exist by which an individual's symptoms or symptom course would disconfirm the existence of FMS. Within the self-help literature, the reader finds a highly permissive narrative that offers many points of entry, tremendous flexibility, and few thresholds of exclusion. This unspecified or unbound narrative therefore creates flexibility to account for the uniqueness of an individual's life, a unique narrative of selfhood.

On the other hand, this unbound nature gets collapsed and dissimilar experiences get organized under a unified diagnosis of FMS.

> Forty-one-year old Janis told of hurting everywhere on her body; even sitting in a straight-back chair brought tears to her eyes. Sarah, a young mother of two, felt throbbing pain all over her body as well as disturbances in deep-level, restful sleep, accompanied by sadness or depression. Mike felt a piercing pain in his neck and shoulder, accompanied by sluggishness that came on suddenly after a car accident. While these patients had different manifestations of pain and fatigue, the symptoms were all the result of fibromyalgia (McIlwain and Bruce 1996:8).

The FMS illness narrative presented in the self-help literature is, thus, simultaneously a permissive and homogenizing narrative. Dissimilar experiences are tied together under the diagnostically bound narrative of FMS, which, in turn, allows individuals to embrace a common identity as fibromyalgic. In other words, self-help literature, as a public narrative, facilitates the construction of a distinctly *collective* FMS illness identity that links an individual to others through a set of FMS symptoms and channels them into a new subjectivity focused on their illness and its management.

THE INTERVIEWS: READING FMS SELF-HELP BOOKS

I now turn to interviews with women diagnosed with FMS to address how FMS sufferers read these texts into their lived illness experiences and how their lived experiences are read onto these texts. Interviews took two forms. Six women attending a regular support-group meeting were interviewed in one focus group in which questions were limited to their reading of FMS self-help literature generally, and *A Survival Manual* in particular. Twenty women (one of whom also participated in the focus group) were interviewed about their FMS experience generally in which questions about the role this literature played in their illness experience were but a small component.[8] Ten of these were contacted through FMS support groups listed with the state Arthritis Foundation; eight responded to a flyer distributed at a conference co-sponsored by the foundation and a university-based fibromyalgia research organization; and two were referred by a nurse practitioner who attended the conference. The sample includes women from diverse communities, including a large metropolitan area, a mid-sized university town, and several small, semi-rural communities. Twelve women had attended FMS support groups regularly, while thirteen had not. Demographically, the sample compares closely in terms of age, race, and education to the distributions reported in previous community prevalence studies (White et al. 1999; Wolfe et al. 1995), suggesting that it is not unrepresentative of the distribution of FMS in the population at large.

The organizing questions of the focus group interview were: "What did you think the first time you read *A Survival Manual*?", "In what ways, if any, did the book help you make sense of or help you deal with your fibromyalgia?", "How well does the book describe your own experience with FMS?", "What other FMS self-help books have you read and how have they helped you make sense of your FMS?" In the semi-structured interviews, the participants were asked if they had read any self-help books, which ones they read, what they got from the books, and which ones they liked and why.[9]

Respondents differed in terms of their level of engagement with self-help literature. Still, only one of the 25 women interviewed said she never read any FMS self-help books (Phyllis, 62). Even this woman said she relied on educational handouts provided by her support group leader, which offered summaries of lay and medical FMS publications. In contrast, most common response to questions concerning FMS self-help books was: "I've read almost everything on the market" (Sally, 36); "I've read just about everything out there" (Wendy, 48); "I read everything I can get my hands on" (Alice, 49); and "I've probably read them all" (Evelyn, 38). Indeed, most of those interviewed had read many self-help literature shaped their own experience with FMS. One woman read several FMS self-help books and were quick to pull several from shelves during the interview. In line with national sales figures, by far the most commonly mentioned book was *A Survival Manual.*

The respondents also differed in terms of how much they thought the self-help books early in her illness, but found them depressing and discouraging and, hence, paid them little attention (Emily, 28). A second routinely read the FMS medical literature and, by comparison, judged most self-help books, with the exception of *The Fibromyalgia Help Book,* to contain misinformation (Paula, 51). Two others (Courtney, 55; Meredith, 55) read several books, but could no longer recall any specific details, lapses they both attributed to their "fibrofog," a term first introduced in *A Survival Manual.* In contrast, most of those spoke about being positively and deeply effected by the FMS self-help literature and focused on the importance of *A Survival Manual* in particular. As a group, the interviewees provided clear evidence of drawing on this text (and others) to organize and give meaning to their own symptoms and to affirm the "realness" of their subjective experience in the face of biomedical uncertainty.

Interviewees were amazed at how well the details in *A Survival Manual* fit their own experiences. Most felt surprisingly understood, as though someone finally witnessed the nature of their experience. One woman concisely captured this common feeling: "Well, parts of the book honestly read as if someone was following me around with a movie camera" (Laura, 48). Others captured the common process of reading through the book, page by page, and finding one's symptoms. "It was funny, when I first got the book I took a highlighter and marked the things that I had and after three pages the whole thing was marked. I'm a classic case" (Alice 49). "There was a lot of stuff in there that I could identify about myself. Like, oh yes! I have this, and I have that, this symptom, and that problem, and so forth" (Ellen, 35).

From the vast list provided in *A Survival Manual,* interviewees identified their unique symptoms. For example, one woman provided insight into how she found her experiences in the text: "Just thumbing through the book while we are talking . . . pages 95 through 122 . . . I have something just like it or similar. Parts of each question I can pick up on. . . . I can see myself in different parts of the book" (Joan, 53). Implicit in this and other statements made by interviewees is how the permissive narrative allowed them to select those symptoms that were most salient to them without excluding themselves for failing to display the vastness of the symptom composite. In large measure this had to do with the widespread understanding that no two people express FMS the same way. This understanding was captured by many: "We don't have the same symptoms. Everyone is different, but we have stuff in common. The book [*A Survival Manual*] explains that" (Sally, 36). Similarly, "I am not saying we all have the same symptoms or even the same symptoms in the same order and that is what is so frustrating to the doctors. You need to find a doctor who will put all your medical history together like Devin does in this book" (Wendy, 48).

Interviewees found symptom after symptom captured on page after page of *A Survival Manual*. But more importantly, the FMS narrative provided them with the tools to organize and make sense of their seemingly unrelated, unexplained, and distressing symptoms; these symptoms are all apart of a coherent whole—FMS.

> For me the image of connect-the-dots comes to mind. She has taken all of these symptoms that you can look at as little dots and she ties them altogether with me at the center. . . . Dry eyes, irritable bowel syndrome, and irritable bladder syndrome. She has taken all of these symptoms and made sense of them (Rachel, 51).

Similarly:

> TMJ, the pain, the concentration, the memory, vision, irritable bowel, irritable bladder, it [*A Survival Manual*] goes on and on and on. Dermatitis, athlete's foot . . . it all connects right back to fibromyalgia. . . . It's stuff that none of us realized was part of it . . . they are all a part of FMS (Wendy, 48).

As revealed in these quotes, the FMS narrative provides a framework for incorporating a large number of common symptoms into a unified whole, and, in the process, gives them meaning. Readers are encouraged to be mindful of the vast number of complaints attributable to FMS, or "stuff that none of us realized was part of it." The following is a powerful example of how this dynamic unfolds:

> I was reading about it one night, about how black flies are attracted to the skin. . . . I was sitting on the couch and I just started crying because I have had that problem for ten years probably. When there are flies in an area, they'll always land on me . . . it just bowled me over. I mean, what a weird thing. . . . I couldn't believe it when I read it after having that problem for so many years (Doris, 61).

As seen in this response, the highly permissive FMS narrative allows a reader tremendous flexibility to organize "symptoms" within its boundaries. In turn, this permissive narrative creates the possibility of mis- and/or over-attribution of normal physical complaints as FMS symptoms. For instance one woman talked about how the book gave her tools to challenge someone who doubted the importance of her seemingly common symptoms. "When someone says 'it is just a bruise' you can say 'no' in your own words by using the book, because the book is your own words" (Joan, 53).

The self-help books taught interviewees that other common complaints such as tripping (Sally, 36), spilling food (Laura, 48), and transposing numbers (Christina, 29) were, indeed, related to their FMS. Likewise, one woman recalled her experience reading *A Survival Manual*: "I had totally forgotten about fibrofog. I just thought I was having a succession of senior moments, . . . but actually there is a reason for this. . . . It is part of FMS" (Pamela, 54). As seen in this comment, the book provides a framework for re-specifying complaints commonly associated with normal aging as FMS symptoms. Another telling example: "Your eyes—everyone says it's just because you're over 40, but that's not it. My vision has changed drastically. . . . She [Devin] goes into all of that in the book" (Wendy, 48).

The women interviewed had years of unexplainable symptoms for which to account. On average they experienced seven years of acute symptoms before being diagnosed,[10] and an average of 16 years separated the onset of their first symptoms and their diagnosis. This reality, read onto the highly ambiguous etiological framework presented in the self-help literature, facilitated the organization of symptoms and experiences into an extensive life-narrative. Many of those interviewed were able to retrospectively see the thread of FMS throughout their lives: "I mean, now that I read things about it, I think this started when I was real little, *real* little" (Phyllis, 62). "Now that I understand fibromyalgia, I think I've probably had it since high school" (Valerie, 49).

The etiological latitude set up in the self-help literature allows individuals to frame years of somatic distress as possible causes for, and outcomes of, their FMS. The following is an illustration of the far-reaching potential the FMS narrative to retrospectively give meaning to years of distress. In reference to *A Survival Manual*:

> It's *me* in that book. My life is that book. It told me so much about myself. I was flabbergasted. . . . I witnessed a traumatic event when I was only ten months old. They say I suffer from PTSD because of this. I don't remember because I was a baby, but I was subconsciously affected. . . . In seventh and eighth grade, I was having a lot of accidents and breaking bones. By the time I was 17 . . . it really intensified. . . . I had lots of injuries, two abusive relationships, had some other traumatic things happen, deaths in the family, so it could've been aggravated by any of that. Then I got real sick. . . . I was sick from December until the end of March with flu and a sinus infection. Exactly four years later, three days after my car accident, the same thing happened. . . . I went through the same thing. I was sick for three months. . . . I went through all these long illnesses and it was because of my FMS (Ellen, 35).

Research on sufferers of multiple chemical sensitivity (MCS) finds that individuals struggle to create a "practical epistemology" or a way of making sense of their "obscure bodies" in the context of professional biomedicine's confusion about the disorder (Kroll-Smith and Floyd 1997:11). As shown by such research, despite the lack of scientific support for MCS, as a cognitive framework it is logically consistent with experienced distress. In a similar fashion, it is evident that FMS offers a practical, subjectively logical, account of somatic distress. One woman offered a particularly telling example of how an extensive history of distress becomes practically framed through the FMS narrative:

> I think I had this when I was a kid. I was abused. I remember telling my mother that I ached and hurt. I did a whole series of paintings when I was a kid about having no arms and legs because I couldn't get comfortable at night. My mother used to say "it's growing pains, you're neurotic, I am going to send you to a psychiatrist." . . . Then I had that back injury and I've been in pain ever since. . . . I've been on the verge of suicide, of wanting to kill myself, but not wanting to die. . . . I've been in pain for years . . . and now I know what it is. . . . The fact there's a book out there validates the things I've been going through for years (Maude, 49).

The FMS public narrative provided a practical, logical, and validating account of readers' symptoms. Seeing their experiences described and explained on the pages of a book was of tremendous importance to nearly all of those interviewed. As noted, most had endured a long period during which no one understood or, indeed, believed their experiences. Moreover, most questioned their own sanity given that no explanation could be given for their deeply felt distress. Not only did the self-help literature make interviewees finally feel understood by someone else (indeed an entire community), it also provided a framework of self-understanding after a long period of self-doubt. Interviewees read *A Survival Manual* and other self-help books as self-validation and confirmation of the realness of FMS: "There were some chapters that would reduce me to tears . . . because this is exactly what my life is like. That helped from the standpoint that this has not been my imagination" (Laura, 48). Similarly:

> I validated that there was something out there. Other people knew what you were going through. . . . There were so many things going on with me that I started to think that maybe I am a hypochondriac. When I read the book, it helped me understand that I am not crazy; I am not imagining this. It is real. It made me feel better to know that it is real and not all just in my head (Christina, 29).

As attested here, there is an important link between self-validation, community, and the "realness" of FMS. This link functions as a resource in remaking the life world in the face of biomedical uncertainty. "It helped me just in terms of my own psychological ability to cope with this because it offers validation that this is real and that you're not nuts and that there are other people that are dealing with it and coping with it" (Hanna, 52). The diagnostic solidarity of symptoms and sufferers forms the basis of FMS illness identity. Readers come to understand that they are linked to others symptomatically and this link offers validation of symptoms and self. Or, as one of the interviewees said of *A Survival Manual,* "I think I speak for all of us when I say . . . it made everything that we have real! Devin's book, and some of the other fibromyalgia books, have brought us all together" (Wendy, 48).

CONCLUSION

Although I have limited my focus to the role of self-help literature in the making of an FMS illness identity, what I have described represents a specific instance of a more general, and increasingly common, phenomenon—namely, the role of self-help communities and resources in illness identity formation. As seen in the case of FMS, an important part of the illness experience is the search to give meaning to symptoms and a recasting of the self in relation to illness. Individuals read their unique personal experiences from and onto the pages of FMS self-help books. While the narrative gives order and meaning to individual suffering, the process of leveling homogenizes varied experiences among individuals into a discrete FMS illness identity. As a public narrative, the FMS self-help literature thus provides a cognitive resource through which individual experience is given meaning and a collective illness identity is established.

There are particular features that characterize the FMS illness experience, but the search for illness coherence and selfhood is culturally pervasive and, therefore, part of the experience of any serious or prolonged illness. Likewise, particular features of the FMS illness experience encourage the coming together of individual sufferers, but this trend, too, is becoming increasingly widespread as self-help communities have grown up around myriad chronic illnesses (Davison, Pennebaker, and Dickerson 2000). This is dramatically seen in the proliferation of Internet newsgroups, bulletin boards, listserves, and chat rooms devoted to illness. Drawing upon these resources, individuals work to remake their life worlds in the face of chronic illness, and, in the process, their search for symptom meaning and self-meaning becomes increasingly collective in nature.

The appeal of self-help communities is not just in avoiding having to face one's illness alone. After all, one can and frequently does draw upon existing support networks when confronting a serious or chronic illness. Rather, the appeal is being able to face one's illness in the company of those who understand one's experience because they share that experience. In this way, illness becomes a bond of affiliation. For example, *WebMD,* one of the most popular health-related Internet sites, provides *Member Columns* where sufferers of common conditions come together to share their firsthand knowledge of living with specific chronic illnesses. *Member Columns* opens:

> It can be of great comfort to know that someone else understands what you're going through—they've "been there," or are there, now. Here you'll find *community* and a personal perspective, as members generously share their stories and insights on what it's like to live with one of the health conditions listed below. Tell us your story! (WebMD 2002, emphasis added).

Visitors to *Member Columns* are invited to affiliate on the basis of illness. They can scroll down to their condition, click on the link, and move through a collection of illness stories into which they can simultaneously locate their individual experience and find an illness community. As this example suggests, the dynamics described in the case of FMS are potentially applicable to illness identity formation more generally. Seeing your experiences described on a book page or computer screen can be of tremendous importance to anyone struggling with the consequences of chronic illness. It signifies being understood by others (a community) and, therefore, offers a forum for self-understanding amidst the "biographical disruptions" (Bury 1982) that chronic illness brings. In this way, self-help resources provide public narratives for the acquisition of collective illness identities.

Given the increasing prevalence of illness affiliation and illness identity within our culture, sociologists would do well to direct their efforts toward understanding the social consequences of this phenomenon. As the case of FMS illustrates, these consequences can be both positive and negative. Specifically, while illness affiliation offers FMS sufferers general support and encouragement, the new subjectivities that it propagates can significantly accelerate the already strong trend toward *medicalization*. As defined by Conrad (1992:209): "Medicalization describes a process by which non-medical problems become defined and treated as medical problems, usually in terms of illnesses or disorders." A compelling argument can be made that FMS represents the medicalization of women's broadly felt distress in a cultural context where distress and illness are understood and experienced as virtually synonymous. By drawing on the case of FMS, we can thus begin to specify the links between self-help communities, illness identities, and medicalization more generally.

The medicalization of experiences that are not fully (or even partially) medical, is not primarily the result of professionalization of "medical imperialism" (Conrad and Potter 2000). As the case of FMS shows, a key element in the process of medicalization is the coming together of sufferers within self-help communities to translate their individual experiences of distress into shared expressions of illness. Because of the benefits of medicalization to the individual (e.g., the extension of cultural meaning and legitimacy to suffering, exemption from personal responsibility, and access to resources that promise to lessen distress) it makes sense that FMS self-help communities would promote medicalization. On the other hand, the medicalization of women's distress may deter us from a developing a more sociologically informed understanding of the embodied nature of gender relations, which is made evident by the feminization of FMS, and, ultimately, from politicizing the broader social forces that contribute to the production and reproduction of women's distress in our society. As Riessman (1983) argues, when women historically have pushed for the medicalization of their needs, this process has most often led to the co-optation and depoliticization of their demands.

As revealed in the case of FMS, the narratives encountered in self-help literature can promote medicalization by encouraging the framing of everyday frustrations as "symptomatic" of illness. Self-help advice can also increase anxiety over minor changes in one's condition, leading to an increase in health care-seeking behavior. A particularly pernicious version of the self-help literature is the "what your doctor may not tell you about your illness" genre. Dozens of best-selling self-help books explain why doctors, for various reasons, are unable or unwilling to tell you (or give you) what you need to protect your own health.[11] Although this builds on a populist impulse and a distrust of experts, the advice promoted rarely suggests that individuals avoid seeking medical care. More often it coaches them to be assertive and demanding consumers of orthodox and alternative health care resources, often promoting a particular treatment regime linked to the author's economic interests. Self-help literature with a "what your doctor may not tell you" focus is likely to further solidify illness identities as individuals come to understand that they are, as a group, oppositionally positioned in relation to doctors who cannot be fully trusted.

In conclusion, through real and virtual self-help communities, sufferers shape the boundaries of their illness experience. They share and define symptoms, assess the merits of competing etiological paradigms and treatment options, make demands for public awareness, fight for public and private funds to advance research and treatment, and support each other by sharing personal struggles and victories. Self-help communities simultaneously give meaning to individual experiences and bind individuals together through diagnoses, symptoms, suffering, and an emerging sense of shared interests. Whether as fibromyalgics, breast cancer survivors, depressives, anorexics, or AIDS survivors, illness identities channel individuals into new subjectivities focused on their illness and its management. We will need to better understand the social consequences of illness identities as the lay public becomes increasingly involved in collectively defining their illnesses. In particular, we will need to be mindful of the potential here for the medicalization of social and personal problems, discontent, and distress. To what extent do self-help communities contribute to a cultural milieu that encourages framing individual hardships and shortcomings as illnesses? In what ways do illness identities run the risk of depoliticizing the forces that create ill health or other distress by locating the origins of our problems within our individual, rather than our social body? These are vital questions for future research.

NOTES

The author thanks Natalie Boero for assisting with interviews and transcriptions, as well as sharing her insights throughout this project. Thanks are also extended to Barbara Seidman for her helpful feedback on an earlier version of this paper. I have benefited greatly from detailed and thoughtful suggestions from the editor, editorial board, and anonymous reviewers at *Social Problems*. Finally, and most important, I thank the women who shared their FMS experiences with me. I hope they understand that I believe their experience is real even while I am critical of its narrow biomedical framing. Please direct all correspondence to Kristin Barker, Dept. of Sociology and Anthropology, Linfield College, McMinnville, OR 97128. E-mail: kbarker@linfield.edu.

1. A leading FMS clinician and researcher, Dr. Robert Bennett of the Oregon Fibromyalgia Foundation (2000), sets the female-to-male ratio of FMS at 20:1. Epidemiological studies done at the community level show less dramatic ratios, ranging from 3:1 (White et al. 1999) to 7:1 (Wolfe et al. 1995).
2. The similarities and overlap between FMS and a host of other functional somatic syndromes or medically unexplainable physical symptoms (irritable bowel syndrome, premenstrual syndrome, repetitive strain injury, multiple chemical sensitivity, and temporomandibular disorder) have been ably documented (Manu 1998; Wessely and Hotopf 1999; Wessely, Nimnuan, and Sharpe 1999). Some argue they are linked by a shared but unknown organic pathology (Russell 1999); others maintain that these disorders are in whole or in part somatic presentations of depression or some other shared psychiatric illness (Manu 1998); still others argue that the specialty of the diagnosing physician determines which diagnosis is evoked to describe what is essentially a shared type of illness behavior (Barsky and Borus 1999; Wessely, Nimnuan, and Sharpe 1999).
3. It is important to make the following distinctions. FMS is biomedically invisible, not invisible in biomedicine. While there are no objective indicators of the disorder, FMS is highly visible in terms of medical publications. Well over 1,000 medical journal articles on FMS have appeared since 1975.
4. Regarding etiology, there is disagreement about the influence of physiological and/or psychiatric factors. Biochemical, hormonal, and neurotransmitter abnormalities, as well as physical injury and viral exposure, are among the identified possible physiological causes (Bennett et al. 1997; Goldenberg 1993; Pillemer et al. 1997). Emotional trauma, anxiety, and affective disorders are among the identified possible psychiatric influences (Hudson and Pope 1989, 1995). There is currently no efficacious treatment for FMS, although some drug, educational/behavioral, and exercise therapies have provided minimal recompense (Goldenberg 1999).
5. There is precedent for using self-help books as primary data in sociological research. For example, Hochschild (1994) provides a systematic analysis of best-selling women's advice books; Ryan, Wentworth, and Chapman (1994) examine top-selling therapeutic books; and Markens (1996) investigators self-help books relating to PMS.
6. These books are ranked based on information provided by a major U.S. book distributor. We have used distribution demand rankings in addition to sales figures provided by publishers because one publisher refused to provide sales data. Additionally, marketing incentives sometimes lead publishers to inflate reported sales. Distributors are not influenced by such incentives since the books they distribute are not their own. Distributors provide data that reflect not sales per se, but the distribution of books (presumably a response to demand). As seen in Table 1, there is general agreement between distribution demand and sales figures, the main exception being the placement of Elrod's, *Reversing Fibromyalgia* (ranked higher in distribution demand than in sales).
7. Williamson (1996) lists metabolic dysfunction, immune disorder, heredity, illness or injury, and prolonged stress as possible causes. McIlwain and Bruce (1996) mention a cycle of disturbed sleep, reduced physical activity, depression, and pain, as well as menopause, aging, serotonin deficiency, and post-viral effects. The most medically orthodox of the texts primarily addresses neurotransmitter abnormalities that may explain the distortion of pain perception characteristic of FMS, but also mentions muscle abnormalities,

physical trauma, emotional trauma, depression and stress (Fransen and Russell 1996:18–30).

8. The author and Natalie Boero jointly conducted two of the interviews. Boero did nine interviews independently. The author conducted the remaining interviews, including the focus group interview.
9. Although not the empirical approach used in the paper, one can also see parallels between the stories told by the women interviewees and the narratives presented in best-selling books. The telling of experiences within the cyclical framework of intense "flares" brought on by "triggers" is an obvious case in point. For example, the following description of flares in *A Survival Manual* closely parallels two of the women's accounts. "Flares are usually triggered by one or more activities or stressors. It might be something microscopically small, such as a virus . . . or something large and dramatic, such as a traffic accident" (Starlanyl and Copeland 1996: 127). From Sally: "It was my first flare. I don't know what caused it. It was such a long time ago, but it can be anything like the flu or a injury, like from a car accident." From Suzanne: "Sometimes it doesn't take anything real big and sometimes it is something big and traumatic, a car accident or different things." There are many similar examples in which women are clearly appropriating the narrative framework presented in the self-help books to organize their own FMS story.
10. This finding is consistent with other research indicating an average of five to seven years of acute symptoms prior to be diagnosed with FMS (Goldenberg 1999).
11. A few titles include: *What Your Doctor May Not Tell You about Living with Fibromyalgia; What Your Doctor May Not Tell You about Menopause;* and *What Your Doctor May Not Tell You about Breast Cancer.*

REFERENCES

Appeldoorn, Marit Elise. (1996). The Curious Paradox of Pain: An Exploratory Study of the Use of Mutual Aid Groups by Women Living with Fibromyalgia Syndrome. M.A. Thesis, Department of Social Work, Smith College, Northhampton, MA.

Aronowitz, Robert A. (1992). "From myalgic encephalitis to yuppie flu: A history of chronic fatigue syndromes." In *Framing Disease: Studies in Cultural History,* Charles E. Rosenberg and Janet Golden, eds., 155–181. New Brunswick, NJ: Rutgers University Press.

Banks, Jonathan, and Lindsay Prior. (2001). "Doing things with illness: the micro politics of the CFS clinic." *Social Science and Medicine* 52:11–23.

Barsky, Arthur J., and Jonathen F. Borus. (1999). "Functional somatic syndromes." *Annuals of Internal Medicine* 130:910–921.

Bennett Robert M., David M. Cook, Sharon R. Clark, Carol S. Burckhardt, and Stephen M. Campbell. (1997). "Hypothalamic-pituitary-insulin-like growth factor-I axis dysfunction in patients with fibromyalgia." *Journal of Rheumatology* 24:1384–1389.

Bohr, Thomas. (1995). "Fibromyalgia syndrome and myofascial pain syndrome: Do they exist?" *Neurological Clinics* 13:365–384.

———. (1996). "Problems with myofascial pain syndrome and fibromyalgia syndrome." *Neurology* 46:593–597.

Borkman, Thomasina. (1999). *Understanding Self-help/Mutual Aid: Experiential Learning in the Commons.* New Brunswick, NJ: Rutgers University Press.

Bourdieu, Pierre. (1984). *Distinctions: A Social Critique of Judgment and Taste.* Cambridge, MA: Harvard University Press.

Broom, Dorothy, and Roslyn Woodward. (1996). "Medicalisation reconsidered: Toward a collaborative approach to care." *Sociology of Health and Illness* 18, 3:357–378.

Brumberg, Joan Jacobs. (1992). "From psychiatric syndrome to 'communicable' disease: The case of anorexia nervosa." In *Framing Disease: Studies in Cultural History,* Charles Rosenberg and Janet Golden, eds., 134–154. New Brunswick, NJ: Rutgers University Press.

Burrows, Roger, Sarah Nettleton, Nicholas Pleace, Brian Loader, and Steven Muncer. (2000). "Virtual community care? Social policy and the emergence of computer mediated social support." *Information, Communication and Society* 3, 1:95–121.

Bury, Michael. (1982). "Chronic illness as biographical disruption." *Sociology of Health and Illness* 4, 2:167–182.

Cain, Carole (1991). "Personal stories: Identity acquisition and self-understanding in Alcoholics Anonymous." *Ethos* 19, 2:210–253.

Cerulo, Karen. (1997). "Identity construction: New issues, new directions." *Annual Review of Sociology* 23:385–409.

Charmaz, Kathy. (1991). *Good Days, Bad Days: The Self in Chronic Illness and Time.* New Brunswick, NJ: Rutgers University Press.

Clauw, Daniel J. (1995). "The pathogenesis of chronic pain and fatigue syndromes, with special reference to fibromyalgia." *Medical Hypotheses* 44, 5:369–378.

Conrad, Peter. (1987). "The experience of illness: Recent and new directions." *Research in the Sociology of Health Care* 6:1–31.

———. (1992). "Medicalization and social control." *Annual Review of Sociology* 18:209–232.

Conrad, Peter, and Deborah Potter. (2000). "From hyperactive children to ADHD adults: Observations on the expansion of medical categories." *Social Problems* 447, 4:559–582.

Cooper, Lesley. (1997). "Myalgic encephalomyelitis and the medical encounter." *Sociology of Health and Illness* 19, 2:186–207.

Copenhagen Declaration. (1992). "Fibromyalgia: The Copenhagen Declaration." *Lancet* 340, 8827:1103.

Davison, Kathryn, James Pennebaker, and Sally Dickerson. (2000). "Who talks: The social psychology of illness support groups." *American Psychologist* 55, 2:205–217.

Elrod, Joe. (1997). *Reversing Fibromyalgia*. Pleasant Grove, UT: Woodland Publishing.

Eng, Thomas. (2001). *The Ehealth Landscape: A Terrain Map of Emerging Information and Communication Technologies in Health and Health Care.* Princeton, NJ: Robert Wood Johnson Foundation.

Ezzy, Douglas. (2000). "Illness narratives: Time, hope and HIV." *Social Science and Medicine* 50:605–617.

Foucault, Michel. (1973). *The Birth the Clinic: An Archaeology of Medical Perception.* New York: Vintage Books.

Frank, Arthur W. (1991). *At the Will of the Body: Reflections on Illness.* Boston, Houghton Mifflin.

———. (1995). *The Wounded Storyteller: Body, Illness, and Ethics.* Chicago: University of Chicago Press.

Fransen, Jenny, and I. Jon Russell. (1996). *The Fibromyalgia Help Book: Practical Guide to Living Better with Fibromyalgia.* St. Paul, MN: Smith House Press.

Garro, Linda. (1992). "Chronic illness and the construction of narratives." In *Pain as Human Experience: An Anthropological Perspective,* Mary-Jo DelVecchio Good, Paul E. Brodwin, Byron J. Good, and Arthur Kleinman, eds., 100–137. Berkeley: University of California Press.

———. (1994). "Narrative representations of chronic illness experience: Cultural models of illness, mind, and body in stories concerning the temporomandibular joint (TMJ)." *Social Science and Medicine* 38, 6:775–788.

Guston-Johansson, Fannie, Marianne, Gustafsson, Ruth Felldin, and Harold Sanne. (1990). "A comparative study of feelings, attitudes and behaviors of patients with fibromyalgia and rheumatoid arthritis." *Social Science and Medicine* 31, 8:941–947.

Goldenberg, Don L. (1993). "Do infections trigger fibromyalgia?" *Arthritis and Rheumatism* 36:1489–1492.

———. (1999). "Fibromyalgia syndrome a decade later: What have we learned?" *Archives of Internal Medicine* 159:777–785.

Goldenberg, Don L., Robert W. Simms, A. Geiger, and Anthony L. Komaroff. (1990). "High frequency of fibromyalgia in patients with chronic fatigue seen in a primary care practice." *Arthritis and Rheumatism* 33:381–387.

Good, Byron. (1994). *Medicine, Rationality, and Experience: An Anthropological Perspective.* New York: Cambridge University Press.

Good, Mary-Jo DelVecchio, Paul E. Brodwin, Byron Good, and Arthur Kleinman, eds. (1992). *Pain as Human Experience: An Anthropological Perspective.* Berkeley: University of California Press.

Helistrom, Olle, Jennifer Bullington, Gunnar Karlsson, Per Lindqvist, and Bengt Mattsson. (1999). "A phenomenological study of fibromyalgia: Patient perspectives." *Scandanavian Journal of Primary Health Care* 17, 1:11–16.

Hilbert, Richard. (1984). "The acultural dimensions of chronic pain: flawed reality construction and the problem of meaning." *Social Problems* 31, 4:365–378.

Hochschild, Arlie Russell. (1994). "The commercial spirit of intimate life and the abduction of feminism: Signs from women's advice books." *Theory, Culture and Society* 11, 2:1–24.

Hudson, James I., and Harrison G. Pope, Jr. (1989). "Fibromyalgia and psychopathology: Is fibromyalgia a form of affective spectrum disorder?" *Journal of Rheumatology Supplement* 19:15–22.

———. (1995). "Does childhood sexual abuse cause fibromyalgia?" *Arthritis and Rheumatism* 38:161–163.

Hyden, Lars-Christer, and Lisbeth Sachs. (1998). "Suffering, hope and diagnosis: On the negotiation of chronic fatigue syndrome." *Health* 2, 2:175–193.

Irvine, Leslie. (1999). *Codependent Forevermore: The Invention of Self in a Twelve Step Group.* Chicago: University of Chicago Press.

Kleinman, Arthur. (1986). *Social Origins of Distress and Disease: Neurasthenia, Depression, and Pain in Modern China.* New Haven, CT: Yale University Press.

———. (1988). *The Illness Narratives: Suffering, Healing, and the Human Condition.* New York: Basic Books.

Kleinman, Arthur, and Norma C. Ware. (1992). "Culture and somatic experience: The social course of illness in neurasthenia and chronic fatigue syndrome." *Psychosomatic Medicine* 54:546–560.

Kroll-Smith, Steve, and H. Huge Floyd. (1997). *Bodies in Protest: Environmental Illness and the Struggle over Medical Knowledge.* New York: New York University Press.

Kugelmann, Robert. (1999). "Complaining about chronic pain." *Social Science and Medicine* 49, 1663–1676.

Lamont, Michele. (1992). *Money, Morals, and Manners: The Culture of the French and the American Upper Middle Class.* Chicago: University of Chicago Press.

Manu, Peter, ed. (1998). *Functional Somatic Syndromes: Etiology, Diagnosis and Treatment.* New York: Cambridge University Press.

Markens, Susan. (1996). "The problematic of experience: A political and cultural critique of PMS." *Gender and Society* 10, 1:42–58.

Mathews, Holly F., Donald Lannin, and James Mitchell. (1994). "Coming to terms with advanced breast cancer: Black women's narratives from eastern North Carolina." *Social Science and Medicine* 38, 6:789–800.

McIlwain, Harris, and Debra Fulghum Bruce. (1996). *The Fibromyalgia Handbook.* New York: Henry Holt.

Melucci, Alberto. (1988). "Getting involved: Identity and mobilization in social movements." *From Structure to Action: Comparing Social Movement Research Across Cultures.* In Bert Klandermans, Kriesi Hanspeter, and Sidney Tarrow, eds., 329–348. Greenwich, CT: JAI Press.

———. (1989). *Nomads of the Present: Social Movements and Individuals Needs in Contemporary Society.* Philadelphia: Temple University Press.

Morris, David. (1991). *The Culture of Pain.* Berkeley: University of California Press.

Oravec, Jo Ann A. (2001). "On the 'proper use' of the Internet: Self-help medical information and on-line health care." *Journal of Health and Social Policy* 14, 1:37–60.

Oregon Fibromyalgia Foundation. (2000). http://www.myalgia.com.

Parsons, Talcott. (1951). *The Social System.* Glencoe, IL: The Free Press.

Phillips, Marilynn. (1990). "Damaged goods: Oral narratives of the experience of disability in American culture." *Social Science and Medicine* 30, 8: 849–857.

Pillemer, Stanley R., Laurence A. Bradley, Leslie J. Crofford, Harvey Moldofsky, and George P. Chrousos. (1997). "Conference summary: The neuroscience and endocrinology of fibromyalgia." *Arthritis and Rheumatism* 40:1928–1939.

Rafalovich, Adam. (1999). "Keep coming back! Narcotics Anonymous narrative and recovering-addict identity." *Contemporary Drug Problems* 26, 1:131–157.

Rhodes, Lorna, Carol McPhillips-Tangum; Christine Markham, and Rebecca Klenk. (1999). "The power of the visible: The meaning of diagnostic tests in chronic back pain." *Social Science and Medicine* 48, 9:1189–1203.

Riessman, Catherine. (1983). "Women and medicalization: A new perspective." *Social Policy* 14, 1:3–18.

———. (1990). "The strategic uses of narrative in the presentation of self and illness." *Social Science and Medicine* 30, 1:1195–1200.

Russell, I. John. (1999). "Is fibromyalgia a distinct clinical entity? The clinical investigator's evidence." *Balliere's Clinical Rheumatology* 13, 3:445–454.

Ryan, John, William M. Wentworth, and Gabrielle Chapman. (1994). "Models of emotions in therapeutic self-help books." *Sociological Spectrum* 12:241–255.

Scarry, Elane. (1985). *The Body in Pain: The Making and Unmaking of the World.* New York: Oxford University Press.

Showalter, Elaine. (1997). *Hystories: Hysterical Epidemics and Modern Media.* New York: Columbia University Press.

Somers, Margret. (1994). "The narrative constitution of identity: A relationship and network approach." *Theory and Society* 23:605–649.

Starlanyl, Devin J., and Mary Ellen Copeland, contributor. (1996). *Fibromyalgia and Chronic Myofascial Pain Syndrome: A Survival Manual.* Oakland, CA: New Harbinger.

Starr, Paul. (1982). *The Social Transformation of American Medicine.* New York: Basic Books.

Strauss, Stephen E., ed. (1994). *Chronic Fatigue Syndrome.* New York: Marcel Dekker.

Taylor, Verta, and Nancy Whittier. (1992). "Collective action in social movements communities: Lesbian feminist mobilization." In *Frontiers in Social Movement Theory,* Aldon Morris and Carol McClurg Mueller, eds. 104–129. New Haven, CT: Yale University Press.

Wallace, Daniel J., and Janice Brock Wallace. (1999). *Making Sense of Fibromyalgia: A Guide for Patients and Their Families.* New York: Oxford University Press.

Ware, Norma. (1999). "Toward a model of social course in chronic illness: The example of chronic

fatigue syndrome." *Culture, Medicine and Psychiatry* 23:303–331.
WebMD. (2002). "*Member columns.*" http://webmd.lycos.com/member–columns.
Wessely, Simon, and Matthew Hotopf. (1999). "Is fibromyalgia a distinct clinical entity? Historical and epidemiological evidence." *Bailliere's Clinical Rheumatology* 12, 3:427–436.
Wessely, Simon, C. Nimnuan, and M. Sharpe. (1999). "Functional somatic syndromes: One or many?" *Lancet* 354, 9182:936–939.
White, Kevin P., Mark Speechley, Manfred Harth, and Truls Ostbye. (1999). "The London fibromyalgia epidemiology study: The prevalence of fibromyalgia syndrome in London, Ontario." *Journal of Rheumatology* (July) 26:1570–1576.
Williams, Gareth. (1984). "The genesis of chronic illness: Narrative re-construction." *Sociology of Health and Illness* 6, 2:175–200.
Williamson, Miryam. (1996). *Fibromyalgia: A Comprehensive Approach.* New York: Walker and Company.
Wituk, Scott, Matthew D. Shepherd, Susan Slavich, Mary L. Warren, and Greg Meissen. (2000). "A typography of self-help groups: An empirical analysis." *Social Work* 45, 2:157–165.
Wolfe, Frederick, Kathryn A. Ross, Janice Anderson, I. John Russell, and Liesi Hebert. (1995) "The prevalence and characteristics of fibromyalgia in the general population." *Arthritis and Rheumatism* 38, 1:19–28.
Wolfe, Frederick, Huge Symthe, Muhammad Yunus, Robert Bennett, Claire Bombardier, Don Goldenberg, Peter Tugwell, Stephen Campbell, Micha Abeles, Patricia Clark, Robert Gatter, Daniel Hamaty, James Lessard, Alan Lichtbrown, Alfonse Masi, Glenn McCain, W. John Reynolds, Thomas Tomano, I. John Russell, and Robert Sheon. (1990). "The American College of Rheumatology 1990 criteria for the classification of fibromyalgia." *Arthritis and Rheumatism* 33, 2:160–172.
Yunus, Muhammad, Alfonse T. Masi, John J. Calabro, Kenneth A. Miller, and Seth L. Feigenbaum Yunus, Muhammad, Alfonse T. Masi, John J. Calabro, Kenneth A. Miller, and Seth L. Fiegenbaum. (1981). "Primary fibromyalgia (fibrositis): Clinical study of 50 patients with matched normal controls." *Seminars in Arthritis and Rheumatism* 11, 1:151–171.
Zola, Irving Kenneth. (1982). *Missing Pieces: A Chronicle of Living with a Disability.* Philadelphia: Temple University Press.

14 The Meaning of Medications: Another Look at Compliance

Peter Conrad

Compliance with medical regimens, especially drug regimens, has become a topic of central interest for both medical and social scientific research. By compliance we mean "the extent to which a person's behavior (in terms of taking medications, following diets, or executing lifestyle changes) coincides with medical or health advice" [1]. It is noncompliance that has engendered the most concern and attention. Most theories locate the sources of noncompliance in the doctor–patient interaction, patient knowledge or beliefs about treatment and, to a lesser extent, the nature of the regimen or illness.

This paper offers an alternative perspective on noncompliance with drug regimens, one situated in the patient's experience of illness. Most studies of noncompliance assume the centrality of patient–practitioner interaction for compliance. Using data from a study of experience of epilepsy, I argue that from a patient-centered perspective the meanings of medication in people's everyday lives are more salient than doctor-patient interaction for understanding why people alter their prescribed medical regimens. The issue is more one of self-regulation than compliance. After reviewing briefly various perspectives on compliance and presenting a synopsis of our method and sample, I develop the concept of medication practice to aid in understanding patients' experiences with medication regimens. This perspective enables us to analyze "noncompliance" among our sample of people with epilepsy in a different light than the usual medically-centered approach allows.

PERSPECTIVES ON COMPLIANCE

Most studies show that at least one-third of patients are noncompliant with drug regimens; i.e., they do not take medications as prescribed or in their correct doses or sequences [2–4]. A recent review of methodologically rigorous studies suggests that compliance rates with medications over a large period tend to converge at approximately 50% [5].

Literally hundreds of studies have been conducted on compliance. Extensive summaries and compilations of this burgeoning literature are available [1, 6, 7]. In this section I will note some of the more general findings and briefly summarize the major explanatory perspectives. Studies have found, for example, that noncompliance tends to be higher under certain conditions: when medical regimens are more complex [8]; with asymptomatic or psychiatric disorders [9]; when treatment periods last for longer periods of time [5]; and when there are several troublesome drug side effects [4]. Interestingly, there seems to be little consistent relationship between noncompliance and such factors as social class, age, sex, education and marital status [8].

Two dominant social scientific perspectives have emerged that attempt to explain variations in compliance and noncompliance. One locates the source of the problem in doctor–patient interaction or communication while the other postulates that patients' health beliefs are central to understanding noncompliant behavior. These perspectives each are multicausal and in some ways are compatible.

There have been a series of diverse studies suggesting that noncompliance is a result of some problem in doctor–patient interaction (see [10]). Researchers have found higher compliance rates are associated with physicians giving explicit and appropriate instructions, more and clearer information, and more and better feedback [2, 11]. Other researchers note that noncompliance is higher when patients' expectations are not met or their physicians are not behaving in a friendly manner [12, 13]. Hulka *et al.* [3], Davis [2] and others suggest that the physician and his or her style of communicating may affect patient compliance. In short, these studies find the source of noncompliance in doctor–patient communication and suggest that compliance rates can be improved by making some changes in clinician–patient interaction.

The importance of patient beliefs for compliant behavior is highlighted by the "health-belief model." The health-belief model is a social psychological perspective first developed to explain preventative health behavior. It has been adapted by Becker [14–16] to explain compliance. This perspective is a "value-expecting model in which behavior is controlled by rational decisions taken in the light of a set of subjective probabilities" [17]. The health-belief model suggests that patients are more likely to comply with doctors' orders when they feel susceptibility to illness, believe the illness to have potential serious consequences for health or daily functioning, and do not anticipate major obstacles, such as side effects or cost. Becker [15] found general support for a relationship between compliance and patients' beliefs about susceptibility, severity, benefits and costs.

Both perspectives have accumulated some supporting evidence, but make certain problematic assumptions about the nature and source of compliant behavior. The whole notion of "compliance" suggests a medically centered orientation; how and why people follow or deviate from doctors orders. It is a concept developed from the doctor's perspective and conceived to solve the provider defined problem of "noncompliance." The assumption is the doctor gives the orders; patients are expected to comply. It is based on a consensual model of doctor–patient relations, aligning with Parsons' [18] perspective, where noncompliance is deemed a form of deviance in need of explanation. Compliance/noncompliance studies generally assume a moral stance that not following medical regimens is deviant. While this perspective is reasonable from the physicians' viewpoint, when social scientists adopt this perspective they implicitly reinforce the medically centered perspective.

Some assumptions of each perspective are also problematic. The doctor–patient interaction perspective points to flaws in doctor–patient communication as the source of noncompliance. It is assumed that the doctor is very significant for compliance and the research proceeds from there. Although the health belief model takes the patient's perspective into account, it assumes that patients act from a rational calculus based on health-related beliefs. This perspective assumes that health-related beliefs are the most significant aspects of subjective experience and that compliance is a rational decision based on these beliefs. In an attempt to create a succinct and straightforward model, it ignores other aspects of experience that may affect how illness and treatment are managed.

There is an alternative, less-developed perspective that is rarely mentioned in studies of compliance. This patient-centered perspective sees patients as active agents in their treatment rather than as "passive and obedient recipients of medical instructions" [19]. Stimson [19] argues that to understand noncompliance it is important to account for several factors that are often ignored in compliance studies. Patients have their own ideas about taking medication which only in part come from doctors that affect their use of medications. People evaluate both doctors' actions and the prescribed drugs in comparison to what they themselves know about illness and medication. In a study of arthritis patients Arluke [20] found that patients evaluate also the therapeutic efficacy of drugs against the achievement of specific outcomes. Medicines are judged ineffective when a salient outcome is not achieved, usually in terms of the patient's expected time frames. The patient's decision to stop taking medications is a rational-empirical method of testing their views of drug efficacy. Another study found some patients augmented or diminished their treatment regimens as an attempt to assert control on the doctor–patient relationship [21]. Hayes-Bautista [21] notes, "The need to modify treatment arises when it appears the original treatment is somehow not totally appropriate" and contends noncompliance may be a form of patient bargaining with doctors. Others [22] have noted that noncompliance may be the result of particular medical regimens that are not compatible with contexts of people's lives.

These studies suggest that the issue of noncompliance appears very different from a patient-centered perspective than a medically centered one. Most are critical of traditional compliance studies, although still connecting compliance with doctor–patient interactions [19, 21] or with direct evaluation of the drug itself [19, 20]. Most sufferers of illness, especially chronic illness, spend a small fraction of their lives in the "patient role" so it is by no means certain that the doctor–patient relationship is the only or even most significant factor in their decisions about drug-taking. A broader perspective suggests that sufferers of illness need to manage their daily existence of which medical regimens are only a part (cf. [23]). Such a perspective proposes that we examine the meaning of medications as they are manifested in people's everyday lives.

This paper is an attempt to further develop a patient- or sufferer-centered perspective on adhering to medical regimens. We did not set out to study compliance *per se;* rather this paper reflects themes that emerged from our larger study of people's experiences of epilepsy [24]. We examine what prescribed medications mean to the people with epilepsy we interviewed; and how these meanings are reflected in their use.

METHOD AND SAMPLE

The larger research project from which these data are drawn endeavors to present and analyze an "insider's" view of what it is like to have epilepsy in our society. To accomplish this we interviewed 80 people about their life experiences with epilepsy. Interviews were conducted over a three-year period and respondents were selected on the basis of availability and willingness to participate. We used a snowball sampling technique, relying on advertisements in local newspapers, invitation letters passed anonymously by common acquaintances, and names obtained from local social agencies, self-help groups and health workers. No pretense to statistical representativeness is intended or sought. Our intention was to develop a sample from which theoretical insight would emerge and a conceptual understanding of epilepsy could be gained (see [25]).

We used an interview guide consisting of 50 open-ended questions and interviewed most of our respondents in their homes. The interviews lasted 1–3 hours and were tape-recorded. The recordings were transcribed and yielded over 2000-single-spaced typed pages of verbatim data.

Our sample ranged in age from 14 to 54 years (average age 28) and included 44 women and 36 men. Most respondents came from a metropolitan area in the midwest; a small number from a major city on the east coast. Our sample could be described as largely lower-middle class in terms of education and income. None of our respondents were or had been institutionalized for epilepsy; none were interviewed in hospitals, clinics or physicians' offices. In short, our sample and study were independent of medical and institutionalized settings. More detail about the method and sample is available elsewhere [24].

EPILEPSY, MEDICATION AND SELF-REGULATION

The common medical response to a diagnosis of epilepsy is to prescribe various medications to control seizures. Given the range of types of epilepsy and the variety of physiological reactions to these medications, patients often see doctors as having a difficult time getting their medication "right." There are starts and stops and changes, depending on the degree of seizure control and the drug's side effects. More often than not, patients are stabilized on a medication or combination at a given dosage or regimen. Continuing or altering medications is the primary if not sole medical management strategy for epilepsy.

Medications are important to people with epilepsy. They "control" seizures. Most take this medication several times daily. It becomes a routine part of their everyday lives. Although all of our respondents were taking or had taken these drugs, their responses to them varied. The effectiveness of these drugs in controlling seizures is a matter of degree. For some, seizures are stopped completely; they take pills regularly and have no seizures. For most, seizure frequency and duration are decreased significantly, although not reduced to zero. For a very few of our respondents, medications seem to have little impact; seizures continue unabated.

Nearly all our respondents said medications have helped them control seizures at one time or another. At the same time, however, many people changed their dose and regimen from those medically prescribed. Some stopped altogether. If medications were seen as so helpful, why were nearly half of our respondents "noncompliant" with their doctors' orders?

Most people with illnesses, even chronic illnesses such as epilepsy, spend only a tiny fraction of their lives in the "patient role." Compliance assumes that the doctor–patient relationship is pivotal for subsequent action, which may be the case. Consistent with our perspective, we conceptualize the issue as one of developing a *medication practice.* Medication practice offers a patient-centered perspective of how people manage their medications, focusing on the meaning and use of medications. In this light we can see the doctor's medication orders as the "prescribed medication practice" (e.g., take a 20 mg pill four times a day). Patients interpret the doctor's prescribed regimen and create a medication practice that may vary decidedly from the prescribed practice. Rather than assume the patient will follow prescribed medical rules, this perspective allows us to explore the kinds of practices patients create.[1] Put another way, it sees patients as active agents rather than passive recipients of doctors' orders.

Although many people failed to conform to their prescribed medication regimen, they did not define this conduct primarily as noncompliance with doctors' orders. The more we examined the data, the clearer it was that from the patient's perspective, doctors had very little impact on people's decisions to alter their medications. It was, rather, much more a question of regulation of control. To examine this more closely we developed criteria for what we could call self-regulation. Many of our respondents occasionally missed taking their medicine, but otherwise were regular in their medication practice. One had to do more than "miss" medications now and again (even a few times a week) to be deemed self-regulating. A person had to (1) reduce or raise the daily dose of prescribed drugs for several weeks or more or (2) skip or take extra doses regularly under specific circumstances (e.g., when drinking, staying up late or under "stress") or (3) stop taking the drugs completely for three consecutive days or longer. These criteria are arbitrary, but they allow us to estimate the extent of self-regulation. Using this definition, 34 of our 80 respondents (42%) self-regulated their medication.[2]

To understand the meaning and management of medications we need to look at those who follow a prescribed medications practice as well as those who create their own variations. While we note that 42% of our respondents are at variance with medical expectations, this number is more suggestive than definitive. Self-regulators are not a discrete and separate group. About half the self-regulators could be defined as regular in their practice, whatever it might be. They may have stopped for a week once or twice, or take extra medication only under "stressful" circumstances; otherwise, they are regular in their practice. On the other hand, perhaps a quarter of those following the prescribed medical practice say they have seriously considered changing or stopping their medications. It is likely there is an overlap between self-regulating and medical-regulating groups. While one needs to appreciate and examine the whole range of medication practice, the self-regulators provide a unique resource for analysis. They articulate views that are probably shared in varying degree by all people with epilepsy and provide an unusual insight into the meaning of medication and medication practice. We first describe how people account for following a prescribed medication practice; we then examine explanations offered for altering prescribed regimens and establishing their own practices. A final section outlines how the meaning of medications constructs and reflects the experience of epilepsy.

A TICKET TO NORMALITY

The availability of effective seizure control medications early in this century is a milestone in the treatment of epilepsy (Phenobarbital was introduced in 1912; Dilantin in 1938). These drugs also literally changed the experience of having epilepsy. To the extent the medications controlled seizures, people with epilepsy suffered fewer convulsive disruptions in their lives and were more able to achieve conventional social roles. To the extent doctors believed medications effective, they developed greater optimism about their ability to treat epileptic patients. To the degree the public recognized epilepsy as a "treatable" disorder, epileptics were no longer segregated in colonies and less subject to restrictive laws regarding marriage, procreation and work [24]. It is not surprising that people with epilepsy regard medications as a "ticket" to normality. The drugs did not, speaking strictly, affect anything but seizures. It was the social response to medications that brought about these changes. As one woman said: "I'm glad we've got [the medications] . . . you know, in the past people didn't and they were looked upon as lepers."

For most people with epilepsy, taking medicine becomes one of those routines of everyday life we engage in to avoid unwanted circumstances or improve our health. Respondents compared it to taking vitamins, birth control pills or teeth brushing. It becomes almost habitual, something done regularly with little reflection. One young working man said: "Well, at first I didn't like it, [but] it doesn't bother me anymore. Just like getting up in the morning and brushing your teeth. It's just something you do."

But seizure control medications differ from "normal pills" like vitamins or contraceptives. They are prescribed for a medical disorder and are seen both by the individual and others, as indicators or evidence of having epilepsy. One young man as a child did not know he had epilepsy "short of taking [his] medication." He said of this connection between epilepsy and medication: "I do, so therefore I have." Medications represent epilepsy: Dilantin or Phenobarbital are quickly recognized by medical people and often by others as epilepsy medications.

Medications can also indicate the degree of one's disorder. Most of our respondents do not know any others with epilepsy; thus they examine changes in their own epilepsy biographies as grounds for conclusions about their condition. Seizure activity is one such sign; the amount of medications "necessary" is another. A decrease or increase in seizures is taken to mean that epilepsy is getting better or worse. So it is with medications. While the two may be related—especially because the common medical response to more seizures is increased medication—they may also operate independently. If the doctor reduces the dose or strength of medication, or vice versa, the patient may interpret this as a sign of improvement or worsening. Similarly, if a person reduces his or her own dose, being able to "get along" on this lowered amount of medication is taken as evidence of "getting better." Since for a large portion of people with epilepsy seizures are considered to be well-controlled, medications become the only readily available measure of the "progress" of the disorder.

TAKING MEDICATIONS

We tried to suspend the medical assumption that people take medications simply because they are prescribed, or because they are supposed to control seizures, to examine our respondents' accounts of what they did and why.

The reason people gave most often for taking medication is *instrumental:* to control seizures, or more generally, to reduce the likelihood of body malfunction. Our respondents often drew a parallel to the reason people with diabetes take insulin. As one woman said, "If it does the trick, I'd rather take them [medications] than not." Or, as a man who would "absolutely not" miss his medications explained, "I don't want to have seizures" (although he continued to have 3 or 4 a month). Those who deal with their medication on instrumental grounds see it simply as a fact of life, as something to be done to avoid body malfunction and social and personal disruption.

While controlling body malfunction is always an underlying reason for taking medications, psychological grounds may be equally compelling. Many people said that medication *reduces worry,* independent of its actually decreasing seizures. These drugs can make people feel secure, so they don't have to think about the probability of seizures. A 20-year-old woman remarked: "My pills keep me from getting hysterical." A woman who has taken seizure control medication for 15 years describes this "psychological" function of medication: "I don't know what it does, but I suppose I'm psychologically dependent on it. In other words, if I take my medication, I feel better." Some people actually report "feeling better"—clearer, more alert and energetic—when they do not take these drugs, but because they begin to worry if they miss, they take them regularly anyhow.

The most important reason for taking medication, however, is to insure "normality." People said specifically that they take medications to be more "normal": The meaning here is normal in the sense of "leading a normal life." In the words of a middle-aged public relations executive who said he does not restrict his life because of epilepsy: "Except I always take my medication. I don't know why. I figure if I took them, then I could do anything I wanted to do." People believed taking medicine reduces the risk of having a seizure in the presence of others, which might be embarrassing or frightening. As a young woman explained:

> I feel if it's going to help, that's what I want because you know you feel uncomfortable enough anyway that you don't want anything like [a seizure] to happen around other people; so if it's going to help, I'll take it.

This is not to say people with epilepsy like to take medications. Quite the contrary. Many respondents who follow their medically prescribed medication practice openly say they "hate" taking medications and hope someday to be "off" the drugs. Part of this distaste is related to the dependence people come to feel. Some used the metaphor of being an addict: "I'm a real drug addict"; "I was an addict before it was fashionable"; "I'm like an alcoholic without a drink; I *have* to have them [pills]"; and "I really don't want to be hooked for the rest of my life." Even while loathing the pills or the "addiction" people may be quite disciplined about taking these drugs.

The drugs used to control seizures are not, of course, foolproof. Some people continue to have seizures quite regularly while others suffer only occasional episodes. Such limited effectiveness does not necessarily lead these people to reject medication as a strategy. They continue, with frustration, to express "hope" that "they [doctors] will get it [the medication] right." For some, then, medications are but a limited ticket to normality.

SELF-REGULATION: GROUNDS FOR CHANGING MEDICATION PRACTICE

For most people there is not a one-to-one correspondence between taking or missing medications and seizure activity. People who take medications regularly may still have seizures, and some people who discontinue their medications may be seizure-free for months or longer. Medical experts say a patient may well miss a whole day's medication yet still have enough of the drug in the bloodstream to prevent a seizure for this period.

In this section we focus on those who deviate from the prescribed medication practice and variously regulate their own medication. On the whole, members of this subgroup are slightly younger than the rest of the sample (average age 25 vs 32) and somewhat more likely to be female (59–43%), but otherwise are not remarkably different from our respondents who follow the prescribed medication practice. Self-regulation for most of our respondents consists of reducing the dose, stopping for a time, or regularly skipping or taking extra doses of medication depending on various circumstances.

Reducing the dose (including total termination) is the most common form of self-regulation. In this context, two points are worth restating. First, doctors typically alter doses of medication in times of increased seizure activity or troublesome drug "side effects." It is difficult to strike the optimum level of medication. To people with epilepsy, it seems that doctors engage in a certain amount of trial and error behavior. Second, and more important, medications are defined, both by doctors and patients, as an indicator of the degree of disorder. If seizure activity is not "controlled" or increases, patients see that doctors respond by raising (or changing) medications. The more medicine prescribed means epilepsy is getting worse; the less means it is getting better. What doctors do does not necessarily explain what patients do, but it may well be an example our respondents use in their own management strategies. The most common rationales for altering a medication practice are drug related: the medication is perceived as ineffective or the so-called side effects become too troublesome.

The efficacy of a drug is a complex issue. Here our concern is merely with perceived efficacy. When a medication is no longer seen as efficacious it is likely to be stopped. Many people continue to have seizures even when they follow the prescribed medication practice. If medication seemed to make no difference, our respondents were more likely to consider changing their medication practice. One woman who stopped taking medications for a couple of months said, "It seemed like [I had] the same number of seizures without it." Most people who stop taking their medicine altogether eventually resume a medication practice of some sort. A woman college instructor said, "When I was taking Dilantin, I stopped a number of times because it never seemed to *do* anything."

The most common drug-related rationale for reducing dose is troublesome "side effects." People with epilepsy attribute a variety of side effects to seizure control medications. One category of effects includes swollen and bleeding gums, oily or yellow skin, pimples, sore throat and a rash. Another category includes slowed mental functioning, drowsiness, slurred speech, dullness, impaired memory, loss of balance and partial impotence.[3] The first category, which we can call body side effects, were virtually never given as an account for self-regulation. Only those side effects that impaired social skills, those in the second category, were given as reasons for altering doctors' medication orders.

Social side effects impinge on social interaction. People believed they felt and acted differently. A self-regulating woman described how she feels when she takes her medication:

> I can feel that I become much more even. I feel like I flatten out a little bit. I don't like that feeling. . . . It's just a feeling of dullness, which I don't like, almost a feeling that you're on the edge of laziness.

If people saw their medication practice as hindering the ability to participate in routine social affairs, they were likely to change it. Our respondents gave many examples such as a college student who claimed the medication slowed him down and wondered if it were affecting his memory, a young newspaper reporter who reduced his medication because it was putting him to sleep at work; or the social worker who felt she "sounds smarter" and more articulate when "off medications."

Drug side effects, even those that impair social skills, are not sufficient in themselves to explain the level of self-regulation we found. Self-regulation was considerably more than a reaction to annoying and uncomfortable side effects. It was an active and intentional endeavor.

SOCIAL MEANINGS OF REGULATING MEDICATION PRACTICE

Variations in medication practice by and large seem to depend on what medication and self-regulation mean to our respondents. Troublesome relationships with physicians, including the perception that they have provided inadequate medical information [14], may be a foundation on which alternative strategies and practices are built. Our respondents, however, did not cite such grounds for altering their doctors' orders. People vary their medication practice on grounds connected to managing their everyday lives. If we examine the social meanings of medications from our respondents' perspective, self-regulation turns on four grounds: testing; control of dependence; destigmatization; and practical practice. While individual respondents may cite one or more of these as grounds for altering medication practice, they are probably best understood as strategies common among those who self regulate.

Testing

Once people with epilepsy begin taking seizure-control medications, given there are no special problems and no seizures, doctors were reported to seldom change the medical regimen. People are likely to stay on medications indefinitely. But how can one know that a period without seizures is a result of medication or spontaneous remission of the disorder? How long can one go without medication? How "bad" is this case of epilepsy? How can one know if epilepsy is "getting better" while still taking medication? Usually after a period without or with only a few seizures, many reduced or stopped their medicine altogether to test for themselves whether or not epilepsy was "still there."

People can take themselves off medications as an experiment, to see "if anything will happen." One woman recalled:

> I was having one to two seizures a year on phenobarb . . . so I decided not to take it and to see what would happen . . . so I stopped it and I watched and it seemed that I had the same amount of seizures with it as without it . . . for three years.

She told her physician, who was skeptical but "allowed" her this control of her medication practice. A man who had taken medication three times a day for 16 years felt intuitively that he could stop his medications:

> Something kept telling me I didn't have to take [medication] anymore, a feeling or somethin'. It took me quite a while to work up the nerve to stop takin' the pills. And one day I said, "One way to find out . . ."

After suffering what he called drug withdrawal effects, he had no seizures for 6 years. Others tested to see how long they can go without medication and seizures.

Testing does not always turn out successfully. A public service agency executive tried twice to stop taking medications when he thought he had "kicked" epilepsy. After two failures, he concluded that stopping medications "just doesn't work." But others continue to test, hoping for some change in their condition. One middle-aged housewife said:

> When I was young I would try not to take it . . . I'd take 'em for a while and think, "Well, I don't need it anymore," and I would not take it for, deliberately, just to see if I could do without. And then [in a few days] I'd start takin' it again because I'd start passin' out . . . I will still try that now, when my husband is out of town . . . I just think, maybe I'm still gonna grow out of it or something.

Testing by reducing or stopping medication is only one way to evaluate how one's disorder is progressing. Even respondents who follow the prescribed medication regimen often wonder "just what would happen" if they stopped.

Controlling Dependence

People with epilepsy struggle continually against becoming too dependent on family, friends, doctors or medications. They do, of course, depend on medications for control of seizures. The medications do not necessarily eliminate seizures and many of our respondents resented their dependence on them. Another paradox is that although medications can increase self reliance by reducing seizures, taking medications can be *experienced* as a threat to self-reliance. Medications seem almost to become symbolic of the dependence created by having epilepsy.

There is a widespread belief in our society that drugs create dependence and that being on chemical substances is not a good thing. Somehow, whatever the goal is, it is thought to be better if we can get there without drugs. Our respondents reflected these ideas in their comments.

A college junior explained: "I don't like it at all. I don't like chemicals in my body. It's sort of like a dependency only that I have to take it because my body forced me to . . ." A political organizer who says medications reduce his seizures commented: "I've never enjoyed having to depend on anything . . . drugs in particular." A nurse summed up the situation: "The *drugs* were really a kind of dependence." Having to take medication relinquished some degree of control of one's life. A woman said:

> I don't like to have to *take* anything. It was, like, at one time birth control pills, but I don't like to take anything *everyday.* It's just like, y'know, controlling me, or something.

The feeling of being controlled need not be substantiated in fact for people to act upon it. If people *feel* dependent on and controlled by medication, it is not surprising that they seek to avoid these drugs. A high school junior, who once took medicine because he feared having a seizure in the street, commented:

> And I'd always heard medicine helps and I just kept taking it and finally I just got so I didn't depend on the medicine no more, I could just fight it off myself and I just stopped taking it in.

After stopping for a month he forgot about his medications completely.

Feelings of dependence are one reason people gave for regulating medicine. For a year, one young social worker took medication when she felt it was necessary; otherwise, she tried not to use it. When we asked her why, she responded, "I regulate my own drug . . . mostly because it's really important for me not to be dependent." She occasionally had seizures and continued to alter her medication to try to "get it right":

> I started having [seizures] every once in a while. And I thought wow, the bad thing is that I just haven't regulated it right and I just need to up it a little bit and then, you know, if I do it just right, I won't have epilepsy anymore.

This woman and others saw medications as a powerful resource in their struggle to gain control over epilepsy. Although she no longer thinks she can rid herself of epilepsy, this woman still regulates her medication.

In this context, people with epilepsy manipulate their sense of dependence on medications by changing medication practice. But there is a more subtle level of dependence that encourages such changes. Some reported they regulated their medication intake in direct response to interventions of others, especially family members. It was as if others *wanted* them to be more dependent by coaxing or reminding them to take their medications regularly. Many responded to this encouraged greater dependence by creating their own medication practice.

A housewife who said she continues regularly to have petit mal seizures and tremors along with an occasional grand mal seizure, remarked:

> Oh, like most things, when someone tells me I have to do something, I basically resent it. . . . If it's my option and I choose to do it, I'll probably do it more often than not. But if you tell me I have to, I'll bend it around and do it my own way, which is basically what I have done.

Regardless of whether one feels dependent on the drug or dependent because of others' interventions around drug taking, changing a prescribed medication practice as well as continuing self-regulation serve as a form of *taking control* of one's epilepsy.

Destigmatization

Epilepsy is a stigmatized illness. Sufferers attempt to control information about the disorder to manage this threat [38]. There are no visible stigmata that make a person with epilepsy obviously different from other people, but a number of aspects of having epilepsy can compromise attempts at information control. The four signs that our respondents most frequently mentioned as threatening information control were seizures in the presence of others, job or insurance applications, lack of a driver's license and taking medications. People may try to avoid seizures in public, lie or hedge on their applications, develop accounts for not having a driver's license, or take their medicine in private in order to minimize the stigma potential of epilepsy.

Medication usually must be taken three or four times daily, so at least one dose must be taken away from home. People attempt to be private about taking their medications and/or develop "normal" pill accounts ("it's to help my digestion"). One woman's mother told her to take medications regularly, as she would for any other sickness:

> When I was younger it didn't bother me too bad. But as I got older, it would tend to bother me some. Whether it was, y'know, maybe somebody seeing me or somethin', I don't know. But it did.

Most people develop skills to minimize potential stigmatization from taking pills in public.

On occasion, stopping medications is an attempt to vacate the stigmatized status of epileptic. One respondent wrote us a letter describing how she tried to get her mother to accept her by not taking her medications. She wrote:

> This is going to sound real dumb, but I can't help it. My mother never accepted me when I was little because I was "different." I stopped taking my medication in an attempt to be normal and accepted by her. Now that I know I need medication it's like I'm completely giving up trying to be "normal" so mom won't be ashamed of me. I'm going to accept the fact that I'm "different" and I don't really care if mom gives a damn or not.

Taking medications in effect acknowledges this "differentness."

It is, of course, more difficult to hide the meaning of medications from one's self. Taking medication is a constant reminder of having epilepsy. For some it is as if the medication itself represents the stigma of epilepsy. The young social worker quoted above felt if she could stop taking her medications she would no longer be an epileptic. A young working woman summed up succinctly why avoiding medications would be avoiding stigma: "Well, at least I would not be . . . generalized and classified in a group as being an epileptic."

Practical Practice

Self-regulators spoke often of how they changed the dose or regimen of medication in an effort to reduce the risk of having a seizure, particularly during "high stress" situations. Several respondents who were students said they take extra medications during exam periods or when they stay up late studying. A law student who had not taken his medication for 6 months took some before his law school exams: "I think it increases the chances [seizures] won't happen." A woman who often participated in horse shows said she "usually didn't pay attention" to her medication in practice but takes extra when she doesn't get the six to eight hours of sleep she requires: "I'll wake up and take two capsules instead of one . . . and I'll generally take it like when we're going to horse shows. I'll take it pretty consistently." Such uses of medication are common ways of trying to forestall "possible trouble."

People with epilepsy changed their medication practice for practical ends in two other kinds of circumstances. Several reported they took extra medication if they felt a "tightening" or felt a seizure coming on. Many people also said they did not take medications if they were going to drink alcohol. They believed that medication (especially Phenobarbital) and alcohol do not mix well.

In short, people change their medication practice to suit their perceptions of social environment. Some reduce medication to avoid potential problems from mixing alcohol and drugs. Others reduce it to remain "clear-headed" and "alert" during "important" performances (something of a "Catch-22" situation). Most, however, adjust their medications practically in an effort to reduce the risk of seizures.

CONCLUSION: ASSERTING CONTROL

Regulating medication represents an attempt to assert some degree of control that appears at times to be completely beyond control. Loss of control is a significant concern for people with epilepsy. While medical treatment can increase both the sense and the fact of control over epilepsy, and information control can limit stigmatization, the regulation of medications is one way people with epilepsy struggle to gain some personal control over their condition.

Medication practice can be modified on several different grounds. Side effects that make managing everyday social interaction difficult can lead to the reduction or termination of medication. People will change their medication practice, including stopping altogether, in order to "test" for the existence or "progress" of the disorder. Medication may be altered to control the perceived level of dependence, either on the drugs themselves or on those who "push" them to adhere to a particular medication practice. Since the medication can represent the stigma potential of epilepsy, both literally and symbolically, altering medication practice can be a form of destigmatization. And finally, many people modify their medication practice in anticipation of specific social circumstances, usually to reduce the risk of seizures.

It is difficult to judge how generalizable these findings are to other illnesses. Clearly, people develop medication practices whenever they must take medications regularly. This is probably most true for long-term chronic illness where medication becomes a central part of everyday life, such as diabetes, rheumatoid arthritis, hypertension and asthma. The degree and amount of self-regulation may differ among illnesses—likely to be related to symptomatology, effectiveness of medications and potential of stigma—but I suspect most of the meanings of medications described here would be present among sufferers of any illness that people must continually manage.

In sum, we found that a large proportion of the people with epilepsy we interviewed said they themselves regulate their medication. Medically-centered compliance research presents a skewed and even distorted view of how and why patients manage medication. From the perspective of the person with epilepsy, the issue is more clearly one of responding to the meaning of medications in everyday life than "compliance" with physicians' orders and medical regimens. Framing the problem as self-regulation rather than compliance allows us to see modifying medication practice as a vehicle for asserting some control over epilepsy. One consequence of such a reframing would be to reexamine the value of achieving "compliant" behavior and to rethink what strategies might be appropriate for achieving greater adherence to prescribed medication regimens.

ACKNOWLEDGMENT

My thanks and appreciation to Joseph W. Schneider, my co-investigator in the epilepsy research, for his insightful comments on an earlier version of this paper. This research was supported in part by grants from the Drake University Research Council, the Epilepsy Foundation of America and the National Institute of Mental Health (MH 30818-01).

NOTES

1. Two previous studies of epilepsy which examine the patients' perspective provide parallel evidence for the significance of developing such an approach in the study of "noncompliance" (see [26] and [27]).
2. Reports in the medical literature indicate that noncompliance with epilepsy regimens is considered a serious problem [28–32]. One study reports that 40% of patients missed the prescribed medication dose often enough to affect their blood-level medication concentrations [33]; an important review article estimates noncompliance with epilepsy drug regimens between 30 and 40%, with a range from 20 to 75% [34]. Another study suggests that noncompliant patients generally had longer duration of the disorder, more complicated regimens and more medication changes [35]. Attempts to increase epilepsy medication compliance include improving doctor–patient communication, incorporating patients more in treatment programs, increasing patient knowledge and simplifying drug regimens. Since noncompliance with anti-convulsant medication regimens is deemed the most frequent reason why patients suffer recurrent seizures [30], some researchers suggest, "If the patient understands the risks of stopping medication, he *will not stop*" [36]. Yet there also have been reports of active noncompliance with epilepsy medications [37]. In sum, epilepsy noncompliance studies are both typical of and reflect upon most other compliance research. In this sense, epilepsy is a good example for developing an alternative approach to understanding how people manage their medications.
3. These are reported side effects. They may or may not be drug related, but our respondents attribute them to the medication.

REFERENCES

1. Haynes R. B., Taylor D. W. and Sackett D. L. (Eds) *Compliance in Health Care*. Johns Hopkins University Press, Baltimore, 1979.
2. Davis M. Variations in patients' compliance with doctor's advice: an empirical analysis of patterns of communication. *Am J. Publ. Hlth* **58,** 272, 1968.
3. Hulka B. S., Kupper L. L., Cassel J. LC. and Barbineau R. A. Practice characteristics and quality of primary medical care: the doctor–patient relationship. *Med Care* **13,** 808–820, 1975.
4. Christenson D. B. Drug-taking compliance: a review and synthesis. *Hlth. Serv. Res.* **6,** 171–187, 1978.
5. Sackett D. L. and Snow J. C. The magnitude of compliance and non-compliance. In *Compliance in Health Care* (Edited by Haynes R. B. *et al.*), pp. 11–22. Johns Hopkins University Press, Baltimore, 1979.
6. Sackett D. L. and Haynes R. B. (Eds.) *Compliance with Therapeutic Regimens*. Johns Hopkins University Press, Baltimore, 1976.
7. DiMatteo M. R. and DiNicola D. D. *Achieving Patient Compliance*. Pergamon Press, New York, 1982.
8. Hingson R., Scotch N. A., Sorenson J. and Swazey J. P. *In Sickness and in Health: Social Dimensions of Medical Care*. C. V. Mosby, St. Louis, 1981.
9. Haynes R. B. Determinants of compliance: the disease and the mechanics of treatment. In *Compliance in Health Care* (Edited by Haynes R. B. *et al.*), pp. 49–62. Johns Hopkins University Press, Baltimore, 1979.
10. Garrity T. F. Medical compliance and the clinician–patient relationship: a review. *Soc. Sci. Med.* **15E,** 215–222, 1981.
11. Svarstad B. L. Physician–patient communication and patient conformity with medical advice. In *Growth of Bureaucratic Medicine* (Edited by Mechanic D.), pp. 220–238. Wiley, New York, 1976.
12. Francis V., Korsch B. and Morris M. Gaps in doctor–patient communication: patients' response to medical advice. *New Engl. J. Med.* **280,** 535, 1969.
13. Korsch B., Gozzi E. and Francis V. Gaps in doctor–patient communication I. Doctor–patient interaction and patient satisfaction. *Pediatrics* **42,** 885, 1968.
14. Becker M. H. and Maiman L. A. Sociobehavioral determinants of compliance with health and medical care recommendations. *Med Care* **13,** 10–24.
15. Becker M. H. Sociobehavioral determinants of compliance. In *Compliance With Therapeutic Regimens* (Edited by Sackett D. L. and Haynes R. B.), pp. 40–50. Johns Hopkins University Press, Baltimore, 1976.

16. Becker M. H., Maiman L. A., Kirscht J. P., Haefner D. L., Drachman R. H. and Taylor D. W. Patient perceptions and compliance: recent studies of the health belief model. In *Compliance in Health Care* (Edited by Haynes, R. B. *et al.*), pp. 79–109. Johns Hopkins University Press, Baltimore, 1979.
17. Berkanovic E. The health belief model and voluntary health behavior. Paper presented to Conference on Critical issues in Health Delivery Systems, Chicago, 1977.
18. Parsons T. *The Social System.* Free Press, Glencoe, 1951.
19. Stimson G. V. Obeying doctor's orders: a view from the other side. *Soc. Sci. Med.* **8**, 97–104, 1974.
20. Arluke A. Judging drugs: patients' conceptions of therapeutic efficacy in the treatment of arthritis. *Hum. Org.* **39**, 84–88, 1980.
21. Hayes-Battista D. E. Modifying the treatment: patient compliance, patient control and medical care. *Soc. Sci. Med.* **10**, 233–238, 1976.
22. Zola I. K. Structural constraints in the doctor–patient relationship: the case of non-compliance. In *The Relevance of Social Science for Medicine* (Edited by Eisenberg L. and Kleinman A.), pp. 241–252. Reidel, Dordrecht, 1981.
23. Strauss A. and Glaser B. *Chronic Illness and the Quality of Life,* pp. 21–32. C. V. Mosby, St. Louis, 1975.
24. Schneider J. and Conrad P. *Having Epilepsy: The Experience and Control of Illness.* Temple University Press, Philadelphia, 1983.
25. Glaser B. and Strauss A. *The Discovery of Grounded Theory.* Aldine, Chicago, 1967.
26. West P. The physician and the management of childhood epilepsy. In *Studies in Everyday Medicine* (Edited by Wadsworth M. and Robinson D.), pp. 13–31. Martin Robinson, London, 1976.
27. Trostle J. *et al.* The logic of non-compliance: management of epilepsy from a patient's point of view. *Cult. Med. Psychiat.* **7**, 35–56, 1983.
28. Lund M., Jurgensen R. S. and Kuhl V. Serum diphenylhydantoin in ambulant patients with epilepsy. *Epilepsia* **5**, 51–58, 1964.
29. Lund M. Failure to observe dosage instructions in patients with epilepsy. *Acta Neurol. Scand.* **49**, 295–306, 1975.
30. Reynolds E. H. Drug treatment of epilepsy. *Lancet* **II**, 721–725, 1978.
31. Browne T. R. and Cramer I. A. Antiepileptic drug serum concentration determinations. In *Epilepsy: Diagnosis and Management* (Edited by Browne T. R. and Feldman R. G.). Little, Brown, Boston, 1982.
32. Pryse-Phillips W., Jardine F. and Bursey F. Compliance with drug therapy by epileptic patients. *Epilepsia* **23**, 269–274, 1982.
33. Eisler J. and Mattson R. H. Compliance with anticonvulsant drug therapy. *Epilepsia* **16**, 203, 1975.
34. The Commission for the Control of Epilepsy and Its Consequences. The literature on patient compliance and implications for cost-effective patient education programs with epilepsy. In *Plan for Nationwide Action on Epilepsy,* Vol. II, Part 1, pp. 391–415. U.S. Government Printing Office, Washington, DC, 1977.
35. Bryant S. G. and Ereshfsky L. Determinants of compliance in epileptic conditions. *Drug Intel. Clin. Pharmac.* **15**, 572–577, 1981.
36. Norman S. E. and Browne T. K. Seizure disorders. *Am. J. Nurs.* **81**, 893, 1981.
37. Desei B. T., Reily T. L., Porter R. J. and Penry J. K. Active non-compliance as a cause of uncontrolled seizures. *Epilepsia* **19**, 447–452, 1978.
38. Schneider J. and Conrad P. In the closet with illness: epilepsy, stigma potential and information control. *Soc. Probl.* **28**, 32–44, 1980.

15 *The Remission Society*

Arthur W. Frank

The possibility, even the necessity, of ill people telling their own stories has been set in place by the same modernist medicine that cannot contain these stories. At the end of the story that I wrote about my own experience of having cancer, I used the term "remission society" to describe all those people who, like me, were effectively well but could never be considered cured.[1] These people are all around, though often invisible. A man standing behind me in an airport security check announces that he has a pacemaker; suddenly his invisible "condition" becomes an issue. Once past the metal detector, his "remission" status disappears into the background.

Members of the remission society include those who have had almost any cancer, those living in cardiac recovery programs, diabetics, those whose allergies and environmental sensitivities require dietary and other self-monitoring, those with prostheses and mechanical body regulators, the chronically ill, the disabled, those "recovering" from abuses and addictions, and for all these people, the families that share the worries and daily triumph of staying well.

Cathy Pearse writes in middle-age about having a bleeding cerebral aneurysm—a stroke—when she was twenty.[2] During the operation, a cranial nerve was damaged. She still suffers from double vision, which she reports is "an ever present reminder" of her near-death experience. Her body is now beginning to feel the long-term effects of muscle asymmetry and favoring her "good side." But her illness history would be invisible to most people she meets, and she is long since considered "cured" by medicine. Cathy is a member of the remission society. Years after her hospitalization and treatment, she can still describe what happened in exquisite detail; she recalls the hurt caused by a nurse's casual comment as if it had been spoken yesterday. She refers to being a "recovered stroke patient" as one aspect of her "ethnicity," a word suggesting an irrevocable identity.

The physical existence of the remission society is modern: the technical achievements of modernist medicine make these lives possible. But people's self-consciousness of what it means to live in the wake of illness is postmodern. In modernist thought people are well *or* sick. Sickness and wellness shift definitively as to which is foreground and which is background at any given moment. In the remission society the foreground and background of sickness and health constantly shade into each other. Instead of a static picture on the page where light is separated from dark, the image is like a computer graphic where one shape is constantly in process of becoming the other.

Parsons's modernist "sick role" carries the expectation that ill people get well, cease to be patients, and return to their normal obligations. In the remission society people return, but obligations are never again what used to be normal. Susan Sontag's metaphor of illness as travel is more subtle than Parsons's sick role. We are each citizens of two kingdoms, Sontag writes, the kingdom of the well and that of the sick. "Although we all prefer to use only the good passport, sooner or later each of us is obliged, at least for a spell, to identify ourselves as citizens of that other place."[3] Sontag's notion of dual citizenship suggests a separation of these two kingdoms. The remission society is left to be either a demilitarized zone in between them, or else it is a secret society within the realm of the healthy.

To adapt Sontag's metaphor, members of the remission society do not use one passport *or* the other. Instead they are on permanent visa status, that visa requiring periodic renewal. The triumph of modernist medicine is to allow increasing numbers of people who would have been dead to enjoy this visa status, living in the world of the healthy even if always subject to expulsion. The problem for these people is that modernist medicine lacked a story appropriate to the experience it was setting in place. People like Judith Zaruches were left needing a new map for their lives.

The postmodernity of the remission society is more than a self-consciousness that has not been routinely available to the ill. Many members of the remission society feel a need to claim their visa status in an active voice. Those who work to express this voice are not only postmodern but, more specifically, *post-colonial* in their construction of self. Just as political and economic colonialism took over geographic areas, modernist medicine claimed the body of its patient as its territory, at least for the duration of the treatment. "When we're admitted to a hospital or even visiting a doctor," writes Dan Gottlieb, who as a quadriplegic has extensive experience with such visits, "the forms ask for 'Patient Name.' We stop being people and start being patients. . . . Our identity as people and the world we once knew both are relinquished; we become their patients and we live in their hospital."[4] Gottlieb's anger reflects a widespread resentment against medical colonization.

For those whose diseases are cured, more or less quickly and permanently, medical colonization is a temporary indignity. This colonization becomes an issue in the remission society when some level of treatment extends over the rest of a person's life, whether as periodic check-ups or as memories. The least form of treatment, periodic check-ups, are not "just" monitoring. "The fear comes and goes," writes Elizabeth Tyson, a breast cancer survivor, "but twice a year, at checkup time, it's ferocious."[5] For the person being checked, these check-ups represent the background of illness shading back into the foreground. Even for those whose visa is stamped expeditiously, the reality of lacking permanent citizenship is reaffirmed.

Colonization was central to the achievement of modernist medicine. Claudine Herzlich and Janine Pierret describe the "sick person" emerging as a recognizable social type in the early modern period, during the eighteenth century. The condition necessary for the emergence of this type was that "the diversity of suffering be reduced by a unifying general view, which is precisely that of clinical medicine."[6] This reducing of the particular to the general provided for scientific achievements, but the clinical reduction created a benevolent form of colonialism.

The ill person who plays out Parsons's sick role accepts having the particularity of his individual suffering reduced to medicine's general view. Modernity did not question this reduction because its benefits were immediate and its cost was not yet apparent. The colonization of experience was judged worth the cure, or the attempted cure. But illnesses have shifted from the acute to the chronic, and self-awareness has shifted. The post-colonial ill person, living with illness for the long term, wants her own suffering recognized in its individual particularity; "reclaiming" is the relevant postmodern phrase.

In postmodern times more and more people, with varying degrees of articulation and action, express suspicion of medicine's reduction of their suffering to its general unifying view. Members of the remission society, who know medicine from the inside out, question their place in medical narratives. What they question can be clarified by drawing an analogy to people who were politically colonized. Gayatri Chakravorty Spivak speaks of colonized people's efforts "to see how the master texts need us in [their] construction . . . without acknowledging that need."[7] What do the master texts of medicine need but not acknowledge?

I met a man who had a cancer of the mouth that required extensive reconstructive surgery to his jaw and face. His treatment had been sufficiently extraordinary for his surgeon to have published a medical journal article about it, complete with pictures showing the stages of the reconstructive process. When he told me about the article and offered to show it to me, I imagined the article might actually be about *him:* his suffering throughout this mutilating, if life-saving, ordeal. As I looked at the article I realized his name was not mentioned. Probably the surgeon and the journal would have considered it unethical to name him, even though pictures of the man were shown. Thus in "his" article he was systematically ignored as anyone actually anything other than a body. But for medical purposes it was not his article at all; it was his surgeon's article. This is exactly the colonization that Spivak speaks of: the master text of the medical journal article needs the suffering person, but the individuality of that suffering cannot be acknowledged.

Most ill people remain willing to continue to play the medical "patient" game by modernist rules without question, and almost all do so when required. But post-colonial members of the remission society are demanding, in various and often frustrated ways, that medicine recognize its need for them. Refusing to be reduced to "clinical material" in the construction of the medical text, they are claiming voices.

Because illness, following medicine, is effectively privatized, this demand for voice rarely achieves a collective force. Feminist health activists are a major exception. Susan Bell writes about the attempts by members of the Cambridge Women's Community Health Center (WCHC) to change the role played by women who were recruited by Harvard Medical School to serve as paid "pelvic models" for medical students to learn to perform gynecological examinations.[8] Bell tells of the women's escalating demands to participate in a full teaching role rather than serve as inert bodies to be taught upon. Women negotiated for their own class time with medical students, they sought to demonstrate how women could perform their own gynecological examinations using a mirror, and they injected political issues into the medical curriculum.

The medical school finally rejected WCHC demands that teaching be limited to women (since the experience of being examined should be, in principle, reciprocal), that non-student hospital personnel and other consumers be included in the teaching sessions, and that more political discussion contextualize the medical teaching. The specifics of the WCHC demands are less important than their basic post-colonial stance: women wanted to have their necessity acknowledged in the construction of medical knowledge and practice. They claimed an active voice in that knowledge and practice.[9]

Post-colonialism in its most generalized form is the demand to speak rather than being spoken for and to represent oneself rather than being represented or, in the worst cases, rather than being effaced entirely. But in postmodern times pressures on clinical practice, including the cost of physicians' time and ever greater use of technologies, mean less time for patients to speak.[10] People then speak elsewhere. The post-colonial impulse is acted out less in the clinic than in stories that members of the remission society tell each other about their illnesses.[11]

The post-colonial stance of these stories resides not in the content of what they say about medicine. Rather the new feel of these stories begins in how often medicine and physicians do *not* enter the stories. Postmodern illness stories are told so that people can place themselves outside the "unifying general view." For people to move their stories outside the professional purview involves a profound assumption of personal responsibility. In Parsons's sick role the ill person as patient was responsible only for getting well; in the remission society, the post-colonial ill person takes responsibility for what illness means in his life.

NOTES

1. Arthur W. Frank, *At the Will of the Body: Reflections on Illness* (Boston: Houghton Mifflin, 1991), 138ff.
2. Personal communication.
3. Susan Sontag, *Illness as Metaphor* (New York: Vintage, 1978), 3.
4. Dan Gottlieb, "Patients must insist that Doctors see the Face behind the Ailment," *The Philadelphia Inquirer,* July 4, 1994.
5. Elizabeth Tyson, "Heal Thyself," *Living Fit,* Winter 1994, 38.
6. Claudine Herzlich and Janine Pierret, *Illness and Self in Society* (Baltimore: Johns Hopkins University Press, 1987), 23. Stanley Joel Reiser quotes the Victorian physician Thomas Syderham, "Nature, in the production of disease is uniform and consistent; so much so, that for the same disease in different persons the symptoms are for the most part the same; and the self-same phenomena you would observe in the sickness of a Socrates you would observe in the sickness of a simpleton." The unavoidable implication is that all patients, for diagnostic purposes, might as well be simpletons. Reiser's conclusion is more moderated: "Thus the symptoms that combine patients into populations have become more significant to physicians than the symptoms that separate patients as individuals." ("Science, Pedagogy, and the Transformation of Empathy in Medicine," in Spiro et al., *Empathy and the Practice of Medicine,* 123–24.)
7. Gayatri Chakravorty Spivak, *The Post-Colonial Critic: Interviews, Strategies, and Dialogues,* ed. Sarah Harasym (New York: Routledge, 1990), 3.
8. Susan Bell, "Political Gynecology: Gynecological Imperialism and the Politics of Self-Help," in Phil Brown, ed., *Perspectives in Medical Sociology* (Prospect Heights, Ill: Waveland Press, 1992), 576–86.
9. For another story of lay narratives achieving a collective voice in opposition to orthodox medicine, see Martha Balshem, *Cancer in the Commu-*

nity: Class and Medical Authority (Washington: Smithsonian Institution Press, 1993).

10. Physicians, who certainly have their own stories, express their version of post-colonialism when they object to having their experiences of caring for patients taken away from them. A physician employed by an HMO says, "I don't want to *manage clients,* I want to *care for patients.* I don't want to hide behind bureaucratic regs and physician assistants. I want to do the caring." Quoted by Kleinman, *The Illness Narratives,* 219 (cf. Preface, n. 2).
11. One indicator of the need for storytelling about illness are "grass roots" publications such as *Expressions: Literature and Art by People with Disabilities and Ongoing Health Problems* (Sefra Kobrin Pitzele, editor; P.O. Box 16294, St. Paul, Minn. 55116-0294) and *Common Journeys* (Leslie Keyes, editor; 4136 43rd Avenue South, Minneapolis, Minn. 55406). Storytelling also takes place in numerous journal writing workshops conducted in all illness support centers I have visited or received information from. The truly postmodern form of storytelling among the ill are electronic messages exchanged in media such as the Internet. An increasing number of specialized "nets" exist for illness stories. On Internet stories, see Faith McLellan, "From Book to Byte: Narratives of Physical Illness," *Medical Humanities Review* 8 (Fall 1994): 9–21.

PART 2 The Social Organization of Medical Care

In Part 2, we turn from the production of disease and illness to the social organizations created to treat it. Here we begin to examine the institutional aspects of health and illness the medical care system. We look at the social organization of medical care historically, structurally, and, finally, interactionally. We seek to understand how this complex system operates and how its particular characteristics have contributed to the current health care crisis.

The Rise and Fall of the Dominance of Medicine

Physicians have a professional monopoly on medical practice in the United States. They have an exclusive state-supported right, manifested in the "licensing" of physicians, to medical practice. With their licenses, physicians can legally do what no one else can, including cutting into the human body and prescribing drugs.

Until the latter part of the nineteenth century, various groups and individuals (e.g., homeopaths, midwives, botanical doctors) competed for the "medical turf." By the second decade of this century, virtually only M.D. physicians had the legal right to practice medicine in this country. One might suggest that physicians achieved their exclusive rights to the nation's medical territory because of their superior scientific and clinical achievements, a line of reasoning which suggests that physicians demonstrated superior healing and curative skills, and the government therefore supported their rights against less effective healers and quacks. But this seems not to have been the case. As we noted earlier, most of the improvement in the health status of the population resulted from social changes, including better nutrition, sanitation, and a rising standard of living rather than from the interventions of clinical medicine. Medical techniques were in fact rather limited, often even dangerous, until the early twentieth century. As L. J. Henderson observed, "somewhere between 1910 and 1912 in this country, a random patient, with a random disease, consulting a doctor chosen at random, had, for the first time in the history of mankind, a better than fifty-fifty chance of profiting from the encounter" (Blumgart, 1964).

The success of the American Medical Association (AMA) in consolidating its power was central to securing a monopoly for M.D. physicians. In recent years the AMA has lost some power to the "corporate rationalizers" in medicine (e.g., health insurance industry, hospital organizations, HMOs [Alford, 1972]). While physicians still maintain a monopoly over medical practice, the "corporatization" of medicine has sharply reduced their control over medical organizations (see also selection 28 by Stone).

By virtue of their monopoly over medical practice, physicians have exerted an enormous influence over the entire field of medicine, including the right to define what constitutes disease and how to treat it. Friedson's (1970a: 251) observation is still valid: "The medical profession has first claim to jurisdiction over the label illness and *always* to how it can be attached, irrespective of its capacity to deal with it effectively."

Physicians also gained "professional dominance" over the organization of medical services in the United States (Friedson, 1970b). This monopoly gave the medical profession functional autonomy and a structural insulation from outside evaluations of medical practice. In addition, professional dominance includes not only the exclusive right to treat disease but also the right to limit and evaluate the performance of most other medical care workers. Finally, the particular vision of medicine that became institutionalized included a "clinical mentality" (Friedson, 1970a) that focused on medical responsibility to *individual* patients rather than to the community or public.

Physicians' professional dominance has been challenged in the past two decades. The rise of corporate and bureaucratic medicine, the emphasis on cost containment by third-party payers, the complexity of medical technology, and the dramatic increase in malpractice suits have left the medical profession feeling besieged (Stoeckle, 1988). There is evidence that professional sovereignty is declining and commercial interest in the health sector is increasing. One analyst has suggested that this is partly due to the actual "surplus" of doctors in this country and the increasing power of "third parties" in financing medicine (Starr, 1982). A lively debate exists over whether professional dominance has waned to the point that physicians are relegated to the position of other workers, a kind of professional "proletariat" (McKinlay and Arches, 1985), or whether professional dominance itself begot the changes that are challenging medical sovereignty (Light and Levine, 1989). In the changing medical environment, professional dominance is clearly changing and is reshaping the influence and authority over medical care. While medicine maintains some of its monopoly, its dominance over the health care system has clearly declined.

In the first selection, "Professionalization, Monopoly, and the Structure of Medical Practice," Peter Conrad and Joseph W. Schneider present a brief review of the historical development of this medical monopoly. They examine the case of abortion in the nineteenth century to highlight how specific medical interests were served by a physician-led crusade against abortion. By successfully outlawing abortion and institutionalizing their own professional ethics, "regular" physicians were able to eliminate effectively some of their competitors and secure greater control of the medical market.

Richard W. Wertz and Dorothy C. Wertz expanded on this theme of monopolization and professional dominance in "Notes on the Decline of Midwives and the Rise of Medical Obstetricians." They investigate the medicalization of childbirth historically and the subsequent decline of midwifery in this country. Female midwifery, which continues to be practiced in most industrialized and developing countries, was virtually eliminated in the United States. Wertz and Wertz show that it was not merely professional imperialism that led to the exclusion of midwives (although this played an important role), but also a subtle and profound sexism within and outside the medical profession. They postulate that the physicians' monopolization of childbirth resulted from a combination of a change in middle-class women's views of birthing, physicians' economic interests, and the development of sexist notions that suggested that women weren't suitable for attending births. Physicians became increasingly interventionist in their childbirth practice partly due to their training (they felt they had to "do" something) but also due to their desire to use instruments "to establish a superior status" and treat childbirth as an illness rather than a natural event. In recent years we have seen the reemergence of nurse midwives, but their work is usually limited to hospitals under medical dominance (Rothman, 1982). Also, there are presently a small number of "lay" midwives whose practice is confined to limited and sometimes illegal situations outside of medical control (See Sullivan and Weitz, 1988).

In the past few decades, analysts have suggested that the power of the medical profession has declined and that we have seen a "corporatization" and "bureaucratization" of medicine (e.g., Starr, 1982; McKinlay and Stoeckle, 1988). There is little doubt that the role of government, the growth of the health insurance industry, and the rise of managed care have played an important role in this change. But this transformation is complex, leaving the medical profession in a very different place than it was in mid-century. In the third article, "The End of the Golden Age of Doctoring," John B. McKinlay and Lisa D. Marceau point to many of the social factors involved in the erosion of professional dominance and the rise of corporate dominance in the twenty-first century. They analyze eight interrelated factors that contributed to the decline of the "golden age of doctoring." It is clear that these changes have profoundly altered the medical profession and doctoring in the current era.

Donald W. Light, in the fourth selection, "Countervailing Power," posits a changing balance of power among professions and related social institutions. "The notion of countervailing powers locates professions within a field of institutional and cultural forces in which one party may gain dominance by subordinating the needs of significant other parties, who, in time, mobilize to counter this dominance" (Hafferty and Light, 1995: 135). In American society, professional medicine historically dominated health care, but we now see "buyers" (e.g., corporations who pay for employees' medical insurance, along with other consumers); "providers" (e.g., physicians, hospitals, HMOs, nursing homes, and other medical care providers); and "payers" (e.g., insurance companies and governments) all vying for power and influence over medical care. This changes the nature of professional power and dominance. Light points out that as medical care evolves more into a buyer-driven system, fundamental tenets of professionalism—including physicians' autonomy over their work and their monopoly over knowledge—are thrown into question. At the dawn of the new millennium, physicians certainly maintain aspects of their dominance and sovereignty, but it is clearly a situation undergoing dynamic changes.

In the final selection, "Changing Medical Organization and the Erosion of Trust," David Mechanic shows how the changes in the medical organization are affecting the patient's relationship with physicians. The doctor-patient relationship was long held in high regard and even considered "sacred." The decline of professional authority and rise of managed health care have eroded the public's trust in the medical profession and undermined patients' trust in doctors. To maintain the sanctity of the doctor-patient relationship in the twenty-first century, physicians are going to have to create ways to reinvent and reinstitutionalize trust. Given the organization and financing (see next section) of the medical care system, this will not be easy.

REFERENCES

Alford, Robert. 1972. "The political economy of health care: Dynamics without change." Politics and Society. 2: 127–164.

Blumgart, H. L. 1964. "Caring for the patient." New England Journal of Medicine. 270: 449–56.

Friedson, Eliot. 1970a. Profession of Medicine. New York: Dodd, Mead.

. 1970b. Professional Dominance. Chicago: Aldine.

Hafferty, Fredric W., and Donald W. Light. 1995. "Professional dynamics and the changing nature of medical work." Journal of Health and Social Behavior. Extra issue: 132–153.

Light, Donald, and Sol Levine. 1988. "The changing character of the medical profession." Milbank Quarterly. 66 (Suppl. 2): 1–23.

McKinlay, John B. and Joan Arches. 1985. "Toward the proletarianization of physicians." International Journal of Health Services. 15: 161–95.

McKinlay, John B., and John Stoeckle. 1988. "Corporatization and the social transformation of doctoring." International Journal of Health Services. 18:191–205.

Rothman, Barbara Katz. 1982. In Labor. New York: Norton.

Starr, Paul. 1982. The Social Transformation of American Medicine. New York: Basic Books.

Stoeckle, John D. 1988. "Reflections on modern doctoring." Milbank Quarterly. 66 (Suppl. 2): 76–91.

Sullivan, Deborah A., and Rose Weitz. 1988. Labor Pains: Modern Midwives and Home Birth. New Haven: Yale University Press.

16 PROFESSIONALIZATION, MONOPOLY, AND THE STRUCTURE OF MEDICAL PRACTICE

Peter Conrad and Joseph W. Schneider

. . . Medicine has not always been the powerful, prestigious, successful, lucrative, and dominant profession we know today. The status of the medical profession is a product of medical politicking as well as therapeutic expertise. This discussion presents a brief overview of the development of the medical profession and its rise to dominance.

EMERGENCE OF THE MEDICAL PROFESSION: UP TO 1850

In ancient societies, disease was given supernatural explanations, and "medicine" was the province of priests or shamans. It was in classical Greece that medicine began to emerge as a separate occupation and develop its own theories, distinct from philosophy or theology. Hippocrates, the great Greek physician who refused to accept supernatural explanations or treatments for disease, developed a theory of the "natural" causes of disease and systematized all available medical knowledge. He laid a basis for the development of medicine as a separate body of knowledge. Early Christianity depicted sickness as punishment for sin, engendering new theological explanations and treatments. Christ and his disciples believed in the supernatural causes and cures of disease. This view became institutionalized in the Middle Ages, when the Church dogma dominated theories and practice of medicine and priests were physicians. The Renaissance in Europe brought a renewed interest in ancient Greek medical knowledge. This marked the beginning of a drift toward natural explanations of disease and the emergence of medicine as an occupation separate from the Church (Cartwright, 1977).

But European medicine developed slowly. The "humoral theory" of disease developed by Hippocrates dominated medical theory and practice until well into the 19th century. Medical diagnosis was impressionistic and often inaccurate, depicting conditions in such general terms as "fevers" and "fluxes." In the 17th century, physicians relied mainly on three techniques to determine the nature of illness: what the patient said about symptoms; the physician's own observations of signs of illness and the patient's appearance and behavior; and more rarely, a manual examination of the body (Reiser, 1978, p. 1). Medicine was by no means scientific, and "medical thought involved unverified doctrines and resulting controversies" (Shryock, 1960, p. 52). Medical practice was a "bedside medicine" that was patient oriented and did not distinguish the illness from the "sick man" (Jewson, 1976). It was not until Thomas Sydenham's astute observations in the late 17th century that physicians could begin to distinguish between the patient and the disease. Physicians possessed few treatments that worked regularly, and many of their treatments actually worsened the sufferer's condition. Medicine in colonial America inherited this European stock of medical knowledge.

Colonial American medicine was less developed than its European counterpart. There were no medical schools and few physicians, and because of the vast frontier and sparse population, much medical care was in effect self-help. Most American physicians were educated and trained by apprenticeship; few were university trained. With the exception of surgeons, most were undifferentiated practitioners. Medical practices were limited. Prior to the revolution, physicians did not commonly attend births; midwives, who were not seen as part of the medical establishment, routinely attended birthings (Wertz and Wertz, 1977). William Rothstein (1972) notes that "American colonial medical practice, like European practice of the period, was characterized by the lack of any substantial body of usable scientific knowledge" (p. 27). Physicians, both educated and otherwise, tended to treat their patients pragmatically, for medical theory had little to offer. Most colonial physicians practiced medicine only part-time, earning their livelihoods as clergymen, teachers, farmers, or in other occupations. Only in the early 19th century did medicine become a full-time vocation (Rothstein, 1972).

The first half of the 19th century saw important changes in the organization of the medical profession. About 1800, "regular," or educated, physicians convinced state legislatures to pass laws limiting the practice of medicine to practitioners of a certain training and class (prior to this nearly anyone could claim the title "doctor" and practice medicine). These state licensing laws were not particularly effective, largely because of the colonial tradition of medical self-help. They were repealed in most states during the Jacksonian period (1828–1836) because they were thought to be elitist, and the temper of the times called for a more "democratic" medicine.

The repeal of the licensing laws and the fact that most "regular" (i.e., regularly educated) physicians shared and used "a distinctive set of medically invalid therapies, known as 'heroic' therapy," created fertile conditions for the emergence of *medical sects* in the first half of the 19th century (Rothstein, 1972, p. 21). Physicians of the time practiced a "heroic" and invasive form of medicine consisting primarily of such treatments as bloodletting, vomiting, blistering, and purging. This highly interventionist, and sometimes dangerous, form of medicine engendered considerable public opposition and resistance. In this context a number of medical sects emerged, the most important of which were the homeopathic and botanical physicians. These "irregular" medical practitioners practiced less invasive, less dangerous forms of medicine. They each developed a considerable following, since their therapies were probably no less effective than those of regulars practicing heroic medicine. The regulars attempted to exclude them from practice; so the various sects set up their own medical schools and professional societies. This sectarian medicine created a highly *competitive* situation for the regulars (Rothstein, 1972). Medical sectarianism, heroic therapies, and ineffective treatment contributed to the low status and lack of prestige of early 19th-century medicine. At this time, medicine was neither a prestigious occupation nor an important economic activity in American society (Starr, 1977).

The regular physicians were concerned about this situation. Large numbers of regularly trained physicians sought to earn a livelihood by practicing medicine (Rothstein, 1972, p. 3). They were troubled by the poor image of medicine and lack of standards in medical training and practice. No doubt they were also concerned about the competition of the irregular sectarian physicians. A group of regular physicians founded the American Medical Association (AMA) in 1847 "to promote the science and art of medicine and the betterment of public health" (quoted in Coe, 1978, p. 204). The AMA also was to set and enforce standards and ethics of "regular" medical practice and strive for exclusive professional and economic rights to the medical turf.

The AMA was the crux of the regulars' attempt to "professionalize" medicine. As Magali Sarfatti Larson (1977) points out, professions organize to create and control *markets*. Organized professions attempt to regulate and limit the competition, usually by controlling professional education and by limiting licensing. Professionalization is, in this view, "the process by which producers of special services sought to constitute *and control* the market for their expertise" (Larson, 1977, p. xvi). The regular physicians and the AMA set out to consolidate and control the market for medical services. As we shall see in the next two sections, the regulars were successful in professionalization, eliminating competition and creating a medical monopoly.

CRUSADING, DEVIANCE, AND MEDICAL MONOPOLY: THE CASE OF ABORTION

The medical profession after the middle of the 19th century was frequently involved in various activities that could be termed social reform. Some of these reforms were directly related to health and illness and medical work; others were peripheral to the manifest medical calling of preventing illness and healing the sick. In these reform movements, physicians became medical crusaders, attempting to influence public morality and behavior. This medical crusading often led physicians squarely into the moral sphere, making them advocates for moral positions that had only peripheral relations to medical practice. Not infrequently these reformers sought to change people's values or to impose a set of particular values on others. . . . We now examine one of the more revealing examples of medical crusading: the criminalization of abortion in American society.[1]

Most people are under the impression that abortion was always defined as deviant and illegal in America prior to the Supreme Court's landmark decision in 1973. This, however, is not the case. American abortion policy, and the attendant defining of abortion as deviant, were specific products of medical crusading. Prior to the Civil War, abortion was a common and largely legal medical procedure performed by various types of physicians and midwives. A pregnancy was not considered confirmed until the occurrence of a phenomenon called "quickening," the first perception of fetal movement. Common law did not recognize the fetus before quickening in criminal cases, and an unquickened fetus was deemed to have no living soul. Thus most people did not consider termination of pregnancy before quickening to be an especially serious matter, much less murder. Abortion before quickening created no moral or medical problems. Public opinion was indifferent, and for the time it was probably a relatively safe medical procedure. Thus, for all intents and purposes, American women were free to terminate their pregnancies before quickening in the early 19th century. Moreover, it was a procedure relatively free of the moral stigma that was attached to abortion in this century.

After 1840 abortion came increasingly into public view. Abortion clinics were vigorously and openly advertised in newspapers and magazines. The advertisements offered euphemistically couched services for "women's complaints," "menstrual blockage," and "obstructed menses." Most contemporary observers suggested that more and more women were using these services. Prior to 1840 most abortions were performed on the unmarried and desperate of the "poor and unfortunate classes." However, beginning about this time, significantly increasing numbers of middle- and upper-class white, Protestant, native-born women began to use these services. It is likely they either wished to delay childbearing or thought they already had all the children they wanted (Mohr, 1978, pp. 46–47). By 1870 approximately one abortion was performed for every five live births (Mohr, 1978, pp. 79–80).

Beginning in the 1850s, a number of physicians, especially moral crusader Dr. Horatio Robinson Storer, began writing in medical and popular journals and lobbying in state legislatures about the danger and immorality of abortion. They opposed abortion before and after quickening and under Dr. Storer's leadership organized an aggressive national campaign. In 1859 these crusaders convinced the AMA to pass a resolution condemning abortion. Some newspapers, particularly *The New York Times*, joined the antiabortion crusade. Feminists supported the crusade, since they saw abortion as a threat to women's health and part of the oppression of women. Religious leaders, however, by and large avoided the issue of abortion, either they didn't consider it in their province or found it too sticky an issue to discuss. It was the physicians who were the guiding force in the antiabortion crusade. They were instrumental in convincing legislatures to pass state laws, especially between 1866 and 1877, that made abortion a criminal offense.

Why did physicians take the lead in the antiabortion crusade and work so directly to have abortion defined as deviant and illegal? Undoubtedly they believed in the moral "rightness" of their cause. But social historian James Mohr (1978) presents two more subtle and important reasons for the physicians' antiabortion crusading. First, concern was growing among medical people and even among some legislators about the significant drop in birthrates. Many claimed that abortion among married women of the "better classes" was a major contributor to the declining birthrate. These middle- and upper-class men (the physicians and legislators) were aware of the waves of immigrants arriving with large families and were anxious about the decline in production of native American babies.

They were deeply afraid they were being betrayed by their own women (Mohr, 1978, p. 169). Implicitly the antiabortion stance was classist and racist; the anxiety was simply that there would not be enough strong, native-born, Protestant stock to save America. This was a persuasive argument in convincing legislators of the need of antiabortion laws.

The second and more direct reason spurring the physicians in the antiabortion crusade was to aid their own nascent professionalization and create a monopoly for regular physicians. . . . The regulars had formed the AMA in 1847 to promote scientific and ethical medicine and combat what they saw as medical quackery. There were, however, no licensing laws to speak of, and many claimed the title "doctor" (e.g., homeopaths, botanical doctors, eclectic physicians). The regular physicians adopted the Hippocratic oath and code of ethics as their standard. Among other things, this oath forbids abortion. Regulars usually did not perform abortions; however, many practitioners of medical sects performed abortions regularly, and some had lucrative practices. Thus for the regular AMA physicians the limitation of abortion became one way of asserting their own professional domination over other medical practitioners. In their crusading these physicians had translated the social goals of cultural and professional dominance into moral and medical language. They lobbied long and hard to convince legislators of the danger and immorality of abortion. By passage of laws making abortion criminal any time during gestation, regular physicians were able to legislate their code of ethics and get the state to employ sanctions against their competitors. This limited these competitors' markets and was a major step toward the regulars' achieving a monopolization of medical practice.

In a relatively short period the antiabortion crusade succeeded in passing legislation that made abortion criminal in every state. A byproduct of this was a shift in American public opinion from an indifference to and tolerance of abortion to a hardening of attitudes against what had until then been a fairly common practice. The irony was that abortion as a medical procedure probably was safer at the turn of the 20th century than a century before, but it was defined and seen as more dangerous. By 1900 abortion was not only illegal but deviant and immoral. The physicians' moral crusade had successfully defined abortion as a deviant activity. This definition remained largely unchanged until the 1973 Supreme Court decision, which essentially returned the abortion situation to its pre-1850 condition. . . .

GROWTH OF MEDICAL EXPERTISE AND PROFESSIONAL DOMINANCE

Although the general public's dissatisfaction with heroic medicine remained, the image of medicine and what it could accomplish was improving by the middle of the 19th century. There had been a considerable reduction in the incidence and mortality of certain dread diseases. The plague and leprosy had nearly disappeared. Smallpox, malaria, and cholera were less devastating than ever before. These improvements in health engendered optimism and increased people's faith in medical practice. Yet these dramatic "conquests of disease" were by and large *not* the result of new medical knowledge or improved clinical medical practice. Rather, they resulted from changes in social conditions: a rising standard of living, better nutrition and housing, and public health innovations like sanitation. With the lone exception of vaccination for smallpox, the decline of these diseases had nearly nothing to do with clinical medicine (Dubos, 1959; McKeown, 1971). But despite lack of effective treatments, medicine was the beneficiary of much popular credit for improved health.

The regular physicians' image was improved well before they demonstrated any unique effectiveness of practice. The AMA's attacks on irregular medical practice continued. In the 1870s the regulars convinced legislatures to outlaw abortion and in some states to restore licensing laws to restrict medical practice. The AMA was becoming an increasingly powerful and authoritative voice representing regular medical practice.

But the last three decades of the century saw significant "breakthroughs" in medical knowledge and treatment. The scientific medicine of the regular physicians was making new medical advances. Anesthesia and antisepsis made possible great strides in surgical medicine and improvements in hospital care. The bacteriological research of Koch and Pasteur developed the "germ theory of disease," which had important applications in medical practice. It was the accomplishments of surgery and bacteriology that put medicine on a scientific basis (Freidson, 1970a, p. 16). The rise of scientific medicine marked a death knell for medical sectarianism (e.g., the homeopathic physicians eventually joined the regulars). The new laboratory sciences provided a way of testing the theories and practices of various sects, which ultimately led to a single model of medical practice. The well-organized regulars were able to legitimate their form of medical practice and support it with "scientific" evidence.

With the emergence of scientific medicine, a unified paradigm, or model, of medical practice developed. It was based, most fundamentally, on viewing the body as a machine (e.g., organ malfunctioning) and on the germ theory of disease (Kelman, 1977). The "doctrine of specific etiology" became predominant: each disease was caused by a specific germ or agent. Medicine focused solely on the internal environment (the body), largely ignoring the external environment (society) (Dubos, 1959). This paradigm proved fruitful in ensuing years. It is the essence of the "medical model." . . .

The development of scientific medicine accorded regular medicine a convincing advantage in medical practice. It set the stage for the achievement of a medical monopoly by the AMA regulars. As Larson (1977) notes, "Once scientific medicine offered sufficient guarantees of its superior effectiveness in dealing with disease, the rate willingly contributed to the creation of a monopoly by means of registration and licensing" (p. 23). The new licensing laws created regular medicine as a *legally enforced monopoly of practice* (Freidson, 1970b, p. 83). They virtually eliminated medical competition.

The medical monopoly was enhanced further by the Flexner Report on medical education in 1910. Under the auspices of the Carnegie Foundation, medical educator Abraham Flexner visited nearly all 160 existing medical schools in the United States. He found the level of medical education poor and recommended the closing of most schools. Flexner urged stricter state laws, rigid standards for medical education, and more rigorous examinations for certification to practice. The enactment of Flexner's recommendations effectively made all nonscientific types of medicine illegal. It created a near total AMA monopoly of medical education in America.

In securing a monopoly, the AMA regulars achieved a unique professional state. Medicine not only monopolized the market for medical services and the training of physicians, it developed an unparalleled "professional dominance." The medical profession was *functionally autonomous* (Freidson, 1970b). Physicians were insulated from external evaluation and were by and large free to regulate their own performance. Medicine could define its own territory and set its own standards. Thus, Eliot Freidson (1970b) notes, "while the profession may not everywhere be free to control the *terms* of its work, it is free to control the *content* of its work" (p. 84).

The domain of medicine has expanded in the past century. This is due partially to the prestige medicine has accrued and its place as the steward of the "sacred" value of life. Medicine has sometimes been called on to repeat its "miracles" and successful treatments on problems that are not biomedical in nature. Yet in other instances the expansion is due to explicit medical crusading or entrepreneurship. This expansion of medicine, especially into the realm of social problems and human behavior, frequently has taken medicine beyond its proven technical competence (Freidson, 1970b). . . .

The organization of medicine has also expanded and become more complex in this century. In the next section we briefly describe the structure of medical practice in the United States.

STRUCTURE OF MEDICAL PRACTICE

Before we leave our discussion of the medical profession, it is worthwhile to outline some general features of the structure of medical practice that have contributed to the expansion of medical jurisdiction.

The medical sector of society has grown enormously in the 20th century. It has become the second largest industry in America. There are about 350,000 physicians and over 5 million people employed in the medical field. The "medical industries," including the pharmaceutical, medical technology, and health insurance industries, are among the most profitable in our economy. Yearly drug sales alone are over $4.5 billion. There are more than 7000 hospitals in the United States with 1.5 million beds and 33 million inpatient and 200 million outpatient visits a year (McKinlay, 1976).

The organization of medical practice has changed. Whereas the single physician in "solo practice" was typical in 1900, today physicians are engaged increasingly in large corporate practices or employed by hospitals or other bureaucratic organizations. Medicine in modern society is becoming bureaucratized (Mechanic, 1976). The power in medicine has become diffused, especially since World War II, from the AMA, which represented the individual physician, to include the organizations that represent bureaucratic medicine: the health insurance industry, the medical schools, and the American Hospital Association (Ehrenreich and Ehrenreich, 1970). Using Robert Alford's (1972) conceptualizations, corporate rationalizers have taken much of the power in medicine from the professional monopolists.

Medicine has become both more specialized and more dependent on technology. In 1929 only 25 percent of American physicians were fulltime specialists; by 1969 the proportion had grown to 75 percent (Reiser, 1978). Great advances were made in medicine, and many were directly related to technology: miracle medicines like penicillin, a myriad of psychoactive drugs, heart and brain surgery, the electrocardiograph, CAT scanners, fetal monitors, kidney dialysis machines, artificial organs, and transplant surgery, to name but a few. The hospital has become the primary medical workshop, a center for technological medicine.

Medicine has made a significant economic expansion. In 1940, medicine claimed about 4 percent of the American gross national product (GNP); today it claims about 9 percent, which amounts to more than $150 billion. The causes for this growth are too complex to describe here, but a few factors should be noted. American medicine has always operated on a "fee-for-service" basis, that is, each service rendered is charged and paid for separately. Simply put, in a capitalist medical system, the more services provided, the more fees collected. This not only creates an incentive to provide more services but also to expand these medical services to new markets. The fee-for-service system may encourage unnecessary medical care. There is some evidence, for example, that American medicine performs a considerable amount of "excess" surgery (McCleery and Keelty, 1971); this may also be true for other services. Medicine is one of the few occupations that can create its own demand. Patients may come to physicians, but physicians tell them what procedures they need. The availability of medical technique may also create a demand for itself.

The method by which medical care is paid for has changed greatly in the past half-century. In 1920 nearly all health care was paid for directly by the patient-consumer. Since the 1930s an increasing amount of medical care has been paid for through "third-party" payments, mainly through health insurance and the government. About 75 percent of the American population is covered by some form of medical insurance (often only for hospital care). Since 1966 the government has been involved directly in financing medical care through Medicare and Medicaid. The availability of a large amount of federal money, with nearly no cost controls or regulation of medical practice, has been a major factor fueling our current medical "cost crisis." But the ascendancy of third-party payments has affected the expansion of medicine in another way: more and more human problems become defined as "medical problems" (sickness) because that is the only way insurance programs will "cover" the costs of services. . . .

In sum, the regular physicians developed control of medical practice and a professional dominance with nearly total functional autonomy. Through professionalization and persuasion concerning the superiority of their form of medicine, the medical profession (represented by the AMA) achieved a legally supported monopoly of practice. In short, it cornered the medical market. The medical profession has succeeded in both therapeutic and economic expansion. It has won the almost exclusive right to reign over the kingdom of health and illness, no matter where it may extend.

NOTE

1. We rely on James C. Mohr's (1978) fine historical account of the origins and evolution of American abortion policy for data and much of the interpretation in this section.

REFERENCES

Alford, R. The political economy of health care: dynamics without change. *Politics and Society,* 1972, 2 (2), 127–64.

Cartwright, F. F. *A Social History of Medicine.* New York: Longman, 1977.

Coe, R. *The Sociology of Medicine.* Second edition. New York: McGraw-Hill, 1978.

Dubos, R. *Mirage of Health.* New York: Harper and Row, 1959.

Ehrenreich, B., and Ehrenreich, J. *The American Health Empire.* New York: Random House, 1970.

Freidson, E. *Profession of Medicine.* New York: Dodd, Mead, 1970a.

Freidson, E. *Professional Dominance.* Chicago: Aldine, 1970b.

Jewson, N. D. The disappearance of the sick-man from medical cosmology, 1770–1870. *Sociology,* 1976, 10, 225–44.

Kelman, S. The social nature of the definition of health. In V. Navarro, *Health and Medical Care in the U.S.* Farmingdale, N.Y.: Baywood, 1977.

Larson, M. S. *The Rise of Professionalism.* Berkeley: California, 1977.

McCleery, R. S., and Keelty, L. T. *One Life-One Physician: An Inquiry into the Medical Profession's Performance in Self-regulation.* Washington, D.C.: Public Affairs Press, 1971.

McKeown, T. A historical appraisal of the medical task. In G. McLachlan and T. McKeown (eds.), *Medical History and Medical Care: A Symposium of Perspectives.* New York: Oxford, 1971.

McKinlay, J. B. The changing political and economic context of the physician-patient encounter. In E. B. Gallagher (ed.), *The Doctor-Patient Relationship in the Changing Health Scene.* Washington, D.C.: U.S. Government Printing Office, 1976.

Mechanic, D. *The Growth of Bureaucratic Medicine.* New York: Wiley, 1976.

Mohr, J. C. *Abortion in America.* New York: Oxford, 1978.

Reiser, S. J. *Medicine and the Reign of Technology.* New York: Cambridge, 1978.

Rothstein, W. G. *American Physicians in the Nineteenth Century: From Sects to Science.* Baltimore: Johns Hopkins, 1972.

Shryock, R. H. *Medicine and Society in America: 1660–1860.* Ithaca, N.Y.: Cornell, 1960.

Starr, P. Medicine, economy and society in nineteenth-century America. *Journal of Social History,* 1977, 10, 588–607.

Wertz, R., and Wertz, D. *Lying-In: A History of Childbirth in America.* New York: Free Press, 1977.

17 NOTES ON THE DECLINE OF MIDWIVES AND THE RISE OF MEDICAL OBSTETRICIANS

Richard W. Wertz and Dorothy C. Wertz

. . . The Americans who were studying medicine in Great Britain [in the late eighteenth century] discovered that men could bring the benefits of the new midwifery to birth and thereby gain income and status. In regard to the unresolved question of what medical arts were appropriate, the Americans took the view of the English physicians, who instructed them that nature was usually adequate and intervention often dangerous. From that perspective they developed a model of the new midwifery suitable for the American situation.

From 1750 to approximately 1810 American doctors conceived of the new midwifery as an enterprise to be shared between themselves and trained midwives. Since doctors during most of that period were few in number, their plan was reasonable and humanitarian and also reflected their belief that, in most cases, natural processes were adequate and the need for skilled intervention limited, though important. Doctors therefore envisaged an arrangement whereby trained midwives would attend normal deliveries and doctors would be called to difficult ones. To implement this plan, Dr. Valentine Seaman established a short course for midwives in the New York (City) Almshouse in 1799, and Dr. William Shippen began a course on anatomy and midwifery, including clinical observation of birth, in Philadelphia. Few women came as students, however, but men did, so the doctors trained the men to be man-midwives, perhaps believing, as Smellie had contended, that the sex of the practitioner was less important than the command of new knowledge and skill.[1]

As late as 1817, Dr. Thomas Ewell of Washington, D.C., a regular physician, proposed to establish a school for midwives, connected with a hospital, similar to the schools that had existed for centuries in the great cities of Europe. Ewell sought federal funding for his enterprise, but it was not forthcoming, and the school was never founded. Herein lay a fundamental difference between European and American development of the midwife. European governments provided financial support for medical education, including the training of midwives. The U.S. government provided no support for medical education in the nineteenth century, and not enough of the women who might have aspired to become midwives could afford the fees to support a school. Those who founded schools turned instead to the potentially lucrative business of training the many men who sought to become doctors.[2]

Doctors also sought to increase the supply of doctors educated in America in the new midwifery and thus saw to it that from the outset of American medical schools midwifery became a specialty field, one all doctors could practice.

The plans of doctors for a shared enterprise with women never developed in America. Doctors were unable to attract women for training, perhaps because women were uninterested in studying what they thought they already knew and, moreover, studying it under the tutelage of men. The restraints of traditional modesty and the tradition of female sufficiency for the management of birth were apparently stronger than the appeal of a rationalized system for a more scientific and, presumably, safer midwifery system.

Not only could doctors not attract women for training in the new science and arts, but they could not even organize midwives already in practice. These women had never been organized among themselves. They thought of themselves as being loyal not primarily to an abstract medical science but to local groups of women and their needs. They reflected the tradition of local self-held empiricism that continued to be very strong in America. Americans had never had a medical profession or medical institutions, so they must have found it hard to understand why the European-trained doctors wished to organize a shared, though hierarchical, midwifery enterprise. How hard it was would be shown later, when doctors sought to organize themselves around the new science of midwifery, in which they had some institutional training. Their practice of midwifery would be governed less by science and professional behavior than by empirical practice and economic opportunity.

In the years after 1810, in fact, the practice of midwifery in American towns took on the same unregulated, open-market character it had in England. Both men and women of various degrees of experience and training competed to attend births. Some trained midwives from England immigrated to America, where they advertised their ability in local newspapers.[3] But these women confronted doctors trained abroad or in the new American medical schools. They also confronted medical empirics who presented themselves as "intrepid" man-midwives after having imbibed the instrumental philosophy from Smellie's books. American women therefore confronted a wide array of talents and skills for aiding their deliveries.

Childbirth in America would not have any neat logic during the nineteenth century, but one feature that distinguished it from childbirth abroad was the gradual disappearance of women from the practice of midwifery. There were many reasons for that unusual development. Most obvious was the severe competition that the new educated doctors and empirics brought to the event of birth, an event that often served as entrance for the medical person to a sustained practice. In addition, doctors lost their allegiance to a conservative view of the science and arts of midwifery under the exigencies of practice; they came to adopt a view endorsing more extensive interventions in birth and less reliance upon the adequacy of nature. This view led to the conviction that a certain mastery was needed, which women were assumed to be unable to achieve.

Women ceased to be midwives also because of a change in the cultural attitudes about the proper place and activity for women in society. It came to be regarded as unthinkable to confront women with the facts of medicine or to mix men and women in training, even for such an event as birth. As a still largely unscientific enterprise, medicine took on the cultural attributes necessary for it to survive, and the Victorian culture found certain roles unsuitable for women. Midwives also disappeared because they had not been organized and had never developed any leadership. Medicine in America may have had minimal scientific authority, but it was beginning to develop social and professional organization and leadership; unorganized midwives were an easy competitive target for medicine. Finally, midwives lost out to doctors and empirics because of the changing tastes among middle- and upper-class women; for these women, the new midwifery came to have the promise of more safety and even more respectability.[4]

Midwives therefore largely ceased to attend the middle classes in America during the nineteenth century. Except among ethnic immigrants, among poor, isolated whites, and among blacks, there is little significant evidence of midwifery. This is not to say that there were no such women or that in instances on the frontier or even in cities when doctors were unavailable women did not undertake to attend other women. But educated doctors and empirics penetrated American settlements quickly and extensively, eager to gain patients and always ready to attend birth. The very dynamics of American mobility contributed to the break-up of those communities that had sustained the midwives' practices.

Because of continued ethnic immigration, however, by 1900 in many urban areas half of the women were still being delivered by immigrant midwives. The fact that ethnic groups existed largely outside the development of American medicine during the nineteenth century would pose a serious problem in the twentieth century.

Native-born educated women sought to become doctors, not midwives, during the nineteenth century. They did not want to play a role in birth that was regarded as inferior and largely nonmedical—the midwife's role—but wished to assume the same medical role allowed to men.

It is important to emphasize, however, that the disappearance of midwives at middle- and upper-class births was not the result of a conspiracy between male doctors and husbands. The choice of medical attendants was the responsibility of women, upon whom devolved the care of their families' health. Women were free to choose whom they wished. A few did seek out unorthodox practitioners, although most did not. But as the number of midwives diminished, women of course found fewer respectable, trained women of their own class whom they might choose to help in their deliveries.

In order to understand the new midwifery [i.e. medical obstetrics], it is necessary to consider who doctors were and how they entered the medical profession. The doctors who assumed control over middle-class births in America were very differently educated and organized from their counterparts in France or England. The fact that their profession remained loosely organized and ill-defined throughout most of the nineteenth century helps to explain their desire to exclude women from midwifery, for often women were the only category of people that they could effectively exclude. Doctors with some formal education had always faced competition from the medical empirics—men, women, and even freed slaves—who declared themselves able to treat all manner of illnesses and often publicly advertised their successes. These empirics, called quacks by the orthodox educated doctors, offered herbal remedies or psychological comfort to patients. Orthodox physicians objected that the empirics prescribed on an individual, trial-and-error basis without reference to any academic theories about the origins and treatment of disease. Usually the educated physician also treated his patients empirically, for medical theory had little to offer that was practically superior to empiricism until the development of bacteriology in the 1870s. Before then there was no convincing, authoritative, scientific nucleus for medicine, and doctors often had difficulty translating what knowledge they did have into practical treatment. The fundamental objection of regular doctors was to competition from uneducated practitioners. Most regular doctors also practiced largely ineffective therapies, but they were convinced that their therapies were better than those of the empirics because they were educated men. The uneducated empirics enjoyed considerable popular support during the first half of the nineteenth century because their therapies were as often successful as the therapies of the regulars, and sometimes less strenuous. Like the empirics, educated doctors treated patients rather than diseases and looked for different symptoms in different social classes. Because a doctor's reputation stemmed from the social standing of his patients, there was considerable competition for the patronage of the more respectable families.

The educated, or "regular," doctors around 1800 were of the upper and middle classes, as were the state legislators. The doctors convinced the legislators that medicine, like other gentlemen's professions, should be restricted to those who held diplomas or who had apprenticed with practitioners of the appropriate social class and training. State licensure laws were passed, in response to the Federalist belief that social deference was due to professional men. The early laws were ineffectual because they did not take into account the popular tradition of self-help. People continued to patronize empirics. During the Jacksonian Era even the nonenforced licensing laws were repealed by most states as elitist; popular belief held that the practice of medicine should be "democratic" and open to all, or at least to all men.[5]

In the absence of legal control, several varieties of "doctors" practiced in the nineteenth century. In addition to the empirics and the "regular" doctors there were the sectarians, who included the Thomsonian Botanists, the Homeopaths, the Eclectics, and a number of minor sects of which the most important for obstetrics were the Hydrotherapists.

The regular doctors can be roughly divided into two groups: the elite, who had attended the better medical schools and who wrote the textbooks urging "conservative" practice in midwifery; and the great number of poorly educated men who had spent a few months at a proprietary medical school from which they were graduated with no practical or clinical knowledge. (Proprietary medical schools were profit-making schools owned by several local doctors who also taught there. Usually such schools had no equipment or resources for teaching.) In the eighteenth century the elite had had to travel to London, or more often Edinburgh, for training. In 1765, however, the Medical College of Philadelphia was founded, followed by King's College (later Columbia) Medical School in 1767 and Harvard in 1782. Obstetrics, or "midwifery," as it was then called, was the first medical specialty in those schools, preceding even surgery, for it was assumed that midwifery was the keystone to medical practice, something that every student would do after graduation as part of his practice. Every medical school founded thereafter had a special "Professor of Midwifery." Among the first such professors were Drs. William Shippen at Philadelphia, Samuel Bard at King's College, and Walter Channing at Harvard. In the better schools early medical courses lasted two years; in the latter half of the nineteenth century some schools began to increase this to three, but many two-year medical graduates were still practicing in 1900.

A prestigious medical education did not guarantee that a new graduate was prepared to deal with patients. Dr. James Marion Sims, a famous nineteenth-century surgeon, stated that his education at Philadelphia's Jefferson Medical College, considered one of the best in the country in 1835, left him fitted for nothing and without the slightest notion of how to treat his first cases.[6] In 1850 a graduate of the University of Buffalo described his total ignorance on approaching his first obstetrical case:

> I was left alone with a poor Irish woman and one crony, to deliver her child . . . and I thought it nec-

> essary to call before me every circumstance I had learned from books—I must examine, and I did—But whether it was head or breech, hand or foot, man or monkey, that was defended from my uninstructed finger by the distended membranes, I was as uncomfortably ignorant, with all my learning, as the foetus itself that was making all this fuss.[7]

Fortunately the baby arrived naturally, the doctor was given great praise for his part in the event, and he wrote that he was glad "to have escaped the commission of murder."

If graduates of the better medical schools made such complaints, those who attended the smaller schools could only have been more ignorant. In 1818 Dr. John Stearns, President of the New York Medical Society, complained, "With a few honorable exceptions in each city, the practitioners are ignorant, degraded, and contemptible."[8] The American Medical Association later estimated that between 1765 and 1905 more than eight hundred medical schools were founded, most of them proprietary, money-making schools, and many were short-lived. In 1905 some 160 were still in operation. Neither the profession nor the states effectively regulated those schools until the appearance of the Flexner Report, a professional self-study published in 1910. The report led to tougher state laws and the setting of standards for medical education. Throughout much of the nineteenth century a doctor could obtain a diploma and begin practice with as little as four months' attendance at a school that might have no laboratories, no dissections, and no clinical training. Not only was it easy to become a doctor, but the profession, with the exception of the elite who attended elite patients, had low standing in the eyes of most people.[9] . . .

. . . Nineteenth-century women could choose among a variety of therapies and practitioners. Their choice was usually dictated by social class. An upper-class woman in an Eastern city would see either an elite regular physician or a homeopath; if she were daring, she might visit a hydropathic establishment. A poor woman in the Midwest might turn to an empiric, a poorly educated regular doctor, or a Thomsonian botanist. This variety of choice distressed regular doctors, who were fighting for professional and economic exclusivity. As long as doctors were organized only on a local basis, it was impossible to exclude irregulars from practice or even to set enforceable standards for regular practice. The American Medical Association was founded in 1848 for those purposes. Not until the end of the century, however, was organized medicine able to re-establish licensing laws. The effort succeeded only because the regulars finally accepted the homeopaths, who were of the same social class, in order to form a sufficient majority to convince state legislators that licensing was desirable.

Having finally won control of the market, doctors were able to turn to self-regulation, an ideal adopted by the American Medical Association in 1860 but not put into effective practice until after 1900. Although there had been progress in medical science and in the education of the elite and the specialists during the nineteenth century, the average doctor was still woefully undereducated. The Flexner Report in 1910 revealed that 90 percent of doctors were then without a college education and that most had attended substandard medical schools.[10] Only after its publication did the profession impose educational requirements on the bulk of medical practitioners and take steps to accredit medical schools and close down diploma mills. Until then the average doctor had little sense of what his limits were or to whom he was responsible, for there was often no defined community of professionals and usually no community of patients.

Because of the ill-defined nature of the medical profession in the nineteenth century and the poor quality of medical education, doctors' insistence on the exclusion of women as economically dangerous competitors is quite understandable. As a group, nineteenth-century doctors were not affluent, and even their staunchest critics admitted that they could have made more money in business. Midwifery itself paid less than other types of practice, for many doctors spent long hours in attending laboring women and later had trouble collecting their fees. Yet midwifery was a guaranteed income, even if small, and it opened the way to family practice and sometimes to consultations involving many doctors and shared fees. The family and female friends who had seen a doctor "perform" successfully were likely to call him again. Doctors worried that, if midwives were allowed to deliver the upper classes, women would turn to them for treatment of other illnesses and male doctors would lose half their clientele. As a prominent Boston doctor wrote in 1820, "If female midwifery is again introduced among the rich and influential, it will become fashionable and it will be considered indelicate to employ a physician."[11] Doctors had to eliminate midwives in order to protect the gateway to their whole practice.

They had to mount an attack on midwives, because midwives had their defenders, who argued that women were safer and more modest than the new man-midwives. For example, the *Virginia Gazette* in 1772 carried a "LETTER on the present State of MIDWIFERY," emphasizing the old idea that "Labour is Nature's Work" and needs no more art than women's experience teaches, and that it was safer when women alone attended births.

> It is a notorious fact that more Children have been lost since Women were so scandalously indecent as to employ Men than for Ages before that Practice became so general. . . . [Women midwives] never dream of having recourse to Force; the barbarous, bloody Crochet, never stained their Hands with Murder. . . . A long unimpassioned Practice, early commenced, and calmly pursued is absolutely requisite to give Men by Art, what Women attain by Nature.

The writer concluded with the statement that men-midwives also took liberties with pregnant and laboring women that were "sufficient to taint the Purity, and sully the Chastity, of any Woman breathing." The final flourish, "True Modesty is incompatible with the Idea of employing a MAN-MIDWIFE," would echo for decades, causing great distress for female patients with male attendants. Defenders of midwives made similar statements throughout the first half of the nineteenth century. Most were sectarian doctors or laymen with an interest in women's modesty.[12] No midwives came forward to defend themselves in print.

The doctors' answer to midwives' defenders was expressed not in terms of pecuniary motives but in terms of safety and the proper place of women. After 1800 doctors' writings implied that women who presumed to supervise births had overreached their proper position in life. One of the earliest American birth manuals, the *Married Lady's Companion and Poor Man's Friend* (1808), denounced the ignorance of midwives and urged them to "submit to their station."[13]

Two new convictions about women were at the heart of the doctors' opposition to midwives: that women were unsafe to attend deliveries and that no "true" woman would want to gain the knowledge and skills necessary to do so. An anonymous pamphlet, published in 1820 in Boston, set forth these convictions along with other reasons for excluding midwives from practice. The author, thought to have been either Dr. Walter Channing or Dr. Henry Ware, another leading obstetrician, granted that women had more "passive fortitude" than men in enduring and witnessing suffering but asserted that women lacked the power to act that was essential to being a birth attendant:

> They have not that power of action, or that active power of mind, which is essential to the practice of a surgeon. They have less power of restraining and governing the natural tendencies to sympathy and are more disposed to yield to the expressions of acute sensibility . . . where they become the principal agents, the feelings of sympathy are too powerful for the cool exercise of judgment.[14]

The author believed only men capable of the attitude of detached concern needed to concentrate on the techniques required in birth. It is not surprising to find the author stressing the importance of interventions, but his undervaluing of sympathy, which in most normal deliveries was the only symptomatic treatment necessary, is rather startling. Clearly, he hoped to exaggerate the need for coolness in order to discountenance the belief of many women and doctors that midwives could safely attend normal deliveries.

The author possibly had something more delicate in mind that he found hard to express. He perhaps meant to imply that women were unsuited because there were certain times when they were "disposed to yield to the expressions of acute sensibility." Doctors quite commonly believed that during menstruation women's limited bodily energy was diverted from the brain, rendering them, as doctors phrased it, idiotic. In later years another Boston doctor, Horatio Storer, explained why he thought women unfit to become surgeons. He granted that exceptional women had the necessary courage, tact, ability, money, education, and patience for the career but argued that, because the "periodical infirmity of their sex . . . in every case . . . unfits them for any responsible effort of mind," he had to oppose them. During their "condition," he said, "neither life nor limb submitted to them would be as safe as at other times," for the condition was a "temporary insanity," a time when women were "more prone than men to commit any unusual or outrageous act."[15]

The author of the anonymous pamphlet declared that a female would find herself at times (i.e., during menstruation) totally unable to manage birth emergencies, such as hemorrhages, convulsions, manual extraction of the placenta, or inversion of the womb, when the newly delivered organ externally turned itself inside out and extruded from the body, sometimes hanging to the knees. In fact, an English midwife, Sarah Stone, had described in 1737 how she personally had handled each of these emergencies successfully. But the author's readers did not know that, and the author himself could have dismissed Stone's skill as fortuitous, exercised in times of mental clarity.[16]

The anonymous author was also convinced that no woman could be trained in the knowledge and skill of midwifery without losing her standing as a lady. In the dissecting room and in the hospital a woman would forfeit her "delicate feelings" and "refined sensibility"; she would see things that would taint her moral character. Such a woman would "unsex" herself, by which the doctors meant not only that she would lose her standing as a "lady" but also, literally, that she would be subject to physical exertions and nervous excitements that would damage her female organs irreparably and prevent her from fulfilling her social role as wife and mother.[17] . . .

. . . The exclusion of women from obstetrical cooperation with men had important effects upon the "new practice" that was to become the dominant tradition in American medical schools. American obstetric education differed significantly from training given in France, where the principal maternity hospitals trained doctors clinically alongside student midwives. Often the hospital's midwives, who supervised all normal births, trained the doctors in normal deliveries. French doctors never lost touch with the conservative tradition that said "Dame Nature is the best midwife." In America, where midwives were not trained at all and medical education was sexually segregated, medicine turned away from the conservative tradition and became more interventionist.

Around 1810 the new midwifery in America appears to have entered a new phase, one that shaped its character and problems throughout the century. Doctors continued to regard birth as a fundamentally natural process, usually sufficient by itself to effect delivery without artful assistance, and understandable mechanistically. But this view conflicted with the exigencies of their medical practice, which called upon them to demonstrate skills. Gradually, more births seemed to require aid.

Young doctors rarely had any clinical training in what the theory of birth meant in practice. Many arrived at birth with only lectures and book learning to guide them. If they (and the laboring patient) were fortunate, they had an older, experienced doctor or attending woman to explain what was natural and what was not. Many young men were less lucky and were embarrassed, confused, and frightened by the appearances of labor and birth. Lacking clinical training, each had to develop his own sense of what each birth required, if anything, in the way of artful assistance; each had to learn the consequence of misdirected aids.[18]

If the doctor was in a hurry to reach another patient, he might be tempted to hasten the process along by using instruments or other expedients. If the laboring woman or her female attendants urged him to assist labor, he might feel compelled to use his tools and skills even though he knew that nature was adequate but slow. He had to use his arts because he was expected to "perform." Walter Channing, Professor of Midwifery at Harvard Medical School in the early nineteenth century, remarked about the doctor, in the context of discussing a case in which forceps were used unnecessarily, that he "must do something. He cannot remain a spectator merely, where there are too many witnesses and where interest in what is going on is too deep to allow of his inaction." Channing was saying that, even though well-educated physicians recognized that natural processes were sufficient and that instruments could be dangerous, in their practice they also had to appear to *do* something for their patient's symptoms, whether that entailed giving a drug to alleviate pain or shortening labor by using the forceps. The doctor could not appear to be indifferent or inattentive or useless. He had to establish his identity by doing something, preferably something to make the patient feel better. And if witnesses were present there was perhaps even more reason to "perform." Channing concluded: "Let him be collected and calm, and he will probably do little he will afterwards look upon and regret."[19]

If educated physicians found it difficult in practice to appeal before their patients to the reliability of nature and the dangers of instruments, one can imagine what less confident and less competent doctors did with instruments in order to appear useful. A number of horror stories from the early decades of the century have been retailed by men and women who believed that doctors used their instruments unfairly and incompetently to drive midwives from practice.[20] Whatever the truth may be about the harm done, it is easy to believe that instruments were used regularly by doctors to establish their superior status.

If doctors believed that they had to perform in order to appear useful and to win approval, it is very likely that women, on the other hand, began to expect that more might go wrong with birth processes than they had previously believed. In the context of social childbirth, which . . . meant that women friends and kin were present at delivery, the appearance of forceps in one birth established the possibility of their being used in subsequent births. In short, women may have come to anticipate difficult births whether or not doctors urged that possibility as a means of selling themselves. Having seen the "best," perhaps each woman wanted the "best" for her delivery, whether she needed it or not.

Strange as it may sound, women may in fact have been choosing male attendants because they wanted a guaranteed performance, in the sense of both guaranteed safety and guaranteed fashionableness. Choosing the best medical care is itself a kind of fashion. But in addition women may have wanted a guaranteed audience, the male attendant, for quite specific purposes; namely, they may have wanted a representative male to see their pain and suffering in order that their femininity might be established and their pain verified before men. Women, then, could have had a range of important reasons for choosing male doctors to perform: for themselves, safety; for the company of women, fashion; for the world of men, femininity.

So a curious inconsistency arose between the principle of noninterference in nature and the exigencies of professional practice. Teachers of midwifery continued to stress the adequacy of nature and the danger of instruments. Samuel Bard, Dean of King's College Medical School, wrote a text on midwifery in 1807 in which he refused even to discuss forceps because he believed that interventions by unskilled men, usually inspired by Smellie's writings, were more dangerous than the most desperate case left to nature. Bard's successors made the same points in the 1830s and 1840s. Dr. Chandler Gilman, Professor of Obstetrics at the College of Physicians and Surgeons in New York from 1841 to 1865, taught his students that "Dame Nature is the best midwife in the world. . . . Meddlesome midwifery is fraught with evil. . . . The less done generally the better. Non-interference is the cornerstone of midwifery."[21] This instruction often went unheeded, however, because young doctors often resorted to instruments in haste or in confusion, or because they were poorly trained and unsupervised in practice, but also, as we have indicated, because physicians, whatever their state of knowledge, were expected to do something.

What they could do—the number of techniques to aid and control natural processes—gradually increased. In 1808, for example, Dr. John Stearns of upper New York State learned from an immigrant German midwife of a new means to effect the mechanics of birth. This was ergot, a powerful natural drug that stimulates uterine muscles when given orally. Ergot is a fungus that grows on rye and other stored grains. It causes powerful and unremitting contractions. Stearns stressed its value in saving the doctor's time and in relieving the distress and agony of long labor. Ergot also quickens the expulsion of the placenta and stems hemorrhage by compelling the uterus to contract. Stearns claimed that ergot had no ill effects but warned that it should be given only after the fetus was positioned for easy delivery, for it induced an incessant action that left no time to turn a child in the birth canal or uterus.

There was in fact no antidote to ergot's rapid and uncontrollable effects until anesthesia became available in later decades. So if the fetus did not move as expected, the drug could cause the uterus to mold itself around the child, rupturing the uterus and killing the child. Ergot, like most new medical arts for birth, was a mix of danger and benefit. Critics of meddlesome doctors said that they often used it simply to save time. However true that was, ergot certainly fitted the mechanistic view of birth, posed a dilemma to doctors about wise use, and enlarged the doctors' range of arts for controlling birth. Doctors eventually determined that using ergot to induce labor without an antidote was too dangerous and limited its use to expelling the placenta or stopping hemorrhage.[22]

Despite the theory of the naturalness of birth and the danger of intervention, the movement in midwifery was in the opposite direction, to less reliance on nature and more reliance on artful intervention. The shift appeared during the 1820s in discussions as to what doctors should call themselves when they practiced the new midwifery. "Male-midwife," "midman," "man-midwife," "physician man-midwife," and even "androboethogynist" were terms too clumsy, too reminiscent of the female title, or too unreflective of the new science and skill. "Accoucheur" sounded better but was French. The doctors of course ignored Elizabeth Nihell's earlier, acid suggestion that they call themselves "pudendists" after the area of the body that so interested them. Then an English doctor suggested in 1828 that "obstetrician" was as appropriate a term as any. Coming from the Latin meaning "to stand before," it had the advantage of sounding like other honorable professions, such as "electrician" or "geometrician," in which men variously understood and dominated nature.[23]

The renaming of the practice of midwifery symbolized doctors' new sense of themselves as professional actors. In fact, the movement toward greater dominance over birth's natural processes cannot be understood unless midwifery is seen in the context of general medical practice. In that perspective, several relations between midwifery and general practice become clearly important. In the first place, midwifery continued during the first half of the nineteenth century to be one of the few areas of general practice where doctors had a scientific understanding and useful medical arts. That meant that practicing midwifery was central to doctors' attempts to build a practice, earn fees, and achieve some status, for birth was one physical condition they were confident they knew how to treat. And they were successful in the great majority of cases because birth itself was usually successful. Treating birth was without the risk of treating many other conditions, but doctors got the credit nonetheless.

In the second place, however, birth was simply one condition among many that doctors treated, and the therapeutic approach they took to other conditions tended to spill over into their treatment of birth. For most physical conditions of illness doctors did not know what processes of nature were at work. They tended therefore to treat the patient and the patient's symptoms rather than the processes of disease, which they did not see and were usually not looking for. By treating his or her symptoms the doctors did something for the patient and thereby gained approbation. The doctors' status came from pleasing the patients rather than from curing diseases. That was a risky endeavor, for sometimes patients judged the treatment offered to relieve symptoms to be worthless or even more disabling than the symptoms themselves. But patients expected doctors to do something for them, an expectation that carried into birth also. So neither doctors nor patients were inclined to allow the natural processes of birth to suffice.

There is no need to try to explain this contradiction by saying that doctors were ignorant, greedy, clumsy, hasty, or salacious in using medical arts unnecessarily (although some may have been), for the contradiction reflects primarily the kind of therapy that was dominant in prescientific medicine.

The relations between midwifery and general medical practice become clearer if one considers what doctors did when they confronted a birth that did not conform to their understanding of birth's natural processes. Their mechanistic view could not explain such symptoms as convulsions or high fevers, occasionally associated with birth. Yet doctors did not walk away from such conditions as being mysterious or untreatable, for they were committed to the mastery of birth. Rather, they treated the strange symptoms with general therapies just as they might treat regular symptoms of birth with medical arts such as forceps and ergot.

Bloodletting was a popular therapy for many symptoms, and doctors often applied it to births that seemed unusual to them. If a pregnant woman seemed to be florid or perspiring, the doctor might place her in a chair, open a vein in her arm, and allow her to bleed until she fainted. Some doctors bled women to unconsciousness to counter delivery pains. A doctor in 1851 opened the temporal arteries of a woman who was having convulsions during birth, "determined to bleed her until the convulsion ceased or as long as the blood would flow." He found it impossible to catch the blood thrown about during her convulsions, but the woman eventually completed her delivery successfully and survived. Bloodletting was also initiated when a woman developed high fever after delivery. Salmon P. Chase, Lincoln's Secretary of the Treasury and later Chief Justice, told in his diary how a group of doctors took 50 ounces of blood from his wife to relieve her fever. The doctors gave careful attention to the strength and frequency of her pulse, debating and deliberating upon the meaning of the symptom, until finally Mrs. Chase died.[24]

For localized pain, doctors applied leeches to draw out blood from the affected region. A distended abdomen after delivery might merit the application of twelve leeches; a headache, six on the temple; vaginal pain also merited several.[25]

Another popular therapy was calomel, a chloride of mercury that irritated the intestine and purged it. A woman suffering puerperal fever might be given extended doses to reduce swelling by purging her bodily contents. If the calomel acted too violently, the doctors could retard it by administering opium. Doctors often gave emetics to induce vomiting when expectant women had convulsions, for they speculated that emetics might be specifics for hysteria or other nervous diseases causing convulsions.

An expectant or laboring woman showing unusual symptoms might be subjected to a battery of such agents as doctors sought to restore her symptoms to a normal balance. In a famous case in Boston in 1833 a woman had convulsions a month before her expected delivery. The doctors bled her of 8 ounces and gave her a purgative. The next day she again had convulsions, and they took 22 ounces of blood. After 90 minutes she had a headache, and the doctors took 18 more ounces of blood, gave emetics to cause vomiting, and put ice on her head and mustard plasters on her feet. Nearly four hours later she had another convulsion, and they took 12 ounces, and soon after, 6 more. By then she had lapsed into a deep coma, so the doctors doused her with cold water but could not revive her. Soon her cervix began to dilate, so the doctors gave ergot to induce labor. Shortly before delivery she convulsed again, and they applied ice and mustard plasters again and also gave a vomiting agent and calomel to purge her bowels. In six hours she delivered a stillborn child. After two days she regained consciousness and recovered. The doctors considered this a conservative treatment, even though they had removed two-fifths of her blood in a two-day period, for they had not artificially dilated her womb or used instruments to expedite delivery.[26]

Symptomatic treatment was intended not simply to make the patient feel better—often the treatment was quite violent, or "heroic"—but to restore some balance of healthy appearances. Nor were the therapies given to ailing women more intrusive or different from therapies given to suffering men. The therapies were not, in most instances, forced upon the patients without their foreknowledge or consent. People were often eager to be made healthy and willing to endure strenuous therapies to this end. Doctors did believe, however, that some groups of people were more susceptible to illness than others and that different groups also required, or deserved, different treatments.

These views reflected in large part the doctors' awareness of cultural classifications of people; in other words, the culture's position on the relative social worth of different social classes influenced doctors' views about whose health was likely to be endangered, how their endangered health affected the whole society, and what treatments, if any, were suitable. For birth this meant, for example, that doctors believed it more important for them to attend the delivery of children by middle- and upper-class women than the delivery of children by the poor. It meant that doctors expected "fashionable" women to suffer more difficult deliveries because their tight clothing, rich diet and lack of exercise were unhealthy and because they were believed to be more susceptible to nervous strain. It also meant that doctors thought it fitting for unmarried and otherwise disreputable mothers not to receive charitable care along with other poor but respectable women.

There is abundant evidence that doctors came to believe in time that middle- and upper-class women typically had more difficult deliveries than, for example, farm women. One cannot find an objective measure of the accuracy of their perception, nor, unfortunately and more to the point, can one find whether their perception that some women were having more difficult deliveries led doctors consistently to use more intervention in attending them than in attending poorer women with normal deliveries. Doctors' perception of the relative difficulty of deliveries was part of their tendency to associate different kinds of sickness with different social classes. They expected to find the symptoms of certain illnesses in certain groups of people, and therefore looked for those particular symptoms or conditions. In the nineteenth century upper-class urban women were generally expected to be sensitive and delicate, while farm women were expected to be robust. Some doctors even believed that the evolutionary result of education was to produce smaller pelves in women and larger heads in babies, leading to more difficult births among civilized women. There is no evidence that these beliefs were medically accurate. Whether a doctor considered a patient "sick" or "healthy" depended in part upon class-related standards of health and illness rather than on objective scientific standards of sickness.

Treatment probably varied according to the doctor's perception of a woman's class and individual character. At some times and places the treatment given probably reflected the patient's class as much as her symptoms. Thus some doctors may have withheld the use of instruments from their upper-class patients in the belief that they were too fragile to undergo instrumental delivery. The same doctors may have used instruments needlessly on poor patients, who were considered healthy enough to stand anything, in order to save the doctor's time and permit him to rush off to the bedside of a wealthier patient. On the other hand, some doctors may have used instruments on the upper-class women in order to shorten labor, believing that they could not endure prolonged pain or were too weak to bring forth children unassisted, and also in order to justify higher fees. The same doctors may have withheld forceps from poor women whom they considered healthy enough to stand several days of labor. Unfortunately, there is no way of knowing exactly how treatments differed according to class, for very few doctors kept records of their private patients. The records now extant are for the small number of people, perhaps 5 percent of the population, who were treated in hospitals in the nineteenth century. Only poor women, most unmarried, delivered in hospitals, so the records do not cover a cross-section of classes. These hospital records do indicate a large number of instrumental deliveries and sometimes give the reasons as the patient's own "laziness" or "stupidity" in being unable to finish a birth. It is likely that doctors' expectations of lower-class performance are reflected here. Hospital records also reflect the use of poor patients for training or experimentation, another reason for a high incidence of instrumental deliveries.

The fact that doctors' tendency to classify patients according to susceptibility did not lead to consistent differences in treatment is an important indication that they were not merely slavish adherents to a mechanistic view of nature or to cultural and class interests. Doctors were still treating individual women, not machines and not social types. The possibility of stereotypical classification and treatment, however, remained a lively threat to more subtle discernments of individual symptoms and to truly artful applications of treatment in birth.

At the same time, it was possible that patients would find even unbiased treatments offensively painful, ineffective, and expensive, or would doubt that the doctor had a scientific reason for giving them. Such persons could seek other treatments, often administered by laypeople or by themselves. Yet those treatments, including treatments for birth, were also directed toward symptoms. At a time when diseases were unrecognized and their causes unknown, the test of therapy was the patient's whole response, not the curing of disease. So patients who resented treatments as painful, ineffective, or officious rejected the doctor and the treatments. A woman who gave birth in Ohio in 1846 recalled that the doctor bled her and then gave her ergot even though the birth was proceeding, in her view, quite normally. She thought he was simply drunk and in a hurry and angrily judged him a "bad man."[27]

The takeover of birth by male doctors in America was an unusual phenomenon in comparison to France and England, where traditional midwifery continued as a much more significant part of birth. Practice developed differently in America because the society itself expanded more rapidly and the medical profession grew more quickly to doctor in ever new communities. American mobility left fewer stable communities than in France or England, and thus networks of women to support midwives were more often broken. The standards of the American medical profession were not so high or so strictly enforced as standards in other countries, and thus there were both more "educated" doctors and more self-proclaimed doctors in America to compete with midwives. So American midwives disappeared from view because they had less support from the stable communities of women and more competition from male doctors.

The exclusion of women from midwifery and obstetrics had profound effects upon practice. Most obviously, it gave obstetrics a sexist bias; maleness became a necessary attribute of safety, and femaleness became a condition in need of male medical control. Within this skewed view of ability and need, doctors found it nearly impossible to gain an objective view of what nature could do and what art should do, for one was identified with being a woman and the other with being a man.

The bias identified functions, attributes, and prerogatives, which unfortunately could become compulsions, so that doctors as men may have often felt that they had to impose their form upon the processes of nature in birth. Obstetrics acquired a basic distortion in its orientation toward nature, a confusion of the need to be masterful and even male with the need for intervention.

Samuel Bard, one of the few doctors to oppose the trend, remarked that the young doctor, too often lacking the ability to discriminate about natural processes, often became alarmed for his patient's safety and his own reputation, leading him to seek a speedy instrumental delivery for both. A tragedy could follow, compounded because the doctor might not even recognize that he had erred and might not, therefore, learn to correct his practice. But doctors may also have found the "indications" for intervention in their professional work—to hurry, to impress, to win approval, and to show why men rather than women should attend births.

The thrust for male control of birth probably expressed psychosexual needs of men, although there is no basis for discussing this historically. The doctor appears to history more as a ritualistic figure, a representative man, identifying and enforcing sexual roles in critical life experiences. He also provided, as a representative scientist, important rationalizations for these roles, particularly why women should be content to be wives and mothers, and, as a representative of dominant cultural morality, determined the classifications of women who deserved various kinds of treatment. Thus the doctor could bring to the event of birth many prerogatives that had little to do with aiding natural processes, but which he believed were essential to a healthy and safe birth.

Expectant and laboring women lost a great deal from the exclusion of educated female birth attendants, although, of course, they would not have chosen men if they had not believed men had more to offer, at least in the beginning decades of the century. Eventually there were only men to choose. Although no doubt doctors were often sympathetic, they could never have the same point of view as a woman who had herself borne a child and who might be more patient and discerning about birth processes. And female attendants would not, of course, have laid on the male prerogatives of physical and moral control of birth. . . .

REFERENCES

1. Valentine Seaman, *The Midwives' Monitor and Mother's Mirror* (New York, 1800); Lewis Scheffey, "The Early History and the Transition Period of Obstetrics and Gynecology in Philadelphia," *Annals of Medical History,* Third Series, 2 (May, 1940), 215–224.
2. John B. Blake, "Women and Medicine in Antebellum America," *Bulletin of the History of Medicine* 34, No. 2 (March-April 1965): 108–109; see also Dr. Thomas Ewell, *Letters to Ladies* (Philadelphia, 1817) pp. 21–31.
3. Julia C. Spruill, *Women's Life and Work in the Southern Colonies* (New York: Norton, 1972), pp. 272–274; Jane Bauer Donegan, "Midwifery in America, 1760–1860: A Study in Medicine and Morality." Unpublished Ph.D. dissertation, Syracuse University, 1972, pp. 50–52.
4. Alice Morse Earle (ed.), *Diary of Anna Green Winslow, a Boston Schoolgirl of 1771* (Detroit: Singing Tree Press, 1970), p. 12 and n. 24.
5. William G. Rothstein, *American Physicians in the Nineteenth Century: From Sects to Science* (Baltimore: Johns Hopkins Press, 1970), pp. 47–49.
6. J. Marion Sims, *The Story of My Life* (New York, 1888), pp. 138–146.
7. *Buffalo Medical Journal* 6 (September, 1850): 250–251.
8. John Stearns, "Presidential Address," *Transactions of the New York State Medical Society* 1:139.
9. Sims, *Story of My Life,* pp. 115–116.
10. Abraham Flexner, *Medical Education in the United States and Canada: A Report to the Carnegie Foundation for the Advancement of Teaching* (New York, 1910).
11. Anonymous, *Remarks on the Employment of Females as Practitioners in Midwifery,* 1820, pp. 4–6. See also Samuel Gregory, *Man-Midwifery Exposed and Corrected* (Boston, 1848) pp. 13, 49; Donegan, "Midwifery in America," pp. 73–74, 240; Thomas Hersey, *The Midwife's Practical Directory; or, Woman's Confidential Friend* (Baltimore, 1836), p. 221; Charles Rosenberg, "The Practice of Medicine in New York a Century Ago," *Bulletin of the History of Medicine* 41 (1967):223–253.
12. Spruill, *Women's Life and Work,* p. 275; Gregory, *Man-Midwifery Exposed,* pp. 13, 28, 36.
13. Samuel K. Jennings, *The Married Lady's Companion and Poor Man's Friend* (New York, 1808), p. 105.
14. Anonymous, *Remarks,* p. 12.
15. Horatio Storer, M.D., *Criminal Abortion* (Boston, 1868), pp. 100–101*n.*
16. Sarah Stone, *A Complete Practice of Midwifery* (London, 1737).
17. Anonymous, *Remarks,* p. 7.
18. Harold Speert, M.D., *The Sloane Hospital Chronicle* (Philadelphia: Davis, 1963), pp. 17–19; Donegan, "Midwifery in America," p. 218.
19. Walter Channing, M.D., *A Treatise on Etherization in Childbirth, Illustrated by 581 Cases* (Boston, 1848), p. 229.
20. Gregory, *Man-Midwifery Exposed,* pp. 13, 28, 36; Hersey, *Midwife's Practical Directory,* p. 220; Wooster Beach, *An Improved System of Midwifery Adapted to the Reformed Practice of Medicine* . . . (New York, 1851), p. 115.
21. Speert, *Sloane Hospital Chronicle,* pp. 31–33, 77–78.
22. Palmer Findlay, *Priests of Lucina: The Story of Obstetrics* (Boston, 1939), pp. 220–221.
23. Elizabeth Nihell, *A Treatise on Art of Midwifery: Setting Forth Various Abuses Therein, Especially as to the Practice with Instruments* (London, 1760), p. 325; Nicholson J. Eastmen and Louis M. Hellman, *Williams Obstetrics,* 13th Ed. (New York: Appleton-Century-Crofts, 1966), p. 1.
24. Rothstein, *American Physicians,* pp. 47–49.
25. *Loc. cit.*
26. Frederick C. Irving, *Safe Deliverance* (Boston, 1942), pp. 221–225.
27. Harriet Connor Brown, *Grandmother Brown's Hundred Years, 1827–1927* (Boston, 1929), p. 93.

18 THE END OF THE GOLDEN AGE OF DOCTORING

John B. McKinlay and Lisa D. Marceau

If we want things to stay as they are, things will have to change.

Giuseppe di Lampedusa (1)

There are striking similarities between the rise and fall of religious monasticism during the Middle Ages and the rise and still continuing decline of professionalism around the turn of the 21st century. During the medieval period, groups of monks (religious orders) clustered together in functionally dependent units (monasteries), eschewed worldly interests (commerce), and professed through values, beliefs, and actions their adherence to another world. Monks considered themselves "called" to their special vocation and embarked on a period of sacrifice and training as novices, during which they learned appropriate forms of behavior and an unquestioning deference to a special body of revealed knowledge. Secrecy, elaborate rituals, special costumes, and an exclusive brotherly devotion to others in their religious order (the brotherhood) insulated them from surrounding worldly corruption. They occupied a special position in the social order and enjoyed a protected status as moral arbiters of all that was good and evil. Civilian authorities (wealthy landowners, royalty, or local governments) generally left them to their own devices or used them to legitimate worldly activities (e.g., unfair taxation, repression, exploitation).

Viewed simplistically as a contest between two competing worldviews (monasticism versus civilian authorities) it is now clear who won. Macroeconomic forces transforming the surrounding society made monasteries increasingly untenable economic units. Increasingly considered anachronistic and out of touch, the once powerful monasteries eventually declined. While a few continued to cling to the traditional order, most were swept away with social and economic change. Rigid adherence to an idealized worldview precluded strategic economic and political alliances that might have halted or forestalled their inexorable decline. From our historical vantage point at the beginning of the 21st century, sociologists of religion can look back and examine the rise and fall of medieval monasticism: with appropriate intellectual distance, we can now understand how religious orders acquired and maintained their special position in society, the functions they performed for other established elites, and how their insulated existence eventually led to their decline.

Present-day observers are just too close to late 20th and early 21st century changes in U.S. medical care to enjoy the vantage point of, say, a contemporary historian reviewing medieval societal changes. Not enough time has elapsed for the full social consequences of the late capitalist transformation of U.S. health care to completely unfold. Still, there are remarkable parallels between the rise and fall of monasticism and the rise and continuing fall of professionalism. Inevitably, modern-day commentators are prisoners of the proximate-being so involved in the phenomenon of interest, it is difficult to assume the distance necessary to appreciate the underlying causes and likely consequences of the subject of our inquiry. To understand the consequences of the industrial revolution as it finally caught up with medicine, we can observe effects produced by its earlier impact on other industrial sectors (like farming, banking, and transportation).

Over a decade ago, the first author and a colleague (Dr. John Stoeckle) argued that the corporatization of medical care was transforming the U.S. medical workplace and profoundly altering the everyday work of the doctors (2). We questioned the adequacy of the prevailing view of professionalism (Freidson's notion of professional dominance) and proposed an alternative view more informed by current developments in the U.S. medical care marketplace (2–4). Our work explicitly repudiated "doctor bashing," a popular sport among social scientists at the time, in favor of a theoretically grounded political-economic explanation (historic changes in the mode of medical care production) of the demise of doctoring. It produced a fierce reaction among many physicians and some medical sociologists. We probably added fuel to the flames by initially employing the Marxist notion of proletarianization—a term eventually abandoned in favor of a less threatening term like "corporatization." That much of the reaction resulted from the term "proletarianization" is evident from the fact that nothing else in the paper was changed—not one argument or datum. While strenuously rejecting the claim that doctors were being slowly "proletarianized," many agreed that doctors were indeed being "corporatized." Apparently it was the word "proletarianized" and what it implied that was objectionable, not our underlying thesis. In our view, it was important that the thesis not be dismissed because of a single word (5–7).

While some could not accept the notion of corporatization (or proletarianization) back in the 1980s, there is hardly an objection today (8). In just 25 years, U.S. health care has been historically transformed—from a predominantly fee-for-service system controlled by dominant professionals to a corporatized system dominated by increasingly concentrated and globalized financial and industrial interests (9). Dudley and Luft (10) believe U.S. health care has experienced "a sea change in the past two decades—not just in the financing of health insurance, but also in the way medicine is practiced." With the golden age of medicine now almost behind us, doctors are huddling in their monasteries (hospitals and medical centers) powerlessly awaiting the next corporate onslaught. One unanticipated consequence of the Clinton administration's failed attempt at health care reform in 1994 was to further dissipate the power of doctors and coalesce opposing economic interests (especially the private insurance, pharmaceutical, and hospital sectors) against progressive change.

Professionalism can be defined as a system of values and beliefs and behavior (concerning how things ought to be done) resulting from dedicated commitment usually following a prolonged period of training. Adherents to this system (professionals) have enjoyed a privileged position and status in society, and their activities have typically been protected or sanctioned by the state. Professional activities were often insulated from observability by secrecy, protective subordinates, and impregnable institutions (11). An ethos of professional collegiality and confidentiality (the brotherhood) was hardly conducive to public scrutiny. From such a viewpoint and for much of the 20th century, professionalism was a powerful social force—it encouraged adherents to behave "ethically" and promoted unquestioning trust among the public (*credat emptor*); it institutionalized the conflict within organizations, between bureaucratic authority (based on tenure in a position in a hierarchy) and professional authority (based on a body of knowledge and technical expertise) and worked against dialectical change; it allowed rapacious interests to disguise their activities in good intentions and a transparent beneficence.

The recent (late 20th and early 21st century) decline of the medical profession and of professionalism as a social force undoubtedly results from many different social influences—at least eight of varying importance are discussed in this article. For convenience we organize them into extrinsic factors (which appear outside the control of the profession) and intrinsic factors (which may be amenable to change by the profession itself). Major *extrinsic factors* are (*a*) the changing nature of the state and loss of its partisan support for doctoring; (*b*) the bureaucratization (corporatization) of doctoring; (*c*) the emerging competitive threat from other health care workers; (*d*) the consequences of globalization and the information revolution; (*e*) the epidemiologic transition and changes in public conceptions of the body; and (*f*) changes in the doctor-patient relationship and the erosion of patient trust. Major *intrinsic factors* are (*g*) the weakening of physicians' or market position through oversupply; and (*h*) the fragmentation of the physicians' union (the American Medical Association, AMA).

SHIFTING ALLEGIANCE OF THE STATE

Various studies have described the important role of the state (local and national government structures) as a sponsor for professionalism generally and as a protector of doctoring in particular. The rise of the medical profession during the 20th century was powerfully reinforced by government action (9, 12–16). The state served a legitimating function for many professional activities, accorded select groups (e.g., physicians and attorneys) a monopolistic position and privileged status, and served as a guarantor of their profits (through programs like Medicare and Medicaid). Hardly neutral with respect to the medical profession, the state has through political and legal means unbashedly advanced professional interests and disposed of perceived threats to professional dominance (13, 17, 18). For its rise during the 20th century, the medical profession (among other privileged interest groups) achieved much for which the state can be thanked. Figure 18-1 depicts principal sources of support for the medical profession in the United States during much of the 20th century (with government and the AMA as mainstay institutional supports).

While there is extensive discussion in the social sciences around the changing structure, functioning, and power of the state, this has yet to feature prominently in the major theories of professionalism or in the debate on the decline of professionalism, despite the state's recognized influence on all health-related activities (the nature and financing of our health care system, the power of medical professionals, the legitimation of competing interests, and the level of support for social policies affecting doctoring). The future of the medical profession and the nature of doctoring in the 21st century will depend on, more than any other influence, the changing nature and support of the state (19, 20). We devote more emphasis to this than any other factor.

The "state" can be viewed organizationally as the "apparatus of government in its broadest sense: that is, as that set of institutions that are recognizably 'public' in that they are responsible for the collective organization of social existence

Figure 18-1. *Sources of support for doctoring in the middle of the 20th century.*

and are funded at the public's expense" (21, p. 84). Most observers view the state as consisting of a wide range of institutions, including the government or legislature (which passes laws), the bureaucracy or civil service (which implements government decisions), the courts and police (which are responsible for law enforcement), and the armed forces (whose job it is to protect the state from external threats). Included under this broad definition are such institutions as welfare services, the education system, and the health care establishment (22).

As far as the United States is concerned—as evidenced by the attempt at health care reform in 1994 (23), the defeat of anti-tobacco legislation (24), and the rapid evolution of managed care—the state appears to have lost some of its ability, or willingness, to act on behalf of and protect the profession's interests. Figure 18.2 depicts the way in which, in the United States during the last decades of the 20th century, the state shifted its primary allegiance from the profession's interests to often conflicting private interests. Such a shift will shape the content and sociopolitical context of doctoring during the new millennium (25).

While there are numerous theories of the state, for the purpose of this discussion of the decline of professionalism and the medical profession, it may be useful to distinguish just three general viewpoints.

1. The *Marxist perspective,* which has never been predominant in the United States, views the state as partisan—maintaining the class system by either subordinating certain groups (e.g., racial and ethnic minorities and women) or dissipating class conflict. According to this view, the state cannot be understood separately from the prevailing economic structure of society. Here we have a clear alternative to the popular pluralist view of the state and neutral arbiter or umpire of competing countervailing interests. The Marxist theory of the state has undergone considerable debate and revision, especially with contributions from Gramsci (26), Mosca (27), Miliband (28), Poulantzas (29), Mills (30), and more recently Jessop (31). Neomarxists, while attempting to remain faithful to the classical ideas of Marx, have generally abandoned the idea that the state is merely a reflection of the class system. The original two-class model is now recognized as simplistic, and Poulantzas

Figure 18-2. *Sources of support for doctoring in the early 21st century.*

(29) has identified significant divisions within the ruling elite (e.g., between financial and industrial (manufacturing) capital). Neomarxists have also tried to provide an alternative to the mechanistic and simplistic views of traditional Marxism (often incurring the wrath of the orthodox in the process) and to move beyond crude economic determinism. Jessop (32), for example, views the state not as an instrument wielded by a dominant group but as "the crystallization of political strategies," a dynamic entity that reflects the balance of power within society at any given time, and thus reflects the outcome of an ongoing hegemonic struggle. Current developments with respect to globalization (the subordination of national governments to supranational organizations and agencies) appear to give the Marxist theory of the state increasing currency.

2. The *pluralist perspective,* with origins traceable to the 17th century liberalism of Thomas Hobbes and John Locke and more recently the work of John Rawls (33), views the state as a neutral body that arbitrates between competing interests in society. There is an often unacknowledged assumption of neutrality—the government sets the rules and acts as an umpire or referee in society. It is viewed as acting in the interest of *all* citizens and therefore as representing the common good or public interest. Many pluralists embrace a constant sum concept of power (there is a fixed amount of power that is widely and evenly dispersed) and view the state as having no interest of its own that is separate from society. Heywood (21) identifies two assumptions underlying the pluralist theory of the state: (*a*) the state is effectively subordinated to government (nonelected state bodies such as the civil service are strictly impartial and subjects to the legitimate authority of their political masters); and (*b*) the democratic process is effective and meaningful (party competition and interest-group activity ensure the government remains responsive to public will). With the work of Dahl (34), Lindblom (35), Marsh (36), and Galbraith (37), among others, it is now recognized that the traditional pluralist theory of the state requires some revision, especially to take account of modernizing trends such as globalization and the emergence of postindustrial society. Neopluralists view Western democracies as "deformed polyarchies," in which major multinational corporations and globalized interests now exert disproportionate influence (21). The medical profession thrived during the latter half of the 20th century under a pluralist state (it was a dominant interest group with widespread public support). The theory of countervailing powers advanced by Mechanic (38) and Light (39) in their discussion of the medical profession appears to rest on a now outmoded pluralist view of the state. Historical developments have left these theories (and especially Freidson's notion (40) of professional dominance) with little explanatory currency. Professional powers appear, incidentally, to have countervailed little in the context of changes in the National Health Service in Britain (41).

3. The *New Right perspective* is a recent powerful reaction against the view of the state as "leviathan"—a self-serving monster intent on its own expansion and aggrandizement (21). The two perspectives discussed so far (pluralist and Marxist) have been termed "society centered"—the state and its actions are shaped by external forces in society as a whole. Pluralism views the state's actions as determined by the democratic will of the people; Marxist theory sees its actions as shaped by the interests of an increasingly concentrated cluster of powerful institutions and individuals. Clearly, society can and does influence the structure and functioning of the state, but obviously the reverse can also occur. This possibility has given rise to what are termed "state-centered" approaches to the theory of power and modern society (22). These approaches (and the New Right is but one of them) view the state as acting independently, or autonomously, to shape social behavior. Nordlinger (42) suggests that state itself has acquired three forms of autonomy: (*a*) when the state has preferences that differ from those of major groups in society and implements its preferred policies despite pressure for it not to do so; (*b*) when the state is able to persuade opponents of its policies to change their mind and support the government; and (*c*) when the state follows policies that are supported, or at least not opposed, by the public or powerful interest groups in society (22).

The New Right perspective, which appears to be on the ascendance in the United States, is distinguished by its strong laissez-faire attitude and antipathy toward state intervention in economic and social life (even medical care). Its proponents argue that the state should retreat from responsibility for medical care (and protection of doctoring) and let market forces prevail. Rooted in a radical form of individualism and exemplified in the writings of Robert Nozick (43), the New Right considers the state a parasitic growth that threatens individual liberty and even economic development. The New Right perspective has been described as follows (21, p. 91):

> In this view, the state, instead of being as pluralists suggest, an impartial umpire or arbiter, is an overbearing "nanny," desperate to interfere or meddle in every aspect of human existence. . . . [The] state pursues interests that are separate from those of society (setting it apart from Marxism), and . . . those interests demand an unrelenting growth in the role or responsibilities of the state itself. . . . [The] twentieth century tendency towards state intervention reflects not popular pressure for economic and social security, or the need to stabilize capitalism by ameliorating class tensions, but rather the internal dynamics of the state.

Figure 18.3 summarizes the three perspectives on the modern state.

To most political scientists, the three perspectives identified and discussed here will be a gross simplification of the complex debate occurring over several decades. Since each viewpoint has its own philosophical tradition, efforts to integrate them creatively so as to achieve some overall theoretical synthesis will remain an elusive task. The appropriateness of any theory of the state probably varies *among* countries, although with globalization this may be changing. The role of the state may also change over time *within* a particular country: *in the United States we are witnessing a move from a pluralist to a New Right state.* New society programs (e.g., Medicare and Medicaid) were formulated and implemented during a more liberal pluralist era—the nature of the state then made them possible. Efforts at health care reform in the United States failed in large part because of a well-orchestrated assault on the leviathan state (as Big Government, increased taxation, public dependency, and curtailed freedoms) (23). Likewise, the ability of the New Right (in combination with the business community) to portray physicians as greedy and willing participants in fraud (overbilling for services) has implications for regulation and public trust. The encroachment of the

Figure 18-3. *Theories of the modern state.*

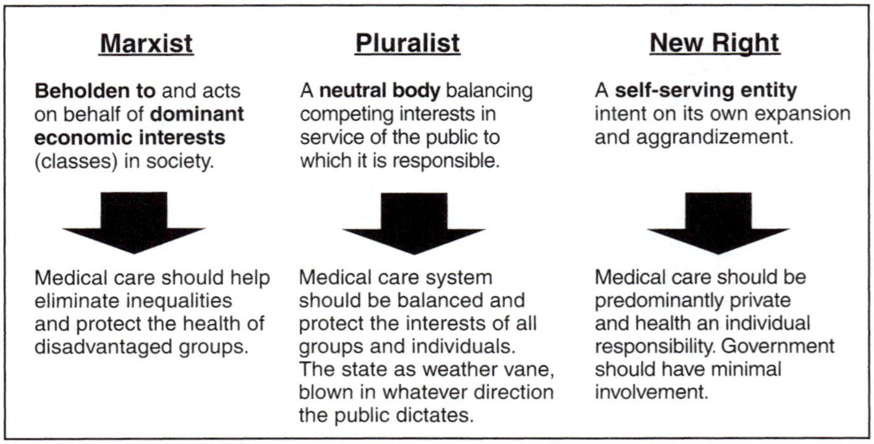

Marxist	Pluralist	New Right
Beholden to and acts on behalf of **dominant economic interests** (classes) in society.	A **neutral body** balancing competing interests in service of the public to which it is responsible.	A **self-serving entity** intent on its own expansion and aggrandizement.
↓	↓	↓
Medical care should help eliminate inequalities and protect the health of disadvantaged groups.	Medical care system should be balanced and protect the interests of all groups and individuals. The state as weather vane, blown in whatever direction the public dictates.	Medical care should be predominantly private and health an individual responsibility. Government should have minimal involvement.

state even on the once-sacred physician-patient relationship (through "gag rules" and court opinions) is discussed below.

The medical profession thrived during the era of the pluralist state: as a major public interest group with considerable public support, the umpire invariably ruled in its favor. Writing in the context of Britain, but with application to the U.S. scene, Klein (44) describes "the politics of the double bed," referring to the way doctors in the United Kingdom were directly involved in policy decisions affecting their activities. While the state (government) is often viewed as an unchanging entity, it is now clear that a subtle change occurred during the last decades of the 20th century: the state is transitioning from a pluralist to an antileviathan New Right viewpoint. Commentators have discussed the transition from a Fordist to a post-Fordist state and what this portends for the medical profession (45–48). Farrell's recent biography (49) of U.S. House Speaker Tip O'Neill describes the nature and focus of government during the late 20th century, ending with a presidential declaration during a State of the Union address that "the era of big government is over." This now dominant New Right perspective has resulted in an important shift in the primary allegiance of the state—from protecting the interests of the medical profession to advancing the interests of the financial and industrial owners of an ever more corporatized U.S. health care system. Figure 18-2 depicts the changes in institutional support for doctoring, with the state shifting its principal allegiance to other interests.

A recent discussion of the implications of the 2000 election for health care in the United States concludes that (50):

> the election of Bush as president has brought a different focus and tone to health policy. . . . Clinton advocated a larger federal role. . . . President Bush has a very different view of the government's role in health care. He emphasizes individual responsibility in making decisions about health care and paying for it, as well as the positive role of the private market place. Bush also believes that local charities should be encouraged to provide needed health care services, that state governments should assume the primary role in many areas of health care policy, and that the federal role should be smaller.

Partisan protection of professional prerogatives now appears secondary to the advancement of global corporate interests. Whereas previously, the state enacted legislation designed to protect physicians, nowadays the New Right state's protective cloak is first used to cover the corporate interests that now determine the structure and content of U.S. health care. Rather than setting the rules and acting as a neutral umpire as Light (51) envisages it, the emerging New Right state is now on the side of and in the service of multinational financial and industrial interests. The gradual shift in the state's principal allegiance (from the medical profession to the corporation and especially its owners) has fostered the erosion of professionalism, leaving the medical profession with little more than ostensible support (see Figure 18-3). Just as the state was important in the earlier rise of the medical profession, so too has its recent protection of corporate interests left the medical profession without a significant source of support, thereby threatening the profession's special position and status. Zola (52) traced the origins of the earlier, special position of physicians as agents of social control to the sponsorship they derived from the state (see also 14). Much of this is now eroding as the state comes increasingly under the control of new global masters. While the decline of the medical profession appears to be a global phenomenon, there is presently no universal explanation for this, but many complex reasons that differ from country to country (53).

BUREAUCRATIZATION (CORPORATIZATION) OF DOCTORING

Using data from the AMA's Socioeconomic Monitoring System (a series of periodic nationally representative samples of the entire U.S. physician population), Kletke and his colleagues (54, 55) report dramatic changes in the nature of physician employment (type of work arrangement) from 1983 to 1997. Between these years, the proportion of patient-care physicians working as employees (with no ownership interest in their practice) rose from 24 to 43 percent, an increase of 19 percentage points (Figure 18-4). Also during this

Figure 18-4. *Distribution of physicians by type of practice, United States, 1983–1997. Source: Kletke et al. (54) and personal communication, 1998.*

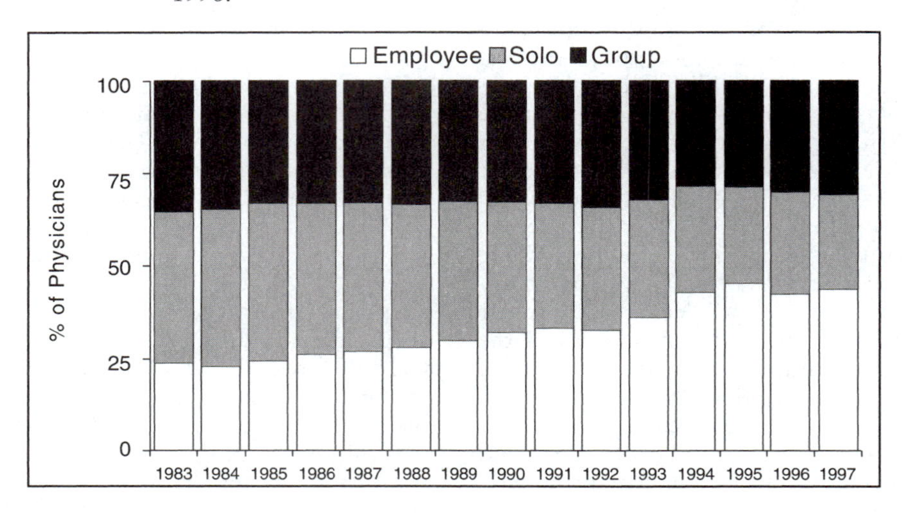

period, the proportion of physician's in *self-employed solo practices* (one-physician practices with an ownership interest) fell from 40 to 26 percent. The proportion of physicians in *self-employed group practices* (multiple-physician practices with an ownership interest) fell from 35 to 31 percent. Kletke and colleagues (54, 55) note that these trends are accelerating—most of them occurring during the latter part of the study period. Moreover, these trends are especially evident among younger physicians (Figure 18-5). Among newly practicing doctors (0 to 5 years in practice), the proportion who were salaried employees increased from 37 to 66 percent between 1983 and 1997. The authors conclude: "These trends are pervasive throughout the patient care physician population, occurring for both male and female physicians, for U.S. medical graduates and international medical graduates, for all specialty groups, and in most parts of the country. . . . That these changes have been especially pronounced among younger physicians suggests that their impact on the delivery of medical care will continue long into the future" (55, p. 559).

Under late 20th century bureaucratized medicine, physicians are *required* (there are now few practice options) to participate in assembly-line medicine. Stoeckle (56) described "working on the factory floor with an M.D. degree." Speed-up of the medical care production process (physicians are "permitted" six to eight minutes with a patient) occurs continuously under the guise of efficiency, or even clinical appropriateness. A report recently suggested that the length of the doctor-patient encounter has not shortened under managed care (57), but its methodology has limitations and its findings differ from the everyday experience of many practicing doctors on the medical care production line. While originally motivated by concern over the quality of care, clinical practice guidelines are welcomed by corporatized medicine and serve to curtail extraneous and costly procedures and to streamline the production process (58). The reward structure for physicians is increasingly tied to exemplary performance of the bureaucratic employee role (the number and types of diagnoses, referrals to other specialties, throughput of patients per practice session). Toward the end of the 20th century, Taylorism appears to have finally caught up with American medical care (59, 60).

Of special concern to some "old-time" doctors is the absence of any real professional resistance to worrisome bureaucratic encroachments. The

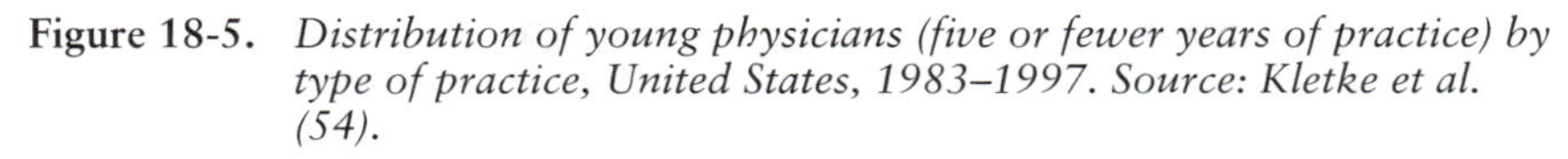

Figure 18-5. *Distribution of young physicians (five or fewer years of practice) by type of practice, United States, 1983–1997. Source: Kletke et al. (54).*

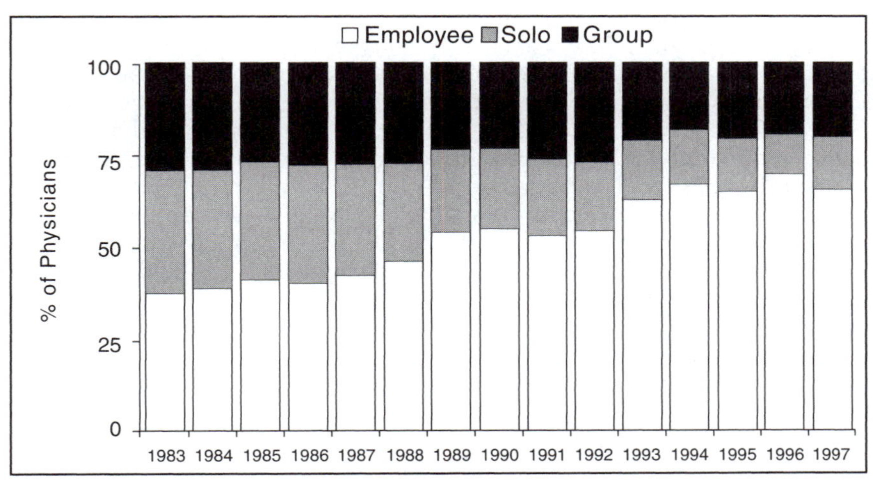

loss of administrative and economic autonomy is understandable and even tolerable; but for many physicians, the loss of clinical autonomy is especially troubling (61, 62). Where they should actually practice (selective contracting) and how much they should be paid are now largely determined by others; but having others determine *how* they should practice (the technical content of care) is just too much (63–65). Sophisticated data-management systems can now track the minutest aspects of care; these systems appear to exist as much to monitor the productivity and costs incurred by providers as to monitor any beneficial clinical outcomes (66). Increasingly, the treatment regimen is formulated before a live case actually presents for medical care. Prior approval is often required from a non–medically qualified reviewer at some geographically distant corporate headquarters before a final decision can be made. The choice of treatment (e.g., which medication can be prescribed) is often determined by what is allowed by a patient's health insurance or by the physician's employer. All clinical actions are scrutinized on a regular basis, and deviant practice behavior is highlighted and corrective steps taken to ensure future conformity with overall practice norms. Older recalcitrant or unproductive practitioners can easily be replaced with younger physicians (oversupply is discussed later) or replaced by less expensive nonphysician clinicians (also described below). As one chief of medicine recently remarked to us, "I listen to all these complaints from the doctors and ask myself, 'But where are they going to go?' " In order to get along under corporatized medicine, it appears that most physicians, for understandable reasons, must be willing to go along.

AN INCREASINGLY CROWDED PLAYING FIELD

During much of the 20th century, physicians gained a privileged position as the principal providers of medical services in the U.S.: the term "monopoly" has been used to characterize their unique situation and behavior (13). Of the many factors that contributed to the emergence of "the golden age" of doctoring, clearly the most influential was the highly supportive action taken by a generally partisan pluralist state described above (9, 12–14, 40). First, early in the century the legitimacy of the medical profession was established through *state licensing and reg-*

ulations—no other group of health care providers could legitimately perform certain tasks. If there were exceptions for particular groups, they had to work under the direct supervision of physicians. Second, during the middle of the 20th century, *third-party reimbursement* enhanced the economic position of the medical profession—they could bill for almost anything and solely determined what was appropriate treatment. Through programs like Medicaid and Medicare (which reimbursed a physician's full costs), the state acted as both an underwriter and a guarantor of professional profits. Third, with considerable support for medical education from government, the medical profession strengthened its position by *training new physicians* in numbers that eclipsed other medically related discipline.

Physicians had the medical playing field to themselves for most of the 20th century, but the last several decades witnessed the arrival of a group of ever more powerful and legitimate new players who are threatening the physician's traditional game. Nonphysician clinicians (NPCs) are responsible for increasing amounts of the medical care that was previously provided almost exclusively by physicians (9, 67–73). With increasing numbers and improvement of their position, NPCs appear to be using the same political game plan that physicians used to secure this special status so successfully in earlier times (70, 74–77).

Cooper and his colleagues (72, 74) have projected the future likely workforce of NPCs and what their rapid increase portends for physicians. Most NPCs are within ten different medical and surgical specialties, which can be classified into three broad groups: (*a*) *the traditional disciplines*—nurse practitioners (NPs), certified nurse-midwives (CNMs), and physician assistants (PAs); (*b*) *the alternative or complementary providers*—chiropractors, naturopaths, acupuncturists, and practitioners of herbal medicine; and (*c*) *specialty disciplines*—optometrists, podiatrists, certified registered nurse anesthetists (CRNAs), and clinical nurse specialists (CNSs).

Through statutes and regulations, states have granted extensive practice prerogatives to *all* the NPCs listed above. The most important of these prerogatives is licensure, which has established the right of these disciplines to practice (although it does not yet assure their autonomy as providers). There are marked differences in the practice perogatives that states grant to NPCs in the various disciplines. For most disciplines, the magnitude of the prerogative correlates with the number of NPCs in each state. In some states, "practice prerogatives [have] authorized a high degree of autonomy and a broad range of authority to provide discrete levels of uncomplicated primary and specialty care" (72, p. 795).

Late 20th century changes in the organization and financing of health care (especially the emergence of profit-driven corporatized care) enhanced the labor market position of NPCs. For a profit-driven organization, the growth of NPCs offers an opportunity to hire appropriate replacements for a physician. Studies comparing the performance of NPCs and physicians show that there are few differences in any clinical outcome, but NPCs are considerably less expensive and patients often prefer the quality of care they offer. Lower costs and customer satisfaction are imperatives in the new medical marketplace.

With respect to the likely magnitude of the threat to physicians posed by NPCs, the aggregate number of NPCs graduating annually in the ten disciplines listed above doubled between 1992 and 1997, and a further increment of 20 percent is projected for 2001 (72). The supply of NPCs is expected to grow from 228,000 in 1995 to 384,000 in 2005, and is likely to continue to expand at a similar rate thereafter. Figures 18-6, 18-7, and 18-8 depict the projected increase in the three broad groups of competing medical care providers.

Competition on the medical playing field is likely to become increasingly intense, especially given the existing oversupply of physicians combined with the national desire to contain health care costs. The size of the overall pie is unlikely to increase, and larger numbers of ever more powerful disciplines are competing for a piece of it. Grumbach and Coffman consider the emerging situation as subject to "Evans Law of Economic Identity" (78), which they describe as follows (79, pp. 825–826):

> . . . total expenditures on professional health care services are by definition equal to the total number

Figure 18-6. *Supply of specialty nonphysician clinicians, United States, 1990–2015. Source: Cooper et al. (72).*

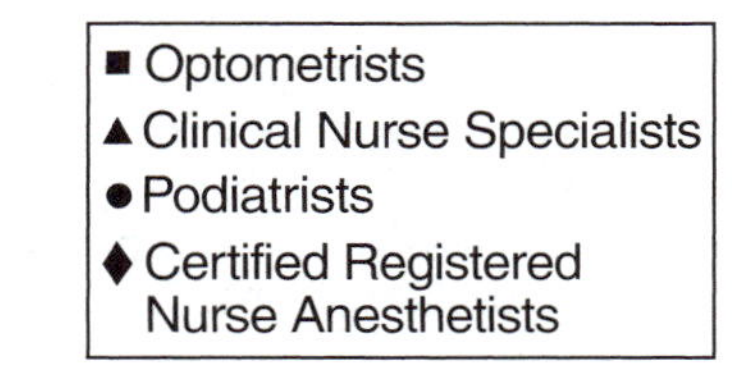

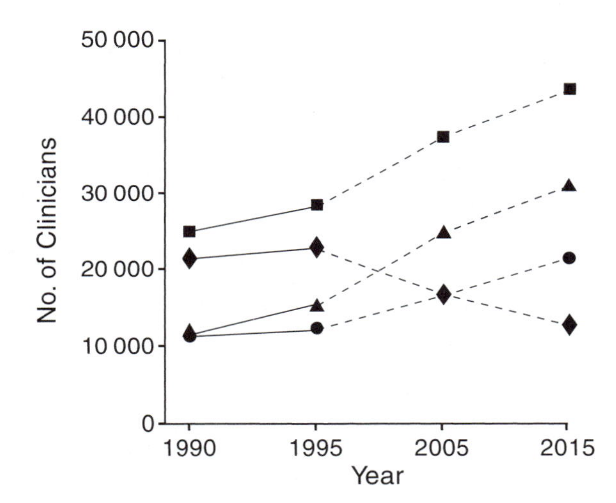

of services provided multiplied by the price of each service, which are in turn equal to the total number of persons earning incomes in health care multiplied by the income of each person. If the supply of health care workers increases and income per worker remains constant, then health expenditures also will increase. To increase the supply of workers without increasing overall costs, either incomes per worker must diminish or new workers must displace other workers. . . . [This] implies either a substantial growth in expenditures for payment of these practitioners or rivalry among physicians and NPCs to protect incomes and jobs in a financially constrained system.

Commenting on the growth of NPCs in relation to the likely supply of physicians over the next decade, Cooper observes (69, p. 1542):

When assessed in terms of physician equivalent effort, the number of NPCs will increase from 51 per 100,000 in 1994, a level equal to 25 percent of pa-

Figure 18-7. *Supply of traditional nonphysician clinicians, United States, 1990–2015. Source: Cooper et al. (72).*

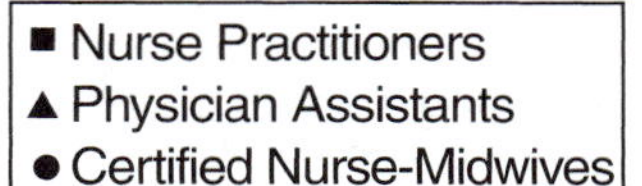

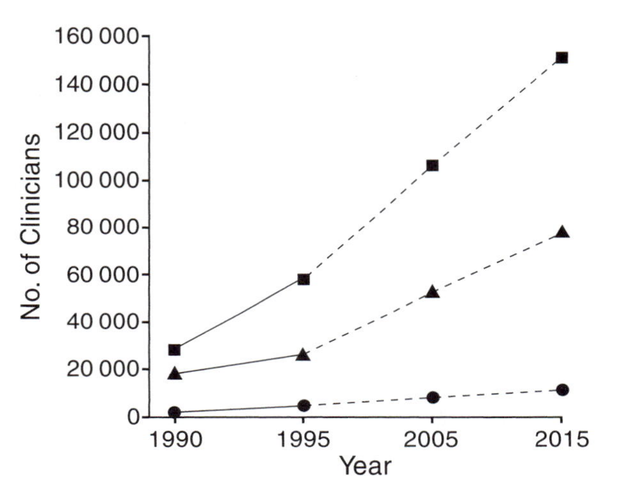

tient care physicians, to 84 per 100,000 in 2010, which is equal to 34 percent of the physician workforce in 2010. The incremental increase of NPCs between 1994 and 2010, expressed as physician equivalents, is 33 percent, which is identical to the increment of physician supply that is projected during the same period. . . . [The] the order of magnitude of the projected growth in their numbers is large in proportion to any estimate of physician surpluses. Moreover, there does not appear to be the capacity to absorb both the increased numbers of physicians that have been projected and a parallel workforce of NPCs of this magnitude.

The recent rapid increase in the number of physicians and other health workers is already creating intradisciplinary (between physicians) and interdisciplinary (between physician and nonphysician clinicians) rivalries. Several observers have noted a decline of intradisciplinary courtesy and reciprocity. Some doctors are barely hanging on, while others are reported to be abandoning a

Figure 18-8. *Supply of alternative or complementary nonphysician clinicians, United States, 1990–2015. Source: Cooper et al. (72).*

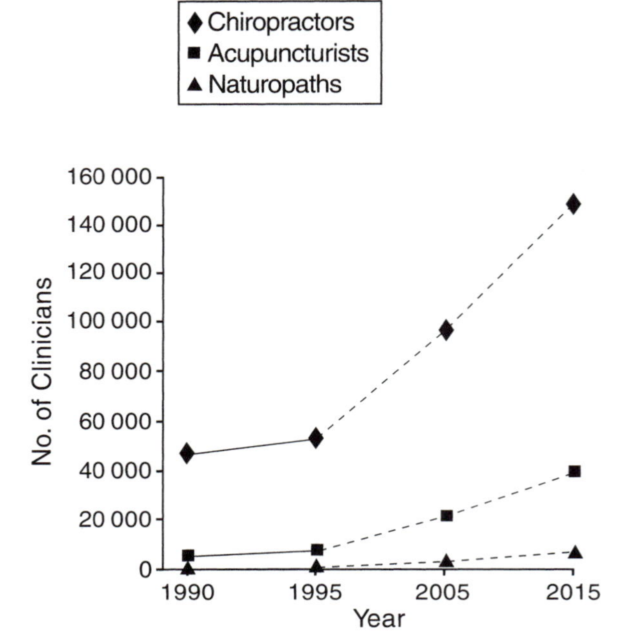

sinking ship (Figure 18-9). All of this is to emphasize that much of the debate over medical workforce trends (oversupply versus undersupply) and their likely consequences appears to be without (political or economic) context or background (80). Discussion of the intrinsic threat to doctoring resulting from statistical oversupply appears myopic and overlooks the even more significant extrinsic threats presented by macroeconomic changes in the surrounding society (e.g., corporatization and the trend to employee status, the changing nature and shifting allegiance of the state, and the erosion of patients' trust). Beneath the threat to doctoring that accompanies statistical oversupply and competition lie even more significant social trends that are undermining the position of physicians in the division of medical labor and the status of doctoring in the surrounding society.

GLOBALIZATION AND THE INFORMATION REVOLUTION

Globalization and the information revolution are also phenomena with potential to alter the social

Figure 18-9. *Increase in supply of nonphysician clinicians, United States, 1994–2010.*

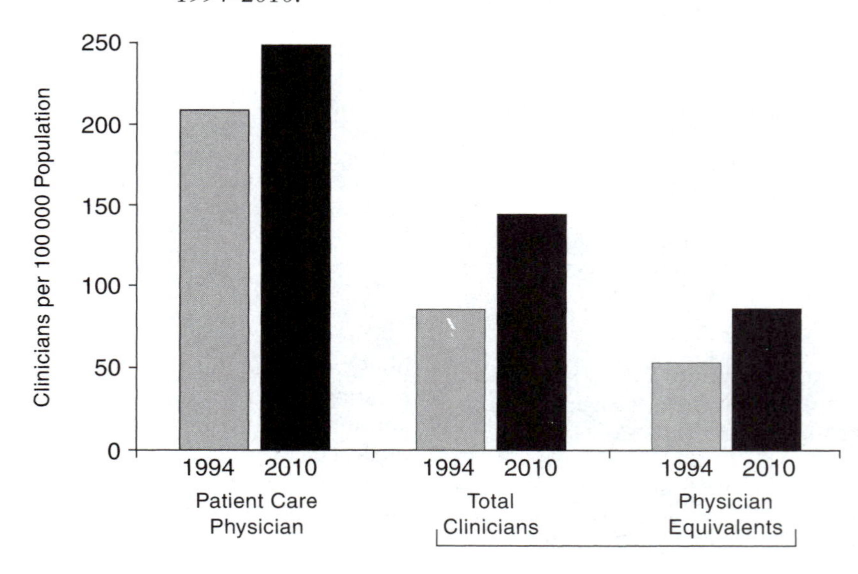

position of doctors worldwide. While globalization may appear only to concern abstract phenomena at the level of nation states and macroeconomics that have little bearing on behavior at the local level (e.g., currency and market fluctuations in one geographic region can force governments in far-off regions to dramatically change local economic policy), nothing could be further from the truth: "it is the very dynamic of globalization that its dimensions operate *both* at the global and local level *at the same time*" (81, p. 55). Giddens observes: "It is wrong to think of globalization as just concerning the big system, like the world financial order. Globalization isn't only about what is 'out there,' remote and far away from the individual. It is an 'in here' phenomena too, influencing intimate and personal aspects of our lives" (82, p. 30). The implications of globalization and the information revolution at the local level for the organization and delivery of health care, for the social position of doctors, and for the content of medical work (doctoring) have received little attention and remain poorly understood.

The term "globalization" refers to the emerging consciousness of the world as a single place and the accompanying process whereby geographically disparate social systems are becoming linked so as to assume a worldwide scale. Modern electronic communications (especially the Internet) provide the lifeblood for emerging global bodies. Globalization is being institutionalized through the activities of transnational corporations and the formation of supranational agencies like the World Bank, the World Trade Organization, and the World Health Organization. Regional affiliations between countries (e.g., the North American Free Trade Agreement and the European Union), which may be termed "intermediate globalization," may eventually result in the formation of worldwide structures. There are several ways in which their activities affect the social position of doctors and the everyday value of doctoring.

Much of the power and position of the medical profession has been traced to the protective activities of professional associations (the doctors' union), often manifest through locally powerful medical societies. As described elsewhere, professional associations like the AMA in the United States and the British Medical Association in Great Britain have exerted considerable influence on the state, shaping legislation affecting their prerogatives. Policies promulgated by supranational organizations and agreements between governments are marginalizing once powerful national and local professional associations, limiting their ability to control licensure and training and shape legislation so as to benefit their constituency. NAFTA is a reciprocal agreement between the United States of America, Mexico, and Canada that provides for the free-trade movement of physicians and other professionals between these three countries. It is expected that other countries will be added to NAFTA in the near future. Similarly, the interests of professional associations in the member countries of the European Union are now subordinated to legislation emanating from Brussels. Despite the local training and licensing requirement of local medical interests, employment mobility of physicians between countries linked through global structures is increasingly common. Illustrative are perhaps the recent reports of South African doctors being lured to work in Canada. South Africa's foreign minister and its ambassador to Canada have said it is unethical for the West to lure doctors from the developing world, which already has too few doctors and struggles to provide medical care for millions of impoverished people and to cope with epidemics such as AIDS and tuberculosis. According to some estimates, 1,500 South African doctors are now working in Canada. Apparently, the president of the Saskatchewan Medical Association (a South African) was able to stand before a group at the association's annual golf tournament last year and tell a joke in Afrikaans (83).

Increasingly widespread use of the Internet, while empowering patients by providing valuable health information, also may have the unanticipated consequence of undermining key aspects of physician authority. For much of the 20th century, the medical profession seemed to exemplify the adage "knowledge is power." Possession of a body of purportedly scientific knowledge about the human body and various methods to possibly prolong life, avoid death, and alleviate suffering contributed to the privileged position of doctors in the social order (described below). Acquisition of technical expertise through prolonged training (professional socialization) was considered a defining characteristic (attribute) of any profession (84). Public access to this highly valued and authoritative medical knowledge was possible only through consultation, usually face-to-face, with a certified (licensed) physician. Any other source of health information was considered suspect and lacking in scientific legitimacy. The ready availability of sophisticated medical information to anyone with Internet access is increasing levels of public medical knowledge, interposing a lay electronic help-seeking system, and changing the structure and content of the doctor-patient relationship.

In contrast with earlier times, newly empowered patients now enter the doctor-patient encounter with (*a*) considerable *up-to-date information* concerning a medical condition and possible types of diagnoses and (*b*) industry-generated *requests* for specific tests or treatments ("ask your doctor about . . .") and expectations concerning what ought to occur during the encounter. And (*c*), subsequent to the encounter, patients now use the Internet to *informally evaluate* the appropriateness of particular treatments and procedures received. The timing of a Web search appears to depend on the person for whom health information is being sought: if for someone else, it usually occurs after a doctor's visit; if for oneself, it tends to occur before a doctor's visit, presumably to see what the diagnosis might be (85).

Physician behavior around the mid-20th century was described as "insulated from observability" (11). Doctors tended to act as independent agents, free from administrative oversight with little formal accountability. As professionals, and again with the acquiescence of the state, doctors acquired a legally sanctioned privilege accorded few occupations—self-regulation. Probably because doctors could "bury their mistakes," professional misconduct appeared to be a rare event, and whenever oversight or investigation was required, it was conducted in closed-door sessions involving only selected members of the profession. With the changes in physician employment described in this article (corporatization), the computerization of medical records, and the on-line availability of data on the comparative performance of medical facilities and particular practitioners, the everyday work situation of doctors is changing dramatically.

Computerized information systems can now capture minute aspects of the clinical encounter (e.g., length of visit, tests ordered, referrals made, prescriptions written, clinical outcomes, patient satisfaction, and costs incurred). Particular providers are now easily compared with each other in terms of patient throughput, productivity, and patient satisfaction, and their performance assessed against officially agreed upon standards of care (practice guidelines). Legal actions against providers for alleged malpractice were once largely based on the testimony (memory) of the parties involved, or required plaintiffs to find a doctor willing to testify against one of their own. Nowadays, the computerized medical record provides an independent contemporaneous record of everything that is done (or not done) during a doctor-patient encounter, and it constitutes evidence thought to be superior to the memory of self-interested parties. Anyone can now go on-line to acquire previously private information on particular providers: their age, educational background, employment history, and the frequency and success of any legal actions. Through the use of the Web, patients today can enter the doctor-patient relationship with up-to-date information on any medical condition, informed expectations about what constitutes appropriate practice, and considerable information on the personal biography of their provider.

Globalization is also having more subtle effects on the position of doctors and the work of doctoring around the world. During the 18th and 19th centuries, British imperialism involved more than only the export of industrial production and products through colonization. Anglo-Saxon culture was also exported. So, too, globalization involves more than just the production, distribution, and exchange of tangible commodities on a worldwide scale. It also involves the development of a worldwide common culture of values, images, and assumptions as to what is modern, stylish, right or wrong, and ideal. For example, a multibillion-dollar diet industry in the United States produces and distributes both pills and diet supplements *and* a demand-producing image of the ideal body (the so-called "tyranny of thinness"). New electronic forms of communication (especially films, television, and the Internet) are greatly facilitating this process.

Transnational corporations involved in the globalization of medicine (pharmaceuticals, services, medical insurance, and biotechnology) generate local demand for services, which indigenous systems are simply unable or unprepared to meet, often widening existing health disparities. In most countries it is usually those who can afford to pay, those who have access to private health care facilities, who receive the benefits of globalized medicine. For the medical profession, being "up to date" or "cutting edge" is highly valued around the world. This usually entails using the latest Western approaches and equipment. In developing countries, scarce resources are often consumed by the latest high-tech equipment and specialties, diverting resources from equipment that is culturally more appropriate, disfiguring indigenous health systems, and disrupting local patterns of medical care. The field of international health is replete with examples of the often unanticipated disfiguring consequences for indigenous systems of globalized health care.

The globalization of medical culture also fosters division within local health care systems. Patients may prefer providers who appear more cosmopolitan, who have "been abroad" and studied at prestigious Western (usually U.S.) medical institutions. Many academic centers now offer distance learning courses for providers in the developing world. The work and status of traditional and indigenous providers, whose orientation is more toward local culture and medical needs, is therefore devalued. Social status within the profession often derives from how Westernized a provider is (educational background, linkage to overseas institutions, regular participation in international symposia), not from the esteem that derives from effectively managing local medical problems. Local medical care systems and the social position of doctors around the world are being insidiously eroded as much by the globalization of Western medical culture as by the globalization of medical care production (manufactured goods and services).

THE EPIDEMIOLOGIC TRANSITION AND CHANGING CONCEPTS OF THE BODY

Sociologists have been engaged for decades in a lively debate on the conceptualization and measurement of occupational status or prestige, and much appears to depend upon the theoretical framework employed (this determines which criteria are given priority) and the purpose for which an occupational classification is developed (the interests of academic researchers and government officials are sometimes at odds). A large body of sociological work on the profession can be reduced to two main schools of thought (although most purists would reject any such simplification): one view (advanced by functionalists) emphasizes the value of "the" professions to society; the other view (advanced by critical theorists and social constructionists) emphasizes the power and self-interest of the professions and the value of their activities to the advancement of their own social position. Both viewpoints may contribute to understanding the changing social position of any occupation. The prestige of any occupation depends to some extent on its contribution to what is valued in any society (e.g., health, the prolongation of life, and the reduction of suffering). There have been changes over time in both the nature of disease and the ability of medical care providers to beneficially alter the natural course of illnesses. Little attention has been devoted to how such epidemiologic changes relate to the changing social position of doctors.

Patterns of mortality, morbidity, and disability obviously change over time: just as each historical epoch has its own predominant form of production (agricultural, industrial, informational), so too does it have its own predominant form of illness (86). Omran (87) suggested that changes in patterns of disease and death can be characterized as moving through three distinct phases.

The *age of pestilence and femine* characterizes premodern and pre-industrial societies. It was characterized by high mortality associated with environmental exposure and accidents and conflict. Total life expectancy was only 20 to 40 years. During the *age of receding pandemics*, improvements in housing, sanitation, and nutrition and public health activities resulted in a decline in deaths from infectious and parasitic diseases. Specific medical measures contributed little to the decline in the diseases (88–91). People began to survive into older age, when they were more likely to die from chronic degenerative diseases. Life expectancy increased to about 50 years. Equilibrium in mortality characterizes the *age of degenerative and human-made diseases*. Overall mortality rates continued to drop and life expectancy increased to about 70 years. A small number of chronic conditions (heart disease, cancer, and stroke) were major contributors to mortality, and (with the exception of cancer) these began an unexpected rapid decline beginning in the mid-1960s. It is common to attribute these improvements to secular changes in lifestyles and improvements in medical care, although the evidence for this remains somewhat inconclusive.

Olshansky and Ault (92) propose a fourth stage of epidemiologic transition, which they term the *age of delayed degenerative diseases*. During this stage the major causes of death remained unchanged, but they became more concentrated in the older age groups. There is evidence that while people may be living longer, they are experiencing increasing periods of disability (93). Palliative care has become an important component of modern medical practice. A fifth stage now appears to be emerging, which can be termed the *age of globalized health threats*. This stage is characterized by (*a*) the emergence of new infectious diseases and the reemergence of old (but newly resistant) foes (e.g., TB and malaria); and (*b*) the emergence of worldwide environmental threats (e.g., pollution, ozone depletion, bioterrorism) (94–96). While these threats have similarities with those of earlier stages, they differ in at least two respects: their global impact and the rapidity of their transmission. With respect to TB for example, the WHO estimates that *Mycobacterium tuberculosis* now infects some two billion people: one in every three worldwide. Approximately 10 percent of these carriers develop the disease and become infectious to an average of 10 to 15 other people. Globally, TB is now the fifth largest cause of death and the major cause of death for women. It is estimated that by 2020 there will be one billion new cases and around 70 million deaths. This new globalized threat of (often drug-resistant) TB obviously requires a globalized public health response—like the Global Alliance for TB Drug Development, involving governments, supranational agencies, transnational corporations, and major philanthropic organizations. Similarly, these emerging worldwide environmental threats will require new forms of sociopolitical intervention as part of a global public health strategy for the 21st century. It is clear that one-on-one curative interventions by health providers (e.g., physicians) will have little impact during the Age of Globalized Health Threats.

The social position of healer in society, only recently termed "the doctor," appears to have changed as the nature of the threat to health has changed over time. Although the evidence is fragmentary, it appears there was little role for a healer during the age of pestilence and famine. During and following the industrial revolution, with its air, water, food, and vector borne diseases, the afflicted either died (in accordance with the will of God) or quickly recovered (as a result of the intervention of a physician). In other words, doctors were perceived to be effective when people survived; failure was attributed to the will of God. Doctoring reached its zenith during the age of degenerative and human-made diseases, when pharmaceuticals and surgery were considered effective cures against the major conditions (heart disease, cancer, and stroke) of the modern era. Curing appears to have been supplanted by caring and pallative measures during the age of delayed degerative diseases. Much of the focus of doctoring has now shifted to regular monitoring of presently incurable conditions (diabetes, hypertension, asthma, arthritis, cancer) and to improving the quality of life. Curing is commonly thought to be a more glamorous and valued activity than caring. Moreover, caring may be more appropriately performed by the many other providers (discussed above) now considered to be equal partners with physicians on the health care team. The emerging threats to health that accompany globalization will likely require entirely different types of interventions, of a more sociopolitical nature.

Several other cultural phenomena have contributed to the erosion of the doctor's social position in the United States. First, increased public access to medical knowledge has resulted in some demystification of the body. The understanding of illness and disease has moved from the metaphysically inexplicable (which once gave providers almost priestly functions) and been reduced to biophysiologic functions. Second, the body is increasingly viewed as a machine that requires regular calibration (weight and diet control) and preventive maintenance (annual physicals). Defective parts like hearts, liver, kidneys, knees, or hips that deteriorate through excessive mileage (aging) are now able to be replaced. Doctoring now shares many similarities with the work of skilled car mechanics. Third, responsibility for personal health has shifted from paternalistic medical care providers: people are now viewed as personally responsible for their own health. Self-care (weight, exercise, diet, stress, self-examination) is beginning to assume the status of a moral obligation. Diagnoses of many medical conditions (diabetes, hypertension, pregnancy, some cancers) can now be made at the kitchen table. Computer-assisted diagnosis and the filling of prescriptions is now possible via the Internet, often rendering a face-to-face encounter with a doctor unnecessary. While such phenomena are increasingly marginalizing the doctor and are a source of some concern for the medical profession, they are often viewed by physician employers as welcome developments likely to reduce costs.

FROM RELATIONSHIP TO ENCOUNTER—THE EROSION OF PATIENTS' TRUST

Macrolevel changes in the content and organization of doctoring and the accompanying decline in the social position and status of doctors bring microlevel changes to the doctor-patient relationship. A measure of the change in this relationship lies in the words now used to describe it: "doctor" has become "provider," the "patient" has become a "client," and the "relationship" is now an "encounter." Recognizing that profound changes are occurring, we have suggested elsewhere the need for new, third-generation studies of the doctor-patient relationship (97). First-generation studies focused on the influence of patients' attributes (age, race, social class, gender, physical attractiveness, and so forth) on the doctor-patient relationship and clinical decision-making. Second-generation studies brought a shift in focus to the characteristics of physicians/providers (age or clinical experience, gender, race/ethnicity, medical specialty). These two types of study tend to employ a closed-system model of the doctor-patient encounter—the exchange is viewed as occurring in a sociological vacuum (a patient interacting with a physician). Our proposed third-generation studies recognize the increasing intrusion of social, economic, and organizational influences on the structure and content of the encounter. Table 18-1 summarizes some differences in the doctor-patient relationship from the mid-20th century to the early 21st century.

During the middle years of the 20th century, physicians acquired a widely discussed position of professional dominance (12, 40), and the doctor-patient relationship was depicted as "asymmetric." While commentators questioned the role of physicians as "medical imperialists" and "agents of social control," still doctors were generally considered to be on the patient's side. There was a coincidence of interest between physicians (who, through autonomous practice on behalf of patients, maximized their income) and patients (who cooperated with their doctor in order to get well). *Credat emptor* was considered an appropriate motto and a necessary condition for an effective encounter (98, 99).

Even the once cherished privacy of the physician-patient relationship is under attack. State encroachment on the relationship is evident in the "gag rule" prohibiting doctors in federally funded clinics from speaking about abortion with their patients. This rule, and the supporting Supreme Court opinion in *Rust* v. *Sullivan*, permitted increased governmental control over

Table 18-1. Some differences in the doctor-patient relationship from mid to late 20th century

	Mid 20th century	Late 20th century
Terminology	Doctor-patient relationship	Client-provider encounter
The state (government) and insurance companies	Recognizes sanctity of "the" relationship	Intrudes on the encounter (e.g., gag rules)
Ownership	Patient is "owned" by the doctor	Client is "owned" by provider's employer
Reference group	Independent physician works for the patient (sole practitioner)	Salaried provider works for an employer
Duration of relationship	Continuity of care (often over many years)	Discontinuity of care (changes with employer and medical staff)
Length of encounter	15–20 minutes	6–8 minutes
Power	Doctor in control (patient has few options)	Client more in control (able to "shop around")
Trust	*Credat emptor*	*Caveat emptor*
Treatment options	Physician does what the patient requests/needs	Provider does what organizational policy permits
Reimbursement	Physician rewarded for doing more (fee-for-service)	Provider rewarded for doing less (salaried employee)
Confidentiality	Held to be inviolable	Threatened by the number of parties involved and computerized medical records.

physicians' speech (100, 101). Testifying before Congress, an AMA representative considered the gag rule would "denigrate the integrity of the doctor-patient relationship and force health care professionals to violate established standards of medical care and professional ethics" (102).

With the phenomenal growth of corporatized medical care the average physician's administrative, economic, and even clinical autonomy has been challenged. Professional dominance has been supplanted by bureaucratic dominance, with the resulting appearance of a conflict of interest for physicians. Physicians now find themselves between a rock and a hard place: there is evidence that many must employ manipulative "covert advocacy" tactics so that patients can receive care that physicians perceive as essential (103). Essentially they must do the wrong thing (lie) to achieve the right outcome (their preferred medical treatment). It is not unreasonable to ask whether physicians are still able to serve the interests of their patients or are required to advance the interests of their employers (104). Physicians have even been referred to as "double agents" (105). Profound changes in the structure and content of late 20th century medical care appear to be eroding the trust that is thought to be a crucial ingredient in the doctor-patient relationship (106–110). Kao and colleagues (104) show that the method of physician payment is related to the level of patients trust. While usually confined to other market transactions (like auto repair, insurance, and the purchase of real estate), the motto *caveat emptor* is now increasingly invoked in the context of the corporate provider-client encounter.

WEAKENING OF MARKET POSITION THROUGH OVERSUPPLY

Much of the decline of modern doctoring can be attributed to influences outside the control of the profession: such *extrinsic factors,* as discussed above, include the bureaucratization of medical care and the decline in public trust, profit-driven corporatization, the erosion of state sponsorship, and the competition presented by other health workers. There are, however, factors *intrinsic* to the medical profession (and certainly under its control) that also are undermining its privileged social position. Of the intrinsic factors, the most important is almost certainly the weakening of physicians' own labor market position by physician oversupply and unwillingness to curtail the overproduction of new medical graduates.

For several decades numerous reports have warned of a looming physician surplus; these worrisome projections are now a reality for the medical profession (111–117). More than 20 years ago (in 1976) it was predicted that by 1990 there would be a surplus of 70,000 active physicians (a 13 percent surplus) and that by 2000 this would increase to 145,000 (22 percent surplus) (111). Weiner (77) projected a surplus of 165,000 physicians (28 percent of practicing physicians) by 2000. He subsequently revised his projected surplus to an oversupply of 270,000 physicians (39 percent of all patient-care physicians) by 2000 (118). These and numerous other projections (and the devil is in the assumptions on which they are based) are the subject of intense debate (119). Despite some disagreement over whether a *national* physician surplus exists there is little doubt that oversupply presents a serious problem in some geographic areas (112, 120–126). The Boston–Washington corridor, for example, accounts for much of the projected surplus (20 percent). One commentator thinks that a decrease of 25,000 physicians (40 percent) and 16,000 residents (40 percent) is necessary to bring this region to the national norm: "it is unlikely that in the near term this region could absorb more physicians per capita than now exist" (69, p. 1541). In the context of national oversupply, there are of course other areas of the country with alarming health inequalities that continue to be severely underdoctored. The most valuable national data on physician supply and demand and their likely consequences for modern doctoring are presented by Cooper (69), who suggests that supply may exceed demand by up to 62,000 physicians (8 percent) through 2010. Cooper predicts that a small deficit may occur by 2020, when the growth rate of physicians is projected to be less than the growth rate of U.S. population (Figure 18-10).

The debate over likely trends will no doubt continue, with different constituencies presenting different scenarios. Practicing physicians are already feeling the squeeze and suggesting that the production of medical graduates should be carefully monitored. But the medical education

Figure 18-10. *Resident-adjusted physician supply and demand, United States, 1993–2020. Source: Cooper (69).*

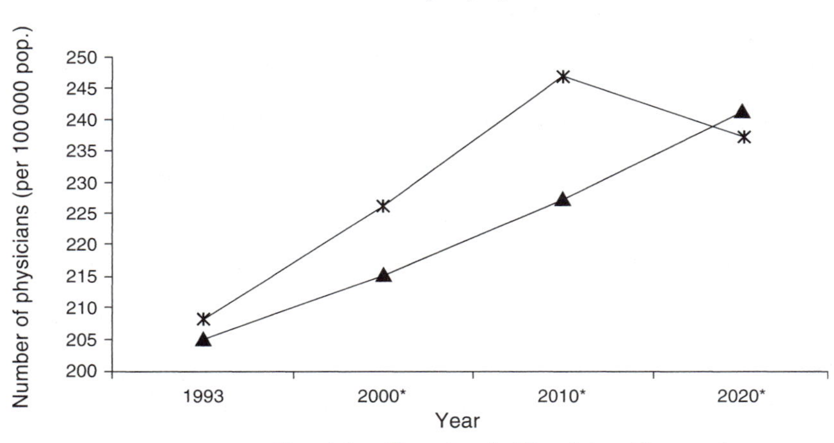

establishment is required to increase the production of medical graduates to justify earlier massive investments in institutional development. No medical school is likely to close its doors in the foreseeable future (the supply of student applicants will continue to exceed the number of available places). If oversupply is a likely scenario, then the medical profession appears to be on a self-destructive course. In our view there is clearly an overproduction of physicians. But current proposals to address the problem, like encouraging specialty and geographic redistribution and some constraints on international medical graduates, appear inadequate and are unlikely to be effective (127, 128). One high-level meeting on this subject (the Trilateral Physician Workforce Conference, held in 1996) concluded that the difficulty of translating the results of workforce research into public policy is more pronounced in the United States than elsewhere (e.g., Canada and the United Kingdom) and that the situation in the United States suffers from "paralysis by analysis" (129).

Until quite recently, a medical degree guaranteed full employment immediately upon graduation from a reputable medical school. Physician unemployment is still rare, but *under*employment appears to be quite common (more than other occupations, physicians are able to supplement their income with non-patient-care activities). Miller and her colleagues (126) reported that one-quarter of newly trained physicians experienced difficulty finding appropriate employment; 67 percent obtained clinical practice positions in their specialties.

Through an inability to even acknowledge let alone control their own worrisome overproduction, physicians appear determined to continue along the path of their own demise—very much like lemmings inexplicably self-destructing into the Arctic Ocean. This erosion of labor market position is, of course, exacerbated by trends in the growth of other health workers as described earlier.

THE DOCTORS' UNION—DIVIDE AND CONQUER

During much of the 20th century, the special position of physicians and the state-supported prerogatives they acquired were engineered and advanced by an ever more powerful union—the American Medical Association. During midcentury, the support or opposition of the AMA determined the success or failure of major national legislation. There was no greater prize for aspiring politicians than some form of support or even endorsement from the AMA. Medical specialization, however, splintered the once unified posture of the AMA. Medical specialization, however, splintered the once unified posture of the AMA; specialty-based societies (unions) replaced the increasingly distant AMA as the primary reference group of many physicians. For example, cardiologists joined the American College of Cardiology and internists joined the Society for General Internal Medicine. These memberships were instead of rather than in addition to membership in the AMA. While the AMA was a dominant institutional force around the middle of the 20th century, probably as influential as the state itself in advancing the prerogatives of "the" profession (Figure 18-1), its influence today is shared with often rival specialist medical societies (Figure 18-2). Its power now appears no greater than that exerted by competing state or specialist societies, and a coincidence of interests cannot be assumed.

Membership in the AMA was never compulsory, but during the middle of the 20th century nearly all physicians joined and paid their dues. It is safe to assume that most physicians still belong to some professional association (or union), but nowadays membership in the AMA is deemed unnecessary by more than half of U.S. physicians. Figure 18.11 shows that at the turn of the 20th century the United States had an estimated 800,000 active physicians, but membership in the AMA had slipped to well under 300,000 (only 40 percent of the nation's doctors).

Particularly disturbing for the AMA is the tendency for younger physicians or new medical graduates not to become members. In other words, the current membership is declining and aging. Previously unheard of divisions within the AMA are now also apparent: an upstart challenge (by Raymond Scaletter) to the usually well-choreographed installation of an heir apparent (Thomas Reardon) reflected discontent within this once unified pressure group (130). A decision by the AMA in 1997 to enter into an exclu-

Figure 18-11. *Physicians in the United States and membership in the AMA, 1960–1999. Source: AMA Physician Masterfile 2000.*

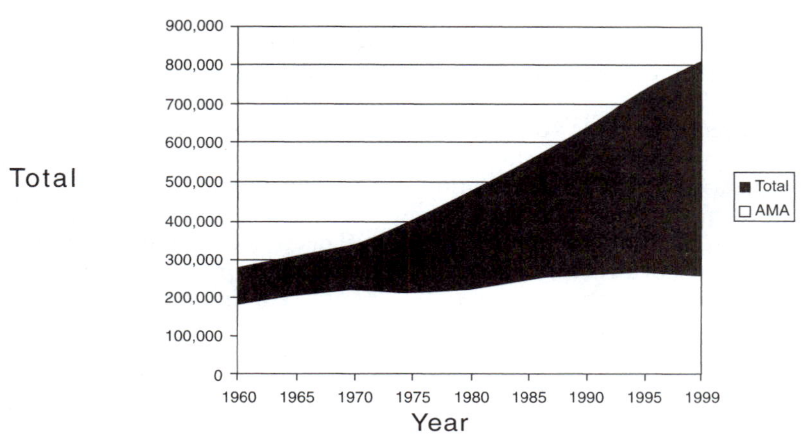

sive trademark licensing agreement with Sunbeam Products, Inc., created turmoil within the organization over the relationship of business and professionalism and particularly disturbed the leadership because it became public: it caused "wrenching public adversity" and "horrendous and well publicized difficulty" (131–133).

The AMA's declining influence on national public policy was evident during the 1994 debate over health care reform—its submission at one early point was given no more time or weight than those of other labor unions and public interest groups. Through its political arm, the American Medical Political Action Committee (AMPAC), the AMA is obviously still a powerful professional interest group—it remains one of the highest-spending lobbying group in the United States (100). Its positions on major issues such as smoking, domestic violence, teen pregnancies, handguns, and the distorting influences of commercialism on medical care are consonant with a majority of public opinion. But the influence of the AMA does appear to have diminished; nowhere is this more evident than in its ability to withstand the movement toward managed care and the corrosive effect of commercialism on professional behavior. Fragmentation of physicians into specialist societies and internal dissention within the AMA itself have created a divide-and-conquer opportunity for both private business interests and the state. Groups of physicians with particular specialty interests can be pitted against each other to achieve an outcome that is sometimes not in the overall or long-term interest of the profession.

CONCLUSION

We have argued in this article that late capitalist changes in the ownership and organization of U.S. health care are eroding the ethos of professionalism, reducing the social status of doctors, and transforming the nature of everyday medical work (doctoring). To underscore the historic magnitude of these changes, we draw parallels with the rise and fall of religious monasticism during the Middle Ages. In just 25 years, U.S. medical care has been transformed from a mainly fee-for-service system controlled by dominant professionals to a corporatized system dominated by increasingly concentrated and globalized financial and industrial interests. Present-day observers are, however, too close to late 20th and early 21st century changes in U.S. medical care to enjoy the vantage point of, say, a modern-day historian studying medieval monasticism. Recognizing the increasing threat to professionalism and doctoring, some commentators have recommended what may be termed intermediate solutions (e.g., more emphasis on a new professional ethic during an already overcrowded medical school curriculum, interventions to increase patients' trust, unionization of discontented doctors, and even a patients' bill of rights). In the context of the global macroeconomic forces now transforming U.S. medical care, such proposals, while well intentioned, appear unfortunately naive.

Freidson (134) has recently made revisions to his earlier work on professional dominance. While recognizing profound changes, he continues to look *inside medicine* to understand the changing status of doctors (training, specialized knowledge, and "the soul of professionalism") rather than *outside medicine,* at more influential surrounding macroeconomic circumstances. He misinterprets and dismisses attempts to look at these latter factors as ideologically inspired attacks and simply shibboleths rather than efforts to understand the more fundamental reasons for the historical decline of doctoring.

We argue that the recent (late 20th century and early 21st century) erosion of professionalism and decline of the medical profession result from many different social influences—at least eight of varying importance are discussed in this article. For convenience we organized these into *extrinsic factors* (six of which appear to be outside the control of the profession) and *intrinsic factors* (two of which may be amenable to change by the medical profession itself). The major extrinsic factors are:

- The changing nature of the U.S. state (from pluralist to New Right) and loss of historically important institutional support for doctoring.
- The bureaucratization (corporation) of doctoring and consequent loss of professional autonomy.
- The emerging competitive threat from other health care workers who provide an opportunity for profit-driven owners to replace doctors with appropriately trained workers at cheaper labor rates.
- Globalization and the information revolution, which are subordinating national and local medical societies, stripping doctors of their monopoly on medical knowledge, and permitting the monitoring of the minutest aspects of the doctor's everyday behavior.
- The epidemiologic transition (to palliative care and global health threats), changing concept of the body (a well-maintained machine), and routinization of the doctor's charisma as an agent of life or death.
- Changes in the nature of the doctor-patient relationship and the erosion of patients' trust, which are corroding the esteem in which the profession is held.

Two intrinsic factors are:

- The weakening of physicians' labor market position through oversupply.
- The continuing fragmentation of the once powerful physicians' union (AMA) through specialty and subspecialty differentiation.

This article is *not* an attempt to assess the strengths and weaknesses of the competing theories of professionalism (dominance, corporatization, deprofessionalism). Its purpose, rather, is to describe the historic magnitude of the changes in the financing and organization of U.S. medical care and their implications for professionalism, the social position of doctors, and the everyday work of doctoring. Just as medieval monks were considered increasingly anachronistic and out of touch, hoping that macroeconomic secular changes in the surrounding society would pass them by, so too do some contemporary observers of medicine cling to the hope that things will eventually get better. With the golden age of medicine now almost behind us, doctors are huddling in their monasteries (hospitals and medical centers) powerlessly awaiting the next corporate onslaught. It is unlikely that the laity (the public) will rise up and save the church (hospital organizations) and the monks (the doctors). In other words, it is unlikely that any actions taken by the institution of medicine—health care organizations, the training and mobilization of doctors—or public protest will have any major effects, given the momentum already in motion. Our only hope probably lies in some form of government action (some fundamental reorganization of the health system to protect the profession and the public). Given the shift in the state's allegiance to the interests that are behind the recent changes in U.S. medical care, whose consequences for doctors we wish to mitigate, the unfortunately must be considered false hope.

ACKNOWLEDGMENTS

Our appreciation to Drs. John Stoeckle (Harvard Medical School), Lee Strunin (Boston University School of Public Health), and Paul Cleary (Harvard Medical School), who provided helpful comments. Nationally syndicated cartoonist Mark Tonra provided valuable assistance with the illustrations.

REFERENCES

1. di Lampedusa, G. *The Leopard.* Parthenon Books, New York, 1960.
2. McKinlay, J. B., and Stoeckle, J. D. Corporatization and the social transformation of doctoring. *Int. J. Health Serv.* 18: 191–205, 1988.
3. McKinlay, J. B., and Arches, J. Towards the proletarianization of physicians. *Int. J. Health Serv.* 15: 161–195, 1985.
4. McKinlay, J. B. The business of good doctoring or doctoring as good business: Reflections on Freidson's view of the medical game. *Int. J. Health Serv.* 8: 459–488, 1978.
5. Navarro, V. Professional dominance or proletarianization? Neither. *Milbank Q.* 66(Suppl. 2): 57–75, 1989.
6. Coburn, D. Canadian medicine: Dominance or proletarianization? *Milbank Q.* 66(Suppl. 2): 92–116, 1988.
7. Scarpachi, J. L. Physician proletarianization and medical care restructuring in Argentina and Uruguay. *Econ. Geography* 6: 362–377, 1990.
8. Wolinsky, F. D. The professional dominance, deprofessionalization, proletarianization and corporatization perspectives: An overview and synthesis. In *The Changing Medical Profession: An International Perspective,* edited by F. W. Hafferty and J. B. McKinlay. Oxford University Press, New York, 1993.
9. Starr, P. *The Social Transformation of American Medicine.* Basic Books, New York, 1982.
10. Dudley, R. A., and Luft, H. S. Managed care in transition. *N. Engl. J. Med.* 344(14): 1087–1091, 2001.
11. Coster, R. L. Insulation from observability and types of social conformity. *Am. Sociol. Rev.* 25: 28–39, February 1961.
12. Freidson, E. *Profession of Medicine.* Dodd, Mead, New York, 1970.
13. Berlant, J. L. *Profession and Monopoly.* University of California Press, Berkeley, 1975.
14. Johnson, T. The state and the professions: Peculiarities of the British. In *Social Class and the Division of Labour,* edited by A. Giddens and G. Mackenzie. Cambridge University Press, Cambridge, 1982.
15. Coburn, D., Torrance, G. M., and Kaufert, J. M. Medical dominance in Canada in historical perspective: The rise and fall of medicine. *Int. J. Health Serv.* 13: 407–432, 1983.
16. Willis, E. *Medical Dominance: The Division of Labour in Australian Health Care.* George Allen and Unwin, Sydney, 1983.
17. Alford, R. *Health Care Politics: Ideological and Interest Group Barriers to Reform.* University of Chicago Press, Chicago, 1975.
18. McKinlay, J. B. On the professional regulation of change. In *Professionalism and Social Change,* edited by P. J. Halmos, pp. 61–84. Sociological Review Monographs, Vol. 20. University of Keele, Keele, U.K., 1973.
19. Fougere, G. Struggling for control: The state and the medical profession in New Zealand. In *The Changing Medical Profession: An International Perspective,* edited by F. W. Hafferty and J. B. McKinlay, pp. 115–123. Oxford University Press, New York, 1993.
20. Krause, E. A. *Death of Guilds, Professions, States, and the Advance of Capitalism, 1930 to the Present.* Yale University Press, New Haven, Conn., 1996.
21. Heywood, A. *Politics.* Macmillan, London, 1997.
22. Haralambos, M., and Holborn, M. *Sociology Themes and Perspectives,* Ed. 4. Collins Educational, London, 1995.
23. Skocpol, T. *Boomerang—Health Care Reform and the Turn against Government.* North, New York, 1997.
24. McKinlay, J. B., and Marceau, L. D. Value for Money in the Battle for the Public Health. Paper presented at the National Institutes of Health, November 6, 1998.
25. Coburn, D. State authority, medical dominance, and trends in the regulation of the health professions: The Ontario case. *Soc. Sci. Med.* 37(2): 129–138, 1993.
26. Gramsci, A. *Selections from the Prison Notebooks,* edited by Q. Hoare and G. Nowell-Smith. International Publishing, Chicago, 1971.
27. Mosca, G. *The Ruling Class,* translated by A. Livingstone. McGraw-Hill, New York, 1939 [1896].
28. Miliband, R. *The State in Capitalist Society.* Weidenfeld and Nicolson, London, 1969.
29. Poulantzas, N. *Political Power and Social Classes.* New Left Books, London, 1968.

30. Mills, C. W. *The Power Elite*. Oxford University Press, New York, 1956.
31. Jessop, B. *State Theory: Putting Capitalist States in Their Place*. Polity Press, Oxford, 1990.
32. Jessop, B. *The Capitalist State*. Martin Robertson, Oxford, 1982.
33. Rawls, J. *A Theory of Justice*. Oxford University Press, Oxford, 1971.
34. Dahl, R. *Modern Political Analysis*, Ed. 4. Prentice-Hall, Englewood Cliffs, N.J., 1984.
35. Lindblom, C. *Politics and Markets*. Basic Books, New York, 1977.
36. Marsh, D. (ed.). *Pressure Politics*. Junction Books, London, 1983.
37. Galbraith, J. K. *The Culture of Contentment*. Sinclair Stevenson, London, 1992.
38. Mechanic, D. Sources of countervailing power in medicine. *J. Health Polit. Policy Law* 16: 485, 1991.
39. Light, D. Professionalism as a countervailing power. *J Health Polit. Policy Law* 16: 499–506, 1991.
40. Freidson, E. *Professional Dominance: The Social Structure of Medical Care*. Aldine, Chicago, 1970.
41. Harrison, S., and Pollitt, C. *Controlling Health Professionals: The Future of Work and Organisation in the NHS*. Open University Press, Buckingham, U.K., 1994.
42. Nordlinger, E. *On the Autonomy of the Democratic State*. Harvard University Press, Cambridge, 1981.
43. Nozick, R. *Anarchy, State, and Utopia*. Basil Blackwell, Oxford, 1974.
44. Klein, R. The state and the profession: The politics of the double bed. *BMJ* 301: 701–702, 1990.
45. Barnett, J. R., Barnett, P., and Kearns, R. A. Declining professional dominance? Trends in the proletarianisation of primary care in New Zealand. *Soc. Sci. Med.* 46(2): 193–207, 1998.
46. Mohan, J. *A National Health Service? The Restructuring of Health Care in Britain since 1979*. Macmillan, Basingstoke, U.K., 1995.
47. Twaddle, A. C. Health system reforms: Toward a framework for international comparisons. *Soc. Sci. Med.* 43: 637–654, 1996.
48. Burrows, R., and Loader, B. (eds.). *Towards a Post Fordist Welfare State*. Routledge, London, 1994.
49. Farrell, J. A. *Tip O'Neill and the Democratic Century*. Little, Brown, Boston, 2001.
50. Blendon, R. J., et al. The implications of 2000 election. *N. Engl. J. Med.* 344(9): 679–684, 2001.
51. Light, D. Comparative models of "health care" systems. In *The Sociology of Health and Illness*, edited by P. Conard and R. Kern. St. Martin's Press, New York, 1994.
52. Zola, I. K. Medicine as an institution of social control. *Sociol. Rev.* 204(4): 487–504, 1972.
53. Hafferty, F., and McKinlay, J. B. (eds.). *The Changing Medical Profession: An International Perspective*. Oxford University Press, New York, 1993.
54. Kletke, P. R., Emmons, D. W., and Gillis, K. D. Current trends in physicians' practice arrangements: From owners to employees. *JAMA* 276(7): 555–560, 1996.
55. Kletke, P. R. The changing proportion of employee physicians: Evidence of new trends. *AHSR FHSR Annual Meeting Abstracts* 11: 68–69, 1994.
56. Stoeckle, J. D. Working on the factory floor. *Ann. Intern. Med.* 107(2): 250–251, 1987.
57. Mechanic, D. Managed care and the imperative for a new professional ethic. *Health Aff. (Millwood)* 19(5): 100–111, 2000.
58. Sandrick, K. Out in front: Managed care helps push clinical guidelines forward. *Hospitals* 67: 30–31, 1993.
59. Bodenheimer, T., and Grumbach, K. The reconfiguration of US medicine. *JAMA* 274: 85–90, 1995.
60. Hunter, D. J. From tribalism to corporatism: The managerial challenge to medical dominance. In *Challenging Medicine*, edited by J. Gabe, D. Kelleher, and G. Williams, pp. 1–22. Routledge, London, 1994.
61. Burdi, M. D., and Baker, L. C. Physicians' perceptions of autonomy and satisfaction in California. *Health Aff. (Millwood)*. July-August 1999, pp. 134–135.
62. Kassirer, J. P. Doctor discontent. *N. Engl. J. Med.* 339(21): 1543, 1998.
63. O'Connor, S. J., and Lanning, J. A. The end of autonomy? Reflections on the post-professional physician. *Health Care Manag. Rev.* 17(63): 63–72, 1992.
64. Calnan, M., and Williams, S. Challenges to professional autonomy in the United Kingdom? The perceptions of general practitioners. *Int. J. Health Serv.* 25: 219–241, 1995.
65. Rappolt, S. G. Clinical guidelines and the fate of medical autonomy in Ontario. *Soc. Sci. Med.* 4: 977–987, 1997.
66. Feinglass, J., and Salmon, J. W. Corporatization of medicine: The use of medical management information systems to increase the clinical pro-

ductivity of physicians. *Int. J. Health Serv.* 20: 233–252, 1990.

67. Brennan, T., and Berwick, D. *Regulation, Markets, and the Quality of American Health Care.* Jossey-Bass, San Francisco, 1996.
68. Cooper, R. A., and Stoflet, S. J. Trends in the education and practice of alternative medicine clinicians. *Health Aff. (Millwood)* 15: 226–238, 1996.
69. Cooper, R. A. Perspectives on the physician workforce to the year 2020. *JAMA* 274(19): 1534–1543, 1995.
70. Osterweis, M., et al. (eds.). *The US Health Workforce: Power, Politics, and Policy.* Association of Academic Health Centers, Washington, D.C., 1996.
71. Safreit, B. J. Impediments to progress in health care workforce policy. *Inquiry* 31: 310–317, 1994.
72. Cooper, R. A., Laud, P., and Dietrich, C. L. Current and projected workforce of nonphysician clinicians. *JAMA* 280(9): 788–794, 1998.
73. Jones, P. E., and Cawley, J. F. Physician assistants and health system reform: Clinical capabilities, practice activities and potential roles. *JAMA* 271(16): 1266–1272, 1994.
74. Cooper, R. A., Henderson, T., and Dietrich, C. L. Roles of nonphysician clinicians as autonomous providers of patient care. *JAMA* 280(9): 795–802, 1998.
75. Lohr, K. N., Vaneslow, N. A., and Detmer, D. E. *The Nation's Physician Workforce: Options for Balancing Supply and Requirements.* National Academy Press, Washington, D.C., 1996.
76. Cohen, J. J., and Todd, J. S. Association of American Medicine Colleges and American Medical Association joint statement on physician workforce planning and graduate medical education reform policies. *JAMA* 272: 712, 1994.
77. Weiner, J. P. Forecasting the effects of health reform on US physician workforce requirement: Evidence from HMO staffing patterns. *JAMA* 272: 222–230, 1994.
78. Evans, R. G. Going for the gold: The redistributive agenda behind market based health care reform. *J. Health Polit. Policy Law* 22: 427–465, 1997.
79. Grumbach, K., and Coffman, J. Physician and nonphysician clinicians: Complements or competitors. *JAMA* 280(9): 825–826, 1998.
80. Greenberg, L., and Cultice, J. M. Forecasting the need for physicians in the United States: The health resources and services administration's physician requirements model. *Health Serv. Res.* 313(6): 723–737, 1997.
81. Bilton, T., et al. *Introducing Sociology,* Ed. 3. Macmillan, London, 1997.
82. Giddens, A. *Consequences of Modernity.* Stanford University Press, Stanford, Calif., 1990.
83. Swarns, R. L. West lures its doctors; South Africa fights back. *New York Times,* February 11, 2001.
84. Goode, W. J. Encroachment, charlatanism, and the emerging profession: Psychology, sociology, and medicine. *Am. Sociol. Rev.* 25: 902–914, 1960.
85. Fox, S., and Rainie, L. The online healthcare revolution: How the Web helps Americans take better care of themselves. November 26, 2000. www.pewinternet.org.
86. Fitzpatrick, R. M. Society and changing patterns of disease. In *Sociology as Applied to Medicine,* Ed. 3, edited by G. Scambler, pp. 3–17. Bailliere Tindall, London, 1991.
87. Omran, A. R. Epidemiologic transition: A theory of the epidemiology of population change. *Milbank Q.* 49: 309–338, 1971.
88. McKeown, T. The direction of medical research. *Lancet* 2(8155): 1281–1284, 1979.
89. Powles, J. On the limits of modern medicine. In *The Challenges of Community Medicine,* edited by R. L. Kane, pp. 89–122. Springer, New York, 1974.
90. Dubos, R. *Mirage of Health.* Harper and Row, New York, 1959.
91. McKinlay, J., and McKinlay, S. The questionable contribution of medical measures to the decline of mortality in the United States in the twentieth century. *Milbank Mem. Fund Q. Health Society* 55(3): 405–428, 1977.
92. Olshansky, S. D., and Ault, A. B. The fourth stage of the epidemiologic transition: The age of delayed degenerative diseases. *Milbank Q.* 64(3): 355–391, 1986.
93. McKinlay, J., McKinlay, S., and Beaglehole, R. Trends in death and disease and the contribution of medical measures. In *Handbook of Medical Sociology,* Ed. 4, edited by H. Freeman and S. Levine. Prentice-Hall, Englewood Cliffs, N.J., 1989.
94. McMichael, A. J., et al. (eds.). *Climate Change and Human Health—An Assessment Prepared by a Task Group on Behalf of the WHO, WMO, and UNEP.* WHO/EHG/96.7. WHO, Geneva, 1996.
95. Kovats, S., et al. Climate change and human health in Europe. *BMJ* 318: 1682–1685, 1999.

96. Githeko, A. K., et al. Climate change and vector borne diseases: A regional analysis. *Bull. World Health Organ.* 78: 1136–1147, 2000.
97. McKinlay, J. B., and Marceau, L. D. U.S. public health and the 21st century: Diabetes mellitus. *Lancet* 356: 757–761, 2000.
98. Thom, D. H., and Campbell, B. Patient-physician trust: An exploratory study. *J. Fam. Pract.* 44: 169–176, 1997.
99. Leopold, N., Cooper, M., and Clancy, C. Sustained partnership in primary care. *J. Fam. Pract.* 42: 129–137, 1996.
100. Sharfstein, J. M., and Sharfstein, S. S. Campaign contributions from the American Medical Political Action Committee to members of Congress. *N. Engl. J. Med.* 330(1): 32–37, 1994.
101. Sugarman, J., and Powers, M. How the doctor got gagged: The disintegrating right of privacy in the physician-patient relationship. *JAMA* 266: 3323–3327, 1991.
102. Scalettar, R. Public Health Services Act, Title X Family Planning Regulations, Statement of the American Medical Association to the Subcommittee on Health and the Environment, Energy and Commerce Committee, United States House of Representatives, March 30, 1992. AMA, Chicago, 1992.
103. Wynia, M. K., et al. Physician manipulation of reimbursement rules for patients. *JAMA* 283(14): 1858–1865, 2000.
104. Kao, A. C., et al. Patients' trust in their physician. *J. Gen. Intern. Med.* 13: 681–686, 1998.
105. Shortell, S. M., et al. Physicians as double agents: Maintaining trust in an era of multiple accountabilities. *JAMA* 280(12): 1102–1108, 1998.
106. Gray, B. H. Trust and trustworthy care in the managed care era. *Health Aff. (Millwood)* 16: 34–49, 1995.
107. Mechanic, D., and Schlesinger, M. The impact of managed care on patients' trust in medical care and their physicians. *JAMA* 275: 1693–1697, 1996.
108. Crawshaw, R., Rogers, D. E., and Pellegrino, E. D. Patient-physician covenant. *JAMA* 273: 1553, 1995.
109. Mechanic, D. Changing medical organization and the erosion of trust. *Milbank Q.* 74: 171–189, 1996.
110. Emanuel, E. J. Managed competition and the patient-physician relationship. *N. Engl. J. Med.* 329: 879, 1993.
111. U.S. Department of Health and Human Services. *Report of the Graduate Medical Education National Advisory Committee: Summary Report.* US DHHS, HAS 81-651. Washington, D.C., 1981.
112. Council on Graduate Medical Education. *Fourth Report: Recommendations to Improve Access to Health Care through Physician Workforce Reform.* U.S. Dept. of Health and Human Services, Rockville, Md., 1994.
113. Gamliel, S., et al. Managed care on the march: Will physicians meet the challenge? *Health Aff. (Millwood)* 14: 131–142, 1995.
114. Tarlov, A. R. The rising supply of physicians and the pursuit of better health. *J. Med. Educ.* 63: 94–107, 1988.
115. Tarlov, A. R. The increasing supply of physicians, the changing structure of the health services system and the future practice of medicine. *N. Engl. J. Med.* 308: 1235–1244, 1983.
116. Physician Payment Review Commission. Training physicians to meet the nation's needs. In *Annual Report to Congress 1992,* Chapt. 11. Washington, D.C., 1992.
117. Physician Payment Review Commission. The changing labor market for physicians. In *Annual Report to Congress 1995,* Chapt. 14. Washington, D.C., 1995.
118. Weiner, J. P. *Assessing Current and Future US Physician Requirements Based on HMO Staffing Rates: A Synthesis of New Sources of Data and Forecasts for the Years 2000 and 2020.* HRSA 94-576 (P). U.S. Dept. of Health and Human Services, Bureau of Health Professions, Washington, D.C., 1995.
119. Tarlov, R. A. Estimating physician workforce requirements: The devil is in the assumptions. *JAMA* 274(19): 1558–1560, 1995.
120. Institute of Medicine. *The Nation's Physician Workforce: Options for Balancing Supply Requirements.* National Academy Press, Washington, D.C., 1996.
121. Pew Health Professions Commission. *Critical Challenges: Revitalizing the Health Professions for the Twenty-first Century.* University of California, San Francisco, Center for the Health Professions, San Francisco, 1995.
122. Council on Graduate Medical Education. *Tenth Report: Physician Distribution and Health Care Challenges in Rural and Inner-City Areas.* U.S. Dept. of Health and Human Services, Rockville, Md., 1998.
123. Bureau of Health Professions. *Seventh Report to the President and Congress on the Status of Health Personnel in the United States.* National Academy Press, Washington, D.C., 1996.

124. Ginsburg, J. A. The physician workforce and financing of graduate medical education. *Ann. Intern. Med.* 128: 142–148, 1998.
125. Reinhardt, U. W. Planning the nation's health workforce: Let the market in. *Inquiry* 31: 250–263, 1994.
126. Miller, R. S., et al. Employment seeking experiences of resident physicians completing training during 1996. *JAMA* 280(9): 777–783, 1998.
127. Fox, D. M. From piety to platitudes to pork: The changing politics of health workforce policy. *J. Health Polit. Policy Law* 21: 825–853, 1996.
128. Foreman, S. Managing the physician workforce: Hands off, the market is working. *Health Aff. (Millwood)* 15: 243–249, 1996.
129. Stoddard, J., Sekscenski, E., and Weiner, J. The physician workforce: Broadening the search for solutions. *Health Aff. (Millwood)* 17(1): 252–257, 1998.
130. Goldstien, A. AMA rejects leadership challenge. *Washington Post,* June 23, 1997.
131. The AMA's appliance sale (editorial). *New York Times,* August 14, 1997.
132. Auctioning a seal of approval (editorial). *Washington Post,* August 20, 1997.
133. Kassirer, J. P., and Angell, M. The high price of product endorsement. *N. Engl. J. Med.* 337: 700–701, 1997.
134. Freidson, E. *Professionalism: The Third Logic.* University of Chicago Press, Chicago, 2001.

19 COUNTERVAILING POWER: THE CHANGING CHARACTER OF THE MEDICAL PROFESSION IN THE UNITED STATES

Donald W. Light

The medical profession appears to be losing its autonomy even as its sovereignty expands. With the more frequent use of physician profiling and other comparative measures of performance, together with the ability of sophisticated programmers to capture the decision-making trees of differential diagnosis on computers so well that they can check out and improve the performance of practitioners, theories of professionalism that rest on autonomy as their cornerstone need to be reconstructed from the ground up (Light 1988).

Although physicians play a central role in developing tools for scrutinizing the core of professional work, they work for purchasers who use them for the external measure of quality and cost-effectiveness. Thus, not only autonomy but also the monopoly over knowledge as the foundation of professionalism is thrown into question. The computerized analysis of practice patterns and decision making, together with the growth of active consumerism, constitute deprofessionalization as a trend (Haug 1973; Haug and Lavin 1983). Patients, governments, and corporate purchasers are taking back the cultural, economic, and even technical authority long granted to the medical profession.

The sovereignty of the profession nevertheless is growing. Evan Willis (1988) was the first to distinguish between autonomy over one's work and sovereignty over matters of illness. The sovereignty of medicine expands with advances in pharmacology, molecular biology, genetics, and diagnostic tools that uncover more and more pathology not known before. Although chronicity is the residue of cure and the growing proportion of insoluble problems is providing a new legitimacy to nonmedical forms of healing, care, and therapy, no other member of the illness trade has a knowledge and skill base that is expanding so rapidly as is the physician's.

This chapter describes the changes in the American medical profession over the past two decades and outlines the concept of countervailing power as a useful way to understand the profession's relations with the economy and the state.

SOME LIMITATIONS OF CURRENT CONCEPTS

In the special issue of the *Milbank Quarterly* . . . Sol Levine and I reviewed the concepts of professional dominance, deprofessionalization, proletarianization, and corporatization (Light and Levine 1988). Each has its truth and limitations. Each captures in its word one characteristic and trend, but this means that each mistakes the part for the whole and for the future. One set predicts the opposite of the other, yet neither can account for reversals. This is best illustrated by the oldest concept among them, professional dominance.

Professional dominance captured in rich complexity the clinical and institutional grip that the profession had over society in the 1960s, a formulation that supplanted Parsons' benign and admiring theoretical reflections of the 1940s and 1950s (Freidson 1970a, 1970b; Light 1989). But the concept of professional dominance cannot account for decline; dominance over institutions and resources leads only to still more dominance. As the very fruits of dominance itself weakened the profession from within and prompted powerful changes from without, the concept has become less useful. In its defense, Freidson (1984, 1985, 1986e, 1989) has been forced to retreat from his original concept of dominance, by which he meant control over the cultural, organizational, economic, and political dimensions of health care, to a much reduced concept that means control over one's work and those involved in it. Even that diminution to the pre-Freidson concept of professionalism may not stand, given the fundamental challenges to autonomy.

Space precludes reiterating the limitations of the other concepts, but it is worth noting the danger of conflating many by-products of professional dominance after World War II (such as increasing complexity, bureaucratization, and rationalization) with recent efforts by investors to corporatize medicine and by institutional payers such as governments and employers to get more effective health care for less money. The concept of corporatization in particular includes five dimensions that characterize medical work today as segmented and directed by the administrators of for-profit organizations that control the facilities, the technology used, and the remuneration of the physician-workers (McKinlay 1988). As the empirical part of this chapter shows, this characterization is not typical and does not capture the complex relations between doctors and corporations.

THE CONCEPT OF COUNTERVAILING POWERS

Sociology needs a concept or framework that provides a way of thinking about the changing relations over time between the profession and the major institutions with which it interacts. The concept of countervailing powers builds on the work of Johnson (1972) and Larson (1977), who analyzed such relations with a dynamic subtlety not found elsewhere. Montesquieu (de Secondat Montesquieu 1748) first developed the idea in his treatise about the abuses of absolute power by the state and the need for counterbalancing centers of power. Sir James Steuart (1767) developed it further in his ironic observations of how the monarchy's promotion of commerce to enhance its domain and wealth produced a countervailing power that tempered the absolute power of the monarchy and produced a set of interdependent relationships. One might discern a certain analogy to the way in which the American medical profession encouraged the development of pharmaceutical and medical supply companies within the monopoly markets it created to protect its own autonomy. They enriched the profession and extended its power, but increasingly on their terms.

The concept of countervailing powers focuses attention on the interactions of a few powerful actors in a field in which they are inherently interdependent yet distinct. If one party is dominant, as the American medical profession has been, its dominance is contextual and likely to elicit countermoves eventually by other powerful actors in an effort not to destroy it but to redress an imbalance of power. "Power on one side of a market," wrote John Kenneth Galbraith (1956: 113) in his original treatise on the dynamics of countervailing power in oligopolistic markets, "creates both the need for, and the prospect of reward to the exercise of countervailing power from the other side." In states where the government has played a central role in nurturing professions within the state structure but has allowed the professions to establish their own institutions and power base, the professions and the state go through phases of harmony and discord in which countervailing actions emerge. In states where the medical profession has been largely suppressed, we now see their rapid reconstitution once governmental oppression is lifted.

Countervailing moves are more difficult to accomplish and may take much longer when political and institutional powers are involved than in an economic market. Nevertheless, dominance tends to produce imbalances, excesses, and neglects that anger other countervailing (latent) powers and alienate the larger public. These imbalances include internal elaboration and expansion that weaken the dominant institution from within, a subsequent tendency to consume more and more of the nation's wealth, a self-regarding importance that ignores the concerns of its clients or subjects and institutional partners, and an expansion of control that exacerbates the impact of the other three. Other characteristics of a profession that affect its relations with countervailing powers are the degree and nature of competition with adjacent professions, about which Andrew Abbott (1988) has written with such richness, the changing technological base of its expertise, and the demographic composition of its membership.

As a sociological concept, countervailing powers is not confined to buyers and sellers; it includes a handful of major political, social, and other economic groups that contend with each other for legitimacy, prestige, and power, as well as for markets and money. Deborah Stone (1988) and Theodore Marmor with Jonathan Christianson (1982) have written insightfully about the ways in which countervailing powers attempt to portray benefits to themselves as benefits for everyone or to portray themselves as the unfair and damaged victims of other powers (particularly the state), or to keep issues out of public view. Here, the degree of power consists of the ability to override, suppress, or render as irrelevant the challenges by others, either behind closed doors or in public.

Because the sociological concept of countervailing powers recognizes several parties, not just buyers and sellers, it opens the door to alliances between two or more parties. These alliances, however, are often characterized by structural ambiguities, a term based on Merton and Barber's (1976) concept of sociological ambivalence that refers to the cross-cutting pressures and expectations experienced by an institution in its relations with other institutions (Light 1983:345–46). For example, a profession's relationships to the corporations that supply it with equipment, materials, and information technology both benefit the profession and make it dependent in uneasy ways. The corporations can even come to control professional practices in the name of quality. Alliances with dominant political parties (Krause 1988b; Jones 1991) or with governments are even more fraught with danger. The alliance of the German medical profession with the National Socialist party, for example, so important to establishing the party's legitimacy, led to a high degree of governmental control over work and even the professional knowledge base (Jarausch 1990; Light, Liebfried, and Tennstedt 1986).

COUNTERVAILING POWERS IN AMERICAN MEDICINE

In the case of the American medical profession, concern over costs, unnecessary and expensive procedures, and overspecialization grew during the 1960s to the "crisis" announced by President Richard Nixon, Senator Edward Kennedy, and many other leaders in the early 1970s. President Nixon attempted to establish a national network of health maintenance organizations (HMOs) bent on efficiency and cost-effectiveness. He and the Congress created new agencies to regulate the spending of capital, the production of new doctors, and even the practice of medicine through institutionalized peer review. All of these were done gingerly at first, in a provider-friendly way. When, at the end of the 1970s, little seemed to have changed, the government and corporations launched a much more adversarial set of changes, depicted in Table 19-1. The large number of unnecessary procedures, the unexplained variations in practice patterns, the unclear answers to rudimentary questions about which treatments were most cost-effective, and the burgeoning bills despite calls for self-restraint had eroded the sacred trust enjoyed by the profession during the golden era of medicine after World War II. To some degree, the dominance of the medical profession had been allowed on the assumption that physicians knew what they were doing and acted in the best interests of society. Unlike the guilds of earlier times, however, the medical profession had failed to exercise controls over products, practices, and prices to ensure uniformly good products at fair prices.

The reassertion of the payers' latent countervailing powers called for a concentration of will and buying power that was only partially achieved. Larger corporations, some states, and particularly the federal government changed from passively paying bills submitted by providers to scrutinizing bills and organizing markets for competitive contracts that covered a range of services for a large pool of people. The health insurance industry, originally designed to reimburse hospitals and doctors, was forcefully notified that it must serve those who pay the premiums or lose business. Today, thousands of insurance sales representatives are now agents of institutional buyers, and insurance companies have developed a complex array of managed care products. Hundreds of utilization management companies and entire divisions of insurance companies devoted to designing these products have arisen (Gray and Field 1989: Ch. 3).

These changes have produced analogous changes among providers: more large groups, vertically integrated clinics, preferred provider organizations (PPOs), health maintenance orga-

Table 19-1. Axes of Change in the American Health Care System

Dimensions	Provider Driven	Buyer Driven
Ideological	Sacred trust in doctors	Distrust of doctors' values, decisions, even competence
Economic	Carte blanche to do what seems best; power to set fees; incentives to specialize, develop techniques	Fixed prepayment or contract with accountability for decisions and their efficacy
	Informal array of cross-subsidizations for teaching, research, charity care, community services	Elimination of "cost shifting"; pay only for services contracted
Political	Extensive legal and administrative power to define and carry out professional work without competition and to shape the organization and economics of medicine	Minimal legal and administrative power to do professional work but not shape the organization and economics of services
Clinical	Exclusive control of clinical decision making	Close monitoring of clinical decisions–their cost and their efficacy
	Emphasis on state-of-the-art specialized interventions; disinterest in prevention, primary care, and chronic care	Emphasis on prevention, primary care, and functioning; minimize high-tech and specialized interventions
Technical	Political and economic incentives to develop new technologies in protected markets	Political and economic disincentives to develop new technologies
Organizational	Cottage industry	Corporate industry
Potential disruptions and dislocations	Overtreatment; iatrogenesis; high cost; unnecessary treatment; fragmentation; depersonalization	Undertreatment; cuts in services; obstructed access; reduced quality; swamped in paperwork

nizations (HMOs), and hospital-doctor joint ventures. When the federal government created and implemented a national schedule of prospective payments for hospital expenses, termed diagnosis related groups (DRGs), doctors and health care managers countered by doing so much more business outside the DRG system that they consumed nearly all the billions saved on inpatient care. Congress more than ever now regards doctors as the culprits, and it has countered by instituting a fee schedule based on costs. In response, the specialties affected have joined hands in a powerful political countermove designed to water down the sharp reductions in the fee schedule for surgeons and technology-based specialists (like radiologists).

Thus, although the buyers' revolt depicted in Table 19-1 spells the end of dominance, it by no means spells the end to professional power. Closely monitored contracts or payments, corporate amalgamation, and significant legal changes to foster competition are being met by responses that the advocates of markets, as the way to make medicine efficient, did not consider. Working together (or, as the other side terms it, collusion), appropriate referrals (known as cost shifting to somebody else's budget), market segmentation, market expansion, and service substitution are all easier and often more profitable than trying to become more efficient, particularly when the work is complex, contingent, and uncertain (Light 1990). Moreover, most inefficiencies in medicine are embedded in organizational structures, professional habits, and power relations so that competitive contracting is unlikely to get at them (Light 1991).

On the buyers' side, the majority of employers and many states have still not been able to take concerted action, much less combine their powers. The utilization management industry has produced a bewildering array of systems and criteria, which are adjusted to suit the preferences of each employer-client. The Institute of Medicine (IOM) study on the subject states that the Mayo Clinic deals with a thousand utilization review (UR) plans (Gray and Field 1989: 59), and large hospitals deal with one hundred to two hundred of them. Who knows which are more "rational" or effective? Moreover, the countervailing efforts of institutional buyers rest on a marshland of data. "Studies continue to document," states the IOM report, "imprecise or inaccurate diagnosis and procedure coding, lack of diagnostic codes on most claim forms, only scattered documentation about entire episodes of treatment or illness, errors and ambiguities in preparation and processing of claims data, and limited information on patient and population characteristics" (Gray and Field 1989:48).

In spite of this morass, a profound restructuring of incentives, payments, and practice environments is beginning to take place, and more solid, coordinated data are rapidly being accumulated. The threat of denial, or of being dropped as a high-cost provider in a market, has probably reduced treatments but in the process increased diagnostic services and documentation, a major vehicle for the expansion of medical sovereignty. Accountability, then, may be the profession's ace card as governments and institutional buyers mobilize to make the profession accountable to their concerns.

CHANGING PRACTICE PATTERNS

Cost and Income

If the first round in the struggle to control rising medical expenditures consisted of tepid and unsuccessful efforts to regulate capital and services in the 1970s, then providers again emerged as the winners of the second round in the 1980s. They expanded services, took market share away from hospitals, packaged services to the most attractive market niches, featured numerous products developed by the highly profitable companies specializing in new medical technology, and advertised vigorously. Eye centers, women's centers, occupational medicine clinics, ambulatory surgical centers, imaging centers, detoxification programs: these and other enterprises caused medical expenditures to rise from $250 billion in 1980 to about $650 billion in 1990. This equals 12 percent of the nation's entire gross national product (GNP), one-third higher than the average for Western Europe. There seems to be no way to avoid health expenditures' rising to 16 percent of GNP by 1995.

At the level of personal income, many physicians tell anyone who will listen that one can no longer make "good money" in medicine, but the facts are otherwise. From 1970 to about 1986, their average income stayed flat after inflation, but since then it has been rising. The era of cost containment and dehospitalization has actually been an opportunity for market expansion. Although physicians' market share of national health expenditures declined from 20 to 17 percent as hospitals' share rose between 1965 and 1984, it has climbed back up to 19 percent since then (Roback, Randolph, and Seidman 1990: Table 105). The profession appears thoroughly commercialized (Potter, McKinlay, and D'Agostino 1991), doing more of what pays more and less of what pays less. Although the profession likes to think it was more altruistic in the golden era of medicine after World War II, this was a time when physicians' incomes rose most rapidly and when it controlled insurance payment committees.

In addition, the range of physicians' incomes has spread. For example, surgeons earned 40 percent more than general practitioners in 1965 but 57 percent more in 1985 (Statistical Abstract 1989). As of 1989, surgeons earned on average $200,500 after expenses but before taxes, while family or general practitioners earned $95,000. All specialties averaged a sixty-hour week. Beleaguered obstetricians, even after their immense malpractice premiums, are doing well. They netted $194,300, up $14,000 from 1988, which was up $17,500 from 1987.

Despite the success so far of the profession in generating more demand, services, and income, the tidal force of population growth is against them. The number of physicians increased from 334,000 in 1970 to 468,000 in 1980 to 601,000 in 1990. By the year 2000, there will be about 722,000 physicians (Roback, Randolph, and Seidman 1990:Table 88). Although about 8.5 percent are inactive or have unknown addresses, the number of physicians in America is growing rapidly nevertheless, as it is in many European countries. There is no slowdown in sight, given the number of doctors graduating from medical schools and the nation's ambivalence about reducing the influx of foreign-trained doctors, many of whom are American born. In fact, between 1970 and 1989, foreign-trained doctors increased 126 percent compared to a 72 percent increase in American-trained doctors, and they constituted 130,000 of the 601,000 doctors in 1990 (Roback, Randolph, and Seidman 1990). As a result, the number of persons per physician is steadily dropping, from around 714 people per doctor thirty years ago to about 417 today and 370 in the year 2000. Will 370 men, women, and children be enough to maintain the average doctor in the style to which he or she is accustomed about five and a half times the average income in the face of countervailing forces? And how will the gross imbalance between the number of specialists and the need for their services play itself out? Today we have what could be called the 80-20 inversion: 80 percent of the doctors are specialists, but only about 20 percent or fewer of the nation's patients have problems warranting the attention of a specialist. Nearly all growth depends on an increasing number of subspecialties in medicine and surgery, and there are now about two hundred specialty societies, many not officially recognized but vying for legitimacy and a market niche (Abbott 1988). Thus, the rapid growth of physicians and their specialty training has set the stage for sharp clashes between countervailing powers.

Trends in the Organization of Practice

The post-Freidson era, from 1970 to the late 1980s, saw a steady trend of dehospitalization and a long-term shift back to office-based care. Most doctors (82%) are involved in patient care, and despite all the talk today about physician-executives, the data show no notable uptrend in numbers (Roback, Randolph, and Seidman 1990: Table A-2). Office-based practice has been rising slowly since 1975 (from 55% to 58.5%), and full-time hospital staff has declined from 10.4 to 8.5 percent in the same period. Hospital-based practice still makes up 23.6 percent of all practice sites because of all the residents and fellows in training. These data underscore the immense role that medical education, practically an industry in itself, plays in staffing and supporting hospital-based practice. The total number of residents has grown since 1970 by 60 percent, and they are a major source of cheap labor. They grew in use during the golden age of reimbursement, and curtailment of the workweek from 100 hours to 80 or fewer is already raising costs.

An increasing number of the 58 percent of doctors practicing in offices (that is, not a hospital or institution) do so in groups. Since the mid-1960s, when private and public insurance became fully established and funded expansion with few restraints, more and more doctors have combined into groups and formed professional corporations. The motives appear largely to have been income and market share. There were 4,300 groups in 1965 (11% of all nonfederal physicians), 8,500 in 1975, and 16,600 in 1988 (30%, or 156,000) (Havlicek 1990:Ch. 8). Supporting this emphasis on economic rather than service motives, an increasing percentage have been single specialty groups, up from 54 percent in 1975 to 71 percent in 1988. They tend to be small, from an average of 5 in 1975 to 6.2 in 1988, and their purpose seems largely to share the financing of space, staff, and equipment and to position themselves for handling larger specialty contracts from institutional buyers.

The future of groups will be affected by demands of the buyers' market. For example, almost all fee-for-service care now is managed by having an array of monitoring activities and cost-containment programs. These complex and expensive controls favor larger groups, and Havlicek (1990:8–38) believes we will see more mergers than new groups in the 1990s. He also suspects there will be more cooperative efforts with hospitals, which have more capital and staff but are subject to more cost controls.

Capitalist Professionals

An important, perhaps even integral, part of the rapid expansion of groups since the mid-1970s has involved doctors' investing in their own clinical laboratories (28% of all groups), radiology laboratories (32%), electrocardiological laboratories (28%), and audiology laboratories (16%). (Additionally, 40 percent of all office-based physicians have their own laboratories.) The larger the group is, the more likely it owns one or more of these facilities. For example, 23 percent of three-person groups own clinical laboratories and 78 percent of all groups with seventy-six to ninety-nine doctors. Large groups also own their own surgical suites: from 15 percent of groups with sixteen to twenty-five people to 41 percent of groups ranging from seventy-six to ninety-nine physicians. The hourly charges are very attractive (Havlicek 1990).

Growth of HMOs, PPOs, and Managed Care

The countervailing power of institutional buyers has forced practitioners to reorganize into larger units of health care that can manage the costs and quality of the services rendered. Health maintenance organizations, first developed in the 1920s, became the centerpiece of President Nixon's 1971 reforms to make American health care efficient and affordable. Medical lobbies fought the reform; when they saw it would pass, they weighed it down with requirements and restrictions. By 1976, there were 175 HMOs with 6 million members, half of them in just six HMOs that had built a solid reputation for good, coordinated care (Gruber, Shadle, and Polich 1988). Among them, PruCare and U.S. Health Care represented the new wave of expansion: national systems of HMOs run by insurers as a key "product" to sell to employers for cost containment or run by investors for the same purpose. Moreover, most of the new HMOs consisted of networks of private practitioners linked by part-time contracts rather than a core dedicated staff.

By December 1987, there were 650 HMOs with about 29 million members. Both Medicare and Medicaid revised terms to favor these groups as a way to moderate costs, as did many revised benefit plans by corporations. HMOs keep annual visits per person down to 3.8 and hospital inpatient bed-days down to 438 per thousand enrollees, well below the figures for autonomous, traditional care (Hodges, Camerlo, and Gold 1990). There were now forty-two national firms, and they enrolled half the total. The proportion of these firms that use networks of independent practitioners rose from 40 percent in 1980 to 62 percent in 1987. To increase their attractiveness, new hybrid HMOs were beginning to form that allowed members to get services outside the HMO's list of physicians if they paid a portion of the bill.

Preferred provider organizations come in many varieties, but all essentially consist of groups of providers who agree to give services at a discount. Employers then structure benefits to encourage employees to use them. For example, they offer to pay all of the fees for PPO providers but only 80 percent of fees from other doctors.

PPOs became significant by the mid-1980s, and by 1988 they had 20 million enrollees (Rice, Gabel, and Mick 1989). This figure is only approximate because patterns of enrollment are constantly changing. Perhaps more reliable are data from employers, who say that 13 to 15 percent of all employees and half their dependents are covered by PPOs (Sullivan and Rice 1991). Increasingly insurers are using PPOs as a managed care product, and they are forming very large PPOs in the range of 200,000 enrollees each with 100 to 200 hospitals and 5,000 to 15,000 physicians involved in their systems. From the other side, physician group practices derive from 13 to 30 percent of their income from PPOs as group size increases. Besides volume discounts on fees, half to three-quarters of the PPOs use physician profiling (to compare the cost-effectiveness of different doctors), utilization review, and preselection of cost-effective providers.

In response to the "buyers' revolt" and the growth of HMOs and PPOs, a growing number of traditional, autonomous, fee-for-service practices have taken on the same techniques of managed care: preadmission review, daily concurrent review to see if inpatients need to stay another day, retrospective review of hospitalized cases, physician profiling to identify high users of costly services, and case management of costly, complex cases. By 1990, the most thorough study of all small, medium, and large employers, including state and local governments, found that only 5 percent of all employees and their families now have traditional fee-for-service physicians without utilization management (Sullivan and Rice 1991).

CONCLUSION

The countervailing power of institutional buyers certainly ends the kind of dominance the medical profession had in 1970, but by no means does it turn doctors into mere corporatized workers. The medical profession's relations with capital are now quite complex. Physicians are investing heavily in their own buildings and equipment, spurred by a refocus of the medical technology industry on office or clinic-based equipment that will either reduce costs or generate more income. Employers and their agents (insurance companies, management companies) are using their oligopolistic market power to restructure medical practice into managed care systems, but physicians have many ways to make those systems work for them. Hospitals are using their considerable capital to build facilities and buy equipment that will attract patients and their physicians, whom they woointensively.

The state is by far the largest buyer and has shown the greatest resolve to bring costs under control. The federal government has pushed through fundamental changes to limit how much it pays hospitals and doctors. Each year brings more stringent or extensive measures. At the same time, the state faces a societal duty to broaden benefits to those not insured and to deepen them to cover new technologies or areas of treatment. And the state is itself a troubled provider through its Veterans Administration health care system and its services to special populations.

Both buyers and providers constantly attempt to use the legal powers of the state to advance their interests. Thus, regulation is best analyzed from this perspective as a weapon in the competition between countervailing powers rather than as an alternative to it. At the same time, competition itself is a powerful form of regulation (Leone 1986). However, Galbraith warned that the self-regulating counterbalance of contending powerblocs works poorly if demand is not limited, because it undermines the bargaining power of the buyers of the agents. This is another basic reason why institutional buyers are, so far, losing.

In response, buyers and the state are using other means besides price and contracts to strengthen their hand. Even as providers keep frustrating the efforts of institutional buyers through "visit enrichment," more bills, and higher incomes, a fundamental change has taken place. The game they are winning (at least so far) has ceased to be their game. Most of the terms are being set by the buyers.

The paradox of declining autonomy and growing sovereignty indicates a larger, more fundamental set of countervailing powers at work than simply the profession and its purchasers. As the dynamic unfolds, capitalism comes face to face with itself, for driving the growing sovereignty or domain of medicine is the medical-industrial complex, perhaps the most successful and largest sector of the entire economy. It is Baxter-Travenol or Humana versus General Motors or Allied Signal, with each side trying to harness the profession to its purposes. Different parts of the profession participate in larger institutional complexes to legitimate their respective goals of "the best medicine for every sick patient" and "a healthy, productive work force at the least cost." The final configuration is unclear, but the concept of professionalism as a countervailing power seems most clearly to frame the interactions.

REFERENCES

Abbott, A. 1988. *The System of Professions: An Essay on the Division of Expert Labor.* Chicago: University of Chicago Press.

de Secondat Montesquieu, C. L. 1748. *De l'Esprit des Loix.* Geneva: Barillot & Sons.

Freidson, E. 1970a. *Professional Dominance: The Social Structure of Medical Care.* Chicago: Aldine.

Freidson, E. 1970b. *Profession of Medicine: A Study of the Sociology of Applied Knowledge.* New York: Dodd, Meed.

Freidson, E. 1984. The Changing Nature of Professional Control. *Annual Review of Sociology* 10:1–20.

Freidson, E. 1985. The Reorganization of the Medical Profession. *Medical Care Review* 42:11–35.

Freidson, E. 1986a. *Professional Powers: A Study of the Institutionalization of Formal Knowledge.* Chicago: University of Chicago Press.

Freidson, E. 1989a. Industrialization or Humanization? In *Medical Work in America.* New Haven: Yale University Press.

Galbraith, J. K. 1956. *American Capitalism: The Concept of Countervailing Power.* Boston: Houghton Mifflin.

Gray, B. H., and M. J. Field, eds. 1989. *Controlling Costs and Changing Patient Care: The Role of Utilization Management.* Washington, D.C.: Institute of Medicine, National Academy Press.

Gruber, L. R., M. Shadle, and C. L. Politch. 1988. From Movement to Industry: The Growth of HMOs. *Health Affairs* 7(3):197–298.

Haug, M. R. 1973. Deprofessionalization. *An Sociological Review Monograph* 20:195–211.

Haug, M. R., and B. Lavin. 1983. *Consumerism in Medicine: Challenging Physician Authority.* Beverly Hills: Sage.

Havlicek, P. L. 1990. *Medical Groups in the U.S.: A Survey of Practice Characteristics.* Chicago: American Medical Association.

Hodges, D., K. Camerlo, and M. Gold. 1990. *HMO Industry Profile.* Vol. 2: *Utilization Patterns, 1988.* Washington, D.C.: Group Health Association of America.

Jarausch, K. H. 1990. *The Unfree Professions: German Lawyers, Teachers, and Engineers, 1900–1950.* New York: Oxford University Press.

Johnson, T. J. 1972. *Professions and Power.* London: Macmillan.

Jones, A., ed. 1991. *Professions and the State: Expertise and Autonomy in the Soviet Union and Eastern Europe.* Philadelphia: Temple University Press.

Krause, E. A. 1988b. Doctors, Partitocrazia, and the Italian State. *Milbank Quarterly* 66(Suppl. 2): 148–66.

Larson, M. S. 1977. *The Rise of Professionalism: A Sociological Analysis.* Berkeley: University of California Press.

Light, D. W. 1983. The Development of Professional Schools in America. In *The Transformation of Higher Learning, 1860–1930,* ed. K. H. Jarausch, 345–66. Chicago: University of Chicago Press.

Light, D. W. 1988. Turf Battles and the Theory of Professional Dominance. *Research in the Sociology of Health Care* 7:203–25.

Light, D. W. 1989. Social Control and the American Health Care System. In *Handbook of Medical Sociology,* ed. H. E. Freeman and S. Levine, 456–74. Englewood Cliffs, N.J.: Prentice-Hall.

Light, D. W. 1990. Bending the Rules. *Health Services Journal* 100(5222):1513–15.

Light, D. W. 1991. Professionalism as a Countervailing Power. *Journal of Health Politics, Policy and Law* 16:499–506.

Light, D. W., and S. Levine. 1988. The Changing Character of the Medical Profession: A Theoretical Overview. *Milbank Quarterly* 66(Suppl. 2): 10–32.

Light, D. W., S. Liebfried, and F. Tennstedt. 1986. Social Medicine vs. Professional Dominance: the German Experience. *American Journal of Public Health* 76(1):78–83.

Marmor, T. R., and J. B. Christianson. 1982. *Health Care Policy: A Political Economy Approach.* Beverly Hills: Sage.

Merton, R. K. and B. Barbar, eds. 1976. Sociological Ambivalence. In *Sociological Ambivalence and Other Essays.* New York: Free Press.

Potter, D. A., J. B. McKinlay, and R. B. D'Agostino. 1991. *Understanding How Social Factors Affect Medical Decision Making: Application of a Factorial Experiment.* Watertown, Mass.: New England Research Institute.
Rice, T., J. Gabel, and S. Mick. 1989. *PPOS: Bigger, Not Better.* Washington, D.C.: HIAA ResearchBulletin.
Roback, G., L. Randolph, and S. Seidman. 1990. *Physician Characteristics and Distribution in the U.S.* Chicago: American Medical Association.
Starr, P. 1982. *The Social Transformation of American Medicine: The Rise of a Sovereign Profession and the Making of a Vast Industry.* New York: Basic Books.
Statistical Abstract of the United States. 1989. Washington, D.C.: Department of Commerce.
Steuart, J. 1767. *Inquiry into the Principles of Political Economy,* vol. 1. London: A. Miller and T. Cadwell.
Stone, D. A. 1988. *Policy Paradox and Political Reason.* Glenview, Ill.: Scott, Foresman.
Sullivan, C., and T. Rice. 1991. The Health Insurance Picture in 1990. *Health Affairs* 10(2):104–15.
Willis, E. 1988. Doctoring in Australia: A View at the Bicentenary. *Milbank Quarterly* 66(Suppl 2): 167–81.

20 Changing Medical Organization and the Erosion of Trust

David Mechanic

Medicine has long been one of our most trusted social institutions. The profession recognized early in its history that public trust was one of its greatest assets, a resource that allowed it to define the scope of medical work and increase the political and clinical autonomy of its practitioners (Starr 1982). The profession achieved this by setting and enforcing high standards of medical and postgraduate education, by promulgating ethical standards that protected the interests of patients, and by controlling entry into the profession (Freidson 1970). The American hospital, developed under religious stewardship and viewed historically as an institution that worked for the public interest, also became a valued community resource (Rosenberg 1987; Stevens 1989).

In recent years, all social institutions, including medicine, have fallen from the public trust (Lipset and Schneider 1987). Confidence in medicine still ranks higher than in education, television, major companies, and Congress, for example (Kasperson, Golding, and Tuler 1992), but confidence in medicine's leaders has fallen from 73 percent in 1965 to 22 percent in 1993, which compares with the degree of trust felt for leaders of other social institutions (Blendon et al. 1993). This trend parallels a general decline in public trust, marked by the proportion of the public that says most people can be trusted falling from 58 percent in 1960 to 37 percent in 1993 (Lipset 1995).

Numerous explanations have been offered for this decline: the cynicism and challenge to expertise resulting from the Vietnam war; the broad and pervasive influence of television and other media on public opinion; the fragmentation of community; the widespread dissemination of information on political and other violations of public trust; and the restructuring of the economy. These general trends have affected trust in medical institutions, but changes in medicine itself also exacerbate the problem. The health sector is increasingly managed by for-profit corporations, which present medicine as a marketplace and view patients as consumers. Although there are many responsible companies, others seek quick profits and engage in dishonest practices like deceptive marketing, kickbacks, and corporate self-dealing (Rodwin 1993). New and unfamiliar arrangements for financing and managing care and new types of incentives that affect how physicians work increasingly place the interests of patients and doctors, and of doctors and insurance programs, in direct conflict (Rodwin 1993).

The situation is made more difficult by tightened restrictions on patient choice. Employers frequently choose insurance for their employees. Facing cost pressures, many employers have constrained employee options and embraced managed care approaches. Managed care in the form of HMOs and utilization management is pervasive, often restricting patients' choices. The need for management of care is undeniable, but limits on allowing patients to change doctors or plans easily when dissatisfied encourages lack of trust. Choice is wisely perceived not only as a personal preference but also as an organizational asset, in that it protects plans against disaffected and complaining patients. Some HMOs historically have welcomed multiple-choice options as a way of allowing patients to select plans that are consistent with their tastes, thus protecting themselves against dissatisfaction and distrust (Saward, Blank, and Greenlick 1968).

Other influences also challenge trust as we have known it. Patients are better educated, and the mass media provide abundant medical information both on new treatments and on physician and hospital errors. Patients are now more aware that some doctors make referrals to laboratories and diagnostic facilities in which they hold a financial interest and that others sign managed-care contracts containing "gag rules." They are urged to be thoughtful and skeptical consumers, ready not only to question their medical treatment but also to scrutinize their medical and hospital bills for signs of fraud and to challenge abuse by their caretakers. Better educated and more sophisticated patients can contribute to meaningful doctor–patient relationships, but some of the information now readily available raises doubts and feelings of insecurity about the motives and behavior of medical providers and institutions.

A NOTE ON THE CONCEPT OF TRUST

To say we trust is to say we believe that individuals and institutions will act appropriately and perform competently, responsibly, and in a manner considerate of our interests (Barber 1983). Although we can test the likelihood of expected behavior in a variety of ways, we have no firm way of knowing the future; thus trust is always accompanied by risk (Luhmann 1989). Trusting is a function of personality traits, the characteristics of the person or entity to be trusted, and the context in which the interaction occurs (Earle and Cvetkovich 1995). Trust is dynamic and fragile, easily challenged by a disconfirming act or by a changing social situation. Slovac (1993) provides empirical support for the view that trust is particularly fragile because negative events are more visible, they carry greater psychological weight, they are perceived as more credible, and they inhibit the kinds of experience needed to overcome distrust.

In this discussion I will address two levels of trust: interpersonal and social. Trust in persons is an intimate form, deriving from earlier experiences with family and other caretakers. Trust forms early in life based on emotional bonds and amplified cognitively over time, and it is one that has important psychological connotations. The most enduring trust relationships are found in families, love relationships, intimate friendships, and other primary-group associations. The doctor–patient relationship often reflects aspects of these bonds and contains strong elements of transference, particularly during times of critical illness when patients are vulnerable and frightened. Social trust, in contrast, is more cognitive and abstract, and typically is based on inferences about shared interests and common norms and values (Kasperson, Golding, and Tuler 1992).

This distinction between interpersonal and social trust is a simple way of characterizing a more complex reality, but empirical research rarely allows us to generalize about more subtle variations. Interpersonal trust refers to several different dimensions that may be more or less consistent. Patients, for example, may trust the competence of their physicians but be less convinced of their personal commitment or caring. Or they may feel secure in their doctor's commitment to their welfare while doubting his or her competence or control over decision-making (as may happen in some managed care situations).

Similarly, institutional trust can be divided into a generalized abstract sense about institutions, like the "health care system" or the "medical profession," and concrete perceptions about institutions with which patients have had experience, like their HMO or community hospital. In the latter case, trust may be cognitively differentiated according to types of personnel or performance. For example, patients may understand that their hospital is excellent for cardiovascular services but poor for urology or psychiatry. Thus, we may trust individuals and institutions in some ways but not in others. Trust is shaped both by media images and by personal experiences. This explains how we can distrust medicine or Congress but trust our doctor or congressman (Blendon and Taylor 1989; Parker and Parker 1993).

Although social and interpersonal trust are separate concepts, they are correlated and mutually supportive (Parker and Parker 1993). High trust in an institution transfers to unknown personnel, and we assume that a highly respected and well-run institution selects its professionals carefully and appropriately supervises and monitors them. Similarly, our trust in doctors and nurses often generalizes to their organizations and affects our willingness to bring our custom to them. Organizations tend to understand these relations and often try to assure the public of the quality of their selection processes and personnel while monitoring their personnel to assure appropriate standards of performance (Schlackman 1989).

Life is impossible without trust, and even the most cynical must depend on it. Trust reduces complexity and the need to plan for innumerable contingencies. Contracts, laws, and other regulatory devices substitute for trust, but even highly formalized systems cannot plan for every contingency and must depend to an important degree on trust. To the extent that high trust can be sustained, it is efficient and reduces the need for costly arrangements. Distrust, therefore, as Luhmann has observed, is not the opposite of trust but is more accurately a functional alternative (Luhmann 1989). Distrust is costly in terms of personnel, monitoring time, and emotional energy.

The downside of trust is risk. Given real variabilities in performance among institutions and professionals, to trust excessively is to endanger oneself. As Hardin (1992) notes, trust can "be stupid and even culpable," leading to dismal results and even quick destruction. Finding the proper balance between trust and distrust, and the appropriate and constructive vehicles to hold institutions and professionals accountable under uncertainty, are particularly challenging tasks. Patients arrive at this balance iteratively, as they experience the doctor–patient relationship over time. By building strong relationships with patients, doctors capitalize on their potential to achieve cooperation under uncertainty (Cassell 1995). Institutions whose relationships with their patients are more impersonal seek to enlist trust by building their reputations and by establishing programs for patient participation in decision-making, quality assurance review, and responsiveness to issues of patient satisfaction.

FACTORS CONTRIBUTING TO TRUST

Social trust of medical institutions reflects the general attitudinal trend in a society and the public's optimism or pessimism (Lipset and Schneider 1987). While social trust is an attitude substantially shaped by media exposure and current events, interpersonal trust is based primarily on social interactions over time. Interpersonal trust builds on the patient's experience of the doctor's competent, responsible, and caring responses. High levels of interpersonal trust can contribute to social trust as well. Medical institutions increasingly advertise to build their public visibility and reputation, but medical leaders understand that the quality of care, and how it is perceived, is critical to their survival.

Physicians commonly link trust to continuity of care, and properly so. New doctor–patient interactions are like other new relationships, in which people use available cues to anticipate the other person's values and likely responses (Thibaut and Kelley 1986). Initially, the doctor's attentiveness, responsiveness, patience, and general demeanor give the patient a sense of what to expect (Roter and Hall 1992). Other cues may be inferred from the quality of the practice setting, the doctor's institutional affiliations, and feedback from other patients. But initial cues are only rough guides to what lies ahead and are only perfected over time as doctor and patient become better acquainted and test the relationship.

Trust can be disconfirmed at any time, even after many years. Although patients discount small lapses because they appreciate that doctors, like others, can have good and bad days, a serious failure to be responsive when needed can shatter even the strongest of relationships. Verghese (1994), in his account of practice in a small town in Tennessee, describes a family that was shocked and appalled when their family doctor, after a close relationship of many years, refused to care for their son who had AIDS. Unless they are seriously ill, people have little opportunity to test the validity of their trust in doctors because of the routine of most medical practice. Typically, the test comes during crises when doctor and patient are already launched on a trajectory of care. People with critical illnesses depend most strongly on their doctors (Cassell 1995), and strong relationships help them to deal with frightening uncertainties.

Trust is multidimensional, and some aspects are more easily tested than others. Patients have little difficulty judging whether they are comfortable with the doctor's manner, whether the encounter is one in which they can disclose private feelings, whether meaningful feedback and useful instructions are elicited, and whether doctors convey a sense of caring (Roter and Hall 1992). They learn less quickly about the doctor's level of dedication and whether the doctor will behave faithfully and responsibly during a time of need. Competence is most difficult for patients to judge, although they often make attributions about this quality based on how doctors proceed in their assessment and physical examination and whether their treatment develops as expected. Trust tends to operate globally, but it can be undermined by evidence of failure on any of its important dimensions.

When they trust, people seek credible cues that such confidence is merited. Physicians who seek to behave competently, responsibly, and in a caring fashion often simply do not know how to convey these attributes in short, episodic encounters. Trusting responses are part of a caring technology that can be taught and even built into the organization of practice in both outpatient and hospital settings (Scott et al. 1995). In a recent communication to his medical staff, the chief medical officer of a major university teaching hospital suggested that physicians give their undivided attention to patients during the first 60 seconds of a visit in order to convey the impression of willingness to spend time with them. He also advised doctors to communicate at the same physical level as the patient (sitting on the bed, for example) and to respond quickly to patient requests. He suggested that they be specific about what is likely to happen and what is expected of the patient, that they write instructions even for simple advice, and that they consider presurgical and follow-up phone calls. These, of course, are no substitute for competence and responsibility, but they help caring doctors convey their concern to the patient.

Trust is typically associated with a high quality of communication and interaction. Good communication increases the likelihood that patients will reveal intimate information and stigmatized conditions, that they will cooperate in treatment and adhere to medical advice, and that they will be open to suggestion about adopting health-promoting behavior, all goals that are important to the emerging health care agenda. Moreover, good communication is linked to shorter hospital stays, improved medical outcomes, and positive physiological changes (Roter and Hall 1992). Trust provides a context in which doctors and patients can work cooperatively to establish care objectives and to seek reasonable ways of achieving them. Eroding social trust in medical institutions forms a threatening backdrop to doctor–patient relationships, but the strength of patients' personal trust in their doctors has until now provided considerable insulation against serious conflict.

CHALLENGES TO TRUST

Emerging structures of care carry the implicit message that the patient must be on guard in the medical marketplace. Managed competition is structured so that patients choose among competing health care plans for their price, coverage, and amenities on the assumption that consumers seeking a best buy among competitors induce greater efficiencies among care providers. Although there are many benefits in this type of competition, its implicit message nevertheless is that medical care resembles other commodities and services and that one must be a prudent purchaser. While the change from "patient" to "consumer" may seem little more than a figure of speech, it is one that suggests a significant change in how we think of health professionals and medical transactions.

A serious challenge to trust comes from the growth of for-profit medicine and the commercial aggressiveness of the medical–industrial complex (Relman 1994). Increasingly, individuals making major social decisions about health and medical care are managers whose background in medicine is limited. When corporations that deliver medical care are primarily motivated to bring generous returns to their stockholders, and when a significant proportion of the medical care dollar goes to investors rather than patient care, then people are inclined to question the motives and decisions of these organizers and providers of care. As provider organizations seek to become more efficient and to reduce expenditures, they introduce incentives that make professional rewards dependent on withholding care, thereby placing the interests of patients and doctors in direct conflict (Hillman 1987). "Gag rules" that limit physicians' ability to discuss these arrangements and treatment options with patients help kindle public distrust (Woolhandler and Himmelstein 1995; Pear 1995).

Some economists and sociologists dismiss the significance of such trends in the belief that dependence on trust in the profession is naive and not in the patient's interest (for example, see Zola 1990). They see trust as a barrier because it allows medicine to define the health paradigm, to dominate the medical division of labor and other health occupations, and to reinforce the medical authority and economic position of doctors and hospitals. They believe that patients should be active and aggressive seekers of information rather than depend on physicians and hospitals to provide it. Their ideal is an active patient who shops among possible providers, who defines her treatment needs and participates actively in treatment, and who is willing to challenge the doctor and take responsibility for her own treatment decisions. Activism is not a bad idea, but it is an illusion to believe that it can reasonably substitute for trust. As Arrow (1963) noted in his classic discussion of the medical marketplace, trust is needed because in much of medical care the activity of production and the product are identical.

The context of medicine has changed dramatically. There are now extraordinary amounts of information about new treatments and medical possibilities. Television, newspapers, and magazines provide enormous coverage to the latest medical advances, quickly reporting the most recent research findings from the *New England Journal of Medicine,* the *Journal of the American Medical Association,* and other major journals. Texts and reference books initially meant for physicians can be found in any large bookstore, and massive amounts of medical information are easily available by surfing the Internet. We know little about how all this potentially conflicting information is digested, but it seems inevitable that the public will be better informed, more aware of uncertainties, and more skeptical of expert opinion. Applied thoughtfully, such knowledge can lead to a strong and meaningful therapeutic alliance. Unwisely applied, it is an additional disruptive force in medical relationships.

MANAGED CARE AND TRUST

Several emerging trends suggest that interpersonal trust will be under assault in coming years. The largest threat comes from increasingly prevalent physician incentives that create opposition between doctors' and patients' interests. When significant proportions of the individual doctor's income depend on meeting goals of reduced utilization, the fiduciary relationship between doctor and patient and the credibility of the doctor's role as the patient's agent are threatened. Although the general public is generally aware of some of the alleged difficulties of managed care, relatively few know the extent of these remunerative arrangements and the degree to which their own doctors are governed by such incentives. Information diffuses slowly, but inevitably patients will become better informed about this situation. Patients are already uncomfortable with the idea that the physician may weigh their needs and interests against the insurance program's budget (Mechanic, Ettel, and Davis 1990). But new arrangements are even more discomforting. Proposals have been made to require physicians to inform their patients about such arrangements and about their ties with other medical profit-making entities to which they refer. This may make patients better informed, but it is unlikely to enhance interpersonal trust.

Perhaps a more damaging aspect of managed care is the push toward greater efficiency and more tightly scheduled doctor–patient interactions. The quality of medical encounters and trust depends on a relationship evolving between doctor and patient. More time also allows for patient instruction, greater participation in treatment choices, and opportunities to give and receive feedback. While the instrumental aspects of care can probably be achieved in short encounters, pressured interactions inhibit patients from revealing concerns and doctors from responding appropriately. Although good data are not available on how time is allocated in varying types of managed care, data from earlier studies show that fee-for-service doctors allot more time to patients, allocate time differently, and typically work longer hours than those on capitation or salary (Mechanic 1975; Freeborn and Pope 1994). To the extent that managed care truncates the encounter, it will have an impact on trust.

The effect of managed care on continuity of care is unclear. In theory, patients in HMOs choose or are assigned to a primary care doctor, who is their link to the system and a gatekeeper to other services. In reality, HMOs often limit available physicians, so that patients have to wait for an unacceptable amount of time to see their designated primary care physician when they feel they need care. Patients often have the option of seeing a doctor on call more immediately, and many do so. To the extent that this is a prevalent practice, it interferes with continuity and the maintenance of a strong trust relationship (Mechanic, Weiss, and Cleary 1983; Freeborn and Pope 1994). Some HMOs have recognized this problem and have taken measures to minimize it.

CONCLUSIONS

Trust building is an iterative process, requiring repeated evidence of competence, responsibility, and caring. Achieving public trust, particularly in an environment of rampant distrust, requires continuing efforts to demonstrate good faith. Medical institutions have fallen dramatically in public trust in recent years. Although this trend is common to all social institutions, many believe that the problem is exacerbated by commercial restructuring of medical care and visible evidence of self-interested and unscrupulous behavior by a segment of programs, institutions, and professionals. Even long-respected and dedicated institutions now function in a climate of suspicion. Maintaining trust requires organizational strategies as well as good intentions (Scott et al. 1995). Institutions can do much to develop and evaluate mechanisms across the wide range of relevant services that demonstrate their commitment to responsive and high-quality care.

NOTES

This article was supported, in part, by an Investigator Award in Health Policy Research from the Robert Wood Johnson Foundation.

REFERENCES

Arrow, K. 1963. Uncertainty and the Welfare Economics of Medical Care. *American Economic Review* 53:941–73.

Barber, B. 1983. *The Logic and Limits of Trust.* New Brunswick, N.J.: Rutgers University Press.

Blendon, R.J., T.S. Hyams, and J.M. Benson. 1993. Bridging the Gap between Expert and Public Views on Health Care Reform. *Journal of the American Medical Association* 269:2573–78.

Blendon, R.J., and H. Taylor. 1989. Views on Health Care: Public Opinion in Three Nations. *Health Affairs* 8:149–57.

Cassell, E.J. 1995. Teaching the Fundamentals of Primary Care. *Milbank Quarterly* 73:373–405.

Earle, T.C., and G.T. Cvetkovich. 1995. *Social Trust: Toward a Cosmopolitan Society.* Westport, Conn.: Praeger.

Freeborn, D.K., and C.R. Pope. 1994. *Promise and Performance in Managed Care.* Baltimore: Johns Hopkins University Press.

Freidson, E. 1970. *Profession of Medicine: A Study of the Sociology of Applied Knowledge.* New York: Dodd, Mead.

Hardin, R. 1992. The Street-Level Epistemology of Trust. *Politics and Society* 21:505–29.

Hillman, A.L. 1987. Financial Incentives for Physicians in HMOs: Is There a Conflict of Interest? *New England Journal of Medicine* 317:1743–8.

Kasperson, R.E., D. Golding, and S. Tuler. 1992. Social Distrust as a Factor in Siting Hazardous Facilities and Community Risks. *Journal of Social Issues* 48:161–87.

Lipset, S.M. 1995. Malaise and Resiliency in America. *Journal of Democracy* 6:4–18.

Lipset, M.L., and W. Schneider. 1987. *The Confidence Gap: Business, Labor and Government in the Public Mind.* Baltimore: Johns Hopkins University Press.

Luhmann, N. 1989. *Trust and Power.* New York: John Wiley.

Mechanic, D., T. Ettel, and D. Davis. 1990. Choosing Among Health Care Options. *Inquiry* 27:14–23.

Mechanic, D., N. Weiss, and P. Cleary. The Growth of HMOs: Issues of Enrollment and Disenrollment. *Medical Care* 21:338–47.

Parker, S.L., and Parker, G.R. 1993. Why Do We Trust Our Congressman? *Journal of Politics* 55:442–53.

Pear, R. 1995. Doctors Say HMOs Limit What They Can Tell Patients. *The New York Times* (December 21).

Relman, A.S. 1994. The Impact of Market Forces on the Physician–Patient Relationship. *Journal of the Royal Society of Medicine* 87(suppl. 22): 22–4.

Rodwin, M. 1993. *Medicine, Money and Morals: Physicians' Conflicts of Interest.* New York: Oxford University Press.

Rosenberg, C.E. 1987. *The Care of Strangers: The Rise of America's Hospital System.* New York: Basic Books.

Roter, D.L., and J.A. Hall. 1992. *Doctors Talking with Patients/Patients Talking with Doctors.* Westport, Conn.: Auburn House.

Saward, E.W., J.D. Blank, and M.R. Greenlick. 1968. Documentation of Twenty Years of Operation and Growth of Prepaid Group Practice Plan. *Medical Care* 6:231–44.

Scott, R.A., L.H. Aiken, D. Mechanic, and C. Moravcsik. 1995. Organizational Aspects of Caring. *Milbank Quarterly* 73:77–95.

Slovac, P. 1993. Perceived Risk, Trust, and Democracy. *Risk Analysis* 13:675–82.

Starr, P. 1982. *The Social Transformation of American Medicine.* New York: Basic Books.

Stevens, R. 1989. *In Sickness and in Wealth: American Hospitals in the Twentieth Century.* New York: Basic Books.

Thibaut, J., and H.H. Kelley. 1986. *The Social Psychology of Groups.* New Brunswick, N.J.: Transaction Publishers.

Verghese, A. 1994. *My Own Country: A Doctor's Story.* New York: Vintage Books.

Woolhandler, S., and D.V. Himmelstein. 1995. Extreme Risk the New Corporate Proposition for Physicians. *New England Journal of Medicine* 333:1706–7.

Zola, I.K. 1990. Medicine as an Institution of Social Control. In *The Sociology of Health and Illness: Critical Perspectives,* 3rd ed., 398–408, eds. P. Conrad and R. Kern. New York: St. Martin's Press.

The Social Organization of Medical Workers

Medical care in the United States is an enormous and complex industry involving thousands of organizations, the expenditure of billions of dollars each year, and the employment of millions of workers. There are discernible patterns in the types and distribution of medical services available in any society. These patterns reflect and reinforce the sociocultural context in which they are found, including the political, economic, and cultural priorities of a society. The composition of the labor force in most sectors of society reflects that society's distribution of power and privilege. This section examines the organization and distribution of medical care services and the nature of the medical care labor force in this country.

Our medical care system has been described as "acute, curative, [and] hospital-based" (Knowles, 1977: 2). That is, we have a *medical* care system (as distinguished from a *health* care system) organized around the cure and/or control of serious diseases and the repairing of physical injuries rather than the "caring" for the sick or the prevention of disease. The American medical care system is highly technological, specialized, and increasingly centralized. More and more medical care is delivered in large bureaucratic institutions. For decades, hospitals dominated medical organizations, employing at one time 75 percent of all medical care workers. With the emergence of managed care, especially of health maintenance organizations (HMOs), the number of hospital workers has declined to 64 percent of the medical work force (DHHS, 1994: 197).

From 1900 to 1975 the number of hospitals in the United States gradually increased, reaching a total of over 6300. Since then there has been a slight decline in the number of hospitals (DHHS, 1994). The seeming trend toward fewer yet larger hospitals threatens the existence of some community hospitals. Approximately 56 percent of all hospitals in 1992 were owned by nonprofit organizations, with another 30 percent owned by federal, state, or local governments. The remaining 13 percent were owned by profit-making organizations; in addition, 81 percent of all nursing homes were profit-making institutions (DHHS, 1994). The number of for-profit hospitals, especially in the form of hospital chains, has increased dramatically in the past decade (see selection 24 by Arnold S. Relman in this volume and Light, 1986).

The medical care system has changed enormously in the past three decades. In 1960 U.S. national health expenditures were 5.2 percent of the gross national product (GNP); in 1996 totaling nearly $1.04 trillion, they made up nearly 14 percent of the GNP. While most of the health policy analysts have focused on the spiraling cost of U.S. medical care, changes in the social organization of the medical system have been equally dramatic. Perhaps no institution in American society is changing as rapidly as the medical system. In 1960 the solo practitioner in private practice was the norm of medical service; by the late 1980s medical care was typically delivered through an organization, be it an HMO, PPO, ambulatory care center, or hospital emergency department. It is also more likely that the physician is a salaried employee rather than an independent professional, and that payment is made by a third party rather than directly by the patient (see also McKinlay and Stoeckle in the previous section).

The first selection, "The US Health Care System," by John Fry and his associates, presents on overview of a changing medical care system, emphasizing its impact on physicians. The authors show the historic impact of the increasing specialization of physicians, including increasing medical costs and physician incomes. They document the shift back from hospital to office-based care, noting how with the rise of "managed care" the demand for primary care physicians is increasing. As we approach the twenty-first century, there will be an increasing demand for primary care physicians, and most of these will be employed by large bureaucratic organizations, especially HMOs and hospitals.

The growth and expansion of medical care institutions has engendered a rapid expansion of the medical labor force. From 1970 to 1998, the number of people employed in the medical care industry in the United States more than doubled from 4.2 million to 11 million. Medical care workers constitute about 8 percent of the total American labor force. Some of these workers are physicians, but the vast majority are not. In fact, physicians make up only 6 percent of the entire medical work force (DHHS, 1994). Nurses make up the largest group of health workers, with over a million registered nurses (RNs) and half a million more licensed practical nurses (LPNs).

Medical care workers include some of the highest paid employees in our nation (physicians) and some of the lowest paid (until the early 1970s, many hospital workers were not even covered by minimum wage laws). More than 75 percent of all medical workers are women, although more than 70 percent of all physicians are men. Many of these women are members of Third World and minority groups, and most come from working-class and lower-middle-class backgrounds. Almost all physicians are white and upper-middle-class. Blacks, for example, account for only 5 percent of physicians (U.S. Department of Labor, 1999). In short, the structure of the medical work force reflects the inequalities of American society in general.

This medical care work-force structure can be pictured as a broad-based triangle, with a small number of highly paid physicians and administrators at the very top. These men and they are mostly men by and large control the administration of medical care services *within* institutions. As one moves toward the bottom of the triangle there are increasing numbers of significantly lower-paid female workers with little or no authority in the medical delivery organization. This triangle is layered with a growing number of licensed occupational categories of workers, a number close to 300 different medical occupations (Caress, 1976: 168). There is practically no movement of workers from one category to another, since each requires its own specialized training and qualifications, requirements that are largely controlled through licensing procedures authorized by the AMA Committee on Education. Professional dominance, as discussed in the previous section, is highly evident throughout the division and organization of medical labor.

The development of a rigidly stratified medical labor force is the result of a complex historical process as deeply connected to the gender and class of those providing services as to the development of organizations themselves. In "A Caring Dilemma: Womanhood and Nursing in Historical Perspective," Susan Reverby traces the emergence of nursing, focusing in particular on how "caring as a duty" was connected to the fact that it was women who were doing the caring. In women, medical administrators could find a caring, disciplined, and cheap labor force. Reverby shows how the dilemmas nurses faced and the struggles they engaged in to improve the image, stature, and authority of nursing were shaped by the gender stratification of society. She argues that this historical past is reflected in nursing's current position in the health care hierarchy and its continuing dilemmas.

In the final selection, "AIDS and Its Impact on Medical Work," Charles L. Bosk and Joel E. Frader present a doctor's view of the medical culture surrounding AIDS in an academic urban hospital. Bosk and Frader see doctors as workers on the "shop floor" of the hospital and examine how AIDS affected the medical work culture of the medical house officers (i.e., residents). The young physicians now perceive themselves at greater risk and their sense of lost invulnerability has engendered rather negative views about treating AIDS patients. While the pressures of work in medical residency often create negative views toward patients (e.g., Mizrahi, 1986), such views are transformed and amplified by the existence of AIDS. As Bosk and Frader note, not all physicians share this view of AIDS patients; the negative attitudes of some physicians are in part a product of their current work situation. It is interesting to note, however, that a recent study found that the "culture of caring" that permeates nursing socialization and work engenders a much more positive view of AIDS patients (Fox, Aiken, and Messikomer, 1991). Nurses see caring for AIDS patients as part of their mission, and many even volunteer to work in AIDS treatment settings. It is thus clear that the cultures of medical workers vary and that the culture of one's work can affect the care that one provides.

REFERENCES

Caress, Barbara. 1976. "The health workforce: Bigger pie, smaller pieces." Pp. 163–170 in David Kotelchuck, Prognosis Negative. New York: Vintage Books. [Reprinted from Health/PAC Bulletin, January/February, 1975.]

Department of Health and Human Services. 1994. Health, United States 1994. Washington, D.C.: U.S. Government Printing Office.

Department of Labor. 1999. Employment and Earnings, Vol. 46, No. 1.

Fox, Reneé C., Linda H. Aiken, and Carlo M. Messikomer. 1991. "The culture of caring: AIDS and the nursing profession." In Dorothy Nelkin, David P. Willis, and Scott V. Parris (eds.), A Disease of Society. New York: Cambridge University Press.

Knowles, John. 1977. "Introduction." John Knowles (ed.), Doing better and feeling worse: Health in the United States. Daedalus. 106, 1: Winter.

Light, Donald W. 1986. "Corporate medicine for profit." Scientific American. 255 (December): 38–45.

Mizrahi, Terry. 1986. Getting Rid of Patients. New Brunswick: Rutgers University Press

21 *The US Health Care System*

John Fry, Donald Light, Jonathan Rodnick, and Peter Orton

INTRODUCTION

The US is a young nation born out of pioneers and with philosophies of equality of opportunities, freedom and democracy, self-reliance and entrepreneurship all of which have been transmitted into the health care system.

There is no single system; health care is provided through a multi-mix of private and public schemes. Private insurance through employment covers most of the population, but it is not full and comprehensive. Publicly funded programs like Medicare (for the elderly), Medicaid (for the poor) and state schemes have slowly filled the gaps over the decades and now generate over 40% of health costs. Personal out-of-pocket payments are the highest of developed countries and make up almost one third of patient expenses, although there are some special, voluntary and charitable programs to help the poor or those without insurance through work, but a sizeable proportion of the population (17%) has no medical insurance.

The US health system is the most expensive at over 14% of GDP, or $3,600 per head in 1993, and may reach 15% of GDP or $5,000 per head, by the year 2000. There is no shortage of physicians and the rate per population is higher than in many other countries. Nor does there appear to be a dearth of primary physicians, but they are distributed unevenly and have poorly defined roles.

While there are recognizable levels of professional care the lines are blurred because of the patient's free choice and access to any physician, the lack of gatekeeping roles for primary physicians, and the mixture of generalists and specialists. Primary care is in crisis with falling recruitment, uncertainty of roles, and low status. The fragmentation of primary care physicians, with family physicians, general internists and general pediatricians having varying responsibilities, leads to unnecessary competition and a waste of resources.

A priority for the future must be to achieve a national health system more appropriate to the needs of the US people and with primary care playing its part to the full.

THE NATION

American policies still reflect the nation's original emphasis on personal freedom and minimal government interference. Such historical factors have been translated into features of its health system and services, largely through the efforts of the medical profession. Thus professional autonomy, free choice and treating citizens as self-reliant individuals until they come in for help, have characterized the US health care system. Private individual charges, voluntary insurance and public support only for the needy and elderly, have been the financial principles underlying the system. Although it is the funding mechanisms and levels that have impeded equal access to services, most Americans believe that governmental programs are inefficient and unresponsive. It has often been noted that the US and South Africa are the only industrialized countries without universal health insurance or a national health system.

The US is a vast, diverse and changing society. About one million new immigrants enter each year, half of them illegally. Its multi-ethnic groups are growing more numerous and more distinct. At present, caucasians of many origins make up 75%, African-Americans 12%, and Hispanics, Asians and others 13% of the population. It is these last groups that are the majority of the new immigrants. More than one in five of the population is under 15 years, but the society is aging fast (13% over 65) because of falling birth rates and longer life (Table 21-1).

Health indices overall are among the lowest of industrialized nations and vary dramatically by educational, income and ethnic group. Paradoxically, this affluent and successful nation is afflicted with many modern social pathologies in its rates of crime, homicide, drug abuse, AIDS

Table 21-1. Demography (US:UK)

	UK	US
Population (millions)	57.5	250
(annual growth)	(0.3%)	(1%)
Population		
Under 15	18.9%	21.4%
Over 65	15.5%	12.6%
Birth rate		
Annual per 1,000 population	13.4	14.1
Cesarean section rate per births	10%	25%
Infant mortality per 1,000 births	8.4	9.0
Legal abortions		
per 1,000 women	11.7	28.0
per 100 births	18.0	29.7
Fertility rate (children per woman 15–45)	1.8	1.9
Life expectancy (at birth)	M 72	M 73
	F 78	F 80
Deaths		
Annual per 1,000	11.4	8.3
Place of death (hospital)	65%	75%
Social		
Unemployed workers	9%	8%
Marriage (annual per 1,000 population)	6.7	9.7
Divorce (annual per 1,000 population)	2.9	4.8
Number persons per household	2.6	2.8
Wealth		
Annual GDP per capita ($)	16,000	21,700
Health expenditure		
% GDP	6.3	12+
(Public)	(5.3)	(4.8)
(Private)	(1.0)	(7.2)

SOURCE: *The Economist,* 1992; Health US, 1990; National Center for Health Statistics, 1991; OHE, 1992.

and poverty, which are substantially higher than in other nations.

With varied health needs, mainly not addressed by the existing health care system, and spiraling medical expenses that exceed 14% of GDP, the nation seeks a new delivery system that can guarantee access for all yet hold costs down.

ORIGINS OF THE HEALTH CARE SYSTEM

The modern American health care system arose from a wide range of therapies practices by large numbers of healers in the late 19th century. This frustrated the American Medical Association (AMA) and its leaders trained in the new scientific medicine. Through a series of remarkably successful campaigns, the AMA and state medical societies gained control of medical education and licensure on behalf of scientific medicine. The systematic improvement in medical education at the beginning of the century was followed by the increasing importance of the hospital, the specialization of most physicians and the rise of the research oriented academic medical center in the mid-century.

The shift in the locus of care and a mounting pile of unpaid bills caused by the Depression led hospitals and then doctors to create provider-run, non-profit health insurance on a voluntary basis. Commercial insurers joined in, and coverage rapidly expanded, providing pass-through reimbursement for hospital and specialty care. The proportion of physicians who were general practitioners (GPs) fell from 75% in 1935, to 45% in 1957, to 34% in 1990.

Between the 1930s and the 1980s the AMA, along with other provider groups, successfully opposed national health insurance and emphasized employer-based insurance that paid for care only when billed by physicians and hospitals (Starr, 1982). Thus most medicine was done by private practitioners, clinics and hospitals who charged fees.

When Congress finally legislated in 1965 coverage for the elderly (Medicare) and the poor (Medicaid), it reinforced the fee for service payments. Direct federal funds were confined largely to capital for building more hospital beds and for research. Thus by the late 1960s, the majority of doctors were specialists, there developed a crisis in primary care, and costs began to rise rapidly. People could see any specialists they wished and did. Few physicians chose to go into general practice and those few were isolated from the mainstream medical community. Hospitals expanded rapidly and competed to offer the latest in technical services, which were generously reimbursed. The term "medical-industrial complex" appeared, and the protected markets of medical services flourished at high profits.

THE STRUCTURE

From this brief history one can see that the organization of the American system is a loose one, emphasizing the hospital and technical services. There is a blurring between all four levels of care, because there is no clear division of labor between generalists and specialists. An arrangement to this end was discussed earlier this century but rejected because GPs wanted to retain hospital privileges (Stevens, 1971).

GENERAL PRACTICE AMONG SPECIALISTS

Since the 1960s, the primary care vacuum has meant in effect that much "primary care" is done by specialists, what Fry (1960) calls "specialoids." To fill the vacuum, internal medicine, pediatrics, obstetrics, and psychiatry each declared themselves to be a "primary care specialty," and all but psychiatry have succeeded. In fact, about 80% of internists and 50% of pediatricians end up in subspecialties, but all American statistics count them as primary care doctors.

Most important, after years of campaigning, general practice attained specialty status by requiring residency training and board certification centered on its new focus, family practice. The Millis Report of 1966 proposed that primary care be recognized as a specialty and receive federal funding and that community health centers be established in poor areas. Both of these changes were made, and the American Board of Family Practice was established in 1969. This change partially stopped the loss of physicians in primary care by encouraging thousands of new doctors to become residency trained. However, as older GPs retire, there has continued to be a significant decrease in the percentage of American physicians in general and family practice.

Family physicians (FPs) and general internists represent the largest groups to whom people turn for primary care. They provide a wide range of services, but a different blend from the British GPs who have access to a broader range of resources through the NHS. Patients go to a wide variety of generalists and specialists for first-contact care, as illustrated in Figure 21-1. With some exceptions, there is no counterpart to community nursing, primary medical teams, and the wide array of services for the disabled, the chronically ill, and the feeble. Home health care is expanding in the US, but largely as a set of high-tech services (such as home intravenous therapy or home physical therapy) provided by for-profit teams. US FPs and internists take care of hospitalized patients and do more procedures (such as sigmoidoscopy) than British GPs.

About 39% of all expenditures go on hospital services, and this percentage has been dropping slightly as insurers and government programs have become much more strict about hospital admissions and length of stay. American hospital lengths of stay are the shortest in the world, but also the most expensive, because those few days are packed with sophisticated procedures, advanced equipment, and highly trained staff

Figure 21-1. *Percent Distribution of US Generalist and Specialty Physicians*

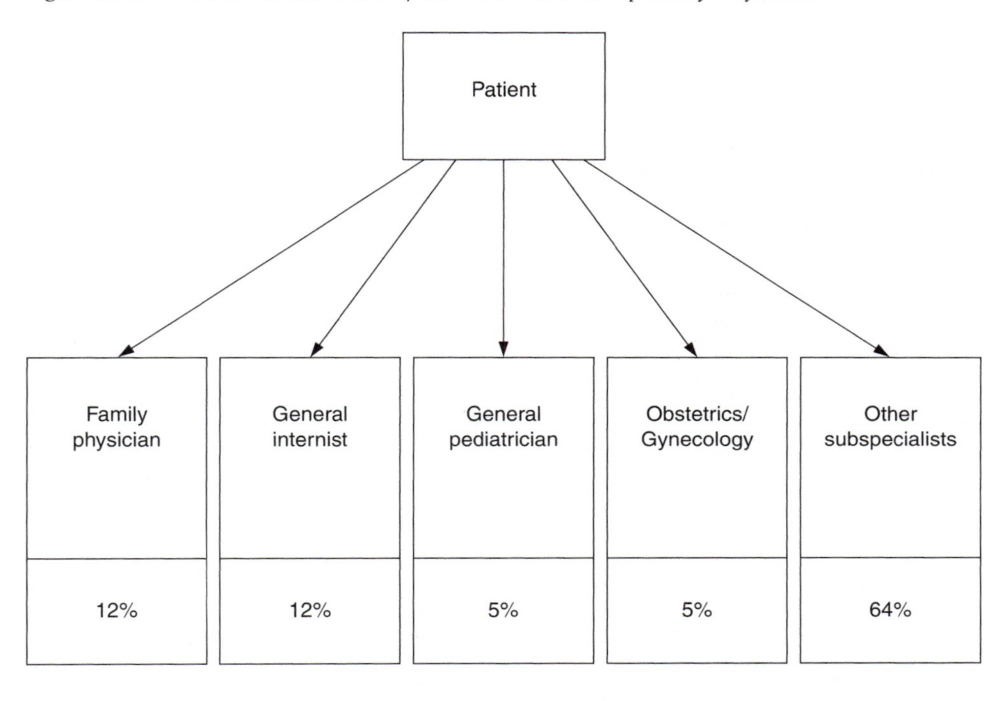

working in expensively built facilities. As more and more complex procedures are done on an outpatient basis, doctors and hospitals have been competing for market share. Many have joined forces to establish surgi-centers, women's centers, imaging centers etc., so that the term "hospital" now includes many facilities and side corporations besides the central building with inpatient beds. Recently there has also been a strong trend to "vertical integration," with hospitals setting up organizations to be involved in and potentially control all aspects of patient care from primary-care practice to nursing homes.

MEDICAL MANPOWER

Surprisingly, the manpower crisis of the late 1960s precipitated a major federal program to expand medical schools. In fact, much of the "crisis" stemmed from there being too few generalists and too many specialists. The number of graduates doubled, and the number of doctors has been expanding rapidly ever since. However, in the absence of an overall manpower plan, most graduates have chosen specialty training. By the mid-1970s, a surplus was predicted in all but a few of the specialties.

From 1965 to 1990, the numbers of family practitioners in the US declined slowly (0.1% per annum), while general internists and general practitioners rose by 6% annually. Specialists rose much faster so that the percentage of primary care doctors fell from 43 in 1965 to 34 in 1990 (Table 21-2).

Many of the new physicians are women, and they now make up 40–60% of medical school classes. Intensive recruitment of minorities has generated only a slowly increasing number of candidates against the many other careers open to the talented. What used to be called "foreign medical graduates" (FMGs) became a significant factor in the 1960s, when rapidly expanding hospital and specialty programs searched for young doctors, who had graduated from non-US medical schools, to fill the more unpopular

Table 21-2. Proliferation of Provider

Practitioners	1960	1980	2000
Physicians (MDs, DOs)	251,200	457,500	704,700
Persons per active physician	735	508	369
Chiropractors	unknown	24,400	88,100
Registered nurses[a]	592,000	1,272,900	1,900,000
Licensed practical nurses[a]	217,000	549,300	724,500
Nurse-midwives[b]	500(?)	2,000	4,800
Physician assistants[c]	0	11,000	32,800
Nurse-practitioners[d]	0	14,700	36,400

[a] The figure for 2000 was an interpolation between high and low estimates.
[b] The figure for 2000 was calculated by assuming 200 graduates per year, with gross attrition rate of 20%.
[c] The figure for 1980 was based on the figure for 1983 minus attrition projected back to 1980; the figure for 2000 was calculated by assuming 1,500 graduates per year, with gross attrition rate of 20%.
[d] The figure for 2000 was calculated by assuming 2,100 graduates per year, with gross attrition rate of 20%.

(inner-city) residencies. After medical schools doubled the national class size, there was increasing pressure to cut back on FMGs. An increasing number of them, however, were Americans who went abroad to obtain a medical degree, and their families mounted a powerful lobby. Subsequent actions have neutralized the term to "international medical graduates" (IMGs) and tightened standards, slowly reducing their proportion from 32% of residents in 1970 to 23% in 1990. IMGs tend to fill empty residency slots, many of them now in internal medicine.

FINANCING MEDICAL CARE

The voluntary health insurance system works best in mid-size and large companies, which provide coverage for employees and their dependents as a benefit. Employers typically pay a "middle-man" insurance company, who then administers the benefits and pays the doctors and hospitals. Some employers offer employees a range of insurance policies to choose from, each administered by a different company. Each policy may cover different services, have different charges and co-payments to the employee and involve different doctors and hospitals. Some companies are "self-insured" and administer the plan themselves or contract with only one insurance company to do so. These policies are "experience-rated," which means that the premiums reflect the health status and illnesses of each employee group. As firm size falls below 50 employees, so the percentage of companies providing health insurance drops rapidly, and staff in these companies must buy insurance on an individual basis (which is very expensive often double or triple the cost to the employer) or through volunteer associations to which they belong (these plans are uncommon and usually involve very large deductibles and co-insurance).

Many large companies also cover employees' dependents, often for an additional charge. Because of the wide variability of medical coverage by employers and the universal exclusion of coverage for pre-existing conditions in new employees, many people are reluctant to change jobs and run the risk of receiving markedly fewer, or no benefits.

Another complicating factor in the American medical care system is that companies are usually searching for a cheaper health plan; they may change the types and numbers of plans offered to employees annually (who may shift plans once a year). Each plan may contract with only a certain number of physicians or hospitals, so that long-term continuity of care is impossible. Both patients and physicians are confused as to what is actually covered and what has been carried out before by other clinicians or facilities. Insurance plans adopt a one-year mentality, in part because employees are likely to change plans, and in part to make a profit by minimizing the amount of medical or hospital bills paid for that year. Thus they are unlikely to invest in preventive care, and they put as many administrative hurdles as possible in the way of getting care (Light, 1993).

Medicare was provided for the elderly, when a plan focused on hospital and specialty care; ironically it covers few home or long-term services for the chronically ill. In addition, Medicare often covers only a portion of physician bills, no drug costs, no other health professions (such as dentists or psychologists), and has significant deductibles before any charges are paid. Because of these gaps in coverage, over 80% of the elderly purchase a supplementary insurance policy for relatively high premiums to help with the uncovered expenses.

Under federal law, the states also provide Medicaid for the poor, with the Federal Government paying about half the costs, more for poorer states and less for affluent ones. The 50 states, however, have made very different decisions about how many services they will cover and about who is eligible. On the whole, they use strict eligibility rules that allow only half or less of those with survival incomes (the poverty line) to be covered primarily poor women with children and poor elderly with chronic disorders who have used up all their life savings paying for what Medicare does not cover. Once their savings are below about $2,000, they become eligible for Medicaid, which does pay for long-term care and a broad range of home services as well as all acute services. In some states, only a third of those on survival incomes are eligible.

Another difficulty is that payment levels for most Medicaid services are set so low that only a few providers will treat Medicaid patients. These providers may "compensate" by treating a high volume of poor patients.

For many years, about 35 million Americans have had no health insurance. Three quarters of these uninsured are in working families. Latinos and African-Americans are twice as likely to be uninsured. When they need care, these citizens (one in every six) use the relatively small and underfunded system of public hospital emergency rooms and clinics, as well as non-physician providers and healers.

An unknown but estimated 40 to 70 million Americans have "Swiss cheese policies" with substantial holes of medical insurance coverage in the middle (exclusion clauses for not covering existing illnesses or high risks, ranging from mental illness to pregnancy, to diabetes), on the front edge (increased deductibles), the sides (copayments), or the back edge (payment caps). No systematic records are kept of these internal policy features, but they have perpetrated a crisis for both physicians and their patients (Light, 1992a). There are over 1200 insurance companies selling medical insurance. Because they compete on price, and because there is no definition of what must be covered by insurance, almost every conceivable and confusing exclusion is used to reduce claims paid. . . .

The US health care financing system is now like a giant shell game, every payer trying to shift costs to other payers, especially back to the patient or to the doctor in the form of unpaid or partially paid bills. In addition, patients pay 30% of all medical costs out of their own pockets. When insurance companies or patients do not pay part or all of a claim, the providers often come after patients through collection agencies, which have the power of ruining their credit for all other financing in their lives.

These problems have led to widespread dissatisfaction of both patients and physicians. The US spends the most money on health care yet registers the highest consumer dissatisfaction with their medical care of any industrialized nation (Blendon and Edwards, 1991).

PHYSICIAN INCOME

Although physician costs are about 20% of total medical costs and half of that goes to overhead expenses, only 10% of all health care dollars go to physicians' "take-home" pay. However, this still amounts to very high incomes; among the highest in the world. Most doctors still bill privately and are paid on a fee-for-service basis. But a growing number work for a salary plus bonuses, for a contract, or on the basis of capitation fees in various managed care organizations. This situation is complex and changing rapidly.

Primary care doctors and a few specialties that involve considerable listening or counselling (such as psychiatry and geriatrics) average about $100,000 per year. Many of the medical subspecialties, such as cardiology, gastroenterology, general surgery and obstetrics and gynecology, average about $200,000, while subspecialty surgeons, such as orthopedics, cardiothoracic and neurosurgery, average over $300,000 (AAFP, 1992 and Light, 1993). These are 1990 figures, and although the mean is about $150,000, there is a long right-handed tail to the distribution stretching out to $800,000 or more. These payment patterns date back to the payments committees of Blue Cross and other insurance plans, which were dominated by hospital-based specialties. They reflect higher charges allowed for new "experimental" procedures, the use of which soon becomes widespread (such as laparoscopy), and also reflect critical moments when, for example, radiologists and pathologists refused to be billed as part of hospital services and set up independent businesses that contract with several hospitals. The so-called competition of the last 15 years has generally not brought down the earnings of these high-end specialties. Indeed, this disparity has been exaggerated. In the 1960s, specialists typically earned 50% more than primary care physicians; now, it is two to three times as much. These drastic inequities in earnings, without any difference in hours worked (about 55 per week) are one of the key reasons for students deciding to pursue subspecialty careers.

ORGANIZATION OF SERVICES

From 1970 to the late 1980s, there was a steady trend of less hospitalization and a shift back to office-based care for patients. Most doctors (82%) are principally involved in patient care (the remainder in teaching, research or administration), and despite all the talk today about physician-executives, the data show no notable increase (Roback, Randolph and Seidman, 1990: Table A-2). The number of physicians in office-based practice (not associated with a hospital) has been rising slowly since 1970 (from 55% to 58.5%), and the percentage of physicians practicing full-time in hospitals has declined from 10.4 to 8.5. However, hospital-based practice makes up 23.6% of all practice sites because of all the residents and fellows in training. This underscores the immense role that medical education, as practically an industry in itself, plays in manning and supporting hospital-based practice. The total number of residents has grown since 1970 by 60%, and they are a major source of "cheap" labor.

An increasing number of the 58% of doctors practicing in "offices" (i.e., not a hospital or institution) do so in groups. Since the mid-1960s, when private and public insurance became fully established and funded expansion with few restraints, more and more doctors have combined into groups to form professional corporations.

While there were 4,300 groups in 1965, this figure rose to 8,500 in 1975 and 16,600 in 1988 (Havlicek, 1990: Chapter 8). This means that while 11% of all non-federal physicians worked in group practice in 1965, 30% did so by 1988. Supporting this emphasis on economic rather than service motives, an increasing percentage practice in single specialty groups, up from 54% in 1975 to 71% in 1988. These groups tend to be small, with an average of 6.2 physicians in 1988, and their purpose is largely to share the financing of space, staff and equipment, and to position themselves for handling larger contracts from institutional payers.

An important, perhaps even integral part of the rapid expansion of groups since the mid-1970s has involved doctors investing in their own clinical laboratories, radiology labs, electrocardiological labs and audiology labs. (In addition, 40% of all office-based physicians have their own labs for blood tests or sample cultures.) The larger the group, the more likely it will own one or more of these facilities.

For example, while 23% of three-person groups own clinical labs, this rises steadily to 78% for groups with more than 75 doctors. Large groups also own their own surgical duties, from 15% of groups size 16–25, to 41% of groups size 76–99. The reason is primarily economic, as current reimbursement levels allow large profits to be made in lab, X-ray and surgical areas. Because the purchase of equipment and staff is so expensive, larger groups are more easily able to afford the initial costs and refer enough patients to keep the facilities busy.

REORGANIZATION TOWARDS MANAGED CARE

In 1970–71, President Richard Nixon, Senator Edward Kennedy (who chaired the Senate Labor and Human Resources Committee), and the business community (which paid and pays most premiums as an employee benefit) all declared that the health care system was in crisis. Problems included:

- weak and dwindling primary care
- too much surgery, hospital care, tests, and specialty visits
- escalating costs that would soon bankrupt the nation
- fragmented, impersonal care
- millions of uninsured citizens, including half the poor who should have been covered by Medicaid.

Each group proposed its own version of national health insurance and met with opposition by doctors, insurance companies and medical supply companies. However, Nixon's proposal for managed competition between hundreds of health maintenance organizations (HMOs) passed into legislation. HMOs provide nearly all medical services for a fixed subscription per annum. One of the key components of the HMO legislation was that all employers with over 25 employees, who offered medical insurance as a benefit (many do not), must offer an HMO as an option if one exists in the nearby region. Overnight, HMOs had a built-in market.

Currently, managed care in the US means essentially that someone in addition to the physician is trying to decrease medical costs by "managing" the patient's care through aggressive contracting or utilization controls (Table 21-3). Typically the primary care physician is the key player and could be rewarded by ordering fewer tests or procedures, i.e., rewarded for more "appropriate" utilization.

Managed care now comes in many variants, but a useful framework is provided by the four basic types of HMOs and PPOs.

1. *Staff or group model HMOs* center around a full-time staff who take care of a defined number of patients (or enrollees). They look like more traditional medical multispecialty groups but with greater numbers of primary care physicians. The groups must figure out how to best serve their subscribers on a fixed budget. These groups are better at holding costs down, primarily by reducing hospital admissions. In staff model HMOs, the plan employs the physicians, while in group models, the plan contracts with medical groups who only take care of that plan's patients.
2. *IPA (Independent Practice Association) HMOs* contract with hundreds of private physicians, each of whom takes on varying numbers of their subscribers in return for a capitation or fee-for-service contract, plus incentives for holding down hospital

Table 21-3. Definitions of Managed Care

Managed care	Any system of health service payment or delivery arrangements where the health plan attempts to control or coordinate use of health services by its enrolled members in order to contain health expenditures, by either improving quality or lowering it.
Managed competition	An approach to health system reform in which health plans compete to provide health insurance coverage and services for enrollees. Typically, enrollees sign up with a health plan purchasing entity and choose a service plan during an open enrollment period.
Managed indemnity	This is traditional private fee for service care with utilization controls and reimbursement of fees by the insurance company.

and specialty costs. Hundreds of new for-profit HMOs have chosen the IPA approach to increase subscribers' choices and therefore market appeal. Typically, lower start-up costs are needed as physicians still have their own offices and staff. But IPA controls over actual practice patterns are tenuous, which often leads to micromanagement by the IPA central staff or the insurance company to control patient utilization.

3. *Network HMOs* lie in between, contracting with many group practices. This means that some of the clinical management can be done within the groups of colleagues, rather than externally by monitors from the central office. Network HMOs try to combine the best of both worlds colleague self-management and wide choice for market appeal.
4. *Preferred Provider Organizations (PPOs)* groups of doctors who offer volume discounts to insurers or employers in return for preferred status (usually by having their reduced fees covered by the subscriber's insurance policy instead of a patient's co-payment). They can be narrow (an obstetrical PPO) or broad (a primary care PPO). Initially hailed as a panacea, they are not proving to save money, and the decrease in fees has been accompanied by an increase in patient volume. PPOs typically do not have a central office to do utilization review; it is more frequently done by the insurance company.

New hybrids have been created to attract more subscribers, such as the Point of Service HMO that allows subscribers to go outside the HMO when they want to see another physician who is not a member of the plan. In that case, the patient ends up paying much more (but not all) of that physician's bill.

Currently, over 50 million Americans get their care from HMOs. This is growing steadily, though much more slowly than envisioned originally. Details of enrollment and disenrollment led some to believe this shows that most Americans have "rejected" the restrictions of HMOs and lead others to believe that Americans are being converted. Managed care in less rigorous forms is part of most health insurance plans. Indeed, in many states Medicaid and Medicare are turning to HMOs to enroll their patients. True endemnity medical insurance, where a portion or all of the physician's fee for each service is paid without a contract or review, is getting rare and very expensive. In some areas of the US, only 5% of medical insurance is the old-style indemnity insurance. . . .

CONCLUSION

The US medical system is in the midst of rapid change. Whether or not the Congress passes sweeping legislation to correct the lack of universal coverage, changes will continue. These changes include:

increasing control by employers of how their medical care dollars are spent
a weakening of hospitals' control over the organization and financing of medical care
increasing formation and growth of physician group practices
increasing managed care (by insurance companies and physicians), with increasing numbers of people taken care of by HMOs and few people insured through plans offering indemnity coverage or contracting with PPOs
less choice (for patients) of doctors and hospitals.

However, without additional national congressional action, these financing and power changes may slow the acceleration in medical costs, but are unlikely to curtail the growth entirely. They fail to address many issues which are a necessary part of reform, including: malpractice and tort reform, simplification of the administration/financing of the medical system, and an over-reliance on technology to diagnose and treat illness.

Only through addressing the basic building block of any medical system medical care can the US make the kind of organizational and philosophical changes that will help the system evolve into one which is more efficient and effective. Primary care physicians are the key to appropriate triage and referrals, to co-ordinated and comprehensive care, and to patient education and community orientation.

REFERENCES

American Academy of Family Physicians. 1992. *Hospital practice characteristics survey.* Kansas City: AAFP.

Blendon, R. J. and Edwards, J. N. 1991. "Utilization of hospital services: A comparison of internal medicine and family practice. *J Fam Prac.* 28: 91–96.

Fry, J. 1969. *Medicine in three societies.* New York: American Elsevier.

Havlicek, P. L. 1990. *Prepaid groups in the U.S.: A survey of practice characteristics.* Chicago: AMA.

Light, D. W. 1992. "The practice and ethics of risk-rated health insurance." *JAMA* 267: 2503–08.

Light, D. W. 1993. "Countervailing power: The changing character of the medical profession in the United States." In Hafferty, F. and McKinlay, J. (eds.) *The changing character of the medical profession: An international perspective.* New York: Oxford University Press.

National Center for Health Statistics. 1991. *Health, United States, 1990.* Hyattsville, Maryland: U.S. Department of Health and Human Resources.

Robeck, G., Randolph, L., and Seidman, B. 1990. *Physician characteristics and distribution in the US.* Chicago: AMA.

Starr, P. 1982. *The social transformation of American medicine.* New York: Basic.

Stevens, R. *American medicine and the public interest.* New Haven: Yale University Press.

22 A Caring Dilemma: Womanhood and Nursing in Historical Perspective

Susan Reverby

"Do not undervalue [your] particular ability to care," students were reminded at a recent nursing school graduation.[1] Rather than merely bemoaning yet another form of late twentieth-century heartlessness, this admonition underscores the central dilemma of American nursing: The order to care in a society that refuses to value caring. This article is an analysis of the historical creation of that dilemma and its consequences for nursing. To explore the meaning of caring for nursing, it is necessary to unravel the terms of the relationship between nursing and womanhood as these bonds have been formed over the last century.

THE MEANING OF CARING

Many different disciplines have explored the various meanings of caring.[2] Much of this literature, however, runs the danger of universalizing caring as an element in female identity, or as a human quality, separate from the cultural and structural circumstances that create it. But as policy analyst Hilary Graham has argued, caring is not merely an identity; it is also work. As she notes, "Caring touches simultaneously on who you are and what you do."[3] Because of this duality, caring can be difficult to define and even harder to control. Graham's analysis moves beyond seeing caring as a psychological trait; but her focus is primarily on women's unpaid labor in the home. She does not fully discuss how the forms of caring are shaped by the context under which they are practiced. Caring is not just a subjective and material experience; it is a historically created one. Particular circumstances, ideologies, and power relations thus create the conditions under which caring can occur, the forms it will take, the consequences it will have for those who do it.

The basis for caring also shapes its effect. Nursing was organized under the expectation that its practitioners would accept a duty to care rather than demand a right to determine how they would satisfy this duty. Nurses were expected to act out of an obligation to care, taking on caring more as an identity than as work, and expressing altruism without thought of autonomy either at the bedside or in their profession. Thus, nurses, like others who perform what is defined as "women's work" in our society, have had to contend with what appears as a dichotomy between the duty to care for others and the right to control their own activities in the name of caring. Nursing is still searching for what philosopher Joel Feinberg argued comes prior to rights, that is, being "recognized as having a claim on rights."[4] The duty to care, organized within the political and economic context of nursing's development, has made it difficult for nurses to obtain this moral and, ultimately, political standing.

Because nurses have been given the duty to care, they are caught in a secondary dilemma: forced to act as if altruism (assumed to be the basis for caring) and autonomy (assumed to be the basis for rights) are separate ways of being. Nurses are still searching for a way to forge a link between altruism and autonomy that will allow them to have what philosopher Larry Blum and others have called "caring-with-autonomy," or what psychiatrist Jean Baker Miller labeled "a way of life that includes serving others without being subservient."[5] Nursing's historical circumstances and ideological underpinnings have made creating this way of life difficult, but not impossible, to achieve.

CARING AS DUTY

A historical analysis of nursing's development makes this theoretical formulation clearer. Most of the writing about American nursing's history begins in the 1870s when formal training for nursing was introduced in the United States. But nursing did not appear de novo at the end of the nineteenth century. As with most medical and health care, nursing throughout the colonial era and most of the nineteenth century took place within the family and the home. In the domestic pantheon that surrounded "middling" and upper-class American womanhood in the nineteenth century, a woman's caring for friends and relatives was an important pillar. Nursing was often taught by mother to daughter as part of female apprenticeship, or learned by a domestic servant as an additional task on her job. Embedded in the seemingly natural or ordained character of women, it became an important manifestation of women's expression of love of others, and was thus integral to the female sense of self.[6] In a society where deeply felt religious tenets were translated into gendered virtues, domesticity advocate Catharine Beecher declared that the sick were to be "commended" to a "woman's benevolent ministries."[7]

The responsibility for nursing went beyond a mother's duty for her children, a wife's for her husband, or a daughter's for her aging parents. It attached to all the available female family members. The family's "long arm" might reach out at any time to a woman working in a distant city, in a mill, or as a maid, pulling her home to care for the sick, infirm, or newborn. No form of women's labor, paid or unpaid, protected her from this demand. "You may be called upon at any moment," Eliza W. Farrar warned in the *The Young Lady's Friend* in 1837, "to attend upon your parents, your brothers, your sisters, or your companions."[8] Nursing was to be, therefore, a woman's duty, not her job. Obligation and love, not the need of work, were to bind the nurse to her patient. Caring was to be an unpaid labor of love.

THE PROFESSED NURSE

Even as Eliza Farrar was proffering her advice, pressures both inward and outward were beginning to reshape the domestic sphere for women of the then-called "middling classes." Women's obligations and work were transformed by the expanding industrial economy and changing cultural assumptions. Parenting took on increasing importance as notions of "moral mothering" filled the domestic arena and other productive labor entered the cash nexus. Female benevolence similarly moved outward as women's charitable efforts took increasingly institutional forms. Duty began to take on new meaning as such women were advised they could fulfill their nursing responsibilities by managing competently those they hired to assist them: Bourgeois female virtue could still be demonstrated as the balance of labor, love, and supervision shifted.[9]

An expanding economy thus had differing effects on women of various classes. For those in the growing urban middle classes, excess cash made it possible to consider hiring a nurse when circumstances, desire, or exhaustion meant a female relative was no longer available for the task. Caring as labor, for these women, could be separated from love.

For older widows or spinsters from the working classes, nursing became a trade they could "profess" relatively easily in the marketplace. A widow who had nursed her husband till his demise, or a domestic servant who had cared for an employer in time of illness, entered casually into the nursing trade, hired by families or individuals unwilling, or unable, to care for their sick alone. The permeable boundaries for women between unpaid and paid labor allowed nursing to pass back and forth when necessary. For many women, nursing thus beckoned as respectable community work.

These "professed" or "natural-born" nurses, as they were known, usually came to their work, as one Boston nurse put it, "laterly" when other forms of employment were closed to them or the lack of any kind of work experience left nursing as an obvious choice. Mehitable Pond Garside, for example, was in her fifties and had outlived two husbands and her children could not, or would not, support her when she came to Boston in the 1840s to nurse. Similarly Alma Frost Merrill, the daughter of a Maine wheelwright, came to Boston in 1818 at nineteen to become a domestic servant. After years as a domestic and seamstress, she declared herself a nurse.[10]

Women like Mehitable Pond Garside and Alma Frost Merrill differed markedly from the Sairy Gamp character of Dickens' novel, *Martin Chuzzlewit.* Gamp was portrayed as a merely besotted representative of lumpen-proletarian womanhood, who asserted her autonomy by daring to question medical diagnosis, to venture her own opinions (usually outrageous and wrong) at every turn, and to spread disease and superstition in the name of self-knowledge. If they were not Gamps, nurses like Garside and Merrill also were not the healers of some more recent feminist mythology that confounds nursing with midwifery, praising the caring and autonomy these women exerted, but refusing to consider their ignorance.[11] Some professed nurses learned their skills from years of experience, demonstrating the truth of the dictum that "to make a kind and sympathizing nurse, one must have waited, in sickness, upon those she loved dearly."[12] Others, however, blundered badly beyond their capabilities or knowledge. They brought to the bedside only the authority that their personalities and community stature could command: Neither credentials nor a professional identity gave weight to their efforts. Their womanhood, and the experience it gave them, defined their authority and taught them to nurse.

THE HOSPITAL NURSE

Nursing was not limited, however, to the bedside in a home. Although the United States had only 178 hospitals at the first national census in 1873, it was workers labeled "nurses" who provided the caring. As in home-based nursing, the route to hospital nursing was paved more with necessity than with intentionality. In 1875, Eliza Higgins, the matron of Boston's Lying-In Hospital, could not find an extra nurse to cover all the deliveries. In desperation, she moved the hospital laundress up to the nursing position, while a recovering patient took over the wash. Higgins' diaries of her trying years at the Lying-In suggest that such an entry into nursing was not uncommon.[13]

As Higgins' reports and memoirs of other nurses attest, hospital nursing could be the work of devoted women who learned what historian Charles Rosenberg has labeled "ad hoc professionalism," or the temporary and dangerous labor of an ambulatory patient or hospital domestic.[14] As in home-based nursing, both caring and concern were frequently demonstrated. But the nursing work and nurses were mainly characterized by the diversity of their efforts and the unevenness of their skills.

Higgins' memoirs attest to the hospital as a battleground where nurses, physicians, and hospital managers contested the realm of their authority. Nurses continually affirmed their right to control the pace and content of their work, to set their own hours, and to structure their relationships to physicians. Aware that the hospital's paternalistic attitudes and practices toward its "inmates" were attached to the nursing personnel as well, they fought to be treated as workers, "not children," as the Lying-In nurses told Eliza Higgins, and to maintain their autonomous adult status.[15]

Like home-based nursing, hospital nurses had neither formal training nor class status upon which to base their arguments. But their sense of the rights of working-class womanhood gave them authority to press their demands. The necessity to care, and their perception of its importance to patient outcome, also structured their belief that demanding the right to be relatively autonomous was possible. However, their efforts were undermined by the nature of their onerous work, the paternalism of the institutions, class differences between trustees and workers, and ultimately the lack of a defined ideology of caring. Mere resistance to those above them, or contending assertions of rights, could not become the basis for nursing authority.

THE INFLUENCE OF NIGHTINGALE

Much of this changed with the introduction of training for nursing in the hospital world. In the aftermath of Nightingale's triumph over the British Army's medical care system in the Crimea, similar attempts by American women during the Civil War, and the need to find respectable work for daughters of the middling classes, a model and support for nursing reform began to grow. By 1873, three nursing schools in hospitals in New York, Boston, and New Haven were opened, patterned after the Nightingale School at St. Thomas' Hospital in London.

Nightingale had envisioned nursing as an art, rather than a science, for which women needed to be trained. Her ideas linked her medical and public health notions to her class and religious beliefs. Accepting the Victorian idea of divided spheres of activity for men and women, she thought women had to be trained to nurse through a disciplined process of honing their womanly virtue. Nightingale stressed character development, the laws of health, and strict adherence to orders passed through a female hierarchy. Nursing was built on a model that relied on the concept of duty to provide its basis for authority. Unlike other feminists of the time, she spoke in the language of duty, not rights.

Furthermore, as a nineteenth-century sanitarian, Nightingale never believed in germ theory, in part because she refused to accept a theory of disease etiology that appeared to be morally neutral. Given her sanitarian beliefs, Nightingale thought medical therapeutics and "curing" were of lesser importance to patient outcome, and she willingly left this realm to the physician. Caring, the arena she did think of great importance, she assigned to the nurse. In order to care, a nurse's character, tempered by the fires of training, was to be her greatest skill. Thus, to "feminize" nursing, Nightingale sought a change in the class-defined behavior, not the gender, of the work force.[16]

To forge a good nurse out of the virtues of a good woman and to provide a political base for nursing, Nightingale sought to organize a female hierarchy in which orders passed down from the nursing superintendent to the lowly probationer. This separate female sphere was to share power in the provision of health care with the male-dominated areas of medicine. For many women in the Victorian era, sisterhood and what Carroll Smith-Rosenberg has called "homosocial networks" served to overcome many of the limits of this separate but supposedly equal system of cultural division.[17] Sisterhood, after all, at least in its fictive forms, underlay much of the female power that grew out of women's culture in the nineteenth century. But in nursing, commonalities of the gendered experience could not become the basis of unity since hierarchial filial relations, not equal sisterhood, lay at the basis of nursing's theoretical formulation.

Service, Not Education

Thus, unwittingly, Nightingale's sanitarian ideas and her beliefs about womanhood provided some of the ideological justification for many of the dilemmas that faced American nursing by 1900. Having fought physician and trustee prejudice against the training of nurses in hospitals in the last quarter of the nineteenth century, American nursing reformers succeeded only too well as the new century began. Between 1890 and 1920, the number of nursing schools jumped from 35 to 1,775, and the number of trained nurses from 16 per 100,000 in the population to 141.[18] Administrators quickly realized that opening a "nursing school" provided their hospitals, in exchange for training, with a young, disciplined, and cheap labor force. There was often no difference between the hospital's nursing school and its nursing service. The service needs of the hospital continually overrode the educational requirements of the schools. A student might, therefore, spend weeks on a medical ward if her labor was so needed, but never see the inside of an operating room before her graduation.

Once the nurse finished her training, however, she was unlikely to be hired by a hospital because it relied on either untrained aides or nursing student labor. The majority of graduate nurses, until the end of the 1930s, had to find work in private duty in a patient's home, as the patient's employee in the hospital, in the branches of public health, or in some hospital staff positions. In the world of nursing beyond the training school, "trained" nurses still had to compete with the thousands of "professed" or "practical" nurses who continued to ply their trade in an overcrowded and unregulated marketplace. The title of nurse took on very ambiguous meanings.[19]

The term, "trained nurse," was far from a uniform designation. As nursing leader Isabel Hampton Robb lamented in 1893, "the title 'trained nurse' may mean then anything, everything, or next to nothing."[20]

The exigencies of nursing acutely ill or surgical patients required the sacrifice of coherent educational programs. Didactic, repetitive, watered-down medical lectures by physicians or older nurses were often provided for the students, usually after they finished ten to twelve hours of ward work. Training emphasized the "one right way" of doing ritualized procedures in hopes the students' adherence to specified rules would be least dangerous to patients.[21] Under these circumstances, the duty to care could be followed with a vengeance and become the martinet adherence to orders.

Furthermore, because nursing emphasized training in discipline, order, and practical skills, the abuse of student labor could be rationalized. And because the work force was almost entirely women, altruism, sacrifice, and submission were expected, encouraged, indeed, demanded. Exploitation was inevitable in a field where, until the early 1900s, there were no accepted standards for how much work an average student should do or how many patients she could successfully care for, no mechanisms through which to enforce such standards. After completing her exhaustive and depressing survey of nursing training in 1912, nursing educator M. Adelaide Nutting bluntly pointed out: "Under the present system the school has no life of its own."[22] In this kind of environment, nurses were trained. But they were not educated.

Virtue and Autonomy

It would be a mistake, however, to see the nursing experience only as one of exploitation and the nursing school as a faintly concealed reformatory for the wayward girl in need of discipline. Many nursing superintendents lived the Nightingale ideals as best they could and infused them into their schools. The authoritarian model could and did retemper many women. It instilled in nurses idealism and pride in their skills, somewhat differentiated the trained nurse from the untrained, and protected and aided the sick and dying. It provided a mechanism for virtuous women to contribute to the improvement of humanity by empowering them to care.

For many of the young women entering training in the nineteenth and early twentieth centuries, nursing thus offered something quite special: both a livelihood and a virtuous state. As one nursing educator noted in 1890: "Young strong country girls are drawn into the work by the glamorer [sic] thrown about hospital work and the halo that sanctifies a Nightingale."[23] Thus, in their letters of application, aspiring nursing students expressed their desire for work, independence, and womanly virtue. As with earlier, nontrained nurses, they did not seem to separate autonomy and altruism, but rather sought its linkage through training. Flora Jones spoke for many such women when she wrote the superintendent of Boston City Hospital in 1880, declaring, "I consider myself fitted for the work by inclination and consider it a womanly occupation. It is also necessary for me to become self-supporting and provide for my future."[24] Thus, one nursing superintendent reminded a graduating class in 1904: "You have become self-controlled, unselfish, gentle, compassionate, brave, capable in fact, you have risen from the period of irresponsible girlhood to that of womanhood."[25] For women like Flora Jones, and many of nursing's early leaders, nursing was the singular way to grow to maturity in a womanly profession that offered meaningful work, independence, and altruism.[26]

Altruism, Not Independence

For many, however, as nursing historian Dorothy Sheahan has noted, the training school, "was a place where . . . women learned to be girls."[27] The range of permissible behaviors for respectable women was often narrowed further through training. Independence was to be sacrificed on the altar of altruism. Thus, despite hopes of aspiring students and promises of training school superintendents, nursing rarely united altruism and autonomy. Duty remained the basis for caring.

Some nurses were able to create what they called "a little world of our own." But nursing had neither the financial nor the cultural power to create the separate women's institutions that provided so much of the basis for women's reform and rights efforts.[28] Under these conditions, nurses found it difficult to make the collective transition out of a woman's culture of obligation into an activist assault on the structure and beliefs that oppressed them. Nursing remained bounded by its ideology and its material circumstances.

THE CONTRADICTIONS OF REFORM

In this context, one begins to understand the difficulties faced by the leaders of nursing reform. Believing that educational reform was central to nursing's professionalizing efforts and clinical improvements, a small group of elite reformers attempted to broaden nursing's scientific content and social outlook. In arguing for an increase in the scientific knowledge necessary in nursing, such leaders were fighting against deep-seated cultural assumptions about male and female "natural" characteristics as embodied in the doctor and nurse. Such sentiments were articulated in the routine platitudes that graced what one nursing leader described as the "doctor homilies" that were a regular feature at nursing graduation exercises.[29]

Not surprisingly, such beliefs were professed by physicians and hospital officials whenever nursing shortages appeared, or nursing groups pushed for higher educational standards or defined nursing as more than assisting the physician. As one nursing educator wrote, with some degree of resignation after the influenza pandemic in 1920: "It is perhaps inevitable that the difficulty of securing nurses during the last year or two should have revived again the old agitation about the 'over-training' of nurses and the clamor for a cheap worker of the old servant–nurse type."[30]

First Steps Toward Professionalism

The nursing leadership, made up primarily of educators and supervisors with their base within what is now the American Nurses' Association and the National League for Nursing, thus faced a series of dilemmas as they struggled to raise educational standards in the schools and criteria for entry into training, to register nurses once they finished their training, and to gain acceptance for the knowledge base and skills of the nurse. They had to exalt the womanly character, self-abnegation, and service ethic of nursing while insisting on the right of nurses to act in their own self-interest. They had to demand higher wages commensurate with their skills, yet not appear commercial. They had to simultaneously find a way to denounce the exploitation of nursing students, as they made political alliances with hospital physicians and administrators whose support they needed. While they lauded character and sacrifice, they had to find a way to measure it with educational criteria in order to formulate registration laws and set admission standards. They had to make demands and organize, without appearing "unlady-like." In sum, they were forced by the social conditions and ideology surrounding nursing to attempt to professionalize altruism without demanding autonomy.

Undermined by Duty

The image of a higher claim of duty also continually undermined a direct assertion of the right to determine that duty. Whether at a bedside, or at a legislative hearing on practice laws, the duty to care became translated into the demand that nurses merely follow doctors' orders. The tradition of obligation almost made it impossible for nurses to speak about rights at all. By the turn of the century necessity and desire were pulling more young women into the labor force, and the women's movement activists were placing rights at the center of cultural discussion. In this atmosphere, nursing's call to duty was perceived by many as an increasingly antiquated language to shore up a changing economic and cultural landscape. Nursing became a type of collective female grasping for an older form of security and power in the face of rapid change. Women who might have been attracted to nursing in the 1880s as a womanly occupation that provided some form of autonomy, were, by the turn of the century, increasingly looking elsewhere for work and careers.

A DIFFERENT VISION

In the face of these difficulties, the nursing leadership became increasingly defensive and turned on its own rank and file. The educators and supervisors who comprised leadership lost touch with the pressing concern of their constituencies in the daily work world of nursing and the belief systems such nurses continued to hold. Yet many nurses, well into the twentieth century, shared the nineteenth-century vision of nursing as the embodiment of womanly virtue. A nurse named Annette Fiske, for example, although she authored two science books for nurses and had an M.A. degree in classics from Radcliffe College before she entered training, spent her professional career in the 1920s arguing against increasing educational standards. Rather, she called for a reinfusion into nursing of spirituality and service, assuming that this would result in nursing's receiving greater "love and respect and admiration."[31]

Other nurses, especially those trained in the smaller schools or reared to hold working-class ideals about respectable behavior in women, shared Fiske's views. They saw the leadership's efforts at professionalization as an attempt to push them out of nursing. Their adherence to nursing skill measured in womanly virtue was less a conservative and reactionary stance than a belief that seemed to transcend class and educational backgrounds to place itself in the individual character and work-place skills of the nurse. It grounded altruism in supposedly natural and spiritual, rather than educational and middle-class, soil. For Fiske and many other nurses, nursing was still a womanly art that required inherent character in its practitioners and training in practical skills and spiritual values in its schools. Their beliefs about nursing did not require the professionalization of altruism, nor the demand for autonomy either at the bedside or in control over the professionalization process.

Still other nurses took a more pragmatic viewpoint that built on their pride in their workplace skills and character. These nurses also saw the necessity for concerted action, not unlike that taken by other American workers. Such nurses fought against what one 1888 nurse, who called herself Candor, characterized as the "missionary spirit . . . [of] self-immolation" that denied that nurses worked because they had to make a living.[32] These worker-nurses saw no contradiction between demanding decent wages and conditions for their labors and being of service for those in need. But the efforts of various groups of these kinds of nurses to turn to hours' legislation, trade union activity, or mutual aid associations were criticized and condemned by the nursing leadership. Their letters were often edited out of the nursing journals, and their voices silenced in public meetings as they were denounced as being commercial, or lacking in proper womanly devotion.[33]

In the face of continual criticism from nursing's professional leadership, the worker-nurses took on an increasingly angry and defensive tone. Aware that their sense of the nurse's skills came from the experiences of the work place, not book learning or degrees, they had to assert this position despite continued hostility toward such a basis of nursing authority.[34] Although the position of women like Candor helped articulate a way for nurses to begin to assert the right to care, it did not constitute a full-blown ideological counterpart to the overwhelming power of the belief in duty.

The Persistence of Dilemmas

By midcentury, the disputes between worker-nurses and the professional leadership began to take on new forms, although the persistent divisions continued. Aware that some kind of collective bargaining was necessary to keep nurses out of the unions and in the professional associations, the ANA reluctantly agreed in 1946 to let its state units act as bargaining agents. The nursing leadership has continued to look at educational reform strategies, now primarily taking the form of legislating for the B.S. degree as the credential necessary for entry into nursing practice, and to changes in the practice laws that will allow increasingly skilled nurses the autonomy and status they deserve. Many nurses have continued to be critical of this educational strategy, to ignore the professional associations, or to leave nursing altogether.

In their various practice fields nurses still need a viable ideology and strategy that will help them adjust to the continual demands of patients and an evermore bureaucratized, cost-conscious, and rationalized work setting. For many nurses it is still, in an ideological sense, the nineteenth century. Even for those nurses who work as practitioners in the more autonomous settings of health maintenance organizations or public health offices, the legacy of nursing's heritage is still felt. Within the last two years, for example, the Massachusetts Board of Medicine tried to push through a regulation that health practitioners acknowledge their dependence on physicians by wearing a badge that identified their supervising physician and stated that they were not doctors.

Nurses have tried various ways to articulate a series of rights that allow them to care. The acknowledgment of responsibilities, however, so deeply ingrained in nursing and American womanhood, as nursing school dean Claire Fagin has noted, continually drown out the nurse's assertion of rights.[35]

Nurses are continuing to struggle to obtain the right to claim rights. Nursing's educational philosophy, ideological underpinnings, and structural position have made it difficult to create the circumstances within which to gain such recognition. It is not a lack of vision that thwarts nursing, but the lack of power to give that vision substantive form.[36]

BEYOND THE OBLIGATION TO CARE

Much has changed in nursing in the last forty years. The severing of nursing education from the hospital's nursing service has finally taken place, as the majority of nurses are now educated in colleges, not hospital-based diploma schools. Hospitals are experimenting with numerous ways to organize the nursing service to provide the nurse with more responsibility and sense of control over the nursing care process. The increasingly technical and machine-aided nature of hospital-based health care has made nurses feel more skilled.

In many ways, however, little has changed. Nursing is still divided over what counts as a nursing skill, how it is to be learned, and whether a nurse's character can be measured in educational criteria. Technical knowledge and capabilities do not easily translate into power and control. Hospitals, seeking to cut costs, have forced nurses to play "beat the clock" as they run from task to task in an increasingly fragmented setting.[37]

Nursing continues to struggle with the basis for, and the value of, caring. The fact that the first legal case on comparable worth was brought by a group of Denver nurses suggests nursing has an important and ongoing role in the political effort to have caring revalued. As in the Denver case, contemporary feminism has provided some nurses with the grounds on which to claim rights from their caring.[38]

Feminism, in its liberal form, appears to give nursing a political language that argues for equality and rights within the given order of things. It suggests a basis for caring that stresses individual discretion and values, acknowledging that the nurses' right to care should be given equal consideration with the physician's right to cure. Just as liberal political theory undermined more paternalistic formulations of government, classical liberalism's tenets applied to women have much to offer nursing. The demand for the right to care questions deeply held beliefs about gendered relations in the health care hierarchy and the structure of the hierarchy itself.

Many nurses continue to hope that with more education, explicit theories to explain the scientific basis for nursing, new skills, and a lot of assertiveness training, nursing will change. As these nurses try to shed the image of the nurse's being ordered to care, however, the admonition to care at a graduation speech has to be made. Unable to find a way to "care with autonomy" and unable to separate caring from its valuing and basis, many nurses find themselves forced to abandon the effort to care, or nursing altogether.

ALTRUISM WITH AUTONOMY

These dilemmas for nurses suggest the constraints that surround the effectiveness of a liberal feminist political strategy to address the problems of caring and, therefore, of nursing. The individualism and autonomy of a rights framework often fail to acknowledge collective social need, to provide a way for adjudicating conflicts over rights, or to address the reasons for the devaluing of female activity.[39] Thus, nurses have often rejected liberal feminism, not just out of their oppression and "false consciousness," but because of some deep understandings of the limited promise of equality and autonomy in a health care system they see as flawed and harmful. In an often inchoate way, such nurses recognize that those who claim the autonomy of rights often run the risk of rejecting altruism and caring itself.

Several feminist psychologists have suggested that what women really want in their lives is autonomy with connectedness. Similarly, many modern moral philosophers are trying to articulate a formal modern theory that values the emotions and the importance of relationships.[40] For nursing, this will require the creation of the conditions under which it is possible to value caring and to understand that the empowerment of others does not have to require self-immolation. To achieve this, nurses will have both to create a new political understanding for the basis of caring and to find ways to gain the power to implement it. Nursing can do much to have this happen through research on the importance of caring on patient outcome, studies of patient improvements in nursing settings where the right to care is created, or implementing nursing control of caring through a bargaining agreement. But nurses cannot do this alone. The dilemma of nursing is too tied to society's broader problems of gender and class to be solved solely by the political or professional efforts of one occupational group.

Nor are nurses alone in benefiting from such an effort. If nursing can achieve the power to practice altruism with autonomy, all of us have much to gain. Nursing has always been a much conflicted metaphor in our culture, reflecting all the ambivalences we give to the meaning of womanhood.[41] Perhaps in the future it can give this metaphor and, ultimately, caring, new value in all our lives.

NOTES

This selection is based on the author's book, *Ordered to Care: The Dilemma of American Nursing,* published in 1987 by Cambridge University Press, New York.

1. Gregory Wticher, "Last Class of Nurses Told: Don't Stop Caring," *Boston Globe,* May 13, 1985, pp. 17–18.
2. See, for examples, Larry Blum et al., "Altruism and Women's Oppression," in *Women and Philosophy,* eds. Carol Gould and Marx Wartofsy (New York: G.P. Putnam's, 1976), pp. 222–247; Nel Noddings, *Caring.* Berkeley: University of California Press, 1984; Nancy Chodorow, *The Reproduction of Mothering.* Berkeley: University of California Press, 1978; Carol Gilligan, *In a Different Voice.* Cambridge: Harvard University Press, 1982; and Janet Finch and Dulcie Groves, eds., *A Labour of Love, Women, Work and Caring.* London and Boston: Routledge, Kegan Paul, 1983.
3. Hilary Graham, "Caring: A Labour of Love," in *A Labour of Love,* eds. Finch and Groves, pp. 13–30.
4. Joel Feinberg, *Rights, Justice and the Bounds of Liberty* (Princeton: Princeton University Press, 1980), p. 141.
5. Blum et al., "Altruism and Women's Oppression," p. 223; Jean Baker Miller, *Toward a New Psychology of Women* (Boston: Beacon Press, 1976), p. 71.
6. Ibid; see also Iris Marion Young, "Is Male Gender Identity the Cause of Male Domination," in

Mothering: Essays in Feminist Theory, ed. Joyce Trebicott (Totowa, NJ: Rowman and Allanheld, 1983), pp. 129–146.

7. Catherine Beecher, *Domestic Receipt-Book* (New York: Harper and Brothers, 1846) p. 214.
8. Eliza Farrar, *The Young Lady's Friend By a Lady* (Boston: American Stationer's Co., 1837), p. 57.
9. Catherine Beecher, *Miss Beecher's Housekeeper and Healthkeeper.* New York: Harper and Brothers, 1876; and Sarah Josepha Hale, *The Good Housekeeper.* Boston: Otis Brothers and Co., 7th edition, 1844. See also Susan Strasser, *Never Done: A History of Housework.* New York: Pantheon, 1982.
10. Cases 2 and 18, "Admissions Committee Records," Volume I, Box 11, Home for Aged Women Collection, Schlesinger Library, Radcliffe College, Cambridge, Mass. Data on the nurses admitted to the home were also found in "Records of Inmates, 1858–1901," "Records of Admission, 1873–1924," and "Records of Inmates, 1901–1916," all in Box 11.
11. Charles Dickens, *Martin Chuzzlewit.* New York: New American Library, 1965, original edition, London: 1865; Barbara Ehrenreich and Deirdre English, *Witches, Nurses, Midwives: A History of Women Healers.* Old Westbury: Glass Mountain Pamphlets, 1972.
12. Virginia Penny, *The Employments of Women: A Cyclopedia of Women's Work* (Boston: Walker, Wise, and Co., 1863), p. 420.
13. Eliza Higgins, Boston Lying-In Hospital, *Matron's Journals,* 1873–1889, Volume I, January 9, 1875, February 22, 1875, Rare Books Room, Countway Medical Library, Harvard Medical School, Boston, Mass.
14. Charles Rosenberg, "'And Heal the Sick': The Hospital and the Patient in 19th Century America," *Journal of Social History* 10 (June 1977):445.
15. Higgins, *Matron's Journals,* Volume II, January 11, 1876, and July 1, 1876. See also a parallel discussion of male artisan behavior in front of the boss in David Montgomery, "Workers' Control of Machine Production in the 19th Century," *Labor History* 17 (Winter 1976):485–509.
16. The discussion of Florence Nightingale is based on my analysis in *Ordered to Care,* chapter 3. See also Charles E. Rosenberg, "Florence Nightingale on Contagion: The Hospital as Moral Universe," in *Healing and History,* ed. Charles E. Rosenberg. New York: Science History Publications, 1979.
17. Carroll Smith-Rosenberg, "The Female World of Love and Ritual," *Signs: Journal of Women in Culture and Society* 1 (Autumn 1975):1.
18. May Ayers Burgess, *Nurses, Patients and Pocketbooks.* New York: Committee on the Grading of Nursing, 1926, reprint edition (New York: Garland Publishing Co, 1985), pp. 36–37.
19. For further discussion of the dilemmas of private duty nursing, see Susan Reverby, "'Neither for the Drawing Room nor for the Kitchen': Private Duty Nursing, 1880–1920," in *Women and Health in America,* ed. Judith Walzer Leavitt. Madison: University of Wisconsin Press, 1984, and Susan Reverby, "'Something Besides Waiting': The Politics of Private Duty Nursing Reform in the Depression," in *Nursing History: New Perspectives, New Possibilities,* ed. Ellen Condliffe Lagemann. New York: Teachers College Press, 1982.
20. Isabel Hampton Robb, "Educational Standards for Nurses," in *Nursing of the Sick 1893* (New York: McGraw-Hill, 1949), p. 11. See also Janet Wilson James, "Isabel Hampton and the Professionalization of Nursing in the 1890s," in *The Therapeutic Revolution,* eds. Morris Vogel and Charles E. Rosenberg. Philadelphia: University of Pennsylvania Press, 1979.
21. For further discussion of the difficulties in training, see JoAnn Ashley, *Hospitals, Paternalism and the Role of the Nurse.* New York: Teachers College Press, 1976, and Reverby, *Ordered to Care,* chapter 4.
22. *Educational Status of Nursing,* Bureau of Education Bulletin Number 7, Whole Number 475 (Washington, D.C.: Government Printing Office, 1912), p. 49.
23. Julia Wells, "Do Hospitals Fit Nurses for Private Nursing," *Trained Nurse and Hospital Review* 3 (March 1890):98.
24. Boston City Hospital (BCH) Training School Records, Box 4, Folder 4, Student 4, February 14, 1880, BCH Training School Papers, Nursing Archives, Special Collections, Boston University, Mugar Library, Boston, Mass. The student's name has been changed to maintain confidentiality.
25. Mary Agnes Snively, "What Manner of Women Ought Nurses To Be?" *American Journal of Nursing* 4 (August 1904):838.
26. For a discussion of many of the early nursing leaders as "new women," see Susan Armeny, "'We Were the New Women': A Comparison of Nurses and Women Physicians, 1890–1915." Paper presented at the American Association for the History of Nursing Conference, University of Virginia, Charlottesville, Va., October 1984.
27. Dorothy Sheahan, "Influence of Occupational Sponsorship on the Professional Development of Nursing." Paper presented at the Rockefeller Archives Conference on the History of Nursing,

Rockefeller Archives, Tarrytown, NY, May 1981, p. 12.
28. Estelle Freedman, "Separatism as Strategy: Female Institution Building and American Feminism, 1870–1930," *Feminist Studies* 5 (Fall 1979):512–529.
29. Lavinia L. Dock, *A History of Nursing,* volume 3 (New York: G.P. Putnam's, 1912), p. 136.
30. Isabel M. Stewart, "Progress in Nursing Education during 1919," *Modern Hospital* 14 (March 1920):183.
31. Annette Fiske, "How Can We Counteract the Prevailing Tendency to Commercialism in Nursing?" *Proceedings of the 17th Annual Meeting of the Massachusetts State Nurses' Association,* p. 8, Massachusetts Nurses Association Papers, Box 7, Nursing Archives.
32. Candor, "Work and Wages," Letter to the Editor, *Trained Nurse and Hospital Review* 2 (April 1888):167–168.
33. See the discussion in Ashley, *Hospitals, Paternalism and the Role of the Nurse,* pp. 40–43, 46–48, 51, and in Barbara Melosh, *"The Physician's Hand": Work Culture and Conflict in American Nursing* (Philadelphia: Temple University Press, 1982), passim.
34. For further discussion see Susan Armeny, "Resolute Enthusiasts: The Effort to Professionalize American Nursing, 1880–1915." PhD dissertation, University of Missouri, Columbia, Mo., 1984, and Reverby, *Ordered to Care,* chapter 6.
35. Feinberg, *Rights,* pp. 130–142; Claire Fagin, "Nurses' Rights," *American Journal of Nursing* 75 (January 1975):82.
36. For a similar argument for bourgeois women, see Carroll Smith-Rosenberg, "The New Woman as Androgyne: Social Disorder and Gender Crisis," in *Disorderly Conduct* (New York: Alfred Knopf, 1985), p. 296.
37. Boston Nurses' Group, "The False Promise: Professionalism in Nursing," *Science for the People* 10 (May/June 1978):20–34; Jennifer Bingham Hull, "Hospital Nightmare: Cuts in Staff Demoralize Nurses as Care Suffers," *Wall Street Journal,* March 27, 1985.
38. Bonnie Bullough, "The Struggle for Women's Rights in Denver: A Personal Account," *Nursing Outlook* 26 (September 1978):566–567.
39. For critiques of liberal feminism see Allison M. Jagger, *Feminist Politics and Human Nature* (Totowa, NJ: Rowman and Allanheld, 1983), pp. 27–50, 173, 206; Zillah Eisenstein, *The Radical Future of Liberal Feminism.* New York and London: Longman, 1981; and Rosalind Pollack Petchesky, *Abortion and Women's Choice* (Boston: Northeastern University Press, 1984), pp. 1–24.
40. Miller, *Toward A New Psychology;* Jane Flax, "The Conflict Between Nurturance and Autonomy in Mother-Daughter Relationships and within Feminism," *Feminist Studies* 4 (June 1978):171–191; Blum et al., "Altruism and Women's Oppression."
41. Claire Fagin and Donna Diers, "Nursing as Metaphor," *New England Journal of Medicine* 309 (July 14, 1983):116–117.

23 AIDS and Its Impact on Medical Work: The Culture and Politics of the Shop Floor

Charles L. Bosk and Joel E. Frader

In 1979 when undergraduates applied in record numbers for admission to medical school, AIDS was not a clinical and diagnostic category. In 1990 when the applications to medical schools are plummeting, AIDS is unarguably with us, and not just as a clinical entity. AIDS has become what the French anthropologist Marcel Mauss called a "total social phenomenon one whose transactions are at once economic, juridical, moral, aesthetic, religious and mythological, and whose meaning cannot, therefore, be adequately described from the point of view of any single discipline" (Hyde 1979). For cultural analysts, present and future, the 1980s and beyond are the AIDS years.

This chapter is about the impact of AIDS on the shop floor of the academic urban hospital, an attempt to understand the impact of AIDS on everyday practices of doctors providing inpatient care. Following Mauss, we wish to view AIDS as a total social phenomenon rather than as a mere disease. Procedurally, we shall concentrate on the house officer (someone who, after graduation from medical school, participates in medical specialty training) and the medical student to see how this new infectious disease changes the content of everyday work and the education of apprentice physicians learning how to doctor and to assume the social responsibilities of the role of the physician. We are going to look at professional and occupational culture as a set of shop-floor practices and beliefs about work.

At the close of this article we will make some generalizations about the impact of AIDS on medical training and reflect on how this affects the professional culture of physicians. This may distort the picture somewhat, as the urban teaching hospital is not representative of the whole world of medical practice. To the degree that AIDS patients are concentrated in them, any inferences drawn from large teaching hospitals overstate or exaggerate the impact of AIDS. At the very least, such sampling fails to catalogue the variety of strategies individual physicians may use to avoid patients with AIDS. It fails, as well, to capture the innovative approaches to AIDS of pioneering health professionals (many of whom also happen to be gay) in nontraditional settings.

This sampling problem notwithstanding, the urban academic teaching hospital is the arena of choice for studying the impact of AIDS on the medical profession. The concentration of cases in urban teaching hospitals means that students and house officers have a high likelihood of treating patients with AIDS. They are the physicians on the clinical front lines, the ones with the heaviest day-to-day operational burdens.

Further, our attention to the house officers and students possesses a secondary benefit for this inquiry into shop-floor or work-place culture: namely, the natural state of the work place in its before-AIDS condition has been extensively documented. We use the terms shop-floor and work-place culture to invoke the sociological tradition for inquiries into work begun by Everett C. Hughes (1971) at the University of Chicago in the post-World War II years. This tradition emphasizes equivalencies between humble and proud occupations, the management of "dirty work," the procedures that surround routines and emergencies, and the handling of mistakes. Above all, the perspective invites us to reverse our "conventional sentimentality" (Becker 1967) about occupations. The idea of the hospital as a shop floor is one rhetorical device for reminding us that house officers and students are workers in a very real and active sense.

Numerous autobiographical accounts beginning with the pseudonymous Dr. X of *Intern*, catalogue the conditions of the shop floor (Dr. X. 1965; a partial list of subsequent narratives includes Nolen 1970; Rubin 1972; Sweeney 1973; Bell 1975; Haseltine and Yaw 1976; Horowitz and Offen 1977; Mullan 1976; Morgan 1980). There have also been similar commentaries on medical schools (Le Baron 1981; Klass 1987; Klein 1981; Konner 1987; Reilly 1987). Novels by former house officers have also described the work-place culture of physicians in training and the tensions inherent in it. (Examples of this genre include Cook 1972; Glasser 1973; and Shem 1978.)

In addition, there is a large literature on the socialization of medical students and house officers; each of these can be viewed as studies of shop-floor culture. (For a critical overview of this literature see Bosk 1985; individual studies of note include Fox 1957; Fox and Lief 1963; Becker et al. 1961; and Coombs 1978.) The literature on house officers is even more extensive. (See Mumford 1970 and Miller 1970 on medical internships; Mizrahi 1986 on internal medicine residencies; Light 1980 and Coser 1979 on psychiatry; Scully 1980 on obstetrics and gynecology; and Bosk 1979 and Millman 1976 on surgery; Burkett and Knafl 1976 on orthopedic surgeons; and Stelling and Bucher 1972 have focused on how house officers either avoid or accept monitoring by superordinates.)

We can construct a before-AIDS shop-floor culture as a first step in assessing what difference

AIDS makes in the occupational culture of physicians. Our picture of the after-AIDS shop floor arises from the pictures drawn in the medical literature, our teaching and consulting experience in large university health centers, and 30 interviews with medical personnel caring for AIDS patients in ten teaching hospitals. These interviews were conducted with individuals at all levels of training and provide admittedly impressionistic data, which need more systematic verification. The interviews averaged an hour in length and explored both how workers treated AIDS patients and how they felt about the patients.

SHOP-FLOOR CULTURE BEFORE AIDS: EXPLOITATION AND POWERLESSNESS

The pre-AIDS shop floor in academic medical centers is not a particularly happy place, as depicted in first-hand accounts of medical education. The dominant tone of many of the volumes is a bitter cynicism, captured in two of the dedications: Glasser's work is "For all the Arrowsmiths"; Cook dedicates his volume "to the ideal of medicine we all held the year we entered medical school." The set of everyday annoyances extends considerably beyond the long hours of work, although these alone are burdensome. Beyond that there is the fact that much of the work is without any profit for the house officer; it is "scut" work, essential drudgery whose completion appears to add little to the worker's overall sense of mastery and competence. (Becker et al. 1961 first commented that medical students, like their more senior trainees, disliked tasks that neither allowed them to exercise medical responsibility nor increased their clinical knowledge.) Consider here a resident's reaction to a day in the operating room, assisting on major surgery:

> I urinated, wrote all the preoperative orders, changed my clothes, and had some dinner, in that order. As I walked across to the dining room, I felt as if I'd been run over by a herd of wild elephants in heat. I was exhausted and, much worse, deeply frustrated. I'd been assisting in surgery for nine hours. Eight of them had been the most important in Mrs. Takura's [a patient] life; yet I felt no sense of accomplishment. I had simply endured, and I was probably the one person they could have done without. Sure, they needed retraction, but a catatonic schizophrenic would have sufficed. Interns are eager to work hard, even to sacrifice above all, to be useful and to display their special talents in order to learn. I felt none of these satisfactions, only an empty bitterness and exhaustion (Cook 1972, 74).

The complaint is not atypical.

In all accounts, house officers and students complain about the ways their energies are wasted because they are inundated with scut work of various types. If procedures are to be done on time, house officers have to act as a back-up transport service. If test results are to be interpreted and patients diagnosed, then house officers have to track down the results; they are their own messenger service. In many hospitals house officers and students do the routine venipunctures and are responsible for maintaining the intravenous lines of patients requiring them. Routine bloodwork composes a large amount of the physician-in-training's everyday scut work.

Their inability to control either their own or their patients' lives, their fundamental powerlessness, and the exploitation of their labors by the "greedy" institution (Coser 1979) that is the modern academic hospital are all at the center of physicians' accounts of their training.

CLINICAL COUPS AND DEFEATS

The juxtaposition of labors that are both Herculean and pointless account for the major narrative themes in accounts of patient care. First, there are stories of "clinical coups." These are dramatic instances where the house officer's labors were not pointless, where a tricky diagnostic problem was solved and a timely and decisive intervention to save a life was initiated. Such stories are rare but all the house officer accounts, even the most bitter, tell at least one. These tales reinforce even in the face of the contradictory details of the rest of the narrative that the house officer's efforts make a difference, however small; that the pain and suffering of both doctors and patients are not invariably pointless; and that professional heroism may still yield a positive result, even if only rarely.

More numerous by far in the narratives are accounts of "clinical defeats." A few of these tales concern the apprentice physician's inability to come to the right decision quickly enough; these are personal defeats. The bulk of these tales, however, concern defeat (indexed by death) even though all the right things were done medically. Narratives of clinical defeats generally emphasize the tension in the conflict between care and cure, between quantity and quality of life, between acting as a medical scientist and acting as a human being.

The repeated accounts of clinical defeats reinforce at one level the general pointlessness of much of the house officers' effort. They recount situations in which house officers either are too overwhelmed to provide clinical care or in which the best available care does not ensure a favorable outcome. But the stories of defeat tell another tale as well. Here, house officers describe how they learn that despite the failings of their technical interventions they can make a difference, that care is often more important than cure, and that the human rewards of their medical role are great. Each of the first-hand accounts of medical training features a tale of defeat that had a transformative effect on the physician in training. Each tale of defeat encodes a lesson about the psychological growth of the human being shrouded in the white coat of scientific authority. For example, Glasser's *Ward 402* (1973) centers on the unexpected decline and death, following initial successful treatment, of an eleven-year-old girl with acute leukemia. The interaction with her angry, anxious, and oppositional parents and the futile medical struggle to overcome neurologic complications forces the protagonist to see beyond the narrow medical activism that he had been carefully taught. In the end the interim hero literally pulls the plug on the child's respirator and goes off to see the angry, drunken father vowing, this time, to listen.

PSYCHOLOGICAL DETACHMENT AND ADOLESCENT INVULNERABILITY

The shop-floor culture of house officers and students is largely a peer culture. The senior authority of faculty appears absent, at best, or disruptive and intrusive, at worst, in the first-hand narratives of clinical training. That is to say, the clinical wisdom of faculty is unavailable when house officers need it; when clinical faculty are present, they "pimp" (humiliate by questioning) house officers during rounds with questions on obscure details or order them to perform mindless tasks easily performed by those (nurses, technicians) far less educated about the pathophysiology of disease.

As a result, house officers feel isolated and embattled. Patients, other staff, and attending faculty are the enemy; each is the source of a set of never-ending demands and ego-lacerating defeats. Konner (1987, 375), an anthropologist who acquired a medical degree, is quite eloquent on the theme of the patient as enemy:

> It is obvious from what I have written here that the stress of clinical training alienates the doctor from the patient, that in a real sense the patient becomes the enemy. (Goddamit did she blow her I.V. again? Jesus Christ did he spike a temp?) At first I believed that this was an inadvertent and unfortunate concomitant of medical training, but I now think that it is intrinsic. Not only stress and sleeplessness but the sense of the patient as the cause of one's distress contributes to the doctor's detachment. This detachment is not just objective but downright negative. To cut and puncture a person, to take his or her life in your hands, to pound the chest until ribs break, to decide upon drastic action without being able to ask permission, to render a judgment about whether care should continue or stop these and a thousand other things may require something stronger than objectivity. They may actually require a measure of dislike.

This sentiment is not, of course, unique to Konner. One sociologist, writing about the socialization process in internal medicine, found negative sentiments about patients so rife that she titled her account *Getting Rid of Patients* (Mizrahi 1986).

Feelings about patients are most visibly displayed in the slang that physicians in training use to describe patients. Beyond the well-known "Gomer" (George and Dundes 1978; Leiderman and Grisso 1985), there is a highly articulated language that refers to patients in distress. Along with the slang, there is much black and "gallows" humor. This black humor is a prominent feature of Shem's (1978) *House of God.*

The slang and humor highlight the psychological and social distance between patients and those who care for them medically. This distance is best exemplified in Shem's "Law IV" of the House of God: "The patient is the one with the disease." The reverse, of course, is that the doctor does not have a problem. He or she is invulnerable. In the first-hand accounts of training, physicians' feelings of invulnerability appear and reappear. The doctors treat disease but they are rarely touched by it (save for the occasional exemplary patient with whom physicians make a psychological connection). To these young apprentice physicians, disease is rarely, if ever, personally threatening and rarely, if ever, presented as something that could happen to the physician. (Many doctors reacted with shock to Lear's (1980) account of her urologist-husband's careless and callous treatment. These readers seemed to have assumed their M.D.s protected them somehow.) Moreover, given that hospitals (outside of pediatrics and before AIDS) housed a high proportion of patients substantially older than house officers, patterns of mortality and morbidity themselves reinforced the sense of invulnerability. It is the rare patient close in age to the author who provokes distress and introspection about doctoring on the part of writers of first-hand narratives.

The fantasy of invulnerability takes on an adolescent quality when one notes the cavalier tone used to describe some of life's most awful problems and the oppositional stance taken toward patients and attending faculty. There may be something structural in this; just as adolescence is betwixt and between childhood and adulthood, the physician-in-training is likewise liminal, betwixt studenthood and professional independence.

THE COMING OF AIDS TO THE SHOP FLOOR: RISK AND THE LOSS OF INVULNERABILITY

Before AIDS entered the shop floor, physicians in training had many objections to work-place conditions. Not only that, AIDS entered a shop floor that was in the process of transformation from major political, social, organizational, and economic policy changes regarding health care. These changes have been elaborated in detail elsewhere (Light 1980; Starr 1982; Relman 1980; Mechanic 1986) and need only brief mention here. Acute illnesses, especially infectious diseases, have given way to chronic disorders. The patient population has aged greatly. There has been a relatively new public emphasis on individual responsibility for one's medical problems diet, smoking, nontherapeutic drug use, "excessive" alcohol use, exercise, etc. (Fox 1986).

Of great importance has been the redefinition of medical care as a service *like any other* in the economy with individual medical decisions subject to the kind of fiscal scrutiny applied to the purchase of automobiles or dry cleaning. Achieving reduced costs through shorter hospitalizations and other measures, however, has created more intensive scheduling for those caring for patients on the hospital's wards even if the hospital's capacity shrinks in the name of efficiency. Fewer patients are admitted to the hospital and they stay for shorter periods of time, yet more things are done to and for them, increasing the house officers' clerical, physical, and intellectual work while decreasing the opportunity for trainees to get to know their patients (Rabkin 1982; Steiner et al. 1987). The beds simply fill up with comparatively sicker, less communicative patients who need more intensive care.

All the shifts in the medical care system have changed the reality of hospital practice in ways that may not conform to the expectations of those entering the medical profession. In addition to the usual disillusionment occurring in training, the contemporary urban teaching hospital brings fewer opportunities for hope (Glick 1988). To the extent that AIDS contributes to the population of more desperately ill hospitalized patients, it exacerbates house officers' feelings of exploitation and, because of its fatal outcome, AIDS adds to their sense of powerlessness. We must assess the impact of AIDS against this background of old resentments and new burdens.

AIDS has certainly not improved the work climate of the medical shop floor. The most apparent phenomenon related to AIDS in the contemporary urban teaching hospital is risk or, more precisely, the *perception* of risk. The orthodox medical literature proclaims, over and over, that the AIDS virus does not pass readily from patient to care giver (Lifson et al. 1986; Gerberding et al. 1987). But some medical writing dwells on risks (Gerbert et al. 1988; Becker, Cone, and Gerberding 1989; O'Connor 1990) and observations of behavior make clear that fear on the wards is rampant. Workers of all types, including doctors, have at times sheathed themselves in inappropriate armor or simply refused to approach the patients at all. Klass (1987, 185) put it quite starkly: "We have to face the fact that we are going through these little rituals of sanitary precaution partly because we are terrified of this disease and are not willing to listen to anything our own dear medical profession may tell us about how it actually is or is not transmitted."

Perceptions of risk can and do change with time and experience. Our interviewees and commentators in the literature indicate that as individuals and institutions have more patients with AIDS they begin to shed some of their protective garb. In one hospital we were told that the practice of donning gown, gloves, and masks became less frequent as doctors, nurses, housekeepers, and dietary workers "saw" that they did not get AIDS from their patients. This, of course, raises another interesting question: In what sense did personnel come to this conclusion? After all, the diseases associated with HIV infection typically have long latencies, up to several years, before symptoms develop. None of the institutions where our informants worked conducted routine surveillance to assess development of HIV antibody among personnel. Thus, staff could not really know if they had "gotten" HIV infection. Moreover, reports of individual physicians anxiously awaiting the results of HIV tests after needle sticks have now become a staple of the oral culture of academic medical centers.

On AIDS wards all personnel are far less likely to place barriers between themselves and patients for activities where blood or other body fluids might be transmitted. Beyond subspecialty units, however, medical, nursing, and support staff are far more fearful and employ many more nonrational techniques to prevent contamination. (We refer to simple touching, as in noninvasive patient examinations, back rubs, etc., as well as activities involving no patient contact at all, such as the placing of meal trays on overbed tables or sweeping the floor.) One informant told us that HIV-infected hemophilia patients in one hospital often refuse hospitalization if it means getting a room on certain floors or nursing units. The patients prefer to delay needed treatment until a bed becomes available on a unit where they feel more humanely treated.

Several other curious phenomena have emerged regarding risks and AIDS in the medical work place. While in some locations lack of experience has led to classic reactions of fear and avoidance, in other places the paucity of experience permits denial to dominate. The comments of house staff in a hospital with only an occasional AIDS patient indicated that few residents followed Centers for Disease Control or similar guidelines for "universal precautions." Various explanations were offered, including the conviction that starting intravenous infusions, blood drawing, or similar procedures is more difficult when wearing gloves. When asked how surgeons accomplish complex manual tasks while wearing one or two pairs of gloves, residents usually replied that they had not learned to do things "that way." Here, one kind of inexperience (with gloves) reinforces another (with AIDS), bolstering the feeling of invulnerability that was widespread before AIDS.

Some medical students and physicians have dealt with the problem of risk globally. They want to avoid encountering patients with AIDS altogether. In one medical school where we teach, there is a policy prohibiting students from refusing to care for HIV-infection patients. The policy infuriates many students, a fact we learned in medical-ethics discussion groups that met to discuss an AIDS case. They cited several reasons. The rules, some felt, were changed midstream. Had they known about the policy, they might have chosen another school. They felt they had no role in the formation of the policy and that the tremendous economic investment they made in the institution, in the form of tuition, entitles them to some decision-making authority. They objected to the rule's existence. They said such rules have no place in medicine. Doctors, they believe, should have as much freedom as lawyers, accountants, executives, or others to accept or reject "clients" or "customers."

When presented with the notion of a professional obligation or duty, based upon generally acknowledged moral precepts, they balked. At other institutions we know there has been more controversy among medical students, with some making impassioned statements about the physician's obligation to treat. In this debate we see AIDS as a total social phenomenon acting as a vehicle for debating and defining standards of professional conduct.

Another aspect of medical risk avoidance may be revealed through the changing patterns of residency selection. For some time there has been a shift away from primary care specialties like internal medicine, family practice, and pediatrics toward specialties such as orthopedics, ophthalmology, otolaryngology, and radiology (McCarty 1987). The reasons for this phenomena are not entirely clear, but include the technical, rather than personal, orientation of the medical training system and the higher compensation available in the latter group of specialties, sought, in part, because of staggering educational debts. In the past few years, the trend may have accelerated, with internal medicine (whose house staff and practitioners provide the bulk of the care for AIDS patients) training programs failing to find sufficient qualified applicants (Graettianger 1989; Davidoff 1989). This crisis has been most marked in the cities with large numbers of HIV-infected patients (Ness et al. 1989). A similar trend toward avoiding residencies in AIDS endemic areas may be emerging in pediatrics, according to faculty rumors; a substantial proportion of pediatric house officers, like those in internal medicine, would not care for AIDS patients if given the choice, according to one survey (Link et al. 1988). (This does not imply that defenses such as denial and risk avoidance were not part of the medical educational culture prior to AIDS. Indeed, denial is at the center of the syndrome of adolescent invulnerability. Distinctive now is the appearance of such sentiments in professional journals.)

SURGICAL RISK AND HISTORICAL PRECEDENT

Even more remarkable in the AIDS-risk reaction has been the appearance in prestigious medical journals of complaints, whines, and pleas for understanding from doctors worried about contamination and ruination (Guy 1987; Ponsford 1987; Dudley and Sim 1988; Carey 1988; Guido 1988). These pieces offer various estimates of risk to person, career, family, future patients deprived of the skills of the author or his or her esteemed colleagues, and other justifications for not treating HIV-infected persons. (At last, the attending authors may have forged an alliance with their house officers by championing the cause of self-protection.) The articles proclaim a kind of anticoup, that is, they are declarations of futility, contrasting sharply with the verbal swaggering of pre-AIDS narratives. It is important to note that the medical literature on AIDS is not entirely negative; complaints can be matched against calls to duty (Gillon 1987; Zuger and Miles 1987; Pellegrino 1987; Kim and Perfect 1988; Friedland 1988; Emanuel 1988; Sharp 1988; Peterson 1989). On the shop floor and in the literature, AIDS as a total social phenomenon has become the lens for focusing on the obligations of members of the medical profession.

Surgeons have been particularly outspoken about the extent to which they are threatened, and there *is* reason for their special concerns (Hagen, Meyer, and Pauker 1988; Peterson 1989). After all, these doctors have a high likelihood of contact with the blood of patients. This involves not just working in blood-perfused tissues, but also a risk of having gloves and skin punctured by the instruments of their craft or having blood splash onto other vulnerable areas of the body (mucous membranes in professional parlance). Surgeons, by the very nature of their work, do more of this than many other doctors. But other physicians do find themselves in similar circumstances, depending on their activities. Intensive-care specialists, invasive cardiologists, emergency physicians, pulmonary and gastrointestinal specialists, and others have frequent and/or sustained contact with the blood or other body fluids of patients who may be infected with HIV. House staff, as the foot soldiers doing comprehensive examinations, drawers of blood specimens, inserters of intravenous catheters or other tubes in other places, cleaners of wounds, or simply as those first on the scene of bloody disasters, are particularly likely to be splashed, splattered, or otherwise coated with patients' blood, secretions, or excretions.

We do not have data on the extent to which fears have or have not been translated into changes in behavior in operating and/or procedure rooms. In some communities there may now be fewer operations and these procedures may take longer as extra time is taken to reduce bleeding and avoid punctures. This may not turn out to be as good as it might at first seem. To the extent that high-risk patients have operations delayed or denied or must undergo longer anesthetics and have wounds open longer, patient care may be compromised.

It is interesting to compare the current outcry with what happened when medical science discovered the nature of hepatitis and recognized the medical risks to personnel of serum hepatitis, now known as hepatitis B. As long ago as 1949 (Liebowitz et al. 1949), the medical literature acknowledged that medical personnel coming in contact with blood stood at risk from hepatitis. A debate continued through the 1950s, 1960s, and early 1970s about whether surgeons were especially vulnerable because of their use of sharp instruments, the frequency of accidental puncture of the skin during surgical procedures, and the likelihood of inoculation of the virus into the bloodstream of the wounded party. The risks were felt to be clearly documented in an article (Rosenberg et al. 1973) in the *Journal of the American Medical Association* that commented: "This study demonstrates the distinct occupational hazard to surgeons when they operate on patients who are capable of transmitting hepatitis virus. . . . We believe that serious attempts should be made to prevent future epidemics. . . . Education and constant vigilance in surgical technique are central to any preventive program." Nowhere does the article suggest surgeons should consider not operating on patients at risk for hepatitis.

Of course, hepatitis B is not associated with a fatal prognosis in a large proportion of cases and is not entirely comparable to AIDS. Nonetheless, the epidemiologic evidence gathered in the 1970s suggested that hepatitis B was very prevalent among physicians, especially surgeons (Denes et al. 1978), and that medical personnel seemed especially vulnerable to having severe courses of the disease (Garibaldi et al. 1973). A portion become chronic carriers of the virus, with the added risk later of liver cancer and liver failure from cirrhosis. Moreover, secondary spread from infected medical workers can occur to patients (through small cuts and sores on the workers' skin) and sexual partners (through exchange of bodily fluids). Despite all this, major medical journals did not carry discussions of whether doctors at risk might be excused from professional activities. It may be that our society's general risk aversiveness (Fairlie 1989) and tolerance of self-centeredness have escalated sufficiently to make public renunciation of professional responsibility more acceptable. More likely, the general medical professional ethic has changed to one closer to that of the entrepreneur, as was true for our students. But perhaps something else is going on that, being synergistic with the perceived loss of invulnerability brought on by AIDS, makes the AIDS era distinctive.

AIDS AS A TOTAL SOCIAL PHENOMENON

The reaction to AIDS on the shop floor must be examined in light of the perceptions of risk, the epidemiology of AIDS, and moral judgments some make about activities that lead to acquiring the disease. Most AIDS patients have come from identifiable populations: the gay community, intravenous drug users and their partners, and those who have gotten the disease from medical use of blood and blood products. While hepatitis B infections were prevalent in these populations and also entailed risks to medical personnel, hepatitis in such patients did not cause doctors to deny their professional responsibility to provide treatment. We are arguing that the unique combination of factors associated with AIDS prompts the negative reactions among doctors: changing tolerances of risk, the shift to an occupation bounded by entrepreneurial rules rather than professional duties, a specific fear of the terrible outcome should one acquire AIDS from a patient, objections to some of the specific behaviors that lead to AIDS, and class and racial bias. Below, we discuss some of the social characteristics of AIDS patients that affect the negativity of the professionals.

The demographics of AIDS is striking and flies rudely in the face of the last several decades of medical progress. Most AIDS patients are young adults. This is true of gays, drug users, and even the hemophiliacs, by and large. Most house officers, however naive and unprepared they are to confront devastating illness and death, at least have a general cultural and social expectation of, if not experience with, the death of old people. With AIDS, many of the sickest patients filling teaching hospital wards in high-prevalence cities are in their prime years, similar in age to the house staff providing the front-line care (Glick 1988). People so young are not supposed to die. These deaths challenge the ideology of the coming-if-not-quite-arrived triumph of modern medical science implicitly provided young doctors in medical education. (Two former house officers have written about the effects of AIDS on medical training: Wachter 1986; Zuger 1987.)

We do not want to paint with too broad a brush here. There are some important differences among the groups of AIDS patients, which influence the reactions of resident physicians. Our informants describe three nonexhaustive groups of patients to whom young doctors and students react: hemophiliacs and others who acquired AIDS through transfusion, young gay men, and drug users and their partners. (We have insufficient information to comment on the reaction to the rapidly growing infant AIDS population. Also, we cannot fully assess how attitudes toward any of these groups may have changed from the pre-AIDS era. Clearly, some in the health care system treated gays and IV drug users badly before they perceived a threat from them.)

In many ways, the patients who develop AIDS from blood products constitute a simple set. These patients are clearly seen as innocents, true victims of unfortunate but inevitable delay between recognition of a technical problem bloodborne transmission of a serious disease and its reliable and practical prevention cleaning up of the blood supply. A chief resident commented that her house officers talk differently about patients with AIDS caused by transfusions from the way they speak about other AIDS patients. "The residents see these cases [with blood-product-related disease] as more tragic; their hearts go out to them more." Hemophiliacs have an air of double tragedy about them: an often crippling, always inconvenient genetic disorder made worse as a direct consequence of their medical treatment.

Hemophiliac patients with AIDS in one of the hospitals where we made inquiries went out of their way to make the origins of their disease or other emblems of their identity known. These patients "display" wives and children to differentiate themselves from homosexual patients. One hemophiliac, reflecting on his desire to have others know that his HIV-positive status preceded his drug abuse, commented that this public knowledge was important because there is "always a pecking order" in who gets scarce nursing care. Even though few people hold these patients in any way responsible for their disease, behavior on the wards toward HIV-positive hemophiliacs clearly differs from attention given non-AIDS or non-HIV-infected patients. As mentioned earlier, their hospital rooms are not as clean as the rooms of hemophiliac patients not infected with HIV; the staff does not touch them as often as they once did. (Many of these patients were frequently hospitalized before the HIV epidemic; in effect, they have served as their own controls in a cruel experiment of nature.) Their care is compromised in small but painful ways.

Gay patients with AIDS occupy an intermediate position in the hierarchy. The social characteristics of many of these patients, in the eyes of our informants, were positive ones: the patients were well educated, well groomed, took an active interest in their treatments, had supportive family and/or networks that relieved some of the burdens from their care providers, and the like. Of course, not all medical personnel appreciate all of these features. Interest in care has emerged into social activism about treatment, which some physicians resent. For example, one patient who had developed severe difficulty swallowing, and was starving as a consequence, requested insertion of a feeding tube through his abdominal wall into his intestinal tract. His primary physicians tried to put him off, apparently believing he would succumb soon, no matter what was done. When he persisted, a surgical consultant was called. The surgeon initially treated the request as a joke, finally agreed after an attempt to dissuade the patient ("So, you really want to do this?"), and then provided no follow-up care.

This is but one case, but our general impression is that the "turfing" (transferring) that Shem (1978) described as a major feature of shop-floor culture before AIDS has intensified. Physicians want to shift the burdens and responsibilities of care to others.

From the resident's point of view, there may also be a down side to the extensive support systems many gay patients enjoy. In the final stages of AIDS, little more can be done for patients beyond providing comfort. For the interested and compassionate resident, titration of pain medication and less technical interaction, that is, talking with the patient, can be therapeutic for both. If the patient has become invested in alternative treatments for discomfort, from herbal medicine to medication to imaging, and if the patient is surrounded by loving family and community, the house officer may feel she or he has nothing whatsoever to contribute. This helplessness amplifies the despair and the pointlessness of whatever scut work must be done. Here, there can be no transforming, heroic intervention, no redemption arising from clinical defeat.

The IV-drug-using HIV-infected patients represent one of the fastest growing and most problematic set of patients. Teaching hospitals have always had more than their share of patients who are "guilty" victims of disease, that is, patients whose medical problems are seen as direct consequences of their behavior. Many of our prestigious teaching hospitals have been municipal or county facilities filled with substance-abusing patients with a wide spectrum of problems from which house staff have learned. Our informants suggested that the coming of AIDS to this population had subtly altered the way these patients are regarded. Now, drug users cannot be regarded with mere contempt or simple disrespect: there is fear among doctors who are afraid of acquiring AIDS from the patients. Whereas frustration and anger in some cases (especially when drug users were manipulative or physically threatening) and indifference in others used to constitute much of the response to drug-using patients, fear of AIDS has added a difficult dimension.

One might argue that before HIV, this underclass population had a set of positive social roles to play. Their very presence reminded doctors and nurses, perhaps even other patients, that things might not be as bad as they seemed. The intern might be miserable after staying up an entire weekend, but she/he could look to a better life ahead and know that she/he did not have to face homelessness and desperate poverty when finally leaving the hospital to rest. Moreover, the underclass patients provided chances to learn and practice that private patients could not offer. (The poor often have more complex or advanced medical problems, compared with wealthier patients, because of limited access to care and delays in diagnosis and treatment. In addition, attendings often permit house staff to exercise greater responsibility with "service" patients.) But AIDS seems to have changed the balance for many who might have tolerated or welcomed the opportunities to care for the underserved. For a medical student contemplating a residency, what was previously a chance to gain relative autonomy quickly in an institution with many substance-abusing patients may have become predominantly unwelcome exposure to a dreadful illness. If this is so, AIDS will trigger, in yet another way, a dreadful decline in the availability and quality of care for America's medical underclass.

CONCLUSION

The full impact of AIDS on the modern system of medical care will not be clear for many years. Nevertheless, the disease has already affected the culture of American medicine in a pivotal place: the urban teaching center. Already a scene beset with anger, pain, sadness, and high technology employed soullessly against disease, AIDS has added to the troubles. We cannot know for certain whether this new plague has contributed to the decline in interest in medicine as a career or to the flight from primary care. There is certainly no evidence that AIDS has prompted many to seek out a life of selfless dedication to tending the hopelessly ill.

For those who have chosen to train in hospitals with large numbers of AIDS patients, the disease has added to the burdens of the shop floor. The perception of risk of acquiring AIDS has undermined one of the best-established defenses house officers have relied on: the maintenance of an air of invulnerability. Some doctors are so scared they are abandoning their traditional duty and no longer seem able or willing to try to bring off the heroic coup against daunting clinical odds. To be sure, this fear is fed by other factors on the social scene: the economic changes in medicine, transforming the profession into the province of the entrepreneur; the youth and other characteristics of many AIDS patients; and the willingness of the entire society to turn away from the underclass, especially from those who are seen as self-destructive.

Nothing here suggests that AIDS will spark a turn to a kinder, gentler medical care system. Those in the educational system inclined to seek models providing compassionate medical care will likely find few attractive mentors. Instead, they will meet burned-out martyrs, steely-eyed technicians, and teachers filled with fear. Tomorrow's first-hand accounts of medical education and fictionalized autobiographies may, as a result, be even grimmer than yesterday's.

There is the possibility that this conclusion is too stark, too depressing. For those desperate for a more hopeful scenario, at least one other alternative suggests itself. As the numbers of medical students dwindle, perhaps those who enter will be more committed to ideals of professional service and, among those, some will enter with a missionary zeal for caring for AIDS patients. There is little to suggest this other than the portraits of the few heroic physicians one finds in Shilts's (1987) account of the early years of the AIDS epidemic. If these physicians inspire a new generation of medical professionals, then the tone of future first-hand accounts will be more in line with the highest ideals and aspirations of the medical profession.

NOTE

The listing of the authors reflects the alphabet rather than the efforts of the contributors. This is in every sense an equal collaboration. The authors gratefully acknowledge the contributions of our informants, who must remain nameless. Helpful comments on earlier drafts were made by Robert Arnold and Harold Bershady.

REFERENCES

Becker, H. 1967. Whose Side Are We On? *Social Problems* 14:239–47.

Becker, C.E., J.E. Cone and J. Gerberding. 1989. Occupational Infection with Human Immunodeficiency Virus (HIV): Risks and Risk Reduction. *Annals of Internal Medicine* 110:653–56.

Becker, H., B. Geer, E.C. Hughes, and A. Strauss. 1961. *Boys in White: Student Culture in Medical School.* Chicago: University of Chicago Press.

Bell, D. 1975. *A Time To Be Born.* New York: Dell.

Bosk, C. 1979. *Forgive and Remember: Managing Medical Failure.* Chicago: University of Chicago Press.

———. 1985. Social Controls and Physicians: The Oscillation of Cynicism and Idealism in Sociological Theory. In *Social Controls and the Medical Profession,* ed. J.P. Swazey and S.R. Scherr, 31–52. Boston: Oelgeschlager, Gunn and Hain.

Burkett, G., and K. Knafl. 1974. Judgment and Decision-making in a Medical Specialty. *Sociology of Work and Occupations* 1:82–109.

Carey, J.S. 1988. Routine Preoperative Screening for HIV (Letter to the Editor). *Journal of the American Medical Association* 260:179.

Cook, R. 1972. *The Year of the Intern.* New York: Harcourt Brace Jovanovich.

Coombs, R.H. 1978. *Mastering Medicine: Professional Socialization of Medical School.* New York: Free Press.

Coser, L. 1974. *Greedy Institutions: Patterns of Undivided Commitment.* New York: Free Press.

Coser, R.L. 1979. *Training in Ambiguity: Learning through Doing in a Mental Hospital.* New York: Free Press.

Davidoff, F. 1989. Medical Residencies: Quantity or Quality? *Annals of Internal Medicine* 110:757–58.

Denes, A.E., J.L. Smith, J.E. Maynard, I.L. Doto, K.R. Berquist, and A.J. Finkel. 1978. Hepatitis B Infection in Physicians: Results of a Nationwide Seroepidemiologic Survey. *Journal of the American Medical Association* 239:210–12.

Dudley, H.A.F., and A. Sim. 1988. AIDS: A Bill of Rights for the Surgical Team? *British Medical Journal* 296:1449–50.

Emanuel, E.J. 1988. Do Physicians Have an Obligation to Treat Patients with AIDS? *New England Journal of Medicine* 318:1686–90.

Fairlie, H. 1989. Fear of Living: America's Morbid Aversion to Risk. *New Republic* January 23:14–19.

Fox, D. 1986. AIDS and the American Health Polity: The History and Prospects of a Crisis of Authority. *Milbank Quarterly* 64 (suppl. 1):7–33.

Fox, R.C. 1957. Training for Uncertainty. In *The Student-Physician: Introductory Studies in the Sociology of Medical Education,* ed. R.K. Merton, G.C. Reader, and P.L. Kendall, 207–41. Cambridge: Harvard University Press.

Fox, R.C., and H. Lief. 1963. Training for "Detached Concern" in Medical Students. In *The Psychological Basis of Medical Practice,* ed. H. Lief, V. Lief, and N. Lief, 12–35. New York: Harper and Row.

Friedland, G. 1988. AIDS and Compassion. *Journal of the American Medical Association* 259:2898–99.

Garibaldi, R.A., J.N. Forrest, J.A. Bryan, B.F. Hanson, and W.E. Dismukes. 1973. Hemodialysis-Associated Hepatitis. *Journal of the American Medical Association* 225:384–89.

George, V., and A. Dundes. 1978. The Gomer: A Figure of American Hospital Folk Speech. *Journal of American Folklore* 91:568–81.

Gerberding, J.L., C.E. Bryant-LeBlanc, K. Nelson, A.R. Moss, D. Osmond, H.F. Chambers, J.R. Carlson, W.L. Drew, J.A. Levy, and M.A. Sande. 1987. Risk of Transmitting the Human Immunodeficiency Virus, Cytomegalovirus, and Hepatitis B Virus to Health Care Workers Exposed to Patients with AIDS and AIDS-related Conditions. *Journal of Infectious Diseases* 156:1–8.

Gerbert, B., B. Maguire, V. Badner, D. Altman, and G. Stone. 1988. Why Fear Persists: Health Care Professionals and AIDS. *Journal of the American Medical Association* 260:3481–83.

Gillon, R. 1987. Refusal to Treat AIDS and HIV Positive Patients. *British Medical Journal* 294:1332–33.

Glasser, R.J. 1973. *Ward 402.* New York: George Braziller.

Glick, S.M. 1988. The Impending Crisis in Internal Medicine Training Programs. *American Journal of Medicine* 84:929–32.

Graettinger, J.S. 1989. Internal Medicine in the National Resident Matching Program 1978–1989. *Annals of Internal Medicine* 110:682.

Guido, L.J. 1988. Routine Preoperative Screening for HIV (Letter to the Editor). *Journal of the American Medical Association* 260:180.

Guy, P.J. 1987. AIDS: A Doctor's Duty. *British Medical Journal* 294–445.

Hagen, M.D., K.B. Meyer, and S.G. Pauker. 1988. Routine Preoperative Screening for HIV: Does the Risk to the Surgeon Outweigh the Risk to the Patient? *Journal of the American Medical Association* 259:1357–59.

Haseltine, F., and Y. Yaw. 1976. *Woman Doctor: The Internship of a Modern Woman.* Boston: Houghton Mifflin.

Horowitz, S., and N. Offen. 1977. *Calling Dr. Horowitz.* New York: William Morrow.

Hughes, E.C. 1971. *The Sociological Eye: Selected Papers on Work, Self, and Society.* Chicago: Aldine-Atherton.

Hyde, L. 1979. *The Gift: Imagination and the Erotic Life of Property.* New York: Vintage Books.

Kim, J.H., and J.R. Perfect. 1988. To Help the Sick: An Historical and Ethical Essay Concerning the Refusal to Care for Patients with AIDS. *American Journal of Medicine* 84:135–38.

Klass, P. 1987. *A Not Entirely Benign Procedure: Four Years as a Medical Student.* New York: Putnam.

Klein, K. 1981. *Getting Better: A Medical Student's Story.* Boston: Little, Brown.

Konner, M. 1987. *Becoming a Doctor: A Journey of Initiation in Medical School.* New York: Viking.

Lear, M.W. 1980. *Heartsounds.* New York: Pocket Books.

LeBaron, C. 1981. *Gentle Vengeance: An Account of the First Year at Harvard Medical School.* New York: Richard Marek.

Liebowitz, S., L. Greenwald, I. Cohen, and J. Lirwins. 1949. Serum Hepatitis in a Blood Bank Worker. *Journal of the American Medical Association* 140(17):1331–33.

Liederman, D., and J. Grisso. 1985. The Gomer Phenomenon. *Journal of Health and Social Behavior* 26:222–31.

Lifson, A.R., K.G. Castro, E. McCray, and H.W. Jaffe. 1986. National Surveillance of AIDS in Health Care Workers. *Journal of the American Medical Association* 265:3231–34.

Light, D. 1980. *Becoming Psychiatrists: The Professional Transformation of Self.* New York: W.W. Norton.

Link, R.N., A.R. Feingold, M.H. Charap, K. Freeman, and S.P. Shelov. 1988. Concerns of Medical and Pediatric House Officers about Acquiring AIDS from Their Patients. *American Journal of Public Health* 78:455–59.

McCarty, D.J. 1987. Why Are Today's Medical Students Choosing High-technology Specialties over Internal Medicine? *New England Journal of Medicine* 317:567–69.

Mechanic, D. 1986. *From Advocacy to Allocation: The Evolving American Health Care System.* New York: Free Press.

Miller, S.J. 1970. *Prescription for Leadership: Training for the Medical Elite.* Chicago: Aldine.

Millman, M. 1977. *The Unkindest Cut: Life in the Backrooms of Medicine.* New York: William Morrow.

Mizrahi, T. 1986. *Getting Rid of Patients: Contradictions in the Socialization of Physicians.* New Brunswick: Rutgers University Press.

Morgan, E. 1980. *The Making of a Woman Surgeon.* New York: G.P. Putnam.

Mullan, F. 1976. *White Coat, Clenched Fist: The Political Education of an American Physician.* New York: Macmillan.

Mumford, E. 1970. *Interns: From Students to Physicians.* Cambridge: Harvard University Press.

Ness, R., C.D. Killian, D.E. Ness, J.B. Frost, and D. McMahon. 1989. Likelihood of Contact with AIDS Patients as a Factor in Medical Students' Residency Selections. *Academic Medicine* 64:588–94.

Nolen, W. 1970. *The Making of a Surgeon.* New York: Random House.

O'Connor, T.W. 1990. Do Patients Have the Right to Infect Their Doctors? *Australia and New Zealand Journal of Surgery* 60:157–62.

Pellegrino, E.D. 1987. Altruism, Self-interest, and Medical Ethics. *Journal of the American Medical Association* 258:1939–40.

Peterson, L.M. 1989. AIDS: The Ethical Dilemma for Surgeons. *Law, Medicine, and Health Care* 17 (Summer):139–44.

Ponsford, G. 1987. AIDS in the OR: A Surgeon's View. *Canadian Medical Association Journal* 137: 1036–39.

Rabkin, M. 1982. The SAG Index. *New England Journal of Medicine* 307:1350–51.

Reilly, P. 1987. *To Do No Harm: A Journey through Medical School.* Dover, Mass.: Auburn House.

Relman, A.S. 1980. The New Medical-Industrial Complex. *New England Journal of Medicine* 303: 963–70.

Rosenberg, J.L., D.P. Jones, L.R. Lipitz, and J.B. Kirsner. 1973. Viral Hepatitis: An Occupational Hazard to Surgeons. *Journal of the American Medical Association* 223:395–400.

Rubin, T.I. 1972. *Emergency Room Diary.* New York: Grosset and Dunlap.

Scully, D. 1980. *Men Who Control Women's Health.* Boston: Houghton Mifflin.

Sharp, S.C. 1988. The Physician's Obligation to Treat AIDS Patients. *Southern Medical Journal* 81: 1282–85.

Shem, S. 1978. *The House of God.* New York: Richard Marek.

Shilts, R. 1987. *And the Band Played On.* New York: St. Martins.

Starr, P. 1982. *The Social Transformations of American Medicine.* New York: Basic Books.

Steiner, J.F., L.E. Feinberg, A.M. Kramer, and R.L. Byyny. 1987. Changing Patterns of Disease on an Inpatient Medical Service: 1961–62 to 1981–82. *American Journal of Medicine* 83:331–35.

Stelling, J., and R. Bucher. 1972. Autonomy and Monitoring on Hospital Wards. *Sociological Quarterly* 13:431–47.

Sweeney, III. W. 1973. *Woman's Doctor: A Year in the Life of an Obstetrician-Gynecologist.* New York: Morrow.

Wachter, R.M. 1986. The Impact of the Acquired Immunodeficiency Syndrome on Medical Residency Training. *New England Journal of Medicine* 314: 177–80.

X, Dr. 1965. *Intern.* New York: Harper and Row.

Zuger, A. 1987. AIDS on the Wards: A Residency in Medical Ethics. *Hastings Center Report* 17(3): 16–20.

Zuger, A., and S.H. Miles. 1987. Physicians, AIDS, and Occupational Risk: Historical Traditions and Ethical Obligations. *Journal of the American Medical Association* 258:1924–28.

Medical Industries

The medical industries have "commodified" health in a number of ways. They have turned certain goods and services into products or commodities that can be marketed to meet "health needs" created by the industry itself. A recent and commonplace example of "commodification" was the promotion of Listerine as a cure for the "disease" of "halitosis" (bad breath). A wide range of products have been marketed to meet commodified health needs, such as products designed to alleviate feminine hygiene "problems" and instant milk formulas to meet the "problem" of feeding infants.

In the late twentieth century, medical care is a profitable investment, at least for stockholders and corporations. With the increase in medical technology and the growth of for-profit hospitals, medicine itself is becoming a corporate industry. The 1960s saw the rise of a large nursing home industry (Vladeck, 1980); in the 1970s, there were huge increases in investment in for-profit hospital chains; and in the 1980s, new free-standing emergency rooms began to dot the suburban landscape. The 1990s saw the expansion of corporatized HMOs and medical complexes. The nonprofit, and especially the public, sector of medicine has decreased while the for-profit sector continues to increase. The closing of many urban, public hospitals is a piece of this change (Sager, 1983). As Starr (1982) notes, the corporatization of medicine presents a threat to the long-standing physician sovereignty. This is part of a shift of power in medicine from the "professional monopolists" (AMA physicians) to the "corporate rationalizers" (Alford, 1972).

Technology has long been central to medicine. In recent years, medical technology has become a major industry. Innovations such as CT scanners, hemodialysis machines, electronic fetal monitors, and neonatal infant care units have transformed medical care. Those medical technologies contribute significantly to the increasing costs of medical care, although these are usually justified by claims of saving lives or reducing maladies. But medical technologies usually are adopted before they are adequately tested and become "standard procedures" without sufficient evidence of their efficacy (McKinlay, 1981). This proliferation of medical technology is expensive and often unnecessary. While medical technology is often useful, it changes the relationships among its users (Timmermans, 2003) and sometimes its application becomes on and in itself. It is doubtful that every hospital needs a CT scanner, a cardiac care unit, or an open heart surgery suite, but most states have exerted little control over the spread or such technology. Further, the medical technological imperative of "can do, should do" has frequently bypassed issues of cost-effectiveness or efficacy. The dominance and reliance on medical technology has been termed "biomedicalization" and is discussed in detail in selection 39; see also "Dilemmas of Medical Technology," the final section of Part 2.

The selections in this section examine two predominant examples of change in the medical industries: increasing corporate control of medical care and expanding medical technology. The selections show the importance of the profit motive in the growth of medical industry; the authors see real problems with the increases in profit-making medical care. In a sense, medical care itself is becoming more overtly commodified.

In the first selection, Arnold S. Relman, a physician and former editor of the prestigious *New England Journal of Medicine,* examines the growth of the for-profit health care industry. He reviews the expansion of the commercialization of health care since 1980, when his classic article on "the new medical industrial complex" first focused attention on this development. Relman finds that while the growth of for-profit hospital chains has slowed, many other aspects of the medical–industrial complex are increasing rapidly with revenues now encompassing over 20 percent of our health care expenditures. Moreover, voluntary ("nonprofit") hospitals now also see themselves as businesses and are becoming more entrepreneurial. The orientation of hospitals and medical care institutions is changing from social service to business and shifting in focus from altruism to the bottom line. Advertising health services and "product" competition are now common. The roots of the commercialization of medical care are in the uncontrolled third-party reimbursement system. Little evidence exists as yet that patients benefit more from "for-profit" care and some evidence indicates that they do not (Gray, 1991). For-profit health care puts the incentives in the wrong place on profitability instead of on necessary care. Thus it is very doubtful that corporatization and profit-making of health care are in the public interest.

The pharmaceutical industry has grown enormously in the past few decades. Medications like Prozac and Viagra (and similar drugs they have spawned) have incredibly wide usage and have become everyday terms in our culture. Blockbuster drugs like these bring in billions of dollars for the pharmaceutical companies. In recent years, direct-to-consumer advertising, especially on television, has expanded the markets for a range of medications. Virtually everyone recognizes the "little purple pill" and "Ask your doctor if Viagra is right for you." Drug companies spend about 35% of their income on marketing and administration, much more than they spend on research for new drugs to treat diseases (Relman and Angell, 2002). In "Medications and the Pharmaceutical Industry," David Cohen and his colleagues examine drugs as a social phenomenon, using a framework of "the life cycle of medications." Pharmaceuticals are a part of our particular social and cultural systems. The authors illustrate the social aspects of pharmaceuticals by focusing on the growth and the use of psychoactive medications, especially with children. They also show how innovations in marketing practices and the Internet are changing the social nature of medications. Pharmaceuticals are a part of our social and cultural systems; they reflect it and in turn, affect our cultural values as well. They are among the most profitable aspects of medicine, with the pharmaceutical companies seeking to create and expand their markets. While some treatments are clearly useful, this can also lead to the further medicalization of life (see the two selections in The Medicalization of Society section).

REFERENCES

Alford, Robert L. 1972. "The political economy of health care: Dynamics without changes." Politics and Society. Winter: 127–64.

Bell, Susan. 1985. "A new model of medical technology development: A case study of DES." In Julius Roth and Sheryl Ruzek (eds.), The Adoption and Social Consequences of Medical Technology (Research in the Sociology of Health Care, Volume 4). Greenwich, CT: JAI Press.

Gray, Bradford H. 1991. The Profit Motive and Patient Care: The Changing Accountability of Doctors and Hospitals. Cambridge, MA: Harvard University Press.

McKinlay, John B. 1981. "From 'promising report' to 'standard procedure': Seven stages in the career of a medical innovation." Milbank Memorial Fund Quarterly/Health and Society. 59: 374–411.

Relman, Arnold S., and Marcia Angell. 2002. "America's other drug problem: How the drug industry distorts medicine and politics." The New Republic. December 16:27–41.

Sager, Alan. 1983. "The reconfiguration of urban hospital care: 1937–1980." In Ann Lennarson Greer and Scott Greer (eds.), Cities and Sickness: Health Care in Urban America. Urban Affairs Annual Review, Volume 26, Chapter 3. Beverly Hills, CA: Sage.

Starr, Paul. 1982. The Social Transformation of American Medicine. New York: Basic Books.

Timmermans, Stefan. 2003. "The practice of medical technology." Sociology of Health and Illness, 25: 97–114.

Vladeck, Bruce. 1980. Unloving Care: The Nursing Home Tragedy. New York: Basic Books.

24 *The Health Care Industry: Where Is It Taking Us?*

Arnold S. Relman

Eleven years ago, in the Annual Discourse presented before the Massachusetts Medical Society and later published in the *New England Journal of Medicine,*[1] I first addressed the issue of commercialism in medical care. Referring to what I called "the new medical-industrial complex," I described a huge new industry that was supplying health care services for profit. It included proprietary hospitals and nursing homes, diagnostic laboratories, home care and emergency room services, renal hemodialysis units, and a wide variety of other medical services that had formerly been provided largely by public or private not-for-profit community-based institutions or by private physicians in their offices. The medical-industrial complex had developed mainly as a response to the entrepreneurial opportunities afforded by the expansion of health insurance coverage offering indemnification through Medicare and employment-based plans. Given the open-ended, piecework basis of third-party payment, business ownership of a medical facility virtually guaranteed a profit, provided that practicing physicians could be persuaded to use the facility and that services were limited to fully insured patients.

At that time, I estimated that the new medical-industrial complex had revenues of perhaps $35 to $40 billion, which would have been about 17 to 19 percent of total health expenditures for the calendar year 1979, and I was concerned about the possible consequences of the continued growth of the complex. I suggested that its marketing and advertising strategies might lead to high costs and widespread overuse of medical resources; that it might overemphasize expensive technology and neglect less profitable personal care, that it might skim off paying patients, leaving the poor and uninsured to an increasingly burdened not-for-profit sector; and that it might come to exercise undue influence on national health policy and the attitude of physicians toward their profession. I suggested that physicians should avoid all financial ties with the medical-industrial complex in order to be free to continue acting as unbiased protectors of their patients' interests and critical evaluators of new products and services. Finally, I recommended that the new health care industry be studied carefully to determine whether it was providing services of acceptable quality at reasonable prices and to ensure that it was not having adverse effects on the rest of the American health care system.

Two years later, in a lecture at the University of North Carolina,[2] I expressed increasing concern about the future of medical practice in the new medical marketplace. I said,

> The key question is: Will medicine now become essentially a business or will it remain a profession? . . . Will we act as businessmen in a system that is becoming increasingly entrepreneurial or will we choose to remain a profession, with all the obligations for self-regulation and protection of the public interest that this commitment implies?

In the decade that has elapsed since then, the problems posed by the commercialization of health care have grown. So have the pressures on the private practice of medicine, and now our profession faces an ethical and economic crisis of unprecedented proportions, as it struggles to find its bearings in a health care system that has become a vast and highly lucrative marketplace.

What I want to do here is, first, describe how the commercialization of health care has progressed since 1980, with a brief summary of the initial studies of the behavior of for-profit hospitals. I shall describe how the investor-owned sector has continued to grow, but in new directions. At the same time, our voluntary not-for-profit hospitals have become much more entrepreneurial and have come to resemble their investor-owned competitors in many ways. I shall then consider how the new market-oriented health system has been influencing practicing physicians and how, in turn, the system has been influenced by them. Medical practice inevitably reflects the incentives and orientation of the health care system, but it also plays a critical part in determining how the system works. Finally, I shall briefly analyze the tensions between medical professionalism and the health care market.

THE MEDICAL-INDUSTRIAL COMPLEX SINCE 1980

Turning first to the recent history of the medical-industrial complex, I am glad to report that my earlier concern about the possible domination of the hospital sector by investor-owned chains was not justified by subsequent events. In 1980 there were approximately 1000 investor-owned hospitals. Ten years later their number had increased to barely 1400 of a total of some 5000 hospitals. In the past few years there has been virtually no growth in the chains. The reason is that hospitals are no longer as profitable as they were in the days before the institution of diagnosis-related groups (DRGs) and all the other cost-control measures now used by third-party payers.

Numerous studies published during the past decade have compared the economic behavior of investor-owned hospitals during the early pre-DRG days with that of similar voluntary hospitals.[3] Most reports (including those of the most carefully conducted studies) have found that the investor-owned hospitals charged approximately 15 to 20 percent more per admission, even when similar cases with similar degrees of severity were compared. This difference was largely attributable to increased use of, and higher charges for, ancillary services such as laboratory tests and radiologic procedures. During that earlier period, investor-owned hospitals were no more efficient, as measured by their operating costs per admission; if anything, their costs were a little higher than those of comparable voluntary hospitals. Furthermore, there was strong evidence that the investor-owned hospitals spent substantially less of their resources for the care of uninsured patients than did the voluntary hospitals.[4] There are few or no published data on whether these differences persisted after all hospitals began to face a more hostile and competitive market, but from what we already know it seems clear that for at least the initial phase of their existence, the investor-owned hospitals did not use their alleged corporate advantages for the public benefit. In fact, by seeking to maximize their revenues and avoiding uninsured patients, they contributed to the problems of cost and access our health care system now faces. A few studies have attempted to compare the quality of care in voluntary and investor-owned hospitals, but quality is much more difficult to measure objectively than economic performance, and there is no convincing evidence on this point.

Although the predicted rapid expansion of for-profit hospital chains did not materialize, investor-owned facilities for other kinds of medical care have been growing rapidly. Most of the recent expansion has been in services provided on an ambulatory basis or at home. This is because there has been much less governmental and third-party regulation of those services, and the opportunities for commercial exploitation are still very attractive. Investor-owned businesses have the largest share of this new sector.

Free-standing centers for ambulatory surgery are a good case in point. Ten or 15 years ago, all but the most minor surgery was performed in hospitals. It has now become apparent that at least half of all procedures, even those involving general anesthesia, can be safely performed on an outpatient basis, and in the past decade there has been a rapid proliferation of ambulatory surgery. Some of it is performed in special units within hospitals, but most of it is done in free-standing centers, of which there are now at least 1200. Most of the free-standing facilities are investor-owned, with the referring surgeons as limited partners, and many of the in-hospital units are joint ventures between hospitals and their staff surgeons.

Sophisticated high-technology radiologic services, formerly found only in hospital radiology units, are now provided at hundreds of free-standing facilities called "imaging centers." Most of them feature magnetic resonance imagers and CT scanners. They usually are investor-owned and have business arrangements with practicing physicians who refer patients to the facilities. Diagnostic laboratory services, formerly provided only in hospitals, are now available in thousands of free-standing laboratories, many of which also have physicians as limited partners. Walk-in clinics, offering services such as those provided in hospital emergency rooms and other services formerly provided in doctors' offices, now flourish on street corners and in shopping centers and are operated by investor-owned businesses that employ salaried physicians. Investor-owned companies now provide all sorts of services to patients in their homes that were formerly available only in hospitals. These include oxygen therapy, respiratory therapy, and intravenous treatments.

Health maintenance organizations (HMOs) are another important part of the ambulatory care sector. Over the past decade they have continued to grow at the rate of 4 or 5 percent per year, and now there are an estimated 40 million patients enrolled in some 570 different plans. Approximately two thirds of these plans are investor-owned.[5] Some investor-owned hospital chains have expanded "vertically"—that is, they offer not only inpatient, outpatient, and home services, but also nursing home and rehabilitation services. One or two of the largest chains have even gone into the health insurance business. The largest now insures more than 1.5 million subscribers, under terms that offer financial incentives to use the corporation's own hospitals.

In short, the investor-owned medical-industrial complex has continued to grow, but in new directions. No one has any clear idea of its present size, but I estimate that its revenues during 1990 were probably more than $150 billion, of a total national expenditure for health care of some $700 billion. This would mean that it represents an even larger fraction of total health care expenditures than it did a decade ago. The absence of reliable data on this point reflects the unfortunate consequence of government indifference and proprietary secrecy. And yet we obviously need such information to make future health policy decisions.

THE COMMERCIALIZATION OF VOLUNTARY HOSPITALS

What I had not fully appreciated in 1980 was that the pressures on our voluntary hospitals would lead many of them to behave just like their investor-owned competitors. The growing transfer of diagnostic and therapeutic procedures out of the hospital, the mounting cost-control constraints imposed by third-party payers, which reduced the hospitals' freedom to shift costs, and the general excess of hospital beds resulting from decades of rapid and uncontrolled expansion have all conspired to threaten the economic viability of voluntary hospitals. Philanthropy and community contributions, a mainstay of support when hospital costs were relatively low, are no longer of much help. Hospitals now must pay higher wages and much more money for supplies and equipment, but they cannot count on third-party payers and charitable contributions to cover costs. To compound the problem, those voluntary institutions traditionally committed to caring for large numbers of uninsured patients now find their resources strained to the limit. Private patients covered by the old-fashioned, open-ended kind of indemnity insurance are in ever shorter supply, and the voluntary hospitals now must compete aggressively in an increasingly unfriendly economic climate.

The result of all this has been a gradual shift in the focus of our voluntary hospital system. Altruistic motives that formerly guided the decisions of voluntary hospital management are giving way in many institutions to a primary concern for the bottom line. Hospital administrators have become corporate executives (with business titles such as chairman, chief executive officer, president, and the like) who are required first of all to ensure the economic survival of their institutions. For many hospitals, this means aggressive use of marketing and advertising strategies, ownership of for-profit businesses, and joint ventures with physicians on their staff. Decisions about the allocation of hospital resources, the creation of new facilities, or the elimination of existing ones are now based more on considerations of what is likely to be profitable than on the priorities of community health needs.

Many if not most of our voluntary hospitals now view themselves as businesses competing for paying patients in the health care marketplace. They have, in effect, become part of the medical-industrial complex. Voluntary hospitals have always been tax-exempt because they are not owned by investors and they do not distribute profits to their owners. Because they are tax-exempt, they have been expected to provide necessary community services, profitable or not, and to care for uninsured patients. Many, of course, do exactly that, to the limit of their ability. But, sad to say, many do not, and this has raised questions in some quarters about the justification of their continued tax exemption.[6]

In any case, we are witnessing a pervasive change in the ethos of the voluntary hospital system in America from that of a social service to that of a business. Leaders of hospital associations now commonly refer to themselves as part of an industry, and the management philosophy of private hospitals, investor-owned or not, is increasingly dominated by business thinking. It would be interesting to compare current prices and unreimbursed care in the voluntary and investor-owned hospital sectors. My guess is that much of the earlier difference in price has disappeared, but the voluntary hospitals probably still provide proportionately more uninsured care.

A MARKET-ORIENTED HEALTH CARE SYSTEM

What we see now is a market-oriented health care system spinning out of control. Costs are rising relentlessly in a competitive marketplace heavily influenced by private commerce and still largely dominated by more or less open-ended indemnity insurance and payment by piecework. The financial arrangements in such a system inevitably stimulate the provision of service with little or no regard for cost. Unlike the usual kind of market, in which consumer demand and ability to pay largely determine what is produced and sold, the health care market is not controlled by consumers, because most payment comes from third parties and most decisions are made by physicians.

The fraction of the gross national product devoted to health care has been rising steeply ever since the advent of Medicare and Medicaid in the mid-1960s. In 1965 we spent about 6 percent of our gross national product on health care; in 1975, approximately 8 percent; in 1985, about 10.5 percent; and last year, over 12 percent, or approximately $700 billion.[7] Despite the high cost, or maybe because of it, the system is unable to provide adequate care for all citizens. At least 15 percent of Americans have no health insurance, and probably at least an equal number are inadequately or only intermittently insured. After all, a system that functions as a competitive marketplace has no more interest in subsidizing the uninsured poor than in restricting the revenues generated by services to those who are insured.

Evidence of inefficiency, duplication, and excessive overhead is everywhere apparent. Administrative costs have recently been estimated to make up between 19 and 24 percent of total spending on health care, far more than in any other country.[8] Nearly half of all the beds in investor-owned hospitals and from 35 to 40 percent of all the beds in voluntary hospitals are, on the average, unused. On the other hand, expensive high-technology diagnostic and therapeutic procedures are being carried out in hospitals, doctors' offices, and growing numbers of specialized free-standing facilities at a rate that many studies suggest is excessive among insured patients, though probably inadequate among the poor.

MEDICAL PRACTICE AS A COMPETITIVE BUSINESS

Adding to the competition and cost in our health care system is the recent rapid increase in the number of practicing physicians, most of whom are specialists. In 1970 there were 153 active physicians per 100,000 members of the population; in 1980 there were 192; and the number for 1990 was estimated to exceed 220.[9] Among these new practitioners, the number of specialists is increasing more rapidly than that of primary care physicians. When doctors were in relatively short supply two or three decades ago, they worried less about their livelihood. Now, as the economists would say, we are in a buyer's market, in which not only underused hospitals but also specialists—available in increasing, sometimes even excessive, numbers—are forced to compete for the diminishing number of paying patients who are not already part of the managed care network.

How have all these developments affected the practice of medicine? In the first place, they have resulted in more regulation of the private practice of medicine by third-party payers, who are trying to control costs. There is more interference with clinical practice decisions, more second-guessing and paperwork, and more administrative delays in billing and collecting than ever before, as third-party payers attempt to slow down cost increases through micromanagement of the medical care system.

Second, doctors are increasingly threatened by malpractice litigation as a strictly business relationship begins to replace the trust and mutual confidence that traditionally characterized the doctor–patient relationship.

Third, the courts, which formerly kept the practice of medicine out of the reach of antitrust law, now regard the physician as just another person doing business, no longer immune from antitrust regulation. In 1975 the Supreme Court handed down a landmark decision that found that the business activities of professionals were properly subject to antitrust law.[10] As a consequence, physicians can no longer act collectively on matters affecting the economics of practice, whether their intent is to protect the public or simply to defend the interests of the profession. Advertising and marketing by individual physicians, groups of physicians, or medical facilities, which used to be regarded as unethical and were proscribed by organized medicine, are now protected—indeed, encouraged—by the Federal Trade Commission.

Advertisements now commonly extol the services of individual physicians or of hospital and ambulatory facilities staffed by physicians. Most of them go far beyond simply informing the public about the availability of medical services. Using the slick marketing techniques more appropriate for consumer goods, they lure, coax, and sometimes even frighten the public into using the services advertised.

I recently saw a particularly egregious example of this kind of advertising in the *Los Angeles Times*. A free-standing imaging center in southern California was urging the public to come for magnetic resonance imaging (MRI) studies in its new "open air" imager, without even suggesting the need for previous examination or referral by a physician. The advertisement listed a wide variety of common ailments about which the MRI scan might provide useful information a stratagem calculated to attract large numbers of worried patients whose insurance coverage would pay the substantial fee for a test that was probably not indicated.

Before it was placed under the protection of antitrust law, such advertising would have been discouraged by the American Medical Association (AMA) and viewed with disfavor by the vast majority of physicians. Now it is ubiquitous, on television and radio, on billboards, and in the popular print media. Of course, not all medical advertising is as sleazy. Many respectable institutions and reputable practitioners advertise in order to bring their services to the public's attention. But in medical advertising there is a fine line between informing and promoting; as competition grows, this line blurs. Increasingly, physicians and hospitals are using marketing and public relations techniques that can only be described as crassly commercial in appearance and intent.

Advertising and marketing are just a part of the varied entrepreneurial activities in which practicing physicians are now engaged. Perceiving the trend toward the industrialization of medicine, sensing the threat to their access to paying patients from hospitals, HMOs, and other closed-panel insurance plans, and feeling the pressures of competition from the growing army of medical practitioners, doctors have begun to think of themselves as beleaguered businesspersons, and they act accordingly. I occasionally hear from physicians expressing this view. For example, a doctor from Texas recently sent me a letter saying: "Medicine is a service business, despite the fact that it deals with human beings and their health problems. . . . Physicians are an economic entity, just like the corner service station." Although I suspect many of his colleagues would not appreciate the analogy, I am afraid that too many would agree with the writer's opinion about the primacy of economic considerations in medical practice. In that respect, they would support the oft-expressed views of the leaders of the for-profit hospital industry. For example, the executive director of the Federation of American Hospitals (the trade association of the investor-owned chains) wrote in a letter published in the *New England Journal of Medicine* 10 years ago: "I fail to see a difference between health services and other basic necessities of life food, housing, and fuel all of which are more oriented to the profit motive than is health care."[11]

Of course, the private practice of medicine has always had businesslike characteristics, in that practicing physicians earn their livelihood through their professional efforts. For the vast majority of physicians, however, professional commitments have dominated business concerns. There was always more than enough work for any physician to do, and few physicians had to worry about competition or earning a livelihood. Furthermore, it had long been generally accepted that a physician's income should derive exclusively from direct services to patients or the supervision of such services, not from any entrepreneurial activities.

All that seems to be changing now in this new era of medical entrepreneurialism and health care marketing. Increasing numbers of physicians have economic interests in health care that go beyond direct services to patients or the supervision of such services. The AMA, which formerly proscribed entrepreneurialism by physicians, now expressly allows it, with some caveats, apparently recognizing that a very substantial fraction of practitioners supplement their income by financial interests in all sorts of health care goods, services, and facilities.

The arrangements are too numerous and varied to describe in full here, so I shall simply cite some of them, a few of which I have already alluded to: (1) practitioners hold limited partnerships in for-profit diagnostic-laboratory facilities, to which they refer their patients but over which they exercise no professional supervision; (2) surgeons hold limited partnerships in for-profit ambulatory surgery facilities to which they refer their own patients; (3) office-based practitioners make deals with prescription-drug wholesalers, who supply them with drugs that the physicians prescribe for their patients and for which they charge retail prices; (4) physicians purchase prostheses at reduced rates from manufacturers and make a profit in addition to the professional fees they receive for implanting the prostheses; and (5) practitioners own interests in imaging units to which they refer their patients. Most of the free-standing imaging units are owned by investor-owned businesses, but some were originally owned by radiologists in private practice who have told me that they were persuaded to form joint partnerships with their referring physicians because these physicians threatened to refer their patients elsewhere.

Such arrangements create conflicts of interest that undermine the traditional role of the doctor.[12] In the minds of some physicians, the old Samaritan tradition of our profession has now given way to the concept of a strict business contract between doctor and patient. According to this view, good physicians are simply honest and competent vendors of medical services who are free to contract for whatever services they are willing to provide and patients or their insurers are willing to pay for. Society has no more stake in the practice of medicine than in the conduct of any other business activity, and therefore no right to interfere with the terms of the private contract between doctor and patient.[13,14]

THE THREAT TO THE MORALE OF PHYSICIANS AND THEIR SOCIAL CONTRACT

. . . Today's market-oriented, profit-driven health care industry . . . sends signals to physicians that are frustrating and profoundly disturbing to the majority of us who believe our primary commitment is to patients. Most of us believe we are parties to a social contract, not a business contract. We are not vendors, and we are not merely free economic agents in a free market. Society has given us a licensed monopoly to practice our profession protected in large part against competition from other would-be dispensers of health services. We enjoy independence and the authority to regulate ourselves and set our own standards. Much of our professional training is subsidized, and almost all the information and technology we need to practice our profession have been produced at public expense. Those of us who practice in hospitals are given without charge the essential facilities and instruments we need to take care of our patients. Most of all, we have the priceless privilege of enjoying the trust of our patients and playing a critical part in their lives when they most need help.

All this we are given in exchange for the commitment to serve our patients' interests first of all and to do the very best we can. In my view, that means we should not only be competent and compassionate practitioners but also avoid ties with the health care market, in order to guide our patients through it in the most medically responsible and cost-effective way possible. If the present organization and incentives of our health care system make it difficult or impossible for us to practice in this way (and I believe they do), then we must join with others in examining ways of reforming the system.

What our health care system needs now is not more money, but different incentives and a better organization that will enable us to use available resources in a more equitable and efficient manner to provide necessary services for all who need them. We can afford all the care that is medically appropriate according to the best professional standards. We cannot afford all the care a market-driven system is capable of giving.

REFERENCES

1. Relman AS. The new medical-industrial complex. N Engl J Med 1980; 303:963–70.
2. *Idem.* The future of medical practice. Health Aff (Millwood) 1983; 2(2):5–19.
3. Gray BH, ed. For-profit enterprise in health care. Washington, D.C.: National Academy Press, 1986.
4. Lewin LS, Eckels TJ, Miller LB. Setting the record straight: the provisions of uncompensated care by not-for-profit hospitals. N Engl J Med 1988; 318: 1212–5.
5. Langwell KM. Structure and performance of health maintenance organizations: a review. Health Care Financ Rev 1990; 12(1):71–9.
6. General Accounting Office. Report to the Chairman, Select Committee on Aging, House of Representatives. Nonprofit hospitals: better standards needed for tax exemption. Washington, D.C.: Government Printing Office, 1990. (GAO publication no. (HRD) 90–84.)
7. Levit KR, Lazenby HC, Letsch SW, Cowan CA. National health care spending, 1989. Health Aff (Millwood) 1991; 10(1):117–30.
8. Woolhandler S, Himmelstein DU. The deteriorating administrative efficiency of the U.S. health care system. N Engl J Med 1991; 324: 1253–8.
9. Kletke PR. The demographics of physician supply: trends and projections. Chicago: American Medical Association, 1987.
10. Goldfarb v. Virginia State Bar, 421 U.S. 773, 1975.
11. Bromberg MD. The new medical-industrial complex. N Engl J Med 1981; 304:233.
12. Relman AS. Dealing with conflicts of interest. N Engl J Med 1984; 313:749–51.
13. Sade RM. Medical care as a right: a refutation. N Engl J Med 1971; 285:1288–92.
14. Engelhardt HT Jr, Rie MA. Morality for the medical-industrial complex: a code of ethics for the mass marketing of health care. N Engl J Med 1988; 319:1086–9.

25 MEDICATIONS AND THE PHARMACEUTICAL INDUSTRY

David Cohen, Michael McCubbin, Johanne Collin, and Guilhème Pérodeau

INTRODUCTION

Medication use at the societal level is determined by much more than the occurrence of ailments and the availability of pharmaceutical remedies to deal with these ailments. Numerous biological, psychological, social, economic, and cultural situations, all in constant interaction, affect the use of prescribed medications (Bush and Osterweis, 1978; Vuckovic and Nichter, 1997).[1] Medications themselves are much more than material objects with physiological effects; they are also representations that carry meanings and shape social relations as they evolve in conjunction with individuals and collectivities (Montagne, 1996; Van der Geest et al., 1996). Hence, an attempt to comprehend medications and medication use in societies should be informed by methods able to deal with complexity, given the wide variety of interacting factors; with change, given the volatile nature of these factors; with social construction, given the preponderant role of human beliefs and judgments; and, as we hope to show, with contradiction and paradox. . . .

THE LIFE CYCLE OF MEDICATIONS

As a therapeutic product, a particular drug follows a long and agitated trajectory (Pignarre, 1995). This may be considered its life cycle—from the initial discovery or conception of a molecule to a substance's eventual disuse as a prescribed medication (Van der Geest et al., 1996). Few medications remain in significant use as remedies for the class of problems for which they are initially indicated and marketed, after a few decades. It is not uncommon for medications to experience rebirth as cultural attitudes change or new uses are found for them. For example, once unrivalled as an over-the-counter analgesic, aspirin has been eclipsed by other painkillers—but it now holds a popular niche as a prophylactic agent for cardiovascular disease (Jack, 1997). Even thalidomide, once the world's most reviled medication, recently returned to the market with new therapeutic indications (Raje and Anderson, 1999).

Between conception and death (or rebirth) a medication may be seen to pass through several overlapping steps, including clinical trials, approval for use by regulatory agencies, approval for reimbursement by health and insurance plans, marketing, promotion, prescription, consumption, and post-marketing surveillance (Figure 25.1). In the initial steps of the life cycle as here conceived, a substance is merely a "molecule," then a "drug." Its designation may be more attribute than property. Paradoxically, regardless of its appearance as an ultra-sophisticated, extremely effective product of rational and technological design, the modern drug may only take on the official appellation "medication" or "medicine" once it has proven itself superior to *inert placebo* in a series of so-called "clinical trials." Of course, this speaks more about the nature and power of the "lowly" placebo[2] than about medications per se, though our point merely emphasizes that a substance has to "earn" the status of a medicinal product on the basis of changing scientific and other criteria.

Each step or stage in the life cycle may be conceived as a mini-system with its own dynamics, which involve a context, a group of key actors, and various transactions among these actors. In addition to patients and physicians, pharmacists and nurses, these actors include investors and fi-

Acknowledgment: This work was supported by Grant 99-ER-3107 from Fonds FCAR, Quebec, Canada.

Figure 25-1. *The life cycle of medications*

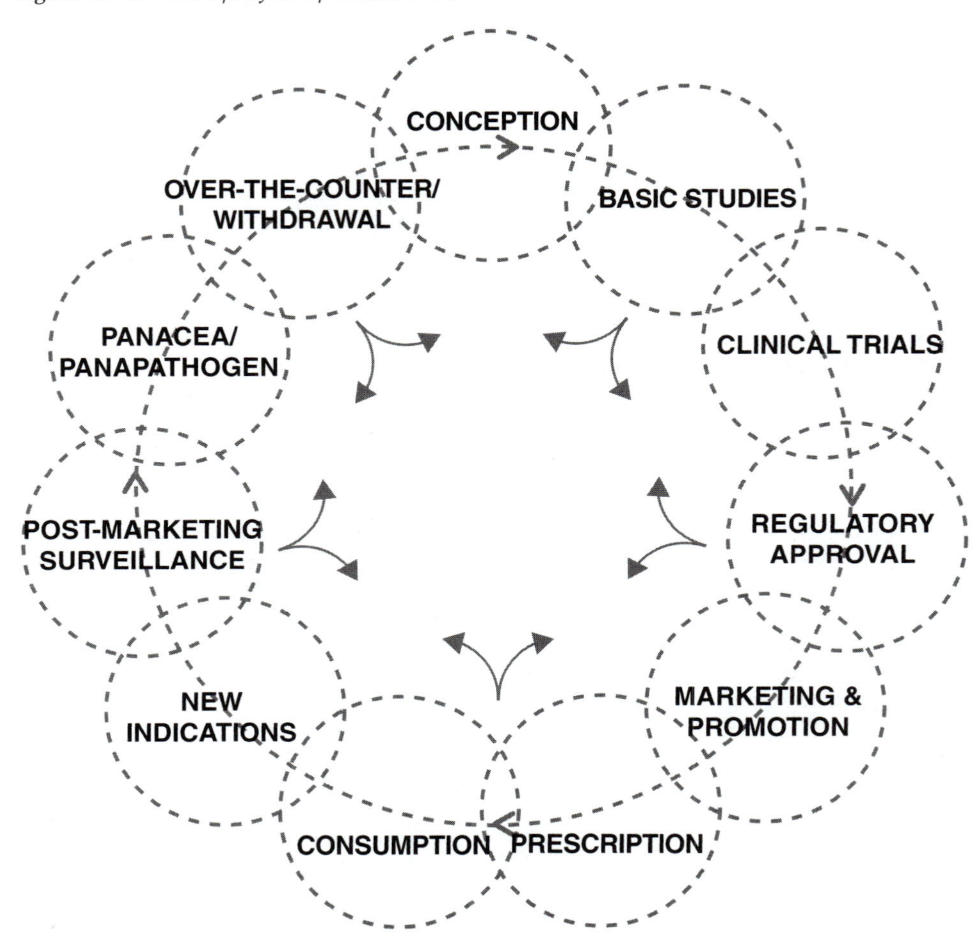

nancial analysts; researchers in industry, academic, or government settings; managers and administrators in insurance and managed care settings; government officials; advertisers; pharmaceutical representatives; journalists and other media personalities; school teachers; non-medical or psychosocial helping professionals; relatives and others in the patient's entourage; and numerous lobby and pressure groups.

Given the dynamic activity at each stage, it is not surprising that different trajectories may emerge: the life cycle involves bifurcations, jumps, improvisations and impasses. These result from difficulties in clinical trials, new indications, withdrawal from the market for various reasons, approval of the medication for over-the-counter sales, etc. Unexpected or predictable events at one or another stage are likely to influence profoundly the nature of the entire life cycle of the medication. Yet, the relationships between such events and the overall fate of medications is little known, in part because researchers have generally failed to adopt such a comprehensive, "biographical" view of medications. In part also, it results from a lack of access to information about the early stages of a drug's life cycle, because of the simple fact that medications are the products of profit-making industries intent on protecting their investments in a fiercely competitive environment. Thus, a very large measure of proprietary activity and secrecy characterizes the early stages of most medications' life cycle, with information on these stages becoming available only at later stages, and then so only partially.

For example, in most countries, negotiations between drug manufacturers and regulatory agencies regarding the actual labeling of a drug and its clinical indications remain essentially inaccessible to researchers, clinicians, or even most public health authorities, except sometimes via freedom of information laws. Although the secrecy is justified as a protection for manufacturers' commercial patents and intellectual property, much of it undoubtedly stems from the well-known culture of secrecy that characterizes government and corporate operations. Undoubtedly, the extremely limited amount of information available about these transactions impacts on how the drug will be perceived and used by physicians and patients in ordinary circumstances.

Another recent development illustrates potential changes in the life cycle of medications. In the last five years, a rapidly increasing proportion of subjects in clinical trials for new drugs are recruited via the offices of private practitioners, who receive financial rewards from drug manufacturers for this purpose. This practice probably results from commercial incentives on manufacturers to introduce products more quickly to the market, for which they must try to circumvent current monitoring and regulation of clinical trials by governments, universities, and ethics committees (Eichenwald and Kolata, 1999). Repercussions of this new trend on other stages of a drug's life cycle, and on other interacting systems such as patient-physician relationships, may be varied and numerous, and could be the subject of future studies.

Finally, as Jacobs (1995) and Zarifian (1996) argue in the case of some newer psychotropics, promotion of a drug by its manufacturer may actually precede the clinical trials where the drug's therapeutic effectiveness is presumably to be established. The promotion may involve funding professional committees working on the creation of a new psychiatric diagnostic category listing specific target symptoms, treatment of which the new drug is then expected to improve. Or the promotion may involve funding a lobby group of consumers or their relatives who will pressure health authorities to ease *future* bureaucratic hurdles which a new product is expected to face (Silverstein, 1999; O'Harrow, 2000). Hence, a model of the life cycle of a medication must include individual behaviors, institutional structures, sociohistorical tendencies—all in interaction over time.

DRUGS AS SOCIAL PHENOMENA

The systemic view sketched above may help researchers detach themselves further from a view of medications as "merely" concrete, material objects. Because they are swallowed or injected inside physical bodies, it is initially difficult to consider how the effects of drugs resonate beyond an individual consumer's body or being, to shape social relations in families, groups, communities and larger societies—and in turn be shaped by these social relations. This insight is well understood in the study of illicit psychoactive substances (Stein, 1990), perhaps because their use is less mediated by professional expertise.

Is the physical/biologistic aspect of drugs' nature fundamental? Perhaps just as we may grasp the "essence" of the body only by considering the exceedingly complex interweaving of agency and structure (e.g. Kelly and Field, 1997), the "essence" of drugs may be grasped by going beyond their material appearance. Studies of the placebo have long made use of this insight (Shapiro and Shapiro, 1997). Of course, the question of the essence of drugs becomes exquisitely complex in the particular case of psychotropic drugs, which by definition influence moods, thoughts, and behaviors of individuals and have long sparked debate on the mind-body question (Huxley, 1954).

One may analyze drugs as *entities*, as *processes*, and as *representations*, each in interaction with drug *effects*. In turn, drug effects might be perceived in the organic, personal, symbolic social, and cultural realms (Bush, 1977; Montagne,

1988, 1997). An analogy may be made with other common but nevertheless "charged" objects, such as money, or automobiles. For example, though automobiles are obviously means of transportation, they are just as evidently and simultaneously strategic commercial products, the planet's worst source of pollution, symbols of freedom and mobility—to name just a few of their intrinsic properties/ascribed attributes. Some authors have explicitly analyzed the functions of written prescriptions, tranquilizer tablets, and vitamins as modern-day talismans or amulets (Sands, 1965; Rome, 1986; Olson, 1994). These analyses express the idea that the material nature of an object may matter less than its meanings in a complex web of historically situated social interactions. A striking contemporary illustration of this idea concerns cocaine and methylphenidate (Ritalin). These two stimulants may be observed to have virtually identical, interchangeable physical and subjective effects in the short and long term on animals and humans who ingest them (Volkow et al., 1995). Yet, they are classified in law, medicine, public policy, and lay knowledge as radically disimilar substances.

Like diamonds reflecting light, the "essence" of medications changes depending on one's standpoint, and cannot quite be captured in a single expression. Thus, recognizing that drugs are concrete material objects does not prevent their simultaneous analysis as complex social phenomena, embedded in the web of individual and collective meanings and interactions. . . .

CHANGES IN PSYCHOACTIVE MEDICATION USAGE PATTERNS

Despite the long-standing centrality of drugs in healing practices in every society, the role of pharmaceuticals in modern medical care in gaining even further prominence. For example, in Canada the proportion of total national health expenditures devoted to medications has risen from less than 9 percent in 1983 to 14.5 percent in 1997, when it surpassed for the first time spending on physician services (Buske, 2000). Yet, such developments should not obscure the fact that the promotion of medications as indispensable products has always been accompanied by doubts about their safety (Vuckovic and Nichter, 1997). Indeed, the contemporary triumph of pharmaceuticals parallels a realization that even their *proper* use causes enough morbidity to rank adverse drug reactions in hospitalized patients as the fourth leading cause of death in North America: Lazarou et al. (1998) estimated that 106,000 patients die and 2.2 million are injured yearly from medication use, excluding errors, in the USA.

Large-scale longitudinal and international psychotropic consumption trend estimates are sparse and mostly document the situation in the USA: overall, they suggest that global and per capita usage in western countries have either remained stationary or decreased modestly during the 1970s and 1980s (Baum et al., 1988; Wysowski and Baum, 1991) but have markedly increased since the mid-1980s (Pincus et al., 1988). In the USA, managed care organizations such as health maintenance organizations (HMO) have probably contributed to this trend, to the extent that they seek to limit their costs and see psychotropic drug use as less expensive than personal contacts with caregivers. In addition, pharmaceutical companies have aggressively moved into the managed care business, where they can promote their own products to HMO members.

At almost each decade since the 1930s, a different psychotropic drug appears to stand out in popularity, until professional disappointments and iatrogenic morbidities become noticeable or significant, and until a different candidate molecule is available to fill the coveted spot (Olivieri et al., 1986; Medawar, 1992; Cohen, 1996). With local variations, the large proportion of elderly and women users of psychotropics has remained stable. The most notable transformations in usage this past decade involve antidepressants and psychostimulants, with a concomitant expansion of the market to children. As noted in the introduction, this expansion clearly distinguishes the use of psychotropics from that of other medications. In the class of antidepressant drugs, the selective serotonin reuptake inhibitors (SSRIs) such as Prozac are beginning to surpass in popularity the benzodiazepines, until recently the most prescribed psychotropics in the world (Pincus et al., 1998). This growth is not attributable to increased efficacy, since considerable evidence has failed to establish that the newer antidepressants are any more effective than the old or are better tolerated by users (Agency for Health Care Policy and Research, 1999). Furthermore, research has also failed to establish more than very modest support in short- and medium-term studies for antidepressants' effectiveness in comparison with psychotherapy (Fisher and Greenberg, 1997; Antonuccio et al., 1999; Spiegel, 1999).

In North America, the 1990s have brought unprecedented growth in prescriptions to children, one sector of the population that appears to have been previously spared major exposure to prescribed psychotropics—though use of over-the-counter analgesics has long been significant (Kogan et al., 1994). Medical visits in the USA resulting in psychostimulant prescriptions (most of which were for children) increased by more than 300 percent between 1985 and 1995 (Pincus et al., 1998). Psychotropic drugs are now being consumed by younger and younger children, for what are clearly unevaluated, "off label" uses. In the USA such prescriptions to 2- to 4-year-old children tripled between 1991 and 1995 (Zito et al., 2000). In that country, citing IMS Health, Diller (2000) reports the use of SSRIs in the 7- to 12-year-old group to be up 151 percent between 1995 and 1999; for those under 6 years, the increase is 580 percent. For children under 18 years, the use of 'mood stabilizers' other than lithium—mostly anticonvulsant drugs—has grown 4000 percent and the use of newer neuroleptics such as risperidone has grown nearly 300 percent. One may confidently estimate that 4 million American youths receive stimulants, 1 million receive antidepressants, and nearly another million receive various other psychotropics.

Ironically, the growth in the consumption by children of *prescribed* stimulants has coincided with an escalation of the "war on drugs" which especially publicizes the dangers of *illicitly used* stimulants. In the USA, even amphetamine, still viewed as a scourge in the drug abuse field (Baberg et al., 1996), is simultaneously one of the fastest-growing prescribed medications for "attention deficit-hyperactivity disorder" in children and adults. This is indicated by the popularity of Adderall, a mixture of pure amphetamine salts. Made widely available on the US market in 1996, almost 3 million prescriptions were dispensed during the first nine months of 1999 only (Witte, 1999). This recalls but does not equal the huge popularity of prescribed stimulants in that country during the 1950s and 1960s, though consumers were mostly adults and "weight loss" was a principal indication, until stimulants' powerful potential to provoke dependence became widely recognized (Grinspoon and Hedblom, 1975). The possible relationship between the resurgence of medical prescription of stimulants and the resurgence of illicit stimulant use (Baberg et al., 1996) has not been explored.

The mass use of behavior-altering drugs with children remains confined essentially to two countries in the world—Canada and the USA—where it may represent an unprecedented experiment in social engineering. To our knowledge, no researchers have investigated the sociocultural determinants of these practices. Rapid growth in stimulant use is now occurring in some other developed countries, especially the UK, though the differences between the USA and Europe remain very large (International Narcotics Control Board, 2000). Interestingly, while the use of stimulants with children in France is extremely rare, studies have shown that the prescription of various tranquilizers to children for "sleep problems" reached prevalence hovering around 10 percent in the 1980s in some regions of that country (Kopferschmitt et al., 1992).

The increased popularity and moral legitimacy of psychotropic drugs as treatments for emotional distress have also sparked developments such as the drive among psychologists (at least in the USA and Canada) to obtain prescription privileges, similar to physicians, but for psychiatric drugs only. This move represents a novel departure for psychology and has led to intense debates within that profession (Adams and Bieliauskas, 1994; Gutierrez and Silk, 1998) as well as fierce opposition from psychiatrists.

With cardiovascular and gastrointestinal medications, psychotropics are among the three most prescribed drug classes is most post-industrial societies.[3] This popularity, and the phenomenal financial returns on investments from a few blockbuster drugs in the SSRI class, has spurred intensive efforts by pharmaceutical companies to market new products: in 2000 some 103 molecules were under development as psychotropic candidates, particularly as anti-dementia drugs, antidepressants, anxiolytics or addiction treatments (Pharmaceutical Research and Manufacturers of America, 2000).

CHANGES IN PHARMACEUTICAL MARKETING PRACTICES

Among the many sociocultural determinants of the popularity of various medications, especially psychotropic medications, pharmaceutical marketing practices have frequently been mentioned, although until a decade ago, there has been surprisingly little study of just how and to what extent these practices have impacted upon physicians (see Prather, 1991; review by Lexchin, 1993). Recently, an exhaustive meta-analysis showed that most gifts and incentives increase physician prescribing for the promoted drug, while simultaneously having a *negative* impact upon physicians' knowledge (Wazana, 2000).

Advertisements in medical journals, visits to physicians using sophisticated persuasion techniques (Roughead et al., 1998), and symposia sponsorship constitute the bulk of promotional activity. More recently, there has been recent growing use of direct-to-consumer advertising (DTCA) in mass-media, a formerly prohibited practice but now fully allowed in the USA and New Zealand and beginning in other western nations. In 1999, the pharmaceutical industry in the USA spent $13.9 billion on drug promotion, one-fifth more than the previous year. Of this amount, $1.8 billion went to DTCA—triple what was spent three years before (IMS Health, 2000b). Despite such estimates, total promotional spending remains unknown because these data—if released by manufacturers—may be classified under other less conspicuous headings; indications exist that promotional spending may approximate or even exceed true research spending.

Direct-to-consumer advertising, via openly persuasive publicity slogans—mostly on television—or industry-funded "educational" campaigns on the identification and lifelong drug treatment of various troubles, is a harbinger for a major transformation in the significations and roles of medications in society—moving them even further out of the domain of medical mystique and into the mass market as lifestyle products. The transformation of a prescription drug from strictly a tool of medical practice to a product that may be sought or declined on the basis not only for "lay knowledge" but, more precisely, *consumer product knowledge*, could have profound implications given the ways in which such knowledge is obtained, perceived, and applied. Direct-to-consumer advertising may also be expected to transform the doctor-patient relationship as increasing numbers of patients arrive at the consultation with not only explanatory frameworks regarding their troubles, but also the proposed solution: a prescription for a drug named by the consumer (Lexchin, 1999). Studies suggest that most physicians respond positively to these requested prescriptions (Wilkes et al., 2000). A marketing executive observes that "DTC advertising is now being used in virtually all phases of a product's life cycle, from launch to patent expiration" (cited in IMS Health, 2000b).

A major part of promotional activity in general is aimed not at consumers or medical prescribers, but at entire institutions: governments and other regulatory agencies, lobby groups concerned with specific illnesses, universities and other research bodies. Rarely is this promotional activity described in the scientific literature though some serious independent or journalistic investigations exist (e.g. Fried, 1998; Medawar, 1999; Silverstein, 1999). The evidence is mounting, however, of persistent and expanding influence of pharmaceutical companies in the formulation of industrial health policies affecting their business, and in influencing what kind of research will be done, how it will be done, and how (or whether) it will be reported (Medawar, 1992; Walker, 1994; Abraham, 1995; Lehrman and Sharav, 1997). The title of a recent editorial in a medical journal illustrates growing medical concern over the issue: "Scientific harassment by pharmaceutical companies: Time to stop" (Hailey, 2000). In these circumstances, it remains an open question whether the pharmaceutical industry serves health systems or whether health systems serve the pharmaceutical industry.

THE INTERNET AND CHANGES IN THE CONSTRUCTION OF KNOWLEDGE ABOUT MEDICATIONS

An exemplary sign of advanced modernity, the Internet has already substantially altered the scientific and commercial stages of the life cycles of medications (Cobert and Silvey, 1999; Henney et al., 1999)—and there is good reason to believe that the interactive information revolution represented by this new technology will alter the meanings and uses of medications beyond current recognition. A major impact of the Internet has been to facilitate the consumer's participation as a prominent actor in the *construction of knowledge* about medications. This represents an enormous change within a health care system where such knowledge was strictly relegated to scientific, health professional, government, and manufacturing experts. This may have been even more so with regard to psychiatric medications, used as they are—especially over the long-term—by emotionally troubled persons who have been particularly powerless compared with other actors (Cohen and McCubbin, 1990; McCubbin and Cohen, 1996).

The Internet has made information from authorized sources increasingly available to the general public, enabling patients to begin dialogue with physicians at a much higher level. Goldsmith even suggests that physicians, who do not have time to search the Internet or analyze information from it, might have to "rely on patients to update them on developments in their own field, [which] is a stunning reversal of the traditional information flow in medicine" (2000: 2). The Internet has also provided a means to create mutual support and interest groups in environments that allow for anonymity and relative safety in comparison with"real-life" social circumstances. Such forums, discussion lists, bulletin boards, news groups, and e-mail chains have clearly contributed to the emergence of the "consumer" class of users of mental health services: people who approach the ideal of informed consumers, who actively seek the best medications and the best physicians for dealing with their complex issues of treatment, advice, care, and support, who can "shop around" for the best service, product, and price. Some Internet groups are categorized according to particular diagnoses and even particular drugs. A participant may be struck by the detailed daily exchange of experiences regarding different drugs, their perceived benefits and side effects, withdrawal problems, and polypharmacy issues. The numbers of such groups, and interlocking participation within them, has exploded into the hundreds, if not thousands.

In this new environment, radical innovations in knowledge construction are possible. For example, within a few weeks following the introduction of a new psychotropic medication, hundreds of ordinary patients widely dispersed geographically will begin to provide their own detailed "product reports." Ironically, within these groups the problems of addiction and withdrawal are extremely well known and a constant topic of discussion, while such issues are virtually unacknowledged by the manufacturers, regulators, and in the scientific literature (Medawar, 1997; Breggin and Cohen, 1999). Only a few years ago, to obtain a small fraction of such data—for example, bearing on withdrawal effects of a new psychiatric drug—would necessitate vast, costly studies in post-marketing surveillance, and only if the scientific, clinical, or public health interest was seriously piqued and sustained in the first place. In sum, not only is knowledge on a medication's effects subject to ongoing revision, but today such knowledge must increasingly accommodate lay knowledge which—far from being hesitantly expressed in dyads of physician–patient or researcher–patient—possesses its own channels for direct, instant, and international diffusion.

This augmented participation of the consumer still is far from reaching equality with the traditional actors, who can mobilize resources far more effectively than consumers (Lenglet and Topuz, 1998). Yet, the traditionally powerless "consumer movement" may be approaching the levers of influence in the mental health and generally in the health care system, which could generate unforeseen changes.

The availability of a multitude of Internet sites that carry various discourses on medications does have a dark side, as members of the public may confuse personal anecdotes and opinions with the results of scientific studies. However, failure to consider scientific data and their uncertainties about the costs and benefits of various medications is not limited to the lay public. Healy (1999), among others, suggests in the case of antidepressants that professionals also may exaggerate the importance of widely disseminated personal narratives of healing and transformation rather than rely primarily upon sober analysis. But even published scientific studies of pharmaceuticals—presumably archetypes of balanced analysis—are regularly found to avoid reporting fundamental information, leading to exaggerated claims of efficacy and minimal adverse effects (Thornley and Adams, 1998). In sum, the Internet's potential to "lead consumers astray" is genuine—but this potential also serves to illustrate that equally "dangerous" though less studied incentives and constraints have always operated and continue to operate upon *all* the actors involved in making decisions about drugs, not merely upon actors traditionally seen as "uninformed."

CONCLUSION: EXPLORING MEDICATIONS AS SOCIAL PHENOMENA

Several research avenues emerge from this framework. One point continually stressed throughout this article concerns the involvement of numerous actors besides doctors and patients in the life cycle of medications, and the fact that these actors' motives and strategies as they interact with each other remain virtually unknown. For example, studies are needed on how individual officials in drug regulatory agencies construct notions such as "risk," "harm," or "therapeutic," and how these personal constructions are associated with various incentives and constraints operating upon these individuals in their networks. Another example concerns the impact of family members or informal caregivers on medication use by the elderly. Countless epidemiological studies indicating high levels of use not always justified by state of health suggest that this avenue of research should be pursued more vigorously. Similarly, studies are needed of non-medical helping professionals' attitudes and feelings about psychotropic medication use, and how these relate to power and ideological struggles in the mental health field, and medication use by their clients.

On a broader level, more investigations are needed into the power of the economic multinationals (such as pharmaceutical companies) to shape social policies in various countries. This power is expanding in a global economy and threatening the capacity of governments to regulate them (McCubbin, 1998). These policies involve drug regulation, access to drugs, drug advertising, and other policies created or altered in order to attract foreign investment. In the climate of globalization, economic power may constitute one of the greatest influences on the entire system of medication use and the life cycle of medications. For example, direct-to-consumer promotion of medications—strongly urged by drug manufacturers in countries where it is not yet fully allowed—has the potential to modify profoundly institutional, professional, and consumer attitudes and behaviors, likely in the direction of increased brand-name medication usage. Many other issues require examination, including the impact of DTCA on the provision of independent information on drugs, on health-related behaviors, on the suppression of alternative treatments, on research funding.

The ideological and cultural dimensions of medication use deserve more study. For example, to what extent do systems of licit and illicit psychoactive drug use feed and impact upon each other. Prohibition of some psychoactives nearly always goes hand in hand with promotion of some other psychoactives. Despite the porous, interactive features of these two seemingly disparate systems, we know of no serious attempts since Szasz (1974) to integrate observations about legal and illegal psychotropic drug use/promotion/prohibition in a single framework.

International differences in use of certain drugs, such as psychostimulants for children, deserve much closer examination than has been the case up to now. These differences highlight how the social system of medication use interacts with other systems, such as public education and child care. In societies where economic development, access to technology, scientific worldviews, and adult psychoactive drug use are comparable—and where claims of concern for the needs and health of children are identical—the magnitude of contemporary differences between countries in the use of behavior-altering drugs among children is extremely intriguing. Within the few societies where such use is common, differences between cultural or minority groups deserve more sophisticated investigations.

The need for well-founded figures on drug consumption is obvious. Currently, researchers, and often, governments, depend on information from commercial sources or use outdated data to estimate prescription or consumption rates despite the rapidly changing patterns of use. In most countries, independent sources of information on these patterns are lacking. This hampers relevant research and public health monitoring.

The veritable impact of iatrogenic effects of drugs is barely known. This ignorance constitutes an inconspicuous but extremely powerful bias toward the "natural" view of medications as primarily essential, lifesaving products and the intent of prescription as necessarily therapeutic. The impact of drug-related injuries in the social realm is also barely known or studied. For example, psychotropic drugs are prescribed in order to modify *behavior* by means of non-specific effects on the central nervous system, yet few researchers have studied the impact of these drugs on interpersonal processes (see Sice et al., 1975; Estroff, 1985; DeGiacomo et al., 1986). Since Illich's (1976) discussions on the institutionalization of iatrogenesis, this topic has also been neglected. Drug-induced iatrogenesis may be conceived as a social system, and may be fruitfully investigated using insights from constructivist and critical perspectives. For example, it is rarely appreciated how even a seemingly fundamental pharmacological term such as "adverse effect" may rest almost entirely on social construction (Cohen, 1997b).

Evaluating the impact of the Internet on numerous phases of the life cycle of medications will undoubtedly spur several interesting studies. Among its many effects, the Internet ostensibly removes an expert intermediary—such as a pharmacist or physician—from the physical, regulatory, and scientific "spaces" between individuals and medications. The Internet (a new technology) helps to level the playing field between professionals and clients, while changing how medications (an old technology) appear to all concerned. More direct access/relationships between individuals and medications raises, as we have suggested, several research questions concerning all actors' participation in the construction of knowledge and expertise about medications and all actors' usages of medications as products and as representations.

In this connection, the role of researchers and scientists in the life cycles of different medications emphatically needs to be made more explicit. Scientists rarely view themselves as actors in the system, which allows them to exclude their own views and roles from their analyses. Given that a large portion of drug research funding emanates directly or indirectly from the pharmaceutical industry, conflicts of interests remain understudied, as is the fact that social researchers typically focus their attention on the *visible* stages and transactions in drugs' life cycles rather than question how and why other stages and transactions are less visible or studied.

In sum, we believe that thinking systemically about medications—described here as a necessarily critical and constructivist endeavor—raises a number of interesting questions for research. A major challenge facing researchers in this field is to relate the motives and reasonings expressed by the different actors involved in the life cycle of medications to observed trends in the conception, promotion, prescription, consumption, and evaluation of medications in society. In turn, such analyses might reach more profound understandings by situating their results within the broader social, cultural, economic, and technological transformations and contradictions at work as we begin another millennium.

NOTES

1. Each of the following factors and situations has been observed, in one or another study, to be a significant predictor of medication use/prescription: age, gender, presenting complaints, physical condition, stress level, and attitudes toward medication (Pérodeau et al., 1992, 1996); perception of social network (Pérodeau and Galbaud du Fort, 2000); family structure (Mishara, 1997); social representations of health and illness (Morant, 1998); personal characteristics of physicians (Davidson et al., 1995);

type of third-party payer (Sclar et al., 1998); cultural preferences for certain diagnoses and medications (Payer, 1990); new technologies and changed political and economic environments which affect medication availability and determine its regulation (Davis, 1996); and promotional practices by pharmaceutical manufacturers which—as we discuss in this article—respond to *and* create professional and consumer demand. . . .

2. The question of the placebo is a most complex one, given the demonstrated efficacy of placebos in numerous ailments, but also given the fact that placebos usually have to be believed in to work. In other words, the drug's impact is not only determined by the interaction of a chemical substance with the body, but also by the expectations of the user and the deceptions of the provider. In this connection, inert placebos (e.g. sugar, yeast) may simply be controls for the "normal state." To study better the effects of medications beyond placebo effects, medications must be compared to "active" placebos (e.g. atropine), substances which produce bodily changes (such as increased heartbeat or sweating) and thus which patients may "actively" believe to be genuine remedies. In the few studies that use active placebos as controls, the relative efficacy of the tested medication is typically much lower than in studies using inert placebos (see, generally, Fisher and Greenberg, 1993).
3. IMS Health (2000a), a commercial company which tracks retail sales of prescription drugs world-wide, lists 16 "therapeutic categories" of medications, in decreasing order of sales in retail pharmacies for 12 months leading up to February 2000: cardiovascular, alimentary/metabolism, central nervous system, anti-infectives, respiratory, genito-urinary, musculo-skeletal, cytostatics, dermatologicals, blood agents, sensory organs, diagnostic agents, hormones, miscellaneous, hospital solutions, parasitology.

REFERENCES

Abraham, J. (1995). *Science, politics and the pharmaceutical industry: Controversy and bias in drug regulation.* London: UCL.

Adams, K.M. and Bieliauskas, L.A. (1994). On perhaps becoming what you had previously despised: Psychologists as prescribers of medication. *Journal of Clinical Psychology in Medical Settings,* 1, 189–97.

Agency for Health Care Policy and Research (AHCPR). (1999). *Treatment of depression: Newer pharmacotherapies. Summary, evidence report/technology assessment* 7. Rockville, MD: AHCPR. Available at: http://www.ahcpr.gov/clinic/deprsumm.htm [accessed 13 July 2001].

Antonuccio, D., Danton, W.G., DeNelsky, G.Y., Greenberg, R.G. and Gordon, J.S. (1999). Raising questions about antidepressants. *Psychotherapy and Psychosomatics,* 68, 3–14.

Baberg, H.T., Nelesen, R.A. and Dimsdale, J.E. (1996). Amphetamine use: Return of an old scourge in a consultation psychiatry setting. *American Journal of Psychiatry,* 153, 789–93.

Baum, C., Kennedy, D.L., Knapp, D.E., Juergens, J.P. and Faich, G.A. (1988). Prescription drug use in 1984 and changes over time. *Medical Care,* 26, 105–14.

Breggin, P.R. and Cohen, D. (1999). *Your drug may be your problem: How and why to stop taking psychiatric medications.* Cambridge, MA: Perseus.

Bush, P.J. (1977). Psychosocial aspects of medicine use. In A.I. Wertheimer and P.J. Bush (Eds.), *Perspectives on medicines in society.* Hamilton, IL: Drug Intelligence.

Bush, P.J. and Osterweis, M. (1978). Pathways to medicine use. *Journal of Health and Social Behavior,* 19, 179–89.

Buske, L. (2000). Drug costs surpass spending on physicians. *Canadian Medical Association Journal,* 162, 405–6.

Cobert, B. and Silvey, J. (1999). The Internet and drug safety? What are the implications for pharmacovigilance? *Drug Safety,* 20, 95–107.

Cohen, D. (1996). Les 'nouveaux' médicaments de l'esprit: Marche avant vers le passé? (The "new" mind drugs: Forward step into the past?) *Sociologie et sociétés,* 28, 17–34.

Cohen, D. (1997b). Psychiatrogenics: Introducing chlorpromazine in psychiatry. *Review of Existential Psychology and Psychiatry,* 23, 206–33.

Cohen, D. and McCubbin, M. (1990). The political economy of tardive dyskinesia: Asymmetries in power and responsibility. *Journal of Mind and Behavior,* 11, 465–88.

Davidson, W., Molloy, W. and Bédard, M. (1995). Physician characteristics and prescribing for elderly people in New Brunswick: Relation to patient outcomes. *Canadian Medical Association Journal,* 152, 1227–34.

Davis, P. (1996). *Contested ground: Public purpose and private interest in the regulation of prescription drugs.* New York: Oxford University Press.

DeGiacomo, P., Silvestri, A., Pierri, G., Lefons, E. and Corfiati, L. (1986). Research on effects of psychodrugs on human interaction. A theoretical/experimental approach. *Acta Psychiatrica Scandinavica,* 74, 417–24.

Diller, L.H. (2000). Kids on drugs: A behavioral pediatrician questions the wisdom of medicating our children. *Salon Health and Body*, 9 March. Available at: http://www.salon.com/health/feature/2000/03/09/kid_drugs/ [accessed 13 July 2001].

Eichenwald, K. and Kolata, G. (1999). Drug trials hide conflicts for doctors. *New York Times*, 16 May, 1.

Estroff, S.E. (1985). *Making it crazy: An ethnography of psychiatric clients in an American community.* Berkeley, CA: University of California Press.

Fisher, S. and Greenberg, R.P. (1993). How sound is the double-blind design for evaluating psychotropic drugs? *Journal of Nervous and Mental Disease*, 181, 345–50.

Fisher, S. and Greenberg, R.P., Eds. (1997). *From placebo to panacea: Putting psychiatric drugs to the test.* New York: Wiley.

Fried, S. (1998). *Bitter pills: Inside the hazardous world of legal drugs.* New York: Bantam.

Goldsmith, J. (2000). How will the Internet change our health system? *Health Affairs*, March/April. Available at: http://www.projhope.org/HA/bonus/190112.htm [accessed 13 July 2001].

Grinspoon, L. and Hedblom, P. (1975). *The speed culture: Amphetamine use and abuse in America.* Cambridge, MA: Harvard University Press.

Gutierrez, P.M. and Silk, K.R. (1998). Prescription privileges for psychologists: A review of the psychological literature. *Professional Psychology-Research and Practice*, 29, 213–22.

Hailey, D. (2000). Scientific harassment by pharmaceutical companies: Time to stop. *Canadian Medical Association Journal*, 162, 212–13.

Healy, D. (1999). The three faces of the antidepressants: A critical commentary on the clinical-economic context of diagnosis. *Journal of Nervous and Mental Disease*, 187, 174–80.

Henney, J.E., Shuren, J.E., Nightingale, S.L. and McGinnis, T.J. (1999). Internet purchases of prescription drugs: Buyer beware. *Annals of Internal Medicine*, 131, 861–2.

Huxley, A. (1954). *The doors of perception.* London: Chatto & Windus.

Illich, I. (1976). *Medical nemesis: The expropriation of health.* New York: Pantheon.

IMS Health. (2000a). *IMS Health reports 10 percent growth in global retail drug sales for 12 month period to February.* Available at http://www.imshealth.com/html/news_arc/04_20_2000_351.htm (accessed 5 September 2000).

IMS Health. (2000b). *IMS Health reports US pharmaceutical promotional spending reached record $13.9 billion in 1999.* Available at: http://www.imshealth.com/html/news_arc/04_20_2000_352.htm (accessed 5 September 2000).

International Narcotics Control Board. (2000). *Report on the International Narcotics Control Board for 1999.* New York: United Nations.

Jack, D.B. (1997). One hundred years of aspirin. *Lancet*, 350, 437–9.

Jacobs, D.J. (1995). Psychiatric drugging: 40 years of pseudo-science, self-interest, and indifference to harm. *Journal of Mind and Behavior*, 16, 421–70.

Kelly, M.P. and Field, D. (1997). Body image and sociology: A reply to Simon Williams. *Sociology of Health and Illness*, 19, 359–66.

Kopferschmitt, J., Meyer, P., Jaeger, A., Mantz, J.M. and Roos, M. (1992). Troubles du sommeil et consommation de médicaments psychotropes chez l'enfant de six ans (Sleep disorders and consumption of psychotropic medications with respect to the six-year-old child). *Revue d'épidémiologique et de Santé Publique*, 40, 467–71.

Lehrman, N.S. and Sharev, V.H. (1997). Ethical problems in psychiatric research. *Journal of Mental Health Administration*, 24, 227–50.

Lenglet, R. and Topuz, B. (1998). *Des lobbies contre la santé* (Lobbies against health). Paris: Syros.

Lexchin, J. (1993). Interactions between physicians and the pharmaceutical industry. *Canadian Medical Association Journal*, 149, 1401–7.

McCubbin, M. (1998). Global anarchy: Market failure, the prisoner's dilemma, and sovereignty over health and social policy. Paper presented at Xth International Conference, International Association of Health Policy, Perugia, Italy. Available at: http://www.mailbase.ac.uk/lists/radical-psychology-network/2000–02/0177.html [accessed 13 July 2001].

McCubbin, M. and Cohen, D. (1996). Extremely unbalanced: Interest divergence and power disparities between clients and psychiatry. *International Journal of Law and Psychiatry*, 19, 1–25.

Medawar, C. (1992). *Power and dependence.* London: Social Audit.

Medawar, C. (1997). The antidepressant web. *International Journal of Risk and Safety in Medicine*, 10, 75–126.

Medawar, C. (1999). *Direct-to-consumer advertising.* Available at: http://www.socialaudit.org.uk/5111-002.htm/#Dear [accessed 13 July 2001].

Montagne, M. (1988). The metaphorical nature of drugs and drug-taking. *Social Science & Medicine*, 26, 417–24.

Montagne, M. (1996). The Pharmakon phenomenon: Cultural conceptions of drugs and drug use. In P. Davis (Ed.), *Contested ground: Public concern and private interest in the regulation of pharmaceuticals.* New York: Oxford University Press.

Montagne, M. (1997). De l'activité pharmacologique à l'usage des drogues: La construction des connaissance sur les psychotropes (From pharmacological activity to the use of drugs: The construction of knowledge about psychotropics). *Santé mentale au Québec,* 22, 149–63.

Morant, N. (1998). The social representations of mental ill-health in communities of mental health practitioners in the UK and France. *Information sur les Sciences Sociales,* 37, 663–85.

O'Harrow, R., Jr (2000). Grass roots seeded by drug-maker. *The Washington Post,* 12 September, A1.

Olivieri, S., Cantopher, T. and Edwards, J.G. (1986). Two hundred years of anxiolytic drug dependence. *Neuropharmacology,* 25, 669–70.

Olson, J.A. (1994). Vitamins: The tortuous path from needs to fantasies. *Journal of Nutrition,* 124, Supplement, S1771–S1776.

Payer, L. (1990). *Medicine and culture: Notions of health and sickness in Britain, the US, France, and West Germany.* London: Gollancz.

Pérodeau, G. and Galbaud du Fort, G. (2000). Psychotropic drug use and the relation between social support, life events and mental health in the elderly. *Journal of Applied Gerontology,* 19, 23–41.

Pérodeau, G., King, S. and Ostoj, M. (1992). Stress and psychotropic drug use among the elderly: An exploratory model. *Canadian Journal on Aging,* 11, 347–69.

Pérodeau, G., Jomphe-Hill, A., Hay-Paquin, L. and Amyot, E. (1996). Les psychotropes et le vieillissement normal: Une perspective psychosociale et socioéconomique (Psychotropics and normal aging: A psychosocial and socioeconomic perspective). *Canadian Journal on Aging,* 15, 559–82.

Pharmaceutical Research and Manufacturers of America. (2000). *New medicines in development for mental illness.* Available at: http://www.phrma.org/searchcures/newmeds/mentalill/surv2000/ [accessed 13 July 2001].

Pignarre, P. (1995). *Les deux médicines: Médicaments, psychotropes et suggestion thérapeutique (The two medicines: Medications, psychotropics, and therapeutic suggesion).* Paris: La Découverte.

Pincus, H.A., Tanielian, T.L., Marcus, S.C., Olfson, M., Zarin, D.A., Thompson, J. et al. (1998). Prescribing trends in psychotropic medications: Primary care, psychiatry, and other medical specialties. *JAMA, 279,* 526–31.

Prather, J. (1991). Decoding advertising: The role of communication studies in explaining the popularity of tranquillisers. In J. Gabe (Ed.), *Understanding tranquilliser use.* London: Tavistock/Routledge.

Raje, N. and Anderson, K. (1999). Thalidomide: A revival story. *New England Journal of Medicine, 341,* 1606–9.

Rome, H.P. (1986). Personal reflections: The Rx as talisman. *Psychiatric Annals,* 16, 566.

Roter, D.L. and Frankel, R. (1992). Quantitative and qualitative approaches to the evaluation of the medical dialogue. *Social Science & Medicine,* 34, 1097–103.

Roughead, E.E., Harvey, K.J. and Gilbert, A.L. (1998). Commercial detailing techniques used by pharmaceutical representatives to influence prescribing. *Australian and New Zealand Journal of Medicine,* 28, 306–10.

Sands, W.L. (1965). The tranquilizer tablet. Talisman for the 1960s. *Psychiatric Quarterly,* 39, 722–6.

Sclar, D.A., Robison, L.M., Skaer, T.L. and Galin, R.S. (1998). What factors influence the prescribing of antidepressant pharmacotherapy? An assessment of national office-based encounters. *International Journal of Psychiatry in Medicine,* 28, 407–19.

Shapiro, A.K. and Shapiro, E. (1997). *The powerful placebo: From ancient priest to modern physician.* Baltimore, MD: Johns Hopkins University Press.

Sice, J., Levine, H.D., Levin, J. and Haertzen, C.A. (1975). Effects of personal interactions and settings on subjective drug responses in small groups. *Psychopharmacologia,* 43, 181–6.

Silverstein, K. (1999). Prozac.org. *Mother Jones,* December, 18–19.

Spiegel, D. (Ed.). (1999). *Efficacy and cost-effectiveness of psychotherapy.* Washington, DC: American Psychiatric Press.

Stein, H.F. (1990). In what systems do alcohol/chemical addictions make sense? Clinical idealogies and practices as cultural metaphors. *Social Science & Medicine,* 30, 987–1000.

Thornley, B. and Adams, C. (1998). Content and quality of 2000 controlled trials in schizophrenia over 50 years. *BMJ,* 317, 1181–4.

Van der Geest, S., Whyte, S.R. and Hardon, A. (1996). The anthropology of pharmaceuticals: A biographical approach. *Annual Review of Anthropology,* 25, 153–78.

Volkow, N.D., Ding, Y., Fowler, J.S., Wang, G., Logan, J., Gatley, J.S., Dewey, S., Ashby, C., Lieberman, J., Hitzemann, R. and Wolf, A.P. (1995). Is methylphenidate like cocaine? Studies on their pharmacokinetics and distribution in the human brain. *Archives of General Psychiatry,* 52, 456–63.

Vuckovic, N. and Nichter, M. (1997). Changing patterns of pharmaceutical practice in the United States. *Social Science & Medicine, 44,* 1285–302.

Walker, M.J. (1994). *Dirty medicine: Science, big business and the assault on natural health care,* revised edn. London: Slingshot.

Witte, B. (1999). *Judge cites hyperactivity drug in homicide acquittal.* Associated Press dispatch, 25 October. Available at: www.abcnews.go.com/sections/living/DailyNews/adderall991025.html [accessed 13 July 2001].

Wysowski, D.K. and Baum, C. (1991). Outpatient use of prescription sedative-hypnotic drugs in the United States, 1970 through 1989. *Archives of Internal Medicine,* 151, 1779–83.

Zarifian, E. (1996). *Le prix du bien-être. Psychotropes et societé* (The price of well-being. Psychotropics and society). Paris: Odile Jacob.

Zito, J.M., Safer, D.J., dosReis, S., Gardner, J.F., Boles, M. and Lynch, F. (2000). Trends in the prescribing of psychotropic medications to preschoolers. *JAMA,* 283, 1025–30.

Financing Medical Care

Medical care is big business in the United States. Billions of dollars are spent each year on medical services, with nearly half of each dollar coming from public funds. Medical costs, a significant factor in the economy's inflationary spiral, were until quite recently practically unregulated. Most of the money spent on medical care in the United States is spent via *third-party payments* on a fee-for-service basis.[1] Unlike *direct* (or *out-of-pocket*) payments, third-party payments are those made through some form of insurance or charitable organization for someone's medical care. Third-party payments have increased steadily over the past forty years. In 1950 a total of 32 percent of personal health care expenditures were made via third-party payments; in 1965 that figure was up to 48 percent; and by 1974 the ratio of third-party payments had increased to 65 percent (*Medical Care Chart Book,* 1976: 117). By 1998 third-party payments represented approximately 81 percent of all medical care expenditures. Almost all third-party payments are made by public or private insurance. The insurance industry is thus central to the financing of medical care services in this country. This section examines the role of insurance in financing medical care and the influence of the insurance industry on the present-day organization of medical services.

The original method of paying for medical services directly or individually, in money or in kind, has today been replaced by payment via insurance. Essentially, insurance is a form of "mass financing" ensuring that medical care providers will be paid and people will be able to obtain and pay for the medical care they need. Insurance involves the regular collection of small amounts of money (premiums) from a large number of people. That money is put into a pool, and when the insured people get sick, that pool (the insurance company) pays for their medical services either directly or indirectly by sending the money to the provider or patient.

Although most Americans are covered by some form of third-party insurance, many millions are not. Over 40 million people are without health insurance and the number is growing (Friedman, 1991; Hadley and Hulahan, 2003); these are mostly young and working people whose employers do not provide insurance, who earn too little to afford the premiums, or who earn too much to be eligible for Medicaid. In addition, having an insurance plan does not mean that all of one's medical costs are paid for.

The United States has both private and public insurance programs. Public insurance programs, including Medicare and Medicaid, are funded primarily by monies collected by federal, state, or local governments in the form of taxes. The nation has two types of private insurance organizations: *nonprofit* tax-exempt Blue Cross and Blue Shield plans and for-profit *commercial* insurance companies.

Blue Cross and Blue Shield emerged out of the Great Depression of the 1930s as mechanisms to ensure the payment of medical bills to hospitals (Blue Cross) and physicians (Blue Shield). The Blues (Blue Cross and Blue Shield) were developed as community plans through which people made small "pre-payments" on a regular basis generally monthly. If they became sick, their hospital bills were paid directly by the insurance plan.

Although commercial insurance companies existed as early as the nineteenth century, only after World War II did they really expand in this country. Blue Cross and Blue Shield originally set the price of insurance premiums by what was called "community rating," giving everybody within a community the chance to purchase insurance at the same price. Commercial insurers, on the other hand, employed "experience rating," which bases the price of insurance premiums on the statistical likelihood of the insured needing medical care. People less likely to need medical care are charged less for premiums than are people more likely to need it. By offering younger, healthier workers lower rates than could the Blues, commercials captured a large segment of the labor union insurance market in the 1950s and 1960s. In order to compete, Blue Cross and Blue Shield eventually abandoned community rating and began using experience rating as well. One unfortunate result of the spread of experience rating has been that those who most need insurance coverage the elderly and the sick are least able to afford or obtain it.

Medicare and Medicaid were passed by Congress in 1965 as amendments to the Social Security Act. Medicare pays for the medical care of people over sixty-five years of age and other qualified recipients of Social Security. Medicaid pays for the care of those who qualify as too poor to pay their own medical costs. However, commercial and nonprofit insurance companies act as intermediaries in these government programs. Providers of medical care are not paid directly by public funds; instead, these funds are channeled through the private insurance industry. The Blues also act as intermediaries in most Medicaid programs, which are state-controlled. Public funding via private insurance companies has resulted in enormous increases in the costs of both of these public insurance programs, high profits for the insurance intermediaries and their beneficiaries physicians and hospitals and near exhaustion of available public funds for the continuation of Medicare and Medicaid. Before 1965, the federal government paid about 10 percent of all medical expenditures. By 1995, it paid for nearly 38 percent of health care costs. The federal contribution to Medicare alone had risen from a couple of billion dollars in 1965 to 400 billion in 2004 and is still rising.

The Medicare-Medicaid response had a number of consequences. Medicare has provided basic medical insurance coverage for 99 percent of Americans over sixty-five. While the elderly still face significant out-of-pocket expenses, this widespread coverage is a stark contrast to their lack of coverage before 1965 (Davis, 1975). Medicaid has been much less comprehensive. Because it is a federal-state matching program, coverage varies from state to state. While many poor people receive greater coverage than they did before Medicaid, severe restrictions in eligibility leave many others with no coverage. Utilization of services has increased under Medicaid so that the poor, who are generally sicker than the nonpoor, visit medical services more frequently. The major impact of Medicaid has been on maternal and child health.

Although federal programs have surely helped some sick people and reduced inequality and inaccessibility of medical services, their effect is limited. The Republican administrations in the 1980s cut back a number of these programs. But even before these cutbacks Medicare covered less than half the elderly's health expenses, and Medicaid covered only a third of those of the poor (Starr, 1982: 374).

The intent of Medicare and Medicaid is certainly worthy, even if the results are limited. But these programs also created new problems. They put billions of new dollars into the health system with no cost controls, so by the 1970s Medicare and Medicaid were clearly fueling escalating health costs, which now comprise nearly 14 percent of the GNP. Some people were reaping enormous profits from the system, especially owners of shoddy nursing homes and so-called Medicaid mills. Tightening restrictions eliminated the worst offenders but medical costs continued to soar.

In the early 1970s the federal government began to mandate a series of programs aimed at reducing spiraling costs, especially with Medicare. In 1972 utilization review boards hospital-based committees were instituted to review the appropriateness of medical utilization. These were followed by Professional Standard Review Organizations (PSROs) set up to monitor both quality and cost of care. In the middle 1970s the nation was divided into dozens of Health System Agencies (HSAs), which were to be regionalized health planning agencies. HSAs attempted to regulate uncontrolled hospital and technological growth by requiring a "certificate of need" approval to justify any new investment over $100,000. There were even attempts to put a "cap" (ceiling) on the total amount that could be allocated to a program. Some cost control programs had limited effects in specific situations, but the federal attempt to control costs has so far been generally a failure.

A recent federal attempt to control costs is a complex reimbursement system called "Diagnostically Related Groups" (DRGs). Mandated in 1984 for Medicare, this program replaces the fee-for-service system with a form of "prospective reimbursement" whereby the government will pay only a specific amount for a specified medical problem. The prices of hundreds of diagnoses are established in advance. Medicare will pay no more, no less. If a hospital spends less than the set amount, it gets to pocket the difference. The idea is to give hospitals the incentive to be efficient and save money. The concern is that patients will get poorer treatment. The rise of managed care as a method for delivering health care (see Selection 21 by Fry et al.) is largely a response to rising costs. Managed care requires pre-approvals for many forms of medical treatment and sets limits on some types of care, in an effort to control medical expenditures. This has given third-party payers more leverage and constrained both the care given by doctors (or providers) and the care received by patients (or subscribers).

This section investigates the origins and consequences of financing medical care in the particular way the American medical system has evolved. In the first selection, "A Century of Failure: Health Care Reform in America," David J. Rothman examines why the United States has not developed a national health insurance plan. Tracing the historical development of private health insurance, Rothman suggests that one key is the absence of the middle class from a coalition favoring government health reform. Both Blue Cross, as the leading insurance company, and physicians, as professionals and business-people, opposed government intervention. Voluntary, private health insurance for the middle class became seen as the best alternative to government involvement in health care.

Thomas Bodenheimer and Kevin Grumbach discuss the historical process of health care financing in "Paying for Health Care," illustrating the impact of shifts in payment mechanisms. Using vignettes as illustrations, they show how each solution for financing health care created a new set of problems. In particular, they examine the emergence of four modes of payment for patients or consumers: out of pocket, individual private health insurance, employment-based group private insurance, and government financing. While private insurance certainly has helped many sick people, it has not been provided in a fair and equitable manner. The shift from community-rated to experience-rated insurance was a regressive policy change and had a negative effect on those who were old, sick, poor, or at risk. In other words, while experience rating gave the commercial insurers a competitive edge (Starr, 1982), it undermined insurance as a principle of mutual aid and eroded any basis of distributive justice in insurance (Stone, 1993). And, as noted earlier, it left approximately 40 million people without any insurance and another 20 million people with insurance that is generally considered inadequate in the face of serious illness (Bodenheimer, 1992).

President Clinton's attempts at national health reform in the early 1990s failed (see Starr, 1995), but the health care system has continued to change through the "market-based reform" of managed care. Currently, nearly 70 million Americans are covered by some kind of managed care system and that number is increasing yearly (Spragins, 1998). Managed care is an attempt to deliver medical care while reducing or controlling health costs. Health Maintenance Organizations (HMOs) are the key to managed care linking hospitals, doctors, and specialists with the goal of delivering more effective care at lower costs and eliminating "unnecessary" or "inappropriate" care (see Wholey and Burns, 2000). While this can create more coordinated care, it also puts restrictions on physician access and available treatments. In an effort to make health care more accountable, patients are concerned that they are treated as "cost units." As discussed in earlier chapters, managed care has eroded physician autonomy (Chapters 18 and 19), endangered "trust" between doctors and patients (Chapter 20), and encouraged new systems for rationing services (see debate "Rationing Medical Care"). In the final article in the section, "Doctoring as a Business: Money, Markets, and Managed Care," Deborah A. Stone shows how the monetary incentives built into managed care can turn doctors into business people, resulting in higher potential incomes but poorer quality care. While the old ideal about clinical care without regard to cost or profit is now unrealistic, the commercial nature of managed care encourages doctors to emphasize profits over patient care.

NOTE

1. Fee-for-service is a central feature of the economic organization of medicine in our society. Since medical providers are paid a fee for every service they

provide, many critics argue that a fee-for-service system creates a financial incentive to deliver unnecessary services, making medical care more profitable and costly.

REFERENCES

Bodenheimer, Thomas. 1992. "Underinsurance in America." New England Journal of Medicine. 327: 274–278.

Davis, Karen. 1975. "Equal treatment and unequal benefits: The Medicare program." Milbank Memorial Fund Quarterly. 53, 4:449–88.

Friedman, Emily. 1991. "The uninsured: From dilemma to crisis." Journal of the American Medical Association. 265: 2491–2495.

Hadley, J., and J. Hulahan. 2003. "Covering the uninsured: How much would it cost?" Health affairs. W3:250–65.

Medical Care Chart Book. Sixth Edition. 1976. School of Public Health, Department of Medical Care Organization, University of Michigan. Data on third-party payments computed from Chart D-15: 117.

Spragins, Ellyn E. 1998. "Does managed care work?" Newsweek, September 28, pp. 61–70.

Starr, Paul. 1982. The Social Transformation of American Medicine. New York: Basic Books.

Starr, Paul. 1995. "What happened to health care reform?" American Prospect. Winter: 20–31.

Stone, Deborah A. 1993. "The struggle for the soul of health insurance." Journal of Health Politics, Policy and Law. 18: 287–317.

Wholey, Douglas R. and Lawton R. Burns. 2000. "Tides of change: The evolution of managed care in the United States." Pp. 217–37 in Chloe Bird, Peter Conrad, and Allen M. Fremont (eds.), Handbook of Medical Sociology, Fifth Edition. Upper Saddle River, NJ: Prentice-Hall.

26 A CENTURY OF FAILURE: HEALTH CARE REFORM IN AMERICA

David J. Rothman

There are some questions that historians return to so often that they become classics in the field, to be explored and reexplored, considered and reconsidered. No inquiry better qualifies for this designation than the question of why the United States has never enacted a national health insurance program. Why, with the exception of South Africa, does it remain the only industrialized country that has not implemented so fundamental a social welfare policy?

The roster of answers that have been provided is impressive in its insights. Some outstanding contributions to our understanding of the issues come from James Morone, Paul Starr, Theodore Marmor, and Theda Skocpol. Their explanations complement, rather than counter, each other. In like manner, the elements that this essay will explore are intended to supplement, not dislodge, their work. A failure in policy that is so basic is bound to be overdetermined, and therefore, efforts to fathom it will inevitably proceed in a variety of directions.

THE LIBERAL STATE

Morone's frame for understanding American health policy in general and the failure of national health insurance in particular centers on the definitions of the proper role of the state, the acceptable limits for all governmental actions. His starting point is with the fact that the medical profession successfully "appropriated public authority to take charge of the health care field," taking for itself the task of defining the content, organization, and, perhaps most important, the financing of medical practice (Morone 1990: 253–84). This accomplishment points to more than the power of the American Medical Association's lobbying machine; AMA rhetoric, which has seemed to other observers to be bombastic, comical, or even hysterical, in Morone's terms was effective precisely because it drew on popularly shared assumptions about the proper relationship between governmental authority, professional capacity, and professional autonomy. By the terms of this consensus, the government's duty was to build up professional capacity without infringing on professional autonomy and as long as the medical profession defined national health insurance as an infringement on its autonomy, such a policy would not be enacted. Government was permitted to build hospitals (witness the implementation of the Hill-Burton Act) and to endow the research establishment (witness the extraordinary growth of the National Institutes of Health), but it was not allowed, at least until very recently, to challenge or subvert professional autonomy.

Paul Starr also focuses on conceptions of state authority to explain health policy. Alert to the markedly different course of national health insurance in European countries, he posits that where a spirit of liberalism and a commitment to the inviolability of private property interests in relation to the state were strongest, movements for social insurance made the least headway. Thus, Bismarck's Germany could accomplish what Theodore Roosevelt's or Franklin Roosevelt's United States could not. Put another way, the fact that socialism never put down strong roots in this country, the absence here of a socialist tradition or threat, obviated the need for more conservative forces to buttress the social order through welfare measures.

Starr is more ready than Morone to credit the raw political power of the AMA, but he also reminds us that the AMA found allies among not only corporations but also labor unions. Union leaders preferred to obtain health care benefits for its members through contract negotiation, not through government largesse even if that meant,

The research for this article was conducted under a grant from the Twentieth Century Fund.

or precisely because that meant, that nonunion members would go without benefits (Starr 1982: part 2).

Paralleling their studies are detailed accounts of the legislative histories of various health insurance proposals, the fate of Progressive, New Deal, and Fair Deal initiatives. The work of Theodore Marmor has clarified the political alliances that came together to enact Medicare and Medicaid (Marmor 1982). So too, the writings of Theda Skocpol place health care legislation more directly in the tradition of American welfare policies (Weir et al. 1988). In all, the existing literature illuminates the effects of both conceptions of governmental authority and the realities of constituent policies to tell us why the United States stands alone in its failure to enact national health insurance.

CO-OPTING THE MIDDLE CLASS

Despite the sophisticated and perceptive quality of these arguments, still other considerations underlie the failure to enact national health insurance. An analysis of them does not subvert the basic contours of the other interpretations but provides a deeper social context for the story.

The starting point for such an analysis is a frank recognition of the fact that what is under discussion is essentially a moral failure, a demonstration of a level of indifference to the well-being of others that stands as an indictment of the intrinsic character of American society. This observation, however, is not meant to inspire a jeremiad on American imperfections as much as to open an inquiry into the dynamics of the failure not only how it occurred but how it was rationalized and tolerated. Americans do not think of themselves as callous and cruel, and yet, in their readiness to forgo and withhold this most elemental social service, they have been so. This question arises: How did the middle class, its elected representatives, and its doctors accommodate themselves to such neglect? To be sure, Morone, Starr, and others have made it clear that ideas on the proper scope of government were powerful determinants of behavior, that leaders like FDR made strategic political calculations that traded off health insurance for other programs, and that the AMA smugly equated physician self-interest with national interest. But given the signal importance of health care and, a minority of commentators aside, the ongoing recognition that it is more than one more commodity to be left to the vagaries of the marketplace there is a need for an even broader framework for understanding these events. The chess moves of politicians, and even the rules of the game of politics, seem somewhat too removed and abstract. Put most succinctly: How could Americans ignore the health needs of so many fellow countrymen and still live with themselves? How could a society that prides itself on decency tolerate this degree of unfairness?

For answers, it is appropriate to look first to the 1930s. As a result of the Great Depression, American social welfare legislation was transformed, as exemplified by the passage of the Social Security Act. Moreover, by the 1930s, the popular faith in the efficacy of medical interventions was firmly established and the consequences of a denial of medical care, apparent. Already by the 1910s, some would-be reformers defined the goal of health insurance not merely as compensation to the sick for wages lost during illness but as the opportunity to obtain curative medical care. Twenty years later, this credo was accepted by almost all reformers, although the efficacy of medical interventions was, at least by current standards, far from impressive. Also by the 1930s, the hospital, which had earlier been almost indistinguishable from the almshouse, had become a temple of science and its leaders, Men in White, widely celebrated. In keeping with these changes, physician visits and hospital occupancy now correlated directly, not inversely, with income.

Why then was national health insurance omitted from the roster of legislation enacted in the 1930s? If medicine was so valued and government so receptive to novel (at least for Americans) social insurance programs, why was health insurance kept off the roster? Although such considerations as FDR's reluctance to do battle with the AMA or to fragment his southern alliance were important, perhaps even more determinative were the tactics, thoroughly self-conscious, that were helping to remove the middle classes from the coalition of advocates for change. And eliminating the middle classes from the alignment successfully deflated the political pressure for national health insurance.

One of the pivotal groups in designing and implementing this strategy was a newly founded, private health insurance company, Blue Cross. Against the backdrop of the report of the Committee on the Costs of Medical Care, urging greater federal intervention in health care, Blue Cross presented itself as the best alternative to government involvement. Its organizers and supporters, such as Rufus Rorem and Walter Dannreuther, held out the promise that enrolling the middle class in its plan would blunt the thrust for national health insurance. Blue Cross, declared Dannreuther, would "eliminate the demand for compulsory health insurance and stop the reintroduction of vicious sociological bills into the state legislature year after year." Blue Cross advertisements, pamphlets, radio programs, and publications insisted that neither the rich nor the poor confronted difficulties in obtaining medical services, the rich because they could easily afford it, the poor because they had ready access to public hospitals. Only the middle classes faced a problem, and unless their needs were met, they were bound to agitate for a change in governmental policy. ("It is the people in the middle income group who often find it most difficult to secure adequate medical and hospital care," declared Louis Pink, president of New York Blue Cross. "It is sometimes said that the very poor and the rich if there are any rich left get the best medical care.")[1] The idea was not to buy the middle classes off by expanding the services of public hospitals and persuading them to take a place on the wards to meet emergency needs. Such a solution, as Blue Cross proponents explained, would not only strain the public hospital system beyond its capacity, but would not work because the middle classes considered the public hospitals to be charity, with all innuendo intended, and they were not about to accept charity. As one Blue Cross official insisted: "The average man, with the average income, has pride. He is not looking for charity; he is not looking for ward care. He wants the best of attention for himself and his family. Yet out of his savings, he is very seldom prepared to meet unexpected sickness or accident expenses." Thus, to use the public hospital was not only to get second-best care but to be stigmatized as dependent, incapable of standing on one's own two feet. Like the dole, the public hospital violated the American way. Were this the only choice, the middle classes would push for, and obtain, national health insurance.

The alternative that embodied the American way was a private subscription plan, which, for as little as three cents a day (the Blue Cross slogan), protected members from the high cost of hospitalization. "The Blue Cross Plans are a distinctly American institution," declared one of its officials, "a unique combination of individual initiative and social responsibility. They perform a public service without public compulsion." Another executive asserted that Blue Cross exemplified "the American spirit of neighborliness and self-help [which] solves the difficult and important problem of personal and national health." All of which led inexorably to the conclusion: "Private enterprise in voluntarily providing hospital care within the reach of everyone is solving the public health problem in the real democratic way. The continued growth of the Blue Cross Movement might well be considered the best insurance against the need of governmental provision for such protection" (quoted in Rothman 1991).

Blue Cross was notably successful in enrolling middle-class subscribers, serving, as intended, to reduce or eliminate their concern over the payment of hospital bills. To be sure, it took some time to build up a membership, but by 1939 there were thirty-nine Blue Cross plans in operation with more than 6 million subscribers. Indeed, the plans became even more over time, with some 31 million subscribers by 1949 (Starr 1982: 298, 327).[2] In fact, from its inception the impact of Blue Cross was probably greater than even the membership statistics indicate. Its extraordinarily active advertising campaigns made a compelling case that private, as against public, initiatives were more than sufficient to meet the problem, so that even those who did not immediately enroll may have accepted the viability of this alternative. There was no reason to press for political change when the private sector seemed to have resolved the issue. Thus both in rhetoric and in reality, Blue Cross helped to undercut middle-class interest in and concern for national health insurance. The result, fully intended, was that they did not join or lend strength to a coalition for change. Politics could do business as usual, allowing a variety of other considerations to outweigh support for such an innovation.[3]

In fact, the dynamic set off by Blue Cross in the 1930s gained strength in the post-1945 period, not only from its own growth but from the labor movement. Not just private insurance but union benefits served to cushion the middle classes from the impact of health care costs. Over these years, contract provisions negotiated with business corporations provided unionized workers with health care benefits, reducing their felt need for government programs. With that many more middle-class households effectively covered, it would require empathy, not self-interest, to push for national health insurance, and that empathy, for reasons that we will explore further below, was in short supply. As a result, public responsibility for health care became linked to the welfare system, serving only the poor, not the respectable. Coverage was something to be provided for "them," not what "we" needed or were entitled to as citizens.

How this divide between "we" and "they" shaped welfare policy emerges with particular vividness in the history of the almshouse in the 1930s. When the decade began, the institution was still one of the mainstays of public welfare policy, particularly for the elderly and for those considered the "unworthy poor." Although the post-World War II generation associates the almshouse with Dickensian England, it was of major importance in this country even at the start of the Great Depression. Only in the mid-1930s did the almshouse begin to lose its hold on welfare programs, moved aside by such New Deal relief programs as the Works Project Administration (WPA) and the Social Security Act. In fact, WPA regulations prohibited the expenditure of funds to build or enlarge these institutions; the WPA was ready to build roads but not to build or refurbish almshouses. Why this distinction? Why the abandonment, at long last, of the almshouse? Because for the first time, almshouse relief would have had to include the middle classes. With state and city budgets staggering under the burden of relief and private charities altogether unequal to the task, absent a WPA or Social Security Act, many of the once-employed would have had to enter the almshouse. The prospect of having respectable middle-class citizens in such a facility was so disturbing as to transform government relief policy.

Imagine this same dynamic at work in health care. Picture the middle classes having no alternative but to crowd into the public hospital, to receive medical services in the twelve-bed wards. It is by no means fanciful to suggest that had this been the case, a different kind of pressure would have been exerted on the government to enact health insurance coverage. Blue Cross, however, self-consciously and successfully short-circuited the process and thereby allowed the play of politics to go on uninterrupted.

THE PHYSICIAN AS ENTREPRENEUR

A second critical element that underlay the American failure to implement national health insurance was the character of its medical profession. The speeches, letters, and writings of American doctors over the period 1920–1950 indicate broad sympathy for the positions of the AMA, perhaps somewhat less dogmatic but fully sharing of the organization's commitment to a fee-for-service system. Although some historians have found significant diversity of medical opinion on national health insurance earlier in the Progressive Era, by the 1920s most physicians were profoundly uncomfortable with proposed government intrusions into health care.

Narrow financial self-interest, the fear of a loss of income through national health insurance, was a force in shaping some doctors' attitudes, but it was far from the only consideration. For one, physicians' earnings were not so large as to turn them necessarily into dogged defenders of the status quo. Physicians' average income, for example, was below that of lawyers and engineers; in 1929, of the 121,000 physicians in private practice, 53 percent had incomes below $4,000, and 80 percent, less than $8,000. To be sure, some 12 percent of physicians had incomes over $11,500, but the profession was far from a lucrative one (President's Research Committee 1933: 1104). In strictly financial terms, it would not have been illogical for doctors generally to have supported national programs, particularly in the 1930s. They might have accepted government intervention with some enthusiasm, on the grounds that it was better to receive some payment from Washington than no payment from a patient. But this was not the position commonly adopted, and to understand why requires an appreciation of the essentially entrepreneurial character of American medicine. In more precise terms, the mindset of physicians was that of the independent proprietor. They identified themselves as businessmen and, as such, shared an aversion to government interference.

It may be that the very differentiation in income among physicians at once reflected and reinforced a scramble for income that is not commonly associated with the practice of medicine. This was the conclusion that the Lynds reached in their portrait of "Middletown" in the 1920s. "The profession of medicine," they wrote, "swings around the making of money as one of its chief concerns. As a group, Middletown physicians are devoting their energies to building up and maintaining a practice in a highly competitive field. Competition is so keen that even the best doctors in many cases supplement their incomes by putting up their own prescriptions" (Lynd and Lynd [1929] 1956: 443). It was not unusual for physicians to invest in proprietary hospitals or to accept fee-splitting arrangements. Doctors also purchased common stocks and invested in local businesses albeit not always very cleverly. By the 1920s, doctors had such a reputation for being suckers that advice books on business addressed to them devoted large sections to discussions of "Why Do Doctors Fail to Choose the Right Investments?" The answers were generally variations on the theme of "There is a host of people who have found out that the doctor likes to take a chance. . . . He has worked so hard to accumulate his small savings and the possibility of making prodigious returns are presented to him so plausibly by some glib talker that all too frequently this nest egg is frittered away on some unsavory scheme, for he seldom has the time, inclination and facilities to make the essential investigation" (Thomas 1923: 174–75). In effect, the financial dealings that occupy physicians today are far less novel than critics like Arnold Relman might like to imagine.

To account for physicians' entrepreneurial perspective, it is vital to remember that their social world overlapped with that of the local business elite, particularly in smaller towns. When one upper-class resident of "Regionville" was asked by sociologist Earl Koos to list the five most important people in the town, he responded: "I put Doc X on that list because . . . he is one of the best-educated men in town, and makes good money—drives a good car, belongs to Rotary, and so forth. . . . Of course, some doctors aren't as important as others, here or anywhere else, but unless they're drunks or drug addicts, they're just automatically pretty top rank in town" (Koos 1954: 54).

The pattern of recruitment to the profession also encouraged this orientation. Medical school classes in the 1920s and 1930s were the almost exclusive preserve of white, upper-middle-class males. From birth, it would seem, physicians were comfortable, socially and ideologically, in the clubhouse locker room. The image is properly one of Wednesday afternoon off, doctor chatting with town banker, lawyer, and principal store owner about investment opportunities and politics, with a shared antagonism to what all of them considered the evil of Government Control.

Physicians voiced their opposition to national health insurance not only collectively through the AMA but individually as well, in the process helping to mold public attitudes. As Koos aptly observed, in towns like Regionville, especially before 1950 (before the rise of a more national media and greater opportunities for travel), doctors were opinion leaders: "In the small town, the doctor is most often 'a big frog in a little puddle'; what he thinks and does can assume an importance in the community not paralleled in the life of his urban counterpart" (Koos 1954: 150). In brief, the entrepreneurial style of American physicians helps explain much of their own and some of their neighbors' disinclination to support national health insurance.

THE ETHOS OF VOLUNTARISM

But then how did Americans live with the consequences of their decision? How did they justify to themselves and to others their unwillingness to provide so essential a service as medical care to those unable to afford it? The need for pragmatism in politics (we dare do no other) and definitions of the boundaries of state authority (we should do no other) surely mattered. So, too, in health care as in matters of social welfare more generally, they could always fall back on such truisms as "The poor have only themselves to blame for their poverty—they should have saved for the rainy day." And middle-class Americans could also invoke the safety net of the public hospital, noting that its services were available to all comers, regardless of income.

But there were other justifications as well, particularly the celebration of the ethos of voluntarism, the credo that individual and organizational charity obviated the need for government intervention. Individual physicians and community charities ostensibly provided the needy with requisite medical care. This idea was not fabricated from whole cloth, for Americans, and their doctors, had good reason to believe that their own initiatives were sufficient to meet the problem.

Physicians, for their part, insisted that they turned no one away from their offices because of an inability to pay for services. They used a sliding scale for setting fees, charging the "haves" more and the "have-nots" less, so as to promote the social good. The claim was incessantly repeated and undoubtedly had some validity to it. "It was probably true," reported Koos, "that no physician in Regionville would leave a worthy case untreated." The physician, claimed the New York Medical Society in 1939, "has socialized his own services. Traditionally, he is at the call of the indigent without recompense. . . . For those who are self-supporting, he graduates his fees to meet the ability to pay, and extends time for payment over long periods." As late as 1951, a survey of physicians in Toledo, Ohio, found overwhelming support for a sliding scale of fees and widespread agreement that, to quote one response: "It's fair, the fairest thing we can do. If a man is wealthy, you certainly would charge him more than if he didn't have a dime. It's not uncommon for a doctor to call me and say, 'These people don't have any money,' or can pay only a little, and I say, 'Sure send 'em on in. I'll take care of 'em' " (Schuler et al. 1952: 60, 69, 85). Thus, physicians justified their opposition to national health insurance by citing their own altruism. Their charity rendered government intervention unnecessary.

By the same token, community philanthropy often stepped in where the circumstances went beyond the scope of individual physicians. It was not only a matter of a voluntary society establishing not-for-profit hospitals or organizing outpatient dispensaries. Voluntarism seemed capable of meeting the most exceptional challenge. To choose one of the most noteworthy examples, in the case of polio, private charitable efforts helped to make certain that no child, whatever the family's income, would lack for access to an iron lung or to rehabilitative services. By November 1931, only two years after Philip Drinker perfected the iron lung, there were 150 respirators to be found in hospitals across the country. Foundations, including Milbank and Harkness, underwrote the cost of some of the machines, and their efforts were supplemented by the fund-raising work of local ladies' auxiliaries. As for patient rehabilitation, the National Foundation for Infantile Paralysis, founded in 1938 by FDR and directed by onetime Wall Street attorney Basil O'Connor, supported both research and the delivery of clinical services. Several thousand local chapters and one hundred thousand volunteers made certain that no person with polio was denied medical assistance because of economic hardship. And the foundation defined "hardship" liberally, to cover the case where medical expenditures would force a family to lower its standard of living.

The polio experience was particularly important in confirming a belief in the adequacy of voluntarism. With a world-famous patient, in the person of President Franklin Roosevelt, and an extraordinarily successful foundation, a compelling case could be made for the capacity of voluntary action to meet the most unusual and costly health care needs. Moreover, the lesson was felt particularly strongly by the middle classes, because polio was in many ways their disease, disproportionately striking children raised in hygienic, uncrowded, and (epidemiologically speaking) protected environments. Those from lower-class and urban backgrounds were more likely to be exposed to the virus at a young age and had thereby built up immunities to it. Thus the foundation, like Blue Cross, served the middle classes so well that it insulated them from the predicament of health care costs. No wonder, then, that they, and their political representatives, to the degree that they looked out on the world from their own experience, found little need for government intervention and were able to maintain this position without either embarrassment or guilt.

THE DUAL MESSAGE OF MEDICARE

Surprising as it may seem, the rhetoric that surrounded the enactment of Medicare reinforced many of these constricted views. The most significant government intervention in health care did not, the wishes of many of its proponents notwithstanding, enlarge the vision of the middle classes or make the case for national health insurance. To the contrary. The debate around Medicare in a variety of ways made it seem as though, the elderly aside, all was well with the provision of medical services.

In the extensive hearings and debates that Congress devoted to Medicare between 1963 and 1965, proponents of the bill, undoubtedly for strategic political reasons, repeatedly distinguished Medicare from a national health insurance scheme. So intent were they on securing the passage of this act that they went to great pains to minimize the need for any additional interventions once Medicare was in place. And as they offered these arguments, perhaps unintentionally but nevertheless quite powerfully, they reinforced very traditional perspectives on poverty and welfare and the special character of middle-class needs.

The opening statement given in November 1963 to the House Committee on Ways and Means by then secretary of Health, Education, and Welfare, Anthony Celebrezze, laid out the themes that other advocates consistently followed. His goal was to demonstrate that the elderly presented "a unique problem," and thereby warranted special support. Just when their postretirement incomes were declining, they faced disproportionately higher health care costs: "People over sixty-five," Celebrezze calculated, "use three times as much hospital care, on the average, as people under sixty-five." Moreover, the private health insurance system that worked so well for others did not meet their needs: the premiums were too expensive (one sixth of their medium income), and the policies often included restrictive clauses (for example, ruling out preexisting conditions). Hence, Celebrezze concluded, "this combination of high health costs, low incomes, and unavailability of group insurance is what clearly distinguishes the situation of the aged as a group from the situation of younger workers as a group" (U.S. Congress 1964: 28).

It was a shrewd argument, but it left open several problems. The first was to justify excluding the young from a federal program. To this end, Celebrezze and the other Medicare proponents frankly and wholeheartedly endorsed the status quo: "The vast majority of young workers can purchase private insurance protection. . . . I think for younger employed people, voluntary private plans can do the job" (U.S. Congress 1964: 36). Those below sixty-five were less likely to require health care interventions, and, should they encounter sudden needs, they could always borrow the sums and pay them back through their future earnings. In effect, the Medicare proponents swept under the table the problems of access to health care for those who were outside the net of employer-provided private insurance.

The second and even tougher issue for the Medicare supporters was to explain why the elderly in need should not be required to rely on the welfare system to meet their health care requirements. After all, as one critic noted, these people had been remiss in not saving for the rainy day, and the government ought not to bail them out. They would not have to forgo health care services. Rather, to the opponents of Medicare, which included to the very end the AMA, the just solution was to aid them through a program like Kerr-Mills. Under its provisions, the needy elderly would demonstrate (to public assistance officials) their lack of resources, take a place on the welfare rolls, and then receive their health care services under a combined federal-state program. The counterargument from the Medicare camp was that to compel the elderly to demonstrate their dependency was too demeaning. "We should take into account the pride and independent spirit of our older people," Celebrezze insisted. "We should do better than say to an aged person that, when he has become poor enough and when he can prove his poverty to the satisfaction of the appropriate public agency, he may be able to get help." But if welfare was so humiliating, why should anyone have to suffer such a process? If welfare demeaned the elderly, why did it not demean the young? To which the tacit answer was that if the young were poor, they had only themselves to blame. Those on welfare, the elderly apart, were so "unworthy" that humiliation was their due, at least until they reached sixty-five (U.S. Congress 1964: 31).

The third and probably most difficult question was whether a federal health insurance program for the elderly ultimately rested, as one opponent put it, on the premise that "the federal government, as a matter of right, owes medical care to elderly people." Again Celebrezze backed off a general principle in order to separate out the case of the elderly. Admittedly, he had opened his testimony with the statement that for the elderly, "the first line of defense is protection furnished as a right." But in response to hostile questions, he retreated, declaring that the federal government did not owe anyone "medical attention as a right." Medicare was to be part of the social security system, which meant that beneficiaries had paid for their benefits. And even if the first recipients would not have done so in strictly actuarial terms, still they had made their contributions "on a total program basis" (U.S. Congress 1964: 158). Although the meaning of that phrase was altogether obscure, the gist of the argument was clear: Medicare would not establish a right to health care. Ostensibly, it was not the opening shot in a larger campaign. In some oblique but still meaningful way, the principle remained that you got what you paid for, more or less.

Clearly, all these maneuvers were part of a strategy to get Medicare enacted, and many proponents insisted after the fact that they had been confident, undoubtedly too confident, that Medicare would be the first step on the road to national health insurance. They were, of course, wrong for all the reasons we have been exploring, along with one other consideration. These Medicare proponents may have been too successful in marking off the case of the elderly. Having taken the pragmatic route, they reinforced older attitudes, afraid to come out in favor of a right to health care, afraid to break out of the mold of a quid pro quo mentality for benefits, afraid to advocate a program in terms that were more universal than middle-class interests. It was the 1930s almshouse dynamic revisited because the worthy middle class could not be expected to go on relief to gain medical benefits, the system had to change. True, others would benefit from the program, including non-middle-class elderly. But that seemed almost serendipitous. Medicare was to protect the elderly middle classes from burdensome health care costs, not break new ground more generally by changing demeaning welfare policies or rethinking health care rights or the limits of private insurance for those under sixty-five. Thus, it should be less surprising that for the next several decades, Medicare did not inspire a new venture in government underwriting of health care.

FUTURE PROSPECTS

In light of a tradition of narrow middle-class self-interest, the entrepreneurial quality of American medicine, and the tradition of voluntarism, what are the current prospects for a national health insurance program?

Perhaps the most encouraging point is that each of the elements that have been discussed here are in flux. The middle classes, by all accounts, are feeling the impact of rising health insurance costs and are becoming increasingly vulnerable (through periodic unemployment or narrowing eligibility requirements of insurance companies) to the loss of insurance benefits. The weaknesses of a private system are in this way becoming quite apparent to them. At the same time, there are signs that American medicine is becoming less entrepreneurial, witness the increased numbers of salaried physicians employed by HMOs, corporations, and hospitals. And by now, the limits of voluntarism are glaringly obvious: whether the case is kidney dialysis or the future of the voluntary hospital, it is practically indisputable that the not-for-profit sector is incapable of shouldering the burden of health care.

All this would be grounds for optimism, were it not for one final element: the persistence of a narrowed vision of middle-class politics. With no largesse of spirit, with no sense of mutual responsibility, the middle classes and their representatives may advocate only minimal changes designed to provide protection only for them, not those in more desperate straits. In policy terms, it may bring changes that are more exclusive than inclusive, serving the employed as against the unemployed, protecting the benefits of those who have some coverage already as opposed to bringing more people to the benefits table. It may also promote schemes that will serve the lower classes in the most expedient fashion. The Oregon model, through which health insurance expands by restricting the benefits that Medicaid patients can receive, may become the standard response. Our past record suggests all too strongly that politics will find a way to protect those several rungs up the social ladder, while doing as little as possible for those at the bottom. Whether we will break this tradition and finally enact a truly national health insurance program remains an open question.

NOTES

1. Statements from Blue Cross representatives are taken from Rothman 1991.
2. In addition, there were another 28 million people enrolled for health care benefits with commercial insurance companies, so the private system was extensive.
3. It may well be that a felt need for health insurance was an acquired, not innate, characteristic. The first Blue Cross advertisements tried to build up a demand for insurance by emphasizing the unexpected character of illness, the sudden and unanticipated strike of disease. One of its popular advertising images represented Blue Cross as a helmet protecting against the club of the hospital bill that lay hidden, waiting to assail the unaware victim; the accompanying slogan read: "You never know what jolt is around the corner." Blue Cross's strategy, to emphasize the unpredictability of health care needs and that illness could strike anyone at any time, suggests that just when it raised consciousness about the need to carry health insurance, it provided an answer as to how best arrange it.

REFERENCES

Koos, E. L. 1954. *The Health of Regionville*. New York: Columbia University Press.

Lynd, R., and H. M. Lynd. [1929] 1956. *Middletown*. New York: Harcourt, Brace & World, Harvest Books.

Marmor, T. 1982. *The Politics of Medicare*. New York: Aldine.

Morone, J. 1990. *The Democratic Wish*. New York: Basic.

President's Research Committee. 1933. *Recent Social Trends in the United States*. 2 vols. New York: McGraw Hill.

Rothman, D. J. 1991. The Public Presentation of Blue Cross, 1935–1965. *Journal of Health Politics, Policy and Law* 16: 672–93.

Schuler, E. A., R. J. Mowitz, and A. J. Mayer. 1952. *Medical Public Relations: A Study of the Public Relations Program of the Academy of Medicine of Toledo and Lucas County, Ohio, 1951*, Detroit, MI: Academy of Medicine of Toledo.

Starr, P. 1982. *The Social Transformation of American Medicine*. New York: Basic.

Thomas, V. C. 1923. *The Successful Physician*. Philadelphia: W. B. Saunders.

U.S. Congress. 1964. *Medical Care for the Aged*. Hearings before the Committee on Ways and Means, House of Representatives, 88th Cong., 1st Sess. 1.

Weir, M., A. Orloff, and T. Skocpol. 1988. *The Politics of Social Policy in the United States*. Princeton, NJ: Princeton University Press.

27 *Paying for Health Care*

Thomas Bodenheimer and Kevin Grumbach

At the center of the debate over health system reform in the United States lies the decision of how to pay for health care. Health care financing in the United States evolved to its current state as a series of social interventions. Each intervention solved a problem but in turn created its own problems requiring further intervention. In this article, we discuss the historical process of health care financing as solution-creating-new-problem-requiring-new-solution. The four basic modes of paying for health care are out-of-pocket payment, individual private insurance, employment-based group private insurance, and government financing. These four modes can be viewed both as an historical progression and as a categorization of current health care financing (Table 27-1).

Table 27-1. Health Care Financing in 1991[4,5]*

Type of Payment	Personal Health Care Expenditures, %
Out-of-pocket	22
Individual private insurance	5
Employment-based private insurance	27†
Government financing	43
Total	97‡
Principal Source of Coverage	**Population, %**
Uninsured	14
Individual private insurance	9
Employment-based private insurance	52†
Government	25
Total	100

* For out-of-pocket payments, the percentage of expenditures is greater than the percentage of the uninsured population, because out-of-pocket dollars are paid not only by the uninsured but also by the insured and medicare populations in the form of deductibles, co-payments, and uncovered services. Because private insurance tends to cover healthier people, the percentage of expenditures is far less than the percentage of population covered. Public expenditures are far higher per population, because the elderly and disabled are concentrated in the public Medicare and Medicaid programs.

† This includes private insurance obtained by federal, state, and local government employees, which is in part purchased by tax funds.

‡ Total expenditures total only 97%; philanthropy and other private funds account for the other 3%.

OUT-OF-POCKET PAYMENTS

> Fred Farmer broke his leg in 1892. His son ran 4 miles to get the doctor who came to the farm to splint the leg. Fred gave the doctor a couple of chickens to pay for the visit.
>
> Fred Farmer's great-grandson, who is uninsured, broke his leg in 1992. He was driven to the emergency department where the physician ordered an X ray and called in an orthopedist who placed a cast on the leg. Mr Farmer was charged $580.

In the 19th century, people like Fred Farmer paid physicians and other health care practitioners in cash or through barter. In the first half of the 20th century, out-of-pocket cash payments were the dominant transaction. Out-of-pocket payment represents the simplest mode of financing: direct purchase by the consumer of goods and services (Figure 27-1).

Figure 27-1. *Direct Purchase. Individuals Pay Out-of-Pocket for Services*

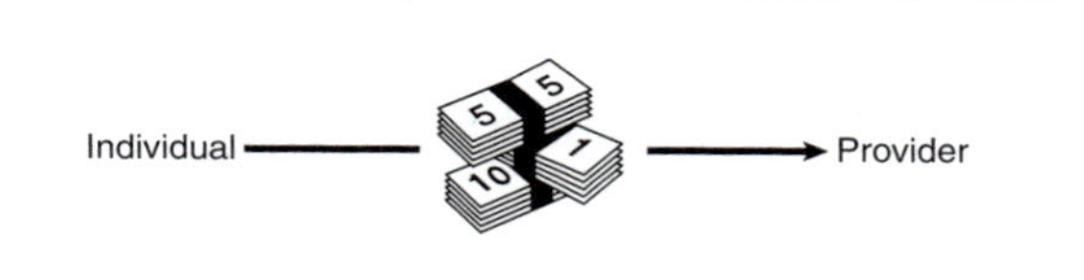

Americans purchase most consumer items, from VCRs to haircuts, through direct out-of-pocket payments. Why has direct out-of-pocket payment been relegated to a lesser role in health care? Economists such as Evans[1] and Arrow[2] have discussed some of the problems with treating health care as a typical consumer item.

First, whereas a VCR is a luxury, the great majority of Americans regard health care as a basic human need.[3]

For 2 weeks, Marina Perez has had vaginal bleeding and is feeling dizzy. She has no insurance and is terrified that medical care might eat up her $250 in savings. She scrapes together $30 to see her doctor, who finds a blood pressure that decreases to 90/50 mm Hg on standing and a hematocrit of 0.26. The doctor calls Ms Perez' sister, Juanita, to drive her to the hospital. Getting into the car, Marina tells Juanita to take her home.

If health care is a basic human need, then people who are unable to afford health care must have a payment mechanism available that is not reliant on out-of-pocket payments.

Second, although the purchase and price of VCRs are relatively predictable (i.e., people can choose whether or not to buy them, and the price is known), the need for and cost of health care services is unpredictable. Most people do not know if or when they may become severely ill or injured or what the cost of care will be.

Jake has a headache and visits the doctor, but Jake does not know whether the headache will cost $35 for a physician visit plus a bottle of aspirin, $1200 for magnetic resonance imaging, or $70,000 for surgery and radiation for a brain tumor.

The unpredictability of many health care needs makes it difficult to plan for these expenses. The medical costs associated with serious illness or injury usually exceed a middle-class family's savings.

Third, unlike purchasers of VCRs, consumers of health care may have little idea what they are buying at the point of needing care.

Jenny develops acute abdominal pain and goes to the hospital to purchase a remedy for her pain. The physician tells her that she has acute cholecystitis or a perforated ulcer and recommends hospitalization, abdominal sonogram, and upper endoscopy. Will Jenny, lying on a gurney in the emergency department and clutching her abdomen with one hand, use her other hand to leaf through her *Textbook of Internal Medicine* to determine whether she really needs these services, and should she have brought along a copy of *Consumer Reports* to learn where to purchase them at the cheapest price?

Health care is the foremost example of an asymmetry of information between providers and consumers.[3] Patients in abdominal pain are in a poor position to question the physician's ordering of laboratory tests, X rays, or surgery. In instances of elective care, health care consumers can weigh the pros and cons of different treatment options, but those options may be filtered through the biases of the physician providing the information. Compared with the voluntary demand for VCRs (the influence of advertising notwithstanding), the demand for health care services may be partially involuntary and physician driven rather than consumer driven.

For these reasons, among others, out-of-pocket payments are flawed as a dominant method of paying for health care services. Because direct purchase of health care services became increasingly difficult for consumers and was not meeting the needs of hospitals and physicians for payment, health insurance came into being.

INDIVIDUAL PRIVATE INSURANCE

Bud Carpenter was self-employed. Mr Carpenter recently purchased a health insurance policy from his insurance broker for his family. To pay the $250 monthly premiums required taking on extra jobs on weekends, and the $2000 deductible meant he would still have to pay quite a bit of his family's medical costs out-of-pocket. But Bud preferred to pay these costs rather than to risk spending his savings for his children's college education on a major illness. When his son was diagnosed with leukemia and ran up a $50,000 hospital bill, Mr Carpenter appreciated the value of health insurance. Nonetheless, he had to wonder when he read a newspaper story that listed his insurance company among those that paid out less than 50 cents in benefits on average for every dollar collected in premiums.

Figure 27-2. *Individual Model of Private Insurance. A Third Party—The Health Insurance Plan—Is Added, Dividing Payment into a Financing Transaction and a Reimbursement Transaction.*

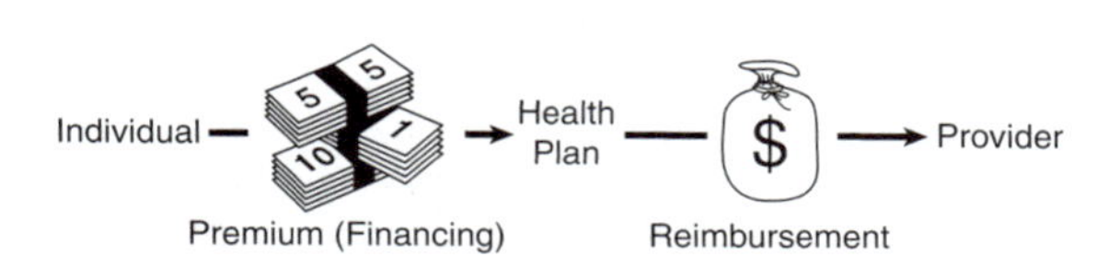

Under private health insurance, a third party, the insurer, is added to the patient and health care provider who comprise the basic two parties of the health care transaction. Although the out-of-pocket mode of payment is limited to a single financial transaction, private insurance requires two transactions: a premium payment from individual to insurance plan and a reimbursement payment from insurance plan to provider (Figure 27-2). (Under indemnity insurance, the process requires three transactions: the premium from individual to insurer, the payment from individual to provider, and the reimbursement from insurer to individual. For simplicity, we will treat health insurance as reimbursement from insurance plan to provider.)

In 19th-century Europe, voluntary benefit funds were established by guilds, industries, and mutual societies. In return for paying a monthly sum, people received assistance in case of illness. This early form of private health insurance was slow to develop in the United States. In the early 20th century, European immigrants established some small benevolent societies in US cities to provide sickness benefits for their members. During the same period, two commercial insurance companies, Metropolitan Life and Prudential, collected from 10 to 25 cents per week from workers for life insurance policies that also paid for funerals and the expenses of a final illness. Because the policies were paid by individuals on a weekly basis, large numbers of insurance agents had to visit their clients to collect the premiums as soon after payday as possible. Because of its huge administrative costs, individual health insurance never became a dominant method of paying for health care.[6]

Currently, individual policies provide health insurance for only 9% of the US population (Table 27-1).

EMPLOYMENT-BASED PRIVATE INSURANCE

Betty Lerner and her schoolteacher colleagues paid $6 per year to Prepaid Hospital in 1929. Ms Lerner suffered a heart attack and was hospitalized at no cost. The following year Prepaid Hospital built a new wing and raised the teachers' prepayment to $12.

Rose Riveter retired in 1961. Her health insurance premium for hospital and physician care, formerly paid by her employer, had been $25 per month. When she called the insurance company to obtain individual coverage, she was told that premiums at age 65 years cost $70 per month. She could not afford the insurance and wondered what would happen if she became ill.

The development of private health insurance in the United States was impelled by the increasing efficacy and cost of hospital care. Hospitals became places not only in which to die, but also in which to get better. Many patients, however, were unable to pay for hospital care, which meant that hospitals were unable to attract customers.[6]

In 1929, Baylor University Hospital agreed to provide up to 21 days of hospital care to 1500 Dallas, Tex, schoolteachers such as Betty Lerner, if they paid the hospital $6 per person per year.[7] As the depression deepened and private hospital occupancy in 1931 decreased to 62%, similar hospital centered private insurance plans spread. These plans (anticipating more modern health maintenance organizations) restricted care to a particular hospital. The American Hospital Association built on this prepayment movement and established statewide Blue Cross hospital insurance plans allowing free choice of hospital. By 1940, 39 Blue Cross plans, controlled by the private-hospital industry, had a total enrollment of more than 6 million people.[6] The Great Depression of the 1930s cut into the amounts patients could pay physicians out-of-pocket, and in 1939 the California Medical Association established the first Blue Shield plan to cover physician services. These plans, controlled by state medical societies, followed Blue Cross in spreading across the nation.[6]

In contrast to the consumer-driven development of health insurance in European nations, US health care coverage was initiated by health care providers seeking a steady source of income. Hospital and physician control over the "Blues," a major sector of the health insurance industry, guaranteed that reimbursement would be generous and that cost control would remain on the back burner.[6,8]

The rapid growth of private insurance was spurred by an accident of history. During World War II, wage and price controls prevented companies from granting wage increases but allowed the growth of fringe benefits. With a labor shortage, companies competing for workers began to offer health insurance to employees such as Rose Riveter as a fringe benefit. After the war, unions picked up on this trend and negotiated for health benefits. The results were dramatic. Enrollment in group hospital insurance plans increased from 12 million in 1940 to 101 million in 1955.[9]

Under employer-sponsored health insurance, employers usually pay all or part of the premium that purchases health insurance for their employees (Figure 27-3). However, the flow of money is not so simple. The federal government views employer-premium payments as a tax-deductible business expense. Moreover, the government does not treat the health insurance fringe benefit as taxable income to the employee, even though the payment of health insurance premiums for employees could be interpreted as a form of employee income. Because each premium dollar of employer-sponsored health insurance results in a reduction in taxes

Figure 27-3. *Employment-Based Model of Private Insurance*

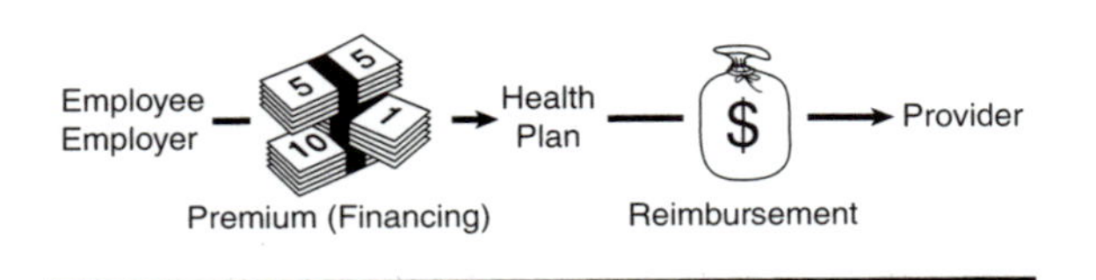

collected, the federal government is in essence subsidizing employer-sponsored health insurance. This subsidy is enormous, estimated at $75 billion in 1991.[10]

The growth of employer-sponsored health insurance attracted commercial insurance companies to the health care field to compete with the Blues for customers. The commercial insurers changed the entire dynamic of health insurance. The new dynamic—which applies to both individual and employment-based health insurance—was called "experience rating."

> Healthy Insurance Company insures three groups of people: (1) a young, healthy group of bank managers; (2) an older, healthy group of truck drivers; and (3) an older group of coal miners with a high rate of chronic illness. Under experience rating, the Healthy Insurance Company sets its premiums according to the experience of each group in using health care services. Since the bank managers rarely use health care, each pays a premium of $100 per month. Because the truck drivers are older, their risk of illness is higher than that of the bankers and their premium is $300. The miners, who have high rates of black lung disease, are charged a premium of $500. The average premium income for the Healthy Insurance Company is $300 per member per month.
>
> Blue Cross insures the same three groups and needs the same $300 per member per month to cover health care plus administrative costs for these groups. Blue Cross sets its premiums by the principle of "community rating." For a given health insurance policy, all subscribers in a community pay the same premium. The bank managers, truck drivers, and mine workers all pay $300 per month.

Health insurance provides a mechanism to distribute health care more in accordance with human need rather than exclusively on the basis of ability to pay. To achieve this goal, health insurance contains a subsidy—a redistribution of funds from the healthy to the sick—that helps pay the health care costs of those unable to purchase services on their own.

Community rating achieves this redistribution in two ways: (1) within each group (bank managers, truck drivers, or mine workers) people who become ill receive health benefits in excess of the premiums they pay, whereas people who remain healthy pay premiums while receiving few or no health benefits; (2) among the three groups, the bank managers, who use a smaller amount of health care than their premiums are worth, help pay for the miners, who use a larger amount of health care than their premiums could buy.

Experience rating is far less redistributive than community rating. Within each group, those who become ill are subsidized by those who remain well. But looking at groups as a whole, healthier groups (bank managers) do not subsidize high-risk groups (mine workers). Thus, the principle of health insurance, to distribute health care more in accordance with human need rather than exclusively on the basis of ability to pay, is diluted by experience rating.[11]

In their early years, Blue Cross plans set insurance premiums by the principle of community rating. Commercial insurers, on the other hand, used experience rating as a weapon to compete with the Blues.[7] Under experience rating, commercials such as the Healthy Insurance Company could offer less expensive premiums to low-risk groups such as bank managers, who would naturally choose a Healthy Insurance Company commercial plan at $100 over the Blue Cross plan at $300. Experience rating helped commercial insurers overtake the Blues in the private-insurance market. In 1945 commercial insurers had only 10 million enrollees compared with 19 million for the Blues; by 1955 the score was commercials, 54 million, vs Blues, 51 million.[9]

Many commercial insurers would not market policies to such high-risk groups as mine workers, who would then be left to Blue Cross. To survive the competition from the commercials, Blue Cross had no choice but to seek younger and healthier groups by abandoning community rating and reducing the premiums for those groups. In this way, most Blue Cross and Blue Shield plans switched to experience rating.[12] Without community rating, older and sicker groups became less and less able to afford health insurance.

From the perspective of the elderly and those with chronic illness, experience rating is discriminatory, but let us view health insurance from the opposite viewpoint. Why would healthy people voluntarily transfer their wealth to sicker people through the insurance subsidy? The answer lies in the unpredictability of health care needs. When purchasing health insurance, individuals do not know if they will suddenly change from their state of good health to one of illness. Thus, within a group, people are willing to risk paying for health insurance even though they may not use the insurance. On the other hand, among different groups, healthy people have no economic incentive to voluntarily pay for community rating and subsidize another group of sicker people. This is why community rating cannot survive in a laissez-faire, competitive, private-insurance environment.[12]

The most positive aspect of health insurance—that it assists people with serious illness to pay for their care—has also become one of its main drawbacks: the difficulty of controlling costs in an insurance environment. Under direct purchase, the "invisible hand" of each individual's ability to pay holds down the price and quantity of health care. Yet a well-insured patient, for whom the cost of care causes no immediate fiscal pain, will use more services than someone who must pay for care out-of-pocket.[7] In addition, health care providers can increase fees far more easily if a third party is available to foot the bill; recall the case of Betty Lerner in which Prepaid Hospital doubled its premium in 1 year.

Health insurance, then, was a social intervention attempting to solve the problem of unaffordable health care under an out-of-pocket payment system; but its capacity to make health care more affordable created a new problem. If people no longer had to pay out-of-pocket for health care, they would use more health care, and if health care providers could charge insurers rather than patients, they could more easily raise prices—especially if the major insurers (the Blues) were controlled by hospitals and physicians. The solution of insurance fueled the problem of rising costs. As private insurance became largely experience rated and employment based, Americans who were low income, chronically ill, or elderly found it increasingly difficult to afford private insurance.

GOVERNMENT FINANCING

In 1984, Rose Riveter developed colon cancer. Because of the enactment of Medicare in 1965, she was no longer uninsured. However, her Medicare premium, hospital deductible, physician co-payments, short nursing-home stay, and uncovered prescriptions cost her $2700 the year she became ill with cancer.

Employer-sponsored private health insurance grew rapidly in the 1950s, helping working Americans and their families afford health care. However, two groups in the population received little or no benefit: the poor and the elderly. The poor were usually unemployed or employed in jobs without the fringe benefit of health insurance; they could not afford insurance premiums. The elderly, who needed health care the most and whose premiums had been partially subsidized by community rating, were hit hard by the tilt toward experience rating. In the late 1950s, less than 15% of the elderly had any health insurance.[13] Only one thing could provide affordable care for the poor and the elderly: tax-financed government health insurance.

The government entered the health care financing arena long before the 1960s through such public programs as municipal hospitals and dispensaries to care for the poor and state-operated mental hospitals. Only with the 1965 enactment of Medicare (for the elderly) and Medicaid (for the poor) did public insurance paying for privately operated health care services become a major feature of American health care.[6]

Medicare Part A is a hospital insurance plan for the elderly financed largely through Social Security taxes from employers and employees. Medicare Part B insures the elderly for physicians' services and is paid for by federal taxes and monthly premiums from the beneficiaries. Medicaid is a program run by the states and funded from federal and state taxes that pays for the care of a portion of the population below the poverty line. Because Medicare has large deductibles, copayments, and gaps in coverage, many Medicare beneficiaries also carry supplemental ("Medigap") private insurance or Medicaid.

Government health insurance for the poor and the elderly added a new factor to the health care financing equation: the taxpayer (Figure 27-4). Under government programs, the taxpayer can interact with the health care consumer in two distinct ways. Under the social insurance model exemplified by Medicare, only those who have paid a certain amount of Social Security taxes are eligible for Part A and only those who pay a monthly premium receive benefits from Part B. As with private insurance, people insured under social insurance must contribute, and those that contribute receive benefits. The contrasting model for government programs is the Medicaid welfare model in which those who contribute (taxpayers) may not be eligible for benefits.[14]

Figure 27-4. *Public Insurance. In the Social Insurance Model of Public Insurance, Individual Eligibility Is Linked to Making Tax Contributions into the Plan (e.g., Medicare Part A). In Other Models, Eligibility Is Uncoupled from Tax Contributions (e.g., Medicaid).*

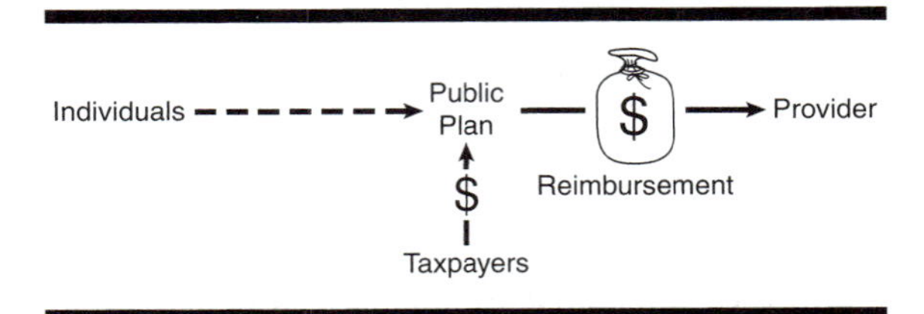

Recall that private insurance contains a subsidy: a redistribution of funds from healthy to sick. Tax-funded insurance has the same subsidy and generally adds another: redistribution of funds from the wealthy to the poor. Under this double subsidy, exemplified by Medicare and Medicaid, healthy middle-income employees generally pay more in Social Security payments and other taxes than they receive in health care services, whereas unemployed, disabled, and lower-income elderly persons tend to receive more in health care services than they contribute in taxes.

The advent of government financing improved financial access to care for some people but in turn aggravated the problem of rising costs. Over time, as costs rose, access declined: Medicaid cutbacks pushed low-income people out of the program, and uncovered services under Medicare left the elderly increasingly unable to pay for prescriptions and long-term care. At the same time, the rising costs of private insurance were placing coverage out of the fiscal reach of more and more employers.

THE BURDEN OF FINANCING HEALTH CARE

Different methods of financing health care place differential burdens on the various income levels of society. Payments are classified as progressive if they take an increasing percentage of income as income increases and regressive if they take a decreasing percentage of income as income increases. Payments are proportional when the ratio of the payment to income is the same for all income classes.[15]

> Mary Blue earns $10,000 per year for her family of four. She develops pneumonia, and her out-of-pocket health care costs come to $1000, 10% of her family income.
>
> Cathy White earns $100,000 per year for her family of four. She develops pneumonia, and her out-of-pocket health care costs come to $1000, 1% of her family income.

Out-of-pocket payments are a regressive mode of financing. The National Medical Care Expenditure Survey confirms that in 1977, direct payments (mainly out-of-pocket payments) took 14.0% of the income of families in the nation's lowest-income decile compared with 1.9% for families in the highest decile.[16] Many economists and health policy experts would consider this regressive burden of payment unfair. Yet out-of-pocket payments constitute fully 22% of total US personal health care expenditures.[4] Aggravating the regressivity of out-of-pocket payments is the fact that lower-income people tend to be sicker[17] and thus have more out-of-pocket payments than the wealthier and healthier.

> John Hale is a young, healthy, self-employed accountant whose monthly income is $6000 with a health insurance premium of $200, or 3% of his income.
>
> Jack Hurt is a disabled mine worker with black lung disease. His income is $1800 per month of which $400 (22%) goes for his health insurance.

Experience-rated private health insurance is a regressive method of financing health care, because increased risk of illness tends to correlate with reduced income.[17] If Mr Hale and Mr Hurt were enrolled in a community-rated plan, each with a premium of $300, they would pay 5% and 17% of their income for health insurance, respectively. Under community rating, the burden of payment is regressive, but less so.

Most private insurance is not individually purchased but obtained through employment. How is the burden of employer-linked health insurance premiums distributed?

> Jill is an assistant hospital administrator. To attract Jill to the job, the hospital offered her a package of salary plus health insurance of $5250 per month. She chose to take $5000 in salary, leaving the hospital to pay $250 for her health insurance.
>
> Bill is a nurse's aide whose union negotiated with the hospital for a total package of $1750 per month; of this, $1500 is salary and $250 pays his health insurance premium.

Do Jill and Bill pay nothing for their health insurance? Not exactly. Employers generally agree on a total package of wages and fringe benefits; if Jill and Bill did not receive health insurance, their pay would probably increase by close to $250 per month. This arrangement is the reason why employer-paid health insurance premiums are generally considered deductions from wages or salary.[16,18] For Jill, health insurance amounts to only 5% of her income. For Bill, the premium is 17% of his income. The National Medical Expenditure Survey corroborates the regressivity of employer-linked health insurance; in 1977, employment-based health insurance premiums took 5.7% of the income of families in the lowest-income decile compared with 1.8% for those in the highest decile.[16]

> John Low earns $10,000 and pays $410 in federal and state income taxes, 4.1% of his income.[16]
>
> Harold High earns $100,000 and pays $12,900 in income taxes, 12.9% of his income.[16]

The largest tax supporting government-financed health care is the progressive individual income tax. Because most other taxes are regressive (e.g., sales and Social Security taxes), the combined burden of all taxes that finance health care is roughly proportional.[15]

About 54% of health care is financed through out-of-pocket payments and premiums, which are regressive, whereas 43% is funded through government revenues,[4] which are proportional. The total of health care financing is regressive. Data from 1977 reveal that the poorest decile of households spent 20% of income on health care, the middle deciles spent 12%, and the highest-income decile paid 8%.[16]

CONCLUSION

Neither Fred Farmer nor his great-grandson had health insurance. Yet the modern-day Mr Farmer's predicament differs drastically from that of his ancestor. Third-party financing of health care has fueled an expansive health care system that offers treatments unimaginable a century ago, but at tremendous expense.

Each of the four modes of financing US health care developed historically as a solution to the inadequacy of the previous modes. Private insurance provided protection to patients against the unpredictable costs of medical care, as well as protection to providers of care against the unpredictable ability of patients to pay. But the private-insurance solution created three new and interrelated problems: (1) the ability of health care providers to increase fees to insurers led to an increasing unaffordability of health care services for those with inadequate insurance or no insurance; (2) the employment-based nature of group insurance placed Americans who were unemployed, retired, or working part-time at a disadvantage for the purchase of insurance and partially masked the true costs of insurance for employees who did receive health benefits at the workplace; and (3) competition inherent in a deregulated private-insurance market en-couraged the practice of experience rating, which made insurance premiums unaffordable to many elderly people and other medically needy groups. To solve these problems, government financing was required. In turn, government financing fueled an even greater inflation in health care costs.

As each solution was introduced, health care financing improved for a time. However, by the 1990s, rising costs were jeopardizing private and public coverage for many Americans and making services unaffordable for those without a source of third-party payment. The problems of each financing mode, and the problems created by each successive solution, had accumulated into a complex crisis characterized by inadequate access for some and rising costs for everyone.

The United States is now deliberating on a new solution to these financing problems, a solution that will undoubtedly beget its own problems. Plans for reforming health insurance in the United States may be characterized by how they propose to rearrange the four basic modes of financing. The plan drafted by the Heritage Foundation, Washington, DC, for example, emphasizes individually purchased private insurance and increased reliance on out-of-pocket payments.[19] Other proposals call for expansion of employment-based financing of private insurance.[20] Single-payer plans would make government financing the dominant mode of payment.[21] . . .

REFERENCES

The authors express their appreciation to Robert G. Evans, PhD, for making health economics intelligible.

1. Evans RG. *Strained Mercy*. Stoneham, Mass: Butterworths; 1984.
2. Arrow KJ. Uncertainty and the welfare economics of medical care. *Am Econ Rev*. 1963;53: 941–973.
3. Shapiro RY, Young JT. The polls: medical care in the United States. *Public Opinion Q*. 1986;50: 418–428.
4. Levit KR, Lazenby HC, Levit KR, Cowan CA. National health expenditures, 1991. *Health Care Financing Rev*. 1992;14(2):1–30.
5. Levit KR, Olin GL, Letsch SW. American's health insurance coverage, 1980–91. *Health Care Financing Rev*. 1992;14(1):31–57.
6. Starr P. *The Social Transformation of American Medicine*. New York, NY: Basic Books; 1982.
7. Fein R. *Medical Care, Medical Costs*. Cambridge, Mass: Harvard University Press; 1986.
8. Law SA. *Blue Cross: What Went Wrong?* New Haven, Conn: Yale University Press; 1974.
9. *Source Book of Health Insurance Data, 1990*. Washington, DC: Health Insurance Association of America; 1990.
10. Reinhardt UE. Reorganizing the financial flows in US health care. *Health Aff (Millwood)*. 1993;12(suppl):172–193.
11. Light DW. The practice and ethics of risk-rated health insurance. *JAMA* 1992;267:2503–2508.
12. Aaron HJ. *Serious and Unstable Condition: Financing America's Health Care*. Washington, DC: The Brookings Institution; 1991.
13. Harris R. *A Sacred Trust*. New York, NY: The New American Library; 1966.
14. Bodenheimer T, Grumbach K. Financing universal health insurance: taxes, premiums, and the lessons of social insurance. *J Health Polit Policy Law*. 1992;17:439–462.

15. Pechman JA. *Who Paid the Taxes, 1966–85*. Washington, DC: The Brookings Institution; 1985.
16. Cantor JC. Expanding health insurance coverage: who will pay? *J Health Polit Policy Law.* 1990;15:755–778.
17. US Dept of Health and Human Services. *Health: United States, 1992*. Washington, DC: US Government Printing Office; 1993.
18. Reinhardt UE. Are mandated benefits the answer? *Health Manage Q*. 1988;10:10–14.
19. Butler SM. A tax reform strategy to deal with the uninsured. *JAMA*. 1991;265:2541–2544.
20. Todd JS, Seekins SV, Krichbaum JA, Harvey LK. Health Access America: strengthening the US health care system. *JAMA*. 1991;265: 2503–2506.
21. Himmelstein DU, Woolhandler S. A national health program for the United States: a phy-sicians' proposal. *N Engl J Med*. 1989;320: 102–108.

28 DOCTORING AS A BUSINESS: MONEY, MARKETS, AND MANAGED CARE

Deborah A. Stone

For more than 150 years, American medicine aspired to an ethical ideal of the separation of money from medical care. Medical practice was a money-making proposition, to be sure, and doctors were entrepreneurs as well as healers. But the lodestar that guided professional calling and evoked public trust was the idea that at the bedside, clinical judgment should be untainted by financial considerations.

Although medicine never quite lived up to that ideal, the new regime of managed care health insurance is an epic reversal of the principle. Today, insurers deliberately try to influence doctors' clinical decisions with money—either the prospect of more of it or the threat of less. What's even more astounding is that this manipulation of medical judgment by money is no longer seen in policy circles as a corruption of science or a betrayal of the doctor–patient relationship. Profit-driven medical decisionmaking is extolled as the path to social responsibility, efficient use of resources, and even medical excellence.

How did such a profound cultural revolution come about? What does the new culture of medicine mean for health care? And where does it leave the welfare state and the culture of solidarity on which it rests when the most respected and essential caregivers in our society are encouraged to let personal financial reward dictate how they pursue patients' welfare?

The title of the selection as originally published was "Bedside Manna: Medicine Turned Upside Down."

MONEY AND MEDICINE

Before the mid-nineteenth century, the business relationship between doctors and patients was simple: The patient paid money in exchange for the doctor's advice, skill, and medicines. However, to win acceptance as professionals and be perceived as something more than commercial salesmen, doctors needed to persuade the public that they were acting out of knowledge and altruism rather than self-interest and profit. Organized medicine built a system of formal education, examinations, licensing, and professional discipline, all meant to assure that doctors' recommendations were based on medical science and the needs of the patient, rather than profit seeking.

In theory, this system eliminated commercial motivation from medicine by selecting high-minded students, acculturating them during medical training, and enforcing a code of ethics that put patients' interests first. In practice, medicine remained substantially a business, and no one behaved more like an economic cartel than the American Medical Association. The system of credentialing doctors eventually eliminated most alternative healers and, by limiting the supply of doctors, enhanced the profitability of doctoring. Nonetheless, medical leaders espoused the ideal and justified these and other market restrictions as necessary to protect patients' health, not doctors' incomes.

It took the growth of health insurance to create a system in which a doctor truly did not need to consider patients' financial means in weighing their clinical needs, so long as the patient was insured. As Columbia University historian David Rothman has shown, private health insurance was advertised to the American middle class on the promise that it would neutralize financial considerations when people needed medical care. Blue Cross ads hinted darkly that health insurance meant not being treated like a poor person—not having to use the public hospital and not suffering the indignity of a ward. Quality of medical care, the ads screamed between the lines, was indeed connected to money, but health insurance could sever the connection.

By 1957, the AMA's Principles of Medical Ethics forbade a doctor to "dispose of his services under terms or conditions that tend to interfere with or impair the free and complete exercise of his medical judgment or skill. . . ." This statement was the apotheosis of the ethical ideal of separating clinical judgment from money. It symbolized the long struggle to make doctoring a scientific and humane calling rather than a commercial enterprise, at least in the public's eyes if not always in actual fact. But the AMA never acknowledged that fee-for-service payment, the dominant arrangement and the only payment method it approved at the time, might itself "interfere with" medical judgment.

Meanwhile, as costs climbed in the late 1960s, research began to show that fee-for-service payment seemed to induce doctors to hospitalize their patients more frequently compared to other payment methods such as flat salaries, and that professional disciplinary bodies rarely, if ever, monitored financial conflicts of interest. Other research showed that the need for medical services in any given population was quite elastic, often a matter of discretion, and that doctors could diagnose enough needs for their own and their hospitals' services to keep everybody running at full throttle.

Still, the cultural premise of these controversies expressed a clear moral imperative: Ethical medicine meant money should not be a factor in medical decisionmaking. The new findings about money's influence on medicine were accepted as muck that needed raking. Occasional exposés of medical incentive schemes—for example, bonuses from drug and device companies for prescribing their products or kickbacks for referrals to diagnostic testing centers—were labeled "fraud and abuse" and branded as outside the pale of normal, ethical medicine.

THE PATH NOT TAKEN

Sooner or later, the ideal of medical practice untainted by financial concerns had to clash with economic reality. Everything that goes into medical care is a resource with a cost, and people's decisions about using resources are always at least partly influenced by cost. By the 1970s, with health care spending hitting 9 percent of the gross national product (GNP) and costs for taxpayers and employers skyrocketing, America perceived itself to be in a medical cost crisis. Doctors and hospitals, however, resisted cost control measures. By the late 1980s, neither the medical profession, the hospitals, the insurers, nor the government had managed to reconcile the traditional fee-for-service system with cost control, even though the number of people without health insurance grew steadily.

During these decades, a pervasive antigovernment sentiment and a resurgence of laissez-faire capitalism on the intellectual right combined to push the United States toward market solutions to its cost crisis. Other countries with universal public-private health insurance systems have watched their spending rise, too, driven by the same underlying forces of demographics and technology. But unlike the U.S., they rely on organized cooperation and planning to contain costs rather than on influencing individual doctors with financial punishment or reward. Some national health systems pay each doctor a flat salary, which eliminates the financial incentive to over-treat, though it might create a mild incentive to under-treat. Systems with more nearly universal health insurance schemes also eliminate expensive competition between insurers, because there is no outlay for risk selection, marketing, or case-by-case pretreatment approval, and far less administrative expense generally.

Countries with comprehensive systems typically plan technology acquisition by doctors and hospitals to moderate one of the chief sources of medical inflation. Most also limit the total supply of doctors, or of specialists, through higher-education policy. They may restrict doctors' geographic location in order to meet needs of rural areas and dampen excess medical provision in cities. Most countries with universal systems have some kind of global budget cap. But the difficult medical trade-offs within that budget constraint are made by clinicians under broad general guidelines, and not on the basis of commercial incentives to individual doctors facing individual patients. Significantly, although government is usually a guiding force in these systems planning is done by councils or commissions that represent and cooperate with doctors, hospitals, other professions, medical suppliers, insurers, unions, and employer associations.

The distinctive feature of the emerging American way of cost control is our reliance on market competition and personal economic incentive to govern the system. For the most part, such incentives are contrived by insurers. In practice, that has meant insurers have far more power in our system than in any other, and it has meant that they insert financial considerations into medical care at a level of detail and personal control unimaginable in any other country.

RECONFIGURING THE ROLE OF MONEY

The theorists of market reform reversed the traditional norm that the doctor–patient relationship should be immune to pecuniary interests. Law professor Clark Havighurst, HMO-advocate Paul Ellwood, and economist Alain Enthoven and their disciples celebrated the power of financial motivation to economize in medical care. In the process, they elaborated a moral justification for restoring money to a prominent place in the doctor's mind.

In what is probably the single most important document of the cultural revolution in medical care, Alain Enthoven began his 1978 Shattuck Lecture to the Massachusetts Medical Society by explaining why he, an economist, should be giving this distinguished lecture instead of a doctor. The central problem of medicine, he said, was no longer simply how to cure the sick, eliminate quackery, and achieve professional excellence, but rather how people could "most effectively use their resources to promote the health of the population." Enthoven dismissed government regulation as ineffective. The key issue was "how to motivate physicians to use hospital and other resources economically." It was time, he concluded, for doctors to look beyond the biological sciences as they crafted the art of medicine, and to draw on cost-effectiveness analysis.

In Enthoven's vision, researchers would incorporate cost-benefit calculations into clinical guidelines: health plans would give doctors incentives to follow these guidelines; and if patients were allowed to shop for plans in an open market, the most efficient plans would win greater market share. We could succeed in "Cutting Costs Without Cutting the Quality of Care," as the title of his lecture promised. The ultimate safeguard against financial temptations to skimp on quality or quantity of care, according to Enthoven, was "the freedom of the dissatisfied patient to change doctors or health plan."

In market theory, consumers are the disciplinary force that keeps producers honest. In applying classical market theory to medicine, theorists such as Havighurst and Enthoven confused consumer with payer. By the late 1970s, when medical care was paid for by private and public insurers or by charity, patient and payer were seldom the same person.

Precisely this ambiguity about the identity of the consumer gave market rhetoric its political appeal. It papered over a deep political conflict over who would control medical care—insurers, patients, doctors, or government. Market imagery suggested to insurers and employers that they, as purchasers of care, would gain control, while it suggested to patients that they, as consumers of care, would be sovereign. For a brief while in the 1970s and 1980s, the women's health movement and a Ralph Nader-inspired health consumer movement adopted market rhetoric, too, thinking that consumer sovereignty would empower patients vis-à-vis their doctors. For their part, many doctors came to accept the introduction of explicit financial incentives into their clinical practice, because, they were told, it was the only alternative to the bogey of government regulation. ("Health care spending will inevitably be brought under control," warned Enthoven in his Shattuck Lecture. "Control could be effected voluntarily by physicians in a system of rational incentives, or by direct economic regulation by the government.")

Enthoven's early approach relied only partly on the discipline of personal reward or punishment for doctors. He also advocated doing more research on cost-effectiveness and educating of doctors to make better use of scarce resources. And like Ellwood, Havighurst, and most advocates of market competition in medicine, Enthoven recognized the differences between medicine and ordinary commerce when he argued that competition had to be regulated in order to limit opportunism and enable patients to discipline insurance plans. But the heavy overlay of regulation originally envisioned by Enthoven and others was not established. While some HMOs have been more diligent than others in bringing quality and outcomes research to bear on medical practice, monetary incentives have become the paramount form of cost discipline.

REMAKING THE DOCTOR AS ENTREPRENEUR

Today, financial incentives on doctors are reversed. Instead of the general incentives of fee-for-service medicine to perform more services and procedures, contractual arrangements between payers and doctors now exert financial pressures to do less. These pressures affect every aspect of the doctor-patient relationship: how doctors and patients choose each other, how many patients a doctor accepts, how much time he or she spends with them, what diagnostic tests the doctor orders, what referrals the doctor makes, what procedures to perform, which of several potentially beneficial therapies to administer, which of several potentially effective drugs to prescribe, whether to hospitalize a patient, when to discharge a patient, and when to give up on a patient with severe illness.

In most HMOs, doctors are no longer paid by one simple method, such as salary, fee-for-service, or capitation (a fixed fee per patient per year). Instead, the doctor's pay is linked to other medical expenditures through a system of multiple accounts, pay withholding, rebates, bonuses, and penalties. Health plans typically divide their budget into separate funds for primary care services, specialists, hospital care, laboratory tests, and prescription drugs. The primary care doctors receive some regular pay, which may be based on salary, capitation, or fee-for-service, but part of their pay is calculated after the fact, based on the financial condition of the other funds. And there's the rub.

Studies of HMOs by Alan Hillman of the University of Pennsylvania found that two-thirds of HMOs routinely withhold a part of each primary care doctor's pay. Of the plans that withhold, about a third withhold less than 10 percent of the doctor's pay and almost half withhold between 11 and 20 percent. A few withhold even more. These "withholds" are the real financial stick of managed care, because doctors are told they may eventually receive all, part, or none of their withheld pay. In some HMOs, the rebate a doctor receives depends solely on his or her own behavior whether he or she sent too many patients to specialists, ordered too many tests, or had too many patients in the hospital. In other plans, each doctor's rebate is tied to the performance of a larger group of doctors. In either case, doctors are vividly aware that a significant portion of their pay is tied to their willingness to hold down the care they dole out.

Withholding pay is itself a strong influence on doctor's clinical decisions, but other mechanisms tighten the screws even further. Forty percent of HMOs make primary care doctors pay for patients' lab tests out of their own payments or from a combined fund for primary care doctors and outpatient tests. Many plans (around 30 percent in Hillman's original survey) impose penalties on top of withholding, and they have invented penalties with Kafka-esque relish: increasing the amount withheld from a doctor's pay in the following year, decreasing the doctor's regular capitation rate, reducing the amount of rebate from future surpluses, or even putting liens on a doctor's future earnings. A doctor's pay in different pay periods can commonly vary by 20 to 50 percent as a result of all these incentives, according to a 1994 survey sponsored by the Physician Payment Review Commission.

Of course, not all HMOs provide financial incentives that reward doctors for denying necessary care. In principle, consumers could punish managed care plans that restricted clinical freedoms, and doctors could refuse to work for them. But as insurers merge and a few gain control of large market shares, and as one or two HMOs come to dominate a local market, doctors and patients may not have much choice about which ones to join. The theorists' safeguards may prove largely theoretical.

In the early managed-market theory of Enthoven and others, the doctor was supposed to make clinical decisions on the basis of cost-effectiveness analysis. That would mean considering the probability of "success" of procedure, the cost of care for each patient, and the benefit to society of spending resources for this treatment on this patient compared to spending them in some other way. But in the new managed care payment systems, financial incentives do not push doctors to think primarily about cost-effectiveness but rather to think about the effect of costs on their own income. Instead of asking themselves whether a procedure is medically necessary for a patient or cost-effective for society, they are led to ask whether it is financially tolerable for themselves. Conscientious doctors may well try to use their knowledge of cost-effectiveness studies to help them make the difficult rationing decisions they are forced to make, but the financial incentives built into managed care do not in themselves encourage anything but personal income maximization. Ironically, managed care returns doctors to the role of salesmen—but now they are rewarded for selling fewer services, not more.

WHO CARES?

Because doctors in managed care often bear some risk for the costs of patient care, they face some of the same incentives that induce commercial health insurance companies to seek out healthy customers and avoid sick or potentially sick ones. In an article in *Health Affairs* last summer, David Blumenthal, chief of health policy research and development at Massachusetts General Hospital, explained why his recent bonuses had varied:

> Last spring I received something completely unexpected: a check for $1,200 from a local health maintenance organization (HMO) along with a letter congratulating me for spending less than predicted on their 100 or so patients under my care. I got no bonus the next quarter because several of my patients had elective arthroscopies for knee injuries. Nor did I get a bonus from another HMO, because three of their 130 patients under my care had been hospitalized over the previous six months, driving my actual expenditures above expected for this group.

Such conscious linking of specific patients to paychecks is not likely to make doctors think that their income depends on how cost-effectively they practice, as market theory would have it. Rather, they are likely to conclude, with some justification, that their income depends on the luck of the draw—how many of their patients happen to be sick in expensive ways. The payment system thus converts each sick patient, even each illness, into a financial liability for doctors, a liability that can easily change their attitude toward sick patients. Doctors may come to resent sick people and to regard them as financial drains.

Dr. Robert Berenson, who subsequently became co-medical director of an HMO, gave a moving account of this phenomenon in the *New Republic* in 1987. An elderly woman was diagnosed with inoperable cancer shortly after she enrolled in a Medicare managed care plan with him as her primary care doctor, and her bills drained his bonus account:

> At a time when the doctor–patient relationship should be closest, concerned with the emotions surrounding death and dying, the HMO payment system introduced a divisive factor. I ended up resenting the seemingly unending medical needs of the patient and the continuing demands placed on me by her distraught family. To me, this Medicare beneficiary had effectively become a "charity patient."

Thus do the financial incentives under managed care spoil doctors' relationships to illness and to people who are ill. Illness becomes something for the doctor to avoid rather than something to treat, and sick patients become adversaries rather than subjects of compassion and intimacy.

Here is also the source of the most profound social change wrought by the American approach to cost containment. Health insur-ance marketing from the 1930s to the 1950s promised subscribers more reliable access to high-quality care than they could expect as charity patients. But as it is now evolving, managed care insurance will soon render all its subscribers charity patients. By tying doctors' income to the cost of each patient, managed care lays bare what was always true about health insurance: The kind of care sick people get, indeed whether they get any care at all, depends on the generosity of others.

Insurance, after all, is organized generosity. It always redistributes from those who don't get sick to those who do. Classic indemnity insurance, by pooling risk anonymously, masking redistribution, and making the users of care relatively invisible to the nonusers, created the illusion that care was free and that no one had to be generous for the sick to be treated. It was a system designed to induce generosity on the part of doctors and fellow citizens. But managed care insurance, to the extent it exposes and highlights the costs to others of sick people's care, is calculated to dampen generosity.

PUTTING THE DOCTOR-BUSINESSMAN TO WORK

The insulation of medical judgment from financial concerns was always partly a fiction. The ideal of the doctor as free of commercial influence was elaborated by a medical profession that sought to expand its market and maintain its political power and autonomy. Now, the opposite ideal—the doctor as ethical businessman whose financial incentives and professional calling mesh perfectly—is promoted in the service of a different drive to expand power and markets.

Corporate insurers use this refashioned image of the doctor to recruit both doctors and patients. The new image has some appeal to doctors, in part because it acknowledges that they need and want to make money in a way the old ethical codes didn't, and in part because it conveys a (false) sense of independence at a time when clinical autonomy is fast eroding. Through financial incentives and requirements for patients to get their treatments and tests authorized in advance, insurers are taking clinical decisions out of doctors' hands. Hospital length-of-stay rules, drug formularies (lists of drugs a plan will cover), and exclusive contracts with medical-device suppliers also reduce doctors' discretion.

In contrast to this reality of diminished clinical authority, images of the doctor as an entrepreneur, as a risk taker, as "the 'general manager' of his patient's medical care" (that's Enthoven's sobriquet in his Shattuck Lecture) convey a message that clinical doctors are still in control. If they practice wisely, in accord with the dictates of good, cost-effective medicine, they will succeed at raising their income without cutting quality. HMOs have long exploited this imagery of business heroism to recruit physicians. Here's Stephen Moore, then medical director of United Health Care, explaining to doctors in the *New England Journal of Medicine* in 1979 how this new type of HMO would help them fulfill "their desire to control costs" while keeping government regulation at bay:

> Incentives encourage the primary-care physician to give serious consideration to his new role as the coordinator and financial manager of all medical care. . . . Because accounts and incentives exist for each primary-care physician, the physician's accountability is not shared by other physicians, even among partners in a group practice. . . . Each physician is solely responsible for the efficiency of his own health care system. . . . In essence, then, the individual primary-care physician becomes a one-man HMO.

The image of entrepreneur suggests that doctors' success depends on their skill and acumen as managers. It plays down the degree to which their financial success and ability to treat all patients conscientiously depend on the mix of sick and costly patients in their practices and the practices of other doctors with whom they are made to share risks.

The once negative image of doctor-as-businessman has been recast to appeal to patients, too, as insurers, employers, and Medicare and Medicaid programs try to persuade patients to give up their old-style insurance and move into managed care plans. Doctors, the public has been told by all the crisis stories of the past two decades, have been commercially motivated all along. They exploited the fee-for-service system and generous health insurance policies to foist unnecessary and excessive "Cadillac" services onto patients, all to line their own pockets. Patients, the story continues, have been paying much more than necessary to obtain adequate, good-quality medical care. But now, under the good auspices of insurers, doctors incentives will be perfectly aligned with the imperatives of scientifically proven medical care, doctors will be converted from bad businessmen to good, and patients will get more value for their money.

If patients knew how much clinical authority was actually stripped from their doctors in managed care plans, they might be more reluctant to join. The marketing materials of managed care plans typically exaggerate doctors' autonomy. They tell potential subscribers that their primary care doctor has the power to authorize any needed services, such as referral to specialists, hospitalization, x-rays, lab tests, and physical therapy. Doctors in these marketing materials "coordinate" all care, "permit" patients to see specialists, and "decide" what care is medically necessary. Meanwhile, the actual contracts often give HMOs the power to authorize medically necessary services, and more importantly to define what services fall under the requirements for HMO approval.

In managed care brochures, doctors not only retain their full professional autonomy, but under the tutelage of management experts, they work magic with economic resources. Through efficient management, they actually increase the value of the medical care dollar. "Because of our expertise in managing health care," a letter to Medicare beneficiaries from the Oxford Medicare Advantage plan promised, "Oxford is able to give you *100% of your Medicare benefits and much, much more*" [emphasis in original]. Not a word in these sales materials about the incentives for doctors to deny expensive procedures and referrals, nor in some cases, the "gag clauses" that prevent doctors from telling patients about treatments a plan won't cover.

In an era when employers and governments are reducing their financial commitments to workers and citizens, the image of the doctor as efficient manager is persuasive rhetoric to mollify people who have come to expect certain benefits. To lower their costs, employers are cutting back on fringe benefits and shifting jobs to part-time and contract employees, to whom they have no obligation to provide health insurance. The federal and state governments are similarly seeking to cut back the costs of Medicare and Medicaid. The image of the doctor as an efficient—manager someone who can actually increase the value to patients of the payer's reduced payments—helps gain beneficiaries' assent to reductions in their benefits. Thus, the cultural icon of doctor-as-businessman has become a source of power for employers and governments as they cut back private and public social welfare commitments.

The old cultural ideal of pure clinical judgment without regard to costs or profits always vibrated with unresolved tensions. It obscured the reality that doctoring was a business as well as a profession and that medical care costs money and consumes resources. But now that commercial managed care has turned doctors into entrepreneurs who maximize profits by minimizing care, the aspirations of the old ideal are worth reconsidering.

In trying to curb costs, we should not economize in ways that subvert the essence of medical care or the moral foundations of community. There is something worthwhile about the ideal of medicine as a higher calling with a healing mission, dedicated to patients' welfare above doctors' incomes and committed to serving people on the basis of their needs, not their status. If we want compassionate medical care, we have to structure both medical care and health insurance to inspire compassion. We must find a way, as other countries have, to insure everybody on relatively equal terms, and thus divorce clinical decisions from the patient's pocketbook and the doctor's personal profit. This will require systems that control expenditures, as other countries do, without making doctor and patient financial adversaries. There is no perfect way to reconcile cost containment with clinical autonomy, but surely, converting the doctor into an entrepreneur is the most perverse strategy yet attempted.

NOTE

This article draws on material that appears in more extended form as "The Doctor as Businessman: Changing Politics of a Cultural Icon," *Journal of Health Politics, Policy and Law,* vol. 22, no. 2, 1997.

Medicine in Practice

The social organization of medicine is manifested on the interactional as well as the structural levels of society. There is an established and rich tradition of studying medical work "firsthand" in medical settings, through participant-observation, interviewing, or both. Researchers go "where the action is"—in this case among doctors and patients—to see just how social life (i.e., medical care) happens. Such studies are time-consuming and difficult (see Danziger, 1979), but they are the only way to penetrate the structure of medical care and reveal the sociological texture of medical practice. For it is here that the structure of medicine shapes the type of care that is delivered.

There are at least three general foci for these qualitative studies. Some studies focus on the organization of the institution itself, such as a mental hospital (Goffman, 1961), a nursing home (Gubrium, 1975), or an intensive care unit (Zussman, 1992). Others examine the delivery of services or practitioner-patient interaction ranging from childbirth (Davis-Floyd, 1992) to dying (Timmermans, 1999). A third general focus is on collegial relations among professionals (e.g., Chambliss, 1996; Bosk, 1979; Guillemin and Holmstrom, 1986). All of these studies give us a window on the backstage world of medical organization. No matter what the focus, they bring to life the processes through which organizations operate and how participants manage in their situations. It is worth noting also that most of these close-up studies end up with the researchers taking a critical stance toward the organization and practice of medicine.

The four selections in this section reveal different aspects of medicine in practice. The readings represent a range of medical settings and situations: outpatient encounters, an emergency room, an intensive-care nursery, and alternative medicine. As well as illuminating the texture of medical practice, the selections individually and together raise a number of significant sociological issues.

In "The Struggle between the Voice of Medicine and the Voice of the Lifeworld," Elliot G. Mishler offers a detailed analysis of the structure of doctor-patient interviews. His analysis allows us to see two distinct "voices" in the interview discourse. In this framework, the "voice of medicine" dominates the interviews and allows physicians to control the interview. When "the voice of the lifeworld"—patients talking "about problems in their lives that were related to or resulted from their symptoms or illness" (Mishler, 1984: 91)—disrupts the voice of medicine, it is often interrupted, silenced, or ignored. This perspective shows how physician dominance is recreated in doctor-patient encounters, and it gives some clues to why patients may say their doctors don't understand them.

In the second selection, "Social Death as Self-Fulfilling Prophecy," Stefan Timmermans demonstrates how staff evaluations of patients' "social worth" affects whether and how the staff will attempt to resuscitate them. Sociologists have frequently shown that medical staff make moral judgments of patients' worthiness based on their evaluations of the patients' social attributes and the "appropriateness" of their demands. Timmermans (1999) observed the use of CPR (cardiopulmonary resuscitation) in two emergency departments and compares his findings to a benchmark study conducted thirty years earlier (Sudnow, 1967). Despite great changes in the health care system and a refinement of CPR techniques, Timmermans found a persistence of social rationing of medical interventions. The allocation of medical care based on perceived social worth not only reflects existing inequalities in society, but creates new ones as well.

Renée R. Anspach, in "The Language of Case Presentation," analyzes the way doctors talk to each other, especially about patients. Based on data collected in a study of neonatal infant-care nurseries, Anspach shows how the language used by medical housestaff in presenting "cases" to their superiors reveals important aspects of physicians' socialization; she also provides insights into assumptions of the medical world view and how physicians mitigate responsibility for errors. She contends that language used in medical work not only communicates information and organizes the task, but reflects underlying attitudes and affects the delivery of patient care (see also Anspach, 1993).

The final selection, "Alternative Health and the Challenges of Institutionalization," by Mathew Scheirov and Jonathan David Geczik is a case study of a complementary medicine clinic in a large urban hospital. Complementary and alternative medicine (CAM) have grown enormously in the past two decades and are increasingly utilized and accepted by patients and providers in American health care. There is a growing body of research suggesting that some types of CAM have considerable treatment efficacy (Goldstein, 2002). The dominant medical system is accepting CAM more often as a part of medical care. Schneirov and Geczik use interviews with clinic staff and patients to understand whether CAM's institutional success is coming at the expense of the ideals of the reformist movement that has brought alternative health to the forefront. The authors conclude that for alternative health to succeed it must establish links with the dominant health-care system, although it needs to be careful to sustain its own identity and not be fully absorbed by biomedicine. It is important for alternative health to maintain a close connection with the lifeworlds of patients.

All four selections highlight the structure of medical practice. Each illustrates how the social organization of medicine constrains and shapes the physician's work. Aside from delivering services, it appears that a very important element of the physician's task is sustaining the medical order in which services are delivered, although there can be meaningful challenges.

REFERENCES

Anspach, Renée. 1993. Deciding Who Lives. Berkeley: University of California Press.

Bosk, Charles. 1979. Forgive and Remember. Chicago: University of Chicago.

Chambliss, Daniel F. 1996. Beyond Caring: Hospitals, Nurses and the Social Organization of Ethics. Chicago: University of California Press.

Danziger, Sandra Klein. 1979. "On doctor watching: Fieldwork in medical settings." Urban Life. 7 (January): 513–31.

Davis-Floyd, Robbie. 1992. Birth as an American Rite of Passage. Berkeley: University of California Press.

Goffman, Erving. 1961. Asylums. New York: Doubleday.

Goldstein, Michael S. 2002. "The emerging socioeconomic and political support for alternative medicine in the United States." The Annals of the American Academy of Political and Social Science. 583(September):44–63.

Gubrium, Jabar. 1975. Living and Dying at Murray Manor. New York: St. Martin's Press.

Guillemin, Jeanne Harley and Linda Lytle Holmstrom. 1986. Mixed Blessings: Intensive Care for Newborns. New York: Oxford.

Mishler, Eliot G. 1984. The Discourse of Medicine: Dialectics of Medical Interviews. Norwood, NJ: Ablex.

Sudnow, David. 1967. Passing On: The Social Organization of Dying. Englewood Cliffs, NJ: Prentice-Hall.

Timmermans, Stefan. 1999. Sudden Death and the Myth of CPR. Philadelphia: Temple University Press.

Zussman, Robert. 1992. Intensive Care. Chicago: University of Chicago Press.

29 *THE STRUGGLE BETWEEN THE VOICE OF MEDICINE AND THE VOICE OF THE LIFEWORLD*

Elliot G. Mishler

INTRODUCTION

The work reported here assumes that the discourse of patients with physicians is central to clinical practice and, therefore, warrants systematic study. . . . Principal features of the approach and the general plan of the study will be outlined briefly in this introductory section.

The inquiry begins with a description and analysis of "unremarkable interviews." This term is applied to stretches of talk between patients and physicians that appear intuitively to be normal and nonproblematic. The interviews are drawn from the large sample collected by Waitzkin and Stoeckle[1] in their study of the informative process in medical care (Waitz-kin & Stoeckle, 1976; Waitzkin et al. 1978). In these interviews patients and physicians talk to each other in ways that we, as members of the same culture, recognize as contextually appropriate. Our sense of appropriateness depends on shared and tacit understandings; on commonly held and often implicit assumptions of how to talk and of what to talk about in this situation.

Our intuitive sense of the unremarkable nature of these interviews merely locates the phenomenon for study. The central task of this chapter is to develop and apply concepts and methods that allow us to go through and beyond our ordinary, implicit, and shared understanding of the "normality" and "unremarkableness" of these interviews. The aim is to make explicit features of the talk that produce and warrant our sense as investigators and, by implication, the sense made by physicians and patients that the talk is unremarkable, and that the interview is going as it "should" go. The investigation proceeds through four analytically distinct but intertwined phases discussed in the review of alternative approaches to the study of discourse: description, analysis, interpretation, and interruption.

An adequate description is a prerequisite to further study. As noted earlier, a transcription of speech is neither a neutral or "objective" description. Transcription rules incorporate models of language in that they specify which features of speech are to be recorded and which are to go unremarked. Thus, they define what is relevant and significant. The typescript notation system used here is a modification and simplification of one developed by Gail Jefferson (1978) and used by many conversation analysts; . . . The general aim is to retain details of the talk believed to be significant for clarifying and understanding the structure and meaning of patient-physician discourse. The relevance of particular details will be demonstrated in the analyses.

In reviewing various approaches to the analysis of discourse, I noted a number of problems in the use of standardized coding systems. A particularly serious limitation is its neglect of the structure and organization of naturally occurring talk between speakers. For this reason alone, this method would be inappropriate to the study of medical interviews which, like other forms of human discourse, is both structured and meaningful. Speaking turns are connected both through the forms of utterances, as in question and answer pairs, and by content. The analyses undertaken here are directed to determining the organization of medical interviews with respect to both form and content.

A structural unit of discourse is proposed that appears to be typical and pervasive in such interviews. It consists of a sequential set of three utterances: Physician Question-Patient Response-Physician Assessment/Next Question. The specific features and functions of this unit will be examined. Problems that arise during the interview are discussed in terms of the disruption and repair of this unit. Finally, the ways in which meaning is developed and organized over the course of the interview are documented and shown to be related to this basic structure.

The effort to make theoretical sense of analytical findings is the work of interpretation, referred to here as the third stage of an investigation. This is usually considered the last stage, but I have adopted a distinction made by Silverman and Torode (1980) between interpretation and interruption. The latter will be discussed below. Interpretations, as would be expected, may take many forms, reflecting different theories of language and of social action. All of them, nonetheless, focus primarily on the questions of "what" is done in and through the talk, and "how" it is done. Thus, in their sociolinguistic analysis of a therapeutic interview, Labov and Fanshel (1977) state their interest as the discovery of "what is being done." They conclude that much of the talk of therapy consists of "requests" and "responses to requests." The framework for the analysis of discourse that they develop and apply is, in large part, a set of definitions, rules, and methods for describing, locating, and interpreting the interactional functions of different types of requests and responses.

The analytic question for ethnomethodologists and conversation analysts shifts toward the "how." For any particular instance of a "request," for example, conversation analysts wish to determine how speakers "do the work" of requesting. That is, how do speakers convey to each other their mutual recognition that what their talk is about is "requesting." But more is involved than a shift from "what" to "how." For conversation analysts, forms of requests and general rules of use cannot be specified and listed in a coding manual, as Labov and Fanshel attempt. The contextual embeddedness of speech would make any such manual a poor guide for conversationalists, and for investigators as well. The "how" of discourse for ethnomethodologists concerns the speaker practices through which "requesting" is routinely done, or "accomplished," to use the ethnomethodologists' term, in any context, despite the problem that a formal rule cannot take into account the specific features of particular contexts.[2]

Much of the work of conversation analysts, like that of sociolinguists, is directed to the study of how general tasks of conversation are accomplished, how conversations are initiated and terminated, how turns are taken, how topics are switched, and how mistakes are repaired. All these conversational tasks are "done" in medical interviews, as in all other types of discourse. One aim of the present study is to determine if there are systematic and typical ways in which patients and physicians accomplish these general tasks of a conversation. For example, there are a number of ways in which speakers may ask and answer questions. How is questioning and answering done by patients and physicians?

Linked to this approach is another level of interpretation that represents a more central topic in our inquiry, namely, the nature of clinical work. Our speakers are physicians and patients, and in how they begin their discourse, take their turns, and take leave of each other they are also doing the work of doctoring and patienting. Interpretation of findings on conversational practices is directed to an understanding of how the work of doctoring and patienting is done. For example, the strong tendency for physicians to ask closed- rather than open-ended questions is interpreted as serving the function of maintaining control over the content of the interview. In turn, this assures the dominance of the biomedical model as the perspective within which patients' statements are interpreted and allows doctors to accomplish the "medical" tasks of diagnosis and prescription. At the same time, the fact that their utterances are almost exclusively in the form of questions gives doctors control of the turn-taking system and, consequently, of the structure and organization of the interview. The interpretation of particular discourse practices developed here will refer to both form and content.

Finally, borrowing from Silverman and Torode, I have referred to a second mode, or line of theorizing, as interruption. Of particular relevance to our purpose is Silverman and Torode's notion of "voices." As I understand it, a voice represents a particular assumption about the relationship between appearance, reality, and language, or, more generally, a "voice" represents a specific normative order. Some discourses are closed and continually reaffirm a single normative order; others are open and include different voices, one of which may interrupt another, thus leading to the possibility of a new "order." There are occasions in medical interviews where the normal and routine practice of clinical work appears to be disrupted. In order to understand both the routine, fluent course of the interview as well as its occasional disruption, a distinction will be introduced between the "voices" representing two different normative orders: the "voice of medicine" and the "voice of the lifeworld." Disruptions of the discourse during interviews appear to mark instances where the "voice of the lifeworld" interrupts the dominant "voice of medicine." How this happens, and whether the discourse is then "opened" or remains "closed" will be of major interest in succeeding analyses.

In sum, the principal aim of this chapter is to develop methods for the study of discourse that are informed by considerations of the research tasks of description, analysis, interpretation, and interruption. The methods are applied to a set of unremarkable interviews to bring out more clearly those features that are associated with our intuitive recognition of the interviews as instances of routine, normal, and ordinary clinical practice. After a close look at how these interviews work to produce a sense of normality and appropriateness, stretches of talk between patients and physicians that depart in some way from the normal and typical pattern will be examined. The departures suggest that something has become problematic. The analysis of problematic interviews is undertaken in the context of the findings from analyses of nonproblematic or unremarkable interviews. This will provide an initial set of contrasting features and their functions for use in further analyses that compare the "voice of medicine" with the "voice of the lifeworld."

UNREMARKABLE MEDICAL INTERVIEWS

Diagnostic Examination (W:02.014)[3]

The excerpt presented as Transcript 29-1 is taken from the beginning of an interview. Through this opening series of exchanges the patient (P) responds to the physician's (D) questions with a report of her symptoms. After each response, the physician asks for further details or other symptoms with the apparent aim of determining the specific nature of the problem and arriving at a diagnosis. On its surface, their talk proceeds as we would expect in a routine medical interview; it is unremarkable.

The physician initiates the interview with a question that Labov and Fanshel (1977, pp. 88–91) would code as a request for information: "What's the problem." Although its syntactic form is that of an open-ended Wh-question, the physician's voice does not carry question intonation. For that reason, the transcript does not show a question mark. The utterance is a request in the imperative mode, a paraphrase of a statement such as, "Tell me what the problem is." The phrasing of a request for action or information as an imperative is not unusual, and Labov and Fanshel argue that "the imperative is the unmarked form of a request for action" and "the central element in the construction of requests" (pp. 77–78).

In his first turn, the physician has set the general topic of discussion, namely, the patient's "problem." Or, more precisely, the physician's request is mutually understood to be germane and to express their joint recognition of the reason for the patient's presence in this setting: she is here because she has, or believes she has, a medically relevant problem. We, as investigators, knowing that this is a medical interview, are able to "read" the physician's utterance in the same way as the patient does. More than simply expressing a mutual understanding of the situation, his request confirms it and by confirming it contributes to the definition of the situation as a medical interview. It is in this sense that the "fact" that a medical interview is taking place is constructed through discourse. Such a definition of the situation excludes others. It is not a social occasion, a casual conversation, or an exchange of gossip, and we do not find initial greetings, an exchange of names, or other courtesies with which such conversations commonly begin. (Their absence must be treated with caution since it may reflect when the tape recorder was turned on).

The patient responds to the physician's request for information; she begins to report her symptoms, when they began, and the change from a

Transcript 29-1

```
W:02.014
      001 D  What's the problem.
  I [                               (Chair noise)
                                              [
    | 002 P                                   (...) had since . last
    | 003    Monday evening so it's a week of sore throat
    | 004 D                                                hm hm
    | 005 P  which turned into a cold .......... uh:m ...........
    | 006    and then a cough.
    | 007 D                   A cold you mean what? Stuffy nose?
    | 008 P  uh Stuffy nose yeah not a chest ........ cold. ..........
    |                                          [
    | 009 D                                    hm hm
    | 010 P  uhm
    |        [
    | 011 D  And a cough.
    | 012 P             And a cough .. which is the most irritating
    | 013    aspect.
    |        [
      014 D  Okay. (hh) uh Any fever?
 II [ 015 P                                ...... Not that I know of.
    | 016    .... I took it a couple of times in the beginning
    | 017    but . haven't felt like-
    |           [
      018 D     hm                   How bout your ears?
III [ 019 P                                                 ........
    | 020 P  (hh) uhm .... Before anything happened .... I thought
    | 021    that my ears ...... might have felt a little bit
    | 022    funny but (....) I haven't got any problem(s).
      023 D                                                 Okay.
 IV [ 024    ..........(hh) Now this uh cough what are you producing
IV' | 025    anything or is it a dry cough?
    | 026 P                                   Mostly dry although
    | 027    ....... a few days . ago it was more mucusy ....
    | 028    cause there was more (cold). Now (there's) mostly cough.
IV" |           [                                              [
      029 D     hm hm                                          What
  V [ 030    about the nasal discharge? Any?
    | 031 P                                       ....A little.
    | 032 D                                                What
    | 033    color is it?
    | 034 P           ...... uh:m ........ I don't really know
    | 035    .... uhm I suppose a whitish- (....)
    |                                       [
    | 036 D                                 hm hm What?
    | 037 P                                            There's been
    | 038    nothing on the hankerchief.
    |                    [
      039 D              hm hm    Okay. .... (hh) Do you have
 VI [ 040    any pressure around your eyes?
    | 041 P                                 No.
```

Transcript 29-1 *(Continued.)*

```
                                                    Okay. How do you feel?
      042 D   .......... uh:m ........ Tired. heh I couldn-(h)
VII  ┌043 P   I couldn't(h) sleep last night(h) uhm
     │044                                            [
     │                                              Because of the . cough.
     │045 D                                                        [
     │                                                              Otherwise-
     │046 P   Yup. Otherwise I feel fine.
     │047                                     Alright. Now . have you .
     └048 D   had good health before (generally).
VIII ┌049                                              Yeah . fine.
     └050 P                   (1′25″)
```

sore throat that began a week ago, "which turned into a cold," "and then a cough." As she gives her account, the physician indicates that he is attending to her, understands, and wants her to continue by a go-ahead signal, "hm hm."

As the patient responds to his opening question, the physician requests further clarification and specification: "A cold you mean what? Stuffy nose?" A little later he asks for confirmation of what he heard her say earlier, "And a cough." Through his questions the physician indicates that although he has asked her to talk about the nature of her "problem," the topic remains under his control. That is, his questions define the relevance of particular features in her account. Further, when the patient mentions a cold, sore throat, and cough as her symptoms, the physician suggests additional dimensions and distinctions that may be of medical relevance that the patient has neglected to report. Thus, a "cold" is not a sufficient description for his purpose; he must know what is "meant" by a cold and what kind of cold it is, "Stuffy nose?" The patient recognizes that there are at least two kinds, nose colds and chest colds, and introduces this contrast pair in order to specify her own: "uh stuffy nose yeah not a chest . . . cold."

The physician acknowledges her distinction, "hm hm," and adds to it the other symptom she has mentioned, "And a cough." The patient reconfirms his addition and goes on to give this symptom particular emphasis: "And a cough . . . which is the most irritating aspect." The physician's "Okay," inserted to overlap with the end of the patient's utterance, terminates the first cycle of the interview. He acknowledges the adequacy of the patient's response to his opening question, "What's the problem," and his "Okay" serves to close this section of the interview; no more is to be said about the problem in general and he will now proceed with more specific questions.

The first cycle is marked on the transcript by a bracket enclosing utterances 001–014 under Roman Numeral I. Its basic structure may be outlined as consisting of: a request/question from the physician, a response from the patient, and a post-response assessment/acknowledgment by the physician, to which is added a new request/question to begin the next cycle. The remainder of the excerpt is made up of seven additional cycles with structures identical to the first one. The first six cycles focus on the "cold" symptoms, the last two open with more general questions.

There are two variants within the basic structure. In the first type, the basic structure is expanded internally by requests from the physician for clarification or elaboration of the patient's response; this occurs in the first, fifth, and seventh cycles. In the second variant, the physician's assessments are implicit. Although his post-response assessments are usually explicit (an "Okay" or "Alright" comment), there are occasions when they are implicitly conveyed by the physician proceeding immediately to a next question. Alternatively, his assessment may occur before the patient's completion of her utterance through an overlapping "hm hm"; this occurs in the linkage between cycles IV and V.

This three-part utterance sequence is a regular and routine occurrence in the talk between patients and physicians. For that reason, I will refer to it as the basic structural unit of discourse in medical interviews. We recognize and accept interviews with these structures as normal, standard, and appropriate—as unremarkable. The medical interview tends to be constituted, overwhelmingly, by a connected series of such structural units. They are linked together through the physician's post-response assessment utterance that serves the dual function of closing the previous cycle and initiating a new one through his next question.

I do not mean to imply that this structure is unique to medical interviews, although it is one of their distinctive features. The same general type of structure appears in other settings of interaction where the aim is assessment, diagnosis, or selection, that is, when one person has the task of eliciting information from another. Thus, the same three-utterance sequence initiated by questions is found in classroom exchanges between teachers and pupils, although these are not interviews and teachers may direct successive questions to different pupils.[4] We might also expect to find it in psychological test situations and personnel interviews. Further work would be needed to determine how these discourses with similar general structures differed in their particular features.

Since I am proposing that this discourse structure is the basic unit of the medical interview and that its pervasive presence in a linked series is what makes this interview unremarkable, it is important to look more closely at how it is constructed and how it functions. The first and most obvious impression is of the physician's strong and consistent control over the content and development of the interview. . . . Here, I am trying to show how physicians exercise control through the structure of their exchanges with patients in the course of an interview.

There are a number of ways in which the physician uses his position as a speaker in this structure to control the interview: he opens each cycle of discourse with his response/question; he assesses the adequacy of the patient's response; he closes each cycle by using his assessment as a terminating marker; he opens the next cycle by another request/question. Through this pattern of opening and terminating cycles the physician controls the turn-taking process; he decides when the patient should take her turn. He also controls the content of what is to be discussed by selectively attending and responding to certain parts of the patient's statements and by initiating each new topic.

The physician's control of content through the initiation of new topics is particularly evident. After the first cycle in which the patient introduces her problem, there are seven new topics, each introduced by the physician through a question that opens a new cycle. In sequence, the physician asks the patient about: presence of fever, ear problems, type of cough, presence and type of nasal discharge, pressure around her eyes, how she feels, and her general state of health. The list is hardly worth noticing; these are the questions we might expect a physician to ask if a patient reports having a sore throat and a cold. The fit between our expectations and the interview is very close, which is why I have referred to it as an unremarkable interview.

We may learn more, however, about the significance and functions of the physician's control if we examine how his questions not only focus on certain topics, but are selectively inattentive to others. Through the questions he asks the physician constructs and specifies a domain of relevance; in Paolo Freire's phrase, he is "naming the world," the world of relevant matters for him and the patient (Freire, 1968).[5] The topics that the patient introduces, all of which are explicit, but not attended to by the physician, are: the history and course of her symptoms, and the effects they have had on her life that the cough is the most irritating aspect, that she's tired and has had a sleepless night. Both of these latter topics, opened up by the patient but not pursued by the physician, bear on a question that remains unasked but whose potential "relevance" is close to the surface: why she has come to see the physician at this point even though the problem began a week before.

In summary, this analysis shows that the physician controls the content of the interview, both through his initiation of new topics and through what he attends to and ignores in the patient's reports. Further, there is a systematic bias to his focus of attention; the patient's reports of how the problem developed and how it affects her the "life contexts" of her symptoms are systematically ignored. The physician directs his attention solely to physical-medical signs that might be associated with her primary symptoms, such as ear or eye problems, or to the further physical specification of a symptom, such as type of cough or color of nasal discharge. . . .

. . . We may now move beyond this level of interpretation to the stage referred to earlier as "interruption." The particular patterning of form and content shown in the analysis documents and defines the interview as "unremarkable," a characterization that was made on intuitive grounds. The clear pattern suggests that the discourse expresses a particular "voice," to use Silverman and Torode's (1980) term. Since the interview is dominated by the physician, I will refer to this as the "voice of medicine."

The topic introduced by the patient in VII, her tiredness and difficulty sleeping, is in another voice; I will call it the "voice of the lifeworld." It is an interruption, or an attempted interruption, of the ongoing discourse being carried on in the "voice of medicine." It is of some interest that the patient's introduction of another voice occurs in response to the open-ended question: "How do you feel?" Except for his initial question, this is the only open-ended question asked by the physician in this excerpt. In this instance, the second voice is suppressed; it does not lead to an opening of the discourse into a fuller and more mutual dialogue between the two voices. Rather, the physician reasserts the dominance of the voice of medicine through his response: "Because of the cough." Interruptions of the discourse and their effects will receive further attention in the following analyses.

It is instructive to examine in some detail the patterns of pauses and hesitations in the respective utterances of physician and patient. The findings of this analysis that pauses are not randomly distributed, but located systematically at certain points, particularly in the transitions between speakers, reinforces the argument made earlier about the importance of including such details of speech in transcripts. If we look at the cycle transition points (that is, from I–II, II–III, etc., that the physician controls through his utterance with a dual function terminating the previous cycle with a post-response assessment and initiating the new cycle with a question), we find a relatively consistent pattern. The physician either breaks into the patient's statement before she has completed it, thus terminating her statement with his own comment an "Okay" or "hm hm" as in I–II, II–III, IV–V, and V–VI, or he takes his next turn without pause as soon as the patient finishes, as in III–IV, VI–VII, and VII–VIII. Often, the assessment-terminating part of his utterance is followed by a pause, filled or unfilled, before the question that begins the next cycle, as in the utterances marking the beginnings of cycles II, III, IV, and VI.

. . . Findings from this analysis of one "unremarkable" interview will be summarized at this point. They provide a characterization, albeit tentative and preliminary, of normal and routine clinical practice, and can be used as a framework for comparing and contrasting analyses of other interviews.

First, the basic structural unit of a medical interview is a linked set of three utterances: a physician's opening question, a patient's response, and the physician's response to the patient which usually, but not always, begins with an assessment followed by a second question. The second utterance of the physician serves the dual function of terminating the first unit, or cycle, and initiating the next. In this way, the separate units are connected together to form the continuous discourse of the interview.

The primary discourse function of the basic structure is that it permits the physician to control the development of the interview. His control is assured by his position as both first and last speaker in each cycle, which allows him to control the turn-taking system and the sequential organization of the interview. This structure of dominance is reinforced by the content of the physician's assessments and questions that he asks, which selectively attend to or ignore particulars of the patient's responses. The physician's dominance is expressed at still another level through the syntactic structure of his questions. These tend to be restrictive closed-end questions, which limit the range of relevance for patient responses. At all these levels, the focus of relevance, that is, of appropriate meaning, is on medically relevant material, as is defined by the physician.

Within utterances, two patterns of pauses were identified that are consistent with the overall structure and its functions. Typically, in physician utterances there is a pause between the assessment and the next question. This serves to mark the termination of the prior unit and the initiation of the next one. The length of initial pauses in patient responses appears to depend on the location of a cycle within a sequence of cycles. Patient utterances in the first cycle of a series are preceded by a short pause, in the second cycle by a long pause, and in the third cycle by no pause. This seems to be related to the degree of disjunction between successive physician questions and whether or not he "helps" the patient prepare for a response by making his next question relevant to her prior response.

Finally, all the features and functions of this unit of discourse have been brought together under a general analytic category referred to as the "voice of medicine." The physician's control of the interview through the structure of turn-taking and through the form and content of his questions expresses the normative order of medicine. The dominance of this voice produces our intuitive impression of the interview as an instance of normal clinical practice, that is, as unremarkable. Patients may attempt to interrupt the dominant voice by speaking in the "voice of the lifeworld." This alternative voice may be suppressed, as it was in this interview, or may open up the interview to a fuller dialogue between voices. Relationships between the two voices will be explored further. . . .

THE INTERRUPTION OF CLINICAL DISCOURSE

The structure of clinical discourse has been explicated through analyses of two unremarkable interviews. The basic three-part unit of such discourse and the ways in which these units are linked together has been described, as well as the functions served by this structure the physician's control of organization and meaning. I referred to this patterned relationship between structure and function as the "voice of medicine," and suggested that it expressed the normative order of medicine and clinical practice. This voice provides a baseline against which to compare other medical interviews that depart in some way from normal and routine practice.

Some preliminary comparisons have already been made. In each of these unremarkable interviews the patient interrupted the flow of the discourse by introducing the "voice of the lifeworld." In both instances, the new voice was quickly silenced and the physician reasserted his dominance and the singularity of the clinical perspective. In the following interview, the patient makes more of an effort to sustain an alternative voice. Examining how the patient does this and how the physician responds will extend our understanding of the specific features and functions of medical interviews and will also alert us to problems that develop when there are departures from normal and routine clinical work. This discussion will also bring forward an issue that will be central to later analyses; the struggle between the voices of medicine and of the lifeworld.

Symptom and Lifeworld Context: Negotiation of Meaning (W: 13.121/01)

The patient is a 26-year-old woman with stomach pains, which she describes as a sour stomach beginning several weeks prior to this medical visit. The excerpt (Transcript 29-2) begins about 3½ minutes into the interview, preceded by a review of her history of peptic ulcers in childhood and the time and circumstances of the present complaint.

In the excerpt, the first four cycles and the beginning of the fifth are similar in structure to the interviews analyzed earlier. Each one begins with the physician's question about the symptom. This is followed by a response from the patient, sometimes preceded by a pause, and is terminated by the physician's next question. His question is sometimes preceded by an assessment, which then initiates the next cycle.

Two other features of the first four cycles may be noted. Although there are occasional pauses

Transcript 29-2

W:13.121/01

```
   ┌001 D  Hm hm .... Now what do you mean by a sour stomach?
 I │002 P  .................. What's a sour stomach? A heartburn
   │003    like a heartburn or something.
   │                                            [
   └004 D                                       Does it burn over here?
II ┌005 P                                                                   Yea:h.
   │006    It li- I think- I think it like- If you take a needle
   │007    and stick ya right .... there's a pain right here ..
   │                        [      [                              [
   │008 D                   Hm hm Hm hm                           Hm hm
   └009 P  and  and then it goes from here on this side to this side.
   ┌010 D  Hm Hm Does it go into the back?
III│                              [
   │011 P                         It's a:ll up here. No. It's all right
   │012    up here in the front.
   │       [
   └013 D  Yeah                    And when do you get that?
IV ┌014 P                                                              ........
   └015    ........... Wel:l when I eat something wrong.
   ┌016 D                                                        How- How
 V │017    soon after you eat it?
V' │018 P                            ............................Wel:l
   │019    ....... probably an hour .... maybe less.
   │                                                 [
   │020 D                                            About an hour?
V" │021 P  Maybe less .............. I've cheated and I've been
   │022    drinking which I shouldn't have done.
   └023 D                                                    ..........
   ┌024    Does drinking making it worse?
VI │       [
   │025 P  (...)                                 Ho ho uh ooh Yes. ....
   └026    ....... Especially the carbonation and the alcohol.
   ┌027 D  ......... Hm hm ........ How much do you drink?
VII│028 P                                                              .....
VII'│029   .................. I don't know. .. Enough to make me
   │030    go to sleep at night ........ and that's quite a bit.
VII"│031 D One or two drinks a day?
   │032 P                                        O:h no no no humph it's (more
   │033    like) ten. ...... at night.
   │                   [
   │034 D              How many drinks- a night.
   │035 P                                                    At night.
   └036 D                                                           .....
   ┌037    ..... Whaddya ta- What type of drinks ....... I (...)-
VIII│                                                              [
   │038 P                                                          Oh vodka
   │039    .. yeah vodka and ginger ale.
   └040 D                                         .......................
```

Transcript 29-2 *(Continued.)*

IX	041	...... How long have you been drinking that heavily?
IX′	042 P	.... Since I've been married.
	043 D	......
IX″	044	.. How long is that?
	045 P	(giggle..) Four years. (giggle)
	046	huh Well I started out with before then I was drinkin
	047	beer but u:m I had a job and I was .... ya know ......
	048	had more things on my mind and ya know I like- but
	049	since I got married I been in and out of jobs and
	050	everything so .... I- I have ta have something to
	051	go to sleep.
	052 D	...... Hm:m.
	053 P	.... I mean I'm not
	054	gonna- ...... It's either gonna be pills or it's
	055	gonna be .. alcohol .... and uh alcohol seems
	056	to satisfy me moren than pills do .... They don't
	057	seem to get strong enough .... pills that I have
	058	got I had- I do have Valium .... but they're two
	059	milligrams .... and that's supposed to
	060	quiet me down during the day but it doesn't.
	061 D	......
X	062	How often do you take them?
		(1′47″)

prior to the patient's responses and some false starts as she appears to search for an appropriate answer, there are few within-utterance pauses and those that occur are of short duration. For the physician, the pattern found earlier of a pause between assessment and question is occasionally present, but there are no false starts or pauses between the patient's responses and the physician's next questions. Again, there is a high degree of fluency in his speech.

The routine breaks down in cycle V. The patient's response to the physician's question with its false start includes a signal of trouble: "How-How soon after you eat it?" The patient's response is preceded by her longest pre-utterance pause (one of 2.5″), and contains two relatively long intra-utterance pauses. A major change comes in her next response, after restating her previous answer, "Maybe less," in response to his clarification question: "About an hour?" This physician question is treated as an internal expansion within V, although it might also be considered as beginning a new cycle, V′. Her answer, "Maybe less," is followed by a moderately long intra-utterance pause of 1.2″, after which she introduces a new topic, her drinking.

This new topic comes in the form of a "tag" comment added to her answer to the physician's question and it has some features that mark it as different from what has previously been said. ". . . I've cheated and I've been drinking which I shouldn't have done," has a quality of intonation that is unusual when compared with her earlier responses. Those who have heard the tape recording easily recognize the difference and describe her speech as "teasing," "flirtatious," or "childish."

The physician's next question, which terminates V and initiates VI, is preceded by his first long pre-question hesitation: ". . . Does drinking make it worse?" This is the first break in the fluency of his pattern of questioning. Further, he talks over the patient's attempt to say something more. His uncertainty, indicated by his pause, reflects two changes in the nature of the interview. The patient's comment introduces her drinking and, since this new topic is not in response to a direct question from the physician, it also shifts the control of the interview from physician to patient. I pointed out in earlier analyses that the basic structure of the medical interview, physician question-patient response-physician (assessment) question, permits the physician to control the form and content of the interview. As the "questioner," the physician controls the turn-taking structure and through the focus of his assessments and questions controls the development of meaning; he defines what is and what is not relevant. By her tag comment, the patient has taken control both of form and meaning; she has introduced another voice.

With this tentative hypothesis that the normal structure of the medical interview has been interrupted and that as a result, the normal pattern of control has also been disrupted, we might expect to find evidence of: (a) other indicators of disruption and breakdown in the continuing exchange, and (b) efforts on the part of the physician to repair the disruption, to restore the normal structure, and to reassert the dominant voice of medicine.

The physician's pre-question hesitation after the patient introduces the new topic has already been noted as a sign of disruption, a change from his usual response timing: ". . . Does drinking make it worse?" Similar and frequently longer pauses appear before all of his succeeding questions initiating new cycles at VII, VIII, IX, and X. The regularity of these pauses is quite striking, particularly when it is contrasted with the equally striking occurrence of no pauses preceding questions in cycles with a normal structure (I–IV).

Throughout the second half of this excerpt, from cycles VI–X, there is a continuing struggle between physician and patient to take control of the interview. The patient tries to maintain her control by restatements of the problem of drinking in her life situation exemplifying the voice of the lifeworld. The physician, on the other, persistently tries to reformulate the problem in narrower, more medically relevant terms. For example, to his question, "How much do you drink?" (the transition between cycles VI and VII), she replies, after a long pause of 2.2", "I don't know . . . Enough to make me go to sleep at night . . . and that's quite a bit." He persists with two further questions, within cycle VII, requesting the specific number of drinks. In this manner, the physician attempts to recapture control of the meaning of her account; he is excluding her meaning of the function of drinking in her life and focusing on "objective" measures of quantity.

The physician persists in this effort. To his question about how long she has been drinking heavily (IX), she responds, "Since I've been married," again preceding her response with a long pause. But this is not considered an adequate or relevant answer from the physician's point of view and he asks for an actual, objective time, "How long is that?" Finally, in a relatively extended account in cycle IX, the patient talks about her drinking, of problems since her marriage, and her preference for alcohol over pills. There is much surplus information in her story to which the physician might respond. He chooses to attend selectively to that part of her account which is of clear medical relevance, the taking of pills, and asks again for a precise, objective, and quantitative answer. "How often do you take them?"

Another way to indicate that a significant change has taken place in the structure of the interview during the fifth cycle is to take note of the difficulty encountered in attempting to describe this interview in terms of the structural units found in the analyses of the first two interviews. Although I have marked the cycles of the interview in the same way, distinguishing such successive series of physician question-patient response-physician (assessment) question exchanges, there are problems in using this unit here. This structural unit assumes that an exchange is initiated by the physician's question and that the three-part exchange cycle is then terminated by the physician as he initiates the next cycle.

The problem may be seen in cycle V, at the point of the patient's comment about her drinking. This statement is not in response to a direct question; rather it is a statement introducing a new topic. The physician's next question refers to this new topic and he thus remains "in role." The reader will note that all of the physician's statements, except for his "Hm" assessments, are questions. The implicit function of questions remains which is to control the form and content of the interview; however, in this instance there is a break in the continuity of the physician's control. As an alternative structure to the one presented, we could ask whether a new cycle should begin with the patient's tag comment. If that were done, the physician's next question would be treated as a "response" to her statement, even though it is framed as a question. I'm not proposing an answer to the problem of structural analysis at this preliminary stage. However, I am suggesting that the change in the interview resulting from the patient's comment introduces problems for analysis. These problems provide another line of evidence for the assertion that there has been a breakdown in the normal structure of the clinical interview. . . .

. . . In this discussion, I have been using the occurrence of a noticeable change in the structure and flow of an interview to raise questions about how to analyze and understand the workings of medical interviews. The introduction of a new topic by the patient altered the routine pattern of the interview found in earlier "unremarkable" interviews. The features of physician and patient utterances varied in specific ways from those found earlier. These changes raised questions about which speaker was controlling the development of the interview, and hence controlling the development of meaning. The idea of "voices," and the distinction between the "voice of medicine" and the "voice of the lifeworld," was introduced to characterize alternative orders of meaning and the struggle between them. . . .

NOTES

1. Waitzkin and Stoeckle's original corpus of nearly 500 interviews included a stratified random sample of physicians in private and clinic sessions in Boston and Oakland. For the present study, a small series of about twenty-five tapes was selected initially from the larger sample. Male and female patients were equally represented in the series, and both single and multiple interviews of a patient with the same physician were included. The original tapes were sequentially ordered by code numbers assigned to physicians and each of their successive patients. The selection procedure was to choose the "next" code number in the sequence where the interview met the criteria noted above until the cells were filled. Although this was not a random sampling procedure it ensured heterogeneity among the interviews and there was no reason to believe that the series was biased in a systematic way with reference to the original sample. The analyses presented here are based on a small number of interviews drawn from this series. Further, analyses are restricted to brief excerpts from the full interviews which exemplify issues of primary theoretical interest. This description of the procedure is intended to clarify the grounds on which the claim is made that the interviews examined in this study are "typical" medical interviews. This claim does not rely on statistical criteria or rules for selecting a "representative" sample. Rather, it rests on a shared understanding and recognition of these interviews as "representative," that is, as displays of normatively appropriate talk between patients and physicians.
2. Examples of these studies may be found in Schenkein (1978); and in Psathas (1979). A perceptive discussion of the way that ethnomethodology approaches the study of talk, and some of its unresolved problems, is found in Wooton (1975).
3. The typescript numbers used here are the codes on the tapes assigned by Waitzkin and Stoeckle; the number is preceded by a "W" to indicate the source.
4. In earlier studies of classroom interaction, I referred to the set of three utterances initiated by a question as an Interrogative Unit. Connections between units through the dual function of the second question were called Chaining (see Mishler 1975a, 1975b, 1978).
5. Another example of the ways in which a physician's selectivity of attention and inattention, through his pattern of questioning, shapes the development of meaning in a medical interview may be found in Paget (1983).

30 SOCIAL DEATH AS SELF-FULFILLING PROPHECY

Stefan Timmermans

Although death is supposedly the great equalizer, social scientists have abundantly documented the social inequality of death via mortality statistics (see e.g., Feinstein 1993; Kittagawa and Hauser 1973; Waldron 1997). Recently researchers have paid less attention to possible social inequality in the dying process itself. One of the most powerful and detailed sociological formulations to account for social inequality in the process of dying is still David Sudnow's classical study *Passing On* (1967). Sudnow argued that the health care staff decided how to administer their care giving based on *the patient's social value:* patients with perceived low social worth were much less likely to be resuscitated aggressively than patients with a perceived high social value. Since Sudnow's study, the health care field has undergone dramatic change (Conrad 1997; Starr 1982). Especially with the advent and widespread use of resuscitation techniques, biomedical researchers have encapsulated medical knowledge about lifesaving in sophisticated protocols, and legislators have instituted legal protections both to encourage resuscitative efforts and to secure patient's autonomy. The objective of this article is to evaluate the extent to which Sudnow's earlier claims about social inequality are still relevant in a transformed health care context that promotes a rational approach to medical practice and is influenced by extensive legal protections.

The purpose of resuscitative interventions is to reverse an ongoing dying process and preserve human lives. In most resuscitative efforts, however, the final result is a deceased patient (Eisenberg, Horwood, Cummins et al. 1990). When this result is the likely outcome of the resuscitative attempt, the staff's task is to avoid prolonged and unnecessary suffering and prepare for the patient's impending death. Saving lives requires an aggressive approach, whereas alleviating suffering demands that the staff intervenes minimally in the dying process and focuses on relieving pain and assisting relatives and friends. An aggressive resuscitative effort for an irreversibly dying (or already biologically dead) patient is not only futile but robs the dying patient of dignity (Callahan 1993; Moller 1996). It becomes a violation of the patient, a caricature of medical acumen (Illich 1976). A low-key resuscitative effort without much conviction for a still viable patient is regarded as passive euthanasia (Siner 1989).

How does the staff—as gatekeepers between life and death (Pelligrino 1986)—decide in the relative short time span of a resuscitative trajectory (Glaser and Strauss 1968) to resuscitate aggressively or to let the patient go with minimal medical interference? In the early 1960s, social scientists demonstrated that those apparently moral questions rest upon deep social foundations (Fox 1976). In death and dying, the fervor of the staff's intervention depends mostly on the patient's perceived social worth (Glaser and Strauss 1964; Sudnow 1967). In one of the first studies of resuscitative efforts in hospitals, Sudnow provided appalling insights into the social rationing[1] of the dying process. He argued that depending on striking social characteristics—such as the patient's age, "moral character," and clinical teaching value—certain groups of people were more likely than others to be treated as "socially dead." According to Sudnow (1967, p. 74), social death is a situation in which "a patient is treated essentially as a corpse, though perhaps still 'clinically' and 'biologically' alive." The most disturbing aspect of Sudnow's analysis was his observation that social death becomes a predictor for biological death during resuscitative attempts. People who were regarded as socially dead by the staff were more likely to die a biological death sooner as well. Under the guise of lifesaving attempts, the staff perpetuated an insidious kind of social inequality.

Zygmunt Bauman has questioned whether Sudnow's observations are still relevant. Bauman (1992, p. 145) postulated that because resuscitative efforts have "lost much of their specularity and have ceased to impress, their discriminating power has all but dissipated."[2] Biomedical researchers and legislators appear to agree by omitting social rationing from a vast medical, legal, and ethical resuscitation literature.[3] The rationalization of medical knowledge was supposed to turn the "art" of medical practice into a "science" (Berg 1997) and eliminate the social problems of a still experimental medical technology. After countless pilot and evaluation studies, national collaborations, and international conferences, medical researchers created uniform and universally employed resuscitation protocols supported by a resuscitation theory (CPR-ECC 1973; 1992). Biomedical researchers have interpreted clinical decision making in terms of formal probabilistic reasoning and algorithms that link clinical data inputs with therapeutic decision outputs (Schwartz and Griffin 1986; Dowie and Elstein 1988). Health care providers reach decisions during lifesaving efforts by simply following the resuscitation protocols until they run into an endpoint. The data taken into consideration consist solely of observable clinical parameters and biomedical test results. In lifesaving, social factors should be irrelevant and filtered out.

In addition, legislators instituted extensive legal protections against any form of discrimination, including social rationing. Legislators made it obligatory for health care providers to initiate cardiopulmonary resuscitation (CPR) in all instances in which it is medically indicated (CPR-ECC 1973). Paramedics and other health care providers have the legal duty to respond and apply all professional and regional standards of care, that is, they should follow the protocols to the end. Consent is implied for emergency care such as resuscitative efforts. To further legally encourage resuscitative measures, first-aid personnel are immune from prosecution for errors rendered in good faith emergency care under the Samaritan laws.[4] Failure to continue treatment, however, is referred to as abandonment that "is legally and ethically the most serious act an emergency medical technician can commit" (Heckman 1992, p. 21). Basically, once the emergency medical system is alerted, the health care providers have the legal and ethical duty to continue resuscitating until the protocols are exhausted.

At the same time, ethicists and legislators have tried to boost and protect patient autonomy. The Patient Self-Determination Act of 1991[5] mandated that patients be given notice of their rights to make medical treatment decisions and of the legal instruments available to give force to decisions made in advance. This attempt at demedicalizing (Conrad 1992) sudden death again is indirectly aimed at diminishing social rationing. When patients have decided that they do not want to be resuscitated, the staff should follow the written directives regardless of the patient's social value.

Did these scientific and medicolegal initiatives remove the social rationing in sudden death exposed by Sudnow, and Glaser and Strauss? I will show that biomedical protocols and legal initiatives did not weaken but reinforced inequality of death and dying. In the emergency department (ED), health care providers reappropriate biomedical theory and advance directives to justify and refine a moral categorization of patients. Furthermore, although the legal protections indeed result in prolonged resuscitative efforts, this does not necessarily serve the patient. The goal of lifesaving becomes subordinated to other objectives. The result is a more sophisticated, theoretically supported, and legally sanctioned configuration of social discrimination when sudden death strikes. The unwillingness of Western societies to accommodate certain marginalized groups and the medicalization of natural processes neutralize the equalizing potential of the rationalization of resuscitation techniques and legal protections.

METHODOLOGY

This article is based on 112 observations of resuscitative efforts over a fourteen-month period in the EDs of two midwestern hospitals: one was a level-1 and the other a level-2 trauma center.[6] I focused my observations on medical out-of-hospital resuscitative efforts. This research was approved by the institutional review board of the two hospitals and by the University of Illinois. I was paged with the other resuscitation team members whenever a resuscitative effort was needed in these EDs. I attended half of the resuscitative efforts that occurred in the two EDs during the observation period.

In addition to the observations, I interviewed forty-two health care providers who work in EDs and routinely participate in resuscitative efforts. This group includes physicians, nurses, respiratory therapists, nurse supervisors, emergency room technicians, social workers, and chaplains. These health care providers came from three hospitals: the two hospitals in which I observed resuscitative efforts and one bigger level-1 trauma center and teaching hospital. All responses were voluntary and kept anonymous. The interviews consisted of fifteen open-ended, semistructured questions. The interview guide covered questions about professional choice, memorable resuscitative efforts, the definition of a "successful" reviving attempt, patient's family presence, teamwork, coping with death and dying, and advanced cardiac life support protocols.

SOCIAL VIABILITY

The ED staff's main task is to find a balance of care that fits the patient's situation (Timmermans and Berg 1997). Based on my observations, whether care providers will aggressively try to save lives still depends on the patient's position in a moral stratification. Certain patient characteristics add up to a patient's presumed social viability, and the staff rations their efforts based on the patient's position in this moral hierarchy (Sudnow 1967; Glaser and Strauss 1964). A significant number of identity aspects that signify a person's social status and overall social worth in the community (e.g., being a volunteer, good speaker, charismatic leader, or effective parent), are irrelevant or unknown during the resuscitation process. In contrast with Sudnow's conceptual preference, I opt for social viability to indicate the grounds of rationing because social worth is too broad to indicate the variations in reviving attempts.

During reviving efforts, *age* remains the most outstanding characteristic of a patient's social viability (Glaser and Strauss 1964; Iserson and Stocking 1993; Kastenbaum and Aisenberg 1972; Sudnow 1967; Roth 1972). The death of young people should be avoided with all means possible. Almost all respondents mentioned this belief explicitly in the interviews. One physician noted, "You are *naturally* more aggressive with younger people. If I had a forty year old who had a massive MI [myocardial infarction], was asystolic for twenty minutes, or something like that, I would be very aggressive with that person. I suppose for the same scenario in a ninety-year-old, I might not be." A colleague agreed, "When you have a younger patient, you try to give it a little bit more effort. You might want to go another half hour on a younger person because you have such a difficult time to let the person go." According to a nurse, dying children "go against the scheme of things. Parents are not supposed to bury their children; the children are supposed to bury their parents." Although respondents hesitated uncomfortably when I asked to give an age cutoff point, the resuscitation of young people triggered an aggressive lifesaving attempt.

A second group of patients for whom the staff was willing to exhaust the resuscitation protocols were patients *recognized* by one or more team members because of their position in the community. During the interview period in one hospital, a well-liked, well-known senior hospital employee was being resuscitated. All the respondents involved made extensive reference to this particular resuscitative effort. When I asked a respiratory therapist how this effort differed from the others, he replied, "I think the routines and procedures were the same, but I think the sense of urgency was a lot greater, the anxiety level was higher. We were more tense. It was very different from, say, a 98-year-old from a nursing home." A nurse explained how her behavior changed after she recognized the patient.

> The most recent one I worked on was one of my college professors. He happened to be one of my favorites and I didn't even realize it was him until we were into the code and somebody mentioned his name. Then I knew it was him. Then all of the sudden it becomes kind of personal, you seem to be really rooting for the person, while as before you were just doing your job . . . trying to do the best

you could, but then it does get personal when you are talking to them and trying to . . . you know . . . whatever you can do to help them through.

When the British Princess Diana died in a car accident, physicians tried external and internal cardiac massage for two hours although her pulmonary vein—which carries half of the blood—was lacerated. Dr. Thomas Amoroso, trauma chief in emergency medicine department at Beth Israel Deaconess Medical Center, reflected, "As with all human endeavors there is emotion involved. You have a young, healthy, vibrant woman with obvious importance to the world at large. You're going to do everything you possibly can do to try and turn the matter around, but I rather suspect, in their hearts, even as her doctors were doing all their work, they knew it would not be successful" (Tye 1997). The interviewed doctors agreed that "most other patients would have been declared dead at the scene, or after arriving at the emergency department. But with a patient as famous as Diana, trauma specialists understandably want to try extraordinary measures" (Tye 1997).

Staff also responded aggressively to patients with whom they *identified.* A nurse reflected, "incidentally, anytime there is an association of a resuscitation with something that you have a close relationship with—your family, the age range, the situation . . . there is more emotional involvement." Another nurse explained how a resuscitative effort became more difficult after she had established a relationship with the patient by talking to her and going through the routine patient assessment procedures.

How do these positive categorizations affect the resuscitation process? Basically, when the perceived social viability of the patient is high, the staff will go all out to reverse the dying process. In the average resuscitative effort, four to eight staff members are involved. In the effort to revive a nine-month-old baby, however, I counted twenty-three health care providers in the room at one point. Specialists from different hospital services were summoned. One physician discussed the resuscitative effort of a patient she identified with: "I even called the cardiologist. I very seldom do call the cardiologist on the scene, and I called him and asked him, 'Is there anything else we can do?'" Often the physician will establish a central line in the patient's neck, and the respiratory therapists will check and recheck the tube to make sure the lungs are indeed inflated. These tasks are part of the protocol, but are not always performed as diligently in resuscitative attempts in which the patient's social viability is viewed as less.

The physician may even go beyond the protocol guidelines to save the patient. For example, at the time of my observations, the amount of sodium bicarbonate that could be administered was limited, and often the paramedics had already exhausted the quota en route to the hospital. The physician was supposed to order more sodium bicarbonate only after receiving lab test results of the patient's blood gases. In the frenzy of one resuscitative effort in which the patient was known to the whole staff, a physician boasted to his colleague, "So much for the guidelines. I gave more bicarb even before the blood gases were back." When the husband of a staff member was being resuscitated, nurses and physicians went out of their way to obtain a bed in intensive care.

How does a resuscitative effort of a highly valued patient end? In contrast with most other reviving attempts, I never saw a physician make a unilateral decision. The physician would go over all the drugs that were given, provide some medical history, mention the time that had elapsed since the patient collapsed, and then turn to the team and ask, "Does anybody have any suggestions?" or "I think we did everything we could. Dr. Martin also agrees—I think we can stop it."

At the bottom of the assumed moral hierarchy are patients for whom death is considered an appropriate "punishment" or a welcome "friend." Death is considered a "friend" or even a "blessing" for *seriously ill* and *older patients.* For those patients, the staff agrees that sudden death is not the worst possible end of life. These patients are the "living dead" (Kastenbaum and Aisenberg 1972). The majority of resuscitation attempts in the ED were performed for elderly patients (Becker, Ostrander, Barrett, and Kondos 1991)—often these patients resided in nursing homes and were confronted with a staff who relied on deeply entrenched ageism. For example, one nurse assumed that older people would want to die. "Maybe this eighty-year-old guy just fell over at home and maybe that is the way he wanted to go. But no, somebody calls an ambulance and brings him to the ER where we work and work and work and get him to the intensive care unit. Where he is poked and prodded for a few days and then they finally decide to let him go." According to a different nurse, older people had nothing more to live for: "When people are in their seventies and eighties, they have lived their lives."

The staff considered death an "appropriate" retaliation for *alcohol-* and *drug-addicted people.* For example, I observed a resuscitative attempt for a patient who had overdosed on heroin. The team went through the resuscitation motions but without much vigor or sympathy. Instead, staff members wore double pairs of gloves, avoided touching the patient, joked about their difficulty inserting an intravenous line, and mentioned how they loathed to bring the bad news to the belligerent "girlfriend" of the patient. Drunks are also much more likely to be nasally intubated rather than administered the safer and less painful tracheal intubation.

These negative definitions affect the course and fervor of the resuscitative effort. For example, patients on the bottom of the social hierarchy were often declared dead in advance. In a typical situation, the physician would tell the team at 7:55 A.M. that the patient would be dead at 8:05 A.M. The physician would then leave to fill out paperwork or talk to the patient's relatives. Exactly at 8:05, the team stopped the effort, the nurse responsible for taking notes wrote down the time of death, and the team dispersed. In two other such resuscitative efforts, the staff called the coroner before the patient was officially pronounced dead.

Even an elderly or seriously ill patient might unexpectedly regain a pulse or start breathing during the lifesaving attempt. This development is often an unsettling discovery and poses a dilemma for the staff: are we going to try to "save" this patient, or will we let the patient die? In most resuscitative efforts of patients with assumed low social viability, these signs were *dismissed or explained away* (Timmermans 1999a). In the drug overdose case, an EKG monitor registered an irregular rhythm, but the physician in charge dismissed this observation with, "This machine has an imagination of its own." Along the same lines, staff who noticed signs of life were considered "inexperienced," and I heard one physician admonish a nurse who noticed heart tones that "she shouldn't have listened." Noticeable signs that couldn't be dismissed easily were explained as insignificant "reflexes" that would disappear soon (Glaser and Strauss 1965). In all of these instances, social death not only preceded but also led to the official pronouncement of death.

Some patient characteristics, such as age and presumed medical history, become "master traits" (Hughes 1971) during the resuscitative effort. The impact of other identity signifiers — such as gender, race, religion, sexual orientation, and socioeconomic status—was more difficult to observe (see also Sudnow 1983, p. 280). The longest resuscitative effort I observed was for a person with presumably low social viability because of his socioeconomic status. He was a white homeless man who had fallen into a creek and was hypothermic.[7] I also noted how the staff made many disturbingly insensitive jokes during the resuscitative effort of a person with a high socioeconomic status: a well-dressed and wealthy elderly white woman who collapsed during dinner in one of the fanciest restaurants in the city. During a particularly hectic day, the staff worked very hard and long to save a middle-aged black teacher who collapsed in front of her classroom, whereas two elderly white men who were also brought in in cardiac arrest were quickly pronounced dead.

Epidemiological studies, however, suggest that race, gender, and socioeconomic status play a statistically significant role in overall survival of patients in sudden cardiac arrest. The emergency medical system is much more likely to be alerted when men die at home than when women experience cardiac arrest; this suggests a selection bias in the system (Joslyn 1994). Women also have much lower survival rates than men. In a Minneapolis study, the survival rate one year after cardiac arrest was 3.5 percent for women and 13.1 percent for men (Tillinghast, Doliszny, Kottke, Gomez-Marin, Lilja, and Campion 1991). A similar relationship has been observed for racial differences. Not only was the incidence of cardiac arrest in Chicago during 1988 significantly higher among blacks in every age group than among whites, but the survival rate of blacks after an out-of-hospital cardiac arrest was only a third of that among whites (1 versus 3 percent) (Becker et al. 1993). Daniel Brookoff and his colleagues (1994) showed that black victims of cardiac arrest receive CPR less frequently than white victims. Using tax assessment data, Alfred Hallstrom's research team (1993) demonstrated that people in lower socioeconomic strata are at greater risk for higher mortality. In addition, lower-class people were also less likely to survive an episode of out-of-hospital cardiac arrest: "An increase of $50,000 in the valuation per unit of the home address increased the patient's chance of survival by 60%" (Hallstrom et al. 1993, p. 247).

Even after twenty-five years of CPR practice, Sudnow's earlier observations still ring true. The social value of the patient affects the fervor with which the staff engages in a resuscitative effort, the length of the reviving attempt, and probably also the outcome. The staff rations their efforts based on a hierarchy of lives they consider worth living and others for which they believe death is the best solution, largely regardless of the patient's clinical viability. Children, young adults, and people who are able to establish some kind of personhood and overcome the anonymity of lifesaving have the best chance for a full, aggressive resuscitative effort. In the other cases, the staff might still "run the code" but "walk it slowly" to the point of uselessness (Muller 1992).

LEGAL PROTECTIONS?

One of the aspects of resuscitation that has changed since Sudnow's ethnography is the drop in the prevalence of DOA or "dead on arrival" cases. Sudnow (1967, p. 100–109) noted that DOA was the most common occurrence in "County" hospital's emergency ward. Ambulance drivers would use a special siren to let the staff know that they were approaching the hospital with a "possible," shorthand for possible DOA. At arrival, the patient was quickly wheeled out of sight to the far end of the hallway. The physician would casually walk into the room, examine the patient, and in most cases confirm the patient's death. Finally, a nurse would call the coroner. Twenty-five years later, I observed DOA only when an extraordinarily long transportation time occurred in which all the possible drugs were given and the patient remained unresponsive. For example,

> Dr. Hendrickson takes me aside before the patient arrives and says, "Stefan, I just want to tell you that the patient has been down for more than half an hour [before the paramedics arrived]. They had a long ride. I probably will declare the patient dead on arrival." When the patient arrives, the paramedic reports, "We had asystole for the last ten minutes. We think he was in V-fib for a while but it was en route. It could have been the movement of the ambulance." The physician replies, "I declare this patient dead."

The DOA scenario has now diminished in importance for legal reasons. When somebody calls 911, a resuscitative effort begins and is virtually unstoppable until the patient is viewed in the ED by a physician. After the call, an ambulance with EMTs or paramedics is dispatched. Unless the patient shows obvious signs of death,[8] the ambulance rescuers start the advanced cardiac treatment as prescribed by their standing orders and protocols. The patient is thus transported to the ED, where the physician with the resuscitation team takes over. Legally, the physician again cannot stop the lifesaving attempt, because the physician needs to make sure that the protocols are exhausted. Stopping sooner would qualify as negligence and be grounds for malpractice. These legal guidelines, more than any magical power inherent to technology, explain the apparent technological imperative and momentum of the resuscitation technology (Koenig 1988; Timmermans 1998).

Patients who in Sudnow's study would be pronounced biologically dead immediately are now much more likely to undergo an extensive resuscitative effort. These patients cluster together in a new group of already presumed low-value patients. They are referred to as *pulseless nonbreathers, goners,* or *flat-liners.* Most of these patients are elderly or suffer from serious illnesses. Sudden infant death syndrome babies and some adults might fulfill the clinical criteria for pulseless nonbreathers, but because they are considered valuable and therefore viable, the staff does not include them in this group.

A respiratory therapist described her reaction to these patients, "If it comes over my beeper that there is a pulseless nonbreather, then I know they were at home, I know that they were down a long time . . . I go and do my thing, [but] it's over when they get here." Some respondents added that this group does not leave a lasting impression: "they all blend together as one gray blur."

Instead of prompting health care workers to provide more aggressive care, the legally extended resuscitative effort has created a situation in which the staff feels obligated to go through some useless motions and they spend the time for other purposes. I observed that while they were compressing the patient's chest and artificially ventilating him or her, the staff's conversation would drift off to other topics such as birthday parties, television shows, hunting events, sports, awful patients, staffing conflicts, and easy or difficult shifts. Besides socializing, the staff also practiced medical techniques on the socially but not yet officially dead patient. I did not observe resuscitative efforts in a teaching hospital but still noticed how occasionally paramedics in training would reintubate the patient for practice.[9]

In addition, instead of attempting to save lives with all means possible, the process of accurately following the protocols became a goal in itself. A resuscitative effort could be rewarding for the staff based on the process of following the different resuscitation steps, regardless of the outcome of the resuscitative effort. A physician confessed, "As bad as it sounds, there are many times when I feel satisfied when it was done very well, the entire resuscitative effort was done very well, very efficiently even though the patient didn't make it." In this bureaucratic mode of thinking, following the legal guidelines à la lettre officially absolved the physician of the blame for sudden death. The physician could face the relatives and sincerely tell them that the staff did everything possible within the current medical guidelines to save the life of their loved one.

Finally, the staff used the mandated resuscitation time to take care of the patient's relatives and friends instead of the patient. A physician explicitly admitted that the current resuscitation set-up was far from optimal for the patient or relatives. He saw it as his responsibility to help the family as best he could:

> Even when I am with the patient for the sixty or ninety seconds, if that, I almost don't think about the patient. I prepare myself for the emotional resuscitation or the emotional guidance of the family in their grief. The patient was gone before they got there [in the ED]. In a better world, they wouldn't be there because there is nothing natural or sanctimonious about being declared dead in a resuscitation. It is far more natural to be declared dead with your own family in your own home. We have now taken that patient out of their environment, away from their family, brought that family to a very strange place that is very unnatural only to be served the news that their loved one has died.

A nurse also shared the preoccupation with the needs of the family:

> My thoughts throughout the entire resuscitative effort, even prior to the arrival, are with the family. Who is going to be with that family? Who is going to support them? And that they are being notified throughout the resuscitative effort what is going on, to prepare them if it is going to be a long haul, or if things are not good and are not going to get better. I think they deserve that. So it is kind of a combined feeling throughout. But I can focus on the one without being bogged down with the emotion of what is going on over there.

The "resuscitation" of the relatives and friends of the patient became more important than the patient's resuscitation attempt. The staff used the resuscitation motions and prescriptions as a platform to achieve other values. They might turn the resuscitative effort into a "good death" ritual in which they prolong the lifesaving attempt to give relatives and friends the option to say goodbye to their dying loved one (Timmermans 1997).

The legal protections guaranteeing universal lifesaving care have not resulted in qualitatively enhanced lifesaving but instead have created a new set of criteria that need to be checked off before a patient can be pronounced dead. In Sudnow's study, social death often preceded and predicted irreversible biological death. The staff of "Cohen" and "County" hospitals did not stretch the lifesaving effort unnecessarily. Once patients of presumed low social value showed obvious signs of biological death, the staff would quickly pronounce them officially deceased. Currently, many patients of presumed low social value in resuscitative efforts are already biologically dead when they are wheeled into the ED. The time it takes to exhaust the resuscitation protocols has created a new temporal interval with *legal death* as the endpoint. Legal requirements form a new instance of what Barney Glaser and Anselm Strauss (1965) originally called the closed awareness and mutual pretense awareness context. The staff is fully aware that the patient was irreversibly dead at arrival in the ED but they go through the motions for legal reasons and to allow the family to come to grips with the suddenness of the situation. If the relatives and friends catch on and know that their loved one is dying, the setup of the reviving attempt encourages them to pretend this is not really happening. This management of sudden death does not reduce any social inequality. The same situational identity features that marginalized certain groups of patients still predict the intensity of lifesaving fervor. As in Glaser and Strauss's and Sudnow's studies, social death now also has become a self-fulfilling prophecy for legal death.

In the wake of the hospice and patient-right movements, ethicists and legislators have also developed legal means such as advance directives, living wills, durable powers of attorney, and do-not-resuscitate orders to empower people to influence their own deaths. These diverse initiatives culminated in the Patient Self-Determination Act of 1991, that mandated that patients be given notice of their rights to make medical treatment decisions and of the legal instruments available to give force to decisions made in advance. The act is intended to enhance patient autonomy, so that if a patient expressed her or his wish not to be resuscitated, a resuscitative effort should be avoided regardless of how the staff perceives the patient's social value. The actual effect, however, is the opposite.

I observed eight resuscitative efforts in which the patient had signed an advance directive. In only two of those eight situations did the advance directive result in a terminated lifesaving attempt. The main problem with the advance directive was that the health care providers who made the initial decision to resuscitate (paramedics) were not authorized to interpret the documents. A chaplain said, "We tell people who have a living will or have been given power of attorney and wish not to be kept alive, if you have a heart attack at home, don't call 911. Don't call the EMTs because they are automatically obligated to do everything they can." To complicate the situation, physicians often did not find out about the living will until well into the lifesaving attempt (Eisendrath and Jonsen 1983). The inefficiency of the advance directive to stop the resuscitative effort has been confirmed in other studies as well. Medical researchers concluded that "advance directives did not affect the rate of resuscitation being tried" (Teno et al. 1997, p. 505). A retrospective study of 694 resuscitative efforts found that 7 percent of all resuscitative efforts were unwanted, and 2 percent of those patients survived to hospital discharge (Dull, Graves, Larson, and Cummins 1993).

Even when the advance directive was present and known, the extent to which the staff followed the written wishes of the advance directive depended mostly on the assumed social viability of the patient. During resuscitative efforts for patients with presumed high social value, I never observed the staff mention the possibility that the patient might have an advance directive. In an interview, a nurse supervisor prided herself on going against the wishes of a patient and his relatives, even though the patient still thought after regaining consciousness that they should not have revived him. A survey of emergency physicians found that 42 percent did not stop a resuscitative effort when an advance directive instructed them to do so (Iserson and Stocking 1993). Health care providers were only willing to accept a living will when the patient fulfilled their criteria for having one; this meant that the patients were seriously ill or old *and* the staff believed that the patient's quality of life suffered. One nurse explained.

> I think if a person has made very clear their wishes beforehand . . . especially in light of a terminal illness, a cancer, or an awful respiratory disease—they know that they don't have long to live and the quality of their life is not very good—then it is very

> appropriate for these people to make their statements when they have a free mind and are conscious that they don't wish to have resuscitations started.

According to the nurse, the staff should always evaluate whether it is appropriate that a patient had an advance directive.

In contrast, the staff blamed patients with presumed low social value (mostly seriously ill patients) for not signing an advance directive. During a resuscitative attempt, the physician entered the room after talking to relatives and asked the nurse, "Got rid of that pulse yet?" When he saw my surprised expression, he added, "She had all kinds of cancer. They were stupid enough not to ask for a red alert and now we have to go through this nonsense." Normally, an advance directive needed to be verified by the physician in charge, but even when no advance directive could be found in the patient's file, the physician still might stop the reviving effort. In the following observation, the team was not sure whether the patient actually had an advance directive or was going to talk to her physician about it.

> The chaplain enters and says, "The neighbor said that she has an aneurysm in her stomach area. She also said that she did not want to be operated. She was going to talk to her doctor tomorrow to discuss this." The physician asks, "Is she a no-code?" "According to the neighbor she is." "Why do we find this out after we have been working on her?" The head nurse takes the patient's file, which the department administrator brought into the room. She looks through it once and looks through it a second time, but she cannot find an advance directive. The physician takes the file, and together they check it again. No advance directive, no official document. The doctor then decides to let the patient go anyway. He considers the patient hopeless unless she wants to have surgery.

Advance directives certainly do not empower the patient. Under the guise of increasing the patient's autonomy, the opposite result—medical paternalism—is obtained (Teaster 1995). Health care providers followed the wishes set forth in the advance directive when these guidelines matched their own assessment of the patient's social value and did not undermine their professional jurisdiction (Abbott 1988).[10]

In general, the legal drive to create a resuscitation-friendly environment and the laws to protect patient autonomy have not abolished the social inequality of sudden death. In certain instances, resuscitative efforts are lengthened or shortened, but these changes occur regardless of the legal intentions. The basic problem of administering resuscitative care based on the social viability of the patient remains uncorrected. The staff works around the legal guidelines to enforce their view of lives worth living and good deaths (Timmermans 1999b).

RESUSCITATION THEORY

Not only does the staff use legal guidelines to perpetuate existing views of social inequality, but health care providers also reappropriate the accumulated medical knowledge about resuscitations to justify withholding care of *new groups with presumed low social value.* For a technique that is not really proved to be effective with national survival rates, the field of resuscitation medicine has a surprisingly high level of agreement as to what constitutes the best chances for survival.[11] From physician to technician to chaplain in the ED, almost all respondents provided a more or less complete reflection of the dominant theory. The basics of resuscitation theory are very simple: the quicker the steps of the "chain of survival" are carried out (Cummins, Ornato, Thies, and Pepe 1991), the better the chances for survival. A weakness in one step will reverberate throughout the entire system and impair optimal survival rates.

The chain of survival is intended as a simple, rational tool for educators, researchers, and policy makers to evaluate whether a community obtains optimal patient survival. In the ED, however, the same theoretical notions underlying the chain of survival serve as a rationalization for *not* trying to resuscitate particular patient groups. The professional rescuers in the ED are acutely aware of their *location* in the chain of survival's temporal framework. The ED is the last link of the survival chain, and many elements need to have fallen in place before the patient reaches the hands of the team. Anything that deviates from the "ideal" resuscitative pattern and causes more time to elapse is a matter of concern for the staff. One technician estimated how important every step in the resuscitation process is for the final outcome,

> One of the most important things would be the time between when the patient actually went down until the first people arrive. That is like, I'd say, 30 percent and then the time that a patient takes to get to the hospital takes another, probably, 30–40 percent. Sixty to 70 percent of it is prehospital time.

A nurse explains the importance of location and timing by contrasting resuscitation of somebody who collapsed inside the ED with somebody who collapsed outside the ED:

> A lot has to do with EMS [Emergency Medical System] and family response and getting them there. If you would drop dead right here, your chances would be pretty good that we would be able to resuscitate you without any brain damage or anything else. If you're at home out on a farm, sixty miles away, and you have to call out for help and that takes fifteen minutes for them to get there and nobody in the house knows CPR, I think your chances are pretty slim.

According to the nurse, if the situation had not been optimal in the first steps, the ED staff could not be expected to rectify the situation. The consequence of this acute awareness about their location in the chain of survival is that the emergency medical hospital staff feels only limited control over the outcome of the resuscitative effort. A physician reiterated this: "for a lot of these people, their outcome is written in stone before I see them." A colleague added "there are certainly many, many instances of cardiac arrest where the end result is predestined, where the chance of resuscitation is very slim." Most respondents echoed the nurse supervisor who remarked, "I think there are always factors involved whether a resuscitation is successful or not. But I don't know if there is any personal or even physical control."

Because of this perceived lack of control, health care providers were less willing to aggressively resuscitate patients who deviate from the ideal scenario. Often such a consensus was reached even before the patient arrived in the ED. I observed how the nurse in charge sent a colleague back to the intensive care unit when paramedics radioed that a patient was found with an unknown downtime, saying, "We will not need you. She'll be dead." Sometimes only the name of the patient's town was sufficient for the staff to know that it probably would be "a short exercise." The town would give an indication of the transportation time and the available emergency care. Once a patient with such low perceived survival chances arrived in the ED, the staff would go through the resuscitation motions without much conviction. A technician noted how in many cases he "start[s] to feel defeated already. To the point now, where it is pretty much decided already, we are not going to get anywhere with this."

The staff interprets the official theory of reviving as a justification for only lukewarmly attempting to resuscitate patients who did not fit the ideal lifesaving scenario. This rationing rests not on biological but on social grounds. Underneath the staff's reluctance to revive patients who deviate from the ideal resuscitative scenario lies the fear that the patient would be only partially resuscitated and suffer from brain damage. According to the dominant resuscitation theory (CPR-ECC 1973), irreversible brain damage occurs after less than five minutes of oxygen deprivation. The staff is concerned that if they revive a patient after this critical time period, the patient might be severely neurologically disabled or comatose. When a nurse got a patient's pulse back, she exclaimed, "Oh no, we can't do that to him. He must be braindead by now." A physician stated, "There have been situations where after a prolonged downtime we get a pulse back. My first feeling is, 'My God, what have I done?' It is a horrible feeling because you know that patient will be put in the unit and ultimately their chances of walking out of the hospital without any neurological deficits are almost zero."

A physician described one scenario to be avoided—a resuscitative effort in which an adult survived in a vegetative state:

> I remember there was a man who was having just an MRI scan done, and while he was in the machine he had a cardiac arrest for who knows what reason. And they brought him to the ER, and we

> started to resuscitate him, and as we did, it looked obvious that he probably wasn't going to survive. And we gave him what we call high-dose epinephrine, and with that high dose he actually returned to a normal heart rhythm. Unfortunately, he had an inadequate blood supply to his brain so he ended up having not too much cognitive function . . . I guess I remember that because I thought he was going to die, and I gave him a little more medicine, and he didn't. And I have always wondered whether that was the right thing to do or not.
>
> [Do you think you did the right thing?]
>
> Well, in retrospect I don't think that I did. The man is alive, but his brain is not alive, so he really is not the same person he was before. I think that from the family's point of view, they probably would have had an easier time dealing with the fact that he was dead and sort of would have gone out of their system instead of in the state he is in right now.

Health care providers generally consider this the ultimate "nightmare scenario," an outcome that will haunt them for years to come.[12] The patient survived in a permanent vegetative state, continuously requiring emotional and financial resources of relatives and society in general.

With those "excesses" in mind, several respondents made thinly veiled arguments in favor of passive euthanasia. A nurse stated that she felt that in many cases attempting to resuscitate patients meant "prolonging their suffering." A technician asserted that "with an extensive medical history it is inhumane to try." Another technician reflected, "Sometimes you wonder if it is really for the benefit of the patient." A chaplain even made a case for suicide (or euthanasia, depending on who the "them" are in his sentence): "I feel a bit of relief knowing that if a person couldn't be resuscitated to a productive life, that it is probably just as well to have them have the right to end life." The principle that guides the rescuer's work is that a quick death is preferable over a lingering death with limited cognitive functioning in an intensive care unit. A nurse said this explicitly, "The child survived with maximum brain injury and has become now, instead of a child that they [the parents] can mourn and put in the ground, a child that they mourn for years."

Although health care providers again hesitated to define a criterion for a quality of life they would find unacceptable, I found implicit in both interviews and observations a view that such lives were not worth living. Drawing from the dominant resuscitation theory, the *prospect* of long-term physical and mental disabilities was reason enough to slow down the lifesaving attempt to the point of uselessness. In an age of disability rights, health care providers reflect and perpetuate the stereotypic assumptions that disability invokes (Fine and Asch 1988; Mairs 1996; Zola 1984). People with disabilities are associated with perpetual dependency and helplessness; they are viewed as victims leading pitiful lives, "damaged creatures who should be put out of their misery" (Mairs 1996, p. 120). Disability symbolizes a lack of control over life, and health care providers fall back on the outcome over which they have the most control. The *possibility* of disability is considered worse than biological death. In a survey of 105 experienced emergency health care providers (doctors, nurses, and EMTs), 82 percent would prefer death for themselves over severe neurological disability (Hauswald and Tanberg 1993).

Along with the dominant resuscitation theory, health care providers support the view that people with disabilities should not be resuscitated. To be fair, the same theory is also invoked as a warning about giving up too soon. Several respondents mentioned that one can never be sure whether a report about downtime and transportation time is accurate. Even if there was a long transportation time, one cannot know for sure when the patient went into cardiac arrest. Exactly because there exists this margin of uncertainty, many respondents considered it worthwhile to at least attempt to resuscitate and follow the protocols. In most observed resuscitative efforts, however, it appeared that the expectations were clearly set and became self-fulfilling prophecies.

SOCIAL RATIONING AND THE MEDICALIZATION OF SUDDEN DEATH

In the conclusion to *Passing On,* David Sudnow discussed the ways in which dying became an institutional routine and a meaningful event for the hospital staff. He emphasized that the staff attempted to maintain an attitude of "appropriate impersonality" toward death and how the organization of the ward and the teaching hospital favored social death preceding biological death. In ethnomethodological fashion, Sudnow (1967, p. 169) underscored how "death" and "dying" emerged out of the interactions and practices of health care providers, "what has been developed is a 'procedural definition of dying,' a definition based upon the activities which that phenomenon can be said to *consist in.*"[13]

My update of Sudnow's study indicates that with the widespread use of resuscitation technologies, health care providers now have to make sense of engaging in a practice with the small chance of saving lives and the potential to severely disable patients. They cope with this dilemma by deliberately not trying to revive certain groups of patients. These groups are not distinguished by their clinical potential but by their social viability. The staff reappropriates biomedical protocols and legal guidelines to further refine a system of implicit social rationing. The bulk of resuscitative efforts are still characterized by a detached attitude toward patients. In most reviving efforts, the staff feels defeated in advance and reviving becomes an empty ritual of going through mandated motions. It is only when patients transcend anonymity and gain a sense of personhood that the staff will aggressively try to revive them.

With regard to the broader institutional context, resuscitation is now, less than in Sudnow's study, marked by the health care provider's desire to "obtain 'experience,' avoid dirty work, and maximize the possibility that the intern will manage some sleep" (Sudnow 1967, p. 170) as well as by the requirements of defensive medicine and managed care. With the gradual erosion of physician autonomy because of peer review and utilization boards, the wave of cost-effectiveness in medicine, the proliferation of medical malpractice suits, and the patient rights movement, physicians' practices have become more externally regulated. As several respondents commented, a resuscitative effort is as much an attempt to avoid a lawsuit as an endeavor to save lives. Health care providers try to maneuver within the boundaries of the law, professional ethics, and biomedical knowledge to maintain lives worth living and proper deaths for their patients. Every resuscitative effort becomes a balancing act of figuring out when "enough is enough" based on the clinical situation and prognosis, legal and ethical guidelines, the wishes of the patient and relatives, and—most importantly—the preferences and emotions of the resuscitation team. The latter are in charge, so ultimately their definitions of the situation and their values will prevail.

After thirty years, Sudnow's main contribution to the sociological literature is his disclosure of how the ED staff rations death and dying based on the presumed social value of the patient. Most studies of social inequality in health care rely on showing statistical race, gender, and socioeconomic variations in the prevalence, incidence, morbidity, and mortality rates of particular conditions (e.g., Wilkinson 1996), however, Sudnow showed that social inequality is an intrinsic part of negotiating and managing death. Surprisingly, though, Sudnow did not question the implications of the rampant social inequality he exposed in *Passing On*. His interpretation of social rationing as a routine institutional coping mechanism for death and dying—not as an important social issue—remains unsatisfactory because the former interpretation implies a theoretical justification of social inequality.

From a contemporary point of view, Sudnow's position has become even more problematic because health care providers keep dismissing similar groups of marginalized patients in a very different health care structure. Policies that should have diminished social inequality have instead strengthened it. Instead of concluding that such rampant social inequality is an inevitable part of the interaction between the patient and the care provider, I suggest that the policy changes did not address the broader societal foundations of social inequality.

Unfortunately, the attitudes of the emergency staff reflect and perpetuate those of a society generally not equipped culturally or structurally to accept the elderly or people with disabilities as people whose lives are valued and valuable (Mulkay and Ernst 1991). As the need for and problems with an Americans with Disabilities Act show, the disabled and seriously ill are not socially dead only in the ED but also in the outside world; this is the original sense in which Erving Goffman first introduced social death (1961). The staff has internalized beliefs about the presumed low worth of elderly and disabled people to the extent that more than 80 percent would rather be dead than live with a severe neurological disability. As gatekeepers between life and death, they have the opportunity to execute explicitly the pervasive but more subtle moral code of the wider society. Just as schools, restaurants, and modes of transportation became the battlegrounds and symbols in the civil rights struggle, medical interventions such as genetic counseling, euthanasia, and resuscitative efforts represent the sites of contention in the disability and elderly rights movements (Fine and Asch 1988; Schneider 1993).

In addition to the fact that social rationing takes place under the guise of a resuscitative effort, the prolonged resuscitation of anyone—including irreversibly dead people—in our emergency systems perpetuates a far-reaching medicalization of the dying process (Conrad 1992). Deceased people are presented more as "not resuscitated" than as having died a sudden, natural death. The resuscitative motions render death literally invisible (Star 1991); the patient and staff are in the resuscitation room while relatives and friends wait in a counseling room. The irony of the resuscitative setup is that nobody seems to benefit from continuing to resuscitate patients who are irreversibly dead. As some staff members commented, the main benefit of the current configuration is that it takes a little of the abruptness of sudden death away for relatives and friends. I doubt, though, that the "front" of a resuscitative effort is the best way to prepare people for sudden death. By engaging and investing in resuscitative efforts, we as a society facilitate the idea that mortality can be deconstructed (Bauman 1992) and that crisis interventions will correct a lack of prevention and healthy life habits (Anspach 1993). The result of engaging in resuscitative efforts on obviously dead patients is structurally sanctioned denial, a paternalistic attitude in which staff members keep relatives and friends in a closed awareness context or engage them in the slippery dance of mutual pretense awareness (Glaser and Strauss 1965). For the sake of preserving hope and softening the blow of sudden death, the staff decides that it is better for relatives not to know that their loved one is dying. Relatives and friends are separated from the dying process and miss the opportunity to say goodbye when it could really matter to them, that is when there is still a chance that their loved one is listening.

Rationalizing medical practice or providing legal accountability only accentuated the medicalization of the dying process and social inequality. The biomedical protocols are part of the problem of the medicalization of death because they promote aggressive care instead of providing means to terminate a reviving attempt (Timmermans forthcoming a), and the staff relies upon those theories to justify not resuscitating people who might become disabled. Legal initiatives mostly stimulated the predominance of resuscitative efforts at the expense of other ways of dying and have been unable to protect marginalized groups.

In the liminal space between lives worth living and proper deaths, resuscitative efforts in the ED crystallize submerged subtle attitudes of the wider society. The ED staff enforces and perpetuates our refusal to let go of life and to accommodate certain groups. Exactly because health care providers implement our moral codes, they are the actors who might be able to initiate a change in attitudes. On a personal level, many health care providers seem to have made up their minds about the limitations of reviving. Medical researchers presented emergency health care providers with a common forty-eight-minute resuscitation scenario with a relatively good prognosis and a reasonable time course. Only 2.9 percent of the respondents would prefer to be resuscitated for the entire episode (Hauswald and Tanberg 1993). If those who are the most informed and have the most personal experience with resuscitative efforts are reluctant to undergo lifesaving attempts, there is a simple solution for the twin problems of social rationing and the medicalization of sudden death. Instead of increasing the access to these technologies, we might want to provide overall less resuscitative efforts. I see two ways that such a goal could be obtained.

The most important step to avoid a resuscitative effort is not to alert the emergency system. I don't believe that more regulations and legal protections will circumvent lifesaving attempts. Even with the best intentions, deciding to let people die in an ED is still too much a violation of core medical values (e.g., the Hippocratic Oath). Discussions about advance directives have an important sensitizing function, but people (and their relatives and caretakers) who choose not to be resuscitated need to realize that the first step of avoiding a resuscitative effort implies not dialing 911. We cannot expect medical restraint from professionals who are socialized and legally obligated to fight death and dying with all means possible.

In addition, relatives and friends should have the opportunity to play a more active role during a resuscitative effort. This occurs already in some midwestern hospitals, where relatives are given the option to attend the resuscitative effort and say goodbye during the last moments that their loved one hovers between life and death. The presence of grieving relatives and friends is a constant reminder for the staff that they are dealing with a person entrenched in a social network and not with a mere body (Timmermans 1997). Such a policy change also entails a more explicit recognition that resuscitative efforts are not only performed for patients but also for relatives and friends who need to make sense of sudden death (Ellis 1993; Rosaldo 1984). These initiatives should stimulate an understanding that "passing on" to the final transition is inevitable and should be the same for everyone, regardless of their presumed social value.

ACKNOWLEDGMENTS

I thank Sharon Hogan, Norm Denzin, Margie Towery, and the anonymous reviewers for their useful comments.

NOTES

1. Social rationing means the withholding of potentially beneficial medical interventions based on social grounds (see Conrad and Brown 1993).
2. Bauman does not argue that resuscitative efforts are not decided upon patients' presumed social worth any longer, but that social discrimination has shifted from "primitive" technologies to more advanced medical technologies such as organ donation and "the electronic computerized gadgetry."
3. Sometimes medical critics will discuss the ethical implications of individualized resuscitation scenarios. Part of Sudnow's contribution, however, was to show that social rationing was not an isolated, individualized event, but a widespread, social practice.
4. Massachusetts General Law c.111C, Paragraph 14 states that "No emergency medical technician certified under the provisions of this chapter . . . who in the performance of his duties and in good faith renders emergency first aid or transportation to an injured person or to a person incapacitated by illness shall be personally in any way liable as a result of transporting such person to a hospital or other safe place . . ."
5. Omnibus Budget Reconciliation Act of 1990 (OBRA-90), Pub. L. 101–508, 4206, and 4751 (Medicare and Medicaid respectively), 42 U.S.C. 1395cc (a) (I) (Q), 1295mm (c) (8), 1395cc (f), 1396a (a) (58), and 1396a (w) (Supp. 1991).
6. Level 1 and level 2 refer to different staffing requirements and to differences in severity of cases. Level 1 hospitals are required to have a neuro, trauma, and cardiac surgeon always on call in the hospital, and these hospitals take more serious cases than level 2 hospitals (the differences are head injuries, gunshot wounds, multiple complex wounds, etc.). The distribution of level 1 and level 2 trauma centers per region is regulated by law.
7. The staff found this resuscitative effort interesting because it involved the first hypothermic person they attempted to revive in a year. They were a little lost about how to warm up the patient. Some patients gain status because they constitute medically challenging or interesting cases.
8. Death is obvious when rigor mortis has set in, decapitation has occurred, the body is consumed by fire, or there is a massive head injury with parts missing.
9. This practice is not as marginal as one would think. Major medical journals regularly publish articles about the ethical implications of practicing intubation and other techniques on the "newly dead" (see for example Burns et al. 1994).
10. There is also some evidence from other research that having an advance directive is in itself related to age, gender, race, socioeconomic status, education. Schonwetter et al. (1994), for example, found a strong relationship between socioeconomic status and the desire for CPR.
11. Partly this is due to the fact that US (and international) resuscitation medicine is dominated by a limited number of research groups who mostly

seem to agree with each other. According to Niemann about 85% of all CPR related research articles in the United States come from a community of 10 research groups (Niemann 1993 p. 8).

12. The physician told me this story six years after it happened. My original question was "Can you give me an example of a resuscitative effort that left a big impression on you?"
13. Although I did not emphasize Sudnow's ethnomethodological legacy in this paper, the idea of life-saving, the technology, and saving lives in itself are jointly accomplished in practice (see Timmermans and Berg 1997). The ironic aspect of resuscitation technology is that resuscitation techniques and practice establish the value of saving lives at all costs while the actual numbers of saved lives remain very low. I discuss this seeming paradox at length in my book (Timmermans forthcoming a). I thank Norm Denzin for drawing my attention to the ethnomethodological importance of Sudnow's study.

REFERENCES

Abbott, Andrew. 1988. *The System of Professions: An Essay on the Division of Expert Labor.* Chicago: University of Chicago Press.

Anspach, Renée R. 1993. *Deciding Who Lives: Fateful Choices in the Intensive-Care Nursery.* Berkeley: University of California Press.

Bauman, Zygmunt. 1992. *Mortality, Immortality and Other Life Strategies.* Stanford, CA: Stanford University Press.

Becker, Lance B., Ben H. Han, Peter M. Meyer, Fred A. Wright, Karin V. Rhodes, David W. Smith, and John Barrett. 1993. "Racial Differences in the Incidence of Cardiac Arrest and Subsequent Survival." *New England Journal of Medicine* 329:600–606.

Becker, Lance, B. M. P. Ostrander, John Barrett, and G. T. Kondos. 1991. "Outcome of CPR in a Large Metropolitan Area: Where Are the Survivors?" *Annals of Emergency Medicine* 20:355–361.

Berg, Marc. 1997. *Rationalizing Medical Work: A Study of Decision Support Techniques and Medical Practices.* Cambridge, MA: MIT Press.

Brookoff, Daniel, Arthur L. Kellermann, Bela B. Hackman, Grant Somes, and Perry Dobyns. 1994. "Do Blacks Get Bystander Cardiopulmonary Resuscitation as Often as Whites?" *Annals of Emergency Medicine* 24:1147–1150.

Burns, J. P., F. E. Reardon, and R. D. Truogh. 1994. "Using Newly Deceased Patients to Practice Resuscitation Procedures." *New England Journal of Medicine* 319:439–441.

Callahan, Daniel. 1993. *The Troubled Dream of Life: Living with Mortality.* New York: Simon and Schuster.

Conrad, Peter. 1992. "Medicalization and Social Control." *Annual Review of Sociology* 18:209– 232.

———, ed. 1997. *Sociology of Health and Illness: Critical Perspectives.* New York: St. Martin's Press.

Conrad, Peter, and Phil Brown. 1993. "Rationing Medical Care: A Sociological Reflection." *Research in the Sociology of Health Care* 10:3–22.

CPR-ECC. 1973. "Standards for Cardiopulmonary Resuscitation and Emergency Cardiac Care." *JAMA* 227:836–868.

———. 1992. "Guidelines for Cardiopulmonary Resuscitation and Emergency Cardiac Care." *JAMA* 268:2171–2295.

Cummins, Richard, Joseph P. Ornato, William H. Thies, and Paul E. Pepe. 1991. "The 'Chain of Survival' Concept." *Circulation* 83:1832–1847.

Dowie, J., and A. Elstein. 1988. *Professional Judgment: A Reader in Clinical Decision Making.* Cambridge: Cambridge University Press.

Dull, Scott M., Judith R. Graves, Mary Pat Larsen, and Richard O. Cummins. 1994. "Expected Death and Unwanted Resuscitation in the Prehospital Setting." *Annals of Emergency Medicine* 23: 997–1001.

Eisenberg, Michael, Bruce T. Horwood, Richard O. Cummins, R. Reynolds-Haertle, and T. R. Hearne. 1990. "Cardiac Arrest and Resuscitation: A Tale of 29 Cities." *Annals of Emergency Medicine* 19: 179–186.

Eisendrath, S. J., and A. R. Jonsen. 1983. "The Living Will: Help or Hindrance?" *JAMA* 249: 2054–2058.

Ellis, Carolyn. 1993. "Telling a Story of Sudden Death." *The Sociological Quarterly* 34:711–731.

Feinstein, Jonathan S. 1993. "The Relationships between Socioeconomic Status and Health." *Milbank Quarterly* 71:279–322.

Fine, Michelle, and Adrienne Asch. 1988. "Disability beyond Stigma: Social Interaction, Discrimination, and Activism." *Journal of Social Issues* 44: 3–21.

Fox, Renée C. 1976. "Advanced Medical Technology: Social and Ethical Implications." *Annual Review of Sociology* 2:231–268.

Glaser, Barney G., and Anselm L. Strauss. 1964. "The Social Loss of Dying Patients." *American Journal of Nursing* 64:119–121.

———. 1965. *Awareness of Dying.* Chicago: Aldine.

———. 1968. *Time for Dying.* Chicago: Aldine.

Goffman, Erving. 1961. *Asylums: Essays on the Social Situation of Mental Patients and Other Inmates.* New York: Doubleday Anchor.

Hallstrom, Alfred, Paul Boutin, Leonard Cobb, and Elise Johnson. 1993. "Socioeconomic Status and

Prediction of Ventricular Fibrillation Survival." *American Journal of Public Health* 83:245–248.

Hauswald, Mark, and Dan Tanberg. 1993. "Out-of-Hospital Resuscitation Preferences of Emergency Health Care Workers." *American Journal of Emergency Medicine* 11:221–224.

Heckman, James D., ed. 1992. *Emergency Care and Transportation of the Sick and Injured.* Dallas: American Academy of Orthopaedic Surgeons.

Hughes, Everett C. 1971. *The Sociological Eye.* Chicago: Aldine.

Illich, Yvan. 1976. *Medical Nemesis: The Expropriation of Health.* New York: Pantheon Books.

Iserson, Kenneth V., and Carol Stocking. 1993. "Standards and Limits: Emergency Physicians' Attitudes toward Prehospital Resuscitation." *American Journal of Emergency Medicine* 11:592–594.

Joslyn, Sue A. 1994. "Case Definition in Survival Studies of Out-of-Hospital Cardiac Arrest." *American Journal of Emergency Medicine* 12:299–301.

Kastenbaum, Robert, and R. Aisenberg. 1972. *The Psychology of Death.* New York: Springer.

Koenig, Barbara A. 1988. "The Technological Imperative in Medical Practice: The Social Creation of a 'Routine' Treatment." Pp. 465–497 in *Biomedicine Examined,* edited by Margaret Lock and Deborah R. Gordon. Dordrecht: Kluwer Academic Publishers.

Mairs, Nancy. 1996. *Waist-High in the World: A Life Among the Nondisabled.* Boston: Beacon Press.

Moller, David Wendell. 1996. *Confronting Death: Values, Institutions, and Human Mortality.* New York: Oxford University Press.

Mulkay, Michael, and John Ernst. 1991. "The Changing Position of Social Death." *European Journal of Sociology* 32:172–196.

Muller, Jessica H. 1992. "Shades of Blue: The Negotiation of Limited Codes by Medical Residents." *Social Science and Medicine* 34:885–898.

Niemann, James T. 1993. "Study Design in Cardiac Arrest Research: Moving from the Laboratory to the Clinical Population." *Annals of Emergency Medicine* 22:8–9.

Pelligrino, Edmund D. 1986. "Rationing Health Care: The Ethics of Medical Gatekeeping." *Journal of Contemporary Health Law and Policy* 2:23–44.

Rosaldo, Renato. 1984. "Grief and a Headhunter's Rage: On the Cultural Force of Emotions." Pp. 178–199 in *Text, Play, and Story: The Construction and Reconstruction of Self and Society,* edited by Edward Bruner. Plainsfield, IL: Waveland Press.

Roth, Julius A. 1972. "Some Contingencies of the Moral Evaluation and Control of Clientele: The Case of the Hospital Emergency Service." *American Journal of Sociology* 77:839–855.

Schneider, Joseph P. 1993. *No Pity: People with Disabilities Forging a New Civil Rights Movement.* New York: Random House.

Schonwetter, Ronald S., Robert M. Walker, David R. Kramer, and Bruce E. Robinson. 1994. "Socioeconomic Status and Resuscitation Preferences in the Elderly." *Journal of Applied Gerontology* 13(2): 157–71.

Schwartz, S., and T. Griffin. 1986. *Medical Thinking: The Psychology of Medical Judgment and Decision Making.* Springer, New York.

Siner, D. A. 1989. "Advance Directives in Emergency Medicine: Medical, Legal, and Ethical Implications." *Annals of Emergency Medicine* 18: 1364–1369.

Star, S. Leigh. 1991. "The Sociology of the Invisible: The Primacy of Work in the Writings of Anselm Strauss." Pp. 265–285 in *Social Organization and Social Process: Essays in Honor of Anselm Strauss,* edited by David Maines. New York: Aldine de Gruyter.

Starr, Paul. 1982. *The Social Transformation of American Medicine.* New York: Basic Books.

Sudnow, David. 1967. *Passing On: The Social Organization of Dying.* Englewood Cliffs, NJ: Prentice-Hall.

———. 1983. "D.O.A." Pp. 275–294 in *Where Medicine Fails,* edited by Anselm Strauss. Lovelorn, NJ: Transaction Books.

Teaster, Pamela B. 1995. "Resuscitation Policy Concerning Older Adults: Ethical Considerations of Paternalism versus Autonomy." *Journal of Applied Gerontology* 14:78–92.

Teno, Joan, Joanne Lynn, Neil Wenger, Russell S. Phillips, Donald P. Murphy, Alfred F. Connors, Norman Desbiens, William Fulkerson, Paul Bellamy, and William Knauss. 1997. "Advance Directives for Seriously Ill Hospitalized Patients: Effectiveness with the Patient Self-Determination Act and the SUPPORT Intervention." *Journal of the American Geriatrics Society* 45:500–507.

Tillinghast, Stanley J., Katherine M. Doliszny, Thomas E. Kottke, Orlando Gomez-Marin, G. Patrick Lilja, and Bian C. Campion. 1991. "Change in Survival from Out-of-Hospital Cardiac Arrest and its Effect on Coronary Heart Disease Mortality." *American Journal of Epidemiology* 134:851–861.

Timmermans, Stefan. 1997. "High Tech in High Touch: The Presence of Relatives and Friends during Resuscitative Efforts." *Scholarly Inquiry for Nursing Practice* 11:153–168.

———. 1998. "Resuscitation Technology in the Emergency Department: Toward a Dignified Death." *Sociology of Health and Illness* 20:144–167.

———. 1999. "When Death isn't Dead: Implicit Social Rationing during Resuscitative Efforts." *Sociological Inquiry* 24:213–214.
———. 1999. *Sudden Death and the Myth of CPR.* Philadelphia: Temple University Press.
Timmermans, Stefan, and Marc Berg. 1997. "Standardization in Action: Achieving Local Universality through Medical Protocols." *Social Studies of Science* 27:273–305.
Tye, Larry. 1997. "Doctor Had Little Hope of Success." *Boston Globe,* September 1, p. A6.
Waldron, Ingrid. 1997. "What Do We Know about Causes of Sex Differences in Mortality?" Pp. 42–55 in *Sociology of Health and Illness:* Cultural Perspectives. New York: St. Martin's Press.
Wilkinson, Richard. 1996. *Unhealthy Societies: The Afflictions of Inequality.* London: Routledge.
Zola, Irving K. 1984. *Missing Pieces: A Chronicle of Living with a Disability.* Philadelphia: Temple University Press.

31 *The Language of Case Presentation*

Renée R. Anspach

This paper examines a significant segment of medical social life: formal presentations of case histories by medical students, interns, and residents. Although physicians in training spend much of their time presenting cases to their superiors (Mizrahi, 1984), little is known about the social and cultural significance of the case presentation.[1] The ostensible purpose of the case history is quite simple: imparting information about patients to peers, superiors, and consultants. However, basing my analysis on case presentations collected in two intensive care nurseries and an obstetrics and gynecology service, I argue that the case presentation does much more than that. It is an arena in which claims to knowledge are made and epistemological assumptions are displayed, a linguistic ritual in which physicians learn and enact fundamental beliefs and values of the medical world. By analyzing the language of this deceptively simple speech event, much can be learned about contemporary medical culture.

APPROACHES TO MEDICAL LANGUAGE

This analysis of case presentations combines the concerns of two traditions in medical sociology: the study of medical discourse and the study of professional socialization. I will summarize briefly the major findings of each approach, in order to discuss how this analysis is informed by their concerns.

Over the past 10 years an extensive literature on doctor–patient interaction has emerged. This literature builds upon the findings of studies which suggest that practitioners restrict the flow of information to patients, often withholding critical facts about their diagnosis and treatment (Davis, 1963; Glaser and Strauss, 1965; Korsch, Gozzi, and Francis, 1968; Korsch and Negrete, 1972; Lipton and Svarstad, 1977; Waitzkin, 1985). Recently, more systematic and detailed studies, often informed by conversation analysis and discourse analysis, have emphasized the following issues. First, the medical interview is a socially structured speech exchange system, organized hierarchically into phases (Drass, 1981) and sequentially into provider-initiated questions, patient responses, and an optional comment by the physician (Fisher, 1979; Mishler, 1985; West, 1983). Second, the interaction between patients and providers is *asymmetrical* (see Fisher and Groce, 1985). Doctors control the medical interview tightly by initiating the topics of conversation (Fisher, 1979), asking the questions (West, 1983), limiting patients' questions, and often deflecting patients' concerns (Beckman and Frankel, 1984; Frankel, forthcoming; West, 1983). Third, medical interaction is shaped by the context in which it takes place: cultural assumptions of providers and patients, the logic of differential diagnosis, and the demands of bureaucratic organizations combine to constrain doctor-patient communications (Cicourel, 1981; Drass, 1981; Fisher and Groce, 1985). Finally, by subordinating the patient's concerns, beliefs, and life world to the demands of medical discourse (Beckman and Frankel, 1984; Cicourel, 1983; Mishler, 1985), the medical interview may become a form of repressive communication which seriously compromises the quality of patient care.

This very extensive literature on medical discourse contains a significant omission. Although much has been written about how doctors talk *to* patients, very little has been written about how doctors talk *about* patients. (Notable exceptions are studies of the written case recorded by Cicourel [1983] and Beckman and Frankel [1984]). This analytic focus on the medical interview occurs even though the way in which physicians talk about patients is a potentially valuable source of information about medical culture. Rarely do doctors directly reveal their assumptions about patients when talking to them; it is in talking and writing to other doctors about patients that cultural assumptions, beliefs, and values are displayed more directly. A consequence of this omission is that with few exceptions, much information about medical culture is inferred directly or introduced ad hoc into discussions of medical discourse.

By contrast, the way in which doctors talk to each other, particularly about patients, is an analytic focus of the second medical sociological tradition: studies of professional socialization. This largely ethnographic literature uses medical language, particularly slang, as a key to understanding the subculture that develops among medical students and residents as a response to problems created by their work environment (Becker, Geer, Hughes, and Strauss, 1961; Coombs and Goldman, 1973; Mizrahi, 1987). This unofficial, subterranean culture that flourishes among physicians in training includes a rich and graphic slang which contains reference to uninteresting work as "scut" (Becker et al., 1961); "gallows humor" in the face of tragedy (Coombs and Goldman, 1973); and the use of strongly pejorative terms to characterize those patients having low social worth (Sudnow, 1967), those with chronic or supposedly self-inflicted illness, those presenting complaints with a suspected psychogenic etiology, or those with diminished mental capacity; such patients are termed respectively "gomers," "turkeys," "crocks," "gorks," or "brain stem preparations" (Becker et al., 1961; Leiderman and Grisso, 1985; Mizrahi, 1984).

Ethnographers of medical socialization have been fascinated by this typing of patients because it flies in the face of the ostensible aim of medical training: to impart humanitarian values or a service orientation (Parsons, 1951). How sociologists assess the ultimate significance of this slang depends partly on their theoretical orientation; that is, whether medical training is seen as partly successful in instilling a collectivity orientation, as it is by functionalists (e.g., Bosk, 1979; Fox, 1957); or whether (alternatively) medical training entails a suspension or relinquishment of idealism, as conflict theorists contend (see, for example, Becker et al., 1961; Light, 1980; Mizrahi, 1984). A more sanguine view holds that these terms are healthy psychosocial mechanisms designed to cope with the limits of medical knowledge or incurable illness which frustrate the active meliorism of the physician (e.g., Leiderman and Grisso, 1985). According to this view, medical slang need not represent a loss of humanitarian values, but may even be beneficial in developing "detached concern" (Fox, 1979; Fox and Lief, 1963). From a more critical perspective, medical slang displays a blunted capacity to care and a deeply dehumanizing orientation to patients which blames them for their illness, views them as potential learning material, and jeopardizes their care (Millman, 1977; Mizrahi, 1984; Schwartz, 1987; Scully, 1980). These ethnographies of socialization, despite their sometimes differing conclusions, treat medical slang as a cultural artifact and analyze its deeper social and cultural significance.

While addressing the cultural meaning of medical language, studies of professional socialization are limited by their exclusive reliance upon ethnographic methods. Medical slang is often presented out of context and is divorced from the actual occasions in which it is used. Moreover, these studies have been confined to slang words and humor, often glaring violations of the service ethnic which are readily apparent to the field worker. Rarely do ethnographers address the more subtle assumptions embedded in physicians' routine talk. For these reasons, the ethnography of professional socialization would be enhanced by the more detailed approach of discourse analysis.

The present analysis of case presentations is informed by both approaches to medical language. As a study of medical discourse, it attempts a detailed analysis of language as it is actually used. Like ethnographers of professional socialization, I emphasize the cultural significance of this language. The approach used here might be termed "symbolic sociolinguistics"; the emphasis is less on the social structure of the case presentation (the hierarchical and sequential organization of speech exchange) and more on the symbolic content of language. I attempt an interpretive analysis of the connotative, cultural meanings of the language of case presentation—meanings which are taken for granted and may not always be readily apparent to those who use it.

Learning to present a case history is an important part of the training of medical students, interns, and residents. Because case histories are presented by subordinates before their superiors, sometimes in front of large audiences, presenting a case skillfully assumes considerable importance in the eyes of physicians in training. The case presentation, then, is a speech event which serves both to impart information and as a vehicle for professional socialization, and herein lies its sociological import. As I will suggest, case presentations, as highly conventionalized linguistic rituals, employ a stylized vocabulary and syntax which reveal tacit and subtle assumptions, beliefs, and values concerning patients, medical knowledge, and medical practice to which physicians in training are covertly socialized. The case presentation, then, provides an opportunity to study an important aspect of professional socialization and is a window to the medical world view.

METHODS

This analysis of case presentations is based on data collected in three settings. I first observed case presentations as part of a 16-month field study of life-and-death decisions in two newborn intensive care units. I spent 12 months in the 20-bed intensive care nursery of Randolph Hospital (a pseudonym), which serves as a referral center for a region that spans fully half the state. Because of the diverse nature of this region, the clientele was heterogeneous from a demographic and socioeconomic standpoint. Because Randolph Hospital is an elite institution and part of a major medical school, competition for its pediatric residency program is rather intense. I also undertook four months of field work in the 40- to 50-bed nursery I will call General, an acute care hospital for the indigent having a largely Hispanic clientele. Although both Randolph and General are teaching hospitals, closely affiliated with major medical schools, the settings contrast sharply with respect to size, prestige, and the demographic composition of their patient populations. In both settings, my observations focused on the pediatric interns and residents and the neonatology fellows who rotated through the nursery and presented cases to attending neonatologists.

In order to compare case presentations in neonatal intensive care to presentations concerning adult patients, I then conducted three months of field work in the obstetrics and gynecology department of the hospital I will call Bennett, a teaching hospital having a demographically and socioeconomically heterogeneous clientele. About 300 infants are delivered each month in the inpatient obstetrics and gynecology ward, which accommodates about 90 obstetrics and 20 gynecology patients. Interns and residents complete rotations in labor and delivery, the gynecology clinic, gynecological oncology, and an affiliated hospital. I observed cases presented by the eight residents and three interns to full-time attending physicians, perinatologists, and part-time clinical faculty members.

In all three settings, participant observation and interviews provided information about the daily life and organizational context of case presentations. I also conducted interviews with residents of Bennett Hospital concerning strategies of presenting cases. The major method of data collection, however, was nonparticipant observation of a total of 50 cases presented by interns, residents, and fellows in daily rounds, consultations, formal conferences, and morbidity and mortality conferences. In Bennett Hospital, my observations focused primarily on formal presentations in weekly "statistical conferences" and on the very formal didactic presentations at breakfast conferences. A total of 15 case presentations were tape recorded, nine from obstetrics and six from neonatology; I transcribed the others in shorthand and attempted to approximate a verbatim transcript.

In addition, I examined nine written histories in handouts and patients' case records. I also obtained and examined 200 admitting, operative, and discharge summaries from Bennett Hospital, and subjected a random sample of 100 summaries to detailed analysis. I coded and content analyzed these field notes, transcripts, and written summaries to reveal the features of case presentations that will be discussed. In order to provide a comparative framework, I analyzed a total of 14 journalistic medical articles from *Time* and *Newsweek* from September 1987 through February 1988. These journalistic accounts, which I selected because they were comparable in content to case presentations, made it possible to determine whether the features of case presentations that will be discussed here are also used in other occupations.

THE CASE PRESENTATION AS A SPEECH EVENT

Occasions

Over the course of his or her career, virtually every resident must present a formal case history. In fact, case presentation is so important to the work routine of the housestaff that, as one researcher notes, "interns spend most of their time keeping charts and presenting cases to senior staff" (Mizrahi, 1984, p. 243). Formal case histories are presented on certain occasions, which include (1) formal conferences (e.g., mortality review, chief of services rounds, statistical rounds, and didactic conferences); (2) daily rounds, when a new patient is admitted to the nursery or when a new attending physician takes charge of the nursery; (3) instances when a specialist is consulted; (4) written summaries distributed in conferences; and (5) certain points in the case record (e.g., on-service notes, off-service notes, and in admission, operative, and discharge summaries). Case presentations vary on a continuum of formality, ranging from relatively informal presentations on daily rounds to formal presentations in large conferences, attended by the senior staff of a department. Although fellows, who are between residents and faculty in the medical hierarchy, occasionally present cases, generally cases are presented by the intern or the resident assigned to the particular case.

Format

Although the specific features of the history vary according to the purpose of the occasion, the case history whether presented in written or in verbal form tends to follow an almost ritualized format, characterized by the frequent use of certain words, phrases, and syntactic forms and by a characteristic organization. Histories presented in rounds generally begin with a sentence introducing the patient and the presenting problem. This is followed by a history of the patient's problem and its management and then by a list and summary of the present problems in each organ system, presented in order of importance. Because social aspects of the case are always presented (if at all) only after medical problems have been discussed, the semantic structure of the base presentation attests to the relatively low priority accorded to social issues in the reward structure of residency programs (Frader and Bosk, 1981).

Evaluation

Case presentations provide attendings (faculty) with an opportunity to evaluate house officers' competency their mastery of the details of the case, clinical judgment, medical management, and conscientiousness. Interns and residents are aware that case presentations are a significant component of the evaluation process; for this reason, presenting skills are part of that elusive quality called "roundsmanship" (for a detailed discussion of roundsmanship see Arluke, 1978). As one resident noted when asked about the importance of presentations:

> Competency or surgical skills carry some weight (in attendings' evaluations); the ability to get along with team members carries even more weight; and the most important is the case presentation.

Although the importance of this evaluative component varies according to the occasion, the evaluative element is a background feature of most case presentations. Even the written case record serves as an informal social control mechanism, which provides physicians with the opportunity to evaluate their colleagues (Mizrahi, 1984)—to say nothing of opening the door to community scrutiny in the case of malpractice suits. At the Bennett obstetrical and gynecology service, the evaluative element looms large, particularly in the weekly statistical conferences, in which residents present cases before 15 or 20 senior staff members.

At any point, attendings can interrupt the resident's presentation to ask questions about the details of the particular case, its clinical management, or general issues of pathophysiology or medical/surgical techniques. Attendings employ a version of the Socratic method, in which the first question invites further questions until a "correct" answer is received and no further questions are deemed necessary. As Bosk notes, this questioning process follows Sacks's chain rule for question-answer sequences in which the floor belongs to the questioner (Bosk, 1979, p. 95); once the process begins, the presenter loses control of the interaction. Any omission of details relevant to the case (e.g., laboratory values), oversights, or displays of ignorance on the part of the resident are occasions for this questioning process to begin.

> During a presentation, a Bennett resident was discussing tocolyzing a preterm labor (administering a drug for the purpose of stopping uterine contractions). An attending asked, "How much ritadine was given?" The resident replied, "Per protocol." The resident, in referring to the nurses' protocol, had displayed his ignorance of the details of the case and implied that he left the details of case management to the nurses. The attending, detecting this thinly disguised ignorance, then asked, "Well, exactly how *many* milliequivalents were given?", forcing the resident to respond that he didn't know, thereby admitting his ignorance.

Attendings' questions, then, are questions in the second sense of the word, designed to call a resident's competency into question rather than to request information. Residents refer to this questioning process as "pimping"; they distinguish between "benign pimping" (helpful and constructive questions, usually by the senior resident) and "malignant pimping" (questioning, usually in the part of the attending, for the purpose of humiliating a resident). Residents are aware that once a resident falters in rounds, he or she will be suspected of incompetence and will be targeted for future questioning.

> Take Melvin, for instance. He really wasn't so dumb, but he got raked over the coals all the time because he just didn't know how to present cases so well that it really sounded like he really knew what he was talking about. They go for the jugular. They'll pick on someone that they don't think knows what's going on, and they get labeled and then picked on, and, once labeled, that's pretty much it unless they invent the Salk vaccine or something.

Case Presentation as Self-Presentation

Because of this evaluative element, as Arluke (1978) also notes, case presentations become self-presentations. Beginning in medical school and continuing throughout their training, physicians develop a set of skills and strategies designed to display competence and to avoid questions from the attendings. Among the most basic of these skills are "dressing professionally" and mastering "the correct medical terminology" and the semantic organization of the case presentation. One of the "rules" by which a successful presentation is judged appears to be "be concise and be relevant"; that is, a history should contain all and only those points deemed to be relevant, with a minimum of wasted words. Interns are instructed by senior residents in the nursery to omit a detailed chronology of the history and to move from detailed account of the delivery, resuscitation, and the infant's first few hours of life to an enumeration of the patient's problems in relevant organ systems that is, to present an analytic summary rather than a chronological account.

More senior residents attend to the issue of a confident style. One resident, when asked about presentation strategies, emphasized the importance of a smooth presentation, avoiding the pauses and hesitations which would display uncertainty and would provide a conversational slot for questions from the attendings.

> Roundsmanship is salesmanship. You gotta put on an air so that you will convince the attendings that you know about the case, and that you're smarter than they are. You've gotta display an air of confidence. (How do you do that?) You show confidence by the way you talk. (How do you talk?) You don't stop between sentences, you don't hesitate. They don't want to see you flipping through the chart. If you make a mistake in the hemoglobin value, don't say it was a mistake. . . . If you have to say "I don't know," don't apologize for it or say it unconfidently. You can say, "I don't know," but it has to be done in the right way, like nobody else would know either, not like you should've known. Just keep up the flow so you don't get interrupted.

Errors of all kinds are occasions for intense questions by the attendings; as Arluke (1978) also notes, skillful presenters employ strategies which anticipate and deftly deflect these questions. In the case of minor errors, these include "covering" to avoid displays of ignorance, presenting justifications for choosing a questionable course of action, and excusing or mitigating responsibility by blaming another department or a physician in the community. (In fact, cases involving errors by outside physicians are selected frequently for presentation.)

> If the attending asks you, "What is the hemoglobin?" don't say, "I don't remember." That's the worst thing you can say—it's blood in the water. If you know it's normal but you can't remember the value, give a normal value. . . . You have to anticipate the questions. If you are asked, "Why wasn't that done?" you can say, "We considered that, but . . ." For instance, in the case of an elective caesarean hysterectomy (a controversial procedure), where blood was transfused, you can anticipate you'll be asked about the caesarean hysterectomy and about the blood transfusions, and you're likely to get raked over the coals. So you bring it up by deflecting or defusing the attending's questions. You say, "This patient received three units of blood. We felt the hematological indices didn't warrant transfusions, but anesthesiology disagreed." This way the attending will get sidetracked (because a discussion of another department's competency would ensue).

Attempts to cover up a major error in medical management, however, represent instances of what Bosk (1979) calls "normative errors," likely to arouse suspicions about the presenter's moral character. Even in such cases, residents, much like the attendings discussed by Bosk, are able to transform a mistake into a moral virtue by a candid admission.

> In the case of the little stuff, you can blame the mistake on someone else, and if not, you can try to cover it up. If you overlook the little details, you can get away with it, as long as it is confidently presented. If it's a major mistake, the worst thing is to cover it up—that's the worst thing you can do. If you're caught trying to cover up, then they'll look upon you as someone who will cover up the next time, and it will follow you around. The way you treat a major mistake can transform you from a villain to a hero by simply stating, "In retrospect, we wish we had done it this way." Then you're a hero—you've showed you've learned from your mistake. They'll admire you and everyone will become your champion. You'll get questioned far less and you won't get pimped by the other attendings. They'll say, "That's OK, it happens to all of us."

This discussion is intended to convey the climate surrounding the case presentation: the importance that case presentations assume in the training of residents; the extent to which case presentations contain an evaluative element; and the fact that case presentations are simultaneously self-presentations. Case presentations, then, are rituals for the display of credibility—a background issue that informs some of the linguistic practices which will be discussed in the following section.

FEATURES OF CASE PRESENTATIONS

In the highly interpretive analysis of case presentations that follows, I will focus on epistemological assumptions and rhetorical features by which claims to knowledge are made and conveyed. I will emphasize four aspects of case presentations, which I call (1) the separation of biological processes from the person (de-personalization); (2) omission of the agent (e.g., use of the passive voice); (3) treating medical technology as the agent; and (4) account markers, such as "states," "reports," and "denies," which emphasize the subjectivity of the patient's accounts. Table 31-1 presents the frequencies with which these features were used in the larger corpus of materials. These features of case presentations are variable, but, as the table suggests, some are employed so frequently as to be considered conventions of the language of case presentation. Although it would be useful to compare the frequency with which these features are used in case presentations to the frequency with which they are used in ordinary speech, unfortunately no study of the use of these features in the vernacular exists. As the table shows, however, most of these features are found more frequently in ordinary speech than in a study of the passive voice in English language novels (Estival and Myhill, 1988) and in journalism, in which the author's goal is to create a heightened sense of agency.

At the conclusion of this paper, I present segments of five case histories. These presentations were selected according to two criteria: (1) the frequency with which the features of case presentations are used, and (2) the extent to which they represent oral and written presentations in neonatology and obstetrics. The first is a summary written by a neonatology fellow for the morbidity and mortality conference which followed the death of Robin Simpson, an infant with serious chronic lung disease of unknown etiology, who died rather unexpectedly. The next two are the initial portions of tape-recorded transcripts of histories in two ethics conferences concerning an infant who had a very unusual brain lesion (Roberta Zapata). One was presented by a fellow and the other by a resident approximately six weeks later. The fourth is an excerpt from a presentation in statistical rounds by a resident in obstetrics and gynecology. This case, which concerns a woman with cervical cancer, involved serious medical mismanagement by an outside community physician. The final case is the history portion of the written admission summary presented by a resident concerning a patient admitted for obstetrical care. A detailed analysis of these case presentations provides the basis for the discussion of the four features of medical language that follows.

De-Personalization

The case history presented in the morbidity and mortality conference which followed Robin Simpson's death begins with the statement: "Baby Girl Simpson was the 1044-gram product of a 27 week gestation." Outside observers of medical settings have commented that physicians sometimes employ an impersonal vocabulary when referring to their patients (Emerson, 1970, pp. 73–100; Lakoff, 1975, p. 65). A clear example of this phenomenon is reference to patients in case presentations. Robin Simpson is identified as a member of a class of baby girls having a particular weight and gestational age. A typical introduction in obstetrics is presented in Line 66: "The patient is a 21-year-old Gravida III, Para I, AbI black female at 32 weeks gestation." This introduction lists the patient's age, previous pregnancies, live births, abortions, race, and weeks of pregnancy. Throughout the presentations, neonatology patients are identified as "the infant" or "the baby" (Lines 4, 23, 25, 35) or "s/he" (Lines 6–10, 13, 15). (Note that the second presenter is mistaken about Roberta's gender.) Obstetrics and gynecology patients are identified as "the patient" (38, 60, 66, 69, 81) or "she" (45, 46, 47, 67, 69, 71, 72, 74, 77, 79). These references invite the audience to see infants or patients rather than individuals; except in the written summary patients are never referred to by their proper names.[2] I will not comment in detail about this phenomenon of no-naming (for a discussion of this issue, see Frader and Bosk, 1981). Nor will I comment extensively on what may appear, from an outsider's perspective, to be the rather impersonal and mechanistic connotative imagery of "expiration date" and "product."

When I speak of de-personalization, I am referring not merely to the use of an impersonal vocabulary but rather to a more subtle set of assumptions: to refer to a baby as a "product" of a "gestation" seems to emphasize that it is the gestation, a biological process, rather than the parents, who produced the baby. Similar formulations are found in all three histories; for example: "the pregnancy was complicated by . . ." (1)

"SROM [spontaneous rupture of membranes] occurred" (2), "the bruit (murmur) has decreased significantly . . ." (16), "the vagina and the cervix were noted to be clear," "the cervix was described . . ." (51). Each of these expressions invites the question "To whom?" or "Whose?" These formulations draw attention to the subject of the sentence: a disease or an organ rather than the patient. Of course the physicians know that parents have babies and that persons become ill, but the use of this language seems to suggest that biological processes can be separated from the persons who experience them. The language I have just described is not confined to physicians; in ordinary conversation we speak of a person "having a disease," thereby separating the disease from the subject. This usage may reflect deeply rooted cultural conceptions of the duality between mind and body. The most egregious examples of de-personalization occur in the everyday

Table 31-1. Frequency of Features of Case Presentation

	Depersonalization	Personalization	Depersonalized[1] References	Personalized[2] References	Reports on Treatments, Procedures, and Actions Which Omit Medical Agent	Reports on Treatments, Procedures, and Actions Which Mention Medical Agent	Claims to Knowledge Which Omit Medical Agent	Claims to Knowledge Which Mention Medical Agent
Obstetrics, Written	3271	92	870	2	1687	29	697	10
Obstetrics, Oral	102	4	92	0	58	3	153	5
Neonatology, Written	160	66	135	4	85	16	178	5
Neonatology, Oral	103	58	129	1	30	35	107	36
Total	3636	220	1226	7	1860[3]	83[4]	1135[5]	56[6]
Number of Presenters Using More Than 60% of Forms	18	3	16	5	15	6	17	4
Comparisons Estival and Myhill (1988) Journalism	69	186	78	49	97	101	193	120
Number of Authors Using 60% of Forms[12]	12	5	3	4	0	5	4	0

[1] De-personalized references are those instances in which the patient is not referred to by name, but as the/this patient, woman, gravida, para, infant, twins, parents, child or by pronouns which refer to the above.

[2] Personalized references are those in which the patient or family is referred to by name.

[3] This includes 1757 agencies passive (e.g., an ultrasound was done), 60 actives with a recipient subject (she had/received an ultrasound), 8 ambiguous without agent (attempts to obtain fetal heart tones were unsuccessful), 6 adverbials (the patient was in the lithotomy position), 4 passive actives (she had an ultrasound done), 2 agentive passives with treatment as agent (this was followed by progesterone), 1 active with the procedure as agent (the surgery removed . . . her disease).

[4] This includes 56 actives, 21 agentive passives (an ultrasound was done by Dr. H.), 2 partial agentive passives (she was followed at the Cancer Center), quasi-agentive declaratives (Her prenatal care was by Dr. H.), and 2 agentive actives (This 29-year-old . . . underwent treatment by the emergency room doctor).

[5] This includes 265 agentless, 114 scores, 111 descriptive statements (she was afebrile), 77 existentials (there was . . .), 66 sponge and needle count were correct, 63 estimated blood loss was, 62 actives with a recipient subject, 46 technology as agent (auscultation revealed), 40 quasi-passives (patient is well-known), 42 consistent with, 28 appeared, seemed, felt (patient appears pale), 26 adverbials (she did well), 25 is (patient is), 24 Apgars, 21 scores and descriptive (electrolytes were within normal limits), 21 exam revealed, 14 organ revealed, 9 presented with, 8 palpable, visible, 6 agentive passives with non-human agent, 5 found to have, 4 results in, 4 improved, worsened, 4 developed, 3 it extrapositions (it extrapositions . . .), 3 required, 3 participles, 13 other actives with non-human agent (the surgery removed the disease), and 28 others.

talk of physicians (and also nurses) when they refer to patients as "the" + "(disease)" (e.g., "the trisomy in Room 311"). On surgical wards and, less frequently, in the intensive care nursery, practitioners sometimes refer to patients as "the" + "(procedure)" (e.g., "the tonsillectomy in 214"). It is debatable whether or not these forms of depersonalization may impel practitioners to adopt certain attitudes toward their patients. By using these designations, however, practitioners leave themselves open to the criticism made by many consumers: that doctors "treat diseases rather than patients."

Omission of the Agent (e.g., Use of the Passive Voice)

Case presentations not only fail to mention the patient's personal identity; they also omit the physician, nurses, or other medical *agents* who perform procedures or make observations, as Table 31-1 suggests. A common example of a

Omission of the Agent: Other Contexts[7]		All Contexts								
Forms Which Omit Medical Agent	*Forms Which Mention Medical Agent*	*Forms Which Omit Medical Agent*	*Forms Which Mention Medical Agent*	(Agentless) Passive Voice	Active Voice	Percent Passive	Technology as Agent	Alternatives	Account Markers Used	Account Markers Not Used
28	229	2412	268	2029	389	83.91	23	105	129	2247
0	4	211	12	64	51	55.65	21	55	11	161
0	10	263	31	101	156	39.30	5	49	N/A	N/A
0	30	137	101	26	161	13.90	9	8	N/A	N/A
28[8]	273[9]	3023	412	2220	757	74.57	58	217[10]	140[11]	2408
1	20	15	2	14 206	7 1940	— 9.60%	4	17	0	21
33	56	1	277	116	390	22.92%	4	3	66	291
2	5	1	4	1	6	—	1	1	0	7

[6] This includes 37 actives, 6 agentive passives, 5 partial agentive passives, 3 descriptive statements (they were in agreement), 2 it extrapositions, and 3 other.
[7] "Other contexts" pertain primarily to instances in which the patient or family is the agent.
[8] This includes 12 descriptives, 5 patient presented, 5 equivalences, 3 agentive passives and 3 existentials.
[9] This includes 205 actives, 46 intrasitives with agentive subjects (the mother died), 11 prepositional verbs (complained of), 8 other intransitives (the infant died), and 3 agentive passives.
[10] These include, most commonly, scores, estimated blood loss, consistent with, and scores and descriptive statements. "Consistent with" was coded as an alternative to technology as agent, since it can designate uncertainty (Prince, Frader, and Bosk, 1982).
[11] Account markers include states, reports, claims, complains of, no known history of, no history was reported, admits, and denies.
[12] Although a total of 14 articles were examined, they were written by a total of seven authors, and anonymously authored articles were excluded from this calculation.

form that omits the agent is the "existential": "There was no mention of bleeding pattern . . ." (41). The canonical form which omits the agent is the "agentless passive." The presenters use the agentless passive voice frequently, and they do so in two contexts. First, they use it when reporting on treatments and procedures; for example: "The infant was transferred . . ." (4), "She was treated with high FiO2's (respirator settings) . . ." (6), "She was extubated" (taken off the respirator) (7), "He was transferred here" (13) and "was put on phenobarb" (30), "The patient was admitted to . . . the hospital" (54), and "was referred to the ___ Cancer Center" (61). In this case the presenters are not omitting reference to the patient on whom the procedures were performed, but rather are omitting the persons who performed the procedures. This omission has the effect of emphasizing what was done rather than who did it or why a decision was made to engage in a given course of action.

This usage becomes particularly significant when the decisions are controversial, problematic, or questionable. For example, in two sentences in the summary concerning Robin Simpson, the use of the passive voice obscures the fact that the actions that were performed resulted from rather problematic and highly significant decisions (in venturing this interpretation, I am going outside the text to interviews and discussions that I observed). For example, "She was extubated" (7) refers to a life-and-death decision, discussed later in the same conference, in which Robin Simpson was weaned from the respirator and was expected to die. Consider also the statement "No betamethasone was given" (3). Bethamethasone is a steroid administered in several large university centers to mothers whose membranes are ruptured prematurely for the purpose of maturing the baby's lungs. In a subsequent interview, a resident who had been present when Robin Simpson was admitted to the Randolph nursery suggested that the failure of physicians at St. Mary's, a small community hospital, to administer betamethasone may have contributed to the severity of Robin's illness. Because betamethasone is given commonly in the Randolph nursery, I am assuming that the fellow alludes to the failure to give betamethasone in an effort to make sense of Robin's illness, and that other participants in the conference understand this implication. Of course it is impossible to discern the fellow's intention in using the passive voice. It seems to me, however, that by divorcing the action from the person who performed the action, the passive voice has the effect of muting an allusion to an unfortunate decision about medical management. (Compare this statement with "The doctors at St. Mary's did not give betamethasone.")

Case D concerns a serious error in medical management on the part of a community physician, a type of case frequently chosen for presentation in rounds. A woman had come to her gynecologist complaining of vaginal bleeding. The physician, noting the enlarged uterus, simply assumed that the patient had fibroid tumors and scheduled her for a total hysterectomy. The gynecologist failed to perform a pap smear during the examination, and, therefore, did not know that, in addition to fibroids, the patient also had cervical cancer. Consequently the physician inadvertently cut into the tumor during surgery, an error which may have seriously compromised the patient's prognosis. As the resident confirmed when interviewed after the presentation, the case was chosen to deflect attendings' questions by emphasizing the error of an outside doctor, while at the same time symbolically affirming superior management at the teaching hospital and the resident's ability to learn from the error. The presentation is constructed as a morality play, a drama beginning with allusions to the errors (40, 52), proceeding to the denouement in which revelations from the pathology report are disclosed (58), and ending with a moral lesson (62). Note the resident's language to describe the errors: "No further details were noted in the history" (40); "No pap smear was performed at the time of this initial visit" (52). By placing the negative at the beginning of the sentence, the resident draws the listener's attention to the errors. Although it is understood clearly that the error was committed by an outside doctor, the passive voice softens the accusation by leaving this implicit and deflecting attention from the perpetrator. (Compare this construction to the active voice in ordinary conversation: "The doctor didn't perform a pap smear." Such a formulation, according to the resident in describing the case to me, "would not have been subtle.")

There is yet another context in which the fellow and the residents use the agentless passive voice: when they refer to observations and make claims to knowledge, as in "Both babies were noted to have respiratory problems on examination" (10), "The baby was noted to have congestive heart failure" (23), "She was found on physical exam . . ." (47), and "The vagina and the cervix were noted to be clear" (50). The use of the passive voice is an extremely common, though not invariant, feature of medical discourse. When one compares this use of the passive voice with its alternative ("They noted that the baby had temporal bruits"), I believe that something can be learned about the epistemological assumptions of the case presentation: to delete mention of the person who made the observation seems to suggest that the observer is irrelevant to what is being observed or "noted," or that anyone would have "noted" the same "thing." In other words, using the passive voice while omitting the observer seems to imbue what is being observed with an unequivocal, authoritative factual status.

Technology as Agent

Physicians occasionally do use the active voice. For example, in Case Histories, B, C, and D, the fellow and the residents make the following statements:

> "Auscultation of the head revealed a very large bruit, and angiography showed a very large arteriovenous malformation in the head . . ." (11, 12)
>
> "Follow-up CT-scans have showed the amount of blood flow to be very minimal . . ." (18)
>
> "The arteriogram showed that this AVM was fed . . ." (26, 27)
>
> "The EEG showed . . . an abnormal . . ." (31–32)
>
> "The path revealed endometrial curettings . . ." (57)

These formulations seem to carry the process of objectification one step farther than the use of the passive voice: not only do the physicians fail to mention the person or persons who performed the diagnostic procedures, but they also omit mention of the often complex processes by which angiograms and CT scans are interpreted. Moreover, these forms actually treat medical technology as though it were the *agent*. (Again, compare these claims with others which seem somewhat less objectified: "Dr. ___ evaluated . . ." (13), "They . . . did an EMI scan (CT-scan)" (25). Moreover, using the terms "revealed" and "showed" seems to suggest that the information received by using the stethoscope, angiogram, or brain scan was obtained by a process of scientific revelation rather than by equivocal interpretation. Having had the opportunity to observe radiology rounds, I was impressed by the considerable amount of negotiation and debate that takes place as the participants come to "see" evidence of lesions on X-rays. Although physicians undoubtedly would acknowledge that this interpretation takes place, they tend to attribute variations in interpretation to the vagaries of "observer error" or "opinion" rather than viewing the process of interpretation as an intrinsic feature of the way in which data obtained via measurement instruments are produced. The use of such formulations as "Auscultation revealed" or "Angiography showed" supports a view of knowledge in which instruments rather than people create the "data."

Account Markers

If physicians imbue the physical examination and diagnostic technology with unquestioned objectivity, they treat the patient's reports with an ethnomethodological skepticism that is, as subjective accounts with only tenuous links to reality. When presenting a clinical history obtained from a patient, the physician has two choices. One is to present events and symptoms reported by the patient as facts, just as physical findings and laboratory results are presented. This is done occasionally, as in the last clinical history: "She takes prenatal vitamins daily" (79), "The patient has a male child with sickle cell trait" (81–82), and "She has had no other surgeries (74)." Alternatively and more commonly, the history is treated as a subjective narrative consisting of statements and reports. For example, the patient "reports" that she was seen in the emergency room (70), "states" that she has been having uterine contractions (67), that there is fetal movement (7), and that she has a history of sickle cell trait (72). "States" and "reports" are markers which signal that we have left the realm of fact and have entered the realm of the subjective account. Note that this information is attributed to the patient, which implies that the physician's knowledge was obtained via hearsay (Prince, Frader, and Bosk 1982, p. 91).

Another frequently used account marker, "denies," actually calls the patient's account into question or casts doubt on the validity of the history. Although sometimes it is used simply when the patient gives a negative answer to the physician's question, "denies" is used most frequently in three other contexts. First, it is almost always used in the context of deviant habits likely to compromise the health of the patient or the unborn child, as in "She denies tobacco, alcohol, coffee, or tea" (78–79). (Compare this statement with the alternative: "She does not use tobacco, alcohol, etc . . ."). In this case, "denies" suggests that the patient may not be telling the truth or may be concealing deviant behavior, and it casts doubt upon her credibility as a historian. Second, "denies" is used frequently in connection with allergies, as in Line 75: "She denies any allergies." Another frequently used phrase is "She has no *known* allergies." In this case I suspect that "denies" has a self-protective function, however unintentional. If the patient were to have an allergic reaction to a drug administered during treatment, the responsibility would rest with the patient's faulty account rather than with the physician. Third, "denies" is used when a patient reports a symptom which usually belongs to a larger constellation of symptoms, but does not report the others that he or she would be likely to have, as in "She denies any dysuria, frequency, or urgency" (76–77).

Physicians "note," "observe," or "find"; patients "state," "report," "claim," "complain of," "admit," or "deny." The first verbs connote objective reality (i.e., only concrete entities can be noted or observed); the second verbs connote subjective perceptions. As Table 31-2 suggests, physicians are inclined to present information obtained from the physician as though it were factual, while treating information from the patient as accounts.

It is significant that medical training teaches physicians to distinguish between *subjective* symptoms, apparent only to the patient, and *objective* signs, apparent to the expert. Moreover, according to the Weed (SOAP) system for recording progress notes, any medical information provided by the patient should be classified as "subjective," while observations by the physician or laboratory studies should be classified as "objective."

The one exception to this rule is the rare occasion on which the presenter calls another physician's account into question. This is precisely what happens in Case History D, which is structured around mismanagement by the community doctor who failed to perform a pap smear.

Table 31-2. Presentation of Information by Source of Information

Presentation of Information	Source of Information: *Information Obtained from Physician*	*Information Obtained from Patient*	*Total*
As Fact (No Account Markers Used)	2009	399	2408
As Account (Account Markers Used)	19	131	151
Total	2028	530	2558

$X^2 = 430.451$.
$df = 1$.
$p = .0001$.

The resident explicitly emphasizes the rather cursory history taken by the community gynecologist, which does not include several pertinent facts.

> No further details were noted in the history. There was no mention of bleeding pattern, frequency duration, female dyspareunia (pain on intercourse), or dysmenorrhea or coital bleeding. . . . In the family history *that was obtained,* her mother was deceased of gastric carcinoma at age 64 (Lines 40–45).

Because a major theme of this history is the physician's cursory examination, which did not include a pap smear, it is not surprising that the resident uses an account marker when relating the physician's physical findings: "The vagina and cervix were noted to be clear, and the cervix *was described as* 'closed'" (50–51). The account marker "described" has the effect of casting doubt on the accuracy of the physician's observations or report and is in keeping with the overall emphasis on a lack of thoroughness. It is significant that in the handwritten notes which the resident used in this history and gave to me, the phrase "noted to be" was crossed out and replaced by "described as." As is the case when used with patients, account markers call attention to the subjective nature of the narrative.

"SO WHAT?" . . . SOCIAL CONSEQUENCES OF THE LANGUAGE OF CASE PRESENTATION

Before discussing the implications of the language of case presentation, I should mention some caveats. In venturing into the realm of connotative meaning, I am aware that I am treading on perilous ground, for these are *my* interpretations of the language of case presentation. Many other interpretations can be made and I will briefly mention two of them. First, some people might suggest that the features of case histories are "merely" instances of "co-occurrence phenomena." Sociolinguists have observed that certain words and phrases tend to "go together" and to be used in certain social situations. Thus formulations such as "This patient is the product of a gestation" and "Auscultation revealed . . ." are parts of a style within an "occupational register." When presenting a case history, the resident simply may slip into this style rather automatically. To be sure, the practices I have just discussed represent instances of linguistic co-occurrence, and may be used without regard for whatever deeper meanings the observer may attribute to them. Yet I am asking a very different set of questions: What assumptions seem to be embodied in this style? What are the possible sociological consequences of this particular form of co-occurrence? The welfare administrator who writes a memo might automatically slip into "bureaucratese," but what does this occupational register tell us about the assumptive world of the bureaucrat?

Second, my interpretation of the language of case presentation is an outsider's interpretation. When questioned about their use of the formulations I have discussed, some physicians agreed with my interpretations; others responded that this style within what linguists call an "occupational register" exists merely for the purpose of imparting information as briefly and concisely as possible (for a discussion of this issue, see Ervin-Tripp, 1971). The characteristic formulations of case presentations, however, may not always be the most parsimonious. (Compare "The baby was noted to have congestive heart failure," Lines 23–24, with "They noted that the baby had temporal bruits," Line 25 an equally succinct formulation.) Although brevity is important in resident culture, the fact that the residents and fellows sometimes use alternative, equally brief, formulations suggests that more may be at issue than the requirement of the brief transmission of information. Moreover, to claim that linguistic forms exist merely for the transmission of information is to subscribe to a rather narrow view of language. Ordinary language philosophers argue that words not only transmit information but accomplish actions and produce certain effects on those who hear them. Although transmitting information is clearly a manifest function of case presentations, the discursive practices I have described may have other consequences which are less obvious, as noted below.

Mitigation of Responsibility

Sociolinguists who have discussed the passive voice note that it is a responsibility-mitigating device. The discursive practices I identified in the previous section minimize responsibility in two ways. First, by suggesting that the observer is irrelevant to what is "observed," "noted," or "found," using the passive voice minimizes the physician's role in producing findings or observations. A similar point can be made about the use of technology as agent ("Auscultation revealed . . ."), which locates responsibility for producing the data in diagnostic technology rather than in the physician's observations and interpretations.

Second, the passive voice minimizes the physician's role in medical decision making. When used in reporting on treatments and procedures, the passive voice calls attention to the action and deflects attention from the actors or the decisions which led to the action. This effect becomes particularly significant when the passive voice is used to report problematic decisions, such as life-and-death decisions, obscuring both the decision makers and the controversy surrounding those decisions. Even on those occasions when physicians call attention to mistakes in medical management or clinical judgment, in using the passive voice they blunt the accusation by emphasizing the error rather than the perpetrator. In short, by eliminating both the actor and the element of judgment from medical decision-making, the passive voice places physicians, their knowledge, and their decisions beyond the pale of linguistic scrutiny.

One might ask whether these practices arise out of a structural imperative in the medical profession to protect itself from scrutiny. This is precisely what the professional dominance perspective would suggest (Friedson, 1970). For example, Millman's (1977) study of mortality review in three community hospitals depicts these conferences as rituals designed to neutralize medical mistakes. Writing from a neofunctionalist perspective, Bosk (1979) takes a different view of mortality review in a university-based teaching hospital. According to Bosk, attendings do acknowledge their mistakes, but turn their contrite admissions into displays of authority. This study provides data from a third context: cases presented by housestaff who are being evaluated by their superiors. Like the physicians described by Millman, housestaff openly admit major errors, if only to escape moral censure and to benefit from their candor, and they openly discuss mistakes of community doctors, if only to deflect criticism and to demonstrate the superior management of teaching hospitals. In each instance the intent is the same: to protect their credibility from challenge by the attendings. Because it mitigates responsibility for clinical decisions, the passive voice, while perhaps not used intentionally and strategically for this purpose, clearly serves this aim.

Oral presentations are private affairs open only to physicians. In the written case record, however, the ambit of evaluation widens. Not only is the case record open to evaluation by other physicians; potentially it can become a public record in malpractice suits. In view of the salience of malpractice in medical culture, the rise of so-called "defensive medicine," and the demand for documentation and the use of diagnostic technology, a language that treats findings as unproblematic and minimizes the responsibility of physicians for decision making has the effect of protecting those who use it from public scrutiny.

Passive Persuasion: The Literary Rhetoric of Medical Discourse

The practices I have just mentioned are by no means the exclusive province of physicians. Quite the contrary; some are found commonly in academic prose. For instance, one need look no farther than the two previous sentences for examples of parallel devices: the presentation of practices apart from the persons who engage in them and the use of passive voice ("found" by whom?). Regardless of my intention in using these devices, they do seem to cloak the claims that are made in the garb of objectivity. In an analysis of the academic prose in a well-known paper on alcoholism, Gusfield (1977) suggests that science has a "literary rhetoric." If one accepts this interpretation of academic prose, it might be possible that medicine, too, has its literary rhetoric. Some of the devices I have just mentioned have the effect of convincing the listener or reader of the unequivocal "truth" of the findings. By suggesting that observers are irrelevant to what is observed and that measurement instruments create the data, the language of case presentation approaches rhetoric or the art of persuasion.

Writing from the perspective of ordinary language philosophy, Austin (1975) suggests that every linguistic utterance has three dimensions: a locutionary or referential dimension (it imparts information), an illocutionary dimension (it accomplishes an action), and a perlocutionary dimension (it produces certain effects on the hearer, including convincing and persuading). Some of the practices I have described as part of the language of case presentation may be used by physicians to convince the audience of the credibility of their claims to knowledge, and hence may belong to the "perlocutionary" realm (which is another way of saying that there may be a literary rhetoric of medical discourse). For two reasons I suspect that at least on certain occasions, the language of case presentation may be used precisely because of its persuasive power. First, case histories are presented by medical students, interns, residents, and fellows to status superiors—attending physicians—who are evaluating them. Case presentations, as physicians acknowledge, are self-presentations, displays of credibility. By adopting a mode of presentation in which observations and diagnostic findings are endowed with unequivocal certainty, these younger physicians may be exploiting the persuasive power of words at the very moments when they may feel most uncertain. Second, I observed a very interesting instance of "style switching," in which a resident, when criticized by his attending physician for failing to conduct certain diagnostic tests, switched immediately from the active voice into the language of case presentation ("This infant was the . . . product of a . . . gestation . . . was noted", etc.) Case presentations are not only rituals affirming the value of scientific observation and diagnostic technology, but perlocutionary acts, affirming the speaker's credibility as well. For this reason the epistemology of the case presentation serves the social psychology of self-presentation.

The Surrender of Subjectivity

If information produced by means of diagnostic technology is valued in the language of case presentation, information obtained from the patient is devalued. Technology "reveals" and "shows"; the physician "notes" or "observes"; the patient "reports" and "denies." The language of case presentation reflects a clear epistemological hierarchy in which diagnostic technology is valued most highly, followed in descending order by the physician's observations and finally by the patient's account. The case presentation concerning mismanagement is not only a symbolic affirmation of the superior management by the resident in a teaching hospital, but also a ritual affirming the value of diagnostic technology over the physical examination and the patient's history.

This hierarchy reflects an historical transformation that is described by Reiser (1978). In the early nineteenth century, physicians diagnosed and treated patients in their homes or by mail; the major source of data was the patient's subjective narrative, accepted at face value. As the locale of diagnosis moved to the hospital and the laboratory, medical practice turned away from reliance on the patient's account toward reliance on the physician's clinical perceptions (observation, palpation, and percussion), which in turn gave way to reliance on sophisticated diagnostic technology. Reiser suggests that each juncture in this epistemological evolution was accompanied by an increasing alienation in the doctor-patient relationship. The new diagnostic armamentarium entailed changes in the physician's role, wherein history taking assumed less importance in medical practice. Patients in turn were compelled to surrender their subjective experience of illness to the expert's authority.

There is another sense in which the language of case presentation reflects a culture that objectifies patients and devalues their subjective experience. The discursive practices which I call "depersonalization" refer to patients rather than to people. In fact, the subject of sentences and the real object of medical intervention is not the patient, but diseases and organs (this phenomenon appears to exist in other settings, described by Donnely, 1986 and by Frader and Bosk, 1981).

The ability to "see" diseases, tissues, and organs as entities apart from patients, also a recent historical development, is what Foucault (1975) calls "the clinical mentality."[3] In its most extreme form, the language of case presentation treats the patient as the passive receptacle for the disease rather than as a suffering subject.

Socialization to a World View

Because it is delivered before superordinates, the case presentation serves as an instrument for professional socialization. Because case presentations are self-presentations, interns and residents learn a set of strategies designed to display and protect their own credibility in the eyes of their superiors. Whereas the skills of presentation are conscious and strategic, many of the deeper assumptions of case presentations are tacit and taken for granted; for this reason, much of the learning is unintentional and implicit. In fact, many of the values and assumptions in the language of case presentation contradict the explicit tenets of medical education. Thus, although medical students are taught to attach more weight to the patient's history than to the physical examination or laboratory findings, the language of case presentation devalues patients' accounts. By using this language, physicians learn a scale of values which emphasizes science, technology, teaching, and learning at the expense of interaction with patients.

Whether used intentionally or unwittingly, the language of case presentation contains certain assumptions about the nature of medical knowledge. The practices I have discussed both reflect and create a world view in which biological processes exist apart from persons, observations can be separated from those who make them, and the knowledge obtained from measurement instruments has a validity independent of the persons who use and interpret this diagnostic technology. Inasmuch as presenting a case history is an important part of medical training, those who use the language of case presentation may be impelled to adopt an unquestioning faith in the superior scientific status of measurable information and to minimize the import of the patient's history and subjective experience. In a restatement of the Whorf hypothesis,[4] one linguist comments that "language uses us as much as we use language" (Lakoff 1975, p. 3). This discussion suggests that the medical students, residents, and fellows who present case histories may come to be used by the very words they choose.

EXAMPLES OF CASE PRESENTATIONS

A. WRITTEN SUMMARY FROM MORBIDITY AND MORTALITY CONFERENCE

Simpson, Baby Girl
Birthdate: 5/13/78
Expiration Date: 12/9/78

1 Baby Girl Simpson was the 1044-gram product of a 27-week gestation. The pregnancy was
2 complicated by the mother falling 2 weeks prior to delivery. SROM occurred on 5/9/78
3 and the infant was delivered by repeat C-section on 5/13/78 at St. Mary's. No betame-
4 ethasone was given before delivery. Apgars were 4 and 8. The infant was transferred to
5 Randolph in room air. The infant developed chronic lung disease after being intubated
6 at about 24 hours of age for increasing respiratory distress. She was treated with high
7 F_IO_2's and a course of steroids as well. She was extubated and at the time she ex-
8 pired, she required an F_IO_2 of 1.0 by hood. She was on chronic diuretics and potassium
9 supplement and had problems with hyperkalemia. She expired on 12/9/78.

10 B. NURSERY ETHICS ROUNDS, Fellow: _____ both babies were noted to have respiratory
11 problems on examination and auscultation of the head revealed a very large
12 bruit and angiography showed a very large arterio-venous malformation in the
13 head . . . ah he was transferred here and Dr. S evaluated and decided to
14 introduce the wires and then within 48 hours there was another baby diagnosed

15 as having the same problem. He was transferred here and his physician had
16 the wires inserted into the malformation. Ah post op, the bruit has decreased
17 significantly in the first baby and follow up CT-scans have showed the
18 amount of blood flow to be very minimal at this time. The second baby is due
19 to go through a CT-scan in the very near future, but has had a lot of other
20 neurological problems, and it has also been much more difficult to control
21 the second one's congestive failure post op.

22 C. NURSERY ETHICS ROUNDS, ROBERTA Z. Res: ______ the mother was 44 years old,
23 gravida 10, para 8. At about 24 hours of age, the baby was noted to have
24 congestive heart failure and was transferred to (hospital). At about 48
25 hours of age they noted that the baby had temporal bruits, did an emi scan
26 and found a very large vein of galen malformation. The arteriogram showed
27 that this AVM was fed by both the anterior cerebral arteries, both posterior
28 arteries and the vertebrals and the (hospital) neurosurgeons thought the
29 baby to be inoperable, so the baby was transferred here. The baby had some
30 right sided seizures as of 24 hours of age, the baby was put on phenobarb.
31 The EEG done at that time this was still at (hospital) showed an
32 abnormal it was abnormal in that this was a space occupying lesion, but
33 there were no other abnormalities. Since then the baby has been on and off
34 phenobarb, but has still been on maintenance phenobarb most of the time. The
35 baby was transferred here and on the fourth of December had wires placed in
36 the malformation in hopes of inducing a thrombosis and closing off the
37 malformation.

38 D. OB-GYN ROUNDS The patient is a 43-year-old Taiwanese female Gravida-
39 6, Para-3, Ab-3 initially seen by her gynecologist for about a six-week history
40 of vaginal bleeding. No further details were noted in the history. There
41 was no mention of bleeding pattern, frequency, duration, female dyspareunia,
42 discharge, or dysmenorrhea or coital bleeding. Her past medical history
43 included no hypertension, diabetes mellitus, and blood dyscrasias. In the
44 family history that was obtained, her mother was deceased of gastric car-
45 cinoma at age 64, but it was otherwise non-contributory. She had no previous
46 surgeries. She had been in the U.S. for about five years from Taiwan, and
47 had no pelvic exam during this time. She was found on physical exam to be a
48 well developed, well-nourished, slender Asian female with no acute distress;
49 5′0″ 113 pounds; the blood pressure was 130/70; pulse 80, respirations, 18.
50 The physical exam was unremarkable. The vagina and cervix were noted to be
51 clear, and the cervix was described as "closed." The uterus was a 10 to 12-
52 week size and the adenexa were clear. No pap smear was performed at the time
53 of this initial visit. The hematocrit was 12.9 and the hemoglobin was 36.9.
54 The patient was immediately admitted to the hospital and underwent a D and C,
55 total hysterectomy-left salpingo-oophorectomy with a pre-operative diagnosis
56 of fibroid uterus. The path report of the specimen revealed
57 endometrial curettings-secretory endometrium, the uterus was 180 grams with
58 andenomyosis and a left corpus luteum cyst. Of particular note was the
59 incidental finding of infiltrating squamous cell carcinoma involving the
60 surgical margins that had been cut through. Two weeks later, the patient was
61 referred to the ______Cancer Center for further evaluation and treat-
62 ment. . . . This case was presented to demonstrate the need for systematic
63 evaluation of vaginal bleeding. This patient's prognosis may have been
64 compromised by cutting through the cervical tumor.

65 E.HISTORY (OB)DATE OF ADMISSION: 11/07/84
66 The patient is a 21-year-old Gravida III, Para I, Ab I black female at 32

67 weeks gestation, by her dates. She states that she has been having uterine
68 contractions every thirty minutes, beginning two days prior to admission.
69 The patient has a history of vaginal bleeding on 10/23, at which time she
70 reports she was seen in the ______ Emergency Room and sent home. Additionally,
71 she does state that there is fetal movement. She denies any rupture of
72 membranes. She states that she has a known history of sickle cell trait.
73 PAST MEDICAL HISTORY: Positive only for spontaneous abortion in 1980, at 12
74 weeks gestation. She has had no other surgeries. She denies any trauma.
75 She denies any allergies.
76 REVIEW OF SYSTEMS: Remarkable only for headaches in the morning. She denies
77 any dysuria, frequency, or urgency. She denies any vaginal discharge or
78 significant breast tenderness. HABITS: She denies tobacco, alcohol,
79 coffee, or tea. MEDICATIONS: She takes pre-natal vitamins daily.
80 FAMILY HISTORY: Positive for a mother with sickle cell anemia. It is
81 unknown whether she is still living. The patient also has a male child with
82 sickle cell trait. Family history, is otherwise, non-contributory.

NOTES

I would like to thank Jeanne Efferding, Kirsten Holm, Duane Alwin, Charles Bosk, James S. House, Deborah Keller-Cohen, John Myhill, Polly Phipps, Emmanuel Schegloff, and Howard Schuman for assistance with data analysis. Most significantly, I wish to thank Jane Sparer and Candace West for giving their time, their encouragement, and their ideas, and in so doing, making this paper possible.

1. A notable exception is Arluke's (1980) discussion of the social control functions of roundsmanship.
2. In contrast to the practice in psychiatry, this omission of names is not intended to protect the confidentiality of the patient, whose name is noted in the written summary.
3. Foucault's use of the term "clinical mentality" differs from Friedson's (1970) use of the term to describe an insular, defensive posture on the part of the physician.
4. According to the Whorf hypothesis, language structures, rather than merely reflects, perceptions of reality.

REFERENCES

Arluke, Arnold. 1978. "Roundsmanship: Inherent Control on a Medical Teaching Ward." *Social Science and Medicine* 14A:297–302.

Austin, J.L. *How to Do Things with Words.* Cambridge: Harvard University Press.

Becker, Howard S., Blanche Geer, Everett C. Hughes, and Anselm S. Strauss. 1961. *Boys in White.* Chicago: University of Chicago Press.

Beckman, Howard B. and Richard M. Frankel. 1984. "Effect of Patient Behavior on Collection of Data." *Annals of Internal Medicine* 102:520–28.

Bosk, Charles. 1979. *Forgive and Remember.* Chicago: University of Chicago Press.

Cicourel, Aaron V. 1981. "Notes on the Integration of Micro and Macro Levels of Analysis." Pp. 1–40 in *Advances in Social Theory and Methodology: Toward an Integration of Macro- and Micro-Sociologies,* edited by Karin Knorr-Cetina and Aaron Cicourel. London: Routledge and Kegan Paul.

———. 1983. "Language and the Structure of Belief in Medical Communication." Pp. 221–40 in *The Social Organization of Doctor-Patient Communication,* edited by Sue Fisher and Alexandra Dundas Todd. Washington, DC: Center for Applied Linguistics.

Coombs, Robert H. and Lawrence J. Goldman. 1973. "Maintenance and Discontinuity of Coping Mechanisms in an Intensive Care Unit." *Social Problems* 20:342–55.

Davis, Fred. 1963. *Passage through Crisis.* Indianapolis: Bobbs-Merrill.

Donnely, William J. 1986. "Medical Language as Symptom: Doctor Talk in Teaching Hospitals." *Perspectives in Biology and Medicine* 30.

Drass, Kris A. 1981. "The Social Organization of Mid-Level Provider-Patient Encounters." Ph.D. dissertation, Indiana University.

Emerson, Joan. 1970. "Behavior in Private Places: Sustaining Definitions of Reality in The Gynecological Exam." Pp. 74–97 in *Recent Sociology,* Vol. 2, edited by Hans Peter Dreitzel. New York: Macmillan.

Ervin-Tripp, Susan. 1971. "Sociolinguistics." Pp. 15–91 in *Advances in the Sociology of Language,* Vol. I, edited by Joshua Fishman. The Hague: Mouton.

Estival, Dominique and John Myhill. 1988. "Formal and Functional Aspects of the Development from Passive to Ergative Systems. Typological Studies in Language." Chapter in *Passive and Voice,* edited by

Masayoshi Shibatani. Amsterdam/Philadelphia: John Benjamins.

Fisher, Sue. 1979. "The Negotiation of Treatment Decisions in Doctor/Patient Communication and Their Impact on Identity of Women Patients." Ph.D. dissertation, University of California, San Diego.

Fisher, Sue and Stephen B. Groce. 1985. "Doctor-Patient Negotiation of Cultural Assumptions." *Sociology of Health and Illness* 7:72–85.

Foucault, Michel. 1975. *The Birth of the Clinic*. New York: Vintage.

Fox, Renée C. 1957. "Training for Uncertainty." Pp. 207–41 in *The Student Physician*, edited by Robert K. Merton, George G. Reader, and Patricia L. Kendall. Cambridge: Harvard University Press.

———. 1979. "The Human Condition of Health Professionals." Lecture, University of New Hampshire.

Fox, Renée C. and Harold I. Lief. 1963. "Training for Detached Concern in Medical Students." pp. 12–35 in *The Psychological Basis of Medical Practice*, edited by Harold Lief, Victor F. Lief, and Nina R. Lief. New York: Harper and Row.

Frader, Joel E. and Charles L. Bosk. 1981. "Parent Talk at Intensive Care Rounds." *Social Science and Medicine* 15E:267–74.

Frankel, Richard M. Forthcoming. "Talking in Interviews: A Dispreference for Patient-Initiated Questions in Physician-Patient Encounters." in *Interactional Competence*, edited by Richard Frankel. New York: Irvington.

Friedson, Eliot. 1970. *Profession of Medicine*. Chicago: Aldine.

Glaser, Barney and Anselm Strauss. 1965. *Awareness of Dying*. Chicago: Aldine.

Gusfield, Joseph. 1977. "The Literary Rhetoric of Science: Comedy and Pathos in Drinking Driver Research." *American Sociological Review* 41:16–34.

Korsch, B.M., E.K. Gozzi, and V. Francis. 1968. "Gaps in Doctor-Patient Communication: Doctor-Patient Interaction and Patient Satisfaction." *Pediatrics* 42:855–71.

Korsch, B.M. and V.F. Negrete. 1972. "Doctor-Patient Communication." *Scientific American* 227:66–74.

Lakoff, Robin. 1975. *Language and Woman's Place*. New York: Harper.

Leiderman, Deborah B. and Jean-Anne Grisso. 1985. "The Gomer Phenomenon." *Journal of Health and Social Behavior* 26:222–31.

Light, Donald. 1980. *Becoming Psychiatrists: The Professional Transformation of Self*. New York: Norton.

Lipton, Helene L. and Bonnie Svarstad. 1977. "Sources of Variation in Clinicians' Communication to Parents about Mental Retardation." *American Journal of Mental Deficiency* 82:155–61.

Millman, Marcia. 1977. *The Unkindest Cut*. New York: Morrow.

Mishler, Eliot. 1985. *The Discourse of Medicine*. New York: Ablex.

Mizrahi, Terry. 1984. "Coping with Patients: Subcultural Adjustments to the Conditions of Work among Internists-in-Training." *Social Problems* 32:156–65.

———. 1987. "Getting Rid of Patients: Contradictions in the Socialization of Internists to the Doctor-Patient Relationship." *Sociology of Health and Illness* 7:214–35.

Parsons, Talcott. 1951. *The Social System*. New York: Free Press.

Prince, Ellen F., Joel Frader, and Charles Bosk. "On Hedging in Physician-Physician Discourse." Pp. 83–96 in *Linguistics and the Professions; Proceedings of the Second Annual Delaware Symposium on Language Studies*, edited by Robert J. Di Pietro. Norwood, NJ: Ablex.

Reiser, Stanley. 1978. *Medicine and the Reign of Technology*. Cambridge: Cambridge University Press.

Schwartz, Howard D. 1987. *Dominant Issues in Medical Sociology*, 2nd ed. New York: Random House.

Scully, Diana. 1980. *Men Who Control Women's Health: The Miseducation of Obstetrician-Gynecologists*. Boston: Houghton Mifflin.

Sudnow, David. 1967. *Passing On*. Englewood Cliffs, NJ: Prentice-Hall.

Waitzkin, Howard. 1985. "Information Giving in Medical Care." *Journal of Health and Social Behavior* 26:81–101.

West, Candace. 1983. "Ask Me No Questions . . . An Analysis of Queries and Replies in Physician-Patient Dialogues." Pp. 75–106 in *The Social Organization of Doctor-Patient Communication*, edited by Sue Fisher and Alexandra Dundas Todd. Washington, DC: Center for Applied Linguistics.

32 ALTERNATIVE HEALTH AND THE CHALLENGES OF INSTITUTIONALIZATION

Matthew Schneirov and Jonathan David Geczik[1]

In this article we examine the relationship between two levels of power in the alternative health movement—the formal processes through which alternative health groups pressure for favorable legislation, and seek recognition, inclusion and professional status in the dominant health care system and, on the other hand, the social interactions of activists, practitioners, and patients in the "microsphere of the everyday communication." Social movements can be understood as existing in a tension between an institutional level, and what Melucci (1989, 1996) calls a movement's "submerged networks." In this arena, similar to what Habermas (1987: 113–99) calls the "lifeworld," there are flows of images, information and ideas that can be a source of creativity for a movement. Habermas in fact goes one step further and argues that learning processes occur in the lifeworld which then become in the modern world the source of institutional transformation. In this sense institutions cannot learn but are dependent for their innovation on learning capacities of everyday actors.

In light of Habermas's emphasis on everyday life as the source of innovation, the drying up of a movement's subcultural roots may be as detrimental to a movement as the failure to make itself visible through ongoing political action and through processes of institutionalization. However if a movement only exists as a submerged network the danger is marginalization. In other words, the movement loses touch with the institutional direction of society as a whole. This results in two consequences; the movement, through 'co-aptation' loses its capacity to challenge powerholders (Piven and Cloward, 1977), but, on the other hand, as isolated and marginal, it may develop conspiratorial fantasies and delusions about its own omnipotence. Therefore, we argue, the power of any moment requires a creative tension between its submerged and institutional dimensions. In short, it must become what we call a "dual movement."

As we have argued elsewhere (Schneirov and Geczik, 1996, 1998), alternative health (O'Connor, 1985; Fuller, 1989; Lowenberg, 1989; English-Hueck, 1990; Wolpe, 1990; McGuire, 1991; Frohock, 1992; Goldstein, 1999) can be conceptualized as a "new social movement." For the most part its goal has not been to change institutions but to create and sustain a form of life the lies outside of conventional codes and institutional arrangements; in organic farming, cooperative stores, study groups, health fairs, classes and lectures in which unconventional health information is shared. These and related activities do not require a high degree of solidarity in order to challenge elites or authorities but they are a significant source of new meanings and identities that may have important implications in the more conventionally political arena. We recognize that alternative health also exists in the more conventionally political realm—as professional associations, American Holistic Medical Association (AHMA), lobbying groups, and promotional organizations. These groups contest for resources, form coalitions, influence legislation, reform particular professions, fight for the existence of new professions and educate the public. But we argued that the strength of alternative health is that it has been able to create, through its "submerged networks" a cultural laboratory where patients and health activists can experience new authority

ACKNOWLEDGMENTS
Many thanks to the staff at the complementary medicine clinic who were enthusiastic about this project and gave us many hours of their time. Special thanks to Dr Lewis Madronna for generously allowing us to interview him over many weeks and in a number of locations. Also, thanks to Sharon Nepstad who read and commented on a version of the manuscript and to Duquesne University for supporting this research.

relations, new ideas and new identities that embody a critique of the health care system, medical expertise, the administrative state and consumer culture. The central goal in alternative health is to return to a more organic relationship with vernacular healing traditions and with communities—to reconnect health and illness to the life-world. (On new social movements see Habermas, 1981; Eder, 1982; Cohen, 1985; Larana et al., 1994; Buechler, 1995.)

METHODS AND CONCEPTS

This study of a complementary medicine clinic is part of a larger project in which we interviewed 60 alternative health patients, practitioners, and activists in two communities. The first community consists of the local food co-op, a meeting point for a range of people interested in alternative health. This community also consists of a group called Holistic Living Quest, a loosely organized collective which distributes a monthly newsletter for over 3000 people, informing them of events related to new age spirituality, alternative health care, progressive political causes including environmental issues and social justice concerns. In addition to this community, we studied two groups in a nearby suburb whose members are largely conservative Christians but are committed to alternative treatments for a range of chronic diseases. The Committee for Freedom of Choice in Cancer Treatment and the Natural Living Group meet monthly, offer speakers who explain unorthodox treatments and discuss alternative means for producing and distributing food. Both these communities can be conceived of as "submerged networks." Along with Melucci we conceive of submerged networks as consisting of face-to-face relations, embedded in everyday life and not openly engaged in political acts like demonstrations, sit-ins, petitioning, and the like. They are fragmented in the sense that diverse groups with common goals often have only tenuous relationships with one another and they are temporary in duration. Individuals move in and out of these networks, rather than being totally committed to them. Submerged networks may or may not break out into the political sphere, into open contestation and authorities. In this article we refer to the "new age" and conservative Christian communities we studied as "submerged networks." Along with others, we define "alternative health" as the substance of non-allopathic healing—an approach to healing that emphasizes illness as imbalance, treating the cause of the disease and not symptoms, illness as an opportunity for self-growth and self-discovery, the use of natural and non-pharmaceutical agents, an emphasis on mobilizing the innate healing capacities of the body, and promoting a more egalitarian relationship between patient and practitioner (Lowenberg, 1989: 15–52). We use the term "complementary medicine" to refer to the use of non-allopathic approaches to healing in a medical setting. We use the term "holistic" to refer to the way alternative health practices are understood philosophically.

ALTERNATIVE HEALTH'S INSTITUTIONALIZATION

We explore in this article the growing institutionalization of alternative health and how this bears on the capacity of alternative health to remain a dual movement. It has been approximately eight years since armed FDA agents raided Dr Jonathon Wright's clinic, then president of the National Health Federation and prominent holistic MD. They confiscated bags of vitamins but found no illegal substances. Also during this period the FDA proposed to regulate herbs and vitamins as drugs, a proposal that could not withstand the opposition of pro-alternative health congressmen, both republicans and democrats. At a National Health Federation (NHF) convention held a few years later, speaker after speaker spoke out against federal government repression of the alternative health community and saw this as an expression of an overly intrusive, if not repressive state. During this period there was a widely held suspicion, not only of the medical industrial complex—the close links between the medical profession, hospitals, pharmaceutical and health insurance companies—but of the administrative state which made the practice of alternative medicine by practitioners and patients difficult.

Much has changed in a relatively short period of time. David Eisenberg's now famous surveys (Eisenberg, 1993; Eisenberg et al., 1998) documented the widespread popularity of alternative health products and services and a recent update of this study demonstrates that patients spend well over US$27 billion a year on these products and services, almost all of which is out of pocket. In 1998, two national surveys found that 42 percent of American households had used some form of alternative therapy over the past year (Goldstein, 1999: 5). Largely positive media coverage has also contributed to and reflected this widespread interest. In addition the National Institutes of Health (NIH) created an Office of Alternative Medicine (now the National Center for Complementary and Alternative Medicine) which has a small but growing budget (over US$50 million) to research the effectiveness of non-conventional health modalities. Today, 64 percent of US medical schools have at least one course on alternative medicine (Wetzel, 1998), research institutes and schools specializing in non-allopathic approaches exist throughout the country, and health insurance companies are beginning to cover some alternative health protocols, especially for heart disease. In short, developments within the state and in the "medical industrial complex" have created new political and economic opportunities (Tarrow, 1994) for the alternative health movement to enhance its professional status and establish closer links to conventional medicine.

What are we to make of all of this? The answer seems simple. Alternative medicine is nowhere near as marginalized as it once was. Practitioners and health store owners fear the FDA less while they sell more of their products and services. Inroads in medical school curricula and new complementary medicine clinics create the potential for a mutual enrichment of both conventional and alternative medicine. But in light of the earlier analysis of alternative health's dual movement character, the stakes involved in the process of this growing institutionalization are complex. Is this success coming at the price of the vitality of alternative health's submerged networks and core identity? Is the health care system changing to accommodate the demands of a popular health movement or is the movement accommodating to the requirements of the system? If the former is the case then we have an instance of successful institutionalization. If the latter is the case the movement loses its creative base and dual character. (On the social control functions of holistic health see Kotarba, 1983.)

A good way to explore these issues is to look at what actually happens when holistic MDs and health care practitioners work within the institutional setting of biomedicine. What tensions exist within the alternative health community—between the holistic doctors and practitioners that work within more institutionalized settings and those who remain embedded in its submerged networks? In order to answer these questions we studied a complementary medicine clinic at a prominent hospital. These clinics are becoming quite common throughout the country and are an ideal setting in which to examine the question of the compatibility of alternative medicine and the dominant health care system. Clinic directors as well as doctors and practitioners associated with these clinics must engage in a delicate balance between preserving the core of alternative or "complementary" medicine but also accommodating to the institutional demands of hospitals—the core of the conventional health care system. The clinic in Pittsburgh exists in the largest hospital chain in the city and one of the largest in the country. All of the features of modern medicine against which alternative health has organized can be found there—highly specialized medical expertise, sophisticated medical technology, and complex bureaucratic rules and procedures and the pressure to generate income.

THE COMPLEMENTARY MEDICINE CLINIC

In the spring of 1997 a nurse practitioner with the help of another nurse who had already been practicing therapeutic touch at the hospital, a sympathetic psychiatrist and a few others approached the chief of the department of medicine with a proposal to form a complementary medicine clinic. These clinics were already in place in many hospitals and the Eisenberg article (1993) had given alternative medicine some degree of legitimacy. With some in-house funding and the fortuitous hiring of a prominent holistic physician from another city, the clinic opened a year later. In addition, members of the hospital's board of directors supported the clinic because of personal experiences with alternative medicine.

The clinic now occupies a suite of offices where three holistic physicians, one psychiatrist and 15 practitioners offer patients a wide range of alternative health therapies—natural remedies like botanical medicine, naturopathic counseling, and nutritional medicine; mind–body approaches like biofeedback, EMDR (eye movement desensitization and reprocessing), relaxation therapies, and guided imagery; and finally bodywork therapies like acupuncture, shiatsu, and therapeutic massage. All the practitioners are licensed by the state as this is a requirement for work in the clinic. The clinic also offers wellness classes in yoga, therapeutic touch, massage therapy, and meditation. Patients are required to have a physician referral to obtain any of the health services at the clinic. Since there are three MDs on the staff this is not a problem although the fact that few patients come with a referral from their own doctors is significant. In all likelihood this requirement was instituted to protect the hospital from potential legal action and to enhance the clinic's legitimacy with patients and the larger community. In addition, any new therapy that a practitioner or MD wants to introduce must be approved by a review board and the clinic's steering committee meets with the board on a weekly basis. Hardly any patient has insurance coverage so that payments are out of pocket.

Interviews with the administrative, program and medical directors of the center shed some light on the motivations of the hospital for agreeing to open the clinic but this is still shrouded in mystery. While cautioning us that she was not "privy to the inner thoughts of the administration," the clinical director believes that the clinic creates a "warm and fuzzy feeling" for the hospital, and can provide the hospital with some positive publicity. At any rate, the work done at the clinic is thought to be "harmless." At the same time, the clinic is under increasing pressure to produce academically credible research to justify their clinical practices and to prove to the business side of the hospital that the clinic can be financially stable and self-sufficient within a few years.

The medical director sees the origins of the center as an accident; there were people "with vision" who had an influence on the hospital administration who then "let it happen" without really understanding what they were doing. After it started, the clinic grew in terms of public awareness, patients treated and the number of practitioners employed by the clinic so that now it has become "sort of an embarrassing baby to take care of but you couldn't drop it at this point." Why are complementary medicine clinics opening throughout the country? The medical director believes that there is a lot of NIH research money available (US$60 million) and to get a piece of this you need patients and a clinic which will attract them so that you can establish research protocols. The other is a marketing motivation. The hope is that through advertising their complementary clinics, hospitals can appeal to a wider segment of the medical market.

According to an internal study of clinic patients, 75 percent are women between 45 and 60, and 5 percent racial minorities. Patients tend to be middle to upper middle class since treatments are not covered by insurance. Most patients suffer from chronic illnesses that do not respond well to conventional medicine. Fifteen percent of patients suffer from arthritis, 15 percent from migraines, 10 percent from cancer, 8 percent from heart disease, 13 percent from depression and anxiety and another 13 percent from irritable bowel and other intestinal disorders. All of these problems, according to the medical director "have a huge mental component."

Beyond this demographic and medical profile, it appears that patients who come to the clinic have one of two approaches to conventional medicine. They have either exhausted the therapies offered by conventional medicine (usually chronic pain and terminally ill patients) and are coming to the clinic as a last resort or "want the best of both worlds." These patients, who are often oncology patients who have just been diagnosed are well educated about alternative cancer treatments and are trying to devise a treatment regime that will combine chemotherapy and alternative approaches which emphasize building up the immune system.

THE PATIENT–PRACTITIONER RELATIONSHIP AT THE CLINIC

To what extent is the patient–practitioner relationship at the clinic a departure from the dominant model? The approach of the clinic to their patients is somewhat pragmatic. They have a range of innovative programs, which are available for patients who are comfortable with approaches that depart from the medical model. But at the same time they are willing to provide alternative treatments that do not require a lot of time and patient effort. As one clinic practitioner put it:

> Some patients come here at different levels so you have to approach them on their level. Some just want a pill you know . . . something that you do and it should have an outcome frequently. It's not a transformative process for them. And that's fine. We do that. But the people who want to go beyond that, we introduce them to people who will help them go on in that direction.

The medical director of the clinic, though, is uncomfortable with the tendency to "give patients what they want" even while recognizing the economic pressures to process patients. He worries that

> it would be very easy to corrupt alternative practitioners and the way it would happen is that what will be squeezed out is the part that takes time. One of the most important is mind–body medicine. It doesn't happen in a ten minute visit. But some things can happen quickly like acupuncture needles—you can have fifteen rooms and we have practitioners who do that. You can sell supplements and herbs without any interaction with a patient just like you'd prescribe medicine. These are the approaches which will actually take over.

While these pressures exist, the practitioner–patient relationship does depart from the dominant model in a number of ways. All three directors of the clinic commented on something they called the "patient culture" or the "waiting room culture." One practitioner saw this as the key to the success of the clinic.

> When people enter here they enter a culture and we might try one intervention but that's not what really changes people, it's that they now have entered a culture and they talk to other people and suddenly have a whole window on a new world and they start entering that world and trying different things and it's that experience that ultimately leads people into a healing path. Which door they go through is really not that important, whether they try message or acupuncture or biofeedback or whatever. Once they buy into it they evolve and that's the process that brings upon a transformation.

The clinic has a range of patient programs that go well beyond the one-on-one encounter of doctor and patient found in biomedicine. For example, the clinic runs an asthma study group where patients practice meditation or guided imagery and talk to one another about various aspects of complementary medicine that seem to work for them. So it is not clear when they do show improvement whether it is the meditation or guided imagery or all the other modalities they have been exposed to in this group setting. Moreover, the social support and encouragement received from other patients may also have a therapeutic effect.

Here is certainly a process that departs from the medical model of the doctor as expert and the patient as a diseased body occupying a "sick role." Moreover it is hard to imagine a patient culture in conventional medicine, at least not the type described here. Other doctors and practitioners described a similar process. One used the word "synergy" to account for the way patients learn from one another and then incorporate more alternative therapies into their lives. Needless to say, in this environment, when there are results, it is hard to isolate one factor that is responsible.

One of the more innovative programs at the center is something called a "healing intensive." The former program director, a Native American physician who combines elements of conventional medicine with traditional Native American healing approaches, is the originator of this program. In the healing intensive, patients undergo an intensive experience modeled after Native American healing rituals and philosophies. Patients receive two to seven hours per day of therapeutic attention including journal writing and discussion of what they have written, group discussions with other patients, hypnosis, body therapy, acupuncture, therapeutic touch, cognitive-behavioral therapy, family therapy, projective techniques including the use of Native American images, shields or animal images and ceremony. The intensive concludes on the seventh evening with a sweat lodge ceremony. All throughout this process patients receive guidance from mentors and coaches who "help them to focus on themselves and have a spiritual journey." Patients who participate in the healing intensive stay for a week-long period in a nearby hotel and undergo various therapies in the clinic. The sweat lodge ceremony, though, is held outside the clinic.

Clearly this approach is not for everyone but for those who have experienced it the clinic has received rave reviews. Patients leave the week-long process feeling like their "illness was a teacher" and experiencing fewer symptoms and reduced pain. A number of terminally ill cancer patients experienced a full remission of their cancer. One of these patients wrote about her experiences in a recent *Ladies Home Journal* article.

While none of the 105 patients who have been through a healing intensive complained, the program director who started this program has come under attack from a number of physicians in the hospital—in part because of these healing intensives and their use of Native American ceremonies. The program director has resigned under pressure, despite the fact that it was his reputation and innovative programming that resulted in the growth of the clinic. Currently, according to Jane Dufield (*Pittsburgh Post-Gazette*), a spokeswoman for the hospital, "the investigation into all aspects of alternative medicine [at the hospital] is continuing. Until the study is complete, [the hospital] can't specifically say what the future holds for the [complementary medicine clinic]."

It appears that fundamentally challenging the dominant medical model has its costs. Despite internal records that show that 65 percent of clinic patients report a significant improvement in their condition after treatment at the center, and despite mounting scientific evidence for mind–body effects in illness and healing (Goldstein, 1999: 13–39), opposition to the center from physicians remains strong. Yet pressures come from patients as well, although of a very different kind. One holistic doctor at the clinic remarked with a little tongue in cheek that patients are too assertive and knowledgeable. That is irritating

> because they are telling you what the treatment should be and you feel a little straightjacketed. Sometimes that's not good because you're the doctor. They do need expert advice. It's good for them to be informed and ask questions but they should be open to getting help from another human being. Sometimes we're [the doctors] the ones who feel like machines.

So some practitioners at the clinic feel pulled between the hospital who would like them to adopt a conventional model of medical expertise and stay away from controversial approaches that involve patients, and their more knowledgeable patients who challenge any notion of medical expertise. . . .

THE SUBMERGED NETWORKS AND THE CLINIC

The biographical consequences for doctors and practitioners who work in this setting departs somewhat from the typical pattern you find among practitioners in the submerged networks—most of whom have their own practice or own their own stores. Most of the practitioners we interviewed (1996) who have their own practice described their entry into alternative medicine as something similar to a religious conversion experience. Many were disenchanted with former careers, had experienced divorces, were victims of domestic violence, or had serious illnesses themselves. Alternative medicine represented a new way of living and for practitioners a career that offered a significant amount of autonomy and creativity. But for the physicians and practitioners at the clinic we heard a different story. The administrative director, a nurse practitioner, said that there is a delicate balance between maintaining a holistic lifestyle and keeping up with the stresses and pressures of working in the clinic. In other words, she said, it is difficult at the clinic to practice what you preach. Work-related stress is common among professionals but most alternative health practitioners we interviewed outside the clinic saw their work as integrated in a balanced way into their lives. Typically their entry into alternative medicine was an escape from a former lifestyle that sacrificed health and personal growth to career development.

We also wanted to find out how practitioners at the clinic related to the broader alternative health subculture and what members of the subculture thought of the clinic. We tried contacting people—both alternative health practitioners, activists and patients we had interviewed over the past few years and their responses were mixed. Many saw the clinic as evidence of alternative health's success and were proud of this achievement. But at the same time many were skeptical that alternative medicine could flourish in this setting. Among the proponents of cleansing regimes using herbs, minerals and natural foods the view is that conventional drug-based therapy is fundamentally incompatible with their purposes. In fact the goal of "detoxification" is to in part remove the effects of drugs. In this corner of the alternative health subculture, there is no way for alternative and conventional medicine to coexist.

Among the practitioners in the clinic there was an ambivalent stance toward the broader subculture. The program director at the clinic characterized alternative health activists as "groupie types" and thought that most patients at the clinic had little association with the subculture although they were quite knowledgeable about alternative health approaches to their own illnesses. The "waiting room" and patient culture she described at the clinic seemed to be something quite distinct from the broader subculture of co-op shopping, lectures, study groups, health fairs, cooking classes, and the like. On the other hand, one of the holistic physicians who practices at the clinic also has an office with two massage therapists in a nearby neighborhood. Her identity is more closely associated with ongoing alternative health activities in the local area. She is skeptical about the long-term viability of the clinic because of all the obstacles the hospital administration is placing in its path.

While the analysis presented here points to serious problems of incorporating alternative medicine into a hospital setting, a number of practitioners and holistic physicians told us there are advantages. The chief one is the discipline of having to explain and justify yourself to people who review what you are doing. While quite frustrating at times, the medical director considers it a "healthy process." Record keeping, clinical research, the credentializing and licensing process for practitioners gives the clinic credibility with patients and makes it possible for the clinic leadership to learn from past practices. This systematic learning process as well as the collaboration between a wide range of practitioners and physicians has resulted is some innovative programs—primarily the use of study groups, and healing intensives which incorporate social support, information sharing, and various therapeutic interventions into a comprehensive holistic approach to treating chronic disease. The hospital setting itself gives alternative medicine credibility and there is a subgroup of clinic patients who would not have seen an alternative practitioner outside of this setting.

A CLINIC PATIENT

In order to illustrate the benefits and liabilities of institutionalization we present one example of a patient who spent a considerable amount of time at the clinic. She is representative of clinic patients in terms of gender, age, and level of education. Moreover, her condition, "multiple chemical sensitivity" is a problem that is difficult for conventional medicine to treat which is typical for the larger group of clinic patients.

Aime Bartell describes her condition prior to her trip to Greece in 1993 as "high energy, and in good health" which supported a "high achieving" career and lifestyle. In Greece she was exposed to high levels of air pollution and on a nearby island to high levels of silicon from the sand. Upon her return her office was in the process of being renovated. These three "toxic" exposures sparked a serious allergic reaction. As she put it, "I got allergies to everything." As a result she experienced continuous "migraine headaches." This connection, however, between her headaches and these three toxic exposures came from her holistic physician Dr Madronna who diagnosed her illness as "multiple chemical sensitivity" (conventional medicine rejects this diagnostic category as did Aime's allergist). At work in order to function she had to hold an ice pack on her head continuously. She worked with small children and they got used to seeing her with the ice pack and would laugh and say "Mrs Bartell has a headache today, can I feel your ice pack?"

Her treatment began with an allergist who gave her a series of shots. She then saw a neurologist who prescribed pain medications all the while giving her Magnetic Resonance Imaging (MRIs) and CT scans to determine the cause of her condition. She also saw a psychologist who taught her biofeedback and other pain relief techniques. Eventually she entered a pain clinic in another city where "stronger medicine" was prescribed. Despite all of these efforts, "the more medicine I took the sicker I got." Finally, her allergist, exasperated at his lack of success, told her about a "Native American" doctor who worked at the complementary medicine clinic. While undergoing conventional medical treatment she described herself as a "highly motivated patient" who would "stand on her head, if told by her doctors." Therefore, she listened to her allergist's advice and visited the clinic.

At the clinic she met Dr Madronna who thought that since Aime had undergone all conventional treatment without success and the tests did not show any known biochemical cause, she was a good candidate for a healing intensive. She was excited to get started because she looked forward to getting off all her medications, especially after reading about their toxic effect on the liver and kidneys. But, what caused her some anxiety about this entire process is that elements of it contradict her own Christian religious background. Beyond her religious traditionalism, her family was also conventional in most other ways, so there was little preparation for this experience. As a "devout Christian" the thought of going through a sweat lodge, "blew my mind" and "I thought to myself: how did my allergist get me into this situation?." She did not participate in the sweat lodge because it "was not for her" but recognized its potential value for others.

But nevertheless, out of curiosity and desperation she went through with the overall healing intensive. She stayed at a local hotel, did not watch TV and went to the clinic eight hours a day for an entire week. Each day she would see a range of practitioners and physicians who introduced her to a variety of modalities including, guided imagery, stories and folk tales for therapeutic purposes, relaxation techniques and acupuncture, massage, yoga, Eye Movement Desensitization and Reprocessing (EMDR), and cognitive restructuring to help her handle stress. She had participated in group events where stories were told and people reacted to the stories in terms of their own experiences and medical condition. She found this helpful because she realized she was not alone in experiencing severe pain and that these people grew to care about her. She learned, among other things, "that I have some control over the pain because they taught me techniques that allowed me to raise or lower the pain."

What really made a difference was the intravenous vitamin treatments she received. This treatment was classified as "experimental" and the clinic had to get approval from the hospital. Dr Madronna initially wanted to administer higher dosages but this was rejected. Nevertheless, Aime made rapid progress after receiving this treatment. She kept a "pain journal" in which she would classify the level of pain each day through the use of colors and numbers and then would write about her experiences. During 1998, the year she started at the clinic, her "bad days" in terms of pain fell dramatically so that by December 1998, 27 out of 31 days were described as low and tolerable levels of pain. Aime got the idea of writing a journal from Dr Madronna's Native American stories. She still calls upon many of the images (in this case snakes, a blue mountain that embodies the destination of health among other things) that were suggested in these stories to help her make sense of her illness and give her hope for recovery. In her pain journal, she draws pictures to illustrate her daily experiences and comments on these pictures.

Dr Madronna diagnosed her illness as multiple chemical sensitivity. This was discovered when she went into shock from an antibiotic treatment for bronchitis and received high dosages of steroids which surprisingly eliminated her "migraine headaches." Dr Madronna realized that steroids are not an effective treatment for migraines and therefore her problem must be elsewhere. This led to her successful treatment by intravenous vitamins. Her allergist, nevertheless, resisted this diagnosis as a "faddish" product of a California subculture (Dr Madronna is from California). This collision between the world of alternative and conventional medicine caused her much distress and anxiety since she wished to maintain access to both. She, therefore, wanted both doctors to talk it through and work it out with each other which they eventually did. Eventually, her allergist admitted that her improvement was remarkable but could not explain it. Unfortunately, since undergoing alternative treatment she had to pay out of pocket, a considerable cost. This has forced her to cut back on her treatment and her condition has not continued to improve as dramatically.

Aime came to understand that the severity of her condition was chemically induced but made worse by her behavioral patterns of denial and avoidance—engaging in palliatives like the use of ice packs, and continuing to work even with severe pain. Even more fundamentally, she feels she has changed tremendously. She used to be "a work horse" and tried to please people, exhausting herself in the process and in her words she "lost sight of who I was." Her attitude toward her illness was "this is not going to beat me." Her father had been critically ill and she was taking on all the responsibility for his care. She realized from the healing intensive that it took too much energy to be the stoic person she used to be. Now she finds to easier to ask for help, to say no and rely on other people. She told her brother that she needed help to care for her father and would not do it alone any more. In her own words, she would "no longer be a doormat for her family and their demands." Her experience at the clinic has helped her to come to terms with her fear of death, her own and her parents, so that she could be with her father when he passed away. Family members, in a half-joking way, attributed her new self to the corrupting influence of alternative medicine.

She also valued her experience of being "a partner" with her physician which allowed her to reflect on her life and make appropriate changes. Through her journal (she has completed her seventh) she could share her thought patterns with her holistic physicians and from this they could devise treatment regimes. She has sent videotapes and articles about alternative medicine to her allergist hoping to educate him but to no avail thus far. She has also experimented with different diets and food regimes although she has found it difficult to sustain her commitment in this respect. In response to Dr Madronna's somewhat forced departure from the hospital, she wrote a letter to the editor protesting his firing and said, "how could they take away someone who has done so much good for so many peopel?." She was quite upset about Dr Madronna's departure.

For Aime and other patients we interviewed, it is not likely that she would have ever seen an alternative practitioner if it were not for the complementary medicine clinic's official connection to a hospital. This gave the clinic an imprimatur of legitimacy and scientific standing. It appears that for other patients as well, their willingness to see a practitioner at the clinic rather than a practitioner in one of the submerged networks was because clinic practitioners were part of the hospital setting and therefore soothed the anxieties of patients not familiar with alternative health.

In addition, this also made it easier for doctors at the hospital to refer patients to the clinic. The setting also allows for collaboration between alternative practitioners so that patients may be treated more holistically. For example, Aime said that during her week-long healing intensive she saw many practitioners during each day, each practitioner with a different modality and all in consultation with one another. Moreover, the setting also allows for conventional and holistic physicians and practitioners to discuss and even debate their respective protocols. This institutional proximity between alternative and conventional medicine may also work to the benefit of conventional medicine in that doctors will be exposed and perhaps may be more willing to accept information and protocols that come out of a different setting. After all, patients at the clinic typically suffer from a range of chronic diseases and have had limited success with conventional doctors. If alternative protocols allow some patients to find relief from symptoms then this information may be of interest to doctors and provide a motive to expand the range of his or her treatments. The fact that complementary medicine clinics are asked to engage in institutional research and keep track of their patients and the efficacy of their interventions makes it possible to provide arguments for extending health care insurance to alternative medical treatments.

The problem with the institutional setting, as stated earlier, is that alternative therapies may be limited in the degree of experimentation and innovation because of the requirement of constant review by the hospital and the research methodologies that they impose. For example, Dr Madronna wanted to increase Aime's intravenous dosage of vitamins but was prevented from doing so by the hospital board. More significantly, Dr Madronna who was largely responsible for the popularity and innovative programs at the clinic was forced to leave because of some of his unorthodox techniques like the use of intravenous vitamins, the healing intensive and the sweat lodge. The very fact that there is such a highly visible institutional setting makes alternative medicine a target for being labeled 'quacks' by groups and organizations that are out to impose their view of what science and proper medicine are. Perhaps, what was discussed earlier as an advantage of institutionalization can also be seen from another perspective as a problem. Patients who could find more innovative and aggressive treatments in the larger submerged networks of alternative health may or may not be willing to utilize this resource because of the existence of an alternative health setting with more legitimacy. For example, Aime and most other patients at the clinic, despite their largely positive experiences have had limited contact with the larger alternative health community. They may come to define alternative health as synonymous with the complementary medicine clinic. Aime has become a booster for the clinic because of their successful treatment of her condition but this has not translated, at this point, into becoming an alternative health activist.

Finally, the very label of the clinic as "complementary" may provide the justification for keeping alternative medicine in its place—as if it were as something secondary and even peripheral to the core practice of medicine. For example, another patient was only referred to the clinic after surgery, nerve blocks and physical therapy failed and, as a result, this patient became angry and blamed her doctors. The hope may have been that the clinic would provide a psychological palliative that would diffuse her anger and possibly avert potential legal action. Clearly the physical interventions of biomedicine in this view are seen as primary while alternative medicine becomes akin to the work of religion, providing consolation and therapeutic support.

CONCLUSION

Hospital-based complementary medicine clinics are only one way in which alternative medicine is establishing closer links to the medical profession and dominant or conventional health care system. Alternative health activists across the country are seeking recognition from insurance companies for their protocols, are establishing "integrative" medicine clinics with sympathetic physicians, are pooling their own resources to form alternative Health Maintenance Organizations (HMOs), and in the process may be redefining their collective identity and redrawing old boundaries. But, we have suggested in this article, "integration" or institutionalization must be evaluated not solely in terms of the result, the extent to which alternative health groups achieve the official recognition many of them desire, but additionally, in terms of what is gained or lost in the process. How institutionalization is achieved may be as important as whether it is achieved.

It is not hard to understand some of the reasons why health insurance companies and hospitals are looking more favorably at alternative medicine. The cost-cutting drive of HMOs fits nicely into alternative medicine's emphasis on low-tech treatments and prevention. Hospitals, in a more competitive health care market, may see alternative medicine as a useful "warm and fuzzy" face that could attract a segment of the market and an opportunity to get a piece of government research funding. On the other hand, the source of opposition to incorporating elements of alternative medicine into the dominant health care system seems to be coming from some segments of the medical profession. For the first time since the establishment of the hegemony of the medical profession in the early 20th century (Starr, 1982), doctors feel threatened by the spread of the corporate model of organization into medicine. The fear that their professional autonomy and earnings may be seriously jeopardized may result in a heightened sensitivity to the threat from alternative medicine. Here, the threat is not so much to professional autonomy but to scientific legitimacy. Physicians who are organizing against the complementary medicine clinic argue that there is no solid scientific evidence to support the clinic's approaches. This critique, as discussed earlier, is somewhat disingenuous considering the fact that much evidence already exists of the efficacy of mind–body approaches and there are legitimate questions about the appropriate scientific model to use in doing clinical research. Nevertheless, this critique is an effective strategy for conservative forces within the medical profession to fight off a weaker adversary (JAMA, 1998). It is interesting, in this respect, that support for the clinic comes from a number of prominent members of the board as well as a core of enthusiastic patients.

The practitioners and directors of the complementary medicine clinic are keenly aware that their continued existence is precarious. Like any other bureaucracy the hospital must evaluate the success of each subdivision or department. The problem, though, is that the hospital's standards of efficacy and the clinic's are not compatible. Processing patients through the clinic would require shortening the time patients spend with holistic physicians and practitioners so it is not likely the clinic can pay its own way without sacrificing its mission. Demonstrating the effectiveness of its treatments through the use of double blind randomized studies also runs counter to the holistic emphasis in alternative medicine—the synergy of patient empowerment, individualized treatment regimes and multiple modalities.

In alternative health, faith that alternative medicine is the wave of the future is nearly universal. Much of this faith is grounded in a naïve view that the truth will inevitably triumph and that change occurs in a simple way—from lifeworld to institutions. In other words, as people change the way they think about health and illness, institutions will inevitably follow. But there is another, more limiting, possibility. Only those elements of alternative medicine that are consistent with the health care institutions' commodified, bureaucratic and "scientific" form will be incorporated.

A possible scenario is that more and more people will buy herbs, minerals, and vitamins, and pharmaceutical companies will find a way to profit from this. Complementary medicine clinics, if they are to continue, will focus on profit-making services, like acupuncture, massage and prescribing herbs and vitamins. Alternative health promoters will make more money on books, courses, and services. HMOs will find ways to incorporate elements of alternative medicine that they believe will reduce health care costs. Alternative health practitioners in their continuing efforts to enhance their credentials and status will adopt the model of expertise modeled after the medical system whereby the doctor is the expert and monopolizes medical information. And finally, alternative modalities that are the least holistic are likely to be the only ones to survive the rigors of biomedical research. Branches of alternative medicine that exhibit a fundamental incompatibility with conventional medicine will be marginalized. In other words, alternative health will become absorbed into market relations and structures of bureaucratic power.

The danger here is that alternative health activists will get caught up in this process of institutionalization and as a result lose their movement character as a kind of anarchic flow of information, remedies, and modalities which are potentially innovative, pathbreaking and at times dangerous. In any social movement, as we have mentioned, there is a dialectic between the more institutionalized segments and their "submerged networks." The more the institutionalized segments dominate, the greater the danger of the drying up of creativity and innovation that are rooted in the flows of interaction in the lifeworld. An excess of creativity may result from the other type of imbalance, when non-institutionalized segments dominate. Here a wide range of approaches to health and illness may blossom but the achievement of an ongoing collaboration among practitioners and patients as well as a systematic learning process is problematic. The opportunities for hucksterism (miracle cures), scams and wild conspiratorial theories may blossom under these conditions.

While we have argued that alternative health must remain a dual movement, the power of the movement in the final analysis rests upon the fact that it is embedded in the practices of the lifeworld. It is that level that provides spaces for innovation, and models of interaction that are non-bureaucratic and non-commodified, in other words the basis for a value shift. This value shift creates the potential for translation into institutional and policy changes.

NOTE

1. Jonathan David Geczik died suddenly of a heart attack on 24 September 2001. John was an accomplished teacher, scholar and poet. He spent much of the last seven years writing about the alternative health movement, which was one of his passions. His many friends will miss his passion for life and learning.

REFERENCES

Buechler, Steven M. (1995). New social movement theories. *The Sociological Quarterly,* 36, 441–64.

Cohen, Jean L. (1985). Strategy or identity: New theoretical paradigms and contemporary social movements. *Social Research,* 52, 663–716.

Eder, Klaus. (1982). A new social movement? *Telos,* 52, 5–20.

Eisenberg, David. (1993). Unconventional medicine in the United States. *New England Journal of Medicine,* 328, 246–52.

Eisenberg, David, Davis, R.B., Ettner, S.L., Appel, S., Wilkey, S., Van Rompay, M. and Kessler, R.C. (1998). Trends in alternative medicine use in the United States, 1990–1997: Results of a follow-up national survey. *The Journal of the American Medical Association,* 280, 1569–75.

English-Hueck, J.A. (1990). *Health in the new age: A study in California holistic practices.* Albuquerque: University of New Mexico Press.

Frohock, Fred M. (1992). *Healing powers: Alternative medicine, spiritual communities, and the state.* Chicago, IL: University of Chicago Press.

Fuller, Robert C. (1989). *Alternative medicine and American religious life.* New York: Oxford University Press.

Goldstein, Michael S. (1999). *Alternative health: Medicine, miracle or mirage?* Philadelphia, PA: Temple University Press.

Habermas, Jurgen. (1981). New social movements. *Telos,* 49, 33–7.

Habermas, Jurgen. (1987). *The theory of communicative action, vol. 2.* Cambridge, MA: MIT Press.

JAMA Editorial. (1998). Learning from the past, examining the present, advancing to the future. *JAMA,* 280, 1615–18.

Kotarba, Joseph A. (1983). Social control function of holistic health care in bureaucratic settings. *Journal of Health and Social Behavior,* 24, 275–88.

Larana, Enrique, Johnston, Hank and Gusfield, Joseph, Eds. (1994). *New social movements: From ideology to identity.* Philadelphia, PA: Temple University Press.

Lowenberg, June S. (1989). *Caring and responsibility: The crossroads between holistic practice and traditional medicine.* Philadelphia, PA: Temple University Press.

McGuire, Meredith B. (1991). *Ritual healing in suburban America.* New Brunswick, NJ: Rutgers University Press.

Melucci, Alberto. (1989). *Nomads of the present.* Philadelphia, PA: Temple University Press.

Melucci, Alberto. (1996). *Challenging codes: Collective action in the information age.* Cambridge: Cambridge University Press.

O'Connor, Bonnie Blair. (1985). *Healing traditions: Alternative medicine and the health professions.* Philadelphia, PA: University of Pennsylvania Press.

Piven, Frances Fox and Cloward, Richard. (1977). *Poor people's movements: Why they succeed and how they fail.* New York: Random House.

Schneirov, Matthew and Geczik, Jonathan David. (1996). A diagnosis for our times: Alternative health's submerged networks and the transformation of identities. *The Sociological Quarterly,* 37, 627–44.

Schneirov, Matthew and Geczik, Jonathan David. (1998). Technologies of the self and the aesthetic project of alternative health. *The Sociological Quarterly,* 39, 435–51.

Starr, Paul. (1982). *The social transformation of American medicine.* New York: Basic Books.

Tarrow, Sidney. (1994). *Power in movement: Social movements, collective action and politics.* Cambridge: Cambridge University Press.

Wetzel, Miriam S. (1998). Courses involving complementary and alternative medicine at US medical schools. *JAMA,* 280, 784–7.

Wolpe, P.R. (1990). The holistic heresy: Strategies of ideological challenge in the medical profession. *Social Science & Medicine,* 31, 913–23.

Dilemmas of Medical Technology

Medical technology exemplifies both the promise and the pitfalls of modern medicine. Medical history is replete with technological interventions that have reduced suffering or delayed death. Much of the success of modern medicine, from diagnostic tests to heroic life-saving individual interventions, has its basis in medical technology. For example, new imaging techniques, including CT scans, MRI (magnetic resonance imaging) machines, and ultrasound devices allow physicians to "see" body interiors without piercing the skin; powerful antibiotics and protective vaccinations have reduced the devastation of formerly dreaded diseases; and developments in modern anesthesia, lasers, and technical life-support have made previously unthinkable innovations in surgery possible. Technology has been one of the foundations of the advancement of medicine and the improvement of health and medical care (cf. Timmermans, 2000).

But along with therapeutic and preventive successes, various medical technologies have created new problems and dilemmas. There are numerous recent examples. Respirators are integral to the modern medical armamentarium. They have aided medical treatment of respiratory, cardiac, and neurological conditions and extended anesthetic capabilities, which in turn have promoted more sophisticated surgical interventions. Yet, they have also created a new situation where critically injured or terminally ill persons are "maintained" on machines long after the brain-controlled spontaneous ability to breathe has ceased. These "extraordinary" life-support measures have produced ethical, legal, political, and medical dilemmas that have only been partially resolved by new definitions of death (Zussman, 1992). The technology around neonatal infant care has allowed premature babies less than 500 grams to survive, but has created new problems: great financial burdens (often over $250,000) and the babies' ultimate outcome. While some such babies go on to live a normal life, many die, and others survive with significant and costly disabilities (Guillemin and Holmstrom, 1986). Parental and staff decisions regarding these tiny neonates are often difficult and painful (Anspach, 1987). One tragic example of medical technology is DES (diethylstilbestrol), a synthetic estrogen prescribed to millions of pregnant women up until the 1970s to prevent miscarriages. DES turned out not only to be ineffective but years later to cause cancer and other reproductive disorders in the daughters of the women who took the drug (Bell, 1986; Dutton, 1988).

Perhaps the most interesting example of a recent technological intervention is the case of end-stage renal disease (ESRD), or chronic kidney failure. Before the development of dialysis (an artificial kidney machine) and kidney transplantation, kidney failure was a death warrant. For sufferers of renal failure, these medical technologies are life-saving or at least life-extending. The dialysis machine, for all of its limitations, was probably the most successful of the first generation of artificial organs. Dialysis was expensive, and the choice of who would receive this life-saving intervention was so difficult that the federal government passed a special law in 1972 to include dialysis coverage under Medicare. The number of patients involved and the costs of dialysis have far exceeded what legislators expected: By the middle 1980s, over $2 billion a year is spent on treating a disease that affects 70,000 people (Plough, 1986). The prevalence of ESRD doubled in the 1990s, with total costs estimated to exceed $16.5 billion by 2002 (Ploth et al., 2003). Given the cost containment initiatives that dominate health policy, it is unlikely that any other disease will be specifically funded in the same way.

The issues raised by dialysis treatment are profound. Before federal funding was available, the issue of who should receive treatment was critical and difficult. How should limited resources be allocated? Who would decide and on what grounds (social worth, ability to pay)? Despite the greater availability of funds, important questions remain. Is it economically reasonable to spend billions of dollars on such a relatively small number of patients? Is this an effective way to spend our health dollars? Can we, as a society with spiraling health costs, make this type of investment in every new medical technology? For example, if an artificial heart were ever perfected, would we make it available to all the 100,000 patients a year who might benefit from such a device? With the heart perhaps costing (at $50,000 each) up to $500 billion a year, who would pay for it? Beyond the economic issues is the quality of extended life. Dialysis patients must go three times a week for six- to eight-hour treatments, which means relatively few patients can work a conventional schedule (Kutner, 1987). Quality-of-life issues are paramount, with many patients suffering social and psychological problems; their suicide rate is six times the normal rate. Finally, a large percentage of the dialysis treatment facilities in the United States are owned by profit-making businesses, thus raising the question of how much commercialization should exist in medical care and whether companies should make large profits from medical treatment (Relman and Rennie, 1980; Plough, 1986).

While many social issues surround medical technology, two are particularly important (see also Timmermans, 2002). The first concerns our great faith in technological expertise and the general medical belief in "doing whatever can be done" for the sick and dying, which has created a "can do, should do" ethic. That is, if we can provide some type of medical intervention—something that would keep an individual alive—we ought to do it no matter what the person's circumstances are or how old or infirm he or she may be. This results in increasing the amount of marginal or questionable care, inflating medical expenses, and creating dilemmas for patients and their kin. The second issue is cost. Medical technology is often expensive and is one of the main factors in our rising health-care costs. We may reach a point soon, if we have not already, that as a society we will not be able to afford all of the medical care we are capable of providing. Thus, we need to seriously consider what we can afford to do and what the most effective ways to spend our health care dollars are. This raises the issue of "rationing" (or apportioning) medical care. Do we ration explicitly, on the basis of need or potential effectiveness, or implicitly as we often already do, by the ability to pay? In Great Britain, with more limited resources devoted to medical care, rationing is built into the expectations of health policy (since it is virtually completely government-funded). For example, for many years no one over fifty-five was begun on dialysis; it simply was not considered a suitable treatment for kidney disorders after that age (patients under fifty-five receive treatment comparable to American patients) (Aaron and Schwartz, 1984). In recent years, dialysis is still rationed in the UK, but not so strictly (Stanton, 1999). (See also the debate on "Rationing Medical Care" in Part 3 of this book.)

The first two selections in this section highlight some of the dilemmas of medical technology. Paul D. Simmons ponders, "The Artificial Heart: How Close Are We, and Do We Want to Get There?" He outlines some of the most significant social and ethical issues surrounding the latest total artificial heart technology. He both examines specific medical technological issues and considers what such technological innovations might mean for society. He sees the issues around the artificial heart as an exemplar of human bioengineering and observes: "The twenty-first century will be a world in which differences between the artificial and the natural will be increasingly difficult to discern." This may be disconcerting for some, and for better or worse, medicine will be at the forefront of this. While Simmons focuses on a medical technology that may impact the future, the second selection examines the dilemmas of a current technology. In this reading, "Issues in the Application of High Cost Medical Technology: The Case of Organ Transplantation," Nancy G. Kutner examines the complex social issues that surround the transplantation of organs. She discusses cost effectiveness, the limited supply of organs, the donors, the selection criteria, and the quality of life for recipients. These issues illustrate how the dilemmas of medical technology extend far beyond the challenges of developing the technology and medical expertise needed to deliver satisfactory treatments.

Genetics is the rising paradigm in medicine. The Human Genome Project commenced in 1990 to map the entire human genetic structure in fifteen years. The prime goal is to locate the causes of the thousands of genetically related diseases and ultimately to develop new treatments and interventions. Research has already discovered genes for cystic fibrosis, Huntington's disease, types of breast and colon cancer, and other disorders, although we are clearly in the early stages of genetic research. Beyond diseases, some scientists have applied the genetic paradigm to behavioral traits, presenting claims for genetic predisposition's to alcoholism, homosexuality, obesity, and intelligence. Although genetic discoveries may eventually yield treatments and preventions of diseases, genetic testing as a medical technology raises serious social and ethical issues. Some analysts have warned of the dangers of biological reductionism, especially in terms of "genetic essentialism," as an increasingly pervasive explanation of human problems (Nelkin and Lindee, 1995; see also Dustor, 1990). One critic has suggested, "Genetics is not just a science. . . . It is a way of thinking, an ideology. We're coming to see life through a 'prism of heritability,' a 'discourse of gene action,' a genetic frame. Genetics is the single best explanation, the most comprehensive theory since God" (Rothman, 1998: 13). In the final article in this section, "A Mirage of Genes," Peter Conrad examines why popular conceptions of genetics have become so readily accepted in medicine and public discourse. He compares genetic theory to the well-established germ theory and finds some parallels that help explain the easy acceptance of the new genetics. An appearance and allure of specificity creates a privileged position for genetic explanations in the public discourse; on closer examination, the specificity may prove to be a mirage.

Medical technology continues to expand, bringing new "miracles" and new dilemmas. Most poignantly reflected in the issues of quality of life and costs, the social and economic consequences of medical technology will need to be addressed in the next decade.

REFERENCES

Aaron, Henry J., and William B. Schwartz. 1984. The Painful Prescription: Rationing Hospital Care. Washington, D.C.: Brookings Institution.

Anspach, Renée. 1987. "Prognostic conflict in life and death decisions: The organization as an ecology of knowledge." Journal of Health and Social Behavior. 28: 215–31.

Bell, Susan. 1986. "A new model of medical technology development: A case study of DES." Pp. 1–32 in Julius A. Roth and Sheryl Burt Ruzek (eds.), The Adoption and Social Consequences of Medical Technology (Research in the Sociology of Health Care, Volume 4). Greenwich, CT: JAI Press.

Duster, Troy. 1990. Backdoor to Eugenics. New York: Routledge.

Dutton, Diana B. 1988. Worse than the Disease: Pitfalls of Medical Progress. New York: Cambridge University Press.

Guillemin, Jeanne Harley, and Lynda Lytle Holmstrom. 1986. Mixed Blessings: Intensive Care for Newborns. New York: Oxford University Press.

Kutner, Nancy G. 1987. "Social worlds and identity in end-stage renal disease (ESRD)." Pp. 107–146 in Julius A. Roth and Peter Conrad (eds.), The Experience and Control of Chronic Illness (Research in the Sociology of Health Care, Volume 6). Greenwich, CT: JAI Press.

Nelkin, Dorothy, and M. Susan Lindee. 1995. The DNA Mystique: The Gene as a Cultural Icon. New York: Freeman.

Ploth, D.W., P.H. Shepp, C. Counts, and F. Hutchison. 2003. "Prospective analysis of global costs for maintenance of patients with ESRD." American Journal of Kidney Diseases. 42: 12–21.

Plough, Alonzo L. 1986. Borrowed Time: Artificial Organs and the Politics of Extending Lives. Philadelphia: Temple University Press.

Relman, Arnold S., and Drummond Rennie. 1980. "Treatment of end-stage renal disease: Free but not equal." New England Journal of Medicine. 303: 996–98.

Rothman, Barbara Katz. 1998. Genetic Maps and Human Imaginations. New York: Norton.

Stanton, J. 1999. "The cost of living: Kidney dialysis rationing and health economics in Britain, 1965–1996." Social Science and Medicine. 49: 1169–82.

Timmermans, Stefan. 2000. "Technology and medical practice." Pp. 309–321 in Chloe E. Bird, Peter Conrad, and Allen M. Fremont (eds.), Handbook of Medical Sociology, fifth edition. Upper Saddle River, NJ: Prentice-Hall.

Timmermans, Stefan. 2002. "The impact of medical technology." Sociology of Health and Illness. 25: 97–114.

Zussman, Robert. 1992. Intensive Care. Chicago: University of Chicago Press.

33 The Artificial Heart: How Close Are We, and Do We Want to Get There?

Paul D. Simmons

On July 2, 2001, a medical milestone was reached when Robert Tools received a total artificial heart implant at Jewish Hospital in Louisville, Kentucky. Tools was implanted with an AbioCor artificial heart, one of several brands of new-generation artificial hearts that has been approved by the U.S. Food and Drug Administration (FDA) for clinical trial. The AbioCor heart was developed by Abiomed of Danvers, Massachusetts.

Following the surgery, physicians were guardedly enthusiastic about the device and optimistic about the patient's future. Tools, 59, has had a history of numerous heart attacks and by-pass surgery, as well as diabetes and kidney problems. He met the requirements of the AbioCor protocol because he was not a candidate for transplant, death was otherwise probably within thirty days, and other interventions were deemed ineffective. Researchers hope that strengthening his heart function will result in increased function of his other vital organs, thus prolonging the patient's life and increasing his energy. But because the device is experimental, nothing can be promised.

The total artificial heart implant is intended to assist those patients whose natural heart is failing or who are unable to come off the heart-lung machine. Each year in the United States, heart failure contributes to the deaths of approximately 700,000 people, which is twice the number of those killed by stroke and seven times the number of those who die from breast cancer. Similar statistics are found in other developed countries. As many as 100,000 patients a year in the United States alone could benefit from a total artificial heart implant, if it proves to be safe, effective, and reliable.[1]

Critics of artificial heart implants argue that such implants should be prohibited, regardless of the patient's deteriorating condition or the nearness of death. For them, an implant amounts to a violation of the Nuremberg prohibition against "experiments . . . in which there is *a priori* reason to believe that death or disabling injury will result."[2] In support of their beliefs, they refer to the checkered history of artificial heart research as well as ethical problems associated with the procedure.

My purpose here is to outline the central ethical issues involved in total artificial heart implants and to assess their importance for the future of humanity. These ethical questions initially arose during the days of research and work with the Jarvik-7, the first implanted artificial heart, developed in the 1970s and first implanted into volunteer recipients in the 1980s. Thus, the discussion of AbioCor will use parallels to the Jarvik-7 project as a way of raising issues and mapping the progress made in developing an artificial heart.

Ethical issues are dealt with in two main sections. The first section deals with the technology of the heart, informed consent, risk-benefit calculus, and termination of the experiment. The second section deals with the more global question of the future of humanity in light of technological developments. Fears of a take-over by cyborgs and the loss of a human future have led to a lively debate.

ETHICS, PATIENT CARE, AND THE ARTIFICIAL HEART

Protecting human subjects during experimental research trials is a major concern of medical ethics, as evidenced by the Nuremberg Code, the Declaration of Helsinki, and the Belmont Report. One precept guiding experimental research on humans is that "there are any number of things that we can do that ought not be done."[3] While researchers as well as the general public readily agree on this principle, consensus regarding its practical application to experimental devices has yet to be attained.

In order to understand the perspective of modern critics of artificial heart implants, it is helpful to examine the history of artificial heart research. The federal government has been involved in funding medical research since at least 1940, and by the 1960s, research on an artificial heart was well under way. By early 1965, the combined efforts of the Atomic Energy Commission (AEC) and the National Institutes of Health (NIH) resulted in a federal commitment to develop a fully implantable artificial heart by 1970.[4]

The task proved more daunting than was expected, however, and several prototypes of the artificial heart were discarded along the way. For instance, the AEC had promoted a heart powered by nuclear energy in the hope that it would be totally implantable. In 1973, this research ended, however, amid concerns that radiation from the U-238 would cause leukemia in the patient and would expose a spouse and others near the recipient to unacceptable levels of radiation. The harm being done outweighed the good to be achieved.

In the 1980s, equally serious problems arose with the Jarvik-7. As a result of numerous emboli being thrown into the bloodstream, patients who received the Jarvik-7 often experienced renal failure, pulmonary problems, lung dysfunction, hemorrhage, strokes, seizures, and convulsions. In fact, the damage to the blood, brain, lungs, and kidneys was so extensive that by the end of the decade the FDA and surgeon Dr. William DeVries decided against any further permanent implants.

The artificial heart program itself was almost terminated several times. In 1982, the Office of Technology Assessment raised serious concerns about the artificial heart program when it determined that questions of cost and therapeutic benefit needed resolution following a full social debate.[5] Funding was actually withdrawn from the program in 1988. More recently, however, the expanded role of corporate funding, influential researchers, and the intervention of powerful political leaders have combined to assure continued government funding,[6] and the project has gained significant momentum despite somewhat ambiguous results.

Technical Objectives: The Design and Function of the AbioCor

Recent efforts of the artificial heart project have focused on eliminating the problems associated with the Jarvik-7. Four technical objectives guided the research: (1) the material used must be compatible with human biology; (2) the device must be miniaturized; (3) the artificial heart must be totally implantable; and (4) it must contain a reliable source of power that does not rely on an external drive. Advances in technology have resulted in miniaturized microprocessors and high capacity batteries and have thus made artificial hearts like the AbioCor possible.

The AbioCor weighs about two pounds, and consists of an internal thoracic unit, an implantable rechargeable battery and miniaturized electronics package, and a battery pack strapped to the chest. The transcutaneous energy transfer (TET) device, which runs on external magnetic coils powered by a battery, controls the pumping speed of the heart to accommodate the patient's physiological needs. In addition, since the AbioCor is miniaturized, certain justice issues in distribution may be resolved. Early models of the artificial heart, unlike the AbioCor, would not fit small-framed persons like the Japanese, women, and children.

Beyond such structural features, the device must function therapeutically. Whether the AbioCor meets all of these objectives remains to be seen, although initial tests look promising. Abiomed claims its proprietary manufacturing techniques result in blood contact surfaces that are smooth to the cellular level.[7] This process should reduce, if not eliminate, the problem of blood clots forming from the pumping movement of the heart. The tests have shown, moreover, that critical components could last up to five years.

Results from the dozens of AbioCor implants performed on calves have also been encouraging. While some calves died before resuscitation after implantation, others returned to normal activity, including energetic play. However, long-term studies on the AbioCor implant in calves have not been conducted since the calves are euthanized after about three months when they outgrow the optimal size for the heart. Anatomical differences between a calf and a human can result in different physical responses to an implant. While calves have small vessels at the base of their skull called *rete mirable,* which filter out blood clots, humans do not have this protection. In fact, implantation studies on calves with the Jarvik-7 also produced encouraging results, without the problems of emboli commonly found in the human patients. Thus, while animal background studies on the AbioCor are necessary and have been promising thus far, they are also inconclusive.

Issues of Informed Consent

Consent that is informed and voluntary is vital for experiments involving permanent heart implants. Experimental medicine pushes the boundaries of standard medical procedures and traditional moral formulations. It takes courage to do this, and wisdom to know the appropriate time to move to human trials.

The first problem in seeking informed consent is that of keeping the role of researcher distinct from that of physician. Caring for the patient is and should remain the primary commitment of the clinician. Thus, involving the treating physician in the consent process may compromise the patient advocacy role of the physician.[8] There is also the danger that the physician's commitment to further research and development will get translated as "promise of therapy" to the hopeful and anxious patient.[9] However, keeping the role and goals of the researcher distinct from that of the clinician may be nearly impossible because certain numbers of patients must be enrolled in order to meet the minimum requirements of an experimental program.[10]

In addition to the problem of keeping the role of researcher distinct from that of physician, some critics insist that the imminence of death makes it impossible for a patient to provide free and informed consent. Death is terribly coercive and may drive a person into dangerous procedures out of desperation. As Christiaan Barnard, the surgeon who performed the first-ever heart transplant in December 1967, put it, patients on the brink of death are between a lion and a crocodile.[11] Furthermore, few people have the intellectual stamina, physical energy, or mental discipline to digest the details of a lengthy consent form, much less a patient who is dying from end-stage heart disease and may have diminished capacity as a result of medication or pain. All this underscores the importance of the *process* of procuring informed consent. Respect for patient autonomy requires that researchers not exploit the situation.

In the case of Tools, researchers were careful to obtain his fully informed consent. First, a team trained in informed consent procedures spent three hours going over the details of the procedure with the patient and exploring its risks and benefits. The team also clearly described the experimental nature of the device. Specifically, the patient was informed that "this device is subject to failure at any time from a variety of possible causes," and that there was no guarantee that the heart would function effectively "for any minimum period of time."

Furthermore, an independent advocate for the patient was made available,[12] and a psychiatrist provided an extensive profile of Tools. A careful screening process was used to clarify the patient's mental status and his ability to provide free and uncoerced consent. Such procedures helped assure the patient's autonomy and should be followed for every artificial heart implantation.

Assessing Benefits and Risks

As an experimental device, the AbioCor will be monitored for the impact it makes on its first human recipient. Assessing benefits and risks is necessary for clinical and ethical reasons.[13] The FDA had approved Jarvik-7 implants without the need to show therapeutic benefit in the programs at Humana Heart Institute in Louisville and at other sites in Arizona, Pittsburgh, and Salt Lake City.[14] Even so, current programs using the ventricular assist device (VAD) or a total artificial heart as a bridge to transplant have found that the benefits have outweighed the burdens.[15]

Since the recipients of the Jarvik-7 were not candidates for transplants and death was otherwise imminent, it was assumed that they would be no worse off with an artificial heart. Nonetheless, continual evaluation of what the device does to or for a particular patient is necessary.

As the National Heart, Lung, and Blood Institute (NHLBI) Working Group stated, "such studies should be conducted in a fashion that does not undermine the primarily therapeutic objectives."[16]

No testing of innovative devices would be possible if researchers were required to show therapeutic benefit before the devices could be used. Although the AbioCor is experimental, it has come through rigorous research and development. In contrast, the Jarvik-7 needed "further developments in the field of biomaterial compatibility."[17] It was rough and incomplete when measured by the vision of a sophisticated biomedical device that is totally implantable and reliably therapeutic.[18] The tether and console were terribly restrictive and totally unacceptable for the finished product. Furthermore, the Jarvik-7 heart contributed to other life-threatening problems. For example, Barney Clark, a recipient of the Jarvik-7, was rarely lucid; he suffered severe depression, wanting and requesting to die but unable to use the key to turn off his console. Strokes, apparently related to blood infections and not simply the emboli that resulted from blood clotting, complicated the recovery of all other Jarvik-7 recipients. Thus, while the Jarvik-7 functioned well as a machine, it created terrible problems for the recipients. The device could be used morally only *in extremis* since injuries were predictable.[19]

Early indications are that Tools is doing well after nearly four months on the device. Thus, the technological advances of the AbioCor give us reason to believe that the device may not produce the same types or degree of problems as the Jarvik-7. At this point, the NHLBI Working Group's recommendation that "research on mechanical circulatory support systems (MCSSs) should continue" seems both ethically and medically supportable.[20]

From the artificial heart project, we have learned that the heart is not just a muscle, much less just a pump. It is a sophisticated, even miraculous organ. Designing an artificial device that sufficiently duplicates its functions in the human body is an enormously complicated task. Nonetheless, the terminal condition of Tools, the encouraging research on AbioCor, and the careful process of informed consent make his decision for AbioCor seem reasonable.

The Altruistic Patient

Every recipient of the total artificial heart may be little more than a volunteer in an experimental protocol. Therapeutic benefits may be primarily for those who will be treated by newer, more efficient devices some time in the future. Nonetheless, prohibiting patients from deciding how they will live out their days while dying is condescending and patronizing. The patients are volunteers, accepting risks to themselves knowing that benefits may accrue primarily to others. The research subject is a necessary factor in developing new medical interventions. Without such volunteers, a reliable and effective device will never be developed. A purist, idealistic expectation seems out of place at the rough and jagged edges of the frontiers of medicine.

People like Barney Clark, who volunteer for experimental procedures knowing they will likely not benefit, are some of the true heroes of medical science. Without the learning curve from the Jarvik-7 era, we would not have the hearts now contending for their place among therapeutic devices. Such pioneers enrich our society, add depth to moral ideals, and give perspective to what is worthwhile about living. Permitting people to volunteer for experimental procedures has long-standing support in both medical and religious communities.

Terminating the Experiment

Perhaps the most difficult ethical quandary during the Jarvik-7 era was deciding how to terminate the experiment. For Barney Clark, the heart caused severe neurological complications, which left him comatose and thus without communicative skills or cognition. The consent form signed by Clark didn't prepare for this eventuality; it assumed that he would either be able to make decisions about treatment or that he would die. It made no provision for the possibility that he might survive but with "severe confusion, mental incompetence or coma."[21]

The informed consent document for the AbioCor attempts to correct this problem. Candid discussions were held with Tools about the possibility of complications, and the advocate counseled him to be cautious about agreeing to the implant. Furthermore, Tools was required to have an advance directive, or living will, in case he becomes incompetent. The patient was also assured that he may withdraw from the experiment without loss of standard therapies.

There are those who object to any talk of terminating an experiment that is life sustaining. During the Jarvik-7 era, it was unclear whether a patient had a legal or moral right to refuse life-sustaining treatment or to have it rejected on his or her behalf. The 1985 statement by the NHLBI Working Group seemed to side-step the issue. First, it said the decision was not the patient's acting alone, but would involve "discussion" with health professionals and the patient's family. Second, it said that some "other suitable therapy" might have to be substituted.[22]

The U.S. Supreme Court has since helped resolve this intense debate—at least for patients—and their physicians—over refusal or withdrawal of treatment. In *Cruzan,* the Supreme Court made it clear that patients have a constitutionally protected right to refuse treatment based on the liberty interests of the Fourteenth Amendment.[23] This protection extends even to non-competent patients, says Annas, "because if they were competent, they would have that right, and to deny it to them because they could no longer personally exercise it would devalue their lives."[24] Thus, thanks to the Court and congressional action, those who receive the AbioCor should have a greater degree of patient autonomy than those who received the Jarvik-7. If a patient finds the experience unbearable, he, or his surrogate, may choose against continuing. It would be a gentle death following the disconnection of batteries. As the Working Group concluded, "the patient may choose to discontinue the device, knowing that his act will result promptly and certainly in his or her death."[25]

The key given to Barney Clark continues to have enormous symbolic significance. The key must remain in the hands of the patient. The basic principle of medical ethics is to treat the patient as a person—a free moral agent. The value of life is enhanced by liberty; it is "lessened not by a decision to refuse treatment, but by the failure to allow a competent human being the right of choice."[26]

THE HEART, CYBORGS, AND THE LIKELIHOOD OF A HUMAN FUTURE

A "cyborg" is a robot-like creature that has been given human features. Body parts are all artificial, but they function together to make human-like movement possible. "Cybernetics" is the science of combining computer technology with the neurological capacities of the human brain and nervous system.[27] These definitions may sound quaint, but cyborgs are on the drawing boards of a number of laboratories. In addition, a journal is now devoted to artificial intelligence, and MIT has a department devoted to research and development in this area.

William Gibson, who coined the term "cyberspace," notes that the future will probably see implantations of silicon chips into the human brain that have been modified with DNA. Such "inelegant procedures" will find a rationale for use by the military or mainstream medicine.[28] Models of nanomolecular computing are already emerging, in which brain cells or human DNA are combined with gelatinous computing "goo" to receive all the benefits of both artificial and natural intelligence.

The twenty-first century will be a world in which the differences between the artificial and the natural will be increasingly difficult to discern. We now rely on bioengineered body parts for breathing, cardiovascular and renal functions, and substitute joints and extremities. The great irony is that technology is also changing our humanity. People are already becoming more cyborg-like—more dependent upon their extensions and less able to live as self-contained beings. From the other end of the spectrum, advances in technology will give machines more human qualities, such as intelligent thought, calculation, feelings, and thus concerns for survival, replication, and control of their environment and dominance over competitors.

The New Being: Cyborgs as Human

Rodney Brooks, the director of the Artificial Intelligence Lab at MIT, believes that we are making progress toward machines with human characteristics. Robots are emerging that have human feelings, wants and needs, reflective thinking, and self-perpetuating capacities. Computer programs reproduce and evolve. They exhibit actions and patterns we once expected only from living creatures. They interact with complex environments, chase prey, evade enemies, and compete for space and environment.[29]

To be sure, like the artificial heart, today's robots are incomplete and imperfect. Their technological design still lacks the sophistication that will make them fully acceptable as replacement devices. They are evolving, however, assisted by their curious, inventive, and determined creators who are also their masters at this present stage of technique. Eventually, says Brooks, we may extend to them certain inalienable rights to which people are now entitled. Critics have argued, however, that the robots' eventual intelligence may cause them to one day reject their masters and get on with the business of creating ever new and more amazing creatures.

. . .

SUMMARY AND CONCLUSIONS

The artificial heart appears here to stay, and it will become ever more reliable and therapeutic. In the new age of medicine, the attributes of humanity are blended with the mechanical and artificial. While we express our humanness by seeking new and more creative treatments for illness and delaying death, we are inevitably modifying what it means to be human.

Ethical issues arise from the interface of the physician-patient relationship and the technologies being developed in today's laboratories. The new Luddites may well be too fearful to tackle the challenges of technology wed to humanity. But they rightly say we seem woefully unprepared to deal with human *hubris* and will to power.

REFERENCES

1. Abiomed, *AbioCor Clinical Trial Information: AbioCor Frequently Asked Questions, at* <http://www.abiomed.com/abiocor/faq.html> (last visited August 23, 2001).
2. See principles 5 and 10 of "The Nuremberg Code of Ethics in Medical Research," in *Trials of War Criminals before the Nuremberg Military Tribunals under Control Council Law No. 10,* vol. 2 (Washington, D.C.: U.S. Government Printing Office, 1949): at 181–82.
3. P. Ramsey, "Shall We Reproduce? I: The Medical Ethics of In-Vitro Fertilization." *JAMA,* 220, no. 10 (1972): 1346–50, at 1347.
4. M.J. Strauss, "Special Report: The Political History of the Artificial Heart," *N. Engl. J. Med.,* 310, no. 5 (1984): 332–36, at 334.
5. *Id.* at 335.
6. G. Gill, "The Artificial Heart Juggernaut," *Hastings Center Report,* 19, no. 2 (1989): 27.
7. Abiomed, *AbioCor Clinical Trial Information: Technological Principles, at* <http://www.abiomed.com/abiocor/principles.html> (last visited August 23, 2001).
8. J.L. Metzler, "Ethical Issues in the Implantation of the Total Artificial Heart," *N. Engl. J. Med,* 311, no. 1 (1984): 61–62.
9. J.G. Copeland et al., "The CardioWest Total Artificial Heart Bridge to Transplantation: 1993 to 1996 National Trial," *Annals of Thoracic Surgery,* 66 (1988): 998–1001.
10. Copeland et al., *supra* note 9, at 1662.
11. C. Barnard, *One Life* (Toronto: Macmillan, 1969): at 348.
12. See P.D. Simmons, "Ethical Considerations in Composite Tissue Allotransplantation," *Microsurgery,* 20 (2000): 458–65, at 463.
13. P.D. Simmons, "Ethical Considerations of Artificial Heart Implantations," *Annals of Clinical and Laboratory Science,* 16, no. 1 (1986): 1–12, at 4.
14. Copeland et al., *supra* note 9, at 1662.
15. S.H. Miles et al., "The Total Artificial Heart: An Ethics Perspective on Current Clinical Research and Deployment," *Chest,* 94, no. 2 (1988): 409–13.
16. The Working Group on Mechanical Circulatory Support of the National Heart, Lung, and Blood Institute, *The Artificial Heart and Assist Devices: Directions, Needs, Costs, Societal and Ethical Issues* (1985): at 21 (unpublished report, on file with author) [hereinafter cited as The Working Group].
17. Gill, *supra* note 6, at 25, *quoting* William DeVries, the surgeon for some of the Jarvik-7 recipients.
18. T.A. Preston, "Who Benefits from the Artificial Heart?," *Hastings Center Report,* 15, no. 1 (1985): 5–7.
19. Simmons, *supra* note 13, at 6.
20. The Working Group, *supra* note 16, at 35. See also H. Schwartz, "Don't Pull the Plug on Artificial Heart Tests," *The Wall Street Journal,* September 27, 1985, at 28.

21. G.J. Annas, "Consent to the Artificial Heart: The Lion and the Crocodile," *Hastings Center Report*, 13, no. 2 (1983): 20–22, at 20.
22. The Working Group, *supra* note 16, at 23.
23. *Cruzan by Cruzan v. Director, Missouri Department of Health*, 497 U.S. 261 (1990).
24. G.J. Annas, "Prisoner in the I.C.U.: The Tragedy of William Bartling," *Hastings Center Report*, 14, no. 6 (1984): 28–29, at 29. See G.J. Annas, "Reconciling *Quinlan* and *Saikewicz*: Decision-Making for the Incompetent Patient," *American Journal of Law & Medicine*, 4, no. 4 (1979): 367–96.
25. The Working Group, *supra* note 16, at 23.
26. *Superintendent of Belchertown State School v. Saikewicz*, 370 N.E.2d 417, 426 (Mass. 1977).
27. D.B. Guralnik, ed., "Cybernetics," *Webster's New World Dictionary of the American Language*, 2d ed. (New York: World Publishing Co., 1971).
28. W. Gibson, "Will We Plug Chips into Our Brains? The Writer Who Coined the Word Cyberspace Contemplates a Future Stranger Than His Science Fiction," *Time*, 155, no. 25 (2000): 84–85.
29. R. Brooks, "Will Robots Rise Up and Demand Their Rights?," *Time*, 155, no. 25 (2000): 86.

34 *Issues in the Application of High Cost Medical Technology: The Case of Organ Transplantation*

Nancy G. Kutner

Sophisticated medical technologies save lives that would otherwise be lost, but they also generate complex economic, social, legal and/or ethical problems. Human organ transplantation, for example, is a high-cost technology, not only in the conventional economic sense, but also because it involves a scarce resource donated in life or in death by other human beings and because it can compromise quality of life as well as patient survival. Advances in transplant technology generate a particularly diverse set of questions and issues.

Appropriate resource allocation among alternative health-care needs is an ongoing debate (e.g., Beierle 1985; Fuchs 1984). Is it appropriate for a relatively small number of people to benefit from public financing of an expensive technology when a larger number of people could benefit from expenditures on a broader range of less expensive health problems? Related issues include the extent of the total health-care commitment that society is willing to make and whether a formal rationing policy would be normatively acceptable. Regardless of total cost and cost-effectiveness concerns, when a potentially life-saving technology becomes available it will certainly be used: "there can be no decision not to transplant" (Nightingale 1985, p. 142).

Organ-transplant technology depends on more than sophisticated equipment and the skills of medical personnel; an adequate supply of viable human organs must be available. A critical question is how the public can be encouraged to supply organs to meet the needs of waiting recipients. In order for organ transplantation to fulfill its potential, the cooperation of the general public is essential, which lends a quasi-public health dimension to the establishment of a wide-scale organ-transplant program.

A third set of questions concerns the criteria for allocating a technology to those who could potentially benefit from it. Since an inadequate supply of donor organs limits the availability of the technology, what criteria should be used to select organ transplant recipients, and are these criteria consistent with the values of a democratic society?

Finally, what are the medical and quality-of-life outcomes associated with organ transplantation? It is too soon to know what the long-term health outcomes will be for persons treated with powerful new immunosuppressive drugs or what outcomes are associated with transplanting at different stages in the course of a disease process. Transplant technology is now labeled therapeutic in the case of kidneys, hearts, and livers but the technology remains "experimental" even in these areas. Lives are saved but for how long, and with what outcomes?

Before examining these issues related to use of organ-transplant technology, I provide a brief overview of the emergence and current status of this technology in the United States.

BACKGROUND: ORGAN TRANSPLANTATION IN THE UNITED STATES

This paper focuses on issues surrounding solid organ transplants (kidney, heart, liver, pancreas, lung, heart-lung). Corneal and bone marrow transplants are also important components of transplant technology, however. Medical prerequisites for successful organ transplantation include perfected surgical techniques, adequate organ procurement and preservation systems, methods to prevent rejection of the transplanted organ, and understanding of the role of tissue matching.

Growth and Current Status of Solid Organ Transplant Programs

Organ transplantation was initiated in the United States when the first kidney transplant was performed in 1954. In 1960 a permanent shunt was developed for use in chronic kidney dialysis treatments; this was a significant event for kidney transplantation because it provided a backup procedure to keep patients alive if a transplant failed, and it allowed patients to be kept alive while they waited for a suitable donor kidney to become available. The so-called modern era of solid organ transplants did not begin, however, until the identification in the early 1960s of an effective combination of drugs (azathioprine and steroids) to prevent rejection of the foreign organ. Kidney transplantation and kidney dialysis developed as complementary treatment procedures for persons whose own kidneys no longer fulfill the essential function of removing toxic wastes from the body.[1] By 1971, 150–175 kidney transplants were being performed per year by Veterans Administration medical centers (Rettig 1980). When Medicare funding for kidney transplants and kidney dialysis became available in 1973, the annual number of kidney transplants began to increase dramatically (Figure 34-1). Patient survival at one year following a first kidney transplant is at least 90 percent, and 55 percent or more of patients who undergo kidney transplantation still have the new kidney one year later (Banowsky 1983).[2]

Heart transplantation was initiated in the United States as early as 1968, but early survival rates were poor. For many years, Dr. Norman Shumway's program at Stanford University was virtually alone in the field. In the early 1980s, the introduction of cyclosporine, a new immunosuppressive drug capable of significantly reducing organ rejection, stimulated a dramatic increase in heart transplantation. With cyclosporine, a two-year patient survival of 75 percent became possible, compared to 58 percent with conventional types of immunosuppression (Austen and Cosimi 1984).[3] Five-year survival rates climbed to between 50 and 60 percent (Casscells 1986). By 1985 the total number of heart transplants performed in the United States had risen to almost 1,200 (Seabrook 1985) and more than 80 centers were participating in heart transplantation.

Liver transplantation in the United States is closely associated with the work of one individual, Dr. Thomas Starzl. His teams at the University of Colorado (Denver) and the University of Pittsburgh have performed some 900 transplants since 1963, and he has personally trained most of the other liver-transplant surgeons. Cyclosporine's introduction significantly improved survival rates in liver transplant recipients. With conventional immunosuppression, a patient's chances for living one year after liver transplantation were about one in three, but with cyclosporine therapy, survival chances more than doubled (Starzl, Iwatsuki, Shaw, Gordon, Esquivel, Todo, Kam, and Lynch 1985). An important factor contributing to this improved survival was the aggressive use of retransplantation that cyclosporine made possible.

Figure 34-1. *Number of Kidney Transplants (Medicare and Non-Medicare)*

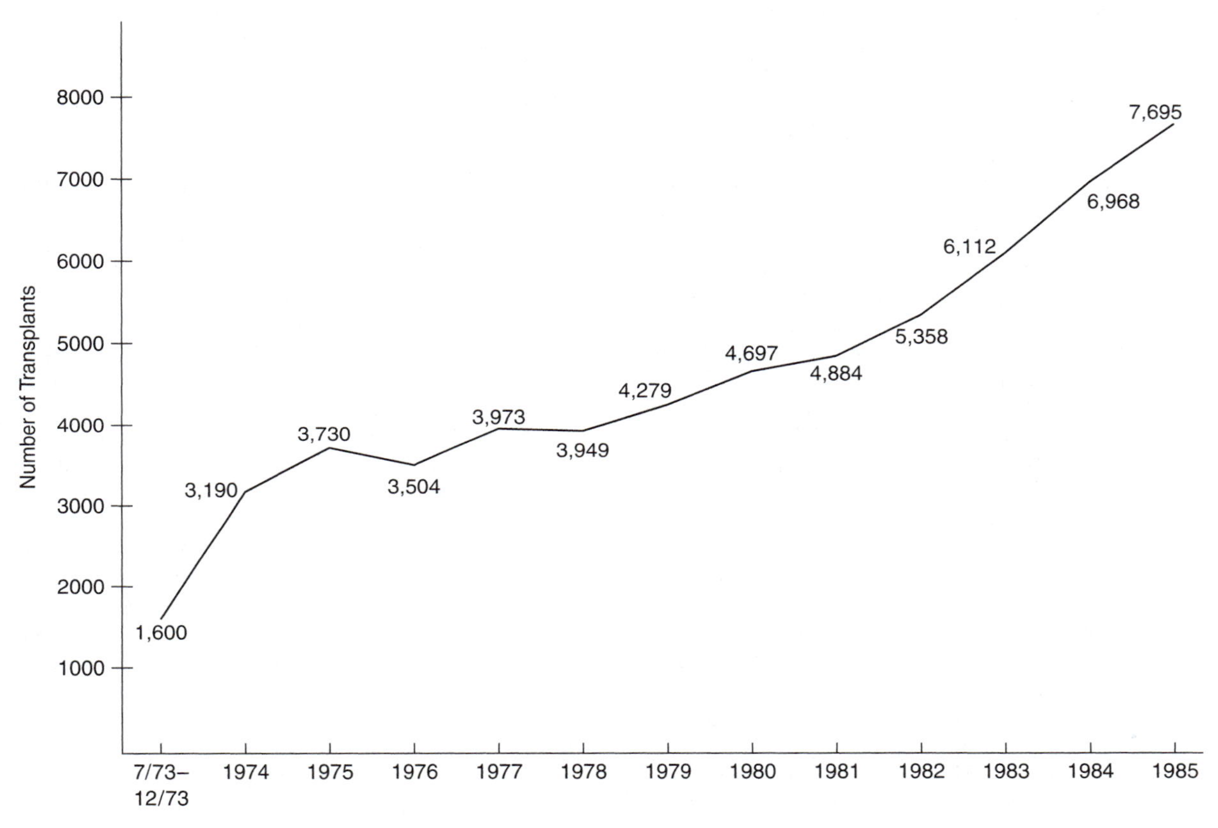

SOURCE: *Dateline 1986*, p. 545.

Pancreas transplantation, the only example of widespread endocrine organ transplantation, was initiated in 1966 at the University of Minnesota. The goal of pancreas transplantation is to provide a self-regulating source of insulin for patients who are insulin-dependent diabetics. Diabetics are overrepresented among kidney failure patients, and for these patients it appears that pancreas transplantation performed in conjunction with kidney transplantation may produce better results than pancreas transplantation by itself (Elick and Sutherland, forthcoming). Although cyclosporine has contributed to improved patient and graft survival rates, results achieved with pancreas transplantation are inferior to those achieved with kidney, heart, or liver transplantation (Pisano 1985; Toledo-Pereyra 1986).

Lung transplants and heart-lung transplants are the least attempted solid organ transplants. Heart-lung transplants, first performed at Stanford University in 1981, are more successful than lung transplants. Again cyclosporine drug therapy appears to promote the success of these procedures. As of 1985, about 140 heart-lung transplants had been performed in the United States.

Legislative Support for Organ Transplantation in the U.S.

In the early 1970s, despite the availability of kidney transplant technology, a number of treatment barriers prevented suitable patients from receiving a new kidney. Only a limited number of medical centers, located in large cities or university areas often geographically distant from where patients lived, were equipped to perform transplants. Moreover, the cost was prohibitive for many patients. Only about eight to ten percent of the American population had adequate insurance coverage for transplantation, and Medicaid coverage was only available to low-income patients. Federal research grants only covered the surgery as long as it was classified "experimental." As legislators were made aware that a shortage of facilities and money was preventing patients from utilizing transplant and dialysis technologies, pressure was generated to attack the problem at the federal level. The result was passage in Fall, 1972, of PL 92–603, an amendment to the Social Security Bill that established the End-Stage Renal Disease (ESRD) Program of Medicare.

Under the amendment Medicare paid 80 percent of the cost of kidney treatment. As a result the number of transplant procedures, transplant centers, and dialysis treatment centers began to increase. The number of transplant candidates maintained by dialysis therapy also increased dramatically. An ironic consequence of PL 92–603 was a growing discrepancy between the number of cadaver kidneys available and the number of potential recipients.

By the early 1980s, advances in immunosuppressive therapy improved the success rates for all types of transplants, and the demand for hearts and livers, as well as kidneys, increased. Equitable distribution of scarce organs became increasingly problematic. Desperate parents of sick children needing liver transplants pleaded with the White House for help, and prominent media coverage increased the pressure on Congress to act. The Organ Procurement and Transplantation Act, PL 98–507, was ready for the president's signature on October 19, 1984. This legislation (1) established a Task Force to examine the medical, legal, ethical, economic and social issues presented by human organ procurement and transplantation (Title I) and to formulate recommendations, (2) authorized assistance for organ procurement agencies in the form of grants (Title II), (3) mandated establishment of an organ procurement and transplantation network and a scientific registry (Title II), and (4) prohibited organ purchases (Title III).

Under PL 98–507, the federal government was authorized to spend up to $25 million during fiscal years 1985–87 to facilitate the planning, establishment, initial operation, or expansion of organ procurement organizations, with special consideration to grant applications from organizations in underserved geographical areas. A national listing of patients in need of organs and a computerized system to match organs and patients, especially patients for whom obtaining a close tissue match is difficult, was to be developed through an organ procurement and transplantation network. This network was directed to maintain a 24-hour telephone service, assist organ procurement organizations in distributing organs that could not be placed within their immediate service areas, and coordinate the actual transporting of organs to transplant centers. These activities would centralize organ procurement and distribution in a manner analogous to the system used in European countries but without actual government involvement. Because of federal cost-cutting policies, funds for the network had not been allocated by mid-1986, and the distribution of scarce organs continued to be influenced by the high visibility of individual cases selected for publicity by the media (Mayfield 1986; Reiner, Eagles, and Watson 1986).

Although the Organ Procurement and Transplantation Act of 1984 signalled federal endorsement of human organ transplants as a component of medical care in the United States, it did not include such definitive steps as establishing the optimal location, number, and program components of transplant centers, or providing for the public funding of expensive medications patients need to take on a long-term basis in order to prevent rejection.

ORGAN TRANSPLANTATION IN THE CONTEXT OF RISING HEALTH COSTS

Health expenditures in 1986 in the United States represented almost 11 percent of the Gross National Product (GNP). Even if it were agreed that a greater share of the GNP should go to health care, American society increasingly faces difficult decisions about how health care dollars should be allocated (Annas 1985a; Culyer and Horisberger 1983; Evans 1983a, b).

Advances in medical technology contribute to rising total health care costs. The cost of a heart transplant and postsurgery care is easily $100,000 or more (Roughton 1986), and the average cost of a liver transplant can be even higher (Table 34-1). The immunosuppressive drugs that patients must take after receiving a transplant are expensive, and there is support at the Congressional level for Medicare to assume this cost (Gore 1986). Finally, transplant rejection episodes are not uncommon—acute rejection episodes were experienced by about 60 percent of the patients who received kidney transplants in 1984—and those episodes involved hospitalization costs.

Cost-effectiveness of a medical therapy is compromised when medical professionals "unconsciously extend the application of care beyond that which is prudent" (Roberts 1980, p. 500). Defining what is "prudent" is very difficult, however. Cost-effectiveness discussions tend to become clouded by the inclusion of different parameters and the application of different data sets (cf. Annas 1985a; Evans 1985; Overcast and Evans 1985). For example, Health Care Financing Administration (HCFA) determined that after four years, a group of kidney transplant patients cost the Medicare Program less than a group of kidney dialysis patients "when considering aggregate costs across the four-year period for the respective groups" (Davis 1983, p. 9). This conclusion, however, did not take into consideration the comparability of these hypothetical groups; regardless of type of therapy, coincident disease (e.g., diabetes) and frequency of hospitalization significantly influence the total costs incurred. Significant costs of failure must also be counted in analyzing the cost-effectiveness of transplantation. The cost of a transplant procedure can also be "one component in the overall cost of treating an end-stage disease. In the absence of a transplant, many end-stage patients incur considerable costs for medical treatment (i.e., the cost of dying)" (Overcast and Evans 1985, p. 107).

There is public support for transplantation regardless of its economic cost, demonstrated, for example, by votes obtained from insurance subscribers. Although there is some public awareness of an increasing strain on Medicare resources, transplantation coverage is not viewed as a major "culprit."

Table 34-1. Estimated Costs Associated with Various Solid Organ Transplant Procedures

	Estimated Cost[a]		
Organ	*Low*	*High*	*Average*
Kidney	$25,000	$45,000	$35,000
Heart	$57,000	$110,000	$95,000
Liver	$68,000	$238,000	$130,000
Pancreas	$18,000	$50,000	$35,000

[a] Total first-year costs including immunosuppressive drugs (Evans, 1985:131). It should be noted that some sources provide even higher estimates, e.g., $170–200,000 for heart transplants and $230–340,000 for liver transplants when "fully-allocated average-one-year-cost" is considered (Massachusetts Task Force on Organ Transplantation, 1985:9).

SUPPLY AND DEMAND IN ORGAN TRANSPLANTATION: LEGAL AND ETHICAL ISSUES

The U.S. Centers for Disease Control have reported the nationwide retrieval rate for cadaver organs as 16.5 percent effective, at maximum (Rapaport and Cortesini 1985). Each year, as many as 75,000 people have conditions that require heart transplantation, but as few as 2,000 donor hearts may be available (Merrikin and Overcast 1985). At least twice as many kidney transplants could be performed annually if organs were available.

Voluntary Organ Donation: A Quasi-Public Health Problem

National survey data indicate that the degree of public support for organ transplantation exceeds the degree of public support for organ donation (Blendon and Altman 1984; Manninen and Evans 1985). Although about 90 percent of Americans express support for continued development of transplantation programs, a smaller percentage (50%–60%) indicate willingness to donate their own organs or those of a relative, and only 19 percent of those who know something about organ transplantation report carrying donor cards (U.S. News 1986).

In a majority of states, surgeons require family approval for removal of organs even when a signed donor card is available and despite the fact that such approval is not required by the Uniform Anatomical Gift Act. It has been argued that "while donor cards are an excellent educational medium and certainly facilitate the activities of transplant coordination, they are not an effective means of substantially increasing the supply of organs for transplantation" (Overcast, Evans, Bowen, Hoe, and Livak 1984, p. 1559). What is needed, according to some observers, is a policy of "presumed consent" under which organs can be legally removed from a brain-dead individual unless the individual carries a refusal card or an objection is raised by a family member (Dukeminier and Sanders 1968; Kaplan 1983). This solution has also been called the "opting out" system; consent for organ retrieval is presumed unless the patient or family explicitly opt out (Strong and Strong 1985). When a presumed consent law allowing removal of eye tissue from autopsy subjects without prior permission from next of kin took effect in Georgia, the number of people receiving corneal transplants increased from 25 in 1983 to more than 1,000 in 1984 (Palmer 1985). As of 1985, thirteen countries in the world had presumed consent laws, and their ability to supply cadaver organs needed for transplants was significantly greater than that of the United States. Less than 10 percent of Americans questioned in a national poll supported the concept of presumed consent, however (Manninen and Evans 1985).

As of 1986, polls indicated that more than 50 percent of Americans supported a policy termed "required [professional] request" (Caplan 1984) or "routine inquiry" (Peele and Salvatierra 1986), requiring hospital personnel to ask next of kin about organ donation when the treating physician determines that brain death has occurred and that medical interventions should cease. This policy can be mandated through legislation or can be made part of a hospital's accreditation criteria (Caplan 1985a). By mid-1986, required request laws had been passed in 25 states. Supporters of the required request policy believe that grieving families can derive significant psychological reward by exercising the organ donation option and that the required request policy can therefore simultaneously serve dual functions. Medical professionals' behavioral and emotional reactions to required request policies represent an unknown variable, however. Physicians and nurses may fear upsetting family members, and they know that organ retrieval will involve them in aggressive procedures that seem inherently disrespectful to the deceased patient. Medical professionals need clear norms about procedures to be followed when organs are retrieved; and they themselves may need emotional support (Corlett 1985; Youngner, Allen, Bartlett, Cascorbi, Hau, Jackson, Mahowald, and Martin 1985). Without a well-developed system of institutional supports, efforts to initiate organ donation may be avoided.

Persistent Ethical Questions Affecting Cadaver and Live-Organ Donation

As Simmons and Simmons (1971) observed, deep-seated ethical questions surround organ donation, e.g. when can a potential donor be defined as dead? What protections are there for the powerless? What are the physician's ethical responsibilities? Questions such as these were widely debated during the early years of kidney-and heart-transplantation (Brewer 1970; Hamburger and Crosnier 1968; Kass 1968; Mc-Geown 1968; Stickel 1966; Wolstenholme andO'Connor 1966).

Transplants from live donors raise a special set of ethical questions. Interestingly, European countries avoid these questions by depending almost totally on cadaver donors in their transplant programs.[4] Approximately 30 percent of all kidneys transplanted annually in the United States are obtained from living-related donors. The likelihood of a close tissue match between donor and recipient is increased when the donor is a relative, thereby increasing the graft survival rate. A small statistical risk to the health of the donor does exist, however, and significant interpersonal strain can arise within a family when relatives who are potentially kidney donors are reluctant to donate (Simmons, Hickey, Kjellstrand, and Simmons, 1971).

Because the rejection rate for organs taken from live donors is less than for organs taken from cadaver donors and because organ shortage has been persistent, attention in recent years has increasingly been given to the use of kidneys from nonrelated living donors (Burley and Stiller 1985; Levey, Hou, and Bush 1986). So-called "emotionally related" donors (spouses, friends, etc.) may derive psychological benefit from donating to a significant other, but without this emotional link, nonrelated living donation becomes more problematic. An international living-related donor and recipient "exchange" has been proposed, using families who have been tissue-typed but who cannot donate to their own family member because the tissue match is not immunologically acceptable. However, it is difficult to imagine that individuals would donate organs within such a system unless they were assured that their family member would benefit within the exchange system or that they themselves might be financially rewarded. The latter possibility, financial compensation for human organs, has been the focus of considerable discussion.

The Market Model and Organ Donation

It is conceivable that a healthy individual, fully informed about the consequences of his/her action, might feel that the financial reward for selling a kidney was worth the personal cost involved. National Kidney Foundation (NKF) chapters have received numerous inquiries from individuals offering to sell a kidney. The possibility of donors selling organs for large fees received media attention during the Congressional hearings that preceded passage of PL 98–507 (Adams 1983), and the resulting legislation specifically stated that organs cannot be transferred for "valuable consideration."

Theoretically, a market system of organ procurement could operate simultaneously with an altruistic system of organ donation, but it is difficult to imagine that individuals or families would not want to receive compensation for organs if others were benefitting financially. An alternative would be to give tax credits to individuals who donate, or to families whose relatives are postmortem donors (Bassett 1985; Sharpe 1985), or to offer "a savings in health care costs for healthy adults who make premortem commitments to cadaveric organ donations" (Surman 1985, p. 318), but even these policies could raise legal, administrative, and social questions that would be difficult to resolve. The market model does not seem to offer a workable solution to the problem of organ shortage in the United States.

Cui Bono? Transplant Recipient Selection

Two important sets of criteria can be identified that shape decisions about which patients are selected to receive scarce organs. One set of criteria is related to the developmental status of the particular transplantation program, i.e. its location on a continuum from experimental to therapeutic. The other set of criteria is related to the individual patient's social background and social characteristics.

Variation in Patient Selection Models

The lower the success rate associated with particular transplant procedures, the more likely it is that patients referred for these procedures have distinctive medical needs (e.g., severe diabetes) or are considered "gravely and irreversibly ill" (Fox and Swazey 1978, p. 308). Pancreas, lung, and heart-lung transplants, therefore, tend to be performed with limited, well-defined categories of patients.

According to the paradigm of therapeutic innovation set forth by Fox and Swazey (1978), as a transplant comes to be regarded as therapeutic in nature, as opposed to an experimental and/or last-chance effort, patient selection criteria begin to enlarge. Liver and heart transplantation moved from an experimental to a therapeutic status in the mid-1980s, and liver transplants were no longer reserved for patients under the age of 18. Both liver and heart transplant programs remained characterized for the most part by well-defined patient selection criteria, however, favoring selection of "best risk" patients in order to maximize use of scarce organs in procedures that remain very expensive.

Patient and graft survival rates characterizing kidney transplantation in the 1980s began to stimulate selection of not only "good risk" patients but also of patients characterized by significant medical risk factors, especially patients with diabetes mellitus, who were virtually excluded from consideration during the early years of kidney transplantation. Because a cadaver donor can provide two kidneys but only one heart or liver, and because living-related donors can provide a kidney, the supply of kidneys is larger than it is for other organs. Despite this, many potential transplant candidates are not able to obtain a transplant because of a shortage of *usable* kidneys. It appears that two factors influencing the receipt of a kidney transplant are patients' socioeconomic status (Kutner, Brogan, and Kutner, forthcoming) and patients' race (Evans, Manninen, Maier, Garrison, and Hart 1985; Hoe, Evans, and Elworth 1984; Kutner 1985).

Social Equity Issues in Transplantation

According to guidelines of the American Medical Association, human organs should be allocated to patients purely on a medical basis; social worth is not an appropriate criterion for organ allocation. The basic prerequisites for transplantation are supposed to be patients' need for the procedure and their ability to "do well" with the particular organ that is available. The latter consideration creates a difficult issue, however. Patients with a history of prior mental, emotional, or family problems are less likely to be selected to receive transplants. It is argued that a stable personal and family life are essential to patient/family compliance with therapeutic regimens and that, without such compliance, transplant success is seriously jeopardized (therefore wasting the organ). This argument received extensive media attention in 1986 when a heart transplant was needed by an infant born to young, unmarried parents. The legality of applying such stringent selection criteria can be questioned:

> It is a legitimate goal to select those candidates judged to have not merely a fair, but the *greatest* probability of surviving transplantation? To what extent should patient-selection decisions be based on general evaluations of emotional stability, as a factor in survivability, or upon specific criteria (such as the presence of a stable home life, or absence of past psychological treatment) that may well exclude some of the handicapped? (Merrikin and Overcast 1985, p. 8).

These are difficult questions which may stimulate legal battles in coming years. In the context of severe organ shortages, however, the transplant gatekeepers are likely to remain committed to reserving this treatment option for patients who do not have characteristics that might prevent them from "doing well."

Differential financial resources at patients' disposal are another source of disparity in access to organ transplants. Although Medicare funding for kidney transplants has existed since 1973, it did not become available for heart transplants until 1986. Medicaid coverage of transplants varies across states. Although the Task Force on Organ Transplantation established by PL 98–507 strongly advocated that transplant centers not give favored access on the basis of a patient's wealth, it has been charged that "flagrant abuse" of this principle occurs, with medical institutions that obtain organs for well-to-do recipients benefitting by receiving large contributions (Johnson 1986; Manne 1985). It is also important to note that, regardless of the availability of Medicare/Medicaid funding for transplants, a patient's financial status can affect transplant success, because financial resources influence a person's ability to travel to, and spend time at, a distant center that is skilled in treating particular types of patients.

Social equity questions also exist in regard to transplant recipients' nationality and race. Making transplants available to nonimmigrant aliens has generated much debate (Anast 1984). Those who argue that scarce organs should be reserved for U.S. citizens feel that this policy is justified because the donors are Americans and because federal tax dollars are used in organ procurement. Those who oppose an exclusionary transplant policy against non-U.S. citizens argue that persons from other countries are willing to spend large sums to receive transplants and thereby benefit the U.S. economy. Furnishing a specialized medical service to patients from countries that lack these services is also viewed as humanitarian and beneficial to the U.S. image abroad. The Task Force on Organ Transplantation finally concluded that 10 percent of the kidneys harvested in the United States should be reserved for nonresident immigrant recipients, but the hearts and livers should be given to foreigners only as a "last resort." The rationale for this decision was that Americans denied access to a heart or liver would die (whereas kidney patients can be maintained on dialysis), that close proximity to the transplant hospital is necessary for follow-up after heart or liver transplant surgery, and that the short period of viability for hearts and livers precludes their exportation to other countries.

Among American transplant candidates, patients' race appears to act as a screening variable. Kidney transplant data indicate that blacks are less likely than whites to be transplant recipients. Approximately 35 percent of the kidney dialysis population in the United States is black (Forum of ESRD Networks 1984), but the percentage of kidney transplant recipients who are black appears to be much lower, perhaps 12 percent (Hoe et al. 1984). It is true that blacks are less likely than whites to donate kidneys, but both black recipients and white recipients fare better when the kidney is from a white donor (Terasaki 1985). In an effort to explore factors that might contribute to the racial differential in kidney transplant rates, the author examined transplant attitudes and experiences in a stratified random sample of 224 never-transplanted chronic kidney dialysis patients in the Atlanta metropolitan area (Kutner 1985). Blacks and whites in the sample were similar in age, total months of dialysis treatment, and perception of overall health status (Garrity, Somes, and Marx 1978), but black patients were significantly less likely to have completed 12 or more years of school and more likely to be unemployed. Black patients (49%) were significantly more likely than whites (36%) to say that no one had mentioned the possibility of their having a transplant. The reasons given by black respondents for not having raised the question themselves suggested that communication barriers, real or perceived, existed, e.g., "I didn't know who to talk to." Similarly, communication barriers regarding kidney donation seemed to exist within black families; black patients (62%) were much more likely than whites (38%) to say that they had never discussed kidney donation with their relatives.

Although the claim has been made that blacks do not get equal access to the kidney transplant system and that "de facto discrimination" exists (Newsclips 1985, p. 9), a variety of factors undoubtedly contribute to a lower kidney transplantation rate in the black population. It would be difficult to establish that discriminatory policies are involved. In the Atlanta sample of dialysis patients, whites (29%) were more likely than blacks (23%) to say that they would like to have a transplant. White patients (14%) were also less likely than blacks (20%) to state that they definitely did not want a transplant. Thus, the attitudes of white patients toward receiving a transplant were more positive than the attitudes of black patients, although they were not significantly different. As noted, black patients were less likely to indicate that they had received sufficient information about transplantation as a treatment option. If blacks tend to be excluded from consideration for kidney and other types of transplantation, socioeconomic factors may be an important reason. Medical professionals may expect higher posttransplant compliance from better educated patients and from patients with strong, intact family support systems. As long as organs remain in scarce supply, patients expected to "do well" are likely to receive preference, but it would be unfortunate if nonmedical criteria were unfairly emphasized in the development of transplant recommendations.

OUTCOME ASSESSMENT: QUALITY-OF-LIFE ISSUES

Although transplantation provides a miraculous "second chance" for patients with end-stage diseases, the long-term immunosuppressive therapy that is required to prevent rejection is associated with physical and psychological problems that can seriously compromise quality of life. For example, it is not uncommon for kidney transplant recipients to experience complications such as cataracts, asepstic necrosis (necessitating hip replacement), and gastrointestinal disorders (peptic ulcer, pancreatitis, liver dysfunction) which may require hospitalization. Severe hypertension is a problem for a subset of kidney transplant recipients (Curtis 1985). If transplant recipients are overwhelmed by their gift of life, wondering how to be "worthy" of their gift or how to ever "pay back" the donor, the new organ can become a psychological burden (Simmons, Klein, and Simmons 1977; Simmons 1985). Fear that the organ will be rejected is another psychological burden.

> . . . The majority of these people usually do not break down, but they do manifest definite psychological needs that must be addressed by the transplant team. . . . Depression, organic brain syndromes, anxiety, compliance problems, and an occasional stress psychosis will surface despite skilled intervention. These will usually respond to a variety of supportive psychotherapies, judicious use of medication, and enlistment of all members of the transplant team in a sensitive, consistent, and caring manner.
>
> Awareness of psychological implications is not a luxury, but is essential if the benefits of transplantation are to be maximized to enhance subsequent life contentment for the patient . . . (Gulledge, Buszta, and Montaque 1983, p. 333).

A number of potential complications can limit heart transplant recipients' long-term survival (Schroeder and Hunt 1986), and these patients seem to have a lower overall quality of life than kidney transplant recipients (Evans et al. 1985). Questions have also been raised about quality of life following liver transplantation:

> . . . a number of problems remain, and new problems are encountered as more patients undergo this procedure at more centers . . . the potential for these patients to have satisfactory quality of life is not clear . . . (Najarian and Ascher 1984, pp. 1180–81).

Assessment of quality-of-life outcomes associated with transplantation is an important area for continuing study. Being given a second chance to live may require much reorganization of individual priorities, styles of relating to others, and own self-image; the availability of psychological support services is obviously very important. An organ transplant does not represent an immediate cure-all for the recipient, either physically or psychologically. Comprehensive (and successful) transplant programs are those that (1) educate patients fully in advance about transplant surgery and its ramifications, especially the risks associated with immunosuppression, and (2) maintain close patient follow-up that deals both with medical and psychological problems posttransplant. Unfortunately, not all transplant centers are willing or able to commit the resources that are required to establish a comprehensive program.

CONCLUSION

Viewed within the broad spectrum of modern medicine, it is probably fair to say that organ transplantation has received an undue amount of attention. Individuals whose survival depends on the timely receipt of a suitable organ quickly become the focus of human-interest media accounts. Physicians remain intrigued by the challenge of trying to outsmart the human body's natural response of rejecting a foreign organ, and successful transplantation represents a "quick fix" (the most satisfying aspect of medical practice to many medical students and physicians). Medical institutions know that transplant center status brings prestige, financial rewards, and the ability to expand related institutional programs such as immunology research.

The issues surrounding application of transplant technology remain complex, despite passage of a national organ transplant act and the deliberations of a national task force. Although the affordability of organ transplant technology can be questioned, we continue to expand entitlement programs, and once established, it is very difficult to consider retreating from these programs because the expected outcome is that people will die. It can also be rationalized that, as Rushing (1985) points out, advances in medical technology represent only one of the factors that contribute to rising total health care costs; other factors include an aging population, inflated prices for health services, health insurance, cultural values associated with industrialization ("the medicalization of society"), and an increase in the supply of physicians.

States that have enacted required request laws have reported an average increase of 100 percent in organ and tissue donations (U.S. News 1986). Whether we will ever reach a point where the supply of organs is reasonably adequate to fill transplant needs is unknown. Because progress toward the goal of preventing traffic accidents and other causes of untimely death would simultaneously decrease the supply of cadaver organs, it is difficult to avoid experiencing mixed feelings about the goal of increasing the supply of cadaver organs suitable for transplantation.

Determining which patients should be recommended for a life-saving therapy, when the therapy cannot be made available to all who might benefit from it, is clearly a "painful prescription." Entitlement programs represent a partial answer to this dilemma. Although criteria for selection of individual recipients still must be employed, in theory the U.S. government made it financially possible in 1972 for any patient to obtain a kidney transplant an option not available anywhere else in the world. A similar program of support for heart and liver transplants is emerging (Casscells 1986).

Quality-of-life outcomes can be maximized for transplant recipients within a comprehensive transplant program that takes into consideration psychosocial as well as medical needs of patients and anticipates potential transplant-related problems. It is difficult, however, for smaller medical centers to support a comprehensive program that provides continuity of care from the transplant work-up stage through ongoing management of outpatient care. The probability of complications is increased if these centers lack expertise in services such as immunology and infectious disease control. Finally, the greater the competition with other centers for scarce organs, the fewer the number of transplant procedures that are likely to be performed at a particular center, which may in turn make it more difficult for the transplant team to maintain a high skill level. All of these factors suggest a need to limit the number of transplant centers and to specify the essential components of transplant programs. More than 80 centers were performing heart transplants in the United States in 1985, but fewer than 40 centers could have handled the available donor supply and performed an optimal number of transplants (Overcast and Evans 1985).

The legislation establishing the ESRD program of Medicare (PL 92–603) and the legislation designed to facilitate organ transplants (PL 98–507) represent unprecedented efforts to structure health care delivery for a particular disease category and a particular medical technology. In the characteristic American pattern, however, both pieces of legislation allowed for operational details to be worked out in a competitive, political context. The proliferation since 1973 of proprietary dialysis centers has been a very important determinant of the nature of dialysis services in this country (cf. Kutner 1982; Plough 1986). Shaped to an important degree by the philosophies of the medical directors who head these centers, the comprehensiveness of the supportive services available to patients varies. An "ESRD network" system was established by HCFA to monitor the quality of kidney dialysis services, but this monitoring process has been carried out with limited and nonuniform success across the 32 HCFA-designated networks, largely because physicians resist monitoring their peers.

The issues reviewed in this paper indicate the need for carefully designed and implemented transplant programs, in order to maximize the efficiency and fairness of organ procurement and distribution systems and the quality of patient outcomes. Reaching decisions about such programs, in the absence of a regulatory system such as is used by Great Britain (Simmons and Marine 1984), is not easy, as illustrated by the lengthy deliberations of a Task Force on Transplantation in Massachusetts and the responses elicited by that Task Force Report (Massachusetts Task Force on Organ Transplantation 1985; Annas 1985a, b; Caplan 1985b; Casscells 1985; Jonsen 1985; Kissick 1985; Miller 1985; Overcast and Evans 1985; Pauly 1985; Skelley 1985). Experience has shown that making kidney dialysis widely available without at the same time taking steps to encourage maximum rehabilitation of patients has resulted in a patient population that is significantly less likely than the pre-Medicare-supported dialysis population to return to productive, gainful activity (Evans, Blagg, and Bryan 1981). When a technology becomes so available that it is no longer necessary to offer it only to those patients most likely to return to active lives (the "best-risk" patients), the patient population becomes a more challenging one to treat and rehabilitate, and the system must include more patient service and dedicated medical personnel in order to further patients' total rehabilitation.

Understandably, we are reluctant to retreat from using technologies that save lives.

> If there is a tenet that forms the bedrock of clinical theory in ESRD (or biomedical science in general), it is the value of increased survival. The ability of a treatment to significantly extend a patient's life where no treatment would surely result in immediate death is almost in itself an operational standard for clinical effectiveness. . . . If a technology extends life, use it! (Plough 1986, p. 39)

We are making a concerted effort to "use" organ transplantation more widely, by expanding entitlement programs and organ procurement programs, and by adopting required request laws to increase organ donation. Greater availability of donated organs may ease the stringent criteria that are currently used in the transplant candidate selection process. If we are also committed to using transplant technology, and the valued resources that are involved, as effectively as possible, we will need so more honestly confront the issues that affect quality-of-life outcomes among organ transplant recipients.

NOTES

Supported in part by the National Institute of Handicapped Research, Grant No. G008006809. An earlier version of this paper was presented at the 1983 Annual Meeting of the Society for the Study of Social Problems in Washington, D.C. I would like to thank J. Michael Henderson and three anonymous reviewers for their valuable comments.

1. Because of the availability of validated back-up procedure, dialysis *via* an artificial kidney, the development of renal transplantation included a dimension of safety not shared by other types of transplantation. The only other types of artificial organs besides the artificial kidney now in routine medical practice are prosthetic heart valves, prosthetic arteries, and the heart-lung machine. However, versions of an artificial liver and an artificial pancreas, in addition to the permanent implantable heart pump (artificial heart), are being tested at several medical centers.
2. Both patient and graft survival rates in kidney transplantation are better when a living-related donor is used instead of a cadaver donor. Transplantation success rates also vary across transplant centers.
3. Unlike other immunosuppressive drugs, cyclosporine appears to inhibit the hormone that controls cells specifically involved in tissue rejection without at the same time destroying the body's immune defenses against infection. However, cyclosporine has also been shown to have undesirable side-effects, especially lymphoma, high blood pressure, and kidney damage, and the dosages given to transplant recipients are tapered off as soon as possible after surgery.
4. In Japan, however, the opposite is true; use of cadaver organs is viewed as a violation of the integrity of the soul.

REFERENCES

Adams, Timothy. 1983. "Debate Over Sale of Transplant Organs." *Atlanta Journal and Constitution,* November 13:sec. C, p. 17.

Anast, David. 1984. "Congressional Hearing on 'Transplantation into Nonimmigrant Aliens.'" *Contemporary Dialysis* 5:18, 20–21, 24.

Annas, George J. 1985a. "Regulating Heart and Liver Transplants in Massachusetts: An Overview of the Report of the Task Force on Organ Transplantation." *Law, Medicine & Health Care* 13:4–7.

———. 1985b. "The Dog and His Shadow: A Response to Overcast and Evans." *Law, Medicine & Health Care* 13:112–29.

Austen, W. Gerald, and A. Benedict Cosimi. 1984. "Heart Transplantation After 16 Years." *New England Journal of Medicine* 311:1436–38.

Banowsky, Lynn H.W. 1983. "Current Results and Future Expectations in Renal Transplantation." *Urologic Clinics of North America* 10:337–46.

Bassett, Beth Dawkins. 1985. "Hearts for Sale?" *Emory Magazine* 61:31.

Beierle, Andrew W.M. 1985. "A Conversation with Harrison Rogers; The President of the AMA Talks About the Problems and Priorities of Organized Medicine." *Emory Magazine* 61:19–23.

Blendon, Robert J., and Drew E. Altman. 1984. "Public Attitudes About Health-Care Costs: A Lesson in National Schizophrenia." *New England Journal of Medicine* 311:613–16.

Brewer, S.P. 1970. "Donors of Organs Seen as Victims." *New York Times,* April 19:36.

Burley, June A., and Calvin R. Stiller. 1985. "Emotionally Related Donors and Renal Transplantation." *Transplantation Proceedings* 17:123–27.

Caplan, Arthur L. 1984. "Ethical and Policy Issues in the Procurement of Cadaver Organs for Transplantation." *New England Journal of Medicine* 311:981–83.

———. 1985a. "Toward Greater Donor Organ Availability for Transplantation." *New England Journal of Medicine* 312:319.

———. 1985b. "If There's a Will, Is There a Way?" *Law, Medicine & Health Care* 13:32–34.

Casscells, Ward. 1985. "A Clinician's View of the Massachusetts Task Force on Organ Transplantation." *Law, Medicine & Health Care* 13:27–28.

———. 1986. "Heart Transplantation: Recent Policy Developments." *New England Journal of Medicine* 315:1365–68.

Corlett, Sue. 1985. "Professional and System Barriers to Organ Donation." *Transplantation Proceedings* 17:111–19.

Culyer, Anthony J., and Bruno Horisberger (eds.). 1983. *Economic and Medical Evaluation of Health Care Technologies*. New York: Springer-Verlag.

Curtis, John J. 1985. "Hypertension: A Common Problem for Kidney Transplant Recipients." *The Kidney* 18:2–8.

Dateline. 1986. "Latest HCFA Statistics Released." *Dialysis & Transplantation* 15:544–45.

Davis, Carolyne K. 1983. *Statement Before the Subcommittee on Investigations and Oversight, House Committee on Science and Technology*. Washington, D.C.: U.S. Department of Health & Human Services.

Dukeminier, Jesse, Jr., and David Sanders. 1968. "Organ Transplantation: A Proposal for Routine Salvaging of Cadaver Organs." *New England Journal of Medicine* 279:413–19.

Elick, Barbara A., and David E.R. Sutherland. Forthcoming. "Renal Transplantation Within A Multi-Organ Transplant System: One Institution's Experience." In *Maximizing Rehabilitation in Chronic Renal Disease*, edited by N.G. Kutner, D.D. Cardenas, and J.D. Bower. New York: SP Medical.

Evans, Roger W. 1983a. "Health Care Technology and the Inevitability of Resource Allocation and Rationing Decisions: Part I." *Journal of the American Medical Association* 249:2047–53.

———. 1983b. "Health Care Technology and the Inevitability of Resource Allocation and Rationing Decisions: Part II." *Journal of the American Medical Association* 249:2208–19.

———. 1985. "The Socioeconomics of Organ Transplantation." *Transplantation Proceedings* 17:129–36.

Evans, Roger W., Christopher R. Blagg, and Fred A. Bryan, Jr. 1981. "Implications for Health Care Policy: A Social and Demographic Profile of Hemodialysis Patients in the United States." *Journal of the American Medical Association* 245:487–91.

Evans, Roger W., Diane L. Manninen, Anthony Maier, Louis P. Garrison, Jr., and L. Gary Hart. 1985. "The Quality of Life of Kidney and Heart Transplant Recipients." *Transplantation Proceedings* 17:1579–82.

Forum of ESRD Networks. 1984. "1983 Program Report." *Contemporary Dialysis & Nephrology* 5(12):56–58.

Fox, Renée C., and Judith P. Swazey. 1978. *The Courage to Fail: A Social View of Organ Transplants and Dialysis*. Chicago: University of Chicago Press.

Fuchs, Victor R. 1984. "The 'Rationing' of Medical Care." *New England Journal of Medicine* 311: 1572–73.

Garrity, Thomas F., Grant W. Sommes, and Martin B. Marx. 1978. "Factors Influencing Self-Assessment of Health." *Social Science & Medicine* 12:77–81.

Gore, Albert, Jr. 1986. "Ignoring the National Organ Transplant Act 'Appears More and More to Be the Administration's Transplant Policy.'" *Contemporary Dialysis & Nephrology* 7:40–41.

Gulledge, A. Dale, Caroline Buszta, and Drogo K. Montague. 1983. "Psychosocial Aspects of Renal Transplantation." *Urologic Clinics of North America* 10:327–35.

Hamburger, Jean, and Jean Crosnier. 1968. "Moral and Ethical Problems in Transplantation." Pp. 37–44 in *Human Transplantation,* edited by F.T. Rapaport and J. Dausset. New York: Grune & Stratton.

Hoe, Marilyn M., Roger W. Evans, and Julie T. Elworth. 1984. *National Kidney Dialysis and Kidney Transplantation Study: A Summary of Results*. Baltimore: Health Care Financing Administration.

Johnson, Roger S. 1986. "Restrictive Policies Voted on by U.S. Task Force on Organ Transplantation." *Contemporary Dialysis & Nephrology* 7:18,20.

Jonsen, Albert R. 1985. "Organ Transplants and the Principle of Fairness." *Law, Medicine & Health Care* 13:37–39.

Kaplan, Arthur. 1983. "Organ Transplants Must Not Be Put on Highest Bidder Basis." *Atlanta Journal and Constitution,* October 2:sec. C, p. 16.

Kass, L.R. 1968. "A Caveat on Transplants." *Washington Post,* January 14:sec. B, p. 1.

Kissick, William L. 1985. "Organ Transplantation and the Art of the Possible." *Law, Medicine & Health Care* 13:34–35.

Kutner, Nancy G. 1982. "Cost-Benefit Issues in U.S. National Health Legislation: The Case of the End-

Stage Renal Disease Program." *Social Problems* 30:51–64.

———. 1985. "Racial Differences in the Transplant Attitudes and Experiences of Chronic Dialysis Patients." Paper presented at annual meeting of National Kidney Foundation, Inc., New Orleans, December 14.

Kutner, Nancy G., Donna Brogan, and Michael H. Kutner. Forthcoming. "ESRD Treatment Modality and Patients' Quality of Life: Longitudinal Assessment." *American Journal of Nephrology.*

Levey, Andrew S., Susan Hou, and Harry L. Bush, Jr. 1986. "Kidney Transplantation from Unrelated Living Donors: Time to Reclaim a Discarded Opportunity." *New England Journal of Medicine* 314:914–16.

Manne, Henry G. 1985. "U.S. Should Allow Sale of Organs for Transplants." *Atlanta Journal and Constitution,* October 20:sec. B, pp. 1,7.

Manninen, Diane L., and Roger W. Evans. 1985. "Public Attitudes and Behavior Regarding Organ Donation." *Journal of the American Medical Association* 253:3111–15.

Massachusetts Task Force on Organ Transplantation. 1985. "Report." *Law, Medicine & Health Care* 13:8–26.

Mayfield, Mark. 1986. "Transplants: Needs Many, Donors Few." *USA Today,* July 24:sec. A, pp. 1–2.

McGeown, Mary G. 1968. "Ethics for the Use of Live Donors in Kidney Transplantation." *American Heart Journal* 75:711–14.

Merriken, Karen J., and Thomas D. Overcast. 1985. "Patient Selection for Heart Transplantation: When Is a Discriminating Choice Discrimination?" *Journal of Health Politics, Policy and Law* 10:7–32.

Miller, Frances H. 1985. "Reflections on Organ Transplantation in the United Kingdom." *Law, Medicine & Health Care* 13:31–32.

Najarian, John S., and Nancy L. Asher. 1984. "Liver Transplantation." *New England Journal of Medicine* 311:1179–81.

Newsclips. 1985. "Blacks Not Getting Fair Share of Transplants." *Renalife* 2:9–10.

Nightingale, Joan E. 1985. "New Organ Transplantation Program: The Decision Tree." *Transplantation Proceedings* 17:137–42.

Overcast, Thomas D., and Roger W. Evans. 1985. "Technology Assessment, Public Policy and Transplantation: A Restrained Appraisal of the Massachusetts Task Force Approach." *Law, Medicine & Health Care* 13:106–11.

Overcast, Thomas D., Roger W. Evans, Lisa E. Bowen, Marilyn M. Hoe, and Cynthia L. Livak. 1984. "Problems in the Identification of Potential Organ Donors." *Journal of the American Medical Association* 251:1559–62.

Palmer, Prentice. 1985. "High Court Upholds Law on Corneal Transplants." *Atlanta Constitution,* October 10:sec. B, p. 9.

Pauly, Mark V. 1985. "Equity and Costs." *Law, Medicine & Health Care* 13:28–31.

Peele, Amy S., and Oscar Salvatierra, Jr. 1986. "Is Routine Inquiry the Answer to Solving the Organ Donor Shortage?" *Contemporary Dialysis & Nephrology* 7:5,43–44.

Pisano, L. 1985. "Critical Comments on Present and Future Possibilities and Advantages of Pancreas Transplantation in Insulin-Dependent Diabetes Mellitus." *Transplantation Proceedings* 17:135.

Plough, Alonzo L. 1986. *Borrowed Time: Artificial Organs and the Politics of Extending Lives.* Philadelphia: Temple University.

Rapaport, Felix T., and Raffaello Cortesini. 1985. "The Past, Present, and Future of Organ Transplantation, with Special Reference to Current Needs in Kidney Procurement and Donation." *Transplantation Proceedings* 17:3–10.

Reiner, Mark, William Eagles, and Ken Watson. 1986. "Organ Bingo: Choice or Chance?" *Dialysis & Transplantation* 15:441–42.

Rettig, Richard A. 1980. *Implementing the End-Stage Renal Disease Program of Medicare.* Santa Monica: Rand Corporation.

Roberts, Stephen D. 1980. "Cost-Effective Oxygen Therapy." *Annals of Internal Medicine* 93:499–500.

Roughton, Bert. 1986. "More than $50,000 Is Pledged to Help 5-Year-Old Heart Patient." *Atlanta Constitution,* March 18:sec. C, p. 7.

Rushing, William A. 1985. "The Supply of Physicians and Expenditures for Health Services with Implications for the Coming Physician Surplus." *Journal of Health and Social Behavior* 26:297–311.

Schroeder, John Speer, and Sharon A. Hunt. 1986. "Cardiac Transplantation: Where Are We?" *New England Journal of Medicine* 315:961–63.

Seabrook, Charles. 1985. "Augusta's Transplant Rate Poor: Survival Record of Heart Recipients Falling Short." *Atlanta Journal and Constitution,* June 9:sec. A, pp. 1,14.

Sharpe, Gilbert. 1985. "Commerce in Tissue and Organs." *Transplantation Proceedings* 17:33–39.

Simmons, Roberta G. 1985. "Social and Psychological Posttransplant Adjustment." Pp. 85–97 in *Rehabilitation and the Chronic Renal Disease Patient,* edited by N.G. Kutner, D.D. Cardenas, and J.D. Bower. New York: SP, Medical.

Simmons, Roberta G., Kathy Hickey, Carl M. Kjellstrand, and Richard L. Simmons. 1971. "Family Tension in the Search for a Kidney Donor." *Journal of the American Medical Association* 215:909–12.

Simmons, Roberta G., Susan D. Klein, and Richard L. Simmons. 1977. *Gift of Life: The Social and Psy-*

chological Impact of Organ Transplantation. New York: Wiley.
Simmons, Roberta G., and Susan Klein Marine. 1984. "The Regulation of High Cost Technology Medicine: The Case of Dialysis and Transplantation in the United Kingdom." *Journal of Health and Social Behavior* 25:320–34.
Simmons, Roberta G., and Richard L. Simmons. 1971. "Organ Transplantation: A Societal Problem." *Social Problems* 19:36–57.
Skelley, Luke. 1985. "Practical Issues in Obtaining Organs for Transplantation." *Law, Medicine & Health Care* 13:35–37.
Starzl, Thomas E., S. Iwatsuki, B.W. Shaw, Jr., R.D. Gordon, C. Esquivel, S. Todo, I. Kam, and S. Lynch. 1985. "Factors in the Development of Liver Transplantation." *Transplantation Proceedings* 17: 107–18.
Stickel, D.L. 1966. "Ethical and Moral Aspects of Transplantation." *Monographs of Surgical Science* 3:267–301.
Strong, Margaret, and Carson Strong. 1985. "The Shortage of Organs for Transplantation." *ANNA Journal* 12:239–42.
Surman, Owen S. 1985. "Toward Greater Donor Organ Availability for Transplantation." *New England Journal of Medicine* 312:318.
Terasaki, Paul. 1985. "Renal Transplantation in Blacks: Special Issues and Challenges." Paper presented at First International Symposium on Renal Failure in Blacks, Washington, D.C., April 29.
Toledo-Pereyra, Luis H. 1986. "Practical Immunologic Aspects of Clinical Pancreas and Islet Cell Transplantation." *Dialysis & Transplantation* 15(a): pp. 514–16, 520, 522.
U.S. News. 1986. "Gallup Organ Survey Results Reported." *Contemporary Dialysis & Nephrology* 7: 15–16.
Wolstenholme, Gordon, Ethelbert Ward, & Maeve O'Connor (eds.). 1966. *Ethics in Medical Progress: With Special Reference to Transplantation.* Boston: Little, Brown.
Youngner, Stuart J., Martha Allen, Edward T. Bartlett, Helmut F. Cascorbi, Toni Hau, David L. Jackson, Mary B. Mahowald, and Barbara J. Martin. 1985. "Psychosocial and Ethical Implications of Organ Retrieval." *New England Journal of Medicine* 313:321–24.

35 A Mirage of Genes

Peter Conrad

INTRODUCTION

In his classic book *Mirage of Health,* Rene Dubos (1959) contends that the ultimate conquest of disease is illusory and that what constitutes health is fundamentally humans adapting to their environments. Because environments continually change, an inevitable amount of maladaptation results, often manifested as disease. Since health consists of adaptation to changing environments, the existence of something approaching a perfect state of health is a mirage.

Dubos' writings have influenced generations of medical sociologists and public health thinkers, and his analysis provided the theoretical underpinnings of the important empirical research of McKeown (1971) and McKinlay and McKinlay (1977). Dubos' work is still prominently cited in textbooks for its seminal contributions to medical sociological thinking.

He was sceptical about the predominant germ theory explanations of the conquest of infectious disease and was among the first to observe that the decrease in incidence of most infectious diseases occurred before the introduction of vaccines and antibiotics. He hypothesised that the reforms inspired by the Sanitation Movement and a rising standard of living were more critical for the reduction of disease mortality in society than the advent of germ theory.[1]

Dubos had studied the history of tuberculosis and observed that mortality rates from the disease were declining prior to the discovery of the TB bacillus and long before the availability of any form of biomedical intervention. He was critical of the belief that germs *cause* disease; they may be necessary but not sufficient causes of most diseases. He noted, for example, that many individuals harboured the TB microbe but did not have tuberculosis. Germ theory as a causal model was too simplistic, and narrowed our vision about disease aetiology. In particular cases, like TB, it was restricting, misleading and at times mistaken. But Dubos' thesis is not widely known outside the medical social science and public health worlds; in many circles germ-theory-based interventions alone are credited with 'conquering' infectious diseases.

In the 20th century, germ theory the notion that microbes cause disease became the dominant popular explanation of disease causation. While the germ theory model is still prevalent, its dominance has been challenged, complemented and supplemented by environmental theories, lifestyle perspectives, alternative medicine and other explanatory frameworks (*cf.* Tesh 1988). Emily Martin (1994) has recently proposed the flexible body with its immune system as another emergent model.

In the past three decades new genetic models have come to the forefront of medical thinking and have become the cutting edge of much research on disease and behaviour. In this paper I build upon Dubos' depiction of germ theory to assess why genetic explanations have been so readily accepted in medicine and the public discourse, even when the evidence in many cases is limited. Moreover, I want to suggest that some of the illusions Dubos pointed out for germ theory have their parallels with genetic explanations. My concern here is the popular image and discourse about genes, essentially how we talk about genes and genetic causation. My interest focuses on the viability of genetic conceptions rather than the validity of particular genetic associations.

The impetus for this paper, and some of the evidence, comes from my current study of how genetics is presented in the news. Specifically, I am examining how findings related to behavioural genetics (alcoholism, homosexuality, depression and schizophrenia, violence and intelligence) have been reported by the American and British press over a 30-year period. Systematic analysis of these data are found elsewhere (Conrad and Weinberg 1996; Conrad 1997; Conrad 1998; Conrad forthcoming). The goal of this paper is more limited: to outline some general features about how genetics is conceptualised in the press and in popular discourse. I use the news media as a vehicle for understanding the public discourse around genetics; I make no claim that this discourse by itself represents "popular thinking" about genetics. But the news medium is the major avenue by which genetic findings and theories get infused into the culture, so it is likely to have a significant impact on popular conceptions of genetics.

THE GERM THEORY MODEL AND THE ACCEPTANCE OF GENETICS

Germ theory is the basis of the clinical medical model that underlies medical and public thinking about disease. This perspective provides an overall lens for seeing and treating disease in modern society. Dubos articulated the structure of the germ theory model as consisting of three interrelated and fundamental assumptions: the doctrine of specific aetiology; a focus on the internal rather than the external environment; and the metaphor of the body as a machine.

The doctrine of specific aetiology contends that every disease has a specific and knowable causal agent. Based on the laboratory work of giants like Koch and Pasteur, the belief is that each disease is caused by a specific microorganism such as a germ or virus. This was not only limited to infectious diseases:

> From the field of infection the doctrine of specific etiology spread rapidly to other areas of medicine . . . Microbial agents, disturbances in essential metabolic processes, deficiencies in growth factors or hormones, and physiological stresses are now regarded as specific causes of disease. (Dubos 1959: 101–2)

Dubos recognised that the doctrine of specific aetiology was a very constructive approach in medical research, but emphasised that "few are the cases in which it has provided a complete account of the causation of disease" (1959: 102). We still see the objective of specific aetiology embraced in various forms in medicine, such as medicine's continual search for *the* cause of cancer.

The second assumption of germ theory is a focus on the internal environment. As Dubos (1959: 101) and others have noted, until the late 19th century, disease had been widely looked upon as an imbalance or disharmony between the sick person and the environment. Thus the aetiological search typically included the environment and disturbances in the individual's relation to it. With the advent of germ theory, however, the clinical focus shifted entirely to the internal environment: How do the microbes affect cells, organs and tissues to produce disease? In the clinical realm, the external environment became largely superfluous for understanding the causes of disease.[2]

The final germ theory assumption, conceptualising the body as a machine, is less explicit in Dubos' writing. This assumption is mechanistic in orientation; that the body is made up of repairable and replaceable parts where problematic functioning can be identified and remedied. Dubos touched on this in his discussion of medicine's pursuit of "magic bullets" to eradicate disease-producing microbes. The machine metaphor is manifested in other clinical interventions including organ transplants, joint replacements, hormone substitutes (*e.g.* insulin for diabetes), supplements for biochemical processes (*e.g.* serotonin levels), or seeking technologies like the artificial heart. I do not mean to suggest that these interventions are not effective; indeed, many are. But the metaphor suggests that by treating the body as a machine we will solve the problem. Frequently the underlying difficulty remains and new problems are created. My point here, however, brackets effectiveness; I simply want to indicate that the dominant model in clinical medicine conceptualises the body as a machine that can be repaired.

My claim is that the public depiction of the new genetics aligns perfectly with the old germ theory model and, independent of scientific validity, fuels the acceptance of genetics in medicine and society. Genetics in the public discourse carries similar and familiar assumptions that are already present in germ theory. I shall briefly outline how the three assumptions of germ theory pertain to the new genetics.

We increasingly hear about discoveries of genes for disease and behaviours; reading the news, it often seems as if announcements of new discoveries appear as frequently as a "gene of the week." The popular conception is really a monogenic model of specific aetiology: a gene or genetic mutation determines a disease or behaviour. While some well-known cases of monogenic causation have been identified, such as cystic fibrosis or Huntington's disease, these are unusual. More typically genes may play a role in aetiology, but are not determinative (Strohman 1993). Single-gene disorders are the exception, yet the model of gene specificity is common, creating an OGOD assumption: one gene, one disease. This is manifested in talking about finding a gene "for" a particular trait or in terming genetic findings as "the breast cancer gene," "the gay gene," or "the obesity gene."

By focusing on genetics, we home in on the internal environment, primarily on the level of DNA. When we talk about discovering a gene for a particular trait or disease, we often make the assumption that the internal environment is the primary causative factor. A gene for alcoholism is more significant than cultural meanings of drinking; a gene for schizophrenia is deemed more primary than family environment. Nature trumps nurture. Rarely is the talk about how genes can be expressed in different environments; the assumption is that genes, like microbes, can be determinant apart from context.

Genes are often pictured as the blueprint for the body as machine. We can see the mechanistic metaphor when genes are depicted as the coding device which determines how some bodily feature or function will be manifested. Genetic testing can sometimes ascertain whether an individual has a faulty part that may lead to disease or debility. The metaphor is evidenced when we talk about gene therapy in terms of replacing faulty genes or selecting particular genes for human enhancement. Change the gene and fix the problem. The field of genetic engineering is based on this assumption. The recent discourse on human cloning reflects the metaphor as well; the assumption that a cloned offspring would grow up virtually identical to its "parent," dispensing with all life experience and effects of social context.

In my view, the close fit between germ theory and gene theory is one of the chief reasons that genetic explanations have been so readily accepted in medicine and the popular discourse. At least on the level of assumptions and structure, gene theory does not challenge common conceptions of aetiology but rather shifts its focus. In this sense at least, genetics is a complementary rather than a challenging paradigm in medicine (see Strohman 1997). Many of Dubos' caveats and criticisms about germ theory similarly pertain to genetics. In the next section I shall examine some of the pitfalls and illusions in the popular conceptions of genetics.

PITFALLS AND ILLUSIONS

Based on the characteristics of germ theory he identified, Dubos outlined some of their pitfalls and limitations in understanding disease causation. We can see some remarkable parallels with genetics.

The Illusion of Specific Aetiology

In scientific announcements, news reports and popular discourse we frequently hear of specific disease or behaviour genes. The image is that this newly discovered gene—its presence or absence—causes a particular trait. The OGOD (one gene, one disease) assumption is the image of specific aetiology.

Until recently human genetics was not interested in particular genes, focusing rather on how traits were heritable. Adoption and twin studies produced heritability estimates and relied on concordance among relatives to measure genetic influence. With the maturation of molecular biology in the last three decades, scientists have begun to identify specific genes associated with human traits and disorders (Billings *et al.* 1992).

Some of the early discoveries were very impressive. Scientists identified specific genes for disorders like cystic fibrosis, Huntington's disease, Duchenne muscular dystrophy, and Fragile X Syndrome. For all practical purposes, in these cases we have specific aetiology. But such single gene disorders are relatively rare; they constitute only two per cent of disease morbidity. Yet discourse about genetics slides almost seamlessly from monogenic disorders to any case of genetic association. It is as if a classic Mendelian model of genetics prevails in the popular discourse.

Over the past decade front page news stories announced the discovery of the "gay gene," "breast cancer gene" and "obesity gene." The imagery of the language suggested that a specific gene had been identified. In each instance, such an interpretation was at best misleading, if not downright wrong. When Dean Hamer identified the Xq28 marker for male homosexuality (Hamer *et al.* 1993), we soon saw depictions and discussions of the implications of discovering a gay gene. What Hamer found, however, was a "marker" associated with male homosexuality—designating an area on the X chromosome containing perhaps hundreds of genes. Thus there was no gene for homosexuality. For breast cancer, scientists did indeed identify a specific gene, BRCA1 (and soon followed by BRCA2) that is associated with breast cancer (Miki *et al.* 1994). Initial reports suggested women with this gene had a 50 per cent chance of developing breast cancer by the age of 50 and an 80 per cent chance by 70 (these estimates have since been reduced). But even here, this could not rightly be termed *the* breast cancer gene, but *a* breast cancer gene. Roughly 5–10 per cent of all breast cancer is hereditary; the BRCA genes did not appear related to 90 per cent of breast cancer. While identifying a specific gene for breast cancer is surely a great breakthrough, it does not mean that most breast cancer is genetic. News about the obesity gene (cutely named by scientists the ob gene or tubby gene) appeared in most major newspapers and magazines. Hope for those struggling with overweight may have been kindled, but the only obesity gene scientists so far have found produces fat mice. The obesity gene, whatever validity it has for mice, has yet to be demonstrated relevant for humans. Moreover, important conceptual and aetiological differences exist between diseases and behaviours, which are subsumed and ignored by depictions of 'the' gene for a particular problem.

Rather than specific aetiology, in the great majority of cases, genes are not directly deterministic, if we mean that if the gene is present an individual will inevitably get the disorder (Rutter and Plomin 1997). For most diseases (*e.g.* hypertension, diabetes, asthma, coronary heart disease), genes are a probabilistic rather than deterministic cause. The language of specific aetiology "disarticulates complex properties of individuals into isolated lumps of biology." (Rose 1995: 301). Dubos' (1959: 102) observations seem suitable for genetics:

> In reality, however, the search for *the* cause may be a hopeless pursuit because most disease is an indirect outcome of a constellation of circumstances rather than a direct result of a single determinant factor.

Beyond the Internal Environment

As with germ theory, genetics focuses the medical gaze on the internal environment. But with genetics, the issue often is framed in terms of nature versus nurture. Most geneticists acknowledge that for many diseases and most behaviours, the issue is nature *and* nurture (Rutter and Plomin 1997), but the question is how much weight to give to each. In the popular discourse genetics is often privileged (Nelkin and Lindee 1995, Conrad 1997), and genes are presented as if they operated independently of their environment.

On one level, we know what DNA does; it codes for proteins. What is frequently unclear are the mechanisms by which genes are implicated with diseases or traits. It is certainly a long way from producing a protein to causing a specific human behaviour. But even with diseases like cystic fibrosis we don't know how the gene works in relation to the manifestation of the disorder (Marks 1996). What is important is how genes are expressed in environments.

In Kitcher's (1996) terms, genes are associated with particular traits in the context of a "standard environment." When geneticists say that people carrying a gene (or more accurately, an 'allele') will develop a particular trait, they mean it will be manifested in a standard environment, not necessarily in all environments. For example, in cases like phenylketonuria (PKU) the genetic propensity for the disease is not manifested under a specific dietary environment. Particular environments may be as necessary as genes, but neither geneticists nor the public talk about an environment for this or that condition.

With behaviour, it is usually clear that the external (social) environment is significant in how genes are expressed. If there were a gene associated with alcoholism, how could we imagine its expression? Would it be a gene that causes an individual to open a bottle and imbibe the drink? How would such a gene fare in a Muslim culture? With homosexuality, studies of identical twins show over a 50 per cent concordance among gay siblings; but what about the other 50 per cent? Even with siblings who had the Xq28 marker associated with homosexuality, more than a third were not gay. Genetics without an external environment is an incomplete explanation.

There is evidence that genes can create environments. Certain characteristics in children (at least partly genetically influenced) can evoke negative responses from family members which in turn affect the children (Patterson 1982, cited in Rutter and Plomin 1997). In this case, nature modifies nurture which may affect how genetic propensities are expressed. Moreover, people's own characteristics play a significant role in selecting and shaping their external environments (Jencks 1980). Attractive or athletic children may receive more attention than awkward or plain children. Children who are bright may be attracted to books; aggressive children may have aggressive friends. At the very least, internal and external environments are interactive. As geneticist Richard C. Lewontin (1991: 30) points out:

> Environmental variation and genetic variation are not independent causal pathways. Genes affect how sensitive one is to the environment and environment affects how relevant one's genetic differences may be.

The environment also can be critical to "turning on and off" genes; for example, the adoption of new exercise regimens can turn on genes that regulate muscle building.

But the focus of the news stories and public discourse is squarely on the internal environment. The BRCA1 gene provides an interesting example. BRCA1 is a tumour suppresser gene. Most women are born with two copies of the gene and have no problem. Those with the inherited BRCA1 mutation have only a single copy. A single copy is sufficient for tumour suppression until, for some reason, it is "knocked out" and a woman is left without the gene. Then she becomes extremely vulnerable to breast or ovarian cancer. The lack of the BRCA1 allele is seen as the cause of breast cancer. Yet could we not also ask, what caused the second copy of the gene to get knocked out? Could not environmental risk factors like a women's past exposure to radiation be critical in understanding how the mutation leads to cancer?

As Dubos (1959: 128) noted:

> . . . the internal environment is constantly responding to the external environment, and history racial, social, as well as individual conditions the manner of response just as much as does the intrinsic nature of the stimulus.

Does it make sense to talk about genes causing particular traits without explicating how they are expressed in the external environment?

Chinks in the Body as a Machine Metaphor

Faulty genes are depicted as causes of disease or behaviour. Fix the gene and the problem will be solved. It is as if genes were a thing that can be separated from the system in which they operate. Such a mechanistic view is an oversimplistic rendition of how genes affect most human traits.

Most geneticists recognise that genetic influences are usually polygenic—traits are determined by many genes acting together—or epigenetic, which involves single-gene or multiple-gene interaction with the environment.

> Epigenesis implies a level of complexity beyond gene-gene interaction and extends to interaction between genes, between genes and gene products (proteins), and between all these and environmental signals, including, of course, individual organismal experience. (Strohman 1993: 114)

The complexity of genetic action belies the scientific utility of the machine metaphor. A single gene may have multiple sites for a mutation.

> A typical gene consists of thousands of base pairs, any one of which is subject to a mutation. In some cases, different mutations in the same gene can lead to very different manifestations of disease. (Alper 1997)

For example, with cystic fibrosis (CF) genes, over 350 mutations are known. This makes genetic testing for CF alleles much more difficult, illustrating that even clearly identified genes are subject to complex interactions. Some forms of CF are so mild that individuals are never aware of it until they undergo genetic testing.

Recent discussions of "shadow syndromes" (Ratey and Johnson 1997) contend that quirky behaviours may actually be mild mental illnesses. Numerous life problems could be included in this model. The brilliant computer geek who can't make conversation has low level autism; the extremely tidy housekeeper has a mild form of obsessive compulsive disorder; the assertive but disorganised salesman has a touch of attention deficit disorder. These alleged shadow syndromes have been tied to genes. This is an additive model; one or two genes give you a little disorder; perhaps three or four creates a serious personality problem; and seven gives you a full-blown illness. Illness and behaviours are seen on a continuum; the arithmetic genetic loading affects the manifestation of the problem. A couple of genes might make one a bit impulsive; a few more leads to a difficulty in controlling impulses; a dozen could make someone into an out-of-control risk seeker. Genes are deemed causative, with their effects incumbent on their cumulative nature. As one psychiatrist noted, genes may be responsible for shadow syndromes, "But as you increase the number of genes you pass over a threshold to a clinical syndrome" (quoted in Bagley 1998: 53). While such an arithmetic model could modify the assumptions of specific aetiology, at the same time it extends the focus on the internal environment and mechanistic metaphor, expanding the conceptual influence of genes.

Discovering genes is of course not the goal of medicine. Medicine is concerned with preventing and treating diseases. As Dubos (1959: 153) notes, medicine's "most important task . . . is to discover some magic bullet capable of reaching and destroying the responsible demon within the body . . ." The promise of magic bullets for genetic disorders is gene therapy. The clinical strategy here is straightforward: identify the bad copy of a gene and replace it with good copy; knock out problem genes and insert new genes. Simple enough in theory, although gene therapy has yet to be accomplished for human ailments.

The discovery of a specific gene does not necessarily lead to successful treatments. Identifying a Huntington's gene or BRCA1 may result in changing individual reproductive or preventative actions, but as yet we have no magic bullets for treatment. It is unclear what future treatments for epigenetic problems might be, given the complexity of causation.

This highlights an interesting difference in comparison to the acceptance of germ theory. Germ theory achieved broad credibility *after* the advent of vaccines and antibiotics. By contrast, it appears genetic explanations have come to be routinely accepted in the absence of gene therapies. While there is yet no "magic bullet," faith in the genetic model remains undimmed.[3]

One disturbing implication of the pervasiveness of the machine metaphor is reductionism (*e.g.* see Rose 1995). This is especially true in the behavioural realm, where complex behaviours are deemed determined by genes. As Richard Horton, the editor of *Lancet,* points out, there exists a

> . . . popular rhetoric of DNA, which supposes an irreducible and immutable unit of the human self. The correlation between potentially active genes and a behavior pattern is assumed to indicate cause and effect. (Horton 1995: 38)

The scientific and public discourse are replete with instances of talking about genes "for" particular traits, such as genes for breast and colon cancer, homosexuality, schizophrenia and even bed-wetting. As Kitcher notes, "genetalk" reflects an image

> of human bodies as built up of DNA laborers, each making an isolated contribution: Here 'the gene for eye color' goes to work injecting a special pigment, there 'the gene for muscles' assembles a host of cells. (1996: 239)

Virtually an army of industrious genes are working to create all variations of human traits.

The machine metaphor helps to sustain the notion that genetics is the primary cause of a phenomenon, which may not be the case. It reinforces ideas of "genetic essentialism" (Nelkin and Lindee 1995), seeing humans as fundamentally products of their DNA. In its extreme, this can become a type of "genetic fatalism," whereby genetic associations to behaviours or conditions are deemed to be deterministic and unchangeable (Alper and Beckwith 1995).

GENETIC DETERMINISM AND SUSCEPTIBILITY

In much scientific and public discourse the complexity of genetics is ignored and genes are represented as if they were the causes of diseases and behaviours. This has spawned a naive form of genetic determinism that assumes (in language at least) that there are specific genes for specific traits under all circumstances.

While undoubtedly genes exert important influences on human life, for the most part they are not deterministic. We would be better served if we consciously recast genetic influence as "genetic susceptibility."[4] This suggests that individuals may have a "genetic loading" for a particular trait, but does not assume determinism. It reflects an understanding that there is a genetic component, but is agnostic about the weight to assign to genetic action. I prefer susceptibility to "predisposition," where the latter reflects more the imagery of a built in mechanism ready to manifest itself, and sounds uncomfortably close to predestination. Susceptibility, like risk, implies probability and interaction, with genes as a contributing rather than determinative factor.

In his discussion of germ theory, Dubos (1959: 66) noted that microbes are not good or bad in themselves yet have a bad reputation for producing disease in humans. He points out, for example, how important micro-organisms are for human digestion or for culturing yoghurt. So it may be with some genetic mutations; particular genetic mutations may actually be beneficial to humans in some environments. It has long been known that the sickle cell trait, common among those with African ancestry, provides a resistance for the carrier to malaria. It has been recently reported that a defective CF gene is likely to benefit the carrier with better resistance to typhoid fever. In both cases disease risk occurs in the offspring of two carriers, but the genetic mutation itself may be protective and evolutionarily adaptive.

Virtually everyone has some genes that make them susceptible to diseases or traits we might find problematic. All of us are genetically liable to some human trouble, be it allergies, nearsightedness, baldness, depression, or forms of heart disease or cancer. The trick is to understand how these susceptibilities interact with particular environments to produce or not produce human traits or disorders. This should be intriguing territory for sociologists interested in genetics and the production of disease (see Richards 1993).

THE ALLURE OF SPECIFICITY AND A MIRAGE OF GENES

Given the growing sophistication of molecular biology and the attendant rising genetic paradigm, it is not surprising that an increasing number of human problems are attributed to the workings of genes. But despite the complexity of human behaviour and disease, the public discourse frequently ascribes undue causal power to genes. It is not that genes have no influence; indeed, often their influence is substantial. Rather, we see a privileging of genetic explanations in the media and public discourse.

A significant attraction of genetic explanations is the allure of specificity. Biological theories of human problems have long been popular (Gould 1981) but genetics has allowed a new focus on the particular. With genes we have a tangible causal agent, a strip of DNA we can point to, rather than messy and slippery epidemiological or social factors. Genes seem to be real "things," with a physical presence. We can have a gene on the short arm of the X chromosome or identified as BRCA1, not "merely" risk factors like radiation exposure or diet, much less intangibles like social class or stress. There is also an aesthetic elegance and simplicity to gene theory. One molecular biologist put it well:

> The theory of the gene is complete and wonderfully so; it is beautiful and magnificent in its utter simplicity. A child could understand it and millions of children now do. But if you mistakenly ask them what it means in terms of function you have shamed them (Strohman 1997: 196).

In the public discourse, simple aetiologies are communicated easily. Too many qualifications and complexities may confuse and undermine an explanation. While genetic causation like germ theory is not as specific as it appears, the appearance of specificity enhances the acceptance of genetic explanations, independent of the validity of scientific findings.

In the next decade, with the completion of the Human Genome Project, we are likely to see an acceleration in discoveries of genes "for" human traits, behaviours and diseases. As Dubos cautioned us for germ theory, we need to be alert that what at first seems to be so clear turns out to be a mirage when we look at it more closely.

The news reporting of genetics and behaviour can create a media version of a mirage of genes. In the past decade there have been numerous announcements by scientists of the discovery of a new gene associated with behaviour—alcoholism, schizophrenia, bipolar illness, thrill-seeking—only to be retracted when the research cannot be replicated by others, or the association disappears upon closer examination. When the genes are found the news is trumpeted on page one, but when the findings cannot be confirmed the stories are buried as a small item in the back pages, if noted at all (Conrad 1997, Conrad forthcoming). These "disconfirmations" are common in science, but it is difficult for the news and public discourse to keep up. The result amplifies finding genes and mutes their subsequent loss, giving the public a false sense of continuous genetic discovery.

I have argued that the cultural resonance with germ theory facilitates the public acceptance and rise of the genetic paradigm. This is not the only sociological reason why genetics has become more popular. As others have pointed out, gene theory also appeals to existing western ideas of individuality and current notions about responsibility for health, and shifts blame for problems from environments and social structures to individuals and biophysiology (Nelkin and Lindee 1995). The huge investment in biomedical funding for genetics and the vast international scientific industry which it supports creates an apparatus continually producing new genetic findings. Professional collaborations between scientists, industry and physicians have put genetics on the cutting edge of me-dical-scientific thinking. But the pitfalls Dubos identified 40 years ago may point to directions where sociologists can provide an intellectual balance and critique of geneticisation (see Conrad 1997).

Perhaps the fate of genetic explanations will parallel that of germ theory; decontextualising aetiological processes, underrepresenting the role of environments, producing some stunning medical interventions, revealing little about the fate of populations, and becoming the most popular explanation for what ails us. The rising influence and ubiquity of the genetic paradigm is already evident in medicine and popular discourse. It is our challenge to continue to explicate the social realities of illness and behaviour in the midst of an enticing and widening genetic mirage.

ACKNOWLEDGMENTS

My thanks to Charles Bosk, Phil Brown, Steven Epstein, Lisa Geller and the anonymous reviewers for comments on an earlier draft of this paper. This research was supported in part by a grant for the section on Ethical, Legal and Social Implications of the Human Genome Project of the National Institutes of Health (1 R55 HGO0849-01A1).

NOTES

1. Nearly two decades after *Mirage of Health* was published, McKeown (1971) and McKinlay and McKinlay (1977) empirically demonstrated Dubos' thesis and applied it to other infectious diseases as well.
2. My emphasis here is on clinical medicine and aetiology. Public health continued to examine the environment, often a vector for the transmission of disease. This approach of course remained critical for preventive strategies, but for proximate cause and clinical interventions, the focus is overwhelmingly on the internal environment.
3. My thanks to Steve Epstein for pointing this out to me.
4. While some geneticists already employ the term susceptibility gene, it is not yet common in the public discourse.

REFERENCES

Alper, J.S. (1997) Complexity. Unpublished paper.

Alper, J.S. and Beckwith, J. (1995) Genetic fatalism and social policy: the implications of behavior genetics research, *Yale Journal of Biology and Medicine*, 66, 511–24.

Bagley, S. (1998) Is everybody crazy? *Newsweek*, 5 January, 50–5.

Billings, P.R., Beckwith, J. and Alper, J.S. (1992) The genetic analysis of human behavior: a new era? *Social Science and Medicine*, 35, 227–38.

Conrad, P. (1997) Public eyes and private genes: historical frames, news constructions, and social problems, *Social Problems*, 44, 139–54.

Conrad, P. (1998) Constructing the 'gay gene': optimism and skepticism in the news. Paper presented at the meeting of the International Sociological Association, Montreal, Canada.

Conrad, P. (forthcoming) Media images, genetics and culture: potential impacts of reporting scientific findings on bioethics. In Hoffmaster, B. and Wylie, A. (eds) *Bioethics in Context*. London and New York: Cambridge University Press.

Conrad, P. and Weinberg, D. (1997) Has the gene for alcoholism been discovered three times since 1980? A news media analysis. *Perspectives on Social Problems*, 8, 3–24.

Dubos, R. (1959) *Mirage of Health*. New York: Harper and Row.

Gould, S.J. (1981) *The Mismeasure of Man*. New York: Norton.

Hamer, D., Hu, S., Magnuson, V.L., Hu, N. and Pattatucci, A.M.L. (1993) A linkage between DNA markers on the X chromosome and male sexual orientation, *Science*, 261, 321–7.

Horton, R. (1995) Is homosexuality inherited? *New York Review of Books*, 13 July, 36–41.

Jencks, C. (1980) Heredity, environment and public policy reconsidered, *American Sociological Review*, 45, 723–36.

Kitcher, P. (1996) *The Lives to Come: The Genetic Revolution and Human Possibilities*. New York: Simon and Schuster.

Lewontin, R.C. (1991) *Biology as Ideology: the Doctrine of DNA*. New York: Harper Perennial.

Marks, J. (1996) Skepticism about behavioral genetics. In Frankel, M.S. (ed) *Exploring Public Policy Issues in Genetics*. American Association for the Advancement of Science.

Martin, E. (1994) *Flexible Bodies: Tracking Immunity in American Culture from the Days of Polio to the Age of AIDS*. Boston: Beacon Press.

McKeown, T. (1971) A historical appraisal of the medical task. In McLachlan, G. and McKeown, T. *Medical History and Medical Care: A Symposium of Perspectives*. New York: Oxford.

McKinlay, J.B. and McKinlay, S.K. (1977) The questionable contribution of medical measures to the decline of mortality in the United States, *Milbank Memorial Fund Quarterly/Health and Society*, 55, 205–28.

Miki, Y., Swanson, J., Shattuck, D., Futreal, P.A. *et al.* (1994) A strong candidate for breast and ovarian cancer susceptibility gene BRCA1, *Science,* 266, 66–71.

Nelkin, D. and Lindee, M.S. (1995) *The DNA Mystique: the Gene as a Cultural Icon.* New York: W.H. Freeman.

Patterson, G.R. (1982) *Coercive Family Process.* Eugene, OR: Castalia Publishing Company.

Ratey, J. and Johnson, C. (1997) *Shadow Syndromes.* New York: Pantheon.

Richards, M.P.M. (1993) The new genetics-issues for social scientists, *Sociology of Health and Illness,* 15, 567–86.

Rose, S. (1995) The Rise of neurogenetic determinism, *Nature,* 373, 380–2.

Rutter, M. and Plomin, R. (1997) Opportunities for psychiatry from genetic findings, *British Journal of Psychiatry,* 171, 209–19.

Strohman, R.C. (1993) Ancient genomes, wise bodies, unhealthy people: limits of a genetic paradigm in biology and medicine, *Perspectives in Biology and Medicine,* 37, 112–45.

Strohman, R.C. (1997) The coming Kuhnian revolution in biology, *Nature Biotechnology,* 15, 194–200.

Tesh, S.N. (1988) *Hidden Arguments: Political Ideology and Disease Prevention.* New Brunswick, NJ: Rutger's University Press.

PART 3 Contemporary Critical Debates

Up until this point, we have presented our analysis of health and medical care as if all critical analysts were more or less in agreement. But in health care, as in any social and intellectual enterprise, controversies rage over the source of problems and over appropriate solutions. In Part 3, we present selections illustrative of contemporary debates on three different but related issues in the sociology of health and illness.

The Relevance of Risk

The focus of medicine is changing. For most of modern history medicine has been concerned with the causes and treatment of *diseases*. In recent years medicine has become much more concerned with the reduction and prevention of *risks*. The forefront of public health medicine and research in the United States attempts to identify *risk factors* associated with various diseases.

Risk factors are usually statistically-based associations derived from epidemiological research. As mentioned in an earlier section, epidemiology is "the study of the distributions and determinants of states of health in human populations" (Susser, 1973). Risk is derived from a multi-dimensional assessment of factors and related to the probability of an event or illness occurring. For example, researchers have found a strong association between cigarette smoking and rates of lung cancer and heart disease; thus we can say cigarette smoking is a risk factor for cancer and heart disease. In a different arena, obesity increases the risk for diabetes. To take another kind of example, women with the BRCA1 or BRCA2 genetic mutation are at higher risk for the development of breast cancer (see "A Mirage of Genes," selection 35).

There are several types of health risks: biological, environmental, and behavioral. Biological risks reside in the body, such as genes or genetic markers that have been shown to be associated with particular diseases. Environmental risks stem from environmental conditions that have been shown to be related to disease, such as toxic wastes or pollutants increasing the risk for cancer (see "Popular Epidemiology," selection 7). Behavioral risks are essentially "lifestyle" factors that have been shown to be associated with an increased incidence of particular diseases: cigarette smoking, alcoholism, obesity, sedentariness, not using seat belts, and so forth. A major distinction among risks is whether or not they are "modifiable." For example, with heart disease, risks present in family history (have there been heart attacks under age 50 in your family?) or genetic structure are not modifiable. On the other hand, risks like smoking, stress, hypertension, high cholesterol, and lack of exercise are all modifiable and can be targeted as risk factors that can be changed to reduce the likelihood of heart disease. Public health medicine has focused on changing modifiable risks as a major initiative toward disease prevention and health promotion, as depicted in the Surgeon General's report, *Healthy People 2000* (Department of Health and Human Services, 1990).

The news media regularly reports new findings about health risks, but these reports can be confusing or even contradictory. One year we read that butter is bad for us (too much cholesterol and fat) and margarine is healthier; another year we read that margarine is bad for us (it has too many artificial additives) and butter is less unhealthy. Alcohol overuse is a health risk, but a glass or two of red wine a day can reduce the risk of heart disease. There are many more such examples about how the air we breathe, food we eat, sex we enjoy, transportation we use, and land we live on all contain health risks; one might even conclude that living is a risk to our health.

While one could debate about the validity of each putative risk factor, or about how ubiquitous risk is in modern society (Beck, 1992), these are not the issues at hand here. This debate is more concerned about the meaning and the relevance of risk in medical discourse and intervention. The first selection in Part 3 is a good example of risk-oriented health research. In "The Prevalence of Risk Factors Among Women in the United States," Robert H. Hahn and his associates present a wide-ranging study of modifiable behavioral risk factors among various racial and ethnic groups of women. One of the major strengths of this study is the very specific measurement and comparison of eleven risk factors among different subgroups of women. The authors found that, overall, women engaged in a variety of behaviors—modifiable risk factors—that increased their risk for morbidity and mortality (e.g., lack of mammograms, smoking, being overweight). The prevalence of these risks varied by race and ethnicity, with blacks and American Indians having the most risks, and Pacific Islanders having the fewest. These differences may be related in part to culture and in part to socioeconomic position, but in either case, remain potentially modifiable if the proper interventions could be mounted. In short, a reduction of risk factors would result in an improvement in women's health.

Deborah Lupton, in "Risk as Moral Danger: The Social and Political Functions of Risk Discourse in Public Health," raises questions about the whole risk factor approach to public health. She suggests that risk is not a simple measure, but is a complex sociocultural concept that often is used in a rhetorical way in the public health discourse. Lupton sees the concept "risk" as ideologically loaded; that in the health discourse it only has negative meanings and that it suggests danger. She is particularly critical about the uses of "lifestyle risk" where risk is moralized (it is often seen as the fault of the person at risk) and there is a certain amount of "victim blaming." The notion of identifying a risk suggests that an individual should do something to modify it. The question becomes who has the power to define risk? How do we know a risk when we see it? Who is deemed at risk? Who is seen as responsible for creating the risk? Who is encouraged or required to do what about the risk, and under what circumstances? Lupton makes it clear that risk is not a neutral term in health and its use has political implications. While scientists have been good at showing us our health risks, they have been less clear about the social meaning of these risks. We should seek modification of health risks that make sense, but be sensitive to the anxiety, guilt, and blame that the risk discourse can produce.

REFERENCES

Beck, Ulrich. 1992. Risk Society. London: Sage Publications.

Department of Health and Human Services. 2000. Healthy People 2010. Washington, DC: U.S. Government Printing Office.

Susser, Mervyn. 1973. Causal Thinking in the Health Sciences: Concepts and Strategies in Epidemiology. New York: Oxford University Press.

36 *The Prevalence of Risk Factors Among Women in the United States*

Robert A. Hahn, Steven M. Teutsch, Adele L. Franks, Man-Huei Chang, and Elizabeth E. Lloyd

Although women in the United States live longer than men,[1] quality of life, as measured by self-report and morbidity, is lower for women than for men.[1,2] Several characteristics of US women, including lower levels of education and lower income per level of education and occupation,[1,3] poverty,[4] and differential medical treatment,[5–7] are likely to adversely affect their health status. Moreover, less is known about women's health, because research has focused on men—sometimes making the questionable assumption that findings are readily transferrable to women. The present study examines risk factors exclusively among women.

The health of women in the United States varies substantially by race/ethnicity and age.[8] Morbidity from many infectious and chronic diseases is generally greater among black, Hispanic, and American Indian women than among Asian and Pacific Islander and white women.[9,10] Mortality rates among women differ as well; reported all-cause, age-adjusted mortality was lowest among Asian/Pacific Islanders (229.3/100,000 population) in 1993–1995, 1.2 times as high among Hispanics, 1.6 times as high among whites and American Indians, and 2.5 times as high among blacks.[1]

Some differences in morbidity and mortality among racial/ethnic groups are associated with socioeconomic characteristics.[11,12] Giles et al[13] found that known biological and demographic risk factors for cerebral infarction each accounted for a substantial portion of the difference in incidence of cerebral infarction between whites and blacks in the United States. Similarly, Orren et al[14] found that six known risk factors accounted for approximately 31% of the excess all-cause mortality among black compared with white adults, and that family income accounted for an additional 38% of the difference.

This report analyzes the prevalence of 11 known risk factors, including nonuse of preventive measures, among US women 18 years and older, by race/ethnicity and age. It also examines the coexistence of multiple risk factors in individual women by race/ethnicity and age. Finally, it examines the hypothesis that racial/ethnic differences in risk factor prevalences can be explained by racial/ethnic differences in socioeconomic status. The object of this report is to increase understanding of morbidity and mortality patterns among US women, to identify populations with higher prevalences of modifiable risk factors for the targeting of health promotion efforts, and to provide baseline measures for risk factor reduction programs.

METHODS

We used the Behavioral Risk Factor Surveillance System (BRFSS) data for 1992 through 1994.[15] Three years of data were included because not all questions of interest were asked in all years or in all states (Arkansas joined BRFSS in 1993 and Wyoming in 1994) and, when multiple years of data were available, to increase the precision of estimates (particularly for the smaller populations, American Indians and Native Alaskans and Asian and Pacific Islanders).

We compared risk factor prevalences in the following racial/ethnic groups: white, black, Asian and Pacific Islander, American Indian and Native Alaskan, and Hispanic origin.

This report provides prevalence estimates and 95% confidence intervals for 11 risk factors, including risk behaviors and preventive health practices, for 1992, 1993, and 1994. We also report demographic and socioeconomic characteristics, including age, family income,

Table 36-1. Prevalence of Risk Factors Among US Women 18 and Older by Race/Ethnicity (BRFSS Data, 1992–1994)

Race/Ethnicity	Obesity[1] (%/CI)	Physical Inactivity[2] (%/CI)	Consumption of Fruits/ Vegetables[3] (%/CI)	Smoking[4] (%/CI)	Heavy Alcohol Consumption[5] (%/CI)	Inadequate Seat Belt Use[6] (%/CI)	Diabetes[7] (%/CI)	Inadequate Pap Smear[8] (%/CI)
White	22.7 (22.4, 23.1)	29.3 (28.9, 29.7)	71.5 (70.9, 72.1)	21.7 (21.4, 22.0)	1.1 (1.0, 1.2)	28.1 (27.7, 28.5)	4.7 (4.6, 4.9)	15.6 (15.3, 15.9)
Black	39.7 (38.6, 40.7)	43.6 (42.3, 44.9)	77.7 (76.3, 79.1)	20.2 (19.4, 21.1)	0.7 (0.5, 0.9)	35.1 (33.8, 36.3)	8.2 (7.6, 8.8)	12.2 (11.4, 13.0)
Asian/Pacific Islander	9.6 (8.1, 11.0)	33.8 (30.7, 36.8)	72.9 (69.0, 76.7)	10.3 (8.9, 11.8)	0.2 (0.1, 0.4)	13.9 (11.7, 16.1)	4.6 (3.3, 5.9)	29.1 (26.4, 31.7)
American Indian/ Alaska Native	35.5 (31.9, 39.1)	34.6 (30.0, 39.2)	72.0 (66.4, 77.5)	30.7 (27.3, 34.2)	1.1 (0.2, 2.0)	29.5 (25.4, 33.6)	9.6 (7.3, 11.8)	16.5 (13.0, 19.9)
Hispanic Origin	26.5 (25.1, 27.8)	41.4 (39.5, 43.3)	72.3 (69.8, 74.8)	14.3 (13.2, 15.3)	0.8 (0.5, 1.1)	27.7 (26.0, 29.5)	6.3 (5.5, 7.0)	21.9 (20.4, 23.4)

[1] Body Mass Index ≥27.3.
[2] No regular physical activity in leisure-time.
[3] Does not eat ≥5 servings of fruits and vegetables per day, information not available for 1993.
[4] Current use of cigarettes by someone who has smoked ≥100 cigarettes in her entire life.
[5] Drinkers who consume two or more drinks of alcohol (approximately ≥1 oz.) of ethanol/per day (60 or more drinks during the past month).
[6] Inadequate seat belt use: does not always use seat belts when driving or riding in a car.
[7] Has ever been told by a physician that she has diabetes.
[8] Inadequate Pap smears: among women ≥20 years of age who have not had a hysterectomy, those who have not had a pap smear test in the last 3 years.

and education, of the race/ethnic subgroups compared.

Using commonly accepted criteria, risk factors were defined as follows and include data for years as listed. Unless indicated otherwise, age was 18 years or older:

Obesity: Body Mass Index (BMI) more than 27.3,[1] 1992 to 1994.

Physical inactivity: a summary index of no regular leisure time physical activity, 1992, 1993.

Inadequate fruit and vegetable consumption: the summary index for servings of fruits and vegetables was defined as less than 5 per day, 1994.

Smoking: current use of cigarettes by someone who has smoked 100 cigarettes or more in her entire life, 1992 to 1994.

Heavy alcohol consumption: drinkers who consume two or more drinks of alcohol (approximately ≥ 1 oz.) of ethanol/per day (60 or

Table 36-2. Prevalence of Inadequate Mammography and Colorectal Screening Among US Women 50 and Older, and Immunization among US Women 65 and Older, by Race/Ethnicity (BRFSS Data, 1993)

Race/Ethnicity	Inadequate Mammography[1] (%/CI)	Inadequate Colorectal Screening[2] (%/CI)	Inadequate Immunization[3] (%/CI)
White	32.9 (32.4, 33.5)	79.0 (78.2, 79.9)	74.1 (72.9, 75.3)
Black	33.3 (31.5, 35.1)	78.8 (76.2, 81.5)	84.2 (80.9, 87.5)
Asian/Pacific Islander	30.5 (25.0, 36.0)	79.7 (71.4, 87.9)	80.0 (68.0, 91.9)
American Indian/ Alaskan Native	34.4 (27.5, 41.4)	80.2 (71.2, 89.1)	78.2 (62.0, 94.5)
Hispanic Origin	37.8 (34.6, 40.9)	81.9 (77.8, 86.1)	81.0 (74.8, 87.3)

[1] Inadequate mammography: among women ≥50 years of age, those who never had a mammogram, or did not have a mammogram within the past 2 years.
[2] Inadequate colorectal screening: among women ≥50 years of age, those who had no sigmoidoscopic exam, or had sigmoidoscopic exam but did not have exam within the past 2 years.
[3] Inadequate immunization: among women ≥65 years of age, those who had no flu shot during the past 12 months or had no pneumococcal disease vaccination.

more drinks during the past month), 1992, 1993.[16]

Diabetes: has ever been told by a physician that she has diabetes, 1992 to 1994.

Inadequate seat belt use: does not always use seat belts when driving or riding in a car, 1992, 1993.

Inadequate pap smear: among women 20 or older who have not had hysterectomies, those who have not had a pap smear test in the last 3 years, 1992 to 1994.

Inadequate mammography: women 50 or older who never had a mammogram or did not have a mammogram within the past 2 years, 1992 to 1994.

Inadequate colorectal screening: women 50 or older who had no sigmoidoscopic exam or did not have an exam within the past 2 years, 1993. (Epidemiologic research has indicated the effectiveness of colorectal screening, but not yet indicated appropriate screening intervals.)

Inadequate immunization: women 65 or older who had no flu shot during the past 12 months or had no pneumococcal disease vaccination, 1993.

Multiple risk factors: age-appropriate risk factors were included for each age. Because BRFSS is a cross-sectional study, only a single year could be examined for this variable. We chose 1993 because it provided data on the greatest number of risk factors and the widest range of applicable ages.

We used multiple logistic regression to examine the hypothesis that racial differences in the coexistence of risk factors (0 v 1–2 risk factors, and 0 v 3 or more risk factors) could be attributed to differences in socioeconomic status. We used education and income as markers of socioeconomic status because they were the only markers routinely available in the data set and because they are commonly used in other studies. We also examined the effect of an interaction term for education and family income.

RESULTS

There were 177,958 women in the BRFSS sample for 1992–1994: 150,807 whites (84.7%), 17,815 blacks (10.0%), 1,917 American Indians (1.1%), 4,081 Asian and Pacific Islanders (2.3%), 3,074 women of other races, and 264 women who refused to answer the question or for whom race was unknown. There were 9,045 Hispanics (5.1%) and 168,496 non-Hispanics (94.7%), and 417 women for whom Hispanic origin was unknown. Overall BRFSS participation rates (including men as well as women) from 1992 through 1994 ranged from 70.0% to 71.4%.

Among all women in the sample, 4,090 (2.3%) were less than 20 years of age, 102,202 (57.4%) were 20 to 49 years of age, 31,589 (21.9%) were 50 to 64, and 38,957 (21.3%) were 65 or older.

Risk Factor Prevalences (see Tables 36-1 and 36-2)

The prevalence of obesity varied 4.1 fold among racial and ethnic groups, from 9.6% among Asian and Pacific Islanders to 39.7% among blacks.

Lack of regular leisure time physical activity varied 1.5 fold among racial and ethnic groups, from 29.3% among whites to 43.6% among blacks.

Consumption of less than 5 servings of fruits and vegetables per day was high and varied little among racial and ethnic groups, from 71.5% among whites and to 77.7% among blacks.

The prevalence of smoking varied 3.0 fold among racial and ethnic groups, from 10.3% among Asian and Pacific Islanders to 30.7% among American Indians and Native Alaskans.

The prevalence of heavy alcohol consumption was low, but varied 5.5 fold among racial and ethnic groups, from 0.2% among Asian and Pacific Islanders to 1.1% among whites and American Indians and Native Alaskans.

The prevalence of inadequate seat belt use varied 2.5 fold among racial and ethnic groups, from 13.9% among Asian and Pacific Islanders to 35.1% among blacks.

The prevalence of self-reported diabetes varied 2.1 fold among racial and ethnic groups, from 4.6% among Asian and Pacific Islanders to 9.6% among American Indians and Native Alaskans.

The prevalence of inadequate pap smear varied 2.4 fold and was lowest (12.2%) among blacks and highest (29.1%) among Asian and Pacific Islanders.

The prevalence of inadequate mammography did not vary substantially by race and Hispanic origin. The prevalence of inadequate colorectal screening was high and likewise varied little by race and Hispanic origin.

The prevalence of inadequate immunization varied somewhat among racial and ethnic populations, from 74.1% among whites to 84.2% among blacks.

Because certain forms of cancer screening and immunization are recommended at different ages, the number of potential risks available for analysis increased from 7 among women under 50 years of age to 9 among women 65 and older. (Information on physical inactivity and fruit and vegetable consumption was not available in 1993, the year for which multiple risk factor prevalence was analyzed.) For all racial and ethnic groups, the prevalence of having no risk factors decreased substantially by age, while the prevalence of having 3 or more risk factors increased substantially with age; an exception was among Asian and Pacific Islanders for whom the prevalence of having no risk factors was greater among women 65 and older than among women 50 to 64. Among women less than 50 years, Asian and Pacific Islanders had the greatest and American Indians the lowest prevalence of no risk factors, and American Indians had the greatest prevalence of 3 or more risk factors. Among women 50 to 64, Hispanics had the highest and American Indians the lowest prevalence of no risk factors, while American Indians again had the highest prevalence of 3 or more risk factors. Among women 65 and older, Asian and Pacific Islanders had the greatest and American Indians and Hispanics the lowest prevalence of no risk factors, whereas blacks had the greatest prevalence of 3 or more risk factors.

To examine the hypothesis that socioeconomic position, as measured by education and income, is the source of differences in risk factor prevalences among racial populations, we compared odds of having a) 1–2 versus 0 risk factors and b) 3 or more versus 0 risk factors among four races included in the study, unadjusted and adjusted for education and family income (see Table 36-3).[3] Hispanics were not included in this analysis, because the analytic method did not allow inclusion of individual women in more than one comparison group. Because Asian and Pacific Islanders generally had the highest preva-

Table 36-3. Effect of Adjustment for Education and Income on Odds Ratio of Multiple Risk Factor Prevalence, by Race/Ethnicity (BRFSS Data, 1993)

Age, Race/Ethnicity	One or Two Versus No Risk Factors		Three or More Versus No Risk Factors	
	Unadjusted (%/CI)	*Adjusted for Education and Income (%/CI)*	*Unadjusted (%/CI)*	*Adjusted for Education and Income (%/CI)*
18–49				
White	1.27* (1.03, 1.57)	1.13 (0.89, 1.44)	2.49* (1.26, 4.90)	1.89 (0.90, 3.94)
Black	2.10* (1.67, 2.65)	1.54* (1.19, 1.99)	4.59* (2.28, 9.26)	2.19* (1.02, 4.70)
American Indian	2.49* (1.64, 3.77)	1.66* (1.08, 1.57)	6.37* (2.56, 15.87)	3.42* (1.29, 9.07)
Asian/Pacific	1.00 1.00	1.00 1.00		
50–64				
White	0.86 (0.37, 1.99)	0.82 (0.30, 2.25)	2.33 (0.94, 5.78)	2.31 (0.91, 5.90)
Black	1.34 (0.49, 3.67)	1.71 (0.53, 5.58)	5.48* (1.89, 15.88)	5.15* (1.66, 16.01)
American Indian	2.49 (0.47, 13.08)	1.58 (0.27, 9.18)	11.71* (2.20, 62.42)	7.04* (1.42, 35.00)
Asian/Pacific	1.00 1.00	1.00 1.00		
65 and older				
White	2.05 (0.47, 8.96)	0.51 (0.18, 1.46)	1.87 (0.42, 8.44)	0.34 (0.12, 1.02)
Black	5.82* (1.12, 30.42)	1.36 (0.38, 4.84)	8.05* (1.51, 42.97)	1.29 (0.35, 4.69)
American Indian	100.05* (20.15, 496.75)	21.10* (5.91, 75.28)	69.81* (14.14, 344.67)	27.89* (7.55, 103.08)
Asian/Pacific	1.00 1.00	1.00 1.00		

*Significant at <0.05 level.

lences of zero risk factors, they were taken as the reference population. Among women 18 to 49, the risk of having a) 1–2 versus 0 risk factors and b) 3 or more versus 0 risk factors was significantly greater for whites, blacks, and American Indians than for Asian and Pacific Islanders. Adjustment for education and family income eliminated the statistical significance of this difference for whites, but not for blacks or American Indians. Among women 50 to 64, only the risk of 3 or more versus 0 risk factors was significantly greater for blacks and American Indians than for Asian and Pacific Islanders. Adjustment for education and family income did not eliminate the statistical significance of these differences. Among women 65 and older, the risk of having a) 1–2 versus 0 risk factors and b) 3 or more versus 0 risk factors was significantly greater for blacks and American Indians than for Asian and Pacific Islanders. Adjustment for education and family income eliminated the statistical significance of thisdifference for blacks, but not for AmericanIndians.

DISCUSSION

This analysis of self-reported risk factors among women in the United States found a high prevalence of modifiable behaviors that place women at risk for many causes of morbidity and mortality. Overall, approximately 14.6% of women 20 and older had not had pap tests within the last three years; 33.0% of women 50 and older had not had mammograms within the past 2 years; and 79.1% of women 50 and older had not had sigmoidoscopic exams within the past 2 years. Substantial proportions of women were overweight, physically inactive, smoked cigarettes, and ate fewer than 5 servings of fruits and vegetables daily.

The analysis also found substantial variation in risk profile among racial/ethnic populations. Asian and Pacific Islanders had the lowest prevalences for 7 of 11 risk factors and the highest prevalence for one (inadequate pap smear screening); blacks had the lowest prevalence for 1 of 11 individual risk factors (inadequate pap smear screening) and the highest prevalence for 5 (obesity, physical inactivity, inadequate consumption of fruits and vegetables, inadequate seat belt use, and inadequate adult immunization). Although some groups, Asian and Pacific Islanders, had relatively low prevalences of most major risk factors, others, particularly blacks and American Indians and Native Alaskans, had relatively high prevalences of many major risk factors.

The US Public Health Service (USPHS) has set health objectives for the nation for the year 2000, including some of the risk factors assessed here.[17] By the period of the study, only Asian and Pacific Islanders had already reached USPHS objectives for the prevalence of obesity and inadequate use of seat belts. And only Asian and Pacific Islanders and Hispanic women had already achieved the objectives for the prevalence of smoking. No group has achieved year 2000 objectives for diabetes, and all must make substantial progress to reduce leisure time physical inactivity and inadequate use of pap smears, mammography, and immunization.

Differences in risk factor profiles among racial/ethnic groups may have several explanations; it should be noted, however, that, as assessed in BRFSS and many other sources, self-identified "race" is only loosely associated with genetic relations within and among populations. Biological explanations have been examined for racial differences in several of the risk factors analyzed here, including diabetes,[18] obesity,[19] and alcohol consumption.[20,21] For other risk factors, such as inadequate seat belt use and cancer screening, biological explanations are improbable. Even where biological differences have been identified, they need not account for all the differences among racial groups; contributions of the social environment have been documented by studies of immigrants within racial/ethnic populations.[22]

Socioeconomic position may also explain racial differences in risk factor prevalence, for example, through effects on access to opportunities to learn about and avoid the hazards of the risk factors examined here.[23–25] Hispanics, American Indians and Native Alaskans, and blacks have less education and lower household incomes than the other groups in the sample. Women of lower socioeconomic position may have a greater sense of inevitability and less sense of "self-efficacy."[26,27] These attitudes may be associated with failure to seek recommended screening[28,29] or to adopt such protective behavior as use of seat belts.[30,31]

Women of racial/ethnic minorities may also face difficulties in access to health care, such as poverty and discrimination.[32,33]

Racial/ethnic groups may differ in their attitudes toward the dangers associated with specific behaviors and their own responsibility for self-protection, independent of socioeconomic position.[34] Our study indicates that statistical adjustment for socioeconomic status, at least as measured by income and education, diminishes, but does not eliminate, differences in the distribution of risk factor prevalences among racial/ethnic populations, thus lending support to the importance of cultural differences among the populations examined.[35] Health habits are shaped by the beliefs, attitudes (including the sense of inevitability and "self-efficacy"), and norms of one's cultural environment, and response to public health campaigns may be affected by the cultural framework of respondents.[36] Evidence indicates, for example, that compared with white women, black women do not believe that moderate obesity is unhealthy; they also believe that it is attractive and are encouraged by their social environment to maintain their weight.[37,38] Other studies have confirmed our findings that adjustment for socioeconomic differences did not eliminate differences in obesity between black and white women[39,40] or between Hispanics and other populations.[41,42] Another cultural characteristic that may affect use of pap smear screening, particularly among Asian and Pacific Islanders and Hispanics, is the "extreme privacy" of the lower torso.[43–45] Racial and ethnic groups also maintain different attitudes toward compliance with legal regulations, such as seat belt laws; whites and non-Hispanics are more likely than other races and Hispanics to conform to seat belt regulations because they are mandatory.[46]

Both psychological and physiological factors may contribute to clustering of relatively high numbers of risk factors. Given that individuals are aware of the risks associated with different behaviors, it may be that psychological characteristics such as fatalism, hedonism, fearlessness, and lack of self-efficacy promote risk-taking behavior. There may be a physiological explanation for certain risk factor combinations, such as obesity and physical inactivity, obesity and diabetes, obesity and consumption of fewer than 5 servings of fruits or vegetables per day. It may be more difficult for obese persons to be active, for example, and activity tends to decrease weight. The physiological explanation seems farfetched, however, for risk factor combinations such as smoking and nonuse of seat belts or inadequate screening and inadequate immunization. Some risk factor combinations, such as heavy drinking and nonuse of seat belts may have both psychological and biological explanations; drinking may impair judgment and both heavy drinking and nonuse of seat belts may be motivated by underlying psychological characteristics.

Evidence indicates that the prevalence of several risk factors—physical inactivity; daily consumption of fewer than five servings of fruits and vegetables; smoking; heavy drinking; and inadequate immunization, mammography, and sigmoidoscopy—have declined in recent years.[47–49] In contrast, the prevalence of other risk factors, such as obesity, has increased in recent years.[50] Cigarette smoking has declined among women, but at slower rates than among men; rates of smoking have increased among white and black women with less than a high school education.[51]

Interventions at the clinical, community, and environmental levels have proved efficacious in reducing the prevalence of some risk factors. Evidence suggests that counseling by clinicians can reduce cigarette smoking and heavy drinking,[52,53] and increase physical activity.[54–56] Programs of dietary control have been shown to be more effective when skills training and social support inside and outside clinical settings are provided along with information, and when attention is paid to follow-up and behavioral reinforcement.[57] Law, education, incentives, monitoring, and reminders have all proved effective in increasing the use of seat belts.[58]

Studies of clinical practice, however, indicate that clinicians have not done as much as they could to reduce risks among their patients. A 1987 survey of US internists found that, while more than 94% asked their patients about smoking and alcohol use, less than 71% asked about pap smears, exercise, diet, and mammography; only 42% asked about immunizations, and only 11% asked about seat belt use.[59] Between 20% and 40% believed that pap smears, mammography, and sigmoidoscopy were only moderately effective. An earlier study reported that more than one-third of physicians were pessimistic about patients' abilities to change, that they gave little credence to the effectiveness of behavior modification programs, and that they claimed not to have enough time or training to counsel patients about their behavior. One-fourth believed that counseling is not appropriate, since behavior is a matter of personal choice.[60]

Prevention has not been a theme in the culture of Western medicine.[61] Changing this pattern will require innovation in the training of clinicians and encouragement of those in practice to incorporate effective risk reduction into their routines.[62] Like the relative ineffectiveness of information alone without modification of the social environment in changing risk behavior, practice guidelines themselves have been shown to be only partially effective in increasing physician use of preventive practices.[63] Assurance of access to and nondiscrimination in health care settings may also improve medical care, particularly for racial/ethnic populations with poorer risk factor profiles.

Public health approaches have had mixed success in changing behavior to date. In the reduction of cardiovascular risk factors, for example, community education has not been consistently successful.[64–67] Some public health education programs have been shown effective in schools, work sites,[68] and communities, however.[69,70] Because habitual behaviors such as smoking and diet are formed in youth, implementation of programs in schools may be important in long-term risk reduction and disease prevention.[71,72]

Just as historical changes in the social environment may be in part responsible for increases in obesity and physical inactivity, so public health policy and environmental change may also affect changes in behavior. An association between seat belt use and state seat belt laws and enforcement suggests that legal regulation and sanction may affect the mandated behavior.[73] Studies of cigarette consumption following media campaigns and increased cigarette taxes in California indicate the effects of both (but principally the latter) in reducing per capita consumption.[74] Nationally, per capita consumption and rates of quitting smoking in states are associated with both the strength of indoor smoking regulation and the amount of excise taxes.[75,76] Alcohol consumption may also be affected by price and taxes.[77]

The risk factors examined in this analysis are responsible for large proportions of mortality, as well as morbidity, among women in the United States. Risk factor profiles among women in US racial/ethnic populations roughly parallel their mortality rates and correspond to the ranking of life expectancy at age 25.[78] There are signs of progress and success in some risk factor trends among women, yet also substantial opportunities for improvement. The risk factor prevalences presented here are guideposts for action, indicating levels and diversity of need and providing baseline measures for programmatic action among racial/ethnic populations of US women.

ACKNOWLEDGMENTS

The authors are grateful for the collaboration of Deborah Holtzman and the BRFSS staff in the provision of data and methodological advice. We are also thankful for the programming help of Nancy Barker.

EDITOR'S NOTE

This article is an abridged and condensed version of the original.

REFERENCES

1. Centers for Disease Control and Prevention. *Health United States 1996–97*. Hyattsville, Md: Department of Health and Human Services; 1995. DHHS publication (PHS)95-1232.
2. CDC. Quality of life as a new public health measure Behavioral Risk Factor Surveillance System, 1993. *MMWR*. 1994;43:375–380.
3. *Statistical Abstract of the United States, 1994*. Washington, DC: US Department of Commerce, 1994.
4. Hahn RA, Eaker E, Barker ND, Teutsch SM, Sosniak W, Krieger N. Poverty and death in the United States 1971 and 1991. *Int J Health Serv.* 1996;26:673–690.
5. Held PJ, Pauly MV, Bovbjerg RR, Newmann J, Salvatierra O, Jr. Access to kidney transplantation. *Arch Intern Med.* 1988;148:1305–1309.
6. Tobin JN, Wassertheil-Smoller S, Wexler JP, et al. Sex bias in considering coronary bypass surgery. *Ann Intern Med.* 1987;107:19–25.

7. American Medical Association Council on Ethical and Judicial Affairs. Gender disparities in clinical decision making. *JAMA*. 1991;266:559–562.
8. Bureau of Health Professions. *Health Status of Minorities and Low Income Groups*. Washington, DC: Health Resources and Services Administration; 1991. DHHS publication (HRSA) HRS-P-DV 85-1.
9. Buehler JW, Stroup DF, Klaucke DN, Berkelman RL. The reporting of race and ethnicity in the National Notifiable Diseases Surveillance System. *Public Health Rep*. 1989;104:457–465.
10. Centers for Disease Control and Prevention. *Chronic Disease in Minority Populations. African-Americans, American Indians and Alaska Natives, Asians and Pacific Islanders, and Hispanic Americans*. Atlanta, Ga: US Public Health Service; 1992.
11. Navarro V. Race or class versus race and class: Mortality differentials in the United States. *Lancet*. 1992;336:1238–1240.
12. Rogers RG. Living and dying in the U.S.A.: Sociodemographic determinants of death among blacks and whites. *Demography*. 1992;29:287–303.
13. Giles WH, Kittner SJ, Hebel R, Losonczy KG, Sherwin RW. Determinants of black-white differences in the risk of cerebral infarction. *Arch Intern Med*. 1993;155:1319–1324.
14. Otten MW, Teutsch SM, Williamson DF, Marks JS. The effect of known risk factors on the excess mortality of black adults in the United States. *JAMA*. 1990;263:854–860.
15. Remington PL, Smith MY, Williamson DF, et al. Design, characteristics, and usefulness of state-based behavioral risk factor surveillance: 1981–1987. *Public Health Rep*. 1988;103:366–375.
16. Dawson DA, Grant BF, Chou PS. Gender differences in alcohol intake. In: Hunt WA, Zakhari S, eds. *Stress, Gender, and Alcohol-Seeking Behavior*. Bethesda, Md: National Institute on Alcohol Abuse and Alcoholism; 1995:3–22. Research Monograph No. 29.
17. US Public Health Service. *Healthy People 2000: National Health Promotion and Disease Prevention Objectives*. Washington, DC: Department of Health and Human Services; 1991. DHHS publication (PHS) 91-50212.
18. National Diabetes Data Group. *Diabetes in America*. Bethesda, Md: National Institute of Diabetes and Digestive and Kidney Diseases; 1995. NIH publication 95-1468.
19. Bouchard C. Current understanding of the etiology of obesity: Genetics and nongenetic factors. *Am J Clin Nutr*. 1991;53:1561s–1565s.
20. Agarwal DP, Godeed HW. Medicobiological and genetic studies on alcoholism. Role of metabolic variation and ethnicity on drinking habits, alcohol abuse and alcohol-related mortality. *Clin Investig*. 1992;70:465–477.
21. Hill SY. Vulnerability to alcoholism in women. Genetic and cultural factors. In: Galanter M, ed. *Recent Developments in Alcoholism*. Vol 12. New York, NY: Plenum; 1995.
22. Kagan A, Harris BR, Winkelstein W Jr, et al. Epidemiologic studies of coronary heart disease and stroke in Japanese men living in Japan, Hawaii, and California: Demographic, physical, dietary, and biochemical characteristics. *J Chronic Dis*. 1974;27:345–364.
23. Clark DO. Racial and educational differences in physical activity among older adults. *Gerontologist*. 1995;35:472–480.
24. Vernon SW, Vogel VG, Halabi S, Jackson GL, Lundy RO, Peters GN. Breast cancer screening behaviors and attitudes in three racial/ethnic groups. *Cancer*. 1992;69:165–174.
25. Jeffrey RW. Population perspectives on the prevention and treatment of obesity in minority populations. *Am J Clin Nutr*. 1991;53:1621s–1624s.
26. Strecher VJ, DeVellis BM, Becker MS, Rosenstock IM. The role of self-efficacy in achieving health behavior change. *Health Educ Q*. 1986; 13:73–91.
27. Perez-Stable EJ, Sabogal F, Otero-Sabogal R, Hiat RA, McPhee SJ. Misconceptions about cancer among Latinos and Anglos. *JAMA*. 1992;268: 3219–3223.
28. Powe BD, Johnson A. Fatalism as a barrier to cancer screening among African-Americans: Philosophical perspectives. *Journal of Religion Health*. 1995;34:119–125.
29. Straughan PT, Seow A. Barriers to mammography among Chinese women in Singapore: A focus group approach. *Health Educ Res*. 1995;10: 431–441.
30. Helsing KH, Comstock GW. What kinds of people do not use seat belts? *Am J Public Health*. 1977;67:1043–1050.
31. Colon I. Race, belief in destiny, and seat belt usage: A pilot study. *Am J Public Health*. 1992; 82:875–877.
32. American Medical Association Council on Ethical and Judicial Affairs. Black-White disparities in health care. *JAMA*. 1990;263:2344–2346.
33. Hahn R. *Sickness and Healing: An Anthropological Perspective*. New Haven, Conn: Yale University Press, 1995.
34. Eiser JR, Sutton SR, Wober M. Smoking, seatbelts, and beliefs about health. *Addict Behav*. 1979;4:331–338.

35. Shea S, Stein AD, Basch CE, et al. Independent associations of educational attainment and ethnicity with behavioral risk factors for cardiovascular disease. *Am J Epidemiology.* 1991;134:567–582.
36. Paul BD, ed. *Health, Culture and Community.* New York, NY: Russell Sage Foundation; 1955.
37. Allan JD, Mayo K, Michel Y. Body size values of white and black women. *Res Nurs Health.* 1993; 16:323–333.
38. Stevens J, Kumanyika SK, Keil JE. Attitudes toward body size and dieting: Differences between elderly black and white women. *Am J Public Health.* 1994;84:1322–1325.
39. Kumanyika S. Obesity in black women. *Epidemiol Rev.* 1987;9:31–50.
40. Rand CSW, Kuldau JM. The epidemiology of obesity and self-defined weight problem in the general population: Gender, race, age, and social class. *Int J Eat Disord.* 1990;9:329–343.
41. Winkleby MA, Gardner CD, Taylor B. The influence of gender and socioeconomic factors on Hispanic/white differences in body mass index. *Prev Med.* 1996;25:203–211.
42. Brown PJ. Cultural perspectives on the etiology and treatment of obesity. In: Stunkard AJ, Wadden TA, eds. *Obesity: Theory and Therapy.* 2nd ed. New York, NY: Raven Press; 1993.
43. Muecke MA. Caring for Southeast Asian refugee patients in the USA. *Am J Public Health.* 1983; 73:431–438.
44. Harwood A, ed. *Ethnicity and Medical Care.* Cambridge, Mass: Harvard University Press; 1981.
45. Harlan LC, Bernstein AB, Kessler LG. Cervical cancer screening: Who is not screened and why? *Am J Public Health.* 1991;81:885–891.
46. Boyle JM. *Motor Vehicle Occupant Safety Survey.* Washington, DC: National Highway Traffic Safety Administration; 1995. Report DOT HS 808 334.
47. Putnam JJ, Allshouse JE. *Food Consumption, Prices, and Expenditures, 1996.* Washington, DC: US Department of Agriculture; 1996. Statistical Bulletin No. 928.
48. CDC. Influenza and pneumococcal vaccination coverage levels among persons aged ≥65 years United States, 1973–1993. *MMWR.* 1995;44: 506–507, 513–515.
49. Siegel PZ, Frazier EL, Mariolis P, Brackbill RM, Smith C. Behavioral Risk Factor Surveillance, 1991: Monitoring progress toward the nation's year 2000 health objectives. *MMWR.* 1993; 42:No. SS-4:1–22.
50. Kuczmarski RJ, Flegal KM, Campbell SM, Johnson CL. Increasing prevalence of overweight among US adults. The National Health and Nutrition Examination Surveys, 1960 to 1991. *JAMA.* 1994;272:238–239.
51. Escobedo LG, Peddicord JP. Smoking prevalence in US birth cohorts: The influence of gender and education. *Am J Public Health.* 1996;86: 231–236.
52. US Preventive Services Task Force. *Guide to Clinical Preventive Services.* Baltimore, Md: Williams and Wilkins; 1996.
53. Thompson RS, Taplin SH, McAfee TA, Mandelson MG, Smith AE. Primary and secondary prevention services in clinical practice. Twenty years' experience in development, implementation, and evaluation. *JAMA.* 1995;273:1130–1135.
54. Harris SS, Caspersen CJ, DeFriese GH, Estes D. Physical activity counseling for healthy adults as a primary prevention in the clinical setting. *JAMA.* 1989;261:3590–3598.
55. Lewis BS, Lynch WD. The effect of physician advice on exercise behavior. *Prev Med.* 1993;22: 110–121.
56. Calfas KJ, Long BJ, Sallis JF, Wooten WJ, Pratt M, Patrick K. A controlled trial of physician counselling to promote the adoption of physical activity. *Prev Med.* 1996;25:225–233.
57. Glanz K. Nutrition education for risk factor reduction and patient education: A review. *Prev Med.* 1985;14:721–752.
58. Johnston JJ, Hendricks SA, Fike JM. Effectiveness of behavioral safety belt interventions. *Accid Anal Prev.* 1994;26:315–323.
59. Schwartz SJ, Lewis CE, Clancy C, Kinosian MS, Radany H, Koplan JP. Internists practices in health promotion and disease prevention. *Ann Intern Med.* 1991;114:46–53.
60. Wechsler H, Levine S, Idelson RK, Pohman M, Taylor JO. The physician's role in health promotion A survey of primary care practitioners. *N Engl J Med.* 1983;308:97–100.
61. Hahn R. The state of federal health statistics on racial and ethnic groups. *JAMA.* 1992;267:268–271.
62. Kottke TE, Brekke MI, Solberg LI. Making "time" for preventive services. *Mayo Clin Proc.* 1993;68:785–791.
63. Grimshaw JM, Russell IT. Effect of clinical guidelines on medical practice: A systematic review of rigorous evaluations. *Lancet.* 1993;432:1317–1322.
64. Kotchen JM, McKean HE, Jackson-Thayer S, Moore RW, Straus R, Kotchen TA. Impact of a rural high blood pressure control program on hypertension control and cardiovascular disease mortality. *JAMA.* 1986;255:2177–2182.
65. Luepker RV, Murray DM, Jacobs DR Jr, et al. Community education for cardiovascular disease

prevention: Risk factor changes in the Minnesota Heart Health Program. *Am J Public Health.* 1994;84:1383–1393.
66. Young DR, Haskell WL, Jatulis DE, Fortmann SP. Associations between changes in physical activity and risk factors for coronary heart disease in a community-based sample of men and women: The Stanford Five-City Project. *Am J Epidemiol.* 1993;138:205–216.
67. Carleton RA, Lasater TM, Assaf AR, Feldman HA, McKinlay S. The Pawtucket Heart Health Program: Community changes in cardiovascular risk factors and projected disease risk. *Am J Public Health.* 1995;85:777–785.
68. Fielding JE. Health promotion and disease prevention at the worksite. *Annu Rev Public Health.* 1984;5:237–265.
69. Kumanyika SK, Charlston JB. Lose weight and win: A church-based program for blood pressure control among black women. *Patient Educ Couns.* 1992;19:19–32.
70. CDC. Worksite and community health promotion/risk reduction project Virginia, 1987–1991. *MMWR.* 1992;41:55–57.
71. US Department of Health and Human Services. *Preventing Tobacco Use Among Young People: A Report of the Surgeon General.* Atlanta, Ga: National Center for Chronic Disease Prevention and Health Promotion, Office on Smoking and Health, Centers for Disease Control and Prevention; 1994.
72. CDC. Guidelines for school health programs to promote lifelong healthy eating. *MMWR.* 1996; 45:No. RR-9:i–41.
73. Escobado LG, Chorba TL, Remington PL, Anda RF, Sanderson S, Zaidi A. The influence of safety belt laws on self-reported safety belt use in the United States. *Accid Anal Prev.* 1992;24:643–653.
74. Hu T, Sung HY, Keeler TE. Reducing cigarette consumption in California: Tobacco taxes vs an anti-smoking media campaign. *Am J Public Health.* 1995;85:1218–1222.
75. Emont SL, Choi WS, Novothy TE, Giovino GA. Clean indoor air legislation, taxation, and smoking behavior in the United States: An ecological analysis. *Tob Control.* 1991;2:13–17.
76. Peterson DE, Zeger SI, Remington PL, Anderson MA. The effect of state cigarette tax increases on cigarette sales, 1955 to 1988. *Am J Public Health.* 1992;82:94–96.
77. Levy D, Sheflin N. New evidence on controlling alcohol use through price. *J Stud Alcohol.* 1983; 44:29–37.
78. Hahn RA, Eberhardt S. Life expectancy in four US racial/ethnic populations: 1990. *Epidemiology.* 1995;6:350–355.

37 Risk as Moral Danger: The Social and Political Functions of Risk Discourse in Public Health

Deborah Lupton

We live in a society that has become more and more aware of risks, especially those caused by technology and "lifestyle" habits. According to Douglas and Wildavsky, modern individuals are afraid of "Nothing much . . . except the food they eat, the water they drink, the air they breathe, the land they live on, and the energy they use" (1, p. 10). Health risks seem to loom around every corner, posing a constant threat to the public (2). They constantly make headlines in the news media and are increasingly the subject of public communication campaigns. Risk assessment and risk communication have become growth industries. In short, the word "risk" itself has acquired a new prominence in western society, becoming a central cultural construct (3, p. 2).

Risk is a concept with different meanings, according to who is using the term. The proliferation of usages of the term in both vernacular and professional applications means that its meanings are both complex and confusing. In its original usage, "risk" is neutral, referring to probability, or the mathematical likelihood of an event occurring. The risk of an event occurring could therefore relate to either a positive or negative outcome, as in the risk of winning the lottery. Used in the more mathematical areas of the growing field of risk analysis, this strict sense of the term is adhered to. Thus, risk analysts speak of the statistical likelihood that an event may occur, and use the mathematical model produced to assist in decision-making in such areas as economics and management. The risk, or likelihood, of an event happening can be calculated to numerical odds—one in fifty chance, one in a hundred, one in a million—as can the magnitude of the outcome should it happen (4, 5).

Most industries devoted to the quantification of risk place a great deal of importance in measuring risk assessment, risk perception, and risk evaluation on the part of individuals in the general population. In the past two decades the field of risk assessment of technologies has grown in prominence in concert with the interest of the public in environmental hazards. Risk assessment applied in this field deals with the complex process of evaluating the hazards of technologies, as well as the communication of information about potential risks and developing appropriate controls (5–8). Risk in this content has been defined as "the probability that a potential harm or undesirable consequence will be realized" (8, p. 321).

This definition points to the new meaning of risk. As Douglas (3) has suggested, the word "risk" has changed its meaning in contemporary western society. No longer a neutral term, risk has come to mean danger; and "high risk means a lot of danger" (3, p. 3). Any risk is now negative; it is a contradiction in terms to speak of something as a "good risk." According to Douglas, the use of "risk" to mean danger is preferred in professional circles because "plain danger does not have the aura of science or afford the pretension of a possible precise calculation" (3, p. 4).

In public health the word "risk" as a synonym for danger is in constant use. A "discourse of risk" has evolved with particular application to health issues. Individuals or groups are labeled as being "at high risk," meaning that they are in danger of contracting or developing a disease or illness. Epidemiologists calculate measures of "relative risk" to compare the likelihood of illness developing in populations exposed to a "risk factor" with the likelihood for populations that have not been thus exposed. State-sponsored health education campaigns in the mass media are conducted to warn the public about health risks, based on the assumption that knowledge and awareness of the danger of certain activities will result in avoidance of these activities.

Risk discourse in public health can be separated loosely into two perspectives. The first views risk as a health danger to populations that is posed by environmental hazards such as pollution, nuclear waste, and toxic chemical residues. In this conceptualization of risk, the health threat is regarded as a hazard that is external, over which the individual has little control. The common response to such risks on the part of the layperson is anger at government authorities, feelings of powerlessness and anxiety, and concern over the seemingly deliberate and unregulated contamination of the environment by industry (9, 10). Risk communication on the part of those in authority is then cynically directed toward defusing community reaction, building trust and credibility for the "risk creator," the "risk regulator," and the "risk analyst," and facilitating "risk acceptance" on the part of the public (11).

Methodologies used to assess health risk perception and acceptance on the part of the layperson are deemed to be objective, systematic, and scientific, able to discern "rational" means to make decisions about health hazards. The layperson's assessment of risk is viewed as a cognitive process that can be measured in the laboratory, divorced from social context. Psychologists in the field of decision analysis employ laboratory experiments, gaming situations, and survey techniques to understand risk perception, attempting to arrive at a quantitative determination of risk acceptance. Individuals are given the names of technologies, activities, or substances and asked to consider the risks each one presents and to rate them (12–14).

The second approach to health risk focuses upon risk as a consequence of the "lifestyle" choices made by individuals, and thus places the emphasis upon self-control. Individuals are exhorted by health promotion authorities to evaluate their risk of succumbing to disease and to change their behavior accordingly. Risk assessment related to lifestyle choices is formally undertaken by means of health risk appraisals and screening programs in which the individual participates and is given a rating. Such health risk appraisals (also termed health risk assessment or health hazard appraisal) are used to counsel individuals about prospective threats to their health that are associated with behaviors deemed to be modifiable. The object is to promote awareness of potential dangers courted by lifestyle choices, and then to motivate individuals to participate in health promotion and health education programs (15, 16).

Research into the layperson's acceptance of personal lifestyle risk again tends to use quantitative methods, usually based upon pen-and-paper questionnaires that incorporate questions such as "How much at risk (from the illness or disease in question) do you think you are personally?", with available responses ranging from "At great risk" to "Not at all at risk." Most questionnaires use only close-ended and pre-categorized items that provide very little opportunity for respondents to give unprompted opinions and to expand upon their answers. These kinds of research methods into risk perception fail to take into account respondents' belief systems relating to causes of disease and health behaviors. Too narrow a range of explanatory variables results in many research studies failing to expose the impact of differing cultural factors upon behavior (17, 18).

As a consequence, the literature on risk acceptance and risk perception in the health domain tends not to account for the influence of the sociocultural contexts within which risk perception takes place and the political uses to which risk discourse is put. Despite the wealth of literature on risk perception, analysis, and assessment, and the extremely common use of the concept of "risk" in public health literature, little critical examination of the meaning and rhetorical use of risk discourse has taken place by scholars within these fields.

In recent years a small number of qualitative sociologists, anthropologists, and philosophers have focused their attention upon other aspects of risk, viewing risk not as a neutral and easily measurable concept, but as a sociocultural concept laden with meaning. The remainder of this article explores this dimension of risk discourse, which has been largely ignored in the public health and risk analysis literature.

EXTERNAL RISK RHETORIC

Interpretive analyses of the meanings of risk discourse in public health argue that there is more to risk than the disclosure of technical information and the mathematical determination of probabilities, and more to the individual's perception of risk than the assimilation and rational weighing up of impartial technical information (1; 3; 7, p. 96; 19; 20). For example, Douglas and Wildavsky (1) contend with respect to external threats that the selection of risks deemed to be hazardous to a population is a social process: the risks that are selected may have no relation to real danger but are culturally identified as important. People's fears about risks can be regarded as ways of maintaining social solidarity rather than as reflecting health or environmental concerns.

Nelkin argues that "definitions of risk are an expression of the tensions inherent in given social and cultural contexts, and that these tensions frequently come to focus on the issue of communication" (7, p. 96). Definitions of risk may serve to identify Self and the Other, to apportion blame upon stigmatized minorities, or as a political weapon. Risk therefore may have less to do with the nature of danger than the ideological purposes to which concerns about risk may be put (7). In history the scapegoating of ethnic minorities when an epidemic such as smallpox or the plague broke out is an example of how the concept of risk has been used for political purposes in public health discourse (21).

The notion of external risk thus serves to categorize individuals or groups into "those at risk" and "those posing a risk." Risk, in modern society, has come to replace the old-fashioned (and in modern secular society, now largely discredited) notion of sin, as a term that "runs across the gamut of social life to moralize and politicise dangers" (3, p. 4). Although risk is a much more "sanitized" concept, it signifies the same meanings, for, as Douglas comments, "the neutral vocabulary of risk is all we have for making a bridge between the known facts of existence and the construction of a moral community" (3, p. 5).

Douglas believes that "being at risk" is the reciprocal of sinning, for the emphasis is placed upon the danger of external forces upon the individual, rather than the dangers afforded the community by the individual: "To be 'at risk' is equivalent to being sinned against, being vulnerable to the events caused by others, whereas being 'in sin' means being the cause of harm" (3, p. 7). Her analysis of the concept of risk is closely tied to the term as it is used in politics, especially with reference to the risks placed by environmental hazards upon individuals who have little personal power to deal with them.

Douglas's distinction, however, while enlightening, is accurate only when applied to risk that is believed to be externally imposed. The theory is less apt when viewed in the light of health risks considered to be the responsibility of the individual to control. When risk is believed to be internally imposed because of lack of willpower, moral weakness, venality, or laziness on the part of the individual, the symbolic relationship of sin and risk is reversed. Those who are deemed "at risk" become the sinners, not the sinned against, because of their apparent voluntary courting of risk. The next section addresses the moral meanings ascribed to health risks deemed to be "voluntary."

HEALTH EDUCATION AND LIFESTYLE RISK DISCOURSE

Ironically, there has been an increasing emphasis upon apprising individuals of their own responsibility for engaging in risky behaviors at the same time as the control of individuals over the risks in their working and living environments has diminished. An important use of risk discourse in the public health arena is that employed in health education, which seeks to create public awareness of the health risks posed by "lifestyle" choices made by the individual.

Cultural theorists interested in risk as a sociocultural phenomenon have tended to focus their speculations upon the moral meanings and political function of external risk. However, I would argue that greater attention needs to be paid to the implicit meanings and functions of lifestyle risk discourse. Just as a moral distinction is drawn between "those at risk" and "those posing a risk," health education routinely draws a distinction between the harm caused by external causes out of the individual's control and that caused by oneself. Lifestyle risk discourse overturns the notion that health hazards in postindustrial society are out of the individual's control. On the contrary, the dominant theme of lifestyle risk discourse is the responsibility of the individual to avoid health risks for the sake of his or her own health as well as the greater good of society. According to this discourse, if individuals choose to ignore health risks they are placing themselves in danger of illness, disability, and disease, which removes them from a useful role in society and incurs costs upon the public purse. Should individuals directly expose others to harm for example, by smoking in a public place, driving while drunk, or spreading an infectious disease there is even greater potential for placing the community at risk.

Why has lifestyle risk discourse gained such cultural resonance in late-capitalist society? There are historico-cultural roots to this discourse. Rosenberg links the public health discourse of risk with the ancient and powerful "desire to explain sickness and death in terms of volition of acts done or left undone" (22, p. 50). He suggests that the decrease in incidence of acute infectious disease in contemporary western society has led to an increasing obsession with regimen, and the control of individuals' diet and exercise, to reduce real or sensed risks, to "redefine the mortal odds that face them" (22, p. 50). The other side of the coin, according to Rosenberg, is a tendency to explain the vulnerability of others to disease and illness in terms of their own acts or lifestyle choices; for example, overeating, alcoholism, or sexual promiscuity.

The modern concept of risk, like that of taboo, has a "forensic" property, for it works backwards in explaining ill-fortune, as well as forwards in predicting future retribution (3). Thus the experience of a heart attack, a positive HIV test result, or the discovery of a cancerous lesion are evidence that the ill person has failed to comply with directives to reduce health risks and therefore is to be blamed for his or her predicament (23–28). As Marantz has commented of health education: "Many within the profession now think that anyone who has a [heart attack] must have lived the life of gluttony and sloth. . . . We seem to view raising a cheeseburger to one's lips as the moral equivalent of holding a gun to one's head" (26, p. 1186).

The current irrational discrimination, fear, and prejudice leveled against people with AIDS is a prime example of the way in which being "at risk" becomes the equivalent of sinning. Research undertaken by the anthropologist McCombie (29) illustrates the moral meanings attributed to the state of being "at risk" in the context of AIDS. She studied the counseling given by health workers to individuals deemed either "high risk" or "low risk" after a test for HIV antibodies had been performed. McCombie noticed that high-risk individuals, whether HIV positive or negative, were treated differently from low-risk individuals: "the high risk person is chastised, admonished and warned, while the low risk person is consoled and reassured" (29, p. 455). She evaluated this behavior in the context of taboo violation, pollution, and punishment for sin. High-risk individuals were being punished for their deviant behavior and were held responsible for their own behavior if HIV positive. By contrast, individuals deemed at low risk were looked upon more as innocent victims. The blood test itself was a ritual, acting an anxiety-reducing measure for those who were concerned that the virus was getting out of control as well as implicitly acting as a tool for detecting social deviance (29).

DEFINING RISK AND THOSE "AT RISK": THE POLITICAL FUNCTION OF RISK DISCOURSE

The rhetoric of risk serves different functions, depending on how personally controllable the danger is perceived as being. Douglas has pointed out that "blaming the victim is a strategy that works in one kind of context, and blaming the outside enemy, a strategy that works in another" (30, p. 59). She believes that both types of attributions of risk serve to maintain the cohesiveness of a society; the first in protecting internal social control, and the second in bolstering loyalty.

The categorization of which risks are deemed to be external and which internal influences the moral judgments made about blame and responsibility for placing health in jeopardy. It is important to consider which institutions have the power to define these categories of risk. Sapolsky (31) suggests that the political system of industrialized countries is responsible for the current obsession with risk. Because members of the general public do not have access to sufficient information to assess environmental risks, they must rely upon intermediaries such as scientists, government officials, environmental campaigners, and the news media to inform them. These intermediaries have their own agenda, and therefore tend to exaggerate and distort the "facts" to further their own cause, making it difficult for the layperson to conceptualize risk in the face of conflicting perspectives (31, p. 90).

The news media, for example, have an integral role in disseminating information about health risks. The news media can have an important influence on shaping public policy and setting the agenda for the public discussion of risks. They are interested in attracting a large audience or readership, and tend to over-dramatize and simplify information about health risks accordingly. If they are relying upon the news media for information and advice, members of the lay audience can be left feeling panicked and confused (32–34). Politicians must react to new risks in a concerned manner, to avoid the backlash of seeming apathy in the face of a new health scare and to bolster their position: "careers are as much at risk in risk controversies as is the public's health" (31, p. 94). They have the power to gain the attention of the news media, and their opinions are therefore privileged over those of the ordinary person.

Personal health risk appraisals have been shown to have serious limitations in their predictive capabilities. These limitations include their use of epidemiological data produced from population research not designed to be applied to personal health risk, and problems with the available statistical methods for estimating risk as a quantitative score using disparate items of measurement (15, 16). Despite these problems, little research has been undertaken into the practical and ethical consequences of such risk appraisals, including their capacity to arouse anxiety in the well and their appropriate use in patient counseling. Some critics have expressed concern that by instituting such programs as health risk appraisals, drug and other screening, and fitness assessments into the workplace, large corporations are able to maintain control over the worker even when she or he is not at the workplace. Programs such as drug screening may be used as tools to identify the "desirable" employees; in other words, those whose lifestyles are deemed acceptable. They also enable employers to determine what workers are doing in their spare time, casting the net of corporate control ever wider (2, 35, 36).

The use of public information campaigns on the part of governments has increased in recent years. According to Wikler (37) there is danger in allowing governments the power to publicize health risks. Knowledge and risk factors may be misinterpreted; interventions may be ineffective or counterproductive. Health education can be coercive when it gives only one side of the argument, and if it attempts to persuade rather than simply give information to aid rational decision-making. Health education campaigns, in their efforts to persuade, have the potential to manipulate information deceptively and to psychologically manipulate by appealing to people's emotions, fears, anxieties, and guilt feelings (38).

Risk definitions may therefore be considered hegemonic conceptual tools that can serve to maintain the power structure of society. The voice of Everyman and Everywoman is rarely accorded equal hearing with that of big business and politicians. The two latter are in a position both to define health risks and to identify their solutions.

People working in the field of health risk communication tend to hold naive views about the ethics and point of such messages. Analysis of the moral and ethical implications of risk communication tends to implicitly accept that public communication of risk is desirable in most circumstances, with no further need to evaluate the ethical implications other than those posed by the involvement of journalists and public relations firms. Public knowledge, or "general edification," as bestowed by the state, is privileged as being in the public's "best interest" (39). The endeavor of risk communication sponsored by the state itself is rarely questioned in the risk communication literature as a political practice that can serve to maintain the interests of the powerful.

More insightful critics have argued that the use of the term "risk" is rarely neutral or devoid of political implications or moral questions. Risk communication, whether it is made by government, industry, or other bodies, can readily be regarded as a "'top-down' justification exercise in which experts attempt to educate an apparently misguided public into the real world of probability and hazard" (11, p. 514).

Government-sponsored arguments for public health education campaigns that employ lifestyle risk discourse include: (*a*) a basic responsibility to protect and promote the nation's health; (*b*) providing resources through collective action to help individuals improve their health; (*c*) containing costs; and (*d*) preventing individuals from harming others through their lifestyle choices (38, pp. 33–34). However, the arguments against government health education campaigns are also compelling. Should the minority be forced to bow to the wishes of the majority? Do health education campaigns constitute paternalism, by telling individuals what they should do with their lifestyle choices and reducing personal autonomy? Moral arguments can be brought to bear against the harm to others and cost-containment justifications (37). Implicated in these arguments is the use of health education campaigns as a cynical means of acting in response to a health problem while perpetuating the structural status quo that helps maintain the problem.

Foucault has remarked that "Every educational system is a political means of maintaining or modifying the appropriation of discourse with the knowledge and powers it carries with it" (40, p. 227). Health education emphasizing risks is a form of pedagogy, which, like other forms, serves to legitimize ideologies and social practices. Risk discourse in the public health sphere allows the state, as the owner of knowledge, to exert power over the bodies of its citizens. Risk discourse, therefore, especially when it emphasizes lifestyle risks, serves as an effective Foucaldian agent of surveillance and control that is difficult to challenge because of its manifest benevolent goal of maintaining standards of health. In doing so, it draws attention away from the structural causes of ill-health.

CONCLUSION

There are ethical questions in the use of risk discourse in public health that have been little questioned. Public health rhetoric has often posited that all individuals should have the right to information about risks. The implication of this assertion is that all individuals should have the right to be warned of the dangers of their behavior. What is left out of this equation is the corollary: that all individuals should have the right *not* to be continually informed of the risks they might be taking when engaging in certain actions, or that they should have the right not to act upon warnings if so preferred. The discourse of risk ostensibly gives people a choice, but the rhetoric in which the choice is couched leaves no room for maneuver. The public is given the statistics of danger, but not the safety margins. The discourse of risk is weighted toward disaster and anxiety rather than peace of mind. Rather than inform the public, for example, that the probability of not contracting HIV in a single sexual encounter is 999 out of 1000, the focus is placed upon the one in 1000 probability that infection will occur.

This emphasis upon a negative outcome, the inducement of anxiety and guilt in those who have received the message about the risks but do not change their behavior, might be said to be unethical. People tend to avoid anxiety by believing that they will not be the victims of a negative outcome. Is the constant assault upon the public's need to feel personally invulnerable ethical? Should employers be allowed to demand health risk appraisals in the name of ameliorating employees' health prospects? Should the discourse of risk give way to more positive statements? Are there ways to induce behavioral change amongst those really at risk other than inciting anxiety?

Risk discourse as it is currently used in public health draws upon the *fin de millennium* mood of the late 20th century, which targets the body as a site of toxicity, contamination, and catastrophe, subject to and needful of a high degree of surveillance and control (41). No longer is the body a temple to be worshipped as the house of God: it has become a commodified and regulated object that must be strictly monitored by its owner to prevent lapses into health-threatening behaviors as identified by risk discourse. For those with the socioeconomic resources to indulge in risk modification, this discourse may supply the advantages of a new religion; for others, risk discourse has the potential to create anxiety and guilt, to promote hopelessness and fear of the future.

There needs to be a move away from viewing risk perception as a rational cognitive process that can and should be influenced by the external efforts of health promotion, to more critical and theoretically informed investigations into the meaning of risk to individuals in contemporary society. Lifestyle risk discourse as it is used in public health should be examined for its ethical, political, and moral subtext. Recent developments in the sociology, anthropology, and philosophy of risk discourse have pointed the way for such investigations.

REFERENCES

1. Douglas, M., and Wildavsky, A. *Risk and Culture.* Basil Blackwell, Oxford, 1982.
2. Stoeckle, J. D. On looking risk in the eye. *Am. J. Public Health* 80: 1170–1171, 1990.
3. Douglas, M. Risk as a forensic resource. *Daedalus*, Fall 1990, pp. 1–16.
4. Starr, C. Social benefit vs. technological risk. *Science* 165: 1232–1238, 1969.
5. Short, J. F. The social fabric at risk: Toward the social transformation of risk analysis. *Am. Soc. Rev.* 49: 711–725, 1984.
6. Fischoff, B., et al. *Acceptable Risk.* Cambridge University Press, New York, 1981.
7. Nelkin, D. Communicating technological risk: The social construction of risk perception. *Annu. Rev. Public Health* 10: 95–113, 1989.
8. National Research Council Committee on Risk Perception and Communication. *Improving Risk Communication.* National Academy Press, Washington, D.C., 1989.

9. Dandoy, S. Risk communication and public confidence in health departments. *Am. J. Public Health* 80: 1299–1300, 1990.
10. Kahn, E., et al. A crisis of community anxiety and mistrust: The Medfly Eradication Project in Santa Clara County, California, 1981–82. *Am. J. Public Health* 80: 1301–1304, 1990.
11. O'Riordan, T., et al. Themes and tasks of risk communication: Report of an international conference held at KFA Julich. *Risk Analysis* 9: 513–518, 1989.
12. Otway, H., and Wynne, B. Risk communication: Paradigm and paradox. *Risk Analysis* 9: 141–145, 1989.
13. Tversky, A., and Kahneman, D. Judgement under uncertainty: Heuristics and biases. *Science* 185: 1124–1131, 1974.
14. Slovic, P. Perception of risk. *Science* 230: 280–285, 1987.
15. De Friese, G. H., and Fielding, J. E. Health risk appraisal in the 1990s: Opportunities, challenges, and expectations. *Annu. Rev. Public Health* 11: 401–418, 1990.
16. Fielding, J. E. Appraising the health of health risk appraisal. *Am. J. Public Health* 72: 337–340, 1982.
17. Kaplan, H. B., et al. The sociological study of AIDS: A critical review of the literature and suggested research agenda. *J. Health Soc. Behav.* 28: 140–157, 1982.
18. Nickerson, C. A. E. The attitude/behavior discrepancy as a methodological artefact: Comment on "Sexually Active Adolescents and Condoms." *Am. J. Public Health* 80: 1174–1179, 1990.
19. Teuber, A. Justifying the risk. *Daedalus,* Fall 1990, pp. 235–254.
20. Douglas, M., and Calvez, M. The self as risk taker: A cultural theory of contagion in relation to AIDS. *Soc. Rev.* 38: 445–464, 1990.
21. Brandt, A. *No Magic Bullet: A Social History of Venereal Disease in the United States since 1880.* Oxford University Press, New York, 1985.
22. Rosenberg, C. E. Disease and social order in America: Perceptions and expectations. *Milbank Mem. Fund. Q.* 64(Suppl.): 34–55, 1986.
23. Sontag, S. *Illness as Metaphor/AIDS and Its Metaphors.* Anchor, New York, 1989.
24. Crawford, R. You are dangerous to your health: The ideology and politics of victim blaming. *Int. J. Health Serv.* 7: 663–680, 1977.
25. Becker, M. H. The tyranny of health promotion. *Public Health Rev.* 14: 15–25, 1986.
26. Marantz, P. R. Blaming the victim: The negative consequence of preventive medicine. *Am. J. Public Health* 80: 1186–1187, 1990.
27. Grace, V. M. The marketing of empowerment and the construction of the health consumer: A critique of health promotion. *Int. J. Health Serv.* 21: 329–343, 1991.
28. Kilwein, J. H. No pain, no gain: A puritan legacy. *Health Ed. Q.* 16: 9–12, 1989.
29. McCombie, S. The cultural impact of the "AIDS" test: The American experience. *Soc. Sci. Med.* 23: 455–459, 1986.
30. Douglas, M. *Risk Acceptability According to the Social Sciences.* Routledge & Kegan Paul, London, 1986.
31. Sapolsky, H. M. The politics of risk. *Daedalus,* Fall 1990, pp. 83–96.
32. Stallings, R. A. Media discourse and the social construction of risk. *Soc. Probl.* 37: 80–95, 1990.
33. Nelkin, D. *Selling Science: How the Press Covers Science and Technology.* W. H. Freeman, New York, 1987.
34. Klaidman, S. How well the media report health risk. *Daedalus,* Fall 1990, pp. 119–132.
35. Stone, D. A. At risk in the welfare state. *Soc. Res.* 56: 591–633, 1989.
36. Conrad, P., and Walsh, D. C. The new corporate health ethic: Lifestyle and the social control of work. *Int. J. Health Serv.* 22: 89–111, 1992.
37. Wikler, D. Who should be blamed for being sick? *Health Ed. Q.* 14: 11–25, 1987.
38. Faden, R. R. Ethical issues in government sponsored public health campaigns. *Health Ed. Q.* 14: 27–37, 1987.
39. Morgan, M. G., and Lave, L. Ethical considerations in risk communication practice and research. *Risk Analysis* 10: 355–358, 1990.
40. Foucault, M. *The Archaeology of Knowledge and the Discourse on Language.* Pantheon, New York, 1972.
41. Kroker, A., and Kroker, M. Panic sex in America. In *Body Invaders: Sexuality and the Postmodern Condition,* edited by A. Kroker and M. Kroker, pp. 1–18. Macmillan Education, London, 1988.

The Medicalization of American Society

Only in the twentieth century did medicine become the dominant and prestigious profession we know today. The germ theory of disease, which achieved dominance after about 1870, provided medicine with a powerful explanatory tool and some of its greatest clinical achievements. It proved to be the key that unlocked the mystery of infectious disease and it came to provide the major paradigm by which physicians viewed sickness. The claimed success of medicine in controlling infectious disease, coupled with consolidation and monopolization of medical practice, enabled medicine to achieve a position of social and professional dominance. Medicine, both in direct and indirect ways, was called upon to repeat its "miracles" with other human problems. At the same time, certain segments of the medical profession were intent on expanding medicine's jurisdiction over societal problems.

By mid-century the domain of medicine had enlarged considerably: childbirth, sexuality, death as well as old age, anxiety, obesity, child development, alcoholism, addiction, homosexuality, amongst other human experiences, were being defined and treated as medical problems. Sociologists began to examine the process and consequences of this *medicalization of society* (e.g., Freidson, 1970; Zola, 1972) and most especially the medicalization of deviance (Conrad and Schneider, 1980/1992; Conrad, 1992). It was clear that the medical model focusing on individual organic pathology and positing physiological etiologies and biomedical interventions was being applied to a wide range of human phenomena. Human life, some critics observed, was increasingly seen as a sickness-wellness continuum, with significant (if not obvious) social consequences (Zola, 1972; Conrad, 1975). The rising genetic paradigm and the growth of managed care are affecting medicalization in complicated ways (Conrad, 2000).

Other sociologists, however, argue that although some expansion of medical jurisdiction has occurred, the medicalization problem is overstated. They contend that we recently have witnessed a considerable *de*medicalization. Strong (1979), for instance, points out that there are numerous factors constraining and limiting medicalization, including restrictions on the number of physicians, the cost of medical care, doctor's primary interests in manifestly organic problems, and the bourgeois value of individual liberty.

Conrad and Schneider (1980b) attempted to clarify the debate by suggesting that medicalization occurs on three levels: (1) the conceptual level, at which a medical vocabulary is used to define a problem; (2) the institutional level, at which medical personnel (usually physicians) are supervisors of treatment organizations or gatekeepers to state benefits; and (3) the interactional level, at which physicians actually treat patients' difficulties as medical problems. While there has been considerable discussion about the types and consequences of medicalization, there has thus far been little research on the actual extent of medicalization and its effects on patients' and other peoples' lives.

In "Medicine as an Institution of Social Control," Irving Kenneth Zola presents the medicalization thesis in terms of the expansion of medicine's social control functions.

Adele Clarke and her colleagues, in "Biomedicalization: Technoscientific Tranformations of Health, Illness, and U.S. Biomedicine," contend that medicalization has broadened and expanded to such a degree that it is now a much more pervasive phenomenon. They see the shift to biomedicalization as moving from medical control over external nature to controlling and transforming inner nature. While they see this as having origins and consequences apart from medicalization itself, one can also wonder whether the notion of biomedicalization may be too encompassing, making it difficult to examine specific consequences.

REFERENCES

Conrad, Peter. 1975. "The discovery of hyperkinesis: Notes on the medicalization of deviant behavior." Social Problems 23 (1): 12–21.

Conrad, Peter. 1992. "Medicalization and Social Control." Annual Review of Sociology 18: 209–32.
Conrad, Peter. 2000. "Medicalization, genetics and human problems." Pp. 322–33 in Chloe E. Bird, Peter Conrad and Allen M. Fremont (eds.), Handbook of Medical Sociology, fifth edition. Upper Saddle River, NJ: Prentice-Hall.
Conrad, Peter, and Joseph W. Schneider. 1980/1992. Deviance and Medicalization: From Badness to Sickness. Expanded edition. Philadelphia: Temple University Press.
———. 1980b. "Looking at levels of medicalization: A comment on Strong's critique of the thesis of medical imperialism." Social Science and Medicine 14A (1): 75–9.
Freidson, Eliot. 1970. Profession of Medicine. New York: Dodd, Mead.
Strong, P. M. 1979. "Sociological imperialism and the profession of medicine: A critical examination of the thesis of medical imperialism." Social Science and Medicine 13A (2): 199–215.
Zola, Irving Kenneth. 1972. "Medicine as an institution of social control." Sociological Review 20 (November): 487–504.

38 MEDICINE AS AN INSTITUTION OF SOCIAL CONTROL

Irving Kenneth Zola

The theme of this essay is that medicine is becoming a major institution of social control, nudging aside, if not incorporating, the more traditional institutions of religion and law. It is becoming the new repository of truth, the place where absolute and often final judgments are made by supposedly morally neutral and objective experts. And these judgments are made, not in the name of virtue or legitimacy, but in the name of health. Moreover, this is not occurring through the political power physicians hold or can influence, but is largely an insidious and often undramatic phenomenon accomplished by "medicalizing" much of daily living, by making medicine and the labels "healthy" and "ill" *relevant* to an ever increasing part of human existence.

Although many have noted aspects of this process, by confining their concern to the field of psychiatry, these criticisms have been misplaced.[1] For psychiatry has by no means distorted the mandate of medicine, but indeed, though perhaps at a pace faster than other medical specialties, is following instead some of the basic claims and directions of that profession. Nor is this extension into society the result of any professional "imperialism," for this leads us to think of the issue in terms of misguided human efforts or motives. If we search for the "why" of this phenomenon, we will see instead that it is rooted in our increasingly complex technological and bureaucratic system—a system which has led us down the path of the reluctant reliance on the expert.[2]

Quite frankly, what is presented in the following pages is not a definitive argument but rather a case in progress. As such it draws heavily on observations made in the United States, though similar murmurings have long been echoed elsewhere.[3]

AN HISTORICAL PERSPECTIVE

The involvement of medicine in the management of society is not new. It did not appear full-blown one day in the mid-twentieth century. As Sigerist[4] has aptly claimed, medicine at base was always not only a social science but an occupation whose very practice was inextricably interwoven into society. This interdependence is perhaps best seen in two branches of medicine which have had a built-in social emphasis from the very start—psychiatry[5] and public health/preventive medicine.[6] Public health was always committed to changing social aspects of life—from sanitary to housing to working conditions—and often used the arm of the state (i.e. through laws and legal power) to gain its ends (e.g. quarantines, vaccinations). Psychiatry's involvement in society is a bit more difficult to trace, but taking the histories of psychiatry as data, then one notes the almost universal reference to one of the early pioneers, a physician named Johan Weyer. His, and thus psychiatry's involvement in social problems lay in the objection that witches ought not to be burned; for they were not possessed by the devil, but rather bedeviled by their problems—namely they were insane. From its early concern with the issue of insanity as a defense in criminal proceedings, psychiatry has grown to become the most dominant rehabilitative perspective in dealing with society's "legal" deviants. Psychiatry, like public health, has also used the legal powers of the state in the accomplishment of its goals (i.e. the cure of the patient through the legal proceedings of involuntary commitment and its concomitant removal of certain rights and privileges).

This is not to say, however, that the rest of medicine has been "socially" uninvolved. For a rereading of history makes it seem a matter of degree. Medicine has long had both a *de jure* and a *de facto* relation to institutions of social control. The *de jure* relationship is seen in the idea of reportable diseases, wherein, if certain phenomena occur in his practice, the physician is required to report them to the appropriate authorities. While this seems somewhat straightforward and even functional where certain highly contagious diseases are concerned, it is less clear where the possible spread of infection is not the primary issue (e.g. with gunshot wounds, attempted suicide, drug use and what is now called child abuse). The *de facto* relation to social control can be argued through a brief look at the disruptions of the last two or three American Medical Association Conventions. For there the American Medical Association members—and really all ancillary health professions—were accused of practicing social control (the term used by the accusers was genocide) in first, *whom* they have traditionally treated with *what*—giving *better* treatment to more favored clientele; and secondly, *what* they have treated—a more subtle form of discrimination in that, with limited resources, by focusing on some diseases others are neglected. Here the accusation was that medicine has focused on the diseases of the rich and the established—cancer, heart disease, stroke—and ignored the diseases of the poor, such as malnutrition and still high infant mortality.

THE MYTH OF ACCOUNTABILITY

Even if we acknowledge such a growing medical involvement, it is easy to regard it as primarily a "good" one—which involves the steady destigmatization of many human and social problems. Thus Barbara Wootton was able to conclude:

> Without question . . . in the contemporary attitude toward antisocial behaviour, psychiatry and humanitarianism have marched hand in hand. Just because it is so much in keeping with the mentalatmosphere of a scientifically-minded age, the medical treatment of social deviants has been a most powerful, perhaps even the most powerful, reinforcement of humanitarian impulses; for today the prestige of humane proposals is immensely enhanced if these are expressed in the idiom of medical science.[7]

The assumption is thus readily made that such medical involvement in social problems leads to their removal from religious and legal scrutiny and thus from moral and punitive consequences. In turn the problems are placed under medical scientific scrutiny and thus in objective and therapeutic circumstances.

The fact that we cling to such a hope is at least partly due to two cultural-historical blindspots—one regarding our notion of punishment and the other our notion of moral responsibility. Regarding the first, if there is one insight into human behavior that the twentieth century should have firmly implanted, it is that punishment cannot be seen in merely physical terms, nor only from the perspective of the giver. Granted that capital offenses are on the decrease, that whipping and torture seem to be disappearing, as is the use of chains and other physical restraints, yet our ability if not willingness to inflict human anguish on one another does not seem similarly on the wane. The most effective forms of brain-washing deny any physical contact and the concept of relativism tells much about the psychological costs of even relative deprivation of tangible and intangible wants. Thus, when an individual because of his "disease" and its treatment is forbidden to have intercourse with fellow human beings, is confined until cured, is forced to undergo certain medical procedures for his own good, perhaps deprived forever of the right to have sexual relations and/or produce children, *then* it is difficult for the patient *not* to view what is happening to him as punishment. This does not mean that medicine is the latest form of twentieth century torture, but merely that pain and suffering take many forms, and that the removal of a despicable inhumane procedure by current standards does not necessarily mean that its replacement will be all that beneficial. In part, the satisfaction in seeing the chains cast off by Pinel may have allowed us for far too long to neglect examining with what they had been replaced.

It is the second issue, that of responsibility, which requires more elaboration, for it is argued here that the medical model has had its greatest impact in the lifting of moral condemnation from the individual. While some sceptics note that while the individual is no longer condemned his disease still *is*, they do not go far enough. Most analysts have tried to make a distinction between illness and crime on the issue of personal responsibility.[8] The criminal is thought to be responsible and therefore accountable (or punishable) for his act, while the sick person is not. While the distinction does exist, it seems to be more a quantitative one rather than a qualitative one, with moral judgments but a pinprick below the surface. For instance, while it is probably true that individuals are no longer directly condemned for being sick, it does seem that much of this condemnation is merely displaced. Though his immoral character is not demonstrated in his having a disease, it becomes evident in what he does about it. Without seeming ludicrous, if one listed the traits of people who break appointments, fail to follow treatment regimen, or even delay in seeking medical aid, one finds a long list of "personal flaws." Such people seem to be ever ignorant of the consequences of certain diseases, inaccurate as to symptomatology, unable to plan ahead or find time, burdened with shame, guilt, neurotic tendencies, haunted with traumatic medical experiences or members of some lower status minority group religious, ethnic, racial or socioeconomic. In short, they appear to be a sorely troubled if not disreputable group of people.

The argument need not rest at this level of analysis, for it is not clear that the issues of morality and individual responsibility have been fully banished from the etiological scene itself. At the same time as the label "illness" is being used to attribute "diminished responsibility" to a whole host of phenomena, the issue of "personal responsibility" seems to be re-emerging within medicine itself. Regardless of the truth and insights of the concepts of stress and the perspective of psychosomatics, whatever else they do, they bring man, *not* bacteria to the center of the stage and lead thereby to a re-examination of the individual's role in his own demise, disability and even recovery.

The case, however, need not be confined to professional concepts and their degree of acceptance, for we can look at the beliefs of the man in the street. As most surveys have reported, when an individual is asked what caused his diabetes, heart disease, upper respiratory infection, etc., we may be comforted by the scientific terminology if not the accuracy of his answers. Yet if we follow this questioning with the probe: "Why did you get X now?", or "Of all the people in your community, family, etc. who were exposed to X, why did you get . . . ?", then the rational scientific veneer is pierced and the concern with personal and moral responsibility emerges quite strikingly. Indeed the issue "why me?" becomes of great concern and is generally expressed in quite moral terms of what they did wrong. It is possible to argue that here we are seeing a residue and that it will surely be different in the new generation. A recent experiment I conducted should cast some doubt on this. I asked a class of forty undergraduates, mostly aged seventeen, eighteen and nineteen, to recall the last time they were sick, disabled, or hurt and then to record how they did or would have communicated this experience to a child under the age of five. The purpose of the assignment had nothing to do with the issue of responsibility and it is worth noting that there was no difference in the nature of the response between those who had or had not actually encountered children during their "illness." The responses speak for themselves.

> The opening words of the sick, injured person to the query of the child were:
>
> "I feel bad"
> "I feel bad all over"
> "I have a bad leg"
> "I have a bad eye"
> "I have a bad stomach ache"
> "I have a bad pain"
> "I have a bad cold"
>
> The reply of the child was inevitable:
>
> "What did you do wrong?"
>
> The "ill person" in no case corrected the child's perspective but rather joined it at that level. On bacteria
>
> "There are good germs and bad germs and sometimes the bad germs . . ."
>
> On catching a cold
>
> "Well you know sometimes when your mother says, 'Wrap up or be careful or you'll catch a cold,' well I . . ."
>
> On an eye sore
>
> "When you use certain kinds of things (mascara) near your eye you must be very careful and I was not . . ."
>
> On a leg injury
>
> "You've always got to watch where you're going and I . . ."
>
> Finally to the treatment phase:
>
> On how drugs work
>
> "You take this medicine and it attacks the bad parts . . ."
>
> On how wounds are healed
>
> "Within our body there are good forces and bad ones and when there is an injury, all the good ones . . ."

On pus
"That's the way the body gets rid of all its bad things . . ."
On general recovery
"If you are good and do all the things the doctor and your mother tell you, you will get better."

In short, on nearly every level, from getting sick to recovering, a moral battle raged. This seems more than the mere anthropomorphising of a phenomenon to communicate it more simply to children. Frankly it seems hard to believe that the English language is so poor that a *moral* rhetoric is needed to describe a supposedly amoral phenomenon—illness.

In short, despite hopes to the contrary, the rhetoric of illness by itself seems to provide no absolution from individual responsibility, accountability and moral judgment.

THE MEDICALIZING OF SOCIETY

Perhaps it is possible that medicine is not devoid of potential for moralizing and social control. The first question becomes: "what means are available to exercise it?" Freidson has stated a major aspect of the process most succinctly:

> The medical profession has first claim to jurisdiction over the label of illness and *anything* to which it may be attached, irrespective of its capacity to deal with it effectively.[9]

For illustrative purposes this "attaching" process may be categorized in four concrete ways: first, through the expansion of what in life is deemed relevant to the good practice of medicine; secondly, through the retention of absolute control over certain technical procedures; thirdly, through the retention of near absolute access to certain "taboo" areas; and finally, through the expansion of what in medicine is deemed relevant to the good practice of life.

1. The Expansion of What in Life Is Deemed Relevant to the Good Practice of Medicine

The change of medicine's commitment from a specific etiological model of disease to a multi-causal one and the greater acceptance of the concepts of comprehensive medicine, psychosomatics, etc., have enormously expanded that which is or can be relevant to the understanding, treatment and even prevention of disease. Thus it is no longer necessary for the patient merely to divulge the symptoms of his body, but also the symptoms of daily living, his habits and his worries. Part of this is greatly facilitated in the "age of the computer," for what might be too embarrassing, or take too long, or be inefficient in a face-to-face encounter can now be asked and analyzed impersonally by the machine, and moreover be done before the patient ever sees the physician. With the advent of the computer a certain guarantee of privacy is necessarily lost, for while many physicians might have probed similar issues, the only place where the data were stored was in the mind of the doctor, and only rarely in the medical record. The computer, on the other hand, has a retrievable, transmittable and almost inexhaustible memory.

It is not merely, however, the nature of the data needed to make more accurate diagnoses and treatments, but the perspective which accompanies it—a perspective which pushes the physician far beyond his office and the exercise of technical skills. To rehabilitate or at least alleviate many of the ravages of chronic disease, it has become increasingly necessary to intervene to change permanently the habits of a patient's lifetime—be it of working, sleeping, playing or eating. In prevention the "extension into life" becomes even deeper, since the very idea of primary prevention means getting there *before* the disease process starts. The physician must not only seek out his clientele but once found must often convince them that they must do something *now* and perhaps at a time when the potential patient feels well or not especially troubled. If this in itself does not get the prevention-oriented physician involved in the workings of society, then the nature of "effective" mechanisms for intervention surely does, as illustrated by the statement of a physician trying to deal with health problems in the ghetto.

> Any effort to improve the health of ghetto residents cannot be separated from equal and simultaneous efforts to remove the multiple social, political and economic restraints currently imposed on inner city residents.[10]

Certain forms of social intervention and control emerge even when medicine comes to grips with some of its more traditional problems like heart disease and cancer. An increasing number of physicians feel that a change in diet may be the most effective deterrent to a number of cardiovascular complications. They are, however, so perplexed as to how to get the general population to follow their recommendations that a leading article in a national magazine was entitled "To Save the Heart: Diet by Decree?"[11] It is obvious that there is an increasing pressure for more explicit sanctions against the tobacco companies and against high users to force both to desist. And what will be the implications of even stronger evidence which links age at parity, frequency of sexual intercourse, or the lack of male circumcision to the incidence of cervical cancer, can be left to our imagination!

2. Through the Retention of Absolute Control over Certain Technical Procedures

In particular this refers to skills which in certain jurisdictions are the very operational and legal definition of the practice of medicine—the right to do surgery and prescribe drugs. Both of these take medicine far beyond concern with ordinary organic disease.

In surgery this is seen in several different subspecialties. The plastic surgeon has at least participated in, if not helped perpetuate, certain aesthetic standards. What once was a practice confined to restoration has now expanded beyond the correction of certain traumatic or even congenital deformities to the creation of new physical properties, from size of nose to size of breast, as well as dealing with certain phenomena—wrinkles, sagging, etc.—formerly associated with the "natural" process of aging. Alterations in sexual and reproductive functioning have long been a medical concern. Yet today the frequency of hysterectomies seems not so highly correlated as one might think with the presence of organic disease. (What avenues the very possibility of sex change will open is anyone's guess.) Transplantations, despite their still relative infrequency, have had a tremendous effect on our very notions of death and dying. And at the other end of life's continuum, since abortion is still essentially a surgical procedure, it is to the physician-surgeon that society is turning (and the physician-surgeon accepting) for criteria and guidelines.

In the exclusive right to prescribe and thus pronounce on and regulate drugs, the power of the physician is even more awesome. Forgetting for the moment our obsession with youth's "illegal" use of drugs, any observer can see, judging by sales alone, that the greatest increase in drug use over the last ten years has not been in the realm of treating any organic disease but in treating a large number of psychosocial states. Thus we have drugs for nearly every mood:

> to help us sleep or keep us awake
> to enhance our appetite or decrease it
> to tone down our energy level or to increase it
> to relieve our depression or stimulate our interest.

Recently the newspapers and more popular magazines, including some medical and scientific ones, have carried articles about drugs which may be effective peace pills or anti-aggression tablets, enhance our memory, our perception, our intelligence and our vision (spiritually or otherwise). This led to the easy prediction:

> We will see new drugs, more targeted, more specific and more potent than anything we have. . . . And many of these would be for people we would call healthy.[12]

This statement incidentally was made not by a visionary science fiction writer but by a former commissioner of the United States Food and Drug Administration.

3. Through the Retention of Near Absolute Access to Certain "Taboo" Areas

These "taboo" areas refer to medicine's almost exclusive license to examine and treat that most personal of individual possessions—the inner workings of our bodies and minds. My contention is that if anything can be shown in some way to affect the workings of the body and to a lesser extent the mind, then it can be labelled an "illness" itself or jurisdictionally "a medical problem." In a sheer statistical sense the import of this is especially great if we look at only four such problems—aging, drug addiction, alcoholism and pregnancy. The first and last were once regarded as normal natural processes and the middle two as human foibles and weaknesses. Now this has changed and to some extent medical specialties have emerged to meet these new needs. Numerically this expands medicine's involvement not only in a longer span of human existence, but it opens the possibility of medicine's services to millions if not billions of people. In the United States at least, the implication of declaring alcoholism a disease (the possible import of a pending Supreme Court decision as well as laws currently being introduced into several state legislatures) would reduce arrests in many jurisdictions by 10 to 50 percent and transfer such "offenders" when "discovered" directly to a medical facility. It is pregnancy, however, which produces the most illuminating illustration. For, again in the United States, it was barely seventy years ago that virtually all births and the concomitants of birth occurred outside the hospital as well as outside medical supervision. I do not frankly have a documentary history, but as this medical claim was solidified, so too was medicine's claim to a whole host of related processes: not only to birth but to prenatal, postnatal, and pediatric care; not only to conception but to infertility; not only to the process of reproduction but to the process and problems of sexual activity itself; not only when life begins (in the issue of abortion) but whether it should be allowed to begin at all (e.g. in genetic counselling).

Partly through this foothold in the "taboo" areas and partly through the simple reduction of other resources, the physician is increasingly becoming the choice for help for many with personal and social problems. Thus a recent British study reported that within a five year period there had been a notable increase (from 25 to 41 percent) in the proportion of the population willing to consult the physician with a personal problem.[13]

4. Through the Expansion of What in Medicine Is Deemed Relevant to the Good Practice of Life

Though in some ways this is the most powerful of all "the medicalizing of society" processes, the point can be made simply. Here we refer to the use of medical rhetoric and evidence in the arguments to advance any cause. For what Wootton attributed to psychiatry is no less true of medicine. To paraphrase her, today the prestige of *any* proposal is immensely enhanced, if not justified, when it is expressed in the idiom of medical science. To say that many who use such labels are not professionals only begs the issue, for the public is only taking its cues from professionals who increasingly have been extending their expertise into the social sphere or have called for such an extension.[14] In politics one hears of the healthy or unhealthy economy or state. More concretely, the physical and mental health of American presidential candidates has been an issue in the last four elections and a recent book claimed to link faulty political decisions with faulty health.[15] For years we knew that the environment was unattractive, polluted, noisy and in certain ways dying, but now we learn that its death may not be unrelated to our own demise. To end with a rather mundane if depressing example, there has always been a constant battle between school authorities and their charges on the basis of dress and such habits as smoking, but recently the issue was happily resolved for a local school administration when they declared that such restrictions were necessary for reasons of health.

THE POTENTIAL AND CONSEQUENCES OF MEDICAL CONTROL

The list of daily activities to which health can be related is ever growing and with the current operating perspective of medicine it seems infinitely expandable. The reasons are manifold. It is not merely that medicine has extended its jurisdiction to cover new problems,[16] or that doctors are professionally committed to finding disease,[17] nor even that society keeps creating disease.[18] For if none of these obtained today we would still find medicine exerting an enormous influence on society. The most powerful empirical stimulus for this is the realization of how much everyone has or believes he has something organically wrong with him, or put more positively, how much can be done to make one feel, look or function better.

The rates of "clinical entities" found on surveys or by periodic health examinations range upwards from 50 to 80 percent of the population studied.[19] The Peckham study found that only 9 percent of their study group were free from clinical disorder. Moreover, they were even wary of this figure and noted in a footnote that, first, some of these 9 percent had subsequently died of a heart attack, and, secondly, that the majority of those without disorder were under the age of five.[20] We used to rationalize that this high level of prevalence did not, however, translate itself into action since not only are rates of medical utilization not astonishingly high but they also have not gone up appreciably. Some recent studies, however, indicate that we may have been looking in the wrong place for this medical action. It has been noted in the United States and the United Kingdom that within a given twenty-four to thirty-six hour period, from 50 to 80 percent of the adult population have taken one or more "medical" drugs.[21]

The belief in the omnipresence of disorder is further enhanced by a reading of the scientific, pharmacological and medical literature, for there one finds a growing litany of indictments of "unhealthy" life activities. From sex to food, from aspirins to clothes, from driving your car to riding the surf, it seems that under certain conditions, or in combination with certain other substances or activities or if done too much or too little, virtually anything can lead to certain medical problems. In short, I at least have finally been convinced that living is injurious to health. This remark is not meant as facetiously as it may sound. But rather every aspect of our daily life has in it elements of risk to health.

These facts take on particular importance not only when health becomes a paramount value in society, but also a phenomenon whose diagnosis and treatment has been restricted to a certain group. For this means that that group, perhaps unwittingly, is in a position to exercise great control and influence about what we should and should not do to attain that "paramount value."

Freidson in his recent book *Profession of Medicine* has very cogently analyzed why the expert in general and the medical expert in particular should be granted a certain autonomy in his researches, his diagnosis and his recommended treatments.[22] On the other hand, when it comes to constraining or directing human behavior *because* of the data of his researches, diagnosis and treatment, a different situation obtains. For in these kinds of decisions it seems that too often the physician is guided not by his technical knowledge but by his values, or values latent in his very techniques.

Perhaps this issue of values can be clarified by reference to some not so randomly chosen medical problems: drug safety, genetic counselling and automated multiphasic testing.

The issue of drug safety should seem straightforward, but both words in that phrase apparently can have some interesting flexibility—namely what is a drug and what is safe. During Prohibition in the United States alcohol was medically regarded as a drug and was often prescribed as a medicine. Yet in recent years, when the issue of dangerous substances and drugs has come up for discussion in medical circles, alcohol has been officially excluded from the debate. As for safety, many have applauded the A.M.A.'s judicious position in declaring the need for much more extensive, longitudinal research on marihuana and their unwillingness to back leglization until much more data are in. This applause might be muted if the public read the 1970 Food and Drug Administration's "Blue Ribbon" Committee Report on the safety, quality and efficacy of *all* medical drugs commercially and legally on the market since 1938.[23] Though appalled at the lack and quality of evidence of any sort, few recommendations were made for the withdrawal of drugs from the market. Moreover there are no recorded cases of anyone dying from an overdose or of extensive adverse side effects from marihuana use, but the literature on the adverse effects of a whole host of "medical drugs" on the market today is legion.

It would seem that the value positions of those on both sides of the abortion issue needs little documenting, but let us pause briefly at a field where "harder" scientists are at work—genetics. The issue of genetic counselling, or whether life should be allowed to begin at all, can only be an ever increasing one. As we learn more and more about congenital, inherited disorders or predispositions, and as the population size for whatever reason becomes more limited, then, inevitably, there will follow an attempt to improve the quality of the population which shall be produced. At a conference on the more limited concern of what to do when there is a documented probability of the offspring of certain unions being damaged, a position was taken that it was not necessary to pass laws or bar marriages that might produce such offspring. Recognizing the power and influence of medicine and the doctor, one of those present argued:

> There is no reason why sensible people could not be dissuaded from marrying if they know that one out of four of their children is likely to inherit a disease.[24]

There are in this statement certain values on marriage and what it is or could be that, while they may be popular, are not necessarily shared by all. Thus, in addition to presenting the argument against marriage, it would seem that the doctor should—if he were to engage in the issue at all—present at the same time some of the other alternatives:

> Some "parents" could be willing to live with the risk that out of four children, three may turn out fine.
> Depending on the diagnostic procedures available they could take the risk and if indications were negative abort.
> If this risk were too great but the desire to bear children was there, and depending on the type of problem, artificial insemination might be a possibility.
> Barring all these and not wanting to take any risk, they could adopt children.
> Finally, there is the option of being married without having any children.

It is perhaps appropriate to end with a seemingly innocuous and technical advance in medicine, automatic multiphasic testing. It has been a procedure hailed as a boon to aid the doctor if not replace him. While some have questioned the validity of all those test-results and still others fear that it will lead to second class medicine for already underprivileged populations, it is apparent that its major use to date and in the future may not be in promoting health or detecting disease but to prevent it. Thus three large institutions are now or are planning to make use of this method, not to treat people, but to "deselect" them. The armed services use it to weed out the physically and mentally unfit, insurance companies to reject "uninsurables" and large industrial firms to point out "high risks." At a recent conference representatives of these same institutions were asked what responsibility they did or would recognize to those whom they have just informed that they have been "rejected" because of some physical or mental anomaly. They calmly and universally stated: none—neither to provide them with any appropriate aid nor even to ensure that they get or be put in touch with any help.

CONCLUSION

C. S. Lewis warned us more than a quarter of a century ago that "man's power over Nature is really the power of some men over other men, with Nature as their instrument." The same could be said regarding man's power over health and illness, for the labels health and illness are remarkable "depoliticizers" of an issue. By locating the source and the treatment of problems in an individual, other levels of intervention are effectively closed. By the very acceptance of a specific behavior as an "illness" and the definition of illness as an undesirable state, the issue becomes not whether to deal with a particular problem, but *how* and *when*.[25] Thus the debate over homosexuality, drugs or abortion becomes focused on the degree of sickness attached to the phenomenon in question or the extent of the health risk involved. And the more principled, more perplexing, or even moral issue, of *what* freedom should an individual have over his or her own body is shunted aside.

As stated in the very beginning this "medicalizing of society" is as much a result of medicine's potential as it is of society's wish for medicine to use that potential. Why then has the focus been more on the medical potential than on the social-desire? In part it is a function of space, but also of political expediency. For the time rapidly may be approaching when recourse to the populace's wishes may be impossible. Let me illustrate this with the statements of two medical scientists who, if they read this essay, would probably dismiss all my fears as groundless. The first was commenting on the ethical, moral, and legal procedures of the sex change operation:

> Physicians generally consider it unethical to destroy or alter tissue except in the presence of disease or deformity. The interference with a person's natural pro-creative function entails definite moral tenets, by which not only physicians but also the general public are influenced. The administration of physical harm as treatment for mental or behavioral problems—as corporal punishment, lobotomy for unmanageable psychotics and sterilization of criminals—is abhorrent in our society.[26]

Here he states, as almost an absolute condition of human nature, something which is at best a recent phenomenon. He seems to forget that there were laws promulgating just such procedures through much of the twentieth century, that within the past few years at least one Californian jurist ordered the sterilization of an unwed mother as a condition of probation, and that such procedures were done by Nazi scientists and physicians as part of a series of medical experiments. More recently, there is the misguided patriotism of the cancer researchers under contract to the United States Department of Defense who allowed their dying patients to be exposed to massive doses of radiation to analyze the psychological and physical results of simulated nuclear fall-out. True, the experiments were stopped, but not until they had been going on for *eleven* years.

The second statement is by Francis Crick at a conference on the implications of certain genetic findings:

> Some of the wild genetic proposals will never be adopted because the people will simply not stand for them.[27]

Note where his emphasis is: on the people, not the scientist. In order, however, for the people to be concerned, to act and to protest, they must first be aware of what is going on. Yet in the very privatized nature of medical practice, plus the continued emphasis that certain expert judgments must be free from public scrutiny, there are certain processes which will prevent the public from ever knowing what has taken place and thus from doing something about it. Let me cite two examples.

> Recently, in a European country, I overheard the following conversation in a kidney dialysis unit. The chief was being questioned about whether or not there were self-help groups among his patients. "No," he almost shouted, "that is the last thing we want. Already the patients are sharing too much knowledge while they sit in the waiting room, thus making our task increasingly difficult. We are working now on a procedure to prevent them from even meeting with one another."

The second example removes certain information even further from public view.

> The issue of fluoridation in the U.S. has been for many years a hot political one. It was in the political arena because, in order to fluoridate local water supplies, the decision in many jurisdictions had to be put to a popular referendum. And when it was, it was often defeated. A solution was found and a series of state laws were passed to make fluoridation a public health decision and to be treated, as all other public health decisions, by the medical officers best qualified to decide questions of such a technical, scientific and medical nature.

Thus the issue at base here is the question of what factors are actually of a solely technical, scientific and medical nature.

To return to our opening caution, this paper is not an attack on medicine so much as on a situation in which we find ourselves in the latter part of the twentieth century; for the medical area is the arena or the example *par excellence* of today's identity crisis—what is or will become of man. It is the battleground, not because there are visible threats and oppressors, but because they are almost invisible; not because the perspective, tools and practitioners of medicine and the other helping professions are evil, but because they are not. It is so frightening because there are elements here of the banality of evil so uncomfortably written about by Hannah Arendt.[28] But here the danger is greater, for not only is the process masked as a technical, scientific, objective one, but one done for our own good. A few years ago a physician speculated on what, based on current knowledge, would be the composite picture of an individual with a low risk of developing atherosclerosis or coronary-artery disease. He would be:

> . . . an effeminate municipal worker or embalmer completely lacking in physical or mental alertness and without drive, ambition, or competitive spirit; who has never attempted to meet a deadline of any kind; a man with poor appetite, subsisting on fruits and vegetables laced with corn and whale oil, detesting tobacco, spurning ownership of radio, television, or motorcar, with full head of hair but scrawny and unathletic appearance, yet constantly straining his puny muscles by exercise. Low in income, blood pressure, blood sugar, uric acid and cholesterol, he has been taking nicotinic acid, pyridoxine, and long term anticoagulant therapy ever since his prophylactic castration.[29]

Thus I fear with Freidson:

> A profession and a society which are so concerned with physical and functional wellbeing as to sacrifice civil liberty and moral integrity must inevitably press for a "scientific" environment similar to that provided laying hens on progressive chicken farms—hens who produce eggs industriously and have no disease or other cares.[30]

Nor does it really matter that if, instead of the above depressing picture, we were guaranteed six more inches in height, thirty more years of life, or drugs to expand our potentialities and potencies; we should still be able to ask: what do six more inches matter, in what kind of environment will the thirty additional years be spent, or who will decide what potentialities and potencies will be expanded and what curbed.

I must confess that given the road down which so much expertise has taken us, I am willing to live with some of the frustrations and even mistakes that will follow when the authority for many decisions becomes shared with those whose lives and activities are involved. For I am convinced that patients have so much to teach to their doctors as do students their professors and children their parents.

NOTE

This paper was written while the author was a consultant in residence at the Netherlands Institute for Preventive Medicine, Leiden. For their general encouragement and the opportunity to pursue this topic I will always be grateful.

It was presented at the Medical Sociology Conference of the British Sociological Association at Weston-Super-Mare in November 1971. My special thanks for their extensive editorial and substantive comments go to Egon Bittner, Mara Sanadi, Alwyn Smith, and Bruce Wheaton.

REFERENCES

1. T. Szasz: *The Myth of Mental Illness,* Harper and Row, New York, 1961; and R. Leifer: *In the Name of Mental Health,* Science House, New York, 1969.
2. E.g. A. Toffler: *Future Shock,* Random House, New York, 1970; and P. E. Slater: *The Pursuit of Loneliness,* Beacon Press, Boston, 1970.
3. Such as B. Wootton: *Social Science and Social Pathology,* Allen and Unwin, London, 1959.
4. H. Sigerist: *Civilization and Disease,* Cornell University Press, New York, 1943.
5. M. Foucault: *Madness and Civilization,* Pantheon, New York, 1965; and Szasz: *op. cit.*
6. G. Rosen: *A History of Public Health,* MD Publications, New York, 1955; and G. Rosen: "The Evolution of Social Medicine," in H. E. Freeman, S. Levine and L. G. Reeder (eds): *Handbook of Medical Sociology,* Prentice-Hall, Englewood Cliffs, N.J., 1963, pp. 17–61.
7. Wootton: *op. cit.,* p. 206.
8. Two excellent discussions are found in V. Aubert and S. Messinger. "The Criminal and the Sick," *Inquiry,* Vol. 1, 1958, pp. 137–160; and E. Freidson: *Profession of Medicine,* Dodd-Mead, New York, 1970, pp. 205–277.
9. Freidson: *op. cit.,* p. 251.
10. J. C. Norman: "Medicine in the Ghetto," *New Engl. J. Med.,* Vol. 281, 1969, p. 1271.
11. "To Save the Heart; Diet by Decree?" *Time Magazine,* 10th January, 1968, p. 42.
12. J. L. Goddard quoted in the *Boston Globe,* August 7th, 1966.
13. K. Dunnell and A. Cartwright: *Medicine Takers, Prescribers and Hoarders,* in press.
14. E.g. S. Alinsky: "The Poor and the Powerful," in *Poverty and Mental Health,* Psychiat. Res. Rep. No. 21 of the Amer. Psychiat. Ass., January 1967; and B. Wedge: "Psychiatry and International Affairs," *Science,* Vol. 157, 1961, pp. 281–285.
15. H. L'Etang: *The Pathology of Leadership,* Hawthorne Books, New York, 1970.
16. Szasz: *op. cit.,* and Leifer: *op. cit.*

17. Freidson: *op. cit.;* and T. Scheff: "Preferred Errors in Diagnoses," *Medical Care,* Vol. 2, 1964, pp. 166–172.
18. R. Dubos: *The Mirage of Health,* Doubleday, Garden City, N.Y., 1959; and R. Dubos: *Man Adapting,* Yale University Press, 1965.
19. E.g. the general summaries of J. W. Meigs: "Occupational Medicine," *New Eng. J. Med.,* Vol. 264, 1961, pp. 861–867; and G. S. Siegel: *Periodic Health Examinations Abstracts from the Literature,* Publ. Hlth. Serv. Publ. No. 1010, U.S. Government Printing Office, Washington, D.C., 1963.
20. I. H. Pearse and L. H. Crocker: *Biologists in Search of Material,* Faber and Faber, London, 1938; and I. H. Pearse and L. H. Crocker: *The Peckham Experiment,* Allen and Unwin, London, 1949.
21. Dunnell and Cartwright: *op. cit.;* and K. White, A. Andjelkovic, R. J. C. Pearson, J. H. Mabry, A. Ross and O. K. Sagan: "International Comparisons of Medical Care Utilization," *New Engl. J. of Med.,* Vol. 277, 167, pp. 516–522.
22. Freidson: *op. cit.*
23. *Drug Efficiency Study Final Report to the Commissioner of Food and Drugs,* Food and Drug Adm. Med. Nat. Res. Council, Nat. Acad. Sci., Washington, D.C., 1969.
24. Reported in L. Eisenberg: "Genetics and the Survival of the Unfit," *Harper's Magazine,* Vol. 232, 1966, p. 57.
25. This general case is argued more specifically in I. K. Zola: *Medicine, Morality, and Social Problems Some Implications of the Label Mental Illness,* Paper presented at the Amer. Ortho-Psychiat. Ass., March 20–23, 1968.
26. D. H. Russell: "The Sex Conversion Controversy", *New Engl. J. Med.,* Vol. 279, 1968, p. 536.
27. F. Crick reported in *Time Magazine,* April 19th, 1971.
28. H. Arendt: *Eichmann in Jerusalem A Report on the Banality of Evil,* Viking Press, New York, 1963.
29. G. S. Myers quoted in L. Losagna: *Life, Death and the Doctor,* Alfred Knopf, New York, 1968, pp. 215–216.
30. Freidson: *op. cit.,* p. 354.

39 Biomedicalization: Technoscientific Transformations of Health, Illness, and U.S. Biomedicine*

Adele E. Clarke, Janet K. Shim, Laura Mamo, Jennifer Ruth Fosket, and Jennifer R. Fishman

INTRODUCTION

Medicalization—processes through which aspects of life previously outside the jurisdiction of medicine come to be construed as medical problems—has constituted one of the most potent social transformations of the last half of the twentieth century in the West (Clarke and Olesen 1999; Conrad 1992; 2000; Morgan 1998). Recently, medicalization is intensifying in new ways. Biomedicine is being reorganized through the remaking of the technical, informational, organizational, and hence institutional infrastructures of the life sciences and medicine, largely via the incorporation of computer and information technologies (e.g., Bowker and Star 1999). Such meso-level (i.e. organizational/institutional) changes are cumulative over time and have now reached critical infrastructural mass. Further, capacities for clinical diagnosis and treatment are being technoscientifically transformed. We argue, therefore, that biomedicalization—which we define as the increasingly technoscientific, com-

*This is a condensed version of a much longer article that was published in *The American Sociological Review,* 68:161–94, 2003. Thanks to the authors for preparing this version for this volume.

plex, multi-sited, multi-directional processes of medicalization—is now transforming the twenty-first century.

Biomedicalization processes are situated within a dynamic and expanding political, economic, and sociocultural biomedical sector. The U.S. health sector has more than tripled in size over the last fifty years, from 4 to 13% of GNP, and is anticipated to exceed 20% by 2040 (Leonhardt 2001). At the same time, Western biomedicine has become a distinctive sociocultural world, ubiquitously webbed throughout mass culture (e.g., Lupton 1994). Health has been the site of multiple social movements as well as being commodified. Biomedicine has become a highly potent cultural lens through which we interpret, understand, and seek to transform bodies and lives.

A fundamental premise of biomedicalization is that increasingly important sciences and technologies *and* new social forms are *co-produced* within biomedicine and related domains, thereby creating ongoing changes. Biomedicalization is manifest through five major interactive processes: 1) the political economic; 2) the focus on health itself and elaboration of risk and surveillance biomedicines; 3) the technoscientization of biomedicine; 4) transformations of biomedical knowledge production, information management, distribution, and consumption; and 5) transformations of bodies and the production of new individual and collective technoscientific identities. These processes each operate at multiple levels as they both engender biomedicalization and are also (re)produced and transformed through it over time.

FROM MEDICALIZATION TO BIOMEDICALIZATION

Historically, the rise in the U.S. of Western (allopathic) medicine as we know it was accomplished clinically, scientifically, technologically, and institutionally c. 1890–1945. In the decades after World War II, medicine as a political economic institutional sector and a sociocultural "good" grew dramatically in the U.S. through major investments, both private (industry and foundations) and public (e.g., NIH, Medicare, Medicaid). The production of medical knowledges and clinical interventions—goods and services—expanded rapidly.

As medicine grew, sociologists and other social scientists began to attend to its importance, especially as a profession. The concept of medicalization was initially framed by Irving Zola (1972) to theorize the extension of medical jurisdiction, authority, and practices into increasingly broader areas of people's lives. Through the theoretical framework of medicalization, medicine as an institutional sector came to be understood as a social and cultural enterprise as well as a medico-scientific one, and illness and disease came to be understood not as necessarily inherent in any particular behaviors or conditions, but as constructed through human (inter)action.

Gradually the concept of medicalization was extended to all instances when new phenomena were deemed medical problems under medical jurisdiction—from initial expansions around childbirth, death, menopause, and contraception in the 1970s to post-traumatic stress disorder (PTSD), premenstrual syndrome (PMS), and attention deficit hyperactivity disorder (ADHD) in the 1980s/90s and so on. Social and cultural aspects and *meanings* of medicalization were elaborated even further and, as we argue next, largely through technoscientific innovations. For example, conditions understood as undesirable or stigmatizable "differences" were medicalized (e.g., unattractiveness through cosmetic surgery; obesity through diet medications) and medical treatment of them was normalized (e.g., Armstrong 1995; Crawford 1985). These were the beginnings of the medicalization of *health*, in addition to illness and disease—the medicalization of phenomena heretofore within the range of "normal."

Then, beginning c. 1985, we are arguing, the nature of medicalization itself began to change as technoscientific innovations and associated new social forms began to transform biomedicine from the inside out. Conceptually, biomedicalization is predicated on what we see as larger shifts-in-progress from the problems of modernity to the problems of late modernity or post-modernity. Within the framework of the Industrial Revolution, we became accustomed to "big science" and "big technology"—projects such as the atom bomb, electrification and transportation grids. In the current technoscientific revolution, "big science" and "big technology" can sit on your desk, in a pillbox, and inside your body. That is, the shift to biomedicalization is from enhanced control over external nature (i.e., the world around us) to the harnessing and transformation of internal nature (i.e., biological processes of human and nonhuman life forms), often transforming "life itself."

Biomedicalization is distinctively characterized by its greater organizational and institutional reach through the meso-level innovations made possible by computer and information sciences in clinical and scientific settings, including computer-based research and record-keeping. The scope of biomedicalization processes is thus much broader, including conceptual and clinical expansions through the commodification of health; the elaboration of risk and surveillance; and innovative clinical applications of drugs, procedures, and other treatments. Such innovations and technologies pervade more and more aspects of daily life and lived experience of health and illness, creating new biomedicalized subjectivities, identities, and biosocialities (Rabinow 1992).

Table 39-1 offers an overview of the shifts from medicalization to biomedicalization. One overarching analytic shift is from medicine exerting clinical and social *control over* particular conditions to an increasingly technoscientifically constituted biomedicine also capable of effecting the *transformation of* bodies and lives (Clarke 1995). Analytically, the shift from medicalization to biomedicalization occurs unevenly across micro, meso, and macro levels. Biomedicalization is constituted through the transformation of the organization of biomedicine as a knowledge- and technology-producing domain as well as one of clinical application. Computer and information technologies and the new social forms co-produced through their design and implementation are key meso-level mechanisms through which biomedicalization both is produced and transforms the institutions and practices of medicine.

Historical change is not simply driven by technological innovations. While sciences and technologies are very powerful, they do not *determine* futures. Sciences and technologies are made by people *and* things working together (e.g., Clarke 1987; Latour 1987). In daily concrete material practices, biomedicalization processes are not predetermined but quite contingent. In laboratories, schools, homes, and hospitals today, workers and people as patients and as providers/health system workers are responding to and negotiating biomedicalization processes, attempting to shape new technoscientific innovations and organizational forms to pragmatically meet their own needs (e.g., Lock and Kaufert, 1998). As a result, the larger forces of biomedicalization are shaped, deflected, transformed, and even contradicted.

In Table 39-1, the shifts are ones of emphasis—these trends are historical and historically *cumulative* from left to right. Traditional medicalization processes can and do continue tem-

Table 39-1. The Shift from Medicalization to Biomedicalization

Medicalization	Biomedicalization
Control Institutional expansion of professional medical jurisdiction into new domains	Transformation Expansion also through technoscientific transformations of biomedical organizations, infrastructures, knowledges, and clinical treatments
Economics: The U.S. Biomedical TechnoService Complex, Inc.	
Foundation and state (usually NIH) funded biomedical, scientific, and clinical research with accessible/public results	Also increasing privatization of research including through university/industry collaborations with increased privatization and commodification of research results as proprietary knowledge

Table 39-1. *(cont.)*

Medicalization	Biomedicalization
Increased economic organization, ration- alization, corporatization, nationalization	Also increased economic privatization, devolution, transnationalization/globalization
Physician-dominated organizations	Managed care system-dominated organizations
Stratification largely through the dual tendencies of selective medicalization and selective exclusion from care based on ability to pay	Stratification also through stratified rationalization, new population dividing practices, and new assemblages for surveillance and treatment based on new technoscientific identities
The Focus on Health, Risk and Surveillance	
Works through a paradigm of definition, diagnosis (through screening and testing), classification, and treatment of illness and diseases	Works also through a paradigm of definition, diagnosis (through screening and testing), classification, and treatment of risks and commodification of health and lifestyles
Health policy as problem solving	Health governance as problem defining
Diseases conceptualized at level of organs, cells	Risks and diseases conceptualized at level of genes, molecules and proteins
The Technoscientization of Biomedicine	
Highly localized infrastructures with idiosyncratic physician, clinic, and hospital records of patients (photocopy and fax are major innovations)	Increasingly integrated infrastructures with widely dispersed access to highly standardized, digitalized patients' medical records, insurance information processing, and storage
Individual/case-based medicine with local (usually office-based) control over patient information	Outcomes/evidence-based medicine with use of decision-support technologies and computerized patient data banks in managed care systems
Medical science and technological interventions, e.g., antibiotics, chemotherapy, radiation, dialysis, transplantation, new reproductive technologies	Biomedical technoscientific transformations, e.g., molecularization, biotechnologies, geneticization, nanoscience, bioengineering, chemoprevention, genetic engineering, and cloning
New medical specialties based on body parts and processes and disease processes (e.g., cardiology, gynecology, oncology) assumed to be universal across populations and practice settings	New medical specialties based on assemblages—loci of practice and knowledge of accompanying distinctive populations and genres of sciences and technologies (e.g., emergency medicine, hospitalists, prison medicine)
Transformations of Information, Knowledge Production, and Distribution	
Professional control over specialized medical knowledge production and distribution, with highly restricted access usually limited to medical professionals	Heterogeneous production of multiple genres of information/knowledges regarding health, illness, disease, and medicine, widely accessible in bookstores and electronically by Internet, etc.
Largely top-down medical professional-initiated interventions	Also heterogeneously initiated interventions (new actors include, e.g., health social movements, consumers, Internet users, pharmaceutical corporations, advertisements, websites)
Transformations of Bodies and Identities	
Normalization	Customization
Universal tailorized bodies; one-size-fits-all medical devices/technologies and drugs; superficially (including cosmetically) modified bodies	Individualized bodies; niche-marketed and individualized drugs and devices/technologies; customized, tailored, and fundamentally transformed bodies
From badness to sickness; stigmatization of conditions and diseases	Also new technoscientifically based individual and collective identities

porally and spatially at the same time that more technoscientifically based biomedicalization processes are also occurring. Innovations accumulate over time such that older, often "low(er)" technologically based approaches are usually available simultaneously somewhere, while emergent, often "high(er)" technoscientifically based approaches do also tend over time to drive out the old. There is no particular event or phenomenon that signals this shift, but rather a cumulative momentum of increasing technoscientific interventions and reorganization of practices throughout biomedicine since roughly 1985.

KEY PROCESSES OF BIOMEDICALIZATION

Biomedicalization is co-constituted through five central (and overlapping) processes: major political economic shifts; new focusing on health and risk and surveillance biomedicines; the technoscientization of biomedicine; transformations of biomedical knowledge production, distribution, and consumption; and transformations of bodies and identities.

1. Economics: The U.S. Biomedical TechnoService Complex Inc.

One theoretical tool for understanding the shift to biomedicalization is the concept of the "medical industrial complex" put forward in the 1970s, in the midst of the medicalization era. Changes in medicine in that era were critically theorized as reflecting the politico-economic development of a "medical industrial complex." For the current biomedicalization era, we offer the parallel concept of the Biomedical TechnoService Complex, Inc. This concept emphasizes the corporatized and privatized (rather than state-funded) research, products and services made possible by technoscientific innovations that further biomedicalization. The corporations and related institutions that constitute this complex are increasingly multinational and are rapidly globalizing both the Western biomedical model and biomedicalization processes per se.

The size and influence of this Biomedical TechnoService Complex, Inc. are significant and growing. The health-care industry is now 13% of the $10 trillion annual U.S. economy. Pharmaceutical-sector growth is estimated at about 8% per year (Leonhardt 2001). Americans spent more than $100 billion on drugs in 2000, double the amount in 1990 (Wayne and Petersen 2001). Through its sheer economic power, the Biomedical TechnoService Complex, Inc. shapes how we think about social life and problems. Within this sector, the most notable changes indicative of biomedicalization are corporatization and commodification, centralization and devolution, and stratified biomedicalization, as shown in Table 39-1.

First, in biomedicalization, not only are the jurisdictional boundaries of medicine and medical work expanding and being reconfigured, but so too are the frontiers of what is legitimately defined as private as opposed to public medicine, and corporatized versus non-profit medicine. In the U.S., federal and state governments have participated in expanding the private health-care sector by inviting corporations to provide services to federally insured beneficiaries. Since the Social Security Act established the government as a direct provider of medical insurance coverage through the Medicaid and Medicare programs in 1965, most recipients have been treated in public and/or not-for-profit clinics, hospitals, and emergency rooms. However, by the late 1990s, efforts were underway to move beneficiaries into private HMOs, effectively privatizing social programs (e.g., Estes et al. 2000).

Under pressure from powerful biomedical conglomerates, the state is increasingly socializing the costs of medical research by underwriting startup expenses of research and development, yet allowing commodifiable products and processes that emerge to be privatized—that is, patented, distributed, and profited from by private interests (e.g., Gaudilliere and Lowy 1998). The Human Genome Project is one high-profile example. What began as a federally based and funded research effort culminated in the shared success of sequencing the genome between Celera Genomics and government-funded scientists. In related developments, genetic and tissue samples collected from the bodies of individuals and communities have become patented commodities of corporate entities with zero patient or community reimbursement (Rabinow 1996).

Next, centralization of facilities and corporate health care coverage has been on the rise through the merger and acquisition of hospital facilities, insurers, physician groups, and pharmaceutical companies. Simultaneously, there is a steady devolution in health care, through the routinization and standardization of services to the minimum required and efforts to shift the labor of health care to outpatient facilities, home health care, and families. There has been a resulting loss of many community, public, and not-for-profit facilities that either could not compete or were acquired expressly for closure. While such health-care consolidations bring some efficiency, they also pose numerous dangers as a result of corporate concentration. Such problems include inflationary tendencies from the concentration of pricing power, new administrative burdens, and the enhanced political power of conglomerates. Consolidations now exert significant leverage over political and regulatory processes, as well as over decisions that affect provider groups, patient care, and service options in highly stratified ways (Waitzkin and Fishman 1997).

Finally, biomedicalization itself is stratified in increasingly elaborated ways. Medicalization has always exhibited dual tendencies of cooptative medicalization, where medicine expanded into new areas of life especially for the white middle and upper classes, and exclusionary disciplining, where particular individuals and groups such as peoples of color and the poor experience high barriers to access (see e.g., Ehrenreich and Ehrenreich 1978; Riessman 1983). These cooptative and exclusionary tendencies persist but have become increasingly complex, and new modes of stratification are also produced. We term this stratified biomedicalization. Cutbacks in government coverage of medical care are widespread, made in concert with reductions in a range of social services that affect the health status of individuals and groups downstream. At the same time, there are dramatic increases in stratifying fee-for-service options for those who can afford them, creating multiple tiers of service provision for those who can pay. Some plans offer higher-end hospital options; others offer out-of-pocket boutique medicine ranging from cosmetic surgeries to reproductive technologies to "concierge" primary care where patients have unprecedented access.

In sum, the political economic transformations of the biomedical sector are massive and ongoing, ranging from macrostructural moves by industries and corporations to meso- and micro-level changes in the concrete practices of health and medicine. Not only do such transformations produce new and elaborated mechanisms through which biomedicalization can occur, but also biomedicalization in turn drives and motivates many of these economic and organizational changes.

2. The Focus on Health, Risk, and Surveillance

In the biomedicalization era, what is perhaps most radical is the biomedicalization of *health itself*. In commodity cultures, health becomes another commodity, and the biomedically (re)engineered body becomes a prized possession. Health becomes an individual goal, a social and moral responsibility, and site for routine biomedical intervention. Increasingly what is being articulated is the individual moral responsibility to be and remain healthy (e.g., Crawford 1985) and/or very properly manage one's chronic illness(es) (Strauss et al. 1984), rather than merely to attempt to recover from illness or disease when they "strike." In the biomedicalization era, the focus is no longer on illness, disability, and disease as matters of fate, but on health as a matter ongoing moral self-transformation. Health cannot be assumed as merely a base or default state. Instead, health itself becomes something to work *toward* (Conrad 1992; Edgley and Brissett 1990).

In the biomedicalization era, risk and surveillance practices have emerged in new and increasingly consequential ways in terms of achieving and maintaining health. Risk and surveillance concerns shape both the technologies and discourses of biomedicalization as well as the spaces within which biomedicalization processes occur. Risks are calculated and assessed in order to rationalize surveillance, and it is through surveillance that risks are conceptualized and standardized into ever more precise calculations and algorithms (Howson 1998; Lupton 1999).

Further, it is no longer necessary to manifest symptoms to be considered either ill or "at risk." With the "problematization of the normal" and the rise of what Armstrong (1995) calls "surveillance medicine," *everyone* is implicated in the process of eventually "becoming ill" (Petersen 1997). Both individually and collectively, we inhabit tenuous and liminal spaces between illness and health, leading to the emergence of the "worried well" (Williams and Calnan 1994), rendering us ready subjects for health-related discourses, commodities, services, procedures, and technologies.

It is impossible not to be "at risk" for something. Instead, individuals and populations are judged for *degrees* of risk—"low," "moderate," or "high"—vis-à-vis different conditions and diseases, and this then frames what is prescribed to manage or reduce that risk. Thus, biomedicalization elaborates through daily and continuous lived experiences and practices of "health" designed to minimize, manage, and treat "risk" as well as through the interactions associated with illness (Fosket forthcoming; Press et al. 2000).

Of particular salience in the biomedicalization era is the elaboration of standardized risk-assessment tools that take epidemiological risk statistics, ostensibly meaningful only at the population level, and transform them into risk factors that are then deemed meaningful at the individual level. For instance, current breast cancer risk assessment technologies construct a standardized category of "high risk" for breast cancer in the U.S. Women classified as "high risk" today are given the option of taking pharmaceuticals to "treat" that *risk* (Fosket forthcoming). Genomic technologies and profiling techniques mark the next wave in such risk assignments (Shostak 2003).

With the assumption that everyone is potentially ill, the health research task becomes an increasingly refined elaboration of risk factors that might lead to future illnesses and shape the future forms of public health (Shim 2002). Health is thus paradoxically both more biomedicalized through such processes as surveillance, screening, and routine measurements of health indicators done in the home and seemingly less medicalized as the key site of responsibility shifts from the professional physician/provider to include collaboration with or reliance upon the individual patient/user/consumer and their families and friends.

3. The Technoscientization of Biomedicine

The increasingly technoscientific nature of the practices and innovations of biomedicine are key features of biomedicalization. Here, we describe three main, overlapping areas: computerization and data banking; molecularization and geneticization of biomedicine and drug design; and medical technology design, development, and distribution.

First, fundamental to biomedicalization is the power (past, present, and especially future) of computerization and data banking, pivotal to the meso-level (re)organization of biomedicine—from hospital care to clinical trials and beyond. For example, considerable pressure is being brought to bear to completely computerize *all* medical records according to standardized formats that can be webbed across multiple domains. Thus, as noted in Table 39-1, from paper versions of medical records dwelling in individual physicians' offices, clinics and hospitals, common during the era of medicalization, patient information can now be uploaded and accessed via cybersites managed by HMOs, pharmacies, and other third-party entities in far-away places for multiple purposes.

Such new and elaborating meso-level infrastructures facilitate many of the downstream processes of biomedicalization, not only facilitating the expansion of medical jurisdiction, but also producing infrastructures for greater public–private linkages. Computerization allows more and more aspects of life to be scrutinized, quantified, and analyzed for their relationships to health and disease. Integration and compatibility of data across various sites are articulated via specialized software that increasingly imposes standardized categories and forms of information (Bowker and Star 1999). Such formats will make it all but impossible to enter certain kinds of data in the record, especially some of the kinds of highly individualized information common to medical practice on individual and unique bodies. At the same time, they render it all but impossible *not* to record other kinds of data, such as the kinds of information required in order to comply with "clinical decision-support technologies" (Berg 1997) and highly detailed diagnostic and treatment regimens. These are the very meso-level techno-organizational transformative devices that biomedicalization demands and *is*.

"Decision-support technologies" are generated through outcomes research and evidence-based medicine, themselves dependent on major computerized databases, as noted in Table 39-1. As the production of biomedical knowledge is accelerated through the use of computer technologies, both behavioral and outcomes research are increasingly defining new biostatistical criteria for what counts as "scientific." Such research allows for the "objective" statistical identification of "industry standards" (Porter 1995), and insurance companies are moving toward covering only those procedures demonstrated as "valid" through such standardizing research. Such developments will likely cut in many different and even paradoxical directions simultaneously. For example, vis-à-vis women's health, "unnecessary" yet costly hysterectomies and Cesarean sections, so long criticized by feminists (e.g., Ruzek and Hill 1986), will be highlighted for deletion. Other highly vaunted treatments, such as bone-marrow transplants for breast cancer and estrogen replacement therapy for menopausal symptoms, have already been gravely challenged due to such outcomes studies.

Second, the biomedical sciences of the new millennium are being transformed by molecular biological approaches. Developments in basic science and research technologies are now propelling attempts to understand diseases at the (sub)molecular level of proteins and genes (proteomics and genomics). In current treatment and drug development, these have generated a shift from "discovery" of healing properties of "natural" entities to computer-generated molecular and genetic "design" that can be targeted at diseases and conditions likely to generate high profits (e.g., baldness, obesity).

The study of differences among human bodies and physiologies is also devolving to the level of the gene. Pharmacogenomics—the field that examines the interaction of genomic differences with drug function and metabolism—offers the promise that pharmaceutical therapies can be customized for groups and individuals. Such gene therapies and related innovations are in fact beginning to hit the market. Further, reengineering human germlines through choosing and assembling genetic traits for offspring will become possible and desired by some, as a "do-it-yourself evolution" (e.g., Buchanan et al. 2000), while opposed by others as further stratifying reproduction (e.g., Rapp 1999).

Third, medical technology developments of all kinds are being transformed through digitization, miniaturization, and hybridization with other innovations to create whole new genres of technologies. These extend the reach of biomedical interventions and applications in fundamentally novel ways. For instance, new advances in material sciences make possible hybrid and bionic devices. Examples include computer-driven limbs, continuously injecting insulin packs for diabetics, custom grown body parts, heart and brain pacemakers.

Digitization has also transformed medical technologies. In addition to the computerization of patient data including genomic, behavioral, and physiologic information, visual diagnostic technologies are also elaborating rapidly with the technical innovations, at times outpacing local organizational capacities to utilize them safely and effectively (e.g., Kevles 1998). Imaging technologies are increasingly digitized, facilitating their resolution, storage, and mobility among multiple providers, between sites of care expanding the possibilities of telemedicine, and among agencies or entities interested in centralizing medical information. Such moves, moreover, intensify stratified biomedicalization.

In sum, the ongoing and ever-elaborating technoscientization of biomedicine is at the heart of biomedicalization. Theorizing these technoscientific transformations of the practices of biomedicine requires that meanings and materialities, including corporealities, be conjointly studied and analyzed as co-constitutive (Casper and Koenig 1996; Gray et al. 1995; Haraway 1985; Hayles 1999).

4. Transformations of Information, Knowledge Production, and Distribution

Information on health and illness is also proliferating in all kinds of media, especially newspapers, on the Internet, in magazines, and through direct-to-consumer prescription and over-the-counter drug advertising. Thus the production and transmission of health and medical knowledges are key sites of biomedicalization in terms of both the transformation of their sources and distribution channels and the reformulation of who is responsible for grasping and applying such knowledges. Biomedicalization also works through the cooptation of competing knowledge systems, including alternative medicine and "patient-based" social movements.

First, the sources contributing to the production of health-related information have both increased and diversified. In cyberspace, for example, both federally sponsored and private websites are targeted to researchers, health-care providers, and Internet-savvy consumers. The information provided on these websites comes from a variety of sources. While clearly there is still a reliance on medical professionals for answers to health questions, sites often facilitate discussion boards where users exchange their own knowledges and experiences. Another rapidly growing source of medical knowledges emerges from established and newly formed patient advocacy groups, which have their own organizations, newsletters, websites, and very serious stakes in knowledge production and dissemination processes.

In theory, these changes have the potential to democratize production and access to medical and health knowledge in ways previously unknown. It is often difficult to know, however, whether the seemingly "objective" information located on the Internet is produced by medical experts holding professional credentials and/or what kinds of financial and/or scientific stakes they may have in presenting information in a particular way. Corporate agreements with search engine companies have begun to find ways to limit the access of Internet consumers to the diversity of information sites available on the web. Companies can purchase "prime time" and "sole supplier" status from search engines, thereby preempting access to their competition, and consumers are often unaware of such agreements (Rogers 2000). For many, these new modes of access to health information are a welcome change. For others, they confound more than they clarify. For yet others, the "digital divide" is all too real, and access remains elusive and stratified.

Second, biomedical knowledges have been transformed in terms of access, distribution, and in the allocation of *responsibility* for grasping such information. Historically in the U.S., non-experts' ability to obtain biomedical information was severely limited. Such knowledges dwelled almost exclusively in medical libraries and schools that were closed to the public, creating what amounted to a professional monopoly on access to information. Popularized "lay" health information was also scarce. "Health" sections in bookstores were notably rare and tiny compared to today, and remained so until the 1970s, when women's health and consumer health movements began producing self-help books. They challenged the conventional professional monopoly in the production of medical knowledges by insisting on their own participation, acquired and disseminated scientific information, and demanded immediate access to innovative health care. Today, individuals, enabled by computer technologies, are coming together and organizing to articulate new research interests; fund research studies; and, at times, open up entirely new research frontiers (e.g., Brown 1995; Fishman 2000). Because of increasing Congressional responsiveness to their demands, some supposed "patients' groups" are now started by scientists, pharmaceutical companies, and/or medical professional organizations.

While knowledge sources proliferate and streamline access in ways purportedly in the interests of democratizing knowledge, the interests of corporate biomedicine predominate. The loosening in 1997 of the criteria under which direct-to-consumer advertising of prescription pharmaceuticals is allowed by the FDA highlights this point. This was a truly profound shift in social policy on the proper relationship between the public and biomedical knowledge. Previously, provider–patient relationships were based on a notion of protecting "lay" people from knowledge best left to professionals. Now, pharmaceutical companies encourage potential consumers to first acquire drug information and then proactively ask their providers about it, by brand name. In 2001, the industry spent about $2.5 billion on such direct-to-consumer advertising (Freudenheim and Petersen 2001). This both transforms doctor–patient relationships and represents a highly successful attempt to increase the power and profits of the pharmaceutical industry, furthering biomedicalization.

Third, another transformation of knowledge constitutive of biomedicalization is the cooptation of competing knowledge systems and the reconfiguration of health-care provision and organizations in ways originally proposed and implemented by social movements. The last decades of the twentieth century in the U.S. have seen a profound rise in the use of alternative and complementary medicines. In 1993, it was estimated that $10.3 billion a year was spent on alternative medicines in the United States (Eisenberg et al. 1993); in 1998, this estimate rose to $27.0 billion, a figure comparable to the out-of-pocket costs to patients for all physician services (Eisenberg et al. 1998). These findings clearly repositioned alternative medical knowledge systems as legitimate (at least to users/consumers) and increasingly threatening economically to Western biomedicine. In response, Western biomedicine is attempting to coopt and appropriate many elements of alternative medicines. Numerous large-scale clinical trials are currently underway or have been completed to test the "effectiveness" of alternative medical practices and therapies (Adams 2002). Major pharmaceutical companies have begun marketing their own brands of herbal and nutritional supplements and vitamins.

Similarly, biomedicalization includes cooptation of organizational and ideological shifts and innovations brought about by grassroots social movements such as women's health movements, disability rights, AIDS activism, and other disease-specific movements (e.g., Belkin 1996; Worcester and Whatley 1988). For example, early feminist consumer activism centered on expanding patient access to drug information via "patient package inserts" and medical information via readable materials on health and illness (e.g., Boston Women's Health Book Collective 1971; Ruzek 1978) and feminist women's health centers. Displacing feminist centers, biomedicine now offers sleeker versions of women's health (Worcester and Whatley 1988). In all of these ways, biomedicalization offers multiple seemingly new sites and kinds of knowledges, while in practice, much remains the same.

5. Transformations of Bodies and Identities

The fifth and last basic process of biomedicalization is the transformation of bodies and the production of new individual and collective identities. There is an extension of the modes of operation of medical research and clinical practice from attaining "control over" bodies through medicalization techniques of labeling disease and concomitant medical intervention to enabling the "transformation of" bodies to include desired new properties and identities (see Clarke 1995). The body is no longer viewed as relatively static, immutable and the focus of control, but instead as flexible, capable of being reconfigured and transformed. Thus, opportunities for biomedicalization extend beyond merely regulating and controlling what bodies can (and cannot) or should (and should not) do to also focus on assessing, shifting, reshaping, reconstituting, and ultimately transforming bodies for varying purposes, including achieving new identities.

The basic medical assumption about intervention in the U.S. and other highly/over-developed countries will be that it is "better" (faster and more effective though likely not cheaper) to redesign and reconstitute the problematic body than to diagnose and treat specific problems in that body. This is already the situation in infertility medicine where the notion of a sequential ladder of appropriate care from least to most intervention has largely been abandoned in favor of immediate application of high-tech approaches that are more assuredly baby-producing regardless of cost (Becker 2000). For lesbians using assisted reproductive technologies to get pregnant, the social category "lesbian" often serves as a springboard for high-tech infertility treatments, regardless of the complete absence of diagnoses of infertility (Mamo 2002).

Such opportunities and imperatives, however, are stratified in their availability—imposed, made accessible, and/or promoted differentially to different populations and groups. Where medicalization practices seemed driven by desires for normalization and rationalization through homogeneity, techniques of stratified biomedicalization additionally accomplish desired tailor-made differences. Institutionally, customization has been increasingly incorporated into biomedicine through projects including computer-generated images of the possible results of cosmetic surgery, the proliferation of conceptive technologies promoting "rhetorics of choice" (Rothman 1998), the promise of individualized gene therapies and pharmacogenetics, and the fetishization of health products and services. Such desires are concomitant with another trend in stratified biomedicalization: "lifestyle" improvement. The pharmaceutical industry's attention to developing "lifestyle drugs" such as Viagra exemplifies this movement toward enhancement and the concern with "treating" the signs of aging (e.g., Fishman 2003; Mamo and Fishman 2001), targeting the fastest-growing U.S. population segment.

We offer the concept of *technoscientific identities* to refer to new genres of risk-based, genomics-based, epidemiology-based and other technoscience-based identities. Such identities are *constructed through technoscientific means*. That is, technoscientific identities are produced through the application of sciences and technologies to our bodies directly and/or to our histories or bodily products. These new genres of identities are frequently inscribed upon us, often whether we like them or not. For example, individuals today may unexpectedly learn they are genetic carriers of inherited diseases or may choose to seek out such information for themselves. The new subjectivities that arise through the availability of these technosciences do so through a biomedical governmentality that encourages such desire, demand, and need to inscribe ourselves with technoscientific identities. Of course, people negotiate the meanings of such identities in heterogeneous ways.

This is not to say that the identities themselves are all new, but rather that technoscientific applications to bodies allow for new ways to access and perform existing (and still social) identities. There are at least four ways that biomedical technoscience engages in processes of identity formation. First, technoscientific applications can be used as a means to attain a previously unavailable but highly desired social identity. For example, fertility treatments allow one to become a "mother" or "father," while the identity of "infertile" can be strategically taken on by lesbians and single women in order to achieve pregnancy (Mamo 2002). Second, biomedicalization imposes new mandates regarding the biomedical and technoscientific tools necessary to manage risk and maintain health that become incorporated into one's sense of self and what it means to be healthy. Third, biomedical technosciences create new categories of health-related identities and redefine old ones. For example, through use of a risk assessment technique, one's identity can shift from being "healthy" to "sick," or to "low risk" or "high risk" (Fosket 2002). Fourth, biomedicalization also enables the acquisition of identities as patients and communities through new technoscientific modes of interaction, such as telemedicine.

However, on an individual basis, technoscientific identities are selectively taken on, especially when accepting such identities seems worthwhile, including gaining access to what can be experienced as "medical miracles." Such an identity can be handled as a "strategic" identity, seemingly accepted to achieve particular goals, but also (typically in other situations) may be refused. Such identities may also be ignored in favor of other alternatives. Thus, attribution of identity does not equal acceptance of it.

CONCLUSIONS

We have offered an analysis of the historical shift from medicalization to a synthesizing framework of biomedicalization that works through and is mutually constituted by economic transformations that together constitute the Biomedical TechnoService Complex, Inc.: a new focus on health, risk and surveillance; the technoscientization of biomedicine; transformations of knowledge production, distribution, and consumption; and transformations of bodies and identities. Biomedicalization describes the key processes occurring in the domains of health, illness, medicine, and bodies especially but not only in the West. We have asserted that the shifts are those of emphasis: Medicalization processes can and do continue temporally and spatially, if unevenly. Innovations thus are cumulative over time such that older approaches are usually available simultaneously somewhere, while new approaches and technoscientifically based alternatives do also tend to drive out the old over time.

In addition to being temporally uneven, biomedicalization is *stratified*, ranging from the selective corporatization of "boutique" biomedical services and commodities directed toward elite markets to the increasingly exclusionary gatekeeping made possible by new technologies of risk and surveillance to the stratification of rationalized medical care. Through emergent "dividing practices," some individuals, bodies, and populations are perceived to be in particular need of the more disciplinary and invasive technologies of biomedicalization, as defined by their "risky" genetics, demographics, and/or behaviors; others are seen as especially deserving of the customizable benefits of biomedicine provided through innovative assemblages, as defined by their "good" genetics, valued demographics (e.g., insurance and/or income status), and/or "compliant" behaviors.

Stratified biomedicalization both exacerbates *and* reshapes the contours and consequences of the medical divide—the widening gap between biomedical "haves" and "have-nots." Surveillance, health maintenance, increased knowledge, and extended health and biomedical responsibilities for self and others are, however, promoted for all. This imperative to "know and take care of thyself," and the multiple technoscientific means through which to do so, currently have given rise to new genres of identities, captured in our concept of *technoscientific identities*. The ubiquity of the culture of biomedicine renders it almost impossible (and perhaps not even desirable) to avoid such inscriptions.

The transformations of biomedicalization are manifest in large, macro-structural changes such as the transnational corporatization of biomedicine as well as micro level changes such as new personal identities. But it is especially potent at the meso-level in terms of new organizational infrastructures and social forms. Processes and experiences of biomedicalization also illustrate the importance of interaction and contingency in social life. Finally, biomedicalization demonstrates what we see as the *mutual* constitution of political, economic, cultural, organizational, and technoscientific trends and processes. We believe the concept of biomedicalization offers a useful bridging framework for new conversations across specialty divides within sociology and more broadly across disciplinary divides in the social sciences.

REFERENCES

Adams, Vincanne. 2002. Randomized Controlled Crime: Postcolonial Sciences in Alternative Medicine Research. *Social Studies of Science* 32(5–6): 659–690.

Armstrong, David. 1995. The Rise of Surveillance Medicine. *Sociology of Health and Illness* 17 (3): 393–404.

Becker, Gay. 2000. Selling Hope: Marketing and Consuming the New Reproductive Technologies in the United States. *Sciences Sociales et Santé* 18 (4):105–25.

Belkin, Lisa. 1996. Charity Begins at . . . The Marketing Meeting, The Gala Event, The Product Tie-In. *New York Times Magazine*, December 22, 40–58.

Berg, Marc. 1997. *Rationalizing Medical Work: Decision-Support Techniques and Medical Practices.* Cambridge, MA: MIT Press.

Boston Women's Health Book Collective. 1971. *Our Bodies, Ourselves*. Boston: South End Press.

Bowker, Geoffrey C., and Susan Leigh Star. 1999. *Sorting Things Out: Classification and Its Consequences*. Cambridge, MA: MIT Press.

Brown, Phil. 1995. Popular Epidemiology, Toxic Waste and Social Movements. In *Medicine, Health and Risk: Sociological Approaches*, edited by J. Gabe. Oxford, UK: Blackwell.

Buchanan, Allen, Dan W. Brock, Norman Daniels, and Daniel Wikler. 2000. *From Chance to Choice: Genetics and Justice*. Cambridge, UK: Cambridge University Press.

Casper, Monica, and Barbara Koenig. 1996. Reconfiguring Nature and Culture: Intersections of Medical Anthropology and Technoscience Studies. *Medical Anthropology Quarterly* 10 (4):523–36.

Clarke, Adele E. 1987. Research Materials and Reproductive Science in the United States, 1910–1940. In *Physiology in the American Context, 1850–1940*, edited by G. L. Geison. Bethesda, MD: American Physiological Society.

Clarke, Adele E. 1995. Modernity, Postmodernity and Reproductive Processes ca. 1890–1990 or, "Mommy, Where Do Cyborgs Come From Anyway?" In *The Cyborg Handbook*, edited by C. H. Gray, H. J. Figueroa-Sarriera and S. Mentor. New York: Routledge.

Clarke, Adele E., and Virginia L. Olesen. 1999. Revising, Diffracting, Acting. In *Revisioning Women, Health, and Healing: Feminist, Cultural, and Technoscience Perspectives*, edited by A. E. Clarke and V. L. Olesen. New York: Routledge.

Conrad, Peter. 1992. Medicalization and Social Control. *Annual Review of Sociology* 18:209–32.

Conrad, Peter. 2000. Medicalization, Genetics, and Human Problems. In *Handbook of Medical Sociology*, edited by C. E. Bird, P. Conrad, and A. Fremont. Thousand Oaks, CA: Sage.

Crawford, Robert. 1985. A Cultural Account of "Health": Control, Release, and the Social Body. In *Issues in the Political Economy of Health*, edited by J. B. McKinlay. New York: Methuen-Tavistock.

Edgley, Charles, and Dennis Brissett. 1990. Health Nazis and the Cult of the Perfect Body: Some Polemical Observations. *Symbolic Interaction* 31 (2):257–80.

Ehrenreich, Barbara, and John Ehrenreich. 1978. Medicine As Social Control. In *The Cultural Crisis of Modern Medicine*, edited by J. Ehrenreich. New York: Monthly Review Press.

Eisenberg, D. M., R. B. Davis, S. L. Ettner, S. Appel, S. Wilkey, M. Van Rompay, and R. C. Kessler. 1998. Trends in Alternative Medicine Use in the U.S., 1990–1997: Results of a Follow-up National Survey. *Journal of the American Medical Association* 280:1569–75.

Eisenberg, D. M., R. C. Kessler, C. Foster, F. E. Norlock, D. R. Calkins, and T. L. Delbanco. 1993. Unconventional Medicine in the U.S.: Prevalence, Costs, and Patterns of Use. *New England Journal of Medicine* 328:346–52.

Estes, Carroll L., Charlene Harrington, and David N. Pellow. 2000. The Medical Industrial Complex. In *The Encyclopedia of Sociology*, edited by E. F. Borgatta and R. V. Montgomery. Farmington Hills, MI: Gale Group.

Fishman, Jennifer R. 2000. Breast Cancer: Risk, Science, and Environmental Activism in an "At Risk" Community. In *Ideologies of Breast Cancer: Feminist Perspectives*, edited by L. Potts. New York: St. Martin's Press.

Fishman, Jennifer R. 2003. Desire for Profit: Viagra and the Remaking of Sexual Dysfunction, Department of Social and Behavioral Sciences, University of California, San Francisco, San Francisco, CA.

Fosket, Jennifer Ruth. 2002. Breast Cancer Risk and the Politics of Prevention: Analysis of a Clinical Trial, Department of Social and Behavioral Sciences, University of California, San Francisco, San Francisco, CA.

Fosket, Jennifer Ruth. forthcoming. Constructing "High Risk" Women: The Development and Standardization of a Breast Cancer Risk Assessment Tool. *Science, Technology, and Human Values*.

Freudenheim, Milt, and Melody Petersen. 2001. The Drug-Price Express Runs into a Wall. *New York Times*, December 23, BU 1, 13.

Gaudilliere, Jean-Paul, and Ilana Lowy, eds. 1998. *The Invisible Industrialist: Manufacturers and the Construction of Scientific Knowledge*. London: MacMillan Press/St Martin's Press.

Gray, Chris Hables, Heidi J. Figueroa-Sarriera, and Steven Mentor, eds. 1995. *The Cyborg Handbook*. New York: Routledge.

Haraway, Donna. 1985. A Manifesto for Cyborgs: Science, Technology, and Socialist Feminism in the 1980s. *Socialist Review* 80:65–108.

Hayles, N. Katherine. 1999. *How We Became Posthuman: Virtual Bodies in Cybernetics, Literature and Informatics*. Chicago: University of Chicago Press.

Howson, Alexandra. 1998. Embodied Obligation: The Female Body and Health Surveillance. In *The Body in Everyday Life*, edited by S. Nettleton and J. Watson. New York: Routledge.

Kevles, Daniel J. 1998. *The Baltimore Case: A Trial of Politics, Science, and Character*. New York: Norton.

Latour, Bruno. 1987. *Science in Action: How to Follow Scientists and Engineers Through Society*. Cambridge, MA: Harvard University Press.

Leonhardt, David. 2001. Health Care As Main Engine: Is That So Bad? *New York Times*, November 11, 1,12, Money & Business section.

Lock, Margaret, and Patricia A. Kaufert., eds. 1998. *Pragmatic Women and Body Politics*. New York: Cambridge University Press.

Lupton, Deborah. 1994. *Medicine as Culture: Illness, Disease and the Body in Western Society*. London: Sage Publications.

Lupton, Deborah. 1999. *Risk*. London: Routledge.

Mamo, Laura. 2002. Sexuality, Reproduction, and Biomedical Negotiations: Achieving Pregnancy in the Absence of Heterosexuality, Department of Social and Behavioral Sciences, University of California, San Francisco, San Francisco, CA.

Mamo, Laura, and Jennifer Fishman. 2001. Potency in All the Right Places: Viagra as a Technology of the Gendered Body. *Body and Society* 7 (4):13–35.

Morgan, Kathryn Pauly. 1998. Contested Bodies, Contested Knowledges: Women, Health, and the Politics of Medicalization. In *The Politics of*

Women's Health: Exploring Agency and Autonomy, edited by S. Sherwin. Philadelphia: Temple University Press.

Petersen, Alan. 1997. Risk, Governance, and the New Public Health. In *Foucault, Health, and Medicine*, edited by A. Petersen and R. Bunton. New York: Routledge.

Porter, Theodore M. 1995. *Trust in Numbers: The Pursuit of Objectivity in Science and Public Life*. Princeton, NJ: Princeton University Press.

Press, Nancy, Jennifer R. Fishman, and Barbara A. Koenig. 2000. Collective Fear, Individualized Risk: The Social and Cultural Context of Genetic Testing for Breast Cancer. *Nursing Ethics* 7 (3):237–49.

Rabinow, Paul. 1992. Artificiality and Enlightenment: From Sociobiology to Biosociality. In *Incorporations*, edited by J. Crary and S. Kwinter. New York: Zone.

Rabinow, Paul. 1996. *Essays on the Anthropology of Reason*. Princeton, NJ: Princeton University Press.

Rapp, Rayna. 1999. *Testing Women, Testing the Fetus: The Social Impact of Amniocentesis in America*. New York: Routledge.

Riessman, Catherine Kohler. 1983. Women and Medicalization: A New Perspective. *Social Policy* 14 (1):3–18.

Rogers, Richard, ed. 2000. *Preferred Placement: Knowledge Politics on the Web*. Maastrict, Netherlands: Jan van Eyk Editions.

Rothman, Barbara Katz. 1998. *Genetic Maps and Human Imaginations: The Limits of Science in Understanding Who We Are*. New York: Norton.

Ruzek, Sheryl. 1978. *The Women's Health Movement: Feminist Alternatives to Medical Control*. New York: Praeger.

Ruzek, Sheryl B., and J. Hill. 1986. Promoting Women's Health: Redefining the Knowledge Base and Strategies for Change. *Health Promotion* 1 (3):301–9.

Shim, Janet K. 2002. Race, Class, and Gender Across the Science-Lay Divide: Expertise, Experience, and Cardiovascular Disease, Department of Social and Behavioral Sciences, University of California, San Francisco, San Francisco, CA.

Shostak, Sara. 2003. Locating gene-environment interaction: at the intersections of genetics and public health. *Social Science and Medicine* 56(11): 2327–42.

Strauss, Anselm, Juliet Corbin, Fagerhaugh Shizuko, Barney G. Glazer, David Maines, Barbara Suczek, and Carolyn L. Weiner, eds. 1984. *Chronic Illness and the Quality of Life*. 2nd ed. St. Louis and Toronto: C.V. Mosby Co.

Waitzkin, Howard, and Jennifer Fishman. 1997. Inside the System: The Patient-Physician Relationship in the Era of Managed Care. In *Competitive Managed Care: The Emerging Health Care System*, edited by J. D. Wilkerson, K. J. Devers and R. S. Given. San Francisco, CA: Jossey-Bass, Inc.

Wayne, Leslie, and Melody Petersen. 2001. A Muscular Lobby Rolls Up Its Sleeves. *New York Times*, November 4, BU 1, 13.

Williams, Simon J., and Michael Calnan. 1994. Perspectives on Prevention: The Views of General Practitioners. *Sociology of Health and Illness* 16 (3):372–93.

Worcester, Nancy, and Marianne Whatley. 1988. The Response of the Health Care System to the Women's Health Movement: The Selling of Women's Health Centers. In *Feminism Within the Science and Health Care Profession: Overcoming Resistance*, edited by S. V. Rosser. New York: Pergamon.

Zola, Irving Kenneth. 1972. Medicine As an Institution of Social Control. *Sociological Review* 20 (November):487–504.

Rationing Medical Care

Rising health care costs have dominated health policy discussions for two decades. Although numerous attempts have been made to control health costs with some minor successes, overall such measures have not managed to slow rising health care costs. From 1975 to 1980 the percentage of GNP spent on health care rose from 8.3 to 9.1 percent, while from 1980 to 1985 it rose from 9.1 to 10.6 percent. Thus there was a 9.6 percent rise from 1975–80 compared to a 16.5 percent rise in the next five years (Reinhardt, 1987). By the year 2000, the percentage has risen to nearly 14 percent. The subsequent years have been no better. It is hard to draw any conclusion other than that the overall result of cost containment efforts in the past decades has been failure.

In this context numerous policy analysts have suggested "rationing" medical care as a way to control rapidly rising costs. In the United Kingdom rationing specific medical services and technology has been for many years an accepted feature of the national health care system (Aaron and Schwartz, 1984). The issue of rationing or "limiting the use of potentially beneficial [medical] resources" has come to the forefront and may well become the preeminent health policy issue of the new millennium. The introduction to the "Dilemmas of Medical Technology" section in Part 2 briefly discussed this issue from the perspective of ethical and economic considerations for limiting medicine's technological arsenal under certain conditions. Here we focus more directly on the concept of rationing as part of the ongoing debate concerning the future of our nation's health policy.

Numerous health policy analysts argue that resources for medical care are not unlimited and that inevitably medical practitioners will soon be able to provide more medical care than society can afford. Some analysts believe we have reached that point already. While they do not necessarily agree with one another, health economists (e.g., Aaron and Schwartz, 1990), bioethicists (e.g. Callahan, 1987), and physicians (Relman, 1990) have all contributed to the discourse on rationing.

The focus of most of the discussion is whether we ought to consider implementing some type of program to ration or limit access to expensive medical services. Sociologists (Mechanic, 1979; Conrad and Brown, 1993) and others (e.g., Blank, 1988) have pointed out that the real question is not *whether* but *how* we should ration. These analysts contend that we already do ration medical services in the United States on the basis of the ability to pay. Those with access to medical services and insurance or some other means of paying for them receive appropriate care, while others, particularly the uninsured, do not. Perhaps because this form of rationing is not the result of specific policies limiting health care, it is often ignored in discussions on rationing. But in our view it is important not to exclude from such discussions the fact that rationing already occurs in outcome, if not in name. Sociologists have called this phenomenon *implicit rationing* to differentiate it from the proposed more explicit rationing policies that dominate current debate.

A decade ago the state of Oregon developed an explicit rationing plan for its Medicaid program. Recognizing that the state could not fund limitless health care and that many people were not covered by Medicaid or private insurance, Oregon passed a law that sought to ensure health coverage for everyone in the state. To achieve this aim, the "Oregon Health Decisions" project was devised to decide with public input what should be the health priorities for the 1990s. Based on the responses thus obtained and cost-benefit analysis, a state health commission developed an extensive, specific, prioritized list of services. Any services that fell below a certain point on this list would not be paid for by Medicaid (for details, see Crawshaw et al., 1990). In short, the plan allowed for extending Medicaid to all people, including the currently uninsured, in exchange for limitations on the types of services to be made available. Analysts who disapproved of rationing in principle of course opposed the proposed program; others criticized the proposal for targeting only the poor, i.e. Medicaid recipients, and not those with private insurance; and many physicians contended that the list of covered services was too narrow and that the cut-off points would not work. Under the Bush administration, the federal government, which oversees Medicaid programs, did not approve the Oregon proposal; the Clinton administration reversed this decision and allowed Oregon to implement the program. The program was implemented in 1994 and in a few years, Oregon was able to expand its health coverage to include 100,000 more individuals. The program succeeded in reducing the number of uninsured, decreased uncompensated care in hospitals, and reduced use of hospital emergency rooms. By most measures, it has been a success (Leichter, 1999). Though Americans are obviously very uncomfortable with explicit rationing of medical care, it seems clear that in the next few years we must confront the rationing issue directly as we reform our health care system.

In this section's first selection, "Rationing Medical Progress: The Way to Affordable Health Care," bioethicist Daniel Callahan argues that we can only meet basic health needs while living within our societal means. To achieve an equitable base level of health care for all, we must limit ineffective, marginal or overly expensive procedures. While acknowledging medical progress as a great human achievement, Callahan argues that the costs of unlimited progress in medical technology are too high, and that for the sake of justice and equity, we must ration technology's use. In the second selection, "The Trouble with Rationing," physician and health analyst Arnold S. Relman contends that rationing is not necessary if we eliminate "overuse of services, inefficient use of facilities and excessive overhead and administrative expenses." In short, reform the medical system, change the incentives, and cut out unnecessary or inefficient care and we won't need to ration health care. Relman believes physicians can and do ethically allocate services to patients, but opposes explicit rationing policies.

Short of some yet unconsidered resolution of the complex issues involved in health care reform, the debate over rationing is certain to continue throughout the next decade.

REFERENCES

Aaron, Henry, and William B. Schwartz. 1984. The Painful Prescription: Rationing Hospital Care. Washington, D.C.: Brookings Institution.

Aaron, Henry, and William B. Schwartz. 1990. "Rationing health care: The choice before us." Science 247:418–22.

Blank, Robert H. 1988. Rationing Medicine. New York: Columbia University Press.

Callahan, Daniel. 1987. Setting Limits: Medical Goals in an Aging Society. New York: Simon and Schuster.

Conrad, Peter, and Phil Brown. 1993. "Rationing medical care: A sociological reflection." Research in the Sociology of Health Care, Volume 12:3–32.

Crawshaw, Ralph, Michael Garland, Brian Hines, and Betty Anderson. 1990. "Developing principles for prudent health care allocation: The continuing Oregon experiment." Western Journal of Medicine 152:441–6.

Leichter, H. M. 1999. "Oregon's bold experiment: Whatever happened to rationing." Journal of Health Politics, Policy and Law. 24:147–60.

Mechanic, David. 1979. Future Issues in Health Care: Policy and the Rationing of Medical Services. New York: Free Press.

Reinhardt, Uwe E. 1987. Medical Economics. August 24.

Relman, Arnold S. 1990. "Is rationing inevitable?" New England Journal of Medicine 322:1809–10.

40 Rationing Medical Progress: The Way to Affordable Health Care

Daniel Callahan

We are engaged in a great struggle to reform the American health care system, a system addicted to increasing costs and decreasing equity. The first tactic of someone suffering from addictive behavior is twofold: to try to remove the bad habit with the least possible disruption to the ordinary way of life, and to try to change the undesirable behavior in a painless, incremental way.

This tactic rarely works, as any reformed smoker or alcoholic can testify. The price of real change is harsher self-examination and the revision of basic values and habits. With the health care crisis, we have not quite reached that point. As a society we are still playing out the incrementalist tactic, hoping against hope that it will work. But I doubt that it will, and I want to argue that it is time to move on toward deeper change, however uncomfortable the next step may be.

There is considerable agreement on the outline of the problem: we spend an increasingly insupportable amount of money on health care but get neither good value for our money nor better equity in terms of access to health care. Greater efficiency and greater equity are widely accepted as goals in response to our troubles. They are being pursued through cost-containment efforts on the one hand, and proposals for universal health care on the other.

Yet for all the vigor behind these efforts, there seems to be an enormous reluctance to engage in the kind of self-examination that will quickly make these goals realities. There is similar resistance to the even more intimidating task of finding the ingredients needed to sustain a health care system one that can provide decent care in the face of increased demand even when all the necessary efficiencies have been achieved. Such a quest leads to a relatively simple insight, that an economically sound health care system must combine three elements: access for all to a base level of health care (equity), a means of limiting the use of procedures that are ineffective or marginally effective as well as some of the procedures that are effective but too expensive (efficiency), and some consensus on health care priorities, both social and individual (so that we can live within our means while meeting our basic health needs).

Working against those goals are several deeply ingrained values that have come to characterize our system. First, we prize autonomy and freedom of choice and want everyone to have them: patients, physicians and other health care workers, and hospital and health administrators. In the name of freedom we indulge our hostility to governmental control and planning, thus setting ourselves apart from every other developed country. Second, we cherish the idea of limitless medical progress, which has come to mean that every disease should be cured, every disability rehabilitated, every health need met, and every evidence of mortality, especially aging, vigorously challenged. Moreover, we embrace the good living that can be made in the effort to combat mortality. Doing good and doing well have found their perfect meeting place in American health care. Finally, we long for quality in medicine and health care, which in practice we define as the presence of high-class amenities (no gross queuing or open wards for us) and a level of technology that is constantly improving and welcoming innovations. High-quality medicine is understood, in effect, as a kind of medicine that is better today than yesterday and will be even better tomorrow.

I have stressed values that are admirable and progressive on the whole values, in fact, that have given the American health care system many of its characteristic strengths. Choice is better than constraint, individual freedom better than government regulation, progress better than stagnation, capitalism better than socialism, and quality better than mediocrity. Yet one can say all this while noting something else: that the unrestrained embodiment of these values in the system is precisely what creates contradictions and renders meaningful reform so hard.

Cost containment is a striking case in point. Beginning with the efforts of President Nixon in 1970 and continuing in every subsequent administration, one obvious and laudable intention has been to control the constant and unremitting escalation of health care costs, rising well beyond the level of overall inflation. Yet not a single serious observer that I know of has shown that cost containment has come anywhere near reaching its goal, although there have been modest successes here and there. Despite this notable failure, it still is commonly believed that serious cost containment is compatible with our cherished values. If we could only eliminate unnecessary, untested, or wasteful diagnostic devices and medical treatments, do away with excessive malpractice claims, pare away expensive bureaucracy, and so forth, we could avoid rationing (the deliberate withholding of beneficial medical care) and provide efficient, equitable care. Indeed, some believe it would be both a mistake and morally objectionable to ration health care before we have exhausted all means of achieving cost containment and making medical care more efficient.

There is much truth in that contention, and I do not want to deny that there is ample room for efficiency in our present system, much less suggest that we should not pursue a wide range of cost containment efforts. There is much that can and should be done, and the possibilities of savings are enormous and well documented. Will this be enough, however? I doubt it. There is a double error in looking to cost containment to save us from rationing and limit setting. Even if it did not constitute rationing as strictly defined, effective cost containment entails an austerity that would itself have much of the weight and effect of rationing. By that I mean that serious cost containment must compel some degree of externally regulated treatment standards, often called protocol treatment. To control overspending, it must invoke tight regulation, full of sanctions and penalties for failure to conform. It must force unpleasant choices, the kind that compel priority setting. Most of all, it must force us to reconsider our values, so that we either give them up or scale them down when necessary.

If 20 years of failed efforts at cost containment have not convinced us of these realities, we might consider some other troubling thoughts. The most important is this: even if we had the most efficient system of health care in the world, the fact of an aging population and the intensification of services that medical progress ordinarily engenders would still tend to expand costs. This is coming to be the experience of Canada and the European countries, which already have in place many of the very reforms we believe will be our economic salvation; even so, strain is beginning to appear in those systems. They find it increasingly difficult to live within budgets that are fixed or growing only slowly, and even if they can achieve greater efficiency, they are cautiously beginning to talk the language of rationing also. As Dr. Adam L. Linton of the Ontario Medical Association put it recently in these pages, "Perhaps all structural tinkering is doomed to fail. The root causes of the problem are the increase in demand and the explosion of new forms of technology. These make the rationing of health care inevitable and the chief issue we should be addressing publicly."[1]

Why is this so? One aspect of our American effort to contain costs is illuminating in this regard. As fast as we try to remove high costs, we are adding a steady stream of new, usually expensive forms of technology. If one takes 1970 as the base-line year, the number of new forms of technology introduced since then is astonishing; there are so many that I, at least, have not even been able to list them fully. Our commitment to unlimited medical innovation has not been seriously hampered by cost-containment efforts. How, then, are we supposed to hold down costs while constantly adding new forms of technology? What known types of efficiency are designed to take such inherent economic pressure into account?

Assessment of our technology can get us out of such problems, of course, at least insofar as it allows us to discover and eliminate useless or only marginally useful forms of technology. It will do little, however, to solve the most troubling problem of technological medicine that of tests and procedures that are effective, that really work, and yet are costly, either in individual cases or in the aggregate. The great but rarely confronted failing of much of the faith in technology assessment might be called the efficacy fallacy that if it works and is beneficial, it must be affordable, or at least ought to be. That, of course, does not follow at all. Unless we are prepared to spend an unconscionable proportion of our resources on health care—letting schools, roads, housing, and manufacturing investments suffer in comparison—we cannot possibly afford every medical advance that might be of benefit. Nor is there any reason to think we would automatically and proportionately increase our happiness and improve our general welfare by even trying to do so.

The trouble with medical progress, one of our great human glories, is that it is intrinsically limitless in its economic possibilities, and no less so in its capacity for puzzlement and contrariness. For one thing, it is impossible to meet every human need merely by pursuing further progress. In this pursuit, we redefine "need" constantly, escalating and expanding it. For example, we do not think of people 100 years of age as needing artificial hearts. But we should know that if an effective heart is eventually developed and someone will die without it, then there will be a need for it. A medical need is usually understood as a need that if fulfilled, would bring life and health, and there is no end to what we can want for that purpose. The contrariness of the pursuit of progress too often shows itself, however. With the steady decline in death rates for all age groups has come an increase in the incidence of disability and chronic illness, as if the body itself will only stand so much progress.

The quest for greater efficiency, as embodied in successful cost containment, does not in itself provide a sufficient long-term alternative to the limitation of some forms of efficacious health care. Nor is it a good substitute for change in our deepest values and aspirations. We need both an effective, potent, and stringent cost-containment movement and a shift in fundamental values. It is not a matter of "either/or," but of "both/and." By continuing to hope that cost containment alone will do the job, we put off the other task that should be taking place that of changing our values. By thinking that this task should await the outcome of further efforts at cost containment, we underestimate the short-term pressure that serious cost containment places on our values. Such a tactic also distracts us from the most urgent long-term task—best begun at once—of devising and learning to live with a less expansive health care system and a less expansive idea of health.

How can we start thinking differently about our values? We might first distinguish between bringing to everyone the medical knowledge and skills that are already available and pressing forward on the frontiers of medicine to find new ways to save and improve life. If we could make all our present knowledge available to everyone right now, we could achieve substantial improvement in the health of people whose poverty and lack of knowledge put them particularly at risk of avoidable illness. Substantial progress in health could be achieved by increasing equity in the access to care. After that, spending more money on schools and housing would make as good a contribution to improved health, in an indirect fashion, as medical expenditures would directly.

Second, we might remind ourselves that we are the healthiest, longest-living human beings in the history of the human race; healthy enough to run a well-educated, economically prosperous, and culturally vital society. Further progress would help some of us, perhaps many, but we have already come a long way and have sufficient general health for most important human purposes. We can always improve our health and extend our life, but that will be true no matter how much progress we make. This is not to deny the obvious and extraordinary benefits of medical progress or to suggest a return to a pretechnological past. It is only to put the idea of unlimited progress in a more modest, perhaps more affordable, light: we want more progress, but we will not necessarily be in terrible shape as a society if we do not get it.

In any case, we must be prepared to ration medical progress and in particular to forgo potentially beneficial advances in the application and development of new techniques. I am not proposing a diminution of efforts to extend our store of theoretical biologic and medical knowledge. A strong commitment to basic biomedical research remains an attractive and desirable goal. That commitment is not incompatible, however, with several insistent requirements: (1) that clinical applications be subjected to stringent technological assessments before dissemination; (2) that the social and economic standards for the assessment be biased toward restrictiveness ("strait is the gate and narrow the way" might be a pertinent maxim here); and (3) that it is understood and accepted that some, perhaps many, beneficial applications will have to be passed over on grounds of cost and other, more pressing social priorities.

Third, we might come to understand that the demand for autonomy and choice, as well as for high-quality care, represents values that can be scaled back considerably without a serious loss in actual health. The great hazard of American individualism is that if we are patients, we sometimes confuse what we want with what is good for us; and if we are physicians, we confuse the way we would prefer to treat patients with what is actually beneficial to them. This is a delicate point, because there is a profound sense in which the gratification we get from making our own choices or practicing medicine according to our own lights makes our life or profession satisfying. Nonetheless, in the face of economic restraints, it is important to decide what we are after most: better health, greater choice, or some wonderful combination of both. We probably cannot have both in equal degrees, and if we had more health than choice, we would still be reasonably well off.

Finally, we might come to understand that there is a diminishing social return from attempts to make health care a source of expanding profit and personal enrichment. If we make medicine so expensive that we can ill afford even adequate emergency rooms, we have gone backward in providing decent care. If we make the provision of adequate health care to working people too expensive, employers will have to provide inadequate coverage or reduce the workers' pay. If we spend too much on health care in relation to everything else (for instance, spending 11.4 percent of our gross national product on health care but only 6.8 percent on education), we risk becoming a hypochondriacal society, one that has sacrificed much that is good and necessary for a rounded life out of an obsession with health.

Is there a politically acceptable and feasible way to restrain the market forces in our health care system without jeopardizing the centrality of a free market in our political economy? One way is already being tried: government uses its buying power under entitlement programs to control fees and costs and uses its regula-tory power to promote competitiveness among providers. But that may not be sufficient. My own guess is that unless we can come to see health care as being like fire, police, and defense protection—a necessity for the public interest rather than a market commodity—we will not be able to resolve that problem. We must be willing to exempt some health care policies and decisions from the market ideology and to do so in the name of the common good.

Whether we like modifying our basic values or not, it seems impossible to achieve equity and efficiency without doing so. Having a minimal level of adequate care available to all means that if such care is to be affordable, it must be combined with limits on choices, progress, and profit. Setting limits means we cannot have everything we want or dream of. The demand for priorities arises when we try to live with both decent minimal care and limits to care. At that point we must decide what it is about health care that advances us most as a society and as individuals. We have bet that we could have it all. That bet is not paying off. There remains no reason, however, that we cannot have a great deal.

We do not necessarily have to limit decent health care in any serious, drastic fashion. What we do need to do is to restrain our demands for unlimited medical progress, maximal choice, perfect health, and profits and income. This is not the same as rationing good health care.

NOTE

1. Linton AL. The Canadian health care system: a Canadian physician's perspective. N Engl J Med 1990; 322:197–9.

41 *The Trouble with Rationing*

Arnold S. Relman

Suddenly everyone is talking about rationing. First brought to public attention in this country by Schwartz and Aaron's study of the allocation of hospital services in the United Kingdom,[1,2] rationing is now widely advocated as the only effective way to control health care costs.

The argument goes like this: An aging and growing population, rising public expectations, and the continual introduction of new and expensive forms of technology generate a virtually unlimited demand for medical services, which inevitably exhausts the resources we are willing and able to devote to health care. Sooner or later we will be forced to limit expenditures by restricting services, even those that are beneficial. Of course, we are already restricting services through our failure to provide health insurance to many who cannot afford it, but we now must confront the necessity of explicitly denying certain services to insured patients at least to those whose insurance is subsidized by government or business.

On the surface it is a persuasive argument. Many observers now seem convinced that the question is not whether but how we will ration health services.[3] A closer examination of the problem suggests, however, that rationing is not necessary, nor would it be likely to work without major changes in our health care system. Furthermore, as even some of its strongest advocates admit, a fair and workable rationing plan would be, to say the least, difficult to design.

The supposed necessity of rationing rests on the assumption that no other expedient can prevent for long the continued escalation of health costs. Advocates of rationing usually acknowledge the growing evidence of overuse of services, inefficient use of facilities, and excessive overhead and administrative expenses. They may even accept the proposition that substantial elimination of such defects might reduce the cost of health care by as much as 20 or 30 percent. But they maintain that any reforms of this kind would produce only a one-time savings that would soon be nullified by a resumption of the inexorable rise in costs.

This argument, it seems to me, fails to recognize the crux of the problem. New forms of technology and insatiable demand are not the fundamental causes of cost inflation, nor are overuse, inefficiency, duplication, or excessive overhead expenses. They are simply the manifestations of a system that has built-in incentives for waste and inflation. It is the way we organize and fund the delivery of health care that rewards the profligate use of technology and stimulates demand for nonessential services; it is the system that allows duplication and waste of resources and produces excessive overhead costs. Change certain features of the system, and you will not only reduce costs in the short run, but moderate the inherent forces causing inflation. As a result, future costs will rise at a slower, more affordable rate without the need to restrict essential services and without loss of quality. To avoid rationing, what we require most is not more money but the will to change those aspects of the present system that are responsible for the present cost crisis. In a subsequent editorial I will discuss what might be done to control costs and avoid rationing. My purpose here is to explain why, even if there were no alternatives, rationing would probably not be acceptable or workable. I will also suggest that unless the funding of health care were to become far more centralized and prospectively budgeted than at present, rationing would not control costs.

To be seen as fair and therefore have a chance of acceptance by the public and the medical profession, a rationing plan needs to have medical and ethical, not simply economic, justification. To be medically justified, rationing decisions have to be personalized, because no two patients are exactly the same and the anticipated benefits of a given procedure vary from patient to patient. As Schwartz and Aaron[4] have recently pointed out in a convincing critique of the method of rationing initially proposed by the state of Oregon,[5] any plan to assign priorities to specific medical interventions on the basis of cost-benefit considerations must take into account individual circumstances, balancing costs against potential benefits in each patient. Thus, for example, it would make no sense simply to approve or disapprove all kidney transplantations, or to assign the procedure a single overall priority rating. In some patients a kidney transplant might have an excellent chance of substantially extending life and improving its quality while saving money as well, but in others a transplant would be worse than useless. Setting out formal guidelines to cover all the clinical circumstances under which kidney transplantation might or might not be worthwhile would be a complex task. The same would be true of bone marrow transplantations, coronary bypass operations, total parenteral nutrition, magnetic resonance imaging, or any other procedure that might become the object of rationing. With each procedure, the cost-benefit assessment depends so heavily on individual circumstances that it is almost impossible to devise medically sound rules applicable to all patients. In fact, the task is so formidable that no one has yet offered a practical suggestion about how personalized rationing might be carried out systematically and on a wide scale. In a recent interview reported in the *Boston Globe*,[6] Dr. Schwartz said, "I don't know that any scheme [of rationing] will be satisfactory." With that candid opinion by one of the most thoughtful students of the subject I emphatically concur.

Beyond these practical difficulties, attempts to ration medical services in our present health care system would create serious ethical and political problems. Doctors would find themselves in the uncomfortable position of having to deny services to some insured patients they would ordinarily have treated in accordance with accepted medical practice. In a system with a fixed global health care budget established by national policy, as in the United Kingdom, physicians forced to withhold potentially useful services from their patients because of costs at least can be assured that the money saved will be appropriately spent to help other patients and that all publicly financed patients will be treated more or less alike. But this is not so in a disorganized and fragmented health care system like ours, which has multiple programs for the care of publicly subsidized patients and no fixed budget. When medical resources are uniformly limited for all, physicians can ethically and in good conscience allocate services to the patients most likely to benefit, but in the absence of clearly defined limits they feel morally bound to do whatever might be of benefit.[7] For rationing to be perceived as equitable, public insurance programs like Medicare and Medicaid would need to have fixed budgets committed to health care, and a method of allocation that was uniformly applied. Present political realities make these conditions unlikely, and therefore I believe that a public rationing plan would not be ethically or politically acceptable at this time.

Even if a workable, medically sensible, ethically and politically acceptable rationing plan could be devised, it would not save money in the long run. The present health care environment generally encourages—virtually requires—physicians and hospitals to be expansive rather than conservative in providing medical services. Aggressive marketing, not the prudent use of resources, is the prevailing imperative. Any limitation of a medical service by rationing would place economic pressures on health care providers to protect their revenues by expanding the delivery of other services that are not rationed. In an open-ended, competitive system with more and more new physicians, new forms of technology, and new health care facilities entering the market, it is inevitable that costs will continue to escalate despite targeted restrictions on the delivery of certain services. Each decision to restrict services might temporarily reduce costs in one part of the system, but no single decision or group of decisions could stop for long the relentless progress of inflation in the rest of the system. With no overall cap on expenditures there would be no way to keep costs under control except by an endless series of rationing decisions that would cut ever more deeply into the body of accepted medical practice. The gap between optimal care and what the regulations allowed would widen. Sooner or later strong general opposition to further cuts would arise, and it would become apparent that rationing is not the solution to the U.S.

health care crisis—at least not without more fundamental reforms in the system.

Our cost crisis, and the limitations on access that result from high costs, stem from an inherently inflationary and wasteful health care system. Rationing is not likely to be successful in controlling costs unless we deal with that basic problem. Given the huge sums we are now committing to medical care as compared with other developed countries, we should be able to afford all the services we really need, provided we use our resources wisely. Concerted attempts to improve the system rather than ration its services are the next sensible step. Even if reform of the system should prove to be an insufficient remedy, it would still be necessary for the ultimate acceptance and success of any rationing plan.

REFERENCES

1. Schwartz WB, Aaron HJ. Rationing hospital care: lessons from Britain. N Engl J Med 1984;310:52–6.
2. Aaron HJ, Schwartz WB. The painful prescription: rationing hospital care. Washington, D.C.: Brookings Institution, 1984.
3. Roehrig CB. Rationing: not "if" but "how?" The Internist. July–August 1990:5.
4. Schwartz WB, Aaron HJ. The Achilles heel of health care rationing. New York Times. July 9, 1990.
5. Relman AS. Is rationing inevitable? N Engl J Med 1990;332:1809–10.
6. Stein C. Strong medicine for health care costs. Boston Globe. July 24, 1990:21, 23.
7. Daniels N. Why saying no to patients in the United States is so hard: cost containment, justice, and provider autonomy. N Engl J Med 1986;314: 1380–3.

PART 4 Toward Alternatives in Health Care

As part of a critical sociological examination of American health and medical care, it is important that we explore what can be done to create alternatives to improve health in our society. In so doing, we look beyond the "medical model" and the current organization and delivery of medical services. We can conceptualize these alternatives as Community Initiatives, Comparative Health Policies, and Prevention and Society. In the first section of Part 4, we examine several community-based alternatives to existing medical services and discuss their problems and limitations, as well as their potential for improving health care. In the second section, we examine alternatives on the broader, societal level by looking at the health care systems of three other countries. In the final section, we consider the potential of prevention as an alternative way of reorienting our approach to health problems. We cannot claim to provide *the* answer to our "health crisis" here. However, we believe the answers to our health care problems will ultimately be found by searching in the directions pointed out in this part of the book.

Community Initiatives

Several issues emerge when we examine and evaluate community-level efforts to improve medical care. The first such issue pertains to the inherent limitations of such efforts. It is widely argued that the possibilities for change within the existing societal and medical care system are inherently limited. Although some of the most exciting and interesting health innovations have occurred through local efforts on the community level—e.g., women's self-help clinics, neighborhood health centers—these efforts are constantly being shaped and limited by the societal context in which they emerge and in which, often, they must struggle to survive. The realities of the present system (e.g., the professional dominance of physicians, the control of medical payments by the insurance industry and medical care providers, and the limitations imposed by existing medical organizations on access to their services) constitute systemic boundaries to the power of community alternative health-care organizations to effect real change. Some critics even contend that these societal-level constraints will, in the very nature of things, always undermine the progressive potential of alternative services: the medical establishment will either coopt their successes or use their unavoidable difficulties as evidence of their failure.

A central issue related to this entire discussion of community alternatives is the idea of medical "self-help." The 1970s saw a widespread and increasing interest in self-help, or self-care. Self-help groups and other indigenous initiatives in health care emerged as adjuncts and alternatives to medical care. Self-help and mutual aid have a long history in Western society (Katz and Bender, 1976). While critics like Ivan Illich (1976) see self-help as a panacea for our medical ills, most view it as having a more limited role. Self-help groups can provide assistance, encouragement, and needed services to people with chronic and disabling conditions that involve emotional and social problems not provided for by traditional medical care (Borkman, 1990). They can also create alternative services, as in the women's health movement. Equally important, self-help groups can aid in demystifying medicine, build a sense of community among people with similar problems, and provide low-cost services and consumer control of services.

While the idea of self-help is not new, it appears on today's medical scene as a somewhat radical departure from the traditional medical notion of a compliant patient and an expert physician. Self-help organizations such as Alcoholics Anonymous (AA) predate the current self-help wave and have apparently successfully demonstrated the possibility of people helping themselves and one another to better health. Often taken as a model for other groups, AA focuses upon behavior, symptoms, and a perception of alcoholism as a chronic and individual problem. It also insists that alcoholics need the continuous social support of other nondrinking alcoholics to maintain their sobriety. A number of analysts (e.g., Kronenfeld, 1979: 263) have noted that AA and other self-help programs modeled on it are somewhat authoritarian in their structure. For example, AA does not question existing societal and cultural arrangements that may have contributed to the drinking problems of its members.

Partly in response to the recognition of the limitations of modern medicine and in reaction to frustrations with existing medical care options, self-help groups and the ideology of self-help became increasingly popular, not only among former patients of the existing system, but also among professional critics of American medical care (see for example, Illich, 1976; Levin, Katz and Holst, 1976). However, these approaches often focus on individual responsibility for change without stressing simultaneously the difficulties of individual change within existing social arrangements. This has led critics to note the potential for victim-blaming in recommendations for self-help (Kronenfeld, 1979) and the limitations of self-help for many of the health problems of various, especially non–middle-class, populations in the United States.

It is nonetheless clear that the idea of self-help is an exciting prospect, and one would certainly not want to see the energy and excitement contained within it diminished. The self-help movement has given rise to a range of important criticisms of existing medical care and to a number of significant discoveries for improved health. Self-help approaches envision the possibility of people taking control over their own lives as well as of demystifying traditional medical care. However, unless self-help incorporates a strategy for community *and* societal change, it is likely to reduce this potential vision to the simplistic contention that people are responsible for their own stresses and diseases. Although providing mutual support and encouraging individuals to alter their "unhealthy" behaviors, self-help programs only rarely confront the real options of what people can do as individuals. What is needed, then, is a linking together of self-help movements with struggles for community and social change—in essence, a politicization of self-help.

Among the most interesting community health initiatives in the 1980s and 1990s were a number of unconnected social movements that have attempted to change the way we address health issues. Mothers Against Drunk Driving (MADD) has focused on alcohol-related traffic accident injuries. The MADD approach centers on injury prevention, relying on punitive and educational action and depicting drunk drivers as "violent criminals" while still accepting the medicalized disease concept of alcoholism (see Reinarman, 1988). ACTUP (AIDS Coalition to Unleash Power) has become a major force in shaping the response to AIDS. This organization has publicly and often emphatically demanded greater government and institutional support for confronting AIDS and committing more of society's substantial resources towards AIDS prevention and treatment (Gamson, 1989; Crimp, 1990). The Independent Living Movement has attempted to reframe living with disabilities as a personal and political rather than a medical matter (DeJong, 1983). This group seeks to demedicalize disabilities and to create situations and work environments where people with disabilities can live independently and reduce their dependence on medical care. Social movements such as these and community responses to problems like toxic wastes (see Article 7 by Phil Brown) are changing the way our society thinks about and responds to health problems.

One of the most recent community initiatives has been the wide range of groups and on-line communities that have emerged on the Internet. The Internet has become an important locale for patients and consumers obtaining medical information (Hardey, 1999; Baker, et al., 2003), but perhaps more importantly, it has become a place where patients and their families can connect with other individuals suffering from similar problems. Nearly every disease, disorder, or disability has spawned a range of Internet bulletin boards, chat rooms, and web sites where people interact and share information. Illness was long seen by sociologists as a privatizing experience; something spoken about only to family and close relatives. Often individuals didn't know anyone else with the same illness, much less had ever communicated with someone similarly afflicted. That would be increasingly unlikely today. The Internet has created a virtual revoluation among people with illnesses and has become an important dimension of the experience of illness and self-help (e.g., Sharf, 1997).

The first two selections focus directly on self-help, providing quite different examples of people reassessing their own health needs and developing alternative health services through collective, community efforts.

"Politicizing Health Care" by John McKnight, describes a fascinating and innovative community effort to assess health needs and design local medical-care alternatives aimed at improving health in the community. In this project, people discovered a number of important things, including: (1) many "medical" problems had little to do with disease, and could more accurately be termed "social problems"; (2) they could, as a community, take collective action to make real changes in their own health; (3) they could build alternative organizations for meeting their health and social needs and in the process include heretofore ignored groups (e.g., the elderly) as productive contributors to the community's health; and (4) they could develop new "tools" of production that would remain under their own control and serve their own particular needs. Despite these marvelous lessons, McKnight acknowledges the limitations of local efforts to change the basic maldistribution of resources and services and notes the need for self-help efforts to come to grips with "external" authorities and structures.

In the second selection, Ann Withorn, in "Helping Ourselves," discusses the limits and potentials of self-help. Focusing her discussion in part on two of the most influential health-related self-help movements the women's health movement and Alcoholics Anonymous Withorn evaluates the place of self-help in progressive change. For over two decades, the women's health movement has been the most important self-help movement in the health field. It emerged as part of the Women's Movement and in the context of a growing recognition of the role of medicine in the oppression of women. The women's health movement has established gynecological self-help clinics, educated women about their health and bodies (e.g., books like *Our Bodies, Our Selves*), challenged the use of dangerous medicines and procedures (e.g., DES, hormone replacement therapy, Caesarean rates), organized politically to protect the choice of abortion and reproductive rights, and empowered women to question their medical care. As with other community initiatives, there have been struggles. The women's self-help movement has been faced with conflicts arising from its challenge of medical prerogative and has been continually faced with problems in financing its alternative services, particularly for poor women who must rely on public funds and other third-party payments for their medical services. The women's health movement has sometimes imposed limitations on itself by rejecting much of what traditional medicine has to offer.

In the third article in this section, Victoria Pitts examines "Illness and Internet Empowerment: Writing and Reading Breast Cancer in Cyberspace." Pitts explores the personal web pages of women with breast cancer, focusing identity, interaction, and agency. She shows that while the Internet provides support and can be empowering, it can also affirm dominant cultural norms like femininity, consumerism, and individualism. Yet the creation of a cyberspace breast cancer community helps women demystify medicine and potentially transform breast cancer from a personal to a public issue.

REFERENCES

Baker, L., T.H. Wagner, S. Singer, and M. R. Bundorf. 2003. "Use of the Internet and email for health care information." Journal of the American Medical Association 29:2400–06.

Borkman, Thomasina. 1990. "Self-help groups at a turning point." American Journal of Community Psychology 18:321–32.

Crimp, Douglas. 1990. AIDS/DEMOGRAPHICS. San Francisco: Bay Press.

DeJong, Gerben. 1983. "Defining and implementing the Independent Living concept." Pp. 4–27 in Nancy M. Crewe and Irving Kenneth Zola, Independent Living for Physically Disabled People. San Francisco: Jossey-Bass.

Gamson, Josh. 1989. "Silence, death and the invisible enemy: AIDS, activism and social movement 'newness.'" Social Problems 36: 351–67.

Hardey, Michael. 1999. "Doctor in the house: The Internet as a source of health knowledge and the challenge to expertise." Sociology of Health and Illness 21:820–36.

Illich, Ivan. 1976. Medical Nemesis: The Expropriation of Health. New York: Pantheon Books.

Katz, A. H., and E. I. Bender. 1976. "Self-help groups in Western society." Journal of Applied Behavioral Science 12: 265–82.

Kronenfeld, Jennie J. 1979. "Self care as a panacea for the ills of the health care system: An assessment." Social Science and Medicine 13A: 263–7.

Levin, L., A. Katz, and E. Holst. 1976. Self-Care: Lay Initiatives in Health. New York: Prodist.

Reinarman, Craig. 1988. "The social construction of an alcohol problem: The case of Mothers Against Drunken Driving and social control in the 1980s." Theory and Society 17: 91–120.

Sharf, B.F. 1997. "Communicating breast cancer online: Support and empowerment on the Internet." Women and Health 26:65–84.

42 *Politicizing Health Care*

John McKnight

Is it possible that out of the contradictions of medicine one can develop the possibilities of politics? The example I want to describe is not going to create a new social order. It is, however, the beginning of an effort to free people from medical clienthood, so that they can perceive the possibility of being citizens engaged in political action.

The example involves a community of about 60,000 people on the west side of Chicago. The people are poor and Black, and the majority are dependent on welfare payments. They have a voluntary community organization which encompasses an area in which there are two hospitals.

The neighborhood was originally all white. During the 1960s it went through a racial transition and over a period of a few years, it became largely populated with Black people.

The two hospitals continued to serve the white people who had lived in the neighborhood before transition, leaving the Black people struggling to gain access to the hospitals' services.

This became a political struggle and the community organization finally "captured" the two hospitals. The boards of directors of the hospitals then accepted people from the neighborhood, employed Black people on their staffs, and treated members of the neighborhood rather than the previous white clients.

After several years, the community organization felt that it was time to stand back and look at the health status of their community. As a result of their analysis, they found that, although they had "captured" the hospitals, there was no significant evidence that the health of the people had changed since they had gained control of the medical services.

The organization then contacted the Center for Urban Affairs where I work. They asked us to assist in finding out why, if the people controlled the two hospitals, their health was not any better.

It was agreed that the Center would do a study of the hospitals' medical records to see why people were receiving medical care. We took a sample of the emergency room medical records to determine the frequency of the various problems that brought the people into the hospitals.

We found that the seven most common reasons for hospitalization, in order of frequency, were:

1. Automobile accidents.
2. Interpersonal attacks.
3. Accidents (non-auto).
4. Bronchial ailments.
5. Alcoholism.
6. Drug-related problems (medically administered and nonmedically administered).
7. Dog bites.

The people from the organization were startled by these findings. The language of medicine is focused upon disease yet the problems we identified have very little to do with disease. The medicalization of health had led them to believe that "disease" was the problem which hospitals were addressing, but they discovered instead that the hospitals were dealing with many problems which were not disease. It was an important step in increasing consciousness to recognize that modern medical systems are usually dealing with maladies social problems rather than disease. Maladies and social problems are the domain of citizens and their community organizations.

A STRATEGY FOR HEALTH

Having seen the list of maladies, the people from the organization considered what they ought to do, or could do, about them. First of all, as good political strategists, they decided to tackle a problem which they felt they could win. They didn't want to start out and immediately lose. So they went down the list and picked dog bites, which caused about four percent of the emergency room visits at an average hospital cost of $185.

How could this problem best be approached? It interested me to see the people in the organization thinking about that problem. The city government has employees who are paid to be "dog-catchers," but the organization did not choose to contact the city. Instead, they said: "Let us see what we can do ourselves." They decided to take a small part of their money and use it for "dog bounties." Through their block clubs they let it be known that for a period of one month, in an area of about a square mile, they would pay a bounty of five dollars for every stray dog that was brought in to the organization or had its location identified so that they could go and capture it.

There were packs of wild dogs in the neighborhood that had frightened many people. The children of the neighborhood, on the other hand, thought that catching dogs was a wonderful idea so they helped to identify them. In one month, 160 of these dogs were captured and cases of dog bites brought to the hospitals decreased.

Two things happened as a result of this success. The people began to learn that their action, rather than the hospital, determines their health. They were also building their organization by involving the children as community activists.

The second course of action was to deal with something more difficult—automobile accidents. "How can we do anything if we don't understand where these accidents are taking place?" the people said. They asked us to try to get information which would help to deal with the accident problem, but we found it extremely difficult to find information regarding when, where, and how an accident took place.

We considered going back to the hospitals and looking at the medical records to determine the nature of the accident that brought each injured person to the hospital. If medicine was thought of as a system that was related to the possibilities of community action, it should have been possible. It was not. The medical record did not say, "This person has a malady because she was hit by an automobile at six o'clock in the evening on January 3rd at the corner of Madison and Kedzie." Sometimes the record did not even say that the cause was an automobile accident. Instead, the record simply tells you that the person has a "broken tibia." It is a record system that obscures the community nature of the problem, by focusing on the therapeutic to the exclusion of the primary cause.

We began, therefore, a search of the data systems of macroplanners. Finally we found one macroplanning group that had data regarding the nature of auto accidents in the city. It was data on a complex, computerized system, to be used in macroplanning to facilitate automobile traffic! We persuaded the planners to do a printout that could be used by the neighborhood people for their own action purposes. This had never occurred to them as a use for their information.

The printouts were so complex, however, that the organization could not comprehend them. So we took the numbers and transposed them onto a neighborhood map showing where the accidents took place. Where people were injured, we put a blue X. Where people were killed, we put a red X.

We did this for all accidents for a period of three months. There are 60,000 residents living in the neighborhood. In that area, in three months, there were more than 1,000 accidents. From the map the people could see, for example, that within three months six people had been injured, and one person killed, in an area 60 feet wide. They immediately identified this place as the entrance to a parking lot for a department store. They were then ready to act, rather than be treated, by dealing with the store owner because information had been "liberated" from its medical and macroplanning captivity.

The experience with the map had two consequences. One, it was an opportunity to invent several different ways to deal with a health problem that the community could understand. The community organization could negotiate with the department store owner and force a change in its entrance.

Two, it became very clear that there were accident problems that the community organization could not handle directly. For example, one of the main reasons for many of the accidents was the fact that higher authorities had decided to make several of the streets through the neighborhood major throughways for automobiles going from the heart of the city out to the affluent suburbs. Those who made this trip were a primary cause of injury to the local people. Dealing with this problem is not within the control of people at the neighborhood level—but they understood the necessity of getting other community organizations involved in a similar process, so that together they could assemble enough power to force the authorities to change the policies that serve the interests of those who use the neighborhoods as their freeway.

The third community action activity developed when the people focused on "bronchial problems." They learned that good nutrition was a factor in these problems, and concluded that they did not have enough fresh fruit and vegetables for good nutrition. In the city, particularly in the winter, these foods were too expensive. So could they grow fresh fruit and vegetables themselves? They looked around, but it seemed difficult in the heart of the city. Then several people pointed out that most of their houses were two story apartments with flat roofs. "Supposing we could build a greenhouse on the roof, couldn't we grow our own fruit and vegetables?" So they built a greenhouse on one of the roofs as an experiment. Then, a fascinating thing began to happen.

Originally, the greenhouse was built to deal with a health problem—inadequate nutrition. The greenhouse was a tool, appropriate to the environment, that people could make and use to improve health. Quickly, however, people began to see that the greenhouse was also an economic development tool. It increased their income because they now produced a commodity to use and also to sell.

Then, another use for the greenhouse appeared. In the United States, energy costs are extremely high and a great burden for poor people. One of the main places where people lose (waste) energy is from the rooftops of their houses—so the greenhouse on top of the roof converted the energy loss into an asset. The energy that did escape from the house went into the greenhouse where heat was needed. The greenhouse, therefore, was an energy conservation tool.

Another use for the greenhouse developed by chance. The community organization owned a retirement home for elderly people, and one day one of the elderly people discovered the greenhouse. She went to work there, and told the other old people and they started coming to the greenhouse every day to help care for the plants. The administrator of the old people's home noticed that the attitude of the older people changed. They were excited. They had found a function. The greenhouse became a tool to empower older people—to allow discarded people to be productive.

MULTILITY VS. UNITILITY

The people began to see something about technology that they had not realized before. Here was a simple tool—a greenhouse. It could be built locally, used locally and among its "outputs" were health, economic development, energy conservation and enabling older people to be productive. A simple tool requiring a minimum "inputs" produced multiple "outputs" with few negative side effects. We called the greenhouse a "multility."

Most tools in a modernized consumer-oriented society are the reverse of the greenhouse. They are systems requiring a complex organization with multiple inputs that produce only a single output. Let me give you an example. If you get bauxite from Jamaica, copper from Chile, rubber from Indonesia, oil from Saudi Arabia, lumber from Canada, and labor from all these countries, and process these resources in an American corporation that uses American labor and professional skills to manufacture a commodity, you can produce an electric toothbrush. This tool is what we call a "unitility." It has multiple inputs and one output. However, if a tool is basically a labor-saving device, then the electric toothbrush is an anti-tool. If you added up all the labor put into producing it, its sum is infinitely more than the labor saved by its use.

The electric toothbrush and the systems for its production are the essence of the technological mistake. The greenhouse is the essence of the technological possibility. The toothbrush (unitility) is a tool that disables capacity and maximizes exploitation. The greenhouse (multility) is a tool that minimizes exploitation and enables community action.

Similarly, the greenhouse is a health tool that creates citizen action and improves health. The hospitalized focus on health disables community capacity by concentrating on therapeutic tools and techniques requiring tremendous inputs, with limited output in terms of standard health measures.

CONCLUSIONS

Let me draw several conclusions from the health work of the community organization.

First, out of all this activity, it is most important that the health action process has strengthened a community organization. Health is a political issue. To convert a medical problem into a political issue is central to health improvement. Therefore, as our action has developed the organization's vitality and power, we have begun the critical health development. Health action must lead away from dependence on professional tools and techniques, towards community building and citizen action. Effective health action must convert a professional-technical problem into a political, communal issue.

Second, effective health action identifies what you can do at the local level with local resources. It must also identify those external authorities and structures that control the limits of the community to act in the interest of its health.

Third, health action develops tools for the people's use, under their own control. To develop these tools may require us to diminish the resources consumed by the medical system. As the community organization's health activity becomes more effective, the swollen balloon of medicine should shrink. For example, after the dogs were captured, the hospital lost clients. Nonetheless, we cannot expect that this action will stop the medical balloon from growing. The medical system will make new claims for resources and power, but our action will intensify the contradictions of medicalized definitions of health. We can now see people saying: "Look, we may have saved $185 in hospital care for many of the 160 dogs that will not now bite people. That's a lot of money! But it still stays with that hospital. We want our $185! We want to begin to trade in an economy in which you don't exchange our action for more medical service. We need income, not therapy. If we are to act in our health interest, we will need the resources medicine claims for its therapeutic purposes in order to diminish our therapeutic need."

These three principles of community health action suggest that improved health is basically about moving away from being "medical consumers."

The experience I have described suggests that the sickness which we face is the captivity of tools, resources, power, and consciousness by medical "unitilities" that create consumers.

Health is a political question. It requires citizens and communities. The health action process can enable "another health development" by translating medically defined problems and resources into politically actionable community problems.

43 *HELPING OURSELVES: THE LIMITS AND POTENTIAL OF SELF-HELP*

Ann Withorn

Self help has emerged as a widely acclaimed "major thrust" of the eighties. Popular magazines, *The New York Times* and the federal government have all recognized the potential of the "self help movement" to influence human service policies and programs. Hundreds of thousands of self help groups now exist across the country. Some are affiliated with nation-wide organizations while others are more isolated local efforts where people join together to help themselves cope with and cure a wide range of human problems. Ideologically they range from the conservative piety of an Alcoholics Anonymous to the radical feminism of feminist "self-health" activities.[1]

Is this activity simply an extension of the self-absorption of the seventies? Is it a retreat into individual solutions and a ploy to keep people from demanding what they need from the state? Or does it reflect a growing, healthy skepticism of professionals and the welfare state bureaucracy? Could it be a sign of a potentially important rise in commitment to popular democracy?

These questions are of some importance in the United States. The simple magnitude of current self help activity, especially among working class people, calls upon us to have, at least, an analysis of its political implications and an understanding of its appeal. Further, the experience of feminist self help suggests that there may be ways to combine selected self help activity with a broader socialist and feminist strategy. At its best, self help may even serve as one way to formulate a progressive politics which is more grounded in the daily experience of working class life and which thereby helps define socialism more broadly than the economistic formulations which so often characterize it. In addition, an understanding of the power of self help as a means for individual change may also go farther in comprehending the fundamental inadequacies of the social service provided by the modern welfare state.

WHAT IS SELF HELP?

The nature of self help itself gives rise to the contradictory questions raised above. Self help is the effort of people to come together in groups in order to resolve mutual individual needs. Today this activity consists of individuals sharing concerns about personal, emotional, health or family problems. Sometimes community or ethnic groups which organize to improve their neighborhoods or social situations also call themselves self-help groups. The major reasons for defining an activity as self help are that it involves group activity and meetings of the people with the problem, not outside experts or professionals, and that the main means by which difficulties are addressed are mutual sharing, support, advice-giving and the pooling of group resources and information. Members benefit as much from the sharing of their problems and the process of helping others as they do from the advice and resources provided by others. In most cases there is a strong ethic of group solidarity, so that individual members become concerned about the progress of other group members as well as in their own "cure."

Within this broad common definition, however, there is wide variety in focus and emphasis for self help groups. At one end of the spectrum are the politically aware feminist self-help efforts, in health care, rape crisis, battered women shelters and other service areas. Here self help is self-conscious, empowering democratic effort where women help each other and often provide an analysis and an example from which to criticize and make feminist demands on the system. At the other end are groups which focus on the specific problem only, like AA, other "anonymous" groups or disease victim groups, with self help used only as a means for coping with a problem, not an alternative model for society or even service delivery. In between are groups which have selected self help as a means to help themselves but which also come to draw from the process ways to suggest broader changes, often in the social services system and sometimes in the whole social system. While all share key aspects of self help and all may teach certain critical lessons about the importance of social networks and group solidarity, their differences are crucial and need to be understood and evaluated as a part of any critique of self help.

HISTORICAL ROOTS OF SELF HELP

Some of the comforts and supports now provided by self-conscious self help groups have always been available. Prior to industrial development village and family networks were the primary means by which people helped each other survive the economic, health and other social difficulties associated with a hard life. As industrial disruption made such supports less accessible early nineteenth century workers began to band together in new forms of "mutual aid" organizations composed of individual craft workers or, in America especially, of groups of ethnically homogeneous workers. These early groups formed to provide for the basic economic and social needs not available from employers, the state, the church or geographic community. Meager resources were pooled to provide burial and family insurance, limited food, clothing and economic support in times of ill health, disability and family crisis. In Britain and the U.S., the emergence of these "burial societies," "workingmen's aid" associations, "friendly societies" and immigrant aid associations reflected constant efforts by workers to help each other and help themselves to cope with the health and social problems associated with capitalist development. The remaining records of such groups show a growing sense of collective responsibility within the groups and the gradual creation of social networks which performed wider social functions than only the insurance of economic survival.[2]

It is easy to admire these self-conscious workers' efforts, like that of Workmen's Circle, to form "an organization that could come to their assistance in terms of need, and especially in case of sickness, that would provide them and their families with plots and decent burials in case of death and extend some measure of help to their surviving dependents, that would, finally, afford them congenial fellowships and thereby lessen the loneliness of their lives in a strange land."[3] It is important, however, to avoid romanticizing this early self help activity. Some groups were controlled by the more conservative and established elements in the craft or community who kept the groups from gaining a more broad "class" identification. Others served as a base from which to distrust or ignore, rather than identify with, the needs of other workers not in the same craft or ethnic group. And, at best, these early groups could only provide the most minimal assistance to their members, still leaving them with major social disadvantages. All these problems were pointed out at the time by radicals in the labor and black movements, especially. But, in times when public aid was extremely punitive and largely nonexistent even such limited efforts were recognized as crucial to the survival and strength of workers and their families. But they were also, perhaps, the only means of survival. Self help was the only help available. It was not developed as a better, more humane, alternative means of support; originally it was the only means of support. This is a crucial difference between early self help and current efforts.

SELF HELP AS A SERVICE ACTIVITY

There is an interesting parallel to these tensions in the professional developments of the period. Just as the more conservative trade unionists and black leadership supported self help as a means for worker and community independence, so did the more conservative doctors, lawyers and social workers who worked in the private sector. The private health and welfare establishment saw individual and group change coming out of self help activities. More liberal professionals argued that this strategy abandoned the poor and they, therefore, allied with progressive people in demanding more public programs. They argued that it was unrealistic to expect the victims of society to help themselves and that outside intervention—from expert professionals funded by the government—was the only reasonable hope for change. These liberal social workers and medical experts gained power in federal and state programs throughout the 1930s and 40s, so that by the 1950s the public health and welfare establishment had become as critical of self help as a service strategy as leftists were of it as a political tactic.

Yet self help came into its own as a service activity during the 1930s and 40s, in spite (or perhaps because) of increasing professional hostility. As the private and public insurance and welfare establishments grew, self help changed form, moving from group provision of welfare insurance and burial services to a process of social supports for dealing with a range of personal, family and emotional problems. The process of self help became important not for itself, as a model and base for democratic self-support, but as a means to achieve personal goals for change or to come to terms with unavoidable difficulties.

The poverty of the Depression gave rise to many self help service projects. Food, clothing and housing exchanges developed, European refugees and internal immigrants organized mutual aid groups. Most important, however, was the birth of Alcoholics Anonymous (AA) in 1935; it has served as a primary model for self help service activities since its inception. It was founded by a pair of mid-western professionals who found little help in the medical, social work or psychiatric professionals and who began to develop a behavior oriented, religiously imbued, program of group support and pressure for alcoholics. The model consisted of admitting the power of one's problem and drawing help from fellow alcoholics, as well as from a "higher power," in order to learn to stop drinking. This was to be done by developing a network of fellow alcoholics, by attending frequent—even daily—meetings where discussions take place about personal experiences with alcohol and where the goal of sobriety is to be achieved "one day at a time." Drawing upon such basic, simple principles AA grew rapidly, reaching 400,000 by 1947 and currently involving more than 700,000 alcoholics a year.

It is easy for socialists and professionals to criticize Alcoholics Anonymous. Its religious pietism is fundamentalist and limiting. Despite its proclaimed organizational refusal to take federal money or political positions, its veterans have increasingly designed and defined alcholism services across the country in harmony with AA principles. These programs often exclude women and those who have not "hit bottom" with their drinking, as well as a range of people less comfortable with the somewhat simplistic "Twelve Steps." Its appeal has been largely limited to whites. Yet AA does appear to have a higher success rate than other forms of professional help with the complex problems associated with alcoholism. It does attract a largely working-class population who have little recourse to private services. It also offers alcoholics the experience of a non-drinking community where they can learn to like themselves better, admit to their problems, trust others and begin to rebuild their lives.

Other self help services have formed using the Anonymous model, where the focus is on the problem faced and the process of mutual help and support is valued as an effective means to the end, not as a goal in itself. Gamblers Anonymous, Overeaters Anonymous, Parents Anonymous (for people who have abused their children) are only three of the dozens of groups which are modelled closely on AA and attempt to help people admit that they have a problem and get help from others in the same situation to overcome it. All groups rely on "recovering" victims to help others, a helping role which is often a major form of continuing improvement for the old time members. Although some groups make greater use of professionals than others, in all peers assume primary roles and outside social networks often grow out of such groups which provide people with a wide range of supports. While there is no hard data, such anonymous groups (most of which, except AA, have been founded since the mid-fifties) seem to attract a largely white working- and middle-class population and create strong loyalties among those helped.

Since the 1940s other services which use self help as a major means of helping people cope with or resolve personal difficulties have emerged. Many drug programs have used self help activities to create "alternative communities" characterized by mutual disclosure, support and pressure. Since the 1940s (and mushrooming in the 1970s) there has been a steady increase in health-oriented self help programs for the families of victims of cancer and other diseases, and for the victims themselves. Stroke victims, cancer victims, heart disease patients, parents of children with Down's Syndrome (to name only a few of thousands) have come together to discuss their feelings, reactions and symptoms and to help each other emotionally. While these programs are often supported by the medical system they frequently come to share vocal and strong criticisms of professionalism and professional care.

The social welfare and medical establishments have reacted to all this increasing self help activity with different types of responses. Sometimes groups have been criticized (often during the initial phases) for "resisting professional treatment" or for avoiding reality. The more critical the groups become of the quality of professional care (a component of almost all self help groups, no matter what their origins) the more they are resisted by doctors and social workers. However, until this happens they are often supported by professionals as another form of service, especially for people with "difficult" problems, i.e. those problems like alcoholism, drug abuse, "incurable" cancer, senility and other afflictions not amenable to conventional intervention. Indeed, the federal government has become enamoured with self help approaches, providing funds for certain efforts and even identifying the existence of a "continuum of care" including self help at one end and full institutional care at the other, all of which will require some form of public support and monitoring.

As with AA, it is easy to criticize. Most of these self help service efforts can be legitimately viewed as methods by which the established medical, mental health and social work professions get people to provide services to themselves which the professionals won't or can't provide. Cheap care and an avoidance of public responsibility may be obvious. Yet progressives working in these fields also have supported self help services, in recognition of the limits of professional care and in order to support the creation of a stronger, less fearful consumer consciousness, among clients or victims of problems as varied as alcoholism, drug abuse, cancer and chronic disease. In addition, many members of such self help service groups find them much more helpful and acceptable forms of care than other, more professional, services. Such groups may provide release and support which come from sharing and comraderie. These results cannot be disregarded, especially for people who felt desperately alone before the experience. A working class veteran of AA, Overeaters Anonymous and Smoke Enders reflected similarly on what self help meant to her:

> Self help groups really help. They make you feel like you are not alone with yourself on your problem. You share with others and find out you are not the only one who smokes in the shower or bakes two pies for your family and eats one before anyone comes home. I'm not sure how it works, but somehow you feel like trying again.
>
> My sister had, in fact, a daughter that died. She had always laughed at me for my "groups," but after that happened she joined one herself. She just couldn't handle it alone, feeling so guilty and not knowing anyone with the same problem. That's what self help means to me.

Particularly important to many people in self help groups is the opportunity to help others with similar problems. The experience of doing this can be powerful and strengthening, especially for people who have only felt like victims before.

In short, as a form of social service, self help groups have proven themselves to be helpful and empowering to many, despite their potential use as a vehicle for providing cheaper services to unwanted clients. As one aspect of the general social services system, self help services seem a secure and welcome addition. The question remains, however, whether this increased self help activity has any underlying impact for progressive change. For such discussions we must look to recent efforts of the women's movement.

THE IMPORTANCE OF FEMINIST SELF HELP

If it weren't for the development of feminist self help, especially in health, we might be less interested in the whole question of whether self help can be a serious part of a socialist strategy. Self help would be seen as merely a social service with little broader political impact. But the impressive efforts of women around the country to take self help seriously as a healthy form of relationship between women and to wed this with feminist analysis may suggest a more general model for reuniting self help with political practice.

Self help has been a central part of most feminist service work, which has, in turn, been a major area of the feminist movement. Since the late sixties, when women's liberation groups developed "consciousness-raising," the model of women sharing and helping other women has been a basic feminist strategy. Feminist historians looked back and found self help equivalents throughout the history of women who have formed strong self helping women's networks within the family, neighborhoods and community as a means for basic survival and emotional support.

Out of this history, and an emerging understanding that "the personal is political," feminists were able to take the process of self help more seriously, to value the experience of working and sharing together in itself, as well as to appreciate the quality of the product of such work. Women were compelled, then, to be more self-conscious in their self help approaches and to proclaim them as central to feminist goals. In "Jane," an early underground Chicago-based abortion clinic, for example, women developed models of abortion care which included sharing all processes and procedures, discussion of feelings and the trading of mutual experiences among the women abortion-workers and the women seeking abortions. Their approach became standard in many feminist services. *Our Bodies, Our Selves,* the classic women's self health care book offered professional information mixed with personal experiences and has been used as a basis for women's health groups across the country. It too has helped to establish the notion of self help—mutual sharing of feelings, information and skills—as a basic tenet of feminist activity.[4]

As feminist services became a major approach of the women's movement—including everything from women's multi-purpose centers, to day care, health and nutrition services, rape and battered women's programs—self help came along as standard feminist practice. The meaning varied, however. In some places it simply meant collective decision-making by staff and a sharing of feelings and information with women who came for service. It was seen as a natural outgrowth of ideas of sisterhood and feminist theory. In the feminist health clinics, however, feminist self help has been most fully defined, has become in Elizabeth Somer's words "both a philosophy and a practice through which we become active creators of our destinies."[5]

Feminist clinics insisted on education and group involvement of all who came to the clinics. This was viewed as an important antidote to the standard medical model of doctor as god and patient as grateful recipient of his care. Health care workers forged different relationships with women who came for care and also began to explore and share a growing criticism of the medical "knowledge" about women's bodies. The most self-conscious programs, the Feminist Women's Health Centers, led in developing clear guidelines for self help in health care which included pelvic self-examinations, group examinations and discussions. They shared an explicit philosophy that self help is more than, and different from, the traditional "delivery" of service:

> Self help is not being simply service oriented . . . we do not want to be middle women between the MD's and the patients. We want to show women how to do it themselves. . . . We do not examine women. We show women how to examine themselves. . . . We neither sell nor give away self help . . . we share it. (Detroit Women's Clinic, 1974)

Feminist self help in health care and other service areas developed in conjunction with the broader feminist movement. Knowledge of the inadequacies and brutality of male dominated medicine came along with a heightened awareness of the prevalence of rape and women-battering. The system-supporting aspects of all medical and welfare care forced women into developing new models and into looking to each other for information and support. The early successes of many groups in raising the consciousness of women who came for "service" was heartening and sustaining. Sustained practice meant that feminists have been able to put the principles of self help to the test, to explore the need for structure and specialization within a self help framework, to discover the complexities of many health and emotional problems and to determine when professional help may, indeed, be necessary.

All this learning and growth have not been without costs, however. Health centers, particularly, have suffered intense bureaucratic harassment from the medical profession which has been anxious to protect its right to control who practices medicine. Most self help programs have suffered from funding problems of a similar sort. The medical and social welfare establishments demand "legitimacy" before they provide money—through third party payments (Medicaid, private insurance) or direct service contracts. They require, at the very least, a professional "cover" for most alternative services and often refuse funding until bureaucratic, hierarchical structures are actually in place. Some battered women's shelters originally received money, in light of favorable publicity, with minimal hassles, but as time passed welfare agencies pressed to fund a "range" of services (i.e., nonfeminist programs), with more familiar, professional approaches. In addition, inflation and cut backs have also limited the amount of money available.

The problems have not been all external either. The time and emotional demands of most self help services have made it hard for most groups to sustain staff, much less to do the continual political education necessary to make the self help offered truly feminist in content. Women with professional aspirations and a lack of feminist values have been drawn to self help efforts. Their pressure can push already overextended feminists to leave rather than fight creeping bureaucracy, "efficiency" and professionalization in their midst. When this happens the mutual aid, democratic and sharing aspects of the service fade as surely as they do when public bureaucracies directly take over.

When such problems are coupled with current general decline in a broad-based feminist movement, they become even more difficult to endure and struggle with. Even in well-functioning self help projects women feel more isolated and less sure of what it all means, as expressed by a women's health worker in 1979:

> After we finally got our license then we had all this paperwork to do all the time. The women's community seemed less interested because we weren't in crisis anymore. The women who wanted to work in the center are more interested in health care than feminism. It just seems to take more effort to be feminist these days, to raise political issues in the groups or work meetings. We're still trying and do OK but I guess it's a lot harder than it used to be.

Feminist services, then, have not totally solved old problems with self help. They have shown that it is possible for participation in self help to be an effective means for political growth and development. Especially the health services have shown us that self help may often be an intrinsically better model of care and may, thereby, offer an immediate and personal way for people to understand what is wrong with public and private health and welfare services. All have shown the natural links between a democratic feminist movement and the process of self help. Women who have participated in such programs talk about themselves as "permanently changed. I don't think I can ever accept without criticism the old authoritarian models again." But over time the pressures to provide services on a large scale, with adequate funding, work against the ability to work in a self help manner. Is it reasonable to assume that we could really provide feminist self help services to all the battered women who need them, for example? And if it is not, we are always stuck with the limits of even the most effective self help efforts—that the harder we work and the better we function, the greater the demand and the more impossible it is to meet.

PROBLEMS AND POTENTIAL OF SELF HELP

Given all this, how should progressive people respond to the likelihood that self help services are likely to continue to grow and re-form in the future? The current momentum and recognition of existing programs seems unstoppable and will probably be even more appealing to administrators wishing to support an image of continued service provision in times of real cut backs. An increasingly popular answer to anyone with a problem will predictably be: "Join, or form, a self help group."

As advanced capitalism lurches along, services and the service economy will become more important. Self help services may play an increasingly important role in this. On the hopeful side, self help activity has the potential to become a base from which people can criticize, demand and affect the nature of the service system in a positive way and out of which progressive workers and clients can form meaningful alliances. On the negative side, self help services may help to provide an opportunity for another professional cover-up. See, we have a humane system. We even let people take care of each other, after they are near death or incapacitated by emotional and personal problems.

The problem, assuming these options, becomes one of how to assist self help efforts in achieving their potential as a base for criticism and change rather than providing tacit reaffirmation of professional hegemony and the capitalist welfare state.

In promoting the potential of self help we cannot, however, ignore certain limits which may be built into the activity. First, we cannot deny that the nature of self help, and the enormity of the difficulties which bring people to it, often emphasize only the personal dimensions of people's problems. Even if the social components of problems are admitted, as they are in feminist and some other self help efforts, the stress remains on how the victim can change, rather than on the implications for broader social action. There can even be a new form of victim blaming which takes place in self help: "We are so fucked up only we can help each other." Admittedly this is an aspect of all psychological services, but the self help model, with emphasis on social support and reciprocity, may serve to mask the individualistic approach more. It also may make it harder for people to move on to other activities because the self help group may form the only support system people know (AA has a strong history of this: people become professional alcoholics, still centered in the group and their problem, long after drinking has ceased to define their lives). For self help activity to lead to broader criticism of the social service system or the whole of society, these tendencies must be recognized and alternatives made available, at least to those who can make use of them.

Second, even with self help set in a broader context, the questions of scope and relationship to the state will still affect us. Self help activity is probably only a limited service tactic which, while it can form a base for criticizing and pressuring the larger system, can never fully replace the professional, bureaucratized services, at least under capitalism. This is a more difficult proposition to accept in practice than it sounds in theory. We get sucked in, we want to "save the world" and it is difficult to remember the political analysis which tells us that the problems we face are generated by social forces beyond our immediate control. It is hard, as those involved in self help often admit, to have to push the state to provide services which we know will be inferior to what we can do through self help (but on a limited scale). All this leads to burnout and frustration, especially when broader movements are not active enough to help us keep our activity in perspective.

Finally, there are some philosophical problems associated with self help, which are similar to those surrounding many populist efforts. Many self help groups, especially including feminist activities, become so skeptical of organization and expertise that they become almost mystical and anti-intellectual. While the social origins of current organizations and expertise may lead to this, as an overall approach it becomes self-defeating. In the process of self help, some people become "experts" in the problem: must they then leave the group? Or groups tend to "reinvent the wheel," perpetually relearning everything about problems from a feminist, working class, consumer or black perspective. While Barbara Ehrenreich's and Deidre English's suggestion that we "take what we want of the technology without buying the ideology" sounds good, the full criticism of all professionalism which is inherent in healthy self help may make this difficult.[6]

Furthermore, we still have to fight rampant specialization in self help groups. Granted, DES daughters have different needs from mastectomy patients and from ex-mental patients, but to be effective, self help concerns will need to be linked together in broader analysis of processes and problems. All this must be accomplished while recognizing that people in immediate pain may resent any deviation from their immediate problems.

These are serious drawbacks, not to be ignored. Yet current circumstances suggest that progressive people should, still, become involved in many facets of self help. We have the accumulated experience of feminist self help to guide us away from some of the worst pitfalls. We have the undeniable broad public interest in self help to provide a responsive climate for our efforts. Finally, and most importantly, we have a national social and economic situation which may make self help once again a necessity for survival. Inflation and creeping recession have already made daily living more tenuous and pressured. The cut backs in social services make professional supports less available, subject to more competition among those deserving service and more bureaucratization and formalities before services can be delivered. Given such a set of factors, it is not unreasonable to support and initiate self help efforts as both a broad base for criticism and change in the social service system as well as favorable settings for people to become exposed to socialist and feminist ideas and practice.

The primary base for our involvement in self help groups can even be personal. Most of us experience problems in our lives as women, men, parents, children, lovers, survivors, drinkers, procrastinators, shy people, fat people, lonely people. Joining or starting a self help group can help us as people, not just as activists with an agenda. This has been a major source of strength within the women's movement. Women have helped each other and been helped themselves with some real personal and political issues in their lives. The sharing and loss of isolation which comes from self help activity are real and can provide us with tangible energy and strength.

Finally, then, the impulse which brings people, including ourselves, to seek mutual aid instead of professional care is a healthy one. It embodies the faith in oneself and others that is essential if we are ever to achieve a more equal society. We cannot allow the all-too-real limitations of the current practice of self help to obscure the equally real opportunity.

NOTES

1. There is a very large current literature on self help. The leading figures in this area are Frank Riessmann and Alan Gartner, who have written *Self Help in the Human Services* (Jossey-Bass, 1977) and sponsor the National Self Help Clearinghouse (CUNY, 33 West 42nd St., Room 1227, New York, NY 10036).
2. For a useful review of this history see Alfred H. Katz and Eugene I. Bender, "Self Help Groups in Western Society: History and Prospects," in *The Journal of Applied Behavioral Science,* XII, no. 3 (1976).
3. Maximillian C. Hurwitz, *The Workers Circle* (New York, 1936).
4. Pauline B. Bart, "Seizing the Means of Reproduction: An Illegal Feminist Abortion Collective How and Why It Worked," Abraham Lincoln School of Medicine, University of Illinois, Chicago.
5. *Ibid.*
6. Helin I. Marieskind and Barbara Ehrenreich, "Towards Socialist Medicine: The Women's Health Movement," *Social Policy,* September–October, 1975.

POSTSCRIPT, 2000

As I reread this essay after twenty years, I am struck with two changes that might make some of its assumptions difficult to understand. First, the political context within which self help occurs has changed immensely. At the beginning of a new century there can be no automatic presumption that viable progressive social movements exist and struggle with questions regarding how members should live their lives or how best to "serve" their constituencies. Surely there are plenty of people (myself still among them) who define ourselves as feminists, or leftists, or gay activists or what-have-you, but the sense of quietude that I described twenty years ago has grown and limited the totality of the way most people experience politics.

It is simply much harder in the year 2000 for people, without the deeper ideological context that movement identity provides, to know what I meant when I called for progressives to stay involved with self help, and to keep pushing to make it more "political." Just recently I spoke to a graduate class about the need to be more political in the way we approach service work. A brave student raised her hand and asked, "do you really think we should talk about how to vote?" Her question and the ensuing discussion helped me clarify that even though I still think self help especially, and human services generally, are natural occasions for basic political discourse about the social context of "need" and the economic and social roots of inequality, many people just don't think that way without a lot of background discussion.

For a more thorough presentation of my arguments about "political service work" see my book, *Serving the People: Social Services and Social Change* (Columbia University Press, 1984) and also see a recent book by Jerome

Sachs and Fred Newdom, *Clinical Work and Social Action* (Haworth, 1999) for a continuation of the discussion. Second, the broader context for human service work has also changed in ways that limits the positive potential for self help as a politicizing tool, in ways I suggested but could not fully anticipate twenty years ago. The managed care environment has made self help an economically attractive option in many contexts, while the time limited, fee for (approved) service nature of the managed care model has made it much more difficult to achieve any real mutual exploration and collective building toward a politicized interpretation of personal pain. "Self help" and, woefully, "empowerment" are now often terms used by right-wing politicians and writers to provide a rationale for cutting public services, and calling into question the integrity, not just the methods, of professional providers.

John McKnight (see *The Careless Society*, Basic Books, 1995), whose critique of professionalism was so helpful in the early 1980s has unfortunately been used to discredit almost any organized efforts through which people try to help each other. And, just as for-profit social services have become acceptable in a privatized social service climate, so for-profit "self-help" groups, led by motivation gurus and writers like Tony Robbins and Stephen Covey have obliterated the history of self help in mutual aid and solidarity movements. On the other hand, tough critiques like Wendy Kaminer's (*I'm Dysfunctional, You're Disfunctional*, Vintage, 1993) have unfairly painted all self help efforts as objects of scorn, and made it all too easy for educated progressives to forget the value of mutual aid as a basic building block of democracy, and as a buffer against intellectual elitism.

One of my hopes for the next years is that out of all the mentoring, community service, and service learning currently being encouraged in schools at all levels, a cohort of young people will emerge willing to revitalize, and re-politicize self help and other service efforts. It still seems as true now as it ever did that doing any kind of service work means giving oneself the opportunity to see the pain of human existence, with self help encounters offering the most expansive understanding of that pain. And, if young people who are by definition not "experts," engage in such work with an open mind and with real respect for people "in need" they will encounter a mind opening experience, one that has the potential to connect people and expose the power that comes when what was once viewed as resulting from individual misfortune is also understood as a product of societal injustice.

---

44 Illness and Internet Empowerment: Writing and Reading Breast Cancer in Cyberspace

Victoria Pitts

The Internet is increasingly becoming a site where women with breast cancer not only receive information about the illness but also compose and circulate their own stories of breast cancer. Women with breast cancer are often deeply interested in self-definition and empowerment, and I describe in this study how they create personal web pages on the Internet as sites for generating new forms of knowledge, awareness and agency in relation to the illness. Debates about the Internet in feminism and cyberstudies have focused on to what extent "cybersubjects" are free to create new identities, relationships and communities in virtual, disembodied space, or, put more simply, how and to what extent they are empowered by virtual technologies. I suggest here that women's web pages might offer potentially critical opportunities for women's knowledge-making in relation to what are often highly political aspects of the body, gender and illness. However, the Internet is not an inherently empowering technology, and it can be a medium for affirming norms of femininity, consumerism, individualism and other powerful social messages.

CYBERAGENCY: VIRTUAL SPACE AND THE INTERACTIVE BODY/SELF

A debate has been underway since the early 1990s about how identities and definitions of situation emerge out of and operate within disembodied media communities. Theories about the Internet have been variously optimistic and skeptical, suggesting the complexity of what we might call "cyberagency," particularly in relationship to symbolic forms of oppression and constraint. A number of scholars have celebrated the disembodiedness of interaction on the Internet, which may foster a disruption in the ordinary ways in which our senses of self, or our "identities," are shaped (Turkle, 1995; Featherstone, 2000; Leary, 2000; Plant, 2000). Corporeal bodies are absent in cyberspace, and thus individuals are left to represent the body through words, images, codes and symbols. This may leave us with greater freedom to perform our identities, since the states of our bodies are no longer "empirically verifiable." As Waskul et al., describe,

> In these on-line social worlds, traditional assumptions about self and body do not apply: the activities of participants and experiences of self are neither contained by nor affixed to corporeal bodies . . . both bodies and selves exist only as [emergent] socially constructed representations. (2000: 378)

Waskul et al. describe how instead of fixed identities for bodies and selves, new meanings are continually generated by cyberspace that are the product of intersubjective, temporary expressions of on-line individuals and collectivities. Selves appear in cyberspace not as "that which the body contains or holds," but rather as constructs that emerge out of communication. Released from traditional bodily constraints, or "situationally freed from the empirical shell of the body," cybersubjects are left to represent themselves virtually (2000: 378). Thus, *choice* in what our identity is and how others will identify us is part of the promise of the on-line world (Willson, 2000).

Unsurprisingly, then, the Internet has been embraced by a number of theorists for what they see as its radical potential. Some writers have described, for instance, how individuals might create multiple identities and roles within a virtual community, and in so doing de-essentialize fixed, unitary subjectivity (Poster, 1995; Turkle, 1995). Others have explored the particular implications of virtuality for gender and sexuality. In cyberspace, new genders and sexualities can theoretically be imagined and represented outside of physical constraints. Faith Wilding describes the "net utopianism" within cyberfeminism, which expects that cyberspace will be "a free space where gender does not matter—[where] you can be anything you want to be regardless of your "real" age, sex, race, or economic position . . ." (1998: 9). Sadie Plant's writings about cyberspace, for instance, might be described this way. Plant declares not only that women have been using cyberspace in radical ways, but also that the very form of cyberspace interaction is already culturally subversive. Because it promotes fluid notions of self and body, she argues that the Net provides women with a space for deconstructing traditional roles and definitions of self and situation. "There is a virtual reality," she writes, "an emergent process for which identity is not the goal but the enemy, precisely what has kept at bay the matrix of potentialities from which women have always downloaded their roles" (2000: 335). Plant's assertion that the Net is a particularly subversive space for women relies on the idea that women can and will embrace fluid identities, forge new kinds of relational networks with other users and employ what she calls "intuitive leaps and cross-connections" that are not traditionally masculine but rather feminine and empowering.

But the idea of women's cyberliberation has a number of problems. so far, as a number of ethnographies of the Internet suggest, cyberculture has far from achieved freedom from normative gender constraints, or from other oppressions related to embodied identity. Researchers have described how conventional power relations, including those of gender and race, work their way into on-line interactions. As Caroline Bassett suggests in her study of a virtual "city" in which participants can choose their own online genders, *actual* on-line gender performance often involves *both* gender play and "rigid adherence to gender norms" (1997: 549; see also Kendall, 1998; Waskul et al., 2000). For instance, homophobia has not disappeared from the gender-experimental on-line universe, and Bassett finds "extreme conformity" in some of the body images employed. To what extent women's writings on the Web resist these problems remains an important research question.

There are other problems to think about in relation to what we might call "cyberagency," two of which I want to raise here. First, in addition to finding that users might affirm social norms rather than deviate from them, we are increasingly finding that cyberspace itself is not so neutral. While some writers depict it as an ideal site for inventing identities and virtual bodies, cyberspace is hardly free from corporate, media and other consumer influences. Despite the Internet's potential as a forum for diverse viewpoints and interests, it is already highly consumerized and, some argue, homogenized, becoming a "monoculture" colonized by corporate and media interests rather than a network of local, diverse, fluid and shifting ideas, identities and interactions (Bell and Kennedy, 2000; Cartwright, 2000; Sardar, 2000; Stratton, 2000). Critics are increasingly aware of cyberspace's role as a mass media delivery system (Stratton, 2000). Search engines, which are often owned by major media companies and seen as "the best bet for advertising revenue," for instance, are the primary way most users locate World Wide Web sites (Croteau and Hoynes, 2000: 73). I am particularly interested in how along with other industries, health is big business in cyberspace. Companies like AOL, Yahoo and CompuServe run popular women's health sites that are saturated with advertising. For example, in my study of Women.com's BreastFest, a web site dedicated to Breast Cancer Awareness Month, I described how it not only promotes awareness of the illness and circulates information about health resources, but also how it directs readers to a broad range of women's "self-care" and self-improvement issues, defined by a mix of feminist, biomedical and consumerist/beauty aims, including the promotion of Victoria's Secret lingerie and breast-augmentation surgery (Pitts, 2001).[1] Cyberspace is not monolithic though, and is created by and through a number of sources. Women's own personal writings about breast cancer on the Internet, such as can be found on personal web pages, might generate knowledge that is independent from the corporate and advertising interests that are promoted within the for-profit on-line world, but they cannot automatically be assumed to be untouched by these interests.

A second problem with "cyberliberation" is that the very notion of the flexible, elective identity that is celebrated in theories of cyberliberation may not itself be inherently radical. Anthony Giddens and others have described how the individual's sense of self as something to be continually created is fostered by, and benefits, postmodern consumer culture, which frames identity as a personal accomplishment that is achieved through various consumer practices, body projects and lifestyle choices (Giddens, 1991; see also Turner, 1991; Shilling, 1993). In the current social context, the elective-identity model is often hard to extricate from the consumer model of identity (see Balsamo, 1995). That we each have the ability to "choose" our identities, in cyberspace and in "real" space, may actually mean that we each have the social responsibility to consider our selves and bodies as projects that must be continually reworked, improved and upgraded. Norms of female beauty and personal responsibility, for instance, are affirmed even within the women's breast cancer movement, as I describe below. Thus, we need to attend to the ways in which consumerism, beauty norms, individualism and other pressures may be operating in people's experiences of cyberspace, and we need to consider the implications of this for women's agency. While there may be many reasons for feminists to be hopeful about the new technologies, these problems all impact upon cyberspace's promise of empowerment.

ILLNESS, BREAST CANCER AND AGENCY

The question of empowerment and agency are particularly salient issues for women with breast cancer. In addition to the burdens of physical sickness, women with breast cancer face a number of challenges to controlling their own self-definitions and framing their experiences in their own terms. These include the high-tech and masculinist terms in which their bodies are often defined, and how breast cancer has been framed in deeply gendered and ideological ways. For instance, feminists have addressed how women's bodies are subjected to multiple forms of medical surveillance and to powerful social messages in relation to breast cancer detection (see Martin, 1987, 1994; Wilkerson, 1998; Clarke and Olesen, 1999). As feminist scholars have pointed out, the worrisome aspects of surveilling women include the new burdens placed on women to prevent and manage disease. As Jennifer Fosket describes, because the early detection and prevention discourse continually implores them to detect or even prevent the disease, women who do get cancer often feel as if they are blamed by others, or blame themselves (2000; see also Altman, 1996; Fosket et al., 2000; Hallowell, 2000; Potts, 2000; Simpson, 2000; Wilkinson, 2001). Women's experiences of breast cancer have also been shaped by beauty norms and consumerism. Feminist researchers have explored how both the media and medical industries have framed breast cancer in ways that assume hetero-normativity, emphasize women's appearance issues and pressure women to look "normal," erase signs of illness and re-beautify themselves (Lorde, 1980; Fosket, 2000; Saywell, 2000; Wilkinson, 2001). One worrisome example is the "Look Good, Feel Better" (LGFB) campaign co-sponsored by the American Cancer Society and the cosmetics industry. As Sharon Batt (1994) describes, this campaign aims to "teach" women recovering from chemotherapy how to disguise signs of their ill health and beautify themselves with makeup and cosmetic techniques.

These pressures shape women's experiences with breast cancer and have influenced the ways in which women narrate their stories about the disease. As Stuart Hall has pointed out, telling stories about ourselves is a way of constructing our identities. In telling stories, we are able to frame our "certain conditions of existence" (Hall in Thornham, 2000: 3). But *how* we frame our stories is not. Hall argues, wholly a matter of personal choice, but rather influenced by social norms and ideologies and "constructed within the play of power and exclusion" (Hall, 1996: 5). For example, Laura Potts (2000) describes how autobiographical writings about breast cancer, by which she means print-published memoirs, have generally affirmed, rather than challenged, mainstream conceptions of beauty, gender and illness. Breast cancer memoirs are largely framed as healing experiences for both the writer and the reader, and they may generate solidarities among women. They can facilitate the development of new identities, such as the breast cancer survivor, or the "warrior" as Audre Lorde (1980) puts it. And they place women and breast cancer center-stage where they can enter into public consciousness. However, Potts and other feminist scholars argue that many women's autobiographies of breast cancer, at least in the print world, have reproduced heteronormative, consumerist and gendered ideologies regarding women's bodies. While Lorde, Kathy Acker, Susan Sontag and other women have written highly critical accounts, many stories repeat what Dorothy Broom, following Arthur Frank (1995), calls the "restitution narrative," in which women "put on a brave face," remain "relentlessly optimistic" and circulate the "obligatory success stories" (2001: 253, 250; see also Stacey, 1992; Wilkinson, 2001). As Broom describes, women often feel a social duty to hide signs of illness, repress feelings of anger or grief, embrace an optimistic attitude and even focus on beautification techniques. Sociocultural fears and expectations about femininity, women's sexuality and illness encourage a sense of shame and discrediting about breast cancer, and work to "isolate and silence" women about its horrible realities (Broom, 2001: 250). As Cherise Saywell argues, this kind of silencing has also characterized much of the newspaper coverage of the disease (Saywell, 2000).

Although little research has been conducted on women's web narratives of breast cancer, Broom and another writer, Sue Wilkinson, have questioned whether the World Wide Web might be a site where women might repeat the "restitution narrative" about breast cancer, or, instead, make visible the injuries that breast cancer brings. Perhaps, if the champions of Internet empowerment are right, the widespread use of this technology may encourage the telling of a wider range of stories and experiences about breast cancer than are tolerated in print and newspaper accounts. For instance, cyberspace may offer women opportunities to challenge the hegemonic authority of medical experts and to research the medical and social aspects of the disease, and may generate opportunities for women to narrate their experiences and generate new definitions of self and identity. The trend since the 1970s toward a democratization of health care, in particular the leveling of hierarchal relationships between doctor and patient, has been linked to its consumerization (see Haug and Lavin, 1983). We might see, as Michael Hardey suggests, that the Internet might play a major part in accelerating this process of transforming the patient's "sick role" and the doctor's authority. Hardey finds that when they surf the Internet for health information, individuals no longer see themselves as patients (or potential patients), but rather they become "reflexive consumer[s] . . . evaluating and at times challenging expert knowledge" (1999: 820).

In this study I survey women's writings about breast cancer on the Internet, particularly in personal web pages, and find mixed evidence for the notion of women's Internet empowerment. I find some support for the idea that access to the Internet, in particular its wide array of health information, plays a significant role in individuals' definitions of self, as consumers rather than as sick persons. In women's breast cancer pages I also find repeated celebrations of the Internet as an empowering tool for ill women. I also find that women's narratives *do* make "visible," in Wilkinson's terms, painful and difficult aspects of breast cancer. However, I also find that such narratives are not always subversive in the sense that champions of cyber-empowerment might expect them to be. Rather than always forging new ideas about identity, gender and community, personal breast cancer narratives often circulate conventional messages of individualism, personal responsibility and femininity that are troubling from a critical feminist perspective.

RESEARCHING BREAST CANCER WEB PAGES

With the advent of the Internet, women with access to computers and servers can participate in autobiographical story-telling about breast cancer that can reach a public audience. On the Internet, autobiographical stories are often told through the construction of personal web pages. Along with e-mail, newsgroups, listservs, chat rooms and other sites, the Internet includes web pages—including corporate, institutional and "personal" pages—and browsers that can search and find them. *Personal* web pages are usually written by individuals, couples or families and often have little or no fixed institutional or organizational ties (except to the servers that electronically support them). They can disappear overnight (although they usually do not), and often change over time; they are sometimes updated, and the authors often get feedback from readers through electronic guest books. There are hundreds, probably thousands, of breast cancer-related personal web pages. They may include diaries, photographs, personal breast cancer timelines, comments of visitor support and memorials, and are visually varied and illustrated.

Over a period of nine months and with the help of research assistants, I identified 50 personal web sites that claim to be constructed by individual breast cancer survivors in which breast cancer is a primary theme. (Together, these 50 sites comprise hundreds of pages of printed text.) I chose to study 50 because I wanted a large enough group of sites to get some sense of their diversity, but a small enough group to ensure that I had sufficient time and resources to conduct in-depth content analysis of each site. We found the first 10 sites through search engines, but the rest we found through creating a virtual snowball sample from these initial sites. Some writers, for example, advertised their own web pages in the space for "guest book" signatures, and advertised other women's pages through providing links. We documented some of the sites' characteristics and, using a grounded theory approach, generated categories for coding. The pages were collected without any criteria of age/race/class/gender or sexuality, but we explicitly looked for web sites that appeared to be "personal web pages" rather than those constructed by health care or women's organizations.

I can make no claims about the off-time identities of the subjects who wrote the web sites. However, most of the sites we gathered announced themselves as composed by women with breast cancer (others were described as written together with a partner, friend or family members).[2] To the extent that we can estimate off-line identities from the content of the sites, we judged our cyberauthors or "cybersubjects"[3] to be racially diverse but not representative: the majority of photographs in the sites appeared to be of white women, and the majority of subjects presented themselves in their sites as heterosexual. Even though I do not assume that on-line identities are necessarily identical to off-line identities, throughout this analysis, I operate under the assumption that the web pages are in some sense "truthful," in that their authors do indeed have breast cancer or know someone with breast cancer, and that the photographs posted that claim to be of the authors actually are. This assumption is not empirically verified and must be considered a limitation of this research.

This problem of verifiability is one of several issues being debated in the literature about how to do Internet research. In addition to the question of the verifiability of subjects or authors, researchers have also disagreed about when researchers may quote freely from Internet text, whether researchers should disguise the on-line names/identities of the subjects and whether Internet researchers are studying people (whose consent is needed) or texts and other "artifacts" (which are copyright protected). While I cannot exhaustively explore these debates in this article, I want to briefly describe my own position.

That no "bodies" can be seen and that the Internet affords a level of anonymity has led to worries over the possibility of "misrepresentation of identity" (Walther, 2001). In this study, I can make no claims about the off-line identities of the authors who wrote the web sites, and I do not assume that cybersubjects' on-line identities are necessarily identical to their off-line identities. Nonetheless, throughout this analysis, I operate under the assumption that the web pages are indeed, as they claim, authored by someone who has breast cancer or knows someone with breast cancer, and that the issues they raise are real to the writers themselves. That this assumption is not empirically verified must be considered a limitation of this research, but one that I believe is minimal. I take Joseph Walther's view that the worry about overt "misrepresentation" is probably overemphasized in discussions of on-line research. Researchers need to consider that "misrepresentations" on the Internet, while getting a lot of media coverage, have not been explored well as an empirical phenomenon and are "probably highly inflated in public perception," and that other research methods, such as survey responses, are no less wrought with these problems. While I could undertake research to demonstrate the off-line identities of the participants, I believe that this would go against the spirit of personal web pages, which are intended to be public but also to afford varying levels of anonymity and a choice about making personal disclosures, such as one's real name, location, appearance and so on, to readers.[4] . . .

In this study I use content analysis—a method used for hermeneutic, qualitative research aims—to explore the themes that cybersubjects address in their sites. I find that breast cancer cybernarratives raise many important issues about virtual representation of the self, body and illness and I described above. I describe a range of issues that the pages raise, pointing to how they illuminate issues of agency and empowerment. I focus in particular on three issues: (1) how web pages describe the use of the Internet to negotiate medical relationships; (2) how the pages contribute to the development of an on-line breast cancer culture; and (3) the ways in which the ill, female body and identity enter these sites through their textual composition, including through narrations of the body's appearance, gender and phenomenological experiences of illness. All three of these issues speak to how women use virtual technologies to negotiate their definitions of self, identity and situation in the context of gendered illness.

MEDICINE, INFORMATION TECHNOLOGY AND EMPOWERMENT

As I mentioned above, the Internet has created a virtual library of medical information that can be surfed and sorted via search engines; in addition to the general search engines that people use to sort information, there are numerous health and cancer-specific engines that direct users to a whole range of sites, from those of the American Cancer Society to hospitals and cancer centers, which offer information about the disease, treatment, clinical trials, conferences, fundraising events and support groups, among other topics. Many of the narratives in my study describe in detail how finding this information, in particular information about treatment, helps women manage illness. As Regina writes in her account of experiencing breast cancer,

> The Internet became my library. I buried myself in its web site and files, *saving sites that were encouraging, deleting those which were too difficult to handle*. It became my lifeline. There was so much knowledge out there, so much to learn. I wanted to know everything there was to know about cancer and its treatment. *I knew I would have to make choices, informed choices.*[5]

Women's own on-line cancer research involves gathering, sorting and learning copious amounts of information. As Hardey (1999) makes clear, sorting through information is not simply a passive act of reading, but involves numerous choices to trace a path through the Web's seemingly endless possibilities. The paths these women trace are not directed only toward instrumental ends. The women's aims are often decidedly practical, but there is sometimes also an emotional reasoning that guides the process of sorting information. Regina describes, for instance, censoring depressing or difficult information and saving "encouraging" sites. She perceives information that offers encouragement to be as helpful as empirical medical data.

Gaining medical knowledge is also used as a way to level the hierarchal relationships that exist between patient, doctor and the medical industries. Indeed, current debates over the deprofessionalization of medicine address how users of the Internet gain lay knowledge of medicine and access health information for themselves, which may have the effect, as Hardey argues, of demystifying medical expertise (Hardey, 1999; see also Haug and Lavin, 1983). That medicine needs demystifying is an oft-repeated theme in these narratives, which repeatedly describe how the world of medicine can seem alien to laypersons. As one husband named Dean writes in his designated section of "MaryJo And Dean's" site:

> Where to start ["on your research journey"]? When my wife was first diagnosed, I must have felt like a new immigrant. I didn't speak a word of the language (of the doctors) and I had no idea what local customs I was violating.[6]

While Dean puts this in the neutral terms of exploring a new culture, learning medical expertise is often described in these sites as part of an adversarial process. Some women, for instance, describe this process in terms of *arming* themselves with information as they try to negotiate the world of high-tech medicine. Their aim is not only to understand their cancers and choose the best treatments available, but also to demand that doctors share the power over their bodies and health care.

> *Dorit:* I started accumulating information [about Tamoxifen] from the net, the more I read the more I wanted to know . . . *Armed with this information* I went to see my oncologist, *asking him why he had not prescribed Tamoxifen for me* . . . [Later] I found several research papers, on the net, mentioning low-dose Megace (Megestrol Acetate) for treatment of hot flushes after breast cancer. *I consulted with my gynecologist, knowing that my oncologist would not listen. This time my net search was received with open arms.*[7]
>
> *Stephanie:* Charlee and I continue to photograph and document my story [for my web site]. Now we are focusing on my ability as a patient to navigate the medical system. While the individuals that I encounter tend to be very compassionate and sensitive, on many days I feel frustrated that the medical community is not sure about how to treat me. Even

> when doctors do suggest treatment, it's very invasive and hostile to the body (chemotherapy, surgery, radiation), rather than treatment to boost the body's natural line of defense, the immune system.[8]

These narratives describe new aspects of dealing with medicine. In her site, Dorit describes a number of acts of active negotiation of her medical care: she researches the drugs Tamoxifen and Magace, reads medical research published on the Net, confronts her oncologist and chooses her gynecologist as the doctor more open to suggestions. Stephanie openly criticizes western medicine and consciously uses her web page as a place to document her experiences "navigating" the medical system.

Reading and surfing Internet health information is a primary use of virtual technologies related to breast cancer, but *writing* is also important. It is in their own web pages that women publicly relate stories about navigating health care. The narratives women create "out" their efforts to understand and master medical language, which otherwise might have been a "secret" aspect of having breast cancer (see Sedgwick, 1999). These efforts are partly negotiations over the definitions of self and situation; relative fluency in medical language may help women establish their own credibility in defining the meanings of illness and treatment, as Stephanie and Dorit suggest. The sites actually vary widely in how, and how much, they incorporate medical language. Some of the women learn medical jargon primarily in order to inform their own treatment decisions and to level hierarchal relationships with doctors, but others also use it to frame their breast cancer stories. Some sites are saturated with medical jargon, but as if acknowledging differential understandings of medical terms, also have a pedagogical, explanatory tone, constructing their audience as clearly nonmedical. MaryJo's site, like many others, narrates her experience by weaving together ordinary language and medical jargon. In her story about deciding between a lumpectomy and a mastectomy, there are quotation marks around some terms that seem out of place, which in this case are the slang terms she uses, like "tummy tuck," and not the more medical jargon.[9] But she also pokes fun at the jargon. A caption to a photo of her husband wearing her wig reads:

> Dean with MJ's $3000 human hair wig! (Yes they ARE made of human hair and, yes, they DO cost that much!). But the insurance companies pick up SOME of the tab if a doctor prescribes it and calls it a "cranial prosthesis!"

Medical language is used in a more serious tone in Lisa's site, where she posts the pathology report from her lumpectomy under the heading "The official diagnosis is in." She has added her own commentary as a way of explaining it to readers. Here, Lisa uses the highly "credible" language of pathology to explain to visitors the relative seriousness of her bodily situation. Her version of the report reads, in part:

> *Infiltrating Ductal Carcinoma*—simply put, this type of cancer begins in the ducts and breaks through into the fatty tissue of the breast./ The size of the tumor was measured to be 2.6 cm./ *0/14 Lymph Nodes* were found to have cancer cells./
>
> *Histologic Tumor Grade 3 of 3*—basically meaning that these cells look as unlike "normal" cells as possible . . . grade 3 cells tend to spread more rapidly and are more aggressive . . . All of this combined put me at a *Stage IIa* cancer.[10]

Posting this report contributes to Lisa's on-line identity as a well-informed patient by demonstrating an understanding of her medical diagnosis. The report is also a medium for presenting her body and her cancer in this virtual space. Cyberspace presents individuals with opportunities to self-describe, inscribe and "rewrite" their bodies because they are faced with tasks of identifying themselves (Wakeford, 1997). Women with breast cancer make choices about representation that are complicated not only by ordinary issues of difference, but also by their differentiating experiences of illness. Here, Lisa appropriates medical discourse to embody her virtual space, presenting her body through the revelations of a medical lens. Visitors to the site may not know what she looks like (there are no photographs), but we know the size and grade of her tumor, the stage of her cancer and other cellular-level characteristics of her body.

Sometimes, in researching and learning medical information, individuals are taking on an even greater aim than refining their roles as informed consumers, leveling the hierarchies between doctor and patient and framing their experiences in medical terms. For some women, on-line research is perceived as one of the most important tasks they undertake. The Internet is repeatedly presented as a beacon of hope. Many of these narratives suggest, implicitly or explicitly, that becoming fluent in medical language and treatments is a key to actually surviving breast cancer, rather than a tool for decision making, psychological comfort or intellectual understanding. One friend named Robin, writing on the web page dedicated to her friend Patti, says:

> Please read Patti's breast cancer story and see if you can think of any information which might relate to her. Maybe you have a friend, relative, acquaintance or neighbor who has had this specific type of cancer and maybe they were cured. Maybe YOU know the answers we are desperately searching for.[11]

The notion that information to save lives is out there, and that it is up to individual patients to find, sort, understand and use such information to save their own lives, may be one of the negative effects of the consumerization of health care. Consumer ideology is highly individualistic; through their shopping and information-sorting practices consumers are meant to make themselves informed about available products that are life-enhancing. The Internet heightens this sense that we are capable of this, as well as the fear that we may fail in this task. Robin writes,

> *My biggest fear is that something happens to her and then we would find information later that could have saved her life, that it was right there all along.* That fear is what spurred me to make this net wide plea . . . Thank goodness for the internet, with its ability to reach more people in one minute, than we would ever be able to reach in one lifetime. (Emphasis added)

Robin wrote this plea in 1998. Sadly, the web site also announces that Patti died in June 2000. When even life-saving technologies are framed as products that consumers can research and advocate for, they become the responsibility of individual consumers to find and get access to. Like the instances in Jennifer Fosket's study where women blamed themselves for not detecting their tumors early enough through self-exams, such examples may suggest that unrealistic imperatives for individuals to prevent sickness and manage their own treatment, along with feelings of self-blame where they cannot, may be among the outcomes of consumer "empowerment."

CREATING SUPPORT NETWORKS AND GIVING ADVICE

Despite its high value to these women, medical information is only one form of knowledge circulating in cyberspace about breast cancer. Beyond specialist knowledge, many women view their own experiences as important sources of information that should be shared with each other. The Internet offers breast cancer survivors a plethora of ways to "seek connections," to put it in Stephanie's terms. These include listservs, e-mail and chat rooms, but also the network of personal web pages, which often provide links to others' web pages, spaces for visitors' comments about the page and invitations to e-mail the site's author or host. The intersections of all of these have created what many see as a virtual community. Personal web sites are often framed as stories that come from women's own standpoint as breast cancer victims and survivors. Many describe how reading other women's stories ameliorated a sense of loneliness and normalized a process that had felt alienating and isolating. Women's experiences with breast cancer may "fall outside others' common sense," to use Arthur Frank's terms, but their web narratives appear to "establish new terms of common sense" and familiarity (Frank, 2000: 327). As Sally put it:

> It was a relief to read that all I had gone through was *normal* . . . I have decided to put my story out here for others to read, so that others can know that *they aren't alone* in this fight.[12]

Many women describe an ethical imperative to share what they have learned with other women through documenting their own stories on the Web, like Mari: "Why divulge all of this personal information? Because I truly believe *that it is my responsibility* to use the experiences, knowledge, and insight I have to help others."[13]

Frank describes how stories "can remoralize," or make less alienating bureaucratic and "disenchanted" our experiences with illness (2000: 321). In women's web pages, experiences of connection, helping and receiving help are part of the moral of the stories. In "helping" others, women construct their audiences as female, usually as sister survivors and other times as undiagnosed women. The values that are generated within breast cancer cyberculture include what Pat Hill Collins (1991) has called a female ethics of relationality, which emphasizes connectedness and empathy over individual survival. Dorit writes,

> Then I found the "Breast Cancer Listserv" mailing list, a great on-line support group where I found people with whom I could share my feelings and fears, express myself openly, and know that someone was listening. Eventually I started feeling better about myself and was able to provide support for women that were going through the same. By then I had learned to ask questions and not to automatically accept everything a doctor tells me.

In sharing stories, women offer each other mutual support, a forum for exploring issues of the body, psyche, relationships and community that are relevant to them, and a sense that their knowledge and experience are resources for others.

The sites are often advice-laden. For instance, women are eager to warn others about the need to be active in negotiating the hierarchies of the doctor–patient relationship:

> *Kelly:* My advice? Get a second, third, and fourth opinion . . . Don't be afraid to ask your doctor(s) questions. And if you do chemotherapy and/or radiation, *demand what you want,* for instance, additional nausea medication if what you have isn't working. Something out there *will* help you—you just need to find it. Don't be afraid to *be your own advocate.*[14]

One woman, Linda, feels so strongly about this, she says, that she continues to chronicle her experiences on her web page despite feeling too sick to do so. This, in order to help others "be prepared" for some of the "betrayals" of the medical system: "*The knowledge that many of us go through the same anxieties and betrayals by a system we must rely on during serious illness forced me to write this for you, in the hope that others might be better prepared.*"[15] Linda's narrative suggests how writing a web page might be considered a type of activism. Like Mari and Kelly, Linda expresses a moral imperative to reach out to other women over the Web and share her experience and knowledge with them.

Worryingly, though, advice circulated on these sites may include pressure to take responsibility not just for self-advocacy, but *also for beating the cancer itself.* In these 50 sites, I found repeated calls for women to take action to prevent death from breast cancer. Women are urged to know everything they can, be their own "best defense" against cancer, and keep getting tested. Fran writes, "Know your enemy."[16]; Geri argues that "Breast cancer kills the unaware, the innocent, the untested."[17] And Sally argues:

> *Every woman is her own first best defense against breast cancer.* Every woman, starting in her teens, needs to become familiar and comfortable with breast self-exams [hyperlinked here to a site for instructions]. Regular mammograms are a must as well . . . Early detection and early treatment can save a life.[18]

The messages that women can defend themselves against breast cancer and can prevent themselves from dying of the disease are not unique; in fact, they echo the empowerment discourse that circulates in much of the breast cancer movement. These messages have also been circulated by advocates of early detection. But the framing of breast cancer in what Christy Simpson identifies as a kind of personal responsibility ideology, in which "responsibility for diseases are presented in terms of lifestyle choices" (2000: 136), may have worrisome effects from a critical feminist perspective. Asking individual women to be their own primary defense against breast cancer is unrealistic, and displaces responsibility for a large-scale social problem onto the bodies of individual women. (This displacement is linked to a broader trend in contemporary health care that emphasizes risk factor epidemiology. See, for example, Link and Phelan, 1995.) And the idea that breast cancer kills only the unaware is patently wrong—it also kills the aware, the "tested"—and implies that women who do get sick or die could have prevented this fate. The recent debate on the efficacy of mammograms to improve women's chances of surviving breast cancer makes this problem even more pressing. According to some recent studies, the increased use of mammograms to detect breast cancer has not translated into better chances for women to survive the disease. (In my study, women's web pages are silent on this controversy, which may reflect that many of the pages had been published on the Web before the debate received widespread coverage in the news.)

There are also calls to take on others' suffering as well as to prevent one's own. As a woman who calls herself Putsy puts it, "We now need to continue to be *crusaders* who tell others there is life after cancer, that there is life after a mastectomy.[19] This call underscores the other-directedness that characterizes many of these web pages. The advice-and-support focus of women's breast cancer cyberculture suggests that a positive or at least bearable breast cancer experience is a social one that involves making connections with other women. Further, there is an ethics of responsibility: women who are sick try to help other women prevent themselves from getting sick, and those who get well have a responsibility to those who are still sick. The norms of connection, empathy and personal responsibility for others that circulate in these narratives are a stark contrast to women's depictions of medical culture, which is characterized as adversarial, impersonal, bureaucratic and dismissive. From a feminist perspective, women's virtual breast cancer communities might be seen as powerful sources of women-centered knowledge and activism that may help to ameliorate the alienating aspects of medicine.

The imperative to reach out to others in some ways defies the individualism of "personal responsibility ideology," since women are thinking beyond the care of the individual self toward a care for others. Women are framing the prevention of breast cancer not only as a matter of personal lifestyle but as a community-wide issue where care for the self and others are linked. Women's responsibilities here are defined beyond the role of informed, healthy consumer. Women must look out for each other and share the knowledge they have about their own illness to help other women avoid the same fate. To my mind, though, the messages circulated in these sites are not necessarily unproblematic. Even though women are positioning themselves in ethical communities of caring, the advice they give each other ultimately still asks a great deal of women who are sick and recovering, and does not ask much of the social systems that need to be transformed to address women's illness more adequately, such as the more radical breast cancer environmental movements and the AIDS movements have done (Clarke and Olesen, 1999; Klawiter, 2000; Simpson, 2000). A social ideology of breast cancer, in contrast to a personal responsibility one, would shift the focus from lifestyle and informed health consumerism, "from individuals to looking at groups of individuals" and the social, environmental and economic conditions which influence their health and illness prospects (Simpson, 2000: 137).

POLITICS AND PROBLEMS OF WRITING THE BODY-SELF IN CYBERSPACE

Technologies of writing and mapping the identity of the body-self, such as those we use on the Internet, help us feel in control. Information technologies offer us opportunities of body and identity composition: through them, information can be gathered and a self can be represented, imagined and textually documented. I describe here the ways in which women are composing their bodies and identities in their narratives on the Web. Yet, they cannot be seen to be wholly autonomous or politically unproblematic. Virtual technologies can be infused with a discourse of empowerment that may not necessarily translate into power for individual women. Cyberspace, which has been hailed by some as a libertarian utopia of free speech, free virtual bodies and free selves, must be seen instead as a site where definitions of situation, body and identity are both contested and are influenced by power relations. It is important to remember that women's narratives are not immune to powerful systems of representation, including medicine and consumerist popular media, and that cyberspace is not a neutral territory in which to construct these narratives. As Rosie Higgins et al. put it, the "electronic frontier has a history, geography, and demography grounded firmly in the non-virtual realities of gender, class, race and other cultural variables that impact upon our experience of the technological" (1999: 111). Breast cancer is part of the Internet market, responsible for marketing products as well as information. In this sense, breast cancer can be symbolically appropriated by corporate interests and dominant ideologies in cyberspace, such as those invested in gendered notions of beauty and attractiveness. The "Look Good, Feel Better" campaign has its own web site, for instance, which celebrates women's beautification after chemotherapy and hair loss.

We have to ask, then, how powerful forces influence women's on-line experiences. We can see empowerment in women's taking in and re-distributing medical knowledge, but alternatively, we can also see an expansion of medical power. Some of the narratives here conceive bodies almost entirely through the lens of medical jargon, a process that reveals women's learnedness of this language but also might affirm it nearly hegemonic legitimacy and credibility. In a critique of "telemedicine," Lisa Cartwright has described how the Internet may not be forcing a democratization of health care, but rather how it may be *extending* the reach and power of medicine by creating a kind of "indirect management of the population" (2000: 354). This process may be evident in this study. For example, the push for women to take charge of their own health that was described in Jennifer Fosket's research is echoed here in women's advice for each other. Arguments that "women are their own best defense" against breast cancer are highly pressurizing. Here women appear to be passing on advice they have received from the medical industry and the media, which until very recently have been touting early detection as the primary response to breast cancer.[20] In this study, women appear to be at times challenging medical authority and contesting the "sick role," while other times framing themselves and their bodies in wholly medical terms and positioning themselves as vehicles for disseminating medical and media advice. One of the conclusions I make from this is that the prospect of health and illness empowerment through the Internet is far from certain, and calls for more thinking and research about how people actually use the Internet for health "empowerment."

That the Internet is presented in many of the narratives as a beacon of hope demonstrates how information technology is perceived by women themselves to greatly expand the individual's role in both prevention and treatment. That individuals have much more access to medical information through the Internet has been touted as one of the great promises of information technology.[21] But the notion that the Internet allows individuals to control the fate of their bodies and selves through researching information, shopping for treatments and advocating on their own behalf is borrowed wholesale from consumer society. Of course, access to information does not in any way guarantee treatments' availability and effectiveness. Even so, underlying the excitement about empowerment here is that women now have not just a chance, but a *responsibility,* to save themselves. The message that women really have the choice whether or not to be seriously affected by breast cancer is deeply worrisome. This message not only offers unrealistic—not to mention highly individualistic—ideas of hope, but it also implicates women in their own sickness.

Of course, this problem is not limited to cyberdiscourses of women's illness. A whole literature in the sociology of medicine has developed to critique the individual responsibility ethnic that is promoted in many contemporary health care approaches (Link and Phelan, 1995; Hallowell, 2000; Simpson, 2000). But the arrival of the Internet and the celebrations of its empowering possibilities may make these issues even more pressing. Social theories that embrace how it fosters elective identity need to consider ways in which the very projects of re-defining the self, body and identity may not always be liberating, but instead may actually *compound* social pressures that already exist for women to keep inventing and improving themselves. For women with breast cancer, the project of self-invention often involves the roles of "restitution" and recovery, relentless optimism and even survival.

This study, then, raises some serious issues about women's cyberagency. My sense is that the structural and institutional pressures that are sometimes affirmed in these narratives work against women's empowerment in many ways. Even so, I still find some reasons to admire breast cancer cyberculture. First, the intersubjective, dialogic processes that are a part of women's use of information technology have engendered networks of support. The relationship character of these narratives affirms what Laura Potts has written about breast cancer memoirs, that they are written toward connectedness rather than individualism. Perhaps, to some extent even Sadie Plant's excited writings about how women in cyberspace will forge new kinds of connections are also affirmed here. Clearly, the narratives I describe in this study describe a sense of female community women feel as members of the on-line breast cancer world. Second, the networks they create offer a new source of information about breast cancer, much of which goes beyond medical knowledge in its interest in personal and social aspects of the illness, and some of which is directly critical of the power relations of medicine. Although I think there are reasons to be deeply worried about the consumerization of health care via the Internet—particularly that it is embroiled with personal responsibility ideology—I find it hard not to admire the ways women are encouraging each other to demystify medicine and level the hierarchies between doctor and patient.

Finally, women are also creating new forms of knowledge about their ill bodies. On-line women with breast cancer are not necessarily interested in gender-play or too interested in leaving the body behind them. Their public narratives do not "hide" the body, and they generally do not abandon gender, beauty and conventional femininity. However, they do compose bodies and selves that negotiate medicine, treatment, pain, beauty and bodily experience in unsettling and sometimes unexpected ways. They make visible what used to be highly private experiences of women's embodiment. In detailing some of the more unpleasant bodily aspects of sickness and treatment, they present women's bodies as they are really lived. The bodies that are written into these sites do not "look good" in the way that the "Look Good, Feel Better" campaign would have them. They are sometimes beautiful and sometimes not-so-beautiful, but either way, they are sick bodies and getting-better bodies and not-getting-better bodies, and their representation here seems more honest and fair than in most other cultural sites where women's bodies are displayed.

ACKNOWLEDGMENTS

Earlier versions of this article were presented to the ESS and to the Society for the Study of Symbolic Interaction. I would like to thank my research assistants for their vital contributions to this article: Maria Biskup, Theana Cheoltes, Sal Haughie, Jr, Keith Okrosky and Theresa Pergola. I would also like to thank the anonymous reviewers for *health:* for their careful reading and suggestions, as well as Lisa Jean Moore, Stefan Timmermans and Peter Conrad. Awards from the American Sociological Association's Fund for the Advancement of the Discipline and the PSC-CUNY Research Foundation aided this research.

NOTES

1. The site was advertised to CompuServe subscribers on its home page and is copyrighted (2000) by CompuServe.
2. In the search of sites, only one site identified itself as being written by a man with breast cancer. Because I only had one male site, which does not allow me to make comparisons with other male sites, I left this site out of the current analysis.
3. I like this term because it allows me to refer to the people writing the web sites without implying that their on-line identities are the same as their off-line identities. Elsewhere, I refer to the people who authored the sites as "women writing in their web pages" and so on, but I do not mean to suggest that I actually have evidence of their off-line identities.
4. My future research will start from the other direction—from the authors themselves, rather than their writings—and examine how women interpret their own Internet participation and describe it within the context of a research interview.
5. http://www.geocities.com/hotsprings/chalet/1674 (emphasis added).
6. http://www.dmccully.com/mjstory.htm
7. http://www.geocities.com/Wellesley/Garden/1562/bc.html (emphasis added).

8. http://eserver.org/cultronix/stephanie/ (emphasis added).
9. http://www.dmccully.com/mjstory.htm
10. http://www.geocities.com/damarna5/lisa.html (emphasis and ellipses in original).
11. http://www.members.aol.com/pattitate/welcome.html
12. http://server30004freeyellow.com/bcancer.html (emphasis added). This person never mentions her name. Sally is my pseudonym for her.
13. http://www.wakeamerica.com/present/mari/ (emphasis added).
14. http://www.azstarnet.com/~pud/ (emphasis in original).
15. http://bcexperience.com/secondpage.htm (emphasis added). Linda is my alias for her, as she is anonymous in this site.
16. http://www.webwitch.com/survivor/
17. http://www.geocities.com/beckholz/Tribute.html. Geri is my alias for her. She is anonymous in this site.
18. http:///www.server3004freeyellow.com/bcancer.html (emphasis added).
19. http://members.nbci.com/svihlikm1/BreastCancerSoulMatesForLife.html (emphasis added).
20. At the time of this writing, the "mammogram debate" is beginning to gain public attention and newspaper coverage.
21. Access to electronic communications is being perceived as an important factor in individuals' access to optimum health care in the 21st century (Science Panel on Interactive Communication and Health [SciPICH], 1999; Cartwright, 2000).

REFERENCES

Altman, R. (1996). *Waking up/fighting back: The politics of breast cancer.* Boston, MA: Little, Brown & Co.

Balsamo, A. (1995). Forms of technological embodiment: Reading the body in contemporary culture. In J. Price and M. Shildrick (Eds.), *Feminist theory and the body: A reader,* pp. 278–89. London: Sage Publications.

Bassett, C. (1997). Virtually gendered: Life in an online world. In K. Gelder and S. Thorton (Eds.), *The subcultures reader,* pp. 537–50. London: Routledge.

Batt, S. (1994). *Patient no more: The politics of breast cancer.* New York: Gynergy Books.

Bell, D. and Kennedy, B., Eds. (2000). *The cybercultures reader.* London: Routledge.

Broom, D. (2001). Reading breast cancer: Reflections on a dangerous intersection. *Health, 5(2),* 249–68.

Cartwright, L. (2000). Reach out and heal someone: Telemedicine and the globalization of health care. *Health, 4(3),* 347–77.

Clarke, A. and Olesen, V., Eds. (1999). *Revisioning women, health and healing: Feminist, cultural and technoscience perspectives.* New York: Routledge.

Collins, P. Hill. (1991). *Black feminist thought: Knowledges, consciousness and the politics of empowerment.* New York: Routledge.

Croteau, D. and Hoynes, W. (2000). *Media society: Industries, images, and audiences.* Thousand Oaks, CA: Pine Forge Press.

Featherstone, M. (2000). Post-bodies, aging, and virtual reality. In D. Bell and B. Kennedy (Eds.), *The cybercultures reader,* pp. 609–18. London: Routledge.

Fosket, J. (2000). Problematizing biomedicine: Women's constructions of breast cancer knowledge. In L. Potts (Ed.), *Ideologies of breast cancer,* pp. 15–36. New York: St. Martin's Press.

Fosket, J., Karran, A. and LaFia, C. (2000). Breast cancer in popular women's magazines from 1913 to 1996. In A. Kasper and S. Ferguson (Eds.), *Breast cancer: Society shapes an epidemic,* pp. 303–23. New York: St. Martin's Press.

Frank, A. (1995). *The wounded storyteller: Body, illness and ethics.* Chicago, IL: University of Chicago Press.

Frank, A. (2000). Illness and the interactionist vocation. *Symbolic Interaction,* 23(4), 321–33.

Giddens, A. (1991). *Modernity and self-identity.* Cambridge: Polity Press.

Hall, S. (1996). *Representation: Cultural representation and signifying practices.* London: Open University Press.

Hallowell, N. (2000). Reconstructing the body or reconstructing the woman? Problems of prophylactic mastectomy for hereditary breast cancer risk. In L. Potts (Ed.), *Ideologies of breast cancer,* pp. 153–80. New York: St. Martin's Press.

Hardey, M. (1999). Doctor in the house: The Internet as a source of lay health knowledge and the challenge to expertise. *Sociology of Health and Illness,* 21(6), 820–36.

Haug, M. and Lavin, B. (1983). *Consumerism in medicine: Challenging physician authority.* Beverly Hills, CA: Sage Publications.

Higgins, R., Rushaija, E. and Medhurst, A. (1999). Technowhores. In Cutting Edge: The Women's Research Group (Eds.), *Desire by design: Body, territories and the new technologies,* pp. 111–22. London: I.B. Tauris.

Kendall, Lori. (1998). Meaning and identity in "cyberspace": The performance of gender, class, and race online. *Symbolic Interaction,* 21(2), 129–54.

Klawiter, M. (2000). Racing for the cure, walking women and toxic touring: Mapping cultures of action within the bay area terrain of breast cancer. In L. Potts (Ed.), *Ideologies of breast cancer*, pp. 63–97. New York: St. Martin's Press.
Leary, T. (2000). The cyberpunk: The individual as reality pilot. In D. Bell and B. Kennedy (Eds.), *The cybercultures reader*, pp. 529–39. London: Routledge.
Link, B. and Phelan, J. (1995). Social conditions as fundamental causes of disease. *Journal of Health and Social Behavior*, 35(Special Issue), 80–94.
Lorde, A. (1980). *The Audre Lorde compendium: Essays, speeches and journals*. London: HarperCollins.
Martin, E. (1987). *The woman in the body: A cultural analysis of reproduction*. Boston, MA: Beacon Press.
Martin, E. (1994). *Flexible bodies: Tracking immunity in American culture from the days of polio to the age of AIDS*. Boston, MA: Beacon Press.
Pitts, V. (2001). Popular pedagogies, illness and the gendered body: Reading breast cancer discourse in cyberspace. *Popular Culture Review*, 12(2), 21–36.
Plant, S. (2000). On the matrix: Cyberfeminist simulations. In D. Bell and M. Kennedy (Eds.), *The cybercultures reader*, pp. 325–436. London: Routledge.
Poster, M. (1995). *The second media age*. Cambridge: Polity.
Potts, L. (2000). Publishing the personal: Autobiographical narratives of breast cancer and the self. In L. Potts (Ed.), *Ideologies of breast cancer*, pp. 98–127. New York: St. Martin's Press.
Sardar, Z. (2000). Alt.civilizations.FAQ: Cyberspace as the darker side of the West. In D. Bell and B. Kennedy (Eds.), *The cybercultures reader*, pp. 732–52. London: Routledge.
Saywell, C. with Henderson, L. and Beattie, L. (2000). Sexualized illness: The newsworthy body in media representations of breast cancer. In L. Potts (Ed.), *Ideologies of breast cancer*, pp. 37–62. New York: St. Martin's Press.
Science Panel on Interactive Communication and Health. (1999). *Wired for health and well-being: The emergence of interactive health communication*. Washington, DC: US Department of Health and Human Services, US Government Printing Office.
Shilling, C. (1993). *The body and social theory*. London: Sage Publications.
Simpson, C. (2000). Controversies in breast cancer prevention: The discourse of risk. In L. Potts (Ed.), *Ideologies of breast cancer*, pp. 131–52. New York: St. Martin's Press.
Stacey, J. (1992). *Teratologies: A cultural study of cancer*. London: Routledge.
Stratton, J. (2000). Cyberspace and the globalization of culture. In D. Bell and B. Kennedy (Eds.), *The cybercultures reader*, pp. 721–31. London: Routledge.
Thornham, S. (2000). *Feminist theory and cultural studies: Stories of unsettled relations*. London: Arnold.
Turkle, S. (1995). *Life on the screen: Identity in the age of the Internet*. New York: Simon & Schuster.
Turner, B.S. (1991). Recent developments in the theory of the body. In M. Featherstone, M. Hepworth and B.S. Turner (Eds.), *The body: Social process and cultural theory*. pp. 1–35. London: Sage Publications.
Wakeford, N. (1997). Cyberqueer. In D. Bell and B. Kennedy (Eds.), *The cybercultures reader*, pp. 403–15. London: Routledge.
Walther, J.B. (2001). Research ethics in Internet-enabled research: Human subjects issues and methodological myopia. *Internet Research Ethics*. Available at http://www.nyu.edu/projects/nissenbaum/projects ethics.html
Waskul, D., Douglass, M. and Edgley, C. (2000). Cybersex: Outercourse and the enselfment of the body. *Symbolic Interaction*, 23(4), 375–98.
Wilding, Faith. (1998). Where is the feminism in cyberfeminism? *n.paradoxa*, 2, 6–13.
Wilkerson, A.L. (1998). *Diagnosis: Difference: The moral authority of medicine*. Ithaca, NY: Cornell University Press.
Wilkinson, S. (2001). Breast cancer: Feminism, representations and resistance—a commentary on Dorothy Broom's "Reading breast cancer." *health:, 5(2)*, 269–77.
Willson, M. (2000). Community in the abstract: A political and ethical dilemma? In D. Bell and B. Kennedy (Eds.), *The cybercultures reader*, pp. 644–57. London: Routledge.

Comparative Health Policies

When we seek alternatives to our own medical care organization, we do well to look at other societies for comparison and guidance, especially societies that have similar health problems or have developed innovative organizational solutions. While no medical system is without problems and none is completely transferable to the United States, there are lessons to be learned in considering alternative models to our own.

In this section, we briefly examine the health policies of Germany, Canada, and Great Britain. These countries are western, industrialized democracies with powerful and advanced medical professions, which makes them generally comparable to the United States. It should be noted that there are, of course, specific ways in which they are not comparable. Nevertheless, by comparing health systems, we are better able to see the consequences and potentials of different national policies on the provision of medical services.

The United States remains the only industrialized nation without a national health program. Many such proposals have been introduced in Congress in the past seventy-five years only to be ultimately defeated. After the passage of Medicare and Medicaid in 1965, many policymakers felt that national health insurance was an idea whose time had come (Margolis, 1981). Dozens of different proposals were introduced during the 1960s and 1970s, and many analysts believed that we would have a national health insurance program by 1980. With the advent of the Reagan administration and a general orientation toward reductions in government spending on social programs, there was little discussion among American policymakers about national health insurance. It appears that national health insurance is again on the political agenda; President Clinton made health care reform one of his top priorities, but unfortunately this attempt at reform failed to pass Congress (Starr, 1995). While proposals of universal health care are again dormant, the continuing problems with costs and access will not disappear. So the struggle for health care reform will continue.

It is problematic to reform health policies piecemeal as has occurred in the United States. Fixing one problem creates another; for example, Medicare and Medicaid paid for medical services for the elderly and poor but, lacking cost controls, fueled inflationary medical costs. Some type of comprehensive and universal national health system is necessary in the United States to increase equity, improve access to services, and control costs. Hence, we look to other societies for models and guidance. Before proceeding, it is important to make one distinction clear. When we discuss national health policies, we can differentiate between national health *insurance* (NHI) and a national health *service* (NHS). Both assume that adequate health care is a basic right of the population. NHI essentially puts the financing of a medical system under government control, typically by providing some type of health insurance where the premiums are paid by taxes. NHI also pays for medical services, so there is no or minimal direct cost to the patient. Canada and Germany are examples of such policies. An NHS, on the other hand, reorganizes medical services in addition to having the government pay directly for those services. It "socializes" medicine in that it treats medical care as a public utility and places much more control of the medical system in the hands of the government. Great Britain is an example of such a policy.

Donald W. Light, in "Comparative Models of 'Health Care' Systems," presents us with four contrasting models of health care systems. By examining these "ideal-typical" models we can see how different underlying *values* affect the politics, social goals, control, costs, and types of administration and shape the organization and delivery of medical services. Using the case of Germany, Light shows how these models vied with one another, leading to the current strains between the corporatist and professional model. When looking at other health care systems, especially in the context of health care reform, we would do well to consider such a schema for comparison. Light's perspective highlights how the values underlying the different models will be manifested in different types of health care systems, with certain consequences for control, cost, and medical care.

Canada is a country rather similar to the United States, although it has a much smaller population (29 million). Between 1947 and 1971, Canada gradually introduced a national health policy that guaranteed medical care as a right for everyone (as opposed to the fragmented American system, which excludes over 8 percent of the population—over 40 million people). The form of NHI that Canada adopted is financed out of a progressive income tax and results in increased equity of health services and substantial control of health costs.

The NHI policy implemented by the Canadian provinces has largely been able to control health expenditures; while the U.S. currently spends roughly 14 percent of its GNP on health care, Canada spends approximately 10 percent. Canada's cost for a health system that covers everyone is actually over $100 per capita *less* than that of the United States (Fuchs, 1990). This saving results from lowering administrative costs, removing the profitability of selling health insurance, limiting the use of some high-technology diagnostic and surgical procedures, and setting a national policy for cost controls. Although Canada has implemented a progressive financing system, it has maintained a fee-for-service, private enterprise orientation in the delivery of health services. Recent research suggests that physicians are increasingly accommodating to the new system and wouldn't want to return to the older commercially controlled health system (Williams et al., 1995). From all indications, the health status of Canadians is equal to or better than that of Americans. (Evans and Roo, 1999)

Numerous health policy analysts have suggested that the U.S. should look to its northern neighbor as a model of health reform. One of the most compelling favorable reports on the Canadian system came from the United States General Accounting Office (GAO), suggesting that if the U.S. adopted a Canadian-style system, it could extend health insurance to all without any new costs.

> If the universal coverage and single-payer features of the Canadian system were applied to the United States, the savings in administrative costs alone would be more than enough to finance insurance coverage for the millions of Americans who are currently uninsured. There would be enough left over to permit a reduction, or possibly even the elimination of copayments and deductibles, if that were deemed appropriate.
>
> If the single payer also had the authority and responsibility to oversee the system as a whole, as in Canada, it could potentially constrain growth in long-run health care costs. (U.S. General Accounting Office, 1991: 3)

In "Health Care Reform: Lessons from Canada," Raisa Berlin Deber describes some of the strengths and dilemmas of the Canadian health care system. She points out the importance of universal coverage, the significance of a single payer system, and the advantages of a health system organized on a subnational basis (the Canadian system is organized by province). The quality of and satisfaction with health care in Canada is reasonably high, and the costs are relatively well controlled. Despite the fact that health care doesn't follow conventional "laws" of supply and demand, Canada has managed to create a health system that is high quality, universal, and fair. There is much for Americans to learn here.

Another model for health service delivery is Great Britain's National Health Service (NHS). In 1948, Britain reorganized its medical system to create a national health service. (See Stevens, 1966, for an account of NHS's formation and early development.) The NHS is a public system of medicine: hospitals, clinics, physicians, and other medical personnel work under the auspices and control of the Ministry of Health of the British government. The fee-for-service system has all but been eliminated: the NHS is financed by tax revenues (through "progressive taxation"), with essentially no cost to the patient at the time of services and with physicians paid stipulated yearly salaries. This system has reduced the "profit motive" in medicine. For example, it is well known that Great Britain has about half the amount of surgery per capita as does the United States. The incomes of physicians are relatively low by American standards (or, perhaps more correctly, American physicians' incomes are astronomical by international standards). Two levels of physicians exist in the NHS, the community-based GP and the hospital-based consultant. Until recently the higher status and incomes of the hospital consultants were a source of dissatisfaction to GPs. While the rigid two-tier system still exists, some of the inequities have been reduced.

During its forty-year development, the NHS has managed admirable accomplishments, including: (1) eliminating financial barriers to access; (2) making the system more rational and equitable; (3) providing care on a community level with community-based primary physicians; (4) maintaining a high level of medical-care quality; and (5) controlling costs. This final point deserves elaboration.

The NHS seems to be a more cost efficient method of delivering health care than the largely private American system. Great Britain spends about 6 percent of its gross national product on health. Specifically, the British government spent only about $581 per citizen per year in 1986 for health care, compared to $1837 per person for all public and private health care in the United States that same year (McIlrath, 1988: 16). And by most measures, the health status of the populations are roughly equal. Furthermore, there is evidence that the NHS delivers medical care more equitably (Stevens, 1983). The British have controlled costs by "rationing" medical services (Aaron and Schwartz, 1984). While all necessary medical services are more or less readily available, patients who wish elective services must "queue up" for them. There are, in fact, two- and three-year waiting lists for some elective medical care. There is little doubt that we as a nation cannot afford all the medical services we are scientifically capable of providing (Fuchs, 1975), so it is likely we too will have to adopt some type of rationing. It is undoubtedly more humane and just when medical services are rationed on the basis of need rather than on the ability to pay. (See also the critical debate on "Rationing Medical Care" in Part 3.)

The NHS is by no means a medical utopia. As a public service, it must compete for funding with other services (e.g., education) and thus by some accounts is perpertually underfinanced. In the past two decades under conservative governments, the NHS has been literally starved for funds. While inequities have lessened, they have not disappeared. The high status of the hospital consultant is a continuing problem and reinforces NHS emphasis on "sick care" rather than prevention. The NHS has recently engaged in a sweeping set of reforms, largely in an attempt to increase efficiency and reduce costs (Holland and Graham, 1994). In the final analysis, however, the NHS delivers better care to more parts of the population at less cost (and with no discernible difference in "health" status) than is accomplished in the United States, and so it needs to be considered in discussions of health reform.

In "The British National Health Service: Continuity and Change," Jonathan Gabe examines some of the achievements and dilemmas of the NHS. He traces the origins of the NHS and points to some of the continuing problems with persistent inequities. He details some of the major reforms of the past two decades, including shifts in management organization, creation of internal markets and competition, empowering the consumer, and the perils of privatization that changed the way the NHS operates. Throughout these changes, however, the NHS remains a socialized system of health care that is "reasonably successful in providing cost-effective and equitable health care in the face of an aging population, increasingly expensive medical technology and heightened patient expectations." While there are clearly some limits on what medical care is available, it seems clear that the NHS as a health policy results in the provision of more-equitable care at a far lower cost than is currently delivered in the United States.

A fundamental emphasis of all three health policies is that they view health care as a right and develop a universal and comprehensive orientation toward the delivery of medical services. As we struggle to achieve a more equitable and reasonable American health system, we will want to look closely at these other systems for ways of reforming our own. David Himmelstein and his associates (1989) proposed an NHI program, largely based on the Canadian model, that represents the type of restructuring that our own medical system requires. These analyses should be benchmarks against which we can measure progressive reform.

REFERENCES

Aaron, J. Henry, and William B. Schwartz. 1984. The Painful Prescription: Rationing Hospital Care. Washington, DC: The Brookings Institution.

Evans, Robert, and Noralou R. Roos. 1999. "What is right about the Canadian health care system." The Milbank Quarterly 77:393–99.

Fuchs, Victor. 1975. Who Shall Live? New York: Basic Books.

Fuchs, Victor. 1990. "How does Canada do it? A comparison of expenditures for physician services in the United States and Canada." New England Journal of Medicine 323: 884–90.

Himmelstein, David U., Steffie Woolhandler, and the Writing Committee of the Working Group on Program Design. 1989. "A national health program for the United States: A physician's proposal." New England Journal of Medicine 320: 102–8.

Holland, Walter W., and Clifford Graham. 1994. "Recent reforms in the British National Health Service: Lessons for the United States." American Journal of Public Health 84: 186–9.

McIlrath, Sharon. 1988. "NHS concept of equality has undergone change." American Medical News. August 26, 1988: 16.

Margolis, Richard J. 1981. "National Health Insurance—A Dream Whose Time Has Come?" Pp. 486–501 in Peter Conrad and Rochelle Kern (eds.), The Sociology of Health and Illness: Critical Perspectives. New York: St. Martin's.

Stevens, Rosemary. 1966. Medical Practice in Modern England. New Haven: Yale University Press.

Stevens, Rosemary. 1983. "Comparisons in Health Care: Britain as a Contrast to the United States." Pp. 281–304 in David Mechanic (ed.), Handbook of Health, Health Care and the Health Professions. New York: Free Press.

United States General Accounting Office. 1991. Canadian Health Insurance: Lessons for the United States. Washington, DC: U.S. Government Printing Office.

Williams, A. Paul, Eugene Vayda, May L. Cohen, Christel A. Woodward, and Barbara Ferrier. 1995. "Medicine and the Canadian state: From the politics of conflict to the politics of accommodation." Journal of Health and Social Behavior 36: 303–21.

45 COMPARATIVE MODELS OF "HEALTH CARE" SYSTEMS

Donald W. Light

The leaders of virtually every industralized nation think that the cost of medical care is spiraling out of control, and they look abroad for solutions and fresh ideas. In the states of the former Soviet Union and Eastern Europe, the crisis centers on legitimacy: given the rejection and overthrow of centrally planned services, what kind of a system should replace the old one, especially when per capita income is only a fraction of the income available in Western models? In the United States and Western Europe, the crisis centers on money, despite their spending more (often much more) than systems anywhere else in the world. This is somewhat akin to a millionaire on his yacht declaring a crisis in his household budget. It implies that something more profound is at issue, namely the high living of systems centered on high-tech medical repairs that endlessly drive up costs rather than focusing on keeping people healthier in the first place. Moreover, these systems encourage societies to medicalize a wide array of social problems that—as non-diseases—are difficult to "treat" and run up costs even more.[1] The exceptions, perhaps, are delivery systems that center on each person having one primary-care physician who looks after his or her health. Even these have begun to devote modest resources to prevention only in the past decade.

Many policy makers and students today compare the ways in which different nations (or subsystems with nations, like their military) deliver medical services. Milton Roemer[2] suggests several reasons why. First, comparative studies are interesting in their own right, like comparing how different people raise children or design their homes. They are also "at the heart of the scientific enterprise," as a veteran of the comparative analysis, Mark Field, points out.[3] Comparative studies can also help give us perspective on our own system. They may even turn up lessons we can apply to our problems. In particular, the basic problems of inequity, inefficiency, ineffectiveness, and cost overruns may be illuminated by comparative studies. These problems, however, involve the whole society more than the nature of medical services. Roemer and many others are quick to point out that medical care has far less impact on health itself than the culture (or the cult) of medicine has led people to believe. Medicine is largely a repair service that patches up or rescues people *after* they get in trouble. Their relative poverty or affluence; their nutrition and housing; the health hazards of their work, home and community environment; their age, sex, and genetic make-up; and their cultural beliefs and habits are the basic determinants of health. Likewise, inequalities in medical care largely reflect class relations, the structure of the economy, and the degree of political oppression or participation. Thus, comparative studies need to take into account these more basic aspects of the societies in which they operate.

To analyze simultaneously all aspects of medical delivery systems and their societies is such a daunting task that most authorities limit themselves largely to just the systems. Some authors provide no comparative framework and describe each country as they see fit or around a few basic questions.[4,5] Some use a list of factors and choose from them the factors that suit each country.[6] While this is not a comparative framework, it does provide a useful checklist of things to take into consideration. A third approach culls critical questions from a review of the literature. One such effort came up with the six listed in Table 45-1. First, in what ways are services and policies legitimated and regulated? Second, what are the services and benefits? Third, how are they financed? Fourth, what are the rules of eligibility that determine who is covered for what? Fifth, how are services and benefits organized and administered? Finally, what are the benefits and liabilities, for patients, for providers, for suppliers, for the government, and for the public? Some systems, like the American one, seem designed to benefit the army of pro-

Table 45-1. Basic Issues in Comparing Health Care Systems

1. Legitimation and Regulation
2. Services and Benefits
3. Finances
4. Rules of Eligibility
5. Organization and Administration
6. Benefits and Liabilities for different parties

viders, insurers, administrators, monitors, regulators, and corporations that supply it more than the patients treated.

A few authors have provided real comparative frameworks.[3] Roemer,[2] for example, in his massive new study of health care systems around the world, discusses all the socio-political dimensions that affect health and medicine and then presents a framework (Table 45-2) focused on how affluent or poor a nation is and how decentralized or centralized the health care system is. Within this frame one looks at the ways in which different systems organize resources and delivery services. Roemer attempts to capture all of these in five components: resources, economic supports, organization, management, and delivery of services. Their relationships to each other are illustrated in Figure 45-1. This is a useful scheme until one gets into the details of what goes into the five components. There, one finds hospitals and clinics under "resources," but curative services under "organization," and hospital care under "delivery of services." The ministries of health are part of "organization," but regulation is part of "management." Social security is part of "economic supports" but social security programs like disability insurance are part of "organization." When one of the world's most distinguished and experienced scholars of comparative health care systems runs into such problems, it shows how difficult it is to formulate good comparative schemes. Moreover, a scheme like Figure 45-1 is not really comparative as is Table 45-2. Rather, like Table 45-1 it serves as a template to apply to different systems.

One other template that can provide valuable insights lists the various targets and modalities at issue.[3] To what extent are different systems focused on death vs disease vs discomfort, and so forth, as illustrated in Table 45-3? How does the balance of focus change over time? Likewise, how heavily do different systems focus on diagnosis to the finest point, versus prevention, versus rehabilitation, and the like? It would be useful to develop zero-sum weights to these different foci. Finally, how does the proportion of resources vary between systems for different sectors listed in Figure 45-1?

COMPARATIVE MODELS BASED ON VALUES

Ideally, comparative models would take one through a common set of characteristics in paral-

Table 45-2. Health Care Systems by Wealth and Control*

	The Degree of Governmental Control			
	Decentralized			Centralized
Affluence (GNP/capita)	*Private Insurance, Private, Entrepreneurial Services*	*National Insurance, Private, Regulated Services*	*National Insurance, Public, Regulated Services*	*National Insurance State-run System*
Affluent	United States	Germany Canada	Great Britain Norway	former East Germany former Soviet Union
Wealthy but Developing	—	Libya	Kuwait	—
Modest and Developing	Thailand	Brazil	Israel	Cuba
Poor	Ghana	India	Tanzania	China

* Modified from Roemer (1991) Fig. 4.1 and Anderson (1989) Fig. 1, to make the dimensions more internally consistent.

Figure 45-1. *National Health System: Components, Functions, and Their Interdependence*

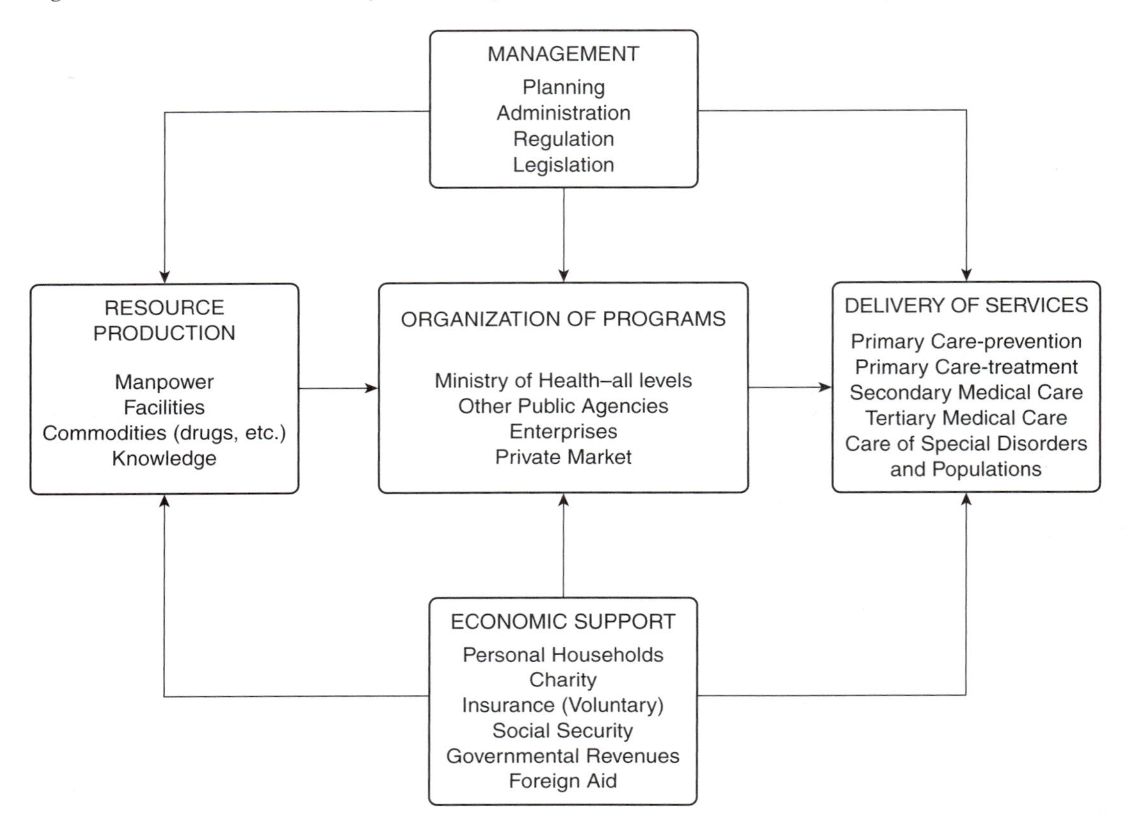

Table 45-3. The Mutual-Aid or Community Model of a Health Care System

Key Values and Goals	*To support fellow members and their families when ill.* To minimize accidents, illness, and unhealthy conditions. To promote ties and mutual support among members. To minimize the financial impact of illness.
Image of the Individual	An active, self-responsible, informed member of the group.
Power	Local control. Mutual decision making. State and profession relatively weak.
Key Institutions	Mutual benefit associations.
Organization	A loose federation of member groups. Administratively collegial. Organized around work or communities. Emphasis on low-tech, primary care and prevention. Strong ties to community programs (educational, occupational, social service).
Division of Labor	Egalitarian. More health care teams. Fewer doctors and specialists.
Finance and Costs	Members contribute to an insurance fund which contracts with doctors and facilities for service. Costs low compared to the Professional model.
Medical Education	Generally not an issue. Logically would favor training health care teams in community-based health care.

lel. Moreover, the characteristics would be connected somehow, so that each model would have a unifying or master characteristic at the same time that it had a comparative parallel structure. Unfortunately, virtually no such models exist, but let us try by identifying what the master characteristic might be. A popular and obvious one is modes of financing, such as general taxes vs employment-based insurance vs earmarked taxes vs out-of-pocket or cash payments, or ways to pay for them such as salary vs contracts vs fee for service. Field,[3] for example, developed such a typology of models along an axis from privately paid services to socialized medicine. More fundamental, we would contend, are values; for values shape financing.[7] They have to change before financing can change.

Political and social values shape not only finances but also the institutional structure of medical services and health care more broadly. They influence how power is exercised. Medicalization itself is an important value. Seemingly neutral acts such as seeking a cure for cancer, treating hypertension with drugs, or dressing rat-bite wounds on patients who return to the same rat-infested apartment building are acts freighted with value judgments about the scope of medicine, the cause of health problems, and the distribution of responsibility. Is the medical issue just the infection of the rat bite, or the infestation of rats in the building, or the neglect of the building by an absentee landlord, or the abject level of poverty allowed in the United States?

From this starting point of values, a set of comparative models have been constructed that show the differences and similarities of the models across several dimensions. These models are *ideal types,* which means they attempt to characterize, not actual delivery systems, but essential and coherent relationships that inform them. Most systems are a mixture of these models, often in tension with one another.

The term *values* means more than "ideology" yet less than "culture." Ideology connotes a logically consistent and coherent set of beliefs. Yet often it cannot fully account for the shape of social welfare institutions such as the health care system. Culture, on the other hand, has such breadth and contains so many elements that it is not useful for analysis. Thus the four models that follow show how values shape the organization, financing, and power of different health care systems.

In order to show the relationship between these comparative models and a real system, we will use Germany as an illustration. We choose Germany not only because all four models clarify the dynamics of its development, but also because the German system has been the most widely emulated in the history of modern health care systems. It may still be. A number of the Eastern bloc countries that have liberated themselves from their Communist past look to "the German model" in designing their medical delivery system for the 21st century. As we shall see, however, what is often called today "the German model" is a post-Nazi model quite different from the original German model, and not well suited to the health needs of industrialized societies in the 21st century.[8]

The Mutual-Aid Model

Long before the world's first national health insurance law was passed in Germany in 1883, groups of people banded together to cope with the impact of accidents, illness, and death on their families' lives. Friendly societies, or fraternal organizations, or mutual-aid societies appear to have started up as early as the 16th century among miners in the Ruhr valley. They pooled small, regular contributions in order to provide funds to members who fell ill or to their families if they died. As early as 1784, sickness funds were protected under Prussian law. By 1854, Prussian law required the workers in all mines and foundries to join either a *freie Hilfskasse* (free help fund) or a *Fabrikkrankenkasse* (factory sickness fund).[9] The main expense and principal benefit was sick pay to compensate for lost wages. Some funds also provided medical services and medications. This movement of workers forming what we shall call generically mutual aid societies became international during the 19th century, spreading to parts of Europe, the United States, and Latin America.[10,11] Employers resisted efforts to make them have such funds, but when they existed, in Germany employees customarily paid two-thirds of the premiums and "managed the sickness funds with the assistance of a master tradesman representing the employer."[12]

Table 45-3 presents the ideal typical model of such mutual-aid health care "systems," centrally driven by the commitment to support fellow members when ill and to minimize illness. Historically, this latter phrase refers to efforts by unions and their sickness funds to advocate for safer working conditions; and by the early 20th century we shall see that some of the most advanced sickness funds also developed programs in disease prevention and health promotion. A corollary goal was to minimize the financial impact of illness. As medical services gained importance in the 20th century, alongside lost wages, mutual aid societies became actively involved in providing or purchasing inexpensive medical services.

The implications of this model for power are local control and mutual decision-making. Perhaps the key word in this model's anchor goal is "*fellow* members." Authority rests in the group as a whole. Social relations are informal and collegial. Social control comes from peer pressure and commitment to the organization's goals. However, as early as 1876 the Prussian state began to lay down regulations concerning contributions and the management of the moneys in order to prevent irregularities and abuses. Otherwise, both the state and the profession take a back seat in this model. The image of the individual implicit in this model is an active, self-responsible, and informed member of the group. Medical services emphasize primary care, and the model implies health care teams that are also egalitarian. Organizationally, the mutual aid features local, small work- and community-based organizations of services and benefits, loosely tied to other similar societies or funds. The society or fund is itself the key institution. As this model began to mature into local health care systems, it tended to emphasize primary care and the use of nonphysicians as well. The mutual aid perspective leads to planning and coordination of services within a consumer-controlled health care system. "Thus," concludes Brian Abel-Smith, "in these countries the consumers of medical care came to be organized before the doctors were effectively organized, and they were in a position to dictate the terms of service of doctors whom they engaged to provide services."[11]

The State Model

States develop national health insurance and/or services for a variety of reasons that center on strengthening the state. In Bismarck's case, he wanted to head off the growing popularity of labor parties by convincing laborers that they could look to the state for social benefits rather than unions or socialist parties. In other cases, political leaders push for health benefits or a health care program to strengthen the workforce and/or the army. In still other cases, national health insurance or services are realized through popular demand, to eliminate the swift impoverishment that illness can bring even to successful families. As Table 45-4 indicates, states exhibit growing interest in minimizing the costs of medical services and likewise minimizing illness in the first place through prevention and health promotion. As an ideal type, the state model reflects the desire of the state to control the health care system, and indeed one is struck by the ways in which different states have taken over and recast the activities of mutual aid groups. Finally, states divide into democratic and autocratic or dictatorial types. The latter often regard health care as a vital political tool for indoctrinating the population. They also use medical services to control dissidents and eliminate "undesirables." Torture and "psychiatric treatment" are examples of the former; the role of medicine in concentration camps, medical "experiments," and genocide are examples of the latter.[13,14]

Power in this model lies with the state and not much with the people, a critical difference between it and the mutual aid model. Even democratic state systems like Britain's National Health Service (NHS) involve little decision-making by the citizens affected. Ironically, their market reforms to make services more "consumer oriented" only do so to the extent that providers and managers act on consumers' behalf. Still, democratic states delegate more and have various systems of councils down to the district or local level. Autocratic states may have such structures but appoint the members and retire them if they do not toe the line. This, for example, is a major concern in Great Britain, where the elimination of civil service protections and the appointment from the center of people

Table 45-4. The Societal or State Model of a Health Care System

Key Values and Goals	*To strengthen the state via a healthy, vigorous population.* To minimize illness and maximize self-care. To minimize the cost of medical services to the state. To provide good, accessible care to all sectors of the population. *To indoctrinate or control, through health care. To enhance loyalty to the state.
Image of the Individual	A member of society. Thus responsibility of the state, but also responsible to stay healthy.
Power	Centered on the governance structure of the society, either democratic or autocratic or a cross-mixture. Secondary power to medical associations.
Key Institutions	The ministry of health and its delegated system of authorities.
Organization	A national, integrated system, administratively centralized and decentralized. Organized around the epidemiological patterns of illness. Organized around primary care. Relatively egalitarian services and recruitment patterns. Strong ties with health programs in other social institutions. Proportionately fewer doctors and more nurses, etc.
Division of Labor	Proportionately fewer specialists, reflecting epidemiology. More teamwork, more delegation.
Finance and Cost	All care free or nearly free. Taxes, premiums, or a mix. Costs relatively low. Doctor's share relatively low.
Medical Education	A state system, free, with extensive continuing education.

* Goals of the autocratic state variation.

who chair regional and local boards mean that the current "decentralization" of the National Health Service (NHS) actually involves more central control than ever before.[15] As these observations imply, a democratically constituted government can be more or less autocratic when it comes to medical services.

The extent of organizational consequences for this model depend on whether the system involves just insurance as a financial mechanism to pay for services that lie outside the state system, or includes medical services as well. It also depends on how autocratic the state is. The key institutions are the ministry of health and the hierarchy of policy-making bodies. The power of the medical and nursing professions seems inversely related to that of the state: the more democratic the state, the more power and influence the professions have. State systems tend to cost less than other systems, and services center around primary care. The NHS, with every citizen having a broadly trained anchor physician, exemplifies this model.

Financially, the ideal typical system would raise funds through general taxes, although often in reality insurance premiums are used or a combination of both. In either case, the state model provides good to excellent overall budgetary control, and it keeps costs within politically acceptable bounds. Granted that six percent of GNP seems high to British politicians, while half again as much defines Germany's sense of an upper limit; when expenditures reach that level, governments take strong measures to cap costs. The United States, by contrast, has neither a budget nor a consensus about the upper bounds of expenditures. It has been declaring a health cost crisis nearly every year since at least 1971, when President Richard Nixon delivered his famous speech to Congress; yet expenditures have kept rising, from six, to nine, to twelve, and now to fifteen percent of GNP. Medical costs now are cutting into such fundamentals as funds for education and into wages.

The world's first national health insurance plan was created by Germany's iron-fisted ruler, Otto von Bismarck, in 1883.[16] In order to quell the Social Democratic Party, which was gaining popularity among dispossessed factory workers who had uprooted themselves from the security of their villages, Bismarck had the police smash 45 of the 47 party newspapers and forbid unions or parties from assembling. Berlin, the seat of both socialism and the largest concentration of Jews in Europe, was put into a minor state of siege. Hatred of socialism and Jews fused in the minds of many, as they would again fifty years later under Hitler. At the same time, Bismarck realized that this suppression did not solve the underlying problems, and therefore he proposed a series of social insurance schemes. He understood the limitations or sickness funds on a voluntary basis and realized that every person at risk must be compelled to join. He seems to have realized the benefits of having employees make premium contributions so that they would share the burden at the same time that official taxes would not have to be increased. Bismarck seems to have favored a state-run system, so workers would realize it was he as the embodiment of the state, and not the unions, to whom they could look for support in times of need.[9,10,17]

Opposing Bismarck were some 20,000 local company, miner, and guild sickness funds averaging 215 members. They appealed to employers and legislators who did not want to see Bismarck and the state gain still more power and patronage. This coalition succeeded in modifying the legislation so that the national health insurance operated through the sickness funds instead of being run by the state. Thus, the final law was a melding of the mutual-aid and the state models, a national set of rules to establish a largely self-funding health insurance scheme to which workers and their employers contributed, but run locally by the sickness funds. Thus, the German system is not "socialist" in the American sense of being state-run or state-financed. Bismarck used the new law "to preserve the existing social order, to minimize social conflicts, and to preserve the state from radical overthrow."[12] Ironically, the operation of the law through the sickness funds enabled workers and union members to retain a good deal of control nevertheless. Bismarck tied the workers more closely to the state but did not alienate them from the unions and the Social Democrats.

Workers in the sickness funds agreed to pay two thirds of the premiums so that they could have two thirds of the seats on the funds' governing boards and thus retain control as they had in the past. Now, however, the workers' mutual aid funds had a stable, much-expanded financial footing, and as the years passed, the legislature steadily widened the circle of workers covered.

The Professional Model

It may seem odd that a study of medical services should only come to a professional model of those services so late, but in fact the medical profession's collective identity and concept of medical services coalesced under the adversity of the other two models.[11] Both the state and mutual aid models tend to draw on doctors when their services are needed and at prices they can afford in their drive to minimize costs. Under German law, doctors were a trade, not a profession, and they were not well organized as national health insurance was being formed. This left sickness funds free to contract with any kind of providers they wished, and they did use a variety of nonphysician providers. Moreover, doctors had to compete for block or volume discount contracts on a *per capita* basis to treat sick fund members, and given the intense competition, the winning bids were low. The impact on local doctors' practices intensified with each round: as more people were covered at less cost per person, it took more business away from private practices at far lower rates.

Perhaps most deeply offensive to gentlemen physicians was being controlled by and answerable to committees of workers with only an elementary school education and from unrecognizable social origins. The committees that reviewed contracts, that investigated patient complaints, and that monitored services were run by workers.

Private practitioners found sickness fund contracts and their clinics politically offensive as well. They stood for a socialist or Marxist concept of health care. Their programs to educate workers about how to manage health problems, their consumer health pamphlets, their programs for off-hours and weekend coverage, their use of nonphysician providers, and their systems for reducing the number of referrals and hospitalizations stuck in their craw. It did not help that the number of physicians more than doubled from 1880 to 1910, putting sickness funds in a buyers' market. Moreover, many of the doctors who helped develop these programs had socialist leanings and were disproportionately Jewish. Their early commitment to developing programs in public health and social medicine is not well known,[18,19,20] though it would become the object of spite by the private practitioners in the years to come.

Little by little, the unsympathetic majority of physicians organized themselves to protect themselves. Only gradually, and after many failed attempts, did physicians succeed in getting one German state after another to change their status from that of a business to a profession. Local medical societies formed committees that insisted on reviewing doctors' contracts with the sickness funds as a condition of membership. These committees focused on strengthening the professional status of the doctors by restricting the criteria for termination, by rejecting a salary if fees had been paid before, and by refusing to work in facilities where unlicensed practitioners were employed. By shaming and/or expelling uncooperative members, medical societies began to bring contract doctors into line.[9,11,17,21]

Then in 1898, a physician, Dr. Landmann, developed a system for reducing medical costs by making drugs available to members directly through the funds at reduced cost, by limiting the number of referrals and admissions to the average rates over the previous three years, and by establishing a system of rotation to expand coverage to nights and weekends. When the doctors under contract with the local sickness fund in Barmen refused to cooperate, they were fired. The doctors protested and went on strike, and eight days later the government intervened on behalf of the doctors. Other strikes followed in towns where the Landmann system was being introduced. In 1900 Dr. Herman Hartmann, concluding that the medical societies were too polite and spineless, formed a militant physicians' union. It launched an all-out attack on the worker-run sickness funds, their contracts, and their clinics. It organized over 200 strikes and boycotts against sickness fund contracts per year. It developed strike funds to provide income to striking doctors. It boycotted employers who tried to bring in "scab" physicians. It set up a job placement service, a credit union, a pension fund, and a burial fund. By 1904, half the private practitioners in Germany belonged to the new union. By 1913, the government stepped in and negotiated equal representation of physicians on all key sickness fund committees. The medical profession, barely visible in the negotiations for national health insurance in 1883, was now a fully equal partner in the sickness funds. It went on to bend them to their interests.

The ideal typical model of a health care system which underlies these and a wide array of other activities by doctors centers, as Table 45-5 illustrates, on providing the best possible clinical care to every sick patient. This means that medicine must be developed to its highest level. This central mission requires professional autonomy and respect. At the collective or organizational level, as Table 45-5 indicates, a central goal is to increase the power, prestige and wealth of the profession.

To achieve these goals, the profession must predominate, and financing must be private or passive so that it interferes as little as possible into clinical judgment and the doctor-patient relationship. Medical services, then, are loosely organized around physicians' practices, hospitals, and other facilities run locally for the benefit of the medical profession. Medical schools play a particularly central role in this model, because they concentrate the effort to improve on the best clinical medicine for every sick patient. The professional model results in an increasingly elaborate division of labor and technical arsenal.

The ideal professional health care system has as few entanglements with other social institutions and community health as is gracefully possible, except to mobilize their enthusiasm and support for professional medical work. It regards the individual as a private person who chooses how to live and then comes in when the

Table 45-5. The Professional Model of a Health Care System

Key Values and Goals	*To provide the best possible clinical care to every sick patient* (who can pay and who lives near where a doctor has chosen to practice). To develop scientific medicine to its highest level. To protect the autonomy of physicians and services. To increase the power and wealth of the profession. To increase the prestige of the profession.
Image of the Individual	A private person who chooses how to live and when to use the medical system.
Power	Centers on the medical profession, and uses state powers to enhance its own.
Key Institutions	Professional associations. Autonomous physicians and hospitals.
Organization	Centered on doctors' preferences of specialty, location, and clinical cases. Emphasizes acute, hi-tech interventions. A loose federation of private practices and hospitals. Weak ties with other social institutions as peripheral to medicine.
Division of Labor	Proportionately more doctors, more specialists. Proportionately more individual clinical work by physicians; less delegation.
Finance and Costs	Private payments by individual or through passive reimbursement by insurance plans. Costs about twice the % GNP of the Societal model. Doctors' share greater than Societal model.
Medical Education	Private, autonomous school with tuition. Disparate, voluntary continuing education.

need arises. To do this, doctors must be free to proceed as they best see fit with as little concern with costs as possible. The nearly exclusive focus on the individual patient contrasts with the state and mutual aid models.

The United States is the purest example of the professional ideal type of a health care system, with all its strengths and weaknesses played out over the past several decades. Its clinical care has risen from the bottom of Western systems to the top. It dominates the world in technical advances, diagnostic sophistication, and esoteric interventions. On the other hand, specialization together with professional autonomy results in fragmented services and spiraling costs. The freedom to practice elaborate medicine and charge fees for it actually weakens the quality of professional work. For fees reward easily countable, technical work over time with the patient and exercising clinical judgment, and they result in many specialists having to take on cases too simple for their training or outside their area of expertise. Besides the maldistribution of specialists and procedures, fees tend to exacerbate geographical and class maldistribution. On another level, the core values of the professional model pay little attention to public health, community medicine, health education, or social inequities. In fact, since the professional model allows doctors to practice what they wish and where and charge whatever fees they can, significant inequities arise between specialties, geographical areas, and particularly social classes.

The pitched battle between the mutual aid and the professional model continued well after the years of physicians' strikes won major concessions in 1913. On one hand, a National Association of German Sick Funds was chartered in 1914 and founded its own publishing company which issued *The Panel Doctor* (*Der Kassenarzt*) a periodical focusing on health reforms and monopolistic actions of medical societies. Based on an analysis of archives in Potsdam, the National Association also published literature on innovative practices in social medicine, sources of cheaper medical equipment and drugs, and lists of generic drugs with sources "to oppose the plethora of drugs and special remedies which had been produced after the war by the chemical industries."[22] Some of the larger sickness funds set up screening clinics, and many were actively involved in public programs or health promotion and prevention. Some established ambulatory clinics, the forerunners of polyclinics. The largest local fund, in Berlin, created an integrated system of health care for over 400,000 members which included two hospitals, 38 clinics, X-ray institutes, dental clinics, pharmaceutical dispensaries, and health baths. Like other larger funds, it offered courses in social hygiene, public lectures, and outreach services. An indication of efficiency comes from records of the sickness fund in the Lehe Quarters of Bremerhaven. Its four physicians treated about one-fourth of all patients in the lower Weser region, while forty-five private physicians treated the other three-quarters. Fund members could choose either the clinic doctors or a private physician.

On the other hand, continued protests and pressure by the militant physicians' union (Hartmannbund) resulted in its becoming in effect the statutory body representing insurance physicians, and the sickness funds had to give them a lump sum for each subscriber for all services, known as a "capitation payment." This effectively eliminated competitive contracting and converted the funds from being *providers* of services to being *payers* of services. Medical societies or physicians' association also took the sickness funds to court many times for practicing medicine in illegal ways or breaching their contracts. The courts generally upheld the funds over the protesting physicians.

Thus, when the National Socialist (Nazi) Party wooed professionals with its anti-union, anti-socialist and anti-Semitic platform, private physicians joined the Party early and in greater numbers than any other profession.[23] The percent of doctors in the Party was almost three times greater than in the population as a whole. This is rarely discussed and not commonly known in Germany, despite all the attention today to the dark history of the Nazi period. Physicians' early support was richly rewarded. Soon after Hitler assumed power in April 1933, he issued two regulations which allowed all "non-Aryan," socialist or communist physicians to be prohibited from practicing in national health insurance panels. The central archives show that physicians' associations did not protect their members from prosecution but instead took up the cause with such zeal that Hitler's Minister of Labor actually threw out a good number of them for lack of sufficient evidence, commenting on the "wantonness" and "enormous sum of injustice and material damage" on excluded doctors.[22,24] Since "non-Aryans" constituted 14 percent of the medical profession, 25–30 percent of the panel doctors in large cities who worked for the sickness fund clinics, and nearly 60 percent of the panel doctors in Berlin, Aryan physicians in private practice stood to benefit from their elimination. Of the 9000 Jewish physicians, only 135 still treated patients (on a private basis) by the end of 1938. How many thousands of other panel doctors deemed "socialist" or "communist" lost their right to practice cannot be easily estimated.

Besides giving private practitioners the "final solution" to their thirty-year-old problem of removing those doctors who supported the mutual-aid model of health care, Hitler also took over control of the sickness funds from their lay boards so they would no longer be "missionary agencies in the area of public health."[22] Ambulatory care centers were closed, because in being more cost-effective, they were "uneconomical." The explanation of this paradox was "that proportional to their expansion, the economic space [in this case of physicians in private practice] is being destroyed. . . ."[25] One physician in an ambulatory clinic cuts into the income of four in private practice. "[These clinics] violate sound economic principles according to which the free enterprise spirit, creativity, individual endeavors and personal responsibility should find roots with a maximum number of citizens."[22] What court battles through the twenties had failed to do was finally accomplished, to shut down what today would be called ambulatory HMOs as the enemy of professionalism and free choice. And finally, Hitler granted doctors the legal status of a profession that they had spent decades pursuing.

The Corporatist Model

This rise to power by the medical profession through the first four decades of the 20th century took place in the context of a fourth model of health care shown in Table 45-6. This model is a synthesis of the other three, a structured counterbalancing of the conflicting priorities and values of citizen/consumers (mutual-aid), providers (profession), and payers (the state and employers). This model is called "corporatist," a European term connoting an independent but publicly constituted body which is not common in the United States.[17] The government sets the rules and acts as umpire; so the corporatist structure is not a welfare body in the American sense of the term. If one party begins to dominate the others, or if the counterbalancing does not work properly, the government may step in and alter the rules. The corporatist model in Table 45-6 centers around the goal of joining together employers, employees, physicians, hospitals, and other providers so that they must negotiate a budget for the medical costs of next year's illnesses. Thus a cardinal goal of the corporatist model is to channel and structure conflict between payers, providers, and patients as they address the problems of meeting demands with limited funds.

In order for the corporatist model to work, each of the major parties must be organized, and as we have seen this happened during the first two decades. An American analogy might be if the medical society, the hospital association, the Chamber of Commerce, a union council, and an insurance council in each state were required by statute to hammer out a total annual budget for all the citizens in that state. Most of the money would come from the premiums of employers and employees (but note that employees pay half the premiums), while the government would cover the unemployed, part-time workers, students, and other individuals who did not fit into the basic employment-based system. This might not be unlike President Clinton's health care purchasing cooperatives.

As one can see, a good deal is subject to negotiation and depends on the balance of power. In the German case, the medical profession institutionalized the goals of the professional model of autonomy, fees, and an emphasis on acute clinical intervention. But this is not inherent in the model itself, and as we shall see, the relentless pressure of costs generated by the professional model eventually has led to some basic restructuring. It is this point which outside admirers of the [postwar] German system have not appreciated.

Table 45-6. The Corporatist Model of a Health Care System

Key Values and Goals	*To join together buyers and sellers, providers and patients in deciding the range and costs of services.* To minimize conflict through mandatory negotiation and consensus. To balance costs against provider interests.
Image of the Individual	Implied in resulting negotiations. Image has been that of a private citizen who comes in when ill.
Power	Countervailing power structure. Subject to imbalance by one party or another. Statutory powers to determine range and costs in the corporatist body itself. State as ultimate setter of rules and referee.
Key Institutions	The corporatist body. Insurers, payers, providers. State as ultimate setter of rules and referee.
Organization	Depends on the organization of the underlying health care system and resulting terms of countervailing negotiations.
Division of Labor	Depends on the organization of the underlying health care system and resulting terms of countervailing negotiations.
Finance and Costs	Depends . . . etc. In German model, employers and employees contribute premiums. Costs depend on results of negotiations and on society's sense of limits. Doctors' share has tended to be high because they run services and dominate negotiations, but not inherent in the model.
Medical Education	Has not been a focus of concern, though model allows for it.

Roots: The Postwar East German System

After 1945 in the Soviet occupied zone, both East German Communists and Russian advisors were eager to correct what they regarded as the abandonment by the German health care system of its original design. It was the concept of social medicine, developed by German pioneers such as Johann Peter Frank, Alfred Grotjahn, Beno Chages, Frank-Karl Meyer-Brodnitz, and others both before Bismarck and in the early days of the sickness fund clinics, that Lenin had emulated to refocus the centralized system he had inherited from the Tsars toward public and occupational health.[26] Faced with mass starvation and epidemics, Lenin established a national system of local health stations.

The East German zone also faced great public health problems from the mass bombings, dismantled economy, and immigrants pouring in from the east. It is notable that one of the first actions by the transition government was to disband organized medical associations. They then set about to establish a network of local clinics and larger polyclinics [multi-specialty group practices] in the cities. They integrated hospital and ambulatory care and hired doctors as civil servants under a central ministry. In short, they created an autocratic state model. As that model indicates, the East German system linked up with other sectors. It established an extensive occupational medicine program, with medical stations at places of work and what we call day care centers for the infants and children of working mothers. A particularly generous system of payments and services was developed for pregnant women and babies, as the single best investment a system can make in preventive medicine.[27,28] The East Germans also recognized women's right to abortion, even though they desparately wanted to replenish the labor force lost to the war's toll through large families and population growth. In general, the public health program was extensive. The East German system also developed an extensive health education program in the public schools, and it made concerted efforts (partially successful) to recruit medical students from working-class backgrounds.

This system manifested several marked differences from the system that continued on its trajectory in the West. First, following the state vs professional models, the East German system regarded individuals as citizens whose health was the responsibility of the state and who had a responsibility to minimize illness, while the West German system tended to regard individuals as private citizens who come in when they want medical services. This led to a second difference, a much greater emphasis on prevention in East Germany. Third, for the East Germans the concept of health was more functional whether you could carry out your domestic duties and work while the West Germans increasingly reflected a concept of health as feeling good. A fourth difference is between physicians as agents of a state ministry versus as autonomous professionals. A resulting fifth difference reflected in the models is that in East Germany more work was done by health care teams and by nonphysician providers. The results were impressive. Starting with significantly worse health statistics after the war, the East German system attained nearly the same level of health status as the West German system for half the money by 1970.

After that, the East German system became more run-down and rigid. Morale dropped, coordination declined, and bureaucratic sclerosis set in. When unification occurred in 1989–90, no one had a kind thing to say about any part of the East German system. As the international analyst, Jeremy Hurst concluded, the system "could also lay some claims to past successes. . . . However, physical standards were low, high technology was lacking, doctors had little autonomy, and such patient choice as existed was not translated into financial incentives for providers. The whole system is discredited by its association with the former GDR."[29] Since similar state models have achieved impressive gains in other nations, one should not let the faulty execution of the system blind one from its merits.

West Germany: Postwar Professional Capture

When the Allied forces took over after 1945, their policy of self-determination contradicted their policy of de-Nazification; for self-determination meant in effect that the advocates professionalizing the delivery system were the only ones left after the panel doctors had been expatriated or killed.[23] They locked in a professional model of health care with measures that prohibited sickness funds from delivering services or running clinics, effectively prohibited group practice, curtailed competition from public health or industrial programs by prohibiting them from treating patients, eliminated the direct election of board members, and required all participating physicians to be members in good standing so that dissidents could be kept from earning a living. As Deborah Stone concluded, "it seems clear from this history that the idea that the medical profession's political strength derives entirely from its special status as a profession or from its monopoly of technical expertise must be dismissed."[17]

There are many parallels in other countries to this striking example of professional dominance from 1900 to the 1960s. In the United States, medical societies mounted fierce campaigns against competitive contracting near the turn of the century and then used a combination of professional pressure, state regulations, and court rulings to oppose any form of prepaid group practice from the end of World War I to the 1960s.[30] The only major difference was that American medicine successfully opposed national health insurance as well.

During the 1960s, the West German system's expenditures rose from 4.7 to 5.5 percent of gross domestic product (GDP), an increase of 17 percent and in line with other countries, but still of some concern.[31] (By comparison, the U.S. system increased by 42 percent, from 5.2 to 7.4.) Then, in just five years, the share of GDP in Germany grew by 42 percent, largely in the hospital sector and through expanded coverage of orthodontic work.[32] The corporatist model engenders consensus and a sense of global responsibility, but here was a case where the government stepped in and changed the rules. The cost containment act of 1977 created a National Health Conference (Konzertierte Aktion) consisting of all stakeholders, state and federal. It mandated that the Conference develop annually a consensus on expenditure caps, by type of service, which would then be monitored by Monitoring Committees in each state. The Committees had to profile the charges of each doctor, and if they were excessive and not warranted, reimbursements could be cut. In the second half of the 1970s, expenditures as a percentage of GDP rose only 1.3 percent.

The government was equally successful in holding down increases during the 1980s, with only a 2.5 percent increase in the percent of GDP from 1980 to 1990.[33] This contrasts with a 31 percent increase for the U.S., from 9.2 to 12.1% GDP. Yet underlying this success was a constant need for the government to intervene because the profession was dominating the corporatist model and creating costly imbalances. The government, as the British so gracefully put it, clawed back many of the profession's postwar prerogatives and attempted through financial reforms to make the German health care system behave less like the hi-tech, highly professionalized system that it is. This was done largely through financial measures that ration providers and suppliers rather than benefits or patients. The Germans seem to understand the basic point that what something costs, or how much providers get paid, is separable from the product or service rendered. Doctors' incomes, or pharmaceutical profits, do not *have* to be at the level they are. The Germans have kept doctors' incomes from rising as fast as average wages for two decades. They also realize that a government does not have to bail out sickness funds when they have cost overruns. Rather, the government's role in a corporatist model is to restructure things so that the funds can control the providers more effectively.

Other reforms suggest the corporatist structure is being shifted towards a state-model system which aims to keep people healthy or get them better by thinking epidemiologically rather than clinically. For example, besides adding copayments for drugs and services as patient disincentives against overuse, the first wave of reforms reintroduced global prospective budgets and set up tougher, more detailed utilization review by payers. Forms of capitation, which the medical profession had beaten back for decades, are back. These changes in effect redefine doctors, from autonomous professionals devoted to providing each patient with the best clinical medicine, to experts on a large team devoted to keeping people well at reasonable cost. In the mid 1980s, a second wave of laws brought hospitals under prospective global budgets and detailed treatment profiles. Even this was not enough, as the professionally driven system kept increasing and elaborating services, and in 1989 the most important law since 1911 was passed. From an historical and systemic point of view, its most important features included (1) breaking down the time-honored separation of hospital from office care in terms of waste and duplication in service and equipment; (2) adding a number of new preventive benefits, and (3) providing people who take care of the long-term sick with both monthly pay and four weeks of paid holiday.

To some with an historical perspective, these echoed some of the changes the East Germans made when they restructured their half of the system after the war. Such an analogy, however, is unthinkable in German policy circles today. Other state-model changes included (4) measures to restrict the number of doctors being admitted to practice with the sickness funds, to force older doctors to retire, and to restrict the number of students trained; (5) moving the service that reviews doctors' practice patterns to an independent, arms-length status and adding more measures of quality/cost review; (6) setting prices for and monitoring drugs; and (7) facilitating the closing of beds and hospitals, including permission for a fund to cancel a contract with an uneconomical hospital.[31,34] There is every sign that the legislative and executive branches, even after these fundamental changes, will intervene again as rule setter and referee, to restructure the German system even more toward the goals and structure of a state rather than a professional model.

Reforms at this basic level indicate that the corporatist model is barely working. Yet under intense pressure from the West German medical profession to bring its professionalized model of health care to the East, together with a general conviction that the West German way is the best way, unification has meant a grand dismantling of the East German system. As of fall 1992, observers reported that about 10,000 of the 14,000 doctors in East Germany were now in solo practice, a decision which almost no independent health care analyst would support given that the German medical profession and training system is not devoted to a sophisticated general practice model like the British. This transformation is heavily subsidized to look successful. Doctors are borrowing heavily to upgrade their facilities through government-sponsored loans with no payback for the first several years. At the same time, they are steadily moving up from receiving 60 percent of West German fees to 80 percent, a major jump in revenues for them.[35] These rates of pay far exceed what East Germans, with up to 30 percent unemployment, can pay in premiums; so operating costs too are heavily supported from the West.

The deeper point here is that the (West) German medical lobby and government are extending to their Eastern half the professionally oriented system which is breaking down in their own backyard and which is ill-suited either to the health needs of East German communities or to the 21st century. Realization is growing in some quarters that the old, quaint mutual-aid or community model may be the one that works best. For example, German citizens have created thousands of community-based, voluntary organizations to provide kinds of care that even their comprehensive medical delivery system does not offer. These center around coping with chronic problems as well as promoting healthier life styles. This is the ingredient which only the mutual-aid model has that fits the needs of future populations, with so many long-term disabilities, problems, and risks through a very long life span: *local involvement.* At its heart are people talking, listening, helping, advocating, and working together so that the culture and way of life changes as well as medical services. This idea is informing the most advanced parts of the NHS reforms in Great Britain, where the purchasing of primary, secondary, and community health care are being combined with a national prevention program around the health needs of communities.[36] In the United States, a similar animus informs such groups as The Healthcare Forum and the communitarian movement.[37,38] Yet professionalized medical care will not yield easily; for it is one of the major growth industries of the 21st century, with heavy commitments from governments and universities. For the long-term success of health care reform, one needs to go beyond financial solutions to the cost containment issues and incorporate the values of the mutual-aid or community model, with a focus on prevention, illness management, and community change.

REFERENCES

1. Conrad P. and Schneider J.W. *Deviance and Medicalization: From Badness to Sickness.* (expanded edition.) Philadelphia: Temple University Press. 1992.
2. Roemer M.I. Introduction, in *National Health Systems of the World* Vol. 1:3–10. Oxford University Press. New York. 1991.
3. Pg. 5 in Field M.G. *Success and Crisis in National Health Systems: A Comparative Approach.* New York: Routledge. 1989.
4. Saltman R.B., ed., *The International Handbook of Health-Care Systems.* Westport, Conn.: Greenwood Press. 1988.
5. Raffel M.W. *Comparative Health Systems.* University Park, Penn.: Pennsylvania State University Press. 1984.
6. Leichter H.M. *A Comparative Approach to Policy Analysis.* New York: Cambridge University Press. 1979.
7. Widman M. and D. W. Light. On Methods: The Paradox of Comparative Policy Research. Pp. 587–595 in Light D.W. and Schuller A.S. eds. *Political Values and Health Care: The German Experience.* Boston: The M.I.T. Press. 1986.
8. Zelizer V. The Social Meaning of Money: 'Special Monies'. *American Journal of Sociology* 95: 614–634. 1989.
9. Peters H. *Geschichte der Sozialversicherung.* Bad Godesberg. 1959.
10. Rimlinger G.V. *Welfare Policy and Industrialization in Europe, America, and Russia.* New York: John Wiley & Sons. 1971.
11. Pg. 9 in Abel-Smith B. *Value for Money in Health Services: A Comparative Study.* New York: St. Martin's Press. 1976.
12. Pg. 110 in Rosenberg P. The origin and the development of compulsory health insurance in Germany. Pp. 105–126 in Light D.W. and Schuller A. eds. *Political Values and Health Care: The German Experience.* Boston: The M.I.T. Press. 1986.
13. Pg. 114 in Jones A. ed. *Professions and the State.* Philadelphia: Temple University Press. 1991.
14. Lifton R.A. *Nazi Doctors: Medical Killing and the Psychology of Genocide.* New York: Basic. 1988.
15. Light D. Learning from their mistakes? *Health Service Journal* 100 (5221), 1740–1472, 1990.
16. Craig G. *Germany: 1860–1945,* Ch. V. New York: Oxford. 1978.
17. See ref. 8, 11, 13, and pg. 53 in Stone D. A. *The Limits of Professional Power: National Health Care and the Federal Republic of Germany.* Chicago: University of Chicago Press. 1980.
18. Plaut T. *Der Gwerkschaftskampf der Deutschen Artze.* Karlsruhe: G. Braunsche. 1913.
19. Kaznelson S. ed. *Juden im deutschen Kulturberich: Ein Sammelwerk.* Berlin: Juedischer verlag. 1962.
20. Acherknecht E.H. German Jews, English dissenters and French protestants as pioneers of modern medicine and science during the 19th century. In Rosenberg C. ed. *Health and Healing: Essays for George Rosen.* New York: Neale Watson. 1979.
21. Naschold F. *Kassenarzte und Krankenversicherungsreform: Zu einer Theorie der Statuspolitik.* Freiberg im Breisgau: Rombach. 1967.
22. *Zentrales Staatsarchiv* RAM. 5361, pp. 317–318. Quoted from archival work done by Leibfried S. and Tennstedt F. See, for example, their essay, "Health-Insurance Policy and Berufsverbote in the Nazi Takeover." Pp. 127–184 in Light D.W. and Schuller A.S. eds. *Political Values and Health Care: The German Experience.* Boston: The M.I.T. Press. 1986.
23. Pg. 157 in Kater M.H. *The Nazi Party: A Social Profile of Members and Leaders 1919–1945.* Cambridge, Mass.: Harvard University Press. 1983.
24. Leibfried S. and Tennstadt F. See ref. in 21 above.
25. Stadtarchiv Bremerhaven: F 288.
26. Rosen G. "The evolution of social medicine." Pp. 23–50 in Freeman H.E., Levine S., Reeder L.G. eds. *Handbook of Medical Sociology.* Englewood Cliffs, NJ: Prentice-Hall. 1979.
27. Henning A. Mother and child care. Pp. 443–468 in Light D. and Schuller A. eds. *Political Values and Health Care: The German Experience.* Boston: M.I.T. Press. 1986.
28. Pg. 84 in Keiner G. The question of induced abortion. Pp. 425–468 in Light and Schuller.
29. Hurst J. Reform of health care in Germany. *Health Care Financing Review* 12(3):84.
30. Starr P. *The Social Transformation of American Medicine.* New York: Basic. 1982.
31. Scheiber G.J., Poullier J-P. International health care expenditures trends: 1987. *Health Affairs* 8(3) 1989: 169–177.
32. Reinhardt U.E. Health insurance and health policy in the federal republic of Germany. *Health Care Financing Review* 3(2) 1981: 1–14.
33. This is based on Scheiber and Poullier's 1989 figure for 1980 (7.9% GDP) and their 1992 figure for

1990 (8.1% GDP). See Scheiber G.J., Poullier J-P, and Greenwald L.M. U.S. health expenditure performance: an international comparison and data update. *Health Care Financing Review* 13(3) 1992: 1–88. However, in the latter article, they put the 1980 figure at 8.4%.
34. Schneider M. Health care cost containment in the Federal Republic of Germany. *Health Care Financing Review* 12(3) 1991: 87–101.
35. Based on interviews with medical sociologists and research physicians who made extensive visits to the Eastern parts of Germany in 1992.
36. North West Thames Regional Health Authority. *Stra-tegic Framework 1993/4–1996/7*. London. 1992.
37. Etzioni A., ed. *The Responsive Community* (a quarterly journal).
38. Shortell S.M. A model for state health care reform. *Health Affairs* 11(1) 1992: 108–127.

46 HEALTH CARE REFORM: LESSONS FROM CANADA

Raisa Berlin Deber

To Americans, Canada resembles the girl next door—familiar but often taken for granted. Despite flurries of interest in the Canadian health care system whenever the United States contemplates implementing universal health insurance, misunderstandings about its nature abound. Indeed, there is no Canadian system; instead, there are a set of publicly financed, provincially run insurance plans covering all legal residents for specified service categories, primarily "medically necessary" physician and hospital care. Neither does Canada have socialized medicine; these services are delivered by private providers. In all industrialized nations, health care seems to be perennially in crisis; however, access and quality in Canada are relatively high, spending relatively well controlled, and satisfaction high, although declining. Canadians remain devoted to their system, but they are increasingly worried that it may not survive.

Recently, several provincial commissions investigated health care and weighed in with their recommendations,[1–3] while the Kirby Senate Committee[4] and the national Romanow Royal Commission[5] are completing extensive research and consultation activities and readying their final reports. What will emerge is unclear, but Canadians have loudly indicated their hopes and fears for the future. Although the Canadian model per se is unlikely to be adopted in the United States, it can provide clear lessons for its neighbor—both positive and negative.

HEALTH SYSTEMS AND THE LIMITS TO MARKETS

Most markets distribute goods on the basis of supply and demand, with price signals used to affect production and consumption decisions. When price drops, demand should increase, with a near-infinite demand for free goods. Conversely, with fixed supply and high demand, price should rise until enough people get priced out of the market to balance supply against this new (lower) level of demand at the new equilibrium price. Yet health care markets stubbornly refuse to follow these economic laws. Economists have debated why this is so and whether they can force health care to behave in accordance with theory. If the discrepancies result only from "asymmetry of information" (because the person who provides services also determines which services must be purchased), providing better information can produce better-informed consumers and allow market forces to prevail. Yet most health economists, particularly outside the United States, recognize that the key problem instead rests with "need." Consider the following scenarios[6]:

1. You want a taxi to take you to a destination across the city but have no money. Should you be taken there anyhow?
2. You win an all-expenses-paid week for two to a destination of your choice, which must be taken within the next 12 months. Do you accept?
3. You enter a hospital emergency room with a ruptured appendix but no money. Should you be treated anyhow?
4. You win free open-heart surgery in the hospital of your choice, which must be performed within the next 12 months. Do you accept?

Although the first 2 scenarios fit the predictions of economic models, the next two do not. Most people agree that the taxi driver need not take you, thus pricing you out of the taxicab market. Yet most also agree that the hospital must treat your appendix, and they would be horrified were you turned away for financial reasons. In economic terms, however, this means that you cannot be priced out of the market for appendix care; attempting to incorporate market forces means that we have set up an economic model in which there is a "floor price" (whatever charity or government will pay) but no ceiling price, because anyone priced out falls back into the publicly funded tier.

Although this model is attractive for providers, who are ensured that they will get at least the floor price, with any additional private charges as a bonus, 2 disquieting consequences follow. First, market forces are less able to achieve cost control. Second, deterioration of publicly funded services is likely because there would be no reason for consumers to pay extra for care unless the publicly funded tier is inadequate (or perceived to be inadequate). Accordingly, Canadian health policy analysts have vehemently defended the principle of "single-tier" publicly funded medicine for "medically necessary" services, not only on the usual grounds of equity but on the grounds of economic efficiency. Multiple payers are seen not only as diminishing equity but also as increasing the burden on business and the economy to pay those extra costs.

Similarly, although most people would be eager to take free trips, few wish open-heart surgery unless they need it. Canadian health policy has rejected the language of consumer sovereignty in favor of the language of need. However, balancing consumerism against need is an ongoing tension. Most recent reform documents—in Canada and abroad—pay deference to both the language of patient rights and the language of evidence-based medicine, with little attention to how these potentially conflicting concepts are to be reconciled.

All health systems must perform similar functions. Mechanisms must be in place to determine how care will be *financed*. Policymakers must determine which costs will remain the responsibility of individuals and which will be *socialized* across many potential recipients. This risk spreading can occur on a voluntary basis or can be mandatory. However, the distribution of risks is not uniform—a very small number of individuals will account for a very large proportion of health expenditures.[7] Accordingly, almost all nations except the United States have recognized that voluntary risk pooling within a competitive market for financing is unlikely to work, precisely because insurers need only avoid a small number of potential clients to avoid a large proportion of health expenditures, often making high risks uninsurable. Canada retains a widespread consensus that a single payer should be retained for core services; the debates are over what counts as core services and how much financing is required.

Systems also vary according to how care is organized and *delivered*. What is the role of the hospital? How will different sectors be coordinated? How much authority rests with physicians?

Finally, systems must pay attention to how resources will flow from those paying for care to those delivering it. This dimension, which we have termed *allocation*, incorporates the incentives guiding the behavior of providers and care recipients.

FEDERALISM AND HEALTH CARE

Because Canada's 1867 constitution assigned most health care responsibilities to provincial jurisdiction,[8] Canadian health policy is inextricably intertwined with federal—provincial relationships. Canada is a federation of 10 provinces plus 3 sparsely populated northern territories. These provinces vary enormously in both size and fiscal capacity, ranging from the Atlantic province of Prince Edward Island, with a 2001 population of 135,000, to the industrial heartland of Ontario, with 11.4 million. The history of the often contentious evolution of the system (and the reactions by physicians) has been told elsewhere.[9–12] From the outset, it represented an attempt to balance the desire of Canadians for national standards of service against the differing fiscal capacities of the various provinces and provincial insistence that their jurisdiction be respected.

Financing the Canadian health care system accordingly evolved incrementally within individual provinces, as they responded to market failure, with national government involvement through a series of programs to share costs with the provinces. Initially, Ottawa provided funding for particular programs, such as public health, hospital construction, and training health personnel. In 1957, the Hospital Insurance and Diagnostic Services Act (HIDS)[13] was passed with all-party approval; it paid approximately half the cost of provincial insurance plans for hospital-based care, as long as the plans complied with specified national conditions. The 1966 Medical Care Act[14] cost-shared provincial insurance plans for physician services under similar provisions. By 1971, all provinces had complying plans insuring their populations for hospital and physician services. Because provinces have jurisdiction, one size does not fit all; there are considerable variations within Canada. In addition, although the financing arrangements were changed in 1977 to a mixture of cash and tax points (reducing the federal tax rates to allow the provinces to take up the resulting "tax room"), the same national terms and conditions initially introduced in HIDS were reinforced in the 1984 Canada Health Act.[15] The system accordingly reflects a hospital/doctor-centered view of health care as practiced in 1957, which is becoming increasingly inadequate.

In order to receive federal money, the provincial insurance plans had only to comply with the following national terms and conditions:

1. Public administration. This frequently misunderstood condition does not mandate public delivery of health services; most care is privately delivered. It represents a reaction to the high overheads associated with private insurance when the system was introduced,[16] and it requires that the health care insurance plan of a province "be administered and operated on a non-profit basis by a public authority appointed or designated by the government of the province"[15] and its activities subject to audit. This administration can be delegated, as long as accountability arrangements are in place.
2. Comprehensiveness. Coverage must include "all insured health services provided by hospitals, medical practitioners or dentists, and where the law of the province so permits, similar or additional services rendered by other health care practitioners."[15] (Insured dental services are defined as those that must be performed within hospitals; practically, less than 1% of dental services so quality.)
3. Universality. The plan must entitle "one hundred per cent of the insured persons of the province to the insured health services provided for by the plan on uniform terms and conditions."[15]
4. Portability. Provisions must be in place to cover insured people when they move between provinces, and to ensure orderly (and uniform) provisions as to when coverage is deemed to have switched. The details are worked out by interprovincial agreements. Although there are some irritants, in general, out-of-province care incurred during short visits (less than 3 months) remains the responsibility of the home province, which can set limitations (e.g., refuse to cover elective procedures). Out-of-country care is reimbursed at the rates payable in the home province. Since these rates are considerably less than what would be charged in the United States, Canadians leaving the country are strongly advised to have supplementary travel health insurance.
5. Accessibility. Provincial plans must "provide for insured health services on uniform terms and conditions and on a basis that does not impede or preclude, either directly or indirectly, whether by charges made to insured persons or otherwise, reasonable access to those services by insured persons."[15] Other provisions require that hospitals and health providers (usually physicians) receive "reasonable compensation," although the mechanisms are not defined.

In practice, this balancing act means that the federal government cannot act as decision-maker, although it may occasionally attempt to influence policy directions through providing money or attempting to suggest guidelines. However, the comprehensiveness definition gives Ottawa a major influence on what services must be insured by provincial governments. The Canadian Institute for Health Information estimates that approximately 99% of expenditures for physician services, and 90% of expenditures for hospital care, come from public sector sources. Insurance coverage for such services is not tied to employment. However, other sectors (especially pharmaceuticals, chronic care, and dental care) are much more heavily funded from the private sector, including reliance on employment-based benefits.[17] Overall, about 70% of Canadian health expenditures comes from public sources, putting it among the *least* publicly financed of industrialized countries.[18]

For decades, delivery was largely unaffected by public financing. Most hospitals were private, not-for-profit organizations with independent boards. Recently, all provinces except Ontario subsumed hospitals into independent (or quasi-independent) regional health authorities, which were given responsibility for delivering an assortment of services.[19,20] (Ontario retains private not-for-profit hospitals, although the provincial government has become increasingly obtrusive, especially for those hospitals running deficits.) Physicians are private small businessmen, largely working fee-for-service, and moving only slowly (and voluntarily) from solo practice into various forms of groups. In some provinces, provincial governments have been attempting to encourage the move toward rostered group practice paid on a capitated basis, with remarkably little success to date.[21] Individual patients have free choice of physicians. Bills are usually submitted directly to the single payer, which means a decided lack of paperwork for either patient or provider. Indeed, in 1991, the US General Accounting Office estimated that, if the United States could get its administrative costs to the Canadian level, it could afford to cover the entire uninsured population.[22]

ISSUES ARISING

Financing the System

In the mid-1980s, Canada faced a deficit trap. To avoid it, they squeezed supply. The federal government unilaterally changed the formula for transfers to the provincial governments, which led to a significant reduction in the cash portion of the transfer. In turn, provincial governments chopped budgets to hospitals, which in turn led to considerable growth in day surgery, reduction in hospital bed numbers, and instability in the nursing employment market.[23] They also attempted to squeeze physician fees. The result was that provincial expenditures per capita for health care, inflation adjusted, were lower in 1997 than they had been in 1989.[6] The search for efficiency proceeded apace, to the point where most hospitals were running at 95% occupancy or greater, and most providers felt that they were overworked and underpaid.[24]

Under the rubric of "sustainability," the pent-up demand for restoring funding (and incomes) to previous levels has dominated recent health policy discussions. Advocates of privatization claim that this increased spending cannot be met from public sources, while health reformers argue that if the issue is the ability to meet total costs (rather than the more political question of who will bear them), a single payer should be retained. Some business leaders, recognizing that the search for alternative sources of revenue may represent a greater burden on payroll, support a single payer. Others retain an ideological objection to government involvement. Providers voice support in theory for public payment, but only if it guarantees that they will receive the resources they require to provide the level of services they feel is necessary. The public agrees; they are highly supportive of a single payer, but not if this means they would be denied care. Although it is not clear the extent to which waiting lists are an actual problem (this varying considerably by procedure and geographic area), they remain a highly potent and symbolic issue.

Another key dilemma is comprehensiveness, spoken of in terms of "defining the basket of services." Although provinces are free to go beyond the federal conditions—which establish a floor rather than a ceiling—in practice, many prefer to cut taxes. As care shifts from hospitals, it can shift beyond the boundaries of public insurance. Patients being treated in a hospital have full coverage for such necessities as pharmaceuticals, physiotherapy, and nursing. Once they are discharged, these costs need no longer be paid for from public funds.[25] Some provinces still pay for such care; others do not. The ongoing debate as to what should be "in" or "out" of the publicly financed services and the role (if any) for user charges, has focused largely but not exclusively on "pharmacare" (coverage for out-patient prescription drugs) and home care.

The "first law of cost containment" states that the easiest way to control costs is to shift them to someone else. These issues have flowed over to massive disputes between levels of government (particularly the federal and provincial governments) and between provincial governments and providers, including some work stoppages by physicians and nurses in certain provinces. These disputes in turn are often resolved by sizeable reimbursement increases, which in turn increases pressure on other provinces to match the enriched contracts.

Delivery

There has been strong pressure to modernize delivery and eliminate "silos," which are seen as impeding smooth delivery and efficient use of resources. The US experience with managed care and the UK experience with general practitioner fundholders are frequently cited examples of what should or should not be achieved, depending on the political and managerial preferences of the observer. The push for integration has been expressed in many ways, including establishing regional health authorities and the ongoing attempt to achieve primary care reform. Physicians within the Canadian clinical workforce are unusual in the degree of autonomy they have enjoyed with respect to where they will work and in the volume and mix of services they choose to deliver.[12] Most other clinicians must be hired by a provider organization and are accordingly subject to labor market forces in determining whether (and where) employment is available. The question of whether this state of affairs should be continued or not is an ongoing source of dispute.

Allocation

Two opposing trends have been evident. Some provinces, for some sectors, have moved toward the planned end of the allocation continuum, usually accompanied by rhetoric about the need for integrated services, better planning, and more efficiency.[19] For other sectors, there has been a movement toward more market-oriented approaches to allocation, usually linked to attempts to encourage competition. For example, Ontario assigned budgets for home care services to a series of regionally based Community Care Access Centres, which in turn are expected to contract out publicly funded services on the basis of "best quality, best price." The competing providers (both for-profit and not-for-profit) respond to each request for proposals; the expectation is that competition will lead to efficiencies (which usually translate into a downward pressure on the wages, skill mix, and working conditions of the nurses, rehabilitation workers, and homemakers employed by these agencies).[26,27] Alberta wants to use competition and for-profit delivery to encourage similar efficiencies in the delivery of clinic services. Some academics suggest setting up competing integrated delivery models.[28]

Considerable attention has been paid to benchmarking, quality assurance, "report cards," and other mechanisms of improving accountability. Those seeking major reform tend to point with glee to any international evidence that Canada is no longer the best system. In that connection, the fact that the World Health Organization, using a controversial methodology that adjusted health system performance for the educational attainment of the population, ranked Canada 30th received considerably more attention than Canada's preadjustment ranking of 7th in the same document.[29] Similarly, considerable attention was paid to Canada's high level of health spending as a proportion of gross domestic product (GDP) (10.1% in 1992), but less to the fact that this reflected the relatively poorer performance of the economy, with actual spending in US dollars per capita being much lower.[30] (Indeed, as the economy did better, the ratio of spending to GDP dropped considerably, reaching 9.2% by 2000.)

LESSONS FOR THE UNITED STATES

Size

A common fear about universal health insurance is that it requires a large and cumbersome bureaucracy. In that connection, it is important to recognize both that single-payer systems yield administrative efficiencies and that Canada's model is organized at the provincial (state) level. Canada's 2001 population was 30 million (vs 284.8 million in the United States); the largest provincial plan (Ontario's) served 11.4 million. In contrast, the largest US insurance plan, Aetna, served 17.2 million health care members, 13.5 million dental members, and 11.5 million group insurance customers. A US model organized at the state (or even substate) level would allow for flexibility to account for local circumstances and would probably result in a less bureaucratic system than at present.

Another feature of size is the recognition that most Canadian communities are not large enough to support competition (particularly for specialized services), even should this be considered desirable.[31] Small size also leads to problems in risk pooling, since one expensive case may place the entire plan at fiscal risk. Single-payer models encouraging cooperation are likely to be particularly applicable to the more rural portions of the United States.

Universal Coverage

A major advantage of a single-payer system is that one can attain universal coverage at a lower cost than is attained by pluralistic funding approaches. Canada has universal coverage, excellent health outcomes, minimal paperwork, and high public satisfaction, although coverage or reimbursement decisions do tend to become political. One key advantage is the avoidance of risk selection; no one is uninsurable. In a pluralistic system, government often ends up with the worst risks, and the high costs associated with them. A single payer allows these costs to be spread more equitably. Canadian health policy largely accepts the limitations of markets in health care, at least for the portions deemed medically necessary.

It is striking that there are more people in the United States without health insurance than the entire population of Canada, with many more in the United States underinsured. Even in 1998, the United States was spending more per capita from public funds for health care than was Canada, in addition to the considerable spending from private sources.[18] Hospitals, physicians, and patients are faced with considerably less administrative costs than in the United States, although this savings may also translate into considerably less administrative data. The one component in Canada that does use a US mix of public and private financing—outpatient pharmaceuticals—is the one part of the system where costs have been rising most quickly, and access is seen as most problematic.

Jurisdiction

Another lesson is that federalism imposes difficulties. Health policy has been damaged by the pitched battles between the national and provincial governments, which have also undermined public confidence in the system. The balance between imposing national standards (and accountability for money spent) and respecting provincial jurisdiction and allowing flexibility is a tricky one, and it would be hard to argue that the present mix is optimal.

CONCLUSION

Despite the angst, the objective evidence suggests that the Canadian model has much to recommend it. Ironically, it is most threatened by proximity to the United States, and the concerted attacks from those favoring for-profit, market-oriented care on both sides of the border.[32,33] The success of earlier reforms may also have produced an excess of "efficiency" at the expense of health care workers and clients alike.[34] Nonetheless, the Romanow Commission has elicited a national, and heartfelt, public reaction. Canadians prize their system of universal coverage. Various changes of the margin are likely. The shape of the overall system, however, will probably remain relatively stable. The major lesson of the Canadian model is precisely the reluctance of Canadians to lose it.

ACKNOWLEDGMENTS

I thank the organizers and participants in the Rekindling Reform conference, particularly Drs

O. Fein and W. Glazer, and the anonymous reviewers of this report.

REFERENCES

1. *Report and Recommendations: Emerging Solutions.* Québec, Québec: Commission d'étude sur les services de santè et les services sociaux (CESSSS); December 18, 2000. Available at: http://www.cessss.gouv.qc.ca/pdf/en/01-109-01a.pdf. Accessed October 11, 2002.
2. *Report of the Premier's Advisory Council on Health. A Framework for Reform.* Edmonton, Alberta: Premier's Advisory Council on Health for Alberta; December 2001. Available at: http://www.gov.ab.ca/home/health_first/documents maz_report.cfm. Accessed October 11, 2002.
3. *Caring for Medicare: Sustaining a Quality System.* Regina, Saskatchewan: Saskatchewan Commission on Medicare; April 6, 2001. Available at: http://www.health.gov.sk.ca/info_center_pub commission_on_medicare_bw.pdf. Accessed October 11, 2002.
4. *The Health of Canadians: The Federal Role.* 6 vol. Ottawa, Ontario: Standing Senate Committee on Social Affairs Science and Technology; 2001–2002. Available at: http://www.parl.gc.ca/37/2/parlbus/commbus/sentate/com-e/soci-e/rep-e/repoct02vol6-e.htm. Accessed November 22, 2002.
5. Commission on the Future of Health Care in Canada. Shape the future of health care: interim report. Available at: http://www.healthcarecommission.ca.gov. Accessed October 11, 2002.
6. Deber RB. Getting what we pay for: myths and realities about financing Canada's health care system. *Health Law Can.* 2000;21(2):9–56. Available at: http://www.utoronto.ca/hpme/dhr/pdf/atrevised3.pdf. Accessed November 22, 2002.
7. Forget EL, Deber RB, Roos LL. Medical savings accounts: will they reduce costs? *Can Med Assoc J.* 2002; 167:143–147.
8. *The Constitution Acts, 1867 to 1982.* Ottawa, Ontario: Government of Canada; 1982.
9. Taylor MG. *Health Insurance and Canadian Public Policy. The Seven Decisions That Created the Canadian Health Insurance System and Their Outcomes.* 2nd ed. Kingston, Ontario: McGill–Queen's University Press; 1987.
10. Maioni A. Parting at the crossroads: the development of health insurance in Canada and the United States. *Comp Polit.* 1997;29:411–432.
11. Naylor CD. *Private Practice, Public Payment: Canadian Medicine and the Politics of Health Insurance 1911–1966.* Kingston, Ontario: McGill–Queen's University Press; 1986.
12. Tuohy CH. *Accidental Logics: The Dynamics of Change in the Health Care Arena in the United States, Britain and Canada.* New York, NY: Oxford University Press; 1999.
13. Government of Canada. *Hospital Insurance and Diagnostic* Services Act. Statutes of Canada. 5-6 Elizabeth II (c. 28, S1 1957), 1957.
14. Government of Canada. *Medical Care Act.* Statutes of Canada (c. 64, s 1), 1966–1967.
15. Government of Canada. *Canada Health Act, Bill C-3.* Statutes of Canada, 32-33 Elizabeth II (RSC 1985, c 6; RSC 1989, c C-6), 1984.
16. *Canada Royal Commission on Health Services,* Vol 1. Ottawa, Ontario: Canada Royal Commission on Health Services; 1964.
17. *Preliminary Provincial and Territorial Government Health Expenditure Estimates 1974/1975 to 2001/2002.* Ottawa, Ontario: Canadian Institute for Health Information; October 2001.
18. *OECD Health Data 2001: A Comparative Analysis of 30 OECD Countries* [CD-ROM]. Paris, France: Organization for Economic Cooperation and Development.
19. Church J, Barker P. Regionalization of health services in Canada: a critical perspective. *Int J Health Serv.* 1998;28:467–486.
20. Lomas J, Woods J, Veenstra G. Devolving authority for health care in Canada's provinces, I: an introduction to the issues. *Can Med Assoc J.* 1997;156:371–377.
21. Hutchison B, Abelson J, Lavis J. Primary care in Canada: so much innovation so little change. *Health Aff (Millwood).* 2001;20(3):116–131.
22. *Canadian Health Insurance: Lessons for the United States. Report to the Chairman, Committee on Government Operations. House of Representatives.* Washington, DC: US General Accounting Office; 1991.
23. Naylor CD. Health care in Canada: incrementalism under fiscal duress. *Health Aff (Millwood).* 1999;18(3):9–26.
24. Armstrong P, Armstrong H, Coburn D, eds. *Unhealthy Times: Political Economy Perspectives on Health and Care in Canada.* Don Mills, Ontario: Oxford University Press; 2001.
25. Williams AP, Deber RB, Baranek P, Gildiner A. From Medicare to home care: globalization, state retrenchment and the profitization of Canada's health care system. In: Armstrong P, Armstrong H, Coburn D, eds. *Unhealthy Times: Political Economy Perspectives on Health and Care in Canada.* Don Mills, Ontario: Oxford University Press; 2001: 7–30.

26. Baranek P, Deber RB, Williams AP. Policy trade-offs in "home care": the Ontario example. *Can Public Adm*. 1999;42(1):69–92.
27. Williams AP, Barnsley J, Leggat S, Deber RB, Baranek P. Long term care goes to market: managed competition and Ontario's reform of community-based services. *Can J Aging*. 1999;18(2): 125–151.
28. Leatt P, Pink GH. Towards a Canadian model of integrated healthcare. *HealthcarePapers* 2000;1 (2):13–36.
29. *The World Health Report 2000: Health Systems: Improving Performance*. Geneva, Switzerland: World Health Organization; 2000.
30. Deber RB, Swan B. Canadian health expenditures: where do we really stand internationally? *Can Med Assoc J*. 1999;160:1730–1734.
31. Griffin P, Cockerill R, Deber RB. Potential impact of population-based funding on delivery of pediatric services. *Ann R Coll Physicians Surg Can*. 2001;34:272–279.
32. Evans RG. Going for the gold: the redistributive agenda behind market-based health care reform. *J Health Polit Policy Law*. 1997;22:427–466.
33. Evans RG, Roos NP. What is right about the Canadian health care system? *Milbank Q*. 1999; 77:393–399.
34. Stein JG. *The Cult of Efficiency*. Toronto, Ontario: House of Anansi Press Ltd; 2001.

47 *The British National Health Service: Continuity and Change**

Jonathan Gabe

INTRODUCTION

The British National Health Service (NHS), since its inception over half a century ago, has frequently been recognized as providing an alternative model to the predominantly private health insurance based system found in the United States. For some American commentators the NHS appears to be the answer to escalating health care costs, spiraling medical negligence cases, and gross inequalities in access to health care. For others it represents the worst aspects of centralized planning and collectivism, restricted by underfunding, an inability to keep pace with the latest medical advances, and a lack of responsiveness to consumer demand.

This chapter will attempt to provide an account of the British model of health care organization and, in so doing, offer a basis for assessing these competing versions of reality. It will start by briefly documenting the origins of the NHS and the way in which its structure derived from attempts to resolve the competing claims of different interest groups. Consideration will then be given to the achievements and failures of the health service, especially prior to its reorganization in the late 1980s. The consequences of this reorganization for the social relations of health care within the NHS and for the boundary between public and private health care provision will then be assessed.

THE ORIGINS OF THE NHS

The National Health Service became a reality in July 1948, two years after it was established under the NHS Act. It represented a radical departure from the previous system of health care organization in Britain, with health care being provided free to all at the point of delivery and

*Updated for the seventh edition.

funded mainly by direct taxation, with limited finance from social insurance contributions.

The new service rested on four principles—collectivism, comprehensiveness, equality, and universalism.[1] It was accepted that the state should take responsibility for the health of all its citizens and that the service provided should be comprehensive. The new service was also expected to be of a uniformly high standard throughout the country and to be available to everyone, free at the point of use.

Under the new arrangements hospitals were to be nationalized and organized on a regional basis, with consultants and their juniors being paid a salary for the hours worked. Community-based general practitioners (GPs) (and other professionals such as dentists), on the other hand, remained independent entrepreneurs who determined how and where they worked and were to be paid by a capitation fee for each NHS patient on their list. Both consultants and GPs could still undertake private practice, but the conditions under which they did so were somewhat different. A patient consulting a GP privately would have to pay both a fee and the full cost of any prescription. The hospital consultant, on the other hand, having seen a patient privately, could admit him or her as an NHS patient to be treated at the public's expense.[2] The third element of the system, alongside hospitals and general practice, was the local authorities. They were to provide domiciliary care such as health visiting and environmental and preventive services.

These reforms had not been achieved without a struggle. The post-war Labour government, and in particular its Minister of Health, Aneurin Bevan, had had to work hard to persuade the different sections of the medical profession to join the service, and the resulting arrangements reflected the compromises he had had to make. For instance, he won over the influential hospital consultants by giving up plans for local authority control of hospital services and agreeing to their nationalization. This shift to national state ownership was seen by the consultants as the best way of generating the resources needed for the development of scientific medicine.[3] At the same time the teaching hospitals, in which many of the more influential consultants worked, were advantaged by an agreement to finance them directly from the Ministry of Health. These doctors were also persuaded by plans to allow them to maintain a high degree of control over their conditions of employment (e.g., deciding promotions and additional payments through merit awards) and clinical decision making (almost regardless of explicit resource implications) and to continue to undertake private work. As Bevan subsequently put it, he had won the support of the consultants by "stuffing their mouths with gold."[4]

General practitioners, represented by the British Medical Association, were for the most part also persuaded at the eleventh hour by the offer of continuing independent status, free from the constraints of the local authorities. In addition, they retained clinical autonomy to prescribe and refer patients to hospital specialists at their own discretion. This countered the trend to increasing specialization found in the US and elsewhere and made sure that general practice survived in Britain.[1]

In addition to winning the support of most of the medical profession, Bevan was also able to count on the backing of the civil servants and administrators, or "rational paternalists,"[5] who were responsible for negotiating the future form of the health service. Apparently, they favored a move to a National Health Service less on grounds of righting social injustice than because of what they perceived as organizational incompetence and inefficiency.

Moreover, the time was ripe for change. Over the previous two decades dissatisfaction about the funding and organization of the existing National Health Insurance (NHI) based system had grown. In the 1930s the NHI scheme was facing increasing financial difficulties, as those covered found themselves unable to pay their premiums, and influential voices criticized the service's organizational arrangements for being fragmentary and muddled.[6] In addition, there appeared to be widespread public support for change, especially amongst the labour movement, whose support for the war effort between 1939 and 1945 had arguably been underpinned by the promise of a health service (in the Beveridge Report of 1942) that would meet the needs of the people.[7] And the war had already resulted in the government creating a temporary administrative framework for co-ordinating both public and private hospitals on a regional basis. Such an experience was said to have "brought home to all concerned the failings of Britain's hospital system."[8]

These circumstances thus provided a favorable context for the radical changes that the Labour government had proposed. As we have seen, however, they were won at the price of the medical profession's continuing autonomy.

THE STRENGTHS AND WEAKNESSES OF THE NHS

When the NHS was first established, it was naively assumed that it would lead to a reduction in health care costs as avoidable problems of ill health were cleared up and demand declined.[9] In practice, along with other industrialized countries, the NHS soon found that demand continued to outstrip supply, partly as a result of an ageing population and heightened patient and doctor expectations following medical advances in diagnosis and treatment.

Against this background, how successful has the NHS been in providing an economical and equitable health service that meets patients' needs? In financial terms the NHS has had some success, although supporters have long argued that it has suffered from underfunding. From the start there was a lack of political will to commit the resources necessary to meet Bevan's remit for the service.[9] With the government determining and controlling the level of overall spending to meet health needs, costs were, for the most part, rigidly contained. By 1960, however, shortcomings in the service such as long waiting lists and dilapidated hospital buildings were so apparent that the Conservative government was forced to increase expenditure, and subsequent governments have followed suit. Between 1960 and 1975 the NHS's share of the Gross National Product (GNP) rose from 3.8% to 5.7%. During the 1980s expenditure stayed at 6.1% but increased to 6.6% in 1991.[10] Despite this increase, the UK still spends significantly less of its GNP on health compared with other OECD countries and in particular Germany and the US (see Table 47–1). Moreover, its administrative costs are said to be substantially less than other countries, amounting to less than 5%, compared with 10% in France and 20% in the US.[12]

In 2000 the Labour government initiated a plan to close the gap in health care spending between the UK and other European countries. It intends to increase its spending annually by 6.1% between April 2000 and March 2004. This will rival the highest annual rate of growth in NHS spending of 6.4% between 1971 and 1976 and, it is claimed, will bring the UK's health expenditure up to the European average by 2004.[13]

The desire to control NHS costs has also resulted in the introduction of direct charges for some services, thereby breaking with the principle of free treatment. In 1951 the Labour government imposed charges for spectacles and dentures, and the Conservatives followed suit later in the year by introducing prescription charges.[9] Thereafter both Labour and Conserva-

Table 47–1. Health Expenditure As a Proportion of Gross Domestic Product

Country	% of GDP on Public and Private Health Care (2000)
Canada	9.1
France	9.5
Germany	10.6
Greece	8.3
Netherlands	8.1
Sweden	8.4
UK	7.3
US	13.0

Source: WHO (2003)[11]

tive governments gradually increased charges, although with varying degrees of enthusiasm. For instance, in the mid-1970s the Labour government held down health charges so that they constituted only 2% of NHS expenditure. Following the election of the Conservatives in 1979, income derived from charges increased to approximately 4% of NHS expenditure, with prescription charges increasing by 2300% between 1979 and 1994.[14] These increases have been offset to some extent by exemptions; for example, in 2002 86% of prescription items were dispensed free to patients in England.[15] However, it is generally accepted that charges have had the effect of reducing service demand, especially by the poor and the elderly.[9]

At the same time, budgetary constraints have helped to explain why the UK has adopted new medical technologies more slowly and in smaller quantities than other countries. Despite being at the forefront of many technological advances, from artificial hips to CT scanners, their uptake in the UK has often been relatively slow when compared with, say, other European countries. For instance, in 1986 there were 2.7 CT scanners per million inhabitants in the UK compared with 6.9 in Germany and 4.6 in Denmark.[16] A similar variability, with the UK low down the league, is found in data for the number of patients receiving kidney dialysis or with functioning kidney transplants. In 1986, 242 patients per million were treated for irreversible kidney failure in the UK, compared with 333 per million in West Germany and 392 per million in Belgium.[17] Likewise, the volume of medicines consumed in the UK is well below the European Community average[18] (see Table 44–2).

It would thus seem that the NHS has been reasonably economical, but what has been the cost in terms of health care provision? How equitable a service has the NHS provided? And has it provided equal access to all citizens regardless of where they live, their class, gender, or race? In terms of equitable spatial distribution, the NHS seems to have had some success. In 1948 one of the most glaring inequalities was in the unequal distribution of GPs, with inner cities and socially isolated rural areas being particularly poorly served. The NHS attempted to tackle the situation by requiring GPs who wanted to set up practice to apply for permission to do so, with those wanting to practice in "over-doctored" areas being turned down. As a result, the proportion of the population in "under-doctored" areas fell sharply from around 50% in 1952 to less than 2% in 1982.[19] Within Inner London, however, access to GPs has remained relatively poor.[20]

Attempts to reduce regional inequalities in access to hospital facilities took rather longer to develop and, as a result, inherited spatial inequalities became "entrenched."[14] It was not until 1975 that the Labour government established the Resource Allocation Working Party (RAWP) to calculate the needs of each region by size of population (controlling for age and gender) and

Table 47–2. Consumption of Pharmaceuticals in the European Community, 1987

Country	Volume of Drugs Consumed Per Person*
Belgium	210
France	292
Greece	74
Netherlands	75
Italy	174
Spain	105
UK	100
West Germany	168
European Community average	149

*The volume of data are scaled so that the UK consumption is defined as 100
Source: Burstall 1990

standardized mortality ratios. The resources required to meet the regions' needs in terms of these criteria were then compared with actual revenue and distributed accordingly. Despite the existence of a formula to calculate and distribute fairly the resources available to health care across the regions, it appears that the NHS is still suffering from an unequal spatial distribution of funds. In 1998–9 eight Health Authorities in England were receiving at least £10 million more than the target, while another nine Health Authorities were receiving at least £10 million below their target level.[13]

In addition to spatial inequality, there is also the question of inequality of access and use by class, gender, and race. Studies concerned with class differences in access and use have presented a rather mixed picture. It seems that working-class people use NHS general practitioners and hospital outpatient services more than those from other social classes, but they also have greater need, as a larger proportion of them are ill at any one time.[21] When it comes to illness prevention and health promotion, however, those in lower occupational groups who are in greatest need make the least use of the services provided. Class differences have been found in the use of family-planning clinics, antenatal classes, immunization, well men clinics, and screening for cervical cancer.[21,22]

There is also some evidence that the quality of care provided varies by class. Studies of general practice consultations indicate that better-off patients have longer consultations and ask for and are given more explanations.[23] Such preferential treatment, however, does not necessarily lead to a better understanding of the information provided by the doctors. One study, which observed GP consultations and then interviewed the patients, found that while better-off patients were slightly less likely to misunderstand what they had been told, their commitment to treatment was similar to that of other social classes.[24]

These class variations are in turn reinforced by gender and racial inequalities. For example, while women have benefited from much greater access to medical care under the NHS, their needs have only been partially met.[25] While they are more likely than men to suffer from chronic, degenerative illnesses, treatment for these illnesses on the NHS has been under-resourced compared with treatments for acute illnesses.[26] At the same time, women tend to find that their experiences continue to be devalued in comparison with the "expert" knowledge of their doctors, and they consequently end up as the passive victims of these doctors' ministrations.[25] This experience is most commonly reported by women in pregnancy and childbirth, although some NHS maternity units have recently developed strategies to enable women to be more active participants in their own labor.[27]

Similarly, class differences in access and use of services are exacerbated by racial factors. On the whole, ethnic minority groups make greater use of the health service than the white majority.[28] However, the services that they do use tend to be of poorer quality. This is because black people are concentrated in inner city areas, where services tend to be more poorly resourced.[29] For example, it is in the inner city that one finds most single-handed GPs, often working from inadequate premises and lacking support from a primary health care team.[30] Indeed, it is the recognition of these inferior services that has lead some black people to seek a second opinion from a private medical practitioner, despite the cost, which they can often ill afford.[31] At the same time, insufficient concern has been shown by the health service for their specific health needs. For instance, the level of service for sickle cell sufferers amongst Afro-Caribbeans remains poor in many places despite persistent lobbying and local activism.[32] In addition to this institutional racism, there is evidence that black people experience personal racism at the hands of NHS health care workers. For example, hospital midwives and GPs have been shown to hold negative stereotypes of South Asian patients as attention seeking and noncompliant, which has affected the quality of care provided.[33]

Despite these inequalities in access and use of the service, the NHS as an institution still remains remarkably popular across all social groups. According to the results of the British Attitude Survey, collective support for the NHS, as for other welfare services, remained high and even increased during the 1980s. At a time when the dominant theme in welfare policy was to constrain public spending, the proportion of people who said that they would be prepared to pay more in taxes to support the welfare state rose from 32% in 1983 to 56% in 1989.[34] The NHS was a particular beneficiary, with 84% stating that they saw it as a priority for extra spending in 1989, compared with 63% in 1983. At the same time, there was increased concern about the quality of NHS provision. The proportion who said that they were satisfied with the service fell from 56% to 36% between 1983 and 1989, while the proportion who claimed they were dissatisfied rose from a quarter to a half.[34] Since then, there has been a gradual increase in satisfaction with both primary and secondary care, with waiting times for hospital appointments remaining a main source of dissatisfaction.[35]

In the 1980s the Conservative government felt the need to respond to the mounting public concern about a favorite institution. It blamed poor management and organization and announced its intention to embark on a major process of restructuring. This involved the application of business ethics to management; the introduction of a distinction between providing and purchasing health care; the advocacy of a consumer-oriented system based on the principles of empowerment and self-help; and the promotion of welfare pluralism, involving cooperation between the NHS and the private health care sector. It is to these developments that we now turn.

THE RESTRUCTURING OF THE NATIONAL HEALTH SERVICE

1. The New Managerialism

Poor NHS management, in one form or another, has long been blamed by governments of all political persuasions for shortcomings in the service. The Conservative administrations of the 1980s, however, attached particular weight to this assessment as it coincided with their ideological attachment to the New Right, with its emphasis on monetarism, political liberalism, professional deregulation, and the application of private-sector business principles to the public sector as a way to control expenditure. Moreover, as noted above, it also served the political function of distancing the Conservatives from the impact that the application of monetarist principles to public spending would have on the level of service. As Klein put it, "to decentralize responsibility is also to disclaim blame."[36]

In 1983 the Conservatives decided to institute change by appointing a businessman, Roy Griffiths—then the managing director of Sainsbury's supermarket chain—to review the management of the NHS. His proposed solution was to alter the organizational culture of the service by introducing features of business management, along the lines suggested particularly by US management theorists.[37] Previously management had been based on consensus teams, involving representatives from medicine, nursing, and administration, each of whom had the power of veto. Griffiths recommended the creation of general managers at each level of the service, in place of consensus teams, who would take responsibility for developing management plans, ensuring quality of care, achieving cost improvements, and monitoring and rewarding staff.[1] At the same time the managers were to be appointed on short-term contracts and to be paid by performance as a spur to good management, as happened in the private sector.[38]

The proposals, which were accepted wholesale by the Government, were designed to alter the balance of power in favor of managers, at the expense of other professionals, especially doctors, whose clinical freedom to make decisions about individual patients regardless of cost had previously been a major determinant of the level of expenditure. In the new system doctors were to be more accountable to managers, who had stricter control over professional and labor costs through a system of management budgets that related workload objectives to the resources available.[39]

Doctors were encouraged to participate in this micromanagement system and help secure and oversee the most effective use of resources. While some doctors applied for and were appointed as general managers and a few experiments were set up involving the delegation of budgetary responsibility to doctors, many were reluctant to give their unequivocal support to these developments.[40] As a result, doctors continued to exercise considerable autonomy and managers continued to lack real control over medical work.

Not to be put off, in 1989 the government published a White Paper, Working for Patients, subsequently enacted through the 1990 NHS and Community Care Act, which attempted, amongst other things, to shift the balance of power more forcefully in the direction of managers. The White Paper recommended that managers should have greater involvement in the specification and policing of consultants' contracts.

At the same time, a plethora of new techniques of managerial evaluation was developed. Quality assurance and performance indicators, made possible by advances in information technology, increased opportunities for the managerial determination of work content, productivity, resource use, and quality standards.[41] In addition, managers now had available a growing body of evidence from the NHS Research and Development program regarding clinical effectiveness and health outcomes, which could be used to challenge clinical autonomy.[42]

Under the current Labour government, managers have been given further powers to challenge such autonomy. The introduction of "clinical governance" as a mechanism to control the health professions, especially doctors, has resulted in hospital Chief Executives becoming responsible for clinical as well as financial performance. From 1999, Chief Executives have been expected to make sure that their clinicians have restricted themselves to treatments recommended on grounds of clinical and cost effectiveness by the National Institute for Clinical Evidence (NICE) and have complied with service guidelines for specified conditions under the National Service Frameworks (NSF). Furthermore, managers have also been required to provide evidence to demonstrate that doctors in their Trusts have been complying with these guidelines for the rolling programme of inspections being conducted by Commission for Health Improvement[43] and its successor (the Commission for Healthcare Audit and Inspection).

Such developments would seem to have given managers the opportunity to constrain British doctors as never before, along the lines identified in the proletarianization thesis. Advocates of this position argue that doctors are being deskilled, are losing their economic independence, and are being required to work in bureaucratically organized institutions under the instruction of managers, in accordance with the requirements of advanced capitalism.[44] However, as Freidson[45] indicates, the widespread adoption of new techniques for monitoring the efficiency of performance and resource allocation does not on its own illustrate reduced professional autonomy. What really matters is whose criteria for evaluation and appraisal are adopted and who controls any actions that are taken.[46] Moreover, doctors are perfectly capable of transforming themselves into managers/clinical directors and have come to see this as a way of retaining control of the service. Having learned the language of management, their bilingual skills have enabled them to interpret and reframe problems, to adopt a clinical perspective on managerial issues and a managerial perspective on clinical matters.[47] Through clinical directors, it can be argued, the medical profession has retained a central position in shaping services and work organization.

In sum, while doctors in the NHS now have to account for their actions in ways that were unthinkable a decade or so ago, it is far from certain that the new managerialism in the NHS will result in a victory for the "corporate rationalizers" over the "professional monopolists."[48] What is certain, however, is that the policy changes outlined above have been good for the managers themselves. Their number increased by 53% between 1975 and 1991[12] and doubled again between 1992 and 2002.[49] Thus numbers have increased substantially over the last 25 years, whatever the political complexion of the government.

2. The Purchaser–Provider Split in Health Care

In addition to enhancing the role of management, Working for Patients and the 1990 NHS and Community Care Act also introduced a market system to the NHS, while reaffirming the principle of providing health care free at the point of use. Premised on the assumption that competition enhances efficiency, it was proposed that the

NHS should be divided into providers and purchasers of services; purchasers, it was assumed, would shop around for the cheapest health care while providers would minimize their price in order to remain competitive in the market.

The idea for an internal market apparently originated with the US economist, Alain Enthoven, who, on a visit to Britain in 1985, declared that the NHS was in a state of "gridlock" or general rigidity and inflexibility and that this could only be broken if the most efficient providers were rewarded with economic incentives.[50] Enthoven's solution, based on experience with US Health Maintenance Organizations,[51,52] proved to be attractive to New Right "think tanks" such as the Centre for Policy Studies, but the government did not take up the idea until the winter of 1987–8, when it faced a political crisis as a result of mounting public and professional concern about the financial problems facing the health service.[53] It was this set of circumstances that triggered Prime Minister Margaret Thatcher's decision to review the NHS, the outcome of which was Working for Patients.

The White Paper and the subsequent Act turned District Health Authorities (DHAs) into purchasers (or commissioning agencies), with capitation budgets, who were responsible for assessing local needs, determining priorities, and buying community services. These services could be bought from either the public or private sector. Larger general practices could also opt to become purchasers, known as fundholders.

Providers of care such as large hospitals and community units were given the opportunity to become self-governing Trusts with the promise of increased financial freedom and greater autonomy. They were to be allowed to set the rate of pay for their staff, invest in capital projects, and alter their service according to the needs of the market. The idea was that self-government would encourage a greater sense of ownership and pride, or corporatism, on the part of those providing services, as well as encouraging local initiative and greater competition.

The reforms were implemented within two years of the publication of Working for Patients. Purchasers found some opportunities for cost savings but were constrained by the lack of choice between service providers (e.g., only one district general hospital in the area) and the need to provide services locally, whatever the savings to be achieved by contracting further afield.[37]

On the supply side, the formation of hospitals and community units into Trusts seemed to provide certain benefits for the service and for patients. Costs were kept down, and the number of patients waiting over a year for hospital treatment was reduced. At the same time, the Trusts' attempts to create a corporate spirit were not entirely successful, and they tended to respond to purchasing power at the expense of social need and concentrated on more profitable areas of work to the detriment of certain categories of patient.[37]

Overall, the internal market seemed to produce a decentralized and fragmented system with numerous buyers and sellers, in place of a centrally planned, uniform, top-down approach. There were certain benefits for patients, but these were offset by a series of problems stemming from a system that put efficiency before equity.

When the self-styled "New Labour" government came into power in 1997, it was determined to find a "third way" between markets and centralized control. It argued that the emphasis on markets had undermined the public service ethos of the NHS and therefore proposed to sweep away the internal market and replace it with a system based on "partnership," collaboration, and networks.[54] Despite this rhetoric, one of New Labour's first decisions was to keep the purchaser–provider split, although extending the length of contracts to three years or more to counter the alleged short-termism of the old internal market. Secondly, and more significantly, the Labour government abolished GP fundholding based on individual practices and replaced it with a collective form of fundholding for all GPs. Under the new system all GPs in an area belong to a Primary Care Trust (PCT), which holds the budget for the patients on their lists and uses it to purchase services on their patients' behalf. The alleged advantages of this approach are that management costs are kept down (because PCTs purchase services for more patients than the old GP fundholders) while GPs' knowledge of their patients' needs can continue to be employed in the purchasing of services. These changes arguably reflect an attempt to learn from the experience of the internal market,[55] building on the positive elements of the purchaser–provider split while changing it where necessary to enhance a sense of partnership and restore the old public service ethos. As such, it illustrates perfectly the pragmatism of the "third way."

3. Empowering the Consumer

Another strand of the health service reforms has involved greater emphasis on consumer choice and redress. The application of consumerist principles to the NHS was given a major impetus with the publication of the 1983 Griffiths Report on management.[55] In line with New Right thinking, with its emphasis on individuals exercising choice through the market, Griffiths stated that managers should give pride of place to "patient," or as they were renamed, "consumer," preferences when making health care decisions. He argued that they should try and establish how well the service for which they were responsible was being delivered by employing market research techniques and other methods to find out the views of their customers. They were then to act on this information by amending policy and monitoring subsequent performance against it. Thereafter, this management-led consumerist approach was promoted vigorously, with Directors of Quality Assurance appointed to Health Authorities to establish users' views and staff sent on customer-relations courses and encouraged to follow newly established "mission statements" outlining their organizations' common goals. However, the benefits to patients seem to have been limited, with managers being mainly concerned with hotel aspects of care, such as cleanliness and food, rather than with patients' views of clinical effectiveness.[55]

Further policy initiatives to enhance consumer choice followed in the 1990s. The 1990 NHS and Community Care Act required Health Authorities, as purchasers, to discuss services with community groups, amongst others, before drawing up contracts. This policy was reinforced in Listening to Local Voices, published by the NHS Management Executive in 1992, which stressed that purchasing authorities should listen to the views of local people about their priorities for health care before making rationing decisions.[1]

The 1990 Act also required GP fundholders to purchase services on their patients' behalf. As Paton states, however, "the fact that the individual was not the purchaser meant that any new consumerism in the NHS was not to be based on the individual's purchasing rights."[56] Rather, GP fundholders, along with Health Authorities, were to be proxy consumers. It was assumed that these fundholders had the incentive to fulfill this role effectively, as otherwise their patients would simply switch to a competing practice.[5] However, as patients lacked the necessary knowledge or inclination to shop around in the medical marketplace and often did not have a great choice of alternative GPs with which to register, critics argued that there was little evidence that this aspect of the reforms markedly increased consumer choice.[57]

In addition, consumerism was promoted by the introduction in 1992 of a Patient's Charter, one of a number planned by the Conservatives to transform the management of the public services. The Patient's Charter was designed to make the health service more responsive to consumers and raise quality overall at nil cost, by setting the rights and service standards that they could expect. New rights were established, such as the right to detailed information about quality standards and waiting lists and having any complaint investigated and dealt with promptly. Critics of the Patient's Charter have argued that while it may have increased users' right to information, it is premised on the dubious assumption that making such information available to the public will of itself change the practice of clinicians and managers. As such, it ignores the vested interests that different health care occupations have in the maintenance of the status quo.[58]

Since 1997, when New Labour came to power, the emphasis has shifted, as we have seen, from one of competition to that of partnership, with PCTs replacing fundholding. Central to these organizational arrangements has been the requirement that users and local people be involved in decision-making. The focus to date seems to be mainly on communication and consultation rather than more participative or community-driven forms of involvement. However, the emphasis on consultation seems to be what lay people prefer, as there is little evidence that there is much enthusiasm for participating in health-related decision-making at service level. This may change with the establishment in 2003 of the Commission for Patient and Public Involvement in Health. The Commission's task is to get as many people as possible involved in decision-making about local health care issues. Its remit includes training people in skills that will maximize the chance of their voice being heard and encouraging Patient Forums to use modern technologies and approaches other than meetings to generate as much interest as possible.

Alongside this concern with public participation at the collective level has been an emphasis on patient partnership at the level of doctor–patient interaction. Under New Labour's NHS Plan of 2000, doctors are being encouraged to share information and decision-making with their patients. Indeed, patients are now being recognized as "experts" in their own care. At present, however, it is unclear to what extent users want to be involved in decision-making about their care. Nor is it clear that doctors will necessarily be willing to share information with patients as the basis for joint decision-making. In some cases they may prefer to limit the nature of the information they impart to patients, thereby maintaining their professional dominance.

While the language of partnership may be the current British government's preferred discourse, consumerism has not been completely displaced. Two recent initiatives—the creation of NHS Direct and NHS walk-in centers—seem to be more in line with increasing individual consumer choice and personal responsibility for care than with joint decision-making. Thus the NHS Direct nurse-led telephone help line is designed to provide faster advice and information about health, illness, and the NHS so that people are better able to care for themselves and their families. And NHS walk-in centers are designed to widen access to primary care services by offering no-appointment consultations in the evening and on weekends as well as during traditional office hours. In both cases the message seems to be that the NHS is accessible, convenient, and customer-focused.[59]

Given the above, how is the popularity of consumerism and, more recently, partnership in policy circles to be explained? One explanation is that the different government initiatives have been driven by ideology. Certainly the policies of the Conservatives seem to have been heavily influenced by a neo-liberal ideology based on a belief in the value of self-reliance, individual responsibility, and the rule of the market, with sovereign consumers expressing demand on the basis of knowledge about the choices available. Yet the Conservatives did not follow this ideology to the letter, as the market they created was internal to the NHS and the service remained free at the point of use. The present Labour government seems to have accepted elements of neo-liberalism (increasing individual and maximizing personal responsibility for health care), combined with a more collective approach, thus reflecting a preference for pragmatism.

An alternative approach is that the emphasis on consumerism reflects more general socio-economic changes, encapsulated in the phrase "post Fordism."[60] From this standpoint the health service reforms described above parallel a shift from Fordist principles (mass production, universalization of welfare, mass consumption) to those of post-Fordism (flexible production techniques designed to take account of rapid changes in consumer demand and fragmented market tastes). In a post-Fordist society it is the consumers rather than the producers who call the tune. While this approach has some value in placing the health policy changes under consideration in a broader context, it fails to distinguish between surface changes in appearance and underlying social relations. While the rhetoric has been about enhanced consumer power or partnership, producers in the form of the medical profession and health service managers arguably continue to hold the upper hand over the users of the service.

4. Promoting Welfare Pluralism

A further principle underpinning the NHS reforms is welfare pluralism. While the health services in Britain, like all others in the developed world,[61] have long been pluralist in the sense of having both public and private funding, planning and provision, the reforms of the 1980s and 1990s have attempted to shift the balance profoundly in favor of greater private-sector involvement.[62,63]

One strategy for shifting the balance between the public and private sector has involved the development of policies to encourage the growth of private medicine. In the 1980s, planning controls were relaxed on the development of private hospitals, and the power of local authorities to object to such developments was curtailed.[64] Furthermore, NHS consultants' contracts were revised to enable them to undertake more private practice in addition to their NHS commitments,[65] and tax changes were introduced to encourage higher levels of private health cover.[66] Together these changes created the climate for private hospital development and provided opportunities that were fully exploited by the private sector. Between 1979 and 1989 the number of private hospitals increased by 30% and the number of private beds by 58%.[66] Many of these hospitals were located in the prosperous South East of England, compounding rather than eliminating the geographical inequalities in the distribution of resources noted earlier. At the same time, the level of private health insurance increased from 5% of the population to a peak of 13% in 1989, with company-purchased schemes being particularly popular.[66] Currently around 11% of the population is covered by private health insurance,[67] with coverage concentrated in London and the southeast of England. Unsurprisingly, those with policies tend to have professional and managerial jobs and to be male, though roughly equal numbers of both sexes are actually covered.[68]

A further strategy to shift the balance between the public and private sector has involved the introduction of reforms that have facilitated greater collaboration between the two sectors. An early attempt was the Conservative government's policy of requiring NHS District Health Authorities to introduce competitive tendering for domestic, catering, and laundry services in 1983. The intention was to challenge the monopoly of the in-house providers of services in the expectation that costs would be reduced and greater "value for money" would be achieved. In practice the financial benefits proved relatively modest, at least to start with, and the savings achieved were said to have been at the expense of quality of service.[12] More recently, the NHS has been encouraged to contract out patient care to the private sector. These cooperative arrangements were initially undertaken on a voluntary basis by individual Health Authorities (HAs) that did not have in-house alternatives, for example, as a result of capacity constraints.[65] Subsequently, HAs were directed by the Conservative government to use private hospitals as a way of reducing NHS waiting lists for non-urgent cases and those waiting more than one year. This policy has since been endorsed by New Labour, who instituted a "concordat" between the NHS and the private sector in 2000, following publication of the NHS plan aimed at revitalizing the health care system and raising it to European Union standards. The concordat allowed patients to be treated at NHS expense in the private sector when there is no spare room in NHS hospitals. The existing, patchy arrangements between the sectors have thus been formalized, allowing NHS managers to plan ahead more effectively to reduce waiting lists.

Another example of collaboration has been the development of the Private Funding Initiative (PFI). The Conservatives launched this initiative in 1992, with the aim of encouraging private capital investment in the NHS, especially with regard to the development of acute hospitals. Under PFI, private companies design, construct, and own and operate services for a 25–30-year period, in return for an annual fee. From 1994 all planned capital development has had to be appraised as to its viability for PFI. The intention of the policy is to increase overall resources in the NHS while avoiding raising taxes or increasing public borrowing. It is also seen as a vehicle for bringing private-sector skills into the NHS, as private-sector managerial and commercial skills are employed to secure "value for money." Despite regular attacks on the PFI before its election victory in 1997 (because of the economic risks and privatizing potential of the approach[59]), New Labour has since embraced the policy enthusiastically on pragmatic rather than ideological grounds. While clinical services remain the responsibility of government, PFI is seen as permitting an element of risk to be transferred to the private sector, as building cost overruns are picked up by the private sector. Arguably it is a win–win situation as the NHS gets improved services while the private sector gets further opportunities to make a profit. Critics argue, however, that there are serious disadvantages associated with PFI-funded projects, including reduced bed numbers (substantially in excess of what would be expected from long term demand trends); the need for a quicker throughput of patients; a significant reduction in spending on clinical staff, especially nurses; and higher interest-rate charges compared to the cost of government borrowing, thereby putting a severe strain on hospital Trust budgets.[69]

The third strategy has been to encourage competition between the NHS and the private sector. This is best illustrated by the Conservative government's willingness to encourage the NHS to expand its pay-bed provision, thereby sharpening competition for private patients and threatening the private providers' profit margins. Originally introduced in 1948 as a concession to hospital consultants, as noted earlier, pay-beds were in decline when the Conservatives came to power in 1979, and their number continued to fall subsequently. In the late 1980s, however, the Conservatives decided to revitalize this provision in the face of increasingly severe financial constraints. The policy was also in line with their belief in generating competition between providers in order to enhance consumer choice and maximize efficiency. In 1988 it therefore used the Health and Medicines Act to relax the rules governing pay-bed charges so that hospitals could make a profit rather than simply cover costs. This propelled hospitals to upgrade their private wings or develop dedicated pay beds on NHS wards. As a result, pay-bed income increased dramatically from £32 million in 1991–2 to nearly £116 million two years later in 1993–4.[70] The NHS now has 20% of the private market and is an important provider of private health care in the UK.

These three strategies illustrate the shift to a new public/private mix of services, a mixed economy of health care. The policy has been driven in part by ideological considerations, especially those of the New Right with its emphasis on individuals exercising choice in the market. Economic and political calculations have also been important, especially the need to maximize efficiency and get value for money from existing tax revenues and the importance of being seen to act to reduce waiting lists. For New Labour these imperatives have, as noted earlier, resulted in the adoption of a pragmatic approach to health policy, in line with "third-way" thinking, and a willingness to embrace those Conservative policies that have been successful, such as PFI.

It has also been suggested that these policies illustrate a shift toward post-Fordism in the sense that Health Authorities have become "flexible firms," concentrating on core functions and buying in peripheral services from outside.[71] While this argument is superficially attractive, it ignores the extent to which the reforms have been the result of deliberate political decisions in the face of external economic considerations and ideological preferences.[12] Rather than simply mirroring structural developments in the economy, the policy of welfare pluralism is best seen as an attempt to erode services that people experience collectively and persuade them to act instead in terms of their own immediate self-interest.

CONCLUSION

This chapter has provided an account of the development of the British National Health Service from its inception in the late 1940s until the present. It has shown that the newly nationalized health service represented a significant departure from the previous system in offering health care free at the point of use, but that the new structure was agreed to at the cost of the medical profession's continuing autonomy.

As we have seen, subsequent events proved this socialized system of health care to be reasonably successful in providing cost-effective and equitable health care in face of an ageing population, increasingly expensive medical technology, and heightened patient and doctor expectations. Costs have been held in check and the spatial distribution of services has become more equitable. However, while greater equality of access and use has been achieved in terms of class, gender, and race, significant disparities continue to exist.

Despite this picture of relative success, both the Conservatives and New Labour have embarked on a series of policy changes in recent years that have had the effect of radically restructuring the NHS while keeping the service free at the point of use. Driven by a deep ideological attachment to the New Right and faced with a financial crisis and public disquiet, the Conservatives introduced managerialism and an internal market into the health service, along with a Patient's Charter and policies to encourage welfare pluralism. Subsequently Labour has modified some of these reforms, on pragmatic grounds, but has not tried to halt the shift toward welfare pluralism.

While these recent policy changes have brought certain benefits such as increasing the accountability of the medical profession, reducing hospital waiting times for patients, making rationing decisions explicit, and creating a more responsive service, there have also been serious disadvantages. Of these perhaps the most significant is the possibility that a two-tier system will develop with the wealthy paying for private care and the NHS providing a safety net for those who cannot afford it. The growth of the private health-care sector, the regeneration of NHS pay beds, and the development of the Private Funding Initiative all make this a realistic prospect. Indeed, they could be seen to reflect a policy of Americanizing health care in the UK[66,72–3] at a time when the US has been looking at the old-style NHS as one possible alternative model of health care. This reference to convergence illustrates the extent to which the NHS has changed in recent times and makes it unlikely that the clock will ever be turned back.

ACKNOWLEDGMENTS

I should like to thank Mike Bury and Mary Ann Elston for their comments on an earlier draft of this chapter. I am also grateful to Brooke Rogers for collecting material to enable me to update the chapter for the seventh edition.

REFERENCES

1. Allsop, J. Health Policy and the NHS. Second Edition. London: Longman, 1995.
2. Stacey, M. The Sociology of Health and Healing. London: Unwin Hyman, 1988.
3. Ginsburg, N. Divisions of Welfare. London: Sage, 1992.
4. Campbell, J. Nye Bevan and the Mirage of British Socialism. London: Weidenfeld and Nicholson, 1987: 168.
5. Klein, R. The Politics of the NHS. Third edition. London: Longman, 1995.
6. Berridge, V., Harrison, M., and Weindling, P. The impact of war and depression, 1918 to 1948. In Caring for Health: History and Diversity. Ed., Webster, C. Buckingham: Open University Press, 1993.
7. Doyal, L., with Pennell, I. The Political Economy of Health. London: Pluto Press, 1979.
8. Abel-Smith, B. The Hospitals 1800–1948. London: Heinemann, 1964: 440.
9. Berridge, V., Webster, C., and Walt, G. Mobilisation for total welfare, 1948 to 1974. In Caring for Health: History and Diversity. Ed., Webster, C. Buckingham: Open University Press, 1993.
10. Abel-Smith, B. Introduction to Health: Policy, Planning and Financing. London: Longman, 1994.
11. World Health Organization(WHO) www.who.int (retrieved on 25/11/2003)
12. Levitt, R., and Wall, A. The Reorganized National Health Service. Fourth edition. London: Chapman and Hall, 1992.
13. Gray, A. International patterns of healthcare, 1960 to 2001. In Caring for Health: History and Diversity. Ed. Webster, C. Buckingham: Open University Press, 2001.
14. Mohan, J. A National Health Service? The Restructuring of Health Care in Britain Since 1979. Basingstoke: Macmillan, 1995.
15. www.info.doh.gov.uk/doh/intpress.nsfpage/2003–0288?Opendocument (Retrieved on 25/11/2003)
16. Stocking, B. The introduction and costs of new technologies. In In the Best of Health. Eds., Beck, E., et al. London: Chapman and Hall, 1992.
17. Mays, N. Innovations in health care. In Dilemmas in Health Care. Eds. Davey, B., and Popay, J. Buckingham: Open University Press, 1993.
18. Burstall, M. 1992 and the Regulation of the Pharmaceutical Industry. IEA Health Series No 9. London: Institute of Economic Affairs, 1990.
19. Gray, A. Rationing and choice. In Dilemmas in Health Care. Eds. Davey, B., and Popay, J. Buckingham: Open University Press, 1993.
20. Jarman, B., and Bosanquet, N. Primary health care in London: Changes since the Acheson Report. British Medical Journal 305, 1130–6, 1992.
21. Townsend, P., and Davidson, N. Inequalities in Health: The Black Report. Harmondsworth: Penguin, 1982.

22. Whitehead, M. The Health Divide. London: Health Education Council, 1987.
23. Pendleton, D., and Bochner, S. The communication of medical information in GP consultations as a function of social class. Social Science and Medicine 14a, 669–73, 1980.
24. Boulton, M., Tuckett, D., Olson, C., and Williams, A. Social class and the general practice consultation. Sociology of Health and Illness 8, 325–50, 1986.
25. Doyal, L. Introduction: women and the health services In Women and the Health Services. Ed. Doyal, L. Buckingham: Open University Press, 1998.
26. Pascall, G. Social Policy: A Feminist Analysis. London: Tavistock, 1986.
27. Doyal, L. Changing medicine? Gender and the politics of healthcare. In Challenging Medicine. Eds. Gabe, J., Kelleher, D. and Williams, G. London: Routledge, 1994.
28. Nazroo, J. The Health of Britain's Ethnic Minorities. London: Policy Studies Institute, 1997.
29. Leese, B., and Bosanquet, N. High and low incomes in general practice. British Medical Journal 298, 932–4, 1989.
30. GLC Health Panel. Ethnic Minorities and the National Health Service in London. London: Greater London Council, 1985.
31. Thorogood, N. Private medicine: "You pay your money and you gets your treatment." Sociology of Health and Illness 14, 1, 23–38, 1992.
32. Anionwu, E. Sickle cell and thalassaemia: community experiences and official responses. In 'Race' and Health in Contemporary Britain. Ed, Ahmad, W.I. Buckingham: Open University Press, 1993.
33. Smaje, C. Health, "Race" and Ethnicity: Making Sense of the Evidence. London: King's Fund Institute, 1995.
34. Taylor-Gooby, P. Social Change, Social Welfare and Social Science. London: Harvester Wheatsheaf, 1991.
35. British Social Attitudes Survey 2000, National Centre for Social Research (www.statiostics.gov.uk/statbase/ssdataset.aspo?vlnk=3509)
36. Klein, R. The Politics of the NHS. Harlow: Longman, 1983, 141.
37. Ranade, W. A Future for the NHS? Harlow: Longman, 1994.
38. Cox, D. Crisis and opportunity in health service management. In Continuity and Crisis in the NHS. Eds. Loveridge, R., and Starkey, K. Buckingham: Open University Press, 1992.
39. Hunter, D. Managing medicine: A response to the crisis. Social Science and Medicine 32, 4, 441–9, 1991.
40. Cox, D. Health service management—a sociological view: Griffiths and the non-negotiated order of the hospital. In The Sociology of the Health Service. Eds. Gabe, J., Calnan, M., and Bury, M. London: Routledge, 1991.
41. Flynn, R. Structures of Control in Health Management. London: Routledge, 1992.
42. Hunter, D. From tribalism to corporatism: The managerial challenge to medical dominance. In Challenging Medicine. Eds. Gabe, J., Kelleher, D., and Williams, G. London: Routledge, 1994.
43. Harrison, S., and Ahmad, W. Medical autonomy and the UK state. Sociology 34, 129–46, 2000.
44. McKinlay, J., and Arches, J. Towards the proletarianization of physicians. International Journal of Health Services 15, 161–95, 1985.
45. Freidson, E. Medical Work in America: Essays in Health Care. New Haven: Yale University Press, 1989.
46. Elston, M. A. The politics of professional power: Medicine in a changing health service. In The Sociology of the Health Service. Eds. Gabe, J., Bury, M., and Calnan, M. London: Routledge, 1991.
47. Thorne, M. Colonizing the new world of NHS management: the shifting power of professionals. Health Services Management Research, 15, 14–26, 2002.
48. Alford, R. Health Care Politics. Chicago: University of Chicago Press, 1975.
49. Department of Health. NHS HCHS and General Practice Workforce Survey, 2002. (www.doh.gov.uk)
50. Enthoven, A. Reflections on the Management of the NHS. London: Nuffield Provincial Hospitals Trust, 1985.
51. Allsop, J., and May, A. Between the devil and the deep blue sea: Managing the NHS in the wake of the 1990 Act. Critical Social Policy 38, 5–22, 1993.
52. The British reforms, however, parted company with the HMOs by splitting purchasers/insurers and providers. See Paton, C. Competition and Planning in the NHS: The Danger of Unplanned Markets. London: Chapman and Hall, 1992.
53. Baggott, R. Health and Health Care in Britain. Basingstoke, Macmillan, 1994.
54. Le Grand, J. Competition, co-operation or control? Tales from the British National Health Service. Health Affairs, 18, 27–39, 1999.
55. Seale, C. The consumer voice. In Dilemmas in Health Care. Eds. Davey, B., and Popay, J. Buckingham: Open University Press, 1993.
56. Paton, C. op. cit.
57. Calnan, M. and Gabe, J. From consumerism to partnership? Britain's National Health Service at

the turn of the century. International Journal of Health Services, 31, 119–31, 2001.
58. Crinson, I. Putting patients first: the continuity of the consumerist discourse in health policy, from the radical right to New Labour. Critical Social Policy, 18, 227–39, 1998.
59. Iliffe, S., and Munro, J. New Labour and Britain's National Health Service: an overview of current reforms. International Journal of Health Services, 30, 309–34, 2000.
60. Nettleton, S. The Sociology of Health and Illness. Cambridge/Oxford: Polity in association with Blackwell Publishers, 1995.
61. Klein, R. Private practice and public policy: Regulating the frontiers. In The Private/Public Mix for Health. Eds. McLachlan, G., and Maynard, A. London: Nuffield Provincial Hospitals Trust, 1982.
62. Davies, C. Things to come: The NHS in the next decade. Sociology of Health and Illness 9, 302–17, 1987.
63. Harrison, S., Hunter, D., and Pollitt, C. The Dynamics of British Health Policy. London: Unwin Hyman, 1990.
64. Mohan, J., and Woods, K. Restructuring health care: The social geography of public and private health care under the British Conservative government. International Journal of Health Services 15, 197–215, 1985.
65. Rayner, G. Lessons from America? Commercialization and growth of private medicine in Britain. International Journal of Health Services 17, 197–216, 1987.
66. Calnan, M., Cant, S., and Gabe, J. Going Private: Why People Pay for Their Health Care. Buckingham: Open University Press, 1993.
67. Humphrey, C., and Russell, J. Private medicine. Working for Health. Eds. Heller, T. et al. London: Open University in association with Sage Publications, 2001.
68. Calnan, M. The NHS and private healthcare. Health Matrix, 10, 3–19, 2000.
69. Mohan, J. Planning, Markets and Hospitals. London: Routledge, 2002.
70. Higgins, J. Goldrush. Health Service Journal 23 November 24–6, 1995.
71. Kelly, A. The enterprise culture and the welfare state: Restructuring the management of health and personal social services. In Deciphering the Enterprise Culture. Ed. Burrows, R. London: Routledge, 1991.
72. Navarro, V. The relevance of the US experience to the reforms in the British National Health Service: The case of general practitioner fund holding. International Journal of Health Services 21, 381–7, 1991.
73. Hudson, D. Quasi-markets in health and social care in Britain: Can the public sector respond? Policy and Politics 20, 131–42, 1992.

Prevention and Society

Prevention became a watchword for health in the 1980s and continues to resonate in society. A number of factors contributed to the renewed interest in prevention. While a few fresh concepts emerged (e.g., focus on lifestyle's effect on health) and a few new discoveries were made (e.g., relating hypertension to heart disease), the current attention paid to prevention has not been spurred by scientific breakthroughs. Rather, it is primarily a response to the situations described in this book: the dominant sick-care orientation of the medical profession; the increase in chronic illness; the continuing uncontrolled escalation of costs; and the influence of third-party payers. And prevention efforts are going beyond the medical profession. Insurance companies give rate reductions to individuals with healthy lifestyles (e.g., nonsmokers) and numerous major corporations have introduced worksite "wellness" and health promotion programs. This new prevention orientation is occurring in a cultural environment that has become sensitized to various forms of health promotion including health foods, health clubs, jogging, and exercise.

If we are serious about reorienting our approach to health from "cure" to prevention of illness, medicine must become more of a "social science." Illness and disease are socially as well as biophysiologically produced. For over a century, under the reign of the germ-theory "medical model," medical research searched for specific etiologies (e.g., germs or viruses) of specific diseases. With the present predominance of chronic disease in American society, the limitations of this viewpoint are becoming apparent. If we push our etiological analysis far enough, as often as not we come to sociological factors as primary causes. We must investigate environments, lifestyles, and social structures in our search for etiological factors of disease with the same commitment and zeal with which we investigate bodily systems, and we must begin to conceptualize preventive measures on the societal level as well as the biophysical. This is not to say that we should ignore or jettison established biomedical knowledge; rather, we need to focus on the production of disease in the interaction of social environments and human physiology.

The Surgeon General's report on disease prevention and health promotion titled *Healthy People* (1979) took steps in this direction. The report recognized the "limitations of modern medicine" and highlighted the importance of behavioral and social factors for health. It deemphasized the role of physicians in controlling health activities and argued persuasively for the need to turn from "sick care" to prevention. Most significantly, the report officially legitimatized the centrality of social and behavioral factors in caring for our health. It argued that people must both take responsibility for changing disease-producing conditions and take positive steps toward good health. In some circles, *Healthy People* was deemed a revolutionary report, more significant even than the 1964 Surgeon General's report on smoking. The fact, however, that many people have not yet heard about this 1979 report, much less are familiar with what it says, raises some questions about its potential impact on health behavior.

Yet from a sociological perspective, the 1991 revision, *Healthy People 2000* (U.S. Department of Health and Human Services, 1991), is also something of a disappointment. While social and behavioral factors are depicted as central in causation and prevention of ill health, a close reading shows that most of these factors are little more than "healthy habits." The report exhorts people to adopt better diets, with more whole grains and less red meat, sugar, and salt; to stop smoking; to exercise regularly; to keep weight down; to seek proper prenatal and postnatal care; and so forth. While these things are surely important to prevention of illness, we must today conceptualize prevention more broadly and as involving at least three levels; medical, behavioral, and structural (see Table 1). Simply put, medical prevention is directed at the individual's body; behavioral prevention is directed at changing people's behav-

Table 1. Conceptualization of Prevention

Level of Prevention	Type of Intervention	Place of Intervention	Examples of Intervention
Medical	Biophysiological	Individual's body	Vaccinations; early diagnosis; medical intervention.
Behavioral	Psychological (and Social Psychological)	Individual's behavior and lifestyle	Change habits or behavior (e.g., eat better, stop smoking, exercise, wear seat belts); learn appropriate coping mechanisms (e.g., meditation).
Structural	Sociological (Social and Political)	Social structure, systems, environments	Legislate controls on nutritional values of food; change work environment; reduce pollution; fluoridate water supplies.

ior; and structural prevention is directed at changing the society or environments in which people work and live.

Healthy People mostly urges us to prevent disease on a behavioral level. While this is undoubtedly a useful level of prevention, some problems remain. For example, social scientists have very little knowledge about *how* to change people's (healthy or unhealthy) habits. The report encourages patient and health education as a solution, but clearly this is not sufficient. Most people are aware of the health risks of smoking or not wearing seat belts, yet more than 25 percent of Americans smoke and 30 percent don't regularly use the seat belts (despite seat belt laws). Sometimes, individual habits are responses to complex social situations, such as smoking as a coping response to stressful and alienating work environments. Behavioral approaches focus on the individual and place the entire burden of change on the individual. Individuals who do not or cannot change their unhealthy habits are often seen merely as "at risk" or non-compliant patients, another form of the blame-the-victim response to health problems. *Healthy People* rarely discusses the structural level of causation and intervention. It hardly touches on significant social structural variables such as gender, race, and class and is strangely silent about the corporate aspects of prevention (Conrad and Schlesinger, 1980).

In "Wellness in the Work Place: Potentials and Pitfalls of Work-Site Health Promotion," Peter Conrad examines a popular corporate strategy for health promotion and disease prevention. This fundamentally behavioral-level intervention grew significantly in the 1980s, largely in response to rising health-care costs and increasing corporate concerns about competitiveness and worker productivity (Conrad and Walsh, 1992). Throughout American industry, many major corporations have introduced health promotion or "wellness" programs at the workplace (Hollander and Lengerman, 1988). While there are broad claims made for these programs and while they are very popular with employees (Sloan, Gruman, and Allegrante, 1987), Conrad argues it is not yet clear whether they are effective in improving health, containing costs, or influencing productivity. When examined in their sociopolitical context, worksite wellness programs have several subtler and potentially disturbing unintended consequences.

In the final selection, "A Case for Refocussing Upstream: The Political Economy of Illness," John McKinlay argues that we need to change the way we think about prevention and start to "refocus upstream," beyond healthy habits to the structure of society. He suggests we should concentrate on and investigate political-economic aspects of disease causation and prevention, paying particular attention to "the manufacturers of illness." McKinlay singles out the food industry as a major manufacturer of illness. However, the major contribution of his selection is to go beyond the conventional view of prevention as a biomedical or lifestyle problem to a conceptualization of prevention as a socioeconomic issue.

Prevention can be a key alternative to our health care dilemma when it focuses at least as directly on the structural as on the behavioral level of intervention.

REFERENCES

Conrad, Peter, and Lynn Schlesinger. 1980. "Beyond healthy habits: Society and the pursuit of health." Unpublished manuscript.

Conrad, Peter, and Diana Chapman Walsh. 1992. "The New Corporate Health Ethic: Lifestyle and the Social Control of Work." International Journal of Health Services 22: 89–111.

Hollander, Roberta B., and Joseph J. Lengermann. 1988. "Corporate characteristics and worksite health promotion programs: Survey findings from Fortune 500 companies." Social Science and Medicine 26: 491–502.

Sloan, Richard P., Jessie C. Gruman, and John P. Allegrante. 1987. Investing in Employee Health. San Francisco: Jossey-Bass.

U.S. Department of Health, Education and Welfare. 1979. Healthy People: The Surgeon General's Report on Health Promotion and Disease Prevention. Washington DC: U.S. Government Printing Office.

48 WELLNESS IN THE WORK PLACE: POTENTIALS AND PITFALLS OF WORK-SITE HEALTH PROMOTION

Peter Conrad

In the past decade work-site health promotion or "wellness" emerged as a manifestation of the growing national interest in disease prevention and health promotion. For many companies it has become an active part of their corporate health care policies. This article examines the potentials and pitfalls of work-site health promotion.

Work-site health promotion is "a combination of educational, organizational and environmental activities designed to support behavior conducive to the health of employees and their families" (Parkinson et al. 1982, 13). In effect, work-site health promotion consists of health education, screening, and/or intervention designed to change employees' behavior in order to achieve better health and reduce the associated health risks.

These programs range from single interventions (such as hypertension screening) to comprehensive health and fitness programs. An increasing number of companies are introducing more comprehensive work-site wellness programs that may include hypertension screening, aerobic exercise and fitness, nutrition and weight control, stress management, smoking cessation, healthy back care, cancer-risk screening and reduction, drug and alcohol abuse prevention, accident prevention, and self-care and health information. Many programs use some type of health-risk appraisal (HRA) to determine employees' health risks and to help them develop a regimen to reduce their risks and improve their health.

Work-site health promotion has captured the imagination of many health educators and corporate policy makers. Workers spend more than 30 percent of their waking hours at the work site, making it an attractive place of health education and promotion. Corporate people are attracted by the broad claims made for work-site health promotion (see O'Donnell 1984). For example:

> Benefits of worksite health promotion have included improvements in productivity, such as decreased absenteeism, increase employee morale, improved ability to perform and the development of high quality staff; reduction in benefit costs, such as decreases in health, life and workers compensation insurance; reduction in human resource development costs, such as decreased turnover and greater employee satisfaction; and improved image for the corporation (Rosen 1984, 1).

If these benefits are valid, probably no company would want to be without a wellness program.

Many major corporations have already developed work-site health promotion programs, including Lockheed, Johnson and Johnson, Campbell Soup, Kimberly-Clark, Blue Cross-Blue Shield of Indiana, Tenneco, AT&T, IBM, Metropolitan Life, CIGNA Insurance, Control Data, Pepsico, and the Ford Motor Company. Nearly all the programs have upbeat names like "Live for Life," "Healthsteps," "Lifestyle," "Total Life Concept," and "Staywell."

The programs' specific characteristics vary in terms of whether they are on- or off-site, company or vendor run, on or off company time, inclusive (all employees eligible) or exclusive, at some or no cost to employees, emphasize health or fitness, year-round classes or periodic modules, have special facilities, and are available to employees only or families as well. All programs are voluntary, although some companies use incentives (from T-shirts to cash) to encourage participation. In general, employees participate on their own time (before and after work or during lunchtime). The typical program is on site, with modest facilities (e.g., shower and exercise room), operating off company time, at a minimal cost to participants and managed by a part-time or full-time health and fitness director.

The number of work-site wellness programs is growing; studies report 21.1 percent (Fielding and Breslow 1983), 23 percent (Davis et al.

1984), 29 percent (Reza-Forouzesh and Ratzker 1984–1985), and 37.6 percent (Business Roundtable Task Force on Health 1985) of surveyed companies had some type of health-promotion program. It is difficult to interpret these figures. Not only are there serious definitional problems as to what counts as a program, but many may yet be only pilot programs and not available to all employees and at all corporate sites. Estimated employee participation rates range from 20 to 40 percent for on-site to 10 to 20 percent for off-site programs (Fielding 1984), but accurate data are very scarce (Conrad 1987a).

Work-site health promotion as a widespread corporate phenomenon only began to emerge in the 1970s and has developed largely outside of the medical care system with little participation by physicians. The dominant stated rationale for work-site health promotion has been containing health care costs by improving employee health. Business and industry pays a large portion (estimated at over 30 percent) of the American national health care bill, and its health insurance costs have been increasing rapidly. By the late 1970s corporate health costs were rising as much as 20 to 30 percent a year (Stein 1985, 14). This has become a corporate concern. In an effort to reduce these costs, corporations have redesigned benefit plans to include more employee "cost-sharing," less coverage of ambulatory surgery, mandated second opinions, increased health care options and alternative delivery plans (e.g., health maintenance organizations and preferred provider organizations), as well as work-site health promotion programs. Although wellness programs are only a piece of a multipronged cost-containment strategy, they may be especially important as a symbolic exchange for employer cost shifting and reductions in other health benefits. They are moderate in cost and very popular with employees.

Corporations are restructuring their benefit packages to shift more cost responsibility to employees in the form of deductibles, cost sharing, and the like. A national survey of over a thousand businesses found that 52 percent of companies provided free coverage to their employees in 1980; by 1984 only 39 percent did so. In 1980 only 5 percent had deductibles over $100; four years later 40 percent had such deductibles (Allegrante and Sloan 1986).

Cost containment may be the most commonly stated goal of wellness programs, but it is not the only one. Reducing absenteeism, improving employee morale, and increasing productivity are also important corporate rationales for work-site health promotion (Hertzlinger and Calkins 1986, 74; Davis et al. 1984, 542). "Hidden" absenteeism can be very costly, especially when skilled labor is involved (Clement and Gibbs 1983). Improved morale is expected to reduce turnover, increase company loyalty, and improve workforce productivity (Bellingham, Johnson, and McCauley 1985). The morale-loyalty-absenteeism-productivity issue may be as important as health costs in the development of work-site wellness. The competitive international economic situation in the 1980s makes the productivity of American workers a critical issue for corporations.

Despite the broad claims for work-site health promotion, the scientific data available to evaluate them are very limited. While more scientific data could better enable us to assess the claims of the promoters of work-site wellness, it is not necessarily helpful for addressing some of the difficult social and health policy issues raised by work-site health promotion. To examine these more policy-oriented dimensions, it is useful to distinguish between potentials and pitfalls potentials roughly aligning with the claims made for work-site programs, the pitfalls with less discussed sociopolitical implications. These distinctions are for analytic purposes and are somewhat arbitrary; there may be downsides to potentials as well as upsides to pitfalls. This framework, however, provides us with a vehicle for examining work-site health promotion that includes yet goes beyond the dominant corporate/medical concerns of reducing individual health risks and containing costs.

POTENTIALS

The Work-Site Locale

More people are in the "public" (i.e., nonhome or farm) work force today than ever before estimated to be 85 million in the United States. Roughly one-third of workers' waking hours are spent in the work place. Work sites are potentially the single most accessible and efficient site for reaching adults for health education. From an employee's perspective, on-site wellness programs may be convenient and inexpensive, thus increasing the opportunities for participation in health promotion. The work site has potentially indigenous social support for difficult undertakings such as quitting smoking, exercising regularly, or losing weight. Work-site programs may raise the level of discourse and concern about health matters, when employees begin to "talk health" with each other. And since corporations pay such a large share of health costs, there is a built-in incentive for corporations to promote health and healthier workers.

One of the most underdeveloped potentials of the work site is possible modification of the "corporate culture." When the term "corporate culture" is used by the health promotion advocates, they generally mean improved health changes in the organizational culture and physical environment. Some also include changing company norms or the creation of the healthy organization (Bellingham 1985), often meaning making healthy behavior a desirable value among employees and management. Such goals, however noble, are vague and difficult to assess. In practice, changing the corporate culture has meant introducing more concrete interventions like company smoking policies (Walsh 1984), "healthy" choices and caloric labeling in cafeterias and vending machines, fruit instead of donuts in meetings, and developing on-site fitness facilities. Very rarely, however, have proposed wellness interventions in the corporate culture included alterations in work organization, such as stressful management styles or the content of boring work, or even shop floor noise.

Health Enhancement

Screening and intervention for risk factors are the most common vehicles for enhancing employee health. Medical screening includes tests for potential physiological problems; interventions are preventive or treatment measures for the putative problem. Medical screening at the work site, including chest X-rays, sophisticated serological (blood) testing, blood pressure and health risk appraisals (HRAs), can identify latent health problems at a presymptomatic stage. To achieve an improvement in health, however, work-site screening must also include appropriate behavioral intervention, medical referral, and back-up when necessary. Thus far, hypertension screening has produced scientific evidence supporting positive work-site results (Foote and Erfurt 1983).

The scientific evidence available to support specific work-site interventions is also, as yet, limited. Examining the extant literature on specific interventions, Fielding (1982) found good evidence for the health effectiveness of work-site hypertension control and smoke-cessation programs. He concluded that the data on physical fitness and weight-reduction were not yet available. Hallet (1986), on the other hand, argued that well-controlled studies of work-place smoking intervention are not yet available. The evidence for physical fitness is still contentious (e.g., Paffenbarger et al. 1984; Solomon 1984) although the health effects of thirty minutes of vigorous exercise three times a week are probably positive, at least for cardiovascular health. There are reports of using work-place competitions (Brownell et al. 1984) or incentives (Forster et al. 1985) for increasing weight reduction, but the studies are short term and lack follow-up.

In the past few years large research projects to study the effects of work-site health promotion were initiated at AT&T (Spilman et al. 1986), Johnson and Johnson (Blair et al. 1986a) and Blue Cross-Blue Shield of Indiana (Reed et al. 1985). Most of the results currently available are from pilot programs or one or two years of work-site health promotion activity (except the Blue Cross-Blue Shield of Indiana study, which is a five year evaluation). In general, these studies show health improvements in terms of exercise (Blair et al. 1986a), reduced blood pressure and cholesterol (Spilman et al. 1986), although the findings are not entirely consistent. The five-year Blue Cross-Blue Shield of Indiana study also found that interventions led to a significant reduction in serum cholesterol and high blood pressure and a lesser reduction in cigarette smoking (Reed et al. 1985). These reductions in risk factors are positive signs of health enhancement, but the studies are too short term to measure actual effect on disease. Limited scientific evidence aside, the interventions are at worst benign, since few appear harmful (save infrequent exercise-related injuries) and likely health effects seem between mildly and moderately positive.

Cost Containment

The effect of work-site health promotion on health costs, while highly touted, is difficult to measure and has engendered little rigorous research. Most companies do not keep records of their health claims in a fashion that is easy for researchers to assess. Since most research in this area tends to be short-term, and cost-containment benefits may be long-term (say five to ten years), the long time frame makes rigorous research on this topic unattractive to corporations and expensive for investigators. Finally, it is difficult to ascertain which, if any, work-site wellness interventions effected any changes in corporate health costs. Many studies of health promotion "project" potential cost savings from reductions in risk, which while unsatisfactory for scientific evaluation often satisfy the corporate sponsors.

There are a few studies of cost benefits that report promising findings. A national survey of 1,500 of the largest United States employers conducted by Health Research Institute found that health care costs for employers with wellness programs in place for four years was $1,311 per employee compared to $1,868 for companies without such programs (*Blue Cross-Blue Shield Consumer Exchange* 1986, 3). Such cross-sectional surveys, however, do not adequately control for confounding variables (e.g., different employee populations or benefit plans) that certainly affect health costs. Blue Cross-Blue Shield of California initiated a single intervention a self-care program through twenty-two California employers, that reduced outpa-tient visits, especially among households with first dollar coverage (Lorig et al. 1985, 1044). The authors don't calculate the estimated cost savings, but since the cost of the intervention was small, the cost-savings potential is high.

The most compelling cost-containment data to date come from the Blue Cross-Blue Shield of Indiana (Reed et al. 1985; Gibbs et al. 1985) and Johnson and Johnson (Bly, Jones, and Richardson 1986) studies. The Blue Cross-Blue Shield study tracked and compared claims data for participants and nonparticipants (N = 2,400) in a comprehensive wellness program for five years. They found that although participants submitted more claims than nonparticipants (i.e., had a higher utilization), the average payment per participant was *lower* throughout the course of the study. When payments were adjusted in 1982 dollars, the mean annual health cost of participants was $227.38 compared to $286.73 for nonparticipants. For five years, the average "savings" per employee was $143.60 compared to the program cost of $98.60 per person, giving a savings to cost ratio of 1.45. A possible selection bias in terms of who is attracted to the program could have affected the results. Overall, the five-year cost of the program was $867,000, with a saving of $1,450,000 in paid claims and an additional $180,000 saved in absence due to illness. The savings is estimated to be 8 to 10 percent of total claims (Mulvaney et al. 1985).

The Johnson and Johnson study compares health care costs and utilization of employees over a five-year period at work sites with or without a health-promotion program (Bly, Jones, and Richardson 1986). Adjusting for differences among the sites, the investigators found that the mean annual per capita inpatient cost increased $42 and $43 at the two sites with the wellness program as opposed to $76 at the sites without one. Health-promotion sites also had lower increases in hospital days and admissions, although there were no significant differences in outpatient or other health costs. The investigators calculate a cost savings of $980,316 for the study period. What is interesting is that this study was based on *all* employees at a work site. The suggestion here is that a work-site wellness program may produce a cost-containing effect on the entire cohort, not just on participants. The "Live for Life" program is an exemplary and unique program in terms of Johnson and Johnson's corporate investment in wellness; the effect of health promotion on an entire employee cohort needs to be replicated in other work-site settings.

Without further prospective studies, cost containment remains a promising but unproven benefit of work-site health promotion. Changes in health status which are more easily measurable do not automatically translate into health cost savings. It is often difficult to quantify health effect and subsequent cost savings. High employee turnover, discovery of new conditions, and other factors may affect actual cost benefits. On the other hand, the usual calculations do not take into account the cost of replacing key employees due to sickness or death. As Clement and Gibbs (1983, 51–52) note, the cost savings may be affected by characteristics of the company:

> For example, more benefits would be achieved by firms with highly compensated, high-risk employees, where turnover is low, recruitment and training costs are high, benefit provisions are generous and employees are likely to participate.

If corporations are serious about using health promotion to contain health costs, programs may need to be reconceptualized and expanded beyond their current scope. An important reality is that roughly *two-thirds* of corporate health costs are paid for spouses and dependents, who are not part of most work-site wellness programs, and that a large portion of health costs is expended for psychiatric care, which may only most indirectly be affected by wellness programs.

Cost containment is an overriding concern for some managers and program evaluators, especially in terms of "cost-benefit ratios." It may be that the current corporate political climate demands such bottom-line rhetoric for the implementation of work-site health promotion, but very few programs have been closed down due to lack of cost effectiveness.

Improving Morale and Productivity

The effects of work-site health promotion on morale and productivity are more difficult to measure than health effects. Participating in wellness activities, especially exercise classes, has several potentially morale-enhancing by-products. Current evidence is only anecdotal, but is generally in a consistent direction. First, there is the "fun" element. In the course of a year's observations at one corporate wellness program, I regularly observed banter, joking, and camaraderie among participants during program activities. There is a sense of people working together to improve their health. Programs that are open to all employees may create a leveling effect; often employees from varying company levels participate in the same classes and corporate hierarchical distinctions make little difference in sweatsuits and gym shorts. As one participant told me, "We all sweat together, including some of the higher ups." But rigorous studies on the effect of the programs on job satisfaction are not yet available.

Despite a legion of claims, virtually no one has even attempted to measure increased productivity as a result of work-site health promotion. Although changes in productivity are difficult to assess, there are two productivity-related effects about which we have some information. Several studies have found a reduction in absenteeism among wellness-program participants (Reed et al. 1985; Baun, Bernacki, and Tsai 1986; Blair et al. 1986b). It is generally believed that a reduction in absenteeism can lead to an increase in overall productivity. Second, several observers have noted that participants often say they "feel" more energetic and productive from participating regularly in the program, especially in terms of exercising (Spilman et al. 1986, 289; Conrad 1987b). This kind of "subjective positivity" that results from wellness participation may be related to improved morale and productivity, although we are not likely to obtain "hard" measures.

The symbolic effects of offering a work-site wellness program should not be underestimated. Work-site health-promotion programs are often among the most visible and popular employee benefits. The mere existence of a program may be interpreted by employees as tangible evidence that the company cares about the health of its workers, and as contributing to company loyalty and morale. Programs are also a plus in recruiting new employees in a competitive market-place.

Individual Empowerment

Work-site promotion presents a positive orientation toward health. Its orientation is promotive and preventative rather than restorative and rehabilitative and provides a general strategy aimed at *all* potential beneficiaries, not only those with problems ("deviants," or troubled or sick employees). This makes participation in wellness nonstigmatizing; in fact, the opposite is possible—participants may be seen as self-actualizing and exemplary.

The ideology of health promotion suggests that people are responsible for their health, that they are or ought to be able to do something about it. This may convey a sense of agency to people's relation with health, by seeing it as something over which individuals can have some personal control. Positive experience with these kinds of activities can be empowering and imbue employees with a sense that they are able to effect changes in their lives.

PITFALLS

In their enthusiasm for the positive potentials of work-site health promotion, the promoters and purveyors of wellness programs usually neglect to consider the subtler, more problematic issues surrounding work-site health promotion. In this section I want to examine some of the limitations and potential unintended consequences of promoting health in the work place.

The Limitations of Prevention

Many wellness activities, such as smoking cessation, hypertension control, and cholesterol reduction, are more accurately seen as prevention of disease than promotion of health. Disease prevention may be useful, but these interventions are not specific to the mission of health promotion (i.e., enhancing positive health).

Research within the lifestyle or "risk factor" paradigm has unearthed convincing evidence that a variety of life "habits" are detrimental to our health (e.g., Breslow 1978; U.S. Department of Health, Education, and Welfare 1979), but it is not always clear that this translates directly to health enhancement. Promoters of health promotion have frequently oversold the benefits of intervention (Goodman and Goodman 1986), which are not always well established (Morris 1982), and have ignored such equivocal evidence as the MRFIT study (Multiple Risk Factor Intervention Trial Group 1982). Moreover, just because a behavior or condition is a "risk factor" does not mean automatically that a change (e.g., a reduction) will lead to a corresponding change in health. In addition, clinicians and social scientists do not yet know very well how to change people's habits—witness the mixed results of various smoking-cessation programs or the high failure rate in diet and weight reduction.

In terms of modifying health risks, over what do people actually have control? Surely, there are some behavioral risk factors, but what about the effects of social structure, the environment, heredity, or simple chance? Clearly, the individual is not solely responsible for the development of disease, yet this is precisely what many work-site health-promotion efforts assume (Allegrante and Sloan 1986).

The overwhelming focus of work-site health promotion on individual lifestyle as the unit of intervention muddles the reality of social behavior. The social reality, including class, gender, and race—all known to affect health as well as lifestyle—is collapsed into handy individual risk factors that can be remedied by changing personal habits. This approach takes behavior out of its context and assumes "that personal habits are discrete and independently modifiable, and that individuals can voluntarily choose to alter such behaviors" (Coriel, Levin, and Jaco 1986, 428). At best this is deceptive; at worst it is misguided and useless.

It is often assumed that prevention is more cost effective than treatment and "cure." As Louise Russell (1986) has persuasively shown, for some diseases prevention may actually add to medical costs, especially when interventions are directed to large numbers of people, only a few of whom would have gotten sick without them. She concludes that prevention and health promotion may be beneficial in their own right, but in general should not be seen as a solution for medical expenditures. Ironically, for corporations for whom cost containment is a major goal, there is an additional problem in that if employees are healthier and live longer (by no means yet proven), corporations will have to pay higher retirement benefits. In any case, prevention seems a limited vehicle for medical cost containment. To the extent that controlling health costs is a major rationale, work-site wellness may seem peripheral when the results are limited.

Blurring the Occupational Health Focus

Work-site health promotion's target for intervention is the individual rather than the organization or environment. While the history of the occupational health and safety movement is replete with examples of corporate denial of responsibility for workers' health and individual interpretations of fault (e.g., "accident prone worker") (Bale 1986), by the 1970s a strong measure was established to change the work environment to protect individual workers from disease and disability. This was both symbolized and in part realized by the existence of the Occupational Safety and Health Administration (OSHA). But the promulgators of wellness are uninterested in the traditional concerns of occupational health and safety and turn attention from the environment to the individual. One virtually never hears wellness people discussing occupational disease or hazardous working conditions. Whether they view it as someone else's domain or as simply too downbeat for upbeat wellness programs is difficult to know. But this may in part explain why work-site health promotion has been greeted with skepticism by occupational health veterans.

The ideology of work-site wellness includes a limited definition of what constitutes health promotion. For example, it does not include improvement of working conditions. As noted earlier, wellness advocates neglect evaluating the work environment and conceptualize "corporate cultures" in a limited way. In fact, the individual lifestyle focus deflects attention away from seriously examining the effects of corporate cultures or the work environment. Little attention is given to how the work-place organization itself might be made more health enhancing. Perhaps it is feared that organizational changes to improve health may conflict with certain corporate priorities. For example, by focusing on individual stress reduction rather than altering a stressful working environment, work-site health promotion may be helping people "adapt" to unhealthy environments.

Moralizing Health Concerns

The ideology of health promotion is creating a "new health morality," based on individual responsibility for health, by which character and moral worth are judged (Becker 1986, 19). This responsibility inevitably creates new "health deviants" and stigmatizes individuals for certain unhealthy lifestyles. While this process is similar to medicalization (Conrad and Schneider 1980) in that it focuses on definitions and interventions on the individual level and fuses medical and moral concerns, it is better thought of as a type of "healthicization." With medicalization we see medical definitions and treatments for previously social problems (e.g., alcoholism, drug addition) or natural events (e.g., menopause); with healthicization, behavioral and social definitions and treatments are offered for previously biomedically defined events (e.g., heart disease). Medicalization proposes biomedical causes and interventions; healthicization proposes lifestyle and behavioral causes and interventions. One turns the moral into the medical; the other turns health into the moral.

The work-site wellness focus on individual responsibility can be overstated and leads to a certain kind of moralizing. For example, although personal responsibility is undeniably an issue with cigarette smoking, social factors like class, stress, and advertising also must be implicated. With other cases like high blood pressure, cholesterol, and stress, attribution of responsibility is even more murky. But when individuals are deemed causally responsible for their health, it facilitates their easily slipping into victim-blaming responses (Crawford 1979). Employees who smoke, are overweight, exhibit "Type A" behaviors, have high blood pressure, and so forth are blamed, usually implicitly, for their condition. Not only does this absolve the organization, society, and even medical care from responsibility for the problem, it creates a moral dilemma for the individual. With the existence of a corporate wellness program, employees may be blamed both for the condition and for not doing something about it. This may be especially true for "high risk" individuals who choose not to participate. And even relatively healthy people may feel uneasy for not working harder to raise their health behavior to the new standards. Thus, work-site health promotion may unwittingly contribute to stigmatizing certain lifestyles and creating new forms of personal guilt.

In a sense, health promotion is engendering a shift in morality in the work place and elsewhere; we need to, at least, raise questions about what value structure is being promoted in the name of health and what consequences might obtain from taking the position that one lifestyle is preferable to another. While it is assumed that work-site wellness is in everyone's interest I've heard it termed a "win-win" situation it is important to examine what we are jeopardizing as well as what is gained (cf. Gillick 1984).

Enhancing the Relatively Healthy

In several ways work-site wellness focuses its attention on relatively healthy individuals. Were we to consider the major global or national health problems from a public health perspective, workers would not be listed among the most needy of intervention. Research for decades has pointed out that lower social class (Syme and Berkman 1976) and social deprivation (Morris 1982), in general, are among the most important contributors to poor health. Workers in spite of having real health problems are a relatively healthy population. Occupational groups have generally lower rates of morbidity and mortality than the rest of the population. This so-called "healthy worker effect" implies that the labor force selects for healthier individuals who are sufficiently healthy to obtain and hold employment (Sterling and Weinkam 1986). There is, furthermore, some evidence suggesting that unemployment may have a detrimental effect on individual health (Liem 1981). The main target of work-site health promotion is a relatively healthy one.

Even within the work-site context, who is it that comes to wellness programs? Although data are limited, a recent review suggests some self-selection occurs:

> Overall, it appears participants are likely to be nonsmokers, more concerned with health matters, perceive themselves in better health, and be more interested in physical activities, especially aerobic exercise, than nonparticipants. There is also some evidence that participants may use less health services and be somewhat younger than nonparticipants (Conrad 1987a, 319).

In general, the data suggest that participants coming to work-site wellness programs may be healthier than nonparticipants (see also Baun, Bernacki, and Tsai 1986).

Finally, the whole health-promotion concept has a middle-class bias (Minkler 1985). Wellness advocates ignore issues like social deprivation and social class, which may have health effects independent of individual behavior (Slater and Carlton 1985), when advocating stress reduction or health enhancement. The health-promotion message itself may have a differential effect on different social classes. As Morris (1982) points out, in 1960 there was little class difference between smokers; by 1980 there were only 21 percent smokers in class I while there were 57 percent smokers in class V. And what little evidence we have suggests that overwhelmingly the participants in work-site wellness programs are management and white-collar workers (Conrad 1987a). For a variety of reasons—including scheduling, time off, and priority setting, blue-collar workers have been less likely to participate (see Pechter 1986). Thus, work-site health-promotion programs may generally be serving the already converted.

Expanding the Boundaries of Corporate Jurisdiction

The boundaries of private and work life are shifting, particularly as to what can legitimately be encompassed under corporate jurisdiction. Work-site programs that screen for drugs, AIDS, or genetic make-up are more obvious manifestations of this, but work-site wellness programs also represent a shift in private corporate boundaries.

Work-site health-promotion programs, with their focus on smoking, exercise, diet, blood pressure, and the like, are entering the domain of what has long been considered private life. Corporations are now increasingly concerned with what employees are doing in off-company time. We have not yet reached a point where corporate paternalism has launched off-site surveillance programs (and this is, of course, highly unlikely), but employers are more concerned about private "habits," even if they do not occur in the work place. These behaviors can be deemd to affect work performance indirectly through a lack of wellness. This raises the question of how far corporations may go when a behavior (e.g., off-hours drug use) or condition (e.g., overweight) does not *directly* affect others or employee job performance. Yet, screening and intervention programs are bringing such concerns into the corporate realm.

With the advent of health insurance, especially when paid for by employers, the boundaries between public and private become less distinct. That is, health-risk behavior potentially becomes a financial burden to others. The interesting question is, however, why are we seeing an increased blurring of boundaries and corporate expansion in the 1980s? The danger of this boundary shift is that it increases the potential for coercion. The current ideology of work-site wellness is one of voluntarism; programs are open to employees who want to participate. But voluntarism needs to be seen in context.

> Bureaucracies are not democracies, and any so-called "voluntary" behavior in organizational settings is likely to be open to challenge. Unlike the community setting, the employer has a fairly long-term contractual relationship with most employees, which in many cases is dynamic with the possibility of raises, promotions, as well as overt and covert demotions. This may result in deliberate or inadvertent impressions that participation in a particular active preventive program is normative and expected (Roman 1981, 40).

Employers and their representatives may now coax employees into participation or lifestyle change, but it is also likely that employers will begin to use incentives (such as higher insurance premiums for employees who smoke or are overweight) to increase health promotion. At some point companies could make wellness a condition of employment or promotion. This raises the specter of new types of job discrimination based on lifestyle and attributed wellness.

In a sense, what we are discussing here is the other side of the "responsible corporation" that cares about the health and well-being of its employees. The crucial question is, are corporations able to represent the individual's authentic interests in work and private life?

CONCLUSION

Work-site health promotion is largely an American phenomenon. Few similar programs exist in Europe or other advanced industrial nations. Work-site wellness is a response to a particular set of circumstances found in the United States: the American cultural preoccupation with health and wellness; the corporate incentive due to the employer-paid health insurance; and the policy concern with spiraling health costs. Its growth is related to a disenchantment with government as a source of health improvement and a retrenchment in the financing of medical services. Its expansion is fueled by the commercialization of health and fitness and the marketing of health-promotion and cost-management strategies (cf. Evans 1982). Moreover, work-site wellness aligns well with the fashion in the 1980s for private-sector "corporate" approaches to health policy.

In their enthusiasm, the promoters of work-site health promotion make excessive claims for its efficacy. The work-site wellness movement has gained momentum, although it may still turn out to be a passing fad rather than a lasting innovation. It seems clear that work-site wellness programs have some potential for improving individual employees' health and will perhaps contribute to reduce the rate of rise in corporate health costs. The scientific data on program effects, however, are by no means in and to a large extent corporations are operating on faith. The actual results are likely to be more modest than the current claims. How much data are necessary for policy implementation is an open question. For despite the rhetoric of cost containment, corporate concern over health costs may be more of a trigger than a drive toward wellness programs. Concern about morale, loyalty, and productivity—corporate competitiveness in the marketplace—may be of greater import than health.

Rigorous scientific evaluation will enable better evaluation of the potentials of work-site health promotion for improving employee health, reducing costs, and improving morale and productivity. But such data remain largely irrelevant for assessing the more sociopolitical pitfalls of work-site wellness. These can be only adequately evaluated in the context of the social organization of the work place, the relation between employers and employees, and as part of an overall health policy strategy. They cannot be simply counted in terms of reduced employee risk factors or saved corporate health dollars.

Work-site health promotion has the appearance of corporate benevolence. Health is a value like motherhood and apple pie. In modern society, health is deemed a gateway to progress, salvation, and productivity. Despite the pitfalls discussed in this article, work-site health promotion does not appear to be an overt extension of corporate control, at least not in terms of so-called technical or bureaucratic control (Edwards 1979). In fact, on the surface work-site wellness appears as more of a throwback to the largely abandoned policies of "welfare capitalism" (Edwards 1979). Whether work-site health promotion is a valuable health innovation, the harbinger of a new type of worker control, or an insignificant footnote in the history of workers' health remains to be seen.

ACKNOWLEDGMENTS

This article was written while the author was a visiting fellow in the Department of Social Medicine and Health Policy at Harvard Medical School, and was partly supported by an NIMH National Research Service Award (1F32MHO333-01). My thanks to Leon Eisenberg, Irving K. Zola, and Diana Chapman Walsh for comments on an earlier draft of this article.

REFERENCES

Allegrante, J.P., and R.P. Sloan. 1986. Ethical Dilemmas in Worksite Health Promotion. *Preventive Medicine* 15:313–20.

Bale, A. 1986. *Compensation Crisis.* Ph.D. diss., Brandeis University (Unpublished).

Baun, W.B., E.J. Bernacki, and Shan P. Tsai. 1986. A Preliminary Investigation: Effect of a Corporate Fitness Program on Absenteeism and Health Care Cost. *Journal of Occupational Medicine* 28:18–22.

Becker, M.H. 1986. The Tyranny of Health Promotion. *Public Health Reviews* 14:15–25.

Bellingham, R. 1985. Keynote address delivered at the 1985 "Wellness in the Workplace" conference, Norfolk, Va., May.

Bellingham, R., D. Johnson, and M. McCauley. 1985. The AT&T Communications Total Life Concept. *Corporate Commentary* 5(4):1–13.

Blair, S.N., P.V. Piserchia, C.S. Wilbur, and J.H. Crowder. 1986a. A Public Health Intervention Model for Work-site Health Promotion: Impact on Exercise and Physical Fitness in a Health Promotion Plan after 24 Months. *Journal of the American Medical Association* 255:921–26.

Blair, S.N., M. Smith, T.R. Collingwood, R. Reynolds, M. Prentice, and C.L. Sterling. 1986b. Health Promotion for Educators: The Impact on Absenteeism. *Preventive Medicine* 16:166–75.

Blue Cross-Blue Shield Consumer Exchange. 1986. Plan Hopes to Spur Worksite Health Promotion and Wellness Programs. May, p. 3.

Bly, J.L., R.C. Jones, and J.E. Richardson. 1986. Impact of Worksite Health Promotion on Health Care Costs and Utilization: Evaluation of Johnson and Johnson's Live for Life Program. *Journal of the American Medical Association* 256:3235–40.

Breslow, L. 1978. Risk Factor Intervention in Health Maintenance. *Science* 200:908–12.

Brownell, K.B., R.Y. Cohen, A.J. Stunkard, and M.R.J. Felix. 1984. Weight Loss Competitions at the Work Site: Impact on Weight, Morale and Cost-Effectiveness. *American Journal of Public Health* 74:1283–85.

Business Roundtable Task Force on Health. 1985. *Corporate Health Care Cost Management and Private-sector Initiatives.* Indianapolis: Lilly Corporate Center.

Castillo-Salgado, C. 1984. Assessing Recent Developments and Opportunities in the Promotion of Health in the American Workplace. *Social Science and Medicine* 19:349–58.

Clement, J., and D.A. Gibbs. 1983. Employer Consideration of Health Promotion Programs: Financial Variables. *Journal of Public Health Policy* 4:45–55.

Conrad, P. 1987a. Who Comes to Worksite Wellness Programs? *Journal of Occupational Medicine* 29: 317–20.

———. 1987b. Health and Fitness at Work: A Participant's Perspective. *Social Science and Medicine* 26:545–50.

Conrad, P., and J.W. Schneider. 1980. *Deviance and Medicalization: From Badness to Sickness.* St. Louis: Mosby.

Coriel, J., J.S. Levin, and E.G. Jaco. 1986. Lifestyle: An Emergent Concept in the Social Sciences. *Culture, Medicine and Psychiatry* 9:423–37.

Crawford, R. 1979. Individual Responsibility and Health Politics in the 1970s. In *Health Care in America,* ed. S. Reverby and D. Rosner, 247–68. Philadelphia: Temple University Press.

Cunningham, R.M. 1982. *Wellness at Work*. Chicago: Blue Cross Association.
Davis, M.K., K. Rosenberg, D.C. Iverson, T.M. Vernon, and J. Bauer. 1984. Worksite Health Promotion in Colorado. *Public Health Reports* 99:538–43.
Edwards, R. 1979. *Contested Terrain: The Transformation of the Workplace in the 20th Century.* New York: Basic Books.
Evans, R. 1982. A Retrospective on the "New Perspective." *Journal of Health Politics, Policy and Law* 7:325–44.
Fielding, J.E. 1982. Effectiveness of Employee Health Programs. *Journal of Occupational Medicine* 24:907–15.
———. 1984. Health Promotion and Disease Prevention at the Worksite. *Annual Review of Public Health* 5:237–65.
Fielding, J.E., and L. Breslow. 1983. Health Promotion Programs Sponsored by California Employers. *American Journal of Public Health* 73:533–42.
Foote, A., and J.C. Erfrut. 1983. Hypertension Control at the Worksite. *New England Journal of Medicine* 308:809–13.
Forster, J.L., R.W. Jeffrey, S. Sullivan, and M.K. Snell. 1985. A Work-site Weight Control Program Using Financial Incentives Collected through Payroll Deductions. *Journal of Occupational Medicine* 27:804–8.
Gibbs, J.O., D. Mulvaney, C. Hanes, and R.W. Reed. 1985. Work-site Health Promotion: Five-year Trend in Employee Health Care Costs. *Journal of Occupational Medicine* 27:826–30.
Gillick, M.R. 1984. Health Promotion, Jogging and the Pursuit of Moral Life. *Journal of Health Politics, Policy and Law* 9:369–87.
Goodman, L.E., and M.J. Goodman. 1986. Prevention: How Misuse of a Concept Undercuts Its Worth. *Hastings Center Report* 16:26–38.
Hallet, R. 1986. Smoking Intervention in the Workplace: Review and Recommendations. *Preventive Medicine* 15:213–31.
Health Research Institute. 1986. *1985 Health Care Cost Containment Survey: Participant Report* (Summary). Walnut Creek, Calif.
Herzlinger, R.E., and D. Calkins. 1986. How Companies Tackle Health Costs: Part 3. *Harvard Business Review* 63(6):70–80.
Liem, R. 1981. Economic Change and Unemployment Contexts of Illness. In *Social Contexts of Health, Illness and Patient Care,* ed. G. Mishler, 55–78. New York: Cambridge University Press.
Levenstein, C., and M. Moret. 1985. Health Promotion in the Workplace. *Journal of Public Health Policy* 6:149–51.
Lorig, K., R.G. Kraines, B.W. Brown, and N. Richardson. 1985. A Workplace Health Education Program that Reduces Outpatient Visits. *Medical Care* 23:1044–54.
Minkler, M. 1985. Health Promotion Research: Are We Asking the Right Questions? Paper presented at the annual meeting of the American Public Health Association, Washington, November 18.
Morris, J.N. 1982. Epidemiology and Prevention. *Milbank Memorial Fund Quarterly/Health and Society* 60(1):1–16.
Multiple Risk Factor Intervention Trial Group. 1982. Multiple Risk Factor Intervention Trial: Risk Factor Changes and Mortality Results. *Journal of the American Medical Association* 248:1465–77.
Mulvaney, D., R. Reed, J. Gibbs, and C. Henes. 1985. Blue Cross and Blue Shield of Indiana: Five Year Payoff in Health Promotion. *Corporate Commentary* 5(1):1–6.
Neubauer, D., and R. Pratt. 1981. The Second Public Health Revolution: A Critical Appraisal. *Journal of Health Politics, Policy and Law* 6:205–28.
O'Donnell, M.P. 1984. The Corporate Perspective. In *Health Promotion in the Work Place,* ed. M.P. O'-Donnell and T.H. Ainsworth, 10–36, New York: Wiley.
Paffenbarger, R.S., R.J. Hyde, A.L. Wing, and C.H. Steinmetz. 1984. A Natural History of Athleticism and Cardiovascular Health. *Journal of the American Medical Association* 252:491–95.
Parkinson, R.S., and Associates (eds.). 1982. *Managing Health Promotion in the Workplace.* Palo Alto: Mayfield.
Pechter, K. 1986. Corporate Fitness and Blue-Collar Fears. *Across the Board* 23(10):14–21.
Reed, R.W., D. Mulvaney, R. Bellingham, and K.C. Huber. 1985. *Health Promotion Service: Evaluation Study.* Indianapolis: Blue Cross-Blue Shield of Indiana.
Reza-Forouzesh, M., and L.E. Ratzker. 1984–1985. Health Promotion and Wellness Programs: An Insight into the Fortune 500. *Health Education* 15(7):18–22.
Roman, P. 1981. *Prevention and Health Promotion Programming in Work Organizations.* DeKalb: Northern Illinois University, Office for Health Promotion.
Rosen, R.H. 1984. Worksite Health Promotion: Fact or Fantasy. *Corporate Commentary* 5(1):1–8.
Russell, L.B. *Is Prevention Better Than Cure?* 1986. Washington: Brookings Institute.
Slater, C., and B. Carlton. 1985. Behavior, Lifestyle and Socioeconomic Variables as Determinants of Health Status: Implications for Health Policy De-

velopment. *American Journal of Preventive Medicine* 1(5):25–33.
Solomon, H.A. 1984. *The Exercise Myth*. New York: Harcourt Brace Jovanovich.
Spilman, M.A., A. Goetz, J. Schultz, R. Bellingham, and D. Johnson. 1986. Effects of a Health Promotion Program. *Journal of Occupational Medicine* 28:285–89.
Stein, J. 1985. Industry's New Bottom Line on Health Care Costs: Is Less Better? *Hastings Center Report* 15(5):14–18.
Sterling, T.D., and J.J. Weinkam. 1986. Extent, Persistence and Constancy of the Healthy Worker or Healthy Person Effect by All and Selected Causes of Death. *Journal of Occupational Medicine* 28:348–53.
Syme, L.S., and L.F. Berkman. 1976. Social Class, Susceptibility and Illness. *American Journal of Epidemiology* 104:1–8.
U.S. Department of Health, Education, and Welfare. 1979. *Healthy People: The Surgeon General's Report on Health Promotion and Disease Prevention.* Washington.
Walsh, D.C. 1984. Corporate Smoking Policies: A Review and an Analysis. *Journal of Occupational Medicine* 26:17–22.

49 A Case for Refocussing Upstream: The Political Economy of Illness

John B. McKinlay

My friend, Irving Zola, relates the story of a physician trying to explain the dilemmas of the modern practice of medicine:

> "You know," he said, "sometimes it feels like this. There I am standing by the shore of a swiftly flowing river and I hear the cry of a drowning man. So I jump into the river, put my arms around him, pull him to shore and apply artificial respiration. Just when he begins to breathe, there is another cry for help. So I jump into the river, reach him, pull him to shore, apply artificial respiration, and then just as he begins to breathe, another cry for help. So back in the river again, reaching, pulling, applying, breathing and then another yell. Again and again, without end, goes the sequence. You know, I am so busy jumping in, pulling them to shore, applying artificial respiration, that I have *no* time to see who the hell is upstream pushing them all in."[1]

I believe this simple story illustrates two important points. *First,* it highlights the fact that a clear majority of our resources and activities in the health field are devoted to what I term "downstream endeavors" in the form of superficial, categorical tinkering in response to almost perennial shifts from one health issue to the next, without really solving anything. I am, of course, not suggesting that such efforts are entirely futile, or that a considerable amount of short-term good is not being accomplished. Clearly, people and groups have important immediate needs which must be recognized and attended to. Nevertheless, one must be wary of the *short-term nature* and *ultimate futility* of such downstream endeavors.

Second, the story indicates that we should somehow cease our preoccupation with this short-term, problem-specific tinkering and begin focussing our attention upstream, where the real problems lie. Such a reorientation would minimally involve an analysis of the means by which various individuals, interest groups, and large-scale, profit-oriented corporations are "pushing people in," and how they subsequently erect, at some point downstream, a health care structure to service the needs which they have had a hand in creating, and for which moral responsibility ought to be assumed.

In this paper two related themes will be developed. *First,* I wish to highlight the activities of the "manufacturers of illness"—those individuals, interest groups, and organizations which, in addition to producing material goods and services, also produce, as an inevitable by-product, widespread morbidity and mortality. Arising out of this, and *second,* I will develop a case for refocussing our attention away from those individuals and groups who are mistakenly held to be responsible for their condition, toward a range of broader upstream political and economic forces.

The task assigned to me for this conference was to review some of the broad social structural factors influencing the onset of heart disease and/or at-risk behavior. Since the issues covered by this request are so varied, I have, of necessity, had to make some decisions concerning both emphasis and scope. These decisions and the reasoning behind them should perhaps be explained at this point. With regard to what can be covered by the term "social structure," it is possible to isolate at least three separate levels of abstraction. One could, for example, focus on such subsystems as the family, and its associated social networks, and how these may be importantly linked to different levels of health status and the utilization of services.[2] On a second level, one could consider how particular organizations and broader social institutions, such as neighborhood and community structures, also affect the social distribution of pathology and at-risk behavior.[3] Third, attention could center on the broader political-economic spectrum, and how these admittedly more remote forces may be etiologically involved in the onset of disease. . . .

. . . [In this paper] I will argue, for example, that the frequent failure of many health intervention programs can be largely attributed to the inadequate recognition we give to aspects of social context. . . . The most important factor in deciding on the subject area of this paper, however, is the fact that, while there appears to be a newly emerging interest in the political economy of health care, social scientists have, as yet, paid little attention to the *political economy of illness.*[4] It is my intention in this paper to begin to develop a case for the serious consideration of this particular area.

A political-economic analysis of health care suggests that the entire structure of institutions in the United States is such as to preclude the adequate provision of services.[5] Increasingly, it seems, the provision of care is being tied to the priorities of profit-making institutions. For a long time, criticism of U.S. health care focussed on the activities of the American Medical Association and the fee for service system of physician payment.[6] Lately, however, attention appears to be refocussing on the relationship between health care arrangements and the structure of big business.[7] It has, for example, been suggested that:

> . . . with the new and apparently permanent involvement of major corporations in health, it is becoming increasingly improbable that the United States can redirect its health priorities without, at the same time, changing the ways in which American industry is organized and the ways in which monopoly capitalism works.[8]

It is my impression that many of the political-economic arguments concerning developments in the organization of health care also have considerable relevance for a holistic understanding of the etiology and distribution of morbidity, mortality, and at-risk behavior. In the following sections I will present some important aspects of these arguments in the hope of contributing to a better understanding of aspects of the political economy of illness.

AN UNEQUAL BATTLE

The downstream efforts of health researchers and practitioners against the upstream efforts of the manufacturers of illness have the appearance of an unequal war, *with a resounding victory assured for those on the side of illness* and the creation of disease-inducing behaviors. The battle between health workers and the manufacturers of illness is unequal on at least two grounds. In the *first* place, we always seem to arrive on the scene and begin to work after the real damage has already been done. By the time health workers intervene, people have already filled the artificial needs created for them by the manufacturers of illness and are habituated to various at-risk behaviors. In the area of smoking behavior, for example, we have an illustration not only of the lateness of health workers' arrival on the scene, and the enormity of the task confronting them, but also, judging by recent evidence, of the resounding defeat being sustained in this area.[9] To push the river analogy even further, the task becomes one of furiously swimming against the flow and finally being swept away when exhausted by the effort or through disillusionment with a lack of progress. So long as we continue to fight the battle downstream, and in such an ineffective manner, we are doomed to frustration, repeated failure, and perhaps ultimately to a sicker society.

Second, the promoters of disease-inducing behavior are manifestly more effective in their use of behavioral science knowledge than are those of us who are concerned with the eradication of such behavior. Indeed, it is somewhat paradoxical that we should be meeting here to consider how behavioral science knowledge and techniques can be effectively employed to reduce or prevent at-risk behavior, when that same body of knowledge *has already* been used to create the at-risk behavior we seek to eliminate. How embarrassingly ineffective are our mass media efforts in the health field (e.g., alcoholism, obesity, drug abuse, safe driving, pollution, etc.) when compared with many of the tax exempt promotional efforts on behalf of the illness generating activities of large-scale corporations.[10] It is a fact that we are demonstrably more effective in persuading people to purchase items they never dreamt they would need, or to pursue at-risk courses of action, than we are in preventing or halting such behavior. Many advertisements are so ingenious in their appeal that they have entertainment value in their own right and become embodied in our national folk humor. By way of contrast, many health advertisements lack any comparable widespread appeal, often appear boring, avuncular, and largely misdirected.

I would argue that one major problem lies in the fact that we are overly concerned with the war itself, and with how we can more effectively participate in it. In the health field we have unquestioningly accepted the assumptions presented by the manufacturers of illness and, as a consequence, have confined our efforts to only downstream offensives. A little reflection would, I believe, convince anyone that those on the side of health are in fact losing. . . . But rather than merely trying to win the war, we need to step back and question the premises, legitimacy and utility of the war itself.

THE BINDING OF AT-RISKNESS TO CULTURE

It seems that the appeals to at-risk behavior that are engineered by the manufacturers of illness are particularly successful because they are constructed in such a way as to be inextricably bound with essential elements of our existing dominant culture. This is accomplished in a number of ways: (a) Exhortations to at-risk behavior are often piggybacked on those legitimized values, beliefs, and norms which are widely recognized and adhered to in the dominant culture. The idea here is that if a person *would only do X,* then they would also be doing Y and Z. (b) Appeals are also advanced which claim or imply that certain courses of at-risk action are subscribed to or endorsed by most of the culture heroes in society (e.g., people in the entertainment industry), or by those with technical competence in that particular field (e.g., "doctors" recommend it). The idea here is that if a person *would only do X,* then he/she would be doing pretty much the same as is done or recommended by such prestigious people as A and B. (c) Artificial needs are manufactured, the fulfilling of which becomes absolutely essential if one is to be a meaningful and useful member of society. The idea here is that if a person *does not do X, or will not do X,* then they are either deficient in some important respect, or they are some kind of liability for the social system.

Variations on these and other kinds of appeal strategies have, of course, been employed for a long time now by the promoters of at-risk behavior. The manufacturers of illness are, for example, fostering the belief that if you want to be an attractive, masculine man, or a "cool," "natural" woman, you will smoke cigarettes; that you can only be a "good parent" if you habituate your children to candy, cookies, etc.; and that if you are a truly loving wife, you will feed your husband foods that are high in cholesterol. All of these appeals have isolated some basic goals to which most people subscribe (e.g., people want to be masculine or feminine, good parents, loving spouses, etc.) and make claim, or imply, that their realization is only possible through the exclusive use of their product or the regular display of a specific type of at-risk behavior. Indeed, one can argue that certain at-risk behaviors have become so inextricably intertwined with our dominant cultural system (perhaps even symbolic of it) that the routine public display of such behavior almost signifies membership in this society.

Such tactics for the habituation of people to at-risk behavior are, perhaps paradoxically, also employed to elicit what I term *"quasi-health behavior."* Here again, an artificially constructed conception of a person in some fanciful state of physiological and emotional equilibrium is presented as the ideal state to strive for, if one is to meaningfully participate in the wider social system. To assist in the attainment of such a state, we are advised to consume a range of quite worthless vitamin pills, mineral supplements, mouthwashes, hair shampoos, laxatives, pain killers, etc. Clearly, one cannot exude radiance and success if one is not taking this vitamin, or that mineral. The achievement of daily regularity is a prerequisite for an effective social existence. One can only compete and win after a good night's sleep, and this can only be ensured by taking such and such. An entrepreneurial pharmaceutical industry appears devoted to the task of making people overly conscious of these quasi-health concerns, and to engendering a dependency on products which have been repeatedly found to be ineffective, and even potentially harmful.[11]

There are no clear signs that such activity is being or will be regulated in any effective way, and the promoters of this quasi-health behavior appear free to range over the entire body in their never-ending search for new areas and issues to be linked to the fanciful equilibrium that they have already engineered in the mind of the consumer. By binding the display of at-risk and quasi-health behavior so inextricably to elements of our dominant culture, a situation is even created whereby to request people to change or alter these behaviors is more or less to request abandonment of dominant culture.

The term "culture" is employed here to denote that integrated system of values, norms, beliefs and patterns of behavior which, for groups and social categories in specific situations, facilitate the solution of social structural problems.[12] This definition lays stress on two features commonly associated with the concept of culture. The *first* is the interrelatedness and interdependence of the various elements (values, norms, beliefs, overt life-styles) that apparently comprise culture. The *second* is the view that a cultural system is, in some part, a response to social structural problems, and that it can be regarded as some kind of resolution of them. Of course, these social structural problems, in partial response to which a cultural pattern emerges, may themselves have been engineered in the interests of creating certain beliefs, norms, life styles, etc. If one assumes that culture can be regarded as some kind of reaction formation, then one must be mindful of the unanticipated social consequences of inviting some alteration in behavior which is a part of a dominant cultural pattern. The request from health workers for alterations in certain at-risk behaviors may result in either awkward dislocations of the interrelated elements of the cultural pattern, or the destruction of a system of values and norms, etc., which have emerged over time in response to situational problems. From this perspective, and with regard to the utilization of medical care, I have already argued elsewhere that, for certain groups of the population, underutilization may be "healthy" behavior, and the advocacy of increased utilization an "unhealthy" request for the abandonment of essential features of culture.[13]

THE CASE OF FOOD

Perhaps it would be useful at this point to illustrate in some detail, from one pertinent area, the style and magnitude of operation engaged in by the manufacturers of illness. Illustrations are, of course, readily available from a variety of different areas, such as: the requirements of existing occupational structure, emerging leisure patterns, smoking and drinking behavior, and automobile usage.[14] Because of current interest, I have decided to consider only one area which is importantly related to a range of large chronic diseases—namely, the 161 billion dollar industry involved in the production and distribution of food and beverages.[15] The present situation, with regard to food, was recently described as follows:

> The sad history of our food supply resembles the energy crisis, and not just because food nourishes our bodies while petroleum fuels the society. We long ago surrendered control of food, a vital resource, to private corporations, just as we surrendered control of energy. The food corporations have shaped the kinds of food we eat for their greater profits, just as the energy companies have dictated the kinds of fuel we use.[16]

From all the independent evidence available, and despite claims to the contrary by the food industry, a widespread decline has occurred during the past three decades in American dietary standards. Some forty percent of U.S. adults are overweight or downright fat.[17] The prevalence of excess weight in the American population as a whole is high—so high, in fact, that in some segments it has reached epidemic proportions.[18] There is evidence that the food industry is manipulating our image of "food" away from basic staples toward synthetic and highly processed items. It has been estimated that we eat between 21 and 25 percent fewer dairy products, vegetables, and fruits than we did twenty years ago, and from 70 to 80 percent more sugary snacks and soft drinks. Apparently, most people now eat more processed and synthetic foods than the real thing. There are even suggestions that a federal, nationwide survey would have revealed how serious our dietary situation really is, if the Nixon Administration had not cancelled it after reviewing some embarrassing preliminary results.[19] The survey apparently confirmed the trend toward deteriorating diets first detected in an earlier household food consumption survey in the years 1955–1965, undertaken by the Department of Agriculture.[20]

Of course, for the food industry, this trend toward deficient synthetics and highly processed items makes good economic sense. Generally speaking, it is much cheaper to make things look and taste like the real thing, than to actually provide the real thing. But the kind of foods that result from the predominance of economic interests clearly do not contain adequate nutrition. It is common knowledge that food manufacturers destroy important nutrients which foods naturally contain, when they transform them into "convenience" high profit items. To give one simple example: a wheat grain's outer layers are apparently very nutritious, but they are also an obstacle to making tasteless, bleached, white flour. Consequently, baking corporations "refine" fourteen nutrients out of the natural flour and then, when it is financially convenient, replace some of them with a synthetic substitute. In the jargon of the food industry, this flour is now "enriched." Clearly, the food industry employs this term in much the same way that coal corporations ravage mountainsides into mud flats, replant them with some soil and seedlings, and then proclaim their moral accomplishment in "rehabilitating" the land. While certain types of food processing may make good economic sense, it may also result in a deficient end product, and perhaps even promote certain diseases. The bleaching and refining of wheat products, for example, largely eliminates fiber or roughage from our diets, and some authorities have suggested that fiber-poor diets can be blamed for some of our major intestinal diseases.[21]

A vast chemical additive technology has enabled manufacturers to acquire enormous control over the food and beverage market and to foster phenomenal profitability. It is estimated that drug companies alone make something like $500 million a year through chemical additives for food. I have already suggested that what is done to food, in the way of processing and artificial additives, may actually be injurious to health. Yet, it is clear that, despite such well-known risks, profitability makes such activity well worthwhile. For example, additives, like preservatives, enable food that might perish in a short period of time to endure unchanged for months or even years. Food manufacturers and distributors can saturate supermarket shelves across the country with their products because there is little chance that they will spoil. Moreover, manufacturers can purchase vast quantities of raw ingredients when they are cheap, produce and stockpile the processed result, and then withhold the product from the market for long periods, hoping for the inevitable rise in prices and the consequent windfall.

The most widely used food additive (although it is seldom described as an additive) is "refined" sugar. Food manufacturers saturate our diets with the substance from the day we are born until the day we die. Children are fed breakfast cereals which consist of 50 percent sugar.[22] The average American adult consumes 126 pounds of sugar each year—and children, of course, eat much more. For the candy industry alone, this amounts to around $3 billion each year. The American sugar mania, which appears to have been deliberately engineered, is a major contributor to such "diseases of civilization" as diabetes, coronary heart disease, gall bladder illness, and cancer—all the insidious, degenerative conditions which most often afflict people in advanced capitalist societies, but which "underdeveloped," nonsugar eaters never get. One witness at a recent meeting of a U.S. Senate Committee, said that if the food industry were proposing sugar today as a new food additive, its "metabolic behavior would undoubtedly lead to its being banned."[23]

In sum, therefore, it seems that the American food industry is mobilizing phenomenal resources to advance and bind us to its own conception of food. We are bombarded from childhood with $2 billion worth of deliberately manipulative advertisements each year, most of them urging us to consume, among other things, as much sugar as possible. To highlight the magnitude of the resources involved, one can point to the activity of one well-known beverage company, Coca-Cola, which alone spent $71 million in 1971 to advertise its artificially flavored, sugar-saturated product. Fully recognizing the enormity of the problem regarding food in the United States, Zwerdling offers the following advice:

> Breaking through the food industry will require government action—banning or sharply limiting use of dangerous additives like artificial colors and flavors, and sugar, and requiring wheat products to contain fiber-rich wheat germ, to give just two examples. Food, if it is to become safe, will have to become part of politics.[24]

THE ASCRIPTION OF RESPONSIBILITY AND MORAL ENTREPRENEURSHIP

So far, I have considered, in some detail, the ways in which industry, through its manufacture and distribution of a variety of products, generates at-risk behavior and disease. Let us now focus on the activities of health workers further down the river and consider their efforts in a social context, which has already been largely shaped by the manufacturers upstream.

Not only should we be mindful of the culturally disruptive and largely unanticipated consequences of health intervention efforts mentioned earlier, but also of the underlying ideology on which so much of this activity rests. Such intervention appears based on an assumption of the *culpability of individuals* or groups who either manifest illness, or display various at-risk behaviors.

From the assumption that individuals and groups with certain illnesses or displaying at-risk behavior are responsible for their state, it is a relatively easy step to advocating some changes in behavior on the part of those involved. By ascribing culpability to some group or social category (usually ethnic minorities and those in lower socio-economic categories) and having this ascription legitimated by health professionals and accepted by other segments of society, it is possible to mobilize resources to change the offending behavior. Certain people are responsible for not approximating, through their activities, some conception of what *ought* to be appropriate behavior on their part. When measured against the artificial conception of what ought to be, certain individuals and groups are found to be deficient in several important respects. They are *either* doing something that they ought not to be doing, *or* they are not doing something that they ought to be doing. If only they would recognize their individual culpability and alter their behavior in some appropriate fashion, they would improve their health status or the likelihood of not developing certain pathologies. On the basis of this line of reasoning, resources are being mobilized to bring those who depart from the desired conception into conformity with what is thought to be appropriate behavior. To use the upstream-downstream analogy, one could argue that people are blamed (and, in a sense, even punished) for not being able to swim after they, perhaps even against their own volition, have been pushed into the river by the manufacturers of illness.

Clearly, this ascription of culpability is not limited only to the area of health. According to popular conception, people in poverty are largely to blame for their social situation, although recent evidence suggests that a social welfare system which prevents them from avoiding this state is at least partly responsible.[25] Again, in the field of education, we often hold "dropouts" responsible for their behavior, when evidence suggests that the school system itself is rigged for failure.[26] Similar examples are readily available from the fields of penology, psychiatry, and race relations.[27]

Perhaps it would be useful to briefly outline, at this point, what I regard as a bizarre relationship between the activities of the manufacturers of illness, the ascription of culpability, and health intervention endeavors. *First,* important segments of our social system appear to be controlled and operated in such a way that people must inevitably fail. The fact is that there is often no choice over whether one can find employment, whether or not to drop out of college, involve oneself in untoward behavior, or become sick. *Second,* even though individuals and groups lack such choice, they are still blamed for not approximating the artificially contrived norm and are treated as if responsibility for their state lay entirely with them. For example, some illness conditions may be the result of particular behavior and/or involvement in certain occupational role relationships over which those affected have little or no control.[28] *Third,* after recognizing that certain individuals and groups have "failed," we establish, at a point downstream, a substructure of services which are regarded as evidence of progressive beneficence on the part of the system. Yet, it is this very system which had a primary role in manufacturing the problems and need for these services in the first place.

It is around certain aspects of life style that most health intervention endeavors appear to revolve and this probably results from the observability of most at-risk behavior. The modification of at-risk behavior can take several different forms, and the intervention appeals that are employed probably vary as a function of which type of change is desired. People can *either* be encouraged to stop doing what they are doing which appears to be endangering their survival (e.g., smoking, drinking, eating certain types of food, working in particular ways); *or* they can be encouraged to adopt certain new patterns of behavior which seemingly enhance their health status (e.g., diet, exercise, rest, eat certain foods, etc.). I have already discussed how the presence or absence of certain life styles in some groups may be a part of some wider cultural pattern which emerges as a response to social structural problems. I have also noted the potentially disruptive consequences to these cultural patterns of intervention programs. Underlying all these aspects is the issue of behavior control and the attempt to enforce a particular type of behavioral conformity. It is more than coincidental that the at-risk life styles, which we are all admonished to avoid, are frequently the type of behaviors which depart from and, in a sense, jeopardize the prevailing puritanical, middle-class ethic of what ought to be. According to this ethic, activities as pleasurable as drinking, smoking, overeating, and sexual intercourse must be harmful and ought to be eradicated.

The important point here is which segments of society and whose interests are health workers serving, and what are the ideological consequences of their actions.[29] Are we advocating the modification of behavior for the *exclusive* purpose of improving health status, or are we using the question of health as a means of obtaining some kind of moral uniformity through the abolition of disapproved behaviors? To what extent, if at all, are health workers actively involved in some wider pattern of social regulation?[30]

Such questions also arise in relation to the burgeoning literature that links more covert personality characteristics to certain illnesses and at-risk behaviors. Capturing a great deal of attention in this regard are the recent studies which associate heart disease with what is termed a Type A personality. The Type A personality consists of a complex of traits which produces: excessive competitive drive, aggressiveness, impatience, and a harrying sense of time urgency. Individuals displaying this pattern seem to be engaged in a chronic, ceaseless and often fruitless struggle with themselves, with others, with circumstances, with time, sometimes with life itself. They also frequently exhibit a free-floating, but well-rationalized form of hostility, and almost always a deep-seated insecurity.[31]

Efforts to change Type A traits appear to be based on some ideal conception of a relaxed, noncompetitive, phlegmatic individual to which people are encouraged to conform.[32] Again, one can question how realistic such a conception is in a system which daily rewards behavior resulting from Type A traits. One can clearly question the ascription of near exclusive culpability to those displaying Type A behavior when the context within which such behavior is manifest is structured in such a way as to guarantee its production. From a cursory reading of job advertisements in any newspaper, we can see that employers actively seek to recruit individuals manifesting Type A characteristics, extolling them as positive virtues.[33]

My earlier point concerning the potentially disruptive consequences of requiring alterations in life style applies equally well in this area of personality and disease. If health workers manage to effect some changes away from Type A behavior in a system which requires and rewards it, then we must be aware of the possible consequences of such change in terms of future failure. Even though the evidence linking Type A traits to heart disease appears quite conclusive, how can health workers ever hope to combat and alter it when such characteristics are so positively and regularly reinforced in this society?

The various points raised in this section have some important moral and practical implications for those involved in health related endeavors. *First,* I have argued that our prevailing ideology involves the ascription of culpability to particular individuals and groups for the manifestation of either disease or at-risk behavior. *Second,* it can be argued that so-called "health professionals" have acquired a mandate to determine the morality of different types of behavior and have access to a body of knowledge and resources which they can "legitimately" deploy for its removal or alteration. (A detailed discussion of the means by which this mandate has been acquired is expanded in a separate paper.) *Third,* [it] is possible to argue that a great deal of health intervention is, perhaps unwittingly, part of a wide pattern of social regulation. We must be clear both as to whose interests we are serving, and the wider implications and consequences of the activities we support through the application of our expertise. *Finally,* it is evident from arguments I have presented that much of our health intervention fails to take adequate account of the social contexts which foster and reinforce the behaviors we seek to alter. The literature of preventive medicine is replete with illustrations of the failure of contextless health intervention programs.

THE NOTION OF A NEED HIERARCHY

At this point in the discussion I shall digress slightly to consider the relationship between the utilization of preventive health services and the concept of need as manifest in this society. We know from available evidence that upper socio-economic groups are generally more responsive to health intervention activities than are those of lower socio-economic status. To partially account for this phenomenon, I have found it useful to introduce the notion of a *need hierarchy.* By this I refer to the fact that some needs (e.g., food, clothing, shelter) are probably universally recognized as related to sheer survival and take precedence, while other needs, for particular social groups, may be perceived as less immediately important (e.g., dental care, exercise, balanced diet). In other words, I conceive of a *hierarchy of needs,* ranging from what could be termed "primary needs" (which relate more or less to the universally recognized immediate needs for survival) through to "secondary needs" (which are not always recognized as important and which may be artificially engineered by the manufacturers of illness). Somewhere between the high priority, primary needs and the less important, secondary needs are likely to fall the kinds of need invoked by preventive health workers. Where one is located at any point in time on the need hierarchy (i.e., which particular needs are engaging one's attention and resources) is largely a function of the shape of the existing social structure and aspects of socioeconomic status.

This notion of a hierarchy of needs enables us to distinguish between the health and illness behavior of the affluent and the poor. Much of the social life of the wealthy clearly concerns secondary needs, which are generally perceived as lower than most health related needs on the need hierarchy. If some pathology presents itself, or some at-risk behavior is recognized, then they naturally assume a priority position, which eclipses most other needs for action. In contrast, much of the social life of the poor centers on needs which are understandably regarded as being of greater priority than most health concerns on the need hierarchy (e.g., homelessness, unemployment). Should some illness event present itself, or should health workers alert people and groups in poverty to possible further health needs, then these needs inevitably assume a position of relative low priority and are eclipsed, perhaps indefinitely, by more pressing primary needs for sheer existence.

From such a perspective, I think it is possible to understand why so much of our health intervention fails in those very groups, at highest risk to morbidity, whom we hope to reach and influence. The appeals that we make in alerting them to possible future needs simply miss the mark by giving inadequate recognition to those primary needs which daily preoccupy their attention. Not only does the notion of a need hierarchy emphasize the difficulty of contextless intervention programs, but it also enables us to view the rejection as a non-compliance with health programs, as, in a sense, rational behavior.

HOW PREVENTIVE IS PREVENTION?

With regard to some of the arguments I have presented, concerning the ultimate futility of downstream endeavors, one may respond that effective preventive medicine does, in fact, take account of this problem. Indeed, many preventive health workers are openly skeptical of a predominantly curative perspective in health care. I have argued, however, that even our best preventive endeavors are misplaced in their almost total ascription of responsibility for illness to the afflicted individuals and groups, and through the types of programs which result. While useful in a limited way, the preventive orientation is itself largely a downstream endeavor through its preoccupation with the avoidance of at-risk behavior in the individual and with its general neglect of the activities of the manufacturers of illness which foster such behavior.

Figure 49-1 is a crude diagrammatic representation of an overall process starting with (1) the activities of the manufacturers of illness, which (2) foster and habituate people to certain at-risk behaviors, which (3) ultimately result in the onset of certain types of morbidity and mortality.[34] The predominant curative orientation in modern medicine deals almost exclusively with the observable patterns of morbidity and mortality, which are the *end-points* in the process. The much heralded preventive orientation focuses on those behaviors which are known to be associated with particular illnesses and which can be viewed as the *midpoint* in the overall process. Still left largely untouched are the entrepreneurial activities of the manufacturers of illness, who, through largely unregulated activities, foster the at-risk behavior we aim to prevent. This *beginning point* in the process remains unaffected by most preventive endeavors, even though it is at this point that the greatest potential for change, and perhaps even ultimate victory, lies.

Figure 49-1.

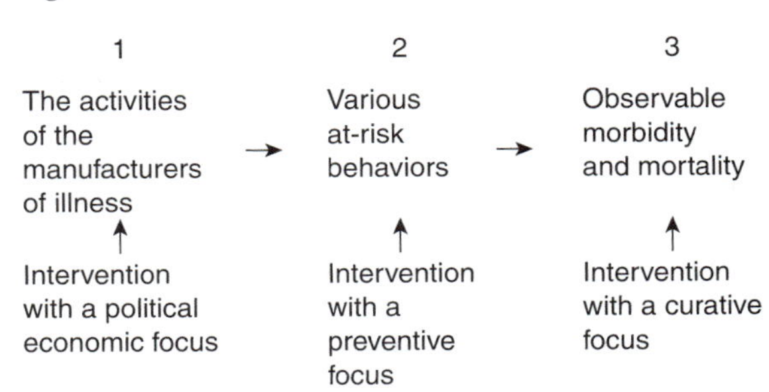

It is clear that this paper raises many questions and issues at a general level—more in fact than it is possible to resolve. Since most of the discussion has been at such an abstract level and concerned with broad political and economic forces, any ensuing recommendations for change must be broad enough to cover the various topics discussed. Hopefully, the preceding argument will also stimulate discussion toward additional recommendations and possible solutions. Given the scope and direction of this paper and the analogy I have employed to convey its content, the task becomes of the order of constructing fences upstream *and* restraining those who, in the interest of corporate profitability, continue to push people in. In this concluding section I will confine my remarks to three selected areas of recommendations.

RECOMMENDED ACTION

a. Legislative Intervention

It is probably true that one stroke of effective health legislation is equal to many separate health intervention endeavors and the cumulative efforts of innumerable health workers over long periods of time. In terms of winning the war which was described earlier, greater changes will result from the continued politicization of illness than from the modification of specific individual behaviors. There are many opportunities for a legislative reduction of at-riskness, and we ought to seize them. Let me give one suggestion which relates to earlier points in this paper. Widespread public advertising is importantly related to the growth and survival of large corporations. If it were not so demonstrably effective, then such vast sums of money and resources would not be devoted to this activity. Moreover, as things stand at present, a great deal of advertising is encouraged through granting it tax exempt status on some vague grounds of public education.[35] To place more stringent, enforceable restrictions on advertising would be to severely curtail the morally abhorrent pushing in activities of the manufacturers of illness. It is true that large corporations are ingenious in their efforts to avoid the consequences of most of the current legislative restrictions on advertising which only prohibit certain kinds of appeals.

As a possible solution to this and in recognition of the moral culpability of those who are actively manufacturing disease, I conceive of a ratio of advertising to health tax or a ratio of risk to benefit tax (RRBT). The idea here is to, in some way, match advertising expenditures to health expenditures. The precise weighting of the ratio could be determined by independently ascertaining the severity of the health effects produced by the manufacture and distribution of the product by the corporation. For example, it is clear that smoking is injurious to health and has no redeeming benefit. Therefore, for this product, the ratio could be determined as say, 3 to 1, where, for example, a company which spends a non-tax deductible $1 million to advertise its cigarettes would be required to devote a non-tax deductible $3 million to the area of health. In the area of quasi-health activities, where the product, although largely useless, may not be so injurious (e.g., nasal sprays, pain killers, mineral supplements, etc.), the ratio could be on, say, a 1 to 1 basis.

Of course, the manufacturers of illness, at the present time, do "donate" large sums of money for the purpose of research, with an obvious understanding that their gift should be reciprocated. In a recent article, Nuehring and Markle touch on the nature of this reciprocity:

> One of the most ironic pro-cigarette forces has been the American Medical Association. This powerful health organization took a position in 1965 clearly favorable to the tobacco interests. . . . In addition, the A.M.A. was, until 1971, conspicuously absent from the membership of the National Interagency Council on Smoking and Health, a coalition of government agencies and virtually all the national health organizations, formed in 1964. The A.M.A.'s largely pro-tobacco behavior has been linked with the acceptance of large research subsidies from the tobacco industry—amounting, according to the industry, to some 18 million dollars.[36]

Given such reciprocity, it would be necessary for this health money from the RRBT to be handled by a supposedly independent government agency, like the FDA or the FTC, for distribution to regular research institutions as well as to consumer organizations in the health field, which are currently so unequally pitted against the upstream manufacturers of illness. Such legislation would, I believe, severely curtail corporate "pushing in" activity and publicly demonstrate our commitment to effectively regulating the source of many health problems.

b. The Question of Lobbying

Unfortunately, due to present arrangements, it is difficult to discern the nature and scope of health lobbying activities. If only we could locate (a) who is lobbying for what, (b) who they are lobbying with, (c) what tactics are being employed, and (d) with what consequences for health legislation. Because these activities are likely to jeopardize the myths that have been so carefully engineered and fed to a gullible public by both the manufacturers of illness *and* various health organizations, they are clothed in secrecy.[37] Judging from recent newspaper reports, concerning multimillion dollar gift-giving by the pharmaceutical industry to physicians, the occasional revelation of lobbying and political exchange remains largely unknown and highly newsworthy. It is frequently argued that lobbying on behalf of specific legislation is an essential avenue for public input in the process of enacting laws. Nevertheless, the evidence suggests that it is often, by being closely linked to the distribution of wealth, a very one-sided process. As it presently occurs, many legitimate interests on a range of health related issues do not have lobbying input in proportion to their numerical strength and may actually be structurally precluded from effective participation. While recognizing the importance of lobbying activity and yet feeling that for certain interests its scope ought to be severely curtailed (perhaps in the same way as the proposed regulation and publication of political campaign contributions), I am, to be honest, at a loss as to what should be specifically recommended. . . . The question is: quite apart from the specific issue of changing individual behavior, *in what ways could we possibly regulate the disproportionately influential lobbying activities of certain interest groups in the health field?*

c. Public Education

In the past, it has been common to advocate the education of the public as a means of achieving an alteration in the behavior of groups at risk to illness. Such downstream educational efforts rest on "blaming the victim" assumptions and seek to *either* stop people doing what we feel they "ought not" to be doing, *or* encourage them to do things they "ought" to be doing, but are not. Seldom do we educate people (especially schoolchildren) about the activities of the manufacturers of illness and about how they are involved in many activities unrelated to their professed area of concern. How many of us know, for example, that for any "average" Thanksgiving dinner, the turkey may be produced by the Greyhound Corporation, the Smithfield Ham by ITT, the lettuce by Dow Chemical, the potatoes by Boeing, the fruits and vegetables by Tenneco or the Bank of America?[38] I would reiterate that I am not opposed to the education of people who are at risk to illness, with a view to altering their behavior to enhance life chances (if this can be done successfully). However, I would add the proviso that if we remain committed to the education of people, we must ensure that they are being told the whole story. And, in my view, immediate priority ought to be given to the sensitization of vast numbers of people to the upstream activities of the manufacturers of illness, some of which have been outlined in this paper. Such a program, actively supported by the federal government (perhaps through revenue derived from the RRBT), may foster a groundswell of consumer interest which, in turn, may go some way toward checking the disproportionately influential lobbying of the large corporations and interest groups.

NOTES AND REFERENCES

1. I.K. Zola, "Helping Does It Matter: The Problems and Prospects of Mutual Aid Groups." Addressed to the United Ostomy Association, 1970.
2. See, for example, M.W. Susser and W. Watson, *Sociology in Medicine,* New York: Oxford University Press, 1971. Edith Chen, et al., "Family Structure in Relation to Health and Disease." *Journal of Chronic Diseases,* Vol. 12 (1960), p. 554–567; and R. Keelner, *Family III Health: An*

Investigation in General Practice, Charles C. Thomas, 1963. There is, of course, voluminous literature which relates family structure to mental illness. Few studies move to the level of considering the broader social forces which promote the family structures which are conducive to the onset of particular illnesses. With regard to utilization behavior, see J.B. McKinlay, "Social Networks, Lay Consultation and Help-Seeking Behavior," *Social Forces,* Vol. 51, No. 3 (March, 1973), pp. 275–292.

3. A rich source for a variety of materials included in this second level is H.E. Freeman, S. Levine, and L.G. Reeder (Eds.), *Handbook of Medical Sociology,* New Jersey: Prentice-Hall, 1972. I would also include here studies of the health implications of different housing patterns. Recent evidence suggests that housing—even when highly dense—may not be directly related to illness.
4. There have, of course, been many studies, mainly by epidemiologists, relating disease patterns to certain occupations and industries. Seldom, however, have social scientists pursued the consequences of these findings in terms of a broader political economy of illness. One exception to this statement can be found in studies and writings on the social causes and consequences of environmental pollution. For a recent elementary treatment of some important issues in this general area, see H. Waitzkin and B. Waterman, *The Exploitation of Illness in Capitalist Society,* New York: Bobbs-Merrill Co., 1974.
5. Some useful introductory readings appear in D.M. Gordon (Ed.), *Problems in Political Economy: An Urban Perspective,* Lexington: D.C. Heath & Co., 1971, and R. C. Edwards, M. Reich and T. E. Weisskopf (Eds.), *The Capitalist System,* New Jersey: Prentice-Hall, 1972. Also, T. Christoffel, D. Finkelhor and D. Gilbarg (Eds.), *Up Against the American Myth,* New York: Holt, Rinehart and Winston, 1970. M. Mankoff (Ed.), *The Poverty of Progress: The Political Economy of American Social Problems,* New York: Holt, Rinehart and Winston, 1972. For more sophisticated treatment see the collection edited by D. Mermelstein, *Economics: Mainstream Readings and Radical Critiques,* New York: Random House, 1970. Additionally useful papers appear in J. B. McKinlay (Ed.), *Politics and Law in Health Care Policy.* New York: Prodist, 1973, and J. B. McKinlay (Ed.), *Economic Aspects of Health Care,* New York: Prodist, 1973. For a highly readable and influential treatment of what is termed "the medical industrial complex," see B. and J. Ehrenreich, *The American Health Empire: Power, Profits and Politics,* New York: Vintage Books, 1971. Also relevant are T. R. Marmor, *The Politics of Medicare,* Chicago: Aldine Publishing Co., 1973, and R. Alford, "The Political Economy of Health Care: Dynamics Without Change," *Politics and Society,* 2 (1972), pp. 127–164.
6. E. Cray, *In Failing Health: The Medical Crisis and the AMA,* Indianapolis: Bobbs-Merrill, 1970. J.S. Burrow, *AMA—Voice of American Medicine,* Baltimore: Johns Hopkins Press, 1963. R. Harris, *A Sacred Trust,* New York: New American Library, 1966. R. Carter, *The Doctor Business,* Garden City, New York: Dolphin Books, 1961. "The American Medical Association: Power, Purpose and Politics in Organized Medicine," *Yale Law Journal,* Vol. 63, No. 7 (May, 1954), pp. 938–1021.
7. See references under footnote 5, especially B. and J. Ehrenreich's *The American Health Empire,* Chapter VII, pp. 95–123.
8. D.M. Gordon (Ed.), *Problems in Political Economy: An Urban Perspective,* Lexington: D.C. Heath & Co., 1971, p. 318.
9. See, for example, D. A. Bernstein, "The Modification of Smoking Behavior: An Evaluative Review," *Psychological Bulletin,* Vol. 71 (June, 1969), pp. 418–440; S. Ford and F. Ederer, "Breaking the Cigarette Habit," *Journal of American Medical Association,* 194 (October, 1965), pp. 139–142; C. S. Keutzer, et al., "Modification of Smoking Behavior: A Review," *Psychological Bulletin,* Vol. 70 (December, 1968), pp. 520–533. Mettlin considers evidence concerning the following techniques for modifying smoking behavior: (1) behavioral conditioning, (2) group discussion, (3) counselling, (4) hypnosis, (5) interpersonal communication, (6) self-analysis. He concludes that:

   > Each of these approaches suggests that smoking behavior is the result of some finite set of social and psychological variables, yet none has either demonstrated any significant powers in predicting the smoking behaviors of an individual or led to techniques of smoking control that considered alone, have significant long-term effects.

   In C. Mettlin, "Smoking as Behavior: Applying a Social Psychological Theory," *Journal of Health and Social Behavior,* 14 (June, 1973), p. 144.
10. It appears that a considerable proportion of advertising by large corporations is tax exempt through being granted the status of "public education." In particular, the enormous media campaign, which was recently waged by major oil companies in an attempt to preserve the public myths they had so carefully constructed con-

cerning their activities, was almost entirely non-taxable.

11. Reports of the harmfulness and ineffectiveness of certain products appear almost weekly in the press. As I have been writing this paper, I have come across reports of the low quality of milk, the uselessness of cold remedies, the health dangers in frankfurters, the linking of the use of the aerosol propellant, vinyl chloride, to liver cancer. That the Food and Drug Administration (F.D.A.) is unable to effectively regulate the manufacturers of illness is evident and illustrated in their inept handling of the withdrawal of the drug, betahistine hydrochloride, which supposedly offered symptomatic relief of Meniere's Syndrome (an affliction of the inner ear). There is every reason to think that this case is not atypical. For additionally disquieting evidence of how the Cigarette Labeling and Advertising Act of 1965 actually curtailed the power of the F.T.C. and other federal agencies from regulating cigarette advertising and nullified all such state and local regulatory efforts, see L. Fritschier, *Smoking and Politics: Policymaking and the Federal Bureaucracy,* New York: Meredith, 1969, and T. Whiteside, *Selling Death: Cigarette Advertising and Public Health,* New York: Liveright, 1970. Also relevant are Congressional Quarterly, 27 (1969) 666, 1026; and U.S. Department of Agriculture, Economic Research Service, *Tobacco Situation,* Washington: Government Printing Office, 1969.
12. The term "culture" is used to refer to a number of other characteristics as well. However, these two appear to be commonly associated with the concept. See J. B. McKinlay, "Some Observations on the Concept of a Subculture." (1970).
13. This has been argued in J. B. McKinlay, "Some Approaches and Problems in the Study of the Use of Services," *Journal of Health and Social Behavior,* Vol. 13 (July, 1972), pp. 115–152; and J. B. McKinlay and D. Dutton, "Social Psychological Factors Affecting Health Service Utilization," chapter in *Consumer Incentives for Health Care,* New York: Prodist Press, 1974.
14. Reliable sources covering these areas are available in many professional journals in the fields of epidemiology, medical sociology, preventive medicine, industrial and occupational medicine and public health. Useful references covering these and related areas appear in J. N. Morris, *Uses of Epidemiology,* London: E. and S. Livingstone Ltd., 1967; and M. W. Susser and W. Watson, *Sociology in Medicine,* New York: Oxford University Press, 1971.
15. D. Zwerling, "Death for Dinner," *The New York Review of Books,* Vol. 21, No. 2 (February 21, 1974), p. 22.
16. D. Zwerling, "Death for Dinner." See footnote 15 above.
17. This figure was quoted by several witnesses at the *Hearings Before the Select Committee on Nutrition and Human Needs,* U.S. Government Printing Office, 1973.
18. The magnitude of this problem is discussed in P. Wyden, *The Overweight: Causes, Costs and Control,* Englewood Cliffs: Prentice-Hall, 1968; National Center for Health Statistics, *Weight by Age and Height of Adults:* 1960–62. Washington: *Vital and Health Statistics,* Public Health Service Publication #1000, Series 11, #14, Government Printing Office, 1966; U.S. Public Health Service, Center for Chronic Disease Control, *Obesity and Health,* Washington: Government Printing Office, 1966.
19. This aborted study is discussed in M. Jacobson, *Nutrition Scoreboard: Your Guide to Better Eating,* Center for Science in the Public Interest.
20. M.S. Hathaway and E. D. Foard, *Heights and Weights for Adults in the United States,* Washington: Home Economics Research Report 10, Agricultural Research Service, U.S. Department of Agriculture, Government Printing Office, 1960.
21. This is discussed by D. Zwerling. See footnote 16.
22. See *Hearings Before the Select Committee on Nutrition and Human Needs,* Parts 3 and 4, "T.V. Advertising of Food to Children," March 5, 1973 and March 6, 1973.
23. Dr. John Udkin, Department of Nutrition, Queen Elizabeth College, London University. See p. 225, *Senate Hearings,* footnote 22 above.
24. D. Zwerling, "Death for Dinner." See footnote 16 above, page 24.
25. This is well argued in F. Piven and R. A. Cloward, *Regulating the Poor: The Functions of Social Welfare,* New York: Vintage, 1971; L. Goodwin, *Do the Poor Want to Work?,* Washington: Brookings, 1972; H. J. Gans, "The Positive Functions of Poverty," *American Journal of Sociology,* Vol. 78, No. 2 (September, 1972), pp. 275–289; R. P. Roby (Ed.), *The Poverty Establishment,* New Jersey: Prentice-Hall, 1974.
26. See, for example, Jules Henry, "American Schoolrooms: Learning the Nightmare," *Columbia University Forum,* (Spring, 1963), pp. 24–30. See also the paper by F. Howe and P. Lanter, "How the School System is Rigged for Failure," *New York Review of Books,* (June 18, 1970).
27. With regard to penology, for example, see the critical work of R. Quinney in *Criminal Justice in*

America, Boston: Little Brown, 1974, and *Critique of Legal Order,* Boston: Little Brown, 1974.

28. See, for example, S. M. Sales, "Organizational Role as a Risk Factor in Coronary Disease," *Administrative Science Quarterly,* Vol. 14, No. 3 (September, 1969), pp. 325–336. The literature in this particular area is enormous. For several good reviews, see L.E. Hinkle, "Some Social and Biological Correlates of Coronary Heart Disease," *Social Science and Medicine,* Vol. 1 (1967), pp. 129–139; F. H. Epstein, "The Epidemiology of Coronary Heart Disease: A Review," *Journal of Chronic Diseases,* 18 (August, 1965), pp. 735–774.
29. Some interesting ideas in this regard are in E. Nuehring and G. E. Markle, "Nicotine and Norms: The Reemergence of a Deviant Behavior" *Social Problems,* Vol. 21, No. 4 (April, 1974), pp. 513–526. Also, J.R. Gusfield, *Symbolic Crusade: Status Politics and the American Temperance Movement,* Urbana, Illinois: University of Illinois Press, 1963.
30. For a study of the ways in which physicians, clergymen, the police, welfare officers, psychiatrists and social workers act as agents of social control, see E. Cumming, *Systems of Social Regulation,* New York: Atherton Press, 1968.
31. R. H. Rosenman and M. Friedman, "The Role of a Specific Overt Behavior Pattern in the Occurrence of Ischemic Heart Disease," *Cardiologia Practica,* 13 (1962), pp. 42–53; M. Friedman and R. H. Rosenman, *Type A Behavior and Your Heart,* Knopf, 1973. Also, S. J. Zyzanski andC. D. Jenkins, "Basic Dimensions Within the Coronary-Prone Behavior Pattern," *Journal of Chronic Diseases,* 22 (1970), pp. 781–795. There are, of course, many other illnesses which have also been related in one way or another to certain personality characteristics. Having found this new turf, behavioral scientists will most likely continue to play it for everything it is worth and then, in the interests of their own survival, will "discover" that something else indeed accounts for what they were trying to explain and will eventually move off there to find renewed fame and fortune. Furthermore, serious methodological doubts have been raised concerning the studies of the relationship between personality and at-risk behavior. See, in this regard, G. M. Hochbaum, "A Critique of Psychological Research on Smoking," paper presented to the American Psychological Association, Los Angeles, 1964. Also B. Lebovits and A. Ostfeld, "Smoking and Personality: A Methodologic Analysis," *Journal of Chronic Diseases (1971).*
32. M. Friedman and R.H. Rosenman. See footnote 31.
33. In the *New York Times* of Sunday, May 26, 1974, there were job advertisements seeking "aggressive self-starters," "people who stand real challenges," "those who like to compete," "career oriented specialists," "those with a spark of determination to someday run their own show," "people with the success drive," and "take charge individuals."
34. Aspects of this process are discussed in J. B. McKinlay, "On the Professional Regulation of Change," in *The Professions and Social Change,* P. Halmos (Ed.), Keele: Sociological Review Monograph, No. 20, 1973, and in "Clients and Organizations," chapter in J.B. McKinlay (Ed.), *Processing People—Studies in Organizational Behavior,* London: Holt, Rinehart, and Winston, 1974.
35. There have been a number of reports recently concerning this activity. Questions have arisen about the conduct of major oil corporations during the so-called "energy crisis." See footnote 10. Equally questionable may be the public spirited advertisements sponsored by various professional organizations which, while claiming to be solely in the interests of the public, actually serve to enhance business in various ways. Furthermore, by granting special status to activities of professional groups, government agencies and large corporations may effectively gag them through some expectation of reciprocity. For example, most health groups, notably the American Cancer Society, did not support the F.C.C.'s action against smoking commercials because they were fearful of alienating the networks from whom they receive free announcements for their fund drives. Both the American Cancer Society and the American Heart Association have been criticized for their reluctance to engage in direct organizational conflict with pro-cigarette forces, particularly before the alliance between the television broadcasters and the tobacco industry broke down. Rather, they have directed their efforts to the downstream reform of the smoker. See E. Nuehring and G. E. Markle, cited in footnote 29.
36. E. Nuehring and G. E. Markle, cited in footnote 29.
37. The ways in which large-scale organizations engineer and disseminate these myths concerning their manifest activities, while avoiding any mention of their underlying latent activities, are discussed in more detail in the two references cited in footnote 34 above.
38. For a popularly written and effective treatment of the relationship between giant corporations and food production and consumption, see W. Robbins, *The American Food Scandal,* New York: William Morrow and Co., 1974.

Credits

John B. McKinlay and Sonja M. McKinlay, "Medical Measures and the Decline of Mortality." Under the title "The Questionable Contribution of Medical Measures to the Decline of Mortality in the United States in the Twentieth Century," this article originally appeared in *Milbank Memorial Fund Quarterly/Health and Sociology,* Summer 1977, pp. 405–428. Reprinted by permission of the Milbank Memorial Fund and John B. McKinlay.

S. Leonard Syme and Lisa F. Berkman, "Social Class, Susceptibility, and Sickness." Reprinted by permission from *The American Journal of Epidemiology,* Vol. 104, pp. 1–8, 1976. Copyright 1976, Oxford University Press.

Colin McCord and Harold P. Freeman, "Excess Mortality in Harlem." Reprinted with permission of the *New England Journal of Medicine* Vol. 322, No. 25, pp. 173–177. Copyright © 1990 Massachusetts Medical Society. All rights reserved.

Ingrid Waldron, "Gender Differences in Mortality: Causes and Variation in Different Societies." Reprinted by permission of the author.

Victor R. Fuchs, "A Tale of Two States." From *Who Shall Live? Health Economics and Social Change.* Wond Scientific Publishing. Copyright 1998. Reprinted with permission of the author.

Victor G. Rodwin and Melanie J. Croce-Galis, "Population Health in Utah and Nevada: An Update on Victor Fuch's Tale of Two States." Reprinted by permission of the authors.

Phil Brown, "Popular Epidemiology: Community Response to Toxic Waste-Induced Disease." Reprinted with permission from *Science, Technology & Human Values,* Vol. 12, 3–4 (Summer/Fall), pp. 78–85. Copyright © 1987. Reprinted by permission of Sage Publications, Inc.

James S. House, Karl R. Landis, and Debra Umberson, "Social Relationships and Health." Reprinted and excerpted with permission of the American Association for the Advancement of Science from *Science,* Vol. 241, July 1988, pp. 540–545. Copyright 1988 AAAS.

Eric Klinenberg, "Dying Alone: The Social Production of Urban Isolation." *Ethnography*, Vol. 2, No. 4, pp. 501–531, copyright © Sage Publications, 2001. Reprinted by permission of Sage Publications, Inc.

Richard Wilkinson, "The Socioeconomic Determinants of Health Inequalities: Relative or Absolute Material Standards?" *British Medical Journal,* Vol. 314, pp. 591–595, February, 1997. Reprinted with permission from the BMJ Publishing Group.

Joan Jacobs Brumberg, "Anorexia Nervosa in Context." Excerpts from *Fasting Girls* by Joan Jacobs Brumberg, pp. 8–18, 31–40, 268–271. Reprinted with permission of the author.

Gregory Herek, "Aids and Stigma." *American Behavioral Scientist*, Vol. 42, No. 7, pp. 1106–1116, copyright © 1999 by Sage Publications, Inc. Reprinted by permission of Sage Publications, Inc.

Kristin Barker, "Self-Help Literature and the Making of an Illness Identity: The Case of Fibromyalgia Syndrome (FMS)." © 2002 by the Society for the Study of Social Problems. Reprinted by permission from *Social Problems*, Vol. 49, No. 3, pp. 279–300.

Peter Conrad, "The Meaning of Medications: Another Look at Compliance." Reprinted from *Social Science and Medicine* Vol. 20, No. 1: pp. 29–37. Copyright 1985, with permission from Elsevier.

Arthur W. Frank, "The Remission Society," from *The Wounded Storyteller: Body, Illness, and Ethics* by Arthur W. Frank, 1995, pp. 8–13. Reprinted by permission of University of Chicago Press.

Peter Conrad and Joseph W. Schneider, "Professionalization, Monopoly, and the Structure of Medical Practice." From *Deviance and Medicalization,* © 1992 Temple University. Reprinted by permission of Temple University Press.

Richard W. Wertz and Dorothy C. Wertz, "Notes on the Decline of Midwives and the Rise of Medical Obstetricians," from *Lying In: A History of Childbirth in America* by Richard W. and Dorothy C. Wertz. Copyright 1989 by Richard W. and Dorothy C. Wertz. Reprinted by permission of the authors and Yale University Press.

John B. McKinlay and Lisa D. Marceau, "The End of the Golden Age of Doctoring." Reprinted with permission of the author and Baywood Publishing Company, Inc. from the *International Journal of Health Services*, Vol. 32, No. 2, pp. 379–416 (2002).

Donald W. Light, "Countervailing Power." From *The Changing Medical Profession: An International Perspective*, edited by Frederic W. Hafferty and John B. McKinlay (pp. 69–79). Copyright 1993 by Oxford University Press, Inc. Used by permission of Oxford University Press, Inc.

David Mechanic, "Changing Medical Organization and the Erosion of Trust." *The Milbank Quarterly,* Vol. 74, No. 2, pp. 171–189, 1996. Reprinted by permission of the Milbank Memorial Fund.

John Fry, Donald Light, Jonathon Rodnick, and Peter Orton, "The US Health Care System." Reprinted with permission from *Reviving Primary Care: A U.S.-U.K. Comparison* (1995), pp. 38–53. Radcliffe Medical Press, Oxford.

Susan Reverby, "A Caring Dilemma: Womanhood and Nursing in Historical Perspective." Copyright 1987 The American Journal of Nursing Company. Reprinted with permission from *Nursing Research,* Jan/Feb, 1987, Vol. 36, No. 1, pp. 5–11.

Charles L. Bosk and Joel E. Frader, "AIDS and Its Impact on Medical Work: The Culture and Politics of the Shop Floor." Reprinted from *Milbank Quarterly* Vol. 68, No. 2, pp. 257–279, 1990. Reprinted with permission of the Milbank Memorial Fund.

Arnold S. Relman, "The Health Care Industry: Where is it Taking Us?" *New England Journal of Medicine* Vol. 325, No. 12, pp. 854–859, 1991. Copyright © 1991 Massachusetts Medical Society. All rights reserved.

David Cohen, Michael McCubbin, Johanne Collin and Guilheme Perdeau, "Medications as Social Phenomena." *Health*, Vol. 5, No. 4, pp. 441–469, copyright © Sage Publications, 2001. Reprinted by permission of Sage Publications, Inc.

David J. Rothman, "A Century of Failure: Health Care Reform in America." *Journal of Health Politics, Policy and Law*, Vol. 18, No. 2, pp. 271–286. Copyright © 1993 Duke University Press. All rights reserved. Used by permission of the publisher.

Thomas Bodenheimer and Kevin Grumbach, "Paying for Health Care." *Journal of the American Medical Association,* Vol. 272, pp. 634–39. Copyright 1994 American Medical Association. Reprinted by permission.

Deborah A. Stone, "Doctoring as a Business: Money, Markets, and Managed Care."

Elliot G. Mishler, "The Struggle Between the Voice of Medicine and the Voice of the Lifeworld." Excerpted and reprinted with permission from *The Discourse of Medicine,* Chapter 3, Copyright © 1984 by Ablex Publishing Co.: Norwood, New Jersey.

Stefan Timmermans, "Social Death as Self-Fulfilling Prophecy: David Sudnow's 'Passing On' Revisited." © 1998 by the Midwest Sociological Society. Reprinted by permission from *The Sociological Quarterly*, Vol. 39, No. 3, pp. 453–472.

Renée R. Anspach, "Notes on the Sociology of Medical Discourse: The Language of Case Presentation." Reprinted and excerpted with permission of the American Sociological Association from the *Journal of Health and Social Behavior,* Vol. 29, No. 4, December 1988.

Matthew Schneirov and Jonathan David Geczik, "Alternative Health and the Challenges of Institutionalization." *Health*, Vol. 6, No. 2, pp. 201–220, copyright © Sage Publications, 2002. Reprinted by permission of Sage Publications, Inc.

Paul D. Simmons, "The Artificial Heart: How Close Are We and Do We Want to Get There?" *The Journal of Law, Medicine and Ethics*, Fall-Winter Vol. 29, No. 3–4, pp. 401–406. © 2001. Reprinted with permission of the American Society of Law, Medicine & Ethics. May not be reproduced without express written consent.

Nancy G. Kutner, "Issues in the Application of High Cost Medical Technology: The Case of Organ Transplantation." Reprinted and excerpted with permission of the American Sociological Association from *Journal of Health and Social Behavior,* Vol. 28, No. March 1987, pp. 23–36.

Peter Conrad, "A Mirage of Genes." *Sociology of Health and Illness,* Vol. 21, No. 2, pp. 228–241, 1999. Reprinted with permission from Blackwell Publishers.

Robert A. Hahn, Steven M. Teutsch, Adele L. Franks, Man-Huei Chang, and Elizabeth Lloyd, "The Prevalence of Risk Factors Among Women in the United States by Race and Age, 1992–1994: Opportunities for Primary and Secondary Prevention." *Journal of the American Medical Women's Association*, Vol. 53, No. 2. Reprinted with permission of the publisher.

Deborah Lupton, "Risk as Moral Danger: The Social and Political Functions of Risk in Public Health." Reprinted with permission of the author and Baywood Publishing Company, Inc. from the *International Journal of Health Services,* Vol. 23, No. 3, pp. 425–435, 1993.

Irving Kenneth Zola, "Medicine as an Institution of Social Control." Reprinted with permission from *Sociological Review,* Vol. 20, pp. 487–504. Copyright © 1972 by The Editorial Board of The Sociological Review.

Adele E. Clark, Laura Mamo, Jennifer R. Fishman, Janet K. Shim, and Jennifer Ruth Fosket, "Biomedicalization: Technoscientific Transformations of Health, Illness, and U.S. Biomedicine." Reprinted and excerpted with permission of the American Sociological Association from *American Sociological Review*, Vol. 68, No. 2 (April 2003).

Daniel Callahan, "Rationing Medical Progress: The Way to Affordable Health Care." Reprinted with permission of the *New England Journal of Medicine*, Vol. 322, pp. 810–813, 1990. Copyright © 1990 Massachusetts Medical Society. All rights reserved.

Arnold S. Relman, "The Trouble with Rationing." Reprinted with permission of the *New England Journal of Medicine* Vol. 323, No. 13, pp. 911–913, 1990. Copyright © 1990 Massachusetts Medical Society. All rights reserved.

Victoria Pitts, "Illness and Internet Empowerment: Writing and Reading Breast Cancer in Cyberspace." *Health*, Vol. 8, No. 2, copyright © Sage Publications, 2004. Reprinted by permission of Sage Publications, Inc.

John McKnight, "Politicizing Health Care." From *Development Dialogue,* 1978:1. Reprinted with permission from the journal of the Dag Hammarskjold Foundation, Uppsala, Sweden.

Ann Withorn, "Helping Ourselves: The Limits and Potential of Self-Help." Reprinted by permission of the author and *Radical America* from *Radical America,* Vol. 14, May/June 1980: pp. 25–59, as edited by the author. *Radical America* is available from the Alternative Education Project, Inc. 1 Summer Street, Somerville, MA 02143.

Donald W. Light, "Comparative Models of 'Health Care' Systems." Reprinted by permission of the author.

Raisa Berlin Deber, "Health Care Reform: Lessons from Canada." Reprinted with permission from *American Journal of Public Health*, Vol. 93, No. 1, pp. 20–24. Copyright, 2003.

Jonathan Gabe, "Continuity and Change in the British National Health Service." Reprinted by permission of the author.

Peter Conrad, "Wellness in the Workplace: Potentials and Pitfalls of Work-Site Health Promotion." Reprinted from *Milbank Quarterly Vol. 65,* No. 2, pp. 255–275, 1987. Reprinted with permission of the Milbank Memorial Fund.

John B. McKinlay, "A Case for Refocussing Upstream: The Political Economy of Illness," from *Applying Behavioral Science to Cardiovascular Risk*. Reproduced with permission. Copyright © 1974, American Heart Association.

Index

B

D

E

F

H

I

J

K

M

N

Q

R